ISBN 978-1-5278-7122-9
PIBN 10888715

1 MONTH OF
FREE
READING

at

www.ForgottenBooks.com

By purchasing this book you are eligible for one month membership to ForgottenBooks.com, giving you unlimited access to our entire collection of over 1,000,000 titles via our web site and mobile apps.

To claim your free month visit:

www.forgottenbooks.com/free888715

English
Français
Deutsche
Italiano
Español
Português

www.forgottenbooks.com

Mythology Photography **Fiction**
Fishing Christianity **Art** Cooking
Essays Buddhism Freemasonry
Medicine **Biology** Music **Ancient
Egypt** Evolution Carpentry Physics
Dance Geology **Mathematics** Fitness
Shakespeare **Folklore** Yoga Marketing
Confidence Immortality Biographies
Poetry **Psychology** Witchcraft
Electronics Chemistry History **Law**
Accounting **Philosophy** Anthropology
Alchemy Drama Quantum Mechanics
Atheism Sexual Health **Ancient History**
Entrepreneurship Languages Sport
Paleontology Needlework Islam
Metaphysics Investment Archaeology
Parenting Statistics Criminology
Motivational

GEORGE HAZZARD
AUTHOR AND PUBLISHER
NEW CASTLE, INDIANA
1906

HAZZARD'S HISTORY

OF

HENRY COUNTY,

INDIANA

1822-1906

MILITARY EDITION

VOLUME II

ILLUSTRATED

GEORGE HAZZARD
AUTHOR AND PUBLISHER
NEW CASTLE, INDIANA
1906

This volume is affectionately dedicated to my wife,

MARIA EUDORA HAZZARD

who yet abides with me, born May 30, A. D. 1849. We were married June 30, A. D. 1870. She is the daughter of the late Reuben and Adaline Tobey. Her father was the minister of the M. E. Church, New Castle, 1869-70.

1139220

GEORGE W. LENNARD POST, NO. 148, G. A. R., NEW CASTLE, INDIANA.

George W. Lennard Post, No. 148, Department of Indiana, Grand Army of the Republic, was organized and instituted at New Castle, Henry County, Indiana, April 1, 1883, in the Knights of Pythias Hall, Murphey Building, and was mustered in by Joseph P. Iliff of Sol Meredith Post, No. 55, Richmond, Indiana, assisted by members of George W. Rader Post, No. 119, Middletown, Indiana. The Post was named for and in honor of the late George W. Lennard, Colonel of the 57th Indiana Infantry, a sketch of whose life and military service is fully set forth at the conclusion of this article.

The following named comrades were present at the organization and became charter members of the Post, viz: John B. Albertson, William H. Albright, Miles E. Anderson, Thomas J. Burchett, Milton Burk, George H. Cain, David W. Chambers, Thaddeus Coffin, David Daniels, William H. Elliott, Owen Evans, George W. Goodwin, Henry C. Gordon, Isaac Grove, Miles Haguewood, Pleasant W. Harvey, Andrew F. Kraner, Louis N. Moore, James I. Newby, Patrick Sullivan, William Thomas.

The regular meetings of the Post are held on Saturday evening of each week. The following were the Post officers from the organization in 1883 down to and including the year 1904. The names of the commanders are arranged in the order in which they served. The names of all other officers are arranged alphabetically.

COMMANDERS.

George H. Cain, Exum Saint, William F. Shelley, William M. Pence, John C. Livezey, Leander P. Mitchell, William S. Bedford, Elihu T. Mendenhall, George W. Burke, Louis N. Moore, Leander S. Denius, Miles E. Anderson, Thomas W. Gronendyke, Thaddeus Coffin, Joseph M. Brown, David W. Chambers, Asa M. Weston, Henry C. Elliott, William B. Bock, Isaac W. Ellis, Richard J. Edleman.

SENIOR VICE COMMANDERS.

William B. Bock, Joseph M. Brown, Thaddeus Coffin, John Curry, Richard J. Edleman, Henry C. Elliott, Isaac W. Ellis, Thomas W. Gronendyke, Mahlon D. Harvey, Louis N. Moore, Henry L. Powell, Obed C. Rife, Albert W. Saint, John Thornburgh, Asa M. Weston.

JUNIOR VICE COMMANDERS.

Miles E. Anderson, William B. Bock, Joseph M. Brown, David W. Chambers, Richard J. Edleman, Henry C. Elliott, Isaac W. Ellis, Daniel Hartman, Mahlon D. Harvey, John C. Murray, Albert W. Saint, George W. Shelley, Lorenzo D. Shepherd, John Thornburgh.

SURGEONS.

William F. Boor, George W. Burke, Thomas W. Gronendyke, Elihu T. Mendenhall.

CHAPLAINS.

William S. Bedford, George W. Bunch, Thomas W. Gronendyke, David T. King.

ADJUTANTS.

William B. Bock, Thaddeus Coffin, Leander S. Denius, William H. Elliott, Elihu T. Mendenhall, Louis N. Moore, Albert W. Saint, Asa M. Weston, Richmond Wisehart.

Andrew F. Kraner, William M. Pence.

Miles E. Anderson, James W. Brodrick, Thaddeus Coffin, William T. Corya, Leander S. Denius, David Modlin, Cornelius M. Moore, Louis N. Moore, John C. Murray, Albert W. Saint, William F. Shelley, Lewis H. Worster.

George H. Cain, Isaac W. Ellis, Richard Hartman, Andrew F. Kraner, Louis N. Moore, John C. Murray, Obed C. Rife, Harvey W. Swaim.

William S. Bedford, Henry C. Elliott, Isaac W. Ellis, Asa W. Hatch, John C. Livezey, William E. Livezey, Louis N. Moore, George B. Robson, Albert W. Saint, Lorenzo D. Shepherd, Richmond Wisehart.

Mathew T. Abbott, Miles E. Anderson, William B. Bock, William T. Corya, Richard J. Edleman, Henry C. Gordon, Leander M. James, Andrew F. Kraner, Peter Michels, Samuel G. Vance.

(Note:—The records of the Post from 1883 to 1888, which contained the minutes of organization, nomination and election of officers, etc., are lost and a strict inquiry and search for the same has been without favorable result.)

Commander, John Thornburgh; Senior Vice-Commander, George W. Shelley; Junior Vice-Commander, Albert W. Saint; Surgeon, Thomas W. Gronendyke; Chaplain, David T. King; Adjutant, Leander S. Denius; Quartermaster, William M. Pence; Officer of the Day, Richard J. Edleman; Officer of the Guard, Isaac W. Ellis; Sergeant Major, Thaddeus Coffin; Quartermaster Sergeant, William T. Corya.

The following is believed to be a complete list or roster of all who have been or are now, members of the Post. In the several alphabetical lists of soldiers and sailors, set out elsewhere in this History, will be found a more detailed statement of the service in the Army and Navy of each comrade who is entitled to further mention in the History of Henry County:

Mathew T. Abbott, Company A, 35th Iowa Infantry.
Thomas Addington, Company C, 87th Indiana Infantry.
John B. Albertson, Company C, 36th Indiana Infantry.
William H. Albright, Company F, 84th Indiana Infantry.
William Alcorn, Company E, 8th Indiana Cavalry.
Miles E. Anderson, Company E, 9th Indiana Cavalry.
Morrow P. Armstrong, Company K and Chaplain, 36th Indiana Infantry.
Samuel Arnold, Company G, 5th Ohio Cavalry.
Samuel Barnard, Company C, 36th Indiana Infantry.
Henry C. Bateman, Company G, 9th Indiana Cavalry.
George P. Beach, Company A, 36th Indiana Infantry.
Thurman H. Beardsley, Company D, 168th New York Infantry.
William S. Bedford, Company E, 8th Indiana Infantry (three years).
Benjamin Bitner, Company H, 147th Indiana Infantry.
William B. Bock, Company G, 84th Indiana Infantry.

William F. Boor, Major and Surgeon, 4th Indiana Cavalry; Brigade Surgeon, 1st Brigade, 2nd Division, Cavalry Corps, Army of the Cumberland.

Moses Bowers, Company F, 57th Indiana Infantry.

John W. Brattain, Company E, 34th Indiana Infantry.

Charles Brenneman, Company B, Benton Cadets, Missouri Volunteers (Fremont's Body Guard).

George Brenneman, Company H, 69th Indiana Infantry.

James W. Brodrick, Company C, 11th Ohio Infantry; Company C, 2nd Indiana Cavalry.

Eli Brookshire, Company G. 84th Indiana Infantry.

William Brookshire, Company D, 36th Indiana Infantry.

Charles Brown, Company E, 13th Indiana Infantry, re-organized.

Francis M. Brown, Company F, 1st U. S. Sharpshooters.

Joseph M. Brown, Company B, 110th Indiana Infantry (Morgan Raid); Company I, 69th Indiana Infantry.

Theodore F. Brown, Company A, 139th Indiana Infantry.

Francis M. Brunner, Company B, 58th Ohio Infantry.

James W. Bunce, Company A, 15th Indiana Infantry.

George W. Bunch, Company B, 19th Indiana Infantry; Company C, 20th Indiana Infantry, re-organized.

Martin L. Bundy, Major and Paymaster and Brevet Lieutenant Colonel, U. S. Volunteers.

William Bunnell, Company D, Benton Cadets, Missouri Volunteers (Fremont's Body Guard); Company D, 39th Ohio Infantry.

Thomas J. Burchett, Company G, 8th Indiana Infantry (three years); Company H, 74th Ohio Infantry.

Milton Burk, Company H, 147th Indiana Infantry.

George W. Burke, Company H, 9th Pennsylvania Infantry; Surgeon, 46th Pennsylvania Infantry, Brevet Lieutenant Colonel.

George H. Cain, Company B, 8th Indiana Infantry (three months); Company G, 84th Indiana Infantry.

Edward H. Campbell, Company D, 147th Indiana Infantry.

Solomon F. Carter, Company A, 30th Indiana Infantry, re-organized.

Daniel C. Catt, Company K, 36th Indiana Infantry; ————, 22nd Indiana Battery.

William F. Catt, Company B, 99th Indiana Infantry.

Andrew J. Chambers, Company D, 113th Ohio Infantry.

David W. Chambers, Company B, 8th Indiana Infantry (three months); Company D, 36th Indiana Infantry.

Harvey B. Chew, Company D, 36th Indiana Infantry; Company E, 9th Regiment, 1st Army Corps (Hancock's Veteran Corps).

Arthur W. Coffin, Company F, 120th Ohio Infantry; Company I, 23rd Ohio Infantry.

Thaddeus Coffin, Company G and Regimental Band, 23rd Ohio Infantry.

Elias Conwell, Company A, 54th Indiana Infantry (one year).

Daniel M. Cooper, Company I, 11th Ohio Infantry; Company K, 87th Ohio Infantry; Company E, 2nd Ohio Heavy Artillery.

William T. Corya, Company D, 54th Indiana Infantry (three months).

Cornelius W. Cosand, ————, 24th Indiana Battery.

James A. Cotton, Company H, 47th Indiana Infantry.

Jacob Courtney, Company H, 69th Indiana Infantry.

Leonard H. Craig, Company K, 105th Indiana Infantry (Morgan Raid); Company H, 140th Indiana Infantry.

William J. C. Crandall, Company G, 1st Tennessee Infantry.

Gilliam L. Craven, Company B, 89th Indiana Infantry.

John C. Curry, Unassigned, 33rd Indiana Infantry.

John L. Custer, Company A, 8th Indiana Infantry (three months).

William H. Dakins, Company F, 57th Indiana Infantry; ——————, 19th Indiana Battery.

David Daniels, Company H, 140th Indiana Infantry.

Milton Davis, Company G, 7th Indiana Cavalry; Company F, 7th Indiana Cavalry, re-organized.

Leander S. Denius, Regimental Band, 35th Ohio Infantry; Company G, 156th Ohio Infantry.

David Dowell, Company C, 12th Missouri Cavalry.

Richard J. Edleman, ——————, 12th Indiana Battery.

Henry C. Elliott, Company B, 8th Indiana Infantry (three months); Company F and Adjutant, 57th Indiana Infantry; Lieutenant Colonel, 118th Indiana Infantry.

William H. Elliott, Lieutenant, U. S. Navy.

Isaac W. Ellis, Company C, 8th Indiana Infantry (three months).

Owen Evans, Company A, 2nd U. S. Sharpshooters.

James P. Ewing, Company B, 18th Ohio Infantry.

James H. E. Feezer, Company I, 1st Maryland Potomac Home Brigade Infantry.

William Fletcher, Company F, 8th U. S. C. T.

James H. S. Ford, Company B, 153rd Indiana Infantry.

Iredell R. Frazier, Company G, 3rd Maryland Cavalry.

James Frazier, Company G, 29th Iowa Infantry.

William Frazier, Company G, 29th Iowa Infantry.

Joseph Funk, Company A, 8th Indiana Infantry (three months); Company I, 36th Indiana Infantry.

George Gaddis, Company B, 130th Indiana Infantry.

Charles N. Gibbs, Company B, 69th Ohio Infantry.

John M. Goar, ——————. Record incomplete in this History.

William O. Gold, Company H, 52nd Indiana Infantry.

George W. Goodwin, Company B, 8th Indiana Infantry (three months); Company C, 36th Indiana Infantry.

Henry C. Gordon, Company B, 19th Indiana Infantry; Principal Musician, 20th Indiana Infantry, re-organized.

James W. Gormon, Company C, 84th Indiana Infantry.

William C. Goudy, Company I, 32nd Ohio Infantry.

Jacob M. Gough, Company B, 8th Indiana Infantry (three months).

Thomas W. Gough, Company K, 19th Indiana Infantry.

David A. Graham, Battery F, 1st West Virginia Light Artillery.

Thomas Gray, ——————, 4th Indiana Battery.

John Griffith, Company H, 140th Indiana Infantry.

Thomas W. Gronendyke, Company K, 105th Indiana Infantry (Morgan Raid); Company H, 69th Indiana Infantry.

William Grose, Colonel, 36th Indiana Infantry; Brigadier General and Brevet Major General, U. S. Volunteers.

Isaac Grove, Company K, 8th Indiana Infantry (three months); Company H, 69th Indiana Infantry; Company F, 124th Indiana Infantry.

Miles Haguewood, Company C, 36th Indiana Infantry.

Henry B. Harter, ——————, 23rd Indiana Battery.

Thomas L. Hartley, Company D, 2nd Indiana Cavalry.

Daniel Hartman, Company E, 8th Indiana Infantry (three years).

Richard Hartman, Company D, 109th U. S. C. T.

Charles W. Harvey, Company D, 79th Ohio Infantry.

John R. Harvey, Company C, 36th Indiana Infantry; Company A, 110th Indana Infantry (Morgan Raid); Company B, 139th Indiana Infantry.

Levi Harvey, Company G, 84th Indiana Infantry.

Mahlon D. Harvey, Company I, 69th Indiana Infantry.

Pleasant W. Harvey, Company I, 69th Indiana Infantry.

Asa W. Hatch, Company F, 2nd Ohio Infantry; Company E, 152nd Ohio Infantry.

James T. J. Hazelrigg, Company D, 4th Kentucky Infantry.

Henry H. Henderson, Company B, 8th Indiana Infantry (three months); Company C, 36th Indiana Infantry.

Isom P. Henderson, Company B, 5th Indiana Cavalry.

Martin L. Henneigh, Company B, 74th Pennsylvania Infantry.

Henry Herliman, Regimental Band, 36th Indiana Infantry; Company A, 110th Indiana Infantry (Morgan Raid).

John W. Hill, Company I, 8th U. S. C. T.

David Hoover, Company B, 110th Indiana Infantry (Morgan Raid); Company B, 139th Indiana Infantry.

Harrison Hoover, Company K, 36th Indiana Infantry; Company G, 84th Indiana Infantry.

Daniel Hoppis, Company A, 19th Indiana Infantry; Company I, 20th Indiana Infantry, re-organized.

Thomas J. Houck, Company B, 8th Indiana Infantry (three months); Company D, 36th Indiana Infantry.

William House, Company B, 110th Indiana Infantry (Morgan Raid); Company A, 30th Indiana Infantry, re-organized.

Charles A. C. Howren, Company A, 84th Indiana Infantry.

John H. Ike, Company E, 71st Ohio Infantry.

James W. Irving, Company H, 3rd Maine Infantry; Company C, 2nd Maine Cavalry.

Presley E. Jackson, Company K, 47th Indiana Infantry.

William H. Jacobs, Company A, 91st Ohio Infantry.

Leander M. James, Company A, 139th Indiana Infantry.

Hiram Julian, Company B, 40th Indiana Infantry.

Milton P. Julian, Company D, 115th Illinois Infantry.

George Kamphere, Company I, 13th Heavy Artillery U. S. C. T.

Adam Kendall, Company K, 57th Indiana Infantry.

David T. King, Company I, 7th Illinois Cavalry.

Alfred M. Kissell, Company G, 84th Indiana Infantry.

Samuel Kissell, Unassigned, 33rd Indiana Infantry.

Andrew F. Kraner, Company G, 8th Indiana Infantry (three months); Company K, 8th Indiana Infantry (three years).

Joseph M. Lacy, Company I, 33rd Indiana Infantry.

William T. Latchaw, Company D, 87th Indiana Infantry; Company D, 42nd Indiana Infantry.

John C. Livezey, Company C, 36th Indiana Infantry; Captain and Commissary of Subsistence and Brevet Major, U. S. Volunteers.

William E. Livezey, Company G, 84th Indiana Infantry.

John Lockridge, Company D, 36th Indiana Infantry.

Pearson Loer, Company A, 54th Indiana Infantry (one year)

Michael Longnecker, Company B, 11th Ohio Infantry; Company B, 94th Ohio Infantry.

David Lowe, Company B, 110th Indiana Infantry (Morgan Raid); Company E, 9th Indiana Cavalry.

Philip Lowery, Company E, 9th Indiana Cavalry.

David M. Luellen, Company E, 147th Indiana Infantry.

Joshua Luthultz, Company D, 36th Indiana Infantry.

John McDivitt, ————, 3rd Indiana Battery.

William H. Macy, Company D, 36th Indiana Infantry.

Elihu T. Mendenhall, Company A, 101st Indiana Infantry.

James M. Mercer, Company A, 54th Indiana Infantry (one year).

Peter Michels, Company K, 72nd Ohio Infantry.

Wilson C. Middaugh, Company C, 1st Michigan Infantry; Company M, 8th Michigan Cavalry.

Leander P. Mitchell, Company B, 139th Indiana Infantry.

David Modlin, Company B, 28th U. S. C. T.

William H. Modlin, Company C, 36th Indiana Infantry.

Cornelius M. Moore, Company B, 8th Indiana Infantry (three months); Company C, 36th Indiana Infantry; Company B, 110th Indiana Infantry (Morgan Raid); Company B, 139th Indiana Infantry.

Gideon Moore, Company H, 59th Indiana Infantry.

Louis N. Moore, Company K, 16th Indiana Infantry.

Hugh L. Mullen, Company C, 36th Indiana Infantry.

Joseph R. Mullen, Company A, 54th Indiana Infantry (one year).

John C. Murray, Company K, 36th Indiana Infantry.

Isaac Needham, Company F, 154th Indiana Infantry.

Winford Needham, Company F and Principal Musician, 57th Indiana Infantry.

James I. Newby, Company D, 36th Indiana Infantry.

John W. Newby, Company D, 36th Indiana Infantry.

Peter Niccum, Company D, 69th Indiana Infantry.

Nathan Nicholson, Company C, 36th Indiana Infantry.

Robert M. Nixon, Regimental Band, 36th Indiana Infantry.

Rhoderick D. Norviel, Company K, 132nd Ohio Infantry.

William O'Neal, Company D, 3rd Indiana Cavalry.

William M. Pence, Seaman, U. S. Navy.

Henry Perry, Company E, 9th Indiana Cavalry.

James B. Philabaum, Company A, 110th Indiana Infantry (Morgan Raid).

Henry L. Powell, Company B, 8th Indiana Infantry (three months); Company A, 110th Indiana Infantry (Morgan Raid).

Henry Pry, Company E, 33rd Ohio Infantry.

George W. Ralston, Company B, 8th Indiana Infantry (three months); Company G, 8th Indiana Infantry (three years).

Martin L. Real, Company D, 9th Indiana Infantry.

John M. Redding, Company F, 57th Indiana Infantry.

Thomas B. Reeder, Company I, 19th Indiana Infantry; Company B and Major, 149th Indiana Infantry.

Henry Reichart, Company C, 36th Indiana Infantry.

John Rhine, Company K, 75th Indiana Infantry.

William Rhinewalt, ————————, 18th Indiana Battery.

Cornelius J. Richardson, Company B, 124th Indiana Infantry.

Obed C. Rife, Company D, 152nd Ohio Infantry; Company H, 154th Indiana Infantry.

George B. Robson, Company A, 86th Ohio Infantry; Company B, 69th Ohio Infantry.

Leonidas Rodgers, Company C, 16th Ohio Infantry; Regimental Band, 13th Missouri Infantry; Company E, 152nd Ohio Infantry.

William H. H. Rohrback, Company E, 1st Maryland Potomac Home Brigade Infantry.

William J. Runyan, Company G, 84th Indiana Infantry.

Dennis Ryan, Company B, 124th Indiana Infantry.

Albert W. Saint, Company D, 36th Indiana Infantry.

Exum Saint, Company E, 4th Iowa Cavalry.

John W. Sanders, Company C, 36th Indiana Infantry.

James M. Semans, Company D, 26th Indiana Infantry.

George W. Shane, Company B, 8th Indiana Infantry (three months); Company K, 54th Indiana Infantry (three months); Company C, 109th Indiana Infantry (Morgan Raid); Company H, 140th Indiana Infantry.

Timothy Shane, Company G, 13th Indiana Cavalry.

Charles C. Shedron, Company H, 69th Indiana Infantry.

George W. Shelley, Company G, 84th Indiana Infantry.

William F. Shelley, Company B, Benton Cadets, Missouri Volunteers (Fremont's

Body Guard); Company B, 19th Indiana Infantry; Company B, 139th Indiana Infantry; Company H, 147th Indiana Infantry.

Lorenzo D. Shepherd, Company C, 36th Indiana Infantry.

David Shields, Company F, 124th Indiana Infantry.

William H. Showalter, Company I, 67th Indiana Infantry.

Henry L. Shopp, Company B, 110th Indiana Infantry (Morgan Raid); Company C. 30th Indiana Infantry, re-organized.

Parvis Sims, Company G, 140th Indiana Infantry.

Frederick Slade, Company F, 64th Ohio Infantry.

Joseph Smith, 5th Independent Battery, Ohio Light Artillery.

Pleasant A. Spain, Company C, 58th Indiana Infantry.

John Speakman, —————, 12th Indiana Battery.

Patrick Sullivan, Company F, 19th Indiana Infantry; Company E, 20th Indiana Infantry, re-organized.

Laban W. Swafford, Company G, 9th Indiana Cavalry.

Harvey W. Swaim, Company F, 6th Indiana Infantry (three months); Company I, 69th Indiana Infantry.

John M. Swaim, Company F, 6th Indiana Infantry (three months); Company A, 36th Indiana Infantry; Company H, 30th Indiana Infantry, re-organized.

James W. Swain, Company B, 81st Ohio Infantry.

Jacob Sweigart, Company C, 36th Indiana Infantry.

Daniel A. Tawney, Chaplain, 179th Ohio Infantry.

James Taylor, Company B, 33rd Ohio Infantry

James W. Thomas, Company A, 36th Indiana Infantry.

James Thornburgh, Company B, 19th Indiana Infantry; Company H, 147th Indiana Infantry.

John Thornburgh, Lieutenant and Quartermaster, 4th Indiana Cavalry.

Isom Thurman, Company F, 14th U. S. C. T.

Moab Turner, Company I, 4th Tennessee, Infantry, re-organized as 1st Tennessee Cavalry.

Nathan Upham, Company G, 84th Indiana Infantry.

Samuel G. Vance, Company F, 146th Indiana Infantry.

Theodore R. Vaughan, Company G, 89th Ohio Infantry.

James L. Waggoner, Company H, 147th Indiana Infantry.

Holman W. Waldron, Company C, 23rd Maine Infantry; Company E, 32nd Maine Infantry.

John C. Wayman, Company C, 36th Indiana Infantry.

Charles H. Weaver, Company K, 17th Indiana Infantry.

Cornelius C. Weaver, Company B, 18th Illinois Infantry.

John S. Weaver, Company K, 17th Indiana Infantry.

James M. Welker, Company K, 54th Indiana Infantry (three months); —————, 15th Indiana Battery.

Jordan Welker, Company H, 140th Indiana Infantry.

Asa M. Weston, Company K and Company E, 50th Ohio Infantry.

Augustus Williams, Company C, 36th Indiana Infantry.

Samuel Winings, Company C, 36th Indiana Infantry.

Richmond Wisehart, Company F, 57th Indiana Infantry.

Samuel Wolf, Company M, 11th Indiana Cavalry.

Pyrrhus Woodward, Company H, 5th Indiana Infantry (Mexican War); Company C, 36th Indiana Infantry.

Lewis H. Worster, Company H, 153rd Indiana Infantry.

David Wrightsman, Company A, 79th Ohio Infantry; Company D, 73rd Ohio Infantry.

BIOGRAPHICAL SKETCH OF GEORGE WASHINGTON LENNARD.

COLONEL 57TH INFANTRY REGIMENT, INDIANA VOLUNTEERS.

Colonel George Washington Lennard, the subject of this sketch, was born near Newark, Licking County, Ohio, March 5, 1825. Deprived by circumstances of early educational advantages, he reached the age of sixteen years without having learned to read or write. By determined energy, which so highly characterized him in later life, he made such use of his meager opportunities that in 1847 he was prepared to commence the study of medicine, a profession to which he then expected to devote his life. In March, 1850, he received the degree of Doctor of Medicine from the Eclectic Medical Institute of Medicine of Cincinnati. He located at New Castle in 1851, to engage in the practice of his profession. Though young in years he became from the first a successful physician. He soon discovered that the practice of medicine did not open to him the field in which to gratify his ambition so he retired from it at the expiration of two years, and purchased the New Castle Courier office, and was connected with this paper as editor and publisher for some eighteen months. He next studied law and graduated with honor at the law school of Cincinnati, in 1855. In this profession he became a successful practitioner. He was married June 10, 1852, at the residence, in New Castle, of Samuel and Vienna (Woodward) Hazzard, parents of the author of this History, to Miss Clarinda Woodward, a noble lady, youngest child of Asahel and Catharine Woodward, the first white settlers of Henry County. She was a sister of Mrs. Samuel Hazzard. In 1861, when the tocsin of war sounded through the land, he was one of the first to respond, and his energy and influence were thrown at once into the cause and his labors from that time forth were earnest and untiring in behalf of his country. He was among the first to volunteer as a private soldier. On the organization of Company C, Thirty Sixth Regiment, he was elected its First Lieutenant, from which position before the company was mustered into service, he was called to the Adjutancy of the regiment. His gentlemanly bearing, prompt attention to duties and fine soldierly qualities soon attracted the attention of his superior officers, and he was tendered by General Thomas J. Wood, a position on his staff with the rank of Captain which was accepted, and for some time filled with such a degree of credit as won for him the unanimous and hearty encomiums of his brother officers. Because of his prompt and manly discharge of every duty, Governor Morton, December 2, 1862, gave him a commission as Colonel and assigned him to the Fifty Seventh Regiment. In all the varied and responsible positions to which he was assigned, his career illustrated the highest type of our citizen soldiery. His duties were performed with skill, bravery and success. In all the engagements in which his regiment participated he was conspicuous for his gallant bearing and was highly complimented. At the battle of Stone's River, December 31, 1862, he was severely wounded in the right leg by a musket shot which resulted in a tedious confinement, but from which he afterward sufficiently recovered to rejoin his regiment. He afterward led his gallant regiment in the hard-fought battles of Missionary Ridge, Rocky Face Ridge and Resaca. At the battle of Resaca, May 14, 1864, he was struck

George W. Lennard

by a shell which shattered his right knee and inflicted a shock from which his system never rallied. Asbury L. Kerwood, one of his soldiers, in a well-written history of the regiment, gives the following account of his death:

"DEATH OF COLONEL LENNARD."

"There were probably few officers connected with the army who were more solicitous or took a deeper interest in every movement in which their command should participate than did Colonel Lennard. Immediately after the last change of position, the Colonel advanced to the open ground in front, dismounted, and was engaged for several minutes in conversation with General Newton and other officers, concerning the disposition of the regiment. The consultation over, he turned to go back to the regiment; and just as he was in the act of mounting his horse a shell from the enemy passed through his right knee, shattering it to pieces and mangling it horribly. The horse, much frightened, dashed on toward the regiment, and in a few moments a pair of stretchers were provided on which to bear away the body of the Colonel. Gloom and sadness took possession of every man as he was borne back to take his farewell of the men who had almost learned to love him. 'Now, take good care of the boys, Major,' were the last words he ever said in hearing of the command. General Wagner, when he heard of the fall of the Colonel, was deeply moved, and was afterwards heard to say he had lost his best man. Soon afterward the Colonel was carried to a house three-quarters of a mile in the rear, and a member of the regiment, Sergeant W. W. Sims, remained with him until after his death.

"At his own request a pallet was laid on the floor, and on that he was placed. The wound produced a wonderful shock on his system, and as yet there was no reaction. From the first he seemed to realize his true situation, and when in conversation with the surgeons spoke coolly and calmly of his wound. He was anxious that amputation should take place just as soon as the system revived. Several hours elapsed from the time he was wounded until the attending surgeon discovered that instead of reviving he was growing weaker. In the meantime he was engaged in conversation on various subjects. He spoke of his experience in the army, and especially since he became connected with the regiment; of a conversation he had with General Whipple about the campaign, and his reply that the enemy would be very obstinate. Then his thoughts would turn toward his family. He requested that his wife might be sent for to come and take care of him; wondering if his little children would always be good children. He spoke of the tender affection which always existed between him and his companion, and talked only as a brave man could, who was so near the hour of dissolution.

"Night was now fast approaching, and a fire of pine knots was kindled on the hearth. About 7 o'clock the surgeons informed the Sergeant that the Colonel would probably never revive; that he was even then sinking; and that he had better speak to him of his danger. When told that he could hardly survive, and that he might die at any moment, his pale features lighted up with a smile as he calmly said, 'What, so soon?' Continuing, he said: 'It is necessary for me to make the sacrifice, and I make it cheerfully, though here I am in Georgia, away from my pleasant home, away from my wife and dear little children. Tonight they don't know that I am dying by the fire of these pine knots.'

"He had given up his regiment. Now he gave up his family, and began to talk of the solemn realities of death. He remarked that he was never a believer in death-bed repentance, and that it was the duty of every one to prepare for death in time of health. One of the surgeons, a pious man, prayed with him, and told him that Jesus died to save him and would hear his prayer. Up to the last moment, the colonel continued to speak of his soul's salvation, and entreated those around him to not postpone the greatest duty of their lives. Before he died, he gave evidence to those around him that he was willing to go, and that he should pass from labor to reward. To the last he was calm and collected. Even the terrors of death did not move him, and he met the grim monster without a shudder. Noble man! Green in our memory will be the remembrance of his name. Encomiums we need not add. We have dropped the tear of sorrow at his untimely death, and we wait in hope of meeting him in a better land. Peace to the ashes of George W. Lennard."

Kind, courteous, and affable with all—one of Nature's own gentlemen. Never was man more popular among his neighbors and acquaintances than was Colonel Lennard. His friends were warmly attached to him and no man ever lived in Henry County who made a deeper impression upon her people, or whose death was more sincerely mourned. He was about five feet and ten inches in height, well proportioned, always appropriately appareled, dark hair, dark gray eyes—a handsome man. Just prior to his death he had been nominated to the State Senate and it was confidently predicted by those who knew him that he would have been transferred from the Senate to a seat in Congress. Hallowed indeed must be the cause which demands the sacrifice of such noble men. It is to be hoped that God in his infinite mercies will never again permit the day to come when our common country shall be divided, section against section, in terrible war. His widow remained single and died of brain fever at her home in New Castle, June 1, 1879, highly respected and loved by all who knew her.

HENRY RUDISEL LENNARD.
(Son.)

Henry Rudisel Lennard, the eldest son of Colonel George W. and Mrs. Clarinda (Woodward) Lennard, was born in New Castle, Henry County, Indiana. August 14, 1853. He was a bright, intelligent youth, possessed of excellent social qualities, who enjoyed the society of his friends and was always full, even to running over, with good humor. He was educated in the public schools of New Castle, and afterwards attended Kentucky University at Lexington, in that State, and Michigan University at Ann Arbor, Michigan.

After completing his education, he took up the study of the law in 1876, at New Castle, having for his preceptor, Judge Joshua H. Mellett, who was never more pleased than when he had under his charge some young man preparing to enter the legal profession. Young Lennard continued to study law during the following two years (1877-78) and was afterwards admitted to the Henry County Bar before Judge Robert L. Polk, presiding judge of the Henry County Circuit Court. He practiced his chosen profession in New Castle for a short time and then turned his attention to mercantile and manufacturing pursuits, which he has since followed, except for a period of several months when he was in the employ of the government as a railway mail clerk, serving from November 13, 1880, to May 5, 1881.

Henry Rudisel Lennard and Letta Gordon, daughter of Milton B. and Sophia Gordon, were married at Metamora, Franklin County, Indiana, January 7, 1880. The parents of Mrs. Lennard are old pioneer residents of Metamora, and the family is probably the most prominent in Franklin County. Mrs. Letta (Gordon) Lennard was born at Metamora and was educated in the public schools of that place and at Asbury, now De Pauw, University, Greencastle, Indiana. After their marriage, Mr. and Mrs. Lennard resided in New Castle, where they had a large circle of relatives and friends, until 1884, when they moved to Mrs. Lennard's old home, Metamora, where they have since resided. They are the parents of two children namely: Edith Gordon, born at New Castle, November 22, 1880; and George Milton, born December 20, 1890. Edith Gordon Lennard, who grew to young womanhood under the watchful care of her devoted parents and who was and is now very prominent in the society of her many friends, at home and abroad, was united in marriage, January 7, 1903, with Frederick H. Wiley, a very active and prominent young business man of Indianapolis, which beautiful, thriving and progressive city is now their home.

Among the chief industries of the timber country of the West, an industry that has assumed great proportions, is the making of handles for shovels, spades, forks, axes, hoes, hammers and numerous other tools and instruments. It is in this business that Mr. Lennard is now engaged, he being the leading member of the Lennard Handle Company, Metamora, Indiana. The product of this factory, which is hardly second to any similar concern in the State, goes mainly under contract to foreign consumers. To the conduct and management of the factory, Mr. Lennard has given and now gives the most assiduous attention but its demands are not allowed to hold him entirely aloof from those affairs which socially and politically engage the efforts of those interested in good government, local, State and National. Hence it is that Mr. Lennard, as a leading Republican of his town, county and district, never fails to participate in the meetings and conventions having for their object the interests and the success of the party.

ASAHEL WOODWARD LENNARD.
(Son.)

One of the most popular of the young men, who figured in the life of New Castle and its immediate neighborhood, was Asahel Woodward Lennard, the second son of Colonel George W. Lennard and Clarinda (Woodward) Lennard, his wife. He was born October 15, 1859, at New Castle and was but a young boy when his lamented father lost his life in the Civil War, at Resaca, Georgia. This boy, "Sale," as he was best known, obtained a part of his education, along with his early associates, in the public schools of New Castle and completed the same at Antioch College, Yellow Springs, Ohio, where he remained as a student for four years.

After finishing his education, he returned to New Castle where he commenced the study of the law with Mellett and Bundy, then one of the leading law firms of Eastern Indiana. He was admitted to the Henry County Bar, December 4, 1880, and in the year 1883 was elected Treasurer of the Corporation of New Castle and was re-elected to the same office in the years 1884 and 1885 without opposition.

He practiced his profession for several years at New Castle and then determined to seek a wider field. After visiting Duluth, Minnesota, and other Northwestern points, he established himself at Pueblo, Colorado, to which growing and prosperous Colorado city he removed in March, 1887. That place has ever since been his home.

On May 21, 1885, he married Anna Agnes Scott, daughter of James Robison and Elizabeth Ann (King) Scott. This lady was born at Champaign, Illinois, June 13, 1862, and was educated at the home schools and in the Chicago Female College, Chicago, Illinois. She is a bright, intelligent woman and the devoted wife of an equally devoted husband.

Mr. Lennard is a prominent and popular citizen of his new home, who holds a warm place in the hearts of a host of friends, and is justly regarded as one of the leading men of the City, County and State. As a lawyer he ranks among the leaders of the bar. He was a member of the Colorado Legislature during the ninth session, 1893, and represented his district, which is one of the most important in Colorado, with credit to himself and honor to his constituents. While a member of the Legislature, he was chairman of the committee on the judiciary and also a member of a number of other leading committees. He has been City Attorney of Bessemer, a manufacturing town adjacent to Pueblo, and was the attorney for the Pueblo Water Trustees. He has also filled several other positions of trust and responsibility. Mr. Lennard was admitted to the Colorado Bar, March 13, 1887. In politics he declares himself to be a high tariff, gold bug, McKinley Republican.

Mr. Asahel W. Lennard is now but little past the meridian of life and is destined probably to become an important factor in the rapid, western civilization with which he has become identified. He seems assured of distinguished civic and political preferment.

LEANDER PERRY MITCHELL.

(Son-in-law.)

Leander Perry Mitchell was born upon his father's farm in Fall Creek Township, Henry County, Indiana, about half way between Mechanicsburg and Middletown, February 5, 1849. His parents were Charles Mitchell and Mary (Black) Mitchell. He worked on his father's farm and attended the public schools in the neighborhood. On May 1, 1864, at the age of fifteen years, he enlisted as a private soldier in Company B, 139th Indiana Infantry, and was mustered into the Army, June 5, 1864. He was mustered out with the regiment September 29, 1864, on account of expiration of term of enlistment. He again enlisted as a private in the 147th Indiana Infantry and went to Richmond, Indiana, for muster in but was rejected on account of his age. This was the last regiment and company which was recruited in Henry County.

In the Winter of 1864-65 he determined to secure, if possible, an education and started to attend the public schools. He taught two Winters at Mechanicsburg; first, as assistant to Walter A. Boor (afterwards a learned and successful physician) of New Castle, who was principal; second, as principal, with William H. Keesling (afterwards the successful merchant, farmer and banker) of Mechanicsburg, as assistant.

Among his students were Erastus L. Elliott, now cashier of the Farmers'

Bank of Middletown, who afterwards served two terms in the General Assembly with honor to himself and to the county; his sister, Ida Elliott, now the wife of Dr. Joseph M. Thurston of Richmond, Indiana; Mattie Jones, now Mrs. Mattie E. S. Charles of Spiceland; Dr. Libbie Weeks, late of Mechanicsburg, deceased; Cassius M. Greenlee, now Judge of the Superior Court of Anderson, Indiana; George L. Swain, attorney-at-law of Middletown; Luther O. Miller of Middletown, a contractor, who built the new Methodist Episcopal Church of New Castle; Lurtin R. Ginn, now an official in the Treasury Department at Washington, D. C., and the present Grand Master of Masons of the District of Columbia; and a number of others who afterwards became useful men and women.

After attending Spiceland Academy for some two years, he entered the Northwestern Christian University (now Butler College) of Indianapolis where he graduated in the Latin-Scientific course. He also graduated in the Law Department of Indiana University at Bloomington. Between terms at college, he rode on horseback once every week from his home in Fall Creek Township to New Castle to recite law to the late Judge Jehu T. Elliott, who had then just retired from the Supreme Bench. In the Fall of 1872 he opened an office at New Castle and began the practice of law, and followed that profession closely until January, 1898. The bar of the Henry Circuit Court was then and has been ever since composed of able lawyers.

On June 4, 1874, he married Bettie E. Woodward, daughter of Dr. Thomas B. and Catharine Woodward, who at that time was a teacher in the public schools of New Castle. On July 31, 1875, but little more than a year after her marriage, Mrs. Mitchell departed this life. The fruit of this marriage was one child who died in infancy. Both mother and child are buried in South Mound Cemetery. Mrs. Mitchell was a bright, sweet, Christian, noble young woman, admired and loved by all who knew her.

On January 6, 1879, he was married to Gertrude Lennard, only daughter of Colonel George W. and Clarinda (Woodward) Lennard. To this union were born two sons, Lennard H., born February 24, 1881, and Bryant S., born December 14, 1887.

In the campaign of 1888, he was the Presidential elector on the Harrison and Morton ticket, for the Sixth Congressional District, which he fully canvassed. In 1890, he was appointed by the Secretary of the Interior, superintendent of the census for the State of Indiana, and had entire charge of the taking of the census of recorded indebtedness of the State, covering the preceding ten years. In 1892 he was an alternate delegate to the national convention which nominated Harrison and Reid. In the campaign of 1896, he was unanimously chosen as member of the Republican State Central Committee from the Sixth Congressional District. In this campaign, after Ex-President Harrison had published his letter stating that he would not be a candidate for President, it is a matter of history that, with the exception of John K. Gowdy, now Consul General at Paris, France, and then State Chairman, Mr. Mitchell did more than any other man in the State to secure in district conventions and in the State convention instructions of delegates to the national convention, for Governor William McKinley. His efforts in that campaign were characterized by energy, zeal and success.

Strange things happen in politics. After Mr. McKinley was elected, Mr.

41

Mitchell became an applicant for appointment to the office of Comptroller of the Treasury. Robert J. Tracewell, then a member of Congress from the Third District, was an applicant for appointment as Associate Justice of the Supreme Court of New Mexico and wrote to Mr. Mitchell for his endorsement for that position, which was given. The President declined to appoint Mr. Tracewell to the position for which he was an applicant on the ground that he would not appoint anyone to that position who was not a resident of the Territory. He declined to appoint Mr. Mitchell, Comptroller of the Treasury, on the ground that he would not appoint anyone to that position who had not been a member of Congress. Both appointments were delayed until the Summer of 1897, when he appointed Mr. Tracewell, without his being an applicant, Comptroller of the Treasury, the position for which Mr. Mitchell was an applicant, and sometime thereafter Mr. Mitchell was tendered the position of Associate Justice of the Supreme Court of New Mexico, the position for which Mr. Tracewell had been an applicant, which was declined. The place was then given to Judge Crumpacker of Indiana and in January, 1898, Mr. Mitchell was appointed Assistant Comptroller of the Treasury, a position corresponding to what was formerly the Second Comptroller of the Treasury. This office he still holds. It is a position of great honor and responsibility and one of the most important offices attached to the Treasury Department. It is practically independent of the Comptroller's Office, has jurisdiction of all fiscal matters pertaining to the War, Navy, and Interior Departments; its decisions are final and no appeal lies from them by the Government; the incumbent should possess legal acumen commensurate with that pertaining to the highest courts in the land. It is a purely judicial position, where legal arguments are made orally or by written briefs, the cases often involving large sums of money. In the discharge of his official duties, Mr. Mitchell has been industrious, painstaking and conscientious and has given good satisfaction.

In November, 1901, the physician attending his wife, who was thought to be slightly indisposed, informed him that she was fatally ill. At first this could scarcely be realized. How often is it true that "In the midst of life we are in death!" She was possessed of a gentle, genial, sunny nature, and her cheerful, hopeful disposition was never more in evidence than during her prolonged struggle with the grim destroyer which continued until the night of April 22, 1902, which brought the end and a release to her warm, sweet spirit. At the time of her decease at her home in Washington, D. C., her husband, her two sons, and her brother Asahel W. Lennard, who had come from Pueblo, Colorado, were with her.

She was born July 22, 1855, at New Castle, which was her home, except when away at college and during her residence in Washington. She was a member of the first class (1875) which graduated from the New Castle Academy. In the Fall of 1875 she entered Antioch College at Yellow Springs, Ohio, at that time ranking in thoroughness and high grade of studies with the best schools in the land, taking the regular classical course. She passed through the Freshman, Sophomore, Junior and the greater part of the Senior year, always standing at the head of her classes, when her health broke down and compelled her, much to her sorrow and that of her friends, to give up her work in college and return to her home. She was a noble woman, possessed of a beautiful Christian character, of strong ability both natural and acquired. No company where she was present could be dull. She was a woman of high ideals, a loyal, generous, sweet-hearted friend, a faithful and devoted wife, an affectionate and indulgent mother. She was admired and loved by all who knew her. Her remains were brought to her home in New Castle, and on Sunday, April 27, 1902, followed by a large assembly of friends who had known her in life, they were laid at rest in South Mound Cemetery. To all who knew her, her life is a sweet and enduring memory.

To Bryant S., the loss of his mother seemed more than he could bear. He could hardly be reconciled to the thought that he would never again see her in this world. On account of his health, after the death of his mother, he went with his uncle to his home in Pueblo, Colorado. On August 1, 1902, he and his father and Lennard H. met in Chicago and together visited the Yellowstone National Park, Salt Lake City, Idaho and other points of interest in the West, and then returned to Pueblo where it was arranged for him to remain and attend a private school during the ensuing year. On September 8th, just three weeks from the day his father and brother left him, word was received that he was dangerously ill. His father started to him immediately but he passed away before he could reach him. By all who knew him he is remembered as of handsome appearance, bright, generous, affectionate, a splendid specimen of a manly boy. His remains were brought to his home in New Castle, where on Monday, September 16th, 1902, they were quietly laid to rest beside his mother.

In a few brief months a pleasant home was shattered, deprived of nearly every ray of sunshine, with no comfort except that which must come from Above.

On page 276 of this History, in the biographical sketch of Samuel Alexander Mitchell, will be found further and fuller reference to Charles and Mary (Black) Mitchell, parents of Leander Perry Mitchell.

LENNARD HARRIS MITCHELL.

(Grandson.)

Lennard Harris Mitchell completed his education at the Dean Academy, Franklin, Massachusetts, twenty seven miles from Boston, where he graduated in June, 1901. In the Fall of the same year he returned to the Academy and took the post graduate course of that institution. On June 23, 1904, he married Bessie Joye, daughter of Judge John M. and Cora (Heritage) Morris, of New Castle. Since his graduation from Dean Academy, he has been connected with the Postoffice Department and he and his wife make their home with his father in Washington, D. C.

In January, 1902, at the request of the Auditor for Cuban affairs at Washington (then in Havana), he was sent to Cuba to assist in straightening out the accounts of the Island. This work had particular reference to the affairs of the Postoffice Department which were being investigated, owing to the peculations of Rathbone and Neely. He remained in Cuba until the following April, when he was called back to Washington on account of the fatal illness of his mother. In the Winter of 1902-3 and again in the Fall of 1903, besides attending to his duties in the Postoffice Department, he found time to attend the law school of the Columbian University (now the George Washington University). He has recently been engaged in the direction and installation of the rural route service in Pennsylvania and Virginia.

CHAPTER XXX

GRAND ARMY POSTS CONTINUED.

ORGANIZATION AND ROSTER OF JOHN R. McCORMACK POST, No. 403, CADIZ—
BIOGRAPHICAL SKETCH OF PRIVATE JOHN ROWDY McCORMACK AND FAMILY
—ORGANIZATION AND ROSTER OF JERRY B. MASON POST, No. 168, KNIGHTS-
TOWN—BIOGRAPHICAL SKETCH OF LIEUTENANT JEROME BONAPARTE MASON
AND FAMILY—ORGANIZATION AND ROSTER OF GEORGE W. RADER POST, No.
110, MIDDLETOWN—BIOGRAPHICAL SKETCH OF SERGEANT GEORGE WASHING-
TON RADER AND FAMILY—ORGANIZATION AND ROSTER OF HARMON RAYL
POST, No. 360, SPICELAND—BIOGRAPHICAL SKETCH OF PRIVATE HARMON
RAYL AND FAMILY—ORGANIZATION AND ROSTER OF THE HENRY COUNTY
ASSOCIATION OF VETERANS OF THE CIVIL WAR.

JOHN R. McCORMACK POST, NO. 403, G. A. R., CADIZ, INDIANA.

John R. McCormack Post, No. 403, Department of Indiana, Grand Army
of the Republic, was organized and instituted at Cadiz, Henry County, Indiana,
June 14, 1885, in Cook's Hall, and was mustered in by Comrade Morrow P. Armstrong of George W. Lennard Post, No. 148, G. A. R., New Castle, Indiana,
mustering officer, assisted by Post Commander, William F. Shelley, who installed
the officers, and George H. Cain, Senior Vice Commander; Asa W. Hatch, Junior
Vice Commander; William S. Bedford, Chaplain; William H. Elliott, Adjutant;
George B. Robson, Officer of the Day; John C. Murray, Officer of the Guard,
and other comrades of George W. Lennard Post, as follows: Thomas J. Burchett,
Henry C. Gordon, Thomas W. Gough, Joseph R. Mullen, Peter Niccum, Lorenzo
D. Shepherd and Harvey W. Swain. The Post was named for and in honor of
the late John Rowdy McCormack of Company I, 69th Indiana Infantry, a sketch
of whose life and military service is fully set forth at the end of this article.

The following named comrades were present at the organization and became
charter members of the Post, viz: Hiram T. Alshouse, Henry Alspaugh, Samuel
Bowers, Samuel Craig, Allen S. Deeter, William M. Gardner, Job B. Ginn,
Patrick H. Hansard, Thomas N. Lewis, Andrew J. McCormack, Noah McCor-
mack, Joseph McKee, Abraham Moore, Joseph O'Neal, John Perry, Henry
Reichart, Ethan S. Taylor and George W. Thompson.

The regular meetings of the Post were held on Wednesday evening of each
week.

The following were the Post officers from the organization in 1885 down to
and including the year 1904. The names of all of the officers are arranged
alphabetically:

COMMANDERS.

Samuel Bowers, Josiah Bradway, George H. Brown, John R. Clevenger, Allen W. Coon, Daniel W. Craig, Samuel Craig, Patrick H. Hansard, Francis M. Lowery, Philander Lowery, John W. McCormack, Noah McCormack, John Perry, Henry Reichart, George W. Thompson.

SENIOR VICE COMMANDERS.

John Baughan, George H. Brown, Abner Cantrell, John R. Clevenger, Allen W. Coon, Samuel Craig, Job B. Ginn, Patrick H. Hansard, Philander Lowery, Abraham Moore, Henry Reichart, Ethan S. Taylor, Henry Thompson.

JUNIOR VICE COMMANDERS.

George H. Brown, Abner Cantrell, John R. Clevenger, Daniel W. Craig. Samuel Craig, Allen S. Deeter, Job B. Ginn, Thomas N. Lewis, Philander Lowery, Samuel McCormack, Henry Reichart, Henry Thompson.

SURGEONS.

John Baughan, Josiah Bradway, John R. Clevenger, Allen W. Coon, Daniel W. Craig, Job B. Ginn, Patrick H. Hansard, John Hill, Alfred Lafferty, Joseph P. McConnell, Abraham Moore, Henry Reichart.

CHAPLAINS.

Josiah Bradway, George H. Brown, Patrick H. Hansard, John Perry.

ADJUTANTS.

Hiram T. Alshouse, Samuel Craig, William M. Gardner, Greenberry W Hedges, Francis M. Lowery, Henry Reichart.

QUARTERMASTERS.

George H. Brown, Josiah Bradway, George W. Thompson.

OFFICERS OF THE DAY.

George H. Brown, Abner Cantrell, Allen W. Coon, Samuel Craig, Allen S. Deeter, Patrick H. Hansard, Philander Lowery, Noah McCormack, Henry Reichart.

OFFICERS OF THE GUARD.

Charles Brown, Daniel W. Craig, William M. Gardner, Job B. Ginn, Francis M. Lowery, Andrew J. McCormack, John W. McCormack, Abraham Moore, John Perry, Henry Reichart, William Shockey, Henry Thompson.

SERGEANTS MAJOR.

Allen W. Coon, Samuel Craig, Patrick H. Hansard, Greenberry W. Hedges, Joseph P. McConnell, Joseph McKee, Henry Reichart, Henry Thompson.

QUARTERMASTER SERGEANTS. ,

Josiah Bradway, Allen W. Coon, Greenberry W. Hedges, Francis M. Lowery, Joseph P. McConnell, Andrew J. McCormack, Henry Reichart, Ethan S. Taylor.

The records of the Department Assistant Adjutant General at Indianapolis show that this Post surrendered its charter, December 16, 1904.

The following is believed to be a complete list or roster of all who have been members of the Post. In the several alphabetical lists of soldiers and sailors, set out elsewhere in this History, will be found a more detailed statement of the service in the Army and Navy of each comrade who is entitled to further mention in the History of Henry County.   An asterisk thus * in front of a name denotes a comrade residing in an adjoining county, therefore there is no further reference to him in the "Alphabetical List" above mentioned.

POST MEMBERS.

Hiram T. Alshouse, Company F, 134th Indiana Infantry.

Henry Alspaugh, Company E, 9th Indiana Cavalry.

Hugh Anderson, Company D, 147th Indiana Infantry.

John Baughan, Company K, 105th Indiana Infantry (Morgan Raid).

Christopher C. M. Bock, Company H, 69th Indiana Infantry; Company H, 147th Indiana Infantry.

Samuel Bowers, Company K, 105th Indiana Infantry (Morgan Raid); Company B, 130th Indiana Infantry.

Josiah Bradway, Company A, 32rd Indiana Infantry.

Charles Brown, Company E, 13th Indiana Infantry, re-organized.

George H. Brown, Company B, 89th Indiana Infantry.

Thomas C. Burton, Company E, 50th Indiana Infantry.

Abner Cantrell, Company A, 2nd West Virginia Infantry.

John R. Clevenger, Company E, 8th Indiana Infantry (three years).

Robert K. Collins, Company B, 8th Indiana Infantry (three months); Company I, 69th Indiana Infantry.

Allen W. Coon, Company D, 36th Indiana Infantry.

Daniel W. Craig, ——————, 15th Indiana Battery.

Samuel Craig, Company E, 8th Indiana Infantry (three years).

Allen S. Deeter, ——————. Record incomplete in this History.

James H. Dowling Company C, 71st New York Infantry.

William M. Gardner, Company G, 69th Indiana Infantry.

Job B. Ginn, Company E, 8th Indiana Infantry (three years).

Jonathan J. Ginn, Company H, 140th Indiana Infantry.

John W. Hammer, Company D, 147th Indiana Infantry.

Patrick H. Hansard, Company F, 14th U. S. C. T.

Lewis Hart, Company K, 105th Indiana Infantry (Morgan Raid).

Greenberry W. Hedges, Company B, 139th Indiana Infantry; Company D, 147th Indiana Infantry.

Joel Hendricks, Company E, 8th Indiana Infantry (three years).

John Hill, Company G, 55th Massachusetts Infantry.

Amos J. Kern, Company B, 42nd Indiana Infantry.

Alfred Lafferty, ——————. Membership honorary on account of having been body servant in the Civil War to Colonel George W. Jackson, 9th Indiana Cavalry.

William Larrowe, Company K, 99th Indiana Infantry.

Thomas N. Lewis, Company A, 36th Indiana Infantry; Company H, 30th Indiana Infantry, re-organized.

Francis M. Lowery, Company I, 69th Indiana Infantry.

Philander Lowery, Company F, 57th Indiana Infantry.

Joseph P. McConnell, Company K, 105th Indiana Infantry (Morgan Raid); Company E, 9th Indiana Cavalry.

Andrew J. McCormack, Company E, 9th Indiana Cavalry.

John W. McCormack, Company D, 147th Indiana Infantry.

Josiah McCormack, Company E, 9th Indiana Cavalry.

*Lafe McCormack, Company I, 111th Indiana Infantry (Morgan Raid).

Noah McCormack, Company C, 36th Indiana Infantry.

Samuel McCormack, Company G, 9th Indiana Cavalry.

Joseph McKee, Company F, 57th Indiana Infantry; Company K, 105th Indiana Infantry (Morgan Raid).

Abraham Moore, Company B, 2nd Indiana Cavalry.

Solomon Myers, Company D, 147th Indiana Infantry.

James L. Newhouse, Company C, 140th Indiana Infantry.

Joseph O'Neal, Company F, 40th Ohio Infantry; Company I. 51st Ohio Infantry

Henry Perry, Company E, 9th Indiana Cavalry.

John Perry, Company B, 5th Indiana Cavalry.

Ezra Pickering, Company B, 130th Indiana Infantry,

Elijah M. Pressnall, Company B, 110th Indiana Infantry (Morgan Raid); Company
A. 30th Indiana Infantry, re-organized.

Henry Reichart, Company C, 36th Indiana Infantry.

William Shockey, —————————. Record incomplete in this History.

Ethan S. Taylor, Company D, 8th Indiana Infantry (three years).

George W. Thompson, Company H, 5th Indiana Infantry (Mexican War); Company C, 36th Illinois Infantry.

Henry Thompson, Company K, 105th Indiana Infantry (Morgan Raid).

Daniel Ulmer, Company I, 79th Pennsylvania Infantry.

Milton Williams, Company B. 139th Indiana Infantry; Company I. 187th Ohio
Infantry.

BIOGRAPHICAL SKETCH OF JOHN ROWDY McCORMACK.

PRIVATE, COMPANY I, 69TH INFANTRY REGIMENT, INDIANA VOLUNTEERS.

John Rowdy McCormack was the eldest son of Melon and Mary McCormack, and was born in Henry County, Indiana, on his father's farm, about two miles west of Cadiz. The parents came from Virginia and settled in Henry County at a very early date.

That the family was full of patriotic blood is shown in the fact that the subject of this sketch was one of four brothers, all of whom served in the Federal Army during the Civil War. The second son, Thomas McCormack, of Company K, 8th Indiana Infantry (three years), was killed at Vicksburg, Mississippi, on the 21st day of May, 1863. The third son, Noah McCormack, of Company C, 36th Indiana Infantry, went through all the campaigns of that well known regiment and upon the muster out of the regiment, September 21, 1864, returned home where he still lives, an honored citizen of the county. The fourth son, Andrew J. McCormack, of Company E, 9th Indiana Cavalry, is a survivor of the ill-fated steamboat, Sultana, which was blown up, set on fire and destroyed on the Mississippi River, April 27, 1865. His recollections of that tragic event are published elsewhere in this work.

John R. McCormack, the subject of this sketch, enlisted in the service of his country in Company I, 69th Indiana Infantry, and was mustered into the service of the United States, August 19, 1862. At the battle of Richmond, Kentucky, August 30, 1862, he was severely wounded and was taken prisoner with the greater part of his regiment. After the regiment had been exchanged and reorganized, it was sent down the Mississippi River to serve under General Grant. After the siege and surrender of Vicksburg, he was taken sick and died at that place, August 11, 1863. His body was buried at Milliken's Bend, Louisiana, but has since been re-interred among the unknown dead in the National Cemetery at Vicksburg.

In 1850 John R. McCormack was married to Nancy Baughan and to them was born one child, now Mrs. Richard Callahan, who lives two and one-half miles southwest of Cadiz. His wife died in 1855. He was a carpenter by trade, honorable and upright, a good citizen, a brave soldier, highly esteemed by all of his friends and neighbors, and his memory preserved and honored by his comrades in arms.

JERRY B. MASON POST, NO. 168, G. A. R., KNIGHTSTOWN, INDIANA.

Jerry B. Mason Post, No. 168, Department of Indiana, Grand Army of the Republic, was organized and instituted at Knightstown, Henry County, Indiana, May 4, 1883, in Bell's Hall, and was mustered in by James R. Carnahan, Department Commander, assisted by Benjamin D. House, Assistant Adjutant General, and Will C. David, Acting Assistant Adjutant General, together with ten or twelve comrades from Samuel H. Dunbar Post, No. 92, Greenfield, Indiana. The Post was named for and in honor of the late Lieutenant Jerome B. Mason (commonly called Jerry B. Mason) of Company F, 84th Indiana Infantry,

John R. McCormack

a sketch of whose life and military service is fully set forth at the conclusion of this article.

The following named comrades were present at the organization and became charter members of the Post, viz: Charles M. Butler, Thomas Clair, Henry M. Crouse, James Daugherty, Francis Dovey, J. Lee Furgason, George P. Graf, Thomas M. Hackleman, John E. Keys, John H. May, George W. Meuser, Harry Watts, Thomas B. Wilkinson and John Wysong.

The regular meetings of the Post are held on the first and third Saturday evenings of each month.

The following were the Post officers from the organization in 1883 down to and including the year 1904. The names of the commanders are arranged in the order in which they served. The names of all other officers are arranged alphabetically.

COMMANDERS.

Thomas B. Wilkinson, John E. Keys, Milton Peden, Harry Watts, Henry M. Crouse. George P. Graf, William H. Edwards, William P. Foulke, Joshua T. C. Welborn, Clinton D. Hawhee, Asa E. Sample, William B. McGavran, Charles M. Butler, Francis Dovey. George P. Graf.

SENIOR VICE COMMANDERS.

De Witt C. Alspaugh, William M. Cameron, Squire Dillee, Francis Dovey, Clinton D. Hawhee, White Heaton, James Hutson, Isaac C. Lemmon, La Fayette Ogborn, Newton Robinson, Albert W. Saint, Asa E. Sample, Joshua T. C. Welborn, Henry C. Woods.

JUNIOR VICE COMMANDERS.

DeWitt C. Alspaugh, Shepperd Bowman, Squire Dillee, William P. Foulke, Thomas M. Hackleman, Clinton D. Hawhee, White Heaton, Joseph P. McConnell, John McNurney. James Steele, Benjamin F. Stratton, Madison Tyer, Henry C. Woods.

SURGEONS.

Henry M. Crouse, William B. McGavran.

CHAPLAINS.

De Witt C. Alspaugh, Robert F. Brewington, William A. Cutler, Francis Dovey. White Heaton, William B. McGavran, John W. Newby.

ADJUTANTS.

John B. Antrim, Charles M. Butler, John A. Craft, William H. Edwards, J. Lee Furgason, Waitsel M. Heaton, Mark M. Morris, Asa E. Sample.

QUARTERMASTERS.

Shepperd Bowman, Francis Dovey, White Heaton, Harry Watts, Henry C. Woods. Robert E. Woods.

OFFICERS OF THE DAY.

Shepperd Bowman, William M. Cameron, George P. Graf, John E. Keys, Levi Kiser, Joseph P. McConnell, Joshua T. C. Welborn.

OFFICERS OF THE GUARD.

James Adams, Squire Dillee, Austin M. Edwards, Leander M. James, Levi Kiser, William F. Lakin, John W. Newby, Benjamin F. Stratton, Madison Tyer, Joshua T. C. Welborn.

SERGEANTS MAJOR.

Charles M. Butler, Amos Crawford, Francis Dovey, George P. Graf, Clinton D. Hawhee. Waitsel M. Heaton, Isaac C. Lemmon, Asa E. Sample, Benjamin F. Stratton, Henry C. Woods, Robert E. Woods, John Wysong.

QUARTERMASTER SERGEANTS.

John B. Antrim, Shepperd Bowman, Charles M. Butler, Waitsel M. Heaton, Isaac C. Lemmon, John McNurney,' John W. Newby, Robert E. Woods.

(Note:—The records of the Post for the years 1892 and 1893 having been lost, it is impossible to give the names of the officers for those two years.)

OFFICERS FOR THE YEAR 1905.

Commander, George P: Graf; Senior Vice-Commander, Francis Dovey; Junior Vice-Commander, John, McNurney; Surgeon, Henry M. Crouse; Chaplain, William B. Mc-Gavran; Adjutant, Asa E. Sample; Quartermaster, Shepperd Bowman; Officer of the Day, Joshua T. C. Welborn; Officer of the Guard, John W. Newby; Sergeant Major, Benjamin F. Stratton; Quartermaster Sergeant, John E. Keys.

The following is believed to be a complete list or roster of all who have been or are now members of the Post. In the several alphabetical lists of soldiers and sailors, set out elsewhere in this History, will be found a more detailed statement of the service in the Army and Navy of each comrade who is entitled to further mention in the History of Henry County. An asterisk, thus *. in front of a name denotes a comrade, residing in an adjoining county, therefore there is no further reference to him in the "Alphabetical List," above mentioned.

POST MEMBERS.

James Adams, Company K, 105th Indiana Infantry (Morgan Raid).

Oliver Allee, Company D, 19th Indiana Infantry; ————, 19th Indiana Battery.

De Witt C. Alspaugh, Company G, 16th Indiana Infantry.

John B. Antrim. Company A, 36th Indiana Infantry.

James Archibald, ————, 23rd Indiana Battery.

Cyrus Armstrong, Company A, 36th Indiana Infantry.

Josiah D. Ayres, Company A, 105th Indiana Infantry (Morgan Raid); Company G, 9th Indiana Infantry.

Warren F. Ballard, Company G, Quartermaster Sergeant, Lieutenant and Quarter-master, 47th Indiana Infantry.

Augustus E. Barrett, Company D, 8th Illinois Infantry (three months); Company D, 8th Illinois Infantry (three years).

*Joseph F. Bartlow, Company C, 9th Indiana Infantry.

Samuel H. Bennett, Company H, 54th Ohio Infantry.

John W. Bishop, Company K, 70th Indiana Infantry; Company B, 33rd Indiana Infantry.

Lycurgus L. Boblett, Company F and Adjutant, 84th Indiana Infantry.

Jacob Bodmer, Company B, 46th New York Infantry; Company C, 32nd Indiana Infantry, re-organized.

James H. Bowles, Company A, 139th Indiana Infantry.

Shepperd Bowman, Company A, 105th Indiana Infantry (Morgan Raid); Company D, 147th Indiana Infantry.

William H. Bowman, Company A, 105th Indiana Infantry (Morgan Raid); Company A, 139th Indiana Infantry.

Robert F. Brewington, Company K, 68th Indiana Infantry.

Daniel Burk, Company A, 57th Indiana Infantry.

Daniel H. Burris, Company A, 105th Indiana Infantry (Morgan Raid); Company A, 139th Indiana Infantry; Unassigned, 22nd Indiana Infantry.

Elwood Burris, Company A, 105th Indiana Infantry (Morgan Raid); Company A, 38th Indiana Infantry.

Charles M. Butler, —————, 19th Indiana Battery.

William R. Callahan, Company A, 36th Indiana Infantry.

John D. Cameron, Company A, 38th Indiana Infantry.

William M. Cameron, Company F, 6th Indiana Infantry (three months); Company F, 84th Indiana Infantry.

Adam P. Campbell, Company C, 147th Indiana Infantry.

James M. Camplin, Company D, 36th Indiana Infantry.

John T. Casely, Company A, 133rd Indiana Infantry.

Daniel C. Catt, Company K, 36th Indiana Infantry; —————, 22nd Indiana Battery.

George Catt, Company I, 3rd Indiana Cavalry.

Thomas Clair, Company I, 3rd Indiana Cavalry.

Timothy Clair, Company K, 36th Indiana Infantry.

Isaac Clevidence, Company E, 13th Maryland Infantry.

Exum Copeland, Company D, 36th Indiana Infantry; Company A, 105th Indiana Infantry (Morgan Raid); Company E, 9th Indiana Cavalry.

John A. Craft, Company A, 57th Indiana Infantry.

Amos Crawford, Company C, 91st Illinois Infantry.

William H. Cross, Company B, 9th Indiana Cavalry.

Henry M. Crouse, Assistant Surgeon, Major and Surgeon, 57th Indiana Infantry.

William A. Cutler, Company C, 145th Illinois Infantry.

Prear Daniel, Company F, 6th Indiana Infantry (three months); Company B, 110th Indiana Infantry (Morgan Raid); Company B, 9th Indiana Cavalry.

*James Daugherty, Company A, 13th Indiana Infantry, re-organized.

Will C. David, Company A, 11th Indiana Infantry.

Amos Davidson, Company D, 147th Indiana Infantry

John E. Deck, Company A, 57th Indiana Infantry.

James I. Dent, Company F, 84th Indiana Infantry.

Luther S. Dillee, Company A, 139th Indiana Infantry.

Squire Dillee, Company A, 57th Indiana Infantry; Company A, 38th Indiana Infantry.

Francis Dovey, —————, 19th Indiana Battery.

Daniel Davidson Duncan, Company A, 105th Indiana Infantry (Morgan Raid); Company A, 139th Indiana Infantry.

George Eagle, Company K, 124th Indiana Infantry.

Austin M. Edwards, Company A, 57th Indiana Infantry.

William H. Edwards, Company B, 19th Indiana Infantry.

William M. Edwards, Company A and Principal Musician, 139th Indiana Infantry.

George D. Englerth, Company D, 36th Indiana Infantry.

·James Fifer, Company K, 105th Indiana Infantry (Morgan Raid); Company B, 130th Indiana Infantry.

John A. Fike, Company F, 20th Indiana Infantry.

Tilghman Fish, Company I, 3rd Indiana Cavalry.

Brice D. Fort, Company A, 105th Indiana Infantry (Morgan Raid); Company A, 139th Indiana Infantry.

William P. Foulke, Company D, 115th Indiana Infantry; Company C, 31st Indiana Infantry.

Henry Frederick, Company C, 9th Indiana Infantry.

J. Lee Furgason, Company A and Quartermaster Sergeant, 139th Indiana Infantry.

Ezra Gillingham, Company I, 21st Regiment, Veteran Reserve Corps.

George P. Graf, Company A, 32nd Indiana Infantry.

Jacob Green, Company A, 57th Indiana Infantry.

Marquis .D. Griffith. Company D, 34th Indiana Infantry.

James Grunden, Company B, 19th Indiana Infantry; Company C. 20th Indiana Infantry, re-organized.

Thomas M. Hackleman. Company F, 84th Indiana Infantry.

James W. Harris, Company H, 2nd Indiana Cavalry.

Martin B. Harris, Company A, 105th Indiana Infantry (Morgan Raid); Company A, 139th Indiana Infantry.

Nathan H. Haskett, Company G, 5th Indiana Cavalry.

Peter Hasting, Company I, 3rd Indiana Cavalry.

Clinton D. Hawhee, Company K, 36th Indiana Infantry.

Waitsel M. Heaton. Company F, 6th Indiana Infantry (three months); Company A and Sergeant Major, 139th Indiana Infantry; Company A. 105th Indiana Infantry (Morgan Raid).

White Heaton, —————, 2nd Indiana Battery.

Charles Hewitt, Company B, 132nd Indiana Infantry.

Orville W. Hobbs, Company G. 133rd Indiana Infantry.

Wilson Hobbs, Major and Surgeon, 85th Indiana Infantry.

John E. Hodson, Company F, 134th Indiana Infantry.

Alonzo Howard, Company L, 16th New York Heavy Artillery; Company L and Company D, 1st New York Mounted Infantry; Company D, 4th New York Cavalry.

Thomas I. Howren, Company D, 36th Indiana Infantry.

Alonzo Hubbard. Company F. 6th Indiana Infantry (three months); Company A. 105th Indiana Infantry (Morgan Raid).

Edwin Hubbard, Company H, 69th Indiana Infantry.

Joseph L. Hubbard, ————————, 19th Indiana Battery.

John W. Hudelson, Company F. 6th Indiana Infantry (three months); Company A, 57th Indiana Infantry.

William H. Hudelson. Company K, 37th Indiana Infantry.

James Hutson, Company G, 5th Indiana Cavalry.

John James, Company A. 57th Indiana Infantry.

Leander M. James. Company A, 139th Indiana Infantry.

Michael Kaltenbach, Company A, 22nd Indiana Infantry.

John E. Keys, Company B, 7th Indiana Cavalry.

William L. Kerr, Company F. 23rd Indiana Infantry; Company B. 13th Indiana Cavalry.

George Kinder. Company A. 57th Indiana Infantry.

Levi Kiser. Company C, 35th Ohio Infantry.

William F. Lakin, Company A, 57th Indiana Infantry.

Isaac C. Lemmon. Company I, 71st Ohio Infantry.

John C. Leonard. Company L, 21st Indiana Infantry re-organized as 1st Heavy Artillery.

William H. Leonard, Company A. 57th Indiana Infantry.

Abraham Level, Company B, 42nd Indiana Infantry.

*John F. McCarty, Company G. 16th Indiana Infantry.

Joseph P. McConnell, Company K. 105th Indiana Infantry (Morgan Raid); Company E, 9th Indiana Cavalry.

Milton McCray. Company K, 132nd Indiana Infantry.

George McDougal, Company A, 30th Indiana Infantry, re-organized.

William B. McGavran. Major and Surgeon, 26th Ohio Infantry.

Samuel H. McGuffin, Company H, 147th Indiana Infantry.

John McNurney. Company A. Major Berry's Battalion. Missouri Cavalry; Company L. 1st Missouri Cavalry.

John H. May. Company A. 57th Indiana Infantry; Company F. 84th Indiana Infantry.

John W. Mayes. Company E. 47th Ohio Infantry.

George W. Meuser, ——————, 2nd Indiana Battery.

Wallace Midkiff, Company B. 156th Indiana Infantry.

William D. Mills, Company A, 105th Indiana Infantry (Morgan Raid); Company A, 139th Indiana Infantry.

David Monticue, Company D, 36th Indiana Infantry.

Solomon R. Monticue, —— ——,——, 4th Indiana Battery.

Abraham Moore, Company B, 2nd Indiana Cavalry.

Mark M. Morris, Company A, 57th Indiana Infantry.

William J. Morris, Company D, 36th Indiana Infantry.

John W. Musselman, Company H, 16th Indiana Infantry.

John W. Newby, Company D, 36th Indiana Infantry.

Thomas E. Niles, Company A, 57th Indiana Infantry.

La Fayette Ogborn, Company G, 12th Illinois Cavalry.

John Oldaker, Company D, 8th Indiana Infantry (three years).

David Osborn, Company D, 147th Indiana Infantry.

George K. Otis, Company I, 54th Indiana Infantry (three months).

Samuel W. Overman, Company B, 42nd Indiana Infantry.

Thomas J. Owens, Company A, 57th Indiana Infantry.

Robert Parker, Company F, 8th Wisconsin Infantry.

Milton Peden, Company K, 36th Indiana Infantry; Colonel, 147th Indiana Infantry.

*Henry Perigo, Company F, 115th Indiana Infantry.

John Perry, Company B, 5th Indiana Cavalry.

*Marion Philpot, Company B, 8th Indiana Infantry (three years).

Elihu Powell, Company F, 6th Indiana Infantry (three months); —— ——. 19th Indiana Battery.

Henry C. Powell, —— ——, 22nd Indiana Battery.

James C. Pratt, Company H, 147th Indiana Infantry.

Isaac Roberts, Company K, 36th Indiana Infantry.

William Roberts, Company C, 120th Indiana Infantry.

Newton Robinson, Company I, 3rd Indiana Cavalry.

Fernandez Rose, Company D, 36th Indiana Infantry; Company H, 30th Indiana Infantry, re-organized.

Albert W. Saint, Company D, 36th Indiana Infantry.

Asa E. Sample, Company B, 54th Indiana Infantry (one year).

Henry Schaffer, Company B, 156th Indiana Infantry.

Jesse R. Schofield, Company F, 69th Ohio Infantry.

Joseph F. Shultz, Company A, 57th Indiana Infantry.

Henry W. Simmons, Company A, 38th Indiana Infantry.

John A. Simmons, Company A, 57th Indiana Infantry; Company K, 132nd Indiana Infantry.

William Simmons, Company A, 57th Indiana Infantry; Company C, 9th Indiana Infantry.

Peter D. Sloat, Company E, 123rd Indiana Infantry.

Thomas M. Smith, Company G, 12th Kentucky Infantry.

James Steele, Company F, 6th Indiana Infantry (three months); Company G, 16th Indiana Infantry.

Valentine Steiner, Company F, 84th Indiana Infantry.

*Corwin Stites, Company K, 31st Indiana Infantry.

*William Stockdale, Company D, 48th Indiana Infantry.

Benjamin F. Stratton, Company A, 105th Indiana Infantry (Morgan Raid); Company A, 139th Indiana Infantry.

Thomas M. Swain, Company D, 36th Indiana Infantry; Company A, 139th Indiana Infantry.

*Martin Trevillian, Company D, 68th Indiana Infantry.

Madison Tyer, Company I, 132nd Indiana Infantry.

Leroy Vallandigham, Company D, 79th Indiana Infantry.

Harry Watts, Company F, 24th Indiana Infantry.

Walter S. Weaver, Company H and Principal Musician, 147th Indiana Infantry.

Joshua T. C. Welborn, Company F, 11th Indiana Infantry; Company F, 84th Indiana Infantry.

Noah B. White, Company A. 57th Indiana Infantry.

James L. Whitesel, Company F, 6th Indiana Infantry (three months); ————————, 2nd Indiana Battery.

Joseph M. Whitesel, Assistant Surgeon, 36th Indiana Infantry.

Thomas B. Wilkinson, Company I, 3rd Indiana Cavalry.

Henry C. Woods, ————————, 19th Indiana Battery.

Jeremiah Woods, Company B, 99th Indiana Infantry.

Robert E. Woods, Company M, 9th Indiana Cavalry.

John Wysong, Company I, 71st Ohio Infantry.

Jerry B. Mason

BIOGRAPHICAL SKETCH OF JEROME BONAPARTE MASON,

SECOND LIEUTENANT COMPANY F, 84TH INFANTRY REGIMENT, INDIANA VOLUNTEERS.

Lieutenant Jerome Bonaparte Mason, son of Daniel and Nellie Mason, was born in the year 1837 at Knightstown, Indiana, but the exact date of his birth is not now obtainable.

He was a brave, intrepid soldier and the first commissioned officer from Knightstown and Wayne Township killed in the Civil War. Because of this fact and to do honor to his name, the G. A. R. Post at Knightstown was named the "Jerry B. Mason Post." "Jerry" being the name by which he was familiarly known, but his correct name was as it appears at the beginning of this sketch. He was instantly killed at the famous battle of Chickamauga, Georgia, on Sunday afternoon, September 20, 1863, at which time, being attached to the staff of General Walter C. Whitaker, who commanded the brigade, be was in the act of carrying a message from the latter's headquarters to the headquarters of the division commander, when he was struck in the forehead by a shell and the top of his head torn off. When at home on furlough a short time before this tragic ending of his life, he told his wife and two or three of his friends a dream he had and at its conclusion stated in bidding them goodbye, "I will never see you again." The vision showed him with particularity the scene of the battle, what he was doing at the time and how he would be killed, and curiously enough was in accordance with the facts as they afterwards transpired.

From boyhood, Mason was interested in military affairs and in 1861 organized a company of zouaves, than which there was no better drilled military organization in the State.

His sword was saved from the battlefield and given into the possession of his widow who died some years ago at Kansas City, Missouri. His wife was a daughter of Dr. Hill who, at the beginning of the Civil War, was a resident of Knightstown. They had but one child, a son, who is still living and engaged in the railroad service in the West. Two of his brothers are also living, Robert W. Mason, who is an inmate of the National Military Home at Danville, Illinois, and George W. Mason, who lives at Edina, Knox County, Missouri. The Post at Knightstown is the owner of an excellent portrait of Lieutenant Mason, whose remains are laid in the National Cemetery at Chattanooga. Tennessee, having been removed there from the battlefield when the National Cemetery was established. Unfortunately, he is among the unknown dead, which results undoubtedly from the fact that he was first buried by the Confederates who occupied the field immediately after the battle.

MASON FAMILY.   **1139220**

The Masons were a martial family. Daniel Mason, Senior, served in the War of 1812-15 with the Virginia Troops and afterwards moved to Indiana, settling at Knightstown. His eight sons were all soldiers of the Civil War. They went into the Federal Army from Knightstown, Ogden and vicinity, except Alexander L. Mason, who at the beginning of the war was in Iowa and entered the army from that State. The record of each is as follows:

Alexander L. Mason, Knightstown. Enlisted at Muscatine, Muscatine County, Iowa. Captain, Company C, First Iowa Infantry. Mustered in May 14, 1861. Killed at Wilson's Creek, Missouri, August 10, 1861.

David A. Mason, Knightstown. Musician, Company F, 84th Indiana Infantry. Mustered in August 26, 1862. Mustered out June 14, 1865.

Daniel Mason, Ogden. Saddler, Company M, 9th Indiana Cavalry. Mustered in March 1, 1864. Mustered out June 9, 1865.

George W. Mason, Knightstown. Private, Company F, 6th Indiana Infantry (three months). Mustered in April 22, 1861. Mustered out August 2, 1861. Again enlisted, Private, Company G, 52nd Indiana Infantry, re-organized. Mustered in February 1, 1862. Veteran. Mustered out September 10, 1865. .

Jerome B. Mason, Knightstown. Second Lieutenant, Company F, 84th Indiana Infantry. Mustered in September 3, 1862. Killed at Chickamauga, Georgia, September 20, 1863.

John Mason, Ogden. Private, Company A, 139th Indiana Infantry. Mustered in June 5, 1864. Appointed Musician. Mustered out September 29, 1864.

Robert W. Mason, Ogden. Private, Company F, 16th Indiana Infantry (one year). Mustered in April 13, 1861. Mustered out May 23, 1862. Again enlisted, Corporal, Company F, 84th Indiana Infantry. Mustered in August 21, 1862. Mustered out June 14, 1865.

Thomas Mason, Knightstown. Private, Company H, 52nd Indiana Infantry, re-organized. Mustered in February 1, 1862. Discharged, disability, September 29, 1862.

GEORGE W. RADER POST, NO. 119, G. A. R., MIDDLETOWN, INDIANA.

George W. Rader Post, No. 119, Department of Indiana, Grand Army of the Republic, was organized and instituted at Middletown, Henry County, Indiana, December 12, 1882, in Odd Fellows Hall, and was mustered in by Joseph P. Iliff, of Sol Meredith Post, No. 55, Richmond, Indiana. The Post was named in honor of the late Sergeant, George W. Rader, of Company E, 8th Indiana Infantry (three years' service), a sketch of whose life and military service is fully set forth at the conclusion of this article.

The following named comrades were present at the organization and became charter members of the Post, viz: John Baker, Samuel Barrett, Jonathan Brattain, Burton W. Castetter, Isaac N. Chenoweth, Enoch Craig, John Dutton, Joseph Dutton, Benjamin H. Davis, Theophilus Everett, James Graham, Joseph Graves, Thomas J. Ginn, Joseph G. Gustin, Abram B. Hopper, David Jones, Josiah McCormack, Peter McKenzie, William M. Moore, Thomas Morton, John A. Mundell, Flemmon T. W. Painter, Collier M. Reed, David Stewart, George W. Tarkleson, Frederick Tykle, Richmond Wisehart, Joseph A. Young.

When the Post was first organized, it held weekly meetings but its ranks have been so thinned by death that only monthly meetings are now held.

The following were the Post officers from the organization in 1882 down to and including the year 1904. The names of the commanders are arranged in the order in which they served. The names of all other officers are arranged alphabetically.

COMMANDERS.

Joseph A. Young, David Jones, Abram B. Hopper, Joseph A. Young, Benjamin H. Davis, Alexander Abernathy, Peter McKenzie, Hiram B. Brattain, Joseph A. Young, John R. Weaver, John Gibson, Isaac H. Miller, Thomas J. Ginn, Jonathan Brattain, Burton W. Castetter, Joseph A. Young, Benjamin H. Davis, Elisha M. Hanby, Andrew J. Fleming, Collier M. Reed.

SENIOR VICE COMMANDERS.

Lafe Bell. Hiram B. Brattain, Jonathan Brattain, Benjamin H. Davis, Andrew J. Fleming, Thomas J. Ginn, Joseph G. Gustin, Elisha M. Hanby, David Jones, Peter McKenzie, Isaac H. Miller, David M. Painter, Collier M. Reed, Sanford Whitworth, Richmond Wisehart.

JUNIOR VICE COMMANDERS.

John Baker, Hiram B. Brattain, Benjamin H. Davis, John Gibson, Thomas J. Ginn, Joseph G. Gustin, Elisha M. Hanby, William H. Morgan, John Mundell, Collier M. Reed, Jacob Warnock.

SURGEONS.

Joseph G. Gustin, Peter McKenzie, Isaac H. Miller, William H. Morgan, Collier M. Reed, James H. Welsh.

CHAPLAINS.

Alexander Abernathy, Perry J. Albright, Benamin H. Davis, John J. Noftsinger, William H. Pierce, George W. Tarkleson.

ADJUTANTS.

Lafe Bell, Burton W. Castetter, Benjamin H. Davis, Abram B. Hopper, David Jones, John R. Weaver, Joseph A. Young, Robert A. Young.

QUARTERMASTERS.

Isaac N. Chenoweth, Benjamin H. Davis, Joseph Dutton, John Gibson, Elisha M. Hanby, Frederick Tykle, John R. Weaver, James H. Welsh, Robert A. Young.

OFFICERS OF THE DAY.

Hiram B. Brattain, Burton W. Castetter, Benjamin H. Davis, John Gibson, Thomas J. Ginn, Elisha M. Hanby, Abram B. Hopper, Thomas Morton, John J. Noftsinger, Charles C. Shedron, John R. Weaver, Richmond Wisehart, Joseph A. Young.

OFFICERS OF THE GUARD.

Jonathan Brattain, George H. Brown, James R. Diltz, Joseph Dutton, John Gibson, Joseph G. Gustin, Amos McGuire, Russell B. Sharp.

SERGEANTS MAJOR.

Isaac H. Miller, William M. Moore, Collier M. Reed, Levi P. Shoemaker, Jacob Warnock.

QUARTERMASTER SERGEANTS.

John Baker, Thomas Morton, Collier M. Reed, Cyrus Van Matre.

OFFICERS FOR THE YEAR 1905.

Commander, Lafe Bell; Senior Vice Commander, Joseph Graves; Junior Vice Commander, Hiram B. Brattain; Surgeon, Peter McKenzie; Chaplain, Cyrus Van Matre; Adjutant, Joseph A. Young; Quartermaster, John R. Weaver; Officer of the Day, Benjamin H. Davis; Officer of the Guard, John J. Noftsinger; Sergeant Major, Jacob Warnock; Quartermaster Sergeant, Collier M. Reed.

42

The following is believed to be a complete list or roster of all, who have been or are now, members 'of the Post. In the several alphabetical lists of soldiers and sailors, set out elsewhere in this History, will be found a more detailed statement of the service in the Army and Navy of each comrade who is entitled to further mention in the History of Henry County.

POST MEMBERS.

Alexander Abernathy, Company G, 21st Indiana Infantry; Company M, 9th Indiana Calvary.

James T. Abshire, Company F, 2nd Indiana Cavalry.

Perry J. Albright, Company B, 110th Ohio Infantry.

Henry Alspaugh, Company E, 9th Indiana Cavalry.

George P. Atkinson, Company C, 36th Indiana Infantry.

John Baker, Company E, 1st Heavy Artillery, U. S. C. T.

Philip Barkdull, Company I, 142nd Indiana Infantry.

Philip N. Barrett, Company I, 193rd Ohio Infantry.

Samuel Barrett, Company B, 118th Indiana Infantry.

John G. Bartow, Company B, 139th Indiana Infantry; Company H, 147th Indiana Infantry.

Benjamin F. Benbow, Company G, 84th Indiana Infantry.

Lafe Bell, Company F, 53rd Kentucky Infantry.

David Bowers, Company H, 147th Indiana Infantry.

Samuel Bowers. Company K, 105th Indiana Infantry (Morgan Raid); Company B, 130th Indiana Infantry.

George W. Brandon, Company C, 109th Indiana Infantry (Morgan Raid); Company G, 7th Indiana Cavalry.

Hiram B. Brattain, Company B, 8th Indiana Infantry (three months); Company H, 69th Indiana Infantry.

Jonathan Brattain, Company E, 34th Indiana Infantry.

Thomas C. Burton. Company E, 50th Indiana Infantry.

Silas Byram, Company K, 34th Ohio Infantry; Company G, 17th Regiment, V. R. Corps.

John B. Campbell, ————, 4th Indiana Battery.

Burton W. Castetter, Company B, 48th Indiana Infantry.

Isaac N. Chenoweth, Company F, 124th Indiana Infantry.

John R. Clevenger, Company E, 8th Indiana Infantry (three years).

Jonathan J. Clevenger, Company G, 134th Indiana Infantry.

Robert K. Collins. Company B, 8th Indiana Infantry (three months); Company I. 69th Indiana Infantry.

Adam Eli Conn. Company F, 57th Indiana Infantry; ————, 25th Indiana Battery.

Imla W. Cooper, Company D, 147th Indiana Infantry.

Enoch Craig, Company K, 105th Indiana Infantry (Morgan Raid); Company E, 8th Indiana Infantry (three years).

Samuel Craig, Company E, 8th Indiana Infantry (three years).

Peter Crasher, Company K, 105th Indiana Infantry (Morgan Raid); Company E. 8th Indiana Infantry (three years).

Benjamin H. Davis, Company C, 155th Indiana Infantry.

James R. Diltz, Company I, 44th Indiana Infantry.

William Downs, Company D, 2nd Indiana Cavalry.

John Dutton, ————, 3rd Ohio Independent Battery.

Joseph Dutton, Company H. 69th Indiana Infantry.

Peter Eaton, Company G, 84th Indiana Infantry.

Richard J. Edleman, ————, 12th Indiana Battery.

Cyrus Ellingwood, Company I, 8th Indiana Cavalry, re-organized.

Theophilus Everett, -————, Magruder's Battery (Mexican War); Company D, 2nd Indiana Cavalry; Company K, 124th Indiana Infantry.

Andrew J. Fleming, Company E, 8th Indiana Infantry (three years).

William R. Fleming, Company E, 8th Indiana Infantry (three years).

William M. Gardner, Company G, 69th Indiana Infantry.

John Gibson. Company K, 12th Indiana Cavalry.

Job B. Ginn, Company E, 8th Indiana Infantry (three years).

Jonathan J. Ginn, Company H, 140th Indiana Infantry.

Thomas J. Ginn, Company F, 57th Indiana Infantry.

Richard S. Gossett, Company G, 17th Indiana Infantry.

William Gossett. Company B, 8th Indiana Infantry (three months); Company E, 8th Indiana Infantry (three years).

James Graham, Company H, 69th Indiana Infantry.

Joseph Graves. Company H. 69th Indiana Infantry.

William Griffith. Company E. 40th Indiana Infantry.

Isaac Grove, Company K, 8th Indiana Infantry (three months); Company H, 69th Indiana Infantry; Company F, 124th Indiana Infantry.

Joseph G. Gustin, Company H. 140th Indiana Infantry.

Elisha M. Hanby, Company F, 53rd Indiana Infantry.

Henry W. Higley, Company G, 3rd Missouri Cavalry.

John Hodson, Company E, 8th Indiana Infantry (three years).

Jacob Holsinger, Company G, 110th Ohio Infantry.

Abram B. Hopper, Company G, 39th Ohio Infantry.

Herbert Hunt, Company C, 57th Indiana Infantry.

Joseph Hurst, Company G, 17th Indiana Infantry.

William H. Jacobs, Company A, 91st Ohio Infantry.

George W. Jennings, Company K, 16th Indiana Infantry.

Gary Jester, Company E, 8th Indiana Infantry (three years).

Stevan John, Company L, 8th Indiana Cavalry, re-organized.

David Jones, Company F, 124th Indiana Infantry.

Richard J. Laboyteaux, Company H, 69th Indiana Infantry.

Elza Lanham, Company K, 105th Indiana Infantry (Morgan Raid).

William Latchaw, Company D. 87th Indiana Infantry; Company D, 42nd Indiana Infantry.

Alfred D. W. Leavens, Company K, 8th Illinois Cavalry.

Thomas N. Lewis. Company A, 30th Indiana Infantry; Company H. 30th Indiana Infantry, re-organized.

Gambral Little, Company B, 130th Indiana Infantry.

Joseph P. McConnell, Company K, 105th Indiana Infantry (Morgan Raid); Company E, 9th Indiana Cavalry.

Andrew J. McCormack, Company E, 9th Indiana Cavalry.

Josiah McCormack, Company E, 9th Indiana Cavalry.

Amos McGuire, Company B, 12th Indiana Infantry.

Peter McKenzie, Company E, 91st Ohio Infantry.

Jonathan May, Company E, 8th Indiana Infantry (three years).

David T. Miller, Company I. 9th New Jersey Infantry.

Isaac H. Miller. ————. Record incomplete in this History.

Samuel H. Mills, Company H. 140th Indiana Infantry.

Andrew J. Minnick, Company H, 69th Indiana Infantry.

Samuel A. Mitchell, Company E, 8th Indiana Infantry (three years).

Abraham Moore, Company B. 2nd Indiana Cavalry.

William M. Moore, Company C. 109th Indiana Infantry (Morgan Raid); Company F, 124th Indiana Infantry.

William H. Morgan, Company E. 38th Illinois Infantry; ————. U. S. Signal Corps.

Thomas Morton, Company F, U. S. Mounted Rifles (Mexican War); Company C and Colonel, 20th Ohio Infantry; Colonel, 81st Ohio Infantry.

John A. Mundell, Company E, 9th Indiana Cavalry.

Lewis E. Myers, Company H, 153rd Indiana Infantry.

Solomon Myers, Company D, 147th Indiana Infantry. .

Isaac Needham, Company G, 7th Indiana Cavalry; Company F, 7th Indiana Cavalry, re-organized.

Joshua Needham, Company E, 19th Indiana Infantry; Company E, 20th Indiana Infantry, re-organized.

William H. Nelson, Company E, 69th Ohio Infantry; Company M, 13th Ohio Cavalry.

Peter Netz, Company A, 54th Indiana Infantry (one year); Company D, 2nd Ohio Heavy Artillery.

Eusebius A. L. Nixon, —————, 13th Indiana Battery.

John J. Noftsinger, Company K, 188th Ohio Infantry.

David M. Painter, Company E, 9th Indiana Cavalry.

Flemmon T. W. Painter, Company E, 8th Indiana Infantry (three years); Company F, 10th Indiana Cavalry.

William M. Paty, Company C, 117th Indiana Infantry; Company D, 35th Indiana Infantry.

Jesse Pearson, Company A, 19th Indiana Infantry; Company I, 20th Indiana Infantry, re-organized.

Alfred M. Pence, Company H, 140th Indiana Infantry.

William H. Pierce, Company H, 84th Indiana Infantry.

Collier M. Reed, Company C, 8th Indiana Infantry (three months).

Daniel Rent, Company E, 8th Indiana Infantry (three years).

George D. Rent, Company A, 139th Indiana Infantry.

John H. Rent, Company F, 57th Indiana Infantry.

Levi Ricks, Company K, 105th Indiana Infantry (Morgan Raid); Company H, 140th Indiana Infantry.

Afred Riggs, Company E, 8th Indiana Infantry (three years).

William H. H. Rohrback, Company E, 1st Maryland Potomac Home Brigade Infantry.

George W. Sanders, —————, 25th Indiana Battery.

Henry Saunders, Company H, 140th Indiana Infantry.

Loveless Seward, Company B, 2nd Indiana Cavalry; Company B, 2nd Indiana Cavalry, re-organized.

Russell B. Sharp, Company F, 66th Ohio Infantry.

Charles C. Shedron, Company H, 69th Indiana Infantry.

John W. Sherry, Company H, 8th Indiana Infantry (three months); Company D, 2nd Indiana Cavalry; Company I, 8th Regiment, 1st Army Corps (Hancock's Veteran Corps).

William P. Sherry, Company K, 36th Indiana Infantry; Company H, 30th Indiana Infantry, re-organized.

John M. Shoemaker, Company H, 69th Indiana Infantry.

John P. Shoemaker, Company C, 109th Indiana Infantry (Morgan Raid); Company B, 134th Indiana Infantry.

Levi P. Shoemaker, Company E, 8th Indiana Infantry (three years).

John W. Shroyer, Company D, 84th Indiana Infantry.

David Stewart, Company G, 17th Indiana Infantry.

William K. Sweet, Company G, 40th Ohio Infantry; Company K, 51st Ohio Infantry.

George W. Tarkleson, Company E, 8th Indiana Infantry (three years).

Ethan S. Taylor, Company D, 8th Indiana Infantry (three years).

Frederick Tykle, Company G and I, 4th Infantry U. S. A. (Mexican War); Company B, 8th Indiana Infantry (three months); Company E, 8th Indiana Infantry (three years); Company C, 109th Indiana Infantry (Morgan Raid).

Cyrus Van Matre, Company B, 8th Indiana Infantry (three months); Company E, 8th Indiana Infantry (three years).

Joseph Walling, Company B, 134th Indiana Infantry.

Noah W. Warner, Company B, 8th Indiana Infantry (three months); Company H, 69th Indiana Infantry.

Jacob Warnock, Company C, 109th Indiana Infantry (Morgan Raid); Company G, 7th Indiana Cavalry.

John R. Weaver, Company E, 9th Indiana Cavalry.

James H. Welsh, Assistant Surgeon U. S. A.; Assistant Surgeon 185th Ohio Infantry.

William H. West, Company E, 8th Indiana Infantry (three years); Company C. 109th Indiana Infantry (Morgan Raid); Company F, 124th Indiana Infantry.

John W. Whitworth, Company E, 8th Indiana Infantry (three years).

Sanford Whitworth, Company G, 7th Indiana Cavalry; Company F, 7th Indiana Cavalry, re-organized.

Robert H. Wilson, Company C, 156th Ohio Infantry.

David E. Windsor, Company I, 99th Indiana Infantry.

Richmond Wisehart, Company F, 57th Indiana Infantry.

William Wisehart, Company H, 69th Indiana Infantry.

Albert N. Yost, Company B, 8th Indiana Infantry (three months); Company G, 84th Indiana Infantry; Company K, 57th Indiana Infantry.

Joseph A. Young, Company C, 109th Indiana Infantry (Morgan Raid); Company G, 7th Indiana Cavalry.

Robert A. Young, Company B, 139th Indiana Infantry; Company H, 147th Indiana Infantry.

BIOGRAPHICAL SKETCH OF GEORGE WASHINGTON RADER.

SERGEANT, COMPANY E, 8TH INFANTRY REGIMENT, INDIANA VOLUNTEERS (THREE
YEARS).

Jesse Rader, the father of the subject of this sketch, was born in Rockingham
County, Virginia, March 4, 1806. In 1832 he was united in marriage with Diana
Hoover, daughter of a wealthy farmer of Rockingham County. In 1835 they
migrated to Indiana and entered one hundred acres of land in Henry County,
immediately south of Middletown. Very little of the land was at that time
cleared, most of it being heavily timbered. Middletown was then composed of a
few log houses, a postoffice, blacksmith shop and a general store. The Raders
commenced housekeeping in a log cabin but soon built a two-story house of
hewed logs, and this in those early days was considered a rather pretentious
dwelling. They both worked at clearing the farm and raising such produce as
they could dispose of, the nearest markets being Columbus and Cincinnati, Ohio.

After their land had been all cleared, forty acres of woodland were added to
it and here they continued to reside, leading quiet and uneventful but honorable
and useful lives. They administered to the sick and assisted in the last rites to
the dead, comforted those in trouble and exercised a broad charity that knew no
distinction of person or creed. Churches and schools were few and scattered but
their children received the best education the locality afforded and the home
was thrown open to worshippers of God and was made the circuit rider's stopping
place at which regular religious services were held.

To the union of Jesse and Diana (Hoover) Rader were born four daughters
and one son. Amanda, the oldest daughter, was married in 1852 to Robert R.
Van Winkle, who lived in the Middletown neighborhood. He became a soldier
of the Civil War, enlisting in Company H, 69th Indiana Infantry. He was
mustered into the service of the United States, as a private, August 19, 1862, and
participated in all the marches, skirmishes and battles of his regiment until
mustered out May 23, 1865. Sarah, the second daughter, was married in 1855
to Dr. David Toops. Mary, the youngest daughter, was married in 1867 to
Madison Grose. The last named was a soldier of the Civil War, whose services
are recounted more at length in connection with the life of his father, General
William Grose, in the chapter of this History relating to General Officers.

Mr. and Mrs. Jesse Rader were members of the United Brethren Church
and devout Christians. After the marriage of their daughters and the death of
their only son in the Civil War, feeling themselves growing too old for the
labors of the farm, they sold it and bought property in Middletown, where they
retired for the remainder of their lives. Jesse Rader died in March, 1885, and
his widow, Diana (Hoover) Rader, died four years later, in May, 1889.

GEORGE WASHINGTON RADER.

George Washington Rader, the subject of this sketch, was the only son of
Jesse and Diana (Hoover) Rader and was born on his parents' farm near Middletown, Henry County, Indiana, August 17, 1841, where he grew to manhood,
assisting in the work of the farm and receiving such education as the schools of

George W. Rader

Middletown afforded. On the threshold of maturity, he was met by the country's call to arms and with the ardor of youth, he plunged into that mighty struggle. He was active in recruiting and organizing what became Company E, 8th Indiana Infantry, three years' service, and was himself mustered into the service of the United States, as a Sergeant of that company, September 5, 1861. He was in ill health during much of his service in the army but never faltered in the performance of duty. He participated in all the marches, skirmishes and battles of his regiment until the 22nd day of May, 1863, when, in the general assault on Vicksburg, one of his legs was broken near the knee by a minie ball. He was taken to the hospital at the Furgason House where the leg was amputated. The injury was mortal and five days later, on May 27, 1863, he passed away and his remains were buried on the battlefield by his comrades. Thus ended the brave and youthful life of one who had been the hope and joy of his parents.

After the war, when a grateful people established the National Cemetery at . Vicksburg as a burial place for the honored dead who had fallen in the struggle for possession of that place, the remains of George Washington Rader were removed from their original burial place and reinterred in the National Cemetery, in Section G, Grave No. 4965.

When the armed hosts of the nation had conquered peace, his returned comrades remembered the gallant young soldier and perpetuated his memory in the name of the George W. Rader Post, No. 119, Grand Army of the Republic.

WILLIAM J. HILLIGOSS.

Connected with the Rader family by marriage was that meritorious soldier of the Civil War, William J. Hilligoss. He was of German-Scotch ancestry but was himself born in Rush County, Indiana, October 3, 1837. He removed to Madison County, Indiana, with his father, where he worked on the farm and was educated in the district schools and at the Marion Academy.

During the Civil War, he enlisted in Company G, 75th Indiana Infantry, and was mustered into the service of the United States, as a Sergeant of the company, July 28, 1862. His regiment was brigaded with the 87th and 101st Indiana Infantry, constituting the famous "Indiana Brigade," which was the 2nd Brigade, 3rd Division, 14th Army Corps, Army of the Cumberland. He participated with his regiment in the Tullahoma Campaign and the march towards Chattanooga and was wounded at Chickamauga, Georgia, September 20, 1863. During the Atlanta Campaign, he especially distinguished himself. He participated in Sherman's "March to the sea," and the campaign through the Carolinas and the final events of the war. April 26, 1864, he was promoted First Lieutenant of his company and was mustered out of the service June 8, 1865.

In August, 1862, a few days after his enlistment in the army, he was united in marriage with Elizabeth Rader, the third daughter of Jesse and Diana (Hoover) Rader. After his return from the war, they resided at Middletown, where for six years Mr. Hilligoss was engaged in business. They then moved to Bluffton, Wells County, where he practiced law. In 1877 he took charge of the Huntington Democrat, as business manager and editor but sold out the business in 1885. In 1882 he was elected to the Indiana State Senate from the district composed of Huntington and Wells counties. In politics he had been a

Republican until 1872 when, in common with many others, during the liberal movement of that time, he joined the Democrats. In 1886 Mr. Hilligoss bought an interest in the Anderson Herald and moved with his family to that city. He was in charge of the paper for a short time only, for in December, 1886, he was appointed Chief of the Eastern Division, in the Pension Department, Washington City, where they went to live. In 1889 Mr. and Mrs. Hilligoss returned to Indiana, where he bought an interest in the Muncie Herald and afterwards engaged in the law and real estate business in that city until his death which occurred January 19, 1901.

During their residence at Middletown, Henry County, two daughters were born to Mr. and Mrs. Hilligoss. Luetta, the younger daughter, was married in January, 1887, to W. G. McEdward, an official of the Erie Railroad. In June of the same year, the elder daughter, De Lenna, died in Washington, D. C.

Mr. Hilligoss was, during his later years, greatly interested in the cause of temperance and religion. He was an earnest and devout member of the Methodist Episcopal Church. Upon his death, the funeral ceremonies were held in that church under the auspices of the Masonic Fraternity and the Grand Army of the Republic, of both of which organizations he was a member. His remains were interred at Anderson.

HARMON RAYL POST, NO. 360, G. A. R., SPICELAND, INDIANA.

Harmon Rayl Post, No. 360, Department of Indiana. Grand Army of the Republic, was organized and instituted at Spiceland, Henry County, Indiana, June 17, 1884, and was mustered in by Colonel Edward H. Wolfe, of Joel Wolfe Post, No. 81, Rushville, Rush County, Indiana, assisted by Thomas J. Lindley, of Lookout Post, No. 133, Noblesville, Hamilton County, Indiana. The Post was named for and in honor of Harmon Rayl, late of Company A, 36th Indiana Infantry, a sketch of whose life and military service is fully set forth at the conclusion of this article.

The following named comrades were present at the organization and became charter members of the Post, viz: Samuel Berry, Jesse Bunker, John F. Camplin, George W. Conrad, Francis M. Crull, James Davy, Martin Deem, John Eastridge, Hugh L. English, Alpheus Fawcett, Andrew Fifer, Nathan Foster, Clarkson Gordon, John N. Leamon, William H. Lewis, Charles H. C. Moore, Louis P. Moore, William A. Pate, William Reynolds, William Rhinewalt, Nelson G. Smith, John A. Spencer, Thomas M. Swain and Thomas B. Van Dyke.

The regular meetings of the Post are held on the first and third Saturday nights of each month.

In February, 1892, the records, paraphernalia and other property of the Post were destroyed by fire. There has been no sergeant major nor quartermaster sergeant of this Post since the fire, which is no doubt owing to the small membership of the Post and for this reason neither of these officers is enumerated in the history of the Post. The fire, unfortunate and disastrous as it was, did not dispel the ardor of its members. The ruins which they sadly contemplated only served to give them fresh strength and from that fatal hour down to the present time, the Post has kept its loyalty and integrity of purpose and today, though small in numbers, it ranks in comparative strength with any other Post in the Department of Indiana.

The following were the Post officers from the organization in 1884 down to and including the year 1904. The names of all of the officers are arranged alphabetically.

COMMANDERS.

George P. Beach. James W. Black. William L. Cooper, Alpheus Fawcett. Nathan Foster, Clarkson Gordon, Micajah C. Gordon, Erie Lamb. Eli F. Millikan, Frank Millis. William Rhinewalt, Albert W. Saint, John A. Spencer. Thomas E. Taylor. Johnson A. White, Richmond Wisehart.

SENIOR VICE COMMANDERS.

George P. Beach, Wesley Copeland, John N. Leamon, Frank Millis, Peter Rifner. John A. Spencer, Thomas E. Taylor.

JUNIOR VICE COMMANDERS.

William D. Ball, James Davy, Alpheus Fawcett, Nathan Foster, Erie Lamb, Peter Rifner. John A. Spencer, Thomas E. Taylor.

SURGEONS.

William D. Ball, George P. Beach, John Eastridge, Andrew J. Sprong, Robert A. Smith. Thomas E. Taylor, Johnson A. White.

CHAPLAINS.

James W. Black, William A. Darling, Clarkson Gordon. Erie Lamb, Nelson G. Smith.

ADJUTANTS.

Clarkson Gordon, Eli F. Millikan, Peter Rifner.

QUARTERMASTERS.

George P. Beach, James W. Black. Clarkson Gordon.

OFFICERS OF THE DAY

Alpheus Fawcett, Nathan Foster.

OFFICERS OF THE GUARD.

Wesley Copeland, John Eastridge. William Jenkins, Erie Lamb. John Millis, John A. Spencer, Thomas E. Taylor.

(The foregoing record of officers is from and including the meeting held in John Eastridge's harness shop, March 26, 1892, and the meeting held in the street, May 14, 1892. Officers for 1892 not given, the records having been destroyed by fire. The commauders, however, are given from the organization of the Post, the same having been compiled from the records of the Department Assistant Adjutant General at Indianapolis).

OFFICERS FOR THE YEAR 1905.

Commander, Erie Lamb; Senior Vice Commander, Thomas E. Taylor; Junior Vice Commander, Frank Millis; Surgeon, Orville W. Hobbs; Chaplain, James W. Black; Adjutant. Eli F. Millikan; Quartermaster, Clarkson Gordon; Officer of the Day. Nathan Foster; Officer of the Guard, John A. Spencer.

The following is believed to be a complete list or roster of all who have been or are now, members of the Post. In the several alphabetical lists of soldiers and sailors, set out elsewhere in this History, will be found a more detailed statement of the service in the Army and Navy of each comrade who is entitled to further mention in the History of Henry County.

POST MEMBERS.

Alexander Abernathy, Company G, 21st Indiana Infantry; Company M, 9th Indiana Calvary.

William T. Addison, Company G, 16th Indiana Infantry.

William D. Ball, Company I, 84th Indiana Infantry.

George P. Beach, Company A, 36th Indiana Infantry

David W. Berry, Company F, 84th Indiana Infantry.

Samuel Berry, Company B, 9th Indiana Cavalry.

James W. Black, Company B, 139th Indiana Infantry; Company H, 147th Indiana Infantry.

Seely A. Black, Company C, 57th Indiana Infantry.

Esley R. Brandon, Company B, 71st Ohio Infantry.

Francis M. Brown, Company F, 1st U. S. Sharpshooters.

George R. Bundy, Company D, 36th Indiana Infantry.

Jesse Bunker, Company A, 36th Indiana Infantry; Company C, 147th Indiana Infantry.

Zachariah Burden, Company F, 8th U. S. C. T.

Cary Campbell, ————————. Record incomplete in this Historq.

John F. Camplin, Company D, 36th Indiana Infantry.

William H. Chance, ————————. Record incomplete in this History.

Joel Collins, Company A, 139th Indiana Infantry.

George W. Conrad, Company A, 36th Indiana Infantry; Company H, 30th Indiana Infantry, re-organized.

Eli Coon, Company H, 72nd Indiana Infantry; Company A, 44th Indiana Infantry.

John Coon, Company I, 3rd Indiana Cavalry.

William L. Cooper, Company A, 105th Indiana Infantry (Morgan Raid); Company A, 139th Indiana Infantry.

Wesley Copeland, Company B, 139th Indiana Infantry.

Thomas J. Cox, Company I, 37th Indiana Infantry.

Francis M. Crull, Company H, 8th Iowa Infantry; Company E, 106th Indiana Infantry (Morgan Raid).

William A. Darling, Company B, 139th Indiana Infantry; Company H, 147th Indiana Infantry.

James Davy, Company C, 47th Indiana Infantry.

Martin Deem, Company A, 36th Indiana Infantry.

Marshall Dill, Company B, 139th Indiana Infantry.

John Eastridge, Company G, 147th Indiana Infantry.

Hugh L. English, Company B, 19th Indiana Infantry.

Alpheus Fawcett, Company G, 84th Indiana Infantry; Company H, 140th Indiana Infantry.

Andrew Fifer, Company B, 89th Indiana Infantry.

Nathan Foster, Company I, 84th Indiana Infantry.

Frederick E. Glidden, Company I, 84th Indiana Infantry.

Truman Goldsbary, Company A, 36th Indiana Infantry.

Clarkson Gordon, Company A, 36th Indiana Infantry; Company A, 4th Regiment, 1st Army Corps (Hancock's Veteran Corps).

Micajah C. Gordon, Company D, 36th Indiana Infantry.

Thomas Gray, ————————, 4th Indiana Battery.

William C. Hall, Company A, 36th Indiana Infantry.

Thomas S. Haugh, Company K, 52nd Indiana Infantry, re-organized.

John R. Henry, Company A, 36th Indiana Infantry.

Branson Hiatt, Company A, 105th Indiana Infantry (Morgan Raid); ————————, 4th Indiana Battery.

Orville W. Hobbs, Company G, 133rd Indiana Infantry.

William Jenkins, Company K, 14th U. S. C. T.

John D. Julian, Company C, 36th Indiana Infantry.
John Kirby, Company E and H, 92nd Ohio Infantry.
Allen M. Kirk, Company B, 98th Ohio Infantry.
Erie Lamb, Company D, 36th Indiana Infantry.
Thomas Lawrence, Company C, 28th U. S. C. T.
John N. Leamon, Company B, 54th Indiana Infantry (one year).
James J. Lewis, ————. Record incomplete in this History.
William H. Lewis, Company A, 36th Indiana Infantry.
Willard H. Loring, ————. Record incomplete in this History.
Dwight G. Loucks, Company H, 112th New York Infantry.
Lambert Macy, ————, 19th Indiana Battery.
William H. Macy, Company D, 36th Indiana Infantry.
Eli F. Millikan, Company C, 36th Indiana Infantry.
Frank Millis, Company A, 139th Indiana Infantry.
Henry Modlin, Company C, 28th U. S. C. T.
Sonney Modlin, Company B, 28th U. S. C. T.
Charles H. C. Moore, Company A, 36th Indiana Infantry; Company K, 11th Indiana
Infantry.
Josiah B. Moore, Company A, 36th Indiana Infantry; Company H. 30th Indiana
Infantry, re-organized.
Louis P. Moore, Company K, 67th Illinois Infantry; Company A, 139th Indiana
Infantry.
William B. Newby, Company D, 36th Indiana Infantry.
King Outland, Company A, 28th U. S. C. T.
William A. Pate, Company H, 69th Indiana Infantry.
Amos E. Pennington, Company B, 110th Indiana Infantry (Morgan Raid); Company A, 139th Indiana Infantry.
Albert W. Poarch, Company D, 33rd Indiana Infantry.
Henry C. Powell, ————, 22nd Indiana Battery.
Amos Ray, ————. Record incomplete in this History.
Henry C. Reece, Company B, 3rd North Carolina Infantry.
William Reynolds, Company I, 69th Indiana Infantry.
William Rhinewalt, ————. 18th Indiana Battery.
Peter Rifner, Company I, 84th Indiana Infantry; Troop G, 6th Cavalry, U. S. A.
Albert W. Saint, Company D, 36th Indiana Infantry.
Nelson G. Smith, Company F, 99th Indiana Infantry; Company F, 48th Indiana
Infantry.
Robert A. Smith, Company A, 57th Indiana Infantry.
David Spencer, Company D, 36th Indiana Infantry.
John A. Spencer, Company D, 36th Indiana Infantry.
Andrew J. Sprong, Company G, 36th Indiana Infantry.
James M. Starbuck, Company D, 147th Indiana Infantry.
Benjamin A. Stewart, Company C, 82nd Indiana Infantry.
John Stigleman, Company A, 36th Indiana Infantry.
Thomas M. Swain, Company D, 36th Indiana Infantry; Company A, 139th Indiana
Infantry.
Thomas E. Taylor, Company K, 54th Indiana Infantry (one year); Company B. 21st
Indiana Infantry re-organized as 1st Heavy Artillery.
William Trail, Company I, 28th U. S. C. T.
Nathan Upham, Company G, 84th Indiana Infantry.
Thomas B. Van Dyke, Company I, 84th Indiana Infantry.
Johnson A. White, Company E, 87th Ohio Infantry.
Henry B. Wiggins, Company K, 37th Indiana Infantry.
Richmond Wisehart, Company F, 57th Indiana Infantry.
John R. Winkler, Company C, 8th Kentucky Infantry.
Isaac N. Wright, Company D, 147th Indiana Infantry.
James S. Young, Company I, 84th Indiana Infantry; Company K, 57th Indiana
Infantry.

BIOGRAPHICAL SKETCH OF HARMON RAYL. •

PRIVATE, COMPANY A, 36TH INFANTRY REGIMENT, INDIANA VOLUNTEERS.

Harmon Rayl was born in Guilford County, North Carolina, October 4, 1839, and in early childhood came with his parents, Zadoc and Delilah Rayl, to Henry County, where he grew to manhood, working on his father's farm, two miles southwest of Spiceland. He attended the country and town schools during the Winter months and obtained a fair education for the time in which he lived. Having become of age a short time prior to the memorable Presidential contest of 1860, he had the privilege of casting his first vote for Abraham Lincoln.

In the Summer of the following year, when President Lincoln called for three hundred thousand volunteers, Harmon Rayl became aroused to the gigantic nature of the struggle to preserve the Union and resolved to give all the aid within his power to the President, whom he had helped to elect. He enlisted in Company A, 36th Indiana Infantry, on September 16, 1861, and participated in all the campaigns of that noted regiment up to and including the battle of Lookout Mountain, Tennessee. Here he was greatly exposed to the inclemency of the weather and subjected to such terrible hardships during the campaign, that he was at last taken ill with brain fever, which terminated his life at Whitesides, Tennessee, December 18, 1863.

His remains were brought home and interred in the old cemetery at Spiceland. A suitable monument marks the last resting place of this genial, whole-souled and patriotic young man. He was a favorite in his social circle, a brave soldier and the light and life of the camp. He yielded up his life, at the age of twenty four years, for the preservation of the Union.

When the Spiceland Post, Grand Army of the Republic, was instituted, it was unanimously agreed to name it Harmon Rayl Post, in honor of the comrade who had shed such lustre upon the annals of his township.

An excellent picture of the deceased was presented to the Post by his father, Zadoc Rayl, but it was destroyed in the fire which consumed the property of the Post in 1892.

Surviving Harmon Rayl, there remain of his family, Alpheus Rayl, a brother, and Mrs. Thomas K. Millikan, a sister, living at Spiceland, and Clarkson Rayl, another brother, who resides at Carmel, Hamilton County, Indiana.

HENRY COUNTY ASSOCIATION OF VETERANS
OF THE CIVIL WAR.

Late in the year 1902, the George W. Lennard Post, Grand Army of the Republic, of New Castle, conceived the idea of a county association of veterans of the Civil War, with the double purpose of recruiting and strengthening the Grand Army and of getting better acquainted with each other, and keeping in closer touch than they had heretofore been able to do.

It was argued in the Post that many soldiers in the county belonged to organizations so widely scattered as to make it impracticable for them to ever meet in regimental or battery re-union with their own comrades and that they

9
H
v

Harmon Rayl

were for that reason liable to drop out and be lost sight of altogether. It was expected that this association would take care of all such soldiers, know who they were, where they were and, if they should die or remove from the county, the vice-president of the township in which they lived would report such fact to the secretary of the association. In this way a complete record would be kept of every soldier in the county.

The argument was so convincing that a committee consisting of William B. Bock, Thomas W. Gronendyke and Henry C. Elliott was appointed to call a meeting. Invitations were issued and the call published in all of the county papers and on Saturday, November 22, 1902, the first meeting was held. The day was an unfavorable one, a rainstorm keeping many away. However, eighty four comrades registered, which, under the circumstances, was considered very encouraging.

William B. Bock called the meeting to order and stated the object of assembling. Thomas W. Gronendyke was elected temporary President and Henry C. Elliott, Secretary. A committee on organization and nomination of officers, consisting of Albert W. Saint, Joseph M. Lacy, Samuel W. Overman, Harvey B. Chew and John H. Templin, was appointed to report after dinner. A number of short speeches, favorable to the new movement, made by different comrades, provoked such enthusiasm that success was assured. Adjournment was then had to the Knights of Pythias Hall where the ladies of the Women's Relief Corps had prepared a grand banquet. The comrades all repaired there and soon convinced the ladies that their efforts were appreciated.

The afternoon session was called to order at 1:30 o'clock and the committee on organization reported as follows:

"We recommend that this organization be known as the 'Henry County Association of Veterans of the Civil War,' and that the officers consist of a President, a Secretary, and a Vice-President from each township in the county, and that we hold meetings annually; that we also recommend Thomas W. Gronendyke for President, to serve one year, and Henry C. Elliott for Secretary, to serve for a like period, and that we recommend the following Vice-Presidents for the several townships:

Blue River Township.....................Henry H. Moore.
Dudley Township........................Joseph M. Lacy.
Fall Creek Township....................Jacob Warnock.
Franklin Township......................John F. Camplin.
Greensboro Township....................Harvey B. Chew.
Harrison Township......................John W. McCormack.
Henry Township.........................William M. Pence.
Jefferson Township.....................John W. Whitworth.
Liberty Township.......................John Perry.
Prairie Township.......................John A. Powers.
Spiceland Township.....................Erie Lamb.
Stony Creek Township...................John H. Templin.
Wayne Township.........................Samuel W. Overman."

On motion of Leander S. Denius, the report of the committee was adopted and a collection, sufficient to defray expenses, was taken up. The exercises of the day followed, consisting of recitations by the Misses Helen Gronendyke, Edythe

King and Harriet Nardin, a song by Edith Gronendyke, and short but lively speeches, after the manner of camp fire talks, by David T. King, Caleb Lamb. Benjamin A. Stewart, George Hazzard (author of this History) and others. On motion of Mahlon D. Harvey, a vote of thanks was tendered the young ladies for their songs and recitations, after which the meeting adjourned to meet on the call of the President.

The "bean supper," prepared by the Women's Relief Corps, was well patronized by the comrades and citizens generally and all left with the feeling that the initial meeting had been a grand success.

The second meeting of the association was held in the G. A. R. Hall, New Castle. on Tuesday, October 6, 1903. At this meeting one hundred ex-soldiers registered. President Thomas W. Gronendyke called the meeting to order at 10:30 o'clock and the session was opened with an invocation by Chaplain David T. King, after which the President appointed the following committee on resolutions: Albert W. Saint, of Henry Township; James M. Mercer, of Liberty Township; John W. McCormack, of Harrison Township; Clarkson Gordon, of Spiceland Township, and Jacob Warnock, of Fall Creek Township. He also appointed the following committee on nominations: Eli F. Millikan, of Spiceland Township; Leonard H. Craig, of Prairie Township, and Isaac N. Wright, of Dudley Township.

Elihu T. Mendenhall made a motion that a committee be appointed to present the matter of a county soldiers' monument to the Board of County Commissioners and the County Council, which was adopted and Elihu T. Mendenhall, Erie Lamb, Jacob Warnock, Pearson Loer and John W. Whitworth were appointed as such committee, after speeches favorable to the project had been made by Richmond Wisehart. Pearson Loer, Leander M. James and Joseph M. Brown. The meeting was then entertained with musical selections by George M. Barnard and Miss Mary Smith. The ladies of the Methodist Church served an excellent dinner in the Knights of Pythias Hall, which was heartily complimented by all. A goodly number of citizens honored the association with their presence and took a lively interest in the proceedings.

At the afternoon session, the committee on resolutions made the following report:

"Resolved, by the Henry County Association of Veterans of the Civil War, that we favor a continuance of this organization of old soldiers to the end that we may keep in touch with each other, renew acquaintances formed in other years and insist that justice be done our comrades in the way of more liberal pensions.

"Resolved, that we favor a pension of not less than twelve dollars per month for all honorably discharged Union soldiers and sailors who have reached the age of sixty years and who served not less than ninety days, and that a like pension be allowed to the widows of such soldiers and sailors, provided they did not marry said soldier later than June 27, 1890.

"Resolved, that we urge our senators and representatives in Congress to do all in their power to secure this much needed legislation for worthy comrades who can never get justice under the existing laws.

"Resolved, that the thanks of this association be tendered the members of the

Knights of Pythias Lodge for the use of their magnificent hall in which to hold its meetings; to George M. Barnard and Miss Mary Smith for the musical entertainment, and to any and all others who aided in carrying out a most successful program."

The committee on nominations reported in favor of Henry C. Elliott for President and Albert W. Saint for Secretary, each to serve for one year, which was concurred in by the meeting.

The session was brought to a close with short speeches, songs and handshaking among the comrades.

The third and last meeting recorded in this History was held in the Court House, New Castle, Tuesday, October 11, 1904. The announcement that Daniel R. Lucas, Department Commander of the G. A. R., would be present served to call out a large crowd of citizens as well as ex-soldiers anxious to honor him by their presence. The attendance of veterans reached high water mark at this meeting, one hundred and ten affixing their names to the register, but the shaky signatures told only too plainly of advancing age and feeble bodies. It may be remarked that a goodly number of comrades, living within sight of the Court House, were by reason of wounds or other disabilities unable to meet their old comrades at this annual gathering.

The meeting was called to order at one o'clock by President Henry C. Elliott and the session opened with an invocation by Department Commander, Daniel R. Lucas. The Secretary, Albert W. Saint, read the minutes of the last meeting which were approved, and a committee on resolutions was appointed consisting of Thomas B. Wilkinson, John W. Whitworth and John Thornburgh. A Vice-President for each township was named as follows:

Blue River Township	Henry C. Bridget.
Dudley Township	Joseph M. Lacy.
Fall Creek Township	Benjamin H. Davis.
Franklin Township	John F. Camplin.
Greensboro Township	Exum Copeland.
Harrison Township	Philander Lowery.
Henry Township	John Thornburgh.
Jefferson Township	John W. Whitworth.
Liberty Township	James M. Mercer.
Prairie Township	William Frazier.
Spiceland Township	George P. Beach.
Stony Creek Township	Franklin W. Murray.
Wayne Township	Clinton D. Hawhee.

These vice-presidents were instructed to report to the secretary any deaths or removals in their respective townships.

The financial report of the secretary showed a balance on hand of $1.15 from the meeting of the previous year. A committee on nominations consisting of. Robert A. Smith, Elihu T. Mendenhall and John Lockridge was appointed. The committee appointed at the preceding session to confer with the Board of County Commissioners and the County Council with regard to aid in erecting a monument to our soldier dead, reported that nothing had as yet been accomplished, owing chiefly to the expense incurred in building the new addition to the Court House, but that the officials were friendly to the proposition and hoped soon to be in shape to aid this much desired object, whereupon the committee was continued.

The chief attraction of this meeting of veterans was the address of Daniel R. Lucas, who proved himself a forceful speaker, a good singer of patriotic songs and a capital story teller. His strong appeal to the veterans to be loyal to each other and to the Grand Army will, no doubt, aid materially in increasing the membership of the organization.

The committee on nominations recommended Robert A. Smith, of Knightstown,, for President and Albert W. Saint, of New Castle, for Secretary, which action of the committee was concurred in.

The committee on resolutions made the following report:

"After a fair trial of the merits of this organization of the veteran soldiers' of Henry County, it is with pleasure that your committee recommends its continuance until the day and the hour when all of the Union ex-soldiers of the county shall have passed away. The organization has fulfilled the fondest hopes of its friends and its several meetings have resulted in strengthening and cementing the ties of comradeship. In the fullness of our hearts, realizing the good of such an organization in this county, we unite in recommending other counties to go and do likewise.

"And it is further resolved, that we reiterate our belief that a pension of not less than twelve dollars per month should be granted to all honorably discharged soldiers and sailors who have reached the age of sixty years and that a like pension should be granted to their widows, and that we heartily approve President Roosevelt's pension order, Number 78.

"Resolved also, that we continue to urge our National Legislature to do all and everything to aid and assist ex-soldiers of the Union, by strengthening our present pension laws and making them more liberal in their intent and purpose."

The third session of annual meetings then came to a close with the singing of patriotic songs.

The following is a list of the members with their addresses, who have attended the several meetings of the association. It is believed that it comprises at least two-thirds of all the ex-soldiers now living in the county. Where the address is in Henry County, the State is omitted. An asterisk * denotes those who are known to have died since joining the association.

Mathew T. Abbott, New Castle. Company A, 35th Iowa Infantry.
William T. Addison, New Castle. Company G, 16th Indiana Infantry.
Miles E. Anderson, New Castle. Company E, 9th Indiana Cavalry.
Samuel Arnold, New Castle. Company G, 5th Ohio Cavalry.
Henry C. Bateman, Lewisville. Company G, 9th Indiana Cavalry.
George P. Beach, Spiceland. Company A, 36th Indiana Infantry.
*William S. Bedford, New Castle. Company E, 8th Indiana Infantry (three years).
Lafe Dell, Middletown. Company F, 53rd Kentucky Infantry.
Benjamin F. Benbow, Sulphur Springs. Company G, 84th Indiana Infantry.
Benjamin Bitner, New Castle. Company H, 147th Indiana Infantry.
James Wesley Black, New Castle, Company B, 139th Indiana Infantry; Company H, 147th Indiana Infantry.
William B. Bock, New Castle. Company G, 84th Indiana Infantry.
William F. Boor, New Castle. Major and Surgeon, 4th Indiana Cavalry. Brigade Surgeon, 1st Brigade, 2nd Division, Cavalry Corps, Army of the Cumberland.
David Bowers, Sulphur Springs. Company H, 147th Indiana Infantry.
John W. Brattain, New Castle. Company E, 34th Indiana Infantry.

George Brenneman, New Castle. Company H, 69th Indiana Infantry.

Henry C. Bridget, Mooreland. Company G, 36th Indiana Infantry. .

George H. Brown, New Castle. Company B, 89th Indiana Infantry.

Joseph M. Brown, New Castle. Company B, 110th Indiana Infantry (Morgan Raid); Company I, 69th Indiana Infantry.

William Brunner, New Castle. Company H, 100th Indiana Infantry.

Martin L. Bundy, New Castle. Major and Paymaster and Brevet Lieutenant Colonel U. S. Volunteers.

William Bunnell, New Castle. Fremont's Body Guard. Company D, Benton Cadets, Missouri Volunteers; Company D, 39th Ohio Infantry.

Thomas J. Burchett, New Castle. Company G, 8th Indiana Infantry (three years); Company H, 74th Ohio Infantry.

Milton Burk, New Castle. Company H, 147th Indiana Infantry.

George Burton, New Castle. Company H, 3rd Indiana Infantry (Mexican War); Company A, 30th Indiana Infantry, re-organized; Company B, 110th Indiana Infantry (Morgan Raid), New Castle Guards, Indiana Legion.

George H. Cain, New Castle. Company B, 8th Indiana Infantry (three months); Company G, 84th Indiana Infantry.

John F. Camplin, Lewisville. Company D, 36th Indiana Infantry.

Solomon F. Carter, New Castle. Company A, 30th Indiana Infantry, re-organized.

David W. Chambers, New Castle. Company B, 8th Indiana Infantry (three months); Company D, 36th Indiana Infantry.

Harvey B. Chew, Kennard. Company D, 36th Indiana Infantry; Company E, 9th Regiment. 1st Army Corps (Hancock's Veteran Corps).

John R. Clevenger, Cadiz. Company E, 8th Indiana Infantry (three years).

Thaddeus Coffin, New Castle. Company G and Regimental Band, 23rd Ohio Infantry.

Joel Collins, Greensboro. Company A, 139th Indiana Infantry.

Allen W. Coon, Cadiz. Company D, 36th Indiana Infantry.

Exum Copeland, Greensboro. Company D, 36th Indiana Infantry; Company A, 105th Indiana Infantry (Morgan Raid); Company E, 9th Indiana Cavalry.

William T. Corya, New Castle. Company D, 54th Indiana Infantry (three months).

Leonard H. Craig, New Castle. Company K, 105th Indiana Infantry (Morgan Raid); Company H, 140th Indiana Infantry.

Samuel Craig, Cadiz. Company E, 8th Indiana Infantry (three years).

William J. C. Crandall, New Castle. Company G, 1st Tennessee Infantry.

Gilliam L. Craven, New Castle. Company B, 89th Indiana Infantry.

Amos Crawford, Knightstown. Company C, 91st Illinois Infantry.

Benjamin Crawford, Losantville, Indiana. Company C, 36th Indiana Infantry.

William C. Crawford, New Lisbon. Company I, 69th Indiana Infantry; Company H, 140th Indiana Infantry.

James Cummins, Daleville, Indiana. Company B, 139th Indiana Infantry.

Benjamin H. Davis, Middletown. Company C, 155th Indiana Infantry.

David F. Davis, Marion, Indiana. Fremont's Body Guard. Company B, Benton Cadets, Missouri Volunteers; Company I, 69th Indiana Infantry.

John Davis, Middletown. Company G, 84th Indiana Infantry.

Sedley A. Deem, Knightstown. Company K, 36th Indiana Infantry.

Leander S. Denius, New Castle. Regimental Band, 35th Ohio Infantry; Company G, 156th Ohio Infantry.

Francis Dovey, Knightstown. 19th Indiana Battery.

David Dowell, New Castle. Company C, 12th Missouri Cavalry.

William Downs, Mount Summit. Company D, 2nd Indiana Cavalry.

Daniel Davidson Duncan, Knightstown. Company A, 105th Indiana Infantry (Morgan Raid); Company A, 139th Indiana Infantry.

Richard J. Edleman, New Castle. 12th Indiana Battery.

Austin M. Edwards, Knightstown. Company A, 57th Indiana Infantry.

Henry C. Elliott, New Castle. Company B, 8th Indiana Infantry (three months);

43

Company F and Adjutant, 57th Indiana Infantry; Lieutenant Colonel, 118th Indiana Infantry.

Isaac W. Ellis, New Castle, Company C, 8th Indiana Infantry (three months).

Joseph H. Fadely, Honey Creek. Company G, 161st Indiana Infantry (Spanish-American War).

Alpheus Fawcett, Spiceland. Company G, 84th Indiana Infantry; Company H, 140th Indiana Infantry.

James L. Filson, New Lisbon. Company G, 161st Indiana Infantry (Spanish-American War).

William Ford, Ashland. U. S. Navy.

Nathan Foster, Spiceland. Company I, 84th Indiana Infantry.

William Frazier, New Castle. Company G, 29th Iowa Infantry.

William J. Frazier, New Castle. Company C, 36th Indiana Infantry.

Joseph Gilbert, New Lisbon. Company G, 8th Indiana Infantry (three years).

*William Gillgeese, Sulphur Springs. Company K, 25th Illinois Infantry; 8th Battery Wisconsin Light Artillery.

Jonathan J. Ginn, Middletown. Company H, 140th Indiana Infantry.

Clarkson Gordon, Spiceland. Company A, 36th Indiana Infantry; Company A, 4th Regiment. 1st Army Corps (Hancock's Veteran Corps).

Thaddeus H. Gordon, Company F, 36th Indiana Infantry.

Jacob M. Gough, New Castle. Company B, 8th Indiana Infantry (three months).

William C. Goudy, New Castle. Company I, 32nd Ohio Infantry.

Thomas W. Gronendyke, New Castle. Company H, 69th Indiana Infantry; Company K, 105th Indiana Infantry (Morgan Raid).

Joseph G. Gustin, Middletown. Company H, 140th Indiana Infantry.

Miles Haguewood, New Castle. Company C, 36th Indiana Infantry.

Patrick H. Hansard, Cadiz. Company F, 14th U. S. C. T.

Frank W. Harris, Kennard. Company L, 38th Infantry, U. S. V. (Spanish-American War).

*Thomas L. Hartley, Oakville, Indiana. Company D, 2nd Indiana Cavalry.

John R. Harvey, New Castle. Company C, 36th Indiana Infantry; Company A, 110th Indiana Infantry (Morgan Raid); Company B, 139th Indiana Infantry.

Mahlon D. Harvey, New Castle. Company I, 69th Indiana Infantry.

Nathan H. Haskett, Knightstown. Company G, 5th Indiana Cavalry.

Clinton D. Hawhee, Knightstown. Company K, 36th Indiana Infantry.

George Hazzard. (Author of this History), Tacoma, Washington. Company C, 36th Indiana Infantry.

Waitsel M. Heaton, Knightstown. Company F, 6th Indiana Infantry (three months); Company A and Sergeant Major, 139th Indiana Infantry; Company A, 105th Indiana Infantry (Morgan Raid).

White Heaton, Knightstown. 2nd Indiana Battery.

Henry H. Henderson, New Castle. Company B, 8th Indiana Infantry (three months); Company C, 36th Indiana Infantry.

Joel Hendricks, Kennard. Company E, 8th Indiana Infantry (three years).

Samuel M. Hockersmith, New Castle. Company D, 47th Ohio Infantry.

David Hoover, New Castle. Company B, 110th Indiana Infantry (Morgan Raid); Company B, 139th Indiana Infantry.

Daniel Hoppis, New Castle. Company A, 19th Indiana Infantry; Company I, 20th Indiana Infantry, re-organized.

William House, New Lisbon. Company B, 110th Indiana Infantry (Morgan Raid); Company A, 30th Indiana Infantry, re-organized.

Thomas I. Howren, New Castle. Company D, 36th Indiana Infantry.

Presley E. Jackson, Kennard. Company K, 47th Indiana Infantry.

John James, Knightstown. Company A, 57th Indiana Infantry.

Leander M. James, New Castle. Company A, 139th Indiana Infantry.

Adam Kendall, New Castle. Company K, 57th Indiana Infantry.

Amos J. Kern, Greensboro. Company B, 42nd Indiana Infantry.

John E. Keys, Knightstown. Company B, 7th Indiana Cavalry.

David T. King, New Castle. Company I, 7th Illinois Cavalry.

Andrew F. Kraner, New Castle. Company G, 8th Indiana Infantry (three months); Company K, 8th Indiana Infantry (three years).

Joseph M. Lacy, New Lisbon. Company I, 33rd Indiana Infantry.

Alfred Lafferty, Cadiz. Honorary member of the Cadiz G. A. R. Post on account of his having been body servant in the Civil War to Colonel George W. Jackson, 9th Indiana Cavalry.

Caleb Lamb, Greensboro. Company A, 19th Indiana Infantry.

Erie Lamb, Spiceland. Company D, 36th Indiana Infantry.

John C. Livezey, New Castle. Company C. 36th Indiana Infantry; Captain and Commissary of Subsistence, U. S. Volunteers; Brevet Major, U. S. Volunteers.

John Lockridge, Shirley., Company D, 36th Indiana Infantry.

Pearson Loer, New Castle. Company A, 54th Indiana Infantry (one year).

Michael Longnecker, Springport. Company B, 11th Ohio Infantry; Company B, 94th Ohio Infantry.

Philander Lowery, Cadiz. Company F, 57th Indiana Infantry.

Philip Lowery, New Castle. Company E, 9th Indiana Cavalry.

Daniel R. Lucas, Indianapolis, Indiana. Chaplain, 99th Indiana Infantry.

Jackson McCormack, Crawfordsville, Indiana. Company H, 140th Indiana Infantry.

John W. McCormack, Cadiz. Company D, 147th Indiana Infantry.

Josiah McCormack, Kennard. Company E, 9th Indiana Cavalry.

Noah McCormack, Knightstown. Company C. 36th Indiana Infantry.

Joseph McKee, Sulphur Springs. Company F, 57th Indiana Infantry; Company K, 105th Indiana Infantry (Morgan Raid).

William H. Macy, New Castle. Company D, 36th Indiana Infantry.

Elihu T. Mendenhall, New Castle. Company A, 101st Indiana Infantry.

James M. Mercer, New Lisbon. Company A, 54th Indiana Infantry (one year).

Peter Michels, New Castle. Company K, 72nd Ohio Infantry.

Wilson C. Middaugh, New Castle. Company C, 1st Michigan Infantry; Company M, 8th Michigan Cavalry.

Eli F. Millikan, Spiceland. Company C, 36th Indiana Infantry.

David Modlin, New Castle. Company B, 28th U. S. C. T.

Henry H. Moore, Mooreland. Company C, 36th Indiana Infantry.

Josiah B. Moore, Spiceland. Company A, 36th Indiana Infantry; Company H, 30th Indiana Infantry, re-organized.

Louis N. Moore, New Castle. Company K, 16th Indiana Infantry.

Hugh L. Mullen, New Castle. Company C. 36th Indiana Infantry.

Franklin W. Murray, Blountsville. Company K, 36th Indiana Infantry.

*John C. Murray, New Castle. Company K, 36th Indiana Infantry.

Alkanah C. Neff, Honey Creek. Company E, 8th Indiana Infantry (three years).

Peter Netz, Sulphur Springs. Company A, 54th Indiana Infantry (one year); Company D, 2nd Ohio Heavy Artillery.

James I. Newby, New Castle. Company D, 36th Indiana Infantry.

Nathan Nicholson, New Castle. Company C, 36th Indiana Infantry.

Samuel W. Overman, Shirley. Company B, 42nd Indiana Infantry.

John Palmer. Winchester, Indiana. U. S. Navy; Company B, 34th New Jersey Infantry.

Franklin N. Pence, Pendleton, Indiana. Company G, 84th Indiana Infantry.

William M. Pence, New Castle. U. S. Navy.

John Perry, New Castle. Company A, 54th Indiana Infantry (one year)

Robert F. Poer, Knightstown. Company F, 6th Indiana Infantry (three months); Company I, 3rd Indiana Cavalry.

Henry L. Powell, New Castle. Company B, 8th Indiana Infantry (three months); Company A, 110th Indiana Infantry (Morgan Raid).

John A. Powers, Springport. Company H, 154th Indiana Infantry.

Elijah M. Pressnall, New Castle. Company B, 110th Indiana Infantry (Morgan Raid); Company A, 30th Indiana Infantry, re-organized.

*John M. Redding, New Castle. Company F, 57th Indiana Infantry.

Collier M. Reed, Middletown, Company C, 8th Indana Infantry (three months).

William Reynolds, Lewisville. Company I, 69th Indiana Infantry.

Peter Ritner, Spiceland. .Company I, 84th Indiana Infantry; Troop G, 6th Cavalry, U. S. A.

Levi Ricks, New Castle. Company K, 105th Indiana Infantry (Morgan Raid); Company H, 140th Indiana Infantry.

Isaac Roberts, Knightstown. Company K, 36th Indiana Infantry.

Leonidas Rodgers, New Castle. Company C, 16th Ohio Infantry; Regimental Band, 13th Missouri Infantry; Company E, 152nd Ohio Infantry.

William H. H. Rohrback, Sulphur Springs. Company E. 1st Maryland Potomac Home Brigade Infantry.

S. A. Rollin, Indianapolis, Indiana. 71st Ohio Infantry.

William J. Runyan, New Castle. Company G, 84th Indiana Infantry.

Albert W. Saint, New Castle. Company D, 36th Indiana Infantry.

Horace M. Saint, Greensboro. Company H, 3rd Battalion, 16th Infantry U. S. A. re-organized as Company H, 34th Infantry, U. S. A.

Charles C. Shedron, Middletown. Company H, 69th Indiana Infantry.

George W. Shelley, New Castle. Company G, 84th Indiana Infantry.

Henry W. Simmons, Springport. .Company A, 38th Indiana Infantry.

James H. Smith, New Castle. Company A, 87th Indiana Infantry; Company A. 42nd Indiana Infantry.

Joseph Smith, New Castle. Record incomplete in this History.

Robert A. Smith, Knightstown. Company A, 57th Indiana Infantry.

John A. Spencer, Spiceland. Company D, 36th Indiana Infantry.

Benjamin A. Stewart, Dunreith. Company C, 82nd Indiana Infantry.

John Stigleman, Spiceland. Company A, 36th Indiana Infantry.

William Sullivan, Dublin, Indiana. Company G. 36th Indiana Infantry.

Samuel V. Swearingen, Mooreland. Company E. 147th Indiana Infantry.

John H. Templin. Losantville, Indiana. Company I, 124th Indiana Infantry.

John Thornburg, New Castle, Lieutenant and Quartermaster, 4th Indiana Cavalry.

William Trail, Kennard, Company I, 28th U. S. C. T.

Moab Turner, New Castle. Company I. 4th Tennessee Infantry, re-organized as 1st Tennessee Cavalry.

Richard H. H. Tyner, Knightstown. Company D, 9th Indiana Infantry.

*Daniel Ulmer, Kennard. Company I, 79th Pennsylvania Infantry.

Samuel G. Vance. New Castle. Company F, 146th Indiana Infantry.

Thomas B. Van Dyke, Lewisville. Company I, 84th Indiana Infantry.

Cyrus Van Matre, Middletown. Company B. 8th Indiana Infantry (three months); Company E, 8th Indiana Infantry (three years).

Thomas Waller, New Lisbon. 3rd Indiana Battery; 14th Indiana Battery.

Noah W. Warner, Sulphur Springs. Company B, 8th Indiana Infantry (three months); Company H, 69th Indiana Infantry.

Jacob Warnock, Honey Creek. Company C, 109th Indiana Infantry (Morgan Raid); Company G, 7th Indiana Cavalry.

Cornelius C. Weaver, New Castle. Company B, 18th Illinois Infantry.

James M. Welker, Millville. Company K, 54th Indiana Infantry (three months); 15th Indiana Battery.

John W. Whitworth. Sulphur Springs. Company E, 8th Indiana Infantry (three years).

Sanford Whitworth. Honey Creek. Company G. 7th Indiana Cavalry; Company F, 7th Indiana Cavalry, re-organized.

Thomas B. Wilkinson, Knightstown. Company I, 3rd Indiana Cavalry.

Richmond Wisehart, New Castle. Company F, 57th Indiana Infantry.

Jeremiah Woods, Knightstown. Company B, 99th Indiana Infantry.

Isaac N. Wright, New Lisbon. Company D, 147th Indiana Infantry.

David Wrightsman. New Castle. Company A, 79th Ohio Infantry; Company D. 73rd Ohio Infantry.

CO.G.161ST.REGT.

CO.G.161ST.REGT.

CORPORAL RAY KEESLING.

CO.G.161ST.REGT.

1ST.LIEUT.J.I.MEYERS.

CO.G.161ST.REGT.

2D.LIEUT.C.M.PITMAN.

CO.H.60TH.REGT.

CAPT.ALBERT OGBORN.

CO.G.161ST.REGT.

CORPORAL H.O.POWELL.

27TH.BATTERY.

CORPORAL M.P.GADDIS.

PRIVATE H.B.MILLIKAN.

SPANISH-AMERICAN WAR.

BRIEF HISTORY OF THE SPANISH AMERICAN WAR—ROSTER OF HENRY COUNTY SOLDIERS IN THE 27TH INDIANA BATTERY—ROSTERS OF HENRY COUNTY SOLDIERS IN THE 158TH INDIANA INFANTRY—159TH INDIANA INFANTRY—160TH INDIANA INFANTRY—ROSTER OF THE 161ST INDIANA INFANTRY—HISTORY OF THE REGIMENT—BIOGRAPHICAL SKETCH OF CAPTAIN ALBERT DURET OGBORN AND FAMILY—RECAPITULATION.

For a period of ten years, from 1868, to 1878, the inhabitants of Cuba were engaged in a struggle to free themselves from the yoke of Spanish tyranny, but were defeated. The Spanish Government made most liberal promises, but failed to keep them. Hostilities were renewed which lasted for three years, from 1895 to 1898. The inhabitants were in a most deplorable condition; the reconcentradoes—men, women, and children non-combatants were by edict of the Spanish Captain General, Weyler, driven from their homes, crowded together without proper food or shelter, and died by thousands of disease and starvation. The attention and sympathy of the American people had several years been attracted to this miserable condition of the Cubans and arguments had been made to relieve their distress.

At the beginning of 1898 about one-third of the inhabitants had perished. At this juncture two events happened which increased the tension in the United States. One was the exposure of a letter written by Senor de Lome, the Spanish Minister to the United States, to a friend grossly reflecting upon the President; the other was a demand by the Spanish Government for the recall from Cuba of Consul General Lee, which was refused. On the 25th of January, 1898, the United States Battleship Maine was ordered to Havana Harbor, on a peaceful mission by the authority of the United States, and on the 15th of February, 1898, between 9 and 10 o'clock p. m., the vessel was blown up by a submarine mine, 266 sailors losing their lives. A searching investigation followed without fixing the responsibility. Congress immediately appropriated $50,000,000 "for the national defense and for each and every purpose connected therewith, to be expended at the discretion of the President."

After fruitless effort to bring about an amicable settlement, on April 11, 1898, the President asked Congress to intervene to stop the Cuban War, and by force establish a stable government on the island. On April 19, 1898, Congress passed resolutions, which were signed by the President at 11:24 a. m. the following day, declaring "that the people of the island of Cuba are, and by right ought to be, free and independent," and demanding that Spain at once relinquish its authority

SPANISH-AMERICAN WAR.

CHAPTER XXXI.

SPANISH-AMERICAN WAR.

BRIEF HISTORY OF THE SPANISH-AMERICAN WAR—ROSTER OF HENRY COUNTY
SOLDIERS IN THE 27TH INDIANA BATTERY—ROSTERS OF HENRY COUNTY
SOLDIERS IN THE 158TH INDIANA INFANTRY—159TH INDIANA INFANTRY—
160TH INDIANA INFANTRY—ROSTER OF THE 161ST INDIANA INFANTRY—HIS-
TORY OF THE REGIMENT—BIOGRAPHICAL SKETCH OF CAPTAIN ALBERT
DURET OGBORN AND FAMILY—RECAPITULATION.

For a period of ten years, from 1868, to 1878, the inhabitants of Cuba were
engaged in a struggle to free themselves from the yoke of Spanish tyranny, but
were defeated. The Spanish Government made most liberal promises, but failed
to keep them. Hostilities were renewed which lasted for three years, from 1895 to
1898. The inhabitants were in a most deplorable condition; the reconcentradoes—
men, women, and children, non-combatants—were by edict of the Spanish Captain
General, Weyler, driven from their homes, crowded together without proper food
or shelter, and died by thousands of disease and starvation. The attention and
sympathy of the American people had for several years been attracted to this
miserable condition of the Cubans, and many attempts had been made to relieve
their distress.

At the beginning of 1898 about 40 per cent. of the inhabitants had perished.
At this juncture two events happened which increased the tension in the United
States. One was the exposure of a letter written by Senor de Lome, the Spanish
Minister to the United States, to a friend, grossly reflecting upon the President;
the other was a demand by the Spanish Government for the recall from Cuba of
Consul General Lee, which was refused. On the 25th of January,
1898, the United States Battleship Maine was ordered to Havana
Harbor, on a peaceful mission, by the authority of the United States,
and on the 15th of February, 1898, between 9 and 10 o'clock p. m., the vessel was
blown up by a submarine mine, 266 sailors losing their lives. A searching investigation followed without fixing the responsibility. Congress immediately appropriated $50,000,000 "for the national defense and for each and every purpose
connected therewith, to be expended at the discretion of the President."

After fruitless effort to bring about an amicable settlement, on April 11,
1898, the President asked Congress to intervene to stop the Cuban War, and by
force establish a stable government on the island. On April 19, 1898, Congress
passed resolutions, which were signed by the President at 11:24 a. m.-the following
day, declaring "that the people of the island of Cuba are, and by right ought to be,
free and independent," and demanding that Spain at once relinquish its authority.

in the island. It also authorized the President to use the entire military force
of the United States to carry the resolution into effect.

The diplomatic relations between the two countries ceased April 21, 1898,
and it was held that a state of war existed from that date. Blockade of the
principal Cuban ports was declared April 22, and on the 23d the President called
for 125,000 volunteers to serve two years, and on May 24 the Spanish Government announced that a state of war between that country and the United States
existed.

The protocol of agreement between the United States and Spain was signed
at Washington, District of Columbia. August 12, 1898, by William R. Day and
Jules Cambon.

The treaty of peace was signed at Paris December 10, 1898, by William R.
Day, Cushman K. Davis, William P. Frye, George Gray, and Whitelaw Reid,
for the United States, and by Eugenio Montero Rios, B. de Abarzuza, J. de Gar-
nica, W. R. de Villa Urrutia, and Rafael Cerero, for the Kingdom of Spain.

Signed at Paris, December 10, 1898; ratification advised by the Senate February 6, 1899; ratified by the President February 6, 1899; ratified by Her Majesty
the Queen Regent of Spain March 19, 1899; ratifications exchanged at Washington April 11, 1899; proclaimed, Washington, April 11, 1899.

TWENTY SEVENTH BATTERY.

This Battery of Light Artillery was formed of Battery A, First Artillery,
Indiana National Guard, and was mustered into the service of the United States
on May 10, 1898. It served at Camp Thomas, Chickamauga Park, Georgia, and
in Porto Rico. It was mustered out November 25, 1898. Henry County had
only three representatives in the Battery.

In the following condensed roster, the name of each soldier is followed by his
postoffice address at the time of enlistment. The date of enrollment is the date of
enlistment, not the date of muster.

William Burton, New Castle. Saddler. Enrolled April 26, 1898. Mustered out
November 25, 1898.

Harry B. Millikan, New Castle. Private. Enrolled April 26, 1898. Discharged,
disability, September 22, 1898.

William F. Rutledge, Mount Summit. Private. Enrolled June 14, 1898. Recruit.
Mustered out November 25, 1898.

ONE HUNDRED AND FIFTY EIGHT INFANTRY.

This regiment was formed of the Second Infantry, Indiana National Guard,
and was mustered into the service of the United States on May 10, 1898. Its
service was confined to Camp Thomas, Chickamauga Park, Georgia, and Camp
Poland, Knoxville, Tennessee. It was mustered out, November 4, 1898. Henry
County had only four representatives in the regiment.

In the following condensed roster, the name of each soldier is followed by
his postoffice address at the time of enlistment. The date of enrollment is the date
of enlistment, not the date of muster.

Frederick Caldwell. Lewisville. Private, Company H. Enrolled April 26, 1898. Mustered out November 4, 1898.

William Netz, 'Ashland. Private, Company E. Enrolled April 26, 1898. Mustered out November 4, 1898.

Daniel E. Shaffer, New Castle. Private, Company B. Enrolled April 26, 1898. Mustered out November 4, 1898.

Homer H. Wrightsman. New Castle. Private, Company H. Enrolled April 26, 1898. Mustered out November 4, 1898.

ONE HUNDRED AND FIFTY NINTH INFANTRY.

This regiment was formed of the First Infantry, Indiana National Guard. and was mustered into the service of the United States on May 12. 1898. Its service was confined to Camp R. A. Alger, Dunn Loring. Virginia ; Thoroughfare Gap, Virginia, and Camp Meade. near Middletown, Pennsylvania. It was mustered out November 23, 1898. Henry County had only one representative in the regiment.

In the following condensed roster, the name of the soldier is followed by his postoffice address at the time of enlistment. The date of enrollment is the date of enlistment, not the date of muster.

William Reed, Mount Summit. Private, Company I. Enrolled April 26, 1898. Appointed Corporal. Mustered out November 23, 1898.

ONE HUNDRED AND SIXTIETH INFANTRY.

This regiment was formed of the Fourth Infantry, Indiana National Guard. and was mustered into the service of the United States on May 12. 1898. It served at Camp Thomas, Chickamauga Park, Georgia ; Camp Hamilton. Lexington, Kentucky, and Matanzas. Cuba. It was mustered out April 25, 1899. Henry County had only two representatives in the regiment.

In the following condensed roster. the name of each soldier is followed by his address at the time of enlistment. The date of enrollment is the date of enlistment, not the date of muster.

William Neff, Honey Creek. Artificer, Company L. Enrolled April 26, 1898. Mustered out April 25, 1899.

Howard O. Powell, New Castle. Corporal, Company K. Enrolled April 26, 1898. Mustered out February 24, 1899.

ONE HUNDRED AND SIXTY FIRST INFANTRY.

This was a volunteer regiment organized for the Spanish-American War to fill the quota of Indiana under the President's second call for troops. It was mustered in by battalions and on July 15, 1898, the regiment as a whole was mustered into the service of the United States. It remained at Camp Mount under instruction until August 11, 1898, when it was ordered to Jacksonville. Florida. where it arrived on August 14 and was assigned to the First Brigade. Third Division, Seventh Army Corps, General Fitzhugh Lee commanding. The brigade was made up of the 2nd Mississippi, the 3rd Nebraska (Colonel William Jennings Bryan) and the 161st Indiana.

During its stay at Jacksonville, the regiment was engaged in numerous regimental drills and brigade and division reviews, and on August 31 took part in a review of the whole corps, in which twenty three regiments and more than twenty eight thousand men were in line. Among this host the 161st Indiana was conspicuous for soldierly appearance, fine marching, full companies and straight lines. ·On October 21, the Seventh Army Corps was re-organized and the 161st Indiana was assigned to the First Brigade, Second Division.

On October 23, 1898, the regiment was moved from Jacksonville to Savannah, Georgia, where it went into camp and once more took up the routine of drills, inspections and reviews, until under orders to proceed to Cuba, the regiment, on December 12, embarked on the transport Mobile, now the Sherman, for Havana, Cuba. Its arrival there was the signal for a notable reception by the Cubans, grateful for long delayed freedom. The Spanish power had not yet turned over its authority in the Island but was to do so under the terms of the treaty of peace negotiated at Paris. The enthusiasm of the people broke all bounds when the Seventh Corps, disembarking at Havana, took up its route for camp through that city.

The regiment went into camp at Camp Columbia, Marianao, Cuba, December 17, 1898, where it remained until ordered home. On January 1, 1899, it participated in the ceremonies marking the relinquishment of Spanish authority in the Antilles and witnessed the raising of the American flag over Morro Castle. an epoch making event, and certainly the most important one in the history of the regiment. While in Cuba, the 161st Indiana gained the reputation of being the finest regiment in the Seventh Army Corps, and the praise awarded it by the commanding officers was a deserved tribute to the intelligent and hard working officers and men of the organization. After the pacification of Cuba, the regiment was ordered home and arrived at Savannah, Georgia, March 31, 1899, where it was mustered out April 30, 1899.

In the following roster, the name of each officer and man is followed by his postoffice address at the time of enlistment. The date of enrollment is the date of enlistment, not the date of muster.

Company G was considered a distinctively Henry County organization, and for that reason the names of all its members are published to complete the roster, whether they lived in Henry County or not. This company was organized by the indefatigable efforts of Captain Albert D. Ogborn and Lieutenant James I. Meyers, who were afterwards joined by Lieutenant Charles M. Pitman. There was great rivalry from all parts of the State to get into this volunteer regiment, and officers and men of this provisional company were alike rejoiced when it was ordered to appear for examination. Defections from the ranks were made good by the acceptance of a number of Delaware County men and the Captain was able to report one hundred and nine men accepted by the local surgeon. Their departure for Indianapolis on July 1, 1898, was celebrated by the closing of the business houses of New Castle, and a great procession, headed by the Grand Army Post, escorted the company to the station. This was the fourth company to arrive in Indianapolis and was the first one ready for muster and was mustered in July 12, 1898. The record of this fine regiment owes much to the soldierly qualities of the officers and men of Company G. In the roster of the company recur the names of many whose fathers fought in the great Civil War, and, remembering the slighter opportunities of the Spanish-American War, they maintained the honor of Henry County in the armies of the Nation with the same loyalty and devotion as their fathers nearly half a century ago.

FIELD OFFICERS AND REGIMENTAL STAFF.

COLONEL.

Winfield T. Durbin. Anderson. Commissioned July 15, 1898. Mustered out April 30, 1899.

LIEUTENANT COLONEL.

Victor M. Backus, Indianapolis. Commissioned July 15, 1898. Mustered out April 30, 1899.

MAJORS.

Harold C. Megrew, Indianapolis. Commissioned July 11, 1898. Mustered out April 30, 1899.

Matt R. Peterson, United States Army. Commissioned July 15, 1898. Resigned November 29, 1898.

SURGEON.

Wickliffe Smith, Delphi. Commissioned June 28, 1898. Mustered out April 30, 1899.

ASSISTANT SURGEONS.

Millard F. Gerrish, Seymour. Commissioned June 28, 1898. Mustered out April 30, 1899.

James Wilson, Wabash. Commissioned June 28, 1898. Mustered out April 30, 1899.

ADJUTANT.

Oliver M. Tichenor, Princeton. Commissioned July 11, 1898. Mustered out April 30 1899.

QUARTERMASTER.

John R. Brunt. Anderson. Commissioned June 30, 1898. Mustered· out April 30, 1899.

CHAPLAIN.

William E. Biederwolf. Logansport. Commissioned July 15, 1898. Mustered out April 30, 1899.

NON-COMMISSIONED STAFF.

SERGEANT MAJOR.

William T. Starr, Richmond. Enrolled July 5, 1898. Mustered out April 30, 1899.

HOSPITAL STEWARDS.

William H. Rathert, Fort Wayne. Enrolled June 30, 1898. Mustered out April 30, 1899.

James G. Espey, Jeffersonville. Enrolled July 12, 1898. Discharged, disability, November 23, 1898.

John I. Lewis. Bedford. Enrolled July 3, 1898. Died September 8, 1898.

QUARTERMASTER SERGEANT.

Baird G. Saltzgaber, Lebanon. Enrolled June 29, 1898. Mustered out April 30, 1899.

CHIEF MUSICIAN.

Edwin White, Waltham, Massachusetts. Enrolled June 24, 1898. Transferred to Company E, December 22, 1898.

PRINCIPAL MUSICIANS.

Charles L. Applegate, Fortville. Enrolled July 12, 1898. Transferred to Company E, July 22, 1898.

Frank F. Webb, Indianapolis. Enrolled July 12, 1898. Transferred to Company E, July 22, 1898.

Anthony A. Montani, Indianapolis. Enrolled August 1. 1898. Recruit. Discharged. disability, November 3, 1898.

Ernest S. Williams, Winchester. Enrolled December 3. 1898. Recruit. Mustered out April 30, 1899.

COMPANY F.

SERGEANT.

John C. Weissgarber, New Castle. Enrolled June 27, 1898. Discharged. disability. January 17, 1899.

PRIVATE.

Frank H. Weissgarber, New Castle. Enrolled June 27, 1898. Appointed Corporal. Mustered out April 30, 1899.

COMPANY G.

CAPTAIN.

Albert D. Ogborn, New Castle. Enrolled June 25, 1898. Mustered out April 30. 1899.

FIRST LIEUTENANT.

James I. Meyers, New Castle. Enrolled June 25, 1898. Mustered out April 30. 1899.

SECOND LIEUTENANT.

Charles M. Pitman, New Castle. Enrolled June 25, 1898. Mustered out April 30. 1899.

FIRST SERGEANT.

Paul Rogers, Muncie, Delaware County. Enrolled June 28, 1898. Reduced to private at his own request, July 31, 1898. Mustered out April 30, 1899.

QUARTERMASTER SERGEANT.

Charles B. Owens, Franklin, Johnson County. Enrolled July 5, 1898. Transferred to Duty Sergeant, December' 22, 1898. Mustered out April 30, 1899

SERGEANTS.

T. William Engle, Indianapolis, Marion County. Enrolled July 5, 1898. Transferred to Hospital Corps.

John Welsbacher, Middletown. Enrolled June 28, 1898. Mustered out April 30. 1899.

Edward McCrea, Muncie,· Delaware County. Enrolled June 28, 1898. Mustered out April 30, 1899.

Claud Bock, New Castle. Enrolled June 27, 1898. Mustered out April 30, 1899.

CORPORALS.

Albert O. Martin, Muncie, Delaware County. Enrolled June 29, 1898. Appointed Sergeant. Mustered out April 30, 1899.

Ray Keesling, Mechanicsburg. Enrolled June 27, 1898. Mustered out April 30, 1899.

Linley W. McKimmey, Muncie, Delaware County. Enrolled June 29, 1898. Mustered out April 30, 1899.

James M. Redding, New Castle. Enrolled June 27, 1898. Mustered out April 30, 1899.

Alonzo Allen, New Castle. Enrolled June 29, 1898. Transferred to Hospital Corps.

George H. Elliott, Mechanicsburg. Enrolled June 27, 1898. Mustered out April 30, 1899.

Joseph H. Fadely, Honey Creek. Enrolled June 27, 1898. Mustered out April 30, 1899.

Charles R. Gontner, Muncie. Delaware County. Enrolled June 29, 1898. Mustered out April 30, 1899.

Ellwood L. Baldwin, Spiceland. Enrolled June 27, 1898. Mustered out April 30, 1899.

Charles M. Nash, Mount Summit. Enrolled June 27, 1898. Mustered out April 30, 1899.

E. Murray Luther, Blountsville. Enrolled June 28, 1898. Appointed Sergeant and Quartermaster Sergeant. Mustered out April 30, 1899.

Harry S. Nugent, Kennard. Enrolled June 28, 1898. Mustered out April 30, 1899.

MUSICIANS.

Henry W. Van Dyke, Lewisville. Enrolled June 27, 1898. Discharged, disability, March 17, 1899.

Ira O. Yates. Middletown. Enrolled June 28, 1898. Discharged, disability. March 17, 1899.

ARTIFICER.

Huston Hutchins, New Castle. Enrolled June 27, 1898. Mustered out April 30, 1899.   ·

WAGONER.

Oscar Livezey, New Castle. Enrolled June 27, 1898. Mustered out April 30, 1899.

PRIVATES.

Joseph Akers, Middletown. Enrolled June 28, 1898. Discharged, disability. February 6, 1899.

Henry Barnes, Muncie, Delaware County. Enrolled June 28, 1898. Mustered out April 30, 1899.

Guy Barnett, New Castle. Enrolled June 27, 1898. Mustered out April 30, 1899.

Edward Beeson, Dalton, Wayne County. Enrolled June 28, 1898. Appointed Musician. Mustered out April 30, 1899.

Roy W. Brown, New Castle. Enrolled June 27, 1898. Transferred to Regimental Band. Transferred from Band to Company L. Mustered out April 30, 1899.

Guy Buckley, New Castle. Enrolled June 27, 1898. Mustered out April 30, 1899.

James Canaday, New Castle. Enrolled July 5, 1898. Mustered out April 30, 1899.

Fred P. Cecil, Muncie, Delaware County. Enrolled July 6, 1898. Mustered out April 30, 1899.

Alva Darling, Spiceland. Enrolled June 27, 1898. Mustered out April 30, 1899.

Harry C. Darnell, Indianapolis, Marion County. Enrolled July 7, 1898. Mustered out April 30, 1899.

Frank N. Davenport, New Castle. Enrolled June 29, 1898. Mustered out April 30, 1899.

George C. Detrich, Muncie, Delaware County. Enrolled June 28, 1898. Discharged, disability, September 28, 1898.

John Dolan, Cambridge City, Wayne County. Enrolled July 6, 1898. Transferred to Hospital Corps.

Benjamin W. Eilar, New Castle. Enrolled June 27, 1898. Appointed Corporal and Sergeant. Mustered out April 30, 1899.

Henry Faulkner, Muncie, Delaware County. Enrolled July 5, 1898. Discharged, disability, January 13, 1899.

James L. Filson, New Lisbon. Enrolled June 28, 1898. Mustered out April 30, 1899.

Frank W. Fisher, New Castle. Enrolled June 29, 1898. Mustered out April 30, 1899.

Frank Foster, Spiceland. Enrolled June 27, 1898. Mustered out April 30, 1899.

Walker Frazee, Byers, Ohio. Enrolled July 6, 1898. Mustered out April 30, 1899.

Perry Freeman, Muncie, Delaware County. Enrolled July 5, 1898. Appointed Cook. Mustered out April 30, 1899. ·   •

Thomas Freeland, New Lisbon. Enrolled June 27, 1898. Mustered out April 30, 1899.

Max P. Gaddis, New Castle. Enrolled June 27, 1898. Appointed Corporal. Mustered out April 30, 1899.

Joseph Goddard, Middletown. Enrolled June 29, 1898. Appointed Corporal. Mustered out April 30, 1899.

Bud Goodman, Muncie, Delaware County. Enrolled June 27, 1898. Mustered out April 30, 1899.

Frank Hale, Springport. Enrolled June 28, 1898. Mustered out April 30, 1899.

Thomas T. Hale, Dublin, Wayne County. Enrolled June 28, 1898. Mustered out April 30, 1899.

Edgar B. Halfaker, Franklin, Johnson County. Enrolled July 5, 1898. Discharged, disability, August 22, 1898.

Benton F. Hamilton, Greensboro. Enrolled June 27, 1898. Mustered out April 30, 1899.

Frank M. Hamilton, New Castle. Enrolled July 6, 1898. Mustered out April 30, 1899.

John W. Hanna, Fort Worth, Texas. Enrolled July 5, 1898. Mustered out April 30, 1899.

Charles Harper, Indianapolis, Marion County. Enrolled July 8, 1898   Mustered out April 30, 1899.

Herbert H. Hickman, Springport. Enrolled June 29, 1898. Discharged, disability, March 13, 1899.

Hoyt A. Holton, Indianapolis, Marion County. Enrolled July 7, 1898. Discharged, disability, January 12, 1899.

Arthur A. Huddleston, Dublin, Wayne County. Enrolled June 29, 1898. Mustered out April 30, 1899.

George Irwin, New York City. Enrolled June 29, 1898. Mustered out April 30, 1899.

William G. Israel, Franklin, Johnson County. Enrolled July 5, 1898. Mustered out April 30, 1899.

Solomon Jackson, Franklin, Johnson County. Enrolled July 5, 1898. Mustered out April 30, 1899.

Oltie F. Lamb, Dalton, Wayne County. Enrolled June 28, 1898. Mustered out April 30, 1899.

Fred Lane, Mooreland. Enrolled June 28, 1898. Mustered out April 30, 1899.

J. Morris F. Leech, Muncie, Delaware County. Enrolled June 28, 1898. Transferred to Hospital Corps.

Arthur Leonard, Muncie, Delaware County. Enrolled June 28, 1898. Mustered out April 30, 1899.

John M. Leonard, Muncie, Delaware County. Enrolled June 28, 1898. Mustered out April 30, 1899.

Sebastian Lykens, Spiceland. Enrolled June 27, 1898. Mustered out April 30, 1899.

Charles McCoy, Muncie, Delaware County. Enrolled June 29, 1898. Mustered out April 30, 1899.

Clarence McCoy, Muncie, Delaware County. Enrolled June 29, 1898. Discharged, disability, September 27, 1898.

Henry C. Martin, Junior, Muncie, Delaware County. Enrolled June 28, 1898. Discharged, disability, February 17, 1899.

George Martindale, Sulphur Springs. Enrolled June 28, 1898. Mustered out April 30, 1899.

James W. Miller, New Castle. Enrolled June 29, 1898. Mustered out April 30, 1899.

Lemuel Mitchell, Middletown. Enrolled June 29, 1898. Mustered out April 30, 1899.

Cliff Morgan, Greensburg, Decatur County. Enrolled July 4, 1898. Mustered out. April 30, 1899.

Charles Netz, Ashland. Enrolled June 28, 1898. Mustered out April 30, 1899.

George W. Newby, Greensboro. Enrolled June 27, 1898. Mustered out April 30, 1899.

Otis C. Newby, Greensboro. Enrolled June 27, 1898. Mustered out April 30, 1899.

Noah A. Nichols, Honey Creek. Enrolled June 27, 1898. Mustered out April 30, 1899.

John J. Paul, Muncie, Delaware County. Enrolled June 29, 1898. Mustered out April 30, 1899.

Joseph M. Pearson, New Castle. Enrolled July 5, 1898. Discharged. disability, December 22, 1898.

James M. Prager, Seattle, Washington. Enrolled July 1, 1898. Transferred to Hospital Corps.

Fred W. Puckett, Muncie, Delaware County. Enrolled June 28, 1898. Appointed First Sergeant. Mustered out April 30, 1899.

Winfield Rawlins, Byers, Ohio. Enrolled July 6, 1898. Mustered out April 30, 1899.

Benjamin F. Reece, Muncie, Delaware County. Enrolled June 28, 1898. Mustered out April 30, 1899.

Elmer Robinson, Fisher's Switch. Hamilton County. Enrolled July 6, 1898. Appointed Corporal. Mustered out April 30, 1899.

Jesse Rothbaust, Franklin, Johnson County. Enrolled July 5, 1898. Discharged. disability, February 4, 1899.

Walton D. Sears, Spiceland. Enrolled June 27, 1898. Mustered out April 30, 1899.

Charles Shellenbarger, Muncie. Delaware County. Enrolled July 4, 1898. Appointed Corporal. Mustered out April 30, 1899.

Albert Sherer, New Castle. Enrolled June 29, 1898. Mustered out April 30, 1899.

William A. Sherman, Middletown. Enrolled August 8, 1898. Recruit. Mustered out April 30, 1899.

Edward C. Shuee. Muncie, Delaware County. Enrolled June 29, 1898. Mustered out April 30, 1899.

Daniel V. Snider, Muncie, Delaware County. Enrolled June 29, 1898. Mustered out April 30, 1899.

Clarence T. Swaim. Dublin, Wayne County. Enrolled June 27, 1898. Mustered out April 30, 1899.

John Sweezy, Franklin, Johnson County. Enrolled July 5, 1898. Mustered out. April 30, 1899.

John Wahl, Indianapolis, Marion County. Enrolled July 8, 1898. Mustered out April 30, 1899.

Edgar O. Walden, Muncie, Delaware County. Enrolled June 28, 1898. Mustered out April 30, 1899.

Arthur Wilmuth, Kennard. Enrolled June 28, 1898. Mustered out April 30, 1899.

John W. Wilson. Muncie, Delaware County. Enrolled June 29, 1898. Mustered out April 30, 1899.

Mark E. Winings, Ashland. Enrolled June 28, 1898. Mustered out April 30, 1899.

Walter A. Winings, Ashland. Enrolled June 28, 1898. Mustered out April 30, 1899.

Minor Wintersteen. New Castle. Enrolled June 28, 1898. Mustered out April 30, 1899.

Edwin Wolfe, Mooreland. Enrolled June 28, 1898. Discharged, disability. February 10, 1899.

Harry Woods, Dublin, Wayne County. Enrolled June 28, 1898. Mustered out April 30. 1899.

COMPANY H.

PRIVATES.

William Bock, New Castle. Enrolled August 9, 1898. Mustered out April 30, 1899.

Ira H. Palmes, Rushville, Rush County. New Castle in 1902. Enrolled June 27, 1898. Mustered out April 30, 1899.

ARTILLERY AND INFANTRY IN THE SPANISH-AMERICAN WAR.

RECAPITULATION.

Captain	1
First Lieutenant	1
Second Lieutenant	1
Quartermaster Sergeant	1
Sergeant	5
Corporal	15
Musician	3
Artificer	2
Saddler	1
Wagoner	1
Privates	89
	——
Total	120

DEDUCTIONS.

Non-resident infantrymen in distinctively Henry County Companies	43	
Duplication of names by reason of promotions and transfers	9	52
		——

Total of artillerymen and infantrymen from Henry County in Indiana Organizations in the Spanish-American War... 68

Albert D. Ogborn

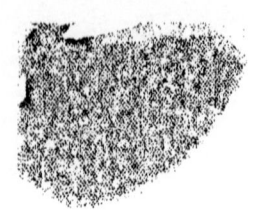

BIOGRAPHICAL SKETCH OF ALBERT DURET OGBORN.

CAPTAIN, COMPANY G, 161ST INFANTRY REGIMENT, INDIANA VOLUNTEERS, SPANISH
AMERICAN WAR; LAWYER AND LEGISLATOR.

It is merit that wins. One may by study fill the mind with knowledge and in theory, at least, know how to do things, but success depends largely upon the application of such knowledge in a practical way. Ability to accomplish results establishes merit and on the strength of merit comes the reward—confidence, commendation and advancement. It is this ability to do things, to accomplish results, that has characterized the life of the subject of this sketch.

In the pioneer days of Eastern Indiana, Wayne County was peopled by large numbers of vigorous, energetic men and women who came mainly from Pennsylvania, old Virginia, North Carolina, Tennessee and Kentucky. Many of these settlers, after a more or less brief residence in Wayne, moved onward to Henry County, and became permanent citizens of that county. Obeying the restless spirit of enterprise and discovery which had carried their parents away from established homes into the wilderness, the descendants of many of the pioneers of "Old Wayne" separated themselves from the parental authority and came to Henry County, where they soon became identified with its people, grew up with its growth and frequently achieved civil, political and social distinction. This early immigration accounts for the close ties of kinship existing between so many of the families of Wayne and Henry counties down to the present time. Descendants of the large Bond family, of the Hoovers, the Elliotts, the Bradburys, the Bransons, the Drapers, the Thornburghs, the Shaffers, the Strattons, the Roofs, the Ezekiel Rogers' branch of the Rogers' family, the Murpheys, the Mendenhalls, the Martindales, the Harveys, the Clifts, the Bundys, and many others, whose names might be mentioned, have spread over Henry County, so that strong ties of blood exist between the two counties, uniting them more closely probably than any other two counties in the State. What is here said of others equally applies to the paternal and maternal families of Albert Duret Ogborn.

His great-great-grandfather, Caleb Ogborn, the first, was born in New Jersey in the year 1729, and his great grandfather, Caleb Ogborn, the second, was born in the same State in the year 1755. Both lived and died in their native State. Caleb Ogborn, the second, married Ann Parker in 1784. She was also a native of New Jersey where she was born in the year 1759. Their son, Samuel Ogborn, the grandfather of Albert D. Ogborn, was born at Egg Harbor, New Jersey, on March 14, 1788. He moved from that State to Ohio in the year 1824 and thence to Wayne County, Indiana, in 1825, settling near Greensfork, where he died July 14, 1839. The grandmother, Esther (Andrews) Ogborn, wife of Samuel Ogborn, was born in New Jersey, November 18, 1784. She died December 19, 1867, and the remains of both herself and husband are buried in the old cemetery at Greensfork. They were all Quakers and their homes in New Jersey were not far from Philadelphia, Pennsylvania, where at that time, the Quaker or Friends' Church was predominant.

Esther Andrews was a descendant of Isaac Andrews, the first, and his wife, Elizabeth Andrews. Their son, Isaac Andrews, the second, born in New Jersey,

September 21, 1749, married in June, 1771, Rebecca Evans, who was born in Eversham, Burlington County, New Jersey, June 19, 1753. To this couple were born November 18, 1784, the twin sisters, Hannah and Esther. Esther was married at Egg Harbor, New Jersey, to Samuel Ogborn in the year 1810, and died in Wayne County, Indiana, December 19, 1867. Of the children born to Samuel and Esther (Andrews) Ogborn, there was Edwin Fothergill Ogborn, father of Albert Duret Ogborn, subject of this sketch; and Allen Ogborn. These were twin brothers, born in New Jersey, August 25, 1816. Edwin Fothergill Ogborn died in New Castle, July 4, 1895, where he had resided for several years during the latter part of his life. His remains lie buried in Sugar Grove Cemetery, near Greensfork, Wayne County, Indiana.

On the maternal side, the great grandfather of Albert Duret Ogborn, was David Bradbury, a native of Elizabeth, New Jersey. He was born October 13, 1760, and in later years moved to Warren County, Ohio, where he died May 7, 1824. He was a soldier of the Revolutionary War, who served five years and among other engagements participated in the historic battles of Staten Island. New York, and Monmouth, New Jersey, and camped with Washington at Valley Forge. He never lived in Indiana except for a brief period in the Wabash Valley. The great grandmother, Susannah (Craig) Bradbury, was born at Elizabeth, New Jersey, April 27, 1762, and it was there she became the wife of David Bradbury. She died in what is now Clay County, Indiana, May 17, 1819. and is buried there.

Daniel Bradbury, the grandfather of Albert Duret Ogborn, was a native of Warren County, Ohio, in the Northwest Territory. He was born September 22, 1800, and died May 29, 1882. He married Mary, daughter of Abraham and Jean (Alexander) Elliott, at Jacksonburg, Wayne County, Indiana, August 13, 1821. She was born November 10, 1804, and died April 4, 1868. They are both buried in the Sugar Grove Cemetery mentioned above. During his lifetime, no man in Wayne County probably was held in higher esteem by the people of Eastern Indiana, among whom he had a wide acquaintance, than Daniel Bradbury. He was prominent in the affairs of the county. Of himself, he says in a brochure, relating to the events of his life, entitled "Memoirs of Daniel Bradbury," published in 1879: "I collected taxes, assessed property and appraised real estate for twenty nine years." Again he says: "I have in my time filled a great many offices of trust and among other things have settled ten estates, as executor and administrator, and was requested to settle many more but declined." Starting out in life for himself at the early age of eighteen years, he determined that his conduct should be governed by the following rule: "I would not keep bad company with male or female; that I would not be a gambler or a drunkard and would lead an honest life, all of which I have kept up to the present time (not even having drunk a dram as a beverage for over forty years) just entering on the eightieth year of my age." He was a man of unusual parts, well informed, earnest in his opinions, firm in his beliefs and possessed of a personal dignity and bearing that won the respect and commendation of all.

His wife, Mary (Elliott) Bradbury, was a fit helpmeet of her husband. She was a sister of the late Judge Jehu T. Elliott, Mrs. Martin L. Bundy, Stephen Elliott, and Elizabeth ("Aunty Betsy") Peed, the mother of Evan Peed, the well known farmer, who is now and has been for several years the superintendent of the Indiana State Agricultural Society. Mrs. Bradbury was quiet in demeanor, possessed of a clear mind (a characteristic of her family), very domestic, very charitable, and to her family, true, loving and devoted. Referring to the death of his wife, Daniel Bradbury in his reminiscences above mentioned says: "She had been an exemplary Christian from her youth, and had been a member of the Old Christian Church since she was sixteen years old." They lived together, a calm, quiet, peaceful life for a period of nearly forty seven years.

Jane (Bradbury) Ogborn, daughter of Daniel and Mary (Elliott) Bradbury, was a native of Wayne County, Indiana, where she was born February 24, 1826; she died September 10, 1882, and lies buried beside her husband in Sugar Grove Cemetery, already mentioned. She was married to Edwin Fothergill Ogborn on April 14, 1850, and to them were born the following named children: Matilda C., now Mrs. Matilda C. Wisehart, of Flagstaff, Arizona; Esther, afterwards Mrs. William R. Wise, now deceased; Daniel B, of Lincoln, Nebraska; Charles S., now deceased; Edwin C., now living in New Castle; Melvina, died in infancy; Albert Duret, the subject of this sketch; Vienna M., a resident of New Castle, and housekeeper for her brother, Albert Duret; and John B., a citizen of Denver, Colorado. These were the children of the second marriage of both parents. The children of Edwin Fothergill Ogborn by a previous marriage were: Mrs. Gulia Weyl, of Economy, Wayne County, Indiana; Mrs. Mary Tingley, of Fairfield, Nebraska; Julia, afterwards Mrs. Samuel McCullough, deceased; and Allen W., deceased. The latter was a member of Company B, 19th Indiana Infantry, and was mortally wounded at the battle of Gettysburg, July 2, 1863; he died in the general hospital at Philadelphia, July 18, 1863. He was a brave and gallant soldier. Jane (Bradbury) Ogborn was first married to James Wilson and they were the parents of one child, a son, named Martin Luther, who was a member of Company A, 36th Indiana Infantry. He died at Buffalo, Kentucky, February 17, 1862, while in the service of his country during the Civil War. Both of these patriotic soldiers are interred in Sugar Grove Cemetery, near Greensfork, Wayne County, Indiana.

ALBERT DURET OGBORN.

Albert Duret Ogborn was born at the old homestead on his father's farm, near Greensfork, Wayne County, Indiana, September 25, 1864, coming upon the stage of life at the time when the United States was engaged in its great conflict for unity and permanency. As child and youth and even to manhood, he remained on the farm and under the parental roof. During those years, he attended regularly, from term to term, the common schools of the neighborhood and acquired the best education afforded by such institutions. On January 14, 1883, he came to New Castle where he engaged in the sale of farm machinery until August, 1884, when he began to clerk in a shoe store. In March, 1886, as he himself says, he "emigrated to Nebraska and returned in four weeks." The remainder of the year 1886, he spent with his brother, Edwin C., who was then engaged in the mercantile business at Arcanum, Ohio. In January, 1887, he took up the study of stenography, pursuing the subject without the aid of a teacher, and in November of that year, through the influence of Judge Eugene H. Bundy, he was appointed storekeeper in the Northern Indiana Hospital for the Insane, at Logansport. He

44

remained with that institution until May, 1889, when he resigned to accept the position of reporter for the Henry Circuit Court. In connection with his duties as reporter, he took up the abstract business and has now the only set of abstract books in the county. He continued to hold the onerous position of reporter until the Spring of 1902, except during the time he was engaged in the Spanish-American War. While attending to his duties as reporter and abstracter, he read law and was in 1894 admitted to the bar of the Henry Circuit Court, Judge Eugene H. Bundy, presiding.

As a reporter, Mr. Ogborn had established an enviable reputation for rapidity and accuracy of service and was in the employ of the State Board of Tax Commissioners of Indiana at four annual sessions; he was the official stenographer for the United States Senate Committee on Territories, of which Senator Beveridge is chairman, during a tour of Arizona, New Mexico, Oklahoma and Indian territories. November, 1902, while they were making a special investigation of those territories with reference to their admission as States of the Union, and in addition on many occasions reported speeches and sermons.

When the Spanish-American War began, Albert D. Ogborn became the prime mover in the recruiting and organizing of what afterwards became Company G. 161st Indiana Infantry. It was mustered into the service of the United States July 12, 1898, and the entire regiment was mustered in at Indianapolis, July 15, 1898. The regiment remained in Camp Mount until August 11, 1898, when under orders it moved to Jacksonville, Florida, where on arrival it was assigned to the First Brigade, Third Division, Seventh Army Corps, under the command of General Fitzhugh Lee. The Third Nebraska, Colonel William Jennings Bryan commanding, was a part of the brigade. The 161st Indiana was afterwards assigned to the First Brigade, Second Division of the Seventh Army Corps. Remaining at Jacksonville until October, 1898, it then moved to Savannah, Georgia, and on December 12th sailed from that point on the transport Sherman to Havana, Cuba, where it landed and marched through the city went into camp at Camp Columbia, Mariano, December 17, 1898, and there the regiment remained until ordered home. It arrived in Savanah, Georgia, March 31, 1899, and was mustered out there on April 30, 1899. A full and complete history of this splendid regiment will be found in chapter XXXI of this work, entitled the "Spanish-American War." The history of the regiment is the military history of Captain Albert D. Ogborn.

In 1900 Captain Ogborn was elected State Senator for the district composed of the counties of Henry, Fayette and Union, and served in the sessions of the General Assembly of 1901 and 1903. He was chairman of the Committee on Military Affairs; also of the Committee on Enrolled Bills; and was a member of the committees on Benevolent Institutions, Public Health, Insurance, Roads, and Congressional Apportionment, during the session of 1901. In the session of 1903, he was chairman of the Committee on Railroads, and a member of the committees on Rules, Finance, Roads, Federal Relations, Public Health, and Legislative Apportionment. Captain Ogborn took a prominent part in the conduct of legislative affairs both in committee and on the floor, every matter coming before the Senate for its action receiving his closest attention.

Prior to the Spanish-American War, Albert D. Ogborn had gained considerable knowledge of military tactics from the fact that he had been for a number of years a member of the Uniformed Rank, Knights of Pythias, which is an organization patterned after that of the United States Army. He commanded, first, the New Castle Company, for a short time, and then for a period of five years was Lieutenant Colonel, and then for four years, Colonel of the Third Indiana Regiment of that organization. He did not surrender his command at the time of entering the United States service during the Spanish-American War, but was simply granted leave of absence, resuming the command on his return from the war. He was afterwards Colonel and Chief of Staff of Brigadier General Harry B. Smith, commanding the Indiana brigade, Uniform Rank, Knights of Pythias. After returning from the Spanish-American War, at the earnest solicitation of Governor James A. Mount, Captain Ogborn organized a company of militia which was mustered into the service of the State on September 26, 1899, and was disbanded at the end of its three years' term of service. He resigned his captaincy in 1900 and went to Chicago to become the confidential secretary of Captain Harry S. New, of the Executive Committee of the Republican National Committee. In the campaign of 1904, Captain Ogborn occupied a like position under Captain New who was vice chairman of the Republican National Committee, and in charge of Western Headquarters.

MILITARY SERVICE OF THE OGBORN FAMILY.

Besides the military service of Captain Albert D. Ogborn as related above, his brother, Daniel Bradbury Ogborn, has followed the colors. He ran away from home, immediately after the Custer Massacre, and enlisted in Troop E, Fifth Cavalry U. S. A., and took part in the relief expedition to the Big Horn Country where the brave General Custer and his entire command had been wiped out by the hostile Indians, lead by the bloodthirsty chief, Sitting Bull.

Mrs. Tingley's son, Edwin Ogborn Tingley, was a member of the First Nebraska Volunteers in the Spanish-American War. He served in the Philippines and was dangerously wounded in one of the battles of the Aguinaldo Insurrection.

Mrs. Weyl's son, John Allen Weyl, enlisted April 26, 1898, in the United States Heavy Artillery and served during the Spanish-American War, being stationed at Fort Myer on the Potomac River, near Washington, D. C. He afterwards enlisted in the Thirty First U. S. Volunteers and served in the Philippines during the insurrection in those islands.

Not to be outdone in loyalty to the flag, Daniel Bradbury Ogborn's son, Clyde C., enlisted in Company G, 161st Indiana Infantry, but much to his regret was rejected by the mustering officer, as he was not able to pass the physical examination.

Besides the foregoing, two uncles and six cousins of Captain Ogborn took part in the Civil War, but at this date the details of their service are not obtainable.

Though the Ogborn family, on the paternal side, is descended from a long line of Quaker ancestors to whom warfare is forbidden, yet their love of country has overtopped the formal dictates of religious faith. They have performed well their part in the service of their common country, like their maternal ancestor, David Bradbury, with his five years of service in the Revolutionary War, that memorable conflict which determined the destiny and civilization of the western world.

CHAPTER XXXII.

ROSTER OF HENRY COUNTY SOLDIERS AND SAILORS IN THE REGULAR ARMY AND NAVY SINCE THE CIVIL WAR, INCLUDING THOSE WHO SERVED DURING THE SPANISH-AMERICAN WAR AND PHILIPPINE INSURRECTION—ROSTER OF HENRY COUNTY SOLDIERS WHO WENT TO OTHER STATES TO ENLIST DURING THE SPANISH-AMERICAN WAR—RECAPITULATION.

REGULAR ARMY AND NAVY.

Soldiers and sailors who have served in the Regular Army or Navy, since the close of the Civil War; also soldiers and sailors who served, during the Spanish-American War and the Philippine Insurrection, in either of the above named branches of the service, and those who have served in either branch, since that time, are included in this list.

The war with Spain was declared April 21, 1898, and amnesty in the Philippines was declared June 20, 1900. Inspection of the date of muster-in and muster-out of any soldier or sailor named in this list will show whether he served at any time during those wars.

James W. Abbott. Spiceland. Private, Company E, 24th Infantry U. S. A. Mustered in July 30, 1881. Appointed Corporal, Regimental Clerk, Sergeant Major, Ordnance Sergeant. The term of his sixth enlistment expired August 6. 1905.

John W. Abbott, Spiceland. Private, Company A, 24th Infantry U. S. A. Mustered in July 30, 1881. Mustered out July 29, 1886.

Burt Albin, Mooreland. Said to have served in the Spanish-American War. Record is incomplete in this History.

Edward R. Alpham, Henry County. Private, Company K, 18th Infantry U. S. A. Mustered in April 24, 1899. Served in the Philippines. Transferred to Company L. 29th Infantry U. S. V. Appointed Corporal. Mustered out April 23, 1902.

Charles A. Armicost. New Lisbon. Rated as Apprentice, U. S. Navy. Enlisted October 26, 1900. Served in U. S. S. Franklin and Lancaster and in U. S. Transport Buffalo. Mustered out July 6, 1901.

George W. Bailey. Greensboro. Private, Company C, 31st Infantry U. S. V. Mustered in July 21. 1899. Served in the Philippines. Mustered out June 18, 1901.

John Baker, Knightstown. Private, Company A, 15th Infantry U. S. A. Mustered in April 25, 1870. Mustered out April 24, 1875.

James A. Berry, New Castle. Private, Company K, 13th Infantry U. S. A. Mustered in May 11, 1870. Mustered out May 10, 1875.

Frederick A. Bills, Lewisville. Private, Company I, 45th Infantry U. S. V. Mustered in September 25, 1899. Appointed Corporal and Sergeant. Served in the Philippines. Mustered out June 3, 1901.

William Bird, Greensboro. Said to have served as private in Company H, 8th Infantry U. S. V. Record is incomplete in this History.

Alva Bowman, Greensboro. Private, Company K, 5th Cavalry U. S. A. Enlisted about 1886. Discharged for disability. Record is incomplete in this History.

Ernest B. Byrket, Ogden. Private, Company M, 10th Infantry U. S. A. Mustered in January 25, 1900. Appointed Corporal. Served in the Philippines. Mustered out January 25, 1903.

Frederick Caldwell, Lewisville. Private, Battery A, 1st Artillery U. S. A. Mustered in November 11, 1898. Transferred to Battery A, 6th Artillery U. S. A. Transferred to Company E, 18th Infanty U. S. A. Served in the Philippines. Mustered out November 10, 1901.

John A. Castetter, Middletown. Private, Company L, 10th Infantry U. S. A. Mustered in October 4, 1899. Served in the Philippines. Mustered out October 10, 1902.

Adelbert B. Cock, Middletown. Private, U. S. Marine Corps. Mustered in November 12, 1902. Serving on U. S. S. Maine. Rated as Ship's Barber. Enlistment will expire November 11, 1906.

Dennis Conner, Mooreland. Private, Company H, 10th Infantry U. S. A. Mustered in January 19, 1893. Appointed Musician. Mustered out May 11, 1895. Re-enlisted as Musician, Company H, 11th Infantry U. S. A. Mustered in January 12, 1897. Appointed Corporal and Sergeant. Served in Porto Rico and in the Philippines. Mustered out January 11, 1903.

George A. Cook, Middletown. Private, Company L, 26th Infantry U. S. V. Mustered in January 10, 1901. Served in the Philippines. Mustered out January 9, 1904.

James E. Cook, Middletown. Private, Company F, 11th Infantry U. S. A. Mustered in January 11, 1897. Served in Porto Rico and in the Philippines. Appointed Corporal and Sergeant. Transferred to Company E, 14th Infantry U. S. A. Now serving his third enlistment.

James O. Crabill, Middletown. Private, Company H, 29th Infantry U. S. V. Mustered in August 6, 1899. Served in the Philippines. Mustered out May 10, 1902.

James F. Dakins, Rogersville. Private, Company G, 16th Infantry U. S. A. Mustered in December 16, 1904. Enlistment will expire December 15, 1907.

Walter Delaware, Millville. Private, Company K, 45th Infantry U. S. V. Mustered in September 18, 1899. Appointed Corporal. Served in the Philippines. Mustered out June 3, 1901.

David P. Denny, Randolph County. Moved to Henry County (Kennard) in 1902. Corporal, Company I, 32nd Infantry U. S. V. Mustered in August 8, 1899. Mustered out August 9, 1902.

John D. Dickerson, New Lisbon. Rated as Machinist, U: S. Navy. Enlisted October 15, 1903. Enlistment will expire October 14, 1907.

James Doggett, Mount Summit. Private, Company F, 31st Infantry U. S. V. Mustered in July 19, 1899. Mustered out June 18, 1901.

Raymond Elliott, Knightstown. Corporal, Company E, 35th Infantry U. S. V. Mustered in August 1, 1899. Served in the Philippines. Mustered out June 18, 1901.

John Estelle, Knightstown. Said to have served in the Spanish-American War. Record is incomplete in this History.

Roy Estelle, Knightstown. Private, Battery D, 6th Artillery U. S. A. Mustered in March 11, 1898. Mustered out March 10, 1901. Enlisted again, as Private, Troop F, 1st Cavalry U. S. A. Mustered in November 29, 1901. Transferred to 12th Cavalry U. S. A., August 14, 1903. Served in the Philippines. Mustered out November 28, 1904.

Robert L. Finnegan, Millville. Private, Troop M, 6th Cavalry U. S. A. Mustered in December 21, 1899. Mustered out December 20, 1902.

Charles E. Fisher, New Castle. Private, Company I, 31st Infantry U. S. V. Mustered in July 27, 1898. Mustered out June 18, 1901.

Homer C. Garriott, Kennard. Private, Troop D, 8th Cavalry U. S. A. Mustered in June 12, 1899. Discharged, disability, August 12, 1899.

Thomas J. Garvis, Millville. Private, Company C, 17th Infantry U. S. A. Mustered in May 11, 1898. Appointed Artificer, Sergeant and Quartermaster Sergeant. Served in Cuba and in the Philippines. Mustered out May 10, 1901.

Heenon Gilbert, New Lisbon. Private, Company K, 22nd Infantry U. S. A. Mustered in May 15, 1899. Served in the Philippines. Discharged, disability, August 29, 1900.

Panander W. Gray, New Castle. Private, Company C, 2nd Infantry U. S. A. Mustered in November 4, 1880. Appointed Corporal, Sergeant and First Sergeant. Mustered out November 4, 1885.

Daniel F. Griffin, Jr., New Castle. Private, Company C, 31st Infantry U. S. V. Mustered in July 13, 1899. Died at Prang Frang., Philippine Islands, December 21, 1900.

William J. P. Halstead, Shirley. Private, Company G, 2nd Infantry U. S. A. Mustered in June 18, 1900. Appointed Artificer, Corporal, Sergeant and Quartermaster Sergeant. Served in the Philippines. Mustered out June 17, 1903.

Ernest Hardway, Christian County, Kentucky. Moved to New Castle. Private, Company F, 24th Infantry U. S. A. Mustered in February 27, 1901. Served in the Philippines. Mustered out February 26, 1904.

Frank W. Harris, Morgan County. Moved to Henry County (Kennard) in 1901. Private, Company L, 38th Infantry U. S. V. Mustered in September 18, 1899. Appointed Corporal. Transferred to the Regimental Band. Served in the Philippines. Mustered out June 30, 1901.

Dallas D. Harry, Mount Summit. Private, Troop H, 13th Cavalry U. S. A. Mustered in July 8, 1901. Re-enlisted April 3, 1903, same Troop and Regiment. Appointed Sergeant and detailed Acting Battalion Sergeant Major. Served in the Philippines. Enlistment will expire April 2, 1906.

Samuel G. Hays, Rogersville. Private, Company I, 21st Infantry U. S. A. Mustered in March 11, 1878. Discharged, disability, March 27, 1880.

Leander E. Hazzard, New Castle. (Brother of the Author of this History). Private, Troop H, 5th Cavalry U. S. A. Mustered in November 25, 1876. Killed by the Indians in Wyoming Territory. Exact date of death and burial place unknown.

Claude H. Heacock, Lewisville. Private, Battery K, 3rd Artillery U. S. A. Mustered in June 12, 1899. Served in the China Relief Expedition and in the Philippines. Transferred to Battery L. Mustered out June 23, 1902.

Emery A. Hilkirk, Knightstown. Private, Company A, 11th Infantry U. S. A. Mustered in September 15, 1897. Appointed Corporal and Sergeant. Mustered out September 15, 1900.

John S. Hill, Rush County. Moved to Henry County (Lewisville) in 1902. Private, Company I, 18th Infantry U. S. A. Mustered in March 6, 1898. Served in the Philippines. Mustered out March 5, 1901.

John Hodson, Middletown. Private, Company A, 45th Infantry U. S. V. Mustered in September 30, 1899. Served in the Philippines. Discharged, disability, February 13, 1901.

Carl L. Holloway, Shirley. Private, Company G, 29th Infantry U. S. V. Mustered in August 8, 1899. Mustered out May 10, 1902.

Louis M. Hoosier, Greensboro. Private, Company C, 24th Infantry U. S. A. Mustered in January 24, 1898. Mustered out March 18, 1899.

William W. Hutson, Knightstown. Private, Company E, 35th Infantry U. S. V. Mustered in August 1, 1900. Served in the Philippines. Mustered out August 1, 1901.

Forest R. Jacobs, Greensboro. Private, Company H, 11th Infantry U. S. A. Mustered in March 18, 1894. Mustered out June 19, 1898. Re-enlisted same company and regiment September 18, 1898. Transferred to Company D. Served in Porto Rico. Mustered out September 17, 1900. Re-enlisted 1st Sergeant, Company H, Porto Rico Provisional Regiment of Infantry. Mustered in August 12, 1901. Appointed Post Quartermaster Sergeant U. S. A. Mustered out August 11, 1904. Re-enlisted for Post Non-Commissioned Staff August 12, 1904. Now serving at Camp Wallace, Union, Philippine Islands, as Post Quartermaster Sergeant.

John N. Jacobs, Greensboro. Private, Troop I, 12th Cavalry U. S. A. Mustered in May 20, 1901. Mustered out May 19, 1904.

Harvey Kahoon, Kennard. Private, Company B, 23rd Infantry U. S. A. Mustered in May 13, 1899. Discharged, disability, February 13, 1900.

Lewis Kelly, Knightstown. Private, Company B, 5th Infantry U. S. A. Mustered In January 23, 1870. Mustered out January 24, 1875.

Elmore F. Keough, St. Louis, Missouri. Moved to Henry County (Greensboro) in 1889. Private, Company E, 15th Infantry U. S. A. Mustered in August 9, 1878. Mustered out August 8, 1883.

Oren E. Lambird, Mooreland. Private, Troop H, 12th Cavalry U. S. A. Mustered in March 13, 1903. Died in the Philippines November 20, 1903.

William Lehman, Wayne County. Moved to Henry County (Sulphur Springs) in 1894. Private, Troop D, 7th Cavalry U. S. A. Mustered in November 8, 1881. Discharged, disability, September 14, 1882. Re-enlisted as private, Troop H, 1st Cavalry U. S. A. Mustered in December 23, 1883. Appointed Sergeant. Mustered out December 21, 1888. Re-enlisted as Sergeant, Troop K, 3rd Cavalry U. S. A. Mustered in January 15, 1889. Mustered out August 28, 1897. Re-enlisted as Sergeant, Troop C, 3rd Cavalry U. S. A. Mustered in November 1, 1897. Appointed 1st Sergeant. Mustered out October 31, 1900. Re-enlisted as Sergeant, Company K, 13th Cavalry U. S. A. Mustered in January 10, 1902. Supposed to be still in the army.

James Lennington, Blountsville. Private, Company H, 23rd Infantry U. S. A. Mustered in May 19, 1899. Served in the Philippines. Mustered out May 18, 1902.

Robert C. McConnell, Knightstown. Private, 25th Company, Coast Artillery U. S. A. Mustered in November 25, 1899. Served in China Relief Expedition. Mustered out November 24, 1902.

William E. McCorkle, Knightstown. Bugler, Company A, 12th Infantry U. S. A. Mustered in September 27, 1897. Died at home in Knightstown, Indiana, October 8, 1898.

Harry F. McGuire, New Lisbon. Rated as Second Class Baker, U. S. Navy. Enlisted October 15, 1903. Enlistment will expire October 14, 1907.

Frank M. Main, Mooreland. Private, Hospital Corps U. S. A. Mustered in December 21, 1898. Served in the Philippines. Mustered out December 20, 1901.

Ross G. Miller, Mooreland. Private, Troop F, 5th Cavalry U. S. A. Mustered in June 13, 1898. Mustered out April 21, 1899. Re-enlisted as private, Troop A, 4th Cavalry U. S. A. Mustered in May 31, 1899. Discharged November 8, 1900, account of wounds received near Santa Crux, Philippine Islands, February, 1900.

Herbert W. Morris, New Castle. Private, Company C, 31st Infantry U. S. V. Mustered in July 11, 1899. Served in the Philippines. Mustered out March 29, 1901.

Otis C. Newby, Greensboro. Corporal, Company C, 45th Infantry U. S. V. Mustered in September 1, 1899. Killed near Bulan, Luzon, Philippine Islands, August 24, 1900.

Boyd Nicholson, New Castle. Private, Company G, 31st Infantry U. S. V. Mustered in July 18, 1899. Served in the Philippines. Mustered out June 18, 1901.

Eugene Otis, Raysville. Said to have served in the Spanish-American War. Record is incomplete in this History.

John E. Paully, Shirley. Private, Company H, 16th Infantry U. S. A. Mustered in July 7, 1897. Mustered out December 19, 1899.

William W. Pence, New Castle. Private, Company K, 7th Infantry U. S. A. Mustered in October 14, 1900. Served in the Philippines. Died at Presidio, San Francisco, California, July 8, 1903.

Herman L. Pitts, Knightstown. Private, 25th Company, Coast Artillery U. S. A. Mustered in November 25, 1899. Served in the China Relief Expedition. Mustered out November 24, 1902.

Walter E. Pitts, Knightstown. Private, 25th Company, Coast Artillery U. S. A. Mustered in November 25, 1899. Served in the China Relief Expedition. Mustered out November 24, 1902.

John J. Powell, New Castle. Private, Reserve Hospital Corps, First Army Corps, U. S. A. Mustered in July 17, 1898. Served in Porto.Rico. Mustered out April 9, 1899.

Leonard M. Reeder, Mount Summit. Private, Company H, 12th Infantry U. S. A. Mustered in May 15, 1898. Killed at Lopez, Philippine Islands, September 10, 1900.

Thomas B. Reeder, Junior, Mount Summit. Private, Company H, 12th Infantry U. S. A. Mustered in August 15, 1897. Mustered out August 14, 1900.

Kalula Riley, Middletown. Private, Company A, 45th Infantry U. S. V. Mustered in September 30, 1899. Served in the Philippines. Mustered out October, 1901. Re-enlisted as Private. Troop E, 5th Cavalry U. S. A. Mustered in May 27, 1904. Enlistment will expire May 26, 1907.

Clarence A. Roberts, Raysville. Private, Company M, 13th Infantry U. S. A. Mustered in August 31, 1900. Appointed Corporal and Sergeant. Served in the Philippines. Mustered out August 30, 1903.

Henry C. Rozell, Blountsville, Private, Company A, 23rd Infantry U. S. A. Mustered in May 16, 1898. Mustered out October 28, 1898. Re-enlisted as private, Company A, 29th Infantry U. S. V. Mustered in March 9, 1901. Transferred to Company H, 5th Infantry U. S. A. March 22, 1901. Transferred to Troop D, 1st Cavalry U. S. A., July 10, 1902. Served in the Philippines. Mustered out March 8, 1904.

William B. Sanders, Middletown. Private, 80th Company, Coast Artillery U. S. A. Mustered in August 15, 1901. Mustered out August 14, 1904.

Frank A. Shepherd, Greensboro. Rated as Apprentice, third class. Enlisted June 11, 1901. Rated as Apprentice, second class and first class. Served in U. S. S. Constellation, Newport, Hartford, Columbia. Wabash and Newark. Enlistment expired July 20, 1905.

Charles Sipes, Middletown. U. S. Hospital Corps. Mustered in December 23, 1898. Served in the Philippines. Mustered out December 19, 1901.

Martin Tarr, Lewisville. Private, Company E, 1st Infantry, U. S. A. Mustered in October 15, 1880. Appointed Corporal, Sergeant and First Sergeant. Mustered out October 15, 1885.

Earl Tipton, Knightstown. Private, Company H. 20th Infantry U. S. A. Mustered in May 11, 1903. Transferred to Company I, 19th Infantry, U. S. A. Enlistment will expire May 10, 1906.

Roy Tipton, Knightstown. Private, 25th Company, Coast Artillery, U. S. A. Mutsered in November 25, 1899. Served in the China Relief Expedition. Mustered out November 24, 1902.

Edwin R. Upham, New Castle. Enlisted at Nashville, Davidson County, Tennessee. as Sergeant, Company L, 2nd Tennessee Infantry. Mustered in May 7, 1898. Transferred to Volunteer Signal Corps. November 17, 1898. Enlisted as Private, Company K, 18th Infantry, U. S. A. Mustered in April 24, 1899. Appointed Corporal. Transferred to Company L, 29th Infantry, U. S. V. Mustered out April 23, 1902. Enlisted again and is now in the army.

Edward Vannatta, Mount Summit. Said to have served during the Spanish-American War in Company I, 18th Infantry, U. S. A. Record is incomplete in this History.

William Vannatta. Mount Summit. Said to have enlisted at Indianapolis, during the Spanish-American War, and is presumed to have served in the Philippines. Record is incomplete in this History.

Ronald B. Veach, Knightstown. Private, Company A, 11th Infantry, U. S. A. Mustered in September 15, 1897. Served in Porto Rico. Mustered out September 15, 1900.

Harry Warnock, Honey Creek. Enlisted at Hudson. St. Croix County, Wisconsin. Private, Company C. 3rd Wisconsin Infantry. Mustered in May 11, 1898. Mustered out January 7, 1899. Enlisted as Private, Company F, 31st Infantry, U. S. V. Mustered in July 19, 1899. Mustered out June 16, 1901.

Jesse Warnock, Honey Creek. Private, Company C and H, 2nd Infantry, U. S. A. Mustered in March 1, 1899. Served in Cuba and in the Philippines. Mustered out March 21, 1902.

Ora J. Warnock. Honey Creek. Private, Troop K, 11th Cavalry, U. S. A. Mustered in May 25, 1904. Enlistment will expire May 24, 1907.

William F. White, Luray. Private. Battery L, 4th Artillery, U. S. A. Mustered in April 28, 1898. Mustered out March 4, 1899.

John L. Willis, Straughn. Private, Company A. 2nd Infantry, U. S. A. Mustered in September 1, 1897. Died July 3, 1898, account of wounds at San Juan Hill, Cuba, July 1, 1898.

Mark E. Winings, Ashland. Embalmer. Entered the service July 10, 1901. Served on U. S. Army Transport McClellan between New York City and the Philippines. Discharged March 20, 1903, by reason of U. S. Army Transport going out of commission.

Frank Woodward, Knightstown. Private, Company L, 31st Infantry, U. S. V. Mustered in July 24, 1899. Mustered out May 18, 1901.

Isaac H. Wrightsman, Mooreland. Private, 12th Battery, U. S. A. Mustered in December 9, 1901. Appointed Corporal. Mustered out December 8, 1904.

HENRY COUNTY SOLDIERS WHO WENT TO OTHER STATES TO ENLIST DURING THE SPANISH-AMERICAN WAR.

Charles H. Barr, New Castle. Enlisted at Benton Harbor, Berrien County, Michigan. Private, Company I, 33rd Michigan Infantry. Mustered in May 16, 1898. Appointed Quartermaster Sergeant. Mustered out January 7, 1899.

Arthur C. Bernard, Knightstown. Enlisted at Hamilton, Butler County, Ohio. Private, Company E, 1st Ohio Infantry. Mustered in April 26, 1898. Mustered out October 25, 1898.

John C. Bright, Cadiz. Enlisted at Horton, Brown County, Kansas. Private, Company G, 22nd Kansas Infantry. Mustered in May 6, 1898. Mustered out November 3, 1898.

Lemuel D. Cummins, Sulphur Springs. Enlisted at Kansas City, Wyandotte County, Kansas. Private, Company B, 20th Kansas Infantry. Mustered in May 9, 1898. Appointed Corporal and Sergeant. Mustered out October 28, 1898.

Percy Donaldson, New Lisbon. Enlisted at Columbus, Ohio. Bugler, Company K, 3rd Tennessee Infantry. Mustered in July 4, 1898. Mustered out January 31, 1899.

William E. Myers, Henry County. Enlisted at San Francisco, California. Private, Company C, 1st Tennessee Infantry. Mustered in June 29, 1898. Mustered out November 23, 1899.

MISCELLANEOUS.

RECAPITULATION.

Sergeant Major	2
Ordnance Sergeant	1
Quartermaster Sergeant	3
First Sergeant	4
Sergeant	12
Corporal	19
Regimental Band	1
Musician	1
Bugler	2
Artificer	2
Regimental Clerk	1
Hospital Corps	1
Embalmer	1
Incomplete	1
Apprentice (Navy)	2
Ship's Barber (Navy)	1
Machinist (Navy)	1
Second Class Baker (Navy)	1
Privates	80
Total	142

DEDUCTIONS.

Soldiers from other counties who have moved to Henry County since expiration of service	6
Duplication of names by reason of promotions and transfers	42 48

Total of soldiers and sailors in the Regular Army and Navy since the Civil War.... 94

CHAPTER XXXIII.

REVOLUTIONARY WAR—WAR OF 1812-15.

SOLDIERS OF THE REVOLUTIONARY WAR—SOLDIERS OF THE WAR OF 1812-15.

SOLDIERS OF THE REVOLUTION IN HENRY COUNTY.

From the close of the War of the Revolution in 1783 until the lands in Henry County, Indiana, were placed on sale by the Government, a period of about forty years had elapsed. Many of the younger patriots, who had taken part in that struggle, were still living and it is definitely known that some of these came into the county soon after its settlement began and here found their last resting place.

Below are given in alphabetical order, the names of soldiers of the Revolution, known to have settled in the county, with the facts of their personal history, so far as known. Others, doubtless, located in Henry County, but by reason of the lapse of time, their names have not been obtainable.

Richard Conway. Settled in Liberty Township in 1821, where he afterwards entered government land. From what Colony he served in the Revolutionary War is not definitely known.

Rhoderick Craig. Settled in Harrison Township. Remains said to be buried in the Reynolds Cemetery, near Cadiz. From what Colony he served in the Revolutionary War and at what time he came to Henry County are not definitely known.

———————— Hubbell. Settled in Liberty Township. Remains said to be buried in the Wisehart Cemetery, near New Lisbon. From what Colony he served in the Revolutionary War and at what time he came to Henry County are not definitely known.

Andrew Ice. Settled in Prairie Township in 1832. Lived to an advanced age and left behind him a long line of descendants, a number of whom are now prominent citizens of the township. He served in a Virginia regiment, during the Revolutionary War, and was the father of Colonel Jesse Ice, a soldier of the War of 1812-1815.

———————— Isham. Settled near the present site of Knightstown, Wayne Township, where he lived and died. From what Colony he served in the Revolutionary War and at what time he came to Henry County are not definitely known.

Christopher Long. A pioneer of Liberty Township. The remains of this venerable soldier of the Revolutionary War, together with those of his wife, lie buried at a point about four and a half miles, south of east, from New Castle, in Liberty Township, near what is known as the "Boyd Schoolhouse", and close to the southeast corner made by the crossing of the two turnpikes. Marking the grave, stands a marble monument, nine feet and six inches high, surrounded by an iron railing, four feet in height, and twelve feet long, north and south, by nine feet wide, east and west. On the west side of the monument, in plain view of the passing traveler, is the following inscription:

"CHRISTOPHER LONG.

"A SOLDIER OF THE REVOLUTION.

"DIED AUGUST 14, 1829, AGED EIGHTY-THREE YEARS AND THREE MONTHS.

"SARAH, HIS WIFE, DIED SEPTEMBER 11, 1822, IN HER 66TH YEAR."

On the base of the monument is another inscription, containing this appeal:

"POSTERITY PRESERVE THESE GRAVES."

Jacob Parkhurst. Settled in Greensboro Township, where he lived and died. From what Colony he served in the Revolutionary War and at what time he came to Henry County are not definitely known.

Orr Scovell . An early settler in Henry County. Served in a New Jersey or Connecticut regiment, during the Revolutionary War. At the time of his death, he lived on what is now known as the Graham Farm, near the "Old Stone Quarry Mill", in Spiceland Township. He was the father of Elisha Scovell, who was the father-in-law of John Morris, of Wayne Township, and therefore the great grandfather of John M. Morris, the present judge of the Henry Circuit Court.

John Shadlow. An early settler in Henry County. Remains are buried in White Union Cemetery, Fall Creek Township. From what Colony he served in the Revolutionary War and at what time he came to Henry County are not definitely known.

James S. Stinson. Settled in Henry Township in 1822. He served in a North Carolina regiment, during the Revolutionary War.

SOLDIERS OF THE SECOND WAR (1812-1815) WITH GREAT BRITAIN IN HENRY COUNTY.

From the time of the treaty of peace in December, 1814, in the second war between the United States and Great Britain, until William Owen had entered the first tract of land in Henry County, but little more than seven years had elapsed. This first entry of land by Owen bears the date of February 4, 1821.

The great majority of the veterans of that war were young men and many of them secured grants of land by reason of their military service. A number sought and found homes in Henry County. One of the most considerable of these was Colonel Jesse Ice, who was a Captain in the army of General Harrison, and who subsequently was promoted to the rank of Colonel, for gallant and meritorious conduct.

The names of all these defenders of the Republic, who came to Henry County, so far as known, are given below, classified by townships. The list is not, perhaps, full and complete, but it contains the names of all that could be found by most diligent search. ' The sources of information from which this list, is compiled are former publications relating to Henry County, lists on file in the different Posts of the Grand Army of the Republic, and personal investigation by the author. The list of soldiers of this war for Wayne is probably more incomplete than that of any other township in the county.

BLUE RIVER TOWNSHIP.

Abraham Corey, Joseph Corey, Jacob Jones, Samuel Marshall, William Moore, Jonathan Pierce, George Rinard.

DUDLEY TOWNSHIP.

Benjamin Dennis, John Jacoby, William Rladon, Merriman Straughn, John Van Buskirk.

FALL CREEK TOWNSHIP.

Solomon Bowers, Isaac Cooper, Charles Cummins, John Fadely, David Fleming, William Graham, Joseph Gossett, Samuel Huston, Henry Isenhour , John Keesling, Reuben

McConnell, Charles Mitchell, William Prigg, Henry Richman, Anthony Sanders, Jacob Shedron. Thomas Windsor, Thomas Wisehart.

FRANKLIN TOWNSHIP.

Jacob Lawson. David Messick, Samuel Templeton.

GREENSBORO TOWNSHIP.

Henry Camplin, Jacob Elliott, John Englerth, John Judge.

HARRISON TOWNSHIP.

Thomas Allen, Israel Jackson. John McCormack, Peter Spencer.

HENRY TOWNSHIP.

David Bowers. Henry Fitch, Alexander Johnson, William McDowell, David Phillips. Levi Shackle. Asahel Woodward.

JEFFERSON TOWNSHIP.

Aaron Ballard, Samuel Beavers. John Cummins, John Hayes.

LIBERTY TOWNSHIP.

Isaac Baker, John Collingsworth, William Grose, John Nicholson, Hiram Perry. Moses Robertson, George Thornton, Ashbury Wood.

PRAIRIE TOWNSHIP.

Michael Brannon, Joseph Cowgill. James Dodd, Robert Downs, Absalom Harvey, Benjamin Harvey, William Hazelton, George Howk, Jesse Ice, William Longfellow, Philip Shively. Alexander Winders.

SPICELAND TOWNSHIP.

Levi Butler, Christian Fout, Jesse L. Smith.

STONY CREEK TOWNSHIP.

Andrew Blount, Bissell Burr, Edward Daugherty, Isaac Daugherty. Peter Davis. Daniel Heffner, John Moore, Jonathan Ross, Nathaniel Thalls. Daniel Trowbridge.

WAYNE TOWNSHIP

Waitsel M. Carey, Major William Doughty, Daniel Mason.

MISCELLANEOUS.

The author has been unable to classify the following by townships: Jacob Chrestner. Enoch Hoglin. David Landis, Martin Oder. David Porter, Humphrey Sutton, James Walters.

, Jacob Elliott, John Englerth, John Judge.

HARRISON TOWNSHIP.

ael Jackson, John McCormack. Peter Spencer.

HENRY TOWNSHIP.

teh, Alexander Johnson, William McDowell, David Phillips, are

JEFFERSON TOWNSHIP.

ar uel Beavers. John Cummins. John Hayes.

LIBERTY TOWNSHIP.

ngsworth. William Grose, John Nicholson, Hiram Perry, ston, Ashbury Wood.

PRAIRIE TOWNSHIP.

h Cowgill, James Dodd, Robert Downs, Absalom Harvey, ckelton, George Howk, Jesse Ice, William Longfellow, Philip

SPICELAND TOWNSHIP.

ther Christian Fout. Jesse L. Smith.

STONY CREEK TOWNSHIP.

Burr. Edward Daugherty, Isaac Daugherty. Peter Davis. Jonathan Ross. Nathaniel Thalls. Daniel Trowbridge.

Asahel Woodward

CHAPTER XXXIV.

THE MEXICAN WAR.

BRIEF HISTORY OF THE MEXICAN WAR—PAPERS RELATING TO THE MEXICAN WAR BY CAPTAIN PYRRHUS WOODWARD—ROSTER OF MEXICAN WAR SOLDIERS NOT MENTIONED BY CAPTAIN WOODWARD—COMPANIES ORGANIZED IN HENRY COUNTY FOR THE MEXICAN WAR, NOT CALLED INTO ACTIVE SERVICE —PERSONAL RECOLLECTIONS OF THE MEXICAN WAR BY DAVID BEARLEY— GEORGE BURTON—RECAPITULATION.

During the administration of Governor James Whitcomb the war with Mexico occurred, which resulted in annexing to the United States vast tracts of land in the South and West. Indiana contributed her full ratio to the troops in that war, and with a remarkable spirit of promptness and patriotism adopted all measures to sustain the general Government. These new acquisitions of territory re-opened the discussion of the slavery question, and Governor Whitcomb expressed his opposition to a further extension of the "national sin."

The causes which led to a declaration of war against Mexico in 1846, must be sought for as far back as the year 1830, when the present State of Texas formed a province of New and Independent Mexico. During the years immediately preceding 1830, Moses Austin, of Connecticut, obtained a liberal grant of lands from the established Government, and on his death his son was treated in an equally liberal manner. The glowing accounts rendered by Austin, and the vivid picture of Elysian fields by visiting journalists, soon resulted in the influx of a large tide of immigrants, nor did the movement to the Southwest cease until 1830. The Mexican province held a prosperous population, comprising 10,000 American citizens. The rapacious Government of the Mexicans looked with greed and jealousy upon their eastern province, and, under the presidency of General Santa Anna, enacted such measures, both unjust and oppressive, as would meet their design of goading the people of Texas on to revolution, and thus afford an opportunity for the infliction of punishment upon subjects whose crime was industry and its accompaniment, prosperity. Precisely in keeping with the course pursued by the British toward the colonists of the Eastern States in the last century, Santa Anna's Government met the remonstrances of the colonists of Texas with threats; and they, secure in their consciousness of right, quietly issued their declaration of independence, and proved its literal meaning on the field of Gonzales in 1835, having with a force of 500 men forced the Mexican army of 1,000 to flee for refuge to their strongholds. Battle after battle followed, bringing victory always to the Colonists, and ultimately resulting in the total rout of the Mexican army and the evacuation of Texas. The routed army after a short term of rest reorganized. and reappeared in the Territory, 8,000 strong. On April 21, a division of this large force under Santa Anna encountered the Texans under General Samuel Houston on the banks of the San Jacinto, and though Houston could only oppose 800 men to the Mexican legions, the latter were driven from the field. nor could they reform their scattered ranks until their General was captured the next day and forced to sign the declaration of 1835. The signature of Santa Anna, though ignored by the Congress of the Mexican Republic, and consequently left unratified on, the part of Mexico, effected so much. that after the second defeat of the army of the Republic all the hostilities of an important nature ceased, the Republic of Texas was recognized by the powers, and subsequently became an integral part of the United States. July 4, 1846. At this period General Herrera was president of Mexico. He was a man of peace, of common sense. and very patriotic; and he entertained, or pretended to entertain, the great neighboring Republic in high esteem. For this reason he grew unpopular with his people, and General Paredes was called to the presidential chair, which he continued to occupy until the breaking out of actual hostilities with the United States, when General Santa Anna was elected thereto.

Captain Pyrrhus Woodward. a soldier of two wars, having served in the Mexican War, as Orderly Sergeant, Company H, 5th Indiana Infantry, and in the Civil War, as Captain, Company C. 36th Indiana Infantry, a full biographical sketch of whom is published in this History (Chapter XVII). left, among his papers relating to the Mexican War, in three parts, a full account of "Henry County's contribution to the history of that sanguinary contest."

Captain Woodward was the paternal uncle of the author of this History, and it was at his house that the latter was making his home when the Civil War began, and became a soldier in the company commanded by Captain Woodward.

The papers relating to the Mexican War, prepared by the last named. have been furnished to the author for publication in this History by the daughter of Captain Woodward, Mrs. Belle Springer, of New Castle. and here follow in their several parts.

PART I.

The admission of Texas, which had previously declared its independence. into the Union in 1845, was the beginning of unfriendly relations between the United States and Mexico. The western boundary of the new State was in dispute. and its annexation to the United States was regarded as an unfriendly act by our neighboring Republic. Our Government sent General Taylor into the newly acquired territory with an army of occupation. On the 28th of March. 1846, General Taylor took up his position on the Rio Grande, opposite Matamoras. On the 12th of April General Ampudia. the Mexican General, notified Taylor to retire beyond the Nueces River. which the Mexican Government claimed was the western boundary of Texas. General Taylor did not heed the notice. but sent a force of sixty three dragoons to ascertain whether the Mexican troops had crossed the Rio Grande. A strong Mexican force fell upon this small body of troops and after killing and wounding seventeen of them, forced the Americans to surrender. This was the first act of bloodshed, and when the news of the affair reached the United States, the excitement rose to a high pitch.

On May 8, 1846, General Taylor fought the battle of Palo Alto and on the day following the battle of Resaca de la Palma. These battles were fought upon Texas soil and in both engagements, the American troops were victorious. On May 16, Congress formally declared war. General Taylor crossed the Rio Grande on May 18, and in September following defeated the Mexicans at Monterey. On the 23d of February, 1847, the American Army, under Taylor, encountered the Mexican Army, commanded by Santa Anna, at Buena Vista, and although the American forces were outnumbered four to one, won a decisive victory, which gave the Americans the possession of the northeastern part of Mexico.

The second American Army consisting of about 13,000 men, under the command of General Scott, landed near Vera Cruz on March 9, 1847, and after a short siege of the city, captured the strong fortress of San Juan de Ulloa on March 27. The Army of General Scott pressed forward towards the City of Mexico, two hundred and sixty miles from the coast, successfully fighting the battles of Cerro Gordo, Contreras, Churubusco, Molino del Rey, and Chapultepec, and on the morning of September 14, the victorious American army entered the City of Mexico and the American flag floated over the National Palace of Mexico.

Under the act of Congress, approved May 13, 1846, providing for the organization of volunteer troops, Governor Whitcomb had issued a proclamation calling for volunteers and the First, Second and Third Regiments of Indiana Volunteers had been organized in 1846, and had promptly gone to the seat of war. The popular sentiment of the North was by no means unanimously favorable to the war, for its was· believed by many that its ultimate object was the acquisition of territory in the interests of slavery. And while the sentiment of Henry County was not strongly favorable to the war, yet early in 1847, a company composed of about sixty members was recruited at New Castle and vicinity. As my grandfather, Thomas Woodward had served in the Revolutionary Army and Asahel Woodward, my father, had been a soldier in Captain Sloan's company, from Ohio, in the War of 1812, it was, perhaps, only natural that I should desire to enter the army, for I was then quite a young man, and I took an active part in recruiting this company, and I might say that I was in about as much danger, on one or two occasions, from angry wives and mothers who thought I was trying to persuade their husbands and sons to volunteer, as I afterwards encountered in Mexico. This company organized by electing, as Captain, Mathew S. Ward, a bright young lawyer of New Castle, who afterwards removed to Mississippi and became a Major of artillery in the Confederate army. Henry Shroyer was elected First Lieutenant and I was chosen Second Lieutenant. The services of the company were not accepted because at the time the State's quota was full.

The Fifth Regiment of Indiana was organized in October, 1847. Captain Ebenezer Cary of Marion had recruited about forty men in Grant County, and on October 4, 1847, this body of men came to New Castle in wagons, en route to Indianapolis. At New Castle, the following persons from Henry County joined Captain Cary's company: Finley Adams, Elam Armfield, James N. Cary, Harvey Copeland, Charles Fifer, Norviel Fleming, Jeremiah Gossett, David Harker, Chapman Mann, William Mann, Abner Phillips, William H. Roby, James A. Schuman, Henry Shank, George Tarkleson, George W. Thompson, David Warner, Richard Webster, Pyrrhus Woodward.

The greater number of those who enlisted in Captain Cary's company, from Henry County, were from Fall Creek Township. George W. Thompson and David Harker were from Harrison Township; James A. Schuman from Prairie Township; 'Elam Armfield from Greensboro Township; Abner Phillips and Harvey Copeland from Henry Township; James N. Cary was from Knightstown. Richard Webster and myself were from New Castle. Amos Brown, a bright young colored man, twenty three years of age, and nearly white, from Fall Creek Township, also joined the company in the capacity of officer's cook. The ages of the men who enlisted from Henry County, as shown by the muster-out rolls now on file in the office of the Adjutant General at Indianapolis, and which have been consulted in the preparation of this article were as follows: Finley Andrews, 20; Elam Armfield, 25; James N. Cary, 24; Harvey Copeland, 19; Charles Fifer, 24; Norviel Fleming, 18; Jeremiah Gossett. 32; David Harker, 19; Chapman Mann, 22; William Mann, 24; Abner Phillips, 21; William H. Roby, 40; James A. Schuman, 18;'Henry Shank, 29; George Tarkleson, 43; George W. Thompson, 21; David Warner, 21; Richard Webster, 21; Pyrrhus Woodward, 25.

Dr. James M. Montgomery, of Lewisville. well known to the older citizens of Franklin Township, had enlisted in another company of the Fifth Regiment and William D. Schuman, of Prairie Township, and a brother of James A. Schuman had previously enlisted in another regiment.

Captain Cary's company remained in New Castle over night, and on October 5, departed for Indianapolis in wagons, going by the way of Knightstown and Greenfield. With the addition of the Henry County recruits the company had about sixty members. On the first night after leaving New Castle we stopped at Greenfield and were taken to the home of the citizens. The next day we reached Indianapolis, where we took the train for Madison, Indiana, going by the new railroad, which had just been completed. Here we went into camp where several companies had preceded us.

The commissioned officers of the company had been selected before the company left Marion and were as follows: Captain, Ebenezer Cary; First Lieutenant. Thomas F. Marshall; Second Lieutenant. David Shunk; additional Second Lieutenant. Joseph W. Holliday. At Madison. about twenty recruits from Jefferson County were assigned to our company which now had its full complement of men. The non-commissioned officers of the company were selected at Madison and I was chosen second, or duty, sergeant and Henry Shank third duty sergeant. Captain Cary's company was mustered into the service of the United States on October 14. 1847, as Company H, of the Fifth Regiment of Indiana Foot Volunteers, as the regiment was designated on the records of the Adjutant General's office. The members of the various companies were in the main young men, and imbued with a lofty spirit of patriotism. The stern realities of war had not yet worn off the glamour which surrounds a soldier's life and every company in camp had chosen a name, illustrating at once the ardor as well as the light hearted enthusiasm of new troops, and by these names the different companies were designated upon the rolls. The Indiana Guards, from Vernon. commanded by Captain Horace Hull. were mustered as Company A; Captain George Greene's Rough and Ready Guards from Charlestown became Company B; the Covington Guards from Madison. commanded by Captain Robert M. Evans, became Company C; the Hancock B'hoys from Greenfield, commanded by Captain James R. Bracken, were mustered as Company D; the Shelbyville Hards from Shelbyville, commanded by Captain Samuel McKinsey, became Company E; the Centre Guards from Madison, commanded by Captain John McDougall, became Company F; Grabbers No. 2, from Lawrenceburg, commanded by Captain Aaron C. Gibbs, were mustered as Company G. Our own Company H, was known as the Washington Guards. The Montgomery boys from Crawfordsville, commanded by Captain Allen May, were mustered as Company I and the Wayne Guards from Madison, commanded by Captain David W. Lewis, as Company K.

The organization of the Fifth Regiment was completed at Madison and our regimental officers were James H. Lane, Colonel; Allen May, Lieutenant Colonel; John M. Myers, Major; James Baker, was Regimental Quartermaster; James S. Athon, Surgeon and John M. Lord Adjutant. Colonel Lane had entered the army as Captain of the Dearborn Volunteers and had seen service in the Third Regiment, before he became Colonel of the Fifth. He was thirty three years old, a handsome man and a gallant soldier. His subsequent brilliant but stormy career in Kansas and Missouri is well known. Captain May of Company I, recruited at Crawfordsville, was promoted to be Lieutenant Colonel and Lieutenant Mahlon D. Manson, afterwards a distinguished officer in the Civil War became Captain of the company. John M. Myers, Major, was twenty-seven years of age, and a very competent officer. A few of the companies were not full and according to E. D. Mansfield's History of the Mexican War, the roster of the Fifth Regiment showed 973 men. The First, Second and Third Regiments of Indiana had enlisted for one year, but the enlistment of the Fourth and Fifth Regiments was for the war.

We remained in camp at Madison about three weeks where we received our uniforms, which were of dark blue cloth, something like those worn in the late war, and we wore caps. The light blue overcoats worn during the late war, were very similar to those issued to our regiment. A letter bearing date October 15, 1857, in the New Albany Democrat and reproduced in the Indiana State Sentinel of October 23, gives a view of the Fifth Regiment at Madison as follows: "Nine companies have arrived and been mustered into the service. The last one, Captain Cary's company from Grant County, was mustered in last evening. All the companies are now in camp and comprise in all something like 700 men, and recruiting for the various companies is going on rapidly. Every one about the camp is in the highest spirits. Every volunteer is elated with the hope of soon leaving that they may aid their fellow soldiers in subduing our treacherous and obstinate foe and share in the revels in the halls of the Montezumas—that all absorbing desire of the volunteer that is now being realized in the City of the Aztecs. The clothing of the different companies is going on rapidly and will be completed by the last of next week at farthest." A contemporary notice of the Fifth Regiment in the Madison Courier is as follows: "During the time this body of men have been encamped here, they have conducted themselves with great propriety, and their conduct has reflected credit on the character of the volunteer. Take them all in all, they are a fine looking body of men and appear competent to do good service in the field."

On Sunday, being the last day of October, or the first day of November, the

45

regiment left Madison for New Orleans. Three steamboats, the Ne Plus Ultra, the Phoenix and the Wave were necessary to transport the regiment down the river. Companies C, H and I, under command of Major Myers, went on the Wave. Company K, not having arrived in camp in time, did not go with the regiment. Our journey of ten days down the Mississippi was a delightful one, in a delightful season of the year, and marred only by the death of our comrade, David Warner, who fell overboard in the night and was drowned. The boat proceeded on its way, and there was much indignation among the men toward the captain of the boat because he did not stop the vessel and allow the body to be recovered. This sad accident brought to our minds some realization of the horrors of war.

Our regiment remained a day and a night at New Orleans. I regret to say, that while here, two members of Company H, from Henry County, deserted. Their names are not included in the list of volunteers from Henry County and are wholly suppressed in this article. One of them was a young painter who had come to New Castle a short time previous to his enlistment. I knew him slightly and while at Greenfield, on our way to Indianapolis, we took a walk together. He called my attention to a ring on his finger and gave me the name and address of a lady, and asked me, if he should be killed in battle, to send her the ring; and if he should be so badly shot to pieces as to be unrecognizable, he stated that I might recognize him by an artificial tooth. I think the fellow so brooded over the possibility of being shot to pieces that he thought the Crescent City an excellent place in which to disappear from sight and avoid such a horrible fate. We never heard of him afterward. The other member of the company who deserted was of a good family and his comrades could never understand why he did so discreditable a thing. At Madison I had been detailed as Commissary Sergeant of the regiment, and at New Orleans, I separated for a time from my company. Several companies of the Fifth Regiment, myself with them, embarked on the steamer Alabama for Vera Cruz. The remaining companies sailed on another vessel. Our voyage across the Gulf of Mexico, lasting some five or six days, was a stormy one. During the height of the storm, there was scarcely a man who did not feel that our vessel would go down. I remember that many of the boys, while the waves surged over the ship, most devoutly prayed, while others sang that good old song, "The Star of Bethlehem." When the waves calmed and the glorious sunshine appeared, I think many good resolutions were forgotten, but it is ever so.

About the middle of November, we came in sight of the grim walls of San Juan de Ulloa, the Mexican fortress defending the city of Vera Cruz, which had been captured by General Scott's army, assisted by the naval forces, seven months before. The sight of land was a joyous one to us after our stormy voyage, even though it was the land of the enemy, but we knew that a friendly garrison was within the walls of the city. Our regiment remained in Vera Cruz several days, and here we received our arms, which were the old flint-lock muskets.

Vera Cruz was an ancient walled city built by the Spanish invader Cortez, the walls of the city being fortified at intervals. On an island about half a mile out in the Gulf stood the famous fortress of San Juan de Ulloa. This was an enclosed fortification of large size, but the fortress had been captured by Scott's army without serious difficulty. Everything was new to us; and here, for the first time, we saw the dark-eyed Mexican senoritas of whom we had heard much. The houses were principally two stories high and the streets narrow. There was a fine cathedral here, and the members of the regiment, when not engaged in military duties, spent the time sight-seeing. Nothing here impressed me so much as the vast, illimitable ocean, and almost daily I walked with comrades out upon the Mole, a structure built of stone and cement and extending into the Gulf. Upon the occasion of our first promenade upon the Mole, not understanding the influence of the tides, we were nearly swept off our feet by the sudden appearance of the waves, to the great amusement of the Mexicans who witnessed our discomfiture. The yellow fever and black vomit prevailed in Vera Cruz almost the entire year, and our regiment was anxious to penetrate the interior.

PART II.

We now began our long march to the City of Mexico which General Scott had occupied six weeks before. The Fifth regiment had been assigned to a brigade with the Third Tennessee regiment, commanded by Colonel Cheatham, afterwards a distinguished officer in the Confederate army. For the first few miles out from Vera Cruz, the scenery was uninteresting. The country was sparsely inhabited, and to our surprise and regret, it was not a land flowing with milk and honey, and the most active foraging parties met with but little success, but pulque, the native drink of the Mexicans, was plentiful and was prescribed by our surgeons. It was mildly intoxicating, and the use of any other kind of liquors was very unsafe for Americans. It was a common saying in our army that the first case of intoxication for a soldier sent him to the hospital and the second case was certain death.

We marched in light marching order, for during the day it was oppressively hot, but the nights were always cool and we slept under our blankets. The country was filled with roving bodies of Mexican cavalry called Lancers and with numerous bands of guerrillas, but the strong holds of the enemy were in possession of our troops. Each company of the regiment had a wagon in which its tents and cooking utensils were conveyed. Our rations were crackers, bacon and coffee. It was asserted that some of the cracker boxes bore the date of 1835, while others contended that the crackers were a remnant left from the battle of New Orleans.

The Fifth Indiana led the advance. Then came the wagon train and the Third Tennessee brought up the rear. No cavalry or artillery accompanied our command. We marched in close order and the two regiments were always within easy supporting distance. This was necessary, for as we proceeded on our march, bodies of Mexican Lancers, sometimes 4,000 or 5,000 in number, often appeared in sight, but as frequently disappeared, without giving us battle. The Lancers were armed with lances and short carbines. They wore gray uniforms, leather leggings and gray *sombreras* and were mounted on sorry little half-starved horses, which bore little comparison with the fine, large horses of our army. They were picturesque horsemen, but poor soldiers. With the enthusiasm of new troops, we were anxious for battle, but before we could effectively fight with our flint-lock muskets, we would have to approach so near the enemy as to see the white of their eyes. The Mexicans, to our regret, never allowed us to get so close.

Our march was over the great national highway from the coast to the interior and over the same road along which General Scott's victorious army had marched. Thirty-five miles from Vera Cruz, we crossed La Puenta Nacional, a splendid bridge, spanning Rio Antiqua. From now on, the scenery was fine, our march being through an undulating country with shade trees and mixed chapparral on either side of the road. We marched from ten to thirty miles a day, depending upon circumstances. If, in the middle of the afternoon, we discovered a fine spring of water near our line of march, we selected a site for a camp near by. Otherwise our march was prolonged until a suitable camping place was found when we pitched our tents and built our camp fires. Strict discipline was maintained, yet the nights in camp were always happy and full of the pleasures and diversions of army camp life.

The first important point we passed through was Jalapa, sixty five miles from the coast. This was a city of about 9,000 inhabitants. It was neat and clean, and there were many handsome buildings here, surrounded with orange groves and lovely gardens filled with fruits and flowers. The climatic fevers which prevail on the coasts, were much less fatal to Americans after reaching Jalapa. Here our regiment and the Third Tennessee went into camp for a week. Cerro Gordo is a high spur of the Cordilleras Mountains, fifteen miles east of Jalapa, and General Santa Anna, commander of the Mexican Army, had selected this point as one having great natural advantages for defense against the invading army, but the battle fought here on the 18th of April had resulted in a decisive victory for the American Army.

After a week in camp, we proceeded on our march. Extensive provision trains, carrying supplies to our army in the City of Mexico, wound their slow length along over the broad macadamized road from the coast to the capital, and we crossed several splendid bridges, magnificent specimens of architecture. The Fifth Indiana and Third Tennessee, marched in friendly concord, little conscious of the fact that in less than fifteen years the North and South would be arrayed against each other in deadly conflict. The country was not populous and the inhabitants lived principally in the pueblos or towns and villages. The grandees or owners of the soil. had comfortable habitations, but the *peons* or slaves, who composed the vast body of the people, and toiled for their masters, lived in mere hovels. The next important town on the line of our march, after leaving Jalapa was Perote. There was a strong fortification here, known as the Castle of Perote, being next in strength to San Juan de Ulloa.

After the capture of the City of Mexico, the Mexican Army was divided into detachments which harrassed our army and endeavored to destroy General Scott's line of communication with Vera Cruz, and in December a Mexican force besieged Puebla then held by our troops. The march of our brigade was now rapid in the direction of the beleaguered city, but before our arrival the garrison had marched out of their fortifications and defeated the Mexicans who hastily withdrew.

The country grew more fruitful as we advanced and occasional foraging parties now went out, but had always to be on the lookout for the Mexican Lancers, who continued to hover on our line of march. I remember that upon one

occasion on our march, Captain Manson of Company I was so ill that he had
been obliged to ride in an ambulance, but when the enemy's cavalry came in sight
and a fight seemed imminent, he alighted from the ambulance with difficulty and
placed himself at the head of his company, much to the disappointment, as I
afterwards heard, of the First Lieutenant, who had hoped to command the company in case of an attack.

After a forced march of several days our brigade marched into Puebla. The
Fourth Indiana Regiment, commanded by Colonel Gorman, and a body of regular
troops were stationed here, and the beleagured garrison had only three or four
days before our arrival repulsed the Mexicans. Here I met Oliver H. P. Carv
and Decatur Cary, brothers and members of the Fourth Regiment, both of whom
I had previously known, for they had both lived at Knightstown and afterwards
removed to Grant County. They were brothers of Captain Ebenezer G. Cary, who
commanded our company and also of James N. Cary, a member of our company
from Henry County. These four brothers held a happy family reunion here.
Later on, I met in the City of Mexico another brother, John T. Cary, who was
serving in the regular army. Fourteen years later, Oliver H. P. Cary and I again
marched under the flag, I, as Captain of Company C of the Thirty Sixth Regiment
of Indiana, and he, as the Lieutenant Colonel of the regiment. He was a brave
and gallant soldier.

The city of Puebla is the capital of the State of Puebla and the second city in
population in the Republic. The city was situated upon a vast plain 7,000 feet
high, and while wholly within the torrid zone is called *tierras frias* or cold lands.
Wheat of fine quality, Indian corn, barley and fruits peculiar to this region, grew
in abundance here. The country around is volcanic and there was little beauty of
foliage. The cactus called the prickly pear was frequent and there were some
palm trees growing along our line of march. In the neighborhood of Puebla
were many cultivated fields, but the methods of farming were most primitive. The
native Mexican plowed with oxen using a plow similar to those used 2,000 years
ago. He seemed to have no desire for better methods and looked with contempt
upon all improvements. We had now reached a volcanic region, and near our
line of march, after leaving Puebla, we passed a slumbering volcano from which
smoke was issuing. Several members of our company ascended the mountain
and looked into the crater, but I did not.

Our march after leaving Puebla was through Plan del Rio Frio. The pass of
Rio Frio afforded excellent opportunities of defence. Neither ancient Greece nor
Switzerland with their mountain defiles offered better opportunities for repelling
an invader. As Mr. Marcy the Secretary of War said: "Perhaps no country
interposed so many and such formidable obstacles to the progress of an invading
army as Mexico." Santa Anna determined to make a stand at the fortified camp
of Contreras and on the heights of Chrurubusco, not far from the City of Mexico.
But, with all the advantages of their position, General Scott attacked the Mexican
strongholds and had won decisive victories at Contreras and Churubusco on the
20th of August.

Shortly after passing through the village of Rio Frio, the plain of Mexico
burst upon our view. In the distance was the historic city with its lofty steeples,
its modern splendor and ancient magnificence. Upon every side were its mag-

nificent lakes. The view was grand and an air of romance gave everything a vivid coloring. The great lake Tezcuco lay to the east. To the south, we beheld in the hazy distance, the extinct volcano of Popocatapetl. We were strangely happy. It was the land of romance surrounded with the glamour of war.

Our regiment had been anxious to reach the City of Mexico before Christmas, and in the afternoon of December 23, our march of two hundred and sixty miles from Vera Cruz to the capital came to an end, and with bayonets gleaming in the sunlight we joyfully entered the historic city of the Aztecs and later of the Spaniard. Our regiment marched to the famous old Convent of Santa Clara, where we were quartered. The convent was a two story building, and occupied, as I now remember, a square. The interior was a court-yard with a fountain, and there were walks lined with flowers. There were numerous apartments in the convent and these were occupied by the different companies, the officers occupying for their quarters, separate apartments. A portion of the convent completely separated from our quarters was occupied by nuns and Sisters of Charity.

Everything, to us, was new and strange. The people, the language, the styles of architecture, the manners and customs, profoundly impressed us. No city upon the continent possessed a history so strange and romantic. Its antiquity was venerable, and long before the discovery of America a high state of civilization had existed here. The history of the city goes back as far as 1325 or 1327, when the Aztecs were directed after their long wanderings to settle here. A century later, with the progress of Aztec culture, the city had greatly improved and the rude habitations of early times were replaced with splendid stone structures built principally upon the small islands of Lake Tezcuco. The Spanish invader Cortes captured the city in 1520. It had then reached its highest splendor and contained 500,000 inhabitants. Numerous canals intersected the city which was connected with the mainland by splendidly constructed causeways. Montezuma, descended from an ancient imperial race, was emperor. Cortes, its conqueror, described the city as "like a fairy creation rather than the work of mortal hands." Two years after its capture the city was almost wholly destroyed. The city as we saw it was rebuilt on the same site, although Lake Tezcuco seems to have greatly subsided. From 1521 to 1821 Mexico was a dependency of Spain. It was a country filled with gold and silver, and its inhabitants were looked upon by their conquerors as slaves fit only to dig the precious metals out of the earth and pour them into the Spanish treasury. For three hundred years viceroys from Spain governed the City of Mexico and the surrounding country, living in kingly splendor; but in 1821 the Mexicans threw off the yoke of Spain. But the Spanish civilization, modified by the traditions and superstitions of the Aztecs, had left its indelible impress upon the great city. It was the romantic history of the Aztecs, and the sight of the mountains and lake in the midst of which they had dwelt, that inspired a young lieutenant of the Third Regiment of Indiana, commissioned as Lewis Wallace, to write the beautiful story of "The Fair God."

The modern City of Mexico as we beheld it contained more than 100,000 inhabitants and was 7,500 feet above the sea-level. Its streets all ran at right angles and its main thoroughfares converged on the central Plaza or Main Square. The plaza contained fourteen acres artistically laid out and filled with trees and flowers and adorned with marble fountains. The public buildings were built upon the plaza, and towering above the government buildings and facing to the North was the great Cathedral, the largest church in America. This magnificent edifice was begun in 1573 and completed in 1657. On the east side of the plaza was the National Palace, with a frontage of 657 feet. This building was formerly the residence of the Spanish viceroys, but was then occupied by the government offices and contained the government archives. The Mexican Congress also convened in the building. One half of the city seemed to be composed of convents, churches and other ecclesiastical structures. But with all the splendor of the buildings on the plaza, the buildings in the outskirts of the city were principally one-story houses and mere hovels. One singular thing which we noticed was that there were no chimneys and I did not see a grate or stove while in the city. The people warmed and cooked by ovens and the smoke escaped through openings in the roof.

There were some fine promenades in the city. One was the famous Alameda, planted with stately beeches. Another fine avenue extended out to the Castle of Chapultepec. Along these promenades and in the plaza the soldiers were accustomed to saunter. The back streets were very narrow and the sidewalks just wide enough for two. It was the custom of the soldiers to go in twos, and when they met a Mexican he was usually shoved into the street. Fully one half of the population were full-blooded Indians, descendants of the aboriginal inhabitants; about a fourth were half-breeds, being half Spanish and half Indian. The remainder were pure whites, descendants of the Spanish conquerors.

Our surroundings at Santa Clara were very pleasant, yet two things made our lot less agreeable. We were unacclimated, and on account of the exhalations from the lakes and the bad sanitary condition of the city, much sickness prevailed, and many members of the regiment were sent to the hospital. Our rations were also far from satisfactory both as to quantity and quality.

For several reasons our army, while in the City of Mexico, was poorly fed and poorly clad. One of the reasons for this state of affairs was the great distance from the base of supplies and the difficulties in the matter of transportation. To our scanty rations of hard bread, bacon and coffee, a limited supply of Mexican beef was added, but we were still inadequately supplied, and there was considerable dissatisfaction throughout the regiment. Colonel Lane was a good officer but a strict disciplinarian, and on this account, was not, in the beginning of our service, altogether popular with the men just out of civil life and unused to military restraints, and while the Colonel was young in years as well as in appearance, he was known throughout the regiment as "Old Jim."

One day the members of Company H held a meeting in the old convent and passed some resolutions respecting our limited supply of rations. While this proceeding was altogether unmilitary, yet the resolutions were respectful and called upon our commanding officer to remedy the evil, if possible. As I was now orderly sergeant I was designated to present the resolutions to Colonel Lane. With a good deal of trepidation, I went to headquarters. Saluting the Colonel, I briefly stated the object of my visit and presented the resolutions. He was rather curt, but read the communication carefully. He then turned the paper over and wrote that he had done everything possible to secure better rations for the men, and had importuned and even demanded of the commissary department better supplies, but without avail. He then ordered me to form the company in line and read his communication to the men. I did so, and reports of the affair spread throughout the regiment, and while our rations were not increased the Colonel's popularity steadily grew.

PART III.

Amos Brown, the young colored man from Fall Creek Township, continued to act as cook for the officers of Company H. He had always desired to be regularly mustered into the service and the officers of the company were not unwilling to have him paid by the Government, rather than out of their own pockets. As I was supposed to have some prejudices on the color line, some of the members of the company, while in the City of Mexico, asked me to interpose no objections to his being mustered into the service, and I made none, and on December 31, as shown by the muster rolls, Brown was mustered into the service of the United States as a member of our company. And thus a colored man from Henry County became a soldier fifteen years before colored men were enlisted in the great Civil War.

On Sundays many members of the regiment attended the old cathedrals and beheld for the first time, the impressive religious ceremonies of the Catholic Church, while others attended in the afternoon the bull fights and witnessed the exciting contests of the arena, which never failed to attract the attendance of the Mexican aristocracy. Many members of the regiment, most of whom were unmarried, cultivated the acquaintance of the *senoritas* many of whom were handsome, with their dark eyes and olive tints, but the freedom of their manners was always a complete surprise to an American. Even the higher classes of Mexican women who were supposed to live most secluded lives, restrained by the traditional customs of the Spanish race and the most punctilious forms of etiquette, were nothing averse to little flirtations with our soldiers.

As upon shipboard, the slightest incidents relieve the monotony, so, unimportant incidents in our garrison life varied the monotony from day to day. While in the City of Mexico, our regiment was paid off, our monthly wages being counted out to us in silver. For risking his life in this dreadful climate, ten fold more destructive than the enemy's bullets, the private soldier received seven dollars per month. Pay day to the soldier was an event of no little importance, and the ill fed soldiers, who a few weeks before, had left comfortable homes in Indiana were wont to frequent the restaurants so long as their money lasted and indulge in Mexican dishes of doubtful origin. We received our mail once a month and news from home was always joyfully received. But the return mails too often carried to homes, in the North, sad tidings of the death of some loved one.

An event which threatened for a time to lead to the most serious consequences now occurred. A portion of the old convent of Santa Clara where the Fifth Regiment was quartered was, as I have before stated, occupied by a body of nuns of the Catholic Church. Their apartments were completely isolated from our quarters and were in a remote part of the convent. A soldier without evil intent, but with a desire to play a practical joke, managed to surreptitiously gain admittance to their apartments, to their great surprise and consternation. The news of this affair, so sacrilegious to a Catholic, spread through the city and profoundly

COMPANY H, 69th INDIANA INFANTRY.

.... He then ordered me to form the company in line
.... I did so, and reports of the affair spread
.... our rations were not increased the Colonel's
....

PART III.

.... the young colored man from Fall Creek Township, continued
.... for the officers of Company H. He had always desired to be regu-
.... into the service and the officers of the company were not unwilling.
.... paid by the Government, rather than out of their own pockets. As
.... to have some prejudices on the color line, some of the members
.... persons, while in the City of Mexico, asked me to interpose no objections
.... mustered into the service, and I made none, and on December 31,
.... the muster rolls, Brown was mustered into the service of the United
States .... of our company. And thus a colored man from Henry
.... years before colored men were enlisted in the
....

.... of the regiment attended the old cathedrals and
.... impressive religious ceremonies of the Catholic
.... in the afternoon the bull fights and witnessed the
.... which never failed to attract the attendance of the
Mexican .... many members of the regiment, most of whom were
unmarried .... acquaintance of the *senoritas* many of whom were
handsome, with their dark eyes and olive tints, but the freedom of their manners
was always a complete surprise to an American. Even the higher classes of
Mexican women who were supposed to live most secluded lives, restrained by
the traditional customs of the Spanish race and the most punctilious forms of
etiquette, were nothing averse to little flirtations with our soldiers.

As upon shipboard, the slightest incidents relieve the monotony, so, unimportant incidents in our garrison life varied the monotony from day to day. While
in the City of Mexico, our regiment was paid off, our monthly wages being counted
out to us in silver. For risking his life in this dreadful climate, ten fold more de-
.... the enemy's bullets, the private soldier received seven dollars per
.... to the soldier was an event of no little importance, and the ill
.... few weeks before, had left comfortable homes in Indiana
.... the restaurants so long as their money lasted and indulge
.... of doubtful origin. We received our mail once a month and
.... was always joyfully received. But the return mails too often
.... North, sad tidings of the death of some loved one.

.... for a time to lead to the most serious consequences
.... the old convent of Santa Clara where the Fifth
.... as I have before stated, occupied by a body of nuns
.... apartments were completely isolated from our
.... part of the convent. A soldier without evil intent,
.... practical joke, managed to surreptitiously gain admit-
.... to their great surprise and consternation. The news of
.... religious to a Catholic, spread through the city and profoundly

COMPANY H, 69th INDIANA INFANTRY.

' excited the populace. The act was regarded as an insult to their religion and a violation of the most sacred of its institutions. The excitement among the Mexicans was very great and there were ominous threats. There were perhaps, not to exceed 10,000 American troops in the city and its suburbs and these were quartered remotely from each other. At the time of the greatest excitement I was in charge of the guard at the Custom House where eight hundred Mexican women were engaged in making clothing for our troops. Half of the guard was withdrawn and ordered to report at the convent where an attack by the infuriated populace was threatened. Fortunately the excitement subsided without serious results.

The rations doled out to the regiment at Santa Clara showed no improvement. All of our money was spent since the last pay day and so with a boldness born of impecuniosity and a hunger never quite satisfied, I entered a bakery and asked for bread. The baker placed several loaves on the counter. With my limited knowledge of Spanish, I said to him, *A poco tiempo*, meaning that I would pay for it in a short time. The baker reached for the bread, but I anticipated him and picked up the loaves. I wrote my name on a slip of paper and handed it to the baker, who placed it in a drawer. I took the bread to our quarters and for two or three days our mess fared sumptuously. A few days afterwards, our regiment was paid off and with my monthly stipend in my pocket, I went to the place of business of my friend, the baker, who remembered me, and to his great surprise, paid for the bread. The news of this little transaction spread among the dealers along the street, and my credit was so well established, that I could, I think, have bought all the bakeries on the street, on time.

Death was decimating the ranks of our army. Men out of an equable climate of the North temperate zone could not withstand the fevers of a plain in the torrid zone, 7,500 feet above the level of the sea. To the dangers of the climate to an American, were added those of the bad sanitary conditions of a great city. Many members of the Fifth Regiment were in the hospital. Captain Cary and Lieutenant Marshall died in the City of Mexico and Lieutenant Shunk was promoted to the captaincy of Company H. The bodies of our dead officers were placed in metallic coffins and taken to Vera Cruz. whence they were to be transported to their homes at Marion, but the superstitious sailors would not allow the corpses to be brought on shipboard, and their remains were buried in the cemetery at Vera Cruz where several hundred American soldiers were buried.

There was an ancient cemetery connected with the convent of Santa Clara, for every ecclesiastical edifice of importance had its burying ground. Here in this cemetery, 2,500 miles from home, many members of the Fifth Regiment were buried. Every cemetery of importance, whether in peace or war, is apt to have its grave robbers. It was discovered that Mexican ghouls were despoiling the graves of our dead comrades. No valuables were ever buried with the bodies of our comrades, but their graves in numerous instances had been opened- and the corpses stripped of their clothing. I was ordered one night to take a squad of men and capture the wretches if possible. We stealthily approached the cemetery under the cover of night, but the ghouls who had opened three graves and stripped two bodies, had confederates, and fled into the chapparral.

After performing garrison duty in the City of Mexico, for a month, the Fifth

Regiment was ordered to Molino del Rey, or The King's Mill, five miles east of the capital and not far from the Castle of Chapultepec. We bade farewell forever to the old convent and marched to our new quarters. Here we selected a pleasant camp and pitched our tents. The Mill of the King from which the place takes its sonorous Spanish name was a stone building several hundred feet long and one story high. Previous to the battle which was fought here, on September 8, the Mexicans had used the mill as a cannon factory. Here the regiment performed ordinary garrison duty and had daily drill. Our regiment had no chaplain, but on Sunday, the members of the regiment were accustomed to attend religious services in a grove near the Castle of Chapultepec.

A Mexican lady of high rank who had known Colonel Lane on the Rio Grande paid him a visit at Molino del Rey. She was mounted on a fine horse and was attended by an escort. There was nothing unusual in her visit and the only thing which attracted our attention was the fact that she rode astride her horse. Her habiliments which came well down on both sides of her horse were modest and decorous and I only recall the incident now to illustrate the fact that the strictest conventionalities of the country permitted her to ride in a manner both comfortable and safe. I afterwards learned that this was the usual way for all Mexican women and people of Spanish extraction to ride, commonly called, "riding Spanish."

An armistice had been agreed upon by the commanders of the American and Mexican armies, August 24, 1847. This armistice provided that "hostilities should instantly and absolutely cease between the armies of the United States of America, and the United Mexican States within thirty leagues of the capital of the latter State." Nicholas P. Trist, the commissioner for the United States, had for a long time been vainly endeavoring to negotiate a treaty of peace with the Mexican Government. Notwithstanding the armistice, bodies of Mexican Cavalry occasionally made dashes within our lines, and the monotony of garrison life at Molino del Rey was varied by an exciting episode one night when our regiment and the Third Tennessee were ordered out to disperse a body of Mexican Cavalry. We hastily formed in line and marched to Guadalupe seven or eight miles distant, only to find the enemy fleeing and hear the splashing of the water as their cavalry plunged into a ditch along the road side.

Our regiment remained at Molino del Rey about six weeks and was then ordered to San Augustin, eleven miles south of the City of Mexico. San Augustin was an aristocratic place with its beautiful residences and lovely orange groves, a suburb of the capital and the home of many wealthy Mexicans and proud hidalgos. Here our regiment was assigned to a brigade with the Fourth Regiment of Tennessee commanded by Colonel Waterhouse. I remember Colonel Waterhouse as an old gray bearded farmer-like gentleman, whose appearance was in marked contrast with that of our handsome colonel.

Our surroundings at San Augustin were very agreeable, and our duties the ordinary and uneventful duties of garrison life. The regiment was quartered in a building used for cocking mains. There was an open space in the center where the cock fights took place and the benches rose one above another as in an amphitheater. Here upon these benches where the Mexican rabble were accustomed to sit, our soldiers slept at night. On the 28th of May, 1848, our comrade William

H. Roby of Fall Creek Township died at San Augustin and his remains repose there in an unknown grave. Life and property were more secure in Mexico, after its occupation by our troops than ever before, and our army furnished an excellent market to the Mexicans for all their products. And while we were invaders of the country and our arms had everywhere been victorious, the Americans were not wholly unwelcome and the people of all classes, descendants of one of the proudest races of Europe treated us with great consideration and with the politeness proverbial among the higher classes of Mexicans.

Soldiers proverbially enjoy favor in feminine eyes and as the most attractive young Mexicans were at the time absent from home, riding over the country as Lancers, *los Americanos,* and the officers especially were in high favor with the Mexican ladies at San Augustin, and many little courtships were carried on under the guise of language schools, in which the Americans taught English to the *senoritas* and in turn received instruction in Spanish. Some amusing stories were in circulation at the time, concerning these international language lessons. One member of our company from Henry County confessed that he had serious intentions of marrying a wealthy Mexican lady and remaining in the country, but a feeling of homesickness so overcame him when the regiment began its homeward march, that he bade farewell forever to the fair lady and soon after his return home, found solace in a Henry County wife.

The reflections made by General Taylor in his official report of the battle of Buena Vista concerning the conduct of the Second Indiana Regiment in this engagement, and the criticisms of Jeff Davis, who commanded the Mississippi Rifles, and others upon the conduct of this regiment, were much discussed throughout the army. The members of the Fifth Regiment were indignant at the reflections upon our State, and while the regiment was stationed at San Augustin Colonel Lane, in order to give us an opportunity of wiping out what we considered an unjust stigma upon the soldiers of Indiana had asked permission to lead the advance of our army in the direction of San Luis Potosi, and as I understand this privilege had been granted, in case hostilities were resumed in that direction.

On February 2, 1848, a treaty of peace had been signed at Guadalupe Hidalgo, by Nicholas P. Trist, commissioner on behalf of the United States. Several months elapsed before the treaty received the approval of the government of the United States. In the latter part of May, however, it became definitely known that hostilities were at an end and the Fifth Regiment received orders to march to Vera Cruz. Leaving forever our pleasant quarters at San Augustin, and casting a last look upon the historic City of Mexico, we set out upon our long march. Our march to the sea was a leisurely and uneventful one over the same route by which we had entered the country. At Puebla, eight recruits joined our company only to return home within a few weeks after their enlistment. Dr. Montgomery of Lewisville, had been promoted to the rank of Assistant Surgeon of the regiment, and on our return march died shortly before we reached Vera Cruz.

About twenty five miles from Vera Cruz our regiment went into camp on the hacienda of General Santa Anna. Here we remained about ten days awaiting a steamer to carry us North. About the first of July we sailed from Vera Cruz. The walls of San Juan de Ulloa slowly faded from our sight and we were homeward bound. On July 4, Levi Donihue, one of the eight recruits who had joined our company at Puebla, died on shipboard. I well remember the event and the muster rolls give the date of Donihue's death. As First Sergeant I had charge of the burial and by my direction, the dead body was sewed up in a blanket with stones placed at the feet, and with the ceremonies attending a sailor's burial, the body was cast into the Gulf. With this exception our voyage across the Gulf was an uneventful one. Joyful anticipations of meeting loved ones at home filled our hearts. But withal we could not wholly escape a feeling of sadness, for many of our comrades were left behind, never to return. The vessel bearing us home steamed up the Mississippi. The regiment disembarked at New Orleans, where, after a delay of a day or two, we took a boat for the North. There had been many changes in our company. Noting the changes among the living, I had been promoted to be first Sergeant; Henry Shank, Second Sergeant; Richard Webster, First Corporal, and Charles Fifer, Fourth Corporal. On July 10, while on the Mississippi, another member of Company H died. About the 25th of July the Fifth Regiment reached Madison in our own beloved State and here on July 28, 1848, where, ten months before, we had been mustered into the service of the United States, we were discharged, and the members of the company regretfully bidding each other goodby, many of them never to meet again, were soon in the bosoms of their respective families.

The war with Mexico was one of conquest undoubtedly, for when the treaty of Guadalupe Hidalgo was ratified, 900,000 square miles of territory were added to the domain of the United States, including California and what is now New Mexico and Arizona. The war in its inception and prosecution had been severely condemned by a large portion of the people of the Northern States. But of the men from Indiana, who marched under the flag, in this struggle, and the same is true of the vast majority of the rank and file of the army, no one, I think, believed he was fighting for conquest, much less for human slavery. The men who confronted the dangers of death from disease and upon the battlefield, saw only the Nation engaged in a struggle with a foreign power, and rallied as patriots and soldiers to the defense of their country and its flag in time of peril.

Men propose but an overruling Providence seems often to dispose of human events. And thus if the war was begun in the interests of human slavery, its purpose wholly failed, for in 1848, California was admitted into the Union as a free State, and its admission gave the free States a preponderance in the affairs of the government. In the same year gold was discovered in the new State and the wealth of the Nation vastly increased. New Mexico and Arizona with their mountainous areas and arid climate yet remain territories, with vast possibilities, but the civilization of the Anglo-Saxon has supplanted that of the Spaniard in all this vast territory. And whatever may have been the motives which led to the Mexican War, there can be no doubt that its results advanced the cause of human freedom, increased the National prosperity and promoted human intelligence and the cause of civilization.

When the Fifth Regiment reached Madison, death had fearfully decimated its ranks. Company H had suffered greatly and twenty one of its members sleep today in unknown graves in a foreign land. Many of its members returned broken in health and Abner Phillips and Jeremiah Gossett died within a short time after their return, victims of an inhospitable climate and as much a sacrifice upon the altar of their country as if they had fallen upon the battlefield. Every man from Henry County, so far as lies within my knowledge, did his whole duty and reflected credit upon his State and county. Some of them afterward did service in the war for the Union. But nearly all of them are now with the silent majority, and after the lapse of almost half a century, it affòrds me pleasure to pay this tribute to all my comrades, living and dead.

Two of the above named Mexican War soldiers had records in the Civil War. Elam Armfield enlisted from Knightstown in Company A, 57th Indiana Infantry, as a private, and was mustered into the service of the United States, December 13, 1861. He was discharged for disability, June 24, 1862. George W. Thompson went from Cadiz to Illinois and enlisted at Young America, Pulaski County, that State, in Company C, 36th Illinois Infantry, as a private, and was mustered into the service of the United States, September 23, 1861. He was captured and held in a Confederate prison, and after his release was mustered out March 15, 1865. After his release from the Confederate prison and when about to be discharged from the army, he purposely refrained from advising his family, which had remained at Cadiz, during his service in the war, of his prospective return home. His purpose was to go direct from Camp Parole, Annapolis, Maryland, to Cadiz and surprise them by his unexpected return. He arrived in Cadiz unannounced and went directly to the house where he supposed his wife to be living and knocked at the door. Alas! his wife had been dead for a week or more. He continued to reside in Cadiz until his death and his remains are buried in the Hess Cemetery, near Cadiz.

MEXICAN WAR SOLDIERS NOT MENTIONED BY CAPTAIN WOODWARD.

David Bearley, born in Warren County, Ohio, August 27, 1829. Moved to New Castle after the Mexican War. Enlisted in what was known as the First Rifles Company, First Ohio Infantry, June 29, 1846. Took part in the siege of Monterey, Mexico, and was mustered out with his regiment, at New Orleans, Louisiana, in the Summer of 1847. He also served in the Civil War, during the Morgan Raid, in Company A, 110th Indiana Infantry.

James Brown, Knightstown. Said to have served in the Mexican War, going from Knightstown. Information furnished by Colonel Milton Peden. Record of military service is not obtainable.

George Burton, born in Jefferson County, Indiana, October 4, 1824. Moved to New Castle after the Mexican War. Served in Company H, 3rd Indiana Infantry, in the Mexican War. Took part in the battle of Buena Vista, Mexico. In the Civil War, enlisted from New Castle in Company A, 30th Indiana Infantry, and was mustered into the service of the United States, as a private, September 22, 1864. Mustered out June 23, 1865. He also served, during the Morgan Raid, as Captain of Company B, 110th Indiana Infantry, identical with the New Castle Guards, Indiana Legion.

John Davis. Said to have served in the Mexican War, later moving to Henry County and living at Greensboro. Information furnished by Daniel W. Saint, now deceased. Record of military service is not obtainable.

Theophilus Everett, born at Wooster, Wayne County, Ohio, in 1806. Moved to Middletown after the Mexican War. Enlisted in Colonel Dodge's regiment of Dragoons when about twenty five years old, and served on the frontier about two years. Enlisted in Magruder's Battery in 1847 and served in the War with Mexico, two years. Enlisted from Middletown in Company D, 2nd Indiana Cavalry, and was mustered into the service of the United States, as Saddler, September 18, 1861, and was discharged for disability,

March 28, 1863; re-enlisted in Company K, 124th Indiana Infantry, and was mustered into the service of the United States, as a private, December 19, 1863, and was mustered out August 31, 1865. He took part in the battles of Shiloh, Atlanta Campaign, Franklin, Nashville and Wise's Forks. Served in the Civil War, forty two months; total service, seven years and six months.

Oliver P. Fort, Knightstown. Served in the Mexican War in the company of the 4th Indiana Infantry, of which Oliver H. P. Cary (afterwards Colonel of the 36th Indiana Infantry) was First Lieutenant. He went to Pike's Peak, Colorado, in 1859, with the Colonel Peden party. He remained in Colorado and, when the Civil War broke out, enlisted in Company K, 2nd Colorado Cavalry, and was mustered into the service of the United States, as a private, January 27, 1863. He died at Benton Barracks, St. Louis, Missouri, January 12, 1864. His remains were taken to his old home at Knightstown and there buried in the Old Cemetery.

Ezra Gillingham, Baltimore, Maryland. Said to have served in the Mexican War. Record of military service in that war not obtainable. In the Civil War he enlisted from Weisburg, Dearborn County, Indiana, in Company I, 21st Regiment, Veteran Reserve Corps and was mustered into the service of the United States, as a private, September 7, 1861. Mustered out September 12, 1864. Moved to Knightstown after the Civil War.

George W. Hazzard, New Castle. . Second Lieutenant, 4th Artillery, U. S. A. (See U. S. Military Academy).

Alexander McAdoo. Said to have served in the Mexican War, later moving to Henry County and living at Greensboro. Information furnished by Daniel W. Saint, now deceased. Record of military service is not obtainable.

Thomas Morton, born in Preble County, Ohio, August 15, 1826. Moved to Middletown after the Civil War. Enlisted in Captain Hawkins' company of Ohio volunteers for the Mexican War, in May, 1846. The company was not accepted and the men were mustered out in June, 1846; re-enlisted in March, 1847, in Company F, United States Mounted Rifles. Took part in the battles of Cerro Gordo, Contreras, Chapultepec and City of Mexico. Severely wounded in the taking of the city, September, 1847. Mustered out in September, 1848. In the Civil War, enlisted at Eaton, Preble County, Ohio, in Company C, 20th Ohio Infantry, and was mustered into the service of the United States as a private April 27, 1861. Promoted Captain and Colonel. Mustered out August 18, 1861. Re-entered the service as Colonel of the 81st Ohio Infantry, August 19, 1861. Resigned July 30, 1864. Took part in the battles of Shiloh, Siege of Corinth, Town Creek, Layton and Corinth. Served in the Mexican War, nineteen months, and in the Civil War, thirty nine months.

Henry Ray, St. Thomas, Franklin County, Pennsylvania. Moved to Henry County, Indiana, in 1852. Said to have served in a Pennsylvania regiment, for eighteen months, as a private, during the Mexican War. Information furnished by Henry L. Powell, of New Castle. Record of military service in that war is not obtainable. In the Civil War, he enlisted from New Castle in Company B, 8th Indiana Infantry (three months' service), and was mustered into the service of the United States, as First Lieutenant, April 25, 1861. Took part in the battle of Rich Mountain, West Virginia, July 11, 1861, and was mustered out August 6, 1861. Re-enlisted as a private in Company B, 5th Indiana Cavalry, and was mustered into the service of the United States, August 6, 1862. Appointed Wagoner. Mustered out June 15, 1865. Buried in Elliott Cemetery, two miles south of New Castle.

Reuben B. Stephenson. Moved to New Castle after the Mexican War. Said to have served in the Mexican War. Information furnished by George Burton, of New Castle. Record of military service in that war is not obtainable. In the Civil War, went to Iowa and enlisted at Des Moines, Polk County, in Company K, 10th Iowa Infantry, and was mustered into the service of the United States, as a private, March 6, 1862. Veteran. Appointed Corporal and Sergeant. Discharged for disability, June 25, 1865.

Frederick Tykle, born in Preble County, Ohio, June 7, 1825. Moved to Middletown after the Mexican War. Enlisted in Captain Hawkins' company of Ohio volunteers for the Mexican War, in May, 1846. The company was not accepted and the men were mustered out in June, 1846. In March, 1847, he enlisted in Company G, 4th Infantry, U. S. A., and on arriving in Mexico was assigned to Company I. Took part in the battles of Churubusco, Molino del Rey, Storming of Chapultepec and the taking of the City of Mexico. Mustered out in August, 1848. General Ulysses S. Grant was at that time First Lieutenant and Quartermaster of the 4th Infantry. In the Civil War, enlisted in Company B, 8th Indiana Infantry (three months' service), and was mustered into the service of the United States, as Captain of the company, April 25, 1861, and took part in the battle of Rich Mountain, West Virginia, July 11, 1861. He was mustered out August 6, 1861. Reentered the service and was mustered in as Captain of Company E, 8th Indiana Infantry (three years' service), September 5, 1861. Resigned October 22, 1861. Served in Mexico, eighteen months, and in the Civil War, six months. He also served during the Morgan Raid as Captain of Company C, 109th Indiana Infantry.

Jacob Wood. Said to have served in the Mexican War. Died and is buried in Liberty Township, near the old town of Chicago. Information furnished by his brothers, living in Liberty Township. Record of his military service is not obtainable.

COMPANIES ORGANIZED IN HENRY COUNTY FOR THE MEXICAN WAR, NOT CALLED INTO ACTIVE SERVICE.

The executive records of the State of Indiana, on deposit in the office of the Secretary of State, at Indianapolis, show that under the Act of Congress, of May 13, 1846, the following provisional companies were organized in Henry County, under the authority of Governor James Whitcomb, none of which were ever called into active service. The first one of these companies is fully described by Captain Woodward, but the other five are not. They are as follows:

Henry County Guards, New Castle. January 18, 1846. Mathew S. Ward, Captain; Henry Shroyer, First Lieutenant; Pyrrhus Woodward, Second Lieutenant.

Lewisville Guards, Lewisville. July 31, 1846. William S. Price, Captain; George W. Truslow, First Lieutenant; Emery Southwick, Second Lieutenant; Joseph Spaw, Ensign.

Middletown Rifle Company, Middletown. August 1, 1846. Simon Summers, Captain; Henry Shank, First Lieutenant; Charles Riley, Second Lieutenant.

Ringgold Troop, Independent Militia, New Castle. August 10, 1846. Richard Goodwin, Captain; John Shroyer, First Lieutenant; George W. Woods, Second Lieutenant.

An unnamed company organized in Prairie Township, August 10, 1846. Jeremiah Veach, Captain; Abraham W. Bouslog, Lieutenant.

Knightstown Grays, Knightstown. September 2, 1846. Solomon McCain, Captain; Gordon Ballard, First Lieutenant; James Tyler, Second Lieutenant.

PERSONAL RECOLLECTIONS OF THE MEXICAN WAR BY DAVID BEARLEY AND GEORGE BURTON.

There are three survivors of the Mexican War, now living in Henry County: Norviel Fleming, of Sulphur Springs, and David Bearley and George Burton, of New Castle. Norviel Fleming served in the same company as Captain Woodward and his personal recollections, so far as they go, are practically covered in Captain Woodward's papers. A condensed statement of the personal recollections of David Bearley and George Burton follow.

DAVID BEARLEY.

David Bearley was born, August 27, 1829, in Warren County, Ohio, about twenty miles from Cincinnati. His parents moved to the city, when he was about six years old, and there he attended school and received such education as the times afforded. At the age of sixteen, he apprenticed himself to A. M. and T. C.

Days, to learn the trade of a confectioner. Twelve months later, the war between the United States and Mexico was declared and, being full of patriotic spirit, it did not take young Bearley long to make up his mind to enlist. He volunteered June 29, 1846, and was assigned to the First Ohio Infantry.

Mr. Bearley was attached to what was called the First Rifles Company, officered by Captain Ramsey, First Lieutenant Isaac Hosea and Second Lieutenant Richard Mason. They went into camp at Camp Washington, near Cincinnati, and from there on July 2, breaking camp, they marched to the city wharf and took steamboats for New Orleans, half of the force, on board the "New World," and the other half on the "Alabama." As the vessels swung into midstream, the bands struck up, "The Girl I Left Behind Me," and a great crowd on the wharf responded to the cheers of the volunteers with, "Good bye, boys," "good luck to you," and "God bless you."

A short run down the Ohio River brought them to Louisville, Kentucky, and after passing the falls, the boats rounded to on the Kentucky shore, where all landed to listen to patriotic speeches and the reading of the Declaration of Independence. Here also all were given an hour to go in swimming and as Mr. Bearley says: "I tell you, it was a great sight to see one thousand people in the water at one time." Once more the journey down the Ohio was resumed and no stops were made until Baton Rouge, Louisiana, was reached. There they received their arms and ammunition and then steamed down the Mississippi River to New Orleans, where they disembarked and were sent to Camp Jackson. The trip from Cincinnati to New Orleans had taken about twelve days. After three or four days at Camp Jackson, they boarded the steamship, "Duke of Orleans," for Mexico. Three stormy days and nights were taken to get to Point Isabel. The troops here went into camp on Brazos Island and after a week's rest took up the line of march for the mouth of the Rio Grande River. After about a week, they marched up that river some twenty miles and went into camp back of the river bluffs. The ground was cleaned for regimental drill, rifle practice and parade purposes, and was called "Camp Belknap." Three weeks were spent here, after which the regiment went to Camargo, on the Tiger River, a tributary of the Rio Grande. Three weeks later they crossed that river and started for Monterey. Passing through a number of important towns, they at last arrived at the famous Walnut Springs, in front of Monterey, Saturday, September 19, 1846. The assault on this strongly fortified city was set for the following Monday.

In his narration of events at this battle, Mr. Bearley says:

"It was in this battle that I received my first 'baptism of fire' and learned something of the realities of war. It was here that the First Ohio Infantry and the First Kentucky Infantry were formed into a brigade under the command of General Thomas L. Hamer, of Ohio, who, while a member of Congress had nominated, for a cadetship at West Point, Ulysses S. Grant. General Hamer died and was buried at Walnut Springs but his remains were afterwards removed to his Ohio home.

"After the battle I was taken with fever and ague, which was further complicated with an attack of dropsy. Because of my illness I was confined to camp and under the surgeon's care for about three months, when the regiment was

George Buston

George Buxton

ordered to Saltillo, as Santa Anna, the Mexican General, was endeavoring to reach and attack that city. When the regiment moved I was sent, with others, on a forced march to the hospital, some distance away. In this hospital I learned some additional facts touching the realities of the life of the soldier. After a few weeks I had so far recovered my health as to warrant rejoining my regiment whch I did at Saltillo. We were at this latter place a week, at the expiration of which time, our regiment was ordered back to Monterey, where we were engaged mostly in performing guard duty and scouting around in that section of Mexico. While so engaged the rumor came to us that the regiment would shortly be placed under orders with instructions to at once return home. This order came after we had been at Monterey for about six weeks and you can imagine with what a joyful shout the welcome news was received. It was not long until we were homeward bound, but our return route to the Rio Grande was over another than that pursued when we entered Mexico.

"We arrived first at Renoso on the Rio Grande where we took boats awaiting our coming and going down the river came to its mouth where we went into camp for a week, then marched to Brazos Island where we embarked on the 'Duke of Orleans' and after an uneventful, but pleasant trip across the gulf, arrived safe and sound at New Orleans. Here we turned over our arms and equipments to the government. After a week's stay at New Orleans we were all rounded up, received our pay and were mustered out of the service. At the conclusion of this final event, and with visions of home filling my mind's eye, I secured passage on a river steamer and in the course of a week or ten days, the journey being a very pleasant one, I landed at Cincinnati and shortly after had the pleasure of meeting and greeting relatives and friends to say nothing of 'The Girl I Left Behind Me.'"

After his return from the war, Mr. Bearley learned the trade of a chairmaker and followed it for a number of years. On December 24, 1849, he married Sarah Jane Bell, of Montgomery County, Indiana, with whom he has lived happily ever since. They have had nine children, six boys and three girls, five of whom are now living. After his marriage, he lived for about a year in Cincinnati and then moved to Cambridge City, Indiana. After a little more than two years, he moved from there to New Castle, where he and his wife have lived for more than fifty years, having arrived there, April 14, 1853.

After the lapse of nearly sixty years, the grizzled veterans of the Mexican War are few in number and soon, very soon, none will be left to answer roll call.

GEORGE BURTON.

George Burton was born in Jefferson County, Indiana, near the city of Madison, October 4, 1824. His parents were Henry and Mary (Alcorne) Burton, natives of Kentucky, who moved to Indiana about the year 1801. He moved to New Castle after the Mexican War and now resides there at the advanced age of eighty one years.

When the call for volunteers for the Mexican War was made, he enlisted in Company H, 3rd Indiana Infantry, under Captain Voorhis Conover, of Shelbyville. The Colonel of the regiment was James H. Lane, who afterwards attained fame during the troubles on the Kansas border. The company was recruited in

46

and around Shelbyville and when organized was sent to New Albany, Indiana, to receive their uniforms, and thence to New Orleans by two boats, the "James Hewitt" and the "Homer." Stopping at Baton Rouge to receive their arms and equipments, they proceeded to New Orleans and went into camp at Camp Jackson, three or four miles below that city. Several days later, they were taken by vessels to Brazos Island, Texas, near the Gulf coast, and thence overland to the Rio Grande and Camp Belknap, where they remained for sometime, drilling and preparing for active service. Thence they marched to Palo Alto and thence in October to Matamoras on the Mexican side of the Rio Grande. Marching to Camargo, they there received mules and wagons for the transportation of regimental supplies and after due preparation, started on the forward march to Montery, one hundred and ninety miles away.

On Christmas Eve, 1846, they arrived at Walnut Springs, four miles from Monterey, and on Christmas day, the soldier boys visited that city. Thence they marched to Saltillo, eighty miles from Monterey, reaching there on New Year's day, 1847. There they remained until the arrival of General Wool, who came from New Mexico, after which they moved twenty miles south to Camp Agua, where they tarried until General Santa Anna drove them out to the battle ground of Buena Vista, about four miles from Saltillo.

In his narrative of his experiences in the Mexican War, Mr. Burton says: "At the battle of Buena Vista, the United States forces were under command of General Zachary Taylor and General Wool. The battle, including preliminary fights and skirmishes, lasted from February 20 to 23, inclusive, 1847, and during that time victory hung in the balance.

"Preliminary to the battle and under order of General Taylor the four rifle companies from the 2nd and 3rd Regiments, Indiana Infantry, were placed on the mountain side, the Sierra Madre, to guard and prevent the Mexicans from outflanking us. These rifle companies were the right wing and left wing companies of the two regiments and were for the time under command of Major Willis A. Gorman. The 2nd Indiana Regiment was placed at the foot of the mountain under Colonel Bowles. At the right of the 2nd Indiana, the 2nd Kentucky, Colonel Gaines, and Lieutenant Colonel Henry Clay, was placed. Colonel Clay was the favorite son of the famous Henry Clay. Both Gaines and Clay were killed in the battle of the 23rd. The 2nd Illinois Infantry, under Colonel Bissel, was to the right of the 2nd Kentucky. At the right of the 2nd Illinois, in the rear of the mountain pass was the 3rd Indiana under command of Colonel Lane. Four pieces of the Washington Battery occupied the pass and were located right in front of the 3rd Indiana. In the rear and to the left of the regiment was General Taylor and his staff.

"On the evening of the 22nd three of General Santa Anna's staff came through the lines and at the fort of our regiment they were met by one of General Taylor's aids de camp. After saluting, one of the Mexican officers said: 'If you will surrender you will be treated as prisoners of war. We have ample force to capture you.' This demand being reported to General Taylor he returned his reply, saying: 'I never surrender.' With this reply the Mexican officers returned to Santa Anna. They were gone but a little while until they again put in an appearance. This time they not only made the former demand but added that if the proposition was declined the battle would be at once resumed and they would not leave, of us, one alive to tell the tale. This altercation was repeated to General Taylor who directed his aid to say to the Mexicans that 'If they want me worse than I do them they will have to come and take me.' There was no further 'dickering' and shortly after the battle was resumed by about 5,000 of the enemy marching out and making their first attack on the 2nd Indiana. The attack was bravely met by the boys of the 2nd who succeeded in driving the enemy back, assisted very materially by a portion of the Washington Battery. Quickly re-organizing their forces which were further augmented by the Mexican Lancers, the enemy once more advanced to the charge, the Lancers making special on-slaught on the four companies of rifle men stationed on the mountain side while the Mexican infantry centered its charge on the 2nd Indiana, but for the second time the enemy was driven back. The Lancers, during the battle made three distinct attacks on the riflemen as did the Mexican Infantry on the 2nd Indiana, but at each succeeding onslaught they were driven back suffering great loss in killed and wounded.

"On the morning of the 23rd Colonel Jefferson Davis came out with six com-panies of Mississippi riflemen, and was ordered by General Taylor, through General Wool, to take them up on the mountain side and relieve the Indiana riflemen who had been so long exposed and who were then without food or drink. While the change was being made the Mexican forces were preparing for another charge. When this was made the Mississippians all fired at once and before they could reload the Lancers were upon them and forced them to retreat down the mountain followed by the Lancers who came to a point in the rear of the 2nd Indiana. Colonel Bowles, two or three times, ordered his men to cease firing and retreat but they refused to do so, and kept on fighting. The Lancers, however, by force of numbers, about five to one, drove the regiment back and following up their advantage, attacked the 2nd Kentucky. It was here that Colonel Gaines and Colonel Clay were killed. The enemy continued its attack, centering finally on the 2nd Illinois, under Colonel Bissel, who succeeded in driving the Mexicans back to the foot of the mountain where they again rallied. During this time, the 3rd Indiana was moving from the extreme right to the extreme left. About half way across the field Colonel Lane brought the com-mand to a halt and brought us to a front face. At this point the 2nd Kentucky being driven back were rallied. We then moved on to the position assigned, the extreme left, where we shortly after attacked the enemy.

"It was here, probably, that the hardest battle of the conflict took place. We drove the enemy back and into a gorge in the mountains. At this time Colonel Jefferson Davis rode up to our regiment and ordered us to charge the enemy, which order, however, General Lane, pointing his sword to Colonel Davis and then to the Lancers, quickly countermanded.

"At this time the 2nd Indiana and the 3rd Indiana were formed somewhat in the shape of an 'S' and the Lancers attacked the first or upper part, coming to the charge twenty abreast. Their charge was heroically met, the three front ranks being killed to a man and the remainder of the command forced to retreat in an utterly demoralized condition. After this, it was, I might say, a continuous fight for the remainder of the day. We had, in the meantime, regained all of our lost ground.

"On the morning of the 24th, sometime before daylight, Colonel Lane ordered Captain Conover to bring in one of our abandoned caissons which had been left on the field during the heavy fighting of the 2nd Indiana. After daylight, looking about to see the situation it was discovered that Santa Anna's camp was deserted and that lying around and about were a good many dead and wounded soldiers. Seeing this and making further investigation we discovered the Mexican Infantry going over the top of the mountain. The victory was won and the battle of Buena Vista, became, from that day and time famous among the annals of war.

"I was engaged in but the one battle. It was fierce and strong while it lasted and the memory of it, in very many respects, is, after a lapse of nearly sixty years, as clear to my mind as if it had occurred but yesterday.

"General Taylor, after the war, became the twelfth President of the United States. I saw him often during the war. He was a plain man, quite unassuming. short in stature, but a brave, intrepid soldier. It was, however, his fame as a hero of the Mexican War, rather than his fitness for the position, which made him the chief magistrate of the nation.

"Jefferson Davis, who had command of the Mississippi Rifles, was, during the Civil War, President of the Southern Confederacy. His history has been written and no words can add to or detract from his name and whatever of fame he may have achieved."

In the roster of Company A, 30th Indiana Infantry, (re-organized), published elsewhere in this History, and again on page 717, is set out the highly creditable part this Mexican War veteran took in the Civil War.

THE MEXICAN WAR.

RECAPITULATION.

Assistant Surgeon.. 1
Second Lieutenant... 1
First Sergeant.. 1
Sergeant 2
Corporal 2
Privates 32
                                                                              ——
    Total 39

DEDUCTIONS.

Soldiers from other counties or states who moved to Henry County after the war.. 6
Duplication of names by reason of promotions or transfers....................... 4 10
                                                                              ——
Total of soldiers from Henry County in the Mexican War..........................29

CHAPTER XXXV

ROLL OF HONOR.

ROSTER OF HENRY COUNTY SOLDIERS AND SAILORS WHO WERE KILLED OR DIED
OF WOUNDS OR DISEASE BEFORE DISCHARGE FROM THE SERVICE—RECAPITU-
LATION—NATIONAL CEMETERIES.

The following is a list of soldiers and sailors of the Civil War, and other
wars, from Henry County, who were killed or died of wounds received in battle,
before discharge from the army; also those who died of disease before discharge,
giving in each instance, the place of first burial and the present place of interment,
so far as the same can be ascertained.

The total actual loss thus shown is four hundred and seventy six. To this
should be added an estimated number equal to twenty five per cent. thereof, or
one hundred and nineteen, for those who have died, after discharge, from wounds
incurred, in battle and disease contracted while in the army, of whom there is
no record. Practically all of this great mortality comes from the Civil War,
as will be shown in the recapitulation following the roll of honor.

From the table of National Cemeteries, at the end of this chapter, it will
be seen that, since the Civil War, the Government has made extraordinary efforts
to gather the scattered remains of its dead soldiers and sailors for appropriate re-
interment. If there is a National Cemetery located at the place where the soldier
died and was buried, it is comparatively easy to locate his place of re-interment,
for it is certain that, if his remains have not after the first interment been removed
to his home in the North, and they are not found among the known dead in that
particular cemetery, then they are there among the unknown.

The difficulty in gathering reliable data has been when the re-interment was
in a National Cemetery, at a point distant from and bearing no similarity in name
to the place of first interment. For example the dead from the battlefields of
Perryville and Richmond, Kentucky, have all been moved to the National Cemetery at Camp Nelson, Jessamine County, Kentucky. The dead from the battlefields of the Atlanta Campaign, from a point about fifty miles distant from Chattanooga, Tennessee, to and around Atlanta, Georgia, have all been gathered into
a National Cemetery at Marietta, Georgia. At Vicksburg, Mississippi, the
National Cemetery contains the dead, not only from Vicksburg proper, but from
Port Gibson, Champion Hills, Jackson, Big Black River, Milliken's Bend,
Young's Point, Arkansas Post and other points in that vicinity. From Chickamauga's bloody field, the dead have all been removed to Chattanooga National
Cemetery. From Franklin and other points in Central Tennessee, the dead have
been gathered and deposited in the National Cemetery, most convenient, either

Nashville or Stone's River (Murfreesboro). The author might proceed to set out with particularity the different National Cemeteries, containing the dead gathered from other and distant points, but it is sufficient to say that in every instance, where a soldier is noted as having been re-interred in a National Cemetery, which bears no relation in name or location to the place of first burial, it has been ascertained by correspondence with the War Department at Washington, District of Columbia, or from other sources of official information, that the dead have been moved from the place of first burial to that stated in this Roll of Honor. After exhausting every avenue of investigation, however, it has been found impossible to locate a number of Henry County soldiers, in any National Cemetery. Presumably their remains have been re-interred in some National Cemetery of which there is no record obtainable. In such cases the entry in this Roll of Honor is as follows: "No record of removal. Remains probably re-interred in some National Cemetery. Unknown list."

In consulting the list of National Cemeteries, it must be borne in mind that the number of dead, reported in the respective cemeteries, is continually increasing, but not to a marked degree, from the fact that it is the right of any person, who ever served in the army or navy of the United States, though not in that service at the time of death, to be buried in a National Cemetery, at the expense of the Government, if he so requests before death or, if his family so request, after his death.

The list of cemeteries, as published by the Government, was made up before the Spanish-American War. Consequently the cemeteries, nearest to Spanish-American War camps and hospitals, have had additions from that cause. Again the cemeteries, contiguous to regular stations, forts, arsenals or general hospitals for United States troops, have received a gradual increase from those sources. The greater number of interments, however, is of the gathered remains of dead soldiers and sailors, made immediately after the establishment of the National Cemeteries, and the list may be considered approximately correct.

At Andersonville, Georgia, Danville, Virginia, and perhaps all other points in the South, where Confederate prisons were maintained during the Civil War, for the confinement of captured Federals, there has been no re-interment, the location and arrangements of the National Cemeteries being made to conform with the place of original interment.

This Roll of Honor contains, not only the names and places of burial of soldiers and sailors from Henry County, who lost their lives in the Civil War, but also of all Henry County soldiers and sailors, who died in the service, during the Mexican War, the Spanish-American War and the Philippine Insurrection; also of soldiers of the regular army who died in the service.

Where an asterisk, thus *, precedes a name, it indicates that the dead soldier, though serving in a distinctively Henry County organization in the Civil War, was not a resident of the county, at the time of his enlistment.

Isaac Abernathy, Company K, 37th Indiana Infantry. Killed at Stone's River, Tennessee, December 31, 1862. Buried on the battlefield. Re-interred in Stone's River (Murfreesboro) National Cemetery. Unknown list.

James Alexander, Company K, 36th Indiana Infantry. Died April 29, 1862, account of wounds at Shiloh, Tennessee, April 7, 1862. Buried on the battlefield. Re-interred in Shiloh National Cemetery. Unknown list.

James W. Alexander, Company E, 8th Indiana Infantry (3 years). Killed at Cedar Creek, Virginia, October 19, 1864. Buried on the battlefield. Re-interred in Winchester National Cemetery. Unknown list.

Amos H. Allee, Company E, 9th Indiana Cavalry. Died at Vicksburg, Mississippi, May 14, 1865. Buried there. Re-interred in Vicksburg National Cemetery. Section L, Grave, No. 6,183.

John W. Allee, Company F, 84th Indiana Infantry. Killed at Kenesaw Mountain, Georgia, June 23, 1864. Buried on the battlefield. Re-interred in Marietta National Cemetery. Section I, Grave, No. 9,403.

Reuben W. Allen, Company D, 36th Indiana Infantry. Died at Murfreesboro, Tennessee, February 22, 1863. Buried there. Re-interred in Hicksite Cemetery, Greensboro, Indiana.

Albert Armstrong, Company B, 130th Indiana Infantry. Died at Anderson, Indiana, January 10, 1864. Buried in Old Cemetery, Anderson, Indiana.

*Riley Bailey, Company K, 36th Indiana Infantry. Died at Murfreesboro, Tennessee, May 4, 1863. Buried there. Re-interred in Stone's River (Murfreesboro) National Cemetery. Section C, Grave, No. 1,282.

*Franklin Bails, Company E, 9th Indiana Cavalry. Died at Indianapolis, Indiana, February 11, 1864. Buried there. Re-interred in Crown Hill Cemetery, Indianapolis, Indiana. Military Plat, Grave, No. 535.

Thomas J. Ball, Company I, 69th Indiana Infantry. Died at Milliken's Bend, Louisiana, June 2, 1863. Buried there. Re-interred in Vicksburg National Cemetery, Section E, Grave, No. 1,795.

James H. Ballard, Company K, 40th Indiana Infantry. Died at Huntsville, Alabama, March 18, 1865. Buried there. Re-interred in Chattanooga National Cemetery. Grave, No. 9,606.

Daniel Baltzley, Company A, 36th Indiana Infantry. Killed at Shiloh, Tennessee, April 7, 1862. Buried on the battlefield. Re-interred in Shiloh National Cemetery. Unknown list.

George H. Bare, Company H, 69th Indiana Infantry. Died on hospital boat, near Vicksburg, Mississippi, January 30, 1863. Buried on the river bank. Re-interred in Vicksburg National Cemetery. Unknown list.

Samuel Barre, Company G, 84th Indiana Infantry. Died at Chattanooga, Tennessee, May 14, 1864, account of wounds in Atlanta Campaign, May 7, 1864. Buried there. Re-interred in Chattanooga National Cemetery. Unknown list.

William Bateman, Company D, 8th Indiana Infantry (three years). Died at Jefferson City, Missouri, March 4, 1862. Buried there. Re-interred in Jefferson City National Cemetery. Unknown list.

Peter Baughan, Company B, 19th Indiana Infantry. Killed at Antietam, Maryland, September 17, 1862. Buried on the battlefield. Re-interred in Antietam National Cemetery. Unknown list.

Benjamin Beaty, Company F, 84th Indiana Infantry. Died at Franklin, Tennessee, February 25, 1863. Buried there. Re-interred in Nashville National Cemetery. Unknown list.

Cornelius Beck, Company F, 84th Indiana Infantry. Died at Chattanooga, Tennessee, July 11, 1864, account of wounds in Atlanta Campaign, June 23, 1864. Buried there. Re-interred in Chattanooga National Cemetery. Section E, Grave, No. 11,851.

Isom Beck, Company F, 84th Indiana Infantry. Killed at Chickamauga, Georgia, September 20, 1863. Buried on the battlefield. Re-interred in Chattanooga National Cemetery. Unknown list.

William T. Beck, Company E, 8th Indiana Infantry (three years). Killed at Vicksburg, Mississippi, May 22, 1863. Buried on the battlefield. Re-interred in Vicksburg National Cemetery. Section G, Grave, No. 4,958.

William H. Beeson, Company I, 69th Indiana Infantry. Died at Memphis, Tennessee, February 10, 1863. Buried there. Re-interred in Memphis National Cemetery. Unknown list.

David R. Bell, 12th Indiana Battery. Died at Nashville, Tennessee, January 2, 1863. Buried there. Re-interred in Nashville National Cemetery. Section B, Grave, No. 6,353.

George W. Bell, 12th Indiana Battery. Died at Honey Creek, Indiana, October 6, 1862. Buried in Miller. Cemetery, Fall Creek Township, Henry County, Indiana.

*Isaac Bell, Company H, 140th Indiana Infantry. Died at Smithfield, North Carolina, February 19, 1865. Buried there. No record of removal. Remains probably re-interred in some National cemetery. Unknown list.

Josiah Bell, Company I, 69th Indiana Infantry. Died at Keokuk, Iowa, February 7. 1863. Buried there. Re-interred in Keokuk National Cemetery. Grave, No. 502.

Noah Bennett, Company F, 57th Indiana Infantry. Died at Louisville, Kentucky. January 17, 1862. Buried in Hess Cemetery, near Cadiz. Indiana.

Anson Bird, Company D, 36th Indiana Infantry. Died at Jeffersonville, Indiana, August 10, 1864, account of wounds at Kenesaw Mountain, Georgia, June 23, 1864. Buried there. Re-interred in New Albany National Cemetery. Section B, Grave, No. 607.

John Bitner, Company B, 5th Indiana Cavalry. Died at Lexington, Kentucky, July 22, 1864. Buried in South Mound Cemetery, New Castle, Indiana.

James J. Black, Company F, 57th Indiana Infantry. Killed at Big Shanty, Georgia, June 18, 1864. Buried on the battlefield. Re-interred in Marietta National Cemetery. Section C. Grave, No. 2,264.

Josiah Blake, Company H, 69th Indiana Infantry. Died at Milliken's Bend, Louisiana, April 2, 1863. Buried there. Re-interred in Vicksburg National Cemetery. Section A, Grave, No. 2,912.

Benjamin F. Bock, Company E, 8th Indiana Infantry (three years). Killed at Winchester, Virginia. September 19, 1864. Buried on the battlefield. Re-interred in Winchester National Cemetery. Unknown list.

Thomas J. Bock, Company B, 21st Indiana Infantry re-organized as 1st Heavy Artillery. Died at New Orleans, Louisiana, January 24, 1865. Buried there. Re-interred in Chalmette National Cemetery. Grave, No. 6,091.

Charles Bogue, Company I, 69th Indiana Infantry. Died at Milliken's Bend, Louisiana. April 2, 1863. Buried there. Re-interred in Vicksburg National Cemetery. Unknown list.

Harmon Boran, Company F, 84th Indiana Infantry. Died at Franklin, Tennessee, February 25, 1863. Buried there. Re-interred in Nashville National Cemetery. Unknown list.

George W. Bowers, Company G, 9th Indiana Cavalry. Died in Cahaba Prison, Alabama. January, 1865. Buried there. Re-interred in Marietta National Cemetery. Unknown list.

John Bowman, Company D, 36th Indiana Infantry. Died at Louisville, Kentucky, April 14, 1862. Buried in Friends' Cemetery, Greensboro. Indiana.

*James T. Bradford, Company F, 57th Indiana Infantry. Died at home, in Marion, Indiana, December 25, 1861. Buried in Morris Chapel Cemetery, near Marion, Indiana.

William S. Bradford, Company F, 57th Indiana Infantry. Died May 14, 1862, at home, in Marion, Indiana, where his family had moved while he was in the army. Buried in Morris Chapel Cemetery, near Marion, Indiana.

John M. Bricker, Company I, 69th Indiana Infantry. Died at Covington, Kentucky. October 30, 1862, account of wounds at Richmond, Kentucky. August 30, 1862. Buried in Lewisville Cemetery, Lewisville, Indiana.

John Bridget, Company A, 36th Indiana Infantry. Died April 19, 1862, account of wounds at Shiloh, Tennessee, April 7, 1862. Buried on the battlefield. Re-interred in Shiloh National Cemetery. Unknown list.

Benjamin Bright, Company I, 69th Indiana Infantry. Died at Milliken's Bend, Louisiana, April 10, 1863. Buried there. Re-interred in Vicksburg National Cemetery. Unknown list.

*Joseph Brooks, Company A, 57th Indiana Infantry. Killed at Stone's River, Tennessee, December 31, 1862. Buried on the battlefield. Re-interred in Stone's River (Murfreesboro) National Cemetery. Unknown list.

124th INDIANA INFANTRY.

?a?id R. Bell, ?.?. ??laaa Battery. Died at Nashville, Tennessee, January 2, ???. Buried there. Re-?.??ed ?. Nashville National Cemetery. Section B, Grave, No. 6,4??

George W. Boit, ?.?t Indiana Battery. Died at Honey Creek, Indiana, October 6, 1862. Buried in ?.?e? ?emetery, Fall Creek Township. Henry County, Indiana.

*Isaac Bell ??m?a?y H. 140th I?.?a?a Infantry. Died at Smithfield, North Carolina, February ?? ??. Buried there. ?o record of removal. Remains probably re-interred in some ?? h.?a? ?emetery. Unknown list.

Josiah Be?? ??m?a?y I, 69th Indiana Infantry. Died a? Keokuk, Iowa, February 7, 1863. Buried ?a ??. Re-interred in Keokuk National Cemetery. Grave. No. 502.

Noah Be?r?? Company F. 57th Indiana Infantry. Died at Louisville, Kentucky, January 17, 18??. Buried in Hess Cemetery. near Cadiz, Indiana.

Anson ??c?. ?ompany D, 36th Indiana Infantry. Died at Jeffersonville, Indiana. August 10, 18?? account of wounds at Kenesaw Mountain. Georgia, June 23, 1864. Buried there. Re-interre? ?i in New Albany National Cemetery. Section B, Grave, No. 607.

John P.?a??. Company B, 5th Indiana Cavalry. Died at Lexington, Kentucky, July 22, 1864. Buried in South Mound Cemetery, New Castle, Indiana.

James ?. ??ack. Company F, 57th Indiana Infantry. Killed at Big Shanty, Georgia, June 1? ??? Buried on the battlefield. Re-interred in Marietta National Cemetery. Section ? ??ave. No. 2,264.

? ??. ??ke. Company H, 69th Indiana Infantry. Died at Milliken's Bend, Louisiana, A?r?? ?, 18??. Buried there. Re-interred in Vicksburg National Cemetery. Section A. G?a?? ?o. ??1?

?a? ??.? ?' Bock. Company E, 8th Indiana Infantry (three years). Killed at Winche??? ?i?g??a? September 19. 1864. Buried on the battlefield. Re-interred in Winchester Nat?o?a? Cemetery. Unknown list.

?b???a? ? Bock. Company B, 21st Indiana Infantry re-organized as 1st Heavy Artil??? ?. Di?d a? New Orleans, Louisiana, January 24. 1865. Buried there. Re-interred in ?.? ?r?e??? National? Cemetery. Grave. No. 6,091.

? Chacles Bo?ne, Company ?, 69th Indiana Infantry. Died at Milliken's Bend, Louisi?r?. ?or?? ? 18?? Buried there. Re-interred in Vicksburg National Cemetery. Un-?.o?w? ?i??

?a?mor Bo?a? Company F, 84th Indiana Infantry. Died at Franklin, Tennessee. ??r?ary 25, 7???. Buried there. Re-interred in Nashville National Cemetery. Unknown ?.?t

?.??? W. Bowen. Company G, 9th Indiana Cavalry. Died in Cahaba Prison, Ala-???. ?a?cary 18??. Buried there. Re-interred in Marietta National Cemetery. Un-? ? ?i?t.

?.? ??a?a? ??m?any ?? 36th Indiana Infantry. Died at Louisville, Kentucky. ???? ?? ???? ?.r??? in Friends' Cemetery, Greensboro, Indiana.

?a??e? ? ?ac?ord ??m?any F, 57th Indiana Infantry. Died at home, in Marion, ??r??. ?.?er ??. ??t?. Buried in Morris Chapel Cemetery. near Mar?on, Indiana.

W.??a ?. ?rac?ord ?ompany F. 57th Indiana Infantry. Died May 14, 1862, at ??. ? Ma??o ?. ?ia?a ?he?e his family had moved while he was in the army. Buried ? ?? ?or??? ?hapel Cemetery. near Marion, Indiana.

?.? ?? ?ricke?. Company I 69th Indiana Infantry. Died ?t Covington, Kentucky. ? ?.??? ?? ?ccou?t ? wounds at Richmond, Kentucky, August 30, 1862. Buried in ??? ?e?etery, Le?iss ?e. Indiana.

??? ?r??er Company A. 36th Indiana Infantry. Died April 19, 1862, account of ? ?h ?. ? Tennessee, April 7, 1862. Buried on the battlefield. Re-interred in ? ???a? Cemetery, Unknown list.

??? ?? ?right Company I 69th Indiana Infantry. Died at Milliken's Bend, ?? ?? 1863. Buried there. Re-interred in Vicksburg National Cemetery.

?? ? ?ooks Company ? ??th Indiana Infantry. Killed at Stone's River, Ten-? ?ec?????? 3i 18?? ?ur??? o? the battlefield. Re-interred in Stone's River (Mur-? ? ?? Na??o?a? Cem?e?? ?n??own list.

SERGEANT CO. I.

DAVID N. KIMBALL

SERGEANT CO. F.

ISAAC N. CHENEWORTH

LIEUTENANT

SERGEANT CO. H.

JOHN Q. A. ROBERTS

PRIVATE CO. I.

AMOS GRONENDYKE

PRIVATE CO. I.

PRIVATE CO. I.

ANTHONY W. JORDAN

JOHN H. TEMPLIN

PRIVATE CO. I.

ERASTUS BURCH

124th INDIANA INFANTRY.

William Bronnenberg, Company H, 69th Indiana Infantry. Died at Milliken's Bend, Louisiana, April, 1863. Buried there. Possibly re-interred near Chesterfield, Madison County, Indiana. Otherwise re-interred in Vicksburg National Cemetery. Unknown list.

John H. Brosius, 2nd Indiana Battery. Died at Fort Smith, Arkansas, April 21, 1864. Buried there. Re-interred in Fort Smith National Cemetery, Section 1, Grave, No. 40.

James A. Brown, Company E, 8th Indiana Infantry (three years). Killed at Vicksburg, Mississippi, May 22, 1863. Buried on the battlefield. Re-interred in Vicksburg National Cemetery. Unknown list.

James M. Brown, Company H, 69th Indiana Infantry. Died on hospital boat, near Vicksburg, Mississippi, February 20, 1863. Buried on the river bank. Re-interred in Vicksburg National Cemetery. Unknown list.

Moses H. G. Brown, Company I, 3rd Indiana Cavalry. Died at Louisville, Kentucky, January, 1862. Buried in Old Cemetery, Knightstown, Indiana.

Riley S. Brown, Company H, 69th Indiana Infantry. Died at Young's Point, Louisiana, January 20, 1863. Buried there. Re-interred in Vicksburg National Cemetery. Unknown list.

George K. Brownfield, 19th Indiana Battery. Died at Chattanooga, Tennessee, September 25, 1863, account of wounds at Chickamauga, Georgia, September 20, 1863. Buried there. Re-interred in Chattanooga National Cemetery. Unknown list.

Francis Buckles, Company C, 36th Indiana Infantry. Died at Nashville, Tennessee, January 10, 1863. Buried there. Re-interred in Nashville National Cemetery. Section A, Grave, No. 4,301.

*Albert Bunker, Company H, 140th Indiana Infantry. Died at Murfreesboro, Tennessee, February 1, 1865. Buried there. Re-interred in Stone's River (Murfreesboro) National Cemetery. Section M, Grave, No. 4,923.

John E. W. Burch, Company H, 140th Indiana Infantry. Died at Murfreesboro, Tennessee, December 18, 1864. Buried there. Re-interred in Stone's River (Murfreesboro) National Cemetery. Unknown list.

*James H. Burk, Company H, 37th Indiana Infantry. Died at Nashville, Tennessee, July 9, 1864, account of wounds in Atlanta Campaign, May 27, 1864. Buried in South Mound Cemetery, New Castle, Indiana.

John Burr, Company G, 17th Indiana Infantry. Died at Evansville, Indiana, December 6, 1864. Buried in Old Cemetery, south of Middletown, Indiana.

William Burt, Company E, 40th Indiana Infantry. Died at Camp Irving, Texas, August 14, 1865. Buried there. No record of removal. Remains probably re-interred in some National cemetery. Unknown list.

Amos Butler, Company F, 84th Indiana Infantry. Died at Franklin, Tennessee, April 22, 1863. Buried there. Re-interred in Nashville National Cemetery. Unknown list.

Hiram Butler, Company D, 36th Indiana Infantry. Died near Jacksonville, Florida, April, 1865, after release from Confederate prison. Buried there. No record of removal. Remains probably re-interred in some National cemetery. Unknown list.

William Butler, Company D, 36th Indiana Infantry. Died near Chattanooga, Tennessee, September 24, 1863, account of wounds at Chickamauga, Georgia, September 20, 1863. Buried there. Re-interred in Masonic Cemetery, Greensboro, Indiana.

John T. Byers, Company F, 84th Indiana Infantry. Died near Chattanooga, Tennessee, October 8, 1863. Buried there. Re-interred in Chattanooga National Cemetery. Unknown list.

Samuel T. Byers, Company F, 84th Indiana Infantry. Died near Chattanooga, Tennessee, date unknown. Buried there. Re-interred in Chattanooga National Cemetery. Unknown list.

William T. Byers, Company A, 57th Indiana Infantry. Died at Big Shanty, Georgia, July 28, 1864, account of wounds at Kenesaw Mountain, Georgia, June 23, 1864. Buried there. Re-interred in Marietta National Cemetery. Unknown list.

Isaiah Byrket, Company F, 84th Indiana Infantry. Died at home, near Knightstown, Indiana, June 1, 1863. Buried in Elm Grove Cemetery, two and a half miles north of Raysville, Indiana.

Peter Byrket, Company E, 9th Indiana Cavalry. Died at Vicksburg, Mississippi, May 19, 1865. Buried there. Re-interred in Vicksburg National Cemetery. Section I, Grave, No. 7,311.

John J. Byrnes, Company I, 69th Indiana Infantry. Killed at Richmond, Kentucky, August 30, 1862. Buried on the battlefield. Re-interred in Camp Nelson National Cemetery. Unknown list.

*Job Cabe, Company F, 57th Indiana Infantry. Died at Nashville, Tennessee, September 21, 1862. Buried there. Re-interred in Nashville National Cemetery. Section A, Grave, No. 4,957.

Henry Caldwell, Company I, 84th Indiana Infantry. Died at Nashville, Tennessee, November 23, 1863, account of wounds at Chickamauga, Georgia, September 20, 1863. Buried there. Re-interred in Nashville National Cemetery. Unknown list.

James E. Calhoun, Company I, 69th Indiana Infantry. Died at Milliken's Bend, Louisiana, June 6, 1863. Buried there. Re-interred in Vicksburg National Cemetery. Section E, Grave. No. 1,813.

John W. Callahan, Junior, Company I, 69th Indiana Infantry. Killed at Richmond, Kentucky, August 30, 1862. Buried on the battlefield. Re-interred in Camp Nelson National Cemetery. Unknown list.

Charles W. Canaday, Company H, 8th Indiana Infantry (three years). Killed at Vicksburg, Mississippi, May 20, 1863. Buried on the battlefield. Re-interred in Vicksburg National Cemetery. Section G, Grave. No. 5,070.

Stansberry Cannon, Company D. 147th Indiana Infantry. Died at Indianapolis, Indiana, March 19, 1865. Buried in Sugar Grove Cemetery, two and a half miles west of New Castle, Indiana.

Milton Carmichael, Company F, 57th Indiana Infantry. Died at Louisville, Kentucky, November 18, 1862. Buried there. Re-interred in Cave Hill (Louisville) National Cemetery. Section B, Grave, No. 41.

Daniel Carr, Company I, 84th Indiana Infantry. Killed at Chickamauga, Georgia. September 20, 1863. Buried on the battlefield. Re-interred in Chattanooga National Cemetery. Unknown list.

Benjamin F. Carter. Company H, 69th Indiana Infantry. Died at. Keokuk, Iowa. January 20, 1863. Buried there. Re-interred in Keokuk National Cemetery. Grave, No. 315.

John J. Carter, Company E, 8th Indiana Infantry (three years). Died at St. Louis, Missouri, August 12, 1863, account of wounds at Vicksburg, Mississippi, May 22, 1863. Buried there. Re-interred in Jefferson Barracks (St. Louis) National Cemetery, but disinterred and removed to place unknown.

Henry Cartwright, Company I, 69th Indiana Infantry. Died at St. Louis, Missouri, February 22, 1864, account of wounds at Matagorda Bay, Texas, December 30, 1863. Buried there. Re-interred in Jefferson Barracks (St. Louis) National Cemetery. Unknown list.

James C. Cartwright, Company D. 36th Indiana Infantry. Died at Nashville, Tennessee, November 9, 1862. Buried there. Re-interred in Nashville National Cemetery. Section B, Grave. No. 6,738.

Daniel D. Case, Company E. 8th Indiana Infantry (three years). Died at St. Louis. Missouri, November 10, 1861. Buried there. No record of removal. Remains probably re-interred in Jefferson Barracks (St. Louis) National Cemetery. Unknown list.

William H. Caster, Company C, 84th Indiana Infantry. Killed at Chickamauga, Georgia, September 20, 1863. Buried on the battlefield. Re-interred in Chattanooga National Cemetery. Unknown list.

Jacob Chappell, Company A, 36th Indiana Infantry. Died at Stevenson, Alabama, March 18, 1864. Buried there. Re-interred in Chattanooga National Cemetery. Unknown list.

John F. Chenoweth. Company F, 57th Indiana Infantry. Lost on Sultana, April 27, 1865. Body never recovered.

John Clapper, Company B, 134th Indiana Infantry. Died at Nashville, Tennessee, July 17, 1864. Buried there. Re-interred in White Branch Cemetery, Blue River Township, Henry County, Indiana. Again re-interred in German Baptist Cemetery, near Hagerstown, Wayne County, Indiana.

George W. Clapsaddle, Company G, 84th Indiana Infantry. Died at Nashville, Tennessee, October 23, 1863, account of wounds at Chickamauga, Georgia, September 20, 1863. Buried there. Re-interred in Nashville National Cemetery. Section E, Grave, No. 131.

Alpheus Clark. Company A, 54th Indiana Infantry (one year). Died in Andersonville Prison, Georgia, August 16, 1864. Buried in Andersonville National Cemetery. Grave, No. 5,901.

Benjamin Clark, Company A, 54th Indiana Infantry (one year). Died in Andersonville Prison, Georgia, date unknown. Buried in Andersonville National Cemetery. Unknown list.

Milton Clark, Company H, 69th Indiana Infantry. Died at Big Black River, near Vicksburg, Mississippi, July 18, 1863, account of wounds received there, May 17, 1863. Buried on the battlefield. Re-interred in Vicksburg National Cemetery. Unknown list.

Nathan M. Clark. Company I, 123rd Indiana Infantry. Died at Nashville, Tennessee, April 12, 1864. Buried there. Re-interred in Nashville National Cemetery. Section H, Grave, No. 9,929.

William C. Clark, Company H, 69th Indiana Infantry. Died on hospital boat, near Memphis, Tennessee, March 18, 1863. Buried on the river bank. Re-interred in Memphis National Cemetery. Grave, No. 131.

James W. Clellan, Company H, 69th Indiana Infantry. . Died at Keokuk, Iowa, March 21, 1863. Buried there. Re-interred in Keokuk National Cemetery. Unknown list.

*David Clements, Company E, 8th Indiana Infantry (three years). Died at St. Louis, Missouri, November 9, 1862. Buried there. Re-interred in Jefferson Barracks (St. Louis) National Cemetery. Section 58, Grave, No. 10,486.

Joshua Clevenger, Company E, 8th Indiana Infantry (three years). Died at Milliken's Bend, Louisiana. April 18, 1863. Buried there. Re-interred in Vicksburg National Cemetery. Unknown list.

Seth Clevenger, Company F. 124th Indiana Infantry. Died at Murfreesboro, Tennessee, April 20, 1864. Buried there. Re-interred in Stone's River (Murfreesboro) National Cemetery. Section M, Grave, No. 5,100.

David S. Cochran, Company F, 57th Indiana Infantry. Died at New Albany. Indiana, June 17, 1862. Buried there. Re-interred in New Albany National Cemetery. Grave, No. 95.

Joseph W. Connell, Company C, 36th Indiana Infantry. Died near Corinth, Mississippi, May 24, 1862. Buried there. Re-interred in Corinth National Cemetery. Unknown list.

Daniel Conner, Company I, 69th Indiana Infantry. Died at Milliken's Bend, Louisiana. July 11, 1863. Buried there. Re-interred in Vicksburg National Cemetery. Section B, Grave, No. 2,710.

Martin V. Conner, Company G, 84th Indiana Infantry. Died at Nashville, Tennessee, March 17, 1863. Buried there. Re-interred in Nashville National Cemetery. Unknown list.

George W. Conwell, Company I, 69th Indiana Infantry. Died on hospital boat, near Helena, Arkansas, February, 1863. Buried on the river bank. Re-interred in Vicksburg National Cemetery. Unknown list.

Noah W. Coon, Company D, 36th Indiana Infantry. Killed at Stone's River, Tennessee, December 31, 1862. Buried on the battlefield. Re-interred in Stone's River (Murfreesboro) National Cemetery. Unknown list..

James M. Cooper, Company D, 19th Indiana Infantry. Died at Baltimore, Maryland, December 17, 1862, account of wounds at Gainesville, Virginia, August 28, 1862. Buried in Shiloh Cemetery, two and a half miles south of Dunreith, Indiana.

John Cracraft, Company K, 36th Indiana Infantry. Died at Louisville, Kentucky,

March 22, 1862. Buried there. Re-interred in Cave Hill (Louisville) National Cemetery. Section A, Grave, No. 10.

Wyatt Crandall, Company E, 9th Indiana Cavalry. Killed at Franklin, Tennessee, December 17, 1864. Buried on the battlefield. Re-interred in Nashville National Cemetery. Unknown list.

George W. Cray, Company I, 69th Indiana Infantry. Died at Young's Point, Louisiana, March 6, 1863. Buried there. Re-interred in Vicksburg National Cemetery. Unknown list.

Jacob Cripe, Company G, 84th Indiana Infantry. Died at Cincinnati, Ohio, December 17, 1862. Buried there. No record of removal. Remains probably re-interred in some National cemetery. Unknown list.

Joseph A. Cross, Company K, 84th Indiana Infantry. Killed at Kenesaw Mountain, Georgia, June 23, 1864. Buried on the battlefield. Re-interred in Marietta National Cemetery. Section I, Grave, No. 9,390.

Samuel G. Culp, 12th Indiana Battery. Died at Nashville, Tennessee, April 30, 1862. Buried there. Re-interred in Nashville National Cemetery. Section A, Grave, No. 4,537.

Calvin Daniel, Company B, 9th Indiana Infantry. Died in Andersonville Prison, Georgia, date unknown. Buried in Andersonville National Cemetery. Unknown list.

Cornelius J. Davis, Company A, 36th Indiana Infantry. Died at Nashville, Tennessee. April 8, 1862. Buried there. Re-interred in Nashville National Cemetery. Unknown list.

Eli Davis, Company E, 9th Indiana Cavalry. Died at Vicksburg, Mississippi, April 13, 1865. Buried there. Re-interred in Vicksburg National Cemetery. Unknown list.

Isaac Davis, Company H, 69th Indiana Infantry. Died at Milliken's Bend, Louisiana, May 11, 1863. Buried there. Re-interred in Vicksburg National Cemetery. Unknown list.

John H. Davis, Company I, 69th Indiana Infantry. Died at Young's Point, Louisiana, February 19, 1863. Buried there. Re-interred in Vicksburg National Cemetery. Unknown list.

Andrew J. Debord, Company F, 84th Indiana Infantry. Died at Nashville, Tennessee. March 27, 1865. Buried there. Re-interred in Nashville National Cemetery. Section J, Grave, No. 14,922.

Robert Deitzer, Company B, 124th Indiana Infantry. Died at Louisville, Kentucky, March 29, 1864. Buried there. Re-interred in Cave Hill (Louisville) National Cemetery. Section B, Grave, No. 46.

Thomas P. Dennis, Company I, 69th Indiana Infantry. Died at Young's Point, Louisiana, March 6, 1863. Buried there. Re-interred in Vicksburg National Cemetery. Section B, Grave, No. 2,816.

Whitesel Dennis, Company I, 3rd Indiana Cavalry. Died at Stevenson, Alabama, September 20, 1863. Buried there. Re-interred in Chattanooga National Cemetery. Unknown list.

Samuel Detrich, Company I, 69th Indiana Infantry. Killed at Richmond, Kentucky. August 30, 1862. Buried on the battlefield. Re-interred in Camp Nelson National Cemetery. Unknown list.

John R. Dillee, Company D, 36th Indiana Infantry. Died at Cleveland, Tennessee, March 4, 1864. Buried there. Re-interred in Chattanooga National Cemetery. Unknown list.

Levi Donihue, Company H, 5th Indiana Infantry (Mexican War). Died on transport ship on Gulf of Mexico, July 4, 1848. Buried at sea.

Thomas J. Dougherty, Company K, 19th Indiana Infantry. Killed at Gettysburg, Pennsylvania, July 1, 1863. Buried on the battlefield. Re-interred in Gettysburg National Cemetery. Indiana Plat, Section A, Grave, No. 2.

*Daniel Doxtader, Company K, 36th Indiana Infantry. Died at Nashville, Tennessee, November 5, 1862. Buried there. Re-interred in Nashville National Cemetery. Section B, Grave, No. 5,653.

John Driver, Company K, 36th Indiana Infantry. Killed at Shiloh, Tennessee, April 7. 1862. Buried on the battlefield. Re-interred in Shiloh National Cemetery. Unknown list.

James A. Drury, Company A, 57th Indiana Infantry. Died at Nashville, Tennessee, December 4, 1862. Buried there. Re-interred in Nashville National Cemetery. Section B, Grave, No. 6,100.

William W. Dubois, Company C, 36th Indiana Infantry. Killed at Shiloh, Tennessee, April 6, 1862. Buried on the battlefield. Re-interred in Shiloh National Cemetery. Unknown list.

Wiley J. Dudley, Company I, 69th Indiana Infantry. Died on hospital boat, near Vicksburg, Mississippi, July 5, 1863. Buried on the river bank. Re-interred in Vicksburg National Cemetery. Unknown list.

John R. Dykes, Company B, 5th Indiana Cavalry. Died in Andersonville Prison, Georgia, November 1, 1864. Buried in Andersonville National Cemetery. Unknown list.

John H. Edwards, Company A, 36th Indiana Infantry. Died at Camp Wickliffe, Kentucky, February 14, 1862. Buried there. No record of removal. Remains probably re-interred in some National cemetery. Unknown list.

Levi S. Edwards, Company D. 36th Indiana Infantry. Died near Chattanooga, Tennessee, September 25, 1863, account of wounds at Chickamauga, Georgia, September 19, 1863. Buried there. Re-interred in Chattanooga National Cemetery. Section B, Grave. No. 815.

Josephus V. Elliott, Company F, 57th Indiana Infantry. Died at home, in Mechanicsburg, March 9, 1863. Buried in Mechanicsburg Cemetery, Mechanicsburg, Indiana.

Jesse S. Ellison, Company H, 69th Indiana Infantry. Died at Richmond, Kentucky, September 12, 1862, account of wounds received there, August 30, 1862. Buried on the battlefield. Re-interred in Camp Nelson National Cemetery. Unknown list.

George Evans, Company H, 140th Indiana Infantry. Died at Nashville, Tennessee, March 21. 1865. Buried there. Re-interred in Nashville National Cemetery. Unknown list.

Henry Evans, Company A, 54th Indiana Infantry (one year). Died at Arkansas Post, Arkansas, January, 1863. Buried there. Re-interred in Vicksburg National Cemefery. Unknown list.

Lemuel Evans, Company F, 57th Indiana Infantry. Died at Nashville, Tennessee, February 5, 1863. Buried there. Re-interred in Nashville National Cemetery. Unknown list.

Samuel Fadely, Company F, 124th Indiana Infantry. Died at Nashville, Tennessee, October 27, 1864. Buried there. Re-interred in Nashville National Cemetery. Section E, Grave, No. 2,663.

Benjamin F. Fawcett, 4th Indiana Battery. Died at Nashville, Tennessee, April 30, 1864. Buried there. Re-interred in Nashville National Cemetery. Section J, Grave, No. 13,707.

William H. Fentress, Company D, 36th Indiana Infantry. Killed in Atlanta Campaign, near Dallas, Georgia, May 31, 1864. Buried in the Masonic Cemetery, Greensboro, Indiana.

William A. Ferry, Company I, 69th Indiana Infantry. Died at Richmond, Kentucky, September 10, 1862, account of wounds received there, August 30, 1862. Buried on the battlefield. Re-interred in Camp Nelson National Cemetery. Unknown list.

Sylvester Fisher, Company E, 130th Indiana Infantry. Died at Chattanooga, Tennessee, June 26, 1864. Buried there. Re-interred in Chattanooga National Cemetery. Section E, Grave, No. 11,486.

Henry Fitch, Company E, 9th Indiana Cavalry. Died at Louisville, Kentucky, February 9, 1865. Buried there. Re-interred in Cave Hill (Louisville) National Cemetery. Section C, Grave, No. 95.

Beniah Fleming, Company E, 8th Indiana Infantry (three years). Died at Middlebrook, Missouri March 9, 1863. Buried in White Union Cemetery, Fall Creek Township, Henry County, Indiana.

Preston Fleming, Company I, 69th Indiana Infantry. Killed at Richmond, Kentucky, August 30, 1862. Buried on the battlefield. Re-interred in Camp Nelson National Cemetery. Unknown list.

*James M. Fletcher, Company A, 57th Indiana Infantry. Lost on Sultana, April 27, 1865. Body never recovered.

*Lorenzo D. Fort, Company A, 57th Indiana Infantry. Died at Stone's River, Tennessee, January 1, 1863, account of wounds received there, December 31, 1862. Buried on the battlefield. Re-interred in Simmons' Cemetery, near Charlottesville, Hancock County, Indiana.

Oliver P. Fort, Company K, 2nd Colorado Cavalry. Died at Benton Barracks, St. Louis, Missouri, January 12, 1864. Buried in Old Cemetery, Knightstown, Indiana.

Randolph Fort, Company B, 19th Indiana Infantry. Killed at Gainesville, Virginia, August 28, 1862. Buried on the battlefield. No record of removal. Remains probably re-interred in some National cemetery. Unknown list.

Robert C. Foster, Company I, 69th Indiana Infantry. Killed at Richmond, Kentucky, August 30, 1862. Buried on the battlefield. Re-interred in Ebenezer Cemetery, Franklin Township, Henry County, Indiana.

Samuel W. Foster, Company A, 36th Indiana Infantry. Died at Stockade No. 3, Nashville and Chattanooga Railroad, June 5, 1863. Buried there. Re-interred in Lewisville Cemetery, Lewisville, Indiana.

John W. Foulks, Company K, 36th Indiana Infantry. Died at Nashville, Tennessee, April 1, 1862. Buried there. Re-interred in Nashville National Cemetery. Section A, Grave. No. 4,417.

John W. Fountain, Company H, 69th Indiana Infantry. Killed at Champion Hills, Mississippi, May 16, 1863. Buried on the battlefield. Re-interred in Vicksburg National Cemetery. Unknown list.

David Franklin, Company H, 69th Indiana Infantry. Died on hospital boat, near Vicksburg, Mississippi, July 2, 1863, of wounds received at Vicksburg, May 22, 1863. Buried on the river bank. Re-interred in Vicksburg National Cemetery. Unknown list.

Washington L. Freeman, Company D, 36th Indiana Infantry. Died at Nashville, Tennessee, December 6, 1863, account of wounds at Chickamauga, Georgia, September 19, 1863. Buried there. Re-interred in Nashville National Cemetery. Unknown list.

*James Gates, Company G, 84th Indiana Infantry. Died at Nashville, Tennessee, August 30, 1863. Buried there. Re-interred in Nashville National Cemetery. Unknown list.

*Richard Gates, Company G, 84th Indiana Infantry. Killed at Chickamauga, Georgia, September 20, 1863. Buried on the battlefield. Re-interred in Chattanooga National Cemetery. Unknown list.

John Gibson, Company D, 2nd Indiana Cavalry. Killed at Pulaski, Tennessee, July 3, 1863. Buried on the battlefield. No record of removal. Remains probably re-interred in some National cemetery. Unknown list.

John M. Ginn, Company I, 69th Indiana Infantry. Killed at Richmond, Kentucky, August 30, 1862. Buried on the battlefield. Re-interred in Camp Nelson National Cemetery. Unknown list.

Joseph Ginn, Company I, 69th Indiana Infantry. Died at Richmond, Kentucky, September, 1862, account of wounds received there, August 30, 1862. Buried on the battlefield. Re-interred in Camp Nelson National Cemetery. Unknown list.

Henry Good, Company E, 8th Indiana Infantry. Killed at Vicksburg, Mississippi, May 22, 1863. Buried on the battlefield. Re-interred in Vicksburg National Cemetery. Unknown list.

Joseph B. Gossett, Company E, 8th Indiana Infantry (three years). Killed at Vicksburg, Mississippi, June 16, 1863. Buried on the battlefield. Re-interred in Vicksburg National Cemetery. Section G, Grave, No. 4,809.

Ferdinand C. Gough, Company D, 2nd Indiana Cavalry. Died at Louisville, Kentucky, May 7, 1864. Buried there. Re-interred in Cave Hill (Louisville) National Cemetery. Unknown list.

Lemuel Gough, Company G, 84th Indiana Infantry. Died at Nashville, Tennessee, May 2, 1863. Buried there. Re-interred in Nashville National Cemetery. Unknown list.

Elijah S. Gowdy, Company I, 69th Indiana Infantry. Killed at Richmond, Kentucky, August 30, 1862. Buried on the battlefield. Re-interred in Camp Nelson National Cemetery. Unknown list.

Francis M. Granger, Company M, 2nd Indiana Cavalry. Died at Columbus, Ohio, March 10, 1865. Buried there. Re-interred in Green Lawn Cemetery, Columbus, Ohio. Soldiers' Circle, Grave, No. 285.

Thomas J. Graves, Company H, 69th Indiana Infantry. Killed at Jackson, Mississippi, July 16, 1863. Buried on the battlefield. Re-interred in Vicksburg National Cemetery. Section K, Grave, No. 5,965.

*Jeremiah Gray, Company F, 57th Indiana Infantry. Died at Nashville, Tennessee, February 5, 1863. Buried there. Re-interred in Nashville National Cemetery. Unknown list.

Edwin A. Gregory, Company F, 57th Indiana Infantry. Killed at Stone's River, Tennessee, December 31, 1862. Buried on the battlefield. Re-interred in Stone's River (Murfreesboro) National Cemetry. Unknown list.

Daniel F. Griffin, Junior, Company C, 31st U. S. V. Died at Prang Prang, Philippine Islands, December 21, 1900. Buried there. Re-interred in Catholic Cemetery, New Castle, Indiana.

Amos Gronendyke, Company F, 124th Indiana Infantry. Died at Nashville, Tennessee, December 27, 1864, account of wounds at Franklin, Tennessee, November 30, 1864. Buried in Painter Cemetery, Fall Creek Township, Henry County, Indiana.

Charles W. Grove, Company F, 124th Indiana Infantry. Died at Nashville, Tennessee, July 17, 1864. Buried there. Re-interred in Nashville National Cemetery. Section H, Grave, No. 10,062.

Edward Gue, Company I, 3rd Indiana Cavalry. Died at Louisville, Kentucky, January, 1862. Buried there. Re-interred in Cave Hill (Louisville) National Cemetery. Unknown list.

Amos R. Gustin, Company H, 69th Indiana Infantry. Died at Evansville, Indiana, June 25, 1863, account of wounds at Champion Hills, Mississippi, May 16, 1863. Buried there. No record of removal. Remains probably re-interred in some National cemetery. Unknown list.

Samuel E. Gustin, Company E, 8th Indiana Infantry (three years). Died at Terre Bonne, Louisiana, June 28, 1864. Buried there. Re-interred in Chalmette National Cemetery. Grave, No. 5,063.

Henry C. Hall, Company F, 84th Indiana Infantry. Died at Nashville, Tennessee, August 26, 1864. Buried there. Re-interred in Nashville National Cemetery. Unknown list.

John D. Hall, Company K, 36th Indiana Infantry. Killed at Stone's River, Tennessee, December 31, 1862. Buried on the battlefield. Re-interred in Stone's River (Murfreesboro) National Cemetery. Unknown list.

William B. Hankins, Company H, 69th Indiana Infantry. Killed at Champion Hills, Mississippi, May 16, 1863. Buried on the battlefield. Re-interred in Vicksburg National Cemetery. Unknown list.

William H. Harris, Company I, 69th Indiana Infantry. Killed at Richmond, Kentucky, August 30, 1862. Buried on the battlefield. Re-interred in Camp Nelson National Cemetery. Unknown list.

Peter Harter, Company G, 84th Indiana Infantry. Killed at Chickamauga, Georgia, September 20, 1863. Buried on the battlefield. Re-interred in Chattanooga National Cemetery. Unknown list.

William A. Haskett, Company I, 69th Indiana Infantry. Died at Memphis, Tennessee, April 1, 1863. Buried there. Re-interred in Memphis National Cemetery. Unknown list.

Isaiah Hawhee, Company K, 36th Indiana Infantry. Killed at Stone's River, Tennessee, December 31. 1862. Buried on the battlefield. Re-interred in Stone's River (Murfreesboro) National Cemetery. Unknown list.

James Hayden, Company C, 5th Indiana Cavalry. Died at Indianapolis, Indiana, October 24, 1862. Buried there. Re-interred in Crown Hill Cemetery, Indianapolis. Indiana. Military Plat, Grave. No. 423.

Wilson Hayden, Company D, 2nd Indiana Cavalry. Died in Andersonville Prison, Georgia, date unknown. Buried in Andersonville National Cemetery. Unknown list.

Jeremiah Hayes, Company E, 36th Indiana Infantry. Died April 30, 1863, account of wounds at Stone's River, Tennessee, December 31, 1862. Buried on the battlefield. Re-interred in Stone's River (Murfreesboro) National Cemetery. Unknown list.

Mahlon Hayes, Company A, 36th Indiana Infantry. Died at Louisville, Kentucky, March 26, 1862. Buried in Lewisville Cemetery, Lewisville, Indiana.

Oliver P. Hayes, Company E, 8th Indiana Infantry (three years). Died at Savannah, Georgia, March 27, 1865. Buried there. No record of removal. Remains probably re-interred in some National cemetery. Unknown list.

Peter Haynes, Company F, 57th Indiana Infantry. Killed at Franklin, Tennessee, November 30, 1864. Buried on the battlefield. Re-interred in Nashville National Cemetery. Unknown list.

George W. Hazzard, (Uncle of the author of this History), Colonel, 37th Indiana Infantry, and Captain. 4th Artillery, U. S. A. Died at Baltimore, Maryland, August 14. 1862, 'account of wounds at White Oak Swamp, Virginia, June 30. 1862. Buried in Cathedral Cemetery, Baltimore, Maryland.

Leander E. Hazzard, (Brother of the author of this History), Troop H, 5th Cavalry, U. S. A. Killed by Indians in Wyoming Territory. Exact date of death and place of burial unknown. Memorial stone erected in South Mound Cemetery, New Castle, Indiana.

Thomas S. Heavenridge, Company A, 36th Indiana Infantry. Killed at Chickamauga, Georgia, September 19, 1863. Buried on the battlefield. Re-interred in Chattanooga National Cemetery. Unknown list.

Joseph Hedrick, Company A, 36th Indiana Infantry. Died at Camp Wickliffe, Kentucky, February 6, 1862. Buried in Lewisville Cemetery, Lewisville, Indiana.

*John P. Heinbaugh, Company G, 84th Indiana Infantry. Killed at Kenesaw, Mountain, Georgia, June 23. 1864. Buried on the battlefield. Re-interred in Marietta National Cemetery. Unknown list.

*Jacob K. Helms. Company K, 36th Indiana Infantry. Died at Nashville, Tennessee, April 27. 1862. Buried there. Re-interred in Nashville National Cemetery. Section A. Grave, No. 1,171.

Mahlon Hendricks, Company C, 36th Indiana Infantry. Killed at Kenesaw Mountain, Georgia, June 23, 1864. Buried on the battlefield. Re-interred in Marietta National Cemetery. Section C, Grave, No. 2,312.

William B. Henshaw, Company H. 69th Indiana Infantry. Killed at Richmond,' Kentucky, August 30, 1862. Buried on the battlefield. Re-interred in Camp Nelson National Cemetery. Unknown list.

George Hess. Company K, 36th Indiana Infantry. Died at Louisville. Kentucky, March 20. 1862. Buried there. Re-interred in Cave Hill (Louisville) National Cemetery. Section A, Grave, No. 5.

Alfred Hewlit. 2nd Indiana Battery. Died at Fort Scott. Kansas, November 27, 1861. Buried there. Re-interred in Old Baptist Cemetery, Knightstown, Indiana.

Henry C. Hiatt, Company G, 9th Indiana Cavalry. Died in Cahaba Prison, Alabama, January, 1865. Buried there. Re-interred in Marietta National Cemetery. Section L, Grave, No. 4,001.

John C. Hiatt, Company A, 19th Indiana Infantry. Killed at North Anna River, Virginia, May 27, 1864. Buried on the battlefield. No record of removal. Remains probably re-interred in some National cemetery. Unknown list.

Joseph Hiatt, Company F, 57th Indiana Infantry. Killed in Atlanta Campaign, May 27, 1864. Buried on the battlefield. No record of removal. Remains probably re-interred in some National cemetery. Unknown list.

COMPANY E, 9th INDIANA CAVALRY.

January 27, 1863. Buried there. No recor
in some National cemetery. Unknown list.

Jesse Hobbs, Company I, 3rd Indiana
ary 1, 1862. Buried in Old Cemetery, Kui

Volney Hobson, Company E. 9th Indi
December 17, 1864. Buried in Batson Cem
ana.

William C. Hoober, Company t 9th
1865. Body never recovered.

Adam Hoombaugh, Company F 139t!
Centreville, Tennessee. November 27, 18.4.
mains probably re-interred in some Nationa

Milton Hooten, Company G. 16th Indi
June 18, 1863. Buried there. Re-interred
list.

Charles B. Hoover, Company K, 36th
tucky, February 16, 1862. Buried there. F
Cemetery. Unknown list.

De Witt C. Hoover, Company H. 69th
isiana, September 14, 1863. Buried there.
Grave, No. 4,427.

John Hoover, Company K. 11th Kui
souri, March 13, 1863. Buried there. Me
Cemetery. Section 14, Grave, No. 795.

Abraham W. Hopper, Company A. 3 i
nessee, June 25, 1863. Buried there. Rea:
tion E. Grave, No. 263.

James Horney, Company 1, 3rd Indi
ville, Virginia. February 15, 1864. Buriei
Section D, Grave, No. 325.

David Houck. Incomplete list. Ui
1878. Buried in Chalmette National Ceme'

John Houser, Company D, 36th Indian
7, 1862. Buried on the battlefield. Re-inte
list.

Nimrod Howren, Company A. 36th
Georgia, September 20, 1863. Buried on it
tional Cemetery. Unknown list.

William A. Howren, Company A. 3'
Virginia, October 18, 1864. Buried on the
probably re-interred in some National cem

Henry Hubbard, Company C. 2nd Ind
December 16, 1864. Buried on the battlefie
Wayne County, Indiana.

James C. Hudelson, Company A, 139t
Kentucky, June 25, 1864. Buried there.
interred in some National cemetery. Unkn

Abraham Huff, Company I, 69th In.
April 7, 1863. Buried there. Re-interred
Cemetery. Grave, No. 19. Remains have
where.

Jacob Huff, Company 1, 69th Indian
January 21, 1863. Buried there. Re-interr
list.

John Hughes, Company A. 54th Indiana

COMPANY E, 9th INDIANA CAVALRY.

*Herman Hines, Company G, 84th Indiana Infantry. Died at Ashland, Kentucky, January 27, 1863. Buried there. No record of removal. Remains probably re-interred in some National cemetery. Unknown list.

Jesse Hobbs, Company I, 3rd Indiana Cavalry. Died at Louisville, Kentucky, January 1, 1862. Buried in Old Cemetery, Knightstown, Indiana.

Volney Hobson, Company E, 9th Indiana Cavalry. Killed at Franklin, Tennessee, December 17, 1864. Buried in Batson Cemetery, Liberty Township, Henry County, Indiana.

William C. Hoober, Company G, 9th Indiana Cavalry. Lost on Sultana, April 27, 1865. Body never recovered.

Adam Hoombaugh, Company F, 130th Indiana Infantry. Killed by guerrillas at Centreville, Tennessee, November 27, 1864. Buried there. No record of removal. Remains probably re-interred in some National cemetery. Unknown list.

Milton Hooten, Company G, 16th Indiana Infantry. Died at Vicksburg, Mississippi, June 18, 1863. Buried there. Re-interred in Vicksburg National Cemetery. Unknown list.

Charles B. Hoover, Company K, 36th Indiana Infantry. Died at Louisville, Kentucky, February 16, 1862. Buried there. Re-interred in Cave Hill (Louisville) National Cemetery. Unknown list.

De Witt C. Hoover, Company H, 69th Indiana infantry. Died at New Orleans, Louisiana, September 14, 1863. Buried there. Re-interred in Chalmette National Cemetery. Grave, No. 4,427.

John Hoover, Company K, 11th Kansas Cavalry. Died at Camp Solomon, Missouri, March 13, 1863. Buried there. Re-interred in Springfield (Missouri) National Cemetery. Section 14, Grave, No. 795.

Abraham W. Hopper, Company A, 36th Indiana Infantry. Died at Nashville, Tennessee, June 25, 1863. Buried there. Re-interred in Nashville National Cemetery. Section E, Grave, No. 263.

James Horney, Company I, 3rd Indiana Cavalry. Died in Danville Prison, Danville, Virginia, February 15, 1864. Buried in Danville (Virginia) National Cemetery. Section D, Grave, No. 325.

David Houck. Incomplete list. Died at New Orleans, Louisiana, September 2, 1878. Buried in Chalmette National Cemetery. Grave, No. 11,792.

John Houser, Company D, 36th Indiana Infantry. Killed at Shiloh, Tennessee, April 7, 1862. Buried on the battlefield. Re-interred in Shiloh National Cemetery. Unknown list.

Nimrod Howren, Company A, 36th Indiana Infantry. Killed at Chickamauga, Georgia, September 20, 1863. Buried on the battlefield. Re-interred in Chattanooga National Cemetery. Unknown list.

William A. Howren, Company A, 20th Indiana Infantry. Killed at Petersburg, Virginia, October 18, 1864. Buried on the battlefield. No record of removal. Remains probably re-interred in some National cemetery. Unknown list.

Henry Hubbard, Company C, 2nd Indiana Cavalry. Killed at Nashville, Tennessee, December 16, 1864. Buried on the battlefield. Re-interred in Friends' Cemetery, Milton, Wayne County, Indiana.

James C. Hudelson, Company A, 139th Indiana Infantry. Died at Mumfordsville, Kentucky, June 25, 1864. Buried there. No record of removal. Remains probably re-interred in some National cemetery. Unknown list.

Abraham Huff, Company I, 69th Indiana Infantry. Died at St. Louis, Missouri, April 7, 1863. Buried there. Re-interred in Jefferson Barracks (St. Louis) National Cemetery. Grave, No. 19. Remains have probably been removed and re-interred elsewhere.

Jacob Huff, Company I, 69th Indiana Infantry. Died at Young's Point, Louisiana, January 21, 1863. Buried there. Re-interred in Vicksburg National Cemetery. Unknown list.

John Hughes, Company A, 54th Indiana Infantry (one year). Died at Young's Point,

47

Louisiana, February 14, 1863. Buried there. Re-interred in Vicksburg National Cemetery. Unknown list.

Joseph Huston, Company F, 57th Indiana Infantry. Died at Nashville, Tennessee, February 5, 1863. Buried there. Re-interred in Mechanicsburg Cemetery, Mechanicsburg, Indiana.

William H. Huston, Company H, 69th Indiana Infantry. Died at Young's' Point, Louisiana, February 20, 1863. Buried there. Re-interred in Mechanicsburg Cemetery, Mechanicsburg, Indiana.

William Hutchins, Company A, 36th Indiana Infantry. Died at Nelson's Furnace, Kentucky, March 1, 1862. Buried there. Re-interred in Flat Rock Cemetery, Liberty Township, Henry County, Indiana.

Jesse A. Ice, Company G, 84th Indiana Infantry. Killed at Kenesaw Mountain, Georgia, June '23, 1864. Buried on the battlefield. Re-interred in Marietta National Cemetery. Section I, Grave, No. 9,365.

Samuel Irvin, Company K, 5th Indiana Cavalry. Died near Jacksonville, Florida, April, 1865, after release from Confederate prison. Buried there. No record of removal. Remains probably re-intered in some National cemetery. Unknown list.

*Jesse Jackson, Company G, 84th Indiana Infantry. Died at Nashville, Tennessee, March 31, 1863. Buried there. Re-interred in Nashville National Cemetery. Section D, Grave, No. 3,495.

Austin W. James, Company D, 36th Indiana Infantry. Killed at Stone's River, Tennessee, December 31, 1862. Buried on the battlefield. Re-interred in Addison Cemetery, Rush County, near Knightstown, Indiana.

James Jarvis, Company G, 84th Indiana Infantry. Killed at·Chickamauga, Georgia, September 20, 1863. Buried on the battlefield. Re-interred in Chattanooga National Cemetery. Unknown list.

Milton Jeffries, Company I, 84th Indiana Infantry. Died at Nashville, Tennessee, February 24, 1863. Buried there. Re-interred in Nashville National Cemetery. Unknown list.

Charles C. Jennings, Company F, 57th Indiana Infantry. Killed at Franklin, Tennessee, November 30, 1864. Buried on the battlefield. Re-interred in Nashville National Cemetery. Unknown list.

William A. Jennings, Company K, 16th Indiana Infantry. Died March 2, 1863. Buried on the battlefield. No record of removal. Remains probably re-interred in some National cemetery. Unknown list.

Josiah A. Jessup, Company I, 84th Indiana Infantry. Died in Danville Prison, Danville, Virginia, March 5, 1864. Buried in Danville (Virginia) National Cemetery. Section D, Grave, No. 463.

Hutchinson Johnson, Company D, 19th Indiana Infantry. Killed at Gainesville, Virginia, August 28, 1862. Buried on the battlefield. No record of removal. Remains probably re-interred in some National cemetery. Unknown list.

John N. Johnson, Company K, 36th Indiana Infantry. Killed at Stone's River, Tennessee, December 31, 1862. Buried on the battlefield. Re-interred in Stone's River (Murfreesboro) National Cemetery. Unknown list.

William·K. Johnson, Company I, 69th Indiana Infantry. Killed at Port Gibson, Mississippi, May 1, 1863. Buried on the battlefield. Re-interred in Vicksburg National Cemetery. Unknown list.

James Jones, Company E, 8th Indiana Infantry (three years). Died in Delaware County, Indiana; December 19, 1863. Buried in Sharp's Cemetery, Salem Township, Delaware County, Indiana.

Henry S. Jordan, Company I, 69th Indiana Infantry. Died at Milliken's Bend, Louisiana, March 15, 1863. Buried there. Re-interred in Vicksburg National Cemetery. Unknown list.

Absalom H. Julian, Company C, 36th Indiana Infantry. Killed at Stone's River, Tennessee, December 31, 1862. Buried on the battlefield. Re-interred in Stone's River (Murfreesboro) National Cemetery. Unknown list.

Isaac B. Keesling, Company H, 69th Indiana Infantry. Died at Young's Point. Louisiana, March 18, 1863. Buried there. Re-interred in Vicksburg National Cemetery. Unknown list.

John H. Kennedy, Company I, 3rd Indiana Cavalry. Died in Andersonville Prison, Georgia, July 8, 1864. Buried in Andersonville National Cemetery. Grave, No. 3,047.

Joseph Kennedy, Company H, 140th Indiana Infantry. Died at Greensboro, North Carolina, June 22, 1865. Buried there. Re-interred in Raleigh National Cemetery. Section 332.

John Kenney, Company F, 57th Indiana Infantry. Killed at Missionary Ridge, Tennessee, November 25, 1863. Buried on the battlefield. Re-interred in Chattanooga National Cemetery. Unknown list.

Henry Kent, Company A, 36th Indiana Infantry. Died at Evansville, Indiana, July 9, 1862. Buried there. No record of removal. Remains probably re-interred in some National cemetery. Unknown list.

John A. Kern, Company D, 36th Indiana Infantry. Killed at Kenesaw Mountain, Georgia, June 23, 1864. Buried on the battlefield. Re-interred in Masonic Cemetery, Greensboro, Indiana.

James L. Kilgore, Company K, 36th Indiana Infantry. Died at Chattanooga, Tennessee, August 5, 1864. Buried there. Re-interred in Chattanooga National Cemetery. Section E, Grave, No. 1,893.

James Kingrey, Company I, 69th Indiana Infantry. Died at Milliken's Bend, Louisiana, April 22, 1863. Buried there. Re-interred in Vicksburg National Cemetery. Section E, Grave, No. 1,571.

Andrew B. Kirkham, Company K, 37th Indiana Infantry. Killed at Stone's River, Tennessee, December 31, 1862. Buried on the battlefield. Re-interred in Shiloh Cemetery, two and a half miles south of Dunreith, Indiana.

Thomas Koons, Company H, 100th Indiana Infantry. Died at Grand Junction, Tennessee, February 1, 1863. Buried there. Re-interred in Corinth National Cemetery. Grave, No. 2,124.

Joseph Laboyteaux, Company H, 69th Indiana Infantry. Died at New Orleans. Louisiana, December, 1863. Buried there. Re-interred in Chalmette National Cemetery. Unknown list.

Thomas Laboyteaux, Company E, 9th Indiana Cavalry. Lost on Sultana, April 27, 1865. Body never recovered.

James C. Lacy, Company B, 69th Indiana Infantry. Died at Indianapolis, Indiana, February, 1864. Buried there. Re-interred in Crown Hill Cemetery, Indianapolis, Indiana. Military Plat, Grave, No. 233.

John L. Lacy, Company B, 69th Indiana Infantry. Died at Jefferson Barracks, Missouri, February 28, 1863. Buried there. Re-interred in Jefferson Barracks (St. Louis) National Cemetery. Grave, No. 10,633.

Wilson P. Lacy, Company B, 69th Indiana Infantry. Died at Young's Point, Louisiana, February 10, 1863. Buried there. Re-interred in Vicksburg National Cemetery. Unknown list.

Oren E. Lambird, Troop H, 12th Cavalry, U. S. A. Died in Philippines, November 20, 1903. Buried there. Re-interred in German Baptist Cemetery, near Hagerstown, Wayne County, Indiana.

Benjamin D. Leavell, Company F, 57th Indiana Infantry. Died at Louisville, Kentucky, February 2, 1862. Buried in Hess Cemetery, near Cadiz, Indiana.

William L. Leavell, Company F, 57th Indiana Infantry. Died at Nashville, Tennessee, December 10, 1862. Buried there. Re-interred in Nashville National Cemetery. Section B, Grave, No. 6,340.

Robert D. F. Lee, Company I, 3rd Indiana Cavalry. Died at Louisville, Kentucky, June 1, 1862. Buried there. Re-interred in Cave Hill (Louisville) National Cemetery. Unknown list.

*William H. Leisure, Company E, 9th Indiana Cavalry. Died in Cahaba Prison,

Alabama. January, 1865. Buried there. Re-interred in Marietta National Cemetery. Unknown list.

William Lemberger, Company D, 11th Indiana Infantry. Killed at Champion Hills, Mississippi, May 16, 1863. Buried on the battlefield. Re-interred in Vicksburg National Cemetery. Unknown list.

George W. Lennard, (Uncle of the author of this History) Colonel, 57th Indiana Infantry. Killed at Resaca, Georgia, May 14, 1864. Buried in South Mound Cemetery, New Castle, Indiana.

James Leonard, Company D, 8th Indiana Infantry (three years). Died at Lewisville, Indiana, October 27, 1862. Buried in New Lisbon Cemetery, New Lisbon, Indiana.

Wilson Lester, Company I, 69th Indiana Infantry. Died at Grand Gulf, Mississippi, May 29, 1863, account of wounds at Port Gibson, Mississippi, May 1, 1863. Buried there. Re-interred in Vicksburg National Cemetery. Unknown list.

Samuel Level, Company E, 7th Indiana Infantry. Died in Confederate prison, Salisbury, North Carolina, April, 1865. Buried in the Salisbury National Cemetery. Unknown list.

Joseph Linens, Company A, 36th Indiana Infantry. Died at Nelson's Furnace, Kentucky, March 1, 1862. Buried there. No record of removal. Remains probably re-interred in some National cemetery. Unknown list.

Elijah H. Lines, Company C, 5th Indiana Cavalry. Died at home, near Luray, Indiana, June 22, 1863. Buried in East Lebanon Cemetery, Prairie Township, Henry County, Indiana.

*Lewis Lock, Company F, 57th Indiana Infantry. Died at Louisville, Kentucky, January 16, 1862. Buried there. Re-interred in Cave Hill (Louisville) National Cemetery. Section A, Grave, No. 12.

George Lockridge, Company F, 84th Indiana Infantry. Died at Franklin, Tennessee, May 25, 1863. Buried there. Re-interred in Nashville National Cemetery. Unknown list.

Lorenzo D. Longfellow, Company I, 69th Indiana Infantry. Killed at Fort Blakely, Alabama, April 9, 1865. Buried on the battlefield. Re-interred in Mobile National Cemetery. Unknown list.

Andrew J. Lucas, Company I, 124th Indiana Infantry. Died at Marietta, Georgia, August 12, 1864. Buried there. Re-interred in Marietta National Cemetery. Grave, No. 7,465.

John J. Luce, Company H, 140th Indiana Infantry. Died at Wilmington, North Carolina, March 4, 1865. Buried there. Re-interred in Wilmington National Cemetery. Unknown list.

Moses Luzadder, Company G, 84th Indiana Infantry. Killed at Chickamauga, Georgia, September 20, 1863. Buried on the battlefield. Re-interred in Chattanooga National Cemetery. Unknown list.

Marcellus Lytle. Company D, 11th Indiana Infantry. Died at Paducah, Kentucky, November 1, 1861. Buried there. No record of removal. Remains probably re-interred in some National cemetery. Unknown list.

John B. McConnell, Company I, 69th Indiana Infantry. Died at Young's Point, Louisiana, February 16, 1863. Buried there. Re-interred in Vicksburg National Cemetery. Unknown list.

Jonathan McConnell, Company H, 140th Indiana Infantry. Died at Wilmington, North Carolina, April 17, 1865. Buried there. Re-interred in Wilmington National Cemetery. Grave, No. 1,719.

William E. McCorkle, Company A, 12th Infantry, U. S. A. Died at home, in Knightstown, Indiana, October 8, 1898. Buried in Friends' Cemetery, near Cadiz, Indiana.

James E. McCormack, Company H, 69th Indiana Infantry. Died at Cairo, Illinois, February 18, 1863, account of wounds at Richmond, Kentucky, August 30, 1862. Buried there. No record of removal. Remains probably re-interred in some National cemetery. Unknown list.

John R. McCormack, Company I, 69th Indiana Infantry. Died at Vicksburg, Mississippi, August 11, 1863. Buried there. Re-interred in Vicksburg National Cemetery. Unknown list.

Thomas McCormack, Company K, 8th Indiana Infantry (three years). Killed at Vicksburg, Mississippi, May 21, 1863. Buried on the battlefield. Re-interred in Vicksburg National Cemetery. Unknown list.

William McCormack, Company H, 69th Indiana Infantry. Died at Indianapolis, Indiana, January 26, 1863, account of wounds at Richmond, Kentucky, August 30, 1862. Buried there. Re-interred in Crown Hill Cemetery, Indianapolis, Indiana. Military Plat. Unknown list.

Thompson W. McCune, Company E, 8th Indiana Infantry (three years), and Company G, First Regiment, Mississippi (River) Marine Brigade. Accidentally drowned in the Mississippi River, April 8, 1863. Buried on Island No. 35, Mississippi River. No record of removal. Remains probably re-interred in some National Cemetery. Unknown list.

Thomas McDowell, Company B, 23rd Iowa Infantry. Died at Eddyville, Iowa, August 26, 1863, account of wounds at Milliken's Bend, Louisiana, June 7, 1863. Buried in Mt. Pleasant Cemetery, Jefferson Township, Polk County, Iowa.

James McFetridge, Company C, 9th Indiana Infantry. Died at New Orleans, Louisiana, June 17, 1865. Buried there. Re-interred in Chalmette National Cemetery. Unknown list.

William H. H. McGuffin, Company I, 3rd Indiana Cavalry. Died at home, near Knightstown, Indiana, January 30, 1862, account of wounds received near Louisville, Kentucky, December, 1861. Buried in Old Cemetery, Knightstown, Indiana.

John McKenzie, Company I, 69th Indiana Infantry. Died at Milliken's Bend, Louisiana, May 24, 1863. Buried there. Re-interred in Vicksburg National Cemetery. Section H. Grave, No. 91.

Eli McLeland, Company G, 84th Indiana Infantry. Died in Danville Prison, Danville, Virginia, date unknown. Buried in Danville (Virginia) National Cemetery. Unknown list.

· Isaac McLeland, Company G, 84th Indiana Infantry. Died at Cleveland, Tennessee, April 2, 1864. Buried there. Re-interred in Hess Cemetery, near Cadiz, Indiana.

Amos Main, Company K, 74th Indiana Infantry. Died at Willett's Point, New York, April 6, 1865. Buried there. No record of removal. Remains probably re-interred in some National cemetery. Unknown list.

James Mallory, Company A, 36th Indiana Infantry. Died at Nashville, Tennessee, February 29, 1864. Buried there. Re-interred in Nashville National Cemetery. Unknown list.

Cyrus Manning, Company A, 54th Indiana Infantry (one year). Died at Columbus, Ohio, May 9, 1863. Buried in New Lisbon Cemetery, New Lisbon, Indiana.

Henry C. Manor, Company A, 36th Indiana Infantry. Killed at Stone's River, Tennessee, December 31, 1862. Buried on the battlefield. Re-interred in Stone's River (Murfreesboro) National Cemetery. Section N. Grave, No. 5,437.

Simeon Marlow, Company A, 36th Indiana Infantry. Died in Henry County, Indiana, April 20, 1862. Buried in Lewisville Cemetery, Lewisville, Indiana.

Alexander L. Mason, Company C, 1st Iowa Infantry. Killed at Wilson's Creek, Missouri, August 10, 1861. Buried on the battlefield. Re-interred in Springfield (Missouri) National Cemetery. Unknown list.

Jerome B. Mason, Company F, 84th Indiana Infantry. Killed at Chickamauga, Georgia, September 20, 1863. Buried on the battlefield. Re-interred in Chattanooga National Cemetery. Unknown list.

Richard May, Company D, 19th Indiana Infantry. Died November 22, 1862, account of wounds at Gainesville, Virginia, August 28, 1862. Buried on the battlefield. No record of removal. Remains probably re-interred in some National cemetery. Unknown list.

Joseph H. Mayes, Band, 1st Brigade, 1st Division, 17th Army Corps. Died near Marietta, Georgia, November 2, 1864. Buried there. Re-interred in Marietta National Cemetery. Unknown list.

Timothy Mead, 19th Indiana Battery. Killed at Perryville, Kentucky, October 8,

1862. Buried on the battlefield. Re-interred in Camp Nelson National Cemetery. Unknown list.

*Kelita Mendenhall, Company E, 9th Indiana Cavalry. Died in Cahaba Prison, Alabama, January, 1865. Buried there. Re-interred in Marietta National Cemetery. Unknown list.

Lewis Micha, Company I, 3rd Indiana Cavalry. Died in Andersonville Prison, Georgia, July 18, 1864. Buried in Andersonville National Cemetery. Grave, No. 3,519.

John W. Miller, Company H, 69th Indiana Infantry. Died at Milliken's Bend, Louisiana, May 9, 1863. Buried there. Re-interred in Vicksburg National Cemetery. Section E, Grave, No. 1,651.

James W. Millikan, Company C, 36th Indiana Infantry. Died at Louisville, Kentucky, February 10, 1862. Buried in Batson Cemetery, Liberty Township, Henry County, Indiana.

*Andrew J. Mills, Company K, 36th Indiana Infantry. Died at New Haven, Kentucky, February 15, 1862. Buried there. No record of removal. Remains probably reinterred in some National cemetery. Unknown list.

Wallenstein Mimmes, Company I, 3rd Indiana Cavalry. Died at Sandtown, Georgia, September, 1864. Buried there. Re-interred in Marietta National Cemetery. Unknown list.

Charles W. T. Minesinger, Company F, 57th Indiana Infantry. Died at Nashville, Tennessee, September 14, 1864, account of wounds at Jonesboro, Georgia, August 31, 1864. Buried in South Mound Cemetery. New Castle, Indiana.

*Abraham G. Misener, Company H, 140th Indiana Infantry. Died at Camp Denison, Ohio, February 2, 1865. Buried there. No record of removal. Remains probably reinterred in some National cemetery. Unknown list.

Perry Mitchell, Company C, 36th Indiana Infantry. Died at Nashville, Tennessee, October 28, 1863, account of wounds at Chickamauga, Georgia, September 19, 1863. Buried there. Re-interred in Nashville National Cemetery. Unknown list.

Thomas Mitchell, Company C, 36th Indiana Infantry. Died at Nashville, Tennessee, October 16, 1863, account of wounds at Chickamauga, Georgia. September 19, 1863. Buried there. Re-interred in Nashville National Cemetery. Unknown list.

John H. Modlin, Company C, 36th Indiana Infantry. Died at Nashville, Tennessee, July 23 ,1864, account of wounds at Resaca, Georgia, May 16, 1864. Buried in South Mound Cemetery, New Castle, Indiana.

Francis M. Moler, Company A, 36th Indiana Infantry. Died in Libby Prison, Richmond, Virginia, February 28, 1863. Buried in Richmond National Cemetery. Unknown list.

James M. Montgomery, Assistant Surgeon, 5th Indiana Infantry (Mexican War). Died near Vera Cruz, Mexico, June, 1848. Buried there in unknown grave.

William Moore, U. S. Navy. Died in hospital at Memphis, Tennessee, January 9, 1865. Buried in South Mound Cemetery, New Castle, Indiana.

Enoch T. Nation, Company G, 9th Indiana Cavalry. Lost on Sultana, April 27, 1865. Body never recovered.

Wallace Nation, 20th Indiana Battery. Died near Atlanta, Georgia, October 28, 1864. Buried there. Re-interred in New Lisbon Cemetery, New Lisbon, Indiana.

James R. Nay, Company E, 9th Indiana Cavalry. Died at home, in New Castle, Indiana, July 30, 1865. Buried in South Mound Cemetery, New Castle, Indiana.

Robert Needham, Company A, 36th Indiana Infantry. Died at Louisville, Kentucky, February 26, 1862. Buried there. Re-interred in Cave Hill (Louisville) National Cemetery. Section A, Grave, No. 26.

Levi Needler, 23rd Indiana Battery. Died at Knoxville, Tennessee, February 21, 1864. Buried there. Re-interred in Knoxville National Cemetery. Grave, No. 646.

William H. Newbold, Company D, 8th Indiana Infantry (three years). Died at home, near New Lisbon, Indiana, January 25, 1862. Buried in Wisehart Cemetery, Liberty Township, Henry County, Indiana.

Isaiah J. Newby, Company C, 87th Indiana Infantry. Died at Chattanooga, Tennessee, October 7, 1863, account of wounds at Chickamauga, Georgia, September 20, 1863. Buried there. Re-interred in Chattanooga National Cemetery. Unknown list.

Otis C. Newby, Company C, 45th Infantry, U. S. V. Killed near Bulan, Luzon, Philippine Islands, August 24, 1900. Buried there. Re-interred in Masonic Cemetery, Greensboro, Indiana.

William H. Newby, Company A, 36th Indiana Infantry. Died near Corinth, Mississippi, May 19, 1862. Buried there. Re-interred in Corinth National Cemetery. Unknown list.

Benjamin F. Newcomer, Company G, 84th Indiana Infantry. Killed at Pine Mountain, Georgia, June 18, 1864. Buried on the battlefield. Re-interred in Marietta National Cemetery. Section H, Grave, No. 8,478.

John Newland, Company F, 57th Indiana Infantry. Died at Shiloh, Tennessee, June 3, 1862. Buried there. Re-interred in Shiloh National Cemetery. Unknown list.

William T. Nicholson, Company G, 84th Indiana Infantry. Died at New Albany, Indiana, May 16, 1863. Buried in South Mound Cemetery, New Castle, Indiana.

George C. Nixon, Company D, 84th Indiana Infantry. Died at Chattanooga, Tennessee, June 3, 1864, account of wounds in Atlanta Campaign. Buried there. Re-interred in Chattanooga National Cemetery. Section D, Grave, No. 12,469.

Barzillai Osborne, Company A, 57th Indiana Infantry. Killed in Atlanta Campaign, June 14, 1864. Buried on the battlefield. Re-interred in Marietta National Cemetery. Section H, Grave, No. 8,870.

George Osborn, Company E, 8th Indiana Infantry (three years). Died at Syracuse, Missouri, December 28, 1861. Buried there. No record of removal. Remains probably re-interred in some National cemetery. Unknown list.

John A. Osborn, Company A, 57th Indiana Infantry. Died at Chattanooga, Tennessee, December 13, 1864, account of wounds at Kenesaw Mountain, Georgia, June 23, 1864. Buried there. Re-interred in Chattanooga National Cemetery. Unknown list.

Gideon H. Padget, Company H, 69th Indiana Infantry. Died at Keokuk, Iowa, January 13, 1863. Buried there. Re-interred in Keokuk National Cemetery. Grave 303.

Samuel C. Page, Company I, 69th Indiana Infantry. Killed at Richmond, Kentucky, August 30, 1862. Buried on the battlefield. Re-interred in Camp Nelson National Cemetery. Unknown list.

Washington Parkhurst, Company I, 3rd Indiana Cavalry. Died at Sandtown, Georgia, September 9, 1864. Buried there. Re-interred in Marietta National Cemetery. Section E, Grave, No. 6,355.

John Pate, Company H, 69th Indiana Infantry. Died at Cairo, Illinois, August 25, 1863, account of wounds at Richmond, Kentucky, August 30, 1862. Buried there. No record of removal. Remains probably re-interred in some National cemetery. Unknown list.

Joseph B. Pate, Company H, 69th Indiana Infantry. Died at Young's Point, Louisiana, February 8, 1863. Buried there. Re-interred in Vicksburg National Cemetery. Unknown list.

James Pattison, Company A, 36th Indiana Infantry. Died at Murfreesboro, Tennessee, September 30, 1864, account of wounds in Atlanta Campaign, May 30, 1864. Buried there. Re-interred in Stone's River (Murfreesboro) National Cemetery. Section F, Grave, No. 2,456.

Daniel H. Paul, Company E, 36th Indiana Infantry. Killed at Kenesaw Mountain, Georgia, June 20, 1864. Buried on the battlefield. Re-interred in Marietta National Cemetery. Unknown list.

Granville Pearson, Company H, 140th Indiana Infantry. Died at Nashville, Tennessee, January 25, 1865. Buried there. Re-interred in Nashville National Cemetery. Unknown list.

Redmond Peed, Company F, 57th Indiana Infantry. Died in Andersonville Prison, Georgia, May 7, 1864. Buried in Andersonville National Cemetery. Grave, No. 944.

William W. Pence, Company K, 7th Infantry, U. S. A. Died at Presidio, San Francisco, California, July 8, 1903. Buried in South Mound Cemetery, New Castle, Indiana.

Abner Perdue, Company E, 8th Indiana Infantry (three years). Died at Otterville, Missouri, January 24, 1862. Buried there. No record of removal. Remains probably re-interred in some National cemetery. Unknown list.

George W. Perdue, Company H, 69th Indiana Infantry. Died at Young's Point, Louisiana, February 15, 1863. Buried there. Re-interred in Vicksburg National Cemetery. Section B, Grave, No. 2,809.

Rufus Perdue, Company H, 69th Indiana Infantry. Died at Memphis, Tennessee, December 27, 1862. Buried there. Re-interred in Memphis National Cemetery. Unknown list.

Mordecai Perry, Company G, 16th Indiana, Infantry. Died at Vicksburg, Mississippi, February 13, 1863. Buried there. Re-interred in Vicksburg National Cemetery. Section A, Grave, No. 3,086.

James Personett, Company G, 84th Indiana Infantry. Died at Marietta, Georgia, July 12, 1864. Buried there. Re-interred in Marietta National Cemetery. Unknown list.

*James F. Petty, Company F, 57th Indiana Infantry. Died at Nashville, Tennessee, March 27, 1862. Buried there. Re-interred in Nashville National Cemetery. Unknown list.

Andrew J. Phillips, Company E, 8th Indiana Infantry (three years). Killed at Vicksburg, Mississippi, May 22, 1863. Buried on the battlefield. Re-interred in Vicksburg National Cemetery. Unknown list.

William A. Pickett, Company F, 84th Indiana Infantry. Died at Catlettsburg, Kentucky. December 16, 1862. Buried in Friends' Cemetery, Greensboro, Indiana.

Hugh Pierce. Company B, 139th Indiana Infantry. Died at Mumfordsville, Kentucky, July 17, 1864. Buried there. No record of removal. Remains probably re-interred in some National cemetery. Unknown list.

Jonathan E. Pierce, Company C, 36th Indiana Infantry. Died near Corinth, Mississippi, July 5, 1862. Buried in Flatrock Cemetery, Liberty Township, Henry County, Indiana.

Joseph H. Pike, Company B, 19th Indiana Infantry. Killed at Gainesville, Virginia, August 28, 1862. Buried on the battlefield. No record of removal. Remains probably re-interred in some National cemetery. Unknown list.

Stanford L. Pike, Company A, 36th Indiana Infantry. Died at Chattanooga, Tennessee, October 13, 1863. account of wounds at Chickamauga, Georgia, September 20, 1863. Buried there. Re-interred in Chattanooga National Cemetery. Unknown list.

Cyrus Pittser, Company E, 8th Indiana Infantry (three years). Died at New Orleans, Louisiana, October 7. 1863. Buried there. Re-interred in Chalmette National Cemetery. Grave, No. 3,751.

Henry C. Polk, Company B, 13th Indiana Infantry. Killed at Petersburg, Virginia, July 30, 1864. Buried on the battlefield. No record of removal. Remains probably re-interred in some National cemetery. Unknown list.

Charles B. Post, Company A, 87th Indiana Infantry. Died at Savannah, Georgia, December 28, 1864. Buried there. No record of removal. Remains probably re-interred in some National cemetery. Unknown list.

Argyle A. Poston, Company F, 84th Indiana Infantry. Died at Catlettsburg, Kentucky, April 14, 1863. Buried there. Re-interred in Nashville National Cemetery. Grave, No. 3,485.

Edenburgh H. Poston, 19th Indiana Battery. Died at Louisville, Kentucky, October 29, 1862. Buried there. Re-interred in Cave Hill (Louisville) National Cemetery. Section A. Grave, No. 28.

Jacob Powell, Company E, 8th Indiana Infantry (three years). Killed at Austin, Mississippi, August 2, 1862. Buried on the battlefield. Re-interred in Vicksburg National Cemetery. Unknown list.

Orlistes W. Powell, Company C, 36th Indiana Infantry. Killed at Chickamauga, Georgia, September 20, 1863. Buried on the battlefield. Re-interred in South Mound Cemetery, New Castle, Indiana.

John W. C. Power. Company F, 84th Indiana Infantry. Died August 15, 1864, account of wounds before Atlanta, Georgia, August 11, 1864. Buried on the battlefield. Re-interred in Marietta National Cemetery. Section I, Grave, No. 9,589.

Robert V. Price, Company H, 69th Indiana Infantry. Killed at Richmond, Kentucky, August 30, 1862. Buried on the battlefield. Re-interred in Camp Nelson National Cemetery. Unknown list.

Oliver D. Protzman, Company F, 57th Indiana Infantry. Killed at Franklin, Tennessee, November 30, 1864. Buried on the battlefield. Re-interred in Nashville National Cemetery. Unknown list.

Daniel Pursley, Company K, 36th Indiana Infantry. Died at Paducah, Kentucky, March 25, 1862. Buried there. No record of removal. Remains probably re-interred in some National cemetery. Unknown list.

Augustus D. Radcliffe, Company D, 36th Indiana Infantry. Killed at Chickamauga, Georgia, September 20, 1863. Buried on the battlefield. Re-interred in Chattanooga National Cemetery. Unknown list.

George W. Rader, Company E, 8th Indiana Infantry (three years). Died at Vicksburg, Mississippi, May 27, 1863, account of wounds received there, May 22, 1863. Buried on the battlefield. Re-interred in Vicksburg National Cemetery. Section G, Grave, No. 4,965.

George Rader, Company G, 84th Indiana Infantry. Died at Catlettsburg, Kentucky, December 16, 1862. Buried there. Re-interred in Nashville National Cemetery. Unknown list.

Henry Ratliff, Company I, 69th Indiana Infantry. Died at Memphis, Tennessee, December 2, 1862. Buried there. Re-interred in Memphis National Cemetery. Unknown list.

Harmon Rayl, Company A, 36th Indiana Infantry. Died at Whitesides, Tennessee, December 18, 1863. Buried there. Re-interred in Friends' Cemetery, Spiceland, Indiana.

Leonard M. Reeder, Company H, 12th Infantry, U. S. A. Killed at Lopez, Philippine Islands, September 10, 1900. Buried on the battlefield. No record of removal. Remains probably re-interred in some National cemetery. Unknown list.

John Reichart, Company C, 36th Indiana Infantry. Died at Athens, Alabama, June 30, 1863. Buried there. Re-interred in Nashville National Cemetery. Unknown list.

Andrew W. Reid, Company A, 11th Indiana Infantry. Died at Carrollton, Louisiana, May 24, 1864. Buried there. Re-interred in Chalmette National Cemetery. Unknown list.

Henry Reynolds, Company I, 69th Indiana Infantry. Died at Milliken's Bend, Louisiana, August 4, 1863. Buried there. Re-interred in Vicksburg National Cemetery. Section B, Grave, No. 2,674.

*Joseph N. Reynolds, Company A, 57th Indiana Infantry. Died at Nashville, Tennessee, June 15, 1863. Buried there. Re-interred in Nashville National Cemetery. Unknown list.

Henry J. Richardson, Company I, 69th Indiana Infantry. Killed at Richmond, Kentucky, August 30, 1862. Buried on the battlefield. Re-interred in Camp Nelson National Cemetery. Unknown list.

James Rickard, Company I, 3rd Indiana Cavalry. Died at Maxwell, Kentucky, October, 1862. Buried there. No record of removal. Remains probably re-interred in some National cemetery. Unknown list.

Benamin F. Ricks, Company E, 9th Indiana Cavalry. Killed at Franklin, Tennessee, December 17, 1864. Buried on the battlefield. Re-interred in Nashville National Cemetery. Unknown list.

Jonathan Ricks, Company I, 69th Indiana Infantry. Killed at Richmond, Kentucky, August 30, 1862. Buried on the battlefield. Re-interred in Camp Nelson National Cemetery. Unknown list.

Mercer Ricks, Company D, 36th Indiana Infantry. Died at Buffalo, Kentucky, February 11, 1862. Buried there. No record of removal. Remains probably re-interred in some National cemetery. Unknown list.

*Avery Riggs, Company E, 8th Indiana Infantry (three years). Died at Markleville,

Indiana, April 14, 1865. Buried in Keesling Cemetery, three fourths of a mile southwest of Mechanicsburg, Indiana.

Charles M. Riley, Company B, 124th Indiana Infantry. Died September 8, 1864. Burial place unknown. No record of removal. Remains probably re-interred in some National cemetery. Unknown list.

William G. Riley, Company I, 69th Indiana Infantry. Died at Young's Point, Louisiana, February 9, 1863. Buried there. Re-interred in Vicksburg National Cemetery. Unknown list.

John H. Rinker, Company F, 57th Indiana Infantry. Died at Shiloh, Tennessee, April 22, 1862. Buried there. Re-interred in Shiloh National Cemetery. Section K, Grave, No. 148.

George Ritchie, Company C, 36th Indiana Infantry. Died at Nashville, Tennessee, November 19, 1862. Buried there. Re-interred in Nashville National Cemetery. Section B, Grave, No. 6,957.

William H. Roby, Company H, 5th Indiana Infantry (Mexican War). Died at San Augustin, Mexico, May 28, 1848. Buried there in unknown grave.

George W. Rogers, Company C, 36th Indiana Infantry. Died at Nashville, Tennessee, February 9, 1864. Buried there. Re-interred in Sugar Grove Cemetery, two and a half miles west of New Castle, Indiana.

Joseph B. Rogers, Company C, 36th Indiana Infantry. Died at home, near Cadiz, Indiana, March 12, 1863. Buried in Sugar Grove Cemetery, two and a half miles west of New Castle, Indiana.

William A. Rogers, Company E, 9th Indiana Cavalry. Died at Baton Rouge, Louisiana, April 28, 1865. Buried there. Re-interred in Baton Rouge National Cemetery. Grave, No. 1,201.

Jonathan Runyan, Company E, 8th Indiana Infantry (three years). Died at St. Louis, Missouri, October 24, 1862. Buried there. Re-interred in Jefferson Barracks (St. Louis) National Cemetery. Unknown list.

Abner P. Saint, Company C, 71st Illinois Infantry. Died at Columbus, Kentucky, August 24, 1862. Buried there. No record of removal. Remains probably re-interred in some National cemetery. Unknown list.

*Charles F. Sanders, Company A, 57th Indiana Infantry. Died June 4, 1862. Burial place unknown. No record of removal. Remains probably re-interred in some National cemetery. Unknown list.

Francis A. Sanders, Company F, 124th Indiana Infantry. Died at Knoxville, Tennessee, June 24, 1864. Buried there. Re-interred in Knoxville National Cemetery. Grave, No. 1,008.

Luther B. Sanders, Company D, 147th Indiana Infantry. Died at Berryville, Virginia, June 22, 1865. Buried there. Re-interred in Winchester National Cemetery. Grave, No. 3,642.

Augustus L. Sayford, Company H, 69th Indiana Infantry. Killed at Port Gibson, Mississippi, May 1, 1863. Buried on the battlefield. Re-interred in Vicksburg National Cemetery. Unknown list.

Henry Scott, 19th Indiana Battery. Killed at Perryville, Kentucky, October 8, 1862. Buried on the battlefield. Re-interred in Camp Nelson National Cemetery. Unknown list.

James M. Scott, Company G, 84th Indiana Infantry. Killed at Chickamauga, Georgia, September 20, 1863. Buried on the battlefield. Re-interred in Chattanooga National Cemetery. Unknown list.

Oliver P. Scott, 12th Indiana Battery. Died at Nashville, Tennessee, March 14, 1862. Buried there. Re-interred in Nashville National Cemetery. Section C, Grave, No. 7,237.

Wesley W. Seward, Company F, 57th Indiana Infantry. Killed at Stone's River, Tennessee, December 31, 1862. Buried on the battlefield. Re-interred in Mechanicsburg Cemetery, Mechanicsburg, Indiana.

Jesse Shackle, Company A, 36th Indiana Infantry. Killed at Stone's River, Ten-

George Shirk

Geo   Shirk

nessee, January 2, 1863. Buried on the battlefield. Re-interred in Stone's River (Murfreesboro) National Cemetery. Section D, Grave, No. 1,548.

Leander Shepherd, Company C, 36th Indiana Infantry. Killed at Chickamauga, Georgia, September 19, 1863. Buried on the battlefield. Re-interred in Chattanooga National Cemetery. Unknown list.

William H. Shepherd, Company G, 84th Indiana Infantry. Killed at Kenesaw Mountain, Georgia, June 23, 1864. Buried on the battlefield. Re-interred in Marietta National Cemetery. Unknown list.

Jacob Shipler, Company C, 5th Indiana Cavalry. Killed in Atlanta Campaign, July 31, 1864. Buried on the battlefield. Re-interred in Marietta National Cemetery. Unknown list.

George Shirk, Company C, 36th Indiana Infantry. Died at home, in New Castle, Indiana, June 6, 1864, account of wounds at Chickamauga, Georgia, September 20, 1863. Buried in South Mound Cemetery, New Castle, Indiana.

Benjamin F. Shockley, Company H, 140th Indiana Infantry. Died at home, in Blue River Township, Henry County, Indiana, December 26, 1864. Buried in Old Cemetery, near Messick, Indiana.

John A. Showers, Company E, 8th Indiana Infantry (three years). Died at St. Louis, Missouri, August 16, 1863. Buried there. Re-interred in Jefferson Barracks (St. Louis) National Cemetery. Section 33, Grave, No. 2,988.

David Shunk, Company I, 69th Indiana Infantry. Died at Evansville, Indiana, August 31, 1863. Buried there. No record of removal. Remains probably re-interred in some National cemetery. Unknown list.

Joel Simons, Company I, 69th Indiana Infantry. Died at St. Louis, Missouri, February 16, 1863. Buried there. Re-interred in Jefferson Barracks (St. Louis) National Cemetery. Section 58, Grave. No. 10,670.

*Nixon Simons, Company F, 57th Indiana Infantry. Died at Louisville, Kentucky, January 17, 1862. Buried there. Re-interred in Cave Hill (Louisville) National Cemetery. Unknown list.

*John L. Skinner, Company E, 8th Indiana Infantry (three years). Died at Memphis, Tennessee, August 30, 1863. Buried there. Re-interred in Memphis National Cemetery. Grave, No. 306.

Abner Sloan, Company M, 21st Indiana Infantry, re-organized as 1st Heavy Artillery. Died at New Orleans, Louisana, January 2, 1865. Buried there. Re-interred in Chalmette National Cemetery. Grave, No. 6,053.

James E. Sloan, Company I, 69th Indiana Infantry. Died at Milliken's Bend, Louisiana, April 10, 1863. Buried there. Re-interred in Vicksburg National Cemetery. Unknown list.

James R. Smith, Company H, 8th Indiana Infantry (three years). Killed at Pea Ridge, Arkansas, March 7, 1862. Buried on the battlefield Re-interred in Fayetteville National Cemetery. Grave, No. 577.

*Jacob Snyder, Company E, 8th Indiana Infantry (three years). Died at St. Louis, Missouri, August 11, 1863. Buried there. Re-interred in Jefferson Barracks (St. Louis) National Cemetery. Section 31, Grave, No. 2,547.

George Spaw, Company A, 36th Indiana Infantry. Killed at Resaca, Georgia, May 15, 1864. Buried on the battlefield. Re-interred in Chattanooga National Cemetery. Section K, Grave, No. 10,206.

Robert O. Spell, Company E, 9th Indiana Cavalry. Killed at Franklin, Tennessee, December 17, 1864. Buried on the battlefield. Re-interred in Nashville National Cemetery. Unknown list.

*Harmon Sphor, Company H, 140th Indiana Infantry. Died at Murfreesboro, Tennessee, December 19, 1864. Buried there. Re-interred in Stone's River (Murfreesboro) National Cemetery. Unknown list.

William Spurry, Company A, 57th Indiana Infantry. Died at Bowling Green, Kentucky, September 21, 1862. Buried there. No record of removal. Remains probably re-interred in some National cemetery. Unknown list.

Zachariah M. Starr, Company D, 36th Indiana Infantry. Died at Wildcat, Kentucky, October 26, 1862, account of wounds received there, October 17, 1862. Buried on the battlefield. Re-interred in Danville (Kentucky) National Cemetery. Unknown list.

Isaac Steele, Company A, 36th Indiana Infantry. Died at Chattanooga, Tennessee, June 23, 1864, account of wounds in Atlanta Campaign, May 30, 1864. Buried there. Re-interred in Chattanooga National Cemetery. Section E, Grave, No. 11,311.

*James A. Steele, Company K, 36th Indiana Infantry. Killed at Stone's River, Tennessee, December 31, 1862. Buried on the battlefield. Re-interred in Stone's River (Murfreesboro) National Cemetery. Unknown list.

Nathaniel Stevens, Company D, 147th Indiana Infantry. Died at Cumberland, Maryland, July 28, 1865. Buried there. No record of removal. Remains probably re-interred in some National cemetery. Unknown list.

Townsend G. Stevens, Troop G, 6th Cavalry, U. S. A. Died at New Orleans, Louisiana, July 29, 1866. Buried there. Re-interred in Chalmette National Cemetery. Grave, No. 7,335.

Samuel L. Stewart, Company F, 84th Indiana Infantry. Died at Nashville, Tennessee, May 4, 1865. Buried there. Re-interred in Nashville National Cemetery. Unknown list.

William Stewart, Company A, 36th Indiana Infantry. Killed at Chickamauga, Georgia, September 19, 1863. Buried on the battlefield. Re-interred in Chattanooga National Cemetery. Unknown list.

William F. Stewart, Company A, 36th Indiana Infantry. Died at Nashville, Tennessee, March 31, 1863. Buried there. Re-interred in Nashville National Cemetery. Unknown list.

John Stinson, Company D, 147th Indiana Infantry. Died at Indianapolis, Indiana, March 16, 1865. Buried in Hess Cemetery, near Cadiz, Indiana.

Moses Straughn, Company D, 8th Indiana Infantry (three years). Died at Memphis, Tennessee, June 7, 1863. Buried there. Re-interred in Memphis National Cemetery. Unknown list.

Peter C. Strickler, Company H, 69th Indiana Infantry. Killed by accident on steamboat, January 7, 1863. Buried on the river bank. No record of removal. Remains probably re-interred in some National cemetery. Unknown list.

Daniel Sullivan, Company F, 1st Battalion, 19th Infantry, U. S. A. Died at U. S. General Hospital, Annapolis, Maryland, July 22, 1864. Buried there. Re-interred in Annapolis National Cemetery. Grave, No. 929.

Jeremiah Sullivan, Company F, 57th Indiana Infantry. Died in field hospital, June 15, 1864, account of wounds in Atlanta Campaign, May 27, 1864. Buried there. Re-interred in Chattanooga National Cemetery. Section E, Grave, No. 11,281.

Elza Swain, Company G, 69th Indiana Infantry. Died May 4, 1863, account of wounds at Port Gibson, Mississippi, May 1, 1863. Buried on the battlefield. Re-interred in Vicksburg National Cemetery. Unknown list.

John K. Swain, Company E, 8th Indiana Infantry (three years). Died at home in Mechanicsburg, Indiana, August 22, 1863. Buried in Mechanicsburg Cemetery, Mechanicsburg, Indiana.

Samuel H. Sweigart, Company E, 9th Indiana Cavalry. Died at St. Louis, Missouri, July 23, 1865. Buried in Elliott Cemetery, two and a half miles south of New Castle, Indiana.

Benjamin F. Symons. Incomplete list. Died in the army. No record of place, date or burial. Remains probably re-interred in some National Cemetery. Unknown list.

David S. Taylor, Company D, 36th Indiana Infantry. Died at Danville, Kentucky, November 17, 1862, account of wounds at Wildcat, Kentucky, October 17, 1862. Buried in Masonic Cemetery, Greensboro, Indiana.

Charles E. Thomas, Company K, 36th Indiana Infantry. Accidentally killed at New Haven, Kentucky, November 18, 1861. Buried there. No record of removal. Remains probably re-interred in some National cemetery. Unknown list.

James Thomas, Company F, 57th Indiana Infantry. Died at Nashville, Tennessee,

April 30, 1863. Buried there. Re-interred in Nashville National Cemetery. Unknown list.

Adolphus G. Thut, Company A, 36th Indiana Infantry. Died at Nashville, Tennessee, May 5, 1862. Buried in Rich Square Cemetery, Franklin Township, Henry County, Indiana.

John W. Timmons, Company C, 147th Indiana Infantry. Died at Indianapolis, Indiana, March 14, 1865. Buried there. Re-interred in Crown Hill Cemetery, Indianapolis, Indiana. Military Plat. Unknown list.

William Topping, Company C, 36th Indiana Infantry. Killed at Chickamauga, Georgia, September 19, 1863. Buried on the battlefield. Re-interred in Chattanooga National Cemetery. Unknown list.

Benjamin F. Trail, Company C, 28th U. S. C. T. Killed at Petersburg, Virginia, July 30, 1864. Buried on the battlefield. No record of removal. Remains probably re-interred in some National cemetery. Unknown list.

James Trail, Company C, 28th U. S. C. T. Died at Corpus Christi, Texas, September 24, 1865. Buried there. No record of removal. Remains probably re-interred in some National cemetery. Unknown list.

William Trout, Company E, 8th Indiana Infantry (three years). Drowned at St. Louis, Missouri, June 17, 1863. Buried there. Re-interred in Jefferson Barracks (St Louis) National Cemetery. Unknown list.

Robert Troxell, Company F, 84th Indiana Infantry. Killed at Chickamauga, Georgia, September 20, 1863. Buried on the battlefield. Re-interred in Chattanooga National Cemetery. Unknown. list.

Robert F. Tuder, Company M, 8th Indiana Cavalry. Killed at Black River, North Carolina, March 16, 1865. Buried on the battlefield. Re-interred in Raleigh National Cemetery. Grave, No. 371.

Sashwell Turner, Company E, 36th Indiana Infantry. Died at St. Louis, Missouri, August 17, 1862. Buried there. Re-interred in Jefferson Barracks (St. Louis) National Cemetery. Unknown list.

Joseph Van Matre, Company F, 57th Indiana Infantry. Died at St. Louis, Missouri, May 10, 1863. Buried in Painter Cemetery, Fall Creek Township, Henry County, Indiana.

Peter Van Matre, Company H, 140th Indiana Infantry. Died at Greensboro, North Carolina, June 27, 1865. Buried there. Re-interred in Painter Cemetery, Fall Creek Township, Henry County, Indiana.

Benjamin Waddell, 19th Indiana Battery. Died at Danville, Kentucky, November 8, 1862. Buried in Holland Cemetery, near Straughn, Indiana.

Luther Waddell, Company A, 36th Indiana Infantry. Died at Nashville, Tennessee, September 16, 1863. Buried in Holland Cemetery, near Straughn, Indiana.

Jehu Waggoner, Company H, 69th Indiana Infantry. Died at New Orleans, Louisiana, September 6, 1863. Buried there. Re-interred in Chalmette National Cemetery. Unknown list.

John S. Wallace, Company B, 54th Indiana Infantry (one year). Died at Memphis, Tennessee, January 21, 1863. Buried there. Re-interred in Memphis National Cemetery. Unknown list.

William H. Ward, Company I, 69th Indiana Infantry. Died at Indianapolis, Indiana, December 27, 1862. Buried in Lewisville Cemetery, Lewisville, Indiana.

Caleb N. Warner, Company A, 57th Indiana Infantry. Died date and place unknown. Remains probably re-interred in some National cemetery. Unknown list.

David Warner, Company H, 5th Indiana Infantry (Mexican War). Drowned in Mississippi River, November, 1847. Body never recovered.

George W. Warner, 12th Indiana Battery. Died at Nashville, Tennessee, April 1, 1862. Buried there. Re-interred in Nashville National Cemetery. Unknown list.

Peter Warner, Company G, 84th Indiana Infantry. Died at Nashville, Tennessee, August 30, 1863. Buried there. Re-interred in Nashville National Cemetery. Unknown list.

George W. Warrick, Company A, 36th Indiana Infantry. Died at Nashville, Tennessee, January 9, 1863, account of wounds at Stone's River, Tennessee, December 31, 1862. Buried there. Re-interred in Nashville National Cemetery. Section A, Grave, No. 5,082.

John D. Wasson, Company I, 124th Indiana Infantry. Died at Chattanooga, Tennessee, June 15, 1864. Buried there. Re-interred in Chattanooga National Cemetery. Section A, Grave, No. 119.

Daniel L. Watkins, Company F, 84th Indiana Infantry. Died in West Virginia, October 17, 1862. Buried there. No record of removal. Remains probably re-interred in some National cemetery. Unknown list.

Francis M. Watkins, Company F, 57th Indiana Infantry. Killed at Resaca, Georgia, May 14, 1864. Buried on the battlefield. Re-interred in South Mound Cemetery, New Castle, Indiana.

Marquis De La Fayette Watkins. Incomplete list. Died at home, near New Castle, February 22, 1865. Buried in South Mound Cemetery, New Castle, Indiana.

Thornton T. Watkins, Company F, 57th Indiana Infantry. Lost on Sultana, April 27, 1865. Body never recovered.

George W. Wean, Company G, 84th Indiana Infantry. Died at Nashville, Tennessee, December 17, 1863. Buried there. Re-interred in Nashville National Cemetery. Section D, Grave, No. 3,205.

Pennel West, Company F, 124th Indiana Infantry. Died in Andersonville Prison, Georgia, June 28, 1864. Buried in Andersonville National Cemetery. Unknown list.

William D. West, Company D, 36th Indiana Infantry. Died at Camp Wickliffe, Kentucky, January 8, 1862. Buried there. No record of removal. Remains probably re-interred in some National cemetery. Unknown list.

William Whitacre, Company E, 9th Indiana Cavalry. Died at Indianapolis, Indiana, May 21, 1864. Buried there. Re-interred in Crown Hill Cemetery, Indianapolis, Indiana. Military plat. Grave, No. 252.

Benjamin Whitelock, Company H, 69th Indiana Infantry. Killed at Richmond, Kentucky, August 30, 1862. Buried on the battlefield. Re-interred in Camp Nelson National Cemetery. Unknown list.

James W. Whitlow, Company B, 19th Indiana Infantry. Died of wounds, date and place unknown. No record of removal. Remains probably re-interred in some National cemetery. Unknown list.

George M. Wilkinson, Company I, 3rd Indiana Cavalry. Died at Louisville, Kentucky, October 18, 1863. Buried in Old Cemetery, Knightstown, Indiana.

George Williams, 15th Indiana Battery. Died in Andersonville Prison, Georgia, October 26, 1864. Buried in Andersonville National Cemetery. Grave, No. 11,497.

Jesse L. Williams, Company I, 69th Indiana Infantry. Died at Milliken's Bend, Louisiana, February 6, 1863. Buried there. Re-interred in Vicksburg National Cemetery. Unknown list.

Joseph Williams, Company H, 69th Indiana Infantry. Died near Vicksburg, Mississippi, January 23, 1863. Buried there. Re-interred in Vicksburg National Cemetery. Unknown list.

Nereus P. Williams, Company C, 36th Indiana Infantry. Killed in Atlanta Campaign, May 31, 1864. Buried on the battlefield. Re-interred in Marietta National Cemetery. Section A, Grave, No. 841.

William Williams, Company B, 139th Indiana Infantry. Died at Mumfordsville, Kentucky, July 20, 1864. Buried there. No record of removal. Remains probably re-interred in some National cemetery. Unknown list.

William O. Williams, Company B, 19th Indiana Infantry. Killed at Gettysburg, Pennsylvania, July 1, 1863. Buried on the battlefield. Re-interred in Gettysburg National Cemetery. Indiana Plat. Unknown list.

John L. Willis, Company A, 2nd Infantry, U. S. A. Died July 3, 1898, account of wounds at San Juan Hill, Cuba, July 1, 1898. Buried on the battlefield. No record of removal. Remains probably re-interred in Arlington National Cemetery. Unknown list.

8th INDIANA INFANTRY.
(THREE MONTHS' SERVICE.)

Joseph S. Winship, Company K, 36th Indiana Infantry. Died in Andersonvill Prison, Georgia. August 3, 1864. Buried in Andersonville National Cemetery. Grav No. 4,639.

William H. Wise, Company F, 124th Indiana Infantry. Died at Indianapolis, Indiana, November 25, 1864. Buried there. Re-interred in Crown Hill Cemetery, Indianapolis, Indiana. Military Plat. Unknown list.

David Wisehart, Company H, 69th Indiana Infantry. Died at Young's Point, Louisiana, March 10, 1863. Buried there. Re-interred in Vicksburg National Cemetery. Unknown list.

Philander Wisehart, Company B, 8th Indiana Infantry (three months). Killed at Rich Mountain, West Virginia, July 11, 1861. Buried on the battlefield. Re-interred i Grafton National Cemetery. Grave, No. 655.

Seth Wood, Company I, 69th Indiana Infantry. Died at Big Black River Bridg Mississippi, July 24, 1863. Buried there. Re-interred in Vicksburg National Cemeter Unknown list.

William F. Wright, Company D, 147th Indiana Infantry. Died at Cumberlan Maryland, April 9, 1865. Buried there. No record of removal. Remains probably re-i terred in some National cemetery. Unknown list.

George H. Zeigler, Company H, 69th Indiana Infantry. Died at New Orleans, Louisana, September 12, 1863. Buried there. Re-interred in Chalmette National Cemeter Unknown list.

RECAPITULATION OF ROLL OF HONOR.

Total known list 4
Total estimated list 1

                                                                        ——

Grand total, including soldiers who served in distinctively Henry County companies 5

DEDUCT.

Soldiers of the Mexican War 4
Soldiers of the Spanish-American War, Philippine Insurrection, and Regular Army. 9

8th INDIANA INFANTRY.
(THREE MONTHS' SERVICE.)

Luther Wilson, Company A, 36th Indiana Infantry. Died at Buffalo, Kentucky, February 17, 1862. Buried there. No record of removal. Remains probably re-interred in some National cemetery. Unknown list.

Enoch M. Windsor, Company G, 7th Indiana Cavalry. Died in Andersonville Prison, Georgia, date unknown. Buried in Andersonville National Cemetery. Unknown list.

James M. Windsor, Company E, 8th Indiana Infantry (three years). Died in Libby Prison, Richmond, Virginia, February 17, 1865. Buried in Richmond National Cemetery. Unknown list.

Joseph S. Winship, Company K, 36th Indiana Infantry. Died in Andersonville Prison, Georgia. August 3, 1864. Buried in Andersonville National Cemetery. Grave, No. 4,639.

William H. Wise, Company F, 124th Indiana Infantry. Died at Indianapolis, Indiana, November 25, 1864. Buried there. Re-interred in Crown Hill Cemetery, Indianapolis, Indiana. Military Plat. Unknown list.

David Wisehart, Company H, 69th Indiana Infantry. Died at Young's Point, Louisiana, March 10, 1863. Buried there. Re-interred in Vicksburg National Cemetery. Unknown list.

Philander Wisehart, Company B, 8th Indiana Infantry (three months). Killed at Rich Mountain, West Virginia, July 11, 1861. Buried on the battlefield. Re-interred in Grafton National Cemetery. Grave, No. 655.

Seth Wood, Company I, 69th Indiana Infantry. Died at Big Black River Bridge, Mississippi, July 24, 1863. Buried there. Re-interred in Vicksburg National Cemetery. Unknown list.

William F. Wright, Company D, 147th Indiana Infantry. Died at Cumberland, Maryland, April 9, 1865. Buried there. No record of removal. Remains probably re-interred in some National cemetery. Unknown list.

George H. Zeigler, Company H, 69th Indiana Infantry. Died at New Orleans, Louisiana, September 12, 1863. Buried there. Re-interred in Chalmette National Cemetery. Unknown list.

RECAPITULATION OF ROLL OF HONOR.

Total known list... 476
Total estimated list.. 119

Grand total, including soldiers who served in distinctively Henry County companies 595

DEDUCT.

Soldiers of the Mexican War.. 4
Soldiers of the Spanish-American War, Philippine Insurrection, and Regular Army. 9 13

Total loss in the Civil War.. 582

NATIONAL CEMETERIES.

September 9, 1861, the Secretary of War directed that the Quartermaster General of the Army should cause to be printed and to be placed in every hospital of the army, blank books and forms for the purpose of preserving accurate and permanent records of deceased soldiers and their place of burial, and that he should provide proper means for a registered head-board to be secured at the head of each soldier's grave.

Act of Congress, approved July 17, 1862, authorizes the President of the United States, whenever, in his opinion, it shall be deemed expedient, to purchase cemetery grounds, and to cause them to be securely enclosed, to be used as a national cemetery for the soldiers who shall die in the service of the country.

April 13, 1866, it was provided by Public Resolution No. 21 "that the Secretary of War be authorized to take immediate measures to preserve from desecration the graves of soldiers of the United States who fell in battle or died of disease during the War of the Rebellion, and to secure suitable burial-places, and to have these grounds enclosed, so that the resting-places of the honored dead may be kept sacred forever."

February 28, 1867, an act to establish and protect national cemeteries was approved, which provided in detail for the purchase of grounds, and the management and inspection of cemeteries; also for the punishment of any person who should mutilate monuments or injure the trees and plants.

In accordance with the foregoing and the orders issued by the War Department from time to time, every effort has been made to collect the remains of the dead, to inter them decently, and to record all the facts known in connection with each grave. After no war, whether of ancient or modern times, have any such systematic exertions been made to secure the collection of the dead and their interment in permanent resting-places, as have been made by the Quartermaster Department of the United States Army under the above provisions of the law.

The latest report of the Quartermaster General on the subject of the Nation's Dead, shows that the following National Cemeteries have been established

| | INTERMENTS. | | |
NAME OF CEMETERY.	Known.	Unknown.	Total.
Annapolis, Maryland.................................	2,285	204	2,489
Alexandria, Louisiana...............................	534	772	1,306
Alexandria, Virginia................................	3,402	120	3,522
Andersonville, Georgia.............................	12,793	921	13,714
Antietam, Maryland.................................	2,853	1,818	4,671
Arlington, Virginia	11,915	4,349	16,264
Ball's Bluff, Virginia.............................	1	24	25
Barrancas, Florida.................................	798	657	1,455
Baton Rouge, Louisiana.............................	2,469	495	2,964
Battle Ground, District of Columbia................	43	....	43
Beaufort, South Carolina...........................	4,748	4,493	9,241
Beverly, New Jersey	145	7	152
Brownsville, Texas.................................	1,417	1,379	2,796
Camp Butler, Springfield, Illinois.................	1,007	355	1,362
Camp Nelson, Jessamine County, Kentucky............	2,477	1,165	3,642
Cave Hill, Louisville, Kentucky....................	3,344	583	3,927
Chalmette, New Orleans, Louisiana..................	6,837	5,674	12,511
Chattanooga, Tennessee.............................	7,999	4,963	12,962
City Point, Virginia...............................	3,778	1,374	5,152
Cold Harbor, Virginia..............................	673	1,281	1,954
Corinth, Mississippi...............................	1,789	3,927	5,716
Crown Hill, Indianapolis, Indiana..................	681	32	713
Culpeper, Virginia	456	911	1,367
Custer Battle Field, Mexican Territory.............	262	....	262
Cypress Hills, New York............................	3,710	76	3,786
Danville, Kentucky	335	8	343
Danville, Virginia.................................	1,172	155	1,327
Fayetteville, Arkansas	431	781	1,212
Finn's Point, Salem, New Jersey....................	....	2,644	2,644

Florence, South Carolina	199	2,799	2,998
Fort Donelson, Tennessee	158	511	669
Fort Gibson, Indian Territory	215	2,212	2,427
Fort Harrison, Virginia	239	575	814
Fort Leavenworth, Kansas	835	928	1,763
Fort McPherson, Lincoln County, Nebraska	152	291	443
Fort Smith, Arkansas	711	1,152	1,863
Fort Scott, Kansas	390	161	551
Fredericksburg, Virginia	2,487	12,770	15,257
Gettysburg, Pennsylvania	1,967	1,608	3,575
Glendale, Virginia	234	961	1,195
Grafton, West Virginia	634	620	1,254
Hampton, Virginia	4,930	494	5,424
Jefferson Barracks, Missouri	8,584	2,906	11,490
Jefferson City, Missouri	349	412	761
Keokuk, Iowa	612	33	645
Knoxville, Tennessee	2,090	1,046	3,136
Laurel, Maryland	232	6	238
Lebanon, Kentucky	591	277	868
Lexington, Kentucky	805	108	913
Little Rock, Arkansas	3,265	2,337	5,602
Loudon Park, Maryland	1,637	166	1,803
Marietta, Georgia	7,188	2,963	10,151
Memphis, Tennessee	5,160	8,817	13,977
Mexico City, Mexico	284	750	1,034
Mills Springs, Somerset, Kentucky	345	366	711
Mobile, Alabama	756	113	869
Mound City, Illinois	2,505	2,721	5,226
Nashville, Tennessee	11,825	4,701	16,526
Natchez, Mississippi	308	2,780	3,088
New Albany, Indiana	2,139	676	2,815
New Berne, North Carolina	2,177	1,077	3,254
Philadelphia, Pennsylvania	1,881	28	1,909
Poplar Grove, Virginia	2,198	4,001	6,199
Port Hudson, Louisiana	596	3,223	3,819
Quincy, Illinois	240	56	296
Raleigh, North Carolina	619	562	1,181
Richmond, Virginia	842	5,700	6,542
Rock Island, Illinois	277	19	296
Salisbury, North Carolina	94	12,032	12,126
San Antonio, Texas	324	167	491
San Francisco, California	4,236	456	4,692
Santa Fe, New Mexico	380	421	801
St. Augustine, Florida	195	73	268
Seven Pines, Virginia	150	1,208	1,358
Shiloh, Hardin County, Tennessee	1,229	2,361	3,590
Soldiers' Home, District of Columbia	5,314	288	5,602
Springfield, Missouri	1,009	740	1,749
Staunton, Virginia	233	520	753
Stone's River, Murfreesboro, Tennessee	3,821	2,324	6,145
Vicksburg, Mississippi	3,896	12,704	16,600
Wilmington, North Carolina	710	1,398	2,108
Winchester, Virginia	2,094	2,365	4,459
Woodlawn, Elmira, New York	3,074	16	3,090
Yorktown, Virginia	748	1,434	2,182
	177,362	149,314	326,676

48

Of the whole number of interments indicated above, there are about 6,900 known and 1,500 unknown civilians, and 6,100 known and 3,200 unknown Confederates. Of these latter, the greater portion are buried at Woodlawn Cemetery, Elmira, New York, and Finn's Point Cemetery, near Salem, New Jersey. The interments at Mexico City are mainly of those who were killed or died in that vicinity during the Mexican War, and include also such citizens of the United States as may have died in Mexico, and who, under treaty provision, have the right of burial therein. From the foregoing, it will appear that, after making all proper deductions for civilians and Confederates, there are gathered in the various places mentioned the remains of nearly 300,000 men who at one time wore the blue during the late war, and who yielded up their lives in defense of the Government which now so graciously cares for their ashes.

CHAPTER XXXVI.

THE MILITIA SYSTEM OF INDIANA.

THE MILITIA SYSTEM OF THE NORTHWEST TERRITORY—THE MUSTER AND THE MILITIA LAWS IN INDIANA TERRITORY—LIST OF MILITIA OFFICERS FROM HENRY COUNTY.

The enforced Militia System which prevailed in Indiana from the first settlement of the Territory by English speaking people until 1844, when a Volunteer System succeeded it, was an inheritance from the old Northwest Territory, for the government of which it was the very first legal enactment. Though often modified and amended by the various Territorial and State Legislatures, it embraced the general principal of enforced military service to the State for the defense of its people, their homes and their property, and the same general requirements for the instruction of the officers and men, and their grouping in Companies, Battalions, Regiments and Brigades, from the first act to the last, except that owing to the narrow limits of the primal settlements, the first law provided for no command larger than a regiment.

The initial militia law for the country north of the Ohio River was published at Marietta, Ohio, on July 25, 1788, by the Governor, Arthur St. Clair, and two of the Territorial Judges, Samuel Holden Parsons and James Mitchell Varnum, almost a year in advance of the meeting of the first Legislative Assembly of the Northwest Territory. It was seemingly the work of the two New England Judges, Parsons and Varnum, and was the form by which the old methods of protecting the early New England settlements from the murderous assaults of the savages and repelling their frequent invasions, were brought into the wilderness, north of the Ohio. The immediate purpose of the enactment was the same as that which inspired the laws from which it was evidently fashioned. Certain clauses of the law itself, show how greatly the need of military preparation for the defense of the new settlements had impressed the men, who were leading the people of the older communities into a wilderness to establish the foundations of great States.

The sweeping and arbitrary character of the first militia law will be more readily understood by the incorporation of its more important sections into the body of this chapter, than by any mere statement of its provisions. The first five sections of the law are as follows:

(1). "All male inhabitants, between the ages of sixteen and fifty, shall be liable to, and perform military duty, and be formed into corps in the following manner:

(2). "Sixty rank and file shall form a company. Eight companies shall form a battalion. Two battalions shall form a regiment. There shall be appointed to each company, one Captain, one Lieutenant, one Ensign, four Sergeants, four Corporals, one Drummer, and one Fifer. To a battalion, there shall be appointed one Lieutenant Colonel, one Major and one Adjutant. To a regiment, one Colonel. The corps shall be divided into Senior and Junior Classes.

(3.) "Whereas, in the infant state of the Country, defense and protection are absolutely essential, all male inhabitants of the age of sixteen years and upwards, shall be armed, equipped, and accoutred in the following manner: with musket and bayonet, or rifle, cartridge box and pouch, or powder horn and bullet pouch, with forty rounds of cartridges, or one pound of powder and four pounds of lead, priming wire and brush and six flints.

(4). "And whereas, for securing principles of defense and protection, it is necessary to be assembled upon certain times and at certain places for examining and inspecting the arms and accoutrements, and for disciplining the men in a soldierly manner; and whereas, the assembling of the community at fixed periods, conduces to health, civilization and morality and such assembling without arms in a newly settled country, may be attended with danger, therefore the corps shall be paraded at ten o'clock in the morning of each first day of the week (Sunday), armed, equipped, and accoutred as aforesaid, in convenient places, next adjacent to the place or places already assigned for public worship. At other times and places, the corps shall be paraded for muster, exercise and review, as the Commander in Chief may direct. And whereas, in the present state of the Territory, it is necessary that guards be established, the Commander in Chief and the commanding officers of counties and smaller districts shall make such detachments for guards and such other military services as the public exigencies may in their opinion, or their opinions, require.

(5). "Those who have borne commissions, civil or military, in the service of the United States, or either of them, or who have been honorably discharged therefrom, and all such as have been graduated in colleges or universities, shall comprise the senior class. Males over the age of fifty shall be liable to military duty in cases of actual invasion only, and then at the direction of the Commander in Chief. Officers of the Civil Government or commissioned by the Governor are exempted from the duties aforesaid."

The remaining six sections of the law provide for its enforcement, establish courts martial, and provide for their method of procedure and determine the penalties such courts may inflict.

The fines for neglect of duty and other violations of the law were at first light, running from a maximum of one dollar down to a minimum of five cents for a trivial offense, twenty five cents being the more usual fine, but all officers were subject to courts martial which seem to have been endowed with almost unlimited powers.

Under an amendment to the law made in November, 1788, fines were assessed and collected against all persons subject to military duty, for neglect or refusal to provide themselves with the equipment required by law and established a fine for each separate offense, ranging from fifty cents for failure to provide a musket or rifle to five cents for failure to provide a priming wire or brush. Arms, accoutrements and ammunition were to be inspected by the officers on the first Sabbath day of each month. Under a subsidiary act passed July 2, 1791, the regular weekly musters were permitted to take place on Saturday instead of Sunday, compelled militiamen to go armed, when attending places of worship, and fixed the fines for neglect; the law to be enforced by distress and sale of property, when necessary.

In 1799 the General Assembly repealed the law of 1788 and all subsequent laws for the establishment of the militia and substituted for them a law of twenty seven articles, including altogether forty three sections and covering twelve pages of closely printed matter. By this law, all able bodied white male citizens, between the ages of eighteen and forty five years, were made subject to militia duty, except civil officers and ministers. It provided for artillery, one battery to be attached to each brigade, an Adjutant General for the territory, and for general, regimental and company officers, as well as non-commissioned officers, much as they exist today in the Army and in the Volunteer Militia. Perhaps the greatest departure from the former law was in the greatly increased severity of the penalties for failure or refusal to obey the provisions of the act, the fines running from five cents to three dollars for enrolled men, up to a maximum fine of one hundred dollars for certain offenses of commissioned officers, while parents and guardians were made responsible for fines assessed against their sons or wards. Fines were to be collected by distress and sale of property or by imprisonment of the offender. Officers and men were to be free from arrest while performing military duty. The men were required to furnish their own arms and accoutrements as under the old law, and the militia was subject to immediate call to repel invasion.

There were various reasons for the increased rigor of this act. The law of 1788 was intended for the organization of the men, young and old, of the Ohio Company's Marietta Colony, for defense against the assaults of Indians, and there was probably not a man or boy in the Company, who was not in accord with the ideas of the leading men of the Colony, on the necessity and duty of self defense imposed on the citizens by the militia law of 1788. But in 1799, thousands of settlers from many parts of America and Europe had come into the Territory and the widely scattered settlements made it a different and more difficult task to provide an efficient militia system for their defense. Besides this, the rapid influx of Quakers and other non-combatants, for conscientious reasons, into the new land, doubtless kindled the old warrior zeal of Puritan and non-conscientious Southron alike, resulting in a determination to make the Quakers train for war or pay the cost of a like number of militiamen.

It is not the author's purpose to discuss the wisdom of the more rigorous law but merely to point out that the law of 1799 and the acts that preceded it, were the foundation upon which all subsequent militia laws, whether coercive or volunteer, have been based. The muster did not originate with the law. In some form it is, doubtless, as old as war itself, but it was this law of the Northwest Territory that brought it into Indiana Territory and State. It was this law also that provoked the long struggle with the Society of Friends and other sects, conscientiously opposed to war. As the danger of invasion passed away, the non-combatants gradually succeeded in their contention for immunity from military duties in times of peace. In 1800 Indiana Territory was established by Act of Congress and in 1802 the new Territorial Government was in full control. The old Northwest Territory had passed into history, but had bequeathed its laws and their spirit to its successor.

THE MUSTER, AND THE MILITIA LAWS IN INDIANA TERRITORY.

The law of 1799 was continued in full force in Indiana Territory, having in order to insure its binding force, been re-enacted by the first Territorial General

Assembly. In 1810 the General Assembly passed an act supplemental to the law of 1799, which made a number of changes in the methods of administration, the most radical of which related to the Society of Friends or Quakers, and their conscientious scruples as to bearing arms. Under the laws of 1799, the Quakers had been the objects of frequent persecution for neglect of military duty, and seizures and sales of their property for the payment of military fines had been of frequent occurrence, for the Quakers held it to be the same in effect to pay fines that went to the support of the militia as to render military service in person. The thirteenth section of the law of 1810 provided as follows:

"Whereas the universal benevolence which governs said society, established by their ample contributions to all charitable and useful institutions, and particularly their exertions to civilize the Indians, a fund having actually been raised to be devoted to that object in this Territory, therefore, for these reasons, as also from the circumstances of the said society being always in the habit of supporting its own poor, although they cheerfully pay their poor tax for the support of those of other denominations, be it enacted that the persons composing said societies shall be, and they are hereby exempted from military duty, provided always, that in time of actual war, they will be subject to such additional tax or contribution in lieu of military service, as the legislature may think proper to impose."

This section constituted one of the first legal acknowledgments of the rights of conscience with reference to military service, that was made in this country. It was, however, of short duration, for the shadows of Indian troubles and the gathering clouds of the Second War with England, known as the War of 1812-15, then beginning to thicken rapidly, caused the repeal of the section at the very next session of the Territorial General Assembly.

The law of 1810 also forbade the sale of intoxicants within two miles of a parade or muster, a provision which seems to have been dropped from the next militia law. The last Territorial law on the subject of the militia was finally passed and approved at the session of 1814. It was an elaborate enactment of no less than seventy nine sections. It retained the principal features of the old law of 1799 but enlarged upon it and brought it down to the needs of the time, which was one of imminent danger from Indian massacres and invasions, while the Treaty of Ghent had not yet brought to a close the Second War with England. It substituted an exemption fee of five dollars for the free exemption given by the preceding law to the Quakers and renewed the old rigorous collection laws. Some changes were made in the titles and duties of officers and the cavalry and artillery branches of the service were better organized. All regiments or parts of regiments were made subject to immediate call by the Commander-in-Chief, to repel invasion or for other specific duties connected with the public safety. Officers and men were still required to equip themselves, and cavalrymen were to furnish their own mounts, but if the animal was killed or rendered worthless when the company was called into active service, the owner was to be paid its appraised value from the Territorial Treasury. Company and battalion musters were to be held in April and September of each year and the regimental musters were to take place in September of each year. The law seems to have been silent as to more frequent company or squad drills; but tradition seems to establish that they were, in most places, matters of monthly occurrence, the hours of muster being from ten o'clock in the morning to three o'clock in the afternoon.

The first Constitution of the State of Indiana provided that "The Militia of Indiana shall consist of all free, able-bodied male persons, negroes, mulattoes and Indians excepted, resident in said State, between the ages of eighteen and forty five years; except such persons as now are or hereafter may be exempted by the laws of the United States or of this State, and shall be armed, equipped and trained as the General Assembly may provide by law."

It made proper exemptions for persons conscientiously scrupulous of bearing arms. Subalterns, captains, majors and colonels were to be elected by those persons subject to military duty in their respective Company, Battalion and Regimental districts; non-commissioned officers of companies were to be appointed by the captains; brigadier generals were to be elected by the commissioned officers in their respective brigades and major generals by the same class of officers in their respective divisions. The manner of forming troops in the several branches of the service was left to the General Assembly. The appointment of an Adjutant General for the State, and of a Quartermaster General and his aids de camp was assigned to the Governor.

While giving the sanction of the State to the rights of conscience in the matter of bearing arms, it still made exemption from military duty on account of conscientious scruples, the subject of a money consideration to be collected by the civil officers. This was materially softened, however, by section three of article nine, which provided that the money which "shall be paid as an equivalent by persons exempt from military duty, except in times of war," should be exclusively and in equal proportion, applied to the support of county seminaries, a class of high schools or academies, for which the constitution elsewhere provided. This did not for many years, even measurably satisfy those who resisted the collection of exemption fees and fines, possibly because the money was applied to special schools rather than to popular schools, in the benefits of which all might partake.

The organization of Henry County was completed June 1, 1822, and the county's connection with the militia system began August 23, 1823. The Adjutant General's office is not in possession of State military documents of any kind that antedate the War with Mexico, which began in 1846. There is, however, a record in the office of the Secretary of State, which contains the names of the militia officers of the State, with the dates of their commissions, and the regiments to which they belonged from 1816 forward. From this record it is found that Elisha Long was commissioned Colonel of the Forty Eighth Regiment of Indiana Militia, on August 28, 1823. So it may be safely assumed that the regiment came into existence in that year, and that the militia system of the county began then. The list of militia officers, who were commissioned at various times, contains the names of many men, who were prominent in the early life and councils of the county, but perhaps no one of them was more distinguished than the first Colonel, Elisha Long. He was the son of a Revolutionary soldier, Christopher Long, whose grave is kept green at the cross roads near the Boyd Schoolhouse in Liberty Township. Colonel Long was a soldier of the War of 1812-15 from Virginia, before coming to Henry County, and played an important part in the affairs of the country as is shown elsewhere in this History.

LIST OF MILITIA OFFICERS FROM HENRY COUNTY.

COMMISSIONED FOR SERVICE IN THE 48TH REGIMENT, INDIANA MILITIA FROM 1823 TO 1846, INCLUSIVE, WITH THE DATES OF THEIR SEVERAL COMMISSIONS.

August 28, 1823.—Elisha Long, Colonel; James Johnson, Lieutenant Colonel; John Dorrah, Major.

November 29, 1823.—Brice Dillee, Captain; George Isham, Lieutenant; Edmund Liston, Ensign.

December 16, 1823.—Achilles Morris, Captain; Michael Swope, Lieutenant; William Huff, Ensign; John Baker, Captain; Anthony Boggs, Lieutenant; Stephen Batson, Ensign; Daniel C. Priddy, Captain; Robert Johnson, Lieutenant; William Wick, Ensign; Jesse Forkner, Captain; George B. Bates, Lieutenant; Thomas Ralston, Ensign; Charles B. Finch, Captain; John Smith, Lieutenant; Asahel Woodward, (Grandfather of the author of this History), Lieutenant; William McDowell, Ensign.

September 13, 1824.—John Odom, Lieutenant.

September 3, 1825.—John Whittaker, Lieutenant; Watson Roe, Lieutenant.

March 11, 1826.—Thomas Porter, Ensign of Riflemen; Mathew McKimmey, Lieutenant of Riflemen.

April 4, 1826.—Brice Dillee, Lieutenant Colonel; Elijah McCray, Captain; Nathan Crawford, Lieutenant.

May 23, 1826.—It was ordered by the Governor and Commander in Chief, that the Militia of the counties of Rush, Decatur and Henry be organized into a brigade to be known as the Eighteenth Brigade, and that it comprise a part of the Seventh Division of the Militia of the State.

August 23, 1826.—Amaziah Morgan, Brigadier General, Eighteenth Brigade; General Morgan lived in Rush County. He represented the district of which Henry County formed a part, in the State Senate, 1826-30.

November 1, 1826.—Michael Swope, Captain; John Shortridge, Lieutenant; Edward Sharp, Ensign; John Keene, Lieutenant; Christopher Hedrick, Ensign; William Ramsey, Lieutenant.

April 17, 1827.—Samuel Howard, Lieutenant Colonel.

August 14, 1827.—John Freeland, Captain; Samuel Griggsby, Lieutenant; John Whittaker, Captain of Riflemen; William Hughes, Lieutenant.

January 14, 1828.—James R. Leonard, Lieutenant; Michael Buck, Ensign.

December 26, 1828.—William Hobson, Lieutenant of Riflemen; John E. Templeton, Lieutenant; William Murphey, Ensign.

August 4, 1829.—Miles Murphey, Major; Samuel Howard, Captain of Cavalry; Jacob Thornburgh, First Lieutenant of Cavalry; William Silver, Second Lieutenant of Cavalry; William Mellett, Cornet of Cavalry; Christopher Hedrick, Captain; Andrew Fletcher, Lieutenant; Joseph Robbins, Captain; Armstead Watkins, Lieutenant; Samuel Marsh, Ensign; Anthony Dunlavy, Captain; Richard Wilson, Lieutenant; Alfred Moore, Ensign; John Odom, Captain; Samuel D. Wells, Lieutenant; William Hill, Ensign; Watson Roe, Captain; John McShirley, Lieutenant; Joel Robinson, Ensign.

February 1, 1830.—Jonathan Bedwell, Captain; Andrew D. Blount, Lieutenant; James Alexander, Ensign.

June 17, 1830.—Richard Wilson, Captain; William B. Wilson, Lieutenant.

August 3, 1830.—John Hill, Lieutenant; Barzillai Rozell, Ensign.

October 11, 1830.—Robert Hudelson, Captain; Alfred M. Brattain, Lieutenant; John Wick, Ensign; Jacob H. Powers, Captain; Edward Jones, Lieutenant; Thomas C. Calkins, Ensign; Thomas B. Miller, Lieutenant; Edmund Liston, Ensign; James Boggs, Ensign.

December 13, 1830.—William Silver, First Lieutenant of Cavalry; Ezekiel T. Hickman, Second Lieutenant of Cavalry.

January 21, 1831.—John Evans, Ensign.

February 10, 1831.—Asa Leonard, Captain; Joseph G. Cooper, Lieutenant; William

LIST OF MILITIA OFFICERS FROM HENRY COUNTY.

COMMISSIONED FOR SERVICE IN THE 48TH REGIMENT, INDIANA MILITIA FROM 1823 TO 1846, INCLUSIVE, WITH THE DATES OF THEIR SEVERAL COMMISSIONS.

August 28, 1823.—Elisha Long, Colonel; James Johnson, Lieutenant Colonel; John Dorrah, Major

November 29, 1823—Brice Dillee, Captain; George Isham, Lieutenant; Edmund Liston Ensign

December 16, 1823.—Achilles Morris, Captain; Michael Swope, Lieutenant; William Huff Ensign; John Baker, Captain; Anthony Boggs, Lieutenant; Stephen Batson, Ensign; Daniel C. Priddy, Captain; Robert Johnson, Lieutenant; William Wick, Ensign; Jesse Forkner, Captain; George B. Bates, Lieutenant; Thomas Ralston, Ensign; Charles R. Finch, Captain; John Smith, Lieutenant; Asahel Woodward, (Grandfather of the author of this History), Lieutenant; William McDowell, Ensign.

September 13 1824.—John Odom. Lieutenant.

September 3, 1825.—John Whittaker, Lieutenant; Watson Roe, Lieutenant.

March 11, 1826—Thomas Porter, Ensign of Riflemen; Mathew McKimmey, Lieutenant of Riflemen.

April 4, 1826—Brice Dillee, Lieutenant Colonel; Elijah McCray, Captain; Nathan Crawford, Lieutenant

May 22, 1826—It was ordered by the Governor and Commander in Chief, that the Militia of the counties of Rush, Decatur and Henry be organized into a brigade to be known as the Eighteenth Brigade, and that it comprise a part of the Seventh Division of the Militia of the State.

August 24, 1826.—Amaziah Morgan, Brigadier General, Eighteenth Brigade; General Morgan lived in Rush County. He represented the district of which Henry County formed a part, in the State Senate, 1826-30.

November 1, 1826.—Michael Swope, Captain; John Shortridge, Lieutenant; Edward Sharp, Ensign; John Keene, Lieutenant; Christopher Hedrick, Ensign; William Ramsey, Lieutenant.

April 17, 1827.—Samuel Howard, Lieutenant Colonel.

August 14, 1827.—John Freeland, Captain; Samuel Griggsby, Lieutenant; John Whittaker, Captain of Riflemen; William Hughes, Lieutenant.

January 14, 1828.—James R. Leonard, Lieutenant; Michael Buck, Ensign.

December 2d, 1828.—William Hobson, Lieutenant of Riflemen; John E. Templeton, Lieutenant; William Murphey, Ensign.

August 1, 1829—Miles Murphey, Major; Samuel Howard, Captain of Cavalry; Jacob Thornburgh, First Lieutenant of Cavalry; William Silver, Second Lieutenant of Cavalry; William Mellett, Cornet of Cavalry; Christopher Hedrick, Captain; Andrew McCaffer, Lieutenant; Joseph Robbins, Captain; Armstead Watkins, Lieutenant; Samuel Marsh, Ensign; Anthony Dunlavy, Captain; Richard Wilson, Lieutenant; Alfred Morris, Ensign; John Odom, Captain; Samuel D. Wells, Lieutenant; William Hill, Ensign; Watson Roe, Captain; John McShirley Lieutenant; Joel Robinson, Ensign.

September 1830—Jonathan Bedwell, Captain; Andrew B. Bloom, Lieutenant; James Alexander, Ensign.

June 17, 1830—Richard Wilson Captain; William B. Wilson Lieutenant.

April 3, 1830—John Hill, Lieutenant; Barzillai Rozell Ensign.

March 31, 1830—Robert Hudelson, Captain; Alfred M. Brotherton, Lieutenant; John West Ensign; Jacob S. Powers, Captain; Edward Jones, Lieutenant; Thomas C. Calkins, Ensign; Cornelius Miller, Lieutenant; Edmund Liston, Ensign, James Boggs, Ensign.

December 1830—William Silver, First Lieutenant of Cavalry; Ezekiel T. Hickman, Second Lieutenant of Cavalry.

January 21, 1831, John Evans, Ensign.

January 10, 183—James Leonard, Captain; Joseph G. Conner, Lieutenant; William

COMPANY C, 36th INDIANA INFANTRY.

Crane, Ensign; Daniel Custard, Lieutenant; Darius Berger, Ensign; William Bruner, Ensign.

April 21, 1831.—Aaron Houghum, Captain; John Wilson, Lieutenant; Ransom Long, Ensign.

May 25, 1831.—Stephen Cory, Ensign.

August 22, 1831.—Miles Murphey, Colonel; Asahel Woodward, (Grandfather of the author of this History), Major.

January 11, 1832.—William Parker, Captain of Riflemen; Jacob Rhinehart, Ensign of Riflemen; John Dennis, Lieutenant; James Holtsclaw, Ensign.

February 27, 1832.—David Fleming, Captain; Valentine Summers, Ensign; John Davidson, Lieutenant; Minor Allee, Ensign.

March 22, 1832.—Ezekiel T. Hickman, Major; William J. Hobson, Lieutenant of Riflemen; Jonathan Pierson, Ensign of Riflemen.

July 30, 1832.—Levi Leakey, Lieutenant.

September 11, 1832.—William S. Bell, Captain; Jacob Donald, Lieutenant; John Millis, Ensign; Jeremiah Veach, Captain; Lemuel Evans, Lieutenant.

October 16, 1832.—William A. Thompson, Captain of Artillery; James Ball, First Lieutenant of·Artillery; Caleb Cope, Second Lieutenant of Artillery; Harris H. Pool, Ensign.

April 13, 1833.—Silas Ruggles, First Lieutenant of Cavalry.

September 19, 1833.—Samuel D. Cory, Ensign.

December 21, 1833.—David D. Priddy, Captain of Riflemen.

February 13, 1834.—William Templeton, Captain; James Carr, Lieutenant; James E. Bell, Ensign; Edward Gillgeese, Ensign.

April 22, 1834.—Joseph Kellum, Captain; Levi Leakey, Captain of Artillery.

March 13, 1836.—William C. Robinson, of Rush County, Brigadier General, Eighteenth Brigade.

November 26, 1840.—George Tarkleson, Captain Light Infantry; Henry Shank, Lieutenant Light Infantry; James C. Murray, Ensign of Light Infantry.

February 17, 1842.—Isaac France, Captain; James M. Whitesel, Lieutenant; Robert G. Emerson, Ensign.

July 15, 1842.—Green T. Simpson, Captain of Riflemen; James Wilson, Lieutenant of Riflemen; Peter Harter, Ensign of Riflemen.

January 18, 1846.—Henry County Guards, New Castle, mustered for the Mexican War, but not called into active service. Mathew S. Ward, Captain; Henry Shroyer, First Lieutenant; Pyrrhus Woodward, (Uncle of the author of this History), Second Lieutenant.

July 31, 1846.—Lewisville Guards mustered for the Mexican War, but not called into active service. William S. Price, Captain; George W. Truslow, First Lieutenant; Emory Southwick, Second Lieutenant; Joseph Spaw, Ensign.

August 1, 1846.—Middletown Rifle Company, mustered for the Mexican War, but not called into active service. Simon Summers, Captain; Henry Shank, First Lieutenant; Charles Riley, Second Lieutenant.

August 10, 1846.—Ringgold Troop, Independent Militia, New Castle. Mustered for the Mexican War, but not called into active service. Richard Goodwin, Captain; John Shroyer, First Lieutenant; George W. Woods, Second Lieutenant.

August 10, 1846.—A company organized in Prairie Township. Mustered for the Mexican War, but not called into active service. Jeremiah Veach, Captain; Abraham W. Bouslog, Lieutenant.

September 2, 1846.—Knightstown Grays, mustered for the Mexican War, but not called into active service. Solomon McCain, Captain; Gordon Ballard, First Lieutenant; James Tyler, Second Lieutenant.

NOTE.—All the companies organized in 1846 were under the Act of Congress of May 13, 1846, and can, therefore, hardly be classed as belonging to the Forty Eighth Regiment. Yet they are so set out on the record in the office of the Secretary of State as above referred to. Further reference to these companies will be found in the Chapter relating to the Mexican War.

A careful study of this list will disclose several matters of interest to the student of our early local history, among which is the fact, that many of the names it contains are the same as those of members of the county's most substantial and honored families of the present time. Another is, that as the years advanced and there came to be less and less danger of Indian outbreaks which might threaten disaster to any of the State's inhabitants, while we were at peace with all civilized nations, the military spirit gradually declined. In the year 1846, when the War with Mexico began, there does not seem to have been an active militia company in the county, until certain companies were formed for service in that war, under an Act of Congress approved May 13, 1846. Prior to the organization of these Mexican War Companies, not one of which was ever called into active service, but three companies of militia had been organized within the county for twelve years; one at Middletown in 1840; one at Knightstown in 1842, and one in Liberty Township in 1842. Practically speaking the Liberty Township Company, of which Green T. Simpson was Captain, was the last ever organized in the county, under the old militia law.

The legislation which affected the militia of Indiana from and after 1823, consisted of the following enactments:

(1.) An Act approved January 11, 1823, which provided that "no major general or brigadier general shall be authorized to take command of any regiment, unless requested by the commandant to do so," and. made it unlawful to contest the election of any militia officer declared elected; changed company musters from April to May, and extended exemptions to all persons who had at any time prior to the former act, or at the date of the act, served five years in the militia.

(2.) An act to regulate the militia of Indiana, approved January 19, 1828, provided for taking account of public arms belonging to the militia, and their distribution to commandants of divisions and making all persons receiving public arms accountable for the same. It also fixed the number of regimental musters, at one for each year, "at such time and place as the brigadier general shall determine," while the company muster was to occur on the second Saturday in April, the captains to give notice to their companies in July of the times and places of muster for the ensuing year.

(3.) An act approved February 2, 1833, provided as its most notable feature that. "Any person subject to military duty, commissioned officers excepted, shall henceforth be annually exempted from such of the fines as may have been imposed on him by law for each annual failure to perform such duty, upon the payment of one dollar to the person having charge of the seminary fund of his county, provided the same be paid before the first day of October in each year."

Section Four of the same act extended, "All and singular, the rights, privileges and benefits, etc.," of said act. "to persons conscientiously scrupulous as to bearing arms, provided that every conscientiously scrupulous person wishing to avail himself thereof shall make the payment in the first section of this act mentioned, to the officer of his county having legal charge of the seminary fund."

Thus did the State essay to build up its seminaries at the expense of its militia, for the evident reason that there existed at that time no prospect of invasion or insurrection, and consequently there was small need of a State militia, while the demand for better schools was most urgent. Under this law, the busy men, the conscientious men and the men who simply disliked militia duties, were each and all released therefrom upon the payment of one dollar each to the seminary fund. This was approaching rapidly to a voluntary militia service and the end of the old system. An act approved February 24, 1840, tended in its general provisions in the same direction. It divided the militia into two classes, active and sedentary. All persons over thirty and under forty to belong to the sedentary militia, and not to be liable to military duty, except in times of war or insurrection. It however repealed that part of an "act for the encouragement of education" which related to fines, except that it continued the part thereof relative to conscientious persons in full force. It returned all fines against members of the militia to the use of the militia and provided for their collection by justices of the peace. The same act provided for voluntary militia companies. Thus with all persons over thirty years of age relieved from active militia service in times of peace, and volunteer military companies provided for, the end of the old coercive system was evidently near at hand.

The end came with an act of the General Assembly, entitled "An Act to amend an Act to Organize the Militia," approved January 13, 1844, which provided for the organization of a volunteer militia and repealed all former laws upon the subject, practically giving the sanction of the law to what the public opinion of the State had several years previously decreed. All militia service in the State has been voluntary since 1844 and there has always been a ready response on the part of the people to the demand of the State authorities for military aid.

It is to be regretted that the companies and battalions into which the Henry County militia was divided for purposes of muster and instruction were not made a matter of public county record. From the meagre data, now obtainable, it is only possible to locate the various companies by the names of the commissioned officers. Taking the first list of officers, as commissioned in 1823, those who remember the early settlers, will realize that the company of which Achilles Morris was Captain; Michael Swope, Lieutenant; and William Huff, Ensign, was organized in the southeastern part of the county in the territory that now comprises Dudley and Franklin townships. While Jesse Forkner was evidently Captain of an east side company, representing the various townships of Liberty, Blue River and Stony Creek. Charles B. Finch, Captain; John Smith, Lieutenant, and William McDowell, Ensign, probably served in a New Castle and Henry Township company. As we continue down the list, the location of the companies by this sort of approximation grows less difficult. If the space at command permitted, a comparison of the names of the commissioned officers on the list with the records of land entries, and the early deed records, town plats, etc., in the Recorder's office, would locate most, if not all of the commissioned officers with reasonable certainty, and the parts of the county represented by the various companies would be approximately determined; but there seems to have been nothing preserved to indicate how they were grouped into battalions or at what places battalion musters were held.

Elisha Long appears to have held the office of Colonel of the Forty Eighth Regiment until 1831. The record does not state but he doubtless resigned in that year, on account of his election to the State Senate, unless he had reached the age limit of sixty years by that time, for on August 22, 1831, Miles Murphey was commissioned Colonel, he having been advanced to the Majorship in 1829. James Johnson was the first Lieutenant Colonel, commissioned at the same time as Colonel Long, August 28, 1823. Brice Dillee, of Wayne Township, was com-. missioned in 1826, and Samuel Howard was commissioned in 1827, but there may have been two battalions in the county by that time. John Dorrah was the first Major, Miles Murphey, the second, and Asahel Woodward (grandfather of the author of this History), the third.

The musters were the occasions upon which the various elements of pioneer society met and mingled upon such terms of fellowship as their various characters, moods and temperaments permitted, tempered only by such discipline as the militia officers might be able to enforce. There was, however, one very prominent element in early Henry County society, that was never in evidence at the musters. It was composed of those who were in the language of the militia law, "Conscientiously scrupulous of bearing arms." The muster days were looked forward to with various anticipations by the "rank and file." To many they were times of pleasant reunion with friends, and were regarded as holidays, but the truth of history compels it to be said that even the most quiet and sober among the young citizens who bore arms, were never wholly without apprehensions of trouble and possible disaster on such occasions.

The fruitful cause was the same which was so prolific of Saturday fist fights and rows in the early villages—"the good, old, unadulterated whiskey that never hurt anybody"—which we have all heard so much about. While the drills were continued and the officers had control of the men, everything was done with a fair degree of decorum and good order. This was the case even when the drills consisted of nothing more than double and single file movements, as tradition tells us was often the case, but after the men were dismissed in the afternoon and the whiskey began to flow freely, as was the all but universal custom, the rougher elements grew boisterous and challenge and counter challenge flew about rapidly, wrestling matches soon ripened into fights and old quarrels were settled with "far and squar" fistic encounters, and many a fight between friends occurred which was impelled wholly by the "good liquor" and the frenzy of the hour.

There was a system of "renowning it," such as Longfellow describes as having prevailed at the drinking places of the students in the German universities, seventy five years ago', which was in vogue in certain neighborhoods of Henry County, on muster days, election days and other public occasions. They differed from the German "renownings" in this, that they were not challenges to deadly combats with the short sword, but to the more indecorous, though less dangerous "fist and skill fights." The "renowner" would take a stick and draw a large circle upon the ground, then stripping himself to the waist, would leap into the ring and with many furious oaths and floods of abuse, dare his enemy, if he had one in the company, to come in and join battle with him, or wanting an enemy, he would simply defy everybody, proclaim himself the champion of the entire countryside or in the usual language of the backwoods ring, "The bully that could whoop any other bully in the county," and dare any man to accept the challenge. Gouged eyes, bitten ears, mashed noses and bruised faces were the usual harvests of the old time muster day; but this state of affairs was more aggravated in some localities than in others. It cannot be regarded as an outgrowth of the militia system or the muster, except in this, that as all able-bodied men, under forty five, in the township or muster districts were required to meet for drills on those days, rare opportunities for settling old grudges and determining important championships were afforded. Doubtless this was the worst foe to military discipline, decorum and training, that the militia officers had to deal with.

The above facts as to the early musters of the county have been largely drawn from the stories told by the pioneers who attended them and kept their heads sufficiently well to remember and retain vivid impressions of the scenes upon the muster grounds. The late Judge Joseph Farley, one of the county's early associate judges, remembered several such scenes as having occurred at "General Musters" on the farm then occupied by Colonel Long. Having been "only fist fights," nobody gave them much attention as being violations of the law of good order, and the young man, who refused to fight when challenged, was generally looked upon as a coward. But on the other hand, the man who attempted to use a pistol, knife or other murderous weapon in such a contest was regarded as a criminal and treated as such.

Judge Martin L. Bundy remembers that General James Noble, who was one of the early United States Senators from Indiana, held a brigade drill, presumably of the Eighteenth Brigade, at New Castle, either in 1827 or 1828. It was so difficult to find a field sufficiently large for the maneuvers of the brigade, on account of the dense forests, that the late Asahel Woodward finally surrendered his new meadow to the "tramp, tramp, tramping" of the men, and the great muster was held there to the demoralization of the meadow, a disaster that the strength and fertility of the newly cleared land soon repaired. It seems reasonably certain that the Eighteenth Brigade consisted of three regiments, one for each of the three counties, Henry, Rush and Decatur, which constituted the brigade district, but if such were not the fact, it is not probable that more than a thousand men took part in the "great general muster" on Woodward's meadow, yet at that time this meadow was the only field suitable to the maneuvers.

Perhaps the last public event in which the old militia was much in evidence in Eastern Indiana, occurred in Cambridge City on July 28, 1842, on the occasion of the great barbecue to celebrate the beginning of work on the Whitewater Valley Canal, at that place. This canal was one of the artificial waterways for internal communication and transportation, undertaken by the joint action of the National and State governments, under the old Internal Improvement System. It was, in the main, completed from Lawrenceburg to Brookville, before the final breakdown of the joint system. After the project of building further was abandoned by the National and State governments, a stock company was organized to complete the work. The stock was taken by the business men, farmers and professional men of the counties and towns most likely to be benefited by the work, which means that most of it was held in Franklin, Fayette, Wayne, Rush and Henry counties. Farms, wild lands, almost everything that could be turned into money, were taken in payment for stock. Men rode from farmhouse to farmhouse and gave such glowing accounts of the good times that were sure to follow the completion of the canal, that the depressed and struggling people were so imbued with the new hope, that they assumed the burden of the proposed work with alacrity. The General Assembly of 1841 chartered the Whitewater Canal Company and it began work as stated.

Andrew Young, in his History of Wayne County, published at Richmond in 1872, says that "Samuel W. Parker, of Connersville, afterwards a member of Congress from this district, took an active part in getting up the company, and in connection with J. G. Marshall and others, secured the granting of the charter by the General Assembly, of which they were active members. One of the principal contractors under the State and company was Thomas N. Tyner."

"The citizens of Cambridge City celebrated the commencement of operations by the company on July 28, 1842, by a barbecue which was attended by about ten thousand people. The first wheelbarrow full of dirt was dug and wheeled by Samuel W. Parker. The second by Judge Jehu T. Elliott, of New Castle. A great flood in 1847 damaged the canal to the amount of one hundred thousand dollars."

It may without much digression be added here that the canal was completed to Cambridge City in 1846, and soon after, perhaps, to Hagerstown, and was the principal means of transportation until the completion of the Indana Central Railway in 1853. On the occasion of the opening of the canal, it is not recalled that there was any special display or parade of the militia; but the presence of such large numbers of citizens who had been trained at various times, as members of the force, made the great parade of horsemen, which was one of the features of the show, one of the finest that ever occurred in the early history of the State. It is remembered that a number of the militia officers were present in the showy military uniforms of the olden times, brilliant scarfs, huge epaulets, gold laced, jauntily fitting coats, fairly glittering with polished brass buttons, and three-cornered hats, rich in flaunting plumes. These officers were in command of the great procession that galloped about on gaily caparisoned steeds, in a way that excited the wonder and admiration of all.

The two most conspicuous figures from Henry County, in that memorable parade, were Colonel Miles Murphey, of New Castle, and Colonel Jesse W. Baldwin, of Lewisville. Both were, at that time, fine, handsome men, to whom the military uniforms gave additional dignity of appearance. Murphey was Colonel of the Forty Eighth Regiment, and was for that reason made Marshal of the Day. Jesse W. Baldwin may have been a Colonel on the staff of Governor Bigger, or may possibly have been a Colonel of militia in his native State before coming to Henry County. There is no record that explains how or where he came by the rank, or at least the title, of Colonel. He represented Henry County in the General Assembly in 1849, having as his colleague, Samuel W. Coffin. Baldwin was, for many years, a man of influence and standing in Henry County. Later he moved to Chicago, where he died at the advanced age of ninety years. At Lewisville and vicinity, many stories and interesting anecdotes are current, regarding him.

GRAND RECAPITULATION.

ARTILLERY, CAVALRY AND INFANTRY.

General Officers (Field and Staff) U. S. Volunteers.............................. 13
General Officers (State of Indiana).. 2
Regimental Officers (Field and Staff) Indiana Vounteers 2
Company Commissioned Officers Indiana Volunteers 223
Non-Commissioned Officers Indiana Volunteers 43
Company Non-Commissioned Officers Indiana Volunteers 748
U. S. Navy and Miscellaneous.. 15
Privates 3408

Total of officers and men furnished by Henry County in the Wars of the Republic
    from the Mexican War through the Spanish-American War.................... 4491

ALPHABETICAL LIST A.

This list includes the names of Henry County soldiers who attained the rank
. of General Officers, Field or Staff. Also Henry County soldiers serving in Indiana
Organizations, in the Regular Army and in the Navy, during the Civil War. Also
soldiers from other counties in the State, who moved to Henry County, after the
Civil War.

Where the number of soldiers from Henry County in any regiment has
justified the same, the full regimental staff is published with the regiment, but only
the names of such of its members, as were from Henry County and such as are
biographically mentioned in this History, are contained in this list.

In the distinctively Henry County companies, the full roster of the company
is given whether the soldiers were from Henry County or not. All non-resident
soldiers, officers and men, whose names appear in this list, are designated by an
asterisk, thus *, before the names. All soldiers from other counties of the State,
who moved to Henry County after the Civil War, are designated by two
asterisks, thus **, before the names.

A

Abbott, Jackson, Private, Corporal, Company E, 9th Indiana Cavalry.

Abbott, Levi, Private, 12th Indiana Battery.

**Abernathy, Alexander, Private, Company G, 21st Indiana Infantry; Sergeant, Company M; Commissary.Sergeant, Non Commissioned Staff, 9th Indiana Cavalry.

Abernathy, Isaac, Second Lieutenant, Company I, First Lieutenant, Company K,
37th Indiana Infantry.

Abernathy, John A., Musician, Company A, 105th Indiana Infantry (Morgan Raid).

Abshire, James T., Private, Company F, 2nd Indiana Cavalry.

Abshire, John, Private, Company F, 74th Indiana Infantry.

Adair, Washington, Private, Company K, 87th Indiana Infantry; Private, Company
K, 42nd Indiana Infantry.

Adams, Alfred E., Private, Company C, 5th Indiana Cavalry.

*Adams, Byron F., Corporal, Company H, 147th Indiana Infantry.

Adams, Isaac H., Private, Company I, 147th Indiana Infantry.

Adams, James, Private, Company K, 105th Indiana Infantry (Morgan Raid).

*Adams, Marcellus M., Private, Company I, 3rd Indiana Cavalry.

Adams, William, Private, Company A, 36th Indiana Infantry; Private, Company
H, 30th Indiana Infantry, re-organized.

Adams, William H., Corporal, Company I, 3rd Indiana Cavalry.

Adamson, Elias H., Private, Wagoner, Company D, 36th Indiana Infantry.

Adamson, Simon P., Private, Company K, 105th Indiana Infantry (Morgan Raid).

**Addington, Thomas, Private, Corporal, Company C, 87th Indiana Infantry.

Addison, William T., Private, Company G, 16th Indiana Infantry.

Addleman, William O., Private, Corporal, Company I, 147th Indiana Infantry.

Ainsworth, Charles, Private, Unassigned, 53rd Indiana Infantry.

Akin, James, Private, Company C, 147th Indiana Infantry.

Albert, Aaron B., Private, Company C, 109th Indiana Infantry (Morgan Raid).

SOLDIERS.
(SEE ALPHABETICAL LIST)

y soldiers who **attained** the rank
ounty soldiers serving in Indiana
avy, during the Civil War. Also
oved to Henry County, after the

v County in any regiment has
ished with the regiment, but only
Henry County and such as are
med in this list.
., the full roster of the company
county or not. All non-resident
n this list, are designated by an
rom other counties of the State.
War. are designated by two

9th Indiana Cavalry.

t Indiana Infantry; Sergeant, Com-
ff, 9th Indiana Cavalr .
I. First Lieutenant. Company K.

Indiana Infantry (Morgan Raid).
na Cavalry.
Infantry.
diana Infantry; Private, Company

iana Cavalry.
Indiana Infantry.
ana Infantry
a Infantry (Morgan Raid).
Indiana Cavalry.
lana Inf ntry; Private, Company

idiana Cavalry.
 86th Indiana Infantry.
idiana Infantry (Morgan Raid).
t' 87th Indiana Infantry.
Indiana Infantry.
iv I, 147th Indiana Infantry.

SOLDIERS.
(SEE ALPHABETICAL LIST.)

Albertson. Daniel C., Private, Company B, 139th Indiana Infantry; Private, Company H, 147th Indiana Infantry.

Albertson, John B., Private, Corporal, Company C. 36th Indiana Infantry.

Albertson, Larkin L., Sergeant. Company F, 57th Indiana Infantry; Private, Company B, 110th Indiana Infantry (Morgan Raid).

Albright, George H., Private, Company H, 140th Indiana Infantry.

Albright. John, Private, Company I. 69th Indiana Infantry.

Albright, Joseph S., Private, Company, I. 69th Indiana Infantry.

Albright, William H., Private, Company F. 84th Indiana Infantry.

**Alcorn, William, Private. Company E, 8th Indiana Cavalry.

Alexander, Cyrus H., Corporal, Company F, 84th Indiana Infantry.

Alexander. Harvey W., Private, Company A, 110th Indiana Infantry (Morgan Raid); Corporal, Company H, 147th Indiana Infantry.

Alexander, James, Private, Company K, 36th Indiana Infantry.

Alexander, James W.. Private. Sergeant, Company E. 8th Indiana Infantry (three years).

Alexander. John M., Private. Sergeant. Company K, 36th Indiana Infantry; Private. Company A. 4th Regiment, 1st Army Corps (Hancock's Veteran Corps).

Alexander. William R., Private. Company H, 69th Indiana Infantry.

Alfred, John W., Private, Company A, 110th Indiana Infantry (Morgan Raid); Private. Company H, 147th Indiana Infantry.

Alger, Isaac, Private. Company H, 69th Indiana Infantry.

Allee, Amos H., Private, Company E, 9th Indiana Cavalry.

Allee. Henry C., Private, Company I, 3rd Indiana Cavalry.

Allee, Jacob W., Private. Company A, 139th Indiana Infantry.

Allee, John W., Corporal, Company F, 84th Indiana Infantry.

Allee. Oliver. Private, Company D, 19th Indiana Infantry; Private, 19th Indiana Battery.

Allee. Taylor. Private, Company A. 139th Indiana Infantry.

Allen, David T., Private, Company D, 147th Indiana Infantry.

Allen, Reuben W., Private, Company D. 36th Indiana Infantry.

Allen, Thomas C., Private, Company D, 147th Indiana Infantry.

Allen, William, Private. Company K, 54th Indiana Infantry (three months); Private. 15th Indiana Battery.

Allis. Joseph, Corporal. Company K. 54th Indiana Infantry (three months).

Allison. Andrew A., Private. Company C. 84th Indiana Infantry.

*Allison, Asa H., Sergeant, Company H. 147th Indiana Infantry.

Allison, Hiram, Private, Corporal, Company G. 9th Indiana Cavalry.

Allison, James R.. Private, Company A, 105th Indiana Infantry (Morgan Raid).

Allison, Jesse, Private. Company A, 105th Indiana Infantry (Morgan Raid).

Allison, Leonidas L.. Musician, Company F. 6th Indiana Infantry (three months).

Allison, Robert, First Lieutenant. Company F. 6th Indiana Infantry (three months); Captain, Company A, 57th Indiana Infantry.

Allison, William M., Musician. Company A. 57th Indiana Infantry.

**Alshouse, Hiram T., Private. Company F. 134th Indiana Infantry

Alspaugh, De Witt C., Private, Company G, 16th Indiana Infantry.

Alspaugh, George W., Private, Company K, 105th Indiana Infantry (Morgan Raid).

Alspaugh, Henry, Private, Company E, 9th Indiana Cavalry.

Alspaugh, Jacob M.. Private, Company H. 69th Indiana Infantry.

**Anderson. Andrew J., Bugler, Company I. 13th Indiana Cavalry.

Anderson, David, Private, Company K, 14th U. S. C. T.

Anderson, Elias, Private. Company I, 69th Indiana Infantry.

Anderson, Hugh, Private, Company D, 147th Indiana Infantry.

Anderson, Isaiah B., Second Lieutenant, Company B. 139th Indiana Infantry.

Anderson, James S., Private, Company A. 105th Indiana Infantry (Morgan Raid); Private, Corporal, Company A, 139th Indiana Infantry.

49

Anderson, John, Private, Company E, 9th Indiana Cavalry.
**Anderson, John B., Corporal, Company I, 67th Indiana Infantry.
Anderson, John M., Private, Corporal, Company F, 84th Indiana Infantry.
Anderson, Miles E., Private, Sergeant, Company E, 9th Indiana Cavalry.
Andrews, John W., Private, Company H, 69th Indiana Infantry.
Antrim, John B, Private, Corporal, Company A, 36th Indiana Infantry.
Archibald, James, Private, 23rd Indiana Battery.
Archibald, Peter, Private, Company E, 106th Indiana Infantry (Morgan Raid);
Private, Company B, 139th Indiana Infantry.
*Arment, James A., Private, Company H, 140th Indiana Infantry.
Armfield, Elam, Private, Company A, 57th Indiana Infantry. (See Mexican War).
Armstrong, Albert, Private, Company B, 130th Indiana Infantry.
Armstrong, Cyrus, Private, Company K, 36th Indiana Infantry.
Armstrong, John, Private, Company C, 36th Indiana Infantry; Corporal, Company
D, 147th Indiana Infantry.
Armstrong, Morrow P.. Captain. Company K; Captain and Chaplain, Staff, 36th In-
diana Infantry.   .
Artherhultz, Leander, Private, Company K, 74th Indiana Infantry; Private, Com-
pany K, 22nd Indiana Infantry.
*Arville, Joseph, Private, Company H, 140th Indiana Infantry.
Atherton, Fenton, Private, Company A, 139th Indiana Infantry.
Atkinson, George P., Private, Company C, 36th Indiana Infantry.
Austin, James E., Private, Company A, 139th Indiana Infantry; Private, Company
H, 147th Indiana Infantry.
*Ayler, Edward, Private, Company H, 147th Indiana Infantry.
Ayres, Josiah D., Private, Company A, 105th Indiana Infantry (Morgan Raid);
Private, Company G, 9th Indiana Infantry.

B

*Babcock, William M., Private, First Sergeant. Company B, 139th Indiana In-
fantry.
*Bailey, Riley, Private, Company K, 36th Indiana Infantry.
Bailey, William, Private, Company K, 36th Indiana Infantry.
Bailey, William, Private, Company B, 124th Indiana Infantry.
*Bails, Franklin, Private, Company E, 9th Indiana Cavalry.
Baker, Amos H., Private, Company K, 36th Indiana Infantry.
Baker. Andrew J., Private, Company A, 110th Indiana Infantry (Morgan Raid).
Baker. George C., Private, Corporal, Company F, 57th Indiana Infantry.
*Baldwin, Calvin, Private, Company H, 140th Indiana Infantry.
*Baldwin, Elias, Private, Company H, 140th Indiana Infantry.
Baldwin, James, Private, Unassigned, 11th Indiana Infantry.
Baldwin, Jonathan, Private, Company F, 84th Indiana Infantry.
Baldwin, Lewis, Private, Company B, 5th Indiana Cavalry.
Bales, Parnel, Private, Company C, 36th Indiana Infantry; Private, Company G,
84th Indiana Infantry; Private, Company E, 9th Indiana Cavalry.
Ball, Henry S., Saddler, Company I, 3rd Indiana Cavalry.
Ball, James W. E., Private, Corporal, 4th Indiana Battery.
Ball, Jerry C., Private, Company C, 147th Indiana Infantry.
Ball, John C., Private, Company I, 84th Indiana Infantry.
Ball, Thomas J., Private, Company I, 69th Indiana Infantry.
Ball, William B, Private, Company I, 147th Indiana Infantry.
Ball, William D., Private, Company I, 84th Indiana Infantry.
Ballard, James H., Private, Company K, 40th Indiana Infantry.
Ballard, Jesse, Private, Company K, 118th Indiana Infantry.
Ballard, Joseph, Corporal, Company I, 69th Indiana Infantry.

*Ballard, Micajah B., Private, Company H; Assistant Surgeon, Staff, 140th Indiana Infantry.

Ballard, Warren F., Private, Company G; Quartermaster Sergeant, Non Commissioned Staff; Lieutenant and Quartermaster, Staff, 47th Indiana Infantry.

Ballenger, Ezra, Private, Company A, 105th Indiana Infantry (Morgan Raid).

Ballenger, Harmon, Private, Company F, 6th Indiana Infantry (three months).

Baltzley, Daniel, Private, Company A, 36th Indiana Infantry.

Bare, George H., Private, Company H, 69th Indiana Infantry.

**Barkdull, Philip, Private, Company I, 142nd Indiana Infantry.

Barnaby, John H., Private, Unassigned. 22nd Indiana Infantry.

Barnard, John, Sergeant, Company F, 124th Indiana Infantry.

Barnard, Samuel, Private, Company C, 36th Indiana Infantry.

Barnell, John W., Private, Company K, 19th Indiana Infantry; Private, Company E, 20th Indiana Infantry, re-organized.

Barnes, Abraham, Private, Company K. 36th Indiana Infantry.

*Barnes, Erastus, Private, Company F, 57th Indiana Infantry.

Barnes, Greenbury, Private, Company K, 36th Indiana Infantry.

*Barnett, Charles W., Private, Company H. 147th Indiana Infantry.

*Barr, Henry, Private, Company H, 147th Indiana Infantry.

Barre, Samuel, Private, Company G, 84th Indiana Infantry.

Barrett, Elijah J., Private, Company E. 8th Indiana Infantry (three years).

Barrett, George W., Private, Company E, 8th Indiana Infantry (three years).

Barrett, Harvey B., Second Lieutenant, Union Guards, Indiana Legion; First Lieutenant, Company A, 105th Indiana Infantry (Morgan Raid).

Barrett, Jeff H., Private, Corporal, Company A, 139th Indiana Infantry.

Barrett, Samuel, Private, Company B, 118th Indiana Infantry.

Bartee, William, Private, Company K, 148th Indiana Infantry.

Bartlow, Cornelius V., Private, Company K, 36th Indiana Infantry; Corporal, Company H, 147th Indiana Infantry.

*Bartlow, Oliver W., Private, Company A, 57th Indiana Infantry.

Bartow, John G., Private, Company B, 139th Indiana Infantry; Private, Company H, 147th Indiana Infantry.

Bateman, Edward, Private, Unassigned. 22nd Indiana Infantry.

Bateman, Henry C., Private, Company G, 9th Indiana Cavalry.

Bateman, William, Private, Company D, 8th Indiana Infantry (three years).

Bates, George W., Private, Company K, 36th Indiana Infantry.

Bates, Sylvester, Private, Company F, 57th Indiana Infantry.

Bates, Thomas, Private, Company E. 106th Indiana Infantry (Morgan Raid).

Baughan, John, Private, Company K, 105th Indiana Infantry (Morgan Raid).

Baughan, Peter, Private, Company B, 19th Indiana Infantry.

Bayse, Noah, Private, Company A, 36th Indiana Infantry; Private, Company A, 4th Regiment, 1st Army Corps (Hancock's Veteran Corps).

Bayse, Thomas F., Hospital Steward, Non Commissioned Staff; Assistant Surgeon, Staff, 36th Indiana Infantry.

Beach, George P., Private, Company A, 36th Indiana Infantry.

Beard, Isaac, Private, Company K, 14th U. S. C. T.

Beard, Joseph, Private, Company A, 105th Indiana Infantry (Morgan Raid).

Bearley, David, Private, Company A, 110th Indiana Infantry (Morgan Raid). (See Mexican War).

Beaty, Benjamin, Private, Company F, 84th Indiana Infantry.

Beaver, George W., Private, Company F, 6th Indiana Infantry (three months).

Bechtelheimer, Samuel, Private, Company E, 147th Indiana Infantry.

Beck, Cornelius, Private, Company F, 84th Indiana Infantry.

Beck, Hamilton, Private, Company A, 110th Indiana Infantry (Morgan Raid).

Beck, Isom, Private, Company F, 84th Indiana Infantry.

Beck, Samuel H., Private, Corporal, Company F, 84th Indiana Infantry.

Beck, Thomas S., Corporal, Company K, 105th Indiana Infantry (Morgan Raid).

Beck, William T., Private, Company E, 8th Indiana Infantry (three years).

Becktell, William M., Private, Sergeant, Company G, 84th Indiana Infantry.

Bedford, Collins T., Corporal, Sergeant, Company E, 8th Indiana Infantry (three years).

Bedford, William S., Private, Company E, 8th Indiana Infantry (three years).

Beeson, William H., Private, Company I, 69th Indiana Infantry.

Bell, David R., Private, 12th Indiana Battery.

Bell, George W., Private, 12th Indiana Battery.

Bell, Henry, Private, Company D, 19th Indiana Infantry.

*Bell, Isaac, Corporal, Company H, 140th Indiana Infantry.

Bell, Josiah, Private, Company I, 69th Indiana Infantry.

Bell, Samuel, Private, Company A, 36th Indiana Infantry; Private, Company H, 30th Indiana Infantry, re-organized.

Bell, Thomas, Private, Company B, 8th Indiana Infantry (three months); Private, Company E, 8th Indiana Infantry (three years).

Bell, William, Corporal, Company K, 36th Indiana Infantry.

Bell, William, Private, Company A, 105th Indiana Infantry (Morgan Raid).

Bement, John J., Private, Company F, 6th Indiana Infantry (three months).

Benbow, Benjamin F., Private, Corporal, Company G, 84th Indiana Infantry.

Benbow, Cyrus W., Private, Company D, 11th Indiana Infantry; Sergeant, Company G, 84th Indiana Infantry; Second Lieutenant, First Lieutenant, Company K, and Adjutant, Staff, 109th U. S. C. T.

Benjamin, Theodore, Private, Company F, 6th Indiana Infantry (three months).

Benjamin, Thomas, Private, Company I, 54th Indiana Infantry (three months).

Bennett, Levi W., Private, Corporal, Company I, 69th Indiana Infantry.

Bennett, Noah, Private, Company F, 57th Indiana Infantry.

Bennett, Ross E., Private, Company A, 139th Indiana Infantry; Private, 2nd Indiana Battery, re-organized.

Bennett, Seth S., Musician, Company C, 128th Indiana Infantry.

*Bennett, Thomas W., Colonel, Staff, 69th Indiana Infantry.

Bennett, Wilberforce, Private, Company D, 36th Indiana Infantry.

Bennett, William H., Private, Company D, 147th Indiana Infantry.

Benson, Andrew J., Private, Company K, 148th Indiana Infantry.

*Benson, George W., Private, Corporal, Company B, 139th Indiana Infantry.

*Benson, John W. M., Private, Sergeant, Company E, 9th Indiana Cavalry.

Bentley, William P., Private, Company C, 36th Indiana Infantry.

*Benton, Joel, Private, Company H, 147th Indiana Infantry.

Berry, Abraham N., Private, Company F, 6th Indiana Infantry (three months).

Berry, Andrew J., Private, Company A, 110th Indiana Infantry (Morgan Raid).

Berry, Charles P., Private, Company H, 147th Indiana Infantry.

Berry, David W., Private, Company F, 84th Indiana Infantry.

Berry, Francis M., Private, Company E, 8th Indiana Infantry (three years).

Berry, Samuel, Private, Company B, 9th Indiana Cavalry.

Bickel, Tobias, Private, Company E, 147th Indiana Infantry.

Bicknall, William E., Musician, Company D, 36th Indiana Infantry.

Biers, Samuel, Private, Company D, 2nd Indiana Cavalry.

*Bigelow, Arthur M., Private, Company H, 147th Indiana Infantry.

Riggers, James A., Private, Company B, 8th Indiana Infantry (three months); Private, Company H, 147th Indiana Infantry.

Bird, Anson, Corporal, Company D, 36th Indiana Infantry.

Bird, Wesley, Private, Corporal, Company D, 36th Indiana Infantry.

**Bishop, John W., Private, Company K, 70th Indiana Infantry; Private, Company B, 33rd Indiana Infantry.

Bitner, Benjamin, Private, Company H, 147th Indiana Infantry.

Bitner, John, Private, Company B, 5th Indiana Cavalry.

Black, James J., Private, Company F, 57th Indiana Infantry.

Black, James Wesley, Private, Company B. 139th Indiana Infantry; Private, Company H, 147th Indiana Infantry.

Black, Levi M., Private, Company F, 57th Indiana Infantry; Private, Company B, 110th Indiana Infantry (Morgan Raid).

**Black, Seely A., Private, Company C, 57th Indiana Infantry.

Black, William, Private, Company I, 69th Indiana Infantry.

Blake, Josiah, Private, Company H, 69th Indiana Infantry.

Blaud, Americus V., Private, Company K, 148th Indiana Infantry.

Bloomfield, Richard, Private, Company F, 6th Indiana Infantry (three months).

Blount, Andrew J. Private, Company B, 26th Indiana Infantry.

Bly, William G., Private, Company K, 148th Indiana Infantry.

Boblett, Lycurgus L., Private, Company F; Adjutant. Staff, 84th Indiana Infantry.

Bock, Benjamin F., Private, Company E, 8th Indiana Infantry (three years).

Bock, Christopher C. M., Private, Company H. 69th Indiana Infantry; Private, Company H, 147th Indiana Infantry.

Bock, James M., Private, Company H; 69th Indiana Infantry.

Bock, John, Private, Company E, 8th Indiana Infantry (three years).

Bock, Milton L., Private, Company B, 8th Indiana Infantry (three months); Private, Company K. 19th Indiana Infantry; Private. Company E. 20th Indiana Infantry, re-organized.

Bock, Thomas J., Private, Company B, 21st Indiana Infantry, re-organized as 1st Heavy Artillery.

Bock, William B., Private, Company G. 84th Indiana Infantry.

Bodmer, Jacob, Private, Company C. 32nd Indiana Infantry, re-organized. (See Alphabetical List C).

Boggs, William, Private, Company K, 36th Indiana Infantry.

Bogue, Benjamin, Private, Company I, 9th Indiana Infantry.

Bogue, Charles, Private, Company I, 69th Indiana Infantry.

Boice, Martin E., Private, Company D, 11th Indiana Infantry.

*Boldriny, Cyrus, Private, Corporal. Company B, 139th Indiana Infantry.

Bole, James M., Private, 25th Indiana Battery.

Bole, William A., Private, Company E, 8th Indiana Infantry (three years).

Bond, Enos, Private, Company I, 69th Indiana Infantry.

Bond, Levi, Private, Company C, 36th Indiana Infantry.

Bonham, Israel W., Fife Major, Non Commissioned Staff. 8th Indiana Infantry (three months); Principal Musician, Non Commissioned Staff, 36th Indiana Infantry

Bonham, Marcus L., Private, Company K, 54th Indiana Infantry (three months).

Bonham, Thomas M., Regimental Band, 36th Indiana Infantry.

Boor, William F., Major and Surgeon. Staff, 4th Indiana Cavalry; Brigade Surgeon, 1st Brigade, 2nd Division, Cavalry Corps, Army of the Cumberland.

Booth, George C., Private, Corporal. Company I, 147th Indiana Infantry.

Boran, Harmon, Private, Company F, 84th Indiana Infantry.

Borroughs, Charles, Private, Company A, 110th Indiana Infantry (Morgan Raid).

Bowers, David, Private, Company H, 147th Indiana Infantry.

Bowers, George W., Private, Company G, 9th Indiana Cavalry.

Bowers, James, Private, Company F, 57th Indiana Infantry.

Bowers, Joseph, Private, Company A, 110th Indiana Infantry (Morgan Raid).

Bowers, Martin L., Private, Company A, 110th Indiana Infantry (Morgan Raid).

Bowers, Michael, Private, 25th Indiana Battery.

Bowers, Moses, Private, Company F, 57th Indiana Infantry.

Bowers, Salathiel, Private, Company E, 8th Indiana Infantry (three years).

Bowers, Samuel, Private, Company K. 105th Indiana Infantry (Morgan Raid); Private, Company B, 130th Indiana Infantry.

Bowers, William H., Private, Company E, 9th Indiana Cavalry.

Bowles, James H., Private, Company A, 139th Indiana Infantry.

Bowman, Edmund R., Private, Company B. 110th Indiana Infantry (Morgan Raid).

Bowman, Jabez H., Private, Corporal, Company D, 36th Indiana Infantry.

Bowman, John, Private, Company D, 36th Indiana Infantry.

Bowman, Oliver H., Sergeant, Company A, 105th Indiana Infantry (Morgan Raid); Private, Sergeant, 4th Indiana Battery;. Second Lieutenant, 4th Indiana Battery, re-organized.

Bowman, Robert B., Private, Company B, 110th Indiana Infantry (Morgan Raid).

Bowman, Shepperd, Private, Company A, 105th Indiana Infantry (Morgan Raid); Corporal, Company D, 147th Indiana Infantry.

Bowman, William H., Private, Company A. 105th Indiana Infantry (Morgan Raid); Second Lieutenant, Company A; 139th Indiana Infantry.

Bowser, Edwin, Private, Company A, 36th Indiana Infantry.

Boyd, Alcander, Private, 20th Indiana Battery.

Boyd, James, Private, Company A, 110th Indiana Infantry (Morgan Raid).

Boyd, William L., Private, Company A, 110th Indiana Infantry (Morgan Raid).

*Boyer, Jeremiah, Private, Company A, 57th Indiana Infantry.

Boyer. Nimrod E., Private, Unassigned, 22nd Indiana Infantry.

*Boyer, William, Private, Company A, 57th Indiana Infantry.

Bradbury, Allison B., Private, Company C, 109th Indiana Infantry (Morgan Raid).

Bradbury, James, Private, Company C. 36th Indiana Infantry.

Bradford, George, Private, Company F, 84th Indiana Infantry.

*Bradford, James T., Private, Company F. 57th Indiana Infantry.

Bradford, William S,. Captain. Company F, 57th Indiana Infantry.

*Bradick, James R., Private, Company I. 3rd Indiana Cavalry.   *

**Bradway, Josiah, Private, Company A, 33rd Indiana Infantry.

Bradway, William, Private, Corporal, Sergeant, Company A, 36th Indiana Infantry.

Brandon, Frank, Private, Company B, 110th Indiana Infantry (Morgan Raid).

*Brandon. George W., Private, Company C. 109th Indiana Infantry (Morgan Raid); Private, Company G, 7th Indiana Cavalry.

Branham, John F., Private, Company A, 11th Indiana Infantry.

Brannon, John. Private, Company K, 36th Indiana Infantry.

Brannon, Thomas, Private. Company A. 4th Regiment. 1st Army Corps (Hancock's Veteran Corps).

Branson. Arthur L., Private, Corporal, Company A, 139th Indiana Infantry; Private, Bugler, 2nd Indiana Battery, re-organized.

Brattain, Hiram B., Private, Company B. 8th Indiana Infantry (three months); Second Lieutenant, Company H, 69th Indiana Infantry

**Brattain, John W., Corporal, Sergeant. Company E, 34th Indiana Infantry.

**Brattain, Jonathan. Private, Company E. 34th Indiana Infantry.

**Brattain, Solomon F., Private. Company E. 33rd Indiana Infantry

Bray, Thomas J., Private, Company K, 148th Indiana Infantry.

Breniser. William, Private, Company I, 9th Indiana Infantry.

Brenneman, Daniel W., Private, Company A, 110th Indiana Infantry (Morgan Raid).

Brenneman, Eli, Musician, Company H. 140th Indiana Infantry.

Brenneman, George. Musician, Company H; Principal Musician, Non Commissioned Staff, 69th Indiana Infantry.

**Brenner, Henry, Private, Company H. 36th Indiana Infantry; Private, Company H. 30th Indiana Infantry, re-organized.

Brewer. Andrew T., Private. Company K, 36th Indiana Infantry.

Brewer. David F., Private, Company A, 36th Indiana Infantry; Sergeant, Company H, 30th Indiana Infantry, re-organized..   · ·

Brewer, John M., Private, Company A, 105th Indiana Infantry (Morgan Raid).

Brewington, Elijah, Private, Company K, 19th Indiana Infantry.

Brewington, John D., Private, Company I, 124th Indiana Infantry.

**Brewington. Robert F., First Lieutenant, Company K, 68th Indiana Infantry.

Bricker, John M., Private, Company I. 69th Indiana Infantry.

**Bridget, Henry C., Private, Corporal, Company G, 36th Indiana Infantry.

Bridget, John, Private. Company A. 36th Indiana Infantry.

Brietenback, George, Private, Company I, 9th Indiana Infantry.

Bright, Alexander, Private, Company K, 105th Indiana Infantry (Morgan Raid).

Bright, Benjamin, Private, Company I, 69th Indiana Infantry.

Bright, Daniel R., Private, Company H, 140th Indiana Infantry.

Bright, Jesse, Private, Company H, 140th Indiana Infantry.

Bright, John J., Private, Company H, 147th Indiana Infantry.

Bristol, Benjamin W., Private, Company H, 69th Indiana Infantry.

**Brodrick, James W., Private, Corporal, Company C, 2nd Indiana Cavalry. (See Alphabetical List C).

Bronnenberg, Carl, Private, Company H, 69th Indiana Infantry. (See Alphabetical List B).

Bronnenberg, William, Private, Company H, 69th Indiana Infantry.

*Brooks, James, Private, Company E, 9th Indiana Cavalry.

*Brooks, Joseph, Private, Company A, 57th Indiana Infantry.

Brooks, Thomas, Private, Company F, 6th Indiana Infantry (three months); Private, Company I, 3rd Indiana Cavalry.

Brookshire, Eli, Private, Company G, 84th Indiana Infantry.

Brookshire, Isham S., First Sergeant, Company C, 28th U. S. C. T.

Brookshire, Thomas J., Corporal, Company B, 110th Indiana Infantry (Morgan Raid); Private, Company E, 9th Indiana Cavalry.

Brookshire, William, Corporal, Company D, 36th Indiana Infantry.

Brosius, Jacob F., Private, Company H, 147th Indiana Infantry.

Brosius, John H., Private, Company F, 6th Indiana Infantry (three months); Second Lieutenant, Company I, 54th Indiana Infantry (three months); Private, 2nd Indiana Battery, re-organized.

Brosius, John M., Private, Company A, 105th Indiana Infantry (Morgan Raid).

Brosius, William, Private, Company K, 36th Indiana Infantry; Private, Company A, 105th Indiana Infantry (Morgan Raid); Private, Company I, 3rd Indiana Cavalry; Private, Company B, 8th Indiana Cavalry, re-organized.

Brown, Archibald, Private, Company C, 36th Indiana Infantry.

Brown, Benjamin F., Private, Company E, 9th Indiana Cavalry.

Brown, Caleb, Private, Company B, 9th Indiana Infantry.

**Brown, Charles, Private, Company E, 13th Indiana Infantry, re-organized.

Brown, George, Private, Company E, 8th Indiana Infantry (three years); Private, Company E, 9th Indiana Cavalry.

**Brown, George H., Corporal, Sergeant, Second Lieutenant, Company B, 89th Indiana Infantry.

Brown, George J., Private, Company E, 8th Indiana Infantry (three years); Corporal, Company K, 54th Indiana Infantry (three months); Sergeant, Company H, 140th Indiana Infantry.

Brown, Harvey F., Farrier and Blacksmith, Company I, 3rd Indiana Cavalry; Sergeant, Company B, 110th Indiana Infantry (Morgan Raid); Private, Sergeant, Company B, 139th Indiana Infantry.

Brown, Henry, Private, Company C, 5th Indiana Cavalry.

Brown, Henry, Private, Company G, 9th Indiana Infantry.

Brown, Isaac, Private, Company B, 147th Indiana Infantry.

Brown, Isaac G., Private, Company D, 36th Indiana Infantry.

Brown, James, Private, Company B, 110th Indiana Infantry (Morgan Raid).

Brown, James A., Corporal, Sergeant, Company E, 8th Indiana Infantry (three years).

Brown, James M., Private, Company H, 69th Indiana Infantry.

Brown, John H., Private, 2nd Indiana Battery, re-organized.

Brown, John H., Private, Company E., 8th Indiana Infantry (three years).

Brown, Joseph M., Private, Company I, 69th Indiana Infantry; Private, Company B, 110th Indiana Infantry (Morgan Raid).

Brown, Levi, Regimental Band, 36th Indiana Infantry.

Brown, Lewis E., Corporal, Company H. 147th Indiana Infantry.
Brown, Milton C, Private, Sergeant, Company G. 16th Indiana Infantry.
Brown, Moses H. G., Private, Company I, 3rd Indiana Cavalry.
Brown, Nathaniel, Private, Company I, 69th Indiana Infantry.
Brown, Nathaniel, Corporal, Company F, 57th Indiana Infantry.
Brown, Oliver S., Private, Company H, 55th Indiana Infantry; Private, Company B, 110th Indiana Infantry (Morgan Raid).
Brown, Riley S., Private, Company H, 69th Indiana Infantry.
Brown, Robert B., Private, Unassigned, 53rd Indiana Infantry.
Brown, Theodore F., Private, Company A, 139th Indiana Infantry.
Brown, William, Private, Company C, 5th Indiana Cavalry.
Brown, William H., Private, Company A. 54th Indiana Infantry, (one year).
Brown, William W., Private, 19th Indiana Battery.
Brownfield, George K., Private, Corporal, 19th Indiana Battery.
Brumfield, Barton, Private, Company E, 11th Indiana Infantry.
Brunner, William, Private, Corporal. Company H, 100th Indiana Infantry.
Bryant, John A., Private, Company A. 36th Indiana Infantry; Private, Company H, 30th Indiana Infantry, re-organized.
Buckles, Francis, Private, Company C, 36th Indiana Infantry.
Buckner, William, Private, Company C. 147th Indiana Infantry.
Budd, Charles C., Private, Company A. 139th Indiana Infantry.
Bufkin, Oliver, Private, Company A, 110th Indiana Infantry (Morgan Raid).
Bulger, Strather J., Private, Company F. 124th Indiana Infantry.
Bullock, John P., Private, Company F, 57th Indiana Infantry.
**Bunce, James W., Private, Company A, 15th Indiana Infantry.
**Bunch, George W., Private, Sergeant, Company B, 19th Indiana Infantry; Sergeant, Second Lieutenant, First Lieutenant, Captain, Company C, 20th Indiana Infantry, re-organized.
Bundy, Charles, Private, Company B, 110th Indiana Infantry (Morgan Raid).
Bundy, Elias M., Private, Company I, 69th Indiana Infantry.
Bundy, George R., Private, Company D, 36th Indiana Infantry.
Bundy, Jordan J., Private, Company A, 110th Indiana Infantry (Morgan Raid).
Bundy, Martin L., Major and Paymaster and Brevet Lieutenant, Colonel, Staff, U. S. Volunteers. (See General Officers, Chapter IX).
Bundy, William W., Private, Company A. 105th Indiana Infantry (Morgan Raid).
*Bunker, Albert, Private, Company H, 140th Indiana Infantry.
Bunker, Jesse, Private, Company A. 36th Indiana Infantry; Private, Sergeant, Company C, 147th Indiana Infantry.
Bunker, Lewis, Private, 19th Indiana Battery.
Bunker, William, Private, Company I. 84th Indiana Infantry; Private, Company K, 57th Indiana Infantry.
Bunner, Christopher, Private, Company H. 147th Indiana Infantry.
Burch, Edwin, Private, Company I. 124th Indiana Infantry.
Burch, Erastus, Private, Company I. 124th Indiana Infantry.
Burch, John E. W., Private, Company H. 140th Indiana Infantry.
Burch, Thomas II. C., Sergeant, Company H. 140th Indiana Infantry.
Burch, Thompson P., Private, Company F, 6th Indiana Infantry (three months).
**Burchett, Thomas J., Private, Company G. 8th Indiana Infantry (three years). (See Alphabetical List B).
Burchman, William J., Private, Company A. 38th Indiana Infantry.
Burden, Zachariah, Private, Company F. 8th U. S. C. T.
Burdette, Joseph B., Private, Company A, 57th Indiana Infantry.
*Burk, Daniel, Private, Sergeant, Company A, 57th Indiana Infantry.
Burk, George W., Private, Company B. 110th Indiana Infantry (Morgan Raid); Private, Company B. 139th Indiana Infantry.

*Burk, James H., First Sergeant, Second Lieutenant, First Lieutenant, Captain, Company H, 37th Indiana Infantry.

Burk, John, Corporal, Company I, 3rd Indiana Cavalry.

Burk, Milton, Private, Company H, 147th Indiana Infantry.

Burks, John, Private, Unassigned, 33rd Indiana Infantry.

Burns, James, Private, Company B, 8th Indiana Infantry (three months).

Burns, Robert, Private, Corporal, Company C, 36th Indiana Infantry.

Burr, Chauncey S., Sergeant, Company E, 8th Indiana Infantry (three years); Second Lieutenant, Company C, 109th Indiana Infantry (Morgan Raid).

Burr, John, Private, Company G, 17th Indiana Infantry.

Burr, Miles H., Private, Company C, 109th Indiana Infantry (Morgan Raid).

Burris, Aaron, Private, Company A, 105th Indiana Infantry (Morgan Raid).

Burris, Arthur M., Private, Company A, 139th Indiana Infantry.

Burris, Asahel, Private, Company B, 110th Indiana Infantry (Morgan Raid).

Burris, Daniel, Private, Company F, 84th Indiana Infantry.

Burris, Daniel H., Private, Knightstown Guards, Indiana Legion; Private, Company A, 105th Indiana Infantry (Morgan Raid); Private, Company A, 139th Indiana Infantry; Private, Unassigned, 22nd Indiana Infantry.

Burris, Daniel L., Private, Company F, 6th Indiana Infantry (three months).

Burris, Elwood, Corporal, Company A, 105th Indiana Infantry (Morgan Raid); Private, Company A, 38th Indiana Infantry.

*Burris, Eden, Private, Company A, 57th Indiana Infantry.

Burris, Henry J., Private, Company F, 84th Indiana Infantry.

Burris, Jacob, Private, Company A, 19th Indiana Infantry.

‘Burris, Mathias, Private, Company A, 105th Indiana Infantry (Morgan Raid); Private, 19th Indiana Battery.

*Burris, Nelson, Private, Company A; Principal Musician, Non Commissioned Staff, 57th Indiana Infantry.

Burt, William, Private, Company E, 40th Indiana Infantry.

Burton, George, Captain, New Castle Guards, Indiana Legion; Captain, Company B, 110th Indiana Infantry (Morgan Raid); Private, Company A, 30th Indiana Infantry, re-organized. (See Mexican War).

*Burton, Marcus M., Private, Company I, 3rd Indiana Cavalry.

**Burton, Thomas C., Private, Company E, 50th Indiana Infantry.

Bush, Amos L., Private, Company A, 36th Indiana Infantry.

Buson, Isaac M., Private, Company A, 110th Indiana Infantry (Morgan Raid).

Butler, Amos, Private, Company F, 84th Indiana Infantry.

Butler, Charles M., Quartermaster Sergeant, Second Lieutenant, 19th Indiana Battery.

Butler, Hiram, Private, Company F, 6th Indiana Infantry (three months); Private, Company D, 36th Indiana Infantry.

Butler, William, Private, Company F, 6th Indiana Infantry (three months); Sergeant, Second Lieutenant, Company D, 36th Indiana Infantry.

Bye, David M., Private, Company A, 147th Indiana Infantry.

Byerly, Wesley, Corporal, Company A, 105th Indiana Infantry (Morgan Raid).

Byers, David S., Corporal, Company D, 36th Indiana Infantry.

Byers, Jacob S., Private, Company A, 105th Indiana Infantry (Morgan Raid); Private, Company A, 139th Indiana Infantry.

Byers, John T., Private, Company F, 84th Indiana Infantry.

Byers, Joseph M., Corporal, Sergeant, Company F, 84th Indiana Infantry.

Byers, Luther J., Private, Company B, 110th Indiana Infantry (Morgan Raid).

Byers, Samuel T., Private, Company F, 84th Indiana Infantry.

Byers, Squire H., Private, Company A, 105th Indiana Infantry (Morgan Raid).

Byers, William T., Private, Company A, 57th Indiana Infantry.

Byrket, Isaiah, Private, Company F, 84th Indiana Infantry.

Byrket, Jacob, Private, Company I, 3rd Indiana Cavalry; Private, Company F, 84th Indiana Infantry.

Byrket, Jesse, Private, Company I, 3rd Indiana Cavalry.

Byrket, Peter, Private, Company E, 9th Indiana Cavalry.

Byrnes, James J., Musician, Company I, 69th Indiana Infantry.

C

*Cabe, Job, Private, Company F, 57th Indiana Infantry.

Cain, George H, Private, Company B, 8th Indiana Infantry (three months); Corporal, First Sergeant, First Lieutenant. Company G, 84th Indiana Infantry.

Cain, Patrick, Private, Company H, 69th Indiana Infantry.

Caldwell, Henry, Corporal, Company I, 84th Indiana Infantry.

Caldwell, Ira, Sergeant. First Sergeant. First Lieutenant, Company I, 84th Indiana Infantry.

Caldwell, Jefferson, Private, Company I, 84th Indiana Infantry; Sergeant, Company K, 57th Indiana Infantry.

Calhoun, James E., Private, Company I, 69th Indiana Infantry.

Callahan, Darilus D., Private, Company K, 105th Indiana Infantry (Morgan Raid).

Callahan, George W., Corporal, Company I, 69th Indiana Infantry.

Callahan, John M., Private, Company K, 105th Indiana Infantry (Morgan Raid).

Callahan, John W., Senior, Private, Company I, 69th Indiana Infantry.

Callahan, John W., Junior, Private, Company I, 69th Indiana Infantry.

Callahan, William R., Private. Company A, 36th Indiana Infantry.

Calvert, Charles L., Cadet. (See U. S. Military Academy).

Camblin, William, Private, Company A, 36th Indiana Infantry.

Cameron, John D., Private, Company A, 38th Indiana Infantry.

Cameron, Joseph B., Private, Company I, 54th Indiana Infantry (three months); Private, Company B, 11th Indiana Infantry.

Cameron, William M., Private, Company F. 6th Indiana Infantry (three months); Sergeant, First Sergeant, First Lieutenant, Company F, 84th Indiana Infantry.

Campbell, Adam P., Private, Company C, 147th Indiana Infantry.

Campbell, Edward H., Sergeant, Company D. 147th Indiana Infantry.

Campbell, John A., Sergeant, First Sergeant, Company K, 36th Indiana Infantry.

Campbell, John B., Private, 4th Indiana Battery.

*Campbell, Thomas J., Private. Company I, 3rd Indiana Cavalry.

Camplin, James M., Musician, Company D, 36th Indiana Infantry.

Camplin, John F., Private, Company D, 36th Indiana Infantry.

Camplin, Thomas H., Private, Company A, 139th Indiana Infantry.

Canaday, Charles W., Private, Company H. 8th Indiana Infantry (three years).

Canaday, John H., Private, Company G, 84th Indiana Infantry.

Canfield, George W., Corporal, Company A, 124th Indiana Infantry.

*Canfield, William, Private, Company H, 147th Indiana Infantry.

Cannon, Stansberry. Private, Company D, 147th Indiana Infantry.

Cantley, George M., Corporal, Sergeant, Second Lieutenant, Company D. 36th Indiana Infantry.

Cantley, William H., Private. Corporal, 4th Indiana Battery.

Carl, Charles, Private, Company K, 13th Indiana Infantry, re-organized.

Carmichael, Milton, Private. Company F, 57th Indiana Infantry.

Carpenter, De Witt C., Private, Company B. 139th Indiana Infantry.

Carpenter, William H., Private. Company B, 139th Indiana Infantry.

Carper, Jacob D., Private, Company C. 147th Indiana Infantry.

Carr, Anthony P., Private, Company B, 19th Indiana Infantry.

Carr, Daniel, Private, Company I, 84th Indiana Infantry.

**Carr, George W., Private, Company A. 11th Indiana Infantry.

Carr, Robert B., First Sergeant, Second Lieutenant. First Lieutenant. Company A, 36th Indiana Infantry.

Carroll, George, Private, Company I, 69th Indiana Infantry.

*Carroll, Henry, Private, Company A, 57th Indiana Infantry.

Carson, Samuel, Private, Company F, 6th Indiana Infantry (three months); Private, 2nd Indiana Battery; Private, Company A, 4th Regiment, 1st Army Corps (Hancock's Veteran Corps).

Carter, Benjamin F., Private, Company H, 69th Indiana Infantry.

Carter, Henry B., Private, Company K, 54th Indiana Infantry (three months).

Carter, Jesse, Private, Company C, 109th Indiana Infantry (Morgan Raid).

Carter, John J., Private, Company E, 8th Indiana Infantry (three years).

Carter, Reece, Private, Company H, 69th Indiana Infantry.

Carter, Solomon F., Private, Company A, 30th Indiana Infantry, re-organized.

Carter, Thomas, Private, Company D, Second Indiana Cavalry.

Cartwright, Henry, Private, Company I, 69th Indiana Infantry.

Cartwright, James C., Private, Company D, 36th Indiana Infantry.

Cartwright, James W., Private, 20th Indiana Battery.

Cary, Oliver H. P., Lieutenant Colonel, Staff, 36th Indiana Infantry. (See Mexican War).

Case, Charles R., Drum Major, Non Commissioned Staff, 8th Indiana Infantry (three months); Second Lieutenant, Captain, Company E, 36th Indiana Infantry.

Case, Daniel D., Private, Company B, 8th Indiana Infantry (three months); Corporal, Company E, 8th Indiana Infantry (three years).

Case, Elijah H., Regimental Band, 36th Indiana Infantry.

Case, John B., Private, Company A, 110th Indiana Infantry (Morgan Raid); Private, Company B, 139th Indiana Infantry.

Case, John`B. S., Private, Company B, 110th Indiana Infantry (Morgan Raid).

Case, John F., Private, Corporal, Company K, 148th Indiana Infantry.

Case, John H., Regimental Band. 36th Indiana Infantry; Private, Sergeant, Company E, 9th Indiana Cavalry.

**Casely, John T., Private, Company A, 133rd Indiana Infantry.

Caster, William H., Private, Company C, 84th Indiana Infantry.

*Casterline, Ziba, Assistant Surgeon, Staff, 84th Indiana Infantry.

**Castetter, Burton W., Private, Company B, 48th Indiana Infantry.

Castor, Lewis, Private, Company K, 54th Indiana Infantry (three months); Corporal, Company A, 54th Indiana Infantry (one year); Private, Company B, 21st Indiana Infantry, re-organized as 1st Heavy Artillery.

Catt, Daniel C., Private, Company K, 36th Indiana Infantry; Private, 22nd Indiana Battery.

Catt, George, Private, Company I, 3rd Indiana Cavalry.

Catt, William F., Private, Company B, 99th Indiana Infantry.

Chalfant, Jonathan, Seaman, U. S. Navy.

Chambers, David W., Private, Company B, 8th Indiana Infantry (three months); First Lieutenant, Captain, Company D, 36th Indiana Infantry.

Chambers, James A., Private, Corporal, Company B, 139th Indiana Infantry.

Champ, George W., Private, Company E, 106th Indiana Infantry (Morgan Raid); Private, Company B, Assistant Surgeon, Staff, 139th Indiana Infantry.

*Chandler, George L., Private, Company A, 57th Indiana Infantry.

Chapman, Joseph, Private, Company G, 147th Indiana Infantry.

Chappell, Jacob, Private, Company A, 36th Indiana Infantry.

Chappell, Milton F., Private, Company A, 105th Indiana Infantry (Morgan Raid).

Charles, John T., Private, Company A, 105th Indiana Infantry (Morgan Raid).

Charles, Oliver, Second Lieutenant, Company I, 3rd Indiana Cavalry.

Charles, Sylvanus, Private, Company A, 36th Indiana Infantry.

Cheeseman, David, Private, Company A, 110th Indiana Infantry (Morgan Raid).

Chenoweth Isaac N., First Sergeant, Company F, 124th Indiana Infantry.

Chenoweth, John F., Private, Company F, 57th Indiana Infantry.

Chew, Harvey B., Private, Corporal, Company D, 36th Indiana Infantry; Private, Company E, 9th Regiment, 1st Army Crops (Hancock's Veteran Corps).

Childers, Shady, Private, 19th Indiana Battery.

Chrisman, Ephraim, Private, 4th Indiana Battery.

Clair, Thomas, Private, Company I, 3rd Indiana Cavalry.

Clair, Timothy, Private, Company K, 36th Indiana Infantry.

Clanton, Pinson W., Private, Company B, 8th Indiana Infantry (three months).

Clapper, John, Private, Company B, 134th Indiana Infantry.

Clapsaddle, George W., Private, Company G, 84th Indiana Infantry.

Clark, Alpheus, Private, Company A, 54th Indiana Infantry (one year).

Clark, Benjamin, Private, Company A, 54th Indiana Infantry (one year).

**Clark, John, Private, 24th Indiana Battery.

Clark, Joseph, Private, Company B, 99th Indiana Infantry.

Clark, Milton, Private, Company H, 69th Indiana Infantry.

Clark, Nathan M, Private, Company I, 123rd Indiana Infantry.

Clark, Simon, Private, Company H, 69th Indiana Infantry.

Clark, William C, Private, Company H, 69th Indiana Infantry.

Clark, William F, Private, Company K, 54th Indiana Infantry (three months).

Clein, Simon, Private Company K, 105th Indiana Infantry (Morgan Raid).

Clellan, James W., Private, Company H, 69th Indiana Infantry.

Clements, Courtland C, Acting Midshipman. (See U. S. Naval Academy).

*Clements, David, Private, Company E, 8th Indiana Infantry (three years).

Clements, Milton F., Private, Company B, 110th Indiana Infantry (Morgan Raid).

Clevenger, John R., Private, Company E, 8th Indiana Infantry (three years).

Clevenger, Jonathan J., Private, Company G, 134th Indiana Infantry.

Clevenger, Joshua, Private, Company E, 8th Indiana Infantry (three years).

Clevenger, Seth, Private, Company C, 109th Indiana Infantry (Morgan Raid); Private, Company F, 124th Indiana Infantry.

Clifford, Cassius B., Private, Company I, 3rd Indiana Cavalry; Private, Company M, 8th Indiana Cavalry, re-organized.

Clifford, David, Private, Company B, 5th Indiana Cavalry.

Clift, James M,. Private, Company A, 110th Indiana Infantry (Morgan Raid); Private, Company A, 30th Indiana Infantry, re-organized.

Clinard, Franklin S., Corporal, Company K, 36th Indiana Infantry.

Cline, Adam H., Private, Company H, 69th Indiana Infantry.

*Cloud, Henry C., Private, Company F, 57th Indiana Infantry.

Cloud, Joseph, Private, Company G, 147th Indiana Infantry.

Cluggish, Robert, Private, Company B, 110th Indiana Infantry (Morgan Raid).

Clutch, George H., Private, Corporal, Sergeant, First Sergeant, 2nd Indiana Battery.

Clymer, John V., Captain, Company B, 156th Indiana Infantry.

Coats, Elijah H., Private, Company F, 6th Indiana Infantry (three months).

Coats, Richard B., Private, 2nd Indiana Battery.

Cochran, Andrew J., Private, Company D, 8th Indiana Infantry (three years).

Cochran, David S., Corporal, Company F, 57th Indiana Infantry.

Coe, John, Private, Company A, 110th Indiana Infantry (Morgan Raid).

Oofa, Nicholas, Private, Company A, 110th Indiana Infantry (Morgan Raid).

Coffman, David, Private, Company E, 8th Indiana Infantry (three years).

*Coffman, William A., Private, Company E, 9th Indiana Cavalry.

*Coke, Jacob J., Private, Company H, 147th Indiana Infantry.

Cole, John, Second Lieutenant, Company F, 6th Indiana Infantry (three months).

Cole, John J., Corporal, Company F, 6th Indiana Infantry (three months); Private, Wagoner, 2nd Indiana Battery; Private, Company A, 4th Regiment, 1st Army Corps (Hancock's Veteran Corps).

Coleman, James, Private, Company E, 9th Indiana Cavalry.

Collins, Andrew J., Private, Company I, 69th Indiana Infantry; Private, Company C, 24th Indiana Infantry.

COMPANY I, 69th INDIANA INFANTRY.

Collins, George W., Private, Company E, 116th Indiana Infantry;
69th Indiana Infantry; Private, Company C, 24th Indiana

Collins, Joel, Private, Company A, 139th Indiana Infantry.

Collins, John W., Corporal, Company F, 124th Indiana Infantry

Collins, Robert A., Private, Company B, 8th Indiana Infantry.
Captain, Company I, 69th Indiana Infantry.

Collins, William B., Private, Company A, 110th Indiana Infantry

Compton, Evan, Private, Company K, 105th Indiana Infantry

Comstock, Daniel W., Private, Company E; Sergeant Major
Staff; First Lieutenant, Company F, and Captain, Company C.

Confare, Ephraim, Private, Quartermaster Sergeant, 2nd
Lieutenant, Company H, Captain, Company K, 2nd Missouri Light

Confrey, Hugh, Private, Unassigned, 22nd Indiana Infantry

Conger, Gresham W., Private, Company I, 3rd Indiana Cavalry
M. 8th Indiana Cavalry, re-organized.

**Conklin, Henry, Private, Company A, 5th Indiana Cavalry

Conklin, John H., Private, Company A, 139th Indiana Infantry
t, 2nd Indiana Infantry.

*Conley, John, Private, Company H, 140th Indiana Infantry

**Conley, Thomas H., Private, Company I, 36th Indiana Infantry

Conn, Adam Eli, Private, Company F, 57th Indiana Infantry
25th Indiana Battery

Connell, Joseph W., Second Lieutenant, Company B, 8th Indiana
months); First Lieutenant, Company C, 36th Indiana Infantry

Connell, Zachariah D., Private, Company B, 139th Indiana Infantry
any H, 147th Indiana Infantry.

Conner, Daniel, Private, Company I, 69th Indiana Infantry

Conner, Daniel M., Private, Company K, 105th Indiana Infantry

Conner, Martin V., Private, Company G, 84th Indiana Infantry

Conniard, George W., Sergeant, Company I, 6th Indiana Infantry

Conrad, George W., Private, Company A, 36th Indiana Infantry
H, 36th Indiana Infantry, re-organized.

Conway, Thomas I., Private, Company B, 110th Indiana Infantry
Private, Company B, 139th Indiana Infantry.

Conway, William S., Private, Corporal, Company A, 124th Indiana Infantry

Conwell, David, Private, Company I, 69th Indiana Infantry

Conwell, Elias, Private, Company A, 54th Indiana Infantry

Conwell, George W., Private, Company I, 69th Indiana Infantry.

Cook, Daniel H., Private, Company K, 105th Indiana Infantry (Morgan

Cook, Elwood, Private, Company B, 139th Indiana Infantry.

Cook, John H., Private, Company F, 6th Indiana Infantry (three months)

Cook, Thomas J., Private, Company C, 109th Indiana Infantry (Morgan
vate, Company D, First Lieutenant, Company K, 147th Indiana Infantry.

Cook, William, Private, Company D, 8th Indiana Infantry (three years)

Cook, William, Private, Company D, 36th Indiana Infantry

Cook, William M., Private, Company H, 140th Indiana Infantry.

Cook, Willis J., Private, Company I, 84th Indiana Infantry.

Cool, John G., Corporal, Company A, 36th Indiana Infantry.

Coon, Allen W., Private, Company D, 36th Indiana Infantry.

Coon, Calvin, Private, Company B, 110th Indiana Infantry (Morgan Raid)

**Coon, Eli, Private, Company H, 72nd Indiana Infantry; Private, Company
Indiana Infantry.

Coon, Isaac, Private, Company B, 110th Indiana Infantry (Morgan Raid);
Company H, 147th Indiana Infantry.

Coon, Job T., Private, Company C, 147th Indiana Infantry.

Coon, John, Private, Company I, 3rd Indiana Cavalry.

COMPANY·I, 69th INDIANA INFANTRY.

Collins, George W., Private ,Company E, 116th Indiana Infantry; Private, Company I, 69th Indiana Infantry; Private, Company C, 24th Indiana Infantry.

Collins, Joel, Private, Company A, 139th Indiana Infantry.

Collins, John W., Corporal. Company F, 124th Indiana Infantry.

Collins, Robert K., Private, Company B, 8th Indiana Infantry (three months); Captain, Company I, 69th Indiana Infantry.

Collins, William B., Private, Company A, 110th Indiana Infantry (Morgan Raid).

Compton, Evan, Private, Company K, 105th Indiana Infantry (Morgan Raid).

Comstock, Daniel W., Private, Company E; Sergeant Major, Non Commissioned Staff; First Lieutenant, Company F, and Captain, Company C, 9th Indiana Cavalry.

Confare, Ephraim, Private, Quartermaster Sergeant, 2nd Indiana Battery; First Lieutenant, Company H, Captain, Company K, 2nd Missouri Light Artillery

Confrey, Hugh, Private, Unassigned, 22nd Indiana Infantry.

Conger, Gresham W., Private, Company ·I, 3rd Indiana Cavalry; Private. Company M, 8th Indiana·Cavalry, re-organized.

**Conklin, Henry, Private, Company A, 9th Indiana Cavalry.

Conklin, John H., Private, Company A, 139th Indiana Infantry; Private, Company I, 42nd Indiana Infantry.

*Conley, John, Private, Company H, 140th Indiana Infantry.

**Conley, Thomas H., Private, Company I. 36th Indiana Infantry.

Conn, Adam Eli, Private, Company F, 57th Indiana Infantry; Private, Corporal, 25th Indiana Battery.

Connell. Joseph W., Second Lieutenant, Company B, 8th Indiana Infantry (three months); First Lieutenant, Company C, 36th Indiana Infantry.

Connell, Zachariah D., Private, Company B. 139th Indiana Infantry; Corporal. Company H, 147th Indiana Infantry.

Conner, Daniel, Private, Company I, 69th Indiana Infantry.

Conner. Daniel M., Private. Company K. 105th Indiana Infantry (Morgan Raid).

Conner, Martin V., Private, Company G, 84th Indiana Infantry.

Conniard, George W., Sergeant, Company F. 6th Indiana Infantry (three months).

Conrad, George W., Private, Company A, 36th Indiana Infantry; Private, Company H, 30th Indiana Infantry, re-organized.

Conway, Thomas L., Private, Company B, 110th Indiana Infantry (Morgan Raid); Private, Company B, 139th Indiana Infantry.

Conway, William S., Private, Corporal, Company A, 124th Indiana Infantry.

Conwell, David, Private, Company I, 69th Indiana Infantry.

Conwell, Elias, Private, Company A, 54th Indiana Infantry (one year).

Conwell, George W., Private, Company I. 69th Indiana Infantry.

Cook, Daniel H., Private, Company K, 105th Indiana Infantry (Morgan Raid).

Cook. Elwood, Private, Company B, 139th Indiana Infantry.

Cook, John H., Private, Company F. 6th Indiana Infantry (three months).

Cook. Thomas J., Private. Company C. 109th Indiana Infantry (Morgan Raid); Private, Company D. First Lieutenant, Company K, 147th Indiana Infantry.

Cook, William, Private, Company D, 8th Indiana Infantry (three years).

Cook, William, Private, Company D, 36th Indiana Infantry.

Cook, William·M., Private. Company H, 140th Indiana Infantry.

Cook, Willis J., Private, Company I, 84th Indiana Infantry.

Cool. John G., Corporal. Company A, 36th Indiana Infantry.

Coon. Allen W., Private, Company D, 36th Indiana Infantry.

Coon. Calvin. Private. Company B. 110th Indiana Infantry (Morgan Raid).

**Coon, Eli. Private. Company H, 72nd Indiana Infantry; Private, Company A, 44th Indiana Infantry.

Coon. Isaac, Private, Company B. 110th Indiana Infantry (Morgan Raid); Private. Company H, 147th Indiana Infantry.

Coon, Job T., Private. Company C, 147th Indiana Infantry.

Coon. John. Private. Company I, 3rd Indiana Cavalry.

Coon, Noah W., Private, Company D, 36th Indiana Infantry.

Cooper, Caleb H., Second Lieutenant, First Lieutenant, Company E, 9th Indiana Cavalry.

*Cooper, Elbert, Private, Company H, 140th Indiana Infantry.

Cooper, Imla W., Sergeant, Company D, 147th Indiana Infantry.

Cooper, James F., Private, Company F, 6th Indiana Infantry (three months); Private, Company A, 36th Indiana Infantry.

Cooper, James M., Private, Company D, 19th Indiana Infantry.

Cooper, John E., Private, Company D, 147th Indiana Infantry.

Cooper, John W., Private, Company A, 110th Indiana Infantry (Morgan Raid).

*Cooper, Richard P., Private, Company F, 84th Indiana Infantry.

Cooper, Thomas P., Private, Company I, 69th Indiana Infantry.

*Cooper, William, Private, Company I, 3rd Indiana Cavalry.

Cooper, William L., Private, Company A, 105th Indiana Infantry (Morgan Raid); Private, Company A, 139th Indiana Infantry.

Copeland, Exum, Private, Company D, 36th Indiana Infantry; Private, Company A, 105th Indiana Infantry (Morgan Raid); Private, Company E, 9th Indiana Cavalry.

Copeland, Levi W., Private, Corporal, Company I, 69th Indiana Infantry.

Copeland, Seth, Private, Company A, 105th Indiana Infantry (Morgan Raid).

Copeland, Wesley, Private, Company B, 139th Indiana Infantry.

*Cornell, John F., Corporal, Company H, 147th Indiana Infantry.

Corwin, William, Private, Company A, 110th Indiana Infantry (Morgan Raid).

**Corya, William T., Private, Company D, 54th Indiana Infantry (three months).

Cosand, Cornelius W., Private, 24th Indiana Battery.

Cotteral, William W., Private, Company C, 109th Indiana Infantry (Morgan Raid).

**Cotton, James A., Private, Company H, 47th Indiana Infantry.

*Cottrell, Charles E., Private, Company C, 109th Indiana Infantry (Morgan Raid); Corporal, Company G, 7th Indiana Cavalry; Commissary Sergeant, Company F, 7th Indiana Cavalry, re-organized.

Cottrell, David W., Private, Company C, 109th Indiana Infantry (Morgan Raid).

Cottrell, Daniel U., Private, 3rd Indiana Battery.

Cottrell, Francis M., Private, Company C, 109th Indiana Infantry (Morgan Raid); Private, Company K, 19th Indiana Infantry; Private, Company E, 20th Indiana Infantry, re-organized.

Cottrell, John O., Private, 3rd Indiana Battery.

Councellor, Elijah, Private, Corporal, Company A, 30th Indiana Infantry, re-organized.

Courtney, Jacob, Private, Company H, 69th Indiana Infantry.

Courtney, Robert, Private, Company C, 36th Indiana Infantry.

Courtney, William C., Private, Company C, 36th Indiana Infantry.

Covalt, Cheniah, Private, Company C, 36th Indiana Infantry.

*Covey, Daniel, Private, Company H, 147th Indiana Infantry.

Covington, William, Private, Unassigned, 16th Indiana Infantry.

Cowgill, James, Private, Company K, 9th Indiana Infantry.

Cowick, Isaac, Private, Company I, 54th Indiana Infantry (one year).

*Cox, Edward, Private, Company H, 147th Indiana Infantry.

*Cox, Edward W., Corporal, Company A, 57th Indiana Infantry.

Cox, George, Private, Company B, 5th Indiana Cavalry.

Cox, Martin, Private, Company A, 110th Indiana Infantry (Morgan Raid).

**Cox, Thomas J., Private, Company I, 37th Indiana Infantry.

Cracraft, John, Private, Company K, 36th Indiana Infantry.

Cracraft, William, Private, Company F, 6th Indiana Infantry (three months); Corporal, Company I, 3rd Indiana Cavalry; Private, Company E, 9th Regiment, 1st Army Corps (Hancock's Veteran Corps).

*Craft, Homer H., Private, Company A, 57th Indiana Infantry.

*Craft. John A.. First Sergeant, First Lieutenant, Captain, Company A, 57th Indiana Infantry.

Craft. Thomas E., Private, Company A, 105th Indiana Infantry (Morgan Raid).

Craig, Caleb. Private, Company B. 139th Indiana Infantry; Private, Company H, 140th Indiana Infantry.

Craig. Daniel W., Private, 15th Indiana Battery.

Craig, Enoch, Private, Company K, 105th Indiana Infantry (Morgan Raid); Private, Company E, 8th Indiana Infantry (three years).

Craig. Hiram, Private, Company K, 54th Indiana Infantry (three months); Sergeant, Company K, 105th Indiana Infantry (Morgan Raid); Private, Company E, 9th Indiana Cavalry.

Craig, Ivason E., Private, Corporal, Company H. 140th Indiana Infantry.

Craig. Leonard H., Corporal, Company K, 105th Indiana Infantry (Morgan Raid); Private, Company H, 140th Indiana Infantry.

Craig, Levi, Private, 23rd Indiana Battery.

Craig. Samuel, Private, Company E, 8th Indiana Infantry (three years).

Craig, William R., Private, Company K, 105th Indiana Infantry (Morgan Raid); Private, Corporal, Company E, 9th Indiana Cavalry.

Crandall, Andrew J., Private, Company E, 9th Indiana Cavalry.

Crandall, James, Private, Company E, 9th Indiana Cavalry.

Crandall. Wyatt, Private, Company B. 110th Indiana Infantry (Morgan Raid); Private, Company E, 9th Indiana Cavalry.

Crasher, Peter, Private, Company K, 105th Indiana Infantry (Morgan Raid); Private, Company E, 8th Indiana Infantry (three years).

**Craven. Gilliam L., Corporal, Company B, 89th Indiana Infantry.

Crawford, Benjamin, Private, Company C, 36th Indiana Infantry.

**Crawford, Cyrus, Private, Company H; Sergeant, Major, Non Commissioned Staff; First Lieutenant, Company D, 16th Indiana Infantry.

*Crawford, Porter A.. Private, Company K, 36th Indiana Infantry

Crawford. William C., Private, Company I, 69th Indiana Infantry; Musician, Company H, 140th Indiana Infantry.

Cray, Daniel W., Private, Company B, 156th Indiana Infantry.

Cray, George W., Wagoner, Company I, 69th Indiana Infantry.

Cray, James M., Private, Company B, 147th Indiana Infantry.

Cray, John H., Private, Unassigned, 53rd Indiana Infantry.

Cray, Richard, Private, Company D, 2nd Indiana Cavalry.

Crews, Francis D., Private, Company K, 36th Indiana Infantry.

Crickmore, John A., Private, Company A, 36th Indiana Infantry.

Cripe. Jacob, Private, Company G, 84th Indiana Infantry.

Cripe. Rudolph. Private, Corporal. Company G, 84th Indiana Infantry.

Cross, Calvin, Private, Company K, 36th Indiana Infantry.

Cross, Ephraim C., Private, Sergeant, Company K, 36th Indiana Infantry.

Cross. Felix G.. First Sergeant, First Lieutenant, Company K, 84th Indiana Infantry.

Cross, Joseph A., Private, Company K, 84th Indiana Infantry.

**Cross. William H., Private, Company B, 9th Indiana Cavalry.

Crossley, Robert, Private, Company E, 8th Indiana Infantry (three years).

Crouse. Henry M.. Assistant Surgeon. Major and Surgeon,. Staff, 57th Indiana Infantry.

Crow. George, Private, Company C. 109th Indiana Infantry (Morgan Raid); Private, Company G, 7th Indiana Cavalry; Private, Company F, 7th Indiana Cavalry, re-organized.

Crull. Francis M., Private, Company E, 106th Indiana Infantry (Morgan Raid). (See Alphabetical List B).

*Culbertson, Alfred, Private, Company G. 7th Indiana Cavalry.

Culbertson, Ambrose. Private, Company D, 147th Indiana Infantry.

Culp, Samuel G., Private. 12th Indiana Battery.

*Cummings, Joel, Private, Company E, 8th Indiana Infantry (three years).
Cummings, John M,. Private, Company I, 69th Indiana Infantry.
Cummings, Thomas B., Private, Company B, 110th Indiana Infantry (Morgan Raid).
*Cummings, William, Private, Company E, 8th Indiana Infantry (three years).
Cummins, James, Private, Company B, 139th Indiana Infantry.
Curry, John C., Private, Unassigned, 33rd Indiana Infantry.
Curry, William, Private, Company F, 6th Indiana Infantry (three months).
Custer, Emmel, Private, Company B, 139th Indiana Infantry.
**Custer, John L., Musician, Company A, 8th Indiana Infantry (three months).

D

Daily, Joseph T,. Private, Company I, 84th Indiana Infantry.
Daily, William, Private, Corporal, Company C, 36th Indiana Infantry.
Dakins, William H., Private, Company F, 57th Indiana Infantry; Private, 19th Indiana Battery.
*Dale, James W., Private, Company B, 139th Indiana Infantry.
Dale, Lewis L., Captain and Chaplain, Staff, 19th Indiana Infantry.
Daniel, Abraham, Private, Unassigned, 22nd Indiana Infantry.
Daniel, Calvin, Private. Company B, 9th Indiana Infantry.
Daniel, Prear, Private, Company F, 6th Indiana Infantry (three months); Corporal, Company B, 110th Indiana Infantry (Morgan Raid); Private, Company B, 9th Indiana Cavalry.
**Daniels, David, Private, Company H., 140th Indiana Infantry.
Darling, William A., Private, Company B, 139th Indiana Infantry; Private, Company H, 147th Indiana Infantry.
Darr, William H., Private, Sergeant, 12th Indiana Battery.
Daugherty, John, Private, Company E, 36th Indiana Infantry.
Davenport, Henry, Private, Company A, 110th Indiana Infantry (Morgan Raid)
Davenport, Henry B., Private, Company B, 110th Indiana Infantry (Morgan Raid).
**David, Will C., Private, Company A, 11th Indiana Infantry.
Davidson, Amos, Private, Company D, 147th Indiana Infantry.
Davis, Abraham, Sergeant, Company A, 57th Indiana Infantry.
Davis, Albert T., Private, Corporal, Company F, 84th Indiana Infantry.
Davis, Alexander, Private, Company D. 2nd Indiana Cavalry.
Davis, Alpheus, Corporal, Company C, 36th Indiana Infantry.
Davis, Amos, Private, Company E, 9th Indiana Infantry.
**Davis, Benjamin H., Private, Company C, 155th Indiana Infantry.
Davis, Charles M., Private, Company F, 6th Indiana Infantry (three months); First Sergeant, First Lieutenant, Company K, 36th Indiana Infantry.
Davis, Charles M., Private, Unassigned, 22nd Indiana Infantry.
Davis, Cornelius J., Private, Company F, 6th Indiana Infantry (three months); Private, Company A, 36th Indiana Infantry.
Davis, David F., Sergeant, First Sergeant, Company I, 69th Indiana Infantry. (See Alphabetical List B).
Davis, Eli, Private, Company E, 9th Indiana Cavalry.
Davis, Isaac, Private, Company B, 8th Indiana Infantry (three months); Corporal, Company H, 69th Indiana Infantry.
Davis, John, Private, Company G, 84th Indiana Infantry.
Davis, John H., Private, Company H, 9th Indiana Infantry.
Davis, John H,. Private, Company I, 69th Indiana Infantry.
**Davis, John S., Musician, Company B, 8th Indiana Infantry (three years); Private, Unassigned, 32nd Indiana Infantry, re-organized.
Davis, John W., Private, Company H, 69th Indiana Infantry.
Davis, John W., Private, Company K, 99th Indiana Infantry; Private, Company B, 110th Indiana Infantry (Morgan Raid); Private, Sergeant, Company B, 139th Indiana Infantry.

Davis, Jonathan. Private, Company I, 3rd Indiana Cavalry.

Davis, Joseph, Private, Company A, 57th Indiana Infantry.

Davis, Lewis W., Private, Company B, 110th Indiana Infantry (Morgan Raid); Private, Company B, 134th Indiana Infantry.

Davis, Michael, Corporal, Company H, 69th Indiana Infantry.

Davis, Milton, Private, Company G, 7th Indiana Cavalry; Private, Company F, 7th Indiana Cavalry, re-organized.

Davis, Reason, Private, Company A, 110th Indiana Infantry (Morgan Raid).

Davis, Ulysses, Private, Company K, 36th Indiana Infantry.

Davis, William, Corporal, Company A, 36th Indiana Infantry; Sergeant, Company B, 110th Indiana Infantry (Morgan Raid).

Davis, William M. C., Private, Company E, 8th Indiana Infantry (three years).

Davis, Zigler, Sergeant, Company A, 110th Indiana Infantry (Morgan Raid).

Davison, Ira H., Private, Unassigned, 22nd Indiana Infantry.

**Davy, James, Private, Sergeant, Company C, 47th Indiana Infantry.

*Dawson, John, Private, Company A, 57th Indiana Infantry.

Dawson, Robert, Private, Company K, 36th Indiana Infantry.

Dean, Solomon, Private, Company B, 149th Indiana Infantry.

Debord, Andrew J., Private, Company F, 84th Indiana Infantry.

Debord, Drury, Private, Company A, 36th Indiana Infantry; Private, Company H, 9th Indiana Infantry.

Deck, John E., Private, First Sergeant, Second Lieutenant, Company A, 57th Indiana Infantry.

Decker, Henry C., Private, Company A, 57th Indiana Infantry.

Decker, William, Private, Company B, 149th Indiana Infantry.

Decker, William J,. Private, Company A, 139th Indiana Infantry.

Deem, Joseph C., Second Lieutenant, Company A, 105th Indiana Infantry (Morgan Raid).

Deem, Martin, Private, Company A, 36th Indiana Infantry.

Deem, Sedley A., Private, Sergeant, Company K, 36th Indiana Infantry.

*Deen, Samuel, Private, Company H, 147th Indiana Infantry.

Deitzer, Robert, Private, Company B, 124th Indiana Infantry.

Delong, Gifford, Private, Company E, 9th Indiana Cavalry.

Delong, Richard, Private, Company B, 139th Indiana Infantry.

Demick, Adolphus, Private, Corporal, Company G, 16th Indiana Infantry.

Demick, Milton, Private, Company G, 16th Indiana Infantry.

Demick, William H., Private, Company D, 19th Indiana Infantry.

**De Moss, William, Private, Company E, 7th Indiana Infantry.

*Demy, Philip J., Private, Company H, 147th Indiana Infantry.

Dennis, Joseph R., Private, Company F, 84th Indiana Infantry.

Dennis, Thomas P., Private, Company I, 69th Indiana Infantry.

Dennis, Van Buren, Private, Company F, 6th Indiana Infantry (three months).

Dennis Whitesel, Private, Company I, 3rd Indiana Cavalry.

Dent, James I., Private, Company F, 84th Indiana Infantry.

**Denton, Benjamin N., Private, Corporal, Company H, 150th Indiana Infantry.

*Denwiddie, Samuel, Sergeant, Company H, 147th Indiana Infantry.

Derickson, Mahlon, Private, Company B, 124th Indiana Infantry.

Deselms, Butler, Private, Company C,. 36th Indiana Infantry.

Deselms, Thomas, Private, Company K, 36th Indiana Infantry.

Detrich, Samuel, Private, Company I, 69th Indiana Infantry.

Dick, Stephen, Private, Company B, 110th Indiana Infantry (Morgan Raid).

*Dickinson, Philemon, First Lieutenant, Company H, 140th Indiana Infantry.

Dickson, Dock, Private, Company F, 8th U. S. C. T.

Diggs, Washington C., Private, Company K, 36th Indiana Infantry.

Dill, Marshall, Private, Company B, 139th Indiana Infantry.

Dillee, Eli H., Private, Company F, 84th Indiana Infantry.

50

*Dillee, George J., Private, Company A, 105th Indiana Infantry (Morgan Raid); Private, Company H, 147th Indiana Infantry.

Dillee, John, Private, Company I, 3rd Indiana Cavalry.

Dillee, John R., Private, Company D, 36th Indiana Infantry.

Dillee, Luther S., Private, Company A, 139th Indiana Infantry.

Dillee, Squire, Sergeant, Company A, 57th Indiana Infantry; Private, Company A. 38th Indiana Infantry.

Dillman, Jesse, Private, Company G, 13th Indiana Infantry, re-organized.

Dillon, Francis, Private, 4th Indiana Battery.

Dillon, John, Private, Company A, 11th Indiana Infantry.

Dillon, Jonathan P., Private, Company A, 105th Indiana Infantry (Morgan Raid); Private, Company A, 139th Indiana Infantry.

**Diltz, James R., Private, Company I, 44th Indiana Infantry.

**Dishman, Nathaniel, Private, Company C, 57th Indiana Infantry.

**Doan, Courtland. (See Incomplete List).

Dobbins, Wilson T., Private, Corporal, Company I, 84th Indiana Infantry.

Doolittle, Eli, Private, Company A, 36th Indiana Infantry.

Doran, George W., Private, Company F, 84th Indiana Infantry; Private, Company C. 1st U. S. Engineers.

Dougherty, Thomas J., Private, Sergeant, Company K, 19th Indiana Infantry.

Dovey, Isaac C., Sergeant, Company A, 105th Indiana Infantry (Morgan Raid).

Dovey, Francis, Private, Corporal, 19th Indiana Battery.

Dowell, Bradford M., Private, Company H, 140th Indiana Infantry.

Dowell, George W., Private, Company A. 139th Indiana Infantry.

Downs, Robert H., Private, 19th Indiana Battery.

Downs, William, Private, Company D, 2nd Indiana Cavalry.

*Doxtader, Albert E., Corporal, Sergeant, Company K, 36th Indiana Infantry.

*Doxtader, Daniel, Private, Company K, 36th Indiana Infantry.

Drake, Winfield H., Private, Company H, 140th Indiana Infantry.

Drear, Valentine, Private, Company I, 147th Indiana Infantry.

*Driscoll, Andrew J., Private, Company K, 36th Indiana Infantry.

Driver, John, Private, Company K, 36th Indiana Infantry.

Drury, James A., Private, Company A, 57th Indiana Infantry.

Dubois, William W., Private, Company C, 36th Indiana Infantry.

Dudley, Anderson R., Private, Company B, 124th Indiana Infantry.

Dudley, Wiley J., Private, Company I, 69th Indiana Infantry.

Duke, Henderson, Private, Company B, 8th Indiana Infantry (three months).

Duncan, Benjamin F., Private, Unassigned, 22nd Indiana Infantry.

Duncan, Daniel Davidson, Private, Company A, 105th Indiana Infantry (Morgan Raid); Private, Company A, 139th Indiana Infantry.

Duncan, John S., Private, Unassigned, 22nd Indiana Infantry.

Dungan, Michael M., Private, Corporal, Company G, 84th Indiana Infantry.

Dungan, Milton R., Private, Company B, 8th Indiana Infantry (three months); Second Lieutenant, Company E, 8th Indiana Infantry (three years).

Dunn, Robert, Private, Company A, 105th Indiana Infantry (Morgan Raid).

Dunnington, Hugh D., Private, Company A, 4th Regiment, 1st Army Corps (Hancock's Veteran Corps).

Dutton, Joseph, Sergeant, Company H, 69th Indiana Infantry.

Dykes, John R., Private, Company B, 5th Indiana Cavalry.

E

Eagle, George, Private, Company K, 124th Indiana Infantry.

*Earl, Isaac T., Private, Corporal, First Lieutenant, Captain, Company A, 57th Indiana Infantry.

Eastman, Lycurgus W., Principal Musician, Non Commissioned Staff, 18th Indiana Infantry.

Eastman, William D., Regimental Band, 8th Indiana Infantry (three years).

**Eastridge, John, Private, Company G, 147th Indiana Infantry.

Eaton, Peter, Private, Company G, 84th Indiana Infantry.

Echelbarger, William, Private, Company F, 57th Indiana Infantry.

Edleman, Richard J., Private, 12th Indiana Battery.

Edmunson, George W., Private, Company B, 139th Indiana Infantry.

Edwards, Albert, Private, Company E, 36th Indiana Infantry.

Edwards, Austin M., Private, Corporal, Company A, 57th Indiana Infantry.

Edwards, James L., Private, Company I, 3rd Indiana Cavalry.

Edwards, Joel B., Private, Company A, 105th Indiana Infantry (Morgan Raid).

Edwards, John H., Private, Company A, 36th Indiana Infantry.

*Edwards, John L., Private, Corporal, Company E, 9th Indiana Cavalry

Edwards, John W., Private, Company D, 36th Indiana Infantry.

Edwards, Levi S., Private, Company D, 36th Indiana Infantry.

Edwards, William H., Private, Company B, 19th Indiana Infantry.

Edwards, William M., Private, Company A, 139th Indiana Infantry; Principal Musician, Non Commissioned Staff, 139th Indiana Infantry.

Ehman, John, Corporal, Sergeant, Company F, 63rd Indiana Infantry.

Elder, Benjamin F., Assistant Surgeon, Staff, 36th Indiana Infantry.

Elder, James P., Private, Company F, 6th Indiana Infantry* (three months); Corporal, 19th Indiana Battery.

Ellinger, Reuben, Private, Corporal, 25th Indiana Battery.

**Ellingwood, Cyrus, Private, Corporal, Company I, 8th Indiana Cavalry.

Elliott, Abraham G., Regimental Band, 36th Indiana Infantry.

Elliott, Calvin, Private, Company A, 105th Indiana Infantry (Morgan Raid).

Elliott, Daniel, Artificer, 19th Indiana Battery.

Elliott, Franklin, Private, Corporal, Company A, 36th Indiana Infantry.

Elliott, Henry C., Sergeant, Company B, 8th Indiana Infantry (three months); Private, Company F, and Adjutant, Staff, 57th Indiana Infantry; Lieutenant Colonel, Staff, 118th Indiana Infantry.

Elliott, Jabez, Private, Company F. 84th Indiana Infantry.

Elliott, James, Private, Company F, 28th U. S. C. T.

Elliott, Jehu T. (son of Stephen Elliott), Private, Company A, 110th Indiana Infantry (Morgan Raid); Private, Sergeant, Company B, 134th Indiana Infantry; Private, Unassigned, 79th Indiana Infantry.

Elliott, Jehu T. (now of Logansport), Private, Company A, 110th Indiana Infantry (Morgan Raid).

Elliott, Jesse, Private, Company A, 110th Indiana Infantry (Morgan Raid).

Elliott, John H., Private, Company E, 9th Indiana Cavalry.

Elliott, John R., First Sergeant, Company H. 69th Indiana Infantry.

Elliott, Josephus V., Private, Company F, 57th Indiana Infantry.

Elliott, Nathan, Private, Company B, 110th Indiana Infantry (Morgan Raid).

Elliott, Richard S., Private, Company K, 105th Indiana Infantry (Morgan Raid); Private, Corporal, Company H, 140th Indiana Infantry.

Elliott, Samuel, Private, 19th Indiana Battery.

Elliott, William, Private, Company A, 105th Indiana Infantry (Morgan Raid).

Elliott, William H., Regimental Band, 18th Indiana Infantry; Sergeant, Company A, 110th Indiana Infantry (Morgan Raid); Private, First Sergeant, Company E, 9th Indiana Cavalry.

Elliott, William H., Lieutenant. (See U. S. Naval Academy).

*Elliott, William S., Private, Company H, 147th Indiana Infantry.

**Ellis, Isaac W., Private, Company C. 8th Indiana Infantry (three months).

Ellis, Simon, Private, Company E, 23rd U. S. C. T.

Ellison, Jesse S., Private, Company H. 69th Indiana Infantry.

Elmore, William P., Private, Company F, 84th Indiana Infantry.

Eitzroth, Eli, Private, Company I, 3rd Indiana Cavalry; Corporal, Company E, 9th Regiment, 1st Army Corps (Hancock's Veteran Corps).

Elwood, Benjamin F., First Sergeant, Company B, 8th Indiana Infantry (three months); First Lieutenant, Captain, Company E, 8th Indiana Infantry (three years).

Emery, Jonathan, Private, Company A, 36th Indiana Infantry.

Englerth, George D., Private, Company D, 36th Indiana Infantry.

English, Hugh L., Private, Company B, 19th Indiana Infantry.

English, James C., Private, Company A, 139th Indiana Infantry.

Enright, Michael, Private, Company D, 8th Indiana Infantry (three years).

Ensminger, Samuel, Private, Company H, 11th Indiana Infantry.

*Erwin, William, Corporal, Company F, 57th Indiana Infantry.

Eshelman, Ira, Private, Company D, 36th Indiana Infantry; Private, Company H, 30th Indiana Infantry, re-organized.

Essenmacher, Charles, Senior, Private, Company B, 124th Indiana Infantry.

Eurick, Isaac, Private, Company C, 36th Indiana Infantry.

Evans, Asbury C., Private, Company F, 19th Indiana Infantry; Private, Company F, 57th Indiana Infantry; Private, Company B, 110th Indiana Infantry (Morgan Raid).

Evans, Ellis E., Private, Company E, 8th Indiana Infantry (three years).

Evans, George, Private, Company A, 54th Indiana Infantry (one year); Private, Company H, 140th Indiana Infantry.

Evans, Henry, Private, Company A, 54th Indiana Infantry (one year).

Evans, Lemuel, Private, Company F, 57th Indiana Infantry.

Everett, Theophilus, Saddler. Company D, 2nd Indiana Cavalry; Private, Company K, 124th Indiana Infantry. (See Mexican War).

Everhard, William, Private, Company F, 6th Indiana Infantry (three months).

F

Fadely, Jacob, Private, Company C, 109th Indiana Infantry (Morgan Raid).

Fadely, Samuel, Private, Company F, 124th Indiana Infantry.

Falls, William D., Private, Company E, 9th Regiment, 1st Army Corps (Hancock's Veteran Corps).

Farmer, Amos, Private, Company F, 84th Indiana Infantry.

Farmer, George W., Private, Company K, 11th Indiana Infantry.

Farmer, John S., Private, Sergeant, Company H, 69th Indiana Infantry.

Farmer, Josiah, Private, Company C, 147th Indiana Infantry.

Farmer, Mahlon A., Private, Company C, 9th Indiana Cavalry.

Farmer, William H., Private, Company A, 36th Indiana Infantry.

Fawcett, Alpheus, Private, Company G, 84th Indiana Infantry; Private, Corporal, Company H, 140th Indiana Infantry.

Fawcett, Benjamin F., Private, 4th Indiana Battery.

Fawcett, Joseph, Hospital Steward, Non Commissioned Staff, 20th Indiana Infantry.

Fellows, James W., Captain, Company I, 84th Indiana Infantry.

Fentress, William H., Sergeant, Second Lieutenant, First Lieutenant, Company D, 36th Indiana Infantry.

Ferris, Warren W., Corporal, Company B, 8th Indiana Infantry (three months).

Ferry, William A., Private, Company I, 69th Indiana Infantry.

Fields, William M., Private, Company A, 105th Indiana Infantry (Morgan Raid).

Fifer, Andrew, Private, Company B, 89th Indiana Infantry.

Fifer, Christopher S., Private, First Sergeant, Company H, 69th Indiana Infantry.

Fifer, James, Private, Company K, 105th Indiana Infantry (Morgan Raid); Private, Company B, 130th Indiana Infantry.

**Fike, John A., Private, Company F, 20th Indiana Infantry.

Filson, Charles, Private, Company D, 8th Indiana Infantry (three years).

Filson, James, Private, Company F, 6th Indiana Infantry (three months).

Finkborn, John, Private, Company B, 124th Indiana Infantry.

Finley, Michael, Private, Company C, 30th Indiana Infantry.
*Firth, Robert, Private, Company B, 139th Indiana Infantry.
Fish, Tilghman, First Lieutenant, Company I, 3rd Indiana Cavalry.
Fish, William S., Private, Company I; Hospital Steward, Non Commissioned Staff, 3rd Indiana Cavalry.
Fisher, Sylvester, Private, Company E, 130th Indiana Infantry.
*Fisk, Americus, Private, Corporal, Company A, 57th Indiana Infantry.
*Fisk, Granville, Private, Company A, 57th Indiana Infantry.
Fitch, Henry, Private, Company E, 9th Indiana Cavalry.
**Fitzhugh, Frank W., Private, Corporal, Sergeant, Company A; Sergeant Major, Non Commissioned Staff; Second Lieutenant, Company A, 11th Infantry U. S. A.
Fitzmorris, Timothy, Private, Company A, 30th Indiana Infantry, re-organized.
Flater, James L., Private, Company C, 147th Indiana Infantry.
Fleming, Andrew J., Private, Company E, 8th Indiana Infantry (three years).
Fleming, Beniah, Private, Company E, 8th Indiana Infantry (three years).
Fleming, Charles A., Private, Company E, 8th Indiana Infantry (three years); Private, Company K, 105th Indiana Infantry (Morgan Raid); Private, Corporal, Company E, 9th Indiana Cavalry.
Fleming, Henry H., Sergeant, Company A, 110th Indiana Infantry (Morgan Raid).
Fleming, Preston, Private, Company I, 69th Indiana Infantry.
Fleming, Stephen, Corporal, Company D, 2nd Indiana Cavalry.
Fleming, William R., Private, Company E, 8th Indiana Infantry (three years).
*Fletcher, James M., Private, Company A, 57th Indiana Infantry.
*Fletcher, John W., Private, Company A, 57th Indiana Infantry.
Fletcher, Robert B., Second Lieutenant, First Lieutenant, Company C, 5th Indiana Cavalry.
**Fletcher, William, Private, Company F, 8th U. S. C. T.
Flynn, Maurice, Private, 2nd Indiana Battery.
Flynn, William, Private, Company K, 36th Indiana Infantry.
*Foland, Jacob S., Private, Company H, 140th Indiana Infantry.
Folkner, James, Private, Company K, 105th Indiana Infantry (Morgan Raid).
*Foraker, Joseph, Private, Company E, 8th Indiana Infantry (three years).
Ford, Frederick, Private, Company I, 3rd Indiana Cavalry.
*Ford, Isaac, Private, Company K, 36th Indiana Infantry.
**Ford, James H. S., Private, Captain, Company B, 153rd Indiana Infantry.
Foreman, David, Private, 4th Indiana Battery.
Foreman, Joseph, Private, 4th Indiana Battery.
Forsha, William, Private, Company B, 8th Indiana Infantry (three months).
Fort, Brice D., Private, Company A, 105th Indiana Infantry (Morgan Raid); Private, Sergeant, Company A, 139th Indiana Infantry.
*Fort, Charles H., Private, Company A, 57th Indiana Infantry.
Fort, David P., Private, Corporal, Company B, 19th Indiana Infantry; Corporal, Sergeant, Company C, 20th Indiana Infantry, re-organized.
Fort, John W., Private, Company I, 3rd Indiana Cavalry; Sergeant, Company A, 105th Indiana Infantry (Morgan Raid); Captain, Company A, 139th Indiana Infantry:
*Fort, Lorenzo D., Private, Company A, 57th Indiana Infantry.
· Fort, Milton, Private, Company A, 105th Indiana Infantry (Morgan Raid).
Fort, Randolph, Private, Company B, 19th Indiana Infantry.
Fort, Thomas C., Private, Unassigned, 33rd Indiana Infantry.
Foster, Gideon W., Private, Company H, 142nd Indiana Infantry.
Foster, John H., Second Lieutenant, Company I, 69th Indiana Infantry.
Foster, John W., Private, Company F, 124th Indiana Infantry.
Foster, Nathan, Private, Company I, 84th Indiana Infantry.
Foster, Robert C., Private, Company I, 69th Indiana Infantry.
Foster, Samuel W., Private, Company A, 36th Indiana Infantry.

**Foulke, William P., Private, Company D, 115th Indiana Infantry; Private, Company C, 31st Indiana Infantry.

Foulk's, John W., Private, Company K, 36th Indiana Infantry.

Fountain, John W., Private, Company H, 69th Indiana Infantry.

Fox, Henry C., Sergeant, Company A, 110th Indiana Infantry (Morgan Raid).

Fox, Leonidas, Second Lieutenant, Company I, 84th Indiana Infantry; Second Lieutenant, Company K, 57th Indiana Infantry.

Foxworthy, Samuel T., Private, Company F, 20th Indiana Infantry.

Frame, William H., Private,. Company D, 36th Indiana Infantry.

Franklin, Andrew D., Private, Company H, 69th Indiana Infantry; Private, Company H, 140th Indiana Infantry.

**Franklin, Columbus, Private. Company B, 7th Indiana Infantry; Private, Sergeant. Company I, 9th Indiana Cavalry.

Franklin, David, Private, Company H. 69th Indiana Infantry.

Franklin, Joseph W., Private. Company H, 140th Indiana Infantry.

Franklin, Milton, Private, Company C, 109th Indiana Infantry (Morgan Raid).

Franklin, Shadrick, Private, Company B, 149th Indiana Infantry.

Frazier, Isaiah, Private, .Company F, 57th Indiana Infantry.

Frazier, William J., Private, Company C, 36th Indiana Infantry.

Frederick, Henry, Private, Company C, 9th Indiana Infantry.

Freedly, Samuel, Private, Company A, 54th Indiana Infantry (one year).

Freeman, Austin S., Private, Company D, 36th Indiana Infantry; Private, 19th Indiana Battery.

Freeman, Christopher C., Private. Company F, 84th Indiana Infantry.

Freeman, George W., Private, Company D. 36th Indiana Infantry.

Freeman, Henry C., Corporal, Company I, 84th Indiana Infantry.

Freeman, Lewis C., First Lieutenant, Captain, Company A; Major, Staff, 36th Indiana Infantry.

Freeman, Lindsey, Private, Company I, 84th Indiana Infantry; Private, 2nd Indiana Battery, re-organized.

Freeman, Washington L., Private, Company D, 36th Indiana Infantry.

**Freeman, William, Private, Company B, 128th Indiana Infantry.

**French, Francis, Second Lieutenant, Company E, 69th Indiana Infantry.

Fricker, John A., Private, Company K, 148th Indiana Infantry.

Fritz, Peter, Private, 2nd Indiana Battery.

Fritzche, Walter, Private, Company C, 36th Indiana Infantry.

Funk, Joseph, Private, Company A, 8th Indiana Infantry (three months); Private, Corporal, Company I, 36th Indiana Infantry.

Fuqua, Burden, Private, Company B, 8th Indiana Infantry (three months).

Fuqua, James, Private, Company B, 8th Indiana Infantry (three months).

Furgason, J. Lee, Private, Company A; Quartermaster Sergeant, Non Commissioned Staff, 139th Indiana Infantry.

Furgeson, Granville S., Private, Company K, 14th U. S. C. T.

Fye, Charles, Private, Company I, 147th Indiana Infantry.

G

Gaddis, George, Private, Company B, 130th Indiana Infantry.

Gailer, Robert P., Private, Company D, 38th Indiana Infantry.

Gales, Charles, Private, Unassigned, 22nd Indiana Infantry.

*Galycon, Milo L., Private, Company H, 140th Indiana Infantry.

Galyean, Allen W., Private, Company K, 19th Indiana Infantry; Private, Company E, 20th Indiana Infantry, re-organized.

**Gardner, William M., Private, Company G, 69th Indiana Infantry.

Garman, Daniel, Private, Company C, 36th Indiana Infantry.

*Garriott, Henry C., Private, Company A, 57th Indiana Infantry.

COMPANY D, 36th INDIANA INFANTRY.

**Foulke, William P., Private, Company D, 115th Indiana Infantry; Private, Company C, 31st Indiana Infantry.

Foulks, John W., Private, Company K, 36th Indiana Infantry.

Fountain, John W., Private, Company H, 69th Indiana Infantry.

Fox, Henry C., Sergeant, Company A, 110th Indiana Infantry (Morgan Raid).

Fox, Leonidas, Second Lieutenant, Company I, 84th Indiana Infantry; Second Lieutenant, Company K, 57th Indiana Infantry.

Foxworthy, Samuel T., Private, Company F, 20th Indiana Infantry.

Frame, William H., Private, Company D, 36th Indiana Infantry.

Franklin, Andrew D., Private, Company H, 69th Indiana Infantry; Private, Company H, 140th Indiana Infantry.

**Franklin, Columbus, Private, Company B, 7th Indiana Infantry; Private, Sergeant, Company I, 9th Indiana Cavalry.

Franklin, David, Private, Company H, 69th Indiana Infantry.

Franklin, Joseph W., Private, Company H, 140th Indiana Infantry.

Franklin, Milton, Private, Company C, 109th Indiana Infantry (Morgan Raid).

Franklin, Shadrick, Private, Company B, 149th Indiana Infantry.

Frazier, Isaiah, Private, Company F, 57th Indiana Infantry.

Frazier, William J., Private, Company C, 36th Indiana Infantry.

Frederick, Henry, Private, Company C, 9th Indiana Infantry.

Freedly, Samuel, Private, Company A, 54th Indiana Infantry (one year).

Freeman, Austin S., Private, Company D, 36th Indiana Infantry; Private, 19th Indiana Battery.

Freeman, Christopher C., Private, Company F, 84th Indiana Infantry.

Freeman, George W., Private, Company D, 76th Indiana Infantry.

Freeman, Henry C., Corporal, Company I, 84th Indiana Infantry.

Freeman, Lewis C., First Lieutenant Captain, Company A; Major, Staff, 36th Indiana Infantry.

Freeman, Lindsey, Private, Company I, 84th Indiana Infantry; Private, 2nd Indiana Battery, re-organized.

Freeman, Washington L., Private, Company D, 36th Indiana Infantry.

**Freeman, William, Private, Company B, 128th Indiana Infantry.

**French, Francis, Second Lieutenant, Company E, 69th Indiana Infantry.

Fricker, John A., Private, Company K, 148th Indiana Infantry.

Fritz, Peter, Private, 2nd Indiana Battery.

Fritzche, Walter, Private, Company C, 36th Indiana Infantry.

Funk, Joseph, Private, Company A, 8th Indiana Infantry (three months); Private, Corporal, Company I, 36th Indiana Infantry.

Fuque, Burden, Private, Company B, 8th Indiana Infantry (three months).

Fuqua, James, Private, Company E, 8th Indiana Infantry (three months).

Furgason, J. Lee, Private, Company A; Quartermaster Sergeant, Non Commissioned Staff, 139th Indiana Infantry.

Furgeson, Granville S., Private, Company K, 14th U. S. I. T.

Fye, Charles, Private, Company I, 147th Indiana Infantry.

G

Goldis, George, Private, Company B, 139th Indiana Infantry.

Gabe, Robert P., Private, Company D, 88th Indiana Infantry.

Gates, Charles, Private, Unassigned, 22nd Indiana Infantry.

Gaigeon, Milo L., Private, Company H, 140th Indiana Infantry.

Galion, Allen W., Private, Company K, 15th Indiana Infantry; Private, Company C, 9th Indiana Infantry, re-organized.

**Gardner, William M., Private, Company G, 69th Indiana Infantry.

Gatman, Daniel, Private, Company C, 36th Indiana Infantry.

**Garriott, Henry C., Private, Company A, 57th Indiana Infantry.

COMPANY D, 36th INDIANA INFANTRY.

Garvis, John A., Private, Company E. 9th Indiana Cavalry.
*Gates, James, Private, Company G, 84th Indiana Infantry.
*Gates, Richard, Private, Company G, 84th Indiana Infantry.
Gearhead, Joseph, Private, Company E, 9th Regiment, 1st Army Corps (Hancock's Veteran Corps).
Gebhart, William S., Private, Unassigned, 22nd Indiana Infantry.
**George, Washington L., Private, Company A, 124th Indiana Infantry.
Gephart, William, First Sergeant, Company A, 105th Indiana Infantry (Morgan Raid).
*Gibbs, John D., Private, Company A, 57th Indiana Infantry.
Gibson, John, Private, Company D, 2nd Indiana Cavalry.
Gibson, John, Private, Company A, 110th Indiana Infantry (Morgan Raid).
**Gibson, John, Private, Company K, 12th Indiana Cavalry.
Gibson, Richard, Private, Company B, 147th Indiana Infantry.
Gibson, Valentine, Private, Company D, 2nd Indiana Cavalry.
Gilbert, Joel M., First Sergeant, Company C, 84th Indiana Infantry.
Gilbert, Jonathan N., Private, Company C, 84th Indiana Infantry.
Gilbert, Joseph, Private, Company G, 8th Indiana Infantry (three years).
Gilbert, Josiah B., Corporal, Company C, 84th Indiana Infantry; Corporal, Company G, 1st U. S. Engineers.
Gilbert, Oliver, Private, Company C. 84th Indiana Infantry.
Gilbreath, John S., Corporal, Sergeant, Second Lieutenant, 19th Indiana Battery.
Gilbreath, Joseph F., Private, Corporal, Company G, 16th Indiana Infantry.
Gilbreath, Robert, Private, Company B, 99th Indiana Infantry.
Gilbreath, Robert W., Private, Company E, 9th Indiana Cavalry.
Gillespie, Charles, Private, Company H, 147th Indiana Infantry.
Gillespie, H. W., Private, Company B, 110th Indiana Infantry (Morgan Raid).
Gillgeese, John, Private, Company C, 36th Indiana Infantry; Private, Company H, 147th Indiana Infantry.
*Gillis, Samuel M., Private, Company H, 140th Indiana Infantry.
**Gilmore, James H., Private, Company F, 57th Indiana Infantry. (The correct name of this soldier is James B. Gilmore).
Ginn, David, Private, Company I, 69th Indiana Infantry; Private, Company H, 140th Indiana Infantry.
Ginn, Ezekiel, Private, Company E, 9th Indiana Cavalry
Ginn, James, Private, Company C, 36th Indiana Infantry.
Ginn, Job, Private, Company K, 105th Indiana Infantry (Morgan Raid).
Ginn, Job B., Private, Company E, 8th Indiana Infantry (three years).
Ginn, John M., Corporal, Company I, 69th Indiana Infantry.
Ginn, Jonathan J., Private, Company H, 140th Indiana Infantry.
Ginn, Joseph, Private, Company I, 69th Indiana Infantry.
Ginn, Nicholas B., Private, Company H, 69th Indiana Infantry.
Ginn, Taber W., Private, Company C, 36th Indiana Infantry.
Ginn, Thomas J., Private, Company F, 57th Indiana Infantry.
**Gipe, Jacob, Private, Company D, 34th Indiana Infantry.
Glass, Francis H., Private, Company A, 139th Indiana Infantry; Private, Company H; Sergeant Major, Non Commissioned Staff, 147th Indiana Infantry.
Glenn, George, Private, Company A, 42nd Indiana Infantry.
Glidden, Augustus, Wagoner, Company A, 36th Indiana Infantry.
Glidden, Frederick E., Corporal, Sergeant, Company I, 84th Indiana Infantry.
Glover, Silas R., Private, Unassigned, 16th Indiana Infantry.
**Goar, Benjamin F., Corporal, Company F, 11th Indiana Infantry (three months).
Goar, John M. (See Incomplete List).
**Goar, Joseph N., Private, Company C, 101st Indiana Infantry.
Goble, Elias, Private, Company I, 3rd Indiana Cavalry.
Goble, Francis M., Private, 22nd Indiana Battery.
**Goff, Joseph, Private, Corporal, Company F, 93rd Indiana Infantry.

**Gold, William O., Private, Company H, 52nd Indiana Infantry.

Goldsbary, Truman, Private, Corporal, Company A, 36th Indiana Infantry.

Good, Abraham, Private, Company C, 147th Indiana Infantry.

Good, Henry, Private, Company E, 8th Indiana Infantry (three years).

Good, Jacob, Private, Company G, 84th Indiana Infantry; Private, Company G, 1st U. S. Engineers.

Good, Jordan, Private, Company C, 147th Indiana Infantry.

Good, Walton P., Corporal, Company A, 110th Indiana Infantry (Morgan Raid).

Goodlander, William H. H., Corporal, 2nd Indiana Battery.

Goodnoe, John, Private, Company F, 6th Indiana Infantry (three months); Sergeant, Company A, 36th Indiana Infantry; First Sergeant, First Lieutenant, Company I, 69th Indiana Infantry; Sergeant, Company A, 4th Regiment, 1st Army Corps (Hancock's veteran Corps).

Goodwin, George W., Private, Company B, 8th Indiana Infantry (three months); Private, Company C, 36th Indiana Infantry.

Goodwin, Isaac, Private, Company C, 8th Indiana Infantry, (three years). (See Alphabetical List B).

Goodwin, Robert, Corporal, Company B, 147th Indiana Infantry.

Goodwin, Wesley R., Private, Company B, 110th Indiana Infantry (Morgan Raid); Private, Company E, 9th Indiana Cavalry.

Gordon, Benjamin, Private, Company A, 11th Indiana Infantry.

Gordon, Clarkson, Private, Company A, 36th Indiana Infantry; Private, Company A, 4th Regiment, 1st Army Corps (Hancock's Veteran Corps).

Gordon, Eli, Private, Company I, 54th Indiana Infantry (three months); Private, Company H, 147th Indiana Infantry.

**Gordon, Henry C., Musician, Company B, 19th Indiana Infantry; Principal Musician, Non Commissioned Staff, 20th Indiana Infantry, re-organized.

Gordon, Micajah C., First Sergeant, Company D, 36th Indiana Infantry.

Gordon, Oliver C., Private, Company E, 69th Indiana Infantry; Private, Company B, 24th Indiana Infantry.

Gordon, Robert, Corporal, Sergeant, Company A, 36th Indiana Infantry.

**Gordon, Robert P., Private, Company I, 8th Indiana Infantry (three months); Sergeant, First Lieutenant, Company F, 36th Indiana Infantry.

**Gordon, Thaddeus H., Corporal, Company F, 36th Indiana Infantry.

Gorgan, Thomas, Musician, Company E, 8th Indiana Infantry (three years).

**Gormon, James W., Private, Corporal, Company C, 84th Indiana Infantry.

Gossett, Joseph B., Private, Company B, 8th Indiana Infantry (three months); Private, Corporal, Company E, 8th Indiana Infantry (three years).

Gossett, Richard S., Private, Corporal, Company G, 17th Indiana Infantry.

Gossett, William, Private, Company B, 8th Indiana Infantry (three months); Private, Company E, 8th Indiana Infantry (three years).

Gotlip, Henry, Private, Company K, 36th Indiana Infantry.

Gough, Augustus F., Corporal, Company I, 69th Indiana Infantry.

Gough, Enoch, Private, Corporal, Company C, 36th Indiana Infantry; Private, 2nd Indiana Battery, re-organized.

Gough, Ferdinand C., Farrier and Blacksmith, Company D, 2nd Indiana Cavalry.

Gough, Hiram, Private, Company E, 106th Indiana Infantry (Morgan Raid).

Gough, Jacob M., Private, Company B, 8th Indiana Infantry (three months).

Gough, Jesse, Private, Company B, 139th Indiana Infantry.

Gough, Lemuel, Private, Company G, 84th Indiana Infantry.

**Gough, Thomas W., Private, Company K, 19th Indiana Infantry.

*Goulman, Thomas J., Wagoner, Company I, 8rd Indiana Cavalry.

Gowdy, Elijah S., Private, Company I, 69th Indiana Infantry.

Graf, George P., Private, Company A, 32nd Indiana Infantry.

Graham, Andrew J., Private, Company F, 6th Indiana Infantry (three months); Corporal, Sergeant, Company G, 16th Indiana Infantry.

*Graham, Henry R., Private, Company E, 8th Indiana Infantry (three years).

Graham, James, Private, Company H, 69th Indiana Infantry. ·

Graham,, Tillman, Private, Company H, 69th Indiana Infantry.

Grandstaff, Lemuel, Private, Company F, 130th Indiana Infantry.

Granger, Francis M., Private, Company M, 2nd Indiana Cavalry; Private, Company D, 2nd Indiana Cavalry, re-organized.

Graves, Joseph, Private, Corporal, Company H, 69th Indiana Infantry.

Graves, Samuel, Private, 4th Indiana Battery.

Graves, Thomas J., Private, Company H, 69th Indiana Infantry.

Graves, William, Private, Company F, 57th Indiana Infantry.

Gray, Charles, Private, Company E, 8th Indiana Infantry (three years).

Gray, Elwood, Private, Company K, 105th Indiana Infantry (Morgan Raid).

Gray, James M., Private, Company B, 8th Indiana Infantry (three months); Private, Company B, 139th Indiana Infantry.

*Gray, Jeremiah, Private, Company F, 57th Indiana Infantry.

Gray, John M., Corporal, Company E, 8th Indiana Infantry (three years).

Gray, Joshua L., Private, Company C, 36th Indiana Infantry.

Gray, Thomas, Private, Corporal, 4th Indiana Battery.

Gray, William, Private, Company C, 5th Indiana Cavalry.

Gregory, Edwin A., Private, Company F, 57th Indiana Infantry.

*Gregory, Henry, Private, Company H, 147th Indiana Infantry.

Green, Alpheus, Sergeant, Second Lieutenant, Company F, 84th Indiana Infantry.

Green, Charles W., Private, Company A, 36th Indiana Infantry.

Green, Jacob, Private, Company A, 57th Indiana Infantry.

Green, Jesse H., Private, 25th Indiana Battery.

Green, John, Private, Company A, 139th Indiana Infantry.

Green, Lawrence, Private, Company H, 69th Indiana Infantry.

Greenwood, Harry, Private, Company H, 147th Indiana Infantry.

Griffin, Andrew J., Private, Sergeant, Company I, 69th Indiana Infantry.

Griffin, Elihu, Major and Paymaster, Staff, U. S. Volunteers. (See General Officers, Chapter IX).

Griffin, Isom, Private, Company B, 110th Indiana Infantry (Morgan Raid).

Griffin, Samuel, Private, Company B, 110th Indiana Infantry (Morgan Raid).

Griffin, William H., Private, Company I, 69th Indiana Infantry.

Griffith, Daniel M., Private, Company F, 6th Indiana Infantry (three months); Private, Company A, 105th Indiana Infantry (Morgan Raid).

*Griffith, Hiram, Private, Company A, 57th Indiana Infantry.

Griffith, John, Private, Company H, 140th Indiana Infantry.

**Griffith, Marquis D., Wagoner, Corporal, Company D, 34th Indiana Infantry.

*Griffith, Thomas H., Private, Corporal, Company A, 57th Indiana Infantry. ·

Griffith, William, Private, Company E, 40th Indiana Infantry.

Griggsby, Samuel, Private, Company D, 36th Indiana Infantry.

Griggsby, William J., Private, Company F, 84th Indiana Infantry.

Grisler, John, Private, Company A, 110th Indiana Infantry (Morgan Raid).

*Grist, John K., Corporal, Sergeant, Company H, 140th Indiana Infantry.

Groler, John, Private, Company A, 57th Indiana Infantry.

Gronendyke, Amos, Second Lieutenant, Middletown Rifles, Indiana Legion; Private, Company C, 109th Indiana Infantry (Morgan Raid); First Lieutenant, Company F, 124th Indiana Infantry.

Gronendyke, Thomas W., Corporal, Company H, 69th Indiana Infantry; Private, Company K, 105th Indiana Infantry (Morgan Raid).

Grose, Abijah, Private, Company E, 106th Indiana Infantry (Morgan Raid).

Grose, Isaac, Captain, New Lisbon Indiana State Guards, Indiana Legion; Corporal, Company A, 110th Indiana Infantry (Morgan Raid).

Grose, John W., Regimental Band, 36th Indiana Infantry.

Grose, Madison, Corporal, Company B, 8th Indiana Infantry (three months);

Principal Musician, Non Commissioned Staff, 36th Indiana Infantry; Private, Second Lieutenant, Company E, 9th Indiana Cavalry.

Grose, Martin L., Private, Company A, 8th Indiana Infantry (three years); Private, Company F, 86th Indiana Infantry.

Grose, William, Colonel, Staff, 36th Indiana Infantry; Brigadier General and Brevet Major General, U. S. Volunteers. (See General Officers, Chapter IX).

Grove, Charles W., Private, Company C, 109th Indiana Infantry (Morgan Raid); Musician, Company F, 124th Indiana Infantry.

Grove, Henry, Private, Company D, 36th Indiana Infantry.

Grove, Isaac, Musician, Company K, 8th Indiana Infantry (three months); Musician, Company H, 69th Indiana Infantry; Musician, Company F. 124th Indiana Infantry.

Grove, Joseph M., Private, Company H, 69th Indiana Infantry; Sergeant, 25th Indiana Battery.

Grover, Andrew, Private, Company F, 124th Indiana Infantry.

*Groves, Stephen, Private, Company B, 139th Indiana Infantry.

Grow, William, Private, Company I, 84th Indiana Infantry.

Grubbs, Benjamin D., Private, Company E, 9th Indiana Cavalry.

Grubbs, Robert M., Captain, Company F; Major, Staff, 84th Indiana Infantry.

Grubbs, Thomas M., First Lieutenant, Company A, 57th Indiana Infantry.

Grunden, James, Private, Company B. 19th Indiana Infantry; Private, Company C, 20th Indiana Infantry, re-organized.

Grunden, William, Private, Company I, 3rd Indiana Cavalry.

Gue, Edward, Private, Company I, 3rd Indiana Cavalry.

Gue, William, Corporal, Company K, 54th Indiana Infantry (three months).

Gunckle, Aaron M., Bugler, 19th Indiana Battery.

Gundrum, Solomon, Private. Company E. 9th Regiment, 1st Army Corps (Hancock's Veteran Corps).

Gurtin, Levi P., Private, Company B, 124th Indiana Infantry.

Gustin, Amos R., Private, Company H. 69th Indiana Infantry.

Gustin, Jeremiah W., Second Lieutenant, Middletown Rifles, Indiana Legion; Private, Company C, 109th Indiana Infantry (Morgan Raid).

Gustin, Joseph G., Private, Company H. 140th Indiana Infantry.

Gustin, Samuel E., Private, Company E. 8th Indiana Infantry (three years).

Guy, Andrew R., Private, Company I, 84th Indiana Infantry.

Gwin, William M., Private, Company K, 124th Indiana Infantry.

H

Hackleman, Darwin. Bugler. Company I, 3rd Indiana Cavalry.

Hackleman, Thomas M., Private. Company F, 84th Indiana Infantry.

Hackman, Samuel, Private. Corporal, Company K, 19th Indiana Infantry; Corporal, Company E. 20th Indiana Infantry, re-organized.

*Hadley, Samuel S., Private, Company H; Quartermaster Sergeant, Non Commissioned Staff. 140th Indiana Infantry.

Haguewood, Isaac, Private. Company A, 110th Indiana Infantry (Morgan Raid); Private, Company E, 9th Indiana Cavalry.

Haguewood, Miles, Private, Company C, 36th Indiana Infantry.

Haguewood, Milton, Private. Company A, 110th Indiana Infantry (Morgan Raid).

Haguewood, Moore, Private, Company A, 42nd Indiana Infantry.

, Haines, Edward, Private, Company A, 105th Indiana Infantry (Morgan Raid).

Haley, Caleb W., Private, Company A, 110th Indiana Infantry (Morgan Raid).

Haley, Thomas L., Private, Company D, 110th Indiana Infantry (Morgan Raid).

Hall, Branson, Private, Company D, 36th Indiana Infantry.

Hall. Ezra, Private, Company G, 84th Indiana Infantry.

Hall, Henry C., Private, Company A, 105th Indiana Infantry (Morgan Raid); Private, Company F, 84th Indiana Infantry.

Hall, John D., Private, Company K, 36th Indiana Infantry.

Hall, Robert, Private, Corporal, Company A, 36th Indiana Infantry.

Hall, Warren, Private. Company A, 139th Indiana Infantry.

Hall, William C., Private, Company A, 36th Indiana Infantry.

Hall, William J., Wagoner, Company D, 36th Indiana Infantry.

*Halley, John B., Private, Company A, 57th Indiana Infantry.

Halpin, Patrick, Private, Company I, 3rd Indiana Cavalry; Private, Company A, 4th Regiment, 1st Army Corps (Hancock's Veteran Corps).

Halsey, Richard, Private. Company A, 139th Indiana Infantry.

*Ham, George W., Private, Company F; Quartermaster Sergeant, Non Commissioned Staff, 57th Indiana Infantry.

Ham, Jacob, Private, Company K, 105th Indiana Infantry (Morgan Raid).

*Ham, Jacob H., Private, Company F, 57th Indiana Infantry.

*Ham, Samuel, Corporal, Company F, 57th Indiana Infantry.

Ham, Samuel, Private, Company K, 105th Indiana Infantry (Morgan Raid).

*Ham, William J., Private, Company F, 57th Indiana Infantry.

Haman, William, Private, Company D, 2nd Indiana Cavalry.

Hammer, John W., Corporal, Company D, 147th Indiana Infantry.

Hammond, William, Private, Company K, 148th Indiana Infantry.

**Hanby, Elisha M., Private, Company F, 53rd Indiana Infantry.

Hanesbrough, William H., Private, Company E, 9th Regiment, 1st Army Corps (Hancock's Veteran Corps).

Hankins, Absalom, Corporal, Company K, 105th Indiana Infantry (Morgan Raid).

Hankins, Daniel, Private, Company K, 105th Indiana Infantry (Morgan Raid).

Hankins, James, Private. Company D, 147th Indiana Infantry.

Hankins, Joseph, Private, Company E, 8th Indiana Infantry (three years).

Hankins, Richard, Private. Company E, 8th Indiana Infantry (three years).

Hankins, William B., Private, Company H, 69th Indiana Infantry.

Hankins, William N,. Private, Company H, 69th Indiana Infantry

**Hansard, Patrick H., Private, Company F, 14th U. S. C. T.

Hanson, John C., Sergeant, Company K, 54th Indiana Infantry (three months); Private. Company G; Sergeant Major, Non Commissioned Staff; Second Lieutenant, Company A, 7th Indiana Cavalry.

Haper, Henry H., Sergeant, Company F, 84th Indiana Infantry.

*Hardin, Albert G., Private, Company F, 57th Indiana Infantry.

·Hardin, Franklin A., Lieutenant Colonel, Staff, 57th Indiana Infantry.

Hardin, Russell B., Corporal, Company C, 84th Indiana Infantry.

Hardin, Samuel, Corporal, Company H, 69th Indiana Infantry; Private, Company K, 105th Indiana Infantry (Morgan Raid).

Hardy, Dennis, Private. 2nd Indiana Battery; Private, 2nd Indiana Battery, reorganized.

Harley, Thomas, Private, Company A, 110th Indiana Infantry (Morgan Raid).

Harmon, Luther H., Second Lieutenant, First Lieutenant, Company H, 8th Indiana Infantry (three years).

Harned, Isaac F., Private, Company C, 109th Indiana Infantry (Morgan Raid).

Harris, Eli, Private, Unassigned. 22nd Indiana Infantry.

**Harris. James W., Private, Corporal. Sergeant. First Lieutenant, Company H. 2nd Indiana Cavalry.

Harris, Martin B., Private, Company A, 105th Indiana Infantry (Morgan Raid); Private, Company A, 139th Indiana Infantry.

*Harris, Meredith, Private, Company F, 57th Indiana Infantry.

Harris, Milton L., Private, Company C, 9th Indiana Cavalry.

Harris, Thomas G., Private, Company I, 69th Indiana Infantry.

Harris, William H., Private, Company I, 69th Indiana Infantry.

Harrold, Abyram. Private. Company F, 84th Indiana Infantry.

Harrold, Andrew, Private. Company B. 110th Indiana Infantry (Morgan Raid).

Harrold, Uriah, Private, Company D, 2nd Indiana Cavalry.

Harry, Martin L., Private, Company G, 84th Indiana Infantry.

Hart, Alfred G. T., Private, Company A, 105th Indiana Infantry (Morgan Raid).

Hart, Elisha, Private, Company B, 8th Indiana Infantry (three months); Private, Corporal, Sergeant, Company F, 57th Indiana Infantry.

**Hart, Harvey. A., Private, Company F, 130th Indiana Infantry.

Hart, John S., Private, 4th Indiana Battery.

Hart, Lewis, Private, Company K, 105th Indiana Infantry (Morgan Raid).

Harter, Henry B., Private, 23rd Indiana Battery.

*Harter, Joseph L., Private, Company H, 147th Indiana Infantry.

Harter, Peter, Private, Company G, 84th Indiana Infantry.

Hartley, John F., Private, Company I, 69th Indiana Infantry.

Hartley, John M., Captain, Union Guards, Indiana Legion; Second Lieutenant, Company E, 16th Indiana Infantry (one year); Lieutenant Colonel, Staff, 105th Indiana Infantry (Morgan Raid); Lieutenant Colonel, Staff, 139th Indiana Infantry.

Hartley, Thomas L., Private, Company D, 2nd Indiana Cavalry.

Hartman, Daniel, Corporal, Sergeant, Company E, 8th Indiana Infantry (three years).

Harvey, Adam, Private, 12th Indiana Battery.

Harvey, Daniel, Private, Company A. 110th Indiana Infantry (Morgan Raid).

Harvey, Henry, Private. Company G. 84th Indiana Infantry.

*Harvey, Isaac W., Private, Company A. 105th Indiana Infantry (Morgan Raid); Private, Company E, 9th Indiana Cavalry.

Harvey, Joel R., Private, 12th Indiana Battery.

Harvey, John R., Private, Company C, 36th Indiana Infantry: Private, Company A. 110th Indiana Infantry (Morgan Raid); Private. Corporal, Company B; 139th Indiana Infantry.

Harvey, Joseph, Private, Company B, 8th Indiana Infantry (three months); Private, Corporal, 12th Indiana Battery.

Harvey, Leander, Private, Company A. 110th Indiana Infantry (Morgan Raid).

Harvey, Levi, Private, Company G, 84th Indiana Infantry.

Harvey, Mahlon D., Corporal, Company I, 69th Indiana Infantry.

Harvey, Miles, Private, 12th Indiana Battery.

Harvey, Milton, Private. Company C, 36th Indiana Infantry.

Harvey, Philander T., Private, 12th Indiana Battery.

Harvey, Pleasant W., Private, Company I, 69th Indiana Infantry.

Harvey, William, Private, Company A, 110th Indiana Infantry (Morgan Raid).

Harwood, Joseph, Private, Company B, 37th Indiana Infantry; Private, Company B. 37th Indiana Infantry, re-organized.

**Haskett. Nathan H., Private, Company G. 5th Indiana Cavalry.

Haskett, Uriah, Private, Company A, 110th Indiana Infantry (Morgan Raid).

Haskett, William A., Private, Company I, 69th Indiana Infantry.

Hasten, Isaac N., Private, Company F, 84th Indiana Infantry; Corporal, Company K, 57th Indiana Infantry.

Hasting, Peter, Private, Company I, 3rd Indiana Cavalry.

Hastings, James J., Private, Company A, 139th Indiana Infantry.

Hasty, George, First Lieutenant, Needmore Rangers, Indiana Legion; First Lieutenant, Company K, 105th Indiana Infantry (Morgan Raid).

Hatch, Henry, First Lieutenant, Union Guards, Indiana Legion; Captain, Company A, 105th Indiana Infantry (Morgan Raid).

Hatfield, Aaron S., Private, Company A, 124th Indiana Infantry. (See Alphabetical List B).

Hatfield, Israel, Private, Company E, 9th Indiana Infantry.

Hatfield, Joseph B., Private, Company A, 139th Indiana Infantry.

**Haugh, Thomas S., Musician, Company K, 52nd Indiana Infantry; Musician. Company K, 52nd Indiana Infantry, re-organized.

Hawhee, Clinton D., Private, Company K, 36th Indiana Infantry.

Hawhee, Isaiah, Private, Company K, 36th Indiana Infantry.

Hawk, Mahlon. Private, Company B, 124th Indiana Infantry.

Hawk, William, Private, Company B, 8th Indiana Infantry (three months); Corporal, Company F, 57th Indiana Infantry.

**Hayden, Benjamin F., Farrier and Blacksmith, Company D, 2nd Indiana Cavalry.

Hayden, James, Private, Company C, 5th Indiana Cavalry.

**Hayden, John, Private, Company H, 139th Indiana Infantry.

Hayden, Wilson, Private, Company D, 2nd Indiana Cavalry.

*Haynes, Milton, Private, Company B, 139th Indiana Infantry.

Haynes, Peter, Private, Company F, 57th Indiana Infantry.

Haynes, Silas, Private, Company E, 9th Indiana Infantry.

Hayes, Alexander P., Private ,Company A, 36th Indiana Infantry; Private, Company I, 84th Indiana Infantry.

Hayes, Bennett, Private, Company E, 9th Indiana Cavalry.

Hayes, Eaton, Private, Company B, 8th Indiana Infantry (three months); Private, Company D, 36th Indiana Infantry; Private, Company H, 140th Indiana Infantry.

Hayes, Jeremiah, Private, Company E, 36th Indiana Infantry.

Hayes, Mahlon, Private, Company A, 36th Indiana Infantry.

Hayes, Noah, Private, Company E, 36th Indiana Infantry; Private, Company A, 30th Indiana Infantry, re-organized.

Hayes, Oliver P., Private, Company E, 8th Indiana Infantry (three years).

Hayes, Quinton B., Private, Company A, 105th Indiana Infantry (Morgan Raid).

Hayes, Theodore, Private, Company K, 105th Indiana Infantry (Morgan Raid).

Hayes, William, Private, Company A, 36th Indiana Infantry.

Hazzard, George, Musician, Company C, 36th Indiana Infantry.

Hazzard, George W., Colonel, Staff, 37th Indiana Infantry. (See U. S. Military Academy).

Hazzard, John W., Private, Company H, 147th Indiana Infantry.

Hazzard, Leander E., Private, Company H, 5th Cavalry U. S. A.

Hazzard, Samuel, Private, Company A, 110th Indiana Infantry (Morgan Raid).

Heacock, Elwood, Private, Company A, 36th Indiana Infantry.

Heaton, Amos, Private, Company A, 11th Indiana Infantry.

Heaton, Eli, Private, Company I, 3rd Indiana Cavalry.

Heaton, Waitsel M., Corporal, Company F, 6th Indiana Infantry (three months); Private, Company A, 105th Indiana Infantry (Morgan Raid); Private, Company A; Sergeant Major, Non Commissioned Staff, 139th Indiana Infantry.

Heaton, White, Corporal, Quartermaster Sergeant, 2nd Indiana Battery.

Heavenridge, Thomas S., Corporal, Company A, 36th Indiana Infantry.

Hedges, Greenberry W., Private, Company B, 139th Indiana Infantry; Private, Corporal, Company D, 147th Indiana Infantry.

Hedrick, Charles, First Sergeant, Second Lieutenant, Captain, Company I, 3rd Indiana Cavalry.

Hedrick, Charles C., Private, 4th Indiana Battery.

Hedrick, George W., Sergeant, Company A, 36th Indiana Infantry.

Hedrick, Joseph, Private, Company A, 36th Indiana Infantry.

Hedrick, Peter, Private, Company B, 99th Indiana Infantry.

Heichert, Henry O., Private, Company K, 72nd Indiana Infantry.

*Heinbaugh, James, Private, Company G, 84th Indiana Infantry.

*Heinbaugh, John P., Private, Company G, 84th Indiana Infantry.

Helman, Michael, Private, Unassigned, 22nd Indiana Infantry.

*Helms, Jacob R., Private, Company K, 36th Indiana Infantry.

*Helms, Peter, Private, Company K, 36th Indiana Infantry.

*Helms, William J., Private, Company K, 36th Indiana Infantry.

Helvey, George P., Private, Sergeant, Company E, 9th Indiana Cavalry.

Hemley, John, Private, Company A, 110th Indiana Infantry (Morgan Raid). (The correct name of this soldier is John R. Hernly).

Henderson, Henry H., Private, Company B, 8th Indiana Infantry (three months); Private, Company C, 36th Indiana Infantry.

Henderson, Isom P., Private, Company B, 5th Indiana Cavalry.

Henderson, Richard T., Private, Sergeant, Company D, 19th Indiana Infantry; Ser-·geant, First Lieutenant, Captain, Company I, 20th Indiana Infantry, re-organized.

Hendricks, Charles, Private, Company F, 6th Indiana Infantry (three months).

Hendricks, Elijah M., Private, Company D, 11th Indiana Infantry; Private, Company K, 105th Indiana Infantry (Morgan Raid).

Hendricks, Joel, Private, Company E, 8th Indiana Infantry (three years).

Hendricks, John P., Private, Company E, 8th ·Indiana Infantry (three years).

Hendricks, Mahlon, Corporal, Sergeant, First Lieutenant, Company C, 36th Indiana Infantry.

Hendricks, Miles, Private, Company H, ·69th Indiana Infantry. (See Alphabetical List B).

Hendricks, Samuel, Private, Sergeant, 12th 'Indiana Battery.

Henry, Edgar, Sergeant, Company I, 3rd Indiana Cavalry.

Henry, John R., Private, Sergeant, Company A, 36th Indiana Infantry.

Henry, William, Private, Company I, 3rd Indiana Cavalry.

Henry, William A., Private, Corporal, Company I, 84th Indiana Infantry.

Henshaw, William B., Private, Company H, 69th Indiana Infantry.

*Henthorne. Adam K., Private, Company B, 139th Indiana Infantry.

*Herford, Hiram B., Private, Company G, 84th Indiana Infantry.

Herliman, Henry, Regimental Band. 36th Indiana Infantry; Private, Company A, 110th Indiana Infantry (Morgan Raid).

Herman, William H., Private, Company B, 8th Indiana Infantry (three months).

Hernley. Henry B., Private. Company A, 110th Indiana Infantry (Morgan Raid).

Hernly, John R. (See Hemley, John).

Hess, George, Private, Company K, 36th Indiana Infantry.

Hess, Luther P., Private, Company H, 8th Indiana Infantry (three years).

Hess, William T., Private, Company H, 8th ·Indiana Infantry (three years).

**Hewitt, Charles, Private, Company B, 132nd Indiana Infantry.

*Hewitt, Joseph, Private, Company K, 36th Indiana Infantry.

*Hewitt, William, Private, Company K, 36th Indiana Infantry.

Hewitt. William, Private. 2nd Indiana Battery; Private, 2nd Indiana Battery, re-organized.

Hewlit, Alfred, Private, 2nd Indiana Battery.

Hiatt, Branson, Private, Company A, 105th Indiana Infantry (Morgan Raid); Private, 4th Indiana Battery.

Hiatt, Daniel, Private. Company A, 105th Indiana Infantry (Morgan Raid).

*Hiatt, Enoch, Private. Company F, 57th Indiana Infantry.

Hiatt, Henry C., Private, Company G, 9th Indiana Cavalry.

Hiatt, Henry (Harry) H., Private, Company B, 19th Indiana Infantry.

*Hiatt. James D., Private, Company F,· 57th Indiana Infantry.

Hiatt. Jesse M., Captain, Company D, 147th Indiana Infantry.

Hiatt, Joel, Private, Company C, 36th Indiana Infantry.

Hiatt, John C., Private, Sergeant, Company A, 19th Indiana Infantry.

Hiatt, Joseph, Private, Company F, 57th Indiana Infantry.

Hiatt. Oliver S., Private, 13th Indiana Battery.

Hiatt, Richard, Private, Company I, 3rd Indiana Cavalry.

Hiatt, Robert C., Private. Company K, 105th Indiana Infantry (Morgan Raid); Private, Company E, 9th Indiana Cavalry.

Hiatt, Seth, Private, Company A, 105th Indiana Infantry (Morgan Raid).

*Hiatt, William H., Private, Corporal, Company F, 57th Indiana Infantry.

Hicklin, Henry H., Private, Company A, 36th Indiana Infantry.

*Hickman, Charles, Private, Company H, 147th Indiana Infantry.

Hicks, Daniel, Private, Company A. 57th Indiana Infantry.

Higgins, James E., Private, Company E, 9th Indiana Cavalry.

Higgins, John E., Private, 22nd Indiana Battery.

Higgins, Joseph, Private, Company I, 3rd Indiana Cavalry.

Higgins. William T., Private, Company I, 3rd Indiana Cavalry.

Hill, Elwood, Private, Company F, 6th Indiana Infantry (three months)

Hill, Henry, Corporal, Company H, 69th Indiana Infantry.

*Hill, James H., Private, Blacksmith, Company E, 9th Indiana Cavalry.

Hill, John A., Private, Musician, Company K, 11th Indiana Infantry.

**Hill, John W., Private, Company I, 8th U. S. C. T.

*Hill, Milton, Private, Company E, 9th Indiana Cavalry.

*Hill, Nathan O., Private, Company E. 9th Indiana Cavalry.

*Hill, Robert H., Private, Company E, 9th Indiana Cavalry.

*Hill, Thomas C., Private, Company E, 9th Indiana Cavalry.

Hill, Thomas G. Private, Company F, 84th Indiana Infantry.

Hill, William, Private, Company A. 110th Indiana Infantry (Morgan Raid).

**Hilligoss, William J., Sergeant, First Lieutenant, Company G, 75th Indiana Infantry.

Hilton, Noah, Private, Corporal, Company K, 148th Indiana Infantry.

*Hines, Herman, Private, Company G, 84th Indiana Infantry.

Hinkle, Joseph, Private, Company A. 57th Indiana Infantry.

Hinshaw, Albert E. Private, Company A, 139th Indiana Infantry.

Hinshaw, Alonzo, Private, 2nd Indiana Battery; Private, 2nd Indiana Battery, re-organized.

Hinshaw, Elias, Private, Company A, 105th Indiana Infantry (Morgan Raid). ,

Hinshaw, Thomas, Private, Company K, 105th Indiana Infantry (Morgan Raid).

Hinshaw, William, Corporal, Company A, 105th Indiana Infantry (Morgan Raid); Private, Company A, 139th Indiana Infantry.

Hobbs, Jesse, Private, Company I, 3rd Indiana Cavalry.

**Hobbs, Orville W., Private, Company G, 133rd Indiana Infantry.

**Hobbs, Wilson, Major and Surgeon, Staff, 85th Indiana Infantry.

Hobson, Volney, Second Lieutenant, Company A, 110th Indiana Infantry (Morgan Raid); Captain, Company E, 9th Indiana Cavalry.

Hockett, Wyatt, Private, Company F, 124th Indiana Infantry.

Hodson, F. H. C., Private, Company B, 8th Indiana Infantry (three years).

Hodson, Hiram, Private, Company K, 105th Indiana Infantry (Morgan Raid); Private, 25th Indiana Battery.

Hodson, John, Private, Company E, 8th Indiana Infantry (three years).

Hodson, Hiram, Private, Company K, 105th Indiana Infantry (Morgan Raid); Private, 25th Indiana Battery.

**Hodson, John E., Private, Company F, 134th Indiana Infantry.

Hoffacker, Daniel, Sergeant, Company E, 106th Indiana Infantry (Morgan Raid).

Holford, Richard A, Private, Company G, 16th Indiana Infantry.

Holland, Adolphus, Private, Company I, 3rd Indiana Cavalry.

Holland, John E. Second Lieutenant, First Lieutenant, Company C, 36th Indiana Infantry. (See U. S. Military Academy).

Holler, Frederick, Corporal, Company G, 84th Indiana Infantry.

Holliday, Benjamin F., Private, Company B, 110th Indiana Infantry (Morgan Raid).

Hollingsworth, Benjamin S., Private, 19th Indiana Battery.

Holloway, David S., Second Lieutenant, First Lieutenant, Captain, Company D, 19th Indiana Infantry.

Holloway, Jonathan D., Private, Company F, 84th Indiana Infantry.

Holloway, Joshua L., Private, Company K, 36th Indiana Infantry.

Holloway, William H. H., Corporal, Company A, 105th Indiana Infantry (Morgan Raid); Private, Company A, 139th Indiana Infantry.

**Holt, John G., Private, Sergeant, Company E, 9th Indiana Cavalry.

Hoober, John B., Private, Company I, 69th Indiana Infantry.

Hoober, William C., Private, Company G, 9th Indiana Cavalry.

Hood, Edward, Private, Company D, 8th Indiana Infantry (three years).

*Hood, Julius G., Private, Company H, 147th Indiana Infantry.

Hoombaugh, Adam, Private, Company F, 130th Indiana Infantry.

Hoostlar, Michael, Private, Company C. 36th Indiana Infantry.

Hooten, John, Private, Company B, 139th Indiana Infantry.

Hooten, Milton, Private, Company G, 16th Indiana Infantry.

Hooten, William F., Private, Company C, 36th Indiana Infantry.

Hoover, Charles B., Private, Company B, 8th Indiana Infantry (three months); Private, Company K, 36th Indiana Infantry.

Hoover, David, Private, Company B, 110th Indiana Infantry (Morgan Raid); Private, Company B, 139th Indiana Infantry.

Hoover, De Witt C., Private, Company B, 8th Indiana Infantry (three months); Sergeant, First Lieutenant, Company H, 69th Indiana Infantry.

Hoover, Frederick, Captain, Company H, 69th Indiana Infantry.

Hoover, Harrison, Musician, Company K, 36th Indiana Infantry; Private, Company G, 84th Indiana Infantry.

Hoover, James M., Private, Company B, 139th Indiana Infantry.

Hoover, John S., Captain and Aid de Camp, Major and Aid de Camp, Brevet Lieutenant Colonel, Brevet Colonel, Staff, U. S. Volunteers. (See Alphabetical List B).

Hoover, Moses, Private, Company A, 110th Indiana Infantry (Morgan Raid).

Hoover, Tobias, Sergeant, Company A, 105th Indiana Infantry (Morgan Raid); Private, Sergeant, Company A, 139th Indiana Infantry.

Hoover, William, Private, Company G, 84th Indiana Infantry.

Hoover, William H., Private, Company B, 8th Indiana Infantry (three months); First Sergeant, Company C, 36th Indiana Infantry; Private, Sergeant, 2nd Indiana Battery, re-organized.

Hopper, Abraham W., Private, Company A, 36th Indiana Infantry.

Hopper, Lewis M., Private, Company A, 36th Indiana Infantry.

Hopper, Samuel, Private, Company A, 36th Indiana Infantry.

Hopper, Theodore, Musician, Company A, 36th Indiana Infantry; Private, 2nd Indiana Battery, re-organized.

**Hoppis, Daniel, Private, Company A, 19th Indiana Infantry; Private, Company I, 20th Indiana Infantry, re-organized.

Horney, James, Private, Company I, 3rd Indiana Cavalry.

Hosier, Bryant, Private, Company D, 147th Indiana Infantry.

**Hosier, Henderson O., Private, 19th Indiana Battery.

Hosier, Isaiah, Private, Company D, 36th Indiana Infantry.

Houck, David. (See Incompete List).

Houck, Leonidas, Private, Company B. 110th Indiana Infantry (Morgan Raid).

Houck, Thomas J., Private, Company B. 8th Indiana Infantry (three months); Private, Company D, 36th Indiana Infantry.

Hough, Ira, Private, Company E, 8th Indiana Infantry (three years).

House, John, Private, Company E, 9th Indiana Cavalry.

House, William, Private, Company B, 110th Indiana Infantry (Morgan Raid); Private, Company A. 30th Indiana Infantry, re-organized.

Houser, John, Private, Company D., 36th Indiana Infantry.

*Howe, Edward P., Second Lieutenant ,First Lieutenant, Captain. Company A, 57th Indiana Infantry.

Howell, John, Private, Company B, 8th Indiana Infantry (three months).

Howren, Charles A. C., Private, Company A, 84th Indiana Infantry; Private, Company E, 106th Indiana Infantry (Morgan Raid).

Howren, Nimrod, Private, Company A, 36th Indiana Infantry.

Howren, Thomas I, Private, Company D. 36th Indiana Infantry.

Howren, William A., Private, Company C, 19th Indiana Infantry; Private, Company A, 20th Indiana Infantry, re-organized.

Hubbard, Alonzo, Private, Company F, 6th Indiana Infantry (three months); Private, Company A, 105th Indiana Infantry (Morgan Raid).

Hubbard, Edwin. Private, Company H, 69th Indiana Infantry.

Hubbard, George, Private, Corporal, Company C, 84th Indiana Infantry.

Hubbard, Henry, Private, Company A, 8th Indiana Infantry (three months); Private, Sergeant, Company C, 2nd Indiana Cavalry; Sergeant, Company C, 2nd Indiana Cavalry, re-organized.

   Hubbard, Joseph B., Sergeant. Second Lieutenant, Company D, 8th Indiana Infantry (three years).

Hubbard, Joseph L., Private, Corporal, 19th Indiana Battery.

Hudelson, James C., Private, Company A, 139th Indiana Infantry.

Hudelson, John W., Sergeant, Company F. 6th Indiana Infantry (three months); Private, Company A, 57th Indiana Infantry.

Hudelson, Martin, Private, Corporal, Company B, 139th Indiana Infantry.

Hudelson, Robert I., Private, Company H, 11th Indiana Infantry; Seaman, U. S. Navy; Private, 2nd Indiana Battery; Private, Corporal, 2nd Indiana Battery, re-organized.

Hudelson, Rufus I., Private, Company K, 37th Indiana Infantry.

Hudelson, Samuel H., Private, Company A. 139th Indiana Infantry.

Hudelson, William H., Private, Company K, 37th Indiana Infantry.

Hudelson, William M., Private, Company A., 105th Indiana Infantry (Morgan Raid).

Huff, Abraham, Private, Company I, 69th Indiana Infantry.

Huff, Jacob, Private. Company I, 69th Indiana Infantry.

Huff, William, Private, Company I, 147th Indiana Infantry

*Huffman, Ezekiel, Private, Company B, 139th Indiana Infantry.

*Huggins, Josiah, Private, Company E, 8th Indiana Infantry (three years).

Hughes, John, Private, Company A. 54th Indiana Infantry (one year).

Hull, George W., Private, Company D, 36th Indiana Infantry; Private, Company A, 139th Indiana Infantry.

Humphrey, Lemuel, Private, Company B. 124th Indiana Infantry.

Humphrey, William, Private, Company G. 16th Indiana Infantry.

*Humphrey, William W., Private, Company A; Sergeant, Major, Non Commissioned Staff; First Lieutenant, Company A, 57th Indiana Infantry.

Hunnicutt, William H., Private, Company A, 57th Indiana Infantry.

Hunt, Edward, Private, Company I, 147th Indiana Infantry.

Hunt, George W., Private, Company H., 147th Indiana Infantry.

**Hunt, Herbert, Private, Company C, 57th Indiana Infantry.

Hunt, Jacob, Private, Company B, 19th Indiana Infantry; Private, Company C, 20th Indiana Infantry, re-organized.

Hunt, Thomas M., Private, Company A, 139th Indiana Infantry.

Hunt, William H., Private, Company D. 19th Indiana Infantry.

*Hunter, Eben B., Private, Sergeant, Company F, 57th Indiana Infantry.

Huntsinger, Daniel. Private, Company I, 36th Indiana Infantry.

Huntsinger, William, Private, Company E, 36th Indiana Infantry.

Hupp, Dewitt C., Sergeant, Company H, 147th Indiana Infantry.

*Hurley, John J., Sergeant, Company G, 7th Indiana Cavalry.

**Hurst, Joseph, Private, Company G, 17th Indiana Infantry.

Hurt, Thomas M., Private, 2nd Indiana Battery, re-organized.

Huston, James, Private. Company K, 105th Indiana Infantry (Morgan Raid).

Huston, Joseph, Private, Company F, 57th Indiana Infantry.

**Huston, Thomas M, Private, Company L, 3rd Indiana Cavalry; Private, Company A. 8th Indiana Cavalry, re-organized.

Huston, Wiliam H., Corporal, Company H, 69th Indiana Infantry.

Hutchins, William, Private, Company A, 36th Indiana Infantry.

**Hutson, James, Private, Company G, 5th Indiana Cavalry.

Hynes, Timothy, Sergeant, Second Lieutenant, Company A, 36th Indiana Infantry.

51

I

Ice, Abraham S., Private, Company H, 147th Indiana Infantry.
Ice, Jesse A., Sergeant, Company G, 84th Indiana Infantry.
*Ingalls, Parker, Private, Company B, 139th Indiana Infantry.
*Inman, John M., Private, Company H, 147th Indiana Infantry.
Irvin, Samuel, Private, Company K, 5th Indiana Cavalry.

J

*Jack, John W., First Lieutenant, Captain, Company E, 9th Indiana Cavalry.
*Jackson, Charles, Private, Company H, 147th Indiana Infantry.
Jackson, Harrison, Musician, Company G, 47th Indiana Infantry; Private, Company C, 109th Indiana Infantry (Morgan Raid); Private, Company E, 9th Indiana Cavalry.
*Jackson, Jesse, Private, Company G, 84th Indiana Infantry.
Jackson, Jesse L., Private, Company E, 11th Indiana Infantry.
**Jackson, Presley E., Private, Corporal, Company K, 47th Indiana Infantry.
*Jackson, William L., Private, Company G, 84th Indiana Infantry.
Jackson, Wilson T, Private, Company I, 84th Indiana Infantry; Private, Company K, 57th Indiana Infantry.
James, Austin W., Private, Company D, 36th Indiana Infantry.
James, Benjamin F., Private, Company A, 105th Indiana Infantry (Morgan Raid).
James, Elwood, Private, Company I, 3rd Indiana Cavalry; Private, Company L, 8th Indiana Cavalry, re-organized.
James, John, Private, Company A, 57th Indiana Infantry.
James, Leander M., Private, Company A, 139th Indiana Infantry.
James, Morgan, Sergeant, Company D; Hospital Steward, Non Commissioned Staff, 36th Indiana Infantry.
James, William, Private, Company·A, 105th Indiana Infantry (Morgan Raid); Private, Company A, 139th Indiana Infantry.
Jamison, William, Private, 19th Indiana Battery.
Jarvis, James, Private, Company G, 84th Indiana Infantry.
Jefferson, Clingman R,. Corporal, Company D, 36th Indiana Infantry.
Jeffries, Milton, Private, Company I, 84th Indiana Infantry.
Jenkins, Alfred, Private, Company G, 84th Indiana Infantry.
Jenkins, William, Private, Company K, 14th U. S. C. T.
Jennings, Charles C., Private, Company F, 57th Indiana Infantry.
Jennings, George W., Corporal, Company K, 16th Indiana Infantry.
Jennings, William A., Corporal, Company K, 16th Indiana Infantry.
Jester, Alexander, Private, Company D, 36th Indiana Infantry; Private, 19th Indiana Battery.
Jester, Avery, Private, Company E, 8th Indiana Infantry (three years).
Jester, Gary, Private, Company E, 8th Indiana Infantry (three years).
*Jester, Isaac L., Private, Company H, 140th Indiana Infantry
Jester, James R., Private, 19th Indiana Battery.
Jester. Philander, Private, Company K, 99th Indiana Infantry; Sergeant, Company H, 140th Indiana Infantry.
Jessup, John A., Private, Company I, 84th Indiana Infantry.
Jessup, Josiah A., Private, Company I, 84th Indiana Infantry.
Jewell, Warren D., Private, Corporal, Company I. 84th Indiana Infantry.
**John, Stevan, Private, Corporal, Company L, 8th Indiana Cavalry, re-organized.
Johnson, Abraham, Private, Company F, 6th Indiana Infantry (three months).
Johnson, Alexander, Private, Company F, 6th Indiana Infantry (three months); Private, Company I, 3rd Indiana Cavalry; Private, Company F, 84th Indiana Infantry; Private, Company K, 57th Indiana Infantry.
Johnson, Caldwell C., Private, Company B, 147th Indiana Infantry.
Johnson, Charles W., Private, Company G, 9th Indiana Cavalry.

Johnson, David, Private, Company K, 36th Indiana Infantry.
**Johnson, George W., Private, Company F, 146th Indiana Infantry.
Johnson, Henry, Private, Company B, 8th Indiana Infantry (three months).
Johnson, Hugh A., Private, Company C, 147th Indiana Infantry.
Johnson, Hutchinson, Corporal, Company D, 19th Indiana Infantry.
Johnson, Israel G., Private, Company A, 110th Indiana Infantry (Morgan Raid).
Johnson, James T., Private, Company G, 9th Indiana Cavalry.
Johnson, John N., Private, Company K, 36th Indiana Infantry.
Johnson, Joseph P., Private, Company C, 109th Indiana Infantry (Morgan Raid).
Johnson, Levi, Private, Company E, 147th Indiana Infantry.
Johnson, Lewis, Private, Company G, 9th Indiana Cavalry.
Johnson, Quincy A., Private, Company B, 147th Indiana Infantry.
Johnson, Robert A., Private, Company E, 147th Indiana Infantry.
Johnson, Samuel J., Private, Company B, 8th Indiana Infantry (three months);
Private, Company H, 69th Indiana Infantry.
Johnson, Silas, Private, Company K, 57th Indiana Infantry; Private, Company B,
134th Indiana Infantry; Sergeant, Company B, 147th Indiana Infantry.
Johnson, Thomas J., Private, Company K, 148th Indiana Infantry.
Johnson, Turner H., Private, Company D, 2nd Indiana Cavalry.
Johnson, William K., Private, Company I, 69th Indiana Infantry.
*Johnston, John D., First Sergeant, Company G, 8th Indiana Infantry (three
months); Sergeant, Second Lieutenant, 18th Indiana Battery.
Jones, Charles W., Private, Company H, 140th Indiana Infantry.
Jones, Clinton, Private, Company K, 99th Indiana Infantry.
Jones, David, Corporal, Company F, 124th Indiana Infantry.
Jones, Ephraim L., Private, Company D, 36th Indiana Infantry; Private, Company
H, 140th Indiana Infantry.
Jones, Hardin, Private, Company C, 147th Indiana Infantry.
Jones, James, Private, Company E, 8th Indiana Infantry (three years).
Jones, James M., Private, 19th Indiana Battery.
Jones, Jenkins, Private, Company K, 105th Indiana Infantry (Morgan Raid).
*Jones, Owen, Private, Company K, 36th Indiana Infantry.
Jones, Philip, Private, Company K, 36th Indiana Infantry.
*Jones, William H., Private, Company A, 57th Indiana Infantry.
Jones, William R., Private, Corporal, 19th Indiana Battery.
Jordan, Anthony W., Private, Company I, 124th Indiana Infantry.
Jordan, B. B., Private, Company A, 110th Indiana Infantry (Morgan Raid).
Jordan, Henry S., Private, Company I, 69th Indiana Infantry.
Judd, James, Private, Company H, 69th Indiana Infantry.
Judd, John, Private, Company K, 105th Indiana Infantry (Morgan Raid); Private,
Company D, 147th Indiana Infantry.
Judd, John D., Private, Company K, 105th Indiana Infantry (Morgan Raid).
Julian, Absalom H., Private, Company B, 8th Indiana Infantry (three months);
Private, Company C, 36th Indiana Infantry.
**Julian, Hiram, Private, Company B, 40th Indiana Infantry.
Julian, John D., Corporal, Company C, 36th Indiana Infantry.
Julian, William S., Private, Company B, 110th Indiana Infantry (Morgan Raid);
Private, Company E; Commissary, Sergeant, Non Commissioned, Staff, 9th Indiana
Cavalry.
Julius, Ferdinand, Private, Company K, 105th Indiana Infantry (Morgan Raid).
**Junken, Henry A., Private, Company D, 19th Indiana Infantry; Private Company
I, 20th Indiana Infantry, re-organized.
**Junken, William A., Private, Company K, 134th Indiana Infantry.

K

**Kaltenbach, Michael, Private, Company A, 22nd Indiana Infantry.

Kaufman, Benjamin, Private, Company A, 139th Indiana Infantry.
*Kays, John, Private, Company E, 9th Indiana Cavalry.
  Keal, Samuel, Private, Company F, 84th Indiana Infantry.
*Keeler, John, Private, Company G, 84th Indiana Infantry.
Keesling, Amos. Private, Company H, 69th Indiana Infantry.
Keesling, Calvin F., Private, Company K, 105th Indiana Infantry (Morgan Raid).
Keesling, Calvin F. B., Private, Company K, 105th Indiana Infantry (Morgan Raid).
Keesling, Calvin L., Private, Company A, 110th Indiana Infantry (Morgan Raid).
Keesling, Eli, Private, Company K, 105th Indiana Infantry (Morgan Raid).
Keesling, Isaac B,. Private, Company H, 69th Indiana Infantry.
Keesling, John W., Private, Company K, 54th Indiana Infantry (three months);
Sergeant, Company K, 105th Indiana Infantry (Morgan Raid).
Keller, Cornelius, Private, Company K, 36th Indiana Infantry.
Keller, Hiram E, Private, 25th Indiana Battery.
*Keller, Jonathan, Private, Company A, 57th Indiana Infantry.
Keller, Jonathan, Private, Company I. 3rd Indiana Cavalry.
Keller, Samuel L., Private, Corporal, 25th Indiana Battery.
Kelley, John W., Private, Company L, 21st Indiana Infantry, re-organized as 1st
Heavy Artillery.
Kelly, James, Private, Company K, 36th Indiana Infantry.
Kelly, Joseph, Private, Company H, 147th Indiana Infantry.
Kelsey, Samuel H,. Private, Company I. 84th Indiana Infantry.
Kelso, Hugh S., Private, Company I, 9th Indiana Infantry.
Kemp, Charles B., Private, Company F. 57th Indiana Infantry.
Kendall, Adam, Private, Company K, 57th Indiana Infantry.
Kendall, Silas, Private, Company K, 148th Indiana Infantry.
Kennedy, John H., Private, Company I, 3rd Indiana Cavalry.
Kennedy, John W., Private, Company F, 6th Indiana Infantry (three months).
Kennedy, Joseph, Private, Company C, 109th Indiana Infantry (Morgan Raid);
Private. Company H, 140th Indiana Infantry.
Kenney, John, Private, Company F, 57th Indiana Infantry.
Kent, Henry, Private, Company A, 36th Indiana Infantry.
Kentley, William H., Private, Company A, 105th Indiana Infantry (Morgan Raid).
Kenyon, William, Private,'Company A, 38th Indiana Infantry.
Kern; Amos J., Private, Company B, 42nd Indiana Infantry.
Kern, John A., Private, Corporal, Sergeant, Company D, 36th Indiana Infantry
Kern, Thomas C., Private, Company A, 105th Indiana Infantry (Morgan Raid);
Private, Sergeant, Company A, 139th Indiana Infantry; Private, Company D; Commis-
sary Sergeant, Non Commissioned Staff, 147th Indiana Infantry.
Kerr, Marcus A., Musician, Company G; Principal Musician, Non Commissioned,
Staff, 84th Indiana Infantry.
Kerr, William H., Private, Company C, 36th Indiana Infantry.
**Kerr, William L., Private, Company F. 23rd Indiana Infantry; Private, Company
B, 13th Indiana Cavalry.
Kersey, Silas, H., Assistant Surgeon and Major and Surgeon, Staff, 36th Indiana
Infantry.
*Kerwood, Asbury L., Sergeant, First Sergeant, Company F, 57th Indiana Infantry.
Keys, John E., Private, Company B. 7th Indiana Cavalry.
Kilgore, James L., Private, Company K, 36th Indiana Infantry.
Kimball, David N., Sergeant, Company I, 124th Indiana Infantry.
Kimmel, Daniel, Private, Corporal, Company H, 69th Indiana Infantry.
Kimmel, Michael, Private, Company C, 109th Indiana Infantry (Morgan Raid).
*Kinder, George, Corporal, Company A, 57th Indiana Infantry.
Kinder, Jefferson, Private, Sergeant, Company B, 19th Indiana Infantry; Sergeant,
Company C, 20th Indiana Infantry, re-organized.

**Kindley, Joseph T., Private, Company D, 124th Indiana Infantry.

Kingrey, James, Private, Company I, 69th Indiana Infantry.

Kinley, Isaac, Captain, Company D; Major, Staff, 36th Indiana Infantry; Provost Marshal, 5th District of Indiana.

Kinley, James W., Private, Unassigned, 22nd Indiana Infantry.

Kinsey, David W., Private, Corporal, Company B, 139th Indiana Infantry.

Kirkham, Andrew B., Private, Company K, 37th Indiana Infantry.

Kirkham, John R., Private, Company A, 105th Indiana Infantry (Morgan Raid).

Kirkham, Samuel, Private, Company G, 16th Indiana Infantry; Private, Company H, 147th Indiana Infantry.

Kirkland, Taylor, Private, Company H, 38th Indiana Infantry.

*Kirkpatrick, Thomas, Private, Company H, 140th Indiana Infantry.

Kirman, William, Private, 19th Indiana Battery.

Kiser, Frank H., Private G, 84th Indiana Infantry.

Kissell, Alfred M., Private, Corporal, Company G, 84th Indiana Infantry.

Kissell, Samuel, Private, Unassigned, 33rd Indiana Infantry.

Kitts, Alfred, Private, Company B, 8th Indiana Infantry (three months).

*Klarman, Nicholas, Private, Company H, 147th Indiana Infantry.

Knight, Ira J., Private, Company H, 8th Indiana Infantry (three years).

Knight, William H., Private, Company H, 8th Indiana Infantry (three years).

Knight, William H., Private, 19th Indiana Battery.

Koons, George W., Private, 19th Indiana Battery.

Koons, Joseph, Private, Company B, 110th Indiana Infantry (Morgan Raid).

Koons, Thomas, Corporal, Company H, 100th Indiana Infantry.

**Kraner, Andrew F., Musician, Company G, 8th Indiana Infantry (three months); Musician, Company K, 8th Indiana Infantry (three years).

Kratzer, Samuel, Private, Company H, 69th Indiana Infantry.

Kunkle, Cyrus, Private, Company E, 8th Indiana Infantry (three years).

L

Laboyteaux, Joseph, Wagoner, Company H, 69th Indiana Infantry.

Laboyteaux, Richard J,. Private, Wagoner, Company H, 69th Indiana Infantry.

Laboyteaux, Stephen A., Private, Company A, 54th Indiana Infantry (one year); Private, Company H, 140th Indiana Infantry.

Laboyteaux, Thomas, Private, Company E, 9th Indiana Cavalry.

Lacy, Alpheus D., Private, Company D, 36th Indiana Infantry.

Lacy, James C., Private, Company B, 69th Indiana Infantry.

Lacy, John L., Private, Company B, 69th Indiana Infantry.

Lacy, Joseph M,. Private, Company I, 33rd Indiana Infantry.

Lacy, William B., Private, Company K, 19th Indiana Infantry; Corporal, Company I, 124th Indiana Infantry.

Lacy, Wilson P., Private, Company B, 69th Indiana Infantry.

Lake, Abner B., Private, Company H, 69th Indiana Infantry.

Lakin, William F., Private, Company A, 57th Indiana Infantry.

*Lamar, Absalom, Private, Company H, 140th Indiana Infantry.

Lamb, Caleb, Private, Company A, 19th Indiana Infantry.

Lamb, Erie, Private, Company D, 36th Indiana Infantry.

Lamb, Isaiah, Private, Company E, 147th Indiana Infantry.

Lamb, Job, Private, Company G, 9th Indiana Cavalry.

Lamb, Richard, Private, Company F, 6th Indiana Infantry (three months).

Landis, Daniel, Private, Company C, 36th Indiana Infantry.

*Landis, George W., Private, Company A, 57th Indiana Infantry.

Landis, John, Private, Company E, 147th Indiana Infantry.

Lane, George A., Private, Company I, 84th Indiana Infantry.

Lane, Jacob, Private, Company K, 105th Indiana Infantry (Morgan Raid).

Lane, John, Private, Company G, 9th Indiana Cavalry.

Lane, Stephen R, Private, Company D., 13th Indiana Infantry, re-organized.

Lane, Thomas B., Private, Sergeant, Company F, 148th Indiana Infantry.

**Langston, Emmett, Sergeant, Company I, 54th Indiana Infantry (one year).

Lanham, Charles, Private, Company K, 105th Indiana Infantry (Morgan Raid); Private, Company A, 87th Indiana Infantry.

Lanham, Elza, Private, Company K, 105th Indiana Infantry (Morgan Raid).

Laremore, James, Private, Company D, 36th Indiana Infantry.

Larrowe, William, Private, Company K, 99th Indiana Infantry.

Latchaw, William T., Private, Company D, 87th Indiana Infantry; Private, Company D, 42nd Indiana Infantry.

Laven, John, Private, Company H, 140th Indiana Infantry.

Lawrence, Thomas, Private, Corporal, Company C, 28th U. S. C. T.

Lawson, Dallas, Private, Company A, 36th Indiana Infantry; Corporal, Company H, 30th Indiana Infantry, re-organized.

Leach, George. Corporal, 12th Indiana Battery.

Leakey, Anthony, Musician, Company A, 8th Indiana Infantry (three years).

Leakey, Arthur M., Musician, Company A, 54th Indiana Infantry (one year); Private, 20th Indiana Battery.

Leakey, Isaac R. R., Private, Company F, 84th Indiana Infantry.

Leakey, Thomas, Private, Company A, 8th Indiana Infantry (three years).

**Leamon, John N., Private, Company B, 54th Indiana Infantry (one year).

Leavell, Benjamin D., Corporal, Company F, 57th Indiana Infantry.

Leavell, John W., First Lieutenant, Needmore Rangers, Indiana Legion.

Leavell, William L., Private, Company F, 57th Indiana Infantry.

Lee, John, Corporal, Company I, 54th Indiana Infantry (three months).

Lee, Robert D. F., Private, Company I, 3rd Indiana Cavalry.

*Leeka, Jesse, Private, Company A, 105th Indiana Infantry (Morgan Raid); Private, Company E, 9th Indiana Cavalry.

**Leffingwell, Jonathan, Private, Company I, 118th Indiana Infantry; Private, Company I, 34th Indiana Infantry.

*Leisure, William H., Private, Company E, 9th Indiana Cavalry.

*Lemay, Charles W., Private, Company A, 57th Indiana Infantry.

Lemberger, William, Private, Company D, 11th Indiana Infantry.

Lemon, Eli J., Private, Company K, 36th Indiana Infantry.

Lemon, Joseph G., Corporal, Sergeant, Company K; Second Lieutenant, First Lieutenant, Company E, 36th Indiana Infantry.

Lemon, Orange V., Senior, Captain and Chaplain, Staff, 36th Indiana Infantry.

Lemon, Orange V., Junior, Musician, Company K, 36th Indiana Infantry.

Lemon, William, Private, Company B, 8th Indiana Infantry (three months); Private, Company E, 8th Indiana Infantry (three years).

Lemon, William H., Private, Company C, 109th Indiana Infantry (Morgan Raid).

*Lemsford, Benjamin F., Private, Company H, 147th Indiana Infantry.

Lennard, George W., Adjutant, Staff, 36th Indiana Infantry; Lieutenant Colonel and Colonel, Staff, 57th Indiana Infantry.

Lennington, Abraham, Corporal, Company K, 36th Indiana Infantry.

Leonard, George W., Corporal, Company A, 57th Indiana Infantry.

Leonard, James, Private, Company D, 8th Indiana Infantry (three years).

**Leonard, John C., Private, Company L, 21st Indiana Infantry re-organized as 1st Heavy Artillery.

Leonard, William H., Second Lieutenant, Company A, 57th Indiana Infantry.

Lesh, Groves, Private, Company D, 36th Indiana Infantry.

Lester, Wilson, Private, Company I, 69th Indiana Infantry.

Level, Abraham, Private, Company B, 42nd Indiana Infantry.

COMPANY C, 36th INDIANA INFANTRY.

COMPANY C, 36th INDIANA INFANTRY.

Level, Samuel, Private, Company F, 7th Indiana Infantry (three months); Corporal, Company E, 7th Indiana Infantry (three years).

Level, Solomon, Private, Company A, 68th Indiana Infantry.

Leweck, Gustave W., Musician, Company F, 84th Indiana Infantry.

Lewellen, John W., Private, Unassigned, 22nd Indiana Infantry.

Lewelling, James M., Private, Unassigned, 22nd Indiana Infantry.

Lewis, James N., Private, Company C, 36th Indiana Infantry; Private, 2nd Indiana Battery, re-organized.

Lewis, John F, Private, Company B, 139th Indiana Infantry; Private, Sergeant, Company H, 147th Indiana Infantry.

*Lewis, Nelson, Private, Company G, 84th Indiana Infantry.

Lewis, Thomas J., Private, Company C, 36th Indiana Infantry.

Lewis, Thomas N., Private, Company A, 36th Indiana Infantry; Private, Company H, 30th Indiana Infantry, re-organized.

*Lewis, William ,Sergeant, Company K, 36th Indiana Infantry.

Lewis, William H., Private, Corporal, Company A, 36th Indiana Infantry.

Linens, Joseph, Private, Company A, 36th Indiana Infantry.

Lines, Elijah H., Private, Company C, 5th Indiana Cavalry.

Linnen, Daniel, Private, Company A, 139th Indiana Iufantry.

**Linville, David C., Private, Company B, 70th Indiana Infantry.

Little, Gambral, Private, Company B, 130th Indiana Infantry.

Livezey, George H., Private, Company G, 84th Indiana Infantry; Private, Company G, 1st U. S. Engineers.

Livezey, John C., Sergeant, Second Lieutenant, Captain, Company C, 36th Indiana Infantry; Captain and Commissary of Subsistence, Brevet Major, Staff, U. S. Volunteers. (See General Officers, Chapter IX).

Livezey, Joseph, Private, Company G, 84th Indiana Infantry.

Livezey, William E., Corporal, Sergeant, Company G, 84th Indiana Infantry.

*Lloyd, Levi, Private, Company F, 57th Indiana Infantry.

*Lock, Lewis, Private, Company F, 57th Indiana Infantry.

Lockridge, George, Private, Company F, 84th Indiana Infantry.

Lockridge, Henry, Private, Company A, 54th Indiana Infantry (one year).

Lockridge, John, Private, Company D, 36th Indiana Infantry.

Lodge, Oliver, Private, Company M, 21st Indiana Infantry re-organized as 1st Heavy Artillery.

Loer, George, Private, Company B, 33rd Indiana Infantry.

Loer, Pearson, Corporal, Company A, 54th Indiana Infantry (one year)

Long, Edward M., Private, Company C, 5th Indiana Cavalry; Second Lieutenant, Company B, 3rd North Carolina Mounted Infantry.

Long, William, Private, Company E, 11th Indiana Infantry.

Longfellow, Lorenzo D., Private, Company I, 69th Indiana Infantry.

Lott, Uriah, Private, Company A, 110th Indiana Infantry (Morgan Raid).

Lovett, Martin D., Private, Company E, 106th Indiana Infantry (Morgan Raid).

Lowe, David, Private, Company B, 110th Indiana Infantry (Morgan Raid); Private, Company E, 9th Indiana Cavalry.

Lowe, George, Private, Company B, 110th Indiana Infantry, (Morgan Raid).

Lowe, George N., Private, Company D, 36th Indiana Infantry; Private, Company D, 147th Indiana Infantry.

Lowe, John, Private, Company K, 105th Indiana Infantry (Morgan Raid).

Lowe, John W., Private, Company A, 110th Indiana Infantry (Morgan Raid).

Lowe, Joseph S., Private, Corporal, Company A, 36th Indiana Infantry.

Lowe, Nixon, Private, Company K, 105th Indiana Infantry (Morgan Raid).

Lowe, William, Private, Company C, 36th Indiana Infantry.

Lowery, Francis M., Private, Company I, 69th Indiana Infantry.

Lowery, Frederick, Private, Company H, 140th Indiana Infantry.

Lowery, Henry, Wagoner, Company C, 36th Indiana Infantry.

Lowery, Jonah, Private, Unassigned, 22nd Indiana Infantry.
Lowery, Philander, Private, Sergeant, Company F, 57th Indiana Infantry.
Lowery, Philip, Private, Company E, 9th Indiana Cavalry.
Lowery, Samuel, Private, Company B, 139th Indiana Infantry.
Lowery, Walter K., Private, Sergeant, Company I, 69th Indiana Infantry.
Lowhead, John W., Private, Company C, 147th Indiana Infantry.
Loy, William L., Private, Company.E, 147th Indiana Infantry.
Lucas, Andrew J., Private, Company I, 124th Indiana Infantry.
**Lucas, David, Private, Company D, 13th Indiana Infantry, re-organized.
Lucas, George, Private, Company D, 8th U. S. C. T.
Luce, Abraham, Private, Company A, 110th Indiana Infantry (Morgan Raid).
Luce, Henry, Sergeant, Company C, 109th Indiana Infantry (Morgan Raid).
Luce, John J., Private, Company H, 140th Indiana Infantry.
Luellen, David M., Private, Corporal, Company E, 147th Indiana Infantry.
Luellen, Oliver F., Private, Company C, 36th Indiana Infantry; Private, Sergeant,
Company A, 147th Indiana Infantry.
**Luther, William J. B., Private, Company E, 132nd Infantry.
Luthultz, Jacob, Private, Company K, 105th Indiana Infantry (Morgan Raid);
Private, Company H, 140th Indiana Infantry.
Luthultz, Joachim, Private, Company D, 36th Indiana Infantry.
Luthultz, Joshua, Private, Company D, 36th Indiana Infantry
Luzadder, Moses, Private, Company G, 84th Indiana Infantry.
Lyman, George, Private, Company I, 3rd Indiana Cavalry.
*Lyman, Perry C., Private, Company H, 147th Indiana Infantry.
Lynch, Edward, Musician, Company E, 8th Indiana Infantry (three years).
Lynch, William A., Private, Company A, 110th Indiana Infantry (Morgan Raid):
*Lynum, John, Private, Company I, 3rd Indiana Cavalry.
Lytle, John D., Private, Company E, 8th Indiana Infantry (three months); Ser-
geant, Company I, 57th Indiana Infantry.
Lytle, Marcellus, Private, Company D, 11th Indiana Infantry.

Mc

McAfee, John F., Private, Company I, 69th Indiana Infantry.
McAfee, Mark,* Private, Company A, 110th Indiana Infantry (Morgan Raid).
McAfee, Nicholas, Private, Company B, 139th Indiana Infantry.
McAlister, Alexander, Private, Company E, 8th Indiana Infantry (three years).
McArthur, Korac, Private, Company B, 8th Indiana Infantry (three months);
First Sergeant, Second Lieutenant, Captain, Company F, 57th Indiana Infantry.
McCance, John, Private, Company E, 8th Indiana Infantry (three years).
McCann, William, Private, Company I, 84th Indiana Infantry.
McCarty, John, Private, Company A, 110th Indiana Infantry (Morgan Raid).
McConnelly, James, Private, Company B, 139th Indiana Infantry.
McConnelly, Jonathan, Private, Company B, 139th Indiana Infantry.
McConnell, James, Private, Company H, 147th Indiana Infantry.
McConnell, John B., Private, Company I, 69th Indiana Infantry.
McConnell, Jonathan, Private, Company H, 140th Indiana Infantry.
McConnell, Joseph P., Private, Company K, 105th Indiana Infantry (Morgan
Raid); Private, Company E, 9th Indiana Cavalry.
McConnell, Robert C., Second Lieutenant, Company H, 140th Indiana Infantry.
McConner, J. P., Private, Company A, 110th Indiana Infantry (Morgan Raid).
*McCorkhill, John, Private, Company A, 57th Indiana Infantry.
**McCorkhill, John H., Private, Company B, 9th Indiana Cavalry.
McCorkle, James, Private, Company B, 42nd Indiana Infantry.
McCormack, Andrew J., Private, Company E, 9th Indiana Cavalry.
McCormack, Isaac N., Musician, Company I; Principal Musician, Non Commis-
sioned, Staff, 69th Indiana Infantry.

McCormack, Jackson, Private, Corporal, Company H, 140th Indiana Infantry.
McCormack, James E., Private, Company H, 69th Indiana Infantry.
McCormack, John, Private, Company H, 69th Indiana Infantry.
McCormack, John R.., Private, Company I, 69th Indiana Infantry.
McCormack, John W., Private, Company D, 147th Indiana Infantry.
McCormack, Josiah, Private, Wagoner, Company E, 9th Indiana Cavalry.
McCormack, Noah, Corporal, Company C, 36th Indiana Infantry.
McCormack, Samuel, Private. Company G, 9th Indiana Cavalry.
McCormack, Thomas, Private, Company K, 8th Indiana Infantry (three years)
McCormack, William, Private, Company H. 69th Indiana Infantry.
**McCray, Milton, Private, Company K, 132nd Indiana Infantry.
*McCullouch, John Q., Private, Company H, 147th Indiana Infantry.
McCullum, Simeon, Private, Company I, 147th Indiana Infantry.
McCune, Henry W., Private, Company G, 84th Indiana Infantry.
McCune, Thompson W., Private, Company E. 8th Indiana Infantry (three years);
First Lieutenant, Company G, 1st Regiment, Mississippi (River) Marine Brigade.
McCurdy, William, Sergeant, Company H, 69th Indiana Infantry.
**McDivitt, John, Private, 3rd Indiana Battery.
McDonald, David, Private, Company K, 36th Indiana Infantry.
McDougall, George, Private, Company A, 30th Indiana Infantry, re-organized..
McDowell, Andrew, Private, Corporal, Company C, 36th Indiana Infantry.
McDowell, John, Private, Company B, 110th Indiana Infantry (Morgan Raid).
McDowell, Peter, Private, Company C, 36th Indiana Infantry.
McFarland, Davis S., Private, Company A, 139th Indiana Infantry.
McFeely, Aaron, Private, Company F, 6th Indiana Infantry (three months).
McFeters, James, Private, Company A, 6th Indiana Infantry (three months).
McFetridge, James, Private, Company C, 9th Indiana Infantry.
*McGeath, Martin, Private, Company F, 57th Indiana Infantry.
McGinnis, James F., Private, Company K, 18th Indiana Infantry.
McGrath, William, Private, Company I. 7th Indiana Cavalry; Private, Company
A, 7th Indiana Cavalry, re-organized.
McGraw, George W., Private, Company G, 84th Indiana Infantry.
McGraw, Richard L., Private, Company G, 84th Indiana Infantry.
McGuffin, Joseph B., Private, Company A, 105th Indiana Infantry (Morgan Raid);
Private, Company A, 4th Indiana Cavalry.
McGuffin, Samuel H., Private, Company H. 147th Indiana Infantry.
McGuffin, William H. H., Private, Company F, 6th Indiana Infantry (three
months); Corporal, Company I, 3rd Indiana Cavalry.
**McGuire, Amos, Private, Company B. 12th Indiana Infantry.
*McGuire, James, Private, Company H, 140th Indiana Infantry.
*McGuire, John, Private, Company K, 36th Indiana Infantry.
McHenry, John A. J., Company I, 147th Indiana Infantry.
McIntosh, William M., Private, Company B, 139th Indiana Infantry.
McInturf, William T., Private, Company B, 124th Indiana Infantry.
McKee, Joseph, Private, Company F, 57th Indiana Infantry; Private, Company K.
105th Indiana Infantry (Morgan Raid).
McKee, William E., Private, Company M, 21st Indiana Infantry re-organized as 1st
Heavy Artillery.
McKenzie, David, Private, Company H, 140th Indiana Infantry.
McKenzie, John, Private, Company I, 69th Indiana Infantry.
McKinney, Wilson H., Private, Corporal. Company A, 36th Indiana Infantry.
McKinzie, Barnabas, Private, Company F, 148th Indiana Infantry.
McLaughlin, Edward L., Private, Company F, 84th Indiana Infantry.
McLaughlin, William H., Sergeant, First Sergeant, Company A, 57th Indiana In-
fantry.

McLeland, Eli, Private, Company G, 84th Indiana Infantry.

McLeland, Isaac, Corporal, Company G, 84th Indiana Infantry.

McMillan, Charles R., Private, Company K, 11th Indiana Infantry.

*McNeese, Alfred, Private, Company K, 36th Indiana Infantry.

*McNeese, Elza, Private, Company K, 36th Indiana Infantry. .

McNew, John H., Private, Company E, 8th Indiana Infantry (three years); Private, Company K, 105th Indiana Infantry (Morgan Raid); Corporal, Company H, 140th Indiana Infantry.   •

McNew, Richard, Private, Company E, 8th Indiana Infantry (three years); Private, Company K, 105th Indiana Infantry (Morgan Raid).

McRoberts, Charles L., Sergeant, Company I, 8th Regiment, 1st Army Corps (Hancock's Veteran Corps).

McSherley, John, Private, Company G, 84th Indiana Infantry.

McSherry, William L., Private, Company H, 147th Indiana Infantry.

M

Macy, Gamaliel B., Private, 19th Indiana Battery.

Macy, George F., Private, Company B, 110th Indiana Infantry (Morgan Raid); Private, Sergeant, 4th Indiana Battery.

Macy, John L., Corporal, Company G, 16th Indiana Infantry.

Macy, Lambert, Private, 19th Indiana Battery.

Macy, William H., Private, Corporal, Sergeant, Company D, 36th Indiana Infantry.

*Madarea, George W., Private, Company H, 147th Indiana Infantry.

Maddy, Isaac S., Private, Company H, 140th Indiana Infantry.

Madison, Charles T., Private, Company F, 6th Indiana Infantry (three months); Corporal, Company A, 36th Indiana Infantry.

Madison, John, Private, Sergeant, Company A, 57th Indiana Infantry

Madison, William, Private, Company F, 84th Indiana Infantry; Private, Company M, 9th Indiana Cavalry.

Madoris, William, Private, Company I, 147th Indiana Infantry.

Magann, E. K., Private, Company A, 110th Indiana Infantry (Morgan Raid).

Magenhart, William, Private, Company A, 11th Indiana Infantry.

Mahan, Wesley D,. Private, Company B, 110th Indiana Infantry (Morgan Raid); Private, Company B, 139th Indiana Infantry.

Main, Amos, Private, Company K, 74th Indiana Infantryy.

Main, Henry, Private, Company K, 124th Indiana Infantry.

Main, Leonard, Private, 23rd Indiana Battery.

Mallory, James, Private, Company A, 36th Indiana Infantry.

Mandlin, David, Private, Company I, 147th Indiana Infantry.

Manis, Curtis, Private, Company A, 36th Indiana Infantry; Private, Company H, 30th Indiana Infantry, re-organized.

Manis, George, Corporal, Company G, 16th Indiana Infantry.

Manis, Isaac G., Private, Company A, 36th Indiana Infantry; Private, Company H, 30th Indiana Infantry, re-organized.

Manlove, Charles, Private, Company D, 36th Indiana Infantry.

Manlove, John, Private, Company D, 36th Indiana Infantry.

Manlove, Pleasant, Private, Company A, 105th Indiana Infantry (Morgan Raid).

Mann, Judson L., Private, Company G, 17th Indiana Infantry.

Manning, Cyrus, Private, Company A, 54th Indiana Infantry (one year).

Manning, John, Private, Company B, 8th Indiana Infantry (three months);· Private, Company E, 8th Indiana Infantry (three years).

Manor, Henry C., Private, Company F, 6th Indiana Infantry (three months); Private, Company A, 36th Indiana Infantry.

*Markle, Dewitt C., Corporal, Company F, 57th Indiana Infantry.

Marley, Ralph, Private, Company A, 36th Indiana Infantry.

Marlow, Simeon, Private, Company A, 36th Indiana Infantry.

Marlow, William, Private, Company A, 36th Indiana Infantry; Private, Company H, 30th Indiana Infantry, re-organized.

Martin, Jefferson, Private, Company F, 84th Indiana Infantry.

Martin, Robert B., Private, Company F, 6th Indiana Infantry (three months).

Martin, Samuel D., Private, Company I, 69th Indiana Infantry.

Martin, Samuel G., Private, Company D, 36th Indiana Infantry.

Martindale, James B., Private, Company A, 110th Indiana Infantry (Morgan Raid).

Martindale, William S., Private, Company A, 110th Indiana Infantry (Morgan Raid).

Marvin, Doctor C., Private, Company B., 139th Indiana Infantry.

Marvin, William, Private, 25th Indiana Battery.

Mason, David A., Musician, Company F, 84th Indiana Infantry.

Mason, Daniel, Saddler, Company M, 9th Indiana Cavalry.

Mason, Daniel W., Private, Company A, 110th Indiana Infantry (Morgan Raid).

Mason, George, Private, Company G, 84th Indiana Infantry.

Mason, George W., Private, Company F, 6th Indiana Infantry (three months); Private, Company G, 52nd Indiana Infantry; Corporal, Company G, 52nd Indiana Infantry, re-organized.

Mason, Jerome B., Second Lieutenant, Company F, 84th Indiana Infantry.

Mason, John, Private, Musician, Company A, 139th Indiana Infantry.

Mason, Robert, Private, Company E, 8th Indiana Infantry (three years).

Mason, Robert W., Private, Company F, 16th Indiana Infantry (one year); Corporal, Company F, 84th Indiana Infantry.

Mason, Thomas, Private, Company H, 52nd Indiana Infantry.

Mathews, Charles, Private, Company E, 8th Indiana Infantry (three years)

**Matthews, Joseph P., Farrier and Blacksmith, Company B, 5th Indiana Cavalry.

Maxwell, Aaron W., Private, Company A, 105th Indiana Infantry (Morgan Raid); Private, Corporal, Company A, 139th Indiana Infantry.

May, Franklin, Private, Company I, 54th Indiana Infantry (three months); Private, 2nd Indiana Battery; Private, 2nd Indiana Battery, re-organized.

May, James, Private, Company F, 20th Indiana Infantry.

May, John H., Corporal, Company A, 57th Indiana Infantry; Private, Company F, 84th Indiana Infantry.

May, Jonathan, Private, Company E, 8th Indiana Infantry (three years).

May, Richard, Private, Company D, 19th Indiana Infantry.

May, William, Private, Unassigned, 18th Indiana Infantry.

May, William, Private, Company A, 30th Indiana Infantry, re-organized.

Mays, Wesley A., Private, Company I, 84th Indiana Infantry.

Mead, Timothy, Private, 19th Indiana Battery.

Meair, Charles L., Artificer, 19th Indiana Battery.

Meek, Irvin R., Private, Corporal, Company F, 8th Indiana Infantry (three years).

Meek, James A., Corporal, Company H, 20th Indiana Infantry.

Meek, William J., Private, Company A, 57th Indiana Infantry.

Meeker, Benjamin F., Private, Company C, 109th Indiana Infantry (Morgan Raid); Private, Company H, 147th Indiana Infantry.

Meeker, Sleaseman, First Sergeant, Company K, 105th Indiana Infantry (Morgan Raid).

Meeker, William, Corporal, Company F, 124th Indiana Infantry.

Mellett, Arthur C., Private, Company H, 9th Indiana Infantry.

Mellett, Joshua H., Private, Company A, 110th Indiana Infantry (Morgan Raid).

Mellette, Randolph H., Seaman, U. S. Navy.

Melross, Adam, Wagoner, Company E, 8th Indiana Infantry (three years); Corporal, Company C, 109th Indiana Infantry (Morgan Raid); Corporal, Company F, 124th Indiana Infantry.

Mendenhall, Daniel, Private, Company A, 147th Indiana Infantry.

**Mendenhall, Elihu T., Private, Company A, 101st Indiana Infantry.

*Mendenhall, Kelita, Private, Company E, 9th Indiana Cavalry.
Mercer, David W., Private, Company H, 140th Indiana Infantry.
Mercer, James M., Private, Company A, 54th Indiana Infantry (one year).
Meuser, George W., Private, Sergeant, 2nd Indiana Battery.
Micha, Lewis, Private, Company I, 3rd Indiana Cavalry.
Michael, Henry, Private, Company A, 110th Indiana Infantry (Morgan Raid).
Mickle, John, Private, Company G, 9th Indiana Infantry.
**Middleton, Joseph L., Private, Company I, 9th Indiana Cavalry.
Midkiff, Wallace, Private, Company B, 156th Indiana Infantry.
*Miller, Abraham, Private, Company H, 147th Indiana Infantry.
Miller, Abraham, Private, Company C, 36th Indiana Infantry.
*Miller, Benjamin, Private, Company A, 57th Indiana Infantry.
Miller, Benjamin A., Private, Company A, 36th Indiana Infantry.
Miller, Benjamin F., Private, Company B, 156th Indiana Infantry.
Miller, Daniel, Private, Company A, 8th Indiana Infantry (three years).
Miller, Francis, Private, Company B, 130th Indiana Infantry.
Miller, George, Private, Company B, 149th Indiana Infantry.
Miller, Henry, Private, Unassigned, 16th Indiana Infantry.
Miller, Henry, Private, Company H, 69th Indiana Infantry.
Miller, James, Private, Company D, 36th Indiana Infantry; Private, Company H, 30th Indiana Infantry, re-organized.
Miller, James, Private, Company F, 84th Indiana Infantry.
Miller, John, Private, Company A, 105th Indiana Infantry (Morgan Raid).
Miller, John W., Private, Company H, 69th Indiana Infantry.
Miller, Peter, Private, Company I, 69th Indiana Infantry.
Miller, Samuel C., Private, Corporal, Company E, 8th Indiana Infantry (three years).
Miller, Sylvester, Private, Company F, 84th Indiana Infantry.
Miller, Thomas, Private, Company I, 3rd Indiana Cavalry.
Miller, William B., Corporal, Company F, 84th Indiana Infantry.
Millikan, Eli F., Private, Company C, 36th Indiana Infantry.
Millikan, James W., Sergeant, Company C, 36th Indiana Infantry.
Millis, Frank, Private, Company A, 139th Indiana Infantry.
Millis, John, Private, Company A, 139th Indiana Infantry.
Millis, Lindsay, Private, Company A, 139th Indiana Infantry.
*Mills, Andrew J., Private, Company K, 36th Indiana Infantry.
Mills, George W., Private, Company K, 36th Indiana Infantry; Private, Company A, 105th Indiana Infantry (Morgan Raid).
*Mills, Leander F., Private, Company E, 9th Indiana Cavalry.
Mills, Pulaski, Private, Company C, 147th Indiana Infantry.
Mills, Robert M., Private, Sergeant, Company E, 9th Indiana Cavalry.
Mills, Samuel H., Corporal, Company H, 140th Indiana Infantry.
Mills, William D., Private, Company A, 105th Indiana Infantry (Morgan Raid); Private, Company A, 139th Indiana Infantry.
Mimmes, Wallenstein, Private, Company I, 3rd Indiana Cavalry.
Mincer, Samuel, Private, Company K, 36th Indiana Infantry.
Minesinger, Charles W. T., Corporal, Second Lieutenant, First Lieutenant, Company F, 57th Indiana Infantry.
Minesinger, Henry M., Musician, Company B, 8th Indiana Infantry (three months).
Minnick, Andrew J., Corporal, Company H, 69th Indiana Infantry.
Minnick, David H., Private, Company E, 36th Indiana Infantry; Private, Company H, 30th Indiana Infantry, re-organized.
*Misener, Abraham G., Private, Company H, 140th Indiana Infantry.
Misener, Joseph W., Private, Company B, 5th Indiana Cavalry.

James W. Millikan

James W. Millikan

Mitcham, Abraham, Private, Company H, 69th Indiana Infantry; Private, Company G, 7th Indiana Cavalry; Private, Company F, 7th Indiana Cavalry, re-organized.

Mitchell, Charles L., Corporal, Company K, 105th Indiana Infantry (Morgan Raid); Private, Company E, 9th Indiana Cavalry.

Mitchell, Daniel, Private, Unassigned, 22nd Indiana Infantry.

Mitchell, Leander P., Private, Company B, 139th Indiana Infantry.

Mitchell, Perry, Private, Company C, 36th Indiana Infantry.

Mitchell, Samuel A., Private, Sergeant, First Sergeant, Second Lieutenant, Company E, 8th Indiana Infantry (three years).

Mitchell, Thomas, Private, Company C, 36th Indiana Infantry.

Mitchell, Thomas J., Private, Company K, 36th Indiana Infantry.

Mitchell, William, Corporal, Company E, 8th Indiana Infantry (three years).

Modlin, David, Private, Company B, 28th U. S. C. T

Modlin, Elias, Private, Company A, 19th Indiana Infantry; Private, Company I, 20th Indiana Infantry, re-organized.

Modlin, Henry, Private, Company C, 28th U. S. C. T.

Modlin, John D., Private, Company E, 9th Indiana Cavalry.

Modlin, John H., Corporal, Company C, 36th Indiana Infantry.

Modlin, Oliver H., Private, Company K, 105th Indiana Infantry (Morgan Raid).

Modlin, Seth, Private, Company A, 139th Indiana Infantry.

Modlin, Sonney, Private, Company B, 28th U. S. C. T.

Modlin, Thomas W., Private, Company I, 69th Indiana Infantry.

Modlin, William H., Private, Corporal, Company C, 36th Indiana Infantry.

Mogle, Benjamin, Private, Company K, 105th Indiana Infantry (Morgan Raid).

Moler, Andrew J., Private, Company A, 36th Indiana Infantry.

Moler, Francis M., Private, Company A, 36th Indiana Infantry.

Montgomery, Alexander C., Private, Company K, 36th Indiana Infantry.

Monticue, Benjamin F., Private, Company A, 105th Indiana Infantry (Morgan Raid); Private, Company D, 36th Indiana Infantry; Corporal, Company H, 30th Indiana Infantry, re-organized.

Monticue, David, Private, Company D, 30th Indiana Infantry.

Monticue, Jesse B., Private, Company D, 36th Indiana Infantry; Private, Company A, 105th Indiana Infantry (Morgan Raid); Private, 4th Indiana Battery.

Monticue, Solomon R., Private, Corporal, 4th Indiana Battery.

*Moon, Benjamin, Private, Company H, 147th Indiana Infantry.

Mooney, Eli B., Private, Company A, 110th Indiana Infantry (Morgan Raid).

Mooney, George, Private, Company B, 139th Indiana Infantry.

Mooney, Robert, Private, Company B, 139th Indiana Infantry.

Moore, Abraham, Private, Company B, 2nd Indiana Cavalry.

Moore, Charles H. C., Private, Company A, 36th Indiana Infantry; Private, Company K, 11th Indiana Infantry.

Moore, Cornelius M., First Lieutenant, New Castle Guards, Indiana Legion; Private, Company B, 8th Indiana Infantry (three months); Sergeant, Company C, 36th Indiana Infantry; First Lieutenant, Company B, 110th Indiana Infantry (Morgan Raid); Captain, Company B, 139th Indiana Infantry.

Moore, Gideon, Private, Company H, 59th Indiana Infantry.

Moore, Henry H., Private, Company C, 36th Indiana Infantry.

Moore, James L., Private, Corporal, Company E, 8th Indiana Infantry (three years).

Moore, James W., Private, Company K, 19th Indiana Infantry; Private, Company E, 20th Indiana Infantry, re-organized.

Moore, John L., Private, Company C, 147th Indiana Infantry.

Moore, John M., First Lieutenant, Company G, 84th Indiana Infantry.

Moore, Josiah B., Private, Company A, 36th Indiana Infantry; Corporal, Company H, 30th Indiana Infantry, re-organized.

**Moore, Louis N., Private, Company K, 16th Indiana Infantry.

Moore, Louis P., Private, Company A, 139th Indiana Infantry. (See Alphabetical List B).

Moore, Miles M., Private, Company C, 36th Indiana Infantry.

Moore, William, Seaman, U. S. Navy.

Moore, William M., Private, Company C, 109th Indiana Infantry (Morgan Raid); Private, Corporal, First Sergeant, Second Lieutenant, Company F, 124th Indiana Infantry.

Moran, John, Private, Company C, 36th Indiana Infantry.

Moreau, William C., Captain, Company F, 6th Indiana Infantry (three months); Captain, Company I, 3rd Indiana Cavalry.

Moreland, David, Junior, Private, Company H, 69th Indiana Infantry.

Morgan, George W., Private, Company H, 69th Indiana Infantry.

Morris, George S., Private, Company E, 8th Indiana Infantry (three years).

Morris, Harriman, Private, 19th Indiana Battery.

Morris, Isaac H., Corporal, Sergeant, Company F, 84th Indiana Infantry.

Morris, Joshua, Private, Company A, 30th Indiana Infantry, re-organized.

Morris, Mark M., Private, Corporal, Sergeant, Second Lieutenant, First Lieutenant, Company A, 57th Indiana Infantry.

Morris, Robert, Private, Company A, 36th Indiana Infantry.

Morris, William, Private, Company A, 36th Indiana Infantry; Private, Company A, 4th Regiment, 1st Army Corps (Hancock's Veteran Corps).

Morris, William J., Private, Company D, 36th Indiana Infantry.

Morris, William W., Private, Company I, 3rd Indiana Cavalry.

Morris, Wilson M., Private, Company D, 36th Indiana Infantry.

*Mosebaugh, George B., Private, Company H, 147th Indiana Infantry.

Moss, Jeremiah, Private, Company D, 8th U. S. C. T.

Mowrey, Elijah, Private, Company K, 105th Indiana Infantry (Morgan Raid).

Mullen, Emery H., Private, Company B, 8th Indiana Infantry (three months); Private, Company I, 36th Indiana Infantry; Private, 2nd Indiana Battery, re-organized.

Mullen, Hugh L., Sergeant, First Sergeant, First Lieutenant, Captain, Company C, 36th Indiana Infantry.

Mullen, Hugh M., Private, Company A, 124th Indiana Infantry.

Mullen, Joseph P., Private, 25th Indiana Battery.

Mullen, Joseph R., Private, Company A, 54th Indiana Infantry (one year).

Mundell, John A., Private, Company E, 9th Indiana Cavalry.

Murphey, Amos D., Private, Company F, 84th Indiana Infantry; Private, Company K, 57th Indiana Infantry.

Murphey, Benjamin F., Captain and Assistant Quartermaster General, State of Indiana. (See General Officers, Chapter IX).

Murphey, Henry C., Private, Company G; Commissary Sergeant, Non Commissioned Staff, 84th Indiana Infantry.

Murphey, Hugh A., Private, Company H, 69th Indiana Infantry.

Murphey, James, Private, Unassigned, 11th Indiana Infantry.

Murphey, James, Private, 25th Indiana Battery.

Murphey, Joel S., First Sergeant, Company A, 110th Indiana Infantry (Morgan Raid).

Murphey, Jonathan, Private, Company B, 8th Indiana Infantry (three months); Private, Corporal, Company F, 124th Indiana Infantry.

Murphey, Jonathan A., Private, Company H, 69th Indiana Infantry.

Murphey, Joseph S., Private, Company H, 140th Indiana Infantry.

Murphey, Miles, Colonel and Inspector General, State of Indiana. (See General Officers, Chapter IX).

Murphey, Miles E., Private, Company A, 110th Indiana Infantry (Morgan Raid).

Murphey, Richard, Private, Corporal, 19th Indiana Battery.

Murphey, William C., Corporal, Company C, 109th Indiana Infantry (Morgan Raid); Private, Corporal, Company B, 139th Indiana Infantry.

Murray, Albert P., Private, Company K, 19th Indiana Infantry; Private, Company E, 20th Indiana Infantry, re-organized.

Murray, Alfred L., Private, Unassigned, 22nd Indiana Infantry.

Murray, Franklin W., Corporal, Sergeant, Company K, 36th Indiana Infantry.

Murray, John C., Wagoner, Company K, 36th Indiana Infantry.

Murray, Ralph V., Corporal, Company D, 36th Indiana Infantry.

Murray, Samuel T., Private, Company C, 101st Indiana Infantry.

Murray, William H., Corporal, Second Lieutenant, Company K, 19th Indiana Infantry.

Musselman, John W., Private, Sergeant, Company H, 16th Indiana Infantry.

Muterspaugh, Jacob, Private, Company A, 105th Indiana Infantry (Morgan Raid).

**Muzzy, William, Private, Company A, 8th Indiana Infantry (three months); Private, 17th Indiana Battery; Private, Company E, 106th Indiana Infantry (Morgan Raid); Private, Company D, 9th Indiana Infantry.

Myers, John B., Private, Company D, 147th Indiana Infantry.

Myers, Joseph, Private, Company I, 57th Indiana Infantry.

**Myers, Lewis E., Private, Company H, 153rd Indiana Infantry.

Myers, Solomon, Private, Company D, 147th Indiana Infantry.

N

Nation, Enoch H., Private, Company E, 106th Indiana Infantry (Morgan Raid).

Nation, Enoch T., Private, Company G, 9th Indiana Cavalry.

Nation, James R., Sergeant, Company A, 8th Indiana Infantry (three years); Captain, Company G; Major, Staff, 9th Indiana Cavalry.

Nation, Seth, Private, Company A, 8th Indiana Infantry (three years).

Nation, Wallace, Private, Company E, 106th Indiana Infantry (Morgan Raid); Private, 20th Indiana Battery.

Nation, William, Private, Company C, 5th Indiana Cavalry.

Nay, James R., Private, Company E, 9th Indiana Cavalry.

Needham, George W., Private, Company G, 7th Indiana Cavalry

Needham, Isaac, Private, Company G, 7th Indiana Cavalry; Private, Company F, 7th Indiana Cavalry, re-organized.

Needham, Isaac, Private, Company F, 154th Indiana Infantry.

Needham, Jesse W., Private, Company C, 36th Indiana Infantry.

**Needham, Joshua, Private, Company E, 19th Indiana Infantry; Private, Company E, 20th Indiana Infantry, re-organized.

Needham, Robert, Private, Company A, 36th Indiana Infantry.

Needham, Winford, Musician, Company F; Principal Musician, Non-Commissioned Staff, 57th Indiana Infantry.

Needler, Levi, Private, 23rd Indiana Battery.

Neely, George P., Private, Company K, 36th Indiana Infantry.

Neff, Alkanah C., Private, Company E, 8th Indiana Infantry (three years).

Nelson, Nathan M., Private, Company A, 36th Indiana Infantry; Private, Company H, 30th Indiana Infantry, re-organized.

Nelson, Wilson, Private, Corporal, Company E, 8th Indiana Infantry (three years); Private, Company H, 147th Indiana Infantry.

Netz, Peter, Private, Company A, 54th Indiana Infantry (one year). (See Alphabetical List B).

Newbold, Samuel, Private, Company A, 8th Indiana Infantry (three years).

Newbold, William H., Private, Company D, 8th Indiana Infantry (three years).

Newby, Benjamin F., Private, Corporal, Company C, 33rd Indiana Infantry.

Newby, Daniel, Corporal, Company A, 36th Indiana Infantry.

Newby, Henry F., Private, Corporal, Company F, 84th Indiana Infantry.

Newby, Isaiah J., Private, Company C, 87th Indiana Infantry.

Newby, James I., Private, Corporal, Company D, 36th Indiana Infantry.

Newby, John W,. Corporal, Company D, 36th Indiana Infantry.
Newby, William B., Private, Company D, 36th Indiana Infantry.
Newby, William H., Private, Company A, 36th Indiana Infantry.
Newcomb, F. H., Private, Company A, 110th Indiana Infantry (Morgan Raid).
Newcomer, Benjamin F., Company G, 84th Indiana Infantry.
Newell, Edmond, Private, Unassigned, 22nd Indiana Infantry.
Newell, Jeremiah, Private, Company F, 20th Indiana Infantry.
**Newhouse, James L., Private, Company C, 140th Indiana Infantry.
Newland, John, Private, Company F, 57th Indiana Infantry.
*Newman, Alexander, Private, Company I, 3rd Indiana Cavalry.
Newman, William L., Private, 12th Indiana Battery.
*Newport, George, Private, Company B, 139th Indiana Infantry.
Niccum, Peter, Private, Company D, 69th Indiana Infantry.
Nicholson, Charles, Private, Company A, 110th Indiana Infantry (Morgan Raid).
Nicholson, John, Private, Company C, 36th Indiana Infantry; Private, Company A,
110th Indiana Infantry (Morgan Raid); Private, Company B, 139th Indiana Infantry.
Nicholson, Luther L., Private, Company A, 36th Indiana Infantry.
Nicholson, Marquis D., Private, Company A, 36th Indiana Infantry.
Nicholson, Merritt N., Private, Company A, 110th Indiana Infantry (Morgan Raid).
Nicholson, Nathan, Private, Corporal, Company C, 36th Indiana Infantry.
Nicholson, Reason, Private, Company A, 110th Indiana Infantry (Morgan Raid).
Nicholson, William T., Sergeant, Company G, 84th Indiana Infantry.
Nicodemus, Isaac, Private, Company F, 57th Indiana Infantry.
Nicodemus, John, Private, Company F, 57th Indiana Infantry.
Nidey, Reason, Private, Company E, 8th Indiana Infantry (three years).
*Niles, Thomas E,. Private, Corporal, Company A, 57th Indiana Infantry; Corporal,
10th Indiana Battery.
*Nixon, Charles O., Private, Company E, 9th Indiana Cavalry.
Nixon, Eusebius A. L., Private, 13th Indiana Battery.
Nixon, George C.,' Corporal, Company D, 84th Indiana Infantry.
Nixon, Robert M., Regimental Band, 36th Indiana Infantry.
Nixon, Sebastian E., Private, Company B, 139th Indiana Infantry.
Noble, Alfred, Private, Bugler, Company I, 3rd Indiana Cavalry; Private, Company
B, 8th Indiana Cavalry, re-organized.
Noland, Michael, Private, Sergeant, Company G, 16th Indiana Infantry.
*Nordbrook, William, Private, Company B, 139th Indiana Infantry.
Norton, Calvin, Private, Company I, 3rd Indiana Cavalry; Private, Unassigned,
22nd Indiana Infantry.
Noyer, Peter, Private, Company K, 105th Indiana Infantry (Morgan Raid).

O

O'Bannion, Cornelius, Private, Company F, 84th Indiana Infantry.
O'Bannion, Joseph, Private, Company F, 84th Indiana Infantry.
O'Connor, Mathew, Private, Company I, 69th Indiana Infantry.
O'Dowell, Philip, Private, Company B, 5th Indiana Cavalry.
O'Harra, Andrew J., Private, Sergeant, Company B, 139th Indiana Infantry.
O'Harra, John, Private, Company K, 36th Indiana Infantry.
O'Harra, Joseph, Private, Company B, 110th Indiana Infantry (Morgan Raid); Pri-
vate, Company E, 9th Indiana Cavalry.
O'Neal, William, Private, Company D, 3rd Indiana Cavalry.
O'Shea, James, Private, Company A, 57th Indiana Infantry.
Odle, Thomas W., Private, Company A, 147th Indiana Infantry.
*Ogborn, Allen W., Corporal, Company B, 19th Indiana Infantry.
Ogle, Lewis A., Private, Company B, 156th Indiana Infantry.
Ogment, Joseph, Private, Company B, 139th Indiana Infantry; Private, Company
H, 147th Indiana Infantry.

*Ohmit, Emanuel,.Private, Corporal, Company H, 147th Indiana Infantry.

Oldaker, John, Private, Company D, 8th Indiana Infantry (three years).

Oliver, William R., Private, Company H, 18th Indiana Infantry.

*Ormsten, Andrew, Private, Company H, 147th Indiana Infantry.

*Orr, Thomas J., Private, Corporal, Company A, 57th Indiana Infantry.

Osborn, David, Private, Company D, 147th Indiana Infantry.

Osborn, George, Private, Company E, 8th Indiana Infantry (three years).

Osborn, Joel, Private, Company E, 8th Indiana Infantry (three years).

Osborn, John A., Private, Company A, 57th Indiana Infantry.

Osborn, Washington, Private, Corporal, Company H, 13th Indiana Infantry, re-organized.

Osborne, Barzillai, Private, Company A, 57th Indiana Infantry.

Osborne, Jacob, Private, Company B, 8th Indiana Infantry (three months).

Osment, John W., Private, Company D, 36th Indiana Infantry.

Otis, George K., Corporal, Company I, 54th Indiana Infantry (three months):

Outland, King, Private, Company A, 28th U. S. C. T.

Overman, Charles W., Private, Corporal, Company F, 84th Indiana Infantry.

Overman, Nathan, Private, Company A, 105th Indiana Infantry (Morgan Raid).

Overman, Samuel W., Private, Company B, 42nd Indiana Infantry.

Owens, Edward R., Private, Company C, 147th Indiana Infantry.

Owens, Jacob, Private, Company A, 105th Indiana Infantry (Morgan Raid).

Owens, Michael J., Private, Company K, 19th Indiana Infantry.

*Owens, Thomas J., Corporal, Sergeant, Second Lieutenant, Company A, 57th Indiana Infantry.

P

Pace, William, Private, Company I, 3rd Indiana Cavalry.

Padget, Gideon H., Private, Company H, 69th Indiana Infantry.

Page, Samuel C., Private, Company I, 69th Indiana Infantry.

*Painter, Alfred, Private, Corporal, Company E, 8th Indiana Infantry (three years).

Painter, David M., Private, Company E, 9th Indiana Cavalry.

Painter, Flemmon T. W., Private, Company E, 8th Indiana Infantry (three years); Private, Company F; Commissary Sergeant, Non Commissioned Staff. 10th Indiana Cavalry.

Palmer, Adoniram, Private, Company I, 147th Indiana Infantry.

Palmer, James, Private, Company A, 110th Indiana Infantry (Morgan Raid).

**Parker, Edwin, Private, Company D, 34th Indiana Infantry.

Parker, Edwin E., Corporal, Company I, 69th Indiana Infantry; Private, Company B, 110th Indiana Infantry (Morgan Raid).

Parker, James C., Private, Corporal, Company G, 16th Indiana Infantry.

**Parker, Samuel J., Private, Company I, 57th Indiana Infantry.

Parker, Thomas, Private, Company G, 9th Indiana Cavalry.

Parker, William B., Private, Company B, 110th Indiana Infantry (Morgan Raid); Private, Company A, 139th Indiana Infantry.

Parkhurst, Adam R., Private, Company B, 54th Indiana Infantry (one year).

Parkhurst, John A., Private, Company D. 36th Indiana Infantry.

Parkhurst, Washington, Private, Company I, 3rd Indiana Cavalry.

Parkinson, Edward W., Corporal, Sergeant, Company E, 36th Indiana Infantry.

*Parris, Lewis B., Private, Company A, 57th Indiana Infantry.

Parrish, Reuben, Private, Company A, 110th Indiana Infantry (Morgan Raid).

Pate, John, Private, Company H, 69th Indiana Infantry.

Pate, Joseph B., Private, Company H, 69th Indiana Infantry.

Pate, William A., Private, Company H, 69th Indiana Infantry.

Pattison, James, Private, Company A, 36th Indiana Infantry.

Patton,.Francis, Private, Company B, 5th Indiana Cavalry.

52

Paty, William M., Corporal, Company C, 117th Indiana Infantry; Private, Company D, 35th Indiana Infantry.

Paul, Daniel H., Private, Company E, 36th Indiana Infantry.

Paxson, Aaron S., Private, Company A, 36th Indiana Infantry.

**Paxson, Benjamin F., Private, Company G, 86th Indiana Infantry.

Payne, Samuel W., First Sergeant, First Lieutenant, Company C, 75th Indiana Infantry.

Peacock, William H., Private, Corporal, Company G, 9th Indiana Cavalry.

*Pearce, Don Francisco, Private, Company H, 140th Indiana Infantry.

Pearson, Daniel, Private, Company H, 140th Indiana Infantry.

Pearson, Enos, Private, Company A, 30th Indiana Infantry, re-organized.

Pearson, Granville, Private, Company H, 140th Indiana Infantry.

Pearson, Jesse, Private, Company A, 19th Indiana Infantry; Private, Corporal, Company I, 20th Indiana Infantry, re-organized.

Pearson, Zeno, Private, Company C, 36th Indiana Infantry; Sergeant, Company D, 147th Indiana Infantry.

Peden, Milton, First Lieutenant, Captain, Company K, 36th Indiana Infantry; Colonel, Staff, 147th Indiana Infantry.

Peed, Albert J., Private, Company A, 110th Indiana Infantry (Morgan Raid).

Peed, James L., Private, Company A, 110th Indiana Infantry (Morgan Raid).

Peed, John R., Private, Company B, 110th Indiana Infantry (Morgan Raid); Private, Unassigned, 79th Indiana Infantry.

Peed, Redmond, Wagoner, Company F, 57th Indiana Infantry.

*Peele, Willis J., Private, Company H, 140th Indiana Infantry.

Pence, Alfred M., Private, Corporal, Company H, 140th Indiana Infantry.

Pence, David, Private, Company C, 109th Indiana Infantry (Morgan Raid).

Pence, Franklin N., Corporal, Company G, 84th Indiana Infantry.

Pence, James M., Private, Corporal, Sergeant, First Lieutenant, Company C, 36th Indiana Infantry.

Pence, William M., Seaman, U. S. Navy.

Pennington, Amos E., First Sergeant, Company B, 110th Indiana Infantry (Morgan Raid); Private, Sergeant, Company A, 139th Indiana Infantry.

Penticost, Andrew F., Private, Company H; Quartermaster Sergeant, Non Commissioned Staff, 147th Indiana Infantry.

Perdue, Abner, Private, Company E, 8th Indiana Infantry (three years).

Perdue, Addison L., Private, Company H, 69th Indiana Infantry.

Perdue, Andrew J. E., Private, Company E, 8th Indiana Infantry (three years).

Perdue, George W., Corporal, Company H, 69th Indiana Infantry.

Perdue, Rufus, Private, Company H, 69th Indiana Infantry.

Perry, Henry, Private, Company E, 9th Indiana Cavalry.

Perry, John, Private, Company A, 54th Indiana Infantry (one year).

Perry, John, Private, Corporal, Company B, 5th Indiana Cavalry.

*Perry, Joseph, Musician, Company F, 57th Indiana Infantry.

Perry, Mordecai, Private, Company G, 16th Indiana Infantry.

Perry, Oran, Adjutant, Lieutenant Colonel and Colonel, Staff, 69th Indiana Infantry.

Perry, William, Private, Corporal, Sergeant, First Lieutenant, Company E, 8th Indiana Infantry (three years).

Personett, James, Private, Company G, 84th Indiana Infantry.

Pettitt, Joseph A., Private, Company A, 36th Indiana Infantry.

*Petty, James F., Private, Company F, 57th Indiana Infantry.

Peyton, William, Private, Company M, 21st Indiana Infantry re-organized as 1st Heavy Artillery.

Pflum, Ferdinand, Private, Company F, 148th Indiana Infantry.

Phelps, Elias. (See Incomplete List).

Philabaum, James B., Private, Company A, 110th Indiana Infantry (Morgan Raid).
Phillips, Andrew J., Private, Company E, 8th Indiana Infantry (three years).
Phillips, John E., Private, Company C, 109th Indiana Infantry (Morgan Raid).
Phillips, John M., Regimental Band, 36th Indiana Infantry.
*Phillips, Orton, Private, Company F, 57th Indiana Infantry.
Pickering, Enos, Private, Company A, 105th Indiana Infantry (Morgan Raid).
**Pickering, Ezra, Private, Company B, 130th Indiana Infantry.
Pickering, Larkin, Private, Company D, 147th Indiana Infantry.
Pickering, Ulysses, Private, Company B, 110th Indana Infantry (Morgan Raid).
Pickett, John, Private, Company I, 69th Indiana Infantry.
Pickett, John, Private, Company D, 36th Indiana Infantry; Private, Company A,
4th Regiment, 1st Army Corps (Hancock's Veteran Corps).
Pickett, Thomas E., Private, Company I, 84th Indiana Infantry.
Pickett, William A., Private, Company F, 84th Indiana Infantry.
Pierce, Benjamin F., Private, Company D, 36th Indiana Infantry.
Pierce, Frank J., Private, Company B, 110th Indiana Infantry (Morgan Raid).
Pierce, Hugh, Private, Company B, 139th Indiana Infantry.
Pierce, James H., Private, Unassigned, 22nd Indiana Infantry.
Pierce, John, Private, Company B, 110th Indiana Infantry (Morgan Raid).
Pierce, John R., Corporal, Company B, 8th Indiana Infantry (three months); First
Sergeant, First Lieutenant, Company E, 8th Indiana Infantry (three years); Sergeant,
25th Indiana Battery.
Pierce, Jonathan E., Private, Company C, 36th Indiana Infantry.
Pierce, Joseph A., Private, Company F, 84th Indiana Infantry.
**Pierce, William H., Private, Company H, 84th Indiana Infantry.
Pierson, Jackson, Private, Company C, 5th Indiana Cavalry.
Pike, Albert H., Corporal, Company I, 3rd Indiana Cavalry.
Pike, Joseph H., Private, Company B, 19th Indiana Infantry.
Pike, Samuel F., Private, Company D, 36th Indiana Infantry.
Pike, Stanford L., Private, Company A, 36th Indiana Infantry.
*Pittman, George W., Private, Company H, 147th Indiana Infantry.
Pittser, Cyrus, Private, Company E, 8th Indiana Infantry (three years).
Pleas, Elwood, Private, Company B, 110th Indiana Infantry (Morgan Raid); Private, Company B, 139th Indiana Infantry.
Pleas, Joseph H., Private, Company A, 139th Indiana Infantry; Corporal, Company
H, 147th Indiana Infantry.
Plummer, William J., First Lieutenant, Company A, 110th Indiana Infantry (Morgan Raid).
Poarch, Albert W., Private, Company D, 33rd Indiana Infantry.
*Poe, Pleasant, Private, Company F, 57th Indiana Infantry.
Poer, Robert F., Private, Company F, 6th Indiana Infantry (three months); Corporal, Company I, 3rd Indiana Cavalry.
Polk, Henry C., Private, Company B, 13th Indiana Infantry.
*Polk, Merriman S., Private, Company H, 140th Indiana Infantry.
Polk, Milton, Private, Unassigned, 22nd Indiana Infantry.
Poor, Edmund, Private, Company F, 124th Indiana Infantry.
Porter, John, Private, Company C, 147th Indiana Infantry.
Porter, William, Private, Company C, 36th Indiana Infantry.
Post, Charles B., Private, Company A, 87th Indiana Infantry.
Post, John M., Private, Company A, 87th Indiana Infantry; Private, Company A,
42nd Indiana Infantry.
Post, Mark T., Private, Company E, 84th Indiana Infantry.
Poston, Argyle A., Private, Company F, 84th Indiana Infantry.
Poston, Edenburgh, H., Private, 19th Indiana Battery.
Powell, Albert W., Private, Company A, 110th Indiana Infantry (Morgan Raid).

Powell, Charles C., Private, Company A, 110th Indiana Infantry (Morgan Raid).

Powell, Elihu, Private, Company F, 6th Indiana Infantry (three months); Private, 19th Indiana Battery.

Powell; Henry C., Private, 22nd Indiana Battery.

Powell, Henry L., Private, Company B, 8th Indiana Infantry (three months); Private, Company A, 110th Indiana Infantry (Morgan Raid).

Powell, Jacob, Private, Company E, 8th Indiana Infantry (three years).

Powell, Oliver, Private, 3rd Indiana Battery.

Powell, Orlistes W., Corporal, Company C; Sergeant Major, Non Commissioned Staff, 36th Indiana Infantry.

Power, John W. C., Corporal, Company F, 84th Indiana Infantry.

Powers, George R., Private, Company B, 156th Indiana Infantry.

Powers, James P., Private, Company G, 7th Indiana Cavalry; Private, Company F, 7th Indiana Cavalry, re-organized.

Powers, John A., Private, Company H, 154th Indiana Infantry.

*Pratt, George W., Private, Company E, 9th Indiana Cavalry.

*Pratt, James C., Musician, Company H, 147th Indiana Infantry.

Pressnall, Dempsey W., Private, Company D, 36th Indiana Infantry.

Pressnall, Elijah M., Private, Company B, 110th Indiana Infantry (Morgan Raid); Private, Company A, 30th Indiana Infantry, re-organized.

Pressnall, Henry, Private, Company C, 36th Indiana Infantry.

Pressnall, Samuel, Private, Company C, 36th Indiana Infantry.

Preston, John V., Private, Company H, 69th Indiana Infantry; Second Lieutenant, Company D, 156th Indiana Infantry.

Preston, Sanford A., Private, Company E, 8th Indiana Infantry (three years).

Price, Robert V., Private, Company H, 69th Indiana Infantry.

Priddy, William, Private, Company G, 84th Indiana Infantry.

Prigg, William H, Private, Company K, 105th Indiana Infantry (Morgan Raid).

Pring, James M., Private, Company E, 8th Indiana Infantry (three years).

*Probasco, John, Private, Company A, 57th Indiana Infantry.

Proctor, Thomas K., Private, Company I, 3rd Indiana Cavalry; Private, Company L, 8th Indiana Cavalry, re-organized.

Protzman, Oliver D., Private, Company F, 57th Indiana Infantry.

Pursley, Daniel, Private, Company K, 36th Indiana Infantry.

*Pyatte, Thomas, Musician, Company A, 57th Indiana Infantry.

R

Radcliffe, Augustus D., Private, Company D, 36th Indiana Infantry.

Radcliffe, Charles F., Private, Company D, 36th Indiana Infantry.

Rader, George, Private, Company G, 84th Indiana Infantry.

Rader, George W., Sergeant, Company E, 8th Indiana Infantry (three years).

Rader, Henry, Private, Company B, 8th Indiana Infantry (three months); Sergeant, First Lieutenant, Company E, 8th Indiana Infantry (three years); Sergeant, Company C, 109th Indiana Infantry (Morgan Raid).

Ralston, George W., Private, Company B, 8th Indiana Infantry (three months); Private, Company G, 8th Indiana Infantry (three years).

Ramsey, James, Private, Company A, 105th Indiana Infantry (Morgan Raid).

Ramsey, Joseph, Private, Company F, 6th Indiana Infantry (three months).

Ranier, Charles T., Private, Company H, 69th Indiana Infantry.

Ranier, Joseph G., Private, Company F, 6th Indiana Infantry (three months).

Ratcliff, Abner, Private, Company K, 105th Indiana Infantry (Morgan Raid).

Ratcliff, John, Private, Company K, 105th Indiana Infantry (Morgan Raid); Private, Wagoner, Company E, 9th Indiana Cavalry.

Ratliff, Calvin, Private, Company H, 140th Indiana Infantry.

Ratliff, Exum P., Private, Company I, 69th Indiana Infantry.

Ratliff, Henry, Private, Company I, 69th Indiana Infantry.

Ratliff, Nathan, Private, Unassigned, 36th Indiana Infantry; Corporal, Company H, 30th Indiana Infantry, re-organized.

Raugett, Josiah, Private, Company K, 105th Indiana Infantry (Morgan Raid).

Ray, Charles A., Sergeant, Company B, 8th Indiana Infantry (three months); Private, Company D, 36th Indiana Infantry; Private, Company H, 30th Indiana Infantry, re-organized.

Ray, Henry, First Lieutenant, Company B, 8th Indiana Infantry (three months); Private, Wagoner, Company B, 5th Indiana Cavalry.

Rayl, Harmon, Private, Company A, 36th Indiana Infantry.

Reagan, Benjamin F., Private, Company B, 110th Indiana Infantry (Morgan Raid).

**Real, Martin L., Private, Company D, 9th Indiana Infantry.

Redding, Jacob, Private, Company A, 110th Indiana Infantry (Morgan Raid); Private, Sergeant, Company B, 139th Indiana Infantry.

Redding, John M., Private, Company F, 57th Indiana Infantry.

Redding, Lemuel, Private, Corporal, Company B, 139th Indiana Infantry.

Reece, Edwin, Private, Unassigned, 22nd Indiana Infantry.

*Reed, Alonzo W., Private, Company H, 140th Indiana Infantry.

**Reed, Collier M., Private, Company C, 8th Indiana Infantry (three months).

Reed, Miles L., Regimental Band, 8th Indiana Infantry (three years); Private, Company K, 1st Artillery, U. S. A.; Surgeon's Nurse, U. S. Navy.

Reed, William C., Second Lieutenant, New Castle Guards, Indiana Legion; Private, Company B, 110th Indiana Infantry (Morgan Raid).

**Reeder, Thomas B., Corporal, Company I, 19th Indiana Infantry; Captain, Company B; Major, Staff, 149th Indiana Infantry.

Reeves, Eli, Private, Company G, 16th Indiana Infantry.

*Reeves, George W., Private, Company H, 140th Indiana Infantry.

*Reeves, John M. H., Private, Company H, 140th Indiana Infantry.

Reeves, Milton M., Private, Corporal, Company A, 139th Indiana Infantry.

Reeves, Nathaniel M., Private, Company E, 11th Indiana Infantry.

Reichart, Henry, Private, Company C, 36th Indiana Infantry.

Reichart, John, Private, Company C, 36th Indiana Infantry.

Reid, Andrew W., Regimental Band, 19th Indiana Infantry; Private, Company A. 11th Indiana Infantry.

*Reid, William C., Private, Corporal, First Sergeant, Second Lieutenant, Company G, 84th Indiana Infantry.

Reid, William E., Principal Musician, Non Commissioned Staff, 19th Indiana Infantry.

Rent, Daniel, Private, Corporal, Company E, 8th Indiana Infantry (three years).

Rent, Frederick, Corporal, Company G, 47th Indiana Infantry.

Rent, George D., Private, Company A, 139th Indiana Infantry.

Rent, John H., Private, Corporal, Sergeant, First Sergeant, First Lieutenant, Captain, Company F, 57th Indiana Infantry.

Reynolds, Andrew, Private, Corporal, 4th Indiana Battery; Private, Troop G, 6th Cavalry, U. S. A.

Reynolds, Calvin W., Private, Company A, 36th Indiana Infantry.

Reynolds, Henry, Private, Company I, 69th Indiana Infantry.

*Reynolds, Hugh, Private, Company H, 147th Indiana Infantry.

Reynolds, Isaac, Private, Company B, 139th Indiana Infantry.

Reynolds, James, Corporal, Company E, 149th Indiana Infantry.

*Reynolds, Joseph N., Private, Company A, 57th Indiana Infantry.

Reynolds, William, Private, Company I, 69th Indiana Infantry.

**Rhine, John, Sergeant, Company K, 75th Indiana Infantry.

**Rhinewalt, William, Private, 18th Indiana Battery.

*Rhody, George, Private, Corporal, Company K, 36th Indiana Infantry.

Riadon, Levi, Private, Company A, 110th Indiana Infantry (Morgan Raid).

*Rich, Elam, Private, Company F, 84th Indiana Infantry.
Richardson, Cornelius J., Private, Company B, 124th Indiana Infantry.
Richardson, Henry J.; Private, Company I, 69th Indiana Infantry. '
Richardson, Isaiah, Private, Unassigned, 22nd Indiana Infantry.
Rickard, James, Private, Company I, 3rd Indiana Cavalry.
Ricketts, James G., Corporal, Company K, 54th Indiana Infantry (three months).
Rickit, John, Farrier and Blacksmith, Company I, 3rd Indiana Cavalry.
Ricks, Benjamin F., Sergeant, Company K, 105th Indiana Infantry (Morgan Raid);
Private, First Sergeant, Company E, 9th Indiana Cavalry.
Ricks, Daniel, Private, Company K, 36th Indiana Infantry.
Ricks, John W., Private, Company D, 36th Indiana Infantry.
Ricks, Jonathan, Private, Company I, 69th Indiana Infantry.
Ricks, Levi, Private, Company K, 105th Indiana Infantry (Morgan Raid.); Private,
Company H, 140th Indiana Infantry.
Ricks, Martin W., Private, Company K, 54th Indiana Infantry (three months);
Second Lieutenant, Needmore Rangers, Indiana Legion; Second Lieutenant, Company
K, 105th Indiana Infantry (Morgan Raid); Private, Company E; Quartermaster Ser-
geant, Non Commissioned Staff, 9th Indiana Cavalry.
Ricks, Mercer, Private, Company D, 36th Indiana Infantry.
Ricks, Peter, Private, Company K, 54th Indiana Infantry (three months).
Ricks, Thomas, Private, Company K, 105th Indiana Infantry (Morgan Raid).
*Ridge, Jacob, Private, Corporal, Company G, 84th Indiana Infantry.
Ridge, Riley, Private, Company H, 140th Indiana Infantry.
Riesner, George A., Private, Company A, 105th Indiana Infantry (Morgan Raid).
Rife, John J., Private, Company B, 8th Indiana Infantry (three months); Private,
Corporal, 12th Indiana Battery. .
Rife, Obed C., Private, Corporal, Company H, 154th Indiana Infantry. (See Alpha-
betical List C).
Rife, William, Private, Sergeant, 12th Indiana Battery.
Rifner, Peter, Private, Company I, 84th Indiana Infantry; Private, Troop G, 6th
Cavalry, U. S. A.
Riggle, Daniel, Private, Company A, 110th Indiana Infantry (Morgan Raid); Pri-
vate, Company B, 139th Indiana Infantry.
Riggle, William, Private, Company I, 3rd Indiana Cavalry.
*Riggs, Alfred, Private, Company E, 8th Indiana Infantry (three years).
*Riggs, Avery, Private, Company E, 8th Indiana Infantry (three years).
Rigin, Martin, Private, Unassigned, 11th Indiana Infantry.
Riley, Charles M., Private, Company B, 124th Indiana Infantry.
Riley, John, Private, Sergeant, Company D, 11th Indiana Infantry.
Riley, William, Private, Company K, 105th Indiana Infantry (Morgan Raid); Pri-
vate, Company H, 140th Indiana Infantry.
Riley, William G., Private, Company I, 69th Indiana Infantry.
Ringo, James M., Private, Company F, 57th Indiana Infantry.
Rinker, Aaron, Private, Company K, 36th Indiana Infantry; Private, Company H,
30th Indiana Infantry, re-organized.
Rinker, John H., Private, Company F, 57th Indiana Infantry.
Risk, John W., Private, Corporal, Sergeant, Company D, 36th Indiana Infantry.
Risk, William B., Private, 2nd Indiana Battery; Corporal, 2nd Indiana Battery,
re-organized.
Ritchie, George, Private, Company C, 36th Indiana Infantry.
Robbins, John, Private, Company D, 8th U. S. C. T.
Robbins, Joseph W., Private, Company K, 105th Indiana Infantry (Morgan Raid).
Robe, Robert, Private, Company D, 2nd Indiana Cavalry.
Roberts, Alexander, Private, Corporal, Company K, 36th Indiana Infantry.
Roberts, Daniel, Private, Company A, 139th Indiana Infantry.

CO. G. 13TH REGT.

TIMOTHY SHANE

CO. D. 2D REGT.

BENJAMIN F. HAYDEN

CO. E. 9TH REGT.

WILLIAM A. ROGERS

CO. E. 9TH REGT.

LIEUT. CALEB W. COOPER

CO. E. 9TH REGT.

EXUM COPELAND

CO. G. 5TH REGT.

JAMES HUTSON

CO. B. 9TH REGT.

JOHN H. McCORKHILL

INDIANA CAVALRY.

Roberts, Edmund, Private, Company H, 147th Indiana Infantry.
Roberts, Elijah I., Unassigned, Indiana Infantry.
Roberts, Isaac. Private, Company K, 36th Indiana Infantry.
Roberts, James, Private, Company I, 36th Indiana Infantry (three months); Private, Company A, 139th Indiana Infantry.
**Roberts, Jeremiah. Company D, 8th Indiana Infantry (three years) organized.

**Roberts, John O., A. Company H, 105th Indiana Infantry.
*Roberts, John S., Private, 105th Indiana Infantry.
**Roberts, John W., Private, Indiana Infantry.
Roberts, Joseph, Private,
Roberts, Leand, Private, Indiana Cavalry, Private Company L, 8th Indiana Cavalry, reorganized.
Roberts, Patrick, Private, Indiana Infantry.
**Roberts, William, Corporal, Indiana Infantry.
Roberts, William, Private, Indiana Infantry (three months); Private, Company E, 8th Indiana Infantry.
**Robinson, John, Private, Company H, 105th Indiana Infantry.
Robinson, Newton, Private, Company 3rd Indiana Cavalry.
Robinson, Peter, Private, Company 4th Indiana Infantry.
*Robinson, Rowland. Private, 139th Indiana Infantry.
Robison, James C., Private, Company 69th Indiana Infantry (Morgan Raid)
Robuck, Henry, Private, Corporal, 148th Indiana Infantry.
*Rock, William H. H. Private, Company A, 105th Indiana Infantry; First Sergeant, Company H, 147th Indiana Infantry. Second Company H, 147th Indiana Infantry.
Rodes, Franklin M., Private,
Rogers, Jerold L., Private,
Rogers, Private,

Rogers, John R., Private,
Rogers, Private,
Rogers, Private,
Rogers, George, Private,
Rogers, William A.,
*Roney, Elias, Private,
Rose, Fernando, Private, Company H, Indiana Infantry, Private Sergeant, Company H, 30th Indiana Infantry, reorganized.
Ross, Henry C., Private, Indiana Battery.
Ross, Hiram C., Private, Company C, 36th Indiana Infantry; Private, Company C, 30th Indiana Infantry, reorganized.
Ross, James, Private, Company C, 3rd Indiana Cavalry.
Ross, Jonathan, Corporal, Sergeant, Second Lieutenant, Company C, 69th Indiana Infantry
Ross, Moses, Private, Company M, 3rd Indiana Cavalry.
Ross, William, Private, Company H, 17th Indiana Infantry, reorganized.
Ross, William A., Private, Company B, 28th U. S. C. T.
*Roszell, John E., Private, Company B, 139th Indiana Infantry.
Routh, Isaac W., Private, Company D, 30th Indiana Infantry.
*Rowland, Joseph, Private, Company A, 57th Indiana Infantry.
Rozier, Jesse, Private, Company E, 8th Indiana Infantry (three years)
Rubush, Paul, Private, 25th Indiana Battery.
*Runnels, Samuel, Private, Company F, 57th Indiana Infantry
Runyan, Abraham, Musician, Company G, 84th Indiana Infantry

INDIÁNA CAVALRY.

Roberts, Edmund, Private, Company H, 147th Indiana Infantry.
Roberts, Elijah P., Private, Unassigned, 22nd Indiana Infantry.
Roberts, Isaac, Private, Company K, 36th Indiana Infantry.
Roberts, James, Private, Company I, 54th Indiana Infantry (three months); Private, Company A, 139th Indiana Infantry.
**Roberts, Jeremiah, Wagoner, Company D, 8th Indiana Infantry (three years).
Roberts, John D., Private, 2nd Indiana Battery; Private, 2nd Indiana Battery, reorganized.
**Roberts, John Q. A., Corporal, Sergeant, Company H, 124th Indiana Infantry.
*Roberts, John S., Private, Company B, 139th Indiana Infantry.
**Roberts, John W., Private, Company F, 117th Indiana Infantry.
Roberts, Joseph, Private, 2nd Indiana Battery, re-organized.
Roberts, Leander, Private, Company I, 3rd Indiana Cavalry; Private, Company L, 8th Indiana Cavalry, re-organized.
Roberts, Patrick, Private, Company H, 147th Indiana Infantry.
**Roberts, William, Corporal, Company C, 120th Indiana Infantry.
Roberts, William, Private, Company F, 6th Indiana Infantry (three months); Private, Company E, 8th Indiana Infantry (three years).
**Robinson, John, Private, Company H, 68th Indiana Infantry.
Robinson, Newton, Private, Company I, 3rd Indiana Cavalry.
Robinson, Peter, Private, Company B, 124th Indiana Infantry.
*Robinson, Rowland, Private, Company B, 139th Indiana Infantry.
Robison, James C., Private, Company B, 110th Indiana Infantry (Morgan Raid).
Robuck, Henry, Private, Company A, 148th Indiana Infantry.
*Rock, William H. H., Private, Company A, 105th Indiana Infantry (Morgan Raid); Private, First Sergeant, Company A, 139th Indiana Infantry; Second Lieutenant, Company H, 147th Indiana Infantry.
Rodes, Franklin M., Private, Unassigned, 22nd Indiana Infantry.
Rogers, David L., Private, Company H, 38th Indiana Infantry.
Rogers, George W., Private, Company C, 36th Indiana Infantry.
Rogers, James, Private, Company H, 51st Indiana Infantry.
Rogers, John W., Private, Company D, 11th Indiana Infantry.
Rogers, Joseph, Corporal, Company E, 13th Indiana Infantry, re-organized.
Rogers, Joseph B., Corporal, Company C, 36th Indiana Infantry.
Rogers, Oscar, Private, Company I, 124th Indiana Infantry.
Rogers, William A., Private, Company E, 9th Indiana Cavalry.
*Roney, Elias M., Private, Company A, 57th Indiana Infantry.
Rose, Fernandez, Private, Company D, 36th Indiana Infantry; Private, Sergeant, Company H, 30th Indiana Infantry, re-organized.
Ross, Henry C., Private, 2nd Indiana Battery.
Ross, Hiram C., Private, Company C, 36th Indiana Infantry; Private, Company H, 30th Indiana Infantry, re-organized.
Ross, James, Private, Company C, 5th Indiana Cavalry.
Ross, Jonathan, Corporal, Sergeant, Second Lieutenant, Company K, 36th Indiana Infantry.
Ross, Moses, Private, Company M, 3rd Indiana Cavalry.
Ross, William, Private, Company H, 13th Indiana Infantry, re-organized.
Ross, William A., Private, Company B, 28th U. S. C. T.
*Roszell, John E., Private, Company B, 139th Indiana Infantry.
Routh, Isaac W., Private, Company D, 36th Indiana Infantry.
*Rowland, Joseph, Private, Company A, 57th Indiana Infantry.
Rozier, Jesse, Private, Company E, 8th Indiana Infantry (three years).
Rubush, Paul, Private, 25th Indiana Battery.
*Runnels, Samuel, Private, Company F, 57th Indiana Infantry.
Runyan, Abraham, Musician, Company G, 84th Indiana Infantry.
Runyan, John, Private, Company E, 9th Indiana Cavalry.

Runyan, Jonathan, Private, Company B, 8th Indiana Infantry (three months); Private, Company E, 8th Indiana Infantry (three years).

Runyan, Marcus L., Private, Company G, 84th Indiana Infantry.

Runyan, William J., Private, Company G, 84th Indiana Infantry.

Russell, Henry, Private, Company G, 84th Indiana Infantry.

Ruth, Jacob, Private, Company H, 5th Regiment, 1st Army Corps (Hancock's Veteran Corps).

Rutledge, William V., Private, Company D, Assistant Surgeon, Staff, 2nd Indiana Cavalry; Assistant Surgeon, Staff, 2nd Indiana Cavalry, re-organized.

**Ryan, Dennis, Private, Company B, 124th Indiana Infantry.

S

Saint, Albert W., Private, First Sergeant, First Lieutenant, Company D, 36th Indiana Infantry.

Saint, Henry H., Private, 19th Indiana Battery.

Saint, Horace M., Private, Company H, 3rd Battalion, 16th Infantry, U. S. A.; Private, Company H, 34th Infantry U. S. A.

Saint, Oliver, P., Private, Company A, 7th Indiana Cavalry; Corporal, Company C, 7th Indiana Cavalry, re-organized.

Saint, William M., Second Lieutenant, Company D; Adjutant, Staff, 147th Indiana Infantry.

Salmon, James, Private, Company B, 8th Indiana Infantry (three months).

Sample, Asa E., Corporal, Sergeant, Company B, 54th Indiana Infantry (one year).

*Sanders, Charles F., Corporal, Company A, 57th Indiana Infantry.

Sanders, David, Private, Company F, 14th U. S. C. T.

Sanders, Francis A., Private, Company F, 124th Indiana Infantry.

Sanders, George W., Private, 25th Indiana Battery.

Sanders, John W., Private, Company C, 36th Indiana Infantry.

Sanders, Luther B., Private, Company B, 139th Indiana Infantry; Private, Company D, 147th Indiana Infantry.

Sapp, Andrew J., Private, Company A, 54th Indiana Infantry (one year).

Sapp, John W., Private, Corporal, Company D, 36th Indiana Infantry.

*Sargent, James L., Private, Company F, 57th Indiana Infantry.

Sater, Noah W., Private, Company D, 36th Indiana Infantry.

Sater, William, Private, Company D, 36th Indiana Infantry; Private, Company A, 4th Regiment, 1st Army Corps (Hancock's Veteran Corps).

Saulsbury, Henry B., Private, Company A, 36th Indiana Infantry.

Saunders, Henry, Private, Company H, 140th Indiana Infantry.

Saunders, John, Private, Corporal, Company K, 36th Indiana Infantry; Corporal, Company H, 30th Indiana Infantry, re-organized.

Saunders, William L., Private, Company A, 6th Indiana Infantry (three months); Private, Company K, 54th Indiana Infantry (three months).

Sayford, Augustus L., Private, Company H, 69th Indiana Infantry.

**Schaffer, Henry, Private, Company B, 156th Indiana Infantry.

Schell, Isaac N., Private, Company D, 147th Indiana Infantry.

Schock, Jacob, Private, Corporal, Company E, 36th Indiana Infantry.

*Scott, Gideon B., Private, Company F, 57th Indiana Infantry.

Scott, Henry, Private, 19th Indiana Battery.

Scott, James M., Private, Company G, 84th Indiana Infantry.

Scott, John H., Private, Company B, 8th Indiana Infantry (three months).

Scott, Oliver P., Private, 12th Indiana Battery.

Sears, Wilson M., Private, Company F, 6th Indiana Infantry (three months); Sergeant, Company I, 3rd Indiana Cavalry.

Seaton, Valentine, Private, Unassigned, 22nd Indiana Infantry.

Seely, George, Private, Corporal, Company G, 84th Indiana Infantry.

**Seamans, James M., Private, Company D, 26th Indiana Infantry.

Settle, Winfield S., Private, Company F, 84th Indiana Infantry; Private, Company K, 57th Indiana Infantry.

**Seward, Loveless, Private, Company B, 2nd Indiana Cavalry; Private, Company B, 2nd Indiana Cavalry, re-organized.

Seward, Thomas, Private, Company F, 57th Indiana Infantry.

Seward, Wesley W., Sergeant, Company F, 57th Indiana Infantry.

*Seward, William T., First Lieutenant, Captain, Company A, 57th Indiana Infantry.

Shackle, Jesse, Private, Company A, 36th Indiana Infantry.

Shackles, Marshall K., Private, Company I, 84th Indiana Infantry.

*Shaffer, Ira, Private, Company A, 57th Indiana Infantry; Private, Company H, 147th Indiana Infantry.

Shaffer, John, Private, Company K, 36th Indiana Infantry.

Shaffer, William W., Private, Company F, 14th U. S. C. T.

Shane, George W., First Lieutenant, Middletown Rifles, Indiana Legion; Sergeant, Company B, 8th Indiana Infantry (three months); First Lieutenant, Company K, 54th Indiana Infantry (three months); First Lieutenant, Company C, 109th Indiana Infantry (Morgan Raid); Captain, Company H, 140th Indiana Infantry.

Shane, Thomas J., Corporal, Sergeant, Company H, 140th Indiana Infantry.

Shane, Timothy, Private, Color Sergeant, Company G, 13th Indiana Cavalry.

Sharp, Cyrus, Private, Company K, 54th Indiana Infantry (three months).

Sharp, John, Private, Company H, 69th Indiana Infantry.

Sharp, Michael, Private, Company A, 110th Indiana Infantry (Morgan Raid).

Sharp, William M., Captain, Needmore Rangers, Indiana Legion; Captain, Company K, 105th Indiana Infantry (Morgan Raid).

*Shatz, William, Private, Company H, 147th Indiana Infantry.

Shaw, Francis Y., Private, Company A, 30th Indiana Infantry, re-organized.

Shaw, Joseph, Private, Company E, 8th Indiana Infantry (three years).

Shearer, Abraham, Private, Unassigned, 13th Indiana Infantry, re-organized.

Shearon, Thomas W., Private, Company C, 36th Indiana Infantry; Private, Company B, 110th Indiana Infantry (Morgan Raid).

Sheckles, John A., Private, Company E, 9th Indiana Cavalry.

Shedron, Charles C., Sergeant, Second Lieutenant, Company H, 69th Indiana Infantry.

Sheehan, William, Private, Unassigned, 11th Indiana Infantry.

Shelley, Benjamin F., Private, Company B, 110th Indiana Infantry (Morgan Raid).

Shelley, George W., Private, Company G, 84th Indiana Infantry.

Shelley, William F., Private, Company B, 19th Indiana Infantry; First Lieutenant, Company B, 139th Indiana Infantry; Captain, Company H, 147th Indiana Infantry. (See Alphabetical List B).

Shelley, Winford W., Sergeant, Company B, 110th Indiana Infantry (Morgan Raid).

Shelton, John J., Private, 19th Indiana Battery.

Shepherd, Daniel, Private, Company B, 8th Indiana Infantry (three months); Private, Corporal, Company E, 9th Indiana Cavalry.

Shepherd, Jeremiah A., Private, Company B, 8th Indiana Infantry (three months).

Shepherd, Leander, Private, Company C, 36th Indiana Infantry.

Shepherd, Lorenzo D., Private, Company C, 36th Indiana Infantry.

Shepherd, Martin, Private, Company A, 110th Indiana Infantry (Morgan Raid); Private, Company H, 147th Indiana Infantry.

Shepherd, William, Private, Company A, 110th Indiana Infantry (Morgan Raid); Private, Corporal, 4th Indiana Battery.

Shepherd, William H., Private, Company B, 8th Indiana Infantry (three months); Corporal, Company G, 84th Indiana Infantry.

**Sheppard, James W., Sergeant, First Sergeant, Company E, 69th Indiana Infantry.

*Shepler, Charles, Private, Company E, 9th Indiana Cavalry.

Sheridan, Calvin, Private, Company B, 8th Indiana Infantry (three months).

Sherry, John W., Private, Company H, 8th Indiana Infantry (three months); Private, Corporal, Company D, 2nd Indiana Cavalry; Private, Company I, 8th Regiment, 1st Army Corps (Hancock's Veteran Corps).

Sherry, William P., Private, Company K, 36th Indiana Infantry; Private, Company H, 30th Indiana Infantry, re-organized.

Shields, David, Private, Company F, 124th Indiana Infantry.

Shipler, Jacob, Private, Company C, 5th Indiana Cavalry.

Shipman, Albert, Musician, Company F, 6th Indiana Infantry (three months); Private, 2nd Indiana Battery; Private, 2nd Indiana Battery, re-organized.

**Shipman, Charles, Private, Company K, 132nd Indiana Infantry.

Shirk, George, Musician, Company C, 36th Indiana Infantry.

*Shirkey, John A., Second Lieutenant, Company G, 84th Indiana Infantry.

Shively, Daniel, Private, Company B, 130th Indiana Infantry.

Shockley, Benjamin F., Private, Company H, 140th Indiana Infantry.

Shockley, Elisha H., Private, Company D, 36th Indiana Infantry; Private, Company E, 9th Indiana Infantry.

Shockley, James, Private, Company B, 147th Indiana Infantry.

Shoemaker, Henry, Private, Company E, 8th Indiana Infantry (three years).

Shoemaker, John M., Private, Company H, 69th Indiana Infantry.

Shoemaker, John P., Private, Company C, 109th Indiana Infantry (Morgan Raid). Private, Company B, 134th Indiana Infantry.

Shoemaker, Joseph R., Private, Company B, 134th Indiana Infantry.

Shoemaker, Levi P., Private, Corporal, Sergeant, Second Lieutenant, Company E, 8th Indiana Infantry (three years).

*Shoemaker, Sanford H., Private, Company G, 7th Indiana Cavalry; Private, Company F, 7th Indiana Cavalry, re-organized.

*Shoemaker, Silas M., Private, Company G, 7th Indiana Cavalry; Private, Company F, 7th Indiana Cavalry, re-organized.

Shopp, Henry L., Corporal, Company B, 110th Indiana Infantry (Morgan Raid); Private, Company C, 30th Indiana Infantry, re-organized.

Shopp, Hershley, Private, Company B, 110th Indiana Infantry (Morgan Raid).

**Showalter, William H., Private, Company I, 67th Indiana Infantry.

Showers, John A., Private, Company E, 8th Indiana Infantry (three years)

Shroyer, Alexander R., Private, Company A, 110th Indiana Infantry (Morgan Raid)

**Shroyer, John W., Private, Company D, 84th Indiana Infantry.

Shroyer, Peter, First Lieutenant, Company F, 57th Indiana Infantry.

Shuderlane, Jeremiah, Private, Company B, 42nd Indiana Infantry.

Shultz, John, Private, Company I, 3rd Indiana Cavalry.

*Shultz, Joseph F., Corporal, Sergeant, Company A, 57th Indiana Infantry

Shunk, David, Private, Company I, 69th Indiana Infantry.

Shurrum, George, Private, Company A, 57th Indiana Infantry.

Silvers, Samuel N., Private, 23rd Indiana Battery.

*Silvey, William T., Private, Corporal, Company G, 84th Indiana Infantry.

Simons, Joel, Corporal, Company I, 69th Indiana Infantry.

*Simons, Nixon, Private, Company F, 57th Indiana Infantry.

Simmons, Henry W., Private, Company A, 38th Indiana Infantry.

Simmons, John A., Private, Company A, 57th Indiana Infantry; Private, Company K, 132nd Indiana Infantry.

Simmons, William, Private, Company A, 57th Indiana Infantry; Private, Company C, 9th Indiana Infantry.

Simmons, William H., Private, Company A, 110th Indiana Infantry (Morgan Raid).

Simpson, Absalom J., Private, Company F, 84th Indiana Infantry.

**Sims, Parvis, Private, Company G, 140th Indiana Infantry.

Sinclair, Wayman, Private, Company A, 11th Indiana Infantry.

Sippy, Nicholas, Private, Company I, 3rd Indiana Cavalry.

Sisson, Marquis L., Private, Corporal, Company A, 139th Indiana Infantry.

Sisson, Perry V., Private, Company F, 6th Indiana Infantry (three months).

Skinner, Jacob, Wagoner, Company G, 84th Indiana Infantry.

*Skinner, John L., Private, Company E, 8th Indiana Infantry (three years).

Skinner, William H., Private, Company E, 8th Indiana Infantry (three years).

Slaviris, Milton, Private, Company B, 148th Indiana Infantry.

Slinger, Andrew J., Regimental Band, 36th Indiana Infantry; First Lieutenant, Company I, 69th Indiana Infantry; Captain, Company A, 110th Indiana Infantry (Morgan Raid); Private, Company B, 26th Indiana Infantry.

Sloan, Abner, Private, Company K, 105th Indiana Infantry (Morgan Raid); Private Company M, 21st Indiana Infantry re-organized as 1st Heavy Artillery.

Sloan, Henry, Private, Company C, 5th Indiana Cavalry.

Sloan, James E., Private, Company I, 69th Indiana Infantry.

Sloat, Peter D., Private, Company E, 123rd Indiana Infantry.

Sloniker, Joseph M., Private, Company K, 36th Indiana Infantry.

*Small, Eli O., Private, Company F, 57th Indiana Infantry.

**Smeltzer, George W., Corporal, Company B, 147th Indiana Infantry.

Smith, Andrew J., Private, Company F, 6th Indiana Infantry (three months).

Smith, David H., Artificer, 23rd Indiana Battery.

Smith, Henry M., Private, Company F, 6th Indiana Infantry (three months); Private, 2nd Indiana Battery.

Smith, Isaac, Private, Company H, 140th Indiana Infantry.

Smith, Isaac P., Corporal, Sergeant, Company F, 84th Indiana Infantry.

Smith, J. C., Private, Company B, 110th Indiana Infantry (Morgan Raid).

*Smith, Jackson, Corporal, Company H, 140th Indiana Infantry.

Smith, Jacob, Private, Company F, 6th Indiana Infantry (three months); Private, Company D, 36th Indiana Infantry; Private, Company H, 30th Indiana Infantry, re-organized.

Smith, James, Private, Company H, 147th Indiana Infantry.

Smith, James H., Private, Company A, 87th Indiana Infantry; Private, Company A, 42nd Indiana Infantry.

Smith, James R., First Sergeant, Second Lieutenant, Company H, 8th Indiana Infantry (three years).

Smith, John, Private, Company E, 9th Indiana Cavalry.

Smith, John F., Private, Company K, 36th Indiana Infantry.

Smith, John H., Private, Company F, 84th Indiana Infantry.

Smith, John P., Private, Company F, 84th Indiana Infantry.

Smith, John T., Private, Company A, 139th Indiana Infantry.

Smith, Joseph D., Private, Company H, 140th Indiana Infantry.

Smith, Joshua, Private, Company C, 5th Indiana Cavalry.

**Smith, Nelson G., Private, Company F, 99th Indiana Infantry; Private, Company F, 48th Indiana Infantry.

Smith, Robert A., Private, Company A, 57th Indiana Infantry

Smith, Robert S., Private, Company A, 110th Indiana Infantry (Morgan Raid).

Smith, Samuel T., Sergeant, Second Lieutenant, First Lieutenant, Company F; Adjutant, Staff, 57th Indiana Infantry.

Smith, Solomon, Private, Company A, 36th Indiana Infantry.

Smith, Stephen, Private, Company A, 139th Indiana Infantry.

Smith, Thomas C., Private, Company E, 9th Indiana Cavalry.

Smith, Thorban W., First Sergeant, Company H, 147th Indiana Infantry.

Smith, William, Corporal, Company I, 3rd Indiana Cavalry.

Snider, Carlisle, Musician, Company F, 130th Indiana Infantry

Snider, William H., Private, Company E, 147th Indiana Infantry.

Snidman, William, Sergeant, Company A, 54th Indiana Infantry (one year).

Snodgrass, Wesley, Corporal, Company A, 110th Indiana Infantry (Morgan Raid).

Snodgrass, Willis, Private, Company C, 11th Indiana Infantry.

Snyder, David, Private, Company F, 11th Indiana Infantry.

*Snyder, Jacob, Private, Company E, 8th Indiana Infantry (three years).

Snyder, Rhynaldo, Private, Company H, 140th Indiana Infantry.

*Soule, William M., Private, Company G; Principal Musician, Non Commissioned Staff, 84th Indiana Infantry.

Sourwine, Isaac, Sergeant, Company G, 7th Indiana Cavalry.

Southard, Asbury, Private, Company I, 3rd Indiana Cavalry.

Spade, Jacob, Private, Company I, 3rd Indiana Cavalry.

**Spain, Pleasant A., Musician, First Sergeant, Company C, 58th Indiana Infantry.

Spaw, George, Private, Company A, 36th Indiana Infantry.

Speakman, John, Corporal, Sergeant, 12th Indiana Battery.

Spell, Robert O., Private, Company B, 110th Indiana Infantry (Morgan Raid); Private, Company E, 9th Indiana Cavalry.

Speese, George W., Private, Company K, 54th Indiana Infantry (three months); Private, Company K, 36th Indiana Infantry; Private, Corporal, Company H, 30th Indiana Infantry, re-organized.

Spencer, Charles, Private, Company A, 110th Indiana Infantry (Morgan Raid); Private, Company B, 139th Indiana Infantry.

Spencer, David, Private, Corporal, Sergeant, Company D, 36th Indiana Infantry.

Spencer, John A., Private, Company D, 36th Indiana Infantry.

Spencer, Lindley H., Private, Company B, 8th Indiana Infantry (three months); Sergeant, Company I, 69th Indiana Infantry.

Spencer, Milton M., Private, Corporal, 4th Indiana Battery.

Sperry, Samuel W., Private, Company I, 42nd Indiana Infantry.

*Sphor, Harmon, Private, Company H, 140th Indiana Infantry.

*Sponsler, Andrew W., Private, Company B, 139th Indiana Infantry.

**Sprong, Andrew J., Wagoner, Company G, 36th Indiana Infantry.

Sprong, James, Private, Company I, 84th Indiana Infantry; Corporal, Company K, 57th Indiana Infantry.

Spurry, William, Private, Company A, 57th Indiana Infantry.

Staff, Frederick, Private, Company A, 105th Indiana Infantry (Morgan Raid).

Staff, Henry, Private, Company F, 20th Indiana Infantry.

Staff, Peter, Private, Company K, 36th Indiana Infantry.

Stafford, Thomas, Private, Company A, 110th Indiana Infantry (Morgan Raid).

Stafford, William H., Private, Company I, 69th Indiana Infantry.

Staht, Christopher, Private, Company B, 149th Indiana Infantry.

Staley, Harrison, Private, Company A, 105th Indiana Infantry, (Morgan Raid).

*Staley, Thomas, Private, Company H, 147th Indiana Infantry.

Stam, William G., Private, Company F, 84th Indiana Infantry.

Stanfield, Clayton, Private, Company K, 105th Indiana Infantry (Morgan Raid).

Stanley, Andrew, Private, Company I, 53rd Indiana Infantry.

Stanley, George W., Private, Company I, 53rd Indiana Infantry.

Stanley, Samuel B., First Sergeant, Company H, 5th Regiment, 1st Army Corps, (Hancock's Veteran Corps)

Stanley, William A., Private, Company F, 6th Indiana Infantry (three months); Private, Company I, 3rd Indiana Cavalry; Private, Company B, 8th Indiana Cavalry, re-organized.

Starbuck, Henry H., Private, Company A, 139th Indiana Infantry.

Starbuck, James M., Private, Company D, 147th Indiana Infantry.

·Starr, Joel, D., Private, Company B, 8th Indiana Infantry (three months); Private, Company D, 2nd Indiana Cavalry; Private, Company D, 147th Indiana Infantry.

**Starr, Leander, Private, Corporal, Company D, 8th Indiana Infantry (three years).

Starr, Zachariah M., Private, Company D, 36th Indiana Infantry.

Steadler, Adam A., First Lieutenant, 12th Indiana Battery.

Steele, Alexander, Private, Company B, 110th Indiana Infantry (Morgan Raid).

Steele, Isaac, Corporal, Company F, 6th Indiana Infantry (three months); First Lieutenant, Company G, 16th Indiana Infantry; Second Lieutenant, Company B, 110th Inuiana Infantry (Morgan Raid); Private, Company A, 36th Indiana Infantry.

Steele, James, Private, Company F, 6th Indiana Infantry (three months); Sergeant, First Lieutenant, Company G, 16th Indiana Infantry.

Steele, James A., Sergeant, Company K, 36th Indiana Infantry.

Steffey, Abraham, Private, Company K, 36th Indiana Infantry.

**Steffey, Joseph, Private, Company H, 147th Indiana Infantry.

Steiner, Valentine, First Lieutenant, Company F, 84th Indiana Infantry.

**Stephens, Charles H., Private, Company A, 153rd Indiana Infantry.

Stephens, William, Private, Company B, 110th Indiana Infantry (Morgan Raid).

Stephenson, Amos, Private, Company F, 6th Indiana Infantry (three.months); Private, Company A, 36th Indiana Infantry.

Stevens, Nathaniel, Private, Company D, 147th Indiana Infantry.

Stevens, Townsend G., Private, 4th Indiana Battery; Private, Troop G, 6th Cavalry U. S. A.

Stevens, William H., Private, Company D, 36th Indiana Infantry.

Stevenson, Weekley M., Corporal, Company B, 110th Indiana Infantry (Morgan Raid).

**Stewart, Benjamin A., Corporal, Company C, 82nd Indiana Infantry.

Stewart, David, Private, Company G, 17th Indiana Infantry.

Stewart, Elijah H., Private, Company F, 84th Indiana Infantry.

*Stewart, Henry R., Private, Company C, 109th Indiana Infantry (Morgan Raid); Private, Company G, 7th Indiana Cavalry.

Stewart, James S., Private, Company F, 84th Indiana Infantry.

Stewart, John, Private, Company F, 6th Indiana Infantry (three months); Sergeant, First Sergeant, Second Lieutenant, Company A, 36th Indiana Infantry; Private, Second Lieutenant, First Lieutenant, 2nd Indiana Battery, re-organized.

Stewart, Leander S., Private, Company A, 105th Indiana Infantry (Morgan Raid).

Stewart, Samuel L., Private, Company F, 84th Indiana Infantry; Private, Company A, 57th Indiana Infantry.

Stewart, Silas, Private, Unassigned, 22nd Indiana Infantry. .

Stewart, William, Private, Company A, 36th Indiana Infantry.

Stewart, William F., Private, Company A, 36th Indiana Infantry.

Stewart, William W., Private, Company F, 84th Indiana Infantry.

Stigleman, John, Private, Company A, 36th Indiana Infantry.

Stilley, James, Private, Company F, 124th Indiana Infantry.

*Stines, Joseph L., Private, Musician, Company I, 69th Indiana Infantry.

Stinson, George, Private, Company C, 36th Indiana Infantry.

Stinson, John, Private, Company D, 147th Indiana Infantry.

Stonebraker, Adam, Private, Corporal, Company E, 147th Indiana Infantry.

Stonebraker, John R., Private, Company E, 147th Indiana Infantry.

*Stonesipher, Thomas J., Sergeant, Company H, 147th Indiana Infantry.

Storms, John M., Private, Sergeant, Company E, 9th Indiana Cavalry.

Stotler, Obediah H., Private, Company H, 69th Indiana Infantry.

Stout, Hezekiah, Private, Company C, 109th Indiana Infantry (Morgan Raid).

Stout, John R., Private, Company E, 8th Indiana Infantry (three years).

Stout, William, Private, Company I, 36th Indiana Infantry.

Stowhig, Daniel, Private, Company I, 37th Indiana Infantry.

**Strahan, David B., Private, Company E, 8th Indiana Infantry (three months); Private, Company C, 69th Indiana Infantry.

Strain, David F., Private, Company I, 9th Indiana Infantry.

Stratton, Albert, Private, Company F, 84th Indiana Infantry.

Stratton, Benjamin F., Private, Company A, 105th Indiana Infantry (Morgan Raid); Private, Company A, 139th Indiana Infantry.

Straughn, Moses, Private, Company F, 6th Indiana Infantry (three months).; Private, Company D, 8th Indiana Infantry (three years).

Stretch, William H., Sergeant, Company G, 84th Indiana Infantry.

Strickler, Peter C., Private, Company H, 69th Indiana Infantry.

Strode,. Robert, Private, Company A, 110th Indiana Infantry (Morgan Raid).

Strohm, Washington L., Private, Company I, 11th Indiana Infantry.

**Strong, Rosey, Private, Company D, 8th Indiana Infantry (three years).

Stuart, Henry, Private, Company A; 139th Indiana Infantry.

Stuart, Ithamer J., Private, Company A, 139th Indiana Infantry.

Stubblefield, James, Private, Company A, 54th. Indiana Infantry (three months).

Stubblefield, Martin, Private, Company H, 147th Indiana Infantry. (See Alphabetical List B).

Stubbs, Clarkson, Private, Company A, 139th Indiana Infantry.

*Studebaker, Daniel, Private, Company E, 8th Indiana Infantry (three years).

Sullivan, Daniel, Private, Company F, 19th Infantry U. S. A.

Sullivan, Jeremiah, Private, Company F, 57th Indiana Infantry.

Sullivan, Patrick, Private, Company F, 19th Indiana Infantry; Private, Company E, 20th Indiana Infantry, re-organized; Private, Company D, 1st Rhode Island Light Artillery.

**Sullivan, William, Private, Company G, 36th Indiana Infantry.

Summers, Henry C., Private, Company C, 109th Indiana Infantry (Morgan Raid)

Summers, Horace, Private, Company C, 109th Indiana Infantry (Morgan Raid).

Swafford, Laban W., Private, Farrier, Company G, 9th Indiana Cavalry.

Swafford. William W., First Lieutenant, New Lisbon Indiana State Guards, Indiana Legion.

Swaim, Elihu, Private, Company F, 6th Indiana Infantry (three months); Private, Company A, 36th Indiana Infantry.

Swaim, Harvey W., Private, Company F, 6th Indiana Infantry (three months); Sergeant, Company I, 69th Indiana Infantry.

Swaim, John M., Private, Company F, 6th Indiana Infantry (three months); Private, Company A, 36th Indiana Infantry; Private, Corporal, Company H, 30th Indiana Infantry, re-organized.

Swain, Elza, Private, Company G, 69th Indiana Infantry.

Swain, George H., Private, Company A, 105th Indiana Infantry (Morgan Raid).

Swain, Henry, Private, Company K, 105th Indiana Infantry (Morgan Raid).

Swain, John K., Private, Company E., 8th Indiana Infantry (three years).

**Swain, John L., Private, Company D, 9th Indiana Cavalry.

Swain, Robert S., Corporal, Company F, 6th Indiana Infantry (three months); Second Lieutenant, Company D, 36th Indiana Infantry.

Swain, Thomas M., Sergeant, Company D, 36th Indiana Infantry; First Lieutenant, Company A, 139th Indiana Infantry.

Swain, William, Private, Company K, 105th Indiana Infantry (Morgan Raid).

Swayne, William T., Private, Unassigned, 22nd Indiana Infantry.

Swartz, George. Private, Company C, 36th Indiana Infantry; Private, 2nd Indiana Battery, re-organized.

Swearingen, Demetrius, Private, Company K, 9th Indiana Infantry.

Swearingen, Samuel V., Private, Company E, 147th Indiana Infantry.

Sweet, Eli M., Corporal, Company D, 36th Indiana Infantry.

Sweigart, Jacob, Private, Corporal, Company C, 36th Indiana Infantry.

Sweigart, Samuel H., Private, Company E, 9th Indiana Cavalry.

Swinney, Henry A., Private, Company I, 3rd Indiana Cavalry.

Swinney, Robert J., Private, Company I, 3rd Indiana Cavalry.

Swope, Joseph A., Private, Company C, 109th Indiana Infantry (Morgan Raid); Private, Company G, 17th Indiana Infantry.

Sydruff, Robert, Private, Company A, 110th Indiana Infantry (Morgan Raid).
Symons, Benjamin F. (See Incomplete List).

T

Tarkleson, George W., Private, Corporal, Sergeant, First Lieutenant, Captain, Company E, 8th Indiana Infantry (three years).
Tarvin, Amzi, Private, Company A, 30th Indiana Infantry, re-organized.
Taylor, David S., Private, Company D, 36th Indiana Infantry.
**Taylor, Ethan S., Private, Company D, 8th Indiana Infantry (three years).
Taylor, George O., Private, Company A, 110th Indiana Infantry (Morgan Raid); Private, Company B, 139th Indiana Infantry.
Taylor, Henry, Private, 19th Indiana Battery.
Taylor, Thomas E., Private, Company K, 54th Indiana Infantry (one year); Private, Company B, 21st Indiana Infantry, re-organized as 1st Heavy Artillery.
Taylor, Wilson, Private, Company I, 84th Indiana Infantry; Private, Company K, 57th Indiana Infantry.
Temple, George, Private, Company F, 84th Indiana Infantry.
Temple, Henry, Private, Company F, 6th Indiana Infantry (three months); Company Quartermaster Sergeant, Company I, 3rd Indiana Cavalry.
Templeton, Charles, Private, Company B, 110th Indiana Infantry (Morgan Raid).
Templin, John H., Private, Company I, 124th Indiana Infantry.
Templin, Samuel V., Private, Corporal, Sergeant, First Lieutenant, Company C, 36th Indiana Infantry; First Lieutenant, Company H, 30th Indiana Infantry, re-organized; Captain and Commissary of Subsistence and Brevet Major, Staff, U. S. Volunteers. (See General Officers, Chapter IX).
Tennell, James B., Second Lieutenant, Middletown Rifles, Indiana Legion; First Sergeant, Company C, 109th Indiana Infantry (Morgan Raid).
Terhune, Albert G., Private, Company F, 57th Indiana Infantry.
Terhune, John H., Private, Sergeant, Company F, 57th Indiana Infantry.
Terrill, Theodore, Private, Company F, 101st Indiana Infantry.
Tharp, Thomas D., Second Lieutenant, First Lieutenant, Company F, 57th Indiana Infantry.
*Thatcher, Edwin, Corporal, Company H, 140th Indiana Infantry.
Thawley, Edward, Private, Company F, 84th Indiana Infantry; Private, Company E, First U. S. Engineers.
Thomas, A. C., Private, Company A, 110th Indiana Infantry (Morgan Raid).
Thomas, Charles E., Private, Company K, 36th Indiana Infantry.
**Thomas, Charles H. B., Private, Company B, 28th U. S. C. T.; Private, Company E. 23rd U. S. C. T.
Thomas, Dock. (See Incomplete List).
*Thomas, James, Private, Company A, 57th Indiana Infantry.
Thomas, James, Private, Company F, 57th Indiana Infantry.
Thomas, James W., Corporal, Company A, 36th Indiana Infantry.
Thomas, Thomas, Private, Company K, 36th Indiana Infantry.
Thomas, William K., Private, Company A, 36th Indiana Infantry; Private, Company H, 30th Indiana Infantry, re-organized.
Thompson, Henry, Private, Company K, 105th Indiana Infantry (Morgan Raid).
Thompson, James, Private, Company E, 36th Indiana Infantry.
Thompson, John, Private, Unassigned, 16th Indiana Infantry.
Thompson, Joseph H., Private, Company G, Quartermaster, Sergeant, Non Commissioned, Staff, 84th Indiana Infantry.
*Thompson, Lewis, Private, Company I, 3rd Indiana Cavalry.
Thompson, Nathan, Private, Company H, 140th Indiana Infantry.
Thornburgh, Alfred M., Musician, Company B, 8th Indiana Infantry (three months); Regimental Band, 18th Indiana Infantry; Private, Company E; Chief Bugler, Non Commissioned Staff, 9th Indiana Cavalry.

Thornburgh, Franklin D., Private, Company B, 110th Indiana Infantry (Morgan Raid); Private, Company E, 9th Indiana Cavalry.

Thornburgh, James, Private, Company B, 19th Indiana Infantry; Private, Company H, 147th Indiana Infantry.

Thornburgh, John, First Lieutenant and Quartermaster, Staff, 4th Indiana Cavalry.

Thornburgh, John M., Regimental Band, 18th Indiana Infantry; First Sergeant, Second Lieutenant, Company H, 140th Indiana Infantry.

*Thornburgh, John W., Private, Corporal, Company K, 36th Indiana Infantry.

Thornburgh, Milton, Sergeant, Company K, 36th Indiana Infantry.

Thornburgh, Weaver, Regimental Band, 18th Indiana Infantry; Sergeant, Company C, 109th Indiana Infantry (Morgan Raid).

Thornburgh, Wilson H., Corporal, Company A, 110th Indiana Infantry (Morgan Raid).

Threewits, Franklin, Private, Company K, 36th Indiana Infantry.

Thurman, Isom, Private, Company F, 14th U. S. C. T.

Thut, Adolphus G., Corporal, Company A, 36th Indiana Infantry.

Tillman, William R., Private, Company I, 84th Indiana Infantry.

Timmons, John W., Private, Company C, 147th Indiana Infantry.

Tinney, James, Sergeant, Company F, 84th Indiana Infantry.

Tolbert, George W., Private, Company I, 69th Indiana Infantry.

Topping, James S., Private, Company I, 54th Indiana Infantry (one year).

Topping, William, Private, Company C, 36th Indiana Infantry.

Tout, Charles, Private, Company A, 110th Indiana Infantry (Morgan Raid).

Trail, Benjamin F., Private, Company C; Sergeant, Major, Non Commissioned Staff, 28th U. S. C. T.

Trail, David, Private, Company F, 14th U. S. C. T.

Trail, James, Private, Company C, 28th U. S. C. T.

Trail, William, Private, Company I, 28th U. S. C. T.

Tribby, James W., Private, Company F, 84th Indiana Infantry; Private, Company K, 57th Indiana Infantry.

Trout, Abraham, Private, Company E, 8th Indiana Infantry (three years); Private, Sergeant, Company E, 9th Indiana Cavalry.

Trout, John L., Private, Company C, 109th Indiana Infantry (Morgan Raid); Corporal, Company F, 124th Indiana Infantry.

Trout, William, Corporal, Company E, 8th Indiana Infantry (three years).

Troxell, Ezra, Private, Company K, 36th Indiana Infantry; Wagoner, Company F, 84th Indiana Infantry.

Troxell, Robert, Private, Company F, 84th Indiana Infantry.

Trumbull, Wescott S., Private, Musician, Company I, 84th Indiana Infantry.

*Trusler, Nelson, Colonel, Staff, 84th Indiana Infantry.

Tucker, George W., Private, Company K, 54th Indiana Infantry (three months).

Tucker, Thomas B., Sergeant, Company C, 109th Indiana Infantry (Morgan Raid); Private, Company F, 124th Indiana Infantry.

Tuder, Robert F., Private, Company M, 8th Indiana Cavalry, re-organized.

Tuft, Andrew, Private, Company B, 110th Indiana Infantry (Morgan Raid).

Turner, Philip, Private, Company B, 147th Indiana Infantry.

Turner, Samuel H., Private, Company A, 139th Indiana Infantry.

Turner, Sashwell, Private, Company E, 30th Indiana Infantry.

Turner, William, Private, Company K, 148th Indiana Infantry.

Tweedy, James L., Private, Company E, 106th Indiana Infantry (Morgan Raid).

Tweedy, James M., Private, Company A, 139th Indiana Infantry.

**Tyer, Madison, Private, Company I, 132nd Indiana Infantry.

*Tygart, Thomas N., Private, Corporal, Company A, 57th Indiana Infantry.

Tykle, Frederick, Captain, Company B, 8th Indiana Infantry (three months); Captain, Company E, 8th Indiana Infantry (three years); Captain, Middletown Rifles, Indiana Legion; Captain, Company C, 109th Indiana Infantry (Morgan Raid). (See Mexican War).

COMPANY E, 8th INDIANA INFANTRY.

COMPANY E. 8th INDIANA INFANTRY.

**Tyner, Richard H. H., Corporal, Sergeant, First Sergeant, First Lieutenant, Company D, 9th Indiana Infantry.

U

Underwood, Enoch, Private, Company K, 36th Indiana Infantry.
*Unthank, Charles R., Private, Company I, 84th Indiana Infantry.
· Upham, Nathan, Private, Corporal, Company G, 84th Indiana Infantry.

VAN

Van Buskirk, John, Sergeant, Company K, 105th Indiana Infantry (Morgan Raid).
Van Buskirk, William H., Private, Company E, 106th Indiana Infantry (Morgan Raid).
Van Dusen, George P. S., Private, Company D, 36th Indiana Infantry.
Van Duyn, Isaac, Private, Company H, 69th Indiana Infantry.
Van Dyke, Marshall, Private, Company A, 57th Indiana Infantry.
Van Dyke, Thomas B., Musician, Company I, 84th Indiana Infantry.
Van Horn, Henry H., Corporal, Sergeant, First Lieutenant, Captain, Company A, 57th Indiana Infantry.
Van Matre, Abner, Private, Company E, 8th Indiana Infantry (three years).
Van Matre, Cyrus, Private, Company B, 8th Indiana Infantry (three months); Sergeant, First Lieutenant, Company E, 8th Indiana Infantry (three years).
Van Matre, David P., Private, Company G, 8th Indiana Cavalry, re-organized.
Van Matre, Jasper, Private, Company D, 2nd Indiana Cavalry; Private, Corporal, Company L, 8th Indiana Cavalry, re-organized.
Van Matre, Joseph, Private, Company F, 57th Indiana Infantry.
Van Matre, Joseph J., Private, · Company C, 109th Indiana Infantry (Morgan Raid); Private, Company G, 7th Indiana Cavalry; Private, Company F, 7th Indiana Cavalry, re-organized.
Van Matre, Joseph W., Private, Company C, 109th Indiana Infantry (Morgan Raid).
Van Matre, Landy, Private, Company B, 8th Indiana Infantry (three months); Private, Company D, 2nd Indiana Cavalry; Private, Company B, 2nd Indiana Cavalry, re-organized.
Van Matre, Luther D., Private, Company D, 36th Indiana Infantry; Private, Company H, 30th Indiana Infantry, re-organized.
Van Matre, Oliver H. P., Private, Company L, 8th Indiana Cavalry, re-organized.
· Van Matre, Peter, Private, Company H, 140th Indiana Infantry.
Van Matre, William J., Private, Company C, 109th Indiana Infantry (Morgan Raid).
Van Matre, William W., Private, Company E, 8th Indiana Infantry (three years).
Van Matre, Winfield S., Private, Company B, 36th Indiana Infantry.
Vanneman, Hiram B., Captain, Company G, 84th Indiana Infantry.
*Vanosdal, Argus D., Captain, Company I, 3rd Indiana Cavalry.
*Vanpelt, John, Private, Company I, 3rd Indiana Cavalry.
Van Winkle, Robert R., Private, Company H, 69th Indiana Infantry.

V

Vail, John M., Private, Company C, 36th Indiana Infantry.
**Vallandigham, Leroy, Private, Sergeant, Company D, 79th Indiana Infantry.
Vance, John H., Private, Company A, 105th Indiana Infantry (Morgan Raid). ✓
Vance, John W., Private, Company B, 110th Indiana Infantry (Morgan Raid).
Vance, John W. H., Private, Corporal, Company A, 139th Indiana Infantry; Private, Company D, 147th Indiana Infantry.
**Vance, Samuel G., Private, Company F, 146th Indiana Infantry.
*Vaughn, Thomas C., Private, Company H, 140th Indiana Infantry.
Veach, Benjamin H., Private, Company G, 84th Indiana Infantry.
*Vest, Arthur E., Private, Sergeant, Company F, 57th Indiana Infantry.

53

*Vest, Rowland, Private, Company F, 57th Indiana Infantry.

Vickrey, James R., Private, Company I, 84th Indiana Infantry.

Vickrey, Rufus W., Private, Company I, 84th Indiana Infantry.

Videto, Willis, Private, Company E, 9th Regiment, 1st Army Corps (Hancock's Veteran Corps).

*Vietch, Henderson, Private, Company G, 84th Indiana Infantry.

Vinson, Charles, Private, Company F, 6th Indiana Infantry (three months).

Vores, James H., Private, Company B, 8th Indiana Infantry (three months); Corporal, Company C, 36th Indiana Infantry.

Voorhees, De Camp B., Private, Company I, 84th Indiana Infantry.

W

Waddell, Benjamin, Private, 19th Indiana Battery.

Waddell, Charles M., Private, 19th Indiana Battery.

Waddell, Henry, Private, Company A, 36th Indiana Infantry.

Waddell, Lorenzo D., Private, 19th Indiana Battery.

Waddell, Luther, Private, Company A, 36th Indiana Infantry.

*Waddy, John B., Private, Company F, 57th Indiana Infantry.

*Waddy, Robert A., Private, Company F, 57th Indiana Infantry.

Waggoner, James L., Private, Company H, 147th Indiana Infantry.

Waggoner, Jehu, Private, Company H, 69th Indiana Infantry.

Walker, Clinton, Private, Company H, 147th Indiana Infantry.

Walker, George D., Private, Company F, 84th Indiana Infantry.

Walker, George W., Private, Company A, 6th Indiana Infantry (three months).

**Walker, Jacob S., Private, Company C, 2nd Indiana Cavalry.

Walker, James A., Private, Company B, 110th Indiana Infantry (Morgan Raid); Private, Company A, 87th Indiana Infantry.

**Walker, John R., Private, Company G, 10th Indiana Cavalry.

Walker, William E., Private, Unassigned, 16th Indiana Infantry; Private, Company G, 13th Indiana Cavalry.

Walker, William F., Private, Company B, 110th Indiana Infantry (Morgan Raid); Private Company B, 139th Indiana Infantry.

*Walker, William H., Private, Corporal, Company G, 84th Indiana Infantry.

Wall, William F. N., Private, Company C, 5th Indiana Cavalry.

Wallace, David, Private, Company G, 84th Indiana Infantry; Private, Company K, 57th Indiana Infantry.

Wallace, John S., Private, Company B, 54th Indiana Infantry (one year).

Waller, David, Private, Company K, 36th Indiana Infantry.

Waller, Thomas, Private, 3rd Indiana Battery; Private, 14th Indiana Battery.

*Wallick, Samuel, Private, Company H, 147th Indiana Infantry.

**Walling, Joseph, Private, Company B, 134th Indiana Infantry.

**Walton, Joseph P., Private, Company B, 5th Indiana Cavalry.

*Wampler, Daniel S., Private, Company H, 147th Indiana Infantry.

Wann, Cyrus, Private, Company E, 8th Indiana Infantry (three years).

Ward, David, Private, Company A, 139th Indiana Infantry.

Ward, John, Private, Company F, 130th Indiana Infantry.

Ward, John S., Private, Company D, 36th Indiana Infantry.

*Ward, Michael, Private, Company A, 57th Indiana Infantry.

Ward, William H., Private, Company I, 69th Indiana Infantry.

Warner, Caleb N., Sergeant, Company A, 57th Indiana Infantry.

Warner, George W., Private, Company B, 8th Indiana Infantry (three months); Private, 12th Indiana Battery.

Warner, John, Private, Company G, 84th Indiana Infantry.

Warner, Noah W., Private, Company B, 8th Indiana Infantry (three months); Private, Company H, 69th Indiana Infantry.

Warner, Peter, Private, Company G, 84th Indiana Infantry.

Warnock, Jacob, Private, Company C, 109th Indiana Infantry (Morgan Raid); Private, Corporal, Sergeant, Company G, 7th Indiana Cavalry.

Warrick, George W., Private, Corporal, Company A, 36th Indiana Infantry.

Wasson, Alexander, Private, Company K, 19th Indiana Infantry; Private, Company E, 20th Indiana Infantry, re-organized.

Wasson, John D., Private, Company I, 124th Indiana Infantry.

Waters, Thomas, Private, Company A, 139th Indiana Infantry.

Waters, William, Private, Company K, 9th Indiana Infantry.

Watkins, Daniel L., Private, Company F, 84th Indiana Infantry.

Watkins, Francis M., Private, Company F, 57th Indiana Infantry.

Watkins, John J., Private, Company B, 110th Indiana Infantry (Morgan Raid).

Watkins, Marquis de L. (See Incomplete List.).

Watkins, Thornton T., Private, Company F, 57th Indiana Infantry.

Watkins, William M., Private, Company B, 110th Indiana Infantry (Morgan Raid); Private, Company G, 17th Indiana Infantry.

Watson, Cervantus S., Private, Company A, 36th Indiana Infantry.

*Watson, William C., Private, Company H, 147th Indiana Infantry.

**Watts, Harry, Private, Company F, 24th Indiana Infantry.

*Way, Armsbee D., Private, Corporal, Company K, 36th Indiana Infantry.

*Way, John S., Second Lieutenant, Company K, 36th Indiana Infantry.

Way, Thomas R., Private, Corporal, Company C, 36th Indiana Infantry.

Wayman, John C., Private, Corporal, Sergeant, Second Lieutenant, Company C, 36th Indiana Infantry.

Wean, George W., Private, Company G, 84th Indiana Infantry.

Weatherald, Thomas R., Private, Company K, 36th Indiana Infantry.

Weaver, Charles H., Private, Company K, 17th Indiana Infantry.

*Weaver, Charles H., Private, Company A, 57th Indiana Infantry.

Weaver, Clement H., Private, Company C, 36th Indiana Infantry; First Sergeant, Second Lieutenant, Company D, 147th Indiana Infantry.

Weaver, David P., Private, Company E, 9th Indiana Cavalry.

Weaver, George C., Private, Company A, 110th Indiana Infantry (Morgan Raid).

Weaver, George T., Private, Company E; Saddler Sergeant, Non Commissioned Staff, 9th Indiana Cavalry.

Weaver, John R., Private, Saddler, Company E, 9th Indiana Cavalry.

Weaver, John S., Private, Company K, 17th Indiana Infantry.

Weaver, Orange R., Private, Company I, 3rd Indiana Cavalry; Private, Company A; Hospital Steward, Non Commissioned, Staff, 139th Indiana Infantry.

Weaver, Thomas D., Private, Company I, 3rd Indiana Cavalry.

Weaver, Walter S., Musician, Company H; Principal Musician, Non Commissioned Staff, 147th Indiana Infantry.

Webb, William, Private, Company E, 8th Indiana Infantry (three years).

Weber, William, Private, Company C, 36th Indiana Infantry.

Weed, Harvey H., Private, Company K, 134th Indiana Infantry.

Weeks, Edward W., Private, Company A, 36th Indiana Infantry.

Weeks, Nathan, Private, Company D, 36th Indiana Infantry; Private B, 110th Indiana Infantry (Morgan Raid).

Weesner, Jesse, Private, Company H, 140th Indiana Infantry.

*Weesner, John S., Private, Company H, 140th Indiana Infantry.

Weesner, William B., Private, Company A, 110th Indiana Infantry (Morgan Raid).

Weesner, William R., Private, Corporal, Company E, 9th Indiana Cavalry.

*Weist, George L., First Lieutenant, Company H, 147th Indiana Infantry.

Welborn, Henry C., Sergeant, Company B, 110th Indiana Infantry (Morgan Raid); Private, Company A, 139th Indiana Infantry.

Welborn, Joshua T. C., Private, Company F, 11th Indiana Infantry; First Sergeant, First Lieutenant, Captain, Company F, 84th Indiana Infantry.

Welborn, Shelby R., Private, Company B, 42nd Indiana Infantry.

Welch, James, Private, Company G, 16th Indiana Infantry.

Welch, Richard, Private, Company F, 124th Indiana Infantry.

Welker, David, Private, Company K, 99th Indiana Infantry.; Wagoner, Company H, 140th Indiana Infantry.

Welker, George W., Private, Company E, 147th Indiana Infantry.

Welker, James M., Private, Company K, 54th Indiana Infantry (three months); Private, 15th Indiana Battery.

Welker, John, Private, Company A, 54th Indiana Infantry (one year).

Welker, Jordan, Private, Company H, 140th Indiana Infantry.

Wells, James A., Private, Company I, 84th Indiana Infantry.

Werking, John, Private, Corporal, Company A, 36th Indiana Infantry.

Werking, Joseph E., Private, Corporal, Company A, 36th Indiana Infantry.

West, Benjamin S., Corporal, Company E, 8th Indiana Infantry (three years).

West, Pennel, Regimental Band, 8th Indiana Infantry (three years); Private, Company F, 124th Indiana Infantry.

West, William D., Private, Company D, 36th Indiana Infantry.

West, William H., Private, Company E, 8th Indiana Infantry (three years); Corporal, Company C, 109th Indiana Infantry (Morgan Raid); Private, Company F, 124th Indiana Infantry.

*Wheeler, Jason, Private, Company F, 57th Indiana Infantry.

Whilton, William A., Private, Company A, 6th Indiana Infantry (three months).

Whippel, David, Private, Company K, 18th Indiana Infantry.

Whitacre, William, Private, Company E, 9th Indiana Cavalry.

White, Aaron. Private, Company D, 28th U. S. C. T.

White, Adam W., Private, Company K, 105th Indiana Infantry (Morgan Raid).

**White, Edgar T., Private, 7th Indiana Battery.

*White, Elisha B., Private, Farrier, Company E, 9th Indiana Cavalry.

White, George O., Private, Company K, 105th Indiana Infantry (Morgan Raid).

White, Harvey, Private, Company H, 140th Indiana Infantry.

White, James M., Private, Unassigned, 33rd Indiana Infantry.

White, Noah B., Private, Company A, 57th Indiana Infantry.

White, William N., Private, Company A, 57th Indiana Infantry.

Whitehead, Jonathan R., Private, Company G, 21st Indiana Infantry, re-organized as 1st Heavy Artillery.

Whitelock, Benjamin, Private, Company H, 69th Indiana Infantry.

Whitesel, James L., First Sergeant, Company F, 6th Indiana Infantry (three months); Sergeant, 2nd Indiana Battery.

Whitesel, Joseph M., Assistant Surgeon, Staff, 36th Indiana Infantry.

Whitlow, James W., Private, Company B, 19th Indiana Infantry.

Whitlow, John W., Corporal, Company I, 3rd Indiana Cavalry.

Whitlow, King S., Private, Company B, 19th Indiana Infantry.

Whitworth, John W., Private, Corporal, Company E, 8th Indiana Infantry (three years).

Whitworth, Sanford, Private, Company G, 7th Indiana Cavalry; Private, Company F, 7th Indiana Cavalry, re-organized.

Wickersham, Caleb J., Private, Company A, 36th Indiana Infantry.

Wickersham, David, Private, Company B, 110th Indiana Infantry (Morgan Raid).

*Widows, William H., Corporal, Company G, 84th Indiana Infantry.

Wigart, Michael S., Private, Company B, 147th Indiana Infantry.

Wiggins, Henry B., Private, Company K, 37th Indiana Infantry.

Wiggins, Walter, Private, Company A, 110th Indiana Infantry (Morgan Raid).

Wiles, Nathan H., Second Lieutenant, Company A, 36th Indiana Infantry.

Wiles, William D., Captain, Company A, 36th Indiana Infantry.

*Wilhelm, Henry, Private, Company E, 9th Indiana Cavalry.

Wilkinson, George M., Private, Company F, 3rd Indiana Cavalry.

Wilkinson, James E., Private, Company A, 105th Indiana Infantry (Morgan Raid).

Wilkinson, Rufus A., Private, Company F, 84th Indiana Infantry.

Wilkinson, Thomas B., Sergeant, First Lieutenant, Company I, 3rd Indiana Cavalry.

Williams, Augustus, Private, Company C, 36th Indiana Infantry.

Williams, Christian M., Private, Company G, 7th Indiana Cavalry; Private, Company F, 7th Indiana Cavalry, re-organized.

Williams, Daniel, Private, Company K, 36th Indiana Infantry.

Williams, Daniel S., Private, Company I, 69th Indiana Infantry.

Williams, David A., Private, Company E, 11th Indiana Infantry.

Williams, George, Private, 15th Indiana Battery.

*Williams, James, Private, Corporal, Company E, 8th Indiana Infantry (three years).

Williams, Jesse L., Sergeant, Company I, 69th Indiana Infantry.

Williams, Jesse R., Private, Company E, 8th Indiana Infantry (three years); Second Lieutenant, Needmore Rangers, Indiana Legion.

Williams, John, Private, Company H, 147th Indiana Infantry.

Williams, John J., Private, Company B, 5th Indiana Cavalry.

Williams, John W., Private, Company F, 6th Indiana Infantry (three months).

Williams, Joseph, Private, Company H, 69th Indiana Infantry.

Williams, Joseph B., Second Lieutenant, New Lisbon Indiana State Guards, Indiana Legion.

Williams, Leander J., Private, Corporal, Company F, 57th Indiana Infantry.

Williams, Lucian B., Private, Company B, 110th Indiana Infantry (Morgan Raid).

Williams, Milton, Private, Company B, 139th Indiana Infantry. (See Alphabetical List B).

Williams, Nereus P., Private, Company C, 36th Indiana Infantry.

*Williams, Richard, Sergeant, Company H, 140th Indiana Infantry.

Williams, Thomas, Private, Corporal, Company F, 36th Indiana Infantry.

Williams, William, Private, Company B, 139th Indiana Infantry.

Williams, William O., Corporal, Company B, 8th Indiana Infantry (three months); Private, Company B, 19th Indiana Infantry.

Williams, William R., Private, Company A, 105th Indiana Infantry (Morgan Raid).

Williams, Yancy, Private, Company A, 110th Indiana Infantry (Morgan Raid).

Williamson, Isaac, Private, Company B, 42nd Indiana Infantry.

Williamson, J. R., Private, Company A, 110th Indiana Infantry (Morgan Raid).

Williamson, James E., Corporal, Company K, 36th Indiana Infantry.

Willis, Zadoc H., Private, Company K, 105th Indiana Infantry (Morgan Raid).

Willits, Irwin, Private, Company A, 30th Indiana Infantry, re-organized.

Wills, John T., Regimental Band, 36th Indiana Infantry.

*Wilmington, Oscar N., Private, Sergeant, First Sergeant, First Lieutenant, Company F, 57th Indiana Infantry.

Wilson, Alpheus A., Private, Company D, 36th Indiana Infantry.

Wilson, Benjamin A., Private, Company B, 110th Indiana Infantry (Morgan Raid).

Wilson, Charles C., Private, Company G, 36th Indiana Infantry.

Wilson, Daniel H., Private, Company F, 36th Indiana Infantry; Private, Company H, 30th Indiana Infantry, re-organized.

Wilson, Jabez, Private, Company A, 105th Indiana Infantry (Morgan Raid); Private, 19th Indiana Battery.

Wilson, James, Private, Company K, 36th Indiana Infantry.

Wilson, John, Private, Company A, 105th Indiana Infantry (Morgan Raid).

Wilson, Leander R., Private, Company F, 6th Indiana Infantry (three months).

Wilson, Luther, Private, Company A, 36th Indiana Infantry.

Wilson, Michael C., Private, Company A, 105th Indiana Infantry (Morgan Raid).

Wilson, Richard, Private, Company B, 139th Indiana Infantry.

Wilson, Shipley S., Sergeant, First Sergeant, First Lieutenant, Captain, Company I, 84th Indiana Infantry.

Wilson, William E., Private, Company A, 105th Indiana Infantry (Morgan Raid).

Winder, Charles, Sergeant, Company I, 3rd Indiana Cavalry.

Windsor, David E., Private, Company I, 99th Indiana Infantry.

Windsor, Enoch M., Private, Company C, 109th Indiana Infantry (Morgan Raid); Private, Company G, 7th Indiana Cavalry.

Windsor, James M., Private, Company E, 8th Indiana Infantry (three years).

Windsor, Zachariah, Private, Company E, 8th Indiana Infantry (three years).

*Wineberg, James A., Private, Company F, 84th Indiana Infantry.

Winings, Lemuel H., Private, Company A, 54th Indiana Infantry (one year).

Winings, Samuel, Private, Corporal, Company C, 36th Indiana Infantry.

Wink, John A., Private, Company F, 84th Indiana Infantry.

Winship, Joseph S., Private, Company K, 36th Indiana Infantry.

Winslow, Davis, Private, Company A, 139th Indiana Infantry.

Winslow, Patrick H., Private, 22nd Indiana Battery.

Wise, William H., Private, Company F, 124th Indiana Infantry.

Wisehart, David, Private, Company H, 69th Indiana Infantry.

Wisehart, Martin, Private, Company K, 105th Indiana Infantry (Morgan Raid).

Wiseheart, Philander, Private, Company B, 8th Indiana Infantry (three months).

Wisehart, Reuben, Private, Company K, 105th Indiana Infantry (Morgan Raid).

Wisehart, Richmond, Private, Sergeant, First Sergeant, Second Lieutenant, Company F, 57th Indiana Infantry.

Wisehart, William, Private, Company H, 69th Indiana Infantry.

*Wolf, Jonathan, Wagoner, Company A, 57th Indiana Infantry.

**Wolf, Samuel, Private, Corporal, Company M, 11th Indiana Cavalry.

*Wolf, William, Private, Company H, 140th Indiana Infantry.

Wood, Seth, Corporal, Company I, 69th Indiana Infantry.

Woodard, William H., Private, Company K, 38th Indiana Infantry.

Wooden, Arthur M., Private, Company B, 110th Indiana Infantry (Morgan Raid).

*Woodring, Benjamin F., Corporal, Company H, 140th Indiana Infantry.

Woodruff, Jerome, Private, Company I, 3rd Indiana Cavalry.

Woodruff, Oliver, Private, Company I, 3rd Indiana Cavalry.

Woods, George W.; Sergeant, 25th Indiana Battery.

Woods, Henry C., Sergeant, 19th Indiana Battery.

**Woods, Jeremiah, Private, Company B, 99th Indiana Infantry.

Woods, Robert E., Private, Corporal, Company M, 9th Indiana Cavalry.

Woods, William H. S., Private, Company K, 36th Indiana Infantry.

Woodward, Alpheus L., Private, Company I, 69th Indiana Infantry.

Woodward, Pyrrhus, Captain, Company C, 36th Indiana Infantry. (See Mexican War).

*Woody, Ancis C., Private, Corporal, Company K, 36th Indiana Infantry.

*Woody, Zenoah B., Private, Company H, 140th Indiana Infantry.

Woolfecker, Francis, Private, Company A, 36th Indiana Infantry; Private, Company H, 30th Indiana Infantry, re-organized.

Woolters, Charles, Private, Company B, 110th Indiana Infantry (Morgan Raid); Private, Company E, 34th Indiana Infantry.

Workman, Henry, Private, Company C, 147th Indiana Infantry.

Workman, Isaac, Private, Company C, 147th Indiana Infantry.

Workman, John, Private, Company C, 147th Indiana Infantry.

*Worle, Alexander, Private, Company H, 147th Indiana Infantry.

**Worster, Lewis H., Private, Company H, 153rd Indiana Infantry.

Woy, George W., Private, 12th Indiana Battery. (See Alphabetical List B).

Wright, Alfred P., Private, Company A, 105th Indiana Infantry (Morgan Raid).

Wright, Henry G., Private, Company A, 105th Indiana Infantry (Morgan Raid).

COMPANY G. 7th INDIANA CAVALRY.

Wright, Isaac N., Private, Musician, Company D. 147th Indiana Infantry.
Wright, John H., Private, Company D, 36th Indiana Infantry.
Wright, Jonathan R., Private, Company I. 3rd Indiana Cavalry.
Wright, William, Private, Unassigned, 22nd Indiana Infantry.
Wright, William B., Private, Company D, 2nd Indiana Cavalry.
Wright, William F., Private, Company D, 147th Indiana Infantry.
Wright, William H., Private, Company I, 3rd Indiana Cavalry.
Wysong, Frederick, Sergeant. Company F. 6th Indiana Infantry (three months).
Wysong, George W., Private, Company A, 105th Indiana Infantry (Morgan Raid);
Private, Company B, 42nd Indiana Infantry.

Y

**Yates, Daniel, Private, Company G, 68th Indiana Infantry.
Yates, William, Private, Company I, 147th Indiana Infantry.
Yetter, Henry, Private, Company A. 105th Indiana Infantry (Morgan Raid); Private, Corporal, Company A, 139th Indiana Infantry.
Yost, Albert N., Private, Company B. 8th Indiana Infantry (three months); Corporal, Company G, 84th Indiana Infantry; First Sergeant, Company K. 57th Indiana Infantry.
Yost, Jacob W., First Sergeant, First Lieutenant, Company G, 84th Indiana Infantry.
Yost, Lewis F., Private, Company G, 84th Indiana Infantry. .
Young, David, Musician. Company A; Principal Musician, Non Commissioned Staff, 36th Indiana Infantry.
Young, James H., Corporal, Company C, 109th Indiana Infantry (Morgan Raid).
**Young, James L., Private, Company K, 53rd Indiana Infantry.
Young, James S., Private, Company I, 84th Indiana Infantry; Private, Company K, 57th Indiana Infantry.
Young, Joseph A., Private. Company C, 109th Indiana Infantry (Morgan Raid); Private, Corporal, Sergeant, Company G, 7th Indiana Cavalry.
Young, Robert A., Private, Company B, 139th Indiana Infantry; Corporal, Company H, 147th Indiana Infantry.
Young, Theodore, Private, Company I. 3rd Indiana Cavalry.
Youngman, Samuel, Private. Company K, 54th Indiana Infantry (three months).
Yount, David S., Regimental Band, 18th Indiana Infantry; First Lieutenant, Captain, Company H, 69th Indiana Infantry.
Yount, William H., Private. Company H, 69th Indiana Infantry; Private, Company C, 109th Indiana Infantry (Morgan Raid); Private, Corporal, Sergeant, Company F, 124th Indiana Infantry. .
Youtsey; Thomas, Private, Company D, 148th Indiana Infantry.

Z

Zeigler, George H., Private. Company H, 69th Indiana Infantry.
Zeigler, Jacob, Private, Company E, 36th Indiana Infantry.
Zimmerly, Edward, Private, Company B, 8th Indiana Infantry (three months).
*Zimmerman, Charles E., Private, Company H; Commissary Sergeant, Non Commissioned Staff, 140th Indiana Infantry.
Zimmerman, Ferris, Private, Company D, 8th Indiana Infantry (three years).
Zimmerman, George W., Private. Company A. 110th Indiana Infantry (Morgan Raid).

OMPANY G, 7th INDIANA CAVALRY.

Wright, Isaac N., Private, Musician, Company D, 147th Indiana Infantry.

Wright, John H., Private, Company D, 36th Indiana Infantry.

Wright, Jonathan R., Private, Company I, 3rd Indiana Cavalry.

Wright, William, Private, Unassigned, 22nd Indiana Infantry.

Wright, William B., Private, Company D, 2nd Indiana Cavalry.

Wright, William F., Private, Company D, 147th Indiana Infantry.

Wright, William H., Private, Company 1, 3rd Indiana Cavalry.

Wysong, Frederick, Sergeant, Company F, 6th Indiana Infantry (three months).

Wysong, George W., Private, Company A, 105th Indiana Infantry (Morgan Raid); Private, Company B, 42nd Indiana Infantry.

. Y

**Yates, Daniel, Private, Company G, 68th Indiana Infantry.

Yates, William, Private, Company I, 147th Indiana Infantry.

Yetter, Henry, Private, Company A, 105th Indiana Infantry (Morgan Raid); Private, Corporal, Company A, 139th Indiana Infantry.

Yost, Albert N., Private, Company B, 8th Indiana Infantry (three months); Corporal, Company G, 84th Indiana Infantry; First Sergeant, Company K, 57th Indiana Infantry.

Yost, Jacob W., First Sergeant, First Lieutenant, Company G, 84th Indiana Infantry.

Yost, Lewis F., Private, Company G, 84th Indiana Infantry.

Young, David, Musician, Company A; Principal Musician, Non Commissioned Staff, 36th Indiana Infantry.

Young, James H., Corporal, Company C, 109th Indiana Infantry (Morgan Raid).

**Young, James L., Private, Company K, 53rd Indiana Infantry.

Young, James S., Private, Company I, 84th Indiana Infantry; Private, Company K, 57th Indiana Infantry.

Young, Joseph A., Private, Company C, 109th Indiana Infantry (Morgan Raid); Private, Corporal, Sergeant, Company G, 7th Indiana Cavalry.

Young, Robert A., Private, Company B, 139th Indiana Infantry; Corporal, Company H, 147th Indiana Infantry.

Young, Theodore, Private, Company I, 3rd Indiana Cavalry.

Youngman, Samuel, Private, Company K, 54th Indiana Infantry (three months).

Yount, David S., Regimental Band, 18th Indiana Infantry; First Lieutenant, Captain, Company H, 69th Indiana Infantry.

Yount, William H., Private, Company H, 69th Indiana Infantry; Private, Company C, 109th Indiana Infantry (Morgan Raid); Private, Corporal, Sergeant, Company F, 124th Indiana Infantry.

Youtsey, Thomas, Private, Company D, 148th Indiana Infantry.

Z

Zeigler, George H., Private, Company H, 69th Indiana Infantry.

Zeigler, Jacob, Private, Company E, 36th Indiana Infantry.

Zimmerly, Edward, Private, Company B, 8th Indiana Infantry (three months).

*Zimmerman, Charles E., Private, Company H; Commissary Sergeant, Non Commissioned Staff, 140th Indiana Infantry.

Zimmerman, Ferris, Private, Company D, 8th Indiana Infantry (three years).

Zimmerman, George W., Private, Company A, 110th Indiana Infantry (Morgan Raid).

ALPHABETICAL LIST B.

This list includes the names of soldiers of the Civil War from Henry County who went to other States to enlist. Soldiers from other counties in the State, who served in other State organizations and moved to Henry County after the Civil War, are also included in this list and are designated by two asterisks, thus **, before the names.

B

**Barnard, Eugene, Private, Company I, 167th Ohio Infantry.

Barrett, Augustus E., Private, Company D, 8th Illinois Infantry (three months); First Sergeant, Second Lieutenant, Company D, 8th Illinois Infantry (three years).

Brenneman, Charles, Private, Company B, Benton Cadets, Missouri Volunteers (Fremont's Body Guard).

Bronnenberg, Carl, Private, Company A, and Private, Company M, 8th Ohio Cavalry. (See Alphabetical List A).

Brunner, Francis M., Private, Company B, 58th Ohio Infantry.

**Burchett, Thomas J., Second Lieutenant, Company H, 74th Ohio Infantry. (See Alphabetical List A).

Burr, Lafe J., Private, Company A, 137th Ohio Infantry.

C

Calvert, Charles L., Private, Company F, 165th New York Infantry. (See U. S. Military Academy).

Confare, Ephraim, First Lieutenant, Captain, Company H, 2nd Missouri Light Artillery. (See Alphabetical List A).

Conn, William D., Captain, Company I, 35th Iowa Infantry.

**Cooper, Daniel M., Sergeant, Company I, 11th Ohio Infantry; First Sergeant, Company K, 87th Ohio Infantry; First Sergeant, Company E, 2nd Ohio Heavy Artillery.

Covey, William, Private, Company B, 23rd Iowa Infantry.

Crull, Francis M., Private, Company H, 8th Iowa Infantry. (See Alphabetical List A).

D

Davis, David F., Private, Company B, Benton Cadets, Missouri Volunteers (Fremont's Body Guard). (See Alphabetical List A).

Dowell, David, Private, Company C, 12th Missouri Cavalry.

E

Evans, Owen, Corporal, First Sergeant, Second Lieutenant, Captain, Company A, 2nd U. S. Sharpshooters.

F

Fort, Oliver P., Private, Company K, 2nd Colorado Cavalry. (See Mexican War).

Frazier, Henry, Private, Company G, 29th Iowa Infantry.

Frazier, James, Private, Company G, 29th Iowa Infantry.

Frazier, Nathan, Private, Company G, 29th Iowa Infantry.
Frazier, William, Private, Company G, 29th Iowa Infantry.

G

Gillgeese, William, Wagoner, Company K, 25th Illinois Infantry; Wagoner, 8th Battery, Wisconsin Light Artillery.
**Gillingham, Ezra, Private, Company I, 21st V. R. Corps. (See Mexican War).
Goodwin, Isaac, Private, Company H, 4th Ohio Cavalry. (See Alphabetical List A).
Gray, James M., Private, Company B, Benton Cadets, Missouri Volunteers (Fremont's Body Guard). (See Alphabetical List A).

H

Hatfield, Aaron S., Private, Company D, 68th Illinois Infantry. (See Alphabetical List A).
Hendricks, Miles, Private, Sergeant, Company I, 187th Ohio Infantry. (See Alphabetical List A).
Hoover, Henry, Private, Company K, 11th Kansas Cavalry.
Hoover, John, Private, Company K, 11th Kansas Cavalry.
Hoover, John S., Private, Company K,; Quartermaster Sergeant, Non Commissioned Staff; First Lieutenant, Company K, 31st Illinois Infantry; Captain and Aid de Camp, Major and Aid de Camp, Brevet Lieutenant Colonel, Brevet Colonel, Staff, U. S. Volunteers. (See General Officers, Chapter IX).

I

Isenhour, Nathan, Private, Corporal, Company K, 34th Illinois Infantry.

L

Long, Edward M., Second Lieutenant, Company B, 3rd North Carolina Mounted Infantry. (See Alphabetical List A).

Mc

McDowell, Thomas, Private, Corporal, Company B, 23rd Iowa Infantry.

M

Mason, Alexander L., Captain, Company C, 1st Iowa Infantry.
Mayes, John, Musician, Brigade Band, 1st Brigade, 1st Division, 17th Army Corps.
Mayes, Joseph H., Musician, Brigade Band, 1st Brigade, 1st Division, 17th Army Corps.
Meek, Sam Carey, Private, Company G, and Private, Company B, 1st California Infantry.
Mills, William, Private, Company D, 6th Minnesota Infantry.
Monticue, William, Private, Company A, 123rd Illinois Infantry.
Moore, Louis P., Private, Company K, 67th Illinois Infantry. (See Alphabetical List A).
Mullen, George E., Private, Company C, 54th Ohio Infantry.
Murray, Alvin R., Private, Company A, 181st Ohio Infantry.

N

Netz, John, Private, Wallace Guards, Ohio Infantry; Private, Wagoner, Corporal, Company I, 2nd Ohio Cavalry.
Netz, Peter, Private, Company D, 2nd Ohio Heavy Artillery. (See Alphabetical List A).

O

**O'Neal, Joseph, Private, Corporal, Company F, 40th Ohio Infantry; Corporal, Company I, 51st Ohio Infantry.

P

Parker, Nathaniel W., Private, Company A, 3rd West Virginia Cavalry.
Parker, Robert, Private, Company F, 8th Wisconsin Infantry.

S

Saint, Abner P., Private, Company C, 71st Illinois Infantry.

Saint, Exum, First Sergeant, Second Lieutenant, First Lieutenant, Captain, Company E, 4th Iowa Cavalry.

Saint, Henry H., Private, Company C, 71st Illinois Infantry. (See Alphabetical List A).

Saint, William M., Private, Sergeant, First Sergeant, Company B, 59th Ohio Infantry. (See Alphabetical List A).

Schildknecht, John, Private, Corporal, Company B, 5th Iowa Cavalry.

Scott, Otho H., Private, Company C, 17th Ohio Infantry; Private, First Sergeant, Company A, 40th Ohio Infantry.

Shelley, William F., Private, Company B, Benton Cadets, Missouri Volunteers (Fremont's Body Guard). (See Alphabetical List A).

Stephenson, Reuben B., Private, Corporal, Sergeant, Company K, 10th Iowa Infantry. (See Mexican War).

Stubblefield, Martin, Private, Company B, Benton Cadets, Missouri Volunteers (Fremont's Body Guard). (See Alphabetical List A).

T

Thompson, George W., Private, Company C, 36th Illinois Infantry.

V

Van Matre, Peter L., Private, Company E, 6th Illinois Cavalry.

W

**Welsh, James H., Assistant Surgeon, Staff, 185th Ohio Infantry.

Williams, Milton, Private, Company I, 187th Ohio Infantry. (See Alphabetical List A).

Woy, George W., First Lieutenant, Captain, Company C, 1st Tennessee Light Artillery. (See Alphabetical List A).

ALPHABETICAL LIST C.

This list includes the names of soldiers of the Civil War from other States who moved to Henry County after the Civil War. The names of soldiers of the Civil War, presumably from other States, whose records are incomplete in this History, are also included in this list. Their services in the Civil War, so far as known, may be found by reference to the "Incomplete List."

A

Abbott, Mathew T., Private, Company A, 35th Iowa Infantry.

Abrams, Joseph W., Private, Company C, 22nd Kentucky Infantry; Private, Company K, 7th Kentucky Infantry.

Abrams, Sylvester, Private, Company E, 18th Missouri Infantry.

Albright, Perry J., Corporal, Company B, 110th Ohio Infantry.

Alexander, William G., Private, Company F, 54th Kentucky Infantry.

Armicost, John W., Private, Company D, 7th Ohio Cavalry.

Arnold, Samuel, Corporal, Sergeant, Company G, 5th Ohio Cavalry.

B

Baker, John, Private, Corporal, Company E, 1st Heavy Artillery, U. S. C. T.

Ball, John D., Private, Company D, 2nd Missouri Cavalry.

Barrett, Philip N., Private, Company I, 193rd Ohio Infantry.

Beardsley, Thurman·H., Private, Company D, 168th New York Infantry.

Bell, Lafe, Private, Sergeant, Company F,·53rd Kentucky Infantry.

Bennett, Samuel H., Private, Company H, 54th Ohio Infantry.

Bodmer, Jacob, Private, Company B, 46th New York Infantry. (See Alphabetical List A).

Brandon, Esley R., Private, Company B, 71st Ohio Infantry.

Brodrick, James W., Private, Company C, 11th Ohio Infantry. (See Alphabetical List A).

Brown, Francis M., Private, Company F, 1st U. S. Sharpshooters.

Bunnell, William, Private, Company D, Benton Cadets, Missouri Volunteers (Fremont's Body Guard); Private, Company D, 39th Ohio Infantry.

Burke, George W., Private, Company H; Hospital Steward, Non Commissioned Staff, 9th Pennsylvania Infantry; Assistant Surgeon, Major and Surgeon, Brevet Lieutenant Colonel, Staff, 46th Pennsylvania Infantry.

Byram, Silas, Private, Company K, 34th Ohio Infantry; Private, Company G, 17th Regiment, V. R. Corps.

C

Campbell, Cary. (See Incomplete List).

Cantrell, Abner, Private, Company A, 2nd West Virginia Infantry.

Chance, William H. (See Incomplete List).

Chambers, Andrew J., Private, Corporal, Company D, 113th Ohio Infantry.

Clevidence, Isaac, Private, Company E, 13th Maryland Infantry.

Cochran, William, Private, Corporal, Company F, 18th Iowa Infantry.

Coffin, Arthur W., Musician, Company F, 120th Ohio Infantry; Musician, Company I, 23rd Ohio Infantry.

Coffin, Thaddeus, Private, Company G; Regimental Band, 23rd Ohio Infantry.

Conner, Patrick, Private, Company K, 66th Ohio Infantry.

Crandall, William J. C., Private, Sergeant, First Lieutenant, Captain, Company' G, 1st Tennessee Infantry.

Crawford, Amos, Private, Sergeant, Company C, 91st Illinois Infantry.

Cutler, William A., Private, Company C, 145th Illinois Infantry.

D

Davis, Joseph S. (See Incomplete List).

Decker, Richard B., Private, Company B, and Private, Company D, 1st New Jersey Light Artillery.

Deeter, A. S. (See Incomplete List.)

Denius, Leander S., Regimental Band, 35th Ohio Infantry; Captain, Company G 156th Ohio Infantry.

De Witt, Abraham, Private, Company D, 37th Kentucky Infantry.

Dill, John W., Private, Company I, 40th Iowa Infantry.

Dodd, William E., Private, Company F, 7th West Virginia Infantry.

Dowling, James H., Private, Company C, 71st New York Infantry.

Dutton, John, Private, 3rd Ohio Independent Battery.

E

Ewing, James P., Private, Company B, 18th Ohio Infantry.

Ewing, James W. (See Incomplete List).

F

Feezer, James H. E., Private, Corporal, Company I, 1st Maryland Potomac Home Brigade Infantry.

Fleming, Andrew J. (See Incomplete List).

Frazier, Iredell R., Private, Company G, 3rd Maryland Cavalry.

G

Gibbs, Charles N., Second Lieutenant, Captain, Company B, 69th Ohio Infantry.

Gillmore, Isaac R., Private, Company I, 30th Illinois Infantry.

Goudy, William C., Private, Company I, 32nd Ohio Infantry.

Graham, David A., Private, Company F, 1st West Virginia Light Artillery.

Griner, Andrew J., Private, Company D, 2nd Ohio Heavy Artillery.

Grunden, Israel H., Private, Company F, 2nd Illinois Cavalry; Private, Company H, 2nd Illinois Cavalry, consolidated.

H

Hansard, Patrick H., Private, Company F, 14th U. S. C. T. (See Alphabetical List A).

Hartman, Richard, Private, Company D, 109th U. S. C. T.

Hartman, Samuel. (See Incomplete List)

Harvey, Charles W., First Sergeant, Company D, 79th Ohio Infantry.

Hatch, Asa W., Private, Company F, 2nd Ohio Infantry; Second Lieutenant, Company E, 152nd Ohio Infantry.

Hazelrigg, James T. J., Private, Sergeant, Company D, 4th Kentucky Infantry.

Heman, Hickok, Private, Corporal, Sergeant, Company B, 3rd Ohio Cavalry.

Henneigh, Martin L., Private, Company B, 74th Pennsylvania Infantry.

Higley, Henry W., Private, Company G, 3rd Missouri Cavalry.

Hill, John, Private, Company G, 55th Massachusetts Infantry.

Hillock, William G., Private, Company E, 5th Ohio Cavalry.

OHIO SOLDIERS IN HENRY COUNTY.

Coffin, Arthur W., Musician, Company F, 120th Ohio Infantry; Musician, Company I, 23rd Ohio Infantry.

Coffin, Thaddeus, Private, Company G; Regimental Band, 23rd Ohio Infantry.

Conner, Patrick, Private, Company K, 66th Ohio Infantry.

Crandall, William J. C., Private, Sergeant, First Lieutenant, Captain, Company G, 1st Tennessee Infantry.

Crawford, Amos, Private, Sergeant, Company C, 91st Illinois Infantry.

Cutler, William A., Private, Company C, 145th Illinois Infantry.

D

Davis, Joseph S. (See Incomplete List).

Decker, Richard B., Private, Company B, and Private, Company D, 1st New Jersey Light Artillery.

Deeter, A. S. (See Incomplete List.)

Denius, Leander S., Regimental Band, 35th Ohio Infantry; Captain, Company G 156th Ohio Infantry.

De Witt, Abraham, Private, Company D, 27th Kentucky Infantry.

Dill, John W., Private, Company I, 40th Iowa Infantry.

Dodd, William E., Private, Company F, 7th West Virginia Infantry.

Dowling, James H., Private, Company C, 71st New York Infantry.

Dutton, John, Private, 3rd Ohio Independent Battery.

E

Ewing, James P., Private, Company B, 18th Ohio Infantry.

Ewing, James W. (See Incomplete List).

F

Feuzer, James H. E., Private, Corporal, Company I, 1st Maryland Potomac Home Brigade infantry.

Fleming, Andrew J. (See Incomplete List).

Frazier, Iredell R., Private, Company G, 3rd Maryland Cavalry.

G

Gibbs, Charles N., Second Lieutenant, Captain, Company B, 69th Ohio Infantry.

Gillmore, Isaac R., Private, Company I, 30th Illinois Infantry.

Goudy, William C., Private Company I, 32nd Ohio Infantry.

Graham, David A., Private, Company F, 1st West Virginia Light Artillery.

Griner, Andrew J., Private, Company D, 2nd Ohio Heavy Artillery.

Grunden, Israel H., Private, Company F, 2nd Illinois Cavalry; Private, Company H, 2nd Illinois Cavalry, consolidated.

H

Hansard, Patrick H., Private, Company F, 14th U. S. C. T. (See Alphabetical List A).

Hartman, Richard, Private, Company D, 109th U. S. C. T.

Hartman, Samuel. (See Incomplete List)

Harvey, Charles W., First Sergeant, Company D, 79th Ohio Infantry.

Hatch, Asa W., Private, Company F, 2nd Ohio Infantry; Second Lieutenant, Company E, 152nd Ohio Infantry.

Hazelrigg, James T. J., Private, Sergeant, Company D, 4th Kentucky Infantry.

Heman, Hickok, Private, Corporal, Sergeant, Company B, 3rd Ohio Cavalry.

Henneigh, Martin L., Private, Company B, 74th Pennsylvania Infantry.

Higley, Henry W., Private, Company G, 3rd Missouri Cavalry.

Hill, John, Private, Company G, 55th Massachusetts Infantry.

Hillock, William G., Private, Company E, 5th Ohio Cavalry.

CO. E. 5TH CAVALRY

CO. G. 5TH CAVALRY

MUSICIAN 23D REGT.

WILLIAM G. HILLOCK

SURGEON 26TH REGT.

SAMUEL ARNOLD

THADDEUS COFFIN

MUSICIAN 23D REGT.

CO. A 137TH REGT.

WILLIAM B. McGAVRAN

ARTHUR W. COFFIN

CAPTAIN 56TH REGIMENT

LAFE J. BURR.

LEANDER S. DENIUS.

OHIO SOLDIERS IN HENRY COUNTY.

Hockersmith, Samuel M., Private, Corporal, Company D, 47th Ohio Infantry.
Holsinger, Jacob, Sergeant, Company G, 110th Ohio Infantry.
Hopper, Abram B., Private, Company G, 39th Ohio Infantry.
Howard, Alonzo, Private, Company L, 16th New York Heavy Artillery; Private, Company L, and Private, Company D, 1st New York Mounted Infantry; Private, Company D, 4th New York Cavalry.
Howe, Charles H. (See Incomplete List).

I

Ike, John H., Private, Company E, 71st Ohio Infantry.
Irving, James W., Private, Company H, 3rd Maine Infantry; Saddler, Company C, 2nd Maine Cavalry.

J

Jacobs, William H., Private, Company A, 91st Ohio Infantry.
Julian, Milton P., Private, Company D, 115th Illinois Infantry.
Justice, John, Corporal, Company K, 40th Kentucky Infantry.

K

Kamphere, George, Private, Company I, 13th Heavy Artillery, U. S. C. T.
King, David T., Bugler, Company I, Chief Bugler, Non Commissioned Staff, 7th Illinois Cavalry.
Kirby, John, Private, Company E, and Private, Company H, 92nd Ohio Infantry.
Kirk, Allen M., Private, Company B, 98th Ohio Infantry.
Kiser, Levi, Private, Company C, 35th Ohio Infantry.

L

Lamb, Jefferson, Private, Company K, 48th Kentucky Infantry.
Leavens, Alfred D. W., Private, Company K, 8th Illinois Cavalry.
Lee, Elihu. (See Incomplete List).
Lemmon, Isaac C., Private, Corporal, Company I, 71st Ohio Infantry.
Lewis, James J. (See Incomplete List).
Longnecker, Michael, Private, Company B, 11th Ohio Infantry; Private, Company B, 94th Ohio Infantry.
Loring, Willard H. (See Incomplete List).
Loucks, Dwight C., Corporal, Company H, 112th New York Infantry.

Mc

McGavran, William B., Major and Surgeon, Staff, 26th Ohio Infantry.
McKenzie, Peter, Private, Company E, 91st Ohio Infantry.
McKinney, Calvin B., Private, Company C, 17th West Virginia Infantry.
McNaught, Gilbert, Private, Company E, 50th New York Engineers.
McNurney, John, Private, Company A, Major Berry's Battalion, Missouri Cavalry; Corporal, Company L, 1st Missouri Cavalry.

M

Malsbary, Thomas L., Private, Company K, 138th Ohio Infantry.
Mayes, John W., Private, Company E, 47th Ohio Infantry.
Michels, Peter, Private, Sergeant, Company K, 72nd Ohio Infantry.
Middaugh, Wilson C., Private, Company C, 1st Michigan Infantry; First Sergeant, Company M, 8th Michigan Cavalry.
Miller, David T., Private, Company I, 9th New Jersey, Infantry.
Miller, Isaac H. (See Incomplete List).
Moore, Joshua C., Private, Company E, 13th Ohio Cavalry.

Morehead, Jacob, Private, Company C, 75th U. S. C. T.

Morgan, William H., Sergeant, Company E, 38th Illinois Infantry.

Morton, Thomas, Private, Captain, Company C; Colonel, Staff, 20th Ohio Infantry; Colonel, Staff, 81st Ohio Infantry. (See Mexican War).

Mulford, John W. (See Incomplete List).

N

Nelson, William H., Private, Company E, 69th Ohio Infantry; Private, Company M, 13th Ohio Cavalry.

Noftsinger, John J., Private, Company K, 188th Ohio Infantry.

Norviel, Rhoderick D., First Sergeant, Company K, 132nd Ohio Infantry.

O

Ogborn, La Fayette, Corporal, Company G, 12th Illinois Cavalry.

P

Palmer, John, Seaman, U. S. Navy; Private, Corporal, Sergeant, Company B, 34th New Jersey Infantry.

Patterson, Amaziah B. (See Incomplete List).

Peyton, Edward, Private, Company I, 74th Ohio Infantry.

Phillips, James, Private, Company D, 2nd Ohio Heavy Artillery.

Potter, Clinton, Private, Company D, 20th Ohio Infantry.

Pry, Henry, Private, Company E, 33rd Ohio Infantry.

R

Ray, Amos. (See Incomplete List).

Reece, Daniel C., Private, Company B, 3rd North Carolina Infantry.

Reece, Henry C., Private, Company B, 3rd North Carolina Infantry.

Rice, John H. C., Private, Company G, 7th Maryland Infantry.

Rife, Obed C., Private, Company D, 152nd Ohio Infantry. (See Alphabetical List A).

Roberson, Caleb J., Sergeant, Company I, 1st Infantry, U. S. A.

Robson, George B., Private, Company A, 86th Ohio Infantry; Private, Corporal, Sergeant, Company B, 69th Ohio Infantry.

Rodgers, Leonidas, Private, Company C, 16th Ohio Infantry; Regimental Band ,13th Missouri Infantry; Private, Company E, 152nd Ohio Infantry.

Rohrback, William H. H., Private, Corporal, Sergeant, Company E, 1st Maryland Potomac Home Brigade Infantry.

Ross, W. J., Private, Company C, 17th West Virginia Infantry.

S

Schofield, Jesse R., Private, Company F, 69th Ohio Infantry.

Sharp, Russell B., Private, Company F, 66th Ohio Infantry.

Sherrod, Frederick, Private, Company M, 102nd Pennsylvania Infantry.

Shockey, William. (See Incomplete List).

Simmons, Robert, Private, Corporal, Sergeant, Company H; Sergeant Major, Non Commissioned Staff, 125th U. S. C. T.

Slade, Frederick, Private, Company F, 64th Ohio Infantry.

Sloan, William C. (See Incomplete List).

Smith, Joseph, 5th Independent Battery, Ohio Light Artillery.

Smith, Thomas M., Private, Company G, 12th Kentucky Infantry.

Smorzka, Joseph, Private, Corporal, Company F, 5th Ohio Infantry.

Stafford, Freeland H. C., Private, Company F, 50th Pennsylvania Militia (State Service).

Stevens, Henry H., Private, Company A, 62nd Illinois Infantry; Private, Company D, 62nd Illinois Infantry, consolidated.

Stuart, Robert, Assistant Surgeon, Staff, 2nd Kentucky Cavalry.

Swain, James W., Private, Company B, 81st Ohio Infantry.

Sweet, William K., Corporal, Company G, 40th Ohio Infantry; Private, Company K, 51st Ohio Infantry.

T

Tawney, Daniel A., Captain and Chaplain, Staff, 179th Ohio Infantry.

Taylor, James, Private, Company B, 33rd Ohio Infantry.

Thomas, Dock. (See Incomplete List).

Turner, Mark. (See Incomplete List).

Turner, Moab, Private, Company I, 4th Tennessee Infantry or 1st Tennessee Cavalry.

U

Ulmer, Daniel, Private, Company I, 79th Pennsylvania Infantry.

Upp, George W., Private, Company E, 1st Ohio Heavy Artillery.

V

Van Fleet, Daniel, Private, Corporal, Company C, 27th New Jersey Infantry.

Vaughan, Theodore R., Private, Company G, 89th Ohio Infantry.

W

Waldron, Holman W., Corporal, Sergeant. Company C, 23rd Maine Infantry; Private, Corporal, Company E, 32nd Maine Infantry.

Watson, James F., Corporal, Company B; Hospital Steward, Non Commissioned Staff; Second Lieutenant, First Lieutenant, Company C, 98th Ohio Infantry; Captain, Company D,' and Captain, Company G, 63rd U. S. C. T.

Weaver, Cornelius, First Lieutenant, Captain, Company B, 18th Illinois Infantry.

Weston, Asa M., Private, Sergeant, Company K; Sergeant Major, Non Commissioned Staff; Second Lieutenant, Company E, 50th Ohio Infantry.

White, Johnson A., Private, Company E, 87th Ohio Infantry.

Willis, James L., Private, Corporal, Sergeant, Company H, 23rd Ohio Infantry.

Wilson, Robert H., Private, Company C, 156th Ohio Infantry.

Winkler, John R., Private, Company C, 8th Kentucky Infantry.

Wrightsman, David, Private, Company A, 79th Ohio Infantry; Private, Company D, 73rd Ohio Infantry.

Wysong, John, Private, Company I, 71st Ohio Infantry.

ALPHABETICAL LIST D.

This list includes the names of Henry County soldiers and sailors who have served in the Regular Army and Navy since the close of the Civil War. Soldiers and sailors who served in the regular Army and Navy and in the United States Volunteer Regiments, during and since the Spanish-American War and the Philippine Insurrection, are classified under this head. The list includes the names of some soldiers, who were not residents of Henry County at the time of enlistment, but who afterwards moved into the County. These are designated by two asterisks, thus **, before the names.

A

Abbott, James W., Private, Corporal, Company E; Sergeant Major and Ordnance Sergeant, Non Commissioned Staff, 24th Infantry, U. S. A.

Abbott, John W., Private, Company A, 24th Infantry, U. S. A.

Albin, Burt. (Record incomplete in this History).

Alpham, Edward R., Private, Company K, 18th Infantry, U. S. A.; Private, Corporal, Company L, 29th Infantry, U. S. V.

Armicost, Charles A., Apprentice, U. S. Navy.

B

· Bailey, George W., Private, Company C, 31st Infantry, U. S. V.

Baker, John, Private, Company A, 15th Infantry, U. S. A.

Berry, James A., Private, Company K, 13th Infantry, U. S. A.

Bills, Frederick A., Private, Corporal, Sergeant, Company I, 45th Infantry, U. S. V.

Bird, William. (Record incomplete in this History).

Bowman, Alva. (Record incomplete in this History).

Bundy, Omar. (See U. S. Military Academy).

Byrket, ᴇrnest B., Private, Corporal, Company M, 10th Infantry, U. S. A.

C

Caldwell, Frederick, Private, Company A, 1st Artillery, U. S. A.; Private, Company A, 6th Artillery, U. S. A.; Private, Company E, 18th Infantry, U. S. A.

Castetter, John A., Private, Company L, 10th Infantry, U. S. A.

Cock, Adelbert B., Private, U. S. Marine Corps; Ship's Barber, U. S. Navy.

Conner, Dennis, Private, Musician, Company H, 10th Infantry, U. S. A.; Musician, Corporal, Sergeant, Company H, 11th Infantry, U. S. A.

Cook, George A., Private, Company L, 26th Infantry, U. S. V.

Cook, James E., Private, Corporal, Sergeant, Company F, 11th Infantry, U .S. A.; Sergeant, Company E, 14th Infantry, U. S. A.

Crabill, James O., Private, Company H, 29th Infantry, U. S. V.

D

Dakins, James F., Private, Company G, 16th Infantry, U. S. A.

Delaware, Walter, Private, Corporal, Company K, 45th Infantry, U. S. V.

**Denny, David P., Corporal, Company I, 32nd Infantry, U. S. V.
Dickerson, John D., Machinist, U. S. Navy.
Doggett, James, Private, Company F, 31st Infantry, U. S. V.

E

Elliott, Raymond, Corporal, Company E, 35th Infantry, U. S. V.
Elliott, William H. (See U. S. Naval Academy).
Estelle, John. (Record incomplete in this History).
Estelle, Roy, Private, Company D, 6th Artillery, U. S. A.; Private, Troop F, 1st Cavalry, U. S. A.; Private, ————————, 12th Cavalry, U. S. A.

F

Finnegan, Robert L., Private, Troop M, 6th Cavalry, U. S. A.
Fisher, Charles E., Private, Company I, 31st Infantry, U. S. V.

G

Garriott, Homer C., Private, Troop D, 8th Cavalry, U. S. A.
Garvis, Thomas J., Private, Artificer, Sergeant, Company C; Quartermaster Sergeant, Non Commissioned Staff, 17th Infantry, U. S. A.
Gilbert, Heenon, Private, Company K, 22nd Infantry, U. S. A.
Gray, Panander W., Private, Corporal, Sergeant, First Sergeant, Company C, 2nd Infantry, U. S. A.
Griffin, Daniel F., Junior, Private, Company C, 31st Infantry, U. S. V.

H

Halstead, William J. P., Private, Artificer, Corporal, Sergeant, Company G; Quartermaster Sergeant, Non Commissioned Staff, 2nd Infantry, U. S. A.
**Hardway, Ernest, Private, Company F, 24th Infantry, U. S. A.
**Harris, Frank W., Private, Corporal, Company L; Regimental Band, 38th Infantry, U. S. V.
Harry, Dallas D., Private, Sergeant, Troop H; Acting Battalion Sergeant Major, Non Commissioned Staff, 13th Cavalry, U. S. A.
Hays, Samuel G., Private, Company I, 21st Infantry, U. S. A.
Hazzard, Leander E., Private, Troop H, 5th Cavalry, U. S. A.
Heacock, Claude H., Private, Company K, 3rd Artillery, U. S. A.
Hilkirk, Emery A., Private, Corporal, Sergeant, Company A, 11th Infantry, U. S. A.
**Hill, John S., Private, Company I, 18th Infantry, U. S. A.
Hodson, John, Private, Company A, 45th Infantry, U. S. V.
Holloway, Carl L., Private, Company G, 29th Infantry, U. S. V.
Hoosier, Louis M., Private, Company C, 24th Infantry, U. S. A.
Hutson, William W., Private, Company E, 35th Infantry, U. S. V.

J

Jacobs, Forest R., Private, Company H, and Private, Company D, 11th Infantry, U. S. A.; First Sergeant, Company H, Porto Rico Provisional Regiment of Infantry; Post Quartermaster Sergeant, Post Non Commissioned Staff, Porto Rico Provisional Regiment of Infantry; Post Quartermaster Sergeant, Post Non Commissioned Staff, U. S. A.
Jacobs, John N., Private, Troop I, 12th Cavalry, U. S. A.

K

Kahoon, Harvey, Private, Company B, 23rd Infantry, U. S. A.
Kelly, Lewis, Private, Company B, 5th Infantry, U. S. A.
**Keough, Elmore F., Private, Company E, 15th Infantry, U. S .A.

L

Lambird, Oren E., Private, Troop H, 12th Cavalry, U. S. A.

**Lehman, William, Private, Troop D, 7th Cavalry, U. S. A.; Private, Sergeant, Troop H, 1st Cavalry, U.S. A.; Sergeant, Troop K, 3rd Cavalry, U. S. A.; Sergeant, First Sergeant, Troop C, 3rd Cavalry, U. S. A.; Sergeant, Troop K, 13th Cavalry, U. S. A.

Lennington, James, Private, Company H, 23rd Infantry, U. S. A.

Mc

McConnell, Robert C., Private, 25th Company, Coast Artillery, U. S. A.

McCorkle, William E., Bugler, Company A, 12th Infantry, U. S. A.

McGuire, Harry F., Second Class Baker, U. S. Navy.

M

Main, Frank M., Private, Hospital Corps, U. S. A.

Miller, Ross G., Private, Troop F, 5th Cavalry, U. S. A.; Private, Troop A, 4th Cavalry, U. S. A.

Morris, Herbert W., Private, Company C, 31st Infantry, U. S. V.

N

Newby, Otis C., Corporal, Company C, 45th Infantry, U. S. V.

Nicholson, Boyd, Private, Company G, 31st Infantry, U. S. V.

O

Otis, Eugene. (Record incomplete in this History).

P

Paully, John E., Private, Company H, 16th Infantry, U. S. A.

Pence, William W., Private, Company K, 7th Infantry, U. S. A.

Pitts, Herman L., Private, 25th Company, Coast Artillery, U. S. A.

Pitts, Walter E., Private, 25th Company, Coast Artillery, U. S. A.

Powell, John J., Private, Reserve Hospital Corps, 1st Army Corps, U. S. A.

R

Reeder, Leonard M., Private, Company H, 12th Infantry, U. S. A.

Reeder, Thomas B., Junior, Private, Company H, 12th Infantry, U. S. A.

Riley, Kalula, Private, Company A, 45th Infantry, U. S. V.; Private, Troop E, 5th Cavalry, U. S. A.

Roberts, Clarence A., Private, Corporal, Sergeant, Company M, 13th Infantry, U. S. A.

Rozell, Henry C., Private, Company A, 23rd Infantry, U. S. A.; Private, Company A, 29th Infantry, U. S. V.; Private, Company H, 5th Infantry, U. S. A.; Private, Troop D, 1st Cavalry, U. S. A.

S

Sanders, William B., Private, 80th Company, Coast Artillery, U. S. A.

Shepherd, Frank A., Apprentice, U. S. Navy.

Sipes, Charles, U. S. Hospital Corps.

T

Tarr, Martin, Private, Corporal, Sergeant, First Sergeant, Company E, 1st Infantry, U. S. A.

Tipton, Earl, Private, Company H, 20th Infantry, U. S. A.; Private, Company I, 19th Infantry, U. S. A.

Tipton, Roy, Private, 25th Company, Coast Artillery, U. S. A.

U

Upham, Edwin R., Sergeant, Company L, 2nd Tennessee Infantry; Private, Corporal, Company K, 18th Infantry, U. S. A.; Corporal, Company L, 29th Infantry, U. S. V.

V

Vannatta, Edward. (Record incomplete in this History).

Vannatta, William. (Record incomplete in this History).

Veach, Ronald B., Private, Company A, 11th Infantry, U. S. A.

W

Warnock, Harry, Private, Company C, 3rd Wisconsin Infantry; Private, Company F, 31st Infantry, U. S. V.

Warnock, Jesse, Private, Company C, and Private, Company H, 2nd Infantry, U. S. A.

Warnock, Ora J., Private, Troop K, 11th Cavalry, U. S. A.

Welborn, Luther S. (See U. S. Military Academy).

White, William F., Private, Company L, 4th Artillery, U. S. A.

Willis, John L., Private, Company A, 2nd Infantry, U. S. A.

Winings, Mark E., Embalmer, U. S. A.

Woodward, Frank, Private, Company L, 31st Infantry, U. S. V.

Wrightsman, Isaac H., Private, Corporal, 12th Battery, U. S. A.

ALPHABETICAL LIST E.

This list includes the names of Henry County soldiers who served in the Spanish-American War and Philippine Insurrection in Indiana regiments and batteries. The names of six Henry County soldiers who enlisted in the military service of other States, during this period, are also included in this list.

Where the number of soldiers from Henry County in any regiment has justified the same, the full regimental staff is published with the regiment, but only the names of such of its members as were from Henry County are contained in this list.

In the distinctively Henry County companies, the full roster of the company is given whether the soldiers were all from Henry County or not. All non-resident soldiers, officers and men, whose names appear in this list, are designated by an asterisk, thus *, before the names.

A

Akers, Joseph, Private, Company G, 161st Indiana Infantry.
Allen, Alonzo, Corporal, Company G, 161st Indiana Infantry.

B

Baldwin, Ellwood L., Corporal, Company G, 161st Indiana Infantry.
*Barnes, Henry, Private, Company G, 161st Indiana Infantry.
Barnett, Guy, Private, Company G, 161st Indiana Infantry.
Barr, Charles H., Private, Company I; Quartermaster Sergeant, Non Commissioned, Staff, 33rd Michigan Infantry.
*Beeson, Edward, Private, Musician, Company G, 161st Indiana Infantry.
Bernard, Arthur C, Private, Company E, 1st Ohio Infantry.
Bock, Claud, Sergeant, Company G, 161st Indiana Infantry.
Bock, William, Private, Company H, 161st Indiana Infantry.
Bright, John C., Private, Company G, 22nd Kansas Infantry.
Brown, Roy W., Private, Company G; Regimental Band; Private, Company L, 161st Indiana Infantry.
Buckley, Guy, Private, Company G, 161st Indiana Infantry.
Burton, William, Saddler, 27th Indiana Battery.

C

Caldwell, Frederick, Private, Company H, 158th Indiana Infantry.
Canaday, James, Private, Company G, 161st Indiana Infantry.
*Cecil, Fred P., Private, Company G, 161st Indiana Infantry.
Cummins, Lemuel D., Private, Corporal, Sergeant, Company B, 20th Kansas Infantry.

D

Darling, Alva, Private, Company G, 161st Indiana Infantry.
*Darnell, Harry C., Private, Company G, 161st Indiana Infantry.

Davenport, Frank N., Private, Company G, 161st Indiana Infantry.
*Detrich, George C., Private, Company G, 161st Indiana Infantry.
*Dolan, John, Private, Company G, 161st Indiana Infantry.
Donaldson, Percy, Bugler, Company K, 3rd Tennessee Infantry.

E

Ellar, Benjamin W., Private, Corporal, Sergeant, Company G, 161st Indiana Infantry.
Elliott, George H., Corporal, Company G, 161st Indiana Infantry.
*Engle, T. William, Sergeant, Company G, 161st Indiana Infantry.

F

Fadely, Joseph H., Corporal, Company G, 161st Indiana Infantry.
*Faulkner, Henry, Private, Company G, 161st Indiana Infantry.
Filson, James L., Private, Company G, 161st Indiana Infantry.
Fisher, Frank W., Private, Company G, 161st Indiana Infantry.
Foster, Frank, Private, Company G, 161st Indiana Infantry.
*Frazee, Walker, Private, Company G, 161st Indiana Infantry.
Freeland, Thomas, Private, Company G, 161st Indiana Infantry.
*Freeman, Perry, Private, Cook, Company G, 161st Indiana Infantry.

G

Gaddis, Max P., Private, Corporal, Company G, 161st Indiana Infantry.
Goddard, Joseph, Private, Corporal, Company G, 161st Indiana Infantry.
*Gontner, Charles R., Corporal, Company G, 161st Indiana Infantry.
*Goodman, Bud, Private, Company G, 161st Indiana Infantry.

H

Hale, Frank, Private, Company G, 161st Indiana Infantry.
*Hale ,Thomas T., Private, Company G, 161st Indiana Infantry.
*Halfaker, Edgar B., Private, Company G, 161st Indiana Infantry.
Hamilton, Benton F., Private, Company G, 161st Indiana Infantry.
Hamilton, Frank M., Private, Company G, 161st Indiana Infantry.
*Hanna, John W., Private, Company G, 161st Indiana Infantry.
*Harper, Charles, Private, Company G, 161st Indiana Infantry.
Hickman, Herbert H., Private, Company G, 161st Indiana Infantry.
*Holton, Hoyt A., Private, Company G, 161st Indiana Infantry.
*Huddleston, Arthur A., Private, Company G, 161st Indiana Infantry.
Hutchins, Huston, Artificer, Company G, 161st Indiana Infantry.

I

*Irwin, George, Private, Company G, 161st Indiana Infantry.
*Israel, Wililiam G., Private, Company G, 161st Indiana Infantry.

J

*Jackson, Solomon, Private, Company G, 161st Indiana Infantry.

K

Keesling, Ray, Corporal, Company G, 161st Indiana Infantry.

L

*Lamb, Oltie F., Private, Company G, 161st Indiana Infantry.
Lane, Fred, Private, Company G, 161st Indiana Infantry.
*Leech, J. Morris F., Private, Company G, 161st Indiana Infantry.

*Leonard, Arthur, Private, Company G, 161st Indiana Infantry.
*Leonard, John M., Private, Company G, 161st Indiana Infantry.
Livezey, Oscar, Wagoner, Company G, 161st Indiana Infantry.
Luther, E. Murray, Corporal, Sergeant, Quartermaster Sergeant, Company G, 161st
Indiana Infantry.
Lykens, Sebastian, Private, Company G, 161st Indiana Infantry.

Mc

*McCoy, Charles, Private, Company G, 161st Indiana Infantry.
*McCoy, Clarence, Private, Company G, 161st Indiana Infantry.
*McCrea, Edward, Sergeant, Company G, 161st Indiana Infantry.
*McKimmey, Linley W., Corporal, Company G, 161st Indiana Infantry.

M

*Martin, Albert O., Corporal, Sergeant, Company G, 161st Indiana Infantry.
*Martin, Henry C., Junior, Private, Company G, 161st Indiana Infantry.
Martindale, George, Private, Company G, 161st Indiana Infantry.
Meyers, James I,. First Lieutenant, Company G, 161st Indiana Infantry.
Miller, James W., Private, Company G, 161st Indiana Infantry.
Millikan, Harry B., Private, 27th Indiana Battery.
Mitchell, Lemuel, Private, Company G, 161st Indiana Infantry.
*Morgan, Cliff, Private, Company G, 161st Indiana Infantry.
Myers, William E., Private, Company C, 1st Tennessee Infantry.

N

Nash, Charles M., Corporal, Company G, 161st Indiana Infantry.
Neff, William, Artificer, Company L, 160th Indiana Infantry.
Netz, Charles, Private, Company G, 161st Indiana Infantry.
Netz, William, Private, Company E, 158th Indiana Infantry.
Newby, George W., Private, Company G, 161st Indiana Infantry.
Newby, Otis C., Private, Company G, 161st Indiana Infantry.
Nichols, Noah A., Private, Company G, 161st Indiana Infantry.
Nugent, Harry S., Corporal, Company G, 161st Indiana Infantry.

O

Ogborn, Albert D., Captain, Company G, 161st Indiana Infantry.
*Owens, Charles B., Quartermaster Sergeant, Company G, 161st Indiana Infantry.

P

Palmes, Ira H., Private, Company H, 161st Indiana Infantry.
*Paul, John J., Private, Company G, 161st Indiana Infantry.
Pearson, Joseph M., Private, Company G, 161st Indiana Infantry.
Pitman, Charles M., Second Lieutenant, Company G, 161st Indiana Infantry.
Powell, Howard O., Corporal, Company K, 160th Indiana Infantry.
*Prager, James M., Private, Company G, 161st Indiana Infantry.
*Puckett, Fred W., Private, First Sergeant, Company G, 161st Indiana Infantry.

R

*Rawlins, Winfield, Private, Company G, 161st Indiana Infantry.
Redding, James M., Corporal, Company G, 161st Indiana Infantry.
*Reece, Benjamin F., Private, Company G, 161st Indiana Infantry.
Reed, William, Private, Corporal, Company I, 159th Indiana Infantry.
*Robinson, Elmer, Private, Corporal, Company G, 161st Indiana Infantry.
*Rogers, Paul, First Sergeant, Company G, 161st Indiana Infantry.

*Rothbaust, Jesse, Private, Company G, 161st Indiana Infantry.
Rutledge, William F., Private, 27th Indiana Battery.

S

Sears, Walton D., Private, Company G, 161st Indiana Infantry.
Shaffer, Daniel E., Private, Company B, 158th Indiana Infantry.
*Shellenbarger, Charles, Private, Corporal, Company G, 161st Indiana Infantry.
Sherer, Albert, Private, Company G, 161st Indiana Infantry.
Sherman, William A., Private, Company G, 161st Indiana Infantry.
*Shuee, Edward C., Private, Company G, 161st Indiana Infantry.
*Snider, Daniel V., Private, Company G, 161st Indiana Infantry.
*Swaim, Clarence T., Private, Company G, 161st Indiana Infantry.
*Sweezy, John, Private, Company G, 161st Indiana Infantry .

V

Van Dyke, Henry W., Musician, Company G, 161st Indiana Infantry.

W

*Wahl, John, Private, Company G, 161st Indiana Infantry.
*Walden, Edgar O., Private, Company G, 161st Indiana Infantry.
Weissgarber, John C., Sergeant, Company F, 161st Indiana Infantry.
Weissgarber, Frank H., Private, Corporal, Company F, 161st Indiana Infantry.
Welsbacher, John, Sergeant, Company G, 161st Indiana Infantry.
Wilmuth, Arthur, Private, Company G, 161st Indiana Infantry.
*Wilson, John W., Private, Company G, 161st Indiana Infantry.
Winings, Mark E., Private, Company G, 161st Indiana Infantry.
Winings, Walter A., Private, Company G, 161st Indiana Infantry.
Wintersteen, Minor, Private, Company G, 161st Indiana Infantry.
Wolfe, Edwin, Private, Company G, 161st Indiana Infantry.
*Woods, Harry, Private, Company G, 161st Indiana Infantry. ·
Wrightsman, Homer H., Private, Company H, 158th Indiana Infantry.

Y

Yates, Ira O., Musician, Company G, 161st Indiana Infantry.

HENRY COUNTY PIONEERS.

ORGANIZATION OF HENRY COUNTY

ITS EARLY HISTORY, DEVELOPMENT AND GROWTH.

ORGANIZATION OF HENRY COUNTY.

ITS EARLY HISTORY, DEVELOPMENT AND GROWTH.

INTRODUCTION.

In the year 1800, "Indiana Territory" was carved out of what was previously known as the "Northwest Territory," and included nearly all of the present States of Indiana, and Michigan, and all of Illinois and Wisconsin, and a portion of Minnesota.

The population of all this vast region, according to the census of 1800, was but 4,875. Michigan was erècted into a separate territory in 1805, and Illinois in 1809. Previous to the separation of Illinois, the territory had been divided into five counties, of which Knox, Dearborn, and Clark were within the present' bounds of Indiana, and St. Clair and Randolph constituted Illinois.

In 1807, an enumeration of the "free white males over twenty one years of age" was had, by which it appears that there were 2,524 within the present limits of the State, which would indicate that the whole population was less than 12,000. Of this number, there were 616 white adult males in what was then Dearborn County, which comprised perhaps one third of the present limits of the State.

The territory of Indiana was organized by act of Congress, May 7, 1800. On the 13th of the same month, General William Henry Harrison was appointed territorial governor and the seat of government was fixed at Vincennes, on the Wabash River, now the county seat of Knox County. The territorial general assembly which convened at Vincennes in February, 1813, changed the territorial capital to Corydon, now the county seat of Harrison County, at which the territorial business seems to have been first transacted in December, 1813. After the territory became a State, the capital was removed in the Winter of 1824-25, from Corydon to Indianapolis. The first entry in the archives of the State on deposit in the office of the State Librarian shows that business was transacted at the new capital on January 10, 1825.

By a joint resolution of Congress of December 11, 1816, Indiana was formally admitted to the sisterhood of States. So rapid had been the influx of population for the ten years preceding that the State was estimated to contain 65,000, and by this time was divided into eighteen counties, although more than three fourths of the State was still in possession of the Indians. Prior to 1810, the Indian boundary ran east of Centreville, Wayne County, and when an additional "Twelve-mile Purchase" extended the limits of civilization so as to include the present sites of Milton, Cambridge City, and almost to Hagerstown, there was quite a flocking to the *new* country, even in advance of the surveyor. So early as 1811, Thomas Symons had settled at the mouth of a small creek that emptied into West River, between Cambridge and Milton, and his brother Nathan fixed his residence at the mouth of another creek that unites with West River above the site of the ancient village of Vandalia which adjoined Cambridge City on the north. Their early possession of the mouths of these creeks (both having their source in Liberty township,) served to attach their names to the streams, and Symons creeks were well known to the early settlers of this county. Indeed it is highly probable that of the whole number of persons who entered this county for the first five years, at least nine tenths crossed the county line between these streams.

The war with Great Britain, from 1812 to 1815, and the consequent alarm occasioned by the hostile attitude of the Indians all along the frontier, partially broke up the settlements along West River. With the return of peace, however, the settlers returned to their homes, and a rapid increase of immigration at once set in, extending to the very limits of the Twelve-mile Purchase, though it is probable that no white family intruded itself upon the almost impenetrable wilds within the present limits of Henry County prior to 1819.

CHAPTER XXXVII.

SETTLEMENT AND ORGANIZATION OF THE COUNTY.

The Indian Treaty of St. Mary's in 1818—Arrival of the First Settlers —Early Settlers in the Different Townships—Land Sales and First Entries—Organization of the County—First County Officers— The Act for the Formation of Henry County Reproduced in Fac- Simile—Boundaries of the County.

The first settlers of whom any reliable information has been obtained, seem to have come to the county in 1819. Prior to this time, many were "waiting and watching over the border," in Wayne County, for the lands between West River and White River to become subject to settlement.

A law of Congress (not very rigidly enforced) forbade the private purchase or occupancy of the "Indian lands". By a treaty negotiated at St. Mary's, near old Fort Wayne, in 1818, by Governor Jonathan Jennings of Indiana, Governor Lewis Chase of Michigan, and Judge Benjamin Parke—former Attorney General of Indiana Territory and afterwards one of Indiana's leading jurists and first United States District Judge for the State of Indiana, for whom Parke County in this State is named—Commissioners on the part of the United States, the Indians relinquished all title to the lands south of the Wabash, except two or three small reservations, and also agreed to vacate the ceded lands within three years. The late David Hoover of Wayne County was secretary to this commission. From this time the whole central portion of the State was looked upon as accessible to the whites, and the settlement of this county began at once, although no titles to land could be obtained for some time.

The earliest titles are under act of Congress of April 24th, 1820, and the work of surveying, etc., consumed another year before they were thrown upon the market. About one hundred and forty persons purchased land in townships sixteen and seventeen north, in the last half of the year 1821. This was in that part of the county embraced in the present townships of Wayne, Spiceland, Franklin, Dudley, Liberty, Henry, Greensboro, and a part of Harrison.

The surveys being incomplete, no lands north of Liberty and Henry townships were sold until the following year. Many had come in prospecting as early as 1818 and 1819. By this means the fame of this magnificent region spread abroad. Its great fertility, magnificent forests, fine streams, numerous springs, abundant game, and its perpetual dedication to the cause of human liberty, pointed it out to many in North Carolina, Virginia, Pennsylvania, Kentucky, and Ohio, as the *Eldorado* of the West.

The early settlers seem to have been attracted principally to three neighborhoods, for a time, and from these *nuclei* spread over the county. These neighbor-

hoods, after a few years, became known as the "Harvey neighborhood," extending from the site of New Castle northward some four or five miles; the "Leavell
neighborhood," which included the southeast part of Liberty and the eastern
portion of Dudley townships; while the region from old West Liberty, on either
side of Blue River, for two or three miles above the site of Knightstown, was
known as the "Heaton neighborhood." These neighborhoods constituted pretty
much all there was of Henry County at the time of its organization, in 1821-22.

It is impossible, at this day, to name all the first "settlers," but the following
facts, though far from being as full as desired, will serve to show something of
the time and order of settlement in the various townships:

HENRY TOWNSHIP.

Early in April, 1819, Asahel Woodward, the maternal grandfather of the
author of this History, put up his cabin just north of New Castle; a Mr. Whittinger and his son-in-law, David Cray, fixed their residence just about the site ot
Joshua Holland's old home; Allen Shepherd settled nearly two miles, north by
east of New Castle, on what is known as the Hudelson farm; Andrew Shannon
located just north of Shepherd, and near the former site of the Hernly Mills;
George Hobson on the farm now owned by Judge Elliott's heirs adjoining New
Castle on the southwest; William Shannon on the Holloway farm, four miles
southwest of New Castle; Joseph Hobson came in not far from the same time,
and settled on the west side of the Stephen Elliott farm, two miles south of town.
At his house the first courts were held, thus making it the county seat *pro tempore.*

George Hobson, Andrew Shannon, Mr. Whittinger, and David Cray,
brought their families with them. Mrs. Asahel Woodward and Mrs. William
Shannon arrived on the thirty first of July following, and Mr. Woodward planted
about two acres of corn, the first crop, he thought, ever raised by a white man in
Henry County. He planted an old Indian field or clearing, and, although he
cultivated with the hoe alone, raised an excellent crop. The Whittingers and
Cray soon left, not liking the country.

PRAIRIE TOWNSHIP.

Benjamin Harvey also came early in the Spring of 1819, with his family, and
settled about three miles north of Asahel Woodward in the Harvey settlement.
Very soon afterward came William Harvey, the farther of Benjamin, with
Uriah Bulla, John Harris, Samuel Howard, and Bartley or Barclay Benbow.
Some of the last named came out in April or May, 1819, but had been out as early
as the February preceding, selected sites, and made some improvements.

WAYNE TOWNSHIP.

Within the limits of this township, a few persons had settled as early as
1820, and probably as early as 1819. Daniel and Asa Heaton were located about
the present site of Raysville, and trading with the Indians as early as 1820.
Samuel Furgason had a double log cabin near the mouth of Montgomery Creek,

i.1 1821, and had made money enough hauling corn from Whitewater and entertaining those in search of lands, to be able to purchase his homestead, August 11,
1821.   Samuel Goble lived just about the site of what was subsequently known
as Church's Mill at the time of the land sale, and had a good cabin and some
eight or ten acres partially cleared and under good fence.   All these improvements were bid from under him by David Lauderback, who so well understood
the estimate in which he would be held by the early settlers that he "made himself
scarce" afterward.   Of those who came in before or just about the time of the
land sale may be mentioned Waitsel M. Cary, Abraham Heaton, Samuel Cary,
Jacob Parkhurst, Joseph Watts, Shaphat McCray, and a few others, the exact
date of whose arrival it is difficult to learn.

SPICELAND TOWNSHIP.

Among the first settlers within the present limits of Spiceland township
were Daniel Jackson and Solomon Byrket, on Blue River, near what is known as
Elm Grove; Thomas Greenstreet, on the Hiatt farm, one half mile southwest of
Spiceland; Samuel Carr, on the Henderson Hosier farm, two miles north of Spiceland, now owned by the Hoover boys; and Allen Hunt, on the Amos Bond place,
two miles west of Spiceland.   These came to their lands immediately after the sale
and very soon after came Samuel Griffin and a few others.

FRANKLIN TOWNSHIP.

Moses Keens, George and Charles See, and Achilles Morris were among the
earliest settlers on Flatrock, within the present limits of Franklin township.
This was about the time of or immediately after the land sale. perhaps in the Fall
of 1821, though the precise date cannot be ascertained.

DUDLEY TOWNSHIP.

John Huff and a Mr. Carter are the only parties ascertained to have resided
within the limits of Dudley, prior to the land sale.   Huff lived near the junction of
the New Castle and Dublin, and Hopewell and Flatrock turnpikes, and Mr.
Carter about one half or three fourths of a mile west from the site of the Hopewell Meeting House.

Josiah Morris, Daniel Paul. Richard Ratliff (father of Cornelius Ratliff),
Richard Thompson, William McKimmey, William Modlin, William Owen, Joseph
R. Leakey, Benjamin Strattan, Thomas Leonard, Thomas Gilbert, Elisha Shortridge, and Jonathan Bundy were among the pioneers of Dudley Township, who
came in the Winter of·1821 or Spring of 1822.

LIBERTY TOWNSHIP.

'Of those who first settled Liberty Township comparatively little has been
learned.   The author of this History is not informed whether any came in before
the land sale, but of those who came in about the time of the sale may be men-

tioned Elisha Long, Moses Robertson, Thomas R. Stanford, David Brower, John Leavell, Robert Thompson, Jesse Forkner, Isaac Forkner, John Baker, and a number of others. Since the purchases made at the land sale exceeded those of any other township, it is fair to suppose that quite a number had already located there.

GREENSBORO TOWNSHIP.

Jacob Woods, Samuel Pickering, and perhaps two or three others first settled here in the Summer of 1821. Samuel and Jonas Pickering, Walker Carpenter, and Benjamin Kirk came through, prospecting in 1820, after visiting Winchester, Anderson, Pendleton, and other points. Jacob Elliott built a cabin about where his son, Jacob S. Elliott, formerly lived, in the Fall of 1821, but did not move into it until the Spring of 1822.

At the time Jacob Woods located where he lived so long, one and one fourth miles east of Greensboro, there were no settlers on Blue River between Daniel Jackson's and Joseph Hobson's, except William Shannon, and for some time there were no neighbors on the east nearer than William Bond, who resided on the old Wickersham farm, now owned by Josiah P. Nicholson, about four miles south of New Castle. A number of persons settled about Greensboro in the following year, and as early as 1823 a Friends' meeting was held at Duck Creek, David Bailey, Joseph Ratcliff, Eli Stafford, Samuel Pickering, and Jacob Woods being among the "charter members."

HARRISON TOWNSHIP.

Dempsey Reece and Roderick Craig settled on Duck Creek in the eastern edge of Harrison Township, in April, 1822. This was on land now known as the Peter Shaffer farm. Reece had raised a crop of corn on White River, about the present site of Indianapolis, the year before.

Phineas Ratliff, Rice Price, and Joseph and Richard Ratliff all settled in the same year within about one and one half miles of Dempsey Reece.

STONY CREEK TOWNSHIP.

Within the present limits of Stony Creek Township there were no settlers prior to the land sale which took place in 1822, and perhaps not until 1823, when John Hodgins, Mr. Schofield, Jonathan Bedwell, and Andrew Blount, the proprietor of Blountsville, settled there. There were but three or four families on Stony Creek, in the Spring of 1826, at which time John Hawk, a cabinet maker of Blountsville, took up quarters there.

FALL CREEK TOWNSHIP.

The settlement of Fall Creek seems not to have begun as early as many other parts of the county. John, Jacob, George, Peter, and David Keesling located near Mechanicsburg, about 1824 or 1825, forming what was known as the "Keesling neighborhood." William Stewart and Joseph Franklin came in about the same time. John Hart, David Van Matre, Adam E. Conn, and the Painters were early settlers in the eastern part of the township, near Middletown.

JEFFERSON TOWNSHIP.

Within the present limits of Jefferson Township, at an early day, perhaps 1824 or 1825, came Samuel Beavers, Anthony Sanders, James Marsh, and the Flemings, with some others. This township constituted a part of Fall Creek and Prairie for many years.

BLUE RIVER TOWNSHIP.

There was considerable progress made in the settlement of Blue River Township (then a part of Stony Creek), in 1823. Michael Conway, Richard and Reuben Wilson, Joseph Cory, John Koons, John P. Johnson, and several others moved to this part of the county as early as 1823, a few, perhaps, having located the year previous, the precise time, however, being difficult to learn.

LAND SALES AND FIRST ENTRIES.

According to the record, William Owen, of Dudley Township, purchased the first tract of land in Henry County; this transaction bearing date of February 4, 1821. David Butler next entered land, August 8, 1821, in the same township, and on the 11th of August, Josiah Morris, of Dudley, and Samuel Furgason of Wayne Township, each entered a tract.

Judging from the number of purchases made, the settlers in Wayne Township must have gone in a body to attend the sale, as of the twenty five purchases made during the year, sixteen were made on the 13th of August. The following is a list of purchases during the year, with date of purchase:

Samuel Furgason, August 11.	David Dalrymple, August 14.
Waitsel M. Cary, August 13.	William Criswell, August 14.
Abraham Heaton, August 13.	Ebenezer Goble, August 14.
Daniel Heaton, August 13.	Joseph Watts, August 14.
Samuel Cary, August 13.	Stephen Cook, August 20.
David Lauderback, August 13.	Samuel Goble, August 20.
Edward Patterson, August 13.	John Daily, August 22.
William Macy, August 13.	Jacob Whitter, August 23.
Jacob Parkhurst, August 13.	John Freeland, September 18.
Thomas Estell, August 13.	Charles Smith, October 13.
Henry Ballenger, August 13.	Edmond Lewis, October 31.
Isaac Pugh, August 13.	John Lewis, October 31.
Shaphat McCray, August 13.	

The 13th of August seems to have been a field day for the people of Wayne Township. On the 14th, nothing seems to have been done. Whether it was Sunday, or was taken up with calling for bids on the tracts of land now in Spiceland and Franklin Townships, is not known. On the 15th, the sale commenced for lands in Henry Township, when seven persons responded to the call of their numbers, and subsequently some ten other purchases were made, as will be seen below:

Allen Shepherd, August 15.	Asahel Woodward, August 20.
William C. Drew, August 15.	Thomas Woodward, August 20.

Thomas Symons, August 15.
Christopher Bundy, August 15.
Joseph Hobson, August 15.
William Shannon, August 15.
Joseph Newby, August 15.
George Hobson, August 16.
Robert Hill, August 21.

Joseph Holman, August 27.
Aaron Mills, August 31.
Ann Ward, September 21.
Caleb Commons, September 21.
Joseph Hiatt, September 24.
William Blount, Senior, October 17.

The auctioneer then passed on to Liberty Township, range eleven east, township seventeen, and found bidders more plentiful. The list and dates below will serve to show something of the tone of the market. We will let William Roe, probably a blood relative of the celebrated Richard Roe, whom school boys will remember as having extensive dealings with John Doe, head the list.

William Roe, August 16.
Andrew Shannon, August 16.
William Yates, August 16.
Thomas Batson, August 16.
Jesse Martindale, August 16.
Moses Robertson, August 16.
John Beard, August 16.
Jeremiah Strode, August 16.
William Bell, August 16.
Daniel Wampler, August 16.
David Brower, August 16.
Joshua Hardman, August 16.
John Leavell, August 16.
George Handley, August 16.
Samuel Southron, August 16.
Robert Thompson, August 16.
Micajah Chamness, August 16.
John Dougherty, August 20.
Henry Brower, August 21.
Thomas Raleston, August 31.
Daniel Miller, August 31.
Prosper Mickels, August 31.

Jacob Rinehart, September 4.
Peter Rinehart, September 4.
Jonathan Pierson, September 4.
John Beaman, September 4.
George Koons, September 12.
Enoch Goff, September 20.
Elisha Long, October 20.
Jerry Long, October 20.
John Baker, October 22.
Keneker Johnson, November 4.
Jesse Forkner, November 12.
Dilwin Bales, November 30.
Jeremiah Hadley, December 5.
Richard Conway, December 5.
Watson Roe, December 5.
John Koons, December 5.
George Hobson, December 6.
John Marshall, December 6.
Thomas Hobson, December 6.
Thomas Mills, December 6.
John Stapler, December 7.
Josiah Clawson, December 20.

In Dudley Township, the purchasers seem to have taken it more leisurely, and strung their purchases out from the time of the land sale to the end of the year, and are as follows:

William Owens, February 4.
David Butler, August 8.
Josiah Morris, August 11.
Stephen Hall, August 16.
Jesse Shortridge, August 16.
Dally Beard, August 16.
Elisha Shortridge, August 17.
John Wilson, August 18.
Jesse Fraizer, August 18.
Jonathan Bundy, August 24.
William Modlin, August 24.
Hampton Green, August 24.
William Seward, August 28.
Joseph Charles, August 30.
Linus French, August 31.

John Gilleland, September 1.
Susanna Leakey, September 8.
Joseph R. Leakey, September 8.
Joseph Cox, October 5.
John Green, October 6.
William Riadon, October 17.
William McKimmey, October 20.
Josiah Gilbert, October 21.
Exum Elliott, October 23.
David Thompson, November 26.
Aaron Morris, November 27.
John Pool, December 1.
John Smith, December 3.
Daniel Paul, December 12.

The following are all the purchasers of land, in 1821, within the present limits of Franklin Township:

William Felton, August 28.
Charles See, September 16.

John Charles, December 28.

Within the present limits of Spiceland Township, there were twelve entries, in that year, as follows:

Daniel Jackson, August 17.
Solomon Byrkett, August 27.
William Felton, August 28.
Allen Hunt, August 30.
Jacob Hall, August 30.
Nathan Davis, August 31.

William Mustard, September 1.
James Carr, September 14.
Jacob Elliott, October 3.
William Elliott, November 6.
William Berry, December 20.
Joseph Charles, December 24.

Within the limits of Greensboro Township, there were eight entries, in that year, namely:

Samuel Hill, August 15.
Thomas McCoy, August 15.
Levi Cook, August 20.
Lewis Hosier, August 20.

John Harvey, Senior, August 21.
Samuel Pickering, August 28.
John Harvey, August 30.
Jacob Eliott, October 3.

In 1822, only three entries were made within the limits of Fall Creek Township, as follows:

Benjamin G. Bristol, August 27.
James W. Wier, September 26.

Reuben Bristol, October 4.

There do not seem to have been any purchases made within the limits of Jefferson Township, during the year 1822, but within the limits of Prairie Township, there was more activity, and the following names appear:

Absalom Harvey, October 22.
Robert Smith, October 25.
Barclay Benbow, October 25.
James Harvey, October 25.
Abijah Cox, October 25.
Benjamin Harvey, October 25.

William Harvey, October 25.
John Harris, October 25.
Jacob Weston, November 12.
Jacob Witter, December 11.
Philip Harkrider, December 22.

These were generally, or all, on Blue River, the bottom and second bottom lands of which seemed very attractive to the early settler. There seems to have been but one entry within the limits of Stony Creek, that of Andrew Blount, Jr., November 11. Within the present limits of Blue River, however, the following secured themselves homesteads:

Richard Wilson, October 28.
Michael Conway, October 28.
George Hobson, October 28.
Joseph Cory, October 31.
Abraham Cory, October 31.
Betsy Cory, October 31.
Reuben Wilson, November 4.
George Koons, November 6.

John Koons, November 11.
Jacob Huston, November 12.
George Hedrick, November 13.
Richard Alsbaugh, November 14.
Henry Metzger, November 14.
Henry Stumph, November 18.
John P. Johnson, November 22.

Dempsey Reece entered a tract of land in Harrison Township, April 29, 1822, which was the only piece purchased in the township, during the year. Zeno Pearson and Richard Ratliff purchased land in January following, and Levi Pearson and Gabriel Ratliff, in June and July, which completed the transactions for the year 1823.

The land office for this district was at Brookville until 1825, when it was transferred to Indianapolis, then a village of little consequence, there being fewer voters in Marion County at that time than there are in Henry Township today.

The manner of the land sale was to commence in a certain township in a certain range, and offer each tract or eighty acre lot, consecutively, till the whole was gone through with. If no one bid, the tract being called by number was soon passed. When a number was called, the "squatter" who, perhaps, had a few acres cleared, or a little cabin on the same, could become the purchaser at one dollar and twenty five cents per acre, the minimum price, unless some one ran it up on him.

Where two persons had the same number and were desirous of entering the same eighty or one hundred and sixty acre lot, it was no uncommon thing for one to buy the other off, with some trifling sum, say ten to twenty five dollars, and, although the law of public opinion was such that neighbors would seldom try to buy each other's improvements from under them, still there were cases in which no little feeling was excited at times, and various little intrigues were resorted to, to bluff or out-wit competitors.

If for any reason a man failed to bid on a piece of land he desired to purchase, it sometimes happened that he could prevail on the auctioneer to call it up "just after dinner," or the "first thing next morning." From and after the land sale, all lands were subject to private entry at the minimum price.

ORGANIZATION OF HENRY COUNTY.

The act referred to as "An act for the fixing of the seats of Justice, in all new counties hereafter to be laid off" in section three (3) of the law authorizing the formation of the county of Henry hereinafter set forth, is Chapter 1, of the "special acts passed and published at the second session of the General Assembly of the State of Indiana, held at Corydon, on the first Monday in December in the year of our Lord, one thousand eight hundred and eighteen." Approved January 2, 1819.

This act is in six sections but the first section is the most important for the purpose of this History. It provided in brief that when a new county was organized that the act creating the same, should appoint five commissioners who "do not reside in said new county, nor hold any real estate therein," thus providing against any real estate speculation on the part of those appointed.

The commissioners so appointed were then instructed "to convene at such time as the General Assembly shall appoint," which in the case of the county of Henry, was "at the Home of Joseph Hobson," who, at the time mentioned, lived about two miles south of the Court House Square in New Castle, on what was subsequently and for a great number of years thereafter, known as the Stephen Elliott farm.

The commissioners named in the act heretofore referred to after having met "at the house of Joseph Hobson," and having been duly sworn, were then directed to "proceed to fix on the most eligible and convenient place for the permanent seat of justice for such new county, taking into view the extent of the county, the quality of the land, and the prospective future, as well as the weight of the present population, together with the probability of future division." They were authorized to acquire the necessary land by either donation or purchase and to take a good and sufficient bond therefor, conditional that the land so acquired, either by donation or purchase, should be duly conveyed to such agent as the Board of County Commissioners might designate as their agent to receive the same.

The remaining five sections of the act relate entirely to the proceedings of Boards of County Commissioners and their duties after the land so acquired was deeded to their agent, as provided in section one of said act.

In the last section, seven (7), of the act creating the county of Henry, hereafter set out, it is provided that the qualified voters of said county shall proceed to hold the first county election in the same manner and under the same conditions as the "qualified voters of Dubois County and others named" were authorized to proceed under an act entitled "An act incorporating a County Library in the counties therein named." Approved, January 28, 1818. The last paragraph of said section seven, (7), provided that the act creating the county of Henry should not be effective until the first day of June, 1822.

Accordingly, under the authority conferred on the commissioners named to organize the county of Henry, acting under the Dubois County act, they must have called a meeting of the qualified voters of the proposed new county to meet "at the home of Joseph Hobson," immediately after the act became operative, for the first entry on the records of the Board of County Commissioners of Henry County is dated June 10, 1822, or ten days after the act creating the county of Henry became effective. This order will be found set out in full in the article treating of the first courts of the county. With this election, which would now be known and recognized as a mass meeting, the duty of the five commissioners named in the act organizing the county of Henry ended and the duties of the Board of County Commissioners and other county officers, began. In short, the county of Henry was organized and ready for business.

As was provided in the act, it was made the duty of the Sheriff of Wayne County to notify the five commissioners appointed to organize the county of Henry, of their appointment and their duties. This mandate seems to have been duly executed as the very early records of the board of commissioners show that "Elias Willets, Sheriff of Wayne County, be allowed fifteen dollars" for the service, which was certainly cheap enough considering the fact that he must have gone into four counties and traveled at least two hundred and fifty miles. On the other hand, it may be considered that the commissioners were liberal as the sum was nearly one tenth of the entire revenue, County and State, collected for the first fiscal year of the life of the county of Henry.

For Congressional purposes, the county was attached to the Third Congressional District, represented by John Test of Brookville, the other counties in the district being Dearborn, Delaware, Fayette, Franklin, Randolph, Ripley, Switzerland, Union and Wayne. For judicial purposes, the county was attached to the Third Judicial District, afterwards the Fifth, of which Miles C. Eggleston of Centreville, was the presiding judge. The other counties of the judicial district being, Dearborn, Fayette, Franklin, Jennings, Randolph, Ripley, Rush, Switzerland, Union and Wayne.

The law must have been that when an act was passed looking to the creation of a new county that it was the duty of the governor to appoint a sheriff and county surveyor for the proposed new county, for the records of the Executive Department of the State on deposit in the offices of the Secretary of State, at Indianapolis, show that on January 1, 1822, the day after the act was approved, creating the county of Henry, it was "ordered that Jesse H. Healey be and he is hereby appointed Sheriff of the county of Henry." The same records show that on May 9, 1822, William McKimmey was appointed Surveyor for the new county. Thus every new county started out from its very inception with a chief peace officer and a county surveyor, which at that time was a highly important office, considering the fact that the boundaries of every piece of land in the county had to be established for the new settlers.

At the election held "at the home of Joseph Hobson" the following add'tional officers were elected, all their commissions dating from July 5, 1822, viz:—Rene Julian, Clerk and Recorder; Thomas R. Stanford and Elisha Long, Associate Judges; Allen Shepherd, Elisha Shortridge, and Samuel Goble, County Commissioners. Subsequently, William Shannon was appointed, by the said Board, the first County Treasurer. The office of County Auditor was not created until 1840, the duties of this office up to that time, devolving upon the County Clerk, who acted as "Clerk to the Board of County Commissioners."

For Senatorial purposes, the new county was attached to the district composed of the counties of Henry, Hamilton, Johnson, Marion, Madison, Rush and Shelby, the Senator being James Gregory of Shelby County. The first session of the General Assembly at which he represented the new county was the eighth regular session which convened at Corydon, (the last held there) "on the first Monday in December, 1823," he having been elected for the term of three years "on the first Monday in August" preceding. For a member of the lower house of the General Assembly, the county was attached to the district composed of the counties of Henry, Decatur, Rush and Shelby, the Representative being Thomas Hendricks, residence probably in Shelby County, who was elected at the same time and sat in the same session with Senator James Gregory.

The first County Coroner was Ezekiel Leavell, who assumed the duties of the office September 8, 1824, and resigned January 24, 1825.

THE LAW CREATING THE COUNTY OF HENRY.

The ancient and musty laws of the State of Indiana in bound volumes, on deposit in the office of the State Librarian at Indianapolis show the following:

CHAPTER LX

AN ACT for the formation of a new county out of the
County of Delaware.*

SEC. 1. *Be it enacted by the General Assembly of the* Names and
State of Indiana, That from and after the first day of June boundaries.
next all that tract of land which is included within the following boundaries shall constitute and form a new county
to be known and designated by the name and style of the
county of Henry, to-wit: Beginning at the southwest corner
of Wayne County; thence west twenty miles; thence north
twenty miles; thence east twenty miles; thence south twenty
miles to the beginning.

SEC. 2. The said new county of Henry shall, from and Privileges,
after the first day of June next enjoy all the rights, privi- &c.
leges and jurisdictions which to separate and independent
counties do or may properly belong and appertain.

SEC. 3. Lawrence H. Brannon and John Bell, of the Commissioners
County of Wayne, John Sample, of the County of Fayette, appointed.
Richard Biem, of the County of Jackson, and James W.
Scott, of the County of Union, are hereby appointed Commissioners agreeably to an act entitled "an act for the fixing the seats of Justice in all new counties hereafter to be
laid off." The Commissioners above named shall meet at When and
the house of Joseph Hobson in the said County of Henry on where to
the first Monday in July next, and shall immediately proceed meet.
to discharge the duties assigned them by law. It is hereby
made the duty of the Sheriff of Wayne County to notify the Sheriff of
said Commissioners either in person or by written notifica- Wayne county
tion of their appointment on or before the fifteenth day of to notify
June next; and the said Sheriff of Wayne County shall be them.
allowed therefor by the County Commissioners of the County
of Henry such compensation as by them shall be deemed
just and reasonable, to be paid out of the county treasury
of said County of Henry in the same manner other allowances are paid.

SEC. 4. The circuit and all other courts of the County Courts,
of Henry shall meet and be holden at the house of Joseph where to be
Hobson until suitable accommodation can be had at the holden.
county seat of said county; and so soon as the courts of said
county are satisfied that suitable accommodations are provided at the county seat of said county, they shall adjourn
thereto after which time all the courts of said county shall
be held at the seat of justice thereof: *Provided,* however,
that the circuit court of said county shall have authority to
remove from the house of said Joseph Hobson, to any more

suitable place in said county previous to the completion of the public buildings if they should deem the same expedient.

10 per cent. reserved.   SEC. 5. The agent who shall be appointed for said county to superintend the sales of lots at the county seat of said county or receive donations for said county, shall reserve ten per cent. out of the proceeds of such sales and donations, which he shall pay over to such person or persons as by law may be authorized to receive the same, for the use of a county library for said county; which he shall pay over at such time or times and manner as shall be directed by law.

Public buildings, when to be erected.   SEC. 6. The Board of County Commissioners of said county shall within twelve months after the permanent seat of justice shall have been selected proceed to erect the necessary public buildings thereon.

SEC. 7. The same powers, privileges and authorities that are granted to the qualified voters of Dubois County and others named in the act entitled "an act incorporating a county library in the counties therein named," approved January the 28th, 1818, to organize, conduct and support a county library, are hereby granted to the qualified voters of said county of Henry; and the same power and authority therein granted to, and the same duties required of, the several officers elected by the qualified voters of the said county of Dubois and other counties named in said act for carrying into effect the provisions thereof according to its true intent and meaning, are hereby granted to and required of the officers who may be elected for the purpose aforesaid by the qualified voters of said County of Henry.

This act shall be in force from and after the first day of June next.

SAMUEL MILROY,

Speaker of the House of Representatives.

RATLIFF BOON,

President of the Senate.

Approved December 31st, 1821.

JONATHAN JENNINGS,

Governor of Indiana.

*Be it remembered that there were two separate and distinct counties, each named Delaware. The first was the "unorganized" county of Delaware, organized January 22, 1820, which embraced all of the "new purchase," being a vast tract of land relinquished by the Indians to the General Government and to the State of Indiana. The second was the present county of Delaware, organized out of a part of the first named county, January 26, 1827. It was from the first mentioned county of Delaware that Henry county was organized. "Unorganized County" means no civil government established.

BOUNDARIES OF HENRY COUNTY.

According to Section one (1) of the act creating the county of Henry, it was made a perfectly square body of territory, twenty miles from east to west and a like distance from north to south. From a glance at the map of the county of Henry or the map of Indiana showing the county, it will be seen that it is not now a body of land twenty miles square, but there is a jog of a mile in the south-west corner on the west side, for six miles. Then on the east side of the county along the center of the county there is a jog of three quarters of a mile for a distance of nine (9) miles. If the county was now twenty miles square as provided in the act creating it, it would contain four hundred square miles of territory.

Section one (1) of the act begins to describe the county of Henry, to-wit: "Beginning at the southwest corner of Wayne County," whereas, the southeastern corner of the county of Henry as now defined is located six miles northwest of the "southwest corner of Wayne County." When the boundaries of the counties of the State were finally adjusted, nearly three Congressional townships of land were attached to the southern tier of Congressional townships in Wayne County, probably taken from Fayette County. Had they extended these townships along the entire southern boundary of Wayne County, Fayette County would not now join the county of Henry. But then, the southeast corner of the county of Henry would be nearly six miles due north of the "southwest corner of Wayne County." The county of Henry—as it exists today, contains about three hundred and ninety square miles and approximately two hundred and fifty thousand acres of land and is bounded on the east by Randolph and Wayne; on the north by Delaware; on the west by Madison and Hancock; and on the south by Rush and Fayette counties.

The actual boundaries of the county of Henry as they exist today and as they have existed probably, for three quarters of a century or more, are defined in the following letter from the County Surveyor, Omar E. Minesinger:

"O. E. MINESINGER,
"COUNTY SURVEYOR.
"HENRY COUNTY.

"NEW CASTLE, INDIANA. September 22, 1905.
"Mr. George Hazzard, New Castle, Ind.:

"SIR: The district of country within the following boundaries constitutes the county of Henry, to-wit: Commencing at the southeast corner of section 31, township 16 north, range 12 east, and running thence north to the township line dividing townships 16 and 17; thence east to the southeast corner of section 32, township 17 north, range 12 east; thence north to the northeast corner of section 20, township 18 north, range 12 east; thence west to the range line dividing ranges 11 and 12; thence north on said range line to the northeast corner of section 25, township 19 north, range 11 east; thence west to the northwest corner of section 25, township 19 north, range 8 east; thence south to the township line dividing townships 16 and 17; thence west to the northwest corner of section 1, township 16 north, range 8 east; thence south to the township line dividing townships 15 and 16; thence east with said township line to the place of beginning.

"Very truly ,
"OMAR E. MINESINGER.
'Surveyor Henry County.'"

CHAPTER XXXVIII.

ORGANIZATION OF THE SEVERAL TOWNSHIPS—POPULATION—ASSESSED VALUA-
TION—TAXATION—ELECTIONS.

At the time of the assembling of the first Commissioners' Court, June 10, 1822, there were no civil townships in existence, within its jurisdiction, and one of its first cares was to provide a few of these indispensable dependencies, "with a local habitation and a name." After describing, in fitting language, the metes and bounds of these "territories," the Commissioners declared that "from and after the first Saturday in July next" they should each *enjoy all the rights and privileges and jurisdictions which to separate and independent townships do or may properly belong or appertain.*

Whether this idea of an independent and separate existence and jurisdiction smacks of "State rights" or not, the reader must judge. The Commissioners were an authority in the land, in those days, and it is quite safe to conclude that they fully intended to carve out of the territorial limits of Henry County several little republics, which were to be fully competent to manage their domestic institutions in their own way.

The townships thus provided were four in number, viz.: Dudley, Wayne, Henry, and Prairie. Dudley and Wayne composed the First Commissioner's District, Henry, the Second, and Prairie, the Third.

The original boundaries of Henry County were not identical with those of the present day, and, as a consequence, the boundaries of the townships lying on the east and west borders of the county underwent some change when the new boundaries were fixed by the General Assembly in the early 'thirties. A township meeting, notwithstanding the size of the township, must have been a small affair in those times. Three years after, when the population had probably more than doubled, the whole vote for Governor was but 366.

DUDLEY TOWNSHIP.

Dudley, the first township called into being by the fiat of the Commissioners, June 11, 1822, began at "the southeast corner of Henry County, of which it is a part," and running thence west on the county line dividing Henry, Fayette and Rush counties, about nine and one fourth miles from the present east line of the county, and was six miles in width. It consequently contained at least fifty five and one half sections of land, and comprised all of its present limits and about four fifths of the present township of Franklin

HENRY COUNTY CITIZENS.

ᴄ of the first Commissioners' Court, June 10,
ᵢₛ in existence, within its jurisdiction, and one
ᵢₑw of these indispensable dependencies, "with
ᵗ ᶠ er describing, in fitting language, the metes
the Commissioners declared that "from and
ᵥᵗ" they should each "*enjoy all the rights and*
ₜₒ separate and independent townships do or

ᵤndent and separate existence and jurisdiction
reader must judge. The Commissioners were
lavs, and it is quite safe to conclude that they
territorial limits of Henry County several little
ompetent to manage their domestic institutions

were four in number, viz.: Dudley, Wayne,
Wayne composed the First Commissioner's Dis-
irie, the Third.
enry County were not identical with those of
ᵉnce, the boundaries of the townships lying on
ᵤnty underwent some change when the new
ᵣₐᵢ Assembly in the early 'thirties. A town-
ᵢze of the township, must have been a small
afₑr, when the population had probably more
overnᵒʳ was but ᴣ⁶

ᵗ ᵧ TOWNSHIP.

ᵈ into being by the fiat of the Commissioners,
ᵣₐₛt corner of Henry County, of which it is a
ₜₕₑ county line dividing Henry, Fayette and
fourth miles from the present east line of the
It consequently contained at least fifty five
ᵗomprised all of its present limits and about

HENRY COUNTY CITIZENS.

At this date, it is estimated that there were not one hundred and fifty persons residing within the limits of the township. A round of log rollings, house raisings, and similar "bees" occupied much of their time, and in talking with one of these veterans you will very likely be told that they enjoyed themselves and felt as hopeful, contented, and happy as at any period since.

A "Friends' Meeting House," a hewed log *edifice*, which stood about one mile southeast of the present site of Hopewell Meeting House, was erected in 1823 or 1824 and was probably the first attempt at church architecture in the township or in the county. The congregation had been in the habit of worshiping at the house of William Charles, north of where Hardin's old tavern stand used to be. An ancient orchard still marks the spot.

A Baptist church, a log building about eighteen by twenty feet, was erected about one and one half miles northeast of Daniel Paul's, so near the same time as to render it difficult to determine which is entitled to the claim of seniority. This church was used as a school house for a number of years.

A school house soon followed, with all the elegant appurtenances and appliances of the times for assisting the "young idea to shoot."

Dudley Township was the gateway of the county, as three principal thoroughfares from the east and southeast led through it. It presents, perhaps, less variety of surface than any other township in the county, being almost entirely table land, lying on "the divide" between Flatrock and West River, with perhaps two thirds of its surface finding drainage to the latter. The passerby of early days regarded it as most unpromisingly wet. Although very little of it can be termed rolling, it is now seen to be sufficiently undulating to permit the most complete drainage of almost every acre, and under improved culture the large average crops and general fertility stamp it as one of the best bodies of land in the county.

Dudley is five and a quarter by six miles in extent, and thus contains about 19,000 acres. According to the census of 1870, it was then divided into 191 farms, an average of about 103 acres each; supporting an almost exclusively rural population of 1,348 souls, about forty three and one half per square mile, divided between 268 families and 267 dwellings. Of this number but thirteen were foreigners—less than one per cent., while the natives of the "Old North State" numbered 126, or nearly ten per cent. of the whole population. The value of the lands and improvements for 1870 was $542,120. The town lots and improvements were valued at $6,300, and the personal property at $249,970, making a total of wealth of $798,390, as shown by the tax duplicate for 1870. The census of 1900 seems to have been taken only by counties; at least the author has been unable to find any subdivision less than the county that would enable him to set out for comparisons, all of the items mentioned above, as taken from the census of 1870; and what is true of Dudley, is true of all the other townships following. The only items of general interest that can be found relating to Dudley and the twelve townships that follow, are those regarding the population, viz.: population, according to the census of 1890, including Straughn, incorporated and New Lisbon not incorporated, 1,395; census of 1900, 1,359; a loss of thirty six in ten years.

The tax duplicate for 1904, the township and towns combined, shows the following: value of lands, $637,600; value of improvements, $111,850; total, $749,450; value of lots, $14,410; value of improvements, $27,560; total, $41,970;

value of personal property of all kinds, $432,240; value of railroad property, including steam and electric lines, $370,720; total value of taxables of all kinds, $1,594.380; less mortgage exemptions, $40,090; leaving the net value of taxables for the year named, $1,554,290.

Total taxes levied on the duplicate for the year 1904, township, Straughn, incorporated, and New Lisbon, not incorporated, combined, which taxes are as follows, viz.:—State tax, for benevolent institutions, State debt sinking fund, State school, State educational institutions, free gravel road repairs, County tax, local tuition, special school, road, township, bridge, court house, and corporation, this last being confined to the corporation of Straughn, $20,254.76. Total polls, being a specified head tax on each male person between the ages of twenty one and fifty, 218; tax on each, distributed through different funds, $2.00; total polls in Straughn, 35; tax on each, $2.00.

From the foregoing, it will be seen that the population of Dudley Township has not been subject to much change since the census of 1870. But a comparison between the tax duplicates of 1870 and 1904, exhibits the fact that the taxable property of Dudley has nearly doubled during that period.

Mortgage exemption is allowed under the law which became effective March 4, 1899. Under this law, an exemption for mortgage on real estate, not in excess of the sum of $700 is allowed, and then only provided the real estate is valued for taxation at twice the sum of the mortgage exemption. Therefore, on all real estate valued for taxation at less than $1,400, the mortgage exemption could not be in excess of one half the value of the property.

The first election was ordered to be held at the house of Daniel Paul, on Saturday, July 6th, 1822, for the purpose of electing one Justice of the Peace, and William McKimmey was appointed Inspector. William McKimmey and Garnette Hayden were appointed first Overseers of the Poor for Dudley Township, and Richard Pearson and Robert Thompson "Fence-viewers." The elections were afterwards held at Benjamin Strattan's for a number of years; about 1840, at Daniel Reynolds; then at New Lisbon. Soon two polls were opened—one at New Lisbon, and the other near Straughn's. Again the polls were united and held at James Macy's. At this time, there are two polls, one at New Lisbon, and the other at Straughn. The vote at the general election, held Tuesday, November 8, 1904, based on the returns for the vote cast for Secretary of State, was: New Lisbon precinct, 200; Straughn precinct, 220; total, 420. The vote set out in the twelve townships following, is for the same election and based on the same returns.

Today, instead of the mere "trace," the "See trail," the blazed bridle path, winding around through the thickets, around or over logs, through "slashes," or high grass and stinging nettles, high as a man's shoulders, so well remembered by the "oldest inhabitant," or over miles and miles of "corduroy road," of which 'internal improvements" Dudley could, fifty or sixty years ago, vie with the world, the township has nearly thirty miles of fine turnpike, splendid and well drained farms and farm houses that equal the best.

WAYNE TOWNSHIP.

The second grand division named in order, on the public records, was to be known and designated by the name and style of Wayne Township. It was originally six miles from north to south, and eleven in length from east to west, including all that territory west of Dudley. It thus included in its fair domain about 42,000 acres of very valuable land, much of it today the most valuable in the county. Its first boundaries included one fifth of the present township of Franklin, all of Spiceland, and one sixth of Greensboro. Although thrice shorn of a portion of its "independent jurisdiction," its present area is a trifle in excess of thirty three square miles.

Wayne township had, at the date of its organization, from thirty to forty families, though the very choice lands, fine springs, and abundant water power of Blue River, Buck and Montgomery creeks, marked it for rapid settlement. A village was projected at the mouth of Montgomery Creek, on the county line, as well as "old State road," at once and known as West Liberty. This became the emporium of trade for the region round about, and rejoiced in all the metropolitan splendors of a "one-eyed grocery" and dry goods store kept by Aaron Maxwell. This "Chamber of Commerce," in 1822, consisted of a very indifferent log cabin, with a wide fire place, flanked on one side by a rude table, where Mrs. Maxwell compounded "red bread," and on the other by a barrel of whisky, and about as many bolts of calico, etc., as could be piled upon a chair.

Raccoon pelts seem to have been the principal circulating medium, and several years afterward, when the stimulus of sharp competition had taxed the energies of the merchant princes of the day, the old ladies were at times under the necessity of sending by the mail boy for a little tea or other luxury, and young ladies in quest of a bridal trousseau would mount their palfreys and make a day's journey to Connersville for the outfit.

The Methodists had preaching at West Liberty, in a very early day, perhaps as early as 1823, Reverend Constant Bliss Jones officiating. The preaching was held at Mr. Hatton's private house for some time. Jones was succeeded by Reverend Mr. Brown, who seems to have resided at West Liberty. Mrs. Eliza Jones (then Miss Cary,) taught a school, in 1825 and 1826, and was the first female teacher in those parts. She, with Mrs. Peggy Jones, the minister's wife, organized the first Sunday school in the township, perhaps in the county.

At the first meeting of the Board of Commissioners, an election was ordered to be held at the house of Joseph Watts, July 6th, for the purpose of electing the one Justice of the Peace for the township. Abraham Heaton was appointed Inspector, and seems to have been elected the first Justice. In August, Elijah McCray and E. Harden were appointed constables of Wayne Township, until the February term, next in course. In November, Daniel Priddy was also appointed constable. Ebenezer Goble and Samuel Furgason were appointed Overseers of the Poor, and Daniel Heaton, Shaphat McCray, and Jacob Parkhurst first "Fence-viewers in and for Wayne Township," and Abraham Heaton was also appointed Superintendent of the school sections in Wayne Township. The elections in this township were afterward held at Prudence Jackson's house, till 1825; changed to Solomon Byrket's, in 1827; then to Jacob Parkhurst's, then to Raysville and Knightstown alternately, and soon afterward fixed permanently at Knightstown.

Abraham Heaton seems to have had, at this early day, a mill erected at the mouth of Buck Creek, a few rods south of what has for many years been known as the "White Mill." John Anderson, afterward "Judge Anderson," then a fresh arrival, dug the race and, receiving $100 for the same, walked to Brookville and entered a part of the present site of Raysville.

Immediately after the organization of the township was effected, the Commissioners ordered the location of a road "to commence at the town of New Castle, and from thence the nearest and best way to Abraham Heaton's mills, and from thence to the county line, where sections thirty three and thirty four corner in township sixteen and range nine, on the line dividing fifteen and sixteen." The terminus was West Liberty, and the route selected was the river route from New Castle via Teas' mill, the stone quarry, and Elm Grove. This was the second ordered in the county, the first being from New Castle via John Baker's and David Thompson's, on Symons Creek, to the county line, on a direct course, to Shook's Mill, in Wayne County, which shows of what importance the opening of the "Cracker line" was to the early settlements. Not to be wondered at either, since "going to mill" required about two to four days out of the month.

In 1870, Wayne was the most populous and wealthy townships of the county, but now Henry Township holds that rank, Wayne being second. According to the census of 1870, its area was divided into 206 farms; an average of about 103 acres each, and had a population of 3,334, or about 100 per square mile. The value of lands and improvements for 1870 was $664,710; of town lots and improvements, $433,120; while personal property footed up to the snug little sum of $682,540, making a total of $1,780,370. Something more than one half its population was then to be found in Knightstown, Raysville, and Grant and Elizabeth cities, 330 of its 680 families residing in Knightstown alone. Dudley and Wayne, with the townships carved out of them, constitute the First Commissioner's District, as they always have and do now.

The population of Wayne Township, according to the census of 1890, including Knightstown incorporated, Raysville, Grant City, and Elizabeth City, not incorporated, was 3,333; census of 1900, 3,370.

The tax duplicate for 1904, township and towns combined, shows the following: Value of lands, $694,530; value of improvements, $119,560; total, $814,090; value of lots, $172,260; value of improvements $357,570; total, $529,830; value of personal property of all kinds, $824,850; value of railroad property including steam and electric lines, $445,620; total value of taxables of all kinds, $2,613,790; less mortgage exemptions, $27,920; leaving net value of taxables for the year named $2,585,870. A comparison of the census figures above set forth, shows that Wayne like Dudley Township, has had a very steady population since 1870.

Total taxes levied on duplicate for the year 1904, township and Knightstown incorporated and Raysville, Grant City, and Elizabeth City, not incorporated, combined, which taxes are all in items set out in Dudley Township, with the addition of township poor, corporation bond, lighting streets, school library and water works, the last four being confined to Knightstown corporation, $50,879.69. Total polls in Wayne Township, 226; tax on each, $2.25; total polls in Knightstown corporation, 283; tax on each, $2.25

Formerly, there were voting precincts at Knightstown, Raysville, Grant City, Elizabeth City and perhaps at other points in the township, but for the general election, held November 8, 1904, the total vote was cast at six precincts, all in

Knightstown. Perhaps one of them was east of Blue River, at Raysville. The vote was, first precinct, 166; second precinct, 134; third precinct, 161; fourth precinct, 154; fifth precinct, 181; sixth precinct, 156; total, 952.

HENRY TOWNSHIP.

Henry, the third township, in the "order of their going," upon the records, was also called up June, 1822, and was a strip of territory six miles wide, extending quite across the county from east to west, and including what is now Liberty, Henry, three fifths of Harrison, and nearly all of Greensboro township. This constituted the Second Commissioner's District. It at first contained 118 square miles, or over 75,000 acres.

Henry Township now contains thirty-six square miles, and is nearly the geographical center of the county, and is the only one in the county in which the Congressional is identical with the civil township. Ten years after the organization of the county, this township had not over 500 inhabitants, while in 1870 it numbered over 2,800, nearly one-half of whom lived in the "rural districts." It contained 135 farms of near 160 acres each, and maintained a population of 78 to the square mile. There were 592 families, 67 colored persons, 121 of foreign birth, and 152 natives of old North Carolina, in the township. The population of Henry Township, according to the census of 1890, including New Castle incorporated, was 4,009; census of 1900, 4,682.

Blue River, dividing the township nearly in the center, is too sluggish to furnish good water power for a mill within the limits of the township. Duck Creek skirts through the northwest corner of the township, and Flatrock through the southeast corner. The table lands between these streams are nearly one hundred feet above the bed of Blue River, and, although there is perhaps as much rolling land in this township as any in the county, there is very little so rolling as to merit the term broken, or too much so to admit of culture. Repeated efforts at ditching and straightening the channel of Blue River have completely redeemed to cultivation the marshy bottom lands which are of inexhaustable fertility.

The county seat being located in Henry Township would of itself (even in the absence of natural advantages), have secured to this township an important position in the county, both financially and politically. The value of the real and personal property in the county, by the assessment of 1870, was shown to be: Lands and improvements, $689,350; lots and improvements, $300,870; personal property, $609,400, making a snug total of $1,599,620.

The tax duplicate for 1904, the township and New Castle, incorporated, combined, shows the following: value of lands, $912,810; value of improvements, $230,020; total, $1,142,830; value of lots, $677,040; value of improvements, $611,130; total, $1,288,170; value of personal property of all kinds, $1,182,720; railroad property including steam and electric lines, $403,890; total value of taxables of all kinds, $4,017,610; less mortgage exemptions, $155,340; total, $3,862,270. Total taxes levied on duplicate for the year 1904, township and New Castle, incorporated, combined, which taxes include all items set forth in Dudley Township with the addition of the township poor tax, corporation, corporation bond, lighting streets, streets, school library, and cemetery, all of which, except township poor tax, are confined to New Castle corporation: total, $82,864.85. Total polls in Henry Township, 202; tax, $2.50 each; New Castle corporation, 912; tax, $2.50 each.

In 1904, the vote of the whole township cast at six precincts, all in New Castle, was as follows: first precinct, 268; second, 287; third, 340; fourth, 200; fifth, 268; sixth, 330; total, 1,693. This total vote indicates a marked increase in the population of Henry Township for 1904 as compared with the census of 1900. In the four years intervening, the population was largely increased by the location of many new manufacturing establishments in New Castle.

The first election was held at the house of Samuel Batson; Charles Jamison, Inspector. Asahel Woodard, Micajah Channess, and Thomas Watkins were appointed Fence-viewers for Henry Township. William Shannon and Samuel Batson were elected first Justices of Peace.

PRAIRIE TOWNSHIP.

The fourth of the original townships, included all the territory lying north of Henry, and was eight miles in width and nearly twenty in length, thus giving it an area of nearly 160 square miles or about 105,000 acres. Within its ample limits were all of the present townships of Blue River, Stony Creek, Prairie, Jefferson, Fall Creek, and about two fifths of Harrison.

In spite of the mutations which have since overtaken it, the township remains five miles in width by eight in length, thus containing over 25,000 acres, which were divided, according to the census of 1870, into 201 farms, averaging about 122 acres each.

The population of Prairie Township according to the census of 1890, including Luray, Springport, Mount Summit, and Hillsboro, not incorporated, was 1,663; census of 1900, 1,662, thus showing that the township, in ten years, lost one inhabitant.

Prairie contains four villages, viz.: Luray, Springport, Mount Summit and Hillsboro. The value of farms and improvements for the year 1870, was $559,210; of town lots and improvements, $10,610; of personal property $258,650; making a total for the township, of $828,470. The tax duplicate for 1904, the township and towns combined, shows the following value of land, $686,730; value of improvements, $70,090; total, $756,820; value of lots, $6,900; value of improvements, $25,470; total, $32,370; value of personal property of all kinds, $287,290; value of railroad property, no electric lines, $222,320; total value of taxables of all kinds, $1,298,800; less mortgage exemptions, $45,700; leaving net value of taxables for the year named, $1,253,100. Total taxes levied on the tax duplicate for 1904, township and towns combined, which taxes include all items enumerated in Dudley Township, except corporation tax, there being no incorporated town in Prairie, $18,750.44; total polls, 293; tax on each, $2.50.

This is a remarkable township in many respects. Situated as it is, on the "divide" between White and Blue Rivers, about one half its surface finds drainage to the north and the remainder southward, and although thus situated on the "water shed," nearly one sixth of its surface consists of low, wet meadows, from fifty to eighty feet below the general level of the table lands. It is from these meadows or prairies that the township takes its name. These "flowery leas" seem ever to have been coveted, although within the memory of the oldest inhabitant large portions of them were so flooded with water much of the year as to be chiefly valuable as the resort of waterfowl. Today, however, under an extensive system of drainage, even the wettest portions of these prairies have been thoroughly redeemed, making farms which for inexhaustible fertility cannot be surpassed.

The first election for Justice of Peace was held July 6, 1822, at the house of Absalom Harvey; William Harvey, Inspector. William Harvey and Abijah Cane were appointed first Overseers of the Poor, and Abraham Harvey, James Massey, and Robert Gordon, Fence-viewers "in and for said township." In 1826, the place of holding elections was changed to Sampson Smith's, afterward to Enoch Dent's, and again to Ezekiel T. Hickman's, where it remained for many years, but, in 1846, was changed to James Harvey's. Later, there were several changes in the voting place, and now there are two voting places, viz.: south precinct, Mount Summit; north precinct, Springport. Vote, 1904, south precinct, 209; north precinct, 232; total, 441.

The first school house in the township was built on Shubal Julian's land, better known of late as the "Shively farm," perhaps in 1824 or 1825. It was a small affair, with split saplings for seats, and a fire-place across the entire end.

The late Dr. Luther W. Hess, of Cadiz, once a State Senator, and ex-County Treasurer, and Emsley Julian, graduated from this school. Milton Wayman, the last Probate Judge for Henry County, was the teacher.

LIBERTY TOWNSHIP.

Liberty was the fifth township organized, this important ceremony bearing date of February 12, 1822. It was a clipping from the east end of Henry Township, and, according to the metes and bounds prescribed, it was at first one mile less in extent from east to west than at present. It is now six miles wide by six and three fourths in length, thus embracing about forty square miles, mostly table land, and of a very fine quality generally. Flatrock, rising in Blue River Township, enters the township near the middle of its northern boundary, passing out near the southwest corner. The valley of this stream is so slightly depressed as to form nothing worthy to be called bluffs, and, although too sluggish to be of much value for hydraulic purposes, it, with its small tributaries, seems in some way connected with the drainage and fertility of a wide belt of superb farming lands. The two Symons creeks, heretofore mentioned, find their sources in Liberty Township, and now furnish ample drainage to many sections of fine land that, doubtless, in the early days of Henry County, passed for very wet land.

The aggregate value of the farms and improvements of Liberty Township exceeds that of the farms of any other township of the county, except Henry, and the evidence of thrift and "farming for profit" are nowhere more generally visible than in Liberty Township. Four villages have been projected in the township— Millville, Ashland, Petersburg, and Chicago, though it is presumed that the proprietors of the two last named, if still living, have long since abandoned the hope of seeing them outstrip their namesakes. Under the old turnpike law, many miles of turnpike sprang into existence, and now the people of this township rejoice in the advantage of traveling to almost any point on good roads.

56

According to the census of 1870, the population numbered 1,868, being almost exclusively rural. Its 24,000 acres were then divided into 203 farms, an average of about 120 acres each. The population then numbered about 49 to the square mile, being divided between 376 families. There were then 6 persons of color, 19 foreigners, 64 North Carolinians, and 32 Virginians, within the township. The population of Liberty Township, township and towns combined, according to the census of 1890, was 1,538; census of 1900, 1,416; showing a loss in ten years of more than one hundred, which is explained by the purchase and consolidation of small farms into large ones.

The wealth of the township was estimated for the purpose of taxation, in 1870, as follows: farms and improvements, $712,430; town lots and improvements, $5,950; personal property, $325,410; total valuation, $1,043,790. The tax duplicate for the year 1904, the township and towns combined, shows the following, viz.: value of lands, $843,720; value of improvements, $104,130; total, $947,850; value of lots, $970; value of improvements, $3,120; total, $4,090; value of personal property of all kinds, $301,607; value of railroad property, no electric lines, $244,-100; total value of taxables of all kinds, $1,497,647; less mortgage exemptions, $42,410; leaving net value of taxables for year named, $1,455,237. Total taxes levied on the tax duplicate for the year 1904, the township and towns combined, which taxes include all items enumerated in Dudley Township, except corporation tax, there being no incorporated town in Liberty Township, $20,854.80; total polls, 241; tax on each, $2.

The first election was held at the house of Ezekiel Leavell, on the first Saturday in May, 1823, for the election of two Justices of the Peace. Ezekiel Leavell was Inspector. John Smith was made Supervisor of all the roads in the township. Jacob Thorp and Cyrus Cotton were appointed Overseers of the Poor. In 1825, the elections were ordered to be held at the house of Samuel D. Wells, and continued to be held at his house for a number of years. After the railroad was built through the township and the town of Millville established, the voting place was moved to that town. There are now two voting precincts in Liberty, one at Millville, the other at Ashland. Vote, 1904, East Liberty precinct, Millville, 209; West Liberty precinct, Ashland, 164; total, 373.

STONY CREEK TOWNSHIP.

This township, the next in order of organization, was established November 11, 1828. By its creation Prairie Township lost about one third of its "independent jurisdiction," as Stony Creek was bounded on the west by the range line separating ranges ten and eleven, and extended to the eastern boundary of the county, including all north of Liberty Township, which made it a region of no small consequence. It was at first eight miles from north to south, six miles wide on the north, and about six and three fourths on its south line, and had in its ample area about forty nine and one half sections of land. A tier of eight sections has since been re-annexed to Prairie to compensate, no doubt, in a measure, for the loss of more than two townships on the west. Blue River Township has also been carved out of Stony Creek, thus reducing it in size to barely twenty square miles, about two fifths of its primal area, and leaving it the smallest of the townships.

COMPANY E, 8th INDIANA INFANTRY.

The township is drained by a creek, which, rising near, runs nearly parallel with its southern border, then runs north across the township and empties into White River. The immense quantities of bowlders or "traveled stones" scattered over some of the highest ridges and points in the township must not only arrest the attention and excite the curiosity of the observer but at once suggest the necessity of inquiry as to the township's name.

This township presents, perhaps, a greater variety of surface and soil than any other equal area in the county, and while there was every variety of timber to be found in the county, there was a larger proportion of oak, beech, and hickory and less poplar, ash and walnut.

There is a portion of two or more prairies in this township similar to those in Prairie. The bottom lands are doubtless equal to any in the county, while the higher lands, which the casual observer would at first sight pronounce poor and only produce abundant crops of the sturdier grasses, when broken up are of more than average size. Blountsville and Rogersville are the only villages. The population, according to the census of 1870, was 634, or an average of 5.7 families. There were then 13 colored persons, 10 foreigners, 40 natives of North Carolina, and 35 Virginians in the township. There were 118 farms, averaging about 78 acres each.

The population of Stony Creek Township, according to the census of 1880, including Blountsville and Rogersville, was 1,088; the census of 1900 shows a less population, the number being 962. Since then, the Chicago, Cincinnati and Louisville Railroad has been built through the township, and now no doubt the township exhibits a marked increase over that of 1000.

The assessed value of farms and improvements for 1870 was $178,940; of town lots, $16,520; and of personal, $112,300; making a total of $297,770. The tax duplicate for the year 1904, township and towns combined, shows the following: value of land, $253,790; value of improvements, $23,300; total, $276,330; value of lots, $3,480; value of improvements, $6,040; total, $9,320; value of personal property of all kinds, $119,590; value of railroad property, including the Big 4, $90,140; total value of taxables of all kinds, $302,420, less mortgage exemptions $25,180; leaving net value of taxables for the year named, $277,340. Total taxes levied on the duplicate for the year 1904, township and towns combined, which taxes include all items enumerated in Dudley Township except corporation tax, there being no incorporated town in Stony Creek Township, $9,883.73; total polls, 179; tax on each, $2.00.

The first election was held at the house of Thomas Hobson, Jr., December 20, 1828, for the purpose of electing one Justice of the Peace; William Wyatt, Inspector. There were formerly two voting precincts, but this was in the days of bad roads, and want of suitable and satisfactory conveyances. Now, since the days of free gravel roads and rubber tired buggies, the two precincts have been consolidated into one, at Blountsville. Vote, 1904, one precinct, Blountsville, 237.

FALL CREEK TOWNSHIP

The next township in order was named Fall Creek, organized August, 1820. This was at first declared to be eight miles in length, from north to south, by seven in width. It thus embraced within its limits fifty six square miles, or 35,840 acres,

The township is fittingly named from a creek, which, rising near, runs nearly parallel with, its southern border, then runs north across the township and finally into White River. The immense quantities of bowlders or "traveled stones" scattered over some of the highest ridges and points in the township must not only arrest the attention and excite the curiosity of the observer, but at once obviate the necessity of inquiry as to the township's name.

This township presents, perhaps, a greater variety of surface and soil than any other equal area in the county, and while there was every variety of timber to be found in the county, there was a larger proportion of oak here than elsewhere, and less poplar, ash and walnut.

There is a portion of two or more prairies in this township, similar to those in Prairie. The bottom lands are doubtless equal to any in the county, while the higher lands, which the casual observer would perhaps, pronounce thin or poor, not only produce abundant crops of the smaller grains, but Indian corn of more than average size. Blountsville and Rogersville are the only villages. The population, according to the census of 1870, was 934; divided between 197 families. . There were then 13 colored persons, 10 foreigners, 21 natives of North Carolina, and 35 Virginians in the township. There were 118 farms, averaging about 109 acres each.

The population of Stony Creek Township, according to the census of 1890, including Blountsville and Rogersville, was 1,088; the census of 1900 shows a less population, the number being 962. Since then, the Chicago, Cincinnati and Louisville Railroad has been built through the township, and now no doubt the township exhibits a marked increase over that of 1900.

The assessed value of farms and improvements for 1870 was $178,940; of town lots, $6,500; and of personal, $112,330; making a total of $297,770. The tax duplicate for the year 1904, township and towns combined, shows the following: value of lands, $333,010; value of improvements, $43,910; total, $376,920; value of lots, $3,480; value of improvements, $10,140; total, $13,620; value of personal property of all kinds, $141,740; value of railroad property, no electric lines, $30,-140; total value of taxables of all kinds, $562,420; less mortgage exemptions, $25,-180; leaving net value of taxables for the year named, $537,240. Total taxes levied on the duplicate for the year 1904, township and towns combined, which taxes include all items enumerated in Dudley Township except corporation tax, there being no incorporated town in Stony Creek Township, $9,383.63; total polls, 179; tax on each, $2.00.

The first election was held at the house of Thomas Hobson, Jr., December 20, 1828, for the purpose of electing one Justice of the Peace; William Wyatt, Inspector. There were formerly two voting precincts, but this was in the days of bad roads, and want of suitable and satisfactory conveyances. Now, since the days of free gravel roads and rubber tired buggies, the two precincts have been consolidated into one, at Blountsville. Vote, 1904, one precinct, Blountsville, 237.

FALL CREEK TOWNSHIP.

The next township in order was named Fall Creek, organized August, 1829. This was at first declared to be eight miles in length, from north to south, by seven in width. It thus embraced within its limits fifty six square miles, or 35,840 acres, and yet with this ample domain the township could only muster twenty nine votes at an exciting election, in 1830, and of these but three were Whig votes, yet now the township is largely Republican. Since the organization of the township a strip two miles in width has been given to Harrison Township, and two miles on the east of Jefferson, leaving the township six miles in length, from north to south, and five miles in width.

Fall Creek is a well watered and very fertile township, and well improved farms and good buildings indicate that the husbandman is being well repaid for his labors. The creek from which the township takes its name, rising near the northeast corner, and meandering through, leaves the township, near the southwest corner. It once had sufficient fall to furnish valuable water power. Deer Creek, a tributary, rising in Harrison Township, near Cadiz, emptying into Fall Creek, about one and one-half miles north of Mechanicsburg, also furnished fair water power. A "corn cracker" was erected on this stream, about the year 1826. Benjamin Franklin, then a boy, afterward a noted preacher, is said to have dug the race. This was the first mill in that part of Henry County.

A very rude log school house, with split pole benches and greased paper windows, did service in the Keesling neighborhood near the present site of Mechanicsburg, as late as 1831 or 1832. Robert Price was the first teacher. Lewis Swain was afterwards principal of this institution. Some of the earlier settlers can remember attending the log rollings every day for weeks together.

Middletown, Mechanicsburg, and Honey Creek, are the towns and villages of the township. The total population of the township, according to the census of 1870, was 2,004, or about 66 to the square mile. Of these 31 were foreigners, 36 North Carolinians, 321 Virginians, and 4 colored persons. There were 197 families living in the town and villages and 209 in the country. The population of Fall Creek Township, according to the census of 1890, including Middletown, Mechanicsburg and Honey Creek, was 2,320; census of 1900, 3,311, the principal gain arising from the increase of the population of Middletown.

The wealth of the township, in 1870, for the purpose of taxation, was as follows: farms, $522,270; town lots, $72,650; personal property, $412,280; total, $1,007,200.

The tax duplicate for the year 1904, township, town and villages combined, shows the following: value of lands, $659,780; value of improvements, $124,090; total, $783,870; value of lots, $79,600; value of improvements, $127,410; total, $207,010; value of personal property of all kinds, $476,850; value of railroad property including steam and electric lines, incomplete, $171,810; total value of taxables of all kinds, $1,639,540; less mortgage exemptions, $37,410, leaving a net value of taxables for the year named, $1,602,130. Total taxes levied on the duplicate for the year 1904, township, town, and villages combined, which taxes include all items enumerated in Dudley Township with the addition of township poor, corporation, bond, lighting streets, and streets, the last named three, being confined to Middletown, $28,404.57. Total polls, the township, 235; tax, $2.50, each. Total polls, Middletown, 241; tax on each $2.50.

All elections were ordered to be held at the house of Abraham Thomas, but in 1832, it was ordered that they thereafter be held at Middletown. Elections are now held at Middletown, Mechanicsburg, and Henry Creek. Vote, 1904, Middletown, precinct "A," 118; "B," 163; "C," 105; "D," 127; Mechanicsburg, 129; Honey Creek, 123; total, 765.

FRANKLIN TOWNSHIP.

Franklin Township was organized on January 5, 1830. It was constructed out of Dudley and Wayne townships, and, from the order making it a township, we learn that the west line was about three fourths of a mile west of the village of Ogden, and continued north to the line dividing townships sixteen and seventeen, which would make the northwest corner of Franklin as it then existed, about one mile west of the Masonic Cemetery, which joins Greensboro on the south. From this point the northern boundary ran east eight miles, or within three fourths of a mile of the present eastern limits of the township. This gave it jurisdiction over nearly all its present territory, all of Spiceland, a small fraction of Wayne (just north of the "Stone Quarry Mill"), and three sections now claimed by Greensboro. In the following year, a change was made in the western boundary, which gave Wayne another tier of sections and made the northwest corner of Franklin Township, just about the location of the Masonic Cemetery, and perhaps, within the corporate limits of Greensboro.

All elections were ordered to be held at the house of Joseph Copeland. John Copeland was appointed Inspector, and Joseph Kellum, Lister; and the first election was ordered on the first Saturday in February, 1830. Upon the setting up of Spiceland Township, in 1842, Franklin, which underwent another mutation, was given a slice off of Dudley, and was then contracted to its present limits of five miles in width, from east to west, by six miles in length.

Flatrock "drags its slow length along" near the middle of the township, and, although at two or three points it was compelled to do duty as a mill stream, it never established much of a character for energy. It, however, is the natural drain of a remarkably fertile body of land. Buck Creek drains the northwest corner of the township.

The present area of the township is about 17,200 acres, which according to the census of 1870, was then divided into 151 farms, an average of about 114 acres each. Lewisville, the only village in the township, then contained 86 families, while 213 families resided in the country. Of the population in 1870, 42 were foreigners, 13 colored, 124 North Carolinians, and 29 Virginians; total population of township for 1870, 1,696; population according to the census of town and township combined, for 1890, 1,330; census of 1900, 1,137; loss in ten years 193. However, the recent improvement in Lewisville, must make a gain in the population of the township for 1905, more than equal to the loss as stated. The loss in population since 1870 must be accounted for in Franklin Township for reasons given in other similar cases, viz.: the consolidation of small farms into large ones.

The wealth of the township, 1870, is reported thus: farms and improvements, $500,750; town lots and improvements, $42,960; personal property, $332,260; total, $875,970.

The tax duplicate for the year 1904, township and Lewisville combined, shows the following: value of lands, $591,920; value of improvements, $88,720; total, $680,640; value of lots, $36,400; value of improvements, $29,330; total, 65,730;

value of personal property of all kinds, $368,870; value of railroad property, including steam and electric lines, $325,240; total value of taxables of all kinds, $1,440,480; less mortgage exemptions, $25,290; leaving net value of taxables for the year named, $1,415,190. Total taxes levied on the duplicate for the year 1904, township and Lewisville incorporated, combined, which taxes include all items enumerated in Dudley Township with addition of township poor, and corporation bond tax for Lewisville corporation, $20,626.66. Total polls in township, 136; tax, $1.50 each; total polls in Lewisville, 72; tax, $2.00 each.

Formerly there was but one voting precinct in the township. Now there are two, both in Lewisville. Vote for 1904, West Franklin precinct, 172; East Franklin precinct, 162; total, 334.

GREENSBORO TOWNSHIP.

Greensboro Township, so named from an ancient village of North Carolina, was organized September 7, 1831. It was at first described as "all that part of the territory of Henry Township west of the range line dividing nine and ten." This made it seven miles from east to west, and six miles from north to south, which would include nearly all of the present area of the township and three fifths of Harrison. In 1838, one half its territory was given to Harrison, and a small addition —four square miles—was made to it, taken from the townships of Wayne and Franklin. This change removed the township line one mile south from the village of Greensboro, and left the township with an area of twenty five square miles, or about 16,000 acres, divided, according to the census of 1870, into 118 farms; an average of about 135 acres each.

Greensboro and Woodville (now extinct), on the line between Harrison and Greensboro Townships, were the only villages. Of the 315 families in 1870 in the township, 70 lived in Greensboro. The population of the township numbered 1,490. Of these six were reported of foreign birth; 81 colored; 221 were North Carolinians; and 52 were natives of Virginia. Population according to the census of 1890: Greensboro, Kennard, and Shirley, in Henry County, combined, 1,612; census for 1900, 1,658.

The tax duplicate for the year 1904, township and towns combined, shows as follows: value of lands, $514,320; value of improvements, $72,760; total, $587,080; value of lots, $16,610; value of improvements, $65,820; total, $82,430; value of personal property of all kinds, $269,850; value of railroad property, no electric lines, $137,020; total value of taxables of all kinds, $1,076,380; less mortgage exemptions, $32,330; leaving net value of taxables for the year named, $1,044,050.

Greensboro is a well watered and fertile township. Blue River, skirting through the southeast corner, and Duck Creek, running across the eastern end, furnish fine water power. Much of the land along these water courses is quite rolling and there are numerous knolls, supplied with excellent gravel. Montgomery Creek, crossing the township near the middle, and Six-mile Creek rising in, and running across, the western part of the township, made the complete drainage of a large and fertile portion of the township (originally counted as wet), a matter of no great difficulty.

The assessed value of Greensboro Township, tax duplicate of 1870, was: farms, $364,850; town lots, $34,190; personal, $196,330; total, $595,370.

Total taxes levied on the duplicate for the year 1904, township and towns combined, which taxes include all items enumerated in Dudley township with the addition of corporation tax, Kennard, Shirley, and Greensboro, and corporation bond, Kennard, and street tax, Shirley; total, $19,259.59. Total polls in township, 154; tax, $3.00 each; Greensboro corporation, 49; tax, $2.50 each; Kennard, 97; tax, $3.00 each; Shirley, 41; tax, $3.50 each.

For many years and until after the building of the Big Four railroad across the northern part of the township, all elections were held in the village of Greensboro. The first election in the township, was held on the fourth Saturday in September, 1831, and Thomas Reagan was made the first inspector of elections. There are now two voting precincts, viz.: Greensboro, and Kennard, all voters living at Shirley, Henry County, voting at Kennard. Vote for 1904, east precinct, Greensboro, 192; west precinct, Kennard, 302; total, 494.

HARRISON TOWNSHIP.

The large and important township of Harrison was formed out of the north half of Greensboro and two tiers of sections off the south side of Fall Creek, November 7, 1838, and all elections were ordered to be held at Cadiz.

The general aspect of this township, which is five miles from north to south and seven miles from east to west, is that of high gently undulating table land, with considerable portions formerly inclined to be wet, but very fertile under a system of intelligent drainage, now practically complete. A larger number of small streams find their head waters in this than any other township of the county. A small portion of the northeast corner of the township finds drainage into Bell Creek, and runs north, and near the same spot rises Honey Creek, also running north. Deer Creek, rising near the center of the township, also runs north by west, and empties into Fall Creek near Mechanicsburg, while two other small tributaries of Fall Creek have their source in the north and northwest portions of the township, and in the central and western portions, Sugar Creek takes its rise and runs west, while Montgomery Creek rises in the south part and runs south, and the west fork of Duck Creek rising near Cadiz, also runs south, while the principal branch of that creek, with some small tributaries, pretty effectually drains the eastern end of the township. A little south and west of Cadiz can doubtless be found some of the highest land in the western part of the county. Cadiz, and a part of Woodville, now extinct, are the only villages of the township.

Harrison Township contains, exclusive of town lots, Cadiz and Woodville, more than 22,000 acres of land, which, according to the census of 1870, was divided into 183 farms, an average of about 122 acres each. The total assessed value of the township, villages included, on the tax duplicate for 1870 was as follows: farms with improvements, $445,010; town lots including improvements, $11,030; total value of personal property of all kinds, $217,390; grand total, $673,430.

The tax duplicate for the year 1904, township and villages combined, shows the following: value of lands, $761,280; value of improvements, $102,200; total, $863,480; value of lots, $4,250; value of improvements, $14,450; total, $18,700; value of personal property of all kinds, $314,560; total value of taxables of all kinds, $1,196,740; less mortgage exemptions, $33,370; leaving net value of taxables for year named, $1,163,370. It will be noted that there is no railroad property, either steam or electric lines included in the above. Harrison township is the only one in the county not touched by a railroad. The total taxes levied on the tax duplicate for 1904, township and villages combined, which taxes include all items enumerated in Dudley Township, with the addition of corporation bond and street tax for Cadiz. Total, $20,828.12. Total polls in Harrison Township, 246; tax, $1.50 each; Cadiz corporation, 33; tax, $2.00 each.

At the first election, on the first Saturday in December, 1838, William Tucker, inspector, there were thirty two votes cast for Justice of the Peace. According to the census of 1870, Harrison had a population of 1,916, of whom 32 were colored, 15 foreign born, 101 natives of North Carolina, and 109 Virginians. Population, according to the census of 1890, township and Cadiz combined, 1,674; census of 1900, 1,488; loss in ten years, 186; loss from 1870 to 1900, 428. The loss in population can be accounted for by the purchase and consolidation of small farms into large ones, and the exodus of farmers and their sons and daughters from country to town life.

The first church and school house was probably at Clear Springs, in the southeast corner of the township, constructed in 1831-2 while it was a part of Greensboro Township.

All elections have been held at Cadiz, from the organization of the township to the present time. Formerly, there was but one voting precinct. Now there are two. Vote for 1904, South Harrison precinct, 196; North Harrison precinct, 170; total, 366.

SPICELAND TOWNSHIP.

This township, the smallest in the county, except Stony Creek, was organized, June, 1842, at which time, Ogden was the principal village. Room for it was found by taking a slice off Wayne and a four mile slip off the west side of Franklin Township. It is of irregular shape, being six miles in length on the eastern side, with an average length of five miles and width of four and one half miles. Blue River forms the boundary for about three miles on the northwest. Its area is a little short of twenty two square miles, or about 13,000 acres, which, according to the census of 1870, was divided into 173 farms, giving an average of only about 75 acres each, the smallest average in the county.

Buck Creek, running in a southwest course, crosses the southeastern corner of the township into Rush, where it makes a short turn and re-enters Henry County about the middle of the south line of the township and bearing in a northwest course, nearly four miles, passes into Wayne Township and falls into Blue River at the old Heaton or White Mills. Blue River on the northwest, and the classic little stream named Brook Bezor, which rises near the center of the township and runs north two and one-half miles with an average descent of about thirty feet to the mile, constitute the only water courses of note in the township.

Notwithstanding the smallness of Spiceland Township in respect to area, it is by no means insignificant in some other respects, being fourth in point of population in the county, and up to the average in point of wealth, while its farm lands are assessed higher for purposes of taxation than many other townships in the county. This is doubtless owing in part to its division into smaller farms and consequent thorough tillage, but much is owing to the high average quality of the land for general farming purposes.

The population of Spiceland Township, according to the census of 1870, numbered 2,020, or about .92 per square mile; of these 334 were born in North Carolina, 45 in Virginia, 17 out of the United States, and 65 were colored persons.

Population of Spiceland Township, including Ogden, Spiceland, and Dunreith according to the census of 1890, 1,823; census of 1900, 1,844; the last census showing a total loss as compared with the census of 1870, of 176. This loss of population, between the years above mentioned, is explained by the improved general school system of the county as compared with the most prosperous days of the Spiceland Academy, under Clarkson Davis, as principal, when it outranked every other school in the county and many people moved to Spiceland to educate their children. The school is yet a most excellent one but the improved educational facilities elsewhere in the county, have stopped the migration to Spiceland as the great educational center.

The first election was held at Ogden, August, 1842. A few years afterwards, the poll was divided and elections held at Spiceland and Ogden. There are now three precincts, two at Spiceland and one at Dunreith. Vote for 1904, West Spiceland precinct, 132; East Spiceland precinct, 196; south precinct, Dunreith, 185; total vote, 513.

The assessed value of the tax duplicate for 1870, in farms was $457,460; town lots, $65,870; personal, $296,310; total, $819,640. The tax duplicate for the year 1904, township and towns combined, shows as follows: value of lands, $453,590; value of improvements, $101,410; total, $555,000; value of lots, $24,550; value of improvements, $60,830; total, $85,380; total value of personal property of all kinds, $393,160; value of railroad property, steam and electric lines, $393,180; total taxables of all kinds, $1,426,720; less mortgage exemptions, $29,410; leaving net value of taxables for the year named, $1,397,310. Total taxes levied on the duplicate for the year 1904, township and towns combined, which taxes include all items enumerated in Dudley Township, with the addition of township poor, lighting streets, corporation and street tax, the last three for Spiceland corporation, and corporation tax for Dunreith, total $21,988.26. Total polls in township, 159; tax, $2.00 each; Spiceland corporation, 81; tax, $2.50 each; Dunreith corporation, 30; tax, $2.50 each.

JEFFERSON TOWNSHIP.

This township was organized September 5, 1843, out of the spare territory of Fall Creek and Prairie. The eastern half of it is eight miles in length, while on the west line it is but six miles. It is four miles in width and contains twenty eight square miles, or nearly 18,000 acres, all passably good land, and much of it very fine farming land. Its principal stream is Bell Creek, which with its tributaries traverses nearly the entire length of the township. Honey Creek is in the southwest; and a branch tributary of Buck Creek, in the northeast corner, carries into White River a portion of its surplus waters. Sulphur Springs is the only village.

The population of the township, according to the census of 1870, numbered 1,234, divided into 230 families, 172 of whom lived in the agricultural districts.

There were 23 foreigners, 12 North Carolinians, and 169 Virginians in the township. The average size of a farm in the township was about 103 acres, and the population numbered about 46 to the square mile.

The farms and improvements on the tax duplicate for 1870 were valued, for the purpose of taxation, at $359,290; town lots, $18,800; personal, $188,050; total, $566,140.

The tax duplicate for the year 1904, townships and town combined, shows the following: value of lands, $543,460; value of improvements, $73,010; total, $616,-470; value of lots, $2,310; value of improvements, $19,840; total, $22,150; total value of personal property of all kinds, $214,200; value of railroad property including steam and unfinished electric line, $143,820; total value of taxables of all kinds, $996,640, less mortgage exemptions, $30,470; leaving net value of taxables for the year named, $966,220. Total taxes levied on the tax duplicate for the year 1904, township and town combined, which taxes include all items enumerated in Dudley Township with the addition of corporation and street tax, Sulphur Springs, $13,269. Total polls in Jefferson Township, 165; tax, $2.50; total polls in Sulphur Springs, 49; tax, $2.25 each.

The elections were first ordered to be held at the house of Michael Swope, on the 2nd day of October, 1843, for the purpose of electing a Justice. Since the building of the Panhandle railroad through the township, 1855-56, and the establishment of Sulphur Springs, the elections have been uniformly held at that place. Formerly, there was but one voting place, now there are two. Vote, for 1904, West Jefferson precinct, 140; East Jefferson precinct, 173; total, 313.

Population, according to the census of 1890, township and town combined, 1,132; census of 1900, 1,144.

BLUE RIVER TOWNSHIP.

This was the last organized, and is one of the smallest townships of the county, and contains a trifle more than twenty two square miles. It was formed from the south half of Stony Creek Township, by act of the Commissioners, on June 6, 1848.

Blue River Township takes its name quite aptly from being the source of both branches of the stream of that name, so intimately connected with the prosperity and history of the county. "Big Blue," as it is often called, rises near the middle of the western portion of the township, and runs nearly north about three and one half miles to within about one half mile of Rogersville, in Stony Creek Township, where it bears to the west and is soon wending its way amid the prairies of Prairie Township. The slashes or head waters of this branch of the river are known in the Duke neighborhood by the classic name of "Goose Creek." The stream has a fall of perhaps twenty feet per mile for the first three and one half or four miles, and, although the volume of water is small, at the ordinary stage there were formerly two pretty valuable mill seats on it before it reached Prairie Township. "Little . Blue" rises near the north line and northeast corner of the township, and running in a general southwest direction into Prairie Township, unites with the main branch about two miles north of New Castle. On this branch of Blue River were formerly situated the flourishing woolen mills of Mowrer and McAfee and later of Ice, Dunn and Company, and the celebrated Hernly Mill, as well as some of the finest farms in the northern part of the county. Flatrock also rises in the northeastern portion of this township, and takes a southerly direction, while a small branch of Stony Creek, almost interlapping with "Little Blue," somehow finds its way through the water shed of this part of the county, and runs north into White River, near the western boundary of Randolph County. From the number of streams having their initial point in the township, and running in opposite directions, the conclusion is easily reached that some of the highest lands in the county are to be found here; but being the highest by no means signifies the dryest. Large portions of the township required drainage to make them available to the husbandman, but being reclaimed are of the very best quality.

The woolen mills mentioned in the preceding paragraph were for many years a land mark in Henry County. There is now no sign of this once flourishing industry except the remnants of a fast disappearing mill race. The factory was first best known as Mowrer and McAfee's and later as Ice, Dunn and Company's. From the destruction of the timber and the drainage of the county and the consequent immediate flow of the waters on their way to the sea, Little Blue River as well as all other rivers and streams in the county have been rendered practically useless, so far as power is concerned, for mill and factory purposes. For the same reason, the Hernly Mill, so long another land mark, was put out of business. This mill and factory stood near each other about three miles northeast of New Castle and not far from the old village of Hillsboro.

This little township was exclusively rural, having neither village nor permanent postoffice within its limits until after the construction of the Big Four railroad through the central part of the county, unless a half interest in the old town site of Centerville, on the line between Blue River and Stony Creek townships, for many years extinct, could have been claimed as a village. Since the building of the Big Four Road, the prosperous and beautiful town of Mooreland has been established and the postoffice has been re-established at what is now the village of Messick, formerly a neighborhood cross roads.

The census of 1870 showed a population of 861, the smallest number at that time, of any of the thirteen civil divisions of the county. Of this population, 13 were colored; 7 foreigners, 25 Virginians; and 70 North Carolinians. The population, according to the census of 1890 including Mooreland, incorporated, and the village of Messick, was 1,032; census of 1900, 1,053.

The farms and improvements on the tax duplicate of 1870, were valued at $269,250, and the personal property at $88,990; total, $358,240. The tax duplicate for the year 1904, township, town, and village combined, shows as follows: value of lands, $458,220; value of improvements, $37,070; total, $495,290; value of lots, $9,160; value of improvements, $32,160; total, $41,320; total value of personal property of all kinds, $190,620; value of railroad property, no electric lines, $98,040; total value of taxables of all kinds, $825,270; less mortgage exemptions, $43,700; leaving net value of taxables for the year named, $781,570. Total taxes levied for the year 1904, township, town and village combined, which taxes include all items enumerated in Dudley Township, with the addition of corporation bond. and street tax for the town of Mooreland, $13,267.09. Total polls in township, 135; tax, $2.50 each; polls in Mooreland, 76; tax, $3.25 each.

At the time the township was established, all elections were ordered to be held at "the home of Philip Moore or at the Meeting House nearby," and they so continued to be held there until after the establishment of Mooreland as above mentioned, since which time the voting has all been done at Mooreland where there are now two precincts. Vote for 1904, West Blue River precinct, 145; East Blue River precinct, 174; total, 319.

CORPORAL CO. D

SHEPPERD BOWMAN

PRIVATE CO. D

JOHN E. COOPER

PRIVATE CO. D

JOHN W. McCORMACK

LIEUTENANT CO. K

THOMAS J. COOK

PRIVATE CO. D

GREENBERRY W. HEDGES

MUSICIAN CO. D

ISAAC N. WRIGHT

PRIVATE CO. D

SOLOMON MYERS

147th INDIANA INFANTRY.

THE FIRST COURT HOUSE—THE SECOND COURT HOUSE—THE PRESENT COURT HOUSE—THE NEW ADDITION TO THE PRESENT COURT HOUSE—EARLIER CLERK'S AND RECORDER'S OFFICE—EARLIER AUDITOR'S AND TREASURER'S OFFICE—THE COURT HOUSE SQUARE—THE FIRST JAIL—THE SECOND JAIL—THE PRESENT JAIL—THE PRESENT JAIL SITE—THE STRAY PEN—THE COUNTY ASYLUM—SUPERINTENDENTS OF THE COUNTY ASYLUM—THE FIRST ORPHANS' HOME AT SPICELAND—THE AGED PERSON'S HOME AND ORPHAN ASYLUM FOR THE GERMAN BAPTIST CHURCH OF THE SOUTHERN DISTRICT OF INDIANA—THE BUNDY HOME AT SPICELAND—THE COUNTY BOARD OF CHARITIES AND CORRECTIONS.

Section six of the act, providing for the organization of the county of Henry, made it the duty of the commissioners to provide for the erection of suitable county buildings within one year after their election.

THE FIRST COURT HOUSE

In obedience to this provision the commissioners, in their own discretion, ordained that:

"The agent of Henry County shall offer for sale the house built in the town of New Castle. the building of the court house of Henry County of the following dimensions. to-wit: being logs twenty feet to be on hewn out, each log to face not less than twelve inches at the little end, being seven inches thick, twelve rounds high, with a cabin roof to consist of eleven joists to be four inches by nine, the joists to be eight feet nine inches from the floor, etc., etc.

The sills of this imposing structure were to be of hard timber one foot from the ground, with a good rock or stone under each corner, a puncheon floor below and plank floor above. with two windows above and three below, consisting of twelve lights each; and they further instructed that the sale of the above described building be on the Wednesday after the second Monday in May next, with a good door three feet wide. six feet. six inches high, etc.

At the May term. following. the board rescinded the above order and at once substituted another with further and more minute specifications. In these specifications, the side logs were to be twenty feet long, and end logs twenty feet, while they were to face at least twelve inches in the middle, and sills and sleepers to be of good durable timber and to be placed on six suitable sized stones; the floor to be of puncheons hewed smooth and solid. and the lower story

147th INDIANA INFANTRY

CHAPTER XXXIX.

COUNTY BUILDINGS AND COUNTY CHARITIES.

The First Court House—The Second Court House—The Present Court House—The New Addition to the Present Court House—Earlier Clerk's And Recorder's Office—Earlier Auditor's And Treasurer's Office—The Court House Square—The First Jail—The Second Jail —The Present Jail—The Present Jail Site—The Stray Pen—The County Asylum — Superintendents of the County Asylum—The First Orphans' Home at Spiceland—The Aged Person's Home and Orphan Asylum for the German Baptist Church of the Southern District of Indiana—The Bundy Home at Spiceland—The County Board of Charities and Corrections.

Section six of the act, providing for the organization of the county of Henry, made it the duty of the commissioners to provide for the erection of suitable county buildings within one year after their election.

THE FIRST COURT HOUSE.

In obedience to this provision, the commissioners, in February, 1823, ordered that:

"The agent of Henry County shall offer for sale to the lowest bidder in the town of New Castle, the building of the court house of Henry County, of the following dimensions, to-wit: being logs twenty two by eighteen feet, each log to face not less than twelve inches at the little end, being seven inches thick, twelve rounds high, with a cabin roof to consist of eleven joists, to be four inches by nine, the joists to be eight feet nine inches from the floor, etc., etc."

The sills of this imposing structure were to be of durable timber, one foot from the ground, with a good rock or stone under each corner, a puncheon floor below and plank floor above, with two windows above and three below, consisting of twelve lights each; and they further instructed that the, "Sale of the above described building be on the Wednesday after the second Monday in May next, with a good door three feet wide, six feet, six inches high."

At the May term following, the board rescinded the above order and at once substituted another with further and more "workmanlike" specifications. In these specifications, the side logs were to be twenty six feet long, and end logs twenty feet, while they were to face at least twelve inches in the middle, and sills and sleepers to be of good durable timber, and to be placed on six suitable sized stones, the floor to be of puncheons hewed smooth and solid, and the lower story to be at least nine feet between joists. The second floor to be of plank, and the second story was to be at least five feet from the floor to the top of the last round of logs, "or square." There were also to be two doors so cut as to make the center of the door "nine feet from the end of the building" (which end is not specified), but they were to be "so hanged as to open on that end of the house intended for spectators," and they were to be hung on strong iron hinges, with a "good lock on what may be considered the front door," and a bar so as to fasten the other. This time there were to be two fifteen-light windows, and a strong partition of banisters, at least four feet high, to separate the court from the spectators, with a strong gate in it, fastening on the inside, and the second floor was to be reached by a "good strong set of straight steps, commonly called mill steps." The building was to be "well chinked and daubed and covered with good oak boards confined with sufficient weight poles."

The order for letting the court house provides that it be "advertised in three of the most public places in the county, and in the Western Times, a paper published at Centreville, Wayne County, Indiana," and it was, in "height, materials and construction, to be similar to the court house in Connersville, Fayette County, Indiana."

This building was ordered to be placed on the southeast corner of lot four, block twelve, which located it near the southwest corner of the new addition to the present court house and immediately across the street, north of the Alcazar theatre. So soon as the building was covered, the contractor was to receive twenty dollars of the "purchase money," and it was also stipulated that it was to be completed before the second Monday in February.

According to arrangement, the Agent did *"sell* the courthouse," on the 14th of May, 1823, to George Barnard, for two hundred and forty seven dollars, and in May following the commissioners adjourned from the house of John Smith to the new court house, which they formally accepted, as it was done according to contract. Once established in a building adequate to the wants and fully comporting with the dignity and wealth of our flourishing county—one that cost them a sum about equal to the tax duplicate for three years, it cannot be doubted but the commissioners felt immeasurable relief. Doubtless the tax-payers grumbled at the extravagance of those fellows who could thus squander two hundred and forty seven dollars, and they were soon rewarded by being permitted to retire to the rest and quietude of private life.

This log building, Henry County's first court house, was ready for occupancy early in the year 1824, and it was used for the transaction of all the business of the county, until after the second court house was ordered constructed in 1831. Between the determination to build a new court house (1831), and the time when it was ready for use, in the Winter of 1836-37, the first court house came to be regarded as unfit in which to hold court, and accordingly in 1834, as related by Judge Martin L. Bundy:

"The Board of County Commissioners procured for a court room. which was so used until the new building was ready for occupancy, the old frame Methodist Church, a small structure which stood where the City Hall (Old Methodist Church), now stands. At the first term of court held in this church, Charles H. Test was the presiding judge and William J. Brown, then of Rushville (Father of Admiral George Brown, of Indianapolis, retired) was the prosecuting attorney. My father-in-law, Abraham Elliott, appeared as counsel for Peter Winslow, a colored man who shot at a constable about to levy an execution on his property. This I think was Abraham Elliott's last appearance in court as attorney."

It is remembered by persons now living in New Castle, that after this first court house was vacated by the county, it was repaired and occupied by Samuel Graham, an English weaver who came to New York in 1833, and soon after to New Castle, where he wove coverlets and where he probably had his place of abode. A number of people in New Castle, and probably elsewhere in the county, now hold as heirlooms, fine, old fashioned coverlets woven in white and blue, with appropriate patterns, and date, the handiwork of Mr. Graham, a well remembered citizen and the father of William D. and the late Thomas R. Graham. After Mr. Graham's vacation of this old log building, remembered as standing as late as 1850, it may have been and probably was used as a residence.

It is mentioned in one of the preceding paragraphs, that the county commissioners in May, 1824, "adjourned from the house of John Smith to the new court house," the first one built. This shows that the board of commissioners had found a new place for business and had moved from the house of Charles Jamison. The history regarding this removal is furnished by Judge Martin L. Bundy who in answer to the inquiry, "Who was John Smith?" says:

"Well, he was the son of John Smith, a little old man who was the proprietor of, and laid out Richmond, Wayne County, Indiana, and whom I remember as far back as 1825. His son, John Smith, built a house and owned the lots where my son, Eugene H. Bundy, and his family now live, opposite, but a near neighbor of Charles Jamison. His house was larger than Jamison's which may have been the reason for the removal. Smith left New Castle, prior to 1833 and settled in Wabash where he lived for many years and where he died. The only two things that I remember about Smith were that he was very deaf and that when he made a visit to a neighbor, his parting salutation was, 'take notice.' I am not sure that he was in any way distinguished, nor do I remember his vocation, if he had one."

The jail, court house, and stray pen, or pound, being completed, a "long spasm of retrenchment and economy" occurred, until the county, fast becoming rich, began to grow proud, and, in 1831, ordered the building of a

SECOND COURT HOUSE (BUILT OF BRICK),

which was to be "forty feet square, walls included," the foundation "to be dug eighteen inches beneath the surface of the ground, the walls to be two feet thick from the foundation three feet up," the lower story to be fifteen feet high, and the upper story to be twelve.

This time, instead of a "cabin roof" sufficiently weighted down with poles, it was to have one of good yellow poplar "join shingles," eighteen inches in length, "to be pitched from each square to the center," the whole to be surmounted with an eight square cupola, eight feet in diameter, to "arise" twenty feet, eight feet of the distance to be enclosed with "Venecian blinds," and said cupola to be surmounted by a suitable cap from which was to be raised a spear bearing a wooden ball, ten inches in diameter, "nicely gilt," and still above this a neat vane and higher yet "a cross with a gilt ball on each end," and the whole surmounted with a "neat cap" on top of the spear.

Let the reader picture to himself the transition from the little cramped up, cabin roofed, puncheon floored, chinked and daubed, poorly lighted, hewed log concern, standing high and dry upon six "nigger heads," and an outside chimney, to this spacious brick, with twenty three windows of twenty four lights each, and a large folding door and "fan light" above, with foundations hidden away the enormous distance of eighteen inches under ground, and the whole surmounted with a cupola, which, for architectural design and finish, must have been the wonder of the age, and he cannot but be struck with the amazing strides in the paths of luxury taken by our forefathers. We are amazed at the old fellows, not one in twenty of whom had anything better than a cabin at home, to be willing to undertake the erection of a "temple of justice" of such proportions and at such an enormous cost, as it seemed at that time, as there were but seventy five dollars and three fourths of a cent in the treasury to commence on.

The building was, nevertheless, sold to one Nathan Crawford, in the latter part of the year 1831, "he being the lowest bidder," for the sum of $5,315, to be paid on the first of January each year, for five years,' as follows: in 1832, $400; in 1833, $700; in 1834, $1,000; in 1835, $1,200; in 1836, the balance. The walls were to be up and covered and all outside wood work was to be completed January 1, 1834, and two years was to be allowed for finishing off the costly interior. In short, it was expected that the contractor would "push things," and spend something like a thousand dollars a year. Robert Murphey was allowed $2.50 for furnishing the design of this elaborate structure. About nine o'clock, on Thursday morning, January 7, 1836, Nathan Crawford moved the commissioners, Robert Murphey, Tabor W. McKee, and John Whittaker to take the job off his hands; which they promptly declined to do, and declared that they had examined the "said court house" and "are of the opinion" that it is deficient in almost every particular, that the "roof leaks," plastering is not neatly done; and carpenter work ditto, and that the "contract is forfeited in toto, and the materials out of which said house is constructed are, in a great many cases, deficient." This was "rough" on the said Crawford, but he had to bear it till the March term, when a compromise was effected, and the building was received at $4,500, which was docking him $815 only.

The second or brick court house was destroyed by fire, about the time of the assembling of a county convention, on February 13, 1864.

After the burning of the second court house in 1864, the commissioners rented the Murphey Hall, now occupied by the Benevolent Protective Order of Elks, which by adoption, became the court house of the county and continued to be so used until the new court house was ready for occupancy in 1869. At the time of the conflagration, some of the public records and a great mass of official papers, stored away in one of the jury rooms, for want of room elsewhere, all more or less valuable, were lost or destroyed.

The commissioners, Morris F. Edwards, John Minesinger, and Elias Phelps at once set to work to devise ways and means for the erection of a new building dedicated to justice. There were several essential points to be secured in this proposed edifice. It must be free from dampness, which would destroy the precious records of the county, on which so much of the "peace and quiet" of our community depends. It must, of course, be fire proof, and sufficiently commodious for all legitimate purposes not only now, but for many years to come; must be of durable materials, and last, if least, it must be "good looking," a monument of the enterprise and taste of the people of one of the wealthy counties of the State. All these prerequisites, when the addition, completed in 1905, is considered in connection with the building, have been faithfully complied with. The main building as completed in 1869 is sixty six feet wide by eighty two feet in length, while the tower, which serves as main entrance and the initial point of the stairway to the court room, jury room, etc., above adds some nineteen feet more, making the extreme length one hundred and one feet. The height of the walls is fifty feet and of the tower one hundred and ten feet from the foundation.

There is a cellar under the building with a labyrinth of arched passages which contain furnaces and flues for heating every part of the building.

Of the capaciousness and convenience of the rooms for the county officers, on the first floor of the building as completed in 1869, it would exceed the limits of this work to speak more minutely. There is a large fire proof and almost burglar proof vault connected with each of the offices for the storage of the abundant and valuable archives on file.

The court rooms for the grand and traverse juries, sheriff's room, &c., as first completed, reached by the main stairway, are all worthy of a more extended notice than this work will allow. The court room itself, about sixty five feet by fifty feet, was in 1869 one of the finest and best appointed in the State, both as to convenience and tasteful ornamentations. The fresco painting on its walls and ceiling alone cost about $1,400 and was at that time regarded as a work of art. In August, 1871, Elwood Pleas, in writing of this court house, said: "The entire cost of this magnificent 'temple of Justice,' so well constructed and of such materials as to withstand the ordinary ravages of the 'tooth of Time,' till several generations shall have passed away, has been about $120,000. This is seemingly a large sum, but it must be remembered that everything used, cost 'war prices,' and already, by comparison with other public buildings, it is coming to be regarded as not too large a sum for such a building. Although there has been no little grumbling by some of the tax-payers, it can safely be predicted that the next generation at least, will thank the commissioners who ordered its erection and give full credit to Morris F. Edwards for having efficiently superintended the construction of the same."

NEW ADDITION TO THE PRESENT COURT HOUSE.

In the Fall of the year 1903, the board of county commissioners, recognizing the inadequate accommodations of the court house, decided to improve the building by an addition to the west end. The contract was let, December 29, 1903, to Patrick H. McCormack and Company, for the erection of the new part. This section of the building is sixty-eight feet, eight inches long, thus lacking but thirteen feet of being equal in length to the original structure, and of the same width. The new part joins flush with the old and from appearance, inside and out, it is hard to imagine that the two sections were not erected at one time. In style of architecture, the new wing is a duplicate of the original. The completed structure occupying the center of the square and surrounded by artistically kept grounds, is massive and imposing.

The work on the new part was begun in the Spring of 1904. The completed building was accepted by the board of commissioners in April, 1905. In comparing the two sections so nearly equal in size, one is impressed with two differences. The first section, a recognized necessity in 1864, was completed in 1869. The other was finished less than eighteen months after the matter was taken up by the commissioners. The new wing cost $44,000, the old section $120,000—Civil War prices.

The two parts have been made symmetrical in interior decoration, the cost for re-decorating the entire structure, being $2,895. About $4,000 worth of new and modern furniture has been purchased giving the offices all the conveniences of the present time and adding the finishing touches to the otherwise handsome quarters.

The new addition with its three floors and basement contains large and commodious public waiting rooms and toilets on the basement floor. The offices of the county assessor, auditor, treasurer, and county surveyor, are on the first floor. The Grand Army room, the law library, judge's library, and private office, two jury rooms, a grand jury apartment and consultation rooms for attorneys, occupy the second floor. Large storage rooms for old documents are on the third floor, which is a subdivision of the second story. It also provides an additional room for the county clerk and permits the establishment of a commissioner's court room in the former recorder's office. the recorder occupying the former auditor's office in the old part. The county superintendent has his office in the old office of the county treasurer in the original building. The sheriff's office still retains its former location in the old building.

Hot water heats the entire structure. Every modern convenience has been installed. Marble wainscotting circles the halls. The walls are calcined and frescoed. The grounds are beautiful. The exterior 150 by 67 feet, is complete and massive, the interior being handsome and convenient.

EARLIER CLERK'S AND RECORDER'S OFFICE.

In the earliest days of the county, the position of a county officer was not a very lucrative one. The records of their transactions were very brief and imperfect, and the business for a whole term of court might have been carried on a few scraps of paper in a vest pocket. One man acted as clerk and recorder and performed many of the duties now devolving upon the auditor, an office not created for twenty years after the county was organized. In this state of affairs, some small room that could be rented for fifteen or twenty dollars per year was all sufficient for one of the officers, and, in fact, there was but little use for a room, except at stated intervals. for a few years, and a party having business with the court would be as likely as any way to find its clerk out in his corn field, with a hoe in his hand. or in his clearing, grubbing.

Of course this sort of thing could not last always, and accordingly the commissioners let the building of a clerk's and recorder's office to Thomas Ginn for the sum of $844. The same was to be a one-story brick building, eighteen feet wide and thirty eight feet in length, divided into two rooms.

EARLIER AUDITOR'S AND TREASURER'S OFFICE.

On the northeast corner of the public square, erected in 1847, by George Lowe, contractor, for the sum of $545, was the counterpart of the last named building in almost every particular.

These little buildings, the first named, immediately south of, and the second, immediately north of the first brick court house and on a line fronting with it, doubtless answered the purpose intended quite well, when first constructed, but the rapid accumulation of records and papers, and the great increase of public business, and number of persons doing business, had, for a number of years, rendered it apparent that their days of usefulness were drawing to a close, when the fire of February 13, 1864, "opened the way," rather unexpectedly, for the building of the present court house.

THE COURT HOUSE SQUARE.

The county of Henry, as the original owner of the townsite of New Castle, reserved the present public square consisting of lots 1, 2, 3, and 4 of block 12 of the original plat for the Court House Square, and at that time for other public uses. Later, it was determined that lots 1, and 2, constituting the east half of the square, would be sufficient for all county purposes, and accordingly an alley way ten feet wide was run through the square, north and south, on the line between lots 2, and 3, thus dividing it into two equal parts.

In November, 1835, there was a subdivision made of lots three and four, dividing the same into five lots, three fronting on Broad Street and two on Race Street, which lots from said subdivision were sold by the county as follows: Lot 1, July 30, 1837, to David Macy for $50; lot 2, October 5, 1837, to George B. Rogers and Alexander Michaels for $50; lot 3, October 25, 1837, to Jehu T. Elliott for $81; lot 4, November 1, 1837, to Ezekiel T. Hickman for $100; lot 5, November 1, 1837, to John Taylor for $117; total for five lots $398. This property underwent many trasfers and when the time came for the county to use the entire present Court House Square for county purposes, the west half of the square was occupied by residences of all the parties below named except in the case of Jacob Mowrer who had a residence and grocery store combined, fronting on Broad Street opposite the site of the present Ward Block.

The county bought the property of the respective owners, allowing them to remove the buildings, as follows: Jacob Mowrer, $1,500; Jacob Byer, $1,000; Helen E. Thornburgh, wife of Alfred M. Thornburgh, $400; Harmon H. Allen, $600; total, $3,500, thus showing a difference of $3,102 between what the county sold the property for in 1837 and what it purchased it back for, less than thirty years after.

THE FIRST JAIL.

At the February term, 1823, the commissioners also ordered the sale of "the jail of Henry County," which, they specify, shall be

"Of the dimensions fourteen feet square, seven feet between the floors, the logs to be square ten inches, to be dovetailed at each corner and pinned; upper and lower floor to consist of logs squared of the same dimensions, the upper floor each log to be pinned down with one inch and one-half auger, one round of logs above the upper floor fit down, the door to be three feet wide, the shutter to be made of two-inch oak plank doubled, and be well spiked and hung with good and sufficient hinges to open outside with a good and sufficient bar with staples and lock, a cabin roof, the lower floor to be laid on two oak sills, and the house to be built on the top thereof, one window one foot square with four-inch square bars of iron to be sufficiently let in."

This was a very imposing structure to a man outside, but once shut in, say in July or August, especially if there were several of the "four inch square" iron bars across the one window (a foot square), all efforts to escape must have soon become quite feeble. The reader of these specifications (which were doubtless clear enough to the commissioners,) may be a little puzzled to determine whether "the house to be built on the top thereof" was to be placed on the lower floor, or whether the house was to have a second story intended for a jailer's residence or some such purpose. It was subsequently ordered that the jail should be completed before the second Monday in August, and that the clerk should issue a county order to the builder for twenty dollars so soon as the building should be "erected to the height of four rounds." Obediah R. Weaver, being the lowest bidder, undertook "the faithful performance" of the contract for $120.

Although this building was to have been completed in August, 1823, it is found that, in May, 1824, the board refused to receive it, "inasmuch as it considered that the same had not been executed according to contract." The building was subsequently received of Mr. Weaver, and forty five dollars paid in full for the work; twenty dollars having been previously advanced, when the structure was but "four rounds high." This jail was soon found to be inadequate, and the growing wants of the times induced the commissioners to order the "selling" of

THE SECOND JAIL.

which was also to be built of timber. It was really to be an extension of the old one, the door of which was to be taken away and the space filled with logs. The addition was to be built adjoining the old part, leaving only eight inches between, which was afterward to be filled with timber. The new part was to have one window like the old one, one foot square, and when carried up to the height of the old one, a second story was to be built on, of logs, extending over both, and to be entered from one end by a "strong stairway," and the only entrance to the lower story was to be through a strong trap door, two feet square, "to be made secure with a strong bar of iron and good and sufficient lock, &c. Once let down into one of these "black holes," the most hardened desperado could dismiss all fears of "the dogs biting him" so long as his incarceration continued. On the 7th of January, 1830, Moses Brown, undertook the reconstruction of said jail, for the sum of $97.50, which was certainly cheap enough even in those days.

The rule that all things earthly must pass away seems to have made no exceptions in favor of Henry County jails. In less than five years from the completion of the second jail or "goal," the commissioners ordered a third to be advertised and erected. This time the external walls were to be of brick. The foundation was to be set in the ground two feet, and to be twenty eight inches in thickness. Above, the wall was to be thirteen inches thick, and eighteen feet by twenty five in dimensions, and two stories in height. The floor of the prisons or "dungeons" was to be of good oak timber ten inches thick, and, on top of this a floor of good oak plank one and one half inches thick. Just inside the brick walls and on top of the floor, was to be "built a log wall" of "hewn timber, ten inches square, to be laid down half dovetailed." and seven feet high. And this was to be lined with one and one half inch beech plank, and "cross lined" and well spiked on with "cut spikes, six inches in length" and not to exceed three inches distant. The wooden walls were to be continued so as to make two tiers of dungeons, but the upper ones were not required to be so well lined, or otherwise made so strong. The upper story was, doubtless, intended for the more corrigible class of culprits, while the more hardened sinners were to be "sent below." The dungeons in the lower story were to be ready for occupants by the third Monday of October, and the whole structure, by the first Monday in May, 1836.

"At a sale held at the court house," to "sell the building of the goals," Miles Murphey "bid off the same for $1,100," $500 to be paid January 1, 1836, and the residue in one year. This work was done according to contract, and the structure, with little amendment, stood the racket until about 1850.

The musty records of the board of commissioners showed that the constant bill of expense for guarding prisoners was such that February 11, 1851, they ordered the building of another jail. Elisha Clift appears to have been the architect and Jacob Elliott was selected to purchase materials and superintend it under the immediate orders of the commissioners. It was two stories in height, and thirty six by forty feet, was of brick with a stone floor, the cell wall being of hewn timber and lined with boiler iron and cost about $3,500. This jail stood until torn down to make room for the present court house.

In locating the site of the last jail, it must be considered that before the building of the present court house (without the new addition) the present public square was cut in two by an alley ten feet wide, running through the center of the square, north and south. Only that part of the square east of the alley was occupied for county purposes, the balance, west of the alley, being used for residences, as is shown, in considering the construction of the present court house. This last mentioned jail stood nearly flush with Broad Street, at the northwest corner of the lot, made by the alley and stood about opposite the present Ward Block. The two preceding jails occupied practically the same ground.

THE PRESENT JAIL.

The present county prison is a fine well built structure, in shape, somewhat like a capital letter "T," with the top of the letter representing the front of the building, which is used as the jailor's residence. The building is complete in all its appointments, is two stories in height, with a cellar underneath, containing a furnace, &c., for warming the whole. Externally the building has the appearance of being all brick, with stone window frames secured with heavy iron rods, behind which are heavy plate glass of such a peculiar make that they do not obstruct the light while they tell none the secrets of the interior. Inside the brick wall is a thick stone one, or rather the wall is half stone and half of brick, and just inside the stone is an iron lining of boiler iron. Next comes a corridor about three feet wide, and then an iron grating, made of heavy iron bars through which pass one and one eighth inch rods of iron. This arrangement extends through both stories. Inside of this formidable grating, is another passage way or corridor entirely surrounding the cells, or strong boxes, which are made of heavy iron grating and boiler iron.

The first floor is of massive stone slabs, about fifteen inches in thickness, and the second floor is of iron. There are eighteen cells in the building, not likely to be all filled at one time.

The structure was built with an eve to the safety of its inmates, and, notwithstanding a mishap or two has occurred, it is not easy to see how a safer trap can reasonably be constructed, and it is the opinion of good judges that, with reasonable care on the part of the keeper to ward off outside influence, the most expert jail-bird could be kept till doomsday.

The cost of the building was about $40,000. Robert Cluggish, most efficiently superintended its erection.

THE PRESENT JAIL SITE.

The present jail site and grounds occupy lot one and the east half of lot two in block five of the original plat of New Castle. The west half of lot two and all of lot three, thus comprising all the lots in block five, is occupied by what is known as the Jacob Brenneman residence. This block is bounded on the east by Twelfth Street, on the north by Vine Street, on the west by Eleventh Street, and on the south by a continuation of Livery Alley. The county was the original owner of this property. Through its agent, Ezekiel Leavell, on May 8, 1834, it sold lots one and three to Samuel Hawn for five dollars. The center lot, number two, was considered so valueless that the county abandoned the same and accordingly on August 25, 1834, it was sold for taxes by Wesley Goodwin, collector of taxes for Henry County, to the said Samuel Hawn for thirty three cents. Thus the county derived a total revenue of $5.33 from the entire block.

That part of the block occupied by the Brenneman residence has changed hands but few times since Hawn bought it, and as far back as the author of this History can remember, more than fifty years, it was in the possession of Jacob Brenneman and is now owned by his heirs.

The east half of the block underwent many transfers and when the time came for the county to buy it for the purpose for which it is now used, it was owned and occupied by Thomas C. Jordan, now and for half a century, past, a resident of New Castle, the county paying him therefor, on March 11, 1868, $1,200. The frame house on this lot was of no particular value to the county and was immediately torn down to make way for the jail. Thus, what the county sold in 1834 for $2.66½ (one half the price of the block) it bought back, thirty four years later at an advance of $1,197.33⅓.

STRAY PEN.

A stray pen or pound, in early days, was considered an indispensable appurtenance of every "well regulated" county. Stock was much more given to straying, no doubt, in early times than at the present. The love of home, or faculty of inhabitiveness, was probably not so well developed then as now, while the powers of locomotion were generally much better, especially with the porkers. The time and money lost in looking up lost stock in this or any other new county, seventy-five years ago, notwithstanding the comparatively small amount kept, was much larger than at present, and, doubtless, led the assembled wisdom of our general assemblies to give it more careful thought than they now apparently devote to some of the great question of the hour.

By an act of the General Assembly, 1824, it was made the duty of the "commissioners in each and every county in the State to cause a pound to be erected at or near the court houses, with a good and sufficient fence, gate, lock, and key, where all stray horses, mules and asses, above two years old, taken up within twenty miles of the court house, shall be kept on the first day of every circuit court, for three succeeding terms, after the same shall be taken up, from eleven until three o'clock in each day, that the owner may have the opportunity of claiming his, her, or their property, and any person having taken up such property, and living more than twenty miles from the court house, shall not be compelled to exhibit it more than once.

In obedience to some such act as this, the Henry County Commissioners ordered to be "sold" the

"Erecting of a pound, commonly called a stray pen, the said pen to be erected in the southwest corner of the public square, the said pen is to be forty feet square, to be erected at least five feet high, and of good and durable timber commonly called a post and rail fence, with a gate and lock to the same."

Minor Fox undertook this great "public enterprise" for the sum of $12.50 and 'gave bond with sureties approved of by the commissioners of Henry County," and faithfully performed the labor within four months in so satisfactory a manner that the commissioners accepted it, and made him the first pound-keeper.

The stray pen or pound was located on the public square, immediately in the rear and south of the jail site which locates it in the center of the present public square, the south end extending to Race Street. The "gate and lock to the same" was on the corner of the alley, near the Race Street side of the pound.

COUNTY ASYLUM.

The buildings and belongings of the establishment where the county's poor are cared for ought to be a matter of more interest to the people of Henry than is generally manifested. Caring for those unfortunate persons who have from any cause, become unable to care for themselves, has been accepted by the county commissioners as a duty, ever since the meeting of the first board, in 1822, and, although the arrangement for the comfort of paupers may have seemed parsimonious at times, surrounding circumstances must be taken into account. It would never do to make the fare, comforts, and general attractiveness of the asylum such that able-bodied, but lazy, shiftless, persons, of whom there are a few in every community, would seek for a residence at the county home, and besides the item, "on account of poor," has ever been a large one in the "budget" of Henry County, and it is largely on the increase.

On March 8, 1839, Commissioners Shawhan, Corwine and Ball, purchased of William Silver a farm of one hundred and sixty acres, about one mile northwest of New Castle, for the sum of $2,000. In May following, a contract was made with John D. Fooshee for keeping the paupers as well as the building of a "poor house," and it was also ordered that "all persons who are now, or may hereafter become, a county charge, shall be removed, as the law directs, to the poor house provided for that purpose."

Just what sort of a house this was to be (probably built of logs) or the price paid to the man who bought it the records do not show, but, on the 4th of January, 1844, a special session of the board was called to receive sealed proposals for the building of another house, which was to be of brick with a cellar under one wing, fourteen by thirty feet. The size of said building is not specified, but it was to have a porch on three sides of the same, with fourteen posts and banisters between from which it may be inferred that it was of considerable size. The brick were to be burned on the place, and all the sills, sleepers, posts, and plates were to be got off the farm. The brick work was to be painted red and penciled with white, and the porch painted drab. John Shroyer, Miles Murphey, and Dr. Joel Reed were appointed to superintend the building of the said house. John H. Polsley undertook the work for $1,100, and was allowed, for extra work, the sum of twenty dollars. The superintendents each received twenty dollars for their services.

This building was burned down and the paupers rendered homeless, May 9, 1855, when the commissioners promptly ordered the building of another and more commodious structure at an expense of about $7,000 which is the present county asylum, since considerably remodeled and enlarged.

Mark Modlin was the superintendent of the county asylum at the time of its destruction by fire. He then moved onto his farm, three and one half miles west of New Castle, the same farm being now occupied by his son, Alcander Modlin, and here under contract with the county commissioners, he kept the county paupers until March, 1860, when the new building was ready for occupancy, and when the unfortunates were brought in and given into the care of the new superintendent, Alvis Haguewood.

For two or three years after the asylum was established, the contract was made with Fooshee to care for the paupers that might, from time to time, be sent to him at the rate of $1.25 per head per week, with some little extra allowance in "extreme cases," he paying $150 for the rent of the farm.

In 1841 the commissioners resolved to turn over a new leaf, and so they let the contract to "board, clothe and feed" all paupers, and "to treat them in a humane manner, and especially to attend to the moral instruction of said paupers," to Samuel Hoover and Mark Modlin, for three years from March 1, 1842, at one dollar per capita per week, they paying $125 for rent of the farm. At the end of this time, they called for "sealed proposals" for keeping the paupers, raising the rent of the farm to $150. The position had come to be looked upon as being so desirable that there was strife over it and Mr. Fooshee instituted an unsuccessful suit to secure possession of it, after the contract was awarded to other parties for three years. In 1844, he was a successful applicant, giving twenty five dollars more than had been previously paid for the use of the farm, and agreeing to take, "board, clothe, feed, and lodge," and morally instruct all paupers, for sixty two and one half cents per head per week, and bring in no other charge whatever. This was quite a coming down, but, after he had given bond to the satisfaction of the board, he seems to have "flew the track," and Mark Modlin was awarded the prize at seventy five cents per head per week, for one year.

Afterward the rent of the farm was reduced to $100 per year, and seventy five cents per week was allowed for keeping the paupers, and to "board, clothe, feed, humanely treat, and morally instruct," &c., which was cheap as dirt.

It is pleasant to know that our late commissioners have turned over still another leaf, and do not let that important charge on the sole condition of economy, and yet there is no loud complaint on this score.

The farm has been enlarged to about three hundred acres, much of the later purchases being first class bottom land. John W. Bell is the present superintendent, having under his charge now, about fifty persons nearly equally divided in sex. The annual average cost for maintenance for each inmate is estimated by Superintendent Bell to be about forty dollars. The value of the land without improvements, is stated by the same authority to be $60 per acre and that the value of the improvements is $12,000, thus making the value of the farm at the rate of one hundred dollars per acre. However, in the opinion of the author of this History, Superintendent Bell's value of the land is entirely too low. The author thinks the land alone, without the buildings is worth $100 per acre. Value of personal property of all kinds is $4,000. The buildings are heated by steam, the county owning and operating its own plant. Mrs. Mary E. Bell, wife of the superintendent, is the matron of the asylum. The annual salaries paid at the present time, are: superintendent, $500; matron, $130, the county paying for the services of extra hands when needed.

SUPERINTENDENTS OF COUNTY ASYLUM.

The following is approximately a correct list of the superintendents of the county asylum and the time for which they served respectively: John D. Fooshee, 1839 to March, 1842; Samuel Hoover and Mark Modlin, March, 1842, to September, 1842; Mark Modlin, September, 1842, to May, 1853; Jacob Batdorf, May, 1853, (short time); Anthony Livezey, 1853 to 1855; Mark Modlin, 1855 to March, 1860; Alvis Haguewood, March, 1860, to March, 1867; Joel R. Hutson, March, 1867, to March, 1869; Mahlon D. Harvey, March, 1869, to March, 1878; Daniel Harvey, March, 1878, to September, 1880; John W. Bell, September, 1880, to September, 1885; Daniel Harvey, September, 1885, to September, 1893; Mahlon D. Harvey, September, 1893, to September, 1897; Joel R. Frazier, September, 1897, to September, 1899; John W. Bell, September, 1899, present incumbent.

William Silver, who sold the first land purchased by the county for the county asylum farm, was a pioneer merchant of New Castle, and Judge Martin L. Bundy, being requested to give his personal recollection of Mr. Silver, says:

"William Silver came to New Castle in 1830 from Warren County, Ohio, and opened a dry goods store. He was then a young married man. He subsequently purchased the lot on which now stands the Shroyer Building and he built thereon a frame building for a store room and residence and continued his business until 1838, when he removed to Pendleton. The carpenter who did the work was Dr. James V. Wayman, then a young man.

"At the time Silver came, Judge Jehu T. Elliott and Miles Murphey were young men and both applicants for a clerkship in his store. Silver chose Murphey because he had $160 which he could lend him and Elliott had no money. This circumstance made Murphey a merchant and Elliott a lawyer in life time business.

"Silver owned and sold to the county, the present poor farm or asylum. Prior to this, paupers were auctioned to the person who would take them for the least price."

THE FIRST ORPHAN'S HOME AT SPICELAND.

Miss Susan Fussell, of Chester County, Pennsylvania, in March, 1877, visited a county home conducted by a family named Johnson at Danville, Indiana, for the care of the county children of Hendricks County, and having under her charge certain soldiers' orphan children, was impressed with the plan employed in Hendricks County. In April of the same year she moved to Spiceland, Henry County, with five of the soldiers' orphan children, these alone remaining of the ten children of whom she had assumed charge in 1865, after the war. The plan for a home similar to that in Hendricks County was formed in her mind.

"In September, 1877, she applied to the county commissioners of Henry county, Cyrus Van Matre, William D. Cooper and Ithamer W. Stuart, for the children then in the county asylum, offering for the sum of twenty five cents per day per child, to feed, clothe, nurse, and educate them, until suitable homes could be found for them.

"The proposition was kept before the commissioners at every session of their court for almost three years before they acceded to it, and then it was accepted on condition that Miss Fussell receive twenty three cents instead of twenty five cents per day for each child.

"So thoroughly convinced was she of the practicability and excellence of the plan, and of the great need of something being done to give these children a chance for an independent and honorable life that she consented to the terms, March, 1880, rented a suitable house at her own expense and at the same time contributed $500 to the institution which was never repaid to her, and received into the home on June 8, 1880, the nine children sent her from the Henry County Asylum."

It was largely due to the efforts of Miss Fussell and others interested in the work that the General Assembly, April 7, 1881, passed a law authorizing the county commissioners in each county to appoint as matron, a woman of good moral character, and judgment, and suitable age, having experience in the care and training of children and to put in her care, at some suitable and convenient place not connected with the county asylum, all pauper children of sound mind between the ages of one and sixteen years. The matron was to be paid not less than twenty five and not more than thirty cents daily for each inmate. Accordingly, after the passage of this law, the commissioners paid Miss Fussell twenty five cents daily per child instead of twenty three cents.

The law made it the duty of the commissioners to appoint a "committee of three competent persons * * * to examine into the condition of the home and the manner in which the children therein are kept and treated by the matron * * * at least once every three months and report to the board the result of their examination. L

The commissioners, June 1882, appointed Mrs. Martha A. White, of Spiceland; Mrs. William M. Ewing, of Knightstown, and Mrs. Sarah A. R. Boor, of New Castle, to serve on this committee, the duties of which in a more limited sphere, were very similar to those of the present county board of charities. Later, Mrs. Ewing, removing to Kansas, Mrs. Maggie Watson, of Dunreith, was appointed to fill her place. When, April 1, 1887, Miss Fussell having become incapaciated through illness and age to act as matron and carry on the heavy duties involved, Mrs. Watson gave up her place as a member of the committee to permit the appointment of Miss Fussell, who lived near the home and was so familiar with the work. Miss Fussell served faithfully as did the other two ladies, until her death, July 19, 1889, when her sister, Ada Fussell, succeeded her. The committee as constituted, continued its service unbrokenly as long as the Spiceland Home was maintained.

After the plan was arranged with Miss Fussell in 1880, the county leased the property in Spiceland where the home was kept during its existence. A year later, June 24, 1881, the property was purchased of Edmund and James White for $2,500. It was rented to Miss Fussell at $144 annually for the house and $25 for the ground which consisted of about seven acres. The house and buildings were continually enlarged and improved. The grounds were beautified with flower beds and walks and with fruit trees and garden. Much of the expense of this was borne by Miss Fussell who frequently contributed from her private purse to the success of her plan and to the welfare of the children. The property acquired by the commissioners, with improvements, grew in value to $4,200. Prior to 1885, the rate per child was raised to thirty cents daily and was so maintained.

Miss Fussell was greatly assisted in her work by her sister, Miss Ada Fussell, who served without compensation and greatly improved the education of the children by her kindergarten work. They were taught useful facts and methods of house work and various out door employments. Instructors were provided for them. The care and attention were of the best.

Under the supervision of the founder and her sister, the home continued to flourish. About ninety children had been cared for and at least two thirds of them had found good homes in the county, up to the year 1887. In this year, in April, failing health made necessary the resignation of Miss Fussell as matron. Miss Martha E. Hadley was appointed to the position and filled the same faithfully and efficiently during the continued existence of the home.

On October 31, 1893, a contract was made by the commissioners, with Julia E. Work, superintendent of the Northern Indiana Orphans' Home at Laporte, Indiana, to deliver to her from the Spiceland Home, twenty two children who were to be cared for by her and placed in private homes, she to receive $35 for each child when placed in a private home. This contract annulled a similar one previously made on September 28, 1893, with the Children's Home Society of Indianapolis, the latter having been for $50 per child instead of $35.

There had been considerable agitation concerning the expense attached to the care of the children and there was a dissension among the commissioners and inter-

ested county officers regarding the advisability of maintaining the County Orphan's Home at Spiceland. The money side prevailed; the conveniences resulting
from years of hard and patient work were overlooked; the congenial surroundings
which made the children, happy and content, completely lost their value. It was
decided that it would be cheaper for the county to enter into the contract with
Mrs. Work.

On December 5, 1893, the commissioners contracted with the German Baptist Home at Honey Creek to care for the dependent children of the county, not then
transferred to Mrs. Work's Home, at the rate of "five children at forty cents each,
daily, ten children at thirty five cents each, daily, fifteen children at thirty cents
each, daily, or forty children at twenty five cents each, daily" that institution to be
free from taxation while acting as servant of the county. This contract removed
the few remaining children from Spiceland and gave the finishing blow to the
Home at that place, which had been in existence for more than thirteen years.

The home at Spiceland was sold for a greatly reduced sum in consideration of
the improvements made on it and the advantages it offered. The work of a noble
woman was brought to naught. Miss Fussell had died before the creation for
which she had labored so unsparingly, was wrecked. She was thus spared the pain
of seeing her life work destroyed. The Home, which had promised so much for
the children and for the county, was no more.

The author of this History acknowledges himself indebted to that noble,
charitable woman, a former member of the committee for the Spiceland Orphans'
Home, Mrs. Sarah A. R. Boor, for the information contained in this article.

AGED PERSON'S HOME AND ORPHAN ASYLUM FOR THE GERMAN BAPTIST CHURCH
OF THE SOUTHERN DISTRICT OF INDIANA.

The beginning of organized effort for the care of aged members and orphan
children of the German Baptist Congregation in the Southern District of Indiana
began to be discussed as early as 1881, and the work began to take form about
that date, by the circulation of subscription papers in the several congregations of
the district and the soliciting of means to secure a site, and funds for building.
In 1883, an amount of sufficient importance had been secured to permit of organization which was effected at a meeting held at Beech Grove in the northern part of
Henry County in 1883. Five trustees were selected into whose hands was placed
the power of taking out articles of association. The names of the first board of
trustees with the length of time for which they were chosen, were as follows:
Jacob W. Yost, five years; James M. Wyatt, four years; John Hart, three years;
John L. Krall, two years; Joseph D. Neher, one year.

On March 1, 1883, Jacob W. Yost, James M. Wyatt, and John L. Krall met
Jacob P. Miller, on the farm near Honey Creek, Henry County, Indiana, where the
home now stands, and completed negotiations for its purchase by which they were
to secure one hundred and forty acres of land for the sum of seven thousand dollars, four thousand of which was paid in cash, Jacob P. Miller, donating one
thousand dollars of this amount.

Articles of association, drawn by Frank W. Fitzhugh, a lawyer of New Castle, were entered into on July 31, 1883, and transcribed into a book which is in pos-

session of the secretary. The corporate seal as set out in article eight of the above mentioned articles of association was designed by David W. Kinsey and others. The legend "Pro Deo, Ecclesia et Re Publica" (For God, The Church and the State) is understood to have been contributed by Adolph Rogers, of New Castle.

The names subscribed to the articles of association are John Hart, of Beechy Mire, Union County, Indiana; Jacob W. Yost, Sulphur Springs, Henry County, Indiana, and James M. Wyatt, Hagerstown, Wayne County, Indiana. In December of the same year in a district meeting held near the home in the Upper Fall Creek Church, David F. Hoover was selected as one of the trustees instead of Joseph D. Neher, deceased.

In 1886, the first building was erected by Waltz and Thornburgh, of Hagerstown, Indiana, at a cost of $3,000. It did its duty well but was considered insufficient for the growing work and in 1901, a second building was erected, Isaac H. Miller, of Middletown, being the architect, which cost about $2,500, and is fitted out for the aged people and is called "The Home," while the old building is called "The Orphanage."

The first superintendent employed by the trustees was John S. McCarty, of Clarksville, Indiana. He remained at the head of the institution for six years, and was succeeded by John Brunk, of Middletown, Indiana, who held the position for five years. Calvin Hooke succeeded John Brunk but gave over the work to his successor at the end of one year. A. C. Snowberger took charge of the work in September, 1898 and continued for four years, when the present superintendent, Moses Smelzer, of Noblesville, took charge.

The first inmate was Jane Orr, of Ladoga, Montgomery County, Indiana, who entered the home, December 30, 1886, and remained there nearly twelve years. Since she entered many have come and gone for whom the final step of life has been made pleasant and happy in this excellent home. Many poor children have been provided with good homes through the agency of this institution, and twice, the county of Henry has contracted with this home to care for its dependent children.

In 1899, the General Assembly passed a law forbidding the detention of dependents between the ages of three and seventeen years for more than ten days in the County Poor Asylum. In 1901, this was amended, increasing the length of time to sixty days.

The first contract made by the Henry County Commissioners with the German Baptist Home to care for its children was made December 5, 1893, as heretofore stated. On April 10, 1901, the second contract was made by the commissioners with the German Baptist Home to care for its dependent children at the rate of twenty five cents per day for each child. This contract continued in force until May 1, 1905, when the Bundy Home at Spiceland, was opened. Part of the children at the Baptist Home and a few still remaining at Plymouth were taken to Spiceland and owing to the greater convenience of the Spiceland Home, the commissioners decided to send all future dependents of proper age to that place.

Following the abandonment of the first County Orphan's Home which had been maintained at Spiceland since 1880, the children dependent on the county were in part taken to a home then superintended by Julia E. Work at Laporte, Indiana, who subsequently removed to Plymouth, Marshall County, Indiana, and has since maintained there the well known Plymouth Home which has grown to such large size. Until April 10, 1901, children continued to be sent to the home of Mrs. Work but the inconvenience of taking children such a distance and the expense attached to the trip decided the board to send all county children to the Baptist institution. Still another advantage sought by the commissioners in making the change to the Baptist establishment was to give the children the benefit of a more individual attention than could be accorded them in the Plymouth Home which had grown very large. The Baptist home not only offered its cleanliness and well kept apartments as an inducement, but in addition, it could give the children more of the home life than could be given them in the larger place where so much routine and system is necessary.

Thus for years the German Baptist Home has been very closely associated with the other benevolent institutions of the county. Many homeless children have found here a good residence or through this institution, have been taken into good homes. Its care has always been of the best and the conditions surrounding the home are very pleasant.

The author of this History acknowledges himself indebted to the Reverend David F. Hoover for the information contained in this article. In the opinion of the author, it is owing to the attention and care that David F. Hoover has devoted to this home that it has reached its present high degree of excellence and has accomplished so much good.

THE BUNDY HOME AT SPICELAND.

On May 1, 1905, for the second time, an institution for the care of orphan and homeless children was opened at Spiceland. The "Children's Home" as it is known, was the result of a joint conference of the commissioners of the counties of Henry and Rush. The joint meeting of the commissioners came after a proposition made by Mrs. Ella Bundy, formerly in charge of the home at Rushville, to establish a home for the dependent children of the two counties. Spiceland was selected by the commissioners as the most desirable location for such a home, on account of its convenient location and the many advantages offered there for the care of children.

Acting largely on the advice of the commissioners of the two counties, Mrs. Bundy purchased the Kersey K. Kirk home in the west part of Spiceland, adjoining the academy on the western boundary. It is a fine piece of land particularly adapted for its present use. It contains six acres and has a large house, barn, and other buildings. The property was purchased for $4,000 and Mrs. Bundy has since greatly improved and added to it, at an additional expense of $1,200. Large dormitories have been arranged for the boys and for the girls. Play rooms and other conveniences for the children have been fitted up. The house now contains fourteen rooms.

The commissioners of the counties of Henry and Rush entered into a three year's contract with Mrs. Bundy, after the purchase of the land, to care for all county children between the ages of two and seventeen at the rate of twenty five cents per day, per child, and for all children under that age at the rate of $3.00 per week. For this price, Mrs. Bundy feeds, clothes, educates and otherwise exercises maternal care over the children, doctoring them when ill, at her own expense, save in case of contagious disease.

The place was bought on March 2, 1905, and was opened for the reception of the children on May 1st. At present there are twenty five children under the care of Mrs. Bundy. Seventeen of these are boys and eight are girls. Twelve of the children are from Henry County and thirteen are from Rush. They range in age from nine months to fifteen years.

Practically the entire ground surrounding the house, with the exception of nearly an acre, which is in grass and is used for a play ground, is under cultivation. Mrs. Bundy raises a great variety of fruits and vegetables and interests the children in the cultivation so that they all have some little task to do each day and not only keep out of mischief but are benefited by the knowledge they gain. The children are also taught in a general way, the work of caring for the house, so that in a short time they acquire a knowledge of practical things which will always be of use to them. The children are kept clean and are apparently happy. Their food is of the best and their dining quarters are light, airy and very clean. Their dormitories and beds are extremely neat and as comfortable as the most fastidious could desire.

Only one inconvenience is now noticeable in the home, this being the ease with which parents from either county may come to see their children. The tendency of such visits is to make the children homesick and dissatisfied. Parents, in some cases too, are inclined to have their children cared for at the expense of the county, if they can see them frequently, whereas if the visit was not so convenient, they would care for them themselves. This difficulty will be overcome soon, however, by the strict enforcement of a ruling limiting the number and frequency of the visits of the parents.

COUNTY BOARD OF CHARITIES AND CORRECTIONS.

The following, from section one of an act passed in 1899, by the General Assembly of the State of Indiana, for the purpose of providing "Boards of County Charities and Corrections," resulted in the appointment, June 19, 1902, of such a board in the county of Henry, by Judge William O. Barnard, then presiding.

"Be it enacted .... that in each county of the State the judge of the circuit court may, and upon the petition of fifteen reputable citizens, shall appoint six persons not more than three of whom shall be of the same political party or belief, and not more than four of whom shall be men, who shall constitute a Board of County Charities and Corrections, to serve without compensation, two of whom, as indicated by the judge of the circuit court, shall serve for one (1) year, two for two (2) years, and two for three (3) years, and upon the resignation or expiration of the term of each, his or her successor shall in like manner be appointed for the term of three (3) years."

The members of this board as constituted by Judge Barnard were John H. Hewitt living east of New Castle, Benjamin S. Parker, and Mrs. Julia A. Loer of New Castle, Mrs. Anna D. Welsh of Middletown, William S. Moffat of Kennard, and Mrs. Richard Wagoner of Knightstown. Mr. Parker and Mrs. Loer served the full three years. Mr. Hewitt and Mrs. Wagoner were appointed for the two-year term. Mr. Moffat and Mrs. Welsh were assigned to the short term, one year. Up to the present time, all members of the board have been re-appointed at the expiration of their respective terms by Judge Barnard's successor, Judge John M. Morris.

The law providing for the creation of the board, directs that a chairman and secretary shall be elected at the first meeting of the board which shall be "within one week after receiving the notice of appointment." At the present time and since the board was organized, the officers have been John H. Hewitt, Chairman, and Mrs. Anna D. Welsh, Secretary.

This board acts as "the eyes and ears of the county." It has no executive power. Its duties consist in visiting the various lockups, county poor asylum, orphan's home, jail, 'and any other charitable or correctional institutions, receiving support from public funds, that may exist in the county .... at least once each quarter," and reporting to the county commissioners once each quarter the results of such visits and investigations. Similar reports are transmitted to the state board of charities which at all times acts as an advisory board and in some measure directs the work and actions of the county board.

The chief benefit of the board is in the publicity it is empowered and authorized to give to the methods used in conducting the county benevolent institutions, and to the condition in which it finds them. It acts as an advisor to the county commissioners and at all times may report to the commissioners such plans for improvement or remedy as it deems advisable. It tends to act as a check on carelessness or mis-management on the part of county officers having charge of these institutions.

The law provides that "the county council in each county shall appropriate and the board of county commissioners shall allow, not to exceed fifty dollars ($50) each year for the actual expenses of said Board of County Charities and Corrections." The economy of the Henry County board is apparent from the fact that the entire expense of the board for the term of its existence has not yet exceeded twenty dollars. The amount is trifling when compared with the possibilities for good which exist in this board.

CHAPTER XL.

The act of the General Assembly organizing the county of Henry provided that the "Circuit Court and all other courts shall meet and be holden at the house of Joseph Hobson, until suitable accommodation can ·be had at the county seat." The same act, however, provided that the Circuit Court might, if in its wisdom it deemed it advisable, remove to some more suitable place.

COMMISSIONERS' COURT.

In accordance with these provisions, the Commissioners' Court assembled "at the house of Joseph Hobson" on June 10, 1822, and we find the following as the first record of an official character ever made in the county of Henry:

"June Term for the year 1822.

"At a meeting of the Board of County Commissioners, in and for the County of Henry, State of Indiana, on Monday, the 10th day of June, A. D. 1822, present Allen Shepherd and Samuel Goble, Esqrs., who produced their respective certificates and were sworn into office by Jesse Healey, Esq., Sheriff of the county aforesaid, as is required by the Constitution and laws of this State."

As the Commissioners meant business, their first act, after taking the oath of office, was the appointment of Rene Julian, Clerk of the Board, he being the Clerk of the Circuit Court elect, and the second order reads:

"Ordered by the Board, that the Court adjourn until to-morrow morning at ten o'clock.   (Signed),

"ALLEN SHEPHERD,
"SAMUEL GOBLE."

Elisha Shortridge, who was doubtless elected at the same time as Shepherd and Goble, did not put in an appearance until the July term, when he "appeared and presented his credentials in due form," and now Goble was absent, from some cause not mentioned. From time to time the record shows that the Board met "at the house of Joseph Hobson" until the May term, 1823, following, when it met at the house of Charles Jamison, in New Castle. Of Charles Jamison, Judge Martin L. Bundy furnishes the only information obtainable which is as follows:

"The house of Charles Jamison was a double cabin, built of round logs, which stood flush with the south side of what is now Church Street, about half way between Main and Twelfth streets, which locates it in rear of the Nixon residence, and diagonally southeast, and across the street from the Presbyterian Church. I do not remember when it disappeared. It was probably built in 1820 and was the first house ever built on the town site of New Castle. It was a most convenient place for the transaction of the business of the new county of Henry, because there was no other house in New Castle.

"Charles Jamison was a small man physically, and was about the size of the late Andrew Nicholson. I do not know from what State he emigrated, probably, however from Tennessee, which was the State from which his son-in-law, Isaac Bedsaul, came. I do not remember his wife, but her daughter, Polly Bedsaul, who died of cholera in 1833, I remember very well, she being so kind to me when I was a small boy. I do not think Charles Jamison had any sons. He died, I think, at the house of Henry Courtney, two miles southeast of New Castle, about 1836. I do not know that he had any regular occupation, and he was rather too old to work when I knew him."

The Board met in June, July, August, and November, 1823, and yet the records of their doings fill but eighteen small pages, while the proceedings of three terms are crowded into eight pages, each one of which was about twice as large as this page. The adopted court house was a "second-hand cabin," which had been moved up from the bottom, west of town, and was, perhaps, twelve by sixteen or sixteen by eighteen feet square, and without chinking or daubing.

The second day of the first term seems to have been a busy day, as William Shannon, Dilwin Bales, and Abraham Heaton were appointed superintendents of several school sections. Shannon was also made Treasurer and John Dorrah was appointed Lister of the county. A poll tax of twenty five cents was levied for county purposes, and Dudley, Wayne, Henry and Prairie townships were created, and elections were ordered to be held in each. Inspectors were appointed for each, after which the Board adjourned "until the first Monday in July next" (1823).

The act of the General Assembly organizing the county provided for the appointment of an agent for the county, who was to receive donations of grounds made for the purpose of a county seat, buildings, etc. The July term was called for the purpose of appointing such agent, and "the lot fell upon" Ezekiel Leavell, of whom biographical mention is made in connection with the location of New Castle. He was duly charged with the duty of superintending the sale of town lots in the New Castle that was to be, the making of deeds, and, in addition, when a court house, a jail, or a stray pen was to be constructed, the Agent was ordered to "offer for sale to the lowest bidder, in the town of New Castle, the building of the court house of Henry County," or the erecting of a "pound, commonly called a stray pen," or the "jail of Henry County," as the case might be.

The Commissioners' Court was a very important institution in early times. Treasurers, Collectors, Listers, Constables, Pound-keepers, Supervisors, Road-viewers, County Agents, Township Agents, Superintendents of school sections (section sixteen of every Congressional township was set aside for school purposes, and the proceeds of the subsequent sale of these sections, is the foundation of our present common school fund), County Commissioners, County Surveyors, Inspectors, etc., were all the creatures of this body. It not only was the keeper of the public funds, levied or remitted the taxes, made the allowances of the other officers, but granted permits to "keep tavern," "keep store," "keep grocery," or "peddle clocks," and with equal facility fixed the price of "liquors, lodgings, horse feed, and stabling." The early commissioner seemed equally at home, whether allowing the treasurer fifteen dollars for his annual services, or regulating the cost of a half pint of whisky, quart of cider or "gallon of oats or corn."

BOARD OF JUSTICES.

On January 31, 1824, the General Assembly enacted that the Justices of the Peace for the several counties should constitute a "Board of Justices" for the transaction of "county business," with all the powers and duties heretofore exercised by the commissioners. It was made the duty of "each and every justice in the several townships to meet" at the seat of Justice on the first Monday in September following, "and then and there to organize themselves into a County Board of Justices, by electing one of their body President," &c., "and to meet on the first Monday of January, March, May, July, September, and November, in each and every year," at such time, unless the circuit court happened to be in session on that day, in which case they were to meet on the Monday after its adjournment. Any three of these justices were competent to transact business, except at the May and November terms, when it should require at least five members, and a less number than a quorum could meet from day to day and compel the attendance of others.

It was made the duty of the justices "to be punctual in their attendance at their January, May, and November sessions, and for every failure thereof, without a reasonable excuse, 'such justice might be indicted or fined not to exceed twenty dollars."

The Clerk of the Circuit Court was required to attend on the sittings of the Board and write up its proceedings. The attendance of the Sheriff, in person or by deputy, was required, and it was made the duty of such officer to execute the decrees of said board.

On January 26, 1827, the Board of Justices was abolished, and the Board of Commissioners revived in the county of Henry and nine other counties lying in the central part of the State. This new arrangement took effect on the first day of August of the same year. The Board of County Commissioners, has, ever since, continued to exist.

CIRCUIT COURT.

The first term of the Circuit Court was held September 30, 1822, by Thomas R. Stanford and Elisha Long, Esqrs., Associate Justices, Miles Eggleston, Presiding Judge of the Circuit Court, not being present. The court assembled, as the law directed, at the house of Joseph Hobson, but availed itself of the privilege of securing better quarters at once, by adopting Charles Jamison's log cabin as the court house, as the following extract from the first record will show:

"At a Henry County Circuit Court, begun at the house of Joseph Hobson, agreeable to an act of the Legislature of the State of Indiana, passed on the 31st day of December, in the year of our Lord, one thousand eight hundred and twenty-one, and adjourned to the house of Charles Jamison, in the county aforesaid, on Monday, the 30th day of September, in the year of our Lord, one thousand eight hundred and twenty-two."

With the exception of the recording of the official bond of Rene Julian, Clerk, on a fly-leaf of the docket, this is the first entry ever made by the Circuit Court of Henry County. After the paragraph above recited is found recorded a copy of the commissions of Judges Stanford and Long, bearing date of July 5, 1822, in which His Excellency Governor Jonathan Jennings sends greetings to all men and "the rest of mankind" that he has commissioned the aforesaid Thomas R. Stanford and the aforesaid Elisha Long, Associate Judges:

"For the county of Henry for and during the term of seven years, and until his successors be appointed and qualified should he so long behave well."

On the back of each commission seems to have been the following endorsement by the Sheriff:

"Be it remembered that, on the 7th day of August A. D. 1822, personally came the within commissioned, Thos. R. Stanford (or Elisha Long), and took the oath against dueling, the oath to support the Constitution of the United States, the oath to support the Constitution of this State, and also the oath of office as an Associate Judge of the Henry Circuit Court. In witness whereof I have hereunto set my hand and seal, this 7th day of August, 1822.   JESSE H. HEALEY, Sheriff of Henry County."

The credentials of the two Judges, of the Sheriff and Clerk being duly disposed of, Jesse H. Healey

"Returned into this court the writ of venire facias heretofore issued out of this court, with the following panel to serve as Grand Jurors, the present term, to-wit: Daniel Heaton, whom the court appoints as foreman, Joseph Watts, Ezekiel Leavell, Absalom Harvey, William Bell, David Baily, John Baker, Jesse Cox, Samuel Dill, John Daugherty, Jacob Parkhurst, Richard Parsons, William Riadon, Dempsey Reece and David Thompson, good and lawful men, and householders of the County of Henry, who, being duly sworn and by the court charged, retired to their room to deliberate."

Of this first Grand Jury consisting of fifteen members there is now no living representative. The room to which they "retired to deliberate" was a convenient log heap hard by. This log heap occupied the ground where is now situated, the Presbyterian Church, distant about one hundred and fifty feet northwest from the house of Charles Jamison. Of this first Grand Jury, William McDowell (Uncle Billy) was the bailiff. He continued as such officer of the Courts of Henry County for a period covering fifty years, when at his own request, he was in 1873, relieved by Judge Joshua H. Mellett, who appointed John Alexander his successor. Lot Bloomfield, producing a license signed by the presiding judge, was permitted to practise in the court, upon taking the necessary oath. He was also made prosecuting attorney for "this and the succeeding term of this court and until a successor be appointed."

The next entry shows that Andrew Shannon so far forgot the dignity and solemnity of the occasion as to "swear two profane oaths in the presence of the court," for which he was promptly fined two dollars, and the clerk ordered to issue an execution for the same.

On the next day the court ordered that the "permanent seal of Henry County shall be engraved on brass, with a vignette of an eagle and stars equal to the number of States in the Union," the size to be about that of a dollar, and around the margin the words, "*Henry Circuit Court.*" An "ink scrawl, with the words Henry County inserted therein," was to be the temporary seal.

On the second day of the term Henry Burkman came into court, and, being duly sworn, declared his intention of becoming a *bona fide* citizen of the United States, and that he "abjures all allegiance to all foreign princes and potentates whatever, and particularly to George IV, King of Great Britain and Ireland, and Prince of Wales."

The Grand Jury then returned into court with the result of their deliberations, which consisted of four bills of indictment for assault and battery, to-wit: One against Solomon Byrket, two against Samuel Batson and one against Peter Smith. Batson then appeared at "the bar of the court" and acknowledged himself guilty as charged in the indictment, and dispensing with a jury, threw himself upon the mercy of the court, "which after due deliberation being had therein," adjudged that he make his fine to the State in the sum of one dollar and stand committed till the same be paid. The judges then allowed themselves four dollars each, and the prosecutor, five dollars, and adjourned till March following; and thus ended the first term of the Circuit Court of Henry County.

At the March term, Bloomfield failed to put in an appearance, and James Gilmore was appointed to prosecute "the pleas of the State."

For this term, the following named grand jurors were selected: William McKimmey, foreman, Solomon Byrket, Abijah Cain, Jacob Elliott, Moses Fink, George Hanby, Daniel Jackson, John K. Nutt, Allen Hunt, Shaphat McCray, William Morris, Thomas Ray and Asahel Woodward, of course all "good and lawful men," although Solomon Byrket was then under indictment for an unlawful act, and was on the same day, brought to the bar of the court, and, to use the quaint language of the record,   ,

"It being forthwith demanded of him how he will acquit himself of the charges set forth in the indictment, for plea says he is not guilty as he stands indicted, and for trial thereof puts himself upon the country, and the said James Gilmore, Prosecutor aforesaid, doth the like; and thereupon came a jury, to-wit: William Shannon, Nathan Pearson, James Rozell, Samuel Batson, Christopher Bundy, Minor Fox, Jacob Richey, Hugh McDaniel, William Row (or Roe), John Blount, Josiah Clawson, and Jacob Witter."

and thus was formed the first traverse jury of Henry County, March 31, 1823, and of the number there is probably not one now alive. William McDowell was also bailiff to this, the first traverse jury that ever sat in Henry County.

Byrket was acquitted, and the court ordered "that he go thereof hence without day."

There was but one civil action tried, during this term, but the Grand Jury returned into court, on the second day, seven indictments: One against the *owner* of the court house, for selling liquor without license; one against Wesley Prior, Eli Ellis, and Charles See, "for rout;" one each against commissioners Elisha Shortridge and Allen Shepherd, for "extortion;" and three cases of assault and battery. The cases for extortion, perhaps, were what would, at this day, be termed taking usurious interest. At least there seems to have been no further notice taken of the matter, the order book not indicating that they were dismissed, quashed, continued or tried.

At this distant day, it will seem a little strange that the best or foremost men of the times should be found among the law-breakers and among the first "hauled over the coals" for it.

This March term of the court fixed a scale of prices for the clerk to be governed by in taking bail of those charged with offenses, as follows: For assault and battery, $100; for routs, $50; for extortion, $100; selling spirituous liquor without license, $20; and subsequently it further instructed that for indictments for perjury the bail should be $300; for violations of the "estray act," $100; for affray, $50; and for robbery on the public highway, the sum of $100. From all of which it would seem that selling liquor without license was a mere peccadillo, that perjury was quite a grave offense and that for two, three, or four men to engage in a nice little "set-to" would require only half the bail demanded of one man who attacked another without first obtaining his consent, and it will be also noticed that assault and battery was placed on a par with highway robbery.

At the March term, the Grand Jury, thirteen in number, were allowed nineteen dollars and fifty cents for their services, and the prosecutor, eight dollars, for prosecuting the pleas of the State and drawing up the seven indictments, and such other services as he could render, and was continued for the next term and until a successor should be appointed, although not at the time a licensed attorney, and the court adjourned, after a three days' session, without disposing of a single case, except the trial of one of the grand jurors heretofore alluded to. It was probably owing to the fact that nothing had been completed that the judges only allowed themselves three dollars for their services.

Following is the substance of an act of the General Assembly of 1822, concerning vagrants: Every person who shall be suspected to get his livelihood by gaming, and every able-bodied person, who is found loitering and wandering about and not having wherewithal to maintain himself by some visible property, and who doth not betake himself to labour or some honest calling to procure a livelihood, and all persons who quit their habitation and leave their wives and children without suitable means of subsistence, whereby they suffer or may become chargeable to the county, and all other idle, vagrant, dissolute persons, rambling about without any visible means of subsistence, shall be deemed and considered as vagrants.—[Revised Laws, 1824, page 421.]

Such person was to give bond in the sum of fifty dollars or be committed to jail, till the meeting of the Circuit Court, and if found to be a vagrant within the meaning of the law, he was, if a minor, to be "bound out," until twenty-one years of age, to some useful trade or occupation, and if over twenty-one years of age, he was to be hired out by the Sheriff for any time not exceeding nine months. The money received for his hire was to be applied to the payment of his debts, and the balance to be given to him at the expiration of his time, provided, however, that, if he had a wife and children, the surplus went to them, and he might also avoid being hired out by giving security that he would return to his family and follow some useful occupation.

In accordance with this act, a special session was called, on April 28, 1823, on account of a charge of vagrancy against a citizen of Henry county. The following panel of sixteen grand jurors, "good and lawful men," were selected to consider whether the person so charged with vagrancy was such "within the meaning of the law": John Dorrah, foreman, Charles Jamison, James Stanford, Samuel Dill, Asahel Woodward, William McDowell, Obediah R. Weaver, Moses Fink, senior, Allen Shepherd, Christopher Bundy, George Hanby, Thomas Watkins, William Bundy, Joshua Welborn, Andrew Shannon, Moses Allis. William McDowell seems to have been a member of this Grand Jury and the bailiff in charge at the same time. Of this jury of lawful men, two were under indictment at the time for violating the laws of the land.

The principal expenses for this term of court were: Sixteen grand jurors, twelve dollars; bailiff, seventy-five cents; prosecutor, two dollars; two judges, four dollars; total, eighteen dollars and seventy-five cents.

Charles Jamison, for selling liquor without license, was tried at the next term of the court, found guilty, and fined three dollars, which was just what he charged the court for the use of the cabin as a court room. As he was afterward granted license to sell liquors, it is evident that the offense consisted not so much in the sale of the liquor, as in having neglected to replenish the almost empty treasury with the five dollars, which was levied solely for purposes of revenue, and not in anywise intended to restrict the traffic.

The August term of the circuit court was held by the associate judges. Miles Eggleston. Presiding Judge, not, as yet, having deigned to visit our county.

To call to the minds of some of the older citizens men once familiar to them, the names of the Grand Jury are given also:

John Dorrah, foreman, as usual, Levi Butler, Ebenezer Goble, Thomas Leonard, Thomas Watkins, John Blount, George Hobson, James McKimmey, Robert Smith, Allen Hunt, Jesse Cox, John Marshall, Nathan Davis, and Josiah Morris.

After a three days' session, the jury returned into court two indictments for assault and battery, three for affray, one for violation of the estray law, one for robbery, and one for perjury. In the five years immediately succeeding the organization of the county, ninety one "true bills" were found for various offenses "against the peace and dignity" of the State of Indiana. Something of the nature of the ills to which society was subjected at that early day will be seen from the character of these presentments as follows, to-wit:

Assault and battery	44	Larceny	2
Affray	24	Lewdness	1
Rout	1	Violating Estray Law	1
Rape	4	Selling Without License	1
Gaming	5	Obstructing Process	1
Extortion	2	Negligence in Office	1
Robbery	1		
Vagrancy	1	Total	91
Perjury	2		

What would our citizens think today of having four fifths of the time of our courts taken up with the adjustment of personal encounters between our citizens? The "fistic" proclivities of our citizens have, without doubt, very much improved in seventy five years.

Miles C. Eggleston, the Presiding Judge for the Third, afterward the Fifth Circuit put in an appearance for the first time November 17, 1823, this being the fifth session since the county was organized. The following order appears on the docket for that day:

"On motion, it is ordered that it be suggested on the records of this court that Reuben Ball, the plaintiff in this cause, is deceased, since the last term of this court."

And, it is supposed, the suggestion was made accordingly. The next cause was "continued till the next term of court," that the court take time until then to consider of the law arising in said case.

The next order was that all indictments found by the Grand Jury, at the August term, be quashed, and the defendants in said indictments be thereof quit and discharged, etc. To this his autograph is appended—the only time it occurs on the order book. The reason for this order seems to have been that the General Assembly had changed the time of holding courts for this circuit, of which our home judges had not been apprised, and so went on with the August term as usual. The indictments were all quashed, but seem to have been immediately revived by the jury then in session.

It would seem that William W. Wick, of Fayette County, was made judge of the circuit, in 1824, but, being elected Secretary of State, Governor Hendricks appointed Bethuel F. Morris, of Marion County, Presiding Judge, "in the room" of said Wick.

In October, 1825, John Anderson succeeded Thomas R. Stanford, as judge. While Anderson was on the bench, an appeal case came up before him and his associate, in which Anderson was defendant, and it is noticeable that the defendant gained the case and his costs off the plaintiff, and then allowed himself two dollars for extra services at that session. It is not to be inferred from this that justice was not done, for the judge soon brought suit in his own court, as Paymaster of the Indiana Militia, against Sheriff Healey, for failure to collect the muster fines off the conscientious people of the county, and, after continuing the case from day to day and term to term, he was finally beaten, Bethuel F. Morris, perhaps, presiding when the decision was reached. Soon after this, one Jacob Thorp filed an information in court to the effect that the said Judge Anderson was an alien, and therefore not competent to fill the position occupied. A rule was granted against the judge to show why he should not be ousted from his seat. This he must have done to the satisfaction of the court, as he continued to hold his position, and at a subsequent term he obtained judgment for costs against Thorp, Anderson and his associate apparently deciding the case, So much for early courts and manner of doing business.

It cannot be doubted that the ends of justice were quite as faithfully subserved in that day as at present, and that it was generally quite as speedily meted out, notwithstanding the quaintness of style and rather 'hifalutin" ring of some of the proceedings.

FIRST ATTORNEYS.

It has already been mentioned that Lot Bloomfield was "sworn in" as the first Prosecutor of "the pleas of the State" for the Henry Circuit Court. There

were but four indictments found, all for assault and battery, and, as one of the
culprits "lit out," another was found not guilty, and still another plead guilty and
was only fined one dollar for two offenses, the Prosecutor, doubtless, felt that
his luck was none of the best. It is said that information was lodged with the
jury that some graceless scamp had been guilty of larceny, but, just before the
finding or returning of a bill, the foreman learned that he had left the county;
so it was concluded that it would be a waste of ammunition to finish proceedings
against him, and they at once dropped the case. This did not suit the attorney,
who grumbled considerably, and called the attention of the jury to the fact that
it cost much labor to draw up the papers in each case, and showed them that
he was at great expense in traveling to and from court, for board, etc., etc. The
court made him the very liberal allowance of five dollars, which was one dollar
more than their honors received, but it does not seem to have been satisfactory,
as he came no more, although appointed for more than one term. James Gilmore,
afterwards a justice of the peace, and not yet a full fledged attorney, was appointed in Bloomfield's place the next term. James Noble, James Rariden, and·
Abraham Elliott, father of Judge Jehu T. Elliott, were admitted to practise in
this first court.

At the August term, 1823, Charles H. Test and Martin M. Ray, of Wayne
County, were admitted as attorneys and counsellors at law, "and thereupon took
the oath of office."

At the April term, 1824, James B. Ray, James Mendall, Calvin Fletcher,
Oliver H. Smith, and Philip Sweetser were admitted to practise.

At the April term, 1825, Harvey Gregg appeared with a regular commission
as prosecuting attorney for the Fifth Judicial Circuit, Henry County had previously been in the Third Circuit. At this term Abraham Elliott was appointed
Master of Chancery and Moses Cox was admitted to the bar. In October of the
same year, Calvin Fletcher presented his credentials as prosecutor for the Circuit.

At the October term, 1826, James Whitcomb appeared with credentials as
prosecutor for the Circuit, and Septimus Smith and Albert G. White were admitted as attorneys. In 1827, Samuel C. Sample, appeared as a licensed attorney
and "took the oath" as "counsellor at law at the bar of the court."

In 1828, on motion of Charles H. Test, Marinus Willitt and David Patton
were admitted. At the October term, 1828, on motion of Samuel C. Sample,
William Daily and Caleb B. Smith, having produced license signed by "two
Presiding Judges of the State of Indiana," were admitted to practise in the Henry
Circuit Court, and, on motion of James Rariden, John S. Newman was in like
manner admitted.

In 1829, William W. Wick, Prosecuting Attorney, and James T. Brown
were admitted to the bar. In 1830, James Perry was prosecutor of the pleas of
the State.

From the foregoing list it will be seen that the early practitioners at the
Henry County Bar included many of the ornaments of the legal profession of
our State. At a later day, came Parker, Julian, Morton, and others scarcely less
noted, to say nothing of resident attorneys, of whom a number have won a name
abroad. Among those who were frequent in their attendance upon our earlier
courts were a number who have distinguished themselves as orators, members
of Congress, governors of our State, and eminent jurists.

It should be borne in mind, however, that the tendency of a general diffusion of knowledge is to lessen the difference between men, growing out of their acquirements, and he who may have seemed almost a prodigy of learning seventy five years ago might not today pass for much more than an ordinary person. Great talents and great learning will, doubtless, be treated with much consideration for all time to come, but the time has long passed when any man can wield such influence over his fellows as did Demosthenes. It is undoubtedly true that greater attainments are expected in many of the stations of life than formerly, and the legal profession is no exception.

CITIZENS.

DISTINCTION BETWEEN VILLAGE AND TOWN—NUMBER OF VILLAGES AND TOWNS IN HENRY COUNTY—FOUNDERS AND EARLY MERCHANTS—ORIGINAL PLATS AND ADDITIONS—BANKS AND NEWSPAPERS—POSTAL AND TRANSPORTATION FACILITIES—POPULATION—ASHLAND—BLOUNTSVILLE — CADIZ — CHICAGO — CIRCLEVILLE — DUNREITH — ELIZABETH CITY FAIRFIELD — GRANT CITY — GREENSBORO — HILLSBORO — HONEY CREEK — KENNARD — KNIGHTSTOWN — LEWISVILLE — LURAY — MECHANICSBURG — MESSICK — MIDDLETOWN — MILLVILLE.

Henry County seems to have been well supplied with villages and town. There is no incorporated city in the county. A place that is not incorporate is referred to as a village. If it is incorporated as a town, then it is re ferred to as a town. This chapter presents a brief official history of forty on villages and towns, past and present, alphabetically arranged, as follows:

Ashland, Blountsville, Cadiz, Chicago, Circleville, Dunreith, Elizabet City, Fairfield, Grant City, Greensboro, Hillsboro, Honey Creek, Kennard Knightstown, Lewisville, Luray, Mechanicsburg, Messick, Middletown, Mil ville, Mooreland, Mount Summit, New Castle, Needmore, New Lisbon, O; den, Petersburg, Pumpkintown, Raysville, Rogersville, Sharington, Shirle Spiceland, Springport, Straughn, Sulphur Springs, Uniontown, West Libert Wheeland, White Raven, Woodville.

The distances to all villages and towns in Henry County are measur from the court house in New Castle, taken as a common center, as shown ! the following letter from the county surveyor:

"O. E. MINESINGER,
"COUNTY SURVEYOR,
"HENRY COUNTY.

"NEW CASTLE, Ind., September 1, 1905

"Mr. George Hazzard, New Castle, Indiana:
"SIR: This will certify that I have made a comparison of the distances on the ' cial map of Henry County with the distances as set out in the following named tov and villages regarding their location from the court house in New Castle and I find same correct as stated. The distances given are approximately from actual meast ments in a straight line and not by the usual traveled roads.
"Very truly,

CITIZENS.

CHAPTER XLI.

HENRY COUNTY VILLAGES AND TOWNS.

DISTINCTION BETWEEN VILLAGE AND TOWN—NUMBER OF VILLAGES AND
TOWNS IN HENRY COUNTY—FOUNDERS AND EARLY MERCHANTS—
ORIGINAL PLATS AND ADDITIONS—BANKS AND NEWSPAPERS—POSTAL
AND TRANSPORTATION FACILITIES—POPULATION—ASHLAND—BLOUNTSVILLE
— CADIZ — CHICAGO — CIRCLEVILLE — DUNREITH — ELIZABETH CITY —
FAIRFIELD — GRANT CITY — GREENSBORO — HILLSBORO — HONEY CREEK —
KENNARD — KNIGHTSTOWN — LEWISVILLE — LURAY — MECHANICSBURG —
MESSICK — MIDDLETOWN — MILLVILLE.

Henry County seems to have been well supplied with villages and towns.
There is no incorporated city in the county. A place that is not incorporated
is referred to as a village. If it is incorporated as a town, then it is referred to as a town. This chapter presents a brief official history of forty one
villages and towns, past and present, alphabetically arranged, as follows:

Ashland, Blountsville, Cadiz, Chicago, Circleville, Dunreith, Elizabeth
City, Fairfield, Grant City, Greensboro, Hillsboro, Honey Creek, Kennard,
Knightstown, Lewisville, Luray, Mechanicsburg, Messick, Middletown. Mill-
ville, Mooreland, Mount Summit, New Castle, Needmore, New Lisbon. Og-
den, Petersburg, Pumpkintown, Raysville, Rogersville, Sharington, Shirley,
Spiceland, Springport, Straughn, Sulphur Springs, Uniontown, West Liberty,
Wheeland, White Raven, Woodville.

The distances to all villages and towns in Henry County are measured
from the court house in New Castle, taken as a common center, as shown by
the following letter from the county surveyor:

"O. E. MINESINGER,
"COUNTY SURVEYOR,
"HENRY COUNTY.

"NEW CASTLE. Ind., September 1, 1905.

"*Mr. George Hazzard, New Castle, Indiana:*

"SIR: This will certify that I have made a comparison of the distances on the official map of Henry County with the distances as set out in the following named towns
and villages regarding their location from the court house in New Castle and I find the
same correct as stated. The distances given are approximately from actual measure-
ments in a straight line and not by the usual traveled roads. .

"Very truly,

"OMAR E. MINESINGER,
"Surveyor of Henry County."

ASHLAND.

The village of Ashland is situated in Liberty Township, three and one half miles east and one half mile south of east from the court house in New Castle, on the Pittsburg, Cincinnati, Chicago and St. Louis railway and one half mile north of the New Castle and Hagerstown Pike. Ashland was never laid out and platted into lots, the real estate in the village being described only by metes and bounds. It was first known as Mullen's Station, taking its name from the well-known family of that name, old pioneers, who were for so many years prominent in eastern Henry and western Liberty townships. Many of their descendants are yet living in Henry, Liberty and perhaps other townships of the county.

Mullen's Station was the first railroad station for New Castle, the old Cincinnati, Logansport and Chicago railway having been completed to this point early in 1854, perhaps late in 1853, and until the road was finally completed to New Castle in the Summer of 1854, all the business for the new railroad, which later came to New Castle, was transacted at Mullen's Station. To this point stock was driven to be shipped to Cincinnati, goods were wagoned from there to be distributed to other points throughout the country and people went there to take the train to Cincinnati and other points. The postoffice was established in 1855, David Millikan being the first postmaster, and the name of the village being changed to Ashland.

Before removal to its present site this postoffice was for many years a country neighborhood affair located at the respective houses of the successive postmasters, near the present location of the station of Messick on the Big Four railway and was then as now called Messick.

Ashland has never been incorporated, therefore its population, as shown by the census of 1900, is included in that of Liberty Township. (See Chapter XXXVIII). The name probably came from Ashland, Ohio, from the fact that, at the time the name was changed, some of the most enterprising citizens of the village had once lived in the town and county of that name in the "Buckeye" State.

A list of the postmasters at Ashland, Messick included, from February 26, 1847, to September 14, 1855, when the office was moved to its present location, will be found on page 34 of this History.

Ashland and Millville are the only postoffices in Liberty Township. Aside from Chicago which was discontinued March 24, 1855, and Devon, which was discontinued February 13, 1868, they are the only postoffices that have ever been in the township.

BLOUNTSVILLE.

Blountsville, situated in Stony Creek Township, twelve miles due northeast from the court house in New Castle, being in the W. ½ of the N. E. ¼ of Sec. 35, Tp. 19 N., R. 11 E., was laid out and platted by Thomas R. Stanford, Surveyor, in July, 1832, and acknowledged by Andrew D. Blount, proprietor, September 5, 1833. The main street running east and west was then designated as "The Logansport and Richmond Road," the road running south on the west line of the town as "The Centreville Road." The original plat contains twenty six lots, no blocks designated.

The first addition, situated immediately south of the original plat, was platted June 14, 1853, and was acknowledged by Beale Manifold, proprietor, January 26, 1854, and contains twelve lots, no blocks designated.

The Northeastern, the second addition, situated immediately east of the original plat and Manifold's addition, was platted and acknowledged by Jonathan Ross, Jesse Cary, William Liser, Daniel Bainter, J. W. Stanley, John Houk and Leander Priest, proprietors, August 19, 1859. It contains twenty six lots and four out-lots, no blocks designated.

Blountsville takes its name from Andrew D. Blount, the original proprietor of the townsite. On the county records showing the filing of the plat, the name is spelled "Blunt," but as far back as the memory of the oldest inhabitant reaches the name has been uniformly used as "Blount." This place from its inception has always been the commercial metropolis of our northeastern township, and on account of its close proximity to Delaware County on the north and Randolph County on the east, its trade has been much increased from those counties.

This place was without railroad facilities until 1902, when the Chicago, Cincinnati and Louisville railway was built, which in a few years must add to the importance of the village.

Blountsville not being incorporated must be content to be known as a village only, and its population, according to the census of 1900, is included in that of Stony Creek Township. (See Chapter XXXVIII.)

A list of the postmasters at Blountsville from the establishment of the postoffice, January 22, 1835, inclusive, to the present time, will be found on pages 34-5 of this History. Also the name of the only rural route carrier.

Blountsville is the only postoffice now in the township. The only other postoffice ever in the township was Rogersville, which was discontinued June 15, 1901.

CADIZ.

The town of Cadiz is situated in Harrison Township, six miles west and one and one fourth miles north of west from the court house in New Castle, being in the S. E. ¼ of Sec. 3, Tp. 17 N., R. 11 E., and was laid out and platted by David Pickering, proprietor, September 11, 1836, and acknowledged March 22, 1837.

The early emigration to that part of Henry County afterwards formed into Harrison Township was largely from Harrison County, Ohio, and the town of Cadiz derives its name from the county seat of that county. In this emigration the Cooper family and their kinsmen, including the Pickerings, were the most numerous, therefore, when it came to establishing a town, what could be more natural than to adopt the name of the chief town of the county from which they emigrated?

The main street running east and west was designated as "The Crawfordsville and New Castle State Road." The original plat contains four and one half blocks, consisting of sixteen lots.

The first addition, situated immediately west of the original plat, was platted March 29, 1849, and was acknowledged by Imla W. Cooper, proprietor, April 7, 1849, and contains four blocks consisting of twelve lots and one out-lot.

The second addition, situated immediately east and north of the original plat, was platted November 7, 1849, and was on the same date acknowledged by David Pickering, proprietor, and contains four blocks, consisting of fifteen lots.

A third addition, situated immediately south of the original plat, was platted February 23, 1855, and was acknowledged by Jonas Pickering, proprietor, August 10, 1860, and contains but two lots, no blocks designated.

The owner of this addition of two lots only was not ambitious to have his small addition to Cadiz speedily a matter of official record, for it took him five years and six months to get the matter properly recorded.

David Pickering, the original proprietor, was the most ambitious of all of the promoters of Cadiz, for the county records show that on March, 23, 1854, he made another addition situated immediately north of his first addition to the original plat, the same containing four blocks, consisting of eight lots, but like his neighbor and kinsman, Jonas Pickering, he was in no hurry to reach the county recorder's office, for it was not until October 3, 1861, seven years and six months later, that it was recorded.

The population of the town of Cadiz, as shown by the census of 1900, was 253. Although surrounded by a fertile country and numbering from time to time as it has, some of Henry County's most enterprising and enlightened citizens, it has never been able to secure railroad facilities. In fact, Harrison Township is the only one of the thirteen in the county not so far traversed by either steam or electric railway. Surely the repeated efforts of the enterprising citizens of the township in this direction will in time bear fruit.

A postoffice was established December 18, 1837. A list of the postmasters from that time to the present will be found on page 35 of this History.

Cadiz is the only postoffice that has ever existed in Harrison Township. There never was a postoffice at the old town of Woodville, the principal street of which was the boundary line between Harrison and Greensboro townships.

CHICAGO.

This proposed town was never laid out and platted. It is situated seven and one half miles east and one mile south from the court house in New Castle, on the New Castle and Hagerstown pike, in Liberty Township. The first transfer, as shown by the records, was for religious purposes and consisted of one acre, transferred by John McSherley and Phebe, his wife, to Christopher Main, George Koons and Jesse K. Platts as Trustees for Liberty Church, November 5, 1827.

The village is located about two miles southeast of the present site of Millville and a mile south of the railroad, the building of which seems to have ruined its prospects. At one time it was an ambitious village, numbering a score or more of houses, one or two stores and two hotels. It is now known as the "Old Chicago Neighborhood." The people who located Chicago were very ambitious and had visions of a great future, therefore, they named this place after the then young giant just coming into prominence at the foot of Lake Michigan.

A postoffice was established May 11, 1852 and discontinued March 24, 1855, which is about the time the postoffice at Millville was established. Three of its prominent citizens served as postmasters. Their names will be found on page 36 of this History.

Chicago is one of the four postoffices that have existed in Liberty Township, the other three being Devon (discontinued), Ashland and Millville.

CIRCLEVILLE.

This village is on the line between Stony Creek and Blue River townships, nine miles due northeast from the court house in New Castle, and one and one half miles due north from the present town of Mooreland. The records do not show that it was ever laid out and platted into town lots.

This place has long since passed from the zenith of its glory and now exists as a village only in the memory of the oldest citizen. Its former site is now commonly known as "Five Forks," for the reason that the turnpikes from here lead to five different points of the compass. Circleville never reached the dignity of a postoffice. Five Forks is adjoined by some of the most fertile and highly improved farms of the county.

The author of this History has been unable to find any old settler who can give a reason why this place was named Circleville.

DUNREITH.

The town of Dunreith is situated in Spiceland Township, nine miles south and three and one half miles west from the court house in New Castle, and five miles east from Knightstown, at the crossing of the Pittsburg, Cincinnati, Chicago and St. Louis railway and the New Castle and Rushville division of the Lake Erie and Western railway, and at the junction of the New Castle branch with the main line of the Indianapolis and Eastern railway (electric line), and in the W. ½ of the N. E. ¼ of Sec. 32, and the W. ½ of the S. E. ¼ of Sec. 29, Tp. 16 N., R. 10 E. It was laid out and platted by James M. Clements, Surveyor, for John W. Griffin, Caleb Johnson and Thomas Evans, proprietors, July 22, 1865, and was acknowledged by them July 25, 1865. The main street running east and west was designated as "The National Road." The original plat contains three blocks consisting of twenty three lots. The town was first known as Coffin's Station.

On the completion of the old Indiana Central railroad to this point a depot was established here and the place named after the proprietor of the land, Emery Dunreith Coffin. Soon there began to spring up a little village around the station. In 1865, when the town was first platted as above shown, those interested, particularly John W. Griffin, decided on a change of name, but out of respect to Mr. Coffin's memory and to preserve his name in connection with the town, it was called Dunreith.

The first addition, situated northwest of the original plat and on the north side of the National Road, was platted August 31, 1866, and was on the same date acknowledged by Thomas Evans, proprietor, and contains six blocks, consisting of thirty six lots.

The second addition, situated immediately north of the original plat, between the National Road and the Pittsburg, Cincinnati, Chicago and St. Louis railway, being the narrow strip of land between the principal street and the railroad and upon which all of the business houses of the town are now situated, was platted and acknowledged by Timothy Wilson, Caleb Johnson and Thomas Evans, December 12, 1866. It contains six lots, no blocks designated.

The Eastern addition, situated immediately north of the Wilson, Johnson and Evans' addition, and east of Evans' addition on the north side of the National Road, was platted November 16, 1867, and was acknowledged by Christopher Wilson, proprietor, December 16, 1867; and by Caleb Johnson on the part of C. Johnson and Company, June 5, 1868. It contains three blocks, consisting of fourteen lots.

An addition, situated immediately north of Evans' addition and east of the turnpike running north to Spiceland, was platted August 29, 1868, and was acknowledged by Caleb Johnson, proprietor, September 14, 1868, and contains two blocks, consisting of eleven lots.

Caleb Johnson, who was one of the chief promoters of the town, was for many years its leading merchant. After leaving the county treasurer's office in August, 1863, he removed to Coffin's Station and established a store. He resided there until 1879 when, having in the meantime entered the ministry of the Friends' Church, he moved to Lynnville, Iowa. Afterwards he was a resident of Wichita, Kansas, and Denver, Colorado. He died at the latter place in 1899 and his remains are buried there.

The next addition, situated immediately west of the original plat and south of the old railway, was platted August 8, 1871, and was acknowledged by John W. Griffin, proprietor, August 17, 1871, and contains eight lots, no blocks designated.

The next ambitious proprietor was James M. Crawford, who had platted May 5, 1883, an addition situated immediately north of Caleb Johnson's addition, on the east side of the pike running north to Spiceland. It was acknowledged by him May 19, 1883, and contains one block of six lots.

Joseph Griffin, father of John W., made an addition, situated immediately west of Evans' addition and west of the pike running north to Spiceland. It was platted July 9, 1883, and was acknowledged by Joseph Griffin, proprietor, December 11, 1883, and contains two blocks, consisting of seven lots.

Robert M. Kenney's north side addition, situated on the extreme north side of the town of Dunreith, between the New Castle and Rushville railway and the road running north to Spiceland, was platted October 20, 1892, and was acknowledged by Kenney July 13, 1893. It contains ten and two thirds acres divided into four blocks, consisting of fifty two lots and two out-lots.

A postoffice was established July 2, 1861, then called Coffin's Station. On pages 36-7 of this History will be found a list of the postmasters for the town as first named and as now named. Also the name of the only rural route carrier.

The only postoffices that have ever existed in Spiceland Township are Dunreith, Ogden and Spiceland, and all are still in existence.

The census of 1900 places the population of the town at 205.

ELIZABETH CITY.

This old village, now much decayed, is situated twelve and one fourth miles southwest from the court house in New Castle, and six miles northwest from Knightstown, and is in Wayne Township, being in the N. W. corner of the S. E. ¼ of Sec. 1, Tp. 16 N., R. 8 E. Elizabeth City was laid out and platted by Robert Overman, proprietor, and acknowledged September 17, 1838, and contains six blocks, consisting of thirty six lots. No addition has ever been filed to the town. It was at an early day, a place of some promise. After the Civil War, Elnathan and Thomas B. Wilkinson, brothers, now of Knightstown, maintained here for several years a general mercantile establishment and did a highly prosperous and satisfactory business. However, no postoffice was established until 1878. It was called "Maple Valley," for the reason that there was a prior postoffice in the State named Elizabeth City.

The construction of the Big Four railway through the county west from New Castle and the establishment of the towns of Kennard in Henry County and Shirley in Henry and Hancock counties, and of Wilkinson in Hancock County, all on the line of the railroad and within a few miles of Elizabeth City, was the death knell of the last named place as a business point. The establishment of the rural free delivery system from Shirley and Wilkinson was another blow to Elizabeth City, for then the postoffice was finally discontinued. On pages 39 and 40 of this History will be found a list of the respective post-masters of "Maple Valley."

Elizabeth City (Maple Valley) is one of the four postoffices that have existed in Wayne Township, the other three being Grant City, (Snyder discontinued), Knightstown and Raysville.

Robert Overman, the proprietor, was from Pasquotank County, North Carolina, of which Elizabeth City is the county town, hence this name.

FAIRFIELD.

This defunct place was situated somewhere on the National Road, The county records do not show where it was located or by whom it was laid out and platted. Henry Lewelling appears to have been the surveyor, who laid out and platted the village about the year 1828. The main street running east and west is designated as "The National Road," and contains four blocks consisting of thirty two lots. Lewis Tacket was the proprietor. Its location was probably east of Lewisville in the neighborhood of the present town of Straughn. It never reached the dignity of a postoffice.

GRANT CITY.

Grant City, so named after our great military chieftain, General Ulysses S. Grant, is situated in Wayne Township, ten and one half miles southwest from the court house in New Castle and five miles north and one mile west from Knightstown. It is located on the E. ½ of the N. E. ¼ and the E. ½ of the S. E. ¼ of Sec. 5 and the W. ½ of the S. W. ¼ of Sec. 4, Tp. 16 N., R. 9 E., and was laid out, platted and acknowledged by Jacob Green, who was a soldier in the Civil War, and by Margaret Green, his wife, October 31, 1868. It contains five blocks, consisting of thirty six lots.

Jacob Green's northern addition, situated immediately north of the original plat, was platted by the same parties March 24, 1869, and was acknowledged July 14, 1869. It contains four blocks, consisting of twenty eight lots.

When Jacob Green returned from the Civil War he was ambitious to found a town, and, being a great admirer of his old commander, named it as above stated. From the fact that there was a prior postoffice in the State of the same name, no postoffice was established until January 26, 1888, when one was established called "Snyder." In the meantime the Big Four railway had been built through the county west from New Castle and the town of Kennard located two and one half miles north and one half mile east of Grant City. Later the rural free delivery system abolished the postoffice. The stores which had been established found their way to the railroad or were discontinued. Thus the glory of Grant City as a business center disappeared. "Jake" Green, the founder of the village, was for many years a well-known character in Henry County. Some years ago he moved to Iowa where he died and is buried.

A list of the postmasters at 'Snyder' will be found on page 45 of this History. Grant City (Snyder discontinued) is one of the four postoffices that have existed in Wayne Township, the other three being Elizabeth City (Maple Valley), Knightstown and Raysville.

GREENSBORO.

This old historic town is situated in Greensboro Township, six and one fourth miles southwest from the court house in New Castle, and is in the E. $\frac{1}{4}$ of the S. E. $\frac{1}{4}$ of Sec. 35 and in the W. $\frac{1}{2}$ of the S. W. $\frac{1}{4}$ of Sec. 36, Tp. 17 N., R. 9 E., and was laid out, platted and acknowledged by Jehu Wickersham, February 27, 1830, and contains six blocks, consisting of forty eight lots.

The first or Eastern addition, situated immediately east of and adjoining the original plat, was platted and acknowledged by Seth Hinshaw, Jonas Pickering, Enoch Wickersham, Abraham Moore, Jehu Wickersham and Mary Wickersham, proprietors, March 26, 1836, and contains six blocks, consisting of twenty eight lots.

The second or Northern addition, situated immediately north of the original plat and east of High Street, was platted and acknowledged by Thomas Reagan, April 13, 1855, and contains one block, consisting of twelve lots.

Reagan's addition to the Northern addition, situated immediately north of the original plat and west of High Street, was platted and acknowledged by Thomas Reagan, October 16, 1866, and contains one block, consisting of six lots.

A plat of the town of Greensboro was surveyed and platted by William R. Harrold, Surveyor, and acknowledged August 6, 1873. This plat includes the original plat and all the additions above mentioned and also out-lots numbering from one to twenty four inclusive; and also out-lots numbers seven to thirteen inclusive, north of Reagan's Northern addition.

Greensboro is situated on the east bank of Duck Creek, about one mile from its junction with Blue River, and nearly seven miles north by east from Knightstown. Being in the midst of a tract of fertile farming lands, it has ever enjoyed a considerable local traffic, though its growth in wealth and importance has not been as rapid as that of some other towns in the county, from the fact that it is not reached by a railroad. Then the construction of the Big Four railroad through the county, two and one half miles north of it, and the establishment of the town of Kennard, two and one half miles northwest of it have drawn from it much of the trade that it once enjoyed.

Greensboro has a number of excellent turnpikes radiating from it; but it was as a "station" on the "underground railroad" that it won a national reputation. As the home of a number of determined and veteran abolition agitators, it had a reputation, fifty years ago, second to no place of its size in the whole country. In those early days a large building, known as 'Liberty Hall," was often filled with enthusiastic audiences, who listened to such apostles of freedom as Arnold Buffum, Abby Kelly, Frederick Douglas, George W. Julian and others of note.

The "underground railroad" was the system employed by abolitionists to transport slaves fleeing from bondage to the land of freedom, principally Canada. The plan was to move them in the night time from the home of an abolitionist, or some other place where they were secreted, called a "station," to some point or "station" further on toward their ultimate destination. This was all done in such a secretive and mysterious way that the term "underground railroad" was applied. Greensboro was known far and wide as a permanent "station," and the abolitionists there were numerous and determined, having at their head the veteran Seth Hinshaw.

The early emigration in and around Greensboro was from Guilford County, North Carolina, of which Greensboro is the county town, and from this fact Greensboro Township and town are so named.

A list of the postmasters from William Reagan, April 18, 1831, to the present time, will be found on page 37 of this History. Greensboro Township has had three postoffices, all of which are retained—Greensboro, Kennard and Shirley. However, at the present time the Shirley postoffice is on the west side of Main Street in Hancock County.

The census of 1900 places the population of the town at 284.

HILLSBORO.

This old village on a hill is situated in the southeast corner of Prairie Township, three and one half miles northeast from the court house in New Castle, and is in the south part of the N. E. ¼ of Sec. 36, Tp. 18 N., R. 10 E., and was laid out, platted and acknowledged by Jacob Huston, Thomas Huston and Samuel Rinehart, proprietors, July 26, 1831, and contains twelve blocks, consisting of sixty lots.

The first addition, situated immediately east of the original plat, was platted March 2, 1852, and acknowledged by Clement Murphey, proprietor, April 19, 1852, and contains twelve lots, no blocks designated.

The second addition, also by Clement Murphey, situated immediately east of his first addition; was platted and acknowledged by him, April 16, 1853, and contains twelve lots, no blocks designated.

The name of the village undoubtedly comes from the fact that one can hardly reach the place from any direction without climbing a hill. It was once a trading point of some consequence. The author of this History well remembers when as a boy he first saw Hillsboro, going there in company with his mother to visit her brother, Franklin Woodward, then residing there. At that time there were three stores, two blacksmith shops, a wagon shop, and a saw mill, with corresponding population. At the foot of the hill on the road leading to New Castle, on Little Blue River, there was then and for many years afterward, the most pretentious woolen mill in the county, known far and wide as the "Mowrer and McAfee Factory," later owned by Ice, Dunn and Company. Before this, at the foot of the hill on the road now leading to Messick, on a little stream that would not now float a duck so thorough has been the drainage, there was a grist mill and still house combined, known as the "Byrket mill." Then on the Little Blue, near the factory there had been a saw mill owned and operated by a man named Neziah Snyder and connected with it he operated one burr for grinding wheat and corn, principally corn. What little flour he ground was bolted by hand. Now these industries have all disappeared and Hillsboro has not only passed into history but almost into oblivion. It was one of the towns projected before the days of railroads and with their coming it began to decay.

A postoffice was established March 10, 1851, named "Dan Webster," from the fact that there was already in Indiana a postoffice called Hillsboro. The first postmaster was Samuel S. Canaday, who moved around a good deal in the county and seemed to be the choice of the people wherever he lived for postmaster, for he served as such at Ashland, Hillsboro and New Castle. A list of the postmasters at "Dan Webster" will be found on page 36 of this History. Prairie Township has had four postoffices—Hillsboro "Dan Webster," Luray, Mount Summit and Springport. The two first named have been discontinued.

HONEY CREEK.

The village of Honey Creek, so named for the little stream near whose banks it is situated, is in Fall Creek Township, nine and one half miles northwest from the court house in New Castle and four miles southeast from Middletown, on the Pittsburg, Cincinnati, Chicago and St. Louis railway. It was founded in 1858 and was called Warnock's Station, after a Henry County pioneer who then owned the land on which Honey Creek is now located, the same being in the N. E. ¼ of Sec. 10, Tp. 18 N., R. 9 E.

The only addition, known as the Western, and situated immediately west of the original village, on the north side of the railroad, and on the west side of the street running north and south, was platted July 28, 1873, for Joseph M. Brown, Commissioner, in the matter of the real estate of John Myers, deceased, of which decedent, Adam Evans was executor, Brown having been appointed Commissioner by the Court to sell the real estate. This addition to Honey Creek was made by the Commissioner to facilitate the sale of said real estate. It contains five acres and seven rods and is divided into three blocks, consisting of twelve lots.

A postoffice was established June 18, 1861, with Zadock G. Tomlinson as postmaster. On pages 37 and 38 of this History will be found a list of the postmasters from Tomlinson to Lertin R. Fadely, the present incumbent.

Honey Creek is one of the three postoffices that were established and that still exist in Fall Creek Township, the other two being Mechanicsburg and Middletown.

Honey Creek not being incorporated the population as given by the census of 1900 is included in that of Fall Creek Township. (See Chapter XXXVIII).

KENNARD.

This town is situated in the northwest part of Greensboro Township, seven and three fourths miles west and two miles south from the court house in New Castle and is on the Peoria and Eastern division of the Cleveland, Cincinnati, Chicago and St. Louis railway, commonly called the Big Four railway. It is located in the E. ¼ of the S. E. ¼ of Sec. 20 and the W. ¼ of the S. W. ¼ of Sec. 21 and the N. E. ¼ of the N. E. ¼ of Sec. 29 and the N. W. ¼ of the N. W. ¼ of Sec. 28, Tp. 17 N., R. 9 E. It was surveyed and platted by Daniel K. Cook, Surveyor, September 6, 1882, and was acknowledged by Cyrus C. Hinshaw, John W. Payne, Westphalia M. Dixon, Charles Hartley and Martha A. Weasner, proprietors, September 6, 1882, and contained twelve blocks, consisting of fifty six lots and ten out-lots.

The first addition, situated immediately north of the original plat and west of Main Street, was platted February 12, 1885, and was acknowledged by Cyrus C. Hinshaw and John W. Payne, proprietors, February 19, 1885, and contains four and sixty-nine hundredths acres, divided into two blocks, consisting of eleven lots.

Then comes Westphalia M. Dixon with an addition which is situated immediately north of the original plat, on the east side of Main Street. It was platted February 8, 1887, and was acknowledged by Dixon March 11, 1887, and contains two blocks, consisting of six lots.

Alexander Younts' addition, situated immediately north of Dixon's addition on the east side of Main Street, was platted April 5, 1888, and was acknowledged by Younts December 22, 1888, and contains three and one half acres, divided into one block, consisting of eight lots.

Alexander Younts was ambitious to add to Kennard's territory for he filed a second addition, situated immediately east of the original plat, on the north side of Broad Street, which was platted in October, 1890. It was acknowledged by Younts November 11, 1890, and contains two and forty five hundredths acres, divided into three lots and one out-lot, no blocks designated.

Martindale, Madison and Hinshaw's addition, situated immediately south of the original plat and south of the Big Four railway, was platted April 27, 1893, and was acknowledged by Frank Martindale, Martha F. Martindale, Cyrus C. Hinshaw, John Madison and Alonzo Hinshaw, proprietors, April 28, 1893, and contains nine and forty seven hundredths acres, divided into forty eight lots, no blocks designated.

George I. Jenckes made the last addition. It is situated immediately west of the original plat and Martindale, Madison and Hinshaw's addition and was platted May 10, 1898, and was acknowledged by Jenckes on the same date. It contains ten and one fourth acres, divided into two blocks, consisting of forty nine lots and one out-lot.

Cyrus C. Hinshaw was instrumental in having the town named for Jenkins Kennard, an old and highly respected citizen of Henry County, a farmer who has lived for many years in the northeastern part of Wayne Township, not far from the Stone Quarry Mill.

A postoffice was established September 12, 1882, with Cyrus C. Hinshaw as postmaster. On page 38 of this History will be found a list of the postmasters from the establishment of the office to the present time. Greensboro Township has had three postoffices, all of which are retained—Greensboro, Kennard and Shirley. However, at the present time the Shirley postoffice is on the west side of Main Street, in Hancock County.

The census of 1900 places the population of the town at 417.

The projected Indianapolis, New Castle and Toledo railway (electric line) passes through Kennard.

KNIGHTSTOWN.

The town of Knightstown is situated in Wayne Township, fourteen miles southwest from the court house in New Castle, on the west bank of Blue River, at the crossing of the Pittsburg, Cincinnati, Chicago and St. Louis railway and the Louisville and Benton Harbor division of the Big Four railway and on the main line of the Indianapolis and Eastern railway, (electric line) and is in the N. E. $\frac{1}{4}$ and the S. E. $\frac{1}{4}$ of Sec. 33 and the W. $\frac{1}{2}$ of the N. W. $\frac{1}{4}$ and the W. $\frac{1}{2}$ of the S. W. $\frac{1}{4}$ of Sec. 34, Tp. 16 N., R. 9 E. It was laid out and platted by Mr. Waitsel M. Cary in 1827, and contains twelve blocks consisting of eighty five lots. Main, or Clay Street, running east and west was then known as "The National Road." The records do not show before whom it was acknowledged, or by whom it was surveyed and platted.

Samuel Brown's plat of out-lots, situated south of the original plat, was platted and acknowledged by him February 7, 1831, and contains thirty three and three fourths acres, consisting of twelve out-lots, no blocks designated.

Waitsel M. Cary's additional plat, situated west of the original plat, was platted and acknowledged by him November 19, 1836, and contains three blocks, consisting of seventeen lots.

Hart's first Southern addition, situated immediately south of the original plat, between Franklin and Adams streets, was platted and acknowledged by Edward K. Hart, April 27, 1837, and contains thirty nine lots, no blocks designated.

The first Eastern addition, situated immediately east and across Blue River from the original plat, was platted March 1, 1839, and was acknowledged by Edward K. Hart and William M. Tate, proprietors, March 2, 1839, and contains eighteen blocks, consisting of one hundred and fifty one lots and one out-lot.

Cary and Church's addition, situated immediately west of Cary's addition, and west of Madison Street, was platted and acknowledged by Waitsel M. Cary and Uzziel Church, March 4, 1839, and contains five blocks consisting of twenty one lots.

The second South addition, situated immediately south of Hart's first Southern addition and east of Jefferson Street, was platted April 11, 1839, and was acknowledged by John Lowrey and Edward K. Hart, proprietors, on the same date and contains six blocks, consisting of thirty eight lots and two out-lots.

Hiram Gaston's addition, situated immediately south of Cary's addition and south of Jackson Street between Madison and Franklin streets, was platted April 12, 1839, and was acknowledged by Gaston, April 13, 1839, and contains two blocks, consisting of ten lots.

An additional plat, block 13, probably a subdivision, situated immediately west of the original plat, between Franklin and Jefferson streets, north of Brown Street, was platted and acknowledged by Waitsel M. Cary, May 28, 1839, and contains one block, consisting of four lots.

A plat of out-lot number two of the Second Southern addition platted and acknowledged by Jesse Charles, proprietor, January 17, 1851, contains four lots, no blocks designated.

The Northern addition, situated immediately north of the original plat, between Franklin and Adams streets, was platted and acknowledged by Robert I. Hudelson, Joseph M. Whitesel, Asa Heaton and Morris F. Edwards, September 6, 1853, and contains three blocks, consisting of twenty-three lots.

White's addition, situated immediately south of Gaston's addition, between Madison and Franklin streets, was platted and acknowledged by Edmund White, Margaret White, Harriet White, Jesse F. Pusey, Jane W. Pusey, Charles White, Lucy H. White, James White and Jemima White, heirs of Caleb White, April 1, 1861, and contains twenty two lots, no blocks designated.

The first Northwestern addition, situated immediately north of Cary and Church's addition, and Cary's additions, between McCullum and Franklin streets, was platted and acknowledged by Mary M. Heaton, Phebe S. Hudelson, Joseph M. Whitesel, Morris F. Edwards, Jesse B. Hinshaw, James T. Hudelson and Ann Maria Hinshaw, proprietors, September 3, 1863, and contains eight blocks, consisting of forty two lots.

Edwards' addition, situated immediately north of the first Northern addition, on the west side of Washington Street, was platted and acknowledged by Morris F. Edwards June 3, 1868, and contains three and one-half acres, divided into two blocks, consisting of twelve lots.

Hudelson's addition, situated north of the First Northwestern addition on the west side of Franklin Street and on the south side of Lincoln Street, was platted and acknowledged by Phebe Hudelson, July 13, 1868, and contains twelve lots, no blocks designated.

Charles' Block, by which name this addition is known, situated immediately east of the first Southern addition and east of Adams Street, was platted August 3, 1868, and was acknowledged by John T. Charles, Oliver Charles and Eunice S. Charles, proprietors, on the same date, and contains two blocks, consisting of twelve lots.

Heaton, Peden and Scovell's addition, situated immediately south of the Panhandle railway, between Madison and Jefferson streets, was platted in October, 1868, and was acknowledged by John W. Heaton, Reuben Peden and Ezra Scovell, proprietors, November 19, 1868, and contains eight blocks, consisting of thirty two lots.

Stuart's addition, situated in the extreme north end of town and east of Franklin Street, was platted and acknowledged by Ithamer W. Stuart, January 14, 1870, and contains ten lots, no blocks designated.

Watts' addition, situated immediately west of White's addition, on the west side of Madison Street and on the south side of Pine Street, was platted and acknowledged by Peter and Harry Watts, June 11, 1870, and contains two blocks, consisting of eight lots.

Lowrey's addition, situated immediately south and west of White's addition, on the east side of Madison Street, was platted in March, 1886, and was acknowledged by John W. Lowrey, July 30, 1886, and contains four lots, no blocks designated.

Harry Watts' North addition, situated immediately north of the Northwestern addition, on the west side of Franklin Street, was platted January 12, 1887, and was acknowledged by Watts, on the same date and contains seventeen lots, no blocks designated.

Green, Allison and Wagoner's addition is a subdivision of lot seven in Stuart's addition and was platted November 4, 1887, and was acknowledged by Alpheus W. Green, Morton Allison and Peter Wagoner, proprietors, November 7, 1887, and contains six lots, no blocks designated.

Barrett's addition, situated immediately north of the Northern addition, between Franklin and Adams streets, was platted May 27, 1889, and was acknowledged by the heirs of Charles A. Barrett, deceased, June 17, 1889, and contains seven and seventy four hundredths acres, divided into four blocks, consisting of twenty four lots.

Noah W. Wagoner's addition, situated immediately north of Harry Watts' addition, between Madison and Franklin streets, was platted January 3, 1890, and was acknowledged by Wagoner on the same day and contains twenty lots, no blocks designated.

James M. Woods' subdivision of a part of out-lot thirty five, situated immediately southwest of Lowrey's addition, on the west side of Madison Street, was platted April 8, 1891, and was acknowledged by Woods, May 8, 1891, and contains ten lots, no blocks designated.

The Knightstown Improvement Company's addition, situated west of the corporate limits of said town, and west of Montgomery Creek, on the south side of Clay or Main Street, was platted March 28, 1892, and was acknowledged by Leonidas P. Newby, Thomas B. Deem, Frank J. Vestal, James Hall, Edward G. Mostler, George W. Williams, William Call, Harry Watts, Shepperd Bowman and Aaron E. Carroll, directors of the Knightstown Land and Improvement Company, April 23, 1892, and contains seventeen and thirty eight hundredths acres, divided into seventy two lots, no blocks designated.

Sadie V. Roberts' addition, situated immediately south of Cary and Church's addition, south of Main Street, between Hill Avenue and Madison Street, was platted September 8, 1892, and was acknowledged by Sadie V. Roberts and Joseph H. Roberts, November 14, 1892, and contains twenty four lots, no blocks designated.

The Merchants' and Manufacturers' Association's addition, situated immediately north of Stuart's addition, in the extreme north end of town, and extending from the Greensboro pike on the east to McCullum Street on the west, was platted October 16, 1902, and was on the same date acknowledged by Robert Silver, President, and John A. Sample, Secretary, of the Merchants' and Manufacturers' Association, and contains one hundred and fifty lots and two out-lots, no blocks designated.

The town of Knightstown is pleasantly situated on Blue River, or rather between that stream and Montgomery Creek. Waitsel M. Cary, the original proprietor, kept the only hotel for some years and built the first frame house in town. The place was named in honor of Jonathan Knight, a United States Engineer, who located the Cumberland, or National Road, through the State. At first the town only extended back two or three tiers of lots from the river bluff.

Levi Griffith and Isaac James owned the first dry goods establishment here about the year 1830. There were about a half dozen houses in the place at that time, and the population was less than three hundred in 1833.

The first church built here was by the Presbyterians, in 1834—a frame, about thirty by forty feet. The Methodists erected a small frame building, about the year 1837. A distillery was erected just over the river, about 1825, by one John Lewis, and about 1828 a carding machine was built near the present Panhandle depot.

About two years after the inception of Knightstown, the Ithamer W. Stuart farm of 160 acres could have been bought for $400. One of the best corner lots sold for $96, which was regarded as a fancy price indeed. Part of this Stuart farm has long since been platted as additions to Knightstown, and one acre of the balance of the unplatted land is now worth what the whole could have been bought for as above stated.

As late as 1830 the country was such a "howling wilderness"—with little more than a bridle-path through the woods—that Dr. Whitesel was badly lost in going to see a patient on Six-Mile Creek, and bears came out of the river bottom and were chased through the streets more than once after that period. A young physician named Hiatt was the first to locate in town; his stay was short. James Wilson was Knightstown's first attorney.

Whisky was in much more general use in early days than at present.

HENRY COUNTY LAWYERS.

... Carpenter's addition, situated immediately north of Harry Watts' addition, between Main and Franklin streets, was platted January 3, 1890, and was acknowledged the same day and contains twenty lots, no blocks designated.

Sadie M. Woods' subdivision of a part of out-lot thirty five, situated immediately ... of Lowrey's addition, on the west side of Madison Street, was platted April 8, 1891, and was acknowledged by Woods, May 8, 1891, and contains ten lots, no blocks designated.

The Knightstown Improvement Company's addition, situated west of the corporate limits of said town, and west of Montgomery Creek, on the south side of Clay or Main Street, was platted March 28, 1892, and was acknowledged by Leonidas P. Newby, Thomas B. Deem, Frank J. Vestal, James Hall, Edward G. Mosler, George W. Williams, William Call, Harry Watts, Shepperd Bowman and Aaron E. Carroll directors of the Knightstown Land and Improvement Company, April 23, 1892 and contains seventeen and thirty eight hundredths acres, divided into seventy two lots, no blocks designated.

Sadie V. Roberts' addition, situated immediately south of Cary and Church's addition, south of Main Street, between Hill Avenue and ... Street, was platted September 8, 1892, and was acknowledged by Sadie V. Roberts and Joseph H. Roberts, November 14, 1892, and contains twenty four lots, no blocks designated.

The Merchants' and Manufacturers' Association addition, situated immediately north of Stuart's addition, in the extreme north end of town and extending from the Greensboro pike on the east to McCullum Street on the west, was platted October 16, 1902, and was on the same date acknowledged by ... Silver, President, and John A. Sample, Secretary, of the Merchants' and Manufacturers' Association, and contains one hundred and fifty lots and two out lots, no blocks designated.

The town of Knightstown is pleasantly situated on Blue River, or rather between that stream and Montgomery Creek. Whitsel M. Cary, the original proprietor, kept the only hotel for some years and built the first frame house in town. The place was named in honor of Jonathan Knight, a United States Engineer, who located the Cumberland, or National Road, through the State. At first the town only extended back two or three tiers of lots from the river bluff.

Levi Griffith and Isaac James owned the first dry goods establishment here about the year 1830. There were about a half dozen houses in the place at that time, and the population was less than three hundred in 1833.

The first church built here was by the Presbyterians; in 1834—a frame, about thirty by forty feet. The Methodists erected a small frame building, about the year 1837. A distillery was erected just over the river, about 1825, by one John Lewis, and about 1828 a carding machine was built near the present ...

... after the inception of Knightstown, the Ethaner W. Stuart farm of 160 acres could have been bought for ... One of the best corner lots sold for $95, which was regarded as a fancy price indeed. Part of this Stuart farm has long since been platted as additions to Knightstown, and one acre of the balance of the unplatted land is worth what the whole could have been bought for as above stated.

As late as 1830 the country was such a "howling wilderness"—with little more than a bridle-path through the woods—that Dr. Whitesel was badly ... in going to see a patient on Six Mile Creek, and bears came out of the ... and were chased through the streets more than once after that ... young physician named Hiatt was the first to locate in town; his

Sta... James Wilson was Knightstown's first attorney.

Whisky ... much more general use in early days than at present.

HENRY COUNTY LAWYERS.

A judge, the "'squire" and all the constables were seen drunk on one or more occasions in early days, and pugilistic encounters were among the cherished amusements. But great changes have been wrought.

Knightstown is in the midst of splendid farming lands, the productions of which find here a ready market.

About 1850 the Knightstown and Shelbyville railroad, the first which reached our county, was completed to Knightstown, and business received a new impetus, and "corner lots" rapidly appreciated in value. This was a primitive railroad, the rails of which were of wood, stripped with flat bar iron. It was abandoned in 1853 but when the present Louisville and Benton Harbor division of the Big Four railway was completed in the summer of 1891, running south through the western part of the county, it followed this old abandoned right of way for a short distance in Rush County.

The Knightstown Academy building is a commodious structure and the graded school has for years ranked high.

The town has two banking institutions, but these are treated of in another part of this History in the chapter entitled, "Banks and Banking." Knightstown is one of the best towns on the line of the old Indiana Central railroad between Richmond and Indianapolis. In the chapter of this History entitled "Newspapers, Past and Present" will be found a full account of the newspapers that have been published and of those now in existence at Knightstown. Knightstown is one of the four postoffices that have existed in Wayne Township, the other three being Elizabeth City (Maple Valley, discontinued), Grant City (Snyder, discontinued) and Raysville. The postoffice at Knightstown was established January 30, 1833, with Joseph McCalley, as postmaster. On page 38 of this history will be found a list of the postmasters to date, with the time served by each. Also the names of the four rural route carriers with the numbers of their respective routes.

The census of 1900 places the population of the town at 1,942.

LEWISVILLE.

Lewisville is situated in Franklin Township, eight and three fourths miles south and one mile east from the court house in New Castle, and nine miles east from Knightstown, on the Pittsburg, Cincinnati, Chicago and St. Louis railway, and the Indianapolis and Eastern railway (electric line), and on the west side of Flatrock. It is in the E. ½ of the S. E. ¼ of Sec. 25, Tp. 16 N., R. 10 E., and the W. ½ of the S. W. ¼ of Sec. 30, Tp. 16 N., R. 11 E. The original plat was laid out and platted by Thomas Brown, Surveyor, and was acknowledged by Lewis C. Freeman and James B. Harris, proprietors, December 25, 1829. The main street running east and west is designated as "The Great National Road." The original plat contains eight blocks, consisting of sixty four lots.

The first Eastern addition, situated immediately east of the original plat, was platted March 2, 1836, and on the same date was acknowledged by Rozel Spencer and William D. Westerfield, proprietors, and contains ten blocks, consisting of eighty four lots.

The first Southern addition, situated immediately south of the original plat, was platted April 28, 1836, and was acknowledged by Dr. M. Strong, proprietor, May 2, 1836, and contains fourteen lots, no blocks designated.

The George B. Morris' addition, situated immediately east of the school lot, on the south side of the National Road, was platted November 26, 1902, and was acknowledged by Morris on the same date and contains four and ninety four hundredths acres, divided into thirty lots, no blocks designated.

It was first proposed to name this town Freemanville, after Lewis C. Freeman, one of the original proprietors, but as it was discovered that there was another town of that name in this State it was finally determined to call it Lewisville, incorporating the first or given name of Mr. Freeman.

Lewisville is today a better town than ever before. No saloon is permitted there, while there are two, perhaps three, fine churches, and many handsome residences. These taken in connection with the excellent business blocks all denote a prosperous and happy community of people.

That the country around Lewisville is in a high state of cultivation is evidenced by the fact that the First National Bank of that town, with a capital of only $25,000, has deposits of about five times that amount. The town only has the one banking institution which is treated of elsewhere in this History in the chapter entitled "Banks and Banking." In the chapter in this history entitled "Newspapers, Past and Present", will be found a full account of the newspapers that have been published and of the one now in existence in Lewisville.

Lewisville is the only town in Franklin Township and is also the only postoffice that was ever established in that township. There is a tradition in South Franklin Township that before the postoffice was established in Lewisville there was a postoffice on the county line a mile and a quarter south of the town kept by Garnette Hayden. However, there is no official record in Washington City of such an office. It is probable that mail was carried from established offices to Hayden's house, which was on the main line of stage travel, for distribution in that neighborhood. Lewis C. Freeman was the first postmaster at Lewisville and opened the office for business, May 27, 1831. On pages 38 and 39 of this history will be found a list of the postmasters, together with the names of the two rural route carriers connected with the office.

The census of 1900 places the population of the town at 404.

LURAY.

This place with only a remnant of its former greatness remaining is situated in Prairie Township, nine and three fourths miles north and one fourth mile east from the court house in New Castle, and is in the N. E. ¼ of Sec. 27, Tp. 19 N., R. 10 E., and was laid out and platted by Lot Hazelton, proprietor, and acknowledged by him, January 19, 1836, and contains six blocks, consisting of eighteen lots. No addition appears to have been filed to the original plat.

The early settlers of Prairie Township came principally from Virginia and named this town Luray, after the county seat of Page County, in the "Old Dominion."

The author of this History well remembers when Luray was the most important point between New Castle and Muncie. At an early day, before the advent of railroads, aside from the fact that New Castle and Muncie were each county seats, Luray was as good a trading point as either and probably did as much business. Some of the most enterprising and prosperous merchants of the county obtained their start in Luray, notably the late Isaac R. Howard, for many years the leading wholesale merchant of Richmond, Indiana, and in whose name the business is yet carried on by his son John; Jeremiah Page, who built the first brick hotel in New Castle, where the Bundy House now stands, was for many years an enterprising citizen of this place. One of the finest flouring mills in the county stood a half mile east of Luray. The building, an imposing structure, still stands and is used as a barn and for other farming purposes.

The decay of Luray began when the Bellefontaine railroad, now a part of the Big Four railway, was built north of it through Delaware County, and when the present Panhandle railroad was built south of it through New Castle; thus the trade was drawn away from it to New Castle and Muncie. Later, when the road was built north from New Castle to Muncie it left Luray one and one half miles to the east, and the establishment of the village of Springport in Henry County and of Oakville in Delaware County, both of which are but two miles distant, was the death knell of the place for business.. The establishment of the rural routes caused the abandonment of the postoffice Now there are less than a dozen houses in the place and one small store operated by a man named McKinley. Thus do the ravages of time tell on towns as well as on individuals.

Prairie Township had four postoffices—Hillsboro (Dan Webster), Luray, Mount Summit and Springport. The two first named have been discontinued. The postoffice at Luray was established May 15, 1838, and was discontinued June 15, 1901. On page 39 of this History will be found a complete list of the postmasters of this place.

MECHANICSBURG.

This village is situated in Fall Creek Township, nine and three fourths miles west and five miles north of west from the court house in New Castle, and three and one half miles south and one mile west of south from Middletown, and is in the S. E. ¼ of Sec. 13 and the N. E. ¼ of Sec. 24, Tp. 18 N., R. 8 E. and the S. W. ¼ of Sec. 18 and the N. W. ¼ of Sec. 19, Tp. 18 N., R. 9 E., and was laid out and platted by Peter Keesling, Margaret Keesling, William Alexander, Frances Alexander, George Keesling and Elizabeth Keesling, proprietors, and was acknowledged by them September 22, 1858, and contains four blocks, consisting of thirty four lots. No addition to the town has ever been filed.

The place is so named from the fact that when the settlement was started there were so many mechanics, representing the different trades, living there that it was determined to recognize them by calling the place Mechanicsburg.

This is the only village or town in the county that was laid off and platted since the advent of railroads that is not located on a railway line. Despite the fact that it has no railroad and that railroads have been built all around it, it has not only maintained but it has also increased its importance as a trading center. Its nearest railroad point and shipping place is Middletown, but the railroad stations of Honey Creek, Sulphur Springs, Kennard and Shirley, in Henry County, and Markleville and Emporia, in Madison County, are easily reached from the 'burg.

Before the days of railroads and steam mills, and before the streams were all reduced to their present diminutive size by ditching and drainage, there were a woolen factory, a grist mill and a saw mill, all adjacent to Mechanicsburg, on Deer Creek; all these have disappeared.

Mechanicsburg is noted for the many exterprising and progressive young men that have gone out in the world from that village. The leading citizen for many years was the late Nimrod R. Elliott, a full biographical sketch of whom will be found elsewhere in this History.

The author of this History in gathering the facts has found that no place in Henry County, according to its population, sent more soldiers to the Civil War than Mechanicsburg and vicinity; in fact its record in this respect is far ahead of many other localities having a much greater population.

Mechanicsburg had an existence as a trading point more than a score of years before it was laid off and platted as a village. The first merchant to establish a store in that neighborhood was Thomas Dunning, who began business about the year 1845, the exact date is disputed. The year named is from the best information obtainable, furnished by William H. Keesling.

A postoffice was established July 14, 1849, and its first postmaster, Thomas B. Keesling, who was born in Preble County, Ohio, May 15, 1824, is still living in San Jose, California. A list of the postmasters will be found on page 40 of this History. Mechanicsburg is one of the three postoffices that have existed and that still exist in Fall Creek Township, the other two being Honey Creek and Middletown. It shares with Cadiz and Greensboro the honor of being the only postoffices in the county not on the line of a railroad.

Notwithstanding its importance, this village has never been incorporated; therefore its population is included only in that of Fall Creek Township. (See Chapter XXXVIII).

MESSICK.

The village of Messick is situated in Blue River Township, four and three-quarter miles northeast from the court house in New Castle, on the Big Four railway. This village was never laid off or platted into town lots by anyone and was founded in the year 1882. The real estate there is described by metes and bounds. Said village is in the S. W. ¼ of Sec. 29 and the N. W. ¼ of Sec. 32, Tp. 18 N., R. 11 E.

It is so named after a well-known family that has for so many years lived there. The place has an existence antedating many years the building of the Big Four railway. Before the building of the Panhandle railway through the county and the establishment of Ashland, there was a postoffice at Messick known by that name which dates back to February 26, 1847. It was a country affair, kept for some time in the respective homes of the successive postmasters and afterward in a country store owned by Millikan and Messick, and perhaps by others. Later, Messick postoffice was discontinued and moved to Ashland, as is recorded in the short description of the last named place found at the beginning of this chapter.

When in 1882 the Big Four railway was completed through the county, east from New Castle, Messick was again given official existence and a postoffice was established, dating from April 7, 1884, and on page 40 of this History will be found a list of the postmasters. However, the postmasters as set out under the head of Ashland in Chapter I of this History from James M. Conner to William Millikan, senior, inclusive, should be considered as at the old country office of Messick. Messick, Mooreland and Rockland are Blue River Township's three postoffices, the last named, however, having been discontinued.

All the population of the village is included in that of Blue River Township, (See Chapter XXXVIII.)

Messick is on the projected line of the Indianapolis, New Castle and Toledo railway (electric line).

MIDDLETOWN.

This town, so named for the reason that it was considered the half way point between New Castle and Anderson, is situated in Fall Creek Township, twelve miles northwest from the court house in New Castle, on the banks of Fall Creek, on the Panhandle railway, on the line of the Union Traction Company from Anderson to New Castle, and is in the S. E. ¼ and the N. E. ¼ of Sec. 31 and the N. W. ¼ of Sec. 32, Tp. 19 N., R. 9 E., and was laid out, platted and acknowledged by Jacob Koontz, October 9, 1829. The main street running north and south was designated as "The New Castle and La Fayette Road," and the original plat contains four blocks consisting of forty lots.

Chauncey H. Burr's addition, situated immediately east of the original plat, was platted August 12, 1839, and was acknowledged by Burr, August 20, 1839, and contains two blocks, consisting of twenty two lots.

Lewis Summers' first and second additions, situated immediately north of the original plat, between Main and Mill streets, were platted the first, March 13, 1834, and the second, March 12, 1840. Both plats were acknowledged by Summers, February 24, 1842. They contain twenty six lots, no blocks designated.

Joseph Yount's addition, situated immediately west of the original plat, on the west side of Church Street, was platted and acknowledged by Joseph Yount, August 23, 1849, and contains five lots, no blocks designated.

Joseph Yount's second addition, situated immediately south and west of Summers' first addition and west of the original plat, and extending west across the Panhandle railway, was platted and acknowledged by Joseph Yount, September 25, 1854, and contains three blocks, consisting of twenty one lots.

Frederick Tykle's addition, situated about twenty four rods east of Summers' first addition, was platted and acknowledged by Frederick Tykle August 22, 1865, and contains thirteen lots, no blocks designated.

Joseph Yount's third addition, situated immediately north of the west part of Yount's second addition and south of the Panhandle railway, was platted March 12, 1866, and was acknowledged by Yount on the same date, and contains three blocks, consisting of twenty one lots.

Willis Wisehart's first addition, situated about two hundred and eighty two feet north of Summers' second addition, on the west side of Main Street and south of Pine Street, was platted April 30, 1881, and was acknowledged by Wisehart on the same date, and contains three blocks, consisting of twenty one lots.

Elizabeth Van Matre's addition, situated immediately north of Summers' second addition, on the west side of Church Street, was platted May 8, 1882, and was acknowledged by Elizabeth Van Matre, May 25, 1882, and contains four lots, no blocks designated.

William M. Moore's addition, situated immediately west of Van Matre's addition, on the east side of Mill Street, was platted June 20, 1883, and was acknowledged by Moore, May 10, 1884, and contains one block, consisting of four lots.

Elizabeth Van Matre's second addition, situated immediately east of Van Matre's first addition, on the east side of Church Street, was platted June 19, 1883, and was acknowledged by Elizabeth Van Matre and Henry Van Matre, July 14, 1883, and contains one block, consisting of four lots.

Willis Wisehart's second addition, situated immediately north of Wisehart's first addition, on the west side of Main Street, and on the north side of Pine Street, was platted June 3, 1885, and was acknowledged by Wisehart on the same date, and contains three blocks, consisting of twenty four lots.

Painter and Watkins' first addition, situated immediately west of Yount's third addition and south of the railroad, was platted July 15, 1890, and was acknowledged by George Davis and Elizabeth Davis, proprietors, on the same date, and contains fifty eight lots, no blocks designated.

Jackson's first addition, situated immediately west of Painter and Watkins' addition and extending north across the Panhandle railway, and lying between Twelfth and Sixteenth streets, was platted February 19. 1894, and was acknowledged by Llewellyn B. Jackson, Nellie J. Jackson, Erastus L. Elliott, Trustee, Andrew S. Miller, President. and George L. Swain, Secretary, of the Indiana Glass Company, on the same date, and contains ninety and twenty three hundredths acres, divided into four hundred and forty one lots, no blocks designated.

The Indiana Glass Company's addition, situated immediately east and north of Jackson's first addition, on the south side of the Panhandle railway, was platted March 26, 1894, and was acknowledged by Andrew S. Miller and George L. Swain, President and Secretary, respectively, of the Indiana Glass Company, on the same date, and contains ten and seventy three hundredths acres, divided into forty seven lots, no blocks designated.

Jackson Wisehart's addition, situated north of Yount's third addition on the north side of High Street and on the east side of Ninth Street, was platted February 27, 1894, and was acknowledged by Willis Wisehart and Elmira Wisehart, proprietors, on the same date, and contains four and forty eight hundredths acres, divided into twenty three lots, no blocks designated.

Willis Wisehart's third addition, situated immediately north of Wisehart's second addition, between Sixth and Eighth streets, was platted April 1, 1894, and was acknowledged by Willis Wisehart, Elmira Wisehart and Overton Cummins, President of the Middletown Butter and Cheese Company, on the same date, and contains six and sixty seven hundredths acres, divided into twenty two lots, no blocks designated.

Tykle's second addition, situated immediately east of Jackson's first addition, and north of the Indiana Glass Company's addition, on the north side of the Panhandle railway, was platted May 11, 1898, and was acknowledged by George E. Tykle and John H. Terhune, Trustees of the estate of Frederick Tykle, deceased, on the same date, and contains fourteen acres, divided into fifty two lots, no blocks designated.

Hedrick's first addition, situated immediately east of Wisehart's first addition, on the north side of Columbia Street, and extending east to Third Street, was platted May 2, 1898, and was acknowledged by John Baker, Jane Baker, J. O. Lambert, Emma Lambert, Berry H. Painter, Jane Sanders, Elizabeth McWilliams, Charles C. Shedron, Mary Shedron, Willis Wisehart, Elmira Wisehart, Lillie Hedrick, John W. Hedrick, John W. Hedrick, guardian of James C. Hedrick, Frank A. Wisehart, Jessie M. Wisehart, Gilbert Watkins and Josie Watkins, heirs of John Hedrick, deceased, on the same date, and contains twenty and ninety eight hundredths acres, divided into seventy five lots and twelve out-lots, no blocks designated.

Jacob Koontz, the original proprietor, had a public sale of lots on December 25, 1829, and it is chronicled that the best prices obtained were very discouraging. At this time there was not a frame house in Fall Creek Township.

In point of population and wealth and as a business point, Middletown has always been considered the third town in the county, ranked only by New Castle and Knightstown. It is surrounded by a fine body of fertile land, all of which has been converted into highly improved farms. The town has always enjoyed a good trade from the southern part of Delaware County, particularly from the "Richwoods" neighborhood, as the county line is only two miles north from the Welsh hotel.

Middletown is noted for its fine private residences, its elegant churches and schools and the high character of its business blocks, particularly the Welsh hotel. It has one bank, known as the Farmers' State Bank of Middletown, with a capital of $30,000, and the thrift and prosperity of its people may be measured from the fact that this bank with so small a capital has carried a deposit account of $200,000. This bank is treated of elsewhere in this History in the chapter entitled "Banks and Banking."

A postoffice was established September 10, 1830, with Jacob Koontz, as postmaster, and on pages 40 and 41 of this History will be found a list of the postmasters together with the names of the four rural route carriers connected with that office. Middletown is one of the three postoffices that have existed and that still exist in Fall Creek Township, the other two being Honey Creek and Mechanicsburg. Its population according to the census of 1900 is given as 1801.

Middletown was incorporated in 1840 by Chauncey H. Burr and fourteen others.

MILLVILLE.

The most eastern village in Henry County on the line of the Panhandle railroad is situated in Liberty Township, six and one fourth miles east and one half mile south of east from the court house in New Castle, and is in the N. E. ¼ of Sec. 15 and the N. W. ¼ of Sec. 14, Tp. 17 N., R. 11 E., and was laid out and platted by John Minesinger, Deputy Surveyor, December 4, 1854, by order of the Court of Common Pleas of Henry County, in January, 1854, from the lands belonging to the estate of John Hershberger, deceased, and contains eight lots, no blocks designated.

Abbott's addition, situated immediately west of the original plat, was platted and acknowledged by Abraham Abbott, August 28, 1856, and contains five blocks, consisting of twenty lots.

Forkner's addition, situated immediately north of the original plat, was platted and acknowledged by Micajah C. Forkner June 20, 1870, and contains five blocks, consisting of twenty one lots.

A plat of Millville, surveyed and platted by William R. Harrold, Surveyor, the same being a re-survey and plat of the original plat and all additions thereto was made and filed in the Recorder's office, August 7, 1873.

The village takes its name from a mill which stood nearby, when the Panhandle railroad was completed to that place, owned by John Hershberger. The railroad established a station there and called it Millville. About this time Hershberger was accidentally killed in the mill, and it being determined to survey and plat the lands into lots, an order of court was obtained therefor as above stated.

The first store room in the town was built by Micajah C. Forkner, father of Judge Mark E. Forkner, of New Castle, who, if he did not start the first store himself, only rented the room for a short time to other parties, and then occupied the store room himself with a stock of general merchandise.

Millville has always been considered a half way point between New Castle and Hagerstown. For many years, as a shipping point, it had the trade of Blue River and Stony Creek townships on the north and of the northern part of Dudley Township on the south, now lost to Millville by the construction of railroads through New Lisbon, Mooreland and Blountsville. It now, as a point for the purchase and shipment of grain and live stock, ranks high from the fact that Samuel D. Wiseheart and Sons, most enterprising merchants in this line, have made it their headquarters for many years.

A postoffice was established June 7, 1855, with Andrew J. Cromer, as postmaster. On page 41 of this history will be found a list of the postmasters. Millville is one of the four postoffices that have existed in Liberty Township, the other three being Chicago (discontinued), Devon (discontinued) and Ashland.

Millville has never been incorporated, and for that reason its population is included in that of Liberty Township. (See Chapter XXXVIII).

CHAPTER XLII.

FOUNDERS AND EARLY MERCHANTS—ORIGINAL PLATS AND ADDITIONS—BANKS
AND NEWSPAPERS—POSTAL AND TRANSPORTATION FACILITIES—POPULATION
—MOORELAND—MOUNT SUMMIT—NEEDMORE—NEW CASTLE—NEW LISBON
— OGDEN — PETERSBURG — PUMPKINTOWN — RAYSVILLE—ROGERSVILLE—
SHARINGTON — SHIRLEY — SPICELAND — SPRINGPORT — STRAUGHN —
SULPHUR SPRINGS—UNIONTOWN—WEST LIBERTY — WHEELAND — WHITE
RAVEN— WOODVILLE—MILES MARSHALL MOORE AND FAMILY.

MOORELAND.

The incorporated town of Mooreland is situated in Blue River Township,
eight miles northeast from the court house in New Castle, on the Big Four rail-
way, and is in the E. $\frac{1}{2}$ of the N. E. $\frac{1}{4}$ of Sec. 22 and the W. $\frac{1}{2}$ of the N. W. $\frac{1}{4}$ and
the W. $\frac{1}{2}$ of the S. W. $\frac{1}{4}$ of Sec. 23, Tp. 18 N., R. 11 E., and was laid out and platted by Daniel K. Cook, Surveyor, and was acknowledged by Miles M. Moore,
proprietor, August 9, 1882, and contains four and eighty seven hundredths acres,
divided into two blocks consisting of sixteen lots and one out-lot.

Mathew Cory's first addition, situated immediately east of the original plat, on the
east side of Broad Street and extending south across the railroad, was platted August
26, 1882, and was acknowledged by Cory on the same date, and contains four blocks, consisting of twenty two lots.

Mathew Cory's second addition, situated immediately east of Cory's first addition,
was platted August 8, 1885, and contains four blocks, consisting of twenty three lots
and one out-lot.

Mathew Cory's third addition, situated immediately north of Cory's first addition,
on the east side of Broad Street, was platted December 28, 1886, and was acknowledged
by Cory on the same date, and contains two blocks, consisting of twelve lots and the
schoolhouse lot.

Mathew Cory's fourth addition, situated north and east of Cory's second addition,
was platted March 13, 1888, and was acknowledged by Cory on the same date, and contains three blocks, consisting of sixteen lots and one out-lot.

Moore's first addition, situated immediately west of the original plat and on the
north side of the Big Four railway, was platted March 28, 1888, and was acknowledged
by Newton B. Davis, administrator of the estate of Miles M. Moore, deceased, on the
same date, and contains three blocks, consisting of twenty six lots.

Mathew Cory's fifth addition, situated immediately south of Cory's second addition, was platted January 22, 1889, and was acknowledged by Cory on the same date,
and contains two blocks, consisting of sixteen lots.

Eli Hardman's first addition, situated immediately north of the original plat and
west of Cory's third addition and north of Charles Street and west of Broad Street,
was platted April 18, 1889, and was acknowledged by Eli Hardman and Mary Jane Hardman, proprietors, on the same date, and contains twelve acres, divided into five blocks,
consisting of forty four lots and one out-lot.

60

Holliday and Koons' addition, situated immediately east of Cory's third addition and north of Block One of Cory's fourth addition, was platted June 12, 1901, and was acknowledged by Eli Holliday, George R. Koons and Benjamin F. Koons, proprietors, on the same date, and contains twenty four lots, no blocks designated.

Mark Huffman's first addition, situated immediately north of Hardman's addition, on the west side of Broad Street, was platted April 25, 1904, and was acknowledged by Mark Huffman and Mary Huffman, proprietors, on the same date, and contains four and thirty one hundredths acres, divided into sixteen lots, no blocks designated.

One of the early settlers of Blue River Township and one of the most successful farmers was Philip Moore, who, dying November 27, 1873, left a valuable estate and a fine farm immediately adjoining the present town of Mooreland. One of his sons, Miles M., by purchase and inheritance, came into possession of that part of the land from which the original plat of Mooreland was surveyed, and it is from these facts that the town is named Mooreland.

A postoffice was established August 21, 1882. On page 41 of this History will be found a list of the postmasters and the names of the two rural route carriers connected with that office, one of whom, Henry H. Moore, is a brother of Miles M., who laid off the town.

Mooreland is surrounded by as fine farming land as there is in Henry County and everything in the town and surrounding country denotes thrift and prosperity. The town has a bank, the history of which will be found in the chapter in this History devoted to "Banks and Banking." The first store was started by Marcus Holliday, son of Oliver Holliday, an early settler, in 1882. The population is given in the census of 1900 at 300. Mooreland is on the projected line of the Indianapolis, New Castle and Toledo electric railway. Mooreland, Messick and Rockland are Blue River Township's three postoffices, the last named having been discontinued.

MILES MARSHALL MOORE.

IN WHOSE HONOR THE TOWN OF MOORELAND WAS NAMED.

Miles Marshall Moore, the third son of Philip and Julia Ann (Wilson) Moore, was born November 18, 1836, on his father's farm in Blue River Township, Henry County, Indiana. He died April 14, 1886, and is buried in Nettle Creek Cemetery, near the old town of Franklin, five miles north of Hagerstown, Wayne County. His father, Philip Moore, was the son of one of the first pioneer settlers of Henry County, William Moore, a native of Tennessee, and his wife, Catharine (Cotener) Moore, who first settled in Preble County, Ohio, where Philip Moore was born April 24, 1812, and who afterwards, when Philip was but fourteen years of age, came to Henry County with his family and settled in Blue River Township. William Moore was a soldier of the War of 1812-15, a record of which fact will be found in another place in this History.

The boyhood days of Miles Marshall Moore were spent in the service of his father and he was a potent helper in clearing the land and cultivating the soil of his father's farm. His education was such as could be secured at the common or district schools of the period. In 1860, with a view to going to some new country, if the outlook proved promising, he took a trip to the Great West from which he soon afterward returned home where he remained with his father until August 27, 1861. The Civil War was then in progress and he enlisted as a private in Company C, 36th Indiana Infantry, and participated in all the engagements of that famous regiment, serving a full enlistment of three years. He was a brave and gallant soldier and the record of his military service will be found in connection with that of his company and regiment in Chapter XVI of this History.

immediately east of Cory's third addition
tion, was platted June 12, 1901, and was ac-
is and Benjamin F. Koons, proprietors, on
3, no blocks designated.
Immediately north of Hardman's addition,
i April 25, 1904, and was acknowledged by
's, on the same date, and contains four and
ixteen lots, no blocks designated.

r Township and one of the most success-
ng November 27, 1873, left a valuable
ng the present town of Mooreland. One
nheritance, came into possession of that
lat of Mooreland was surveved, and it is
Mooreland.
21. 1882. On page 41 of this History
the names of the two rural route carriers
Henry H. Moore, is a brother of Miles

r farming land as there is in Henry

Miles M. Moore

After his honorable discharge from the army at Atlanta, Georgia, September 15, 1864, he returned to his home in Blue River Township, and in the following year, March 26, 1865, was united in marriage with Nancy, daughter of Thomas and Elvira Lamb, of Dalton, Wayne County, Indiana. She was born November 17, 1845.

Immediately after their marriage, Miles M. Moore and his wife went to White County, in the western part of the State of Indiana, where he and his brother, James H. Moore, had purchased for seven thousand five hundred dollars, two hundred and fifty acres of land. After making the first payment on the land, he had thirty dollars left with which he and his wife began housekeeping. She was a very economical woman and a valued helpmeet, using as little as possible of their small store of money for the household but spending the greater part of it for corn, hay and feed for the stock. Mrs. Moore not only performed her duties as the housekeeper but often went into the field and assisted her husband in tilling and cultivating the soil. This double labor, willingly performed, was continued until the birth of their first child, Philip Edgar, born May 12, 1867. He was a very bright and interesting child and was the pride of the household. On January 15, 1869, Thomas Eugene, their second child, was born. From this time the health of Mrs. Moore declined and her husband became correspondingly depressed and discouraged. On May 18, 1872, the eldest son, Philip Edgar, or Eddie as he was familiarly called, was taken down with brain fever from which, after severe pain and suffering, death came to his relief. At the earnest desire of the wife and mother, the remains of the child were taken to Wayne County, Indiana, and were there interred in Nettle Creek Cemetery. He died May 28, 1872.

The husband and wife returned to their desolate home where they remained for a time but the health of the family not improving, Mr. Moore disposed of his interest in the White County farm and in 1874, following the death of his father, purchased a part of the old homestead and on August 18th returned to Henry County, from which time their health improved and their prospects became bright for a prosperous future.

Mr. Moore was for many years, as his widow is now, a member of the United Brethren Church, to which he gave of his strength and means liberally during his life. Politically, Mr. Moore was for a number of years a radical Republican but he subsequently became a "Greenbacker" and gave to that organization, of which he was a leading member in Henry County, his warm and active support. He was a firm believer in the idea that the Government should issue all money and that the same should be a full legal tender for all purposes, public and private.

Miles Marshall Moore was a good citizen and was one of that great number of loyal and patriotic men, who by their acts and deeds during the great Civil War gave honor to the splendid military history of Indiana and Henry County. He was an experienced, practical farmer and by thrift and industry accumulated a life's competency. He was of an energetic and persevering disposition and won and held the regard and esteem of his neighbors and many friends.

Thomas Eugene, the second son of Miles M. Moore and his wife, Nancy (Lamb) Moore, was married September 21, 1889, to Rozella Bird, who was born March 27, 1872. She was the daughter of Joseph and Eliza (Houser) Bird, of the well known family of that name which has been for many years prominent in the affairs of Stony Creek Township, Henry County. They have two children, Ernest Edgar, born August 26, 1890, and Gladys, born September 19, 1896. . Thomas Eugene and his family reside in Muncie, the "magic city" of Delaware County, Indiana, where he is engaged in the natural gas and oil business.

Since the death of Miles Marshall Moore, April 14, 1886, as above stated, his widow, Nancy (Lamb) Moore, has given all of her time to overseeing and managing the property left by her beloved husband. She is a thorough business woman and has conducted the business with great care and prudence, not only keeping the property intact but adding materially to its value. She resides at Mooreland, where she has a fine home and where she owns one hundred and forty two acres of land, adjoining that place on the south, which is highly improved and which is valued at one hundred and fifty dollars per acre. She is a very excellent woman, domestic in her habits, hospitable, of a kindly disposition, charitable, and has the entire respect of the community in which she lives.

The town of Mooreland was laid out by Miles M. Moore and was named in his honor. It is a thriving place, is kept neat and clean, has a provident population, is blessed with good schools, good churches, good society and bears the reputation of being the most beautiful town in Henry County.

MOUNT SUMMIT.

Mount Summit, or Summit as it is generally called, derives its name from the supposition that it occupies one of the highest points of land in the county and is situated in Prairie Township, five miles north and three fourths of a mile west of north from the court house in New Castle and is in the S. E. ¼ of Sec. 16 and the N. E. ¼ of Sec. 21 and the S. W. ¼ of Sec. 15 and the N. W. ¼ of Sec. 22, Tp· 18 N., R. 10 E., and was laid out and platted by Isaac Kinley, Surveyor, and was acknowledged by Jesse Ice, proprietor, July 11, 1854, and contains four blocks, consisting of fifteen lots.

A plat of Mount Summit by Jesse Ice, situated immediately south of the pike leading west to Sulphur Springs and on the east side of the Lake Erie and Western railway was laid out, platted and acknowledged by Jesse Ice, proprietor, July 22, 1857, and contains twenty four lots, no blocks designated.

William West's addition, situated immediately east of the road running north and south from New Castle to Springport and on the north side of the pike running east and west from Mount Summit to Sulphur Springs, was platted April 16, 1869, and was acknowledged by West on the same date, and contains three blocks, consisting of ten lots.

Abel W. Ice's addition, situated immediately east and south of the original plat, on the south side of the pike running east and west and on the west side of the pike running north and south, was platted April 16, 1869, and acknowledged by Ice on the same date, and contains five blocks, consisting of twenty four lots.

Peter P. Rifner's addition, situated on the north side of the pike running east and west, and east of the Lake Erie and Western railway, was platted August 8, 1870, and was acknowledged by Rifner April 1, 1872, and contains two blocks, consisting of fourteen lots.

Abel W. Ice's second addition, situated immediately south of his first addition and between the railroad and the pike running north and south, was platted October 17, 1871, and was acknowledged by Ice, April 26, 1872, and contains three blocks, consisting of eleven lots.

Sarah Ice's addition, situated immediately east of Abel W. Ice's first and second additions and south of West's addition, was platted October 24, 1871, and was acknowledged . by Sarah Ice, October 16, 1872, and contains two blocks, consisting of eight lots.

A plat of Mount Summit made by William R. Harrold, Surveyor, includes all of the foregoing additions and ten out-lots, and was completed May 9, 1873.

Peter P. Rifner's second addition, situated immediately north of Abel W. Ice's first addition, was platted May 24, 1890, and was acknowledged by Rifner on the same date, and contains two blocks, consisting of eight lots.

Ezekiel T. Ice's addition, situated immediately south of Sarah Ice's addition and on the east side of the pike running north and south, was platted June 9, 1891, and was acknowledged by Ezekiel T. Ice and Hester A. Ice, on the same date, and contains seven lots, no blocks designated.

The village was first projected in anticipation of the construction of the north and south railroad before the Civil war. This road collapsed preceding the panic of 1857 and it was not, until more than a dozen years thereafter, completed north from New Castle to Muncie. This accounts for the fact that no postoffice was established until November 25, 1869. Prior to this time the people of the neighborhood got their mail from either New Castle, Sulphur Springs or Luray. The first store was established in 1852 by John Warner.

On pages 41 and 42 of this History will be found a list of all the postmasters, together with the name of the one rural route carrier connected with that office.

As the place has never been incorporated its population, whatever it may be, is included in that of Prairie Township. (See Chapter XXXVIII). Prairie Township has had four postoffices—Hillsboro (Dan Webster), Luray, Mount Summit and Springport. The two first named have been discontinued.

NEEDMORE.

Needmore was an old settlement or village, never platted into lots, situated in Harrison Township, on the road leading due west and distant from Cadiz three and one half miles at a cross roads, and two and one half miles due south of Mechanicsburg. At an early day this village or settlement contained a store, a blacksmith shop, a wagon shop, a shoemaker's shop and a saw mill and possibly other industries which enter into the make-up of a little settlement. It never acquired the distinction of being a postoffice and at this time all evidences of the former village have disappeared.

Needmore's chief claim to fame rests in the fact that a company of the Indiana Legion or Home Guards was organized at Mechanicsburg during the Civil War which was known as the "Needmore Rangers," a goodly number of the members of the organization coming from that particular locality. The author has been unable to ascertain why the name Needmore was given this settlement, but it is possible that it came from some one of that name who lived there at an early day.

NEW CASTLE.

New Castle, named for New Castle, Henry County, Kentucky, is the county seat of Henry County, and is situated in Henry Township, about a mile east of the geographical center of the county on the Panhandle railway, the Peoria and Eastern division of the Big Four railway, the Lake Erie and Western railway, the New Castle and Rushville division of the Lake Erie and Western railway, and the New Castle and Dunreith division of the Indianapolis and Eastern electric railway. It is also the southern terminus of the Anderson and New Castle division of the Union Traction Company's electric line, and of the projected electric railroad from Muncie to New Castle. The projected Indianapolis, New Castle and Toledo electric line will also be an important addition to the railroad facilities of the town, which is in the S. $\frac{1}{2}$ and N. E. $\frac{1}{4}$ of Sec. 10, the S. $\frac{1}{2}$ of Sec. 11, the N. $\frac{1}{2}$ and S. E. $\frac{1}{4}$ of Sec. 15, and the N. $\frac{1}{2}$ and S. W. $\frac{1}{4}$ of Sec. 14, Tp. 17 N., R. 10 E., and the original plat was laid out and platted January 4, 1836, by Thomas Leonard, who had been appointed for that purpose by the Board of County Commissioners, and who took to his aid Thomas R. Stanford, Surveyor. The original plat was made up from the field notes of the town of New Castle, as returned to the Recorder's office by John Dorrah and William McKimmey, Surveyors, and was acknowledged by Ezekiel Leavell, agent for Henry County, April 8, 1823, and contained twenty blocks, consisting of one hundred and forty lots and twenty out-lots. The survey of 1836 above mentioned was a re-establishment of the lines of the original plat.

The west half of the public square was vacated by the board of commissioners at their November term, 1835, and Moses Roberts was appointed to cause a survey or subdivision to be made, and said west half was platted into five lots, three fronting on Broad Street and two on Race Street.

Rue and Holman's addition, situated immediately south of the original plat, on the east side of South Main Street and south of Indiana Avenue, was platted by Richard Rue and Joseph Holman and was acknowledged by Richard Rue, January 26, 1844, and by Joseph Holman February 3, 1844. It contains six blocks, consisting of thirty two lots and four out-lots.

William Murphey's addition, situated immediately south of the original plat and south of Indiana Avenue, on the west side of South Main Street, was platted by Murphey, May 20, 1851, and was acknowledged June 19, 1851, and contains four blocks, consisting of ten lots.

Taylor's addition, situated east and north of the Panhandle railroad, on the south side of East Broad Street, is a subdivision of out-lots 4 and 5 of the original plat and was platted April 6, 1853, and was acknowledged by John Taylor on the same date and contains twenty one lots, no blocks designated.

Thornburgh's addition, situated immediately east of the original plat, on the north side of Broad Street and east of Fifteenth Street, was platted July 18, 1853, and was acknowledged by Hiram Thornburgh and by Hiram Thornburgh, guardian, of John and Jacob Thornburgh, July 20, 1853, and contains two blocks, consisting of thirty five lots.

George W. Lennard's addition, situated immediately west of the original plat, on the north side of West Broad Street and west of Eleventh Street, was platted September 22, 1854, and was acknowledged by Lennard, October 3, 1854, and contains two blocks, consisting of thirty six lots.

Martin L. Powell's first addition, situated immediately east and north of Thornburgh's addition and north of Taylor's addition beginning fifty feet west of Pennsylvania Avenue, now Eighteenth Street, and on the north side of East Broad Street, was platted August 24, 1866, and was acknowledged by Powell, September 10, 1866, and contains five blocks, consisting of thirty two lots.

Hazzard and Shirk's addition, situated two blocks north of Vine Street, at the alley which marks the northern boundary of the original plat, on the west side of North Main Street, was platted March 18, 1867, and was acknowledged by George Hazzard (the author of this History) and Benjamin Shirk on the same date, and contains ten lots ,no blocks designated.

George Lowe's addition, situated immediately south of the Eastern out-lots in the original plat and south of Taylor's addition and east of Rue and Holman's addition, was platted September 28, 1867, and was acknowledged by Lowe, September 30, 1867, and contains five blocks, consisting of forty one lots.

Seth H. Elliott's addition, situated immediately south of Lowe's addition and north of the Lake Erie and Western railway, was platted September 28, 1867, and was acknowledged by Seth H. Elliott and Catharine Elliott, September 30, 1867, and contains four blocks, consisting of twenty two lots and Elliott's reservation, equal to four lots, for a residence.

Nicholson's addition, situated immediately south of Bundy's second addition, between South Eleventh Street and Bundy Avenue, was platted August 3, 1868, and was acknowledged by Andrew Nicholson on the same date, and contains four blocks, consisting of eleven lots.

Miles Murphey's addition, situated immediately south of Rue and Holman's addition, on the east side of South Main Street, was platted April 13, 1868, and was acknowledged by Murphey, April 21, 1868, and contains ten lots, no blocks designated.

Benjamin Elder's addition, situated immediately west and south of the George W. Lennard addition in the west‛part of town, on the north side of West Broad Street between Seventh and Ninth Streets, was platted August 17, 1868, and was acknowledged by Elder, August 21, 1868, and contains four blocks, consisting of thirty two lots.

Martin L. Bundy's addition, situated south of William Murphey's addition, on the west side of South Main Street and on the north side of Lincoln Avenue, was platted September 7, 1868, and was acknowledged by Bundy, September 9, 1868, and contains three blocks, consisting of eleven lots.

Hiram Thornburgh's second addition, situated immediately north of Martin L. Powell's first addition, between the Panhandle railway and Eighteenth Street, was platted by Hiram Thornburgh, March 1, 1869, and was acknowledged March 31, 1869, and contains fifteen blocks, consisting of sixty nine lots and three out-lots.

Martin L. Powell's second addition, situated immediately east of the East School House grounds, on the south side of East Broad Street and extending south of the Panhandle railway, was platted October 11, 1869, and was acknowledged by Powell October 14, 1869, and contains thirteen acres, divided into seven blocks, consisting of forty two lots.

Benjamin Elder's second addition, situated immediately north and west of Elder's first addition, was platted and acknowledged by Benjamin Elder, July 5, 1870, and contains six blocks, consisting of thirty two lots.

Jacob Shopp's addition, situated immediately east of Taylor's addition and on the south side of Shopp Avenue, was platted May 27, 1871, and was acknowledged by Shopp on the same date, and contains ten lots, no blocks designated.

James Loer's addition, situated east of Martin L. Powell's first addition and north of East Broad Street, the homesteads of James Brown and Thomas B. Redding intervening, and on the west side of North Twenty First Street, was platted August 4, 1871, and was acknowledged by Loer, August 14, 1871, and contains four blocks, consisting of twenty one lots.

Eli Murphey's addition, situated immediately west of William Murphey's addition, on the west side of South Twelfth Street, was platted October 16, 1871, and was acknowledged by Murphey September 17, 1872, and contains five lots, no blocks designated.

James Brown's addition, situated immediately east of Thornburgh's second addition and Powell's first addition, on the east side of Nineteenth Street, was platted and acknowledged by James Brown January 27, 1873, and contains seven lots, no blocks designated.

John Rea's addition, situated immediately east of Powell's second addition, between East Broad Street and the Panhandle railway, was platted September 21, 1872, and was acknowledged by Rea, October 30, 1874, and contains five blocks, consisting of fifteen lots.

Elizabeth Murphey's addition, situated east of South Park addition, south of the former General William Grose's homestead, now the home of the Henry County Historical Society, and on the east side of South Fourteenth Street, was platted October 8, 1874, and was acknowledged by Elizabeth Murphey and Miles Murphey, March 15, 1875, and contains two blocks, consisting of twenty four lots.

Bowers' division of out-lots, situated immediately east of Nicholson's addition, between South Main Street and Bundy Avenue, was platted April 24, 1875, by John Unthank, Surveyor, and was acknowledged by said Unthank on the same date, and contains sixteen lots, no blocks designated.

Martin L. Powell's subdivision, situated immediately east and south of Powell's second addition, on the south side of the Panhandle railway (with the exception of nine lots which are north of the railroad), and extending north to the New Castle and Hagerstown turnpike, or East Broad Street, was platted by Martin L. Powell, May 25, 1876, and was acknowledged by him May 26, 1876, and contains nine lots and twelve out-lots, no blocks designated.

Thomas Mullen's addition, situated east of Powell's subdivision, between East Broad Street and the Panhandle railway, was platted March 1, 1877, and was acknowledged by Thomas Mullen, March 10, 1877, and contains three blocks, consisting of twenty eight lots.

James Loer's second addition, situated immediately east of his first addition, was platted and acknowledged by him August 21, 1878, and contains four blocks, consisting of twenty four lots.

William E. and Mary C. Woodward's addition, situated east of Elizabeth Murphey's addition, between Walnut Street and the Lake Erie and Western railway, was platted July 3, 1883, and was acknowledged by Mary C. Woodward and William E. Woodward on the same date, and contains three blocks, consisting of twenty one lots and seven out-lots.

Martin L. Bundy's second addition, situated immediately north of Nicholson's addition and south of Burr's addition, on the west side of South Main Street and Bundy Avenue, was platted June 24, 1881, and was acknowledged by Martin L. Bundy and Amanda, his wife, on the same date, and contains three blocks, consisting of eleven lots and one out-lot.

Mowrer's addition, situated immediately south of Bundy's second addition, on the west side of Bundy Avenue, was platted June 25, 1881, and was acknowledged by James M. Mowrer, Emma C. Mowrer, Mary C. Mowrer, Thomas W. Millikan and Margaret R. Millikan on the same date, and contains two blocks, consisting of six lots and one out-lot.

Thomas B. Reeder's addition, situated immediately south of Mowrer's addition, between Bundy Avenue and South Eleventh Street, was platted June 25, 1881, and was acknowledged by Reeder on the same date, and contains seven lots, no blocks designated.

Lycurgus L. Burr's addition, situated immediately south of Bundy's first addition, on the west side of South Main Street and south side of Lincoln Avenue, was platted June 25, 1881, and was acknowledged by Burr on the same date, and contains two blocks, consisting of eight lots and one out-lot.

James M. Thornton's addition, situated immediately north of George W. Lennard's addition and west of Hazzard and Shirk's addition, between North Ninth and North Eleventh streets, and on the north side of West Spring Street, was platted August 24, 1881, and was acknowledged by Thornton on the same date, and contains four blocks, consisting of thirty two lots.

Hernly and Brown's addition (known as Lockwood), situated immediately north of Woodward's second addition, at the extreme north end of town, on the west side of the Panhandle railway, was platted October 14, 1881, and was acknowledged by Charles S. Hernly and Samuel Hadley Brown, proprietors, on the same date, and contains two blocks, consisting of twenty lots.

Pyrrhus Woodward's addition, situated immediately north of Hazzard and Shirk's addition, on the west side of North Twelfth Street, was platted October 1, 1881, and was acknowledged by Woodward on the same date, and contains three blocks, consisting of twenty four lots and two out-lots.

David W. Chambers' addition, situated immediately south of the original plat, on the east side of South Eleventh Street, was platted April 19, 1882, and was acknowledged by Chambers on the same date, and contains thirteen lots, no blocks designated.

Jacob Brenneman's addition, situated immediately south of out-lots twenty two and twenty three, original plat, on the south side of Indiana Avenue and east side of South Ninth Street, was platted March 23, 1883, and was acknowledged by Brenneman, April 3, 1883, and contains one block, consisting of five lots.

Asahel W. Lennard's addition, situated immediately north of Thornburgh's second addition, on the east side of Columbia Avenue, was platted August 27, 1883, and was acknowledged by Lennard on the same date, and contains eleven and fifty three hundredths acres, divided into four blocks, consisting of thirty five lots.

Martin L. Bundy's third addition, situated south of Bower's addition, on the west side of South Main Street, was platted June 20, 1890, and was acknowledged by Bundy on the same date, and contains five lots, no blocks designated.

James V. Hickman's addition, situated immediately east of Loer's second addition, on the south side of the Brown pike (the old Brown road), was platted September 29,

1890, and was acknowledged by Hickman on the same date and contains twenty two and seventy one hundredths acres, divided into one hundred and four lots, no blocks designated.

Morris and Bundy's South Park addition, situated immediately east of Bower's division, between South Main and South Fourteenth streets, was platted May 2, 1892, and was acknowledged by John M. Morris and Eugene H. Bundy on the same date and contains thirty six lots and one out-lot, no blocks designated.

Vestal's first addition, situated immediately north and west of Powell's subdivision, between East Broad Street and the Panhandle railway, was platted June 3, 1893, and was acknowledged by Milton M. Vestal on the same date, and contains three and one half acres, divided into fifteen lots, no blocks designated.

The Speeder Cycle Company's addition, situated immediately south of South Park addition, between South Main and South Fourteenth streets, was platted August 21, 1894, and was acknowledged by Henry J. Adams, President, and Alman L. Bowman, Secretary of the Speeder Cycle Company on the same date, and contains seventeen and fifty three hundredths acres, divided into seventy five lots and one out-lot, no blocks designated.

The Jehu T. Elliott Heirs' addition, situated immediately west of the original plat, on the south side of West Broad Street between South Fifth and South Ninth streets, was platted April 27, 1895, and was acknowledged by Mark E. Forkner, Attorney in Fact for the Elliott heirs, on the same date, and contains thirteen and ninety three hundredths acres, divided into sixty four lots, no blocks designated.

Woodward's second addition, situated immediately north of Woodward's first addition, between the Panhandle and Big Four railways, was platted May 20, 1896, and was acknowledged by Pyrrhus Woodward, Mary E. Woodward, George Woodward, Lizzie Woodward and Belle Springer on the same date, and contains twenty two and sixty five hundredths acres, divided into seventy seven lots and two out-lots.

The Robert M. Nixon Heirs' addition, situated immediately west of Chambers' addition, on the west side of South Eleventh Street, was platted July 1, 1897, and was acknowledged by Thomas L. Campbell, administrator of the estate of Robert M. Nixon, deceased, and Celestina Nixon, widow, on the same date, and contains thirteen lots, no blocks designated.

Rentzsch's sub-plat, situated in Mowrer's addition, includes out-lot one and lots one, two and three in block one and is between South Eleventh Street and Bundy Avenue. It was platted April 28, 1898, and was acknowledged by Otto Rentzsch on the same date, and contains ten lots, no blocks designated.

Mikels and Ogborn's Cable addition, situated immediately east of John Rea's addition, between East Broad Street and the Panhandle railway, was platted November 18, 1899, and was acknowledged by Charles N. Mikels and Albert D. Ogborn on the same date, and contains eleven acres, divided into fifty lots and one out-lot, no blocks designated.

The American Shovel Company's addition, situated east of Hernly and Brown's addition ·and the north part of Woodward's second addition, between Columbia Avenue and the Panhandle railway, was platted November 28, 1899, and was· acknowledged by George W. Miller, President, and Charles W. Mouch, Secretary, of the American Shovel Company, on the same date, and contains twenty five acres, divided into ninety two lots, no blocks designated.

Charles S. Hernly's first addition, situated south of Powell's subdivision, on the west side of South Twenty Fifth Street, was platted December 30, 1901, and was acknowledged by Charles S. Hernly and Elizabeth Hernly on the same date, and contains four and thirty hundredths acres, divided into twenty four lots, no blocks designated.

The first Industrial addition, situated in the southeast part of town, on the south side of A and Grand avenues and immediately east of the New Castle and Rushville division of the Lake Erie and Western railway, was platted January 14, 1902, and was acknowledged by Lycurgus L. Burr, President, and Charles S. Hernly, Secretary, of The New Castle Industrial Company, on the same date, and contains four hundred and twenty six lots, no blocks designated.

Heller, McIntyre and Dittman's Rosedale addition, situated immediately east of South Park addition, between South Fourteenth Street and the New Castle and Rushville division of the Lake Erie and Western railway, was platted January 11, 1902, and was acknowledged by Myer Heller, Robert H. McIntyre and William Dittman, on the same date and contains fifty five lots, no blocks designated.

Higdon's first addition, situated immediately south of The Speeder Cycle Company's addition, between South Main and South Fourteenth streets, was platted May 12, 1902, and was acknowledged by Emma Higdon and Gilman H. Higdon, on the same date, and contains eight and sixty seven hundredths acres, divided into forty lots, no blocks designated.

Charles S. Hernly's second addition, situated immediately northwest of Hernly's first addition, on the south side of Plum Street and east side of South Twenty Second Street, was platted June 10, 1902, and was acknowledged by Charles S. Hernly, Elizabeth Hernly and Eli Bond, on the same date, and contains forty lots, no blocks designated.

Hartman's first addition, situated immediately north of Elder's second addition, on the west side of North Ninth Street, was platted January 25, 1902, and was acknowledged by Daniel Hartman and Rebecca Hartman, on the same date, and contains seven lots, no blocks designated.

Compton's addition, situated south of the East School House grounds and south of the Panhandle railway, was platted July 22, 1902, and was acknowledged by Sanford W. Compton and Dorcas I. Compton, on the same date, and contains six lots, no blocks designated.

Klein, Heller and Weil's addition, situated in the southwest part of town immediately north of South Mound Cemetery, between South Ninth and South Eleventh streets, was platted August 28, 1902, and was acknowledged by Sallie H. Klein, August 28, 1902, and by Adolph Klein, August 30, 1902, and by Herbert Heller, Herman Weil and Minnie Weil, September 4, 1902, and contains twenty five lots, no blocks designated.

The Simon T. Powell addition, situated immediately south of Rue and Holman's addition and being the Simon T. Powell homestead or out-lot No. 2, Miles Murphey's addition, was platted August 9, 1902, and was acknowledged by Melvina Powell, on the same date, and contains twelve lots, no blocks designated.

Pitman's addition, situated immediately north of Loer's second addition in the northeast part of town, on the north side of East Spring Street, was platted October 21, 1902, and was acknowledged by Edward E. Pitman and Nina L. Pitman, on the same date, and contains forty lots, no blocks designated.

Thomas M. Randle's first addition, situated immediately east of the first Industrial addition, between A. and I avenues, in the southeast part of town, was platted November 19, 1903, and was acknowledged by Thomas M. Randle and Ella A. Randle, on the same date, and contains four hundred and forty lots, no blocks designated.

Newton F. Williams' addition, situated immediately west of the Robert M. Nixon Heirs' addition, on the east side of South Ninth Street, was platted March 12, 1903, and was acknowledged by Newton F. Williams and Blanche Williams, on the same date, and contains four and seventy hundredths acres, divided into twenty one lots, no blocks designated.

The Elliott Farm addition, situated immediately south of the Jehu T. Elliott Heirs' addition in the southwest part of town, on the west side of South Ninth Street, was platted September 8, 1903, and was acknowledged by The Central Trust and Savings Company, by Robert H. McIntyre, Secretary, Attorney in Fact for the Jehu T. Elliott heirs, on the same date, and contains twenty and ninety four hundredths acres, divided into two divisions, consisting of one hundred and four lots.

William H. Elliott's Homestead addition, situated immediately east of the Jehu T. Elliott Heirs' addition and the Elliott Farm addition, on the south side of West Race Street, between South Ninth and South Eleventh streets, was platted Ocober 21, 1903, and was acknowledged by William H. Elliott and Emma E. Elliott, on the same date, and contains twenty eight lots and three out-lots, no blocks designated.

LEADING MANUFACTURERS.

John C. Goodwin's subdivision of part of lot 3 and all of lot 2, in block 2, Elizabeth Murphey's addition, was platted November 3, 1903, and was acknowledged by John C. Goodwin, on the same date, and contains but two lots.

Lycurgus L. Burr's addition, situated in Burr's old addition, on the south side of Lincoln Avenue, between North Main and South Eleventh streets, was platted March 22, 1904, and was acknowledged by Lycurgus L. Burr and Martha Burr, on the same date, and contains fourteen lots, no blocks designated.

Eliza J. Elliott's first addition, situated immediately east of Elder's first addition, on the east side of North Ninth and north side of West Vine streets, was platted June 6, 1904, and was acknowledged by Eliza J. Elliott, on the same date, and contains six lots, no blocks designated.

Mote and Lohr's first addition, situated southwest of Powell's second addition, on the south side of East Price Street, was platted and acknowledged by Ida L. Mote and Cora A. Lohr, January 13, and contains ninety five hundredths acres, divided into five lots, no blocks designated.

When the Legislative commission, already spoken of in Chapter XXXVII of this History, was in quest of a town site, about one hundred acres of land were proffered by public-spirited and interested parties, for the use of the county, on the sole condition that the present site should be chosen. Of this, Absalom Harvey gave twenty eight acres, John Brumfield, twenty eight acres, less two lots; A. Lewis, fourteen acres, shepherd, ten acres, and Rue and Holman, of Wayne County, subsequent proprietors of the first addition to the town of New Castle, twenty four acres less lots reserved.

This nice little patch of wilderness, was placed at the disposal of the County Agent, Ezekiel and was surveyed, and by direction of the commissioners thrown on sale in July, 1822. This first sale could not have been very great, for the money handled by the treasurer for that year amounted to only five and the commissioner showed an appreciation of printer's ink by ordering the agent to advertise in the intelligencer and the Indiana Statesman, a newspaper published in Cincinnati. This was followed in a few months by another sale, and still Castle remained a wilderness, and, in May, 1824, the clearing here was "sold to the lowest bidder." William McKimmey and the surveying, and received twenty five dollars each for this service.

Charles Jamison was the first tavern keeper, and, of course, "gave bond to the satisfaction of the Board. In 1823 Isaac Bedsaul, being able to satisfy the Board of County Commissioners that he was the proper party, was licensed to "keep store. His first store room was a twelve by sixteen cabin, with earthen floor and a shelf and counter resting on stakes driven into the earth. In this region sawmills were as yet unknown and a frame house next to an impossibility. A log cabin was deemed good enough for the proudest. But the town grew apace and by 1833 had three hundred inhabitants, of whom about one tenth died of the cholera in 1833.

The first preaching in the village seems to have been by Father Havens, of the Methodist Episcopal church, and was had in a log house opposite the present residence of Dr. William H. Boor, on North Main Street.

The first railroad, the Chicago and Great Eastern, now a part of the great Pennsylvania system, was completed to New Castle in 1854, and in the language

John C. Goodwin's subdivision of part of lot 3 and all of lot 2, in block 2, Elizabeth Murphey's addition, was platted November 3, 1903, and was acknowledged by John C. Goodwin, on the same date, and contains but two lots.

Lycurgus L. Burr's addition, situated in Burr's old addition, on the south side of Lincoln Avenue, between South Main and South Eleventh streets, was platted March 22, 1904, and was acknowledged by Lycurgus L. Burr and Martha Burr, on the same date, and contains fourteen lots, no blocks designated.

Eliza J. Elliott's first addition, situated immediately east of Elder's first addition, on the east side of North Ninth and north side of West Vine streets, was platted June 6, 1904, and was acknowledged by Eliza J. Elliott, on the same date, and contains six lots, no blocks designated.

Mote and Lohr's first addition, situated southwest of Powell's second addition, on the south side of East Plum Street, was platted and acknowledged by Ida L. Mote and Cora A. Lohr, January 12, 1905, and contains ninety five hundredths acres, divided into five lots, no blocks designated.

When the Legislative Commission, already spoken of in Chapter XXXVII of this History, was in quest of a town site, about one hundred acres of land were proffered by public-spirited and interested parties, for the use of the county, on the sole condition that the present site should be chosen. Of this, Absalom Harvey gave twenty eight acres; John Brumfield, twenty eight acres, less two lots; A. Lewis, fourteen acres, Allen Shepherd, ten acres, and Rue and Holman, of Wayne County, subsequent proprietors of the first addition to the town of New Castle, twenty four acres, less five lots reserved.

This nice little patch in the wilderness was placed at the disposal of the County Agent, Ezekiel Leavell, and at once, surveyed, and, by direction of the commissioners, thrown upon the market in July, 1822. This first sale could not have been a great success, as all the money handled by the treasurer for that year amounted to only $154 all told. In August, 1823, another sale was ordered, and the commissioners showed their appreciation of printer's ink by ordering the agent to advertise in the "Richmond Weekly Intelligencer and the Indiana Statesman, a newspaper printed at Connersville." This was followed in a few months by another sale, and still much of New Castle remained a wilderness, and, in May, 1824, the clearing off of the public square was "sold to the lowest bidder." William McKimmey and John Dorrah did the surveying, and received twenty five dollars each for this service.

Charles Jamison was soon after made the first tavern keeper, and, of course, "gave bond to the satisfaction of the Board." In 1823 Isaac Bedsaul, being able to satisfy the Board of County Commissioners that he was the proper party, was licensed to "keep store." His first store room was a twelve by sixteen cabin, with earthen floor and a clapboard counter, resting on stakes driven into the earth. In this region sawmills were as yet unknown and a frame house next to an impossibility. A log cabin was deemed good enough for the proudest. But the town grew apace and by 1833 had about three hundred inhabitants, of whom about one tenth died of the cholera in 1832-3.

The first preaching in the village seems to have been by Father Havens, of the Methodist Episcopal Church, and was had in a log house opposite the present residence of Dr. William F. Boor, on North Main Street.

The first railroad, the Chicago and Great Eastern, now a part of the great Pennsylvania system, was completed to New Castle in 1854, and in the language of the song of that time—

'In eighteen hundred and fifty four
"The cars ran into the depot door."

Of Ezekiel Leavell, the county agent for the sale of the lots, Judge Martin L.
Bundy, being requested to give his recollections, says: "I knew Ezekiel Leavell
very well; he lived to be an old man. He owned a farm on the Nettle Creek road,
near Jacob Thorp, the old bell maker, and near Jesse Forkner on the north and
south road through Liberty Township, about two miles south of the present village of Millville. I knew him as county agent who sold the lots and afterward as
sheriff of the county. He was a Kentuckian, a warm supporter of Henry Clay,
and in my opinion he was most influential in having the town and county named
after New Castle, Henry County, Kentucky. I have often said the town should
have been named after one of the first settlers, either Woodward, Jamison or
Hobson. When I carried the mail from Centreville to Noblesville, I delivered a
newspaper to old man Leavell and Judge Thorp; that was in 1835, and I think
Leavell lived ten years after that."

' The population of New Castle, according to the census of 1900, was 3,406,
since which time it has largely increased.

There are three banks in the town. In the chapter in this History on "Banks
and Banking" will be found a full account of these together with mention of
others now in existence. In the chapter in this History entitled "Newspapers,
Past and Present" will be found a full account of the three newspapers now published in New Castle, together with the obituaries of several now defunct.

On page 42 of this History will be found a list of the postmasters from
April 12, 1823, to the present time, together with the names of the ten rural
route carriers connected with the postoffice. New Castle is the only postoffice
that has ever existed in Henry Township.

NEW LISBON.

New Lisbon, the oldest village in Dudley Township, is situated seven and
three quarters miles southeast from the court house in New Castle and is in the S.
W. ¼ of the S. W. ¼ of Sec. 1 and the E. ½ of the S. E. ¼ of Sec. 2 and the N.
W. ¼ of the N. W. ¼ of Sec. 12, Tp. 16, N., R. 11 E., on the Lake Erie and Western
railroad and the New Castle and Dublin pike. The original plat was made by
Thomas R. Stanford, Surveyor, July 29, 1833, and acknowledged by James Tomlinson and William Crane, proprietors, August 5, 1833 and contains six blocks,
consisting of forty lots.

An additional plat is situated immediately south of the original plat and was laid
out, platted and acknowledged by John Shortridge, July 2, 1835, and contains two blocks,
consisting of five lots.

The first Northern addition, situated immediately north of the original plat, on
the east side of Broad Street, was platted and acknowledged by Thomas Shearin and
Aaron York, proprietors, November 22, 1836, and contains two blocks, consisting of eighteen lots.

A plat of New Lisbon, laid out and platted by Daniel K. Cook, surveyor, and acknowledged February 2, 1880, includes all of the foregoing additions and thirty three
out-lots.

Cornelius C. and Louisa R. Weaver's addition, situated immediately east of the Northern addition, on the east side of the Lake Erie and Western railroad and south of the pike, was platted and acknowledged by Cornelius C. Weaver and Louisa R. Weaver, August 31, 1886, and contains six blocks, consisting of twenty three lots.

Keller's addition, situated immediately east of Weaver's addition, on the south side of the Millville pike, was platted October 10, 1903, and was acknowledged by John W. Keller and Lydia Keller, October 15, 1903, and contains four blocks, consisting of thirteen lots

This village was originally called Jamestown after the Christian name of one of its original proprietors. Indeed, the designation of the village on the records of Henry County was probably not changed until the consolidated plat was made by Daniel K. Cook, Surveyor, February 2, 1880. On account of its original name the village has from the beginning been commonly known as 'Jimtown."

When, soon after the village was located, it was proposed to have a postoffice established, it was found that there was already a postoffice named Jamestown in Indiana, which necessitated the substitution of another name for the office and accordingly New Lisbon was chosen, this name probably coming from New Lisbon, the county seat of Columbiana County, Ohio.

A postoffice was established December 28, 1836, and on pages 42 and 43 of this History will be found a list of all the postmasters to date, together with the name of the one rural route carrier. One of its early postmasters who served from January 12, 1838, to March 23, 1846, was William Grose, who in the Civil War was Colonel of the 36th Indiana Infantry, and Brigadier General and Brevet Major General United States Volunteers. The place divides with Straughn the honor of being one of the only two postoffices ever established in Dudley Township.

As New Lisbon has never been incorporated such population as it has is included only in that of Dudley Township. (See Chapter XXXVIII).

Caleb B. Smith's Short Line railroad from Cincinnati was projected in the early fifties and most of the work was done on the road in Henry County before the panic of 1857. The ties were placed on the roadbed and the bridges built as far north as New Lisbon. They all rotted away. Fourteen years later the road was again taken up and constructed north to Fort Wayne, and is now known as the Lake Erie and Western.

Before the days of railroads, New Lisbon, being on the main traveled road to Cincinnati and the half way point between New Castle and Cambridge City, was a general stopping place for drovers driving hogs and cattle to Cincinnati and for teamsters hauling supplies from Cincinnati, and later from Cambridge City, after the Whitewater Valley canal was completed to that point. It is the center of as fine a farming region as there is in Henry County or for that matter in Eastern Indiana.

OGDEN.

The village of Ogden is situated in Spiceland Township, seven miles southwest from the court house in New Castle and three miles due east from Knightstown, on the Panhandle railway and the Indianapolis and Eastern railway (electric line) . The main street running east and west was designated as "The National Pike.' It was laid out and platted by Hiram Crum and acknowledged December 18, 1829, and contains four blocks, consisting of thirty two lots.

Lasure and Davis' addition, situated immediately west and south of the original plat, was plattrd and acknowledged by Harvey Lasure and Thomas Davis July 8, 1837, and contains eight blocks, consisting of fifty four lots.

The addition of Elihu Griffin and others, situated immediately north of the original plat and south of the Panhandle railway, was platted March 9, 1853, and acknowledged by Elihu Griffin and Adam Griffin, on the same date, and contains twenty two lots, no blocks designated.

Griffin, Johnson, Hiatt and Company's addition, situated immediately south and east of the original plat, on the south side of the National Road, was platted and acknowledged by Elihu Griffin, for Griffin, Johnson, Hiatt and Company, May 28, 1855, and contains nine blocks, consisting of fifty three lots.

The original plat and all additions are in the N. E. ¼ of Sec. 36, Tp. 16 N., R. 9 E.

Ogden was first named Middletown on account of being the half way point on the old National Road between Richmond and Indianapolis, and was for some time known by the name originally given it. Soon after the place was established it developed that the town of Middletown, in Fall Creek Township, had been laid out and platted October 9, 1829, two months before, therefore it was necessary to select a new name for this village, and it was named Ogden, in honor of a United States Engineer engaged in the construction of the old National Road. It is the oldest village and the first voting precinct in Spiceland Township.

As a village or town Ogden is the second place in Henry County, on the line of the old National Road, to be platted, being preceded only by Knightstown.

In early days Ogden enjoyed a large trade. The development of Knightstown on the west and the establishment of Dunreith on the east and Spiceland on the northeast has taken away all of its trade, as well as its railroad depot. However, since the construction of the electric line through there the village has taken on new life.

A postoffice was established July 15, 1840. On pages 43 and 44 of this History will be found a list of the postmasters.

Ogden not being incorporated, the population of the town is included in that of Spiceland Township. (See Chapter XXXVIII.) The only postoffices that ever existed in Spiceland Township are Dunreith, Ogden and Spiceland, and all are still in existence.

PETERSBURG.

The old village of Petersburg is situated in Liberty Township, eight miles east and one mile north of east from the court house in New Castle and one half mile south of the Daniel Bowman farm, and is in the N. E. ¼ of the N. E. ¼ of Sec. 12, Tp. 17 N., R. 11 E., and the N. W. ¼ of the N. W. ¼ of Sec. 8, Tp. 17 N., R. 12 E., and was founded in about the year 1845.

The village was never laid off and platted into lots but all the real estate descriptions are by metes and bounds of the section, township and range above mentioned. It is one of the old places in the county projected before the days of railroads and canals. The first thing to blight its future ambition was the extension of the old Whitewater Valley canal from Cambridge City to Hagerstown, which latter place is about two and one half miles southeast of Petersburg. This artificial waterway carried most of the trade from Petersburg to Hagerstown.

Later, the construction of the Panhandle railway from Richmond through Hagerstown and on through Henry County, and the establishment of Millville in the same township two and a half miles southwest, marked the final decay of Petersburg.

In an early day there were some stores in the village, but for more than a half century its few straggling houses have simply stood as memories of the past. The place is within one half mile of the Wayne County line and surrounded by some of the most highly improved farm lands in Henry and Wayne counties. No postoffice was ever established there. In an early day mail was carried there from Hagerstown and distributed as a matter of accommodation to the people.

The name comes from Petersburg, Dinwiddie County, Virginia, the place where the Confederate army, under General Robert E. Lee, made its last stand behind entrenchments, preceding the surrender at Appomattox.

PUMPKINTOWN.

Pumpkintown was hardly a village but was a cross roads point in Prairie Township, now known as West Lebanon Church, on the road leading from Mount Summit to Springport, on the east side of the railway, about midway between the two places. In early days and prior to the advent of the railway there was a store located at this point where it remained for a number of years and did a large country trade. It was owned and managed for a long time sy Sampson Jetmore, who afterwards became a leading merchant of New Castle, being a member of the firm of Mowrer, Jetmore and Company.

At one time there was an attempt made to get rid of the name "Pumpkintown" by calling it "Winona," but the name which was given it in derision, because of the fact that a great many pumpkins were raised in the neighborhood, stuck, and the change in name was never effected.

There was no postoffice, but the mail was gathered from New Castle and Luray for the neighborhood and distributed from the store. At this time there is nothing left at Pumpkintown save the West Lebanon Church and one house which was formerly used for a toll gate at the cross roads.

RAYSVILLE.

This village so named for one of Indiana's early Governors, is situated in Wayne Township, thirteen and one half miles southwest from the court house in New Castle and one half mile due east from Knightstown, on the Panhandle railroad and the Indianapolis and Eastern railroad (electric line), and in the N. E. ¼ of Sec. 34, Tp. 16 N., R. 9 E;. and was laid out and platted by Thomas R. Stanford, Surveyor, April 10, 1832, and acknowledged by John Anderson, proprietor, May 7, 1832, and contains one hundred and seven lots, no blocks designated.

The original plat was replatted by Waitsel M. Cary and acknowledged by him August 9, 1838, and includes thirty four lots in the west part of the above plat made by John Anderson and is probably a subdivision of a part of the original plat.

The village does not extend west to Blue River for the reason that east of Blue River and west of Raysville there is an addition to the town of Knightstown, made by 'Edward K. Hart and William M. Tate, March 2, 1839, consisting of one hundred and fifty one lots and one out-lot.

Raysville was for many years a rival of Knightstown, with which place it had an even start in business, and in an early day many of the leading and most enterprising merchants of Southwestern Henry County had their headquarters at Raysville. When the old Indiana Central railroad was constructed east and west through the southern part of Henry County there was for many years a station at Raysville which did as much business as the one at Knightstown.

The decay of Raysville and the successful growth of Knightstown must be attributed partly to the fact that the latter place was on the west side of Blue River and the trade, which came mostly from the west and northwest would not cross the river, and partly to the fact that the mills and warehouses were constructed near the Knightstown railroad station.

Raysville, according to the census of 1870 had a population of 465; now, that it has lost its corporate existence its population is not given in this History save as included in that of Wayne Township. (See Chapter XXXVIII).

A postoffice was established as early as October 30, 1830, nearly three years before one was established at Knightstown. On page 44 of this History will be found a list of the postmasters to date.

Charles S. Hubbard, for many years a leading and influential citizen, a merchant at Knightstown, member of the General Assembly from Henry County, and who now devotes his time and energies to religious and charitable work, has as far back as the author of this History can remember, resided in Raysville.

The "heights" around Raysville furnish quite commanding and picturesque building sites, with advantageous views of the Blue River Valley. Fine springs in the neighboring hills have been tapped and the water conveyed along Main Street for the use of the inhabitants.

James B. Ray, for whom Raysville was named, was the fourth Governor of the State of Indiana, serving as such for nearly seven years. His predecessor, Governor William Hendricks, having been elected a United States Senator, resigned as Governor, February 12, 1825, when he was succeeded by Ray, then the President of the State Senate. Ray was elected Governor at the August election, 1825, and served two full terms of three years each.

Raysville is one of the four postoffices that have existed in Wayne Township, the other three being Elizabeth City (Maple Valley, discontinued), Grant City (Snyder, discontinued) and Knightstown.

ROGERSVILLE.

Rogersville was named after one of the founders of the village and is situated in Stony Creek Township, seven and one half miles north and three and one half miles east from the court house in New Castle and is in the S. ¼ of the N. W. ¼ and the N. ½ of the S. W. ¼ of Sec. 5, Tp. 18 N., R. 11 E., and was laid out and platted by Joseph G. Rogers and John B. Colburn, proprietors, and acknowledged January 16, 1837, and contains twelve blocks, consisting of forty eight lots. No addition has ever been platted.

Rogersville is another one of the early villages of the county located before the days of railroads and whose decay began with the whistling of the locomotive engine. At an early day it had merchants, doctors, and mechanics representing the different trades. Doctor William M. Kerr was for many years its leading citizen, physician and merchant, although he never quite lived in the village, his residence and place of business being one mile south. Lycurgus L. Burr, of New Castle, as a young man, was a clerk in Dr. Kerr's store, afterward marrying his daughter, Martha J. The Luellen family was also prominent, five of its members having served as postmaster.

A postoffice was established November 19, 1849, and on page 44 of this History will be found a list of all the postmasters. The office was finally discontinued in June, 1901, through the establishment of the rural route system.

As a place of business Rogersville, through changed conditions and the ravages of time, has been marked off the map. The village never reached the dignity of a corporation. Such population as it has is included in that of Stony Creek Township. (See Chapter XXXVIII). The discontinuance of Rogersville as a postoffice, as above noted, left Blountsville the only remaining postoffice in Stony Creek Township.

SHARINGTON.

Sharington is another "paper" village of Henry County and is situated in Fall Creek Township, somewhere on the road leading from Sulphur Springs west to Mechanicsburg, probably one half to three fourths of a mile east of College Corner, about nine and one half miles northwest from the court house in New Castle, and three and one half miles south of Middletown, and was laid out and platted by Benjamin Franklin, Abraham Showalter and James Personett, February 23, 1835, and acknowledged March 2, 1835, and contains eighteen lots, no blocks designated.

It is a curious omission on the records of the county that while the official plat shows all the facts requisite for the subdivision of land into lots, yet there is no description of the land from which the lots were made; hence the location of Sharington is fixed by tradition only.

It never had a postoffice and so far as the author of this History has been able to ascertain never had any buildings or population, nor is there any record of the sale of lots in the alleged village. Tradition fails to give any information as to the derivation of the name.

SHIRLEY.

That part of the most recently incorporated town located in Henry County is situated in Greensboro Township, ten and three fourths miles west and two and three fourths miles south from the court house in New Castle and on the line between Henry and Hancock counties at the crossing of the Peoria and Eastern and Louisville and Benton Harbor divisions of the Big Four railway, and on the projected Indianapolis, New Castle and Toledo (electric line), and seven miles north and three miles east from Knightstown. It was laid out and platted by John H. Landis, Surveyor and Civil Engineer, and acknowledged by William D. Thomas and Casinda A. Thomas, November 27, 1890, and contains fourteen lots, no blocks designated.

William D. Thomas' first addition, situated immediately north of the original plat, on the east side of Main Street, was platted March 23, 1897, and was acknowledged by William D. Thomas and Casinda A. Thomas, on the same date, and contains four and fifteen hundredths acres. divided into eighteen lots, no blocks designated.

Woodlawn addition, situated immediately east of the original plat and Thomas' first addition, was platted April 16, 1901, and was acknowledged by William H. Wood and Harriet O. Wood, proprietors, on the same date, and contains thirty two and seventy three hundredths acres, divided into nine blocks, consisting of one hundred and twenty two lots and five out-lots.

SHIRLEY (IN HANCOCK COUNTY).

Main Street of the town of Shirley is the dividing line between Henry and Hancock counties. That part of the town situated in Hancock County is in the S. E. ¼ of the S. E. ¼ and in the N. E. ¼ of the S. E. ¼ of Sec. 26, Tp. 17 N., R. 8 E. It was laid out and platted in October, 1890, by John H. Landis. Surveyor and Civil Engineer, and acknowledged by John W. White and Sylvester Hamilton, proprietors, December 1, 1890, and contains thirty eight lots.

White's addition, situated immediately south and west of the original plat, on the west side of Main treet, was platted May 14, 1894, and was acknowledged by John W. White, proprietor, on the same date, and contains eleven and one fourth acres, divided into forty four lots.

George W. Sowerwine. Trustee's addition, situated west of Main Street and west of both the original plat and White's addition, was platted and acknowledged by George W. Sowerwine, Trustee for John W. White, May 21, 1896, and contains seven hundred and ninety eight lots.

Kuntz and Higi's addition, situated north and west of the original plat, was platted October 30, 1893, and was acknowledged by Charles P. Kuntz, of the Shirley Lumber Company, represented by Kuntz and Higi, on the same date, and contains seven lots.

The town takes its name from Joseph A. Shirley, who at the time was division superintendent of the Ohio, Indiana and Western railway, since taken under control by the Big Four railway and now constituting the Peoria and Eastern division of that line. Mr. Shirley is now a resident of Indianapolis where he is engaged in the real estate business.

In this History, Shirley, which is incorporated as one town in the two counties, is treated of as if it were all in Henry County and as such it is the fourth town in the county in point of importance, being preceded only by New Castle, Knightstown and Middletown.

A postoffice was established June 10, 1891. On page 45 of this History will be found a list of the postmasters to date with the names of the two rural route carriers.

The Big Four railway was built through in 1882. but there was no movement made to establish a town there until after the north and south line of the Big Four railway was in course of construction, which was completed about the time the postoffice was established.

Shirley has two banks. The history of each will be found in the chapter in this History entitled "Banks and Banking." Several newspapers have been started. Only one is now in existence—The Shirley News. In the chapter in this History entitled "Newspapers. Past and Present" will be found proper reference to the press of Shirley.

COMPANY A, 36th INDIANA INFANTRY.

one half mi
Castle and
Dunreith a:
(electric lin
laid out an
and was ac'
Gause. Aar
contained f(

Much natural gas has been developed at Shirley and from that cause and on account of the transportation facilities of the place, coupled with the enterprise of its citizens, it is a manufacturing center of considerable importance.

The postoffice is on the west side of Main Street and therefore in Hancock County, in which county it has probably been since its origin. Shirley, Kennard and Greensboro are the three postoffices in Greensboro Township, and all that have ever been established. Woodville never having had a postoffice.

The population of Shirley, according to the census of 1900, was only 381. The population has more than tripled since that time.

SPICELAND.

The thriving town of Spiceland is situated in Spiceland Township, seven and one half miles west of south from the court house in New Castle, on the New Castle and Rushville branch of the Lake Erie and Western railroad and the Dunreith and New Castle division of the Indianapolis and Eastern railroad (electric line), and includes nearly all of Sec. 17, Tp. 16 N., R. 10 E., and was laid out and platted by Stephen G. Mendenhall, Surveyor, January 22, 1850, and was acknowledged by Peter C. Cloud, Joseph M. Allen, Charles Gordon, Eli Gause, Aaron L. Pleas and Levi Hodson, proprietors, February 12, 1850, and contained forty lots, no blocks designated.

William R. Macy's addition, situated immediately north of the original plat, on the east side of Pearl Street, was platted and acknowledged by William R. Macy September 21, 1850, and contains six lots. no blocks designated.

Pleas' addition, situated immediately north of the original plat, was platted May 24, 1856, and was acknowledged by Charles Gause, administrator of the estate of Aaron L. Pleas, deceased, on the same date, and contains six lots, no blocks designated.

Thomas Cook (and others) Company's addition, situated immediately east of the original plat, on the south side of Main Street, was platted August 20, 1869, and was acknowledged by Josiah P. Bogue, attorney in fact for Thomas Cook (and others), on the same date, and contains four blocks, consisting of twenty eights lots and fourteen out-lots.

Nathan Newby's addition, situated immediately east of William R. Macy's addition, was platted and acknowledged by Nathan Newby, September 20, 1875, and contains twenty two lots, no blocks designated.

Louisa Macy's addition, situated south of the original plat and in the extreme southwest part of the town, on the east side of Academy Avenue, was platted and acknowledged by Louisa Macy, with the consent of her husband, Samuel H. Macy, August 27, 1877, and contains fourteen lots. no blocks designated.

The Southside addition, situated immediately south of Thomas Cook (and others) Company's addition, between South Pearl Street and the Lake Erie and Western railway, was platted September 12, 1890, and was acknowledged by Frank A. Coffin, President, and Oliver H. Nixon, Secretary, of the Spiceland Land Company, September 25, 1890, and contains sixteen blocks, consisting of one hundred and seventy one lots.

Winchester's addition, situated immediately north of the Southside addition, on the east side of Second Street, was platted October 24, 1890, and was acknowledged by Daniel W. Winchester, proprietor, October 28, 1890, and contains two blocks, consisting of forty three lots.

Mordecai White's addition, situated immediately north of the Thomas Cook (and others) Company's addition, on the north side of East Main Street and the east side of North Fourth Street, was platted May 15. 1891. and was acknowledged by Mordecai White, on the same date, and contains one hundred and sixty five lots and eight out-lots, no blocks designated.

Spiceland Township was organized in 1842 and was so named on account of the abundance of "spice brush" that grew in that part of the county. The early settlement and the town take their name from the same cause. There was a settlement where the town stands at a very early day, but it was not until 1847 that Driver Boone began to sell land by metes and bounds for building purposes.

A postoffice was established April 10, 1838, with Thomas Cook as postmaster. On page 45 of this History will be found a list of the postmasters together with the name of the rural route carrier.

The first settlement was distinctively a Friend or Quaker affair, which denomination has always predominated not only in Spiceland but also in Spiceland Township. This denomination erected a log meeting house and school house as early as 1828. The schools of Spiceland have always been among the foremost in the county.

The town was incorporated in 1869. According to the census of 1870 it had a population of 371. In 1900 the population, as reported by the census was 590. Spiceland, Dunreith and Ogden are the only three postoffices that ever existed in Spiceland Township and all are now in existence. There is one bank, the history of which will be found in the chapter of this History entitled "Banks and Banking." Formerly a newspaper was published there called the Spiceland Reporter. Recently the New Castle Tribune was moved there for publication. A history of these newspapers will be found in the chapter entitled "Newspapers Past and Present." There has never been a saloon in Spiceland, nor in fact in Spiceland Township.

SPRINGPORT.

The enterprising village of Springport is situated in Prairie Township, eight miles north and one mile west of north from the court house in New Castle, on the Lake Erie and Western railroad, and is in the S. $\frac{1}{2}$ of the S. E. $\frac{1}{4}$ and the S. E. $\frac{1}{4}$ of the S. W. $\frac{1}{4}$ of Sec. 33, Tp. 19 N., R. 10 E., and was laid out and platted by James M. Clements, Surveyor, in July, 1868, and acknowledged by Jeremiah Veach, proprietor, April 4, 1870, and contains three blocks, consisting of seventeen lots.

Vance's addition, situated immediately north of the original plat, was platted January 1, 1870, and was acknowledged by David Vance, proprietor, January 4, 1870, and contains twelve lots, no blocks designated.

James L. Freeman's addition, situated immediately south of the original plat, on the east side of the Lake Erie and Western railroad, was platted by James L. Freeman, September 10, 1884, and was acknowldged October 18, 1884, and contains eight lots and two out-lots, no blocks designated.

Henry Reiman's addition, situated north of David Vance's addition and north of the school house ground, was platted February 9, 1882, and was acknowledged by Henry Reiman and Sarah E. Reiman February 16, 1884, and contains five lots, no blocks designated.

John M. Vance's addition, situated immediately west of David Vance's addition, on the west side of the Lake Erie and Western railroad, was platted May 11, 1885, and was acknowledged by John M. Vance and Mary E. Vance, January 21, 1886, and contains five and seven hundredths acres, divided into two blocks, consisting of eighteen lots.

The Springport Land Company's first addition, situated immediately south of Vance's addition, on the south side of Main Street and west of the Lake Erie and Western railroad, was platted May 1, 1894, and was acknowledged by Josiah D. Painter, President, and James B. Gilmore, Secretary, of The Springport Land Company, on the same date, and contains fifty six lots and four out-lots, no blocks designated.

The village sprang into existence after the completion of the Fort Wayne, Muncie and Cincinnati railway, now a part of the Lake Erie and Western system, in 1869. The place takes its name from the fine springs located near the railway depot.

A postoffice was established June 29, 1869, with Hiram Allen, as postmaster, he being also probably the first merchant. . On page 46 of this History will be found a list of the postmasters, together with the name of the rural route carrier.

Springport never having been incorporated its population is included in that of Prairie Township. (See Chapter XXXVIII).

The village has succeeded to the remnant of the large trade that formerly found its way to the old town of Luray, and with Mount Summit, Hillsboro and Luray constitute the only postoffices that have existed in Prairie Township. The two last named have been discontinued.

STRAUGHN.

This little town was named in honor of Merriman Straughn, who came to the vicinity in the autumn of 1822 when it was a "howling wilderness." It is situated in Dudley Township, nine and three fourths miles southeast from the court house in New Castle, on the Panhandle railway and Indianapolis and Eastern railway (electric line), and was laid out and platted by John L. Starr, proprietor, in 1868. The main street running east and west is known as "The National Road."

Gauker's addition, situated on the south side of Main or Washington Street, and on the west side of Pike Street, was platted by William H. Gauker and contains twenty six lots, no blocks designated.

McMeans' addition, situated on the north side of Main or Washington Street and on the east side of Pike Street, was platted by Nathaniel S. McMeans and contains eight lots.

Hazelrigg's addition, situated south of Gauker's addition, on the south side of the Panhandle railroad, was platted October 5, 1875, and was acknowledged by John Hazelrigg, proprietor, on the same date, and contains nineteen lots, no blocks designated.

A plat of the town of Straughn, which includes all of the above additions together with twenty eight out-lots, was laid out and platted by Daniel K. Cook, Surveyor, and acknowledged July 3, 1882.

Merriman Straughn, for whom the town was named, was a soldier in the war of 1812-15 and his name is so recorded in the chapter in this History devoted to that war. His son and other descendants are still in Henry County, east of Straughn.

This was the last town or village to be located on the old National Road in Henry County and the most eastern town in the county on that old thoroughfare. A postoffice was established July 15, 1869. On page 46 of this History will be found a list of the postmasters. Straughn and New Lisbon are the only postoffices that were ever established in Dudley Township and both are still in existence.

Straughn is in the southeastern corner of the county, it being only one mile to the Fayette County line and two and one half miles to the Wayne County line. It is the smallest incorporated town in the county, the population according to the census of 1900 being 186.

SULPHUR SPRINGS.

The incorporated town of Sulphur Springs is situated in Jefferson Township, six and one fourth miles northwest from the court house in New Castle, on the Panhandle railway and the Union Traction line from Anderson to New Castle and is in the S. E. $\frac{1}{4}$ of the S. E. $\frac{1}{4}$ of Sec. 13 and the N. E. $\frac{1}{4}$ of the N. E. $\frac{1}{4}$ of Sec. 24, Tp. 18 N., R. 9 E., and in the S. W. $\frac{1}{4}$ of the S. W. $\frac{1}{4}$ of Sec. 18 and the N. W. $\frac{1}{4}$ of the N. W.$\frac{1}{4}$ of Sec. 19, Tp. 18 N., R. 10 E., and was laid out and platted by William S. Yost, proprietor, and acknowledged by him January 7, 1853, and contains four blocks, consisting of forty one lots.

William S. Yost's addition, situated immediately west and north of the original plat, was platted and acknowledged by Elisha Clift, Commissioner appointed by the court in the matter of the estate of William S. Yost, deceased, May 11, 1867, and contains six lots, no blocks designated.

The Northwest addition, situated immediately west of the original plat and William S. Yost's addition, on the north side of West Main Street, was platted by Bushrod W. Scott, guardian of the minor heirs of Samuel L. Yost, deceased, by an order of the Common Pleas Court of Henry County, February 12, 1868, and was acknowledged November 20, 1868, and contains two blocks, consisting of nine lots.

Scott and Yost's first addition, situated immediately east and north of the original plat, between East Main Street and the Panhandle railway, was platted by Bushrod W. Scott, guardian of Samuel L. Yost's heirs and by William E. Yost, and was acknowledged January 27, 1870, and contains seven lots, no blocks designated.

Scott and Yost's second addition, situated immediately west of the Northwest addition, on the north side of West Main Street, was platted by Bushrod W. Scott, guardian of Francis M. and Sarah C. Yost, and by William E. Yost, April 18, 1870, and was acknowledged by Bushrod W. Scott, guardian, May 11, 1870, and by William E. Yost May 18, 1870, and contains eight blocks, consisting of thirty two lots.

Scott and Yost's third addition, situated immediately north of Scott and Yost's second addition, on the north side of Mill Street, was platted by Bushrod W. Scott, guardian of Francis M. and Sarah C. Yost, and by William E. Yost, April 28, 1870, and was acknowledged by William E. Yost, May 15, 1870, and by Bushrod W. Scott, guardian, May 11, 1870, and contains eight lots, no blocks designated.

Jacob W. Yost (and others) addition, situated immediately west and south of the original plat, on the south side of west Main Street, was platted by Jacob W. Yost, Albert N. Yost and Joseph H. Thompson, November 7, 1870, and contains two blocks, consisting of eleven lots.

The town was platted in anticipation of the early completion of the Panhandle railway to that point and takes its name from the springs of the same name within the corporate limits, and before it was officially designated as a town by the filing of a plat, the settlement was called—Sulphur Springs.

A store was established a dozen years before the railroad came by William S. Yost, who was instrumental in having the postoffice established there February 13, 1844, he being the first postmaster. Elsewhere in this History there is a biographical sketch of his son, Jacob Weaver Yost, and incidentally of the family and to this reference is made.

Sulphur Springs is the only postoffice that has ever existed in Jefferson Township. On pages 46 and 47 of this History will be found a list of the postmasters, together with the name of the rural route carrier. The population of the town, according to the census of 1900, was 262.

UNIONTOWN.

This ancient and abandoned village is situated in Dudley Township, about fourteen and three fourths miles southeast from the court house in New Castle and about four miles southeast of Straughn, in the extreme southeastern corner of the county, somewhere near Little Symons Creek, and on the old State Road, which is the boundary between Henry and Fayette counties, leading from the Ohio state line to Indianapolis, and is in Sec. 36, Tp. 16 N., R. 11 E. It was laid out and platted by William McKimmey, Surveyor of Henry County, and asknowledged by William Seward, proprietor, May 27, 1823, and contains six blocks, consisting of twenty two lots.

Uniontown only reached the second or third house before the building of the National Road blighted its prospects. The place was no doubt platted on both sides of the old State Road, thus putting it in two counties. The site of the place has long since been vacated. It never reached the dignity of a postoffice and never had any population other than that included in Dudley Township. The name is no doubt derived from the fact that the village was a union of the two counties.

WEST LIBERTY.

West Liberty is, or rather was, situated in Wayne Township, fourteen and three fourths miles southwest from the court house in New Castle, and three fourths of a mile southwest from Knightstown, and was located on the county line between Henry and Rush counties, and is in the southeast corner of the W. ½ of the S. W. ¼ of Sec. 33, Tp. 16 N., R. 9 E., and was laid out and platted by Samuel Furgason and acknowledged April 18, 1823.

A part of this village was in Rush County. No postoffice was ever established although at an early day mail was carried there from regularly established offices for general distribution. The first mail route established through the county went through West Liberty from Greensburg and Rushville to New Castle and Muncie.

West Liberty was located near the mouth of Montgomery Creek; it grew quite favorably for a few years and had at one time about twenty houses and two or more groceries and dry goods stores. Doctor Elliott, who subsequently died of cholera in New Castle, was the first physician and Aaron Maxwell the first merchant. Unfortunately for the hopes of West Liberty the National Road was located about a mile north and Knightstown thus established. There is nothing now remaining to mark the site of the old village.

Next to New Castle, West Liberty is the oldest town or village in the county. It takes its name from the fact that the people who first settled there came from Liberty in Union County, and, therefore this village was called West Liberty.

WHEELAND.

Wheeland was situated somewhere in Henry County but the records do not show what section, township and range. It was laid out and platted by Caleb Williams, Surveyor, about the year 1833, and contains four blocks, consisting of twenty.four lots. For whom the land was platted does not appear.

The place never successfully passed the paper stage, and further information regarding it has not been obtainable.

WHITE RAVEN.

The first settlers of the region in and around New Castle were the Indians. rior to 1823 the site of the present beautiful county town was a wilderness of forest, almost impenetrable by the foot of man. There were no roads through these vast woods and the first white settlers made pathways through them by cutting away the underbrush and blazing the trees. Early in the nineteenth century a tribe of Indians, probably the Miamis, established a village on the high point northwest of the present town of New Castle, across Blue River, where the county asylum was afterward located and now stands. There they remained and maintained a typical Indian settlement, for several years, called White Raven, after one of the chiefs of the tribe. Other tribes of Indians had established villages at Anderson and Muncie and exchange of visits was frequent between these various tribes. About the year 1823 the advent of white settlers caused the Miamis to abandon their village and move on and they settled at some point in Wisconsin, then a part of the Northwest Territory.

For sometime after this date access to the present site of the county asylum was not possible by direct road from New Castle, on account of the swamp made by the spreading waters of Blue River, but a road was blazed northward past the old Woodward homestead for some distance which then made a circuit to the west, avoiding the marshes in the bottoms. Subsequently the Cadiz road was built running directly west out Broad Street and the county asylum was reached by a road running north. a mile west of New Castle, past the Catholic cemetery and many years later the Northwestern pike was constructed extending in a northwesterly direction through the Blue River bottom and bisecting the land belonging to the county asylum, formerly the Indian village of White Raven.

WOODVILLE.

This old and now obliterated village is situated in Greensboro Township. nine miles west and one mile south of west from the court house in New Castle, and is in the N. W. ¼ of the N. E. ¼ of Sec. 19, Tp. 17 N., R. 9 E., and was laid out and platted by James Atkinson and acknowledged May 30, 1836, and contains eight blocks, consisting of forty eight lots.

John Judge's addition, situated immediately north of the original plat, on the east side of Main Street, was platted August 20, 1855, and was acknowledged by John Judge on the same date and contains two blocks, consisting of six lots. The main street of the village running east and west was and is the boundary line between Harrison and Greensboro townships. Woodville never got beyond two scores of houses and now there remain but two or three dilapidated places to mark its former site.

There never was a postoffice in the village. At one time a store owned by Alfred Jackson and Leonard Fowler flourished there and at the same time a physician named Wilson C. Olden pursued the practise of medicine. Like many other villages located before the days of railroads, Woodville went into decline on their advent to more favored towns. The village probably took its name from the dense forests which surrounded it at the time it was located.

CHAPTER XLIII.

GENERAL STATEMENT OF POLITICAL DIVISIONS AND PARTY LINES—CLERK—
AUDITOR — RECORDER — SHERIFF — TREASURER — ASSESSOR — COLLEC-
TOR — COMMISSIONERS — CORONER — SURVEYOR — SUPERINTENDENTS OF
COUNTY SCHOOLS — COUNTY COUNCIL — TOWNSHIP ADVISORY BOARDS —
COUNTY ATTORNEY—DRAINAGE COMMISSIONERS—COURT HOUSE JANITOR—
COURT BAILIFFS—BIOGRAPHICAL MENTION.

In making up the Official Register of Henry County, showing who have
been its officers from its organization to the present time, it is proper to consider
the political divisions that have existed since the county was formed; and to make
clear the reasons for divisions on party lines, it is necessary to refer briefly to the
political divisions that have existed since the United States became a nation; in
fact to get a clear view of political divisions it is necessary to consider those existing between the colonies and the mother country before the Revolution and
the differences between the colonies during the existence of the confederacy, immediately following the Revolutionary War, as well as the political conditions
which developed after the adoption of the Constitution of the United States. Immediately following the Revolution there was nearly as much difference of material and political interests, real or imaginary, between the thirteen commonwealths forming the confederacy as there had been between the colonies and
England before their separation, and it looked for a time as if the fruits of the
struggle for independence would be lost and the confederacy dissolved by reason
of those conflicting interests.

Several efforts were made to get the colonies to unite in an offensive and de-
fensive alliance and a few of the far-seeing men of the country, notably Benjamin Franklin and Robert Morris, of Pennsylvania, James Madison, of Virginia,
and the Pinckneys, of South Carolina and Maryland, early advocated a general
government for all the colonies. But the rivalries and jealousies which had grown
up between them, especially the rivalries and jealousies between the different sea-
port towns, such as New York, Boston, Providence, Philadelphia, Wilmington,
Baltimore and Charleston, as to which should be the great commercial city long
constituted a formidable obstacle. Each of the colonies was absolutely independent of its neighbors and the colonies in which the cities named were situate
were outbidding each other for foreign trade and by various means and strate-
gems seeking to divert trade to their own ports. It was for this reason that the
clause was introduced into the Constitution of the United States which forbade
any discrimination between the ports of the United States: or, in other words,

s formed; and to make
v to refer briefly to the
es became a nation; in
y to consider those ex-
re the Revolution and
of the confederacy, im-
the political conditions
he United States. Im-
much difference of ma-
the thirteen common-
ween the colonies and
as if the fruits of the
cy dissolved by reason

in an offensive and de-

HENRY COUNTY OFFICIALS.

declaring that duties should be uniform at all of the ports. Another obstacle was the dispute between New York and New Hampshire as to which of the two owned the territory now embraced in the State of Vermont, and a greater obstacle in this direction was the disputes and jealousies existing between New Hampshire, Massachusetts, New Jersey and Delaware on the one side, and the colonies of New York, Pennsylvania, Virginia, North Carolina and Georgia on the other side, on account of the vast public domains claimed by the latter colonies outside of their original boundaries and jurisdiction, thus making the outlook for any unity of action between them very dark. Another serious dispute between the colonies, or at least such of them as contained navigable rivers running through two or more colonies, was the right of complete navigation of the rivers; that is, that a boat bound from a port in one colony should have unrestricted navigation to the ports of another colony. This was denied and vexatious restrict'o-s were place l on vessels bound from the ports of one to the ports of another colony. This question was settled in the convention by that clause of the Constitution giving Congress exclusive power to regulate commerce between the States, which gives the general government absolute control of the navigable waters flowing through two or more States. As the word "State" is now for the first time used in this article, it is proper to say that before the adoption of the Declaration of Independence there were no States, but the thirteen original States were separate and independent sovereign governments, each refusing allegiance to any higher authority. Another fear that arose can be best described by taking the case of Pennsylvania. Her fear was that if she united in a general government with the small colonies, like Delaware, that they might unite in levying a direct tax on her vast empire of unsettled land extending to the head waters of the Ohio River. Still another fear which was common to Georgia, South Carolina, North Carolina and Virginia was that if they went into a general government that the northern colonies might unite and interfere with their great domestic instituion, African slavery, and the distinguished Virginian, Patrick Henry, opposed the formation of the Federal union to the very last, on the ground that the Southern colonies were uniting in a common government which gave Congress the power to abolish slavery, which it did three quarters of a century afterwards. These two last questions were compromised in the Constitution by that clause which bases direct taxation by the general government upon population and not upon property, and by the further compromise which gave to the slave-holding colonies the right to count three-fifths of their slaves as a basis of representation in Congress, and which prohibited interference with the African slave trade before 1808.

But probably the greatest bone of contention was as to the disposal of the vast tracts of land, claimed by some of the colonies, west of the Alleghanies and west and north of the Ohio River, and those which Virginia, North Carolina and Georgia claimed, lying south of the Ohio and east of the Mississippi River. It was contended that all of this land should be ceded to the proposed central government for the benefit of all, and this was finally done. The colonies of Virginia and Connecticut united in ceding all of their western territory for the benefit of the proposed new government, and this vast domain was formed into the Northwest Territory with its seat of government at Marietta, Ohio, and out of which the States of Ohio, Indiana, Illinois, Wisconsin, Michigan, and that part of Minnesota, lying east of the Mississippi River, have since been formed. This territory belonged mainly to Virginia and the colony having the next largest interest was Connecticut, which owned all that part of Ohio bordering on Lake Erie, afterward known as the Western Reserve. New York and Pennsylvania made claim to a part of this territory but it was resisted by Virginia. Then Virginia, always in the advance, under the leadership of James Madison, the protege of Thomas Jefferson, united with North Carolina and Georgia and relinquished their rights to what are now the States of Kentucky, Tennessee, Alabama, Mississippi and all that part of Louisiana east of the Mississippi River to the proposed general government, and this territory was organized into what was known as the Southwest Territory, which was governed from Knoxville, Tennessee. Thus the principal objections being removed and the demand for some central authority becoming more and more imperative and the fact that Great Britain refused to carry out her treaty stipulation regarding the independence of the colonies on the ground that there was no central and binding authority in them, finally brought about the convention which formed the Constitution of the United States. This convention met at Philadelphia on May 25, 1787, and was in session until September 17, 1787. The result of its deliberations was the present Constitution less the fifteen amendments that have since been added. It was under this Constitution that the government was put in operation, March 4' 1789, though Washington was not formally inducted into the office of president until April 30th, following.

One might have thought that after all the labor and patience that had been expended in getting the convention together, in forming the Constitution and in organizing the government under it, that there would have been some unity of opinion as to what the instrument, in its grants, reservations and implied powers, meant; but no sooner had the government been formed than violent discussions and divisions arose over its meaning. Some of the questions then raised have not been settled unto this day, the last discussion of the implied powers occurring in the decision by the Supreme Court, by a vote of five to four, of what are known as the "Insular cases," which defines the present relations of the Philippine Islands to the general government. Two parties at once arose. The one claimed that the Constitution should be liberally construed, and that it was as elastic as if it had been made of India rubber, and that all the power possible should be centered in the general government to the exclusion of the power of the State governments. This party took the name of "Federal" which is in effect the Republican party of to day. They were generally known at first—in fact the term is still applicable—as "Loose Constructionists." The other party claimed that the Constitution should be strictly construed; that the government of the United States and of the States was a government of distributive powers. This party took the name of "Republican," and its adherents were known as "Strict Constructionists," which is in effect the Democratic party of to day, claiming from the very foundation of the government that the central government shall be clothed with as little internal power as possible at the expense of the States. Hence it was that Jefferson, in his first inaugural, said: "We are all Federalists, we are all Republicans."

Washington was a moderate Federalist, but he surrounded himself with the extremes of the two parties. Alexander Hamilton, his first Secretary of the Treasury, led the Federal party, while Thomas Jefferson, his Secretary of State, held the same relation to the Republicans. Washington was succeeded by a Federalist, his vice president during both terms, John Adams, of Massachusetts, who succeeded in making his party so very obnoxious through the Alien and Sedition Laws that the election of 1800 resulted in his defeat and the selection of Thomas Jefferson as President. Shortly after this Hamilton was killed in a duel with Aaron Burr, and thus the party of loose construction and centralized power lost its first and greatest leader. Jefferson succeeded himself. Then came the controversy with England and France over the Berlin and Milan decrees and the great questions relating to our commerce all of which grew out of the wars between England and France. The embargo was laid by Jefferson and this bore most heavily upon the commercial colonies of the North and particularly of New England, which then controlled the deep water tonnage of the United States. Afterward under Madison came the second war with England. To this war all of New England, in fact most of the Federalists were violently opposed, and were called the "Blue Lighted Federalists" from the fact that they were accused of building blue lights on the shores of New England to pilot vessels into port contrary to the embargo. They were also accused of being what was known in the Civil War times as "blockade runners". The governors of Massachusetts and Vermont and, perhaps, of some other States even went so far in their opposition to Mr. Madison and his conduct of the war of 1812-15 that they sought to withdraw their respective State troops, then at the front, from the authority of the general government. The extreme Federalists called a convention at Hartford, Connecticut, the ultimate object of which it was charged was to dissolve the Union. This convention has been known in history ever since as the "Hartford Convention," which drew an address to Congress, demanding certain proposed relief and appointed a committee, the head of which was Timothy Pickering of Massachusetts, Washington's second Secretary of State, to carry the petition to Congress and if the proposed relief therein prayed for was not granted, then it was charged the Hartford Convention was to reassemble and formally proceed to dissolve the American union. This was all in the autumn of 1814. Congress did not meet until December, the committee did not get to Washington until the January following, and when it did arrive, it found that Andrew Jackson had fought and gained the battle of New Orleans and that peace had been declared between Great Britain and the United States. The address to Congress was not delivered. The result was that "Hartford Convention" became a very odious term and the Federalists of that day found themselves in a very unenviable position. They were without political influence, in fact they were held up to universal condemnation and detestation. The result was that in 1816 the Federalist candidate for president, Rufus King, so far as the returns were concerned, hardly knew that he was running for the office. James Monroe was elected president by the first great land-slide majority. So odious was Federalism made through the Hartford Convention and the alleged blue lights on the coast of New England that the party for the time became extinct, and in 1820, Monroe was re-elected president without any opposing candidate against him, and he received every electoral vote cast, except one from New England, which was withheld on the ground that no president other than Washington should be the unanimous choice of the people.

The second term of Monroe, extending from March 4, 1821, to March 4, 1825, was then known and is now commonly referred to as the "Era of

Good Feeling," there being, so far as surface indications were concerned, but one political party in the United States. It was during this era of good feeling in 1822 that Henry County was organized. Hence there were no political divisions in the county. However, the practically unanimous election of Monroe was only a calm preceding the storm. Whereas in 1820 there had been but one presidential candidate and a campaign free from excitement, there were four candidates in 1824, and a campaign full of excitement. Up to this time and until 1832 such a thing as a national convention to nominate candidates for the presidency was unknown. It took nearly half a century of the existence of the government to evolve a national convention. Up to 1828 the candidates for the presidency were put in nomination by a caucus of the members of Congress representing different parties, or by the State legislatures nominating a candidate and commending him to other States.

Under the surface, the conditions had been working during the era of good feeling to bring about in the United States another division on party lines and in 1824, the campaign was what would now be called a "Free for All." The caucuses of the members of Congress broke up into cliques, with the result that there were nominated John Quincy Adams of Massachusetts, Henry Clay of Kentucky, William H. Crawford of Georgia and Andrew Jackson of Tennessee, none of them, however, running as Federalists; at that time at least all professed different shades of the Republican belief. No candidate had a majority, the vote being for Adams 84, for Clay 37, for Crawford 41, for Jackson 99. As a result, the election for the second time went into the house of representatives. The supporters of Adams and Clay united and Adams was elected. In this campaign in Henry County the voters, all classified as Republicans, were divided only as "Adams men," "Clay men," "Jackson men," with possibly an occasional "Crawford man." The vote is not obtainable in the office of the County Clerk nor of the Secretary of State. The adherents of Jackson immediately set up a great cry that their candidate, having received many more electoral votes than Adams, had been defrauded of the office, as John Randolph of Roanoke declared in the halls of Congress, by a coalition between a Puritan (Adams) and a black leg (Clay), Mr. Clay being so stigmatized by the erratic Virginian on account of his fondness for attending the Kentucky horse races and wagering his money on a favorite.

The legislature of Tennessee soon after nominated Jackson for president and he was thus kept continually before the voters until the election of 1828 came around, when he was triumphantly elected, the opposing vote being cast for Adams. The voters in Henry County were classified as either "Adams men" (the followers of Clay were supporters of Mr. Adams) or "Jackson men," but the vote is not obtainable. Mr. Clay, then in the Senate from Kentucky, soon quarreled with Jackson; in fact, the quarrel dated back to 1824 and perhaps before, and it is more proper to say, immediately after Jackson's term of office began, March 4, 1829, Mr. Clay and his supporters began in Congress the formation of an opposition party. However, not much headway at first was made, Jackson being elected over Henry Clay by a large majority in 1832. Jackson was this time nominated by a national convention held in Baltimore, Maryland, the first of its kind in the history of the government. The vote in Henry County was 767 for Clay and 580 for Jackson. The opposition continued formidable. They were not content to be known as

Republicans, so they were given the name "National Republicans," the followers of Mr. Jackson and his administration taking the name of "Democratic Republicans." By 1836 the National Republicans had taken the name of "Whig" and the Democratic Republicans the name of "Democrat." Thus the two great parties were re-established in American politics, and have so continued until the present day, the Republican being the successor of the Whig party, the name Whig losing its popularity, its influence and its party largely through its opposition to the Mexican War. The Republican party was formally organized for the presidential campaign of 1856, its first presidential candidate being General John C. Fremont.

With the campaign of 1836 political division became complete in Henry County, the Whig party being largely in the ascendant. The author has classified the political divisions in the county as dating from 1835-7. Prior to this time candidates were voted for for office without regard to political affiliations, and up to this time no such thing as a nominating convention had ever been heard of in Henry County, the candidates for the different offices being designated usually by conference of some of the leading men of the county, usually headed by Dr. Joel Reed. Since that time (1835-7) no man other than a Whig or Republican has been elevated to office in Henry County, with but very rare exceptions. Miles Murphey, then a Democrat, but after the repeal of the Missouri Compromise in 1854, a Republican, and then again after the Civil War, a Democrat, to the end of his life, was in 1837 elected a member of the lower house of the general assembly. This was an exceptional case, as Mr. Murphey was a very popular man, and, next to Dr. Joel Reed, probably then the leading citizen of the county. In 1839 Thomas Ginn, a Moderate Democrat, was elected sheriff. This was another very exceptional case, Ginn running not upon a party platform but on his personal popularity and the record that he had made in many previous positions of public trust in the county. From the annual election of 1838 in Henry County may date the history of county conventions and the nomination of regular party candidates. Up to about the beginning of the Civil War, the Whigs and Republicans, as well as the Democrats, had always nominated by a delegate convention, but since that time the Republican nominations have been made by a primary election. No other party than the Republican has made its nominations by a primary in Henry County.

The Whigs continued largely in the ascendancy in the county until 1851, when as strange a mixture of political affiliations as was ever known was combined into one convention which nominated what would now be known as fusion candidates, all of whom except one were elected. In that year there were to be elected three delegates to the proposed convention to form a new constitution of the State. The Whigs nominated as delegate to the convention Daniel Mason, of Wayne Township; Isaac Parker, of Franklin; Dr. George H. Ballengall, of Fall Creek; for senator, William A. Rifner, of Prairie; for representative, William W. Williams, of Spiceland; for sheriff, Samuel Hazzard (father of the author of this History), of Henry. In opposition there was a union of the Democrats, Free-soil Whigs (opposed to the extension of slavery), Abolitionists and Prohibitionists, who nominated as delegates, Isaac Kinley and Daniel Mowrer, of Henry Township, and John F. Johnston, of Prairie; for senator, Ezekiel T. Hickman, of Prairie; for representative, Isaac H. Morris, of Wayne; for sheriff, Joshua Johnson, of Henry. Every one of these candidates, except John F. Johnston, was elected, he being defeated by Dr. George H. Ballengall. The Democrats in this fusion took the lion's share, for every candidate on the ticket was a straight out and out Democrat, except Isaac Kinley, who stood as the lone representative of the Abolitionists, the Free-soil Whigs and the Prohibitionists. From that election to the present time not a single man other than a Whig or Republican has ever been elected to office from Henry County alone, and only in four instances has any one except a member of the dominant party been elected from any district in which Henry County formed a part, the exception being in the case of Addison R. A. Thompson and Exum Saint, both fusionists, to the lower house of the general assembly in 1874 and 1878 respectively, as is fully set out in the succeeding chapter where their election is recorded; and Charles M. Butler, of Knightstown, elected prosecuting attorney, and Calvin W. Thompson, of Anderson, elected district attorney for the old common pleas court, as is more fully described under the head of "Henry County Courts" in the succeeding chapter. In 1890 a fusion ticket was nominated by a joint convention of Democrats, Populists and Prohibitionists; while they greatly reduced the usual Republican majority, they failed to elect any of their candidates.

In this connection it may be interesting to consider in detail the vote of Henry County, relating to the formation and adoption of the present constitution of the State.

In 1849 the question was submitted to the voters of Indiana for or against a constitutional convention. The election was held August 6th and Henry County voted 1,507 for and 1,261 against. The proposition carried in the State by a vote of 81,500 for to 57,418 against. Accordingly, a convention consisting of one hundred and fifty members convened at Indianapolis, October 7, 1850, and adjourned February 10, 1851, when the present constitution, less the amendments which have been adopted since the Civil War, was submitted to the voters of Indiana for their adoption or rejection. It was adopted on the "first Monday in August, 1851," and became effective by the proclamation of the governor, November 1st of the same year.

On this question, Henry County voted as follows: "For the constitution," 2,200; "against the constitution," 621; "for exclusion and colonization of negroes," 1,931; "against exclusion and colonization of negroes," 802. In other words, a little more than fifty years ago, nearly two and a half to one, the electors of Henry County voted to exclude all persons of color from Indiana, and not being satisfied with this, they also voted that all persons of color then residing in Indiana should be deported and colonized in Africa or elsewhere outside of the jurisdiction of the United States. The total vote in the State for exclusion, etc., was 109,976; against, 26,066; equal to a majority of 83,910 for legal discrimination against a man on account of his color and for forcible ejection from the State. However, this part of the constitution was always a dead letter and was finally expunged by the fourteenth amendment to the constitution of the United States. The word "white" was stricken from the State constitution by the fifteenth amendment to the Federal instrument.

The delegates from Henry County to this convention were men of capacity and each acquitted himself creditably. Isaac Kinley is still living, at a very advanced age, in Los Angeles, California, and is probably the only surviving member of the convention. Full biographical mention is made of him elsewhere in this History in connection with the history of the 36th Indiana Infantry, in which regiment he reached the rank of major.

Dr. George H. Ballengall lived for many years in Fall Creek Township, where he was not only a physician with a large practise but also a civil engineer of much reputation. He acted for a long time as Surveyor of Henry County and under the title of that office published in this chapter will be found full official reference to him in that capacity.

Daniel Mowrer came to Henry County from Pennsylvania. He was a very enterprising man and was a brother of Nicholas Mowrer, who was so long identified with the woolen mill which stood near Hillsboro, and afterward until his death was a leading merchant in New Castle. Daniel Mowrer soon after the completion of the first railroad to New Castle, the present Panhandle, built the large flouring mill which stood two squares due north from the present union depot. His venture was not successful and later he moved to Marion, Grant County, Indiana, where he resided until his death.

In considering the political divisions that have existed in Henry County, note should be taken of the fact that the early immigration to the county came principally from three States, North Carolina, Kentucky and Virginia, with a sprinkling from Tennessee. A later immigration came from Pennsylvania and Ohio. The political opinions and divisions which these sturdy immigrants brought with them are yet clearly discernible in the politics of the county and may be traced by well defined lines from the original settlements.

COUNTY CLERK.

Under the first constitution of the State which was in force from December 11, 1816, when Indiana Territory became a State (although the State government actually began November 7, 1816) to November 1, 1851, all elections were held annually "on the first Monday of August." The term of office of the county clerk was seven years. Under the present constitution of the State, effective since November 1, 1851, the term of this office was réduced to four years, and it was provided that "all general elections shall be held biennially on the second Tuesday in October, beginning in 1852." The constitution was amended March 14, 1881, to provide that "all general elections shall be held on the first Tuesday after the first Monday in November, but township elections may be held at such times as may be provided by law." This amendment makes the State elections which are biennial fall every fourth year on the same date as the presidential election.

The first constitution provided that "nothing herein contained shall prevent the clerks of the circuit court (county clerk) from holding the office of county recorder." Accordingly Rene Julian was during his term as county clerk, until his death, ex-officio county recorder.

Under the first constitution the county clerk was clerk of the circuit court and probate court and until the office of county auditor was created in 1841, clerk to the board of county commissioners and discharged many of the duties now performed by the county auditor. Under the constitution of 1851 he was also clerk of the court of common pleas until that court was abolished in 1873, thus leaving now the circuit court only.

In the following roster of county clerks and all other county officers the names of the respective incumbents are followed by the dates of their respective terms, which is made up from the official records in the office of the Secretary of State, showing the dates of their respective commissions or the days when their terms of office began; in case of vacancies by resignation or death, then by the records of the board of county commissioners and from official records on file in the office of the county clerk. The variations in the duration of the terms of county clerks and of all other county officers were occasioned by the change from the old to the new constitution and aside from this change the variations were more frequent from vacancies occasioned by death and in early days an occasional resignation, and by the later law making the time of induction into office on the uniform date of January 1. The word "commissioned" implies an election.

CLERKS.

Rene Julian, commissioned from July 5, 1822, to July 5, 1829; died in office August 9, 1828, within a week after he had been elected for another full term from July 5, 1829.

Abraham Elliott, appointed August 11, 1828, *vice* Julian, deceased, serving to August 13, 1829.

John Elliott, commissioned August 13, 1829, to August 13, 1836; died in office, August, 1833.

Thomas Ginn, appointed August 23, 1833, *vice* John Elliott, deceased; served to October 25, 1833, when he resigned, being at that time county recorder.

Eli Murphey, appointed October 25, 1833, serving to August 13, 1836, thus filling the unexpired term of John Elliott, deceased, *vice* Thomas Ginn, resigned. Murphey was elected to the full term of seven years, and commissioned from August 13, 1836, to August 13, 1843.

Samuel Hoover, commissioned from August 13, 1843, to August 13, 1850.

Simon T. Powell, commissioned to serve from August 13, 1850, to August 13, 1857. The constitution of 1851 becoming effective, his term of office was reduced to one full term of four years from November 1, 1851, plus the time he had served under the old constitution; hence Mr. Powell served from August 13, 1850, to November 1, 1855.

John C. Hudelson, commissioned from November 1, 1855, to November 1, 1859.

Benjamin Shirk, commissioned from November 1, 1859, to November 1, 1863; re-elected and commissioned from November 1, 1863, to November 1, 1867.

Harry H. Hiatt, commissioned from November 1, 1867, to November 1, 1871; died in office March 21, 1871, after he had been elected for another full term from November 1, 1871.

David W. Kinsey, appointed *vice* Harry H. Hiatt, deceased, March 21, 1871, serving to October 29, 1872.

Robert B. Carr, commissioned from October 29, 1872, to October 29, 1876.

John S. Hedges, commissioned from October 29, 1876, to October 29, 1880.

Milton Brown, Jr., commissioned from October 29, 1880, to October 29, 1884.

Adolph Rogers, commissioned from October 29, 1884, to October 29, 1888.

Benjamin S. Parker, commissioned from October 29, 1888, to October 29, 1892.

Charles S. Hernly, commissioned from October 29, 1892, to October 29, 1896.

Loring A. Williams, commissioned from October 29, 1896, to October 29, 1900.

George W. Burke, commissioned from October 29, 1900, to October 29, 1904; died in office October 18, 1901.

Joseph M. Brown was appointed *vice* George W. Burke, deceased, October 22, 1901, and served to January 1, 1903; elected and commissioned from January 1, 1903, to January 1, 1907; present incumbent.

BIOGRAPHICAL.

Many of the county's eminent citizens have filled the office of county clerk, namely, Rene Julian, Abraham Elliott, Thomas Ginn, Eli Murphey (afterwards represented Henry County in the State Senate), Samuel Hoover (who was for seven years prior to this probate judge), Simon T. Powell (afterwards for about four years Supervisor of Internal Revenue for the District of Indiana under President Grant), John C. Hudelson (before this county treasurer for six years), Benjamin Shirk (afterwards for four years State Senator), Benjamin S. Parker (who previously was for about four years United States Consul at Sherbrooke, Canada, and afterward served as a member for one term in the lower house of the Indiana General Assembly), and Charles S. Hernly (eminent in promoting the material growth of New Castle and Henry County and who was the originator and successfully accomplished the completion of the Indianapolis, New Castle and Toledo (electric) railway).

Eli Murphey filled the office longer than any other man, serving by appointment and election nine years, nine months and twenty days.

One clerk, Thomas Ginn, resigned. Four clerks, Rene Julian, John Elliott, Harry H. Hiatt and George W. Burke, died in office. Robert B. Carr had served two terms as sheriff before reaching the county clerk's office.

Harry H. Hiatt, David W. Kinsey, Robert B. Carr, George W. Burke and Joseph M. Brown were soldiers in the Civil War whose respective services will be found appropriately set out elsewhere in this History.

Other chapters of this History contain proper biographical reference to Abraham Elliott, Eli Murphey, Samuel Hoover, Simon T. Powell, John C. Hudelson, Benjamin Shirk, David W. Kinsey, Benjamin S. Parker and Charles S. Hernly.

RENE JULIAN, the first county clerk, came at an early day from North Carolina and settled first in Wayne County, Indiana. He came to Henry County in 1821. He was a member of the well-known Julian family that became so prominent in Wayne and Henry counties, being an uncle of George W. Julian, for so many years a member of Congress from the old "burnt dstrict," of which Henry County was always a part. Another nephew, Jacob B. Julian, became very prominent in eastern Indiana. Still another nephew, Emsley Julian, was for four years treasurer of Henry County. Rene Julian had a brother named Shubal who lived for many years in Harrison Township and who was largely known and enjoyed an enviable reputation throughout the county.

JOHN ELLIOTT was not related to his immediate predecessor, Abraham Elliott. He was a young physician of Knightstown, but his knowledge of medicine did not save him from the ravages of cholera, so prevalent throughout the county in 1833.

THOMAS GINN was one of the very early settlers from Kentucky and it must be conceded that he was a very popular man when his name is considered in connection with the register of clerks, recorders and sheriffs, all of which offices he filled. He resigned as county clerk and failed to qualify as recorder for nearly two years after he was elected to that office. He was appointed sheriff in 1825 vice John Dorrah, deceased, and refused to qualify. He was elected sheriff in 1839 and served the full term of two years, soon after the expiration of which he moved to Mount Pleasant, Henry County, Iowa, where

Robert B. Carr, commissioned from October 29, 1872, to October 29, 1876.

John S. Hedges, commissioned from October 29, 1876, to October 29, 1880.

Milton Brown, Jr., commissioned from October 29, 1880, to October 29, 1884.

Adolph Rogers, commissioned from October 29, 1884, to October 29, 1888.

Benjamin S. Parker, commissioned from October 29, 1888, to October 29, 1892.

Charles S Hernly, commissioned from October 29, 1892, to October 29, 1896.

Loring A. Williams, commissioned from October 29, 1896, to October 29, 1900.

George W. Burke, commissioned from October 29, 1900, to October 29, 1904; died in office October 18, 1901.

Joseph M Brown was appointed vice George W. Burke, deceased, October 22, 1901, and served to January 1, 1903, elected and commissioned from January 1, 1903, to January 1, 1907; present incumbent

BIOGRAPHICAL.

Many of the county's eminent citizens have filled the office of county clerk, namely, Rene Julian, Abraham Elliott, Thomas Ginn, Eli Murphey (afterwards represented Henry County in the State Senate), Samuel Hoover (who was for seven years prior to this probate judge), Simon T. Powell (afterwards for about four years Supervisor of Internal Revenue for the District of Indiana under President Grant), John C. Hudelson (before this county treasurer for six years), Benjamin Shirk (afterwards for four years State Senator, Benjamin S. Parker (who previously was for about four years United States Consul at Sherbrooke, Canada and afterward served as a member for one term in the lower house of the Indiana General Assembly), and Charles S. Hernly (eminent in promoting the material growth of New Castle and Henry County and who was the originator and successfully accomplished the completion of the Indianapolis, New Castle and Toledo (electric) railway).

Eli Murphey filled the office longer than any other man, serving by appointment and election nine years, nine months and twenty days.

One of the Thomas Ginn resigned. Four clerks, Rene Julian, John Elliott, Harry S and George W. Burke died in office. Robert B. Carr had served two terms as deputy prior to being the county clerk's office

Milton B. Brown, Daniel W. Kinsey, Robert B. Carr, George W. Burke and Joseph M. Brown are residents of the City, and whose respective services will be found appropriate elsewhere in this History.

Other chapters of this History contain proper biographical reference to Abraham Elliott, Eli Murphey, Samuel Hoover, Simon T. Powell, John C. Hudelson, Benjamin S. Shirk, Daniel W. Kinsey, Benjamin S. Parker and Charles S. Hernly.

The second county clerk came at an early day from North Carolina and was among the settlers. He came to Henry County in 1821. He was a well known man, father and became prominent in Wayne and Henry counties. His son, George W. Julian, for so many years a member of Congress of which Henry County was always a part. Another nephew, Jacob B. Julian, became very prominent in eastern Indiana. Still another one, Wesley Julian, was for four years treasurer of Henry County. Rene Julian had a son named Shubal who lived for many years in Harrison Township and who was known and enjoyed an enviable reputation throughout the county.

It was not decided by his successor, Abraham Elliott. He was a man of education and his knowledge of medicine did not save him as he died near Sulphur in the county in 1833.

He came to the county early, Indians from Kentucky and it must be considered a thoughtful man when his name is considered in connection with the recorders and sheriffs, all of which offices he filled. He resigned as soon as he failed to qualify as recorder for nearly two years after he was elected, and was appointed sheriff in 1825 vice John Dorrah, deceased, and refused, was elected sheriff in 1839 and served the full term of two years, soon after the election of which he moved to Mount Pleasant, Henry County, Iowa, where

INDIANA INFANTRY.

he died and is buried. He built the first brick house erected in New Castle, about 1830, and probably the first one built in the county. It was a one-story structure containing four rooms and stood on Broad Street about fifty feet east of the First National Bank building. This house became the first residence of Samuel Hazzard and in it the author of this History was born July 22, 1845. The Ginns were for a long time very numerous in Harrison Township. They all came from Kentucky and were all related.

HARRY H. HIATT was the third clerk to die in office. He lived at Knightstown and went into the army from there. He was a gallant soldier, serving in Company B, 19th Indiana Infantry in the Army of the Potomac under Colonel (afterwards General) Solomon Meredith. The wounds that he received at one of the desperate battles in Virginia undoubtedly hastened his death. A widow and two daughters survive him. His remains were first buried in the old cemetery and since re-interred in Glencove Cemetery, Knightstown.

ROBERT B. CARR lived in Franklin Township before the war, where he married the daughter of Robert and Elizabeth (Maple) Smith. After his term as clerk had expired he moved to Harper County, Kansas, and became a member of the State Legislature. He now lives in Lebanon, Potter County, South Dakota.

JOHN S. HEDGES was born in Harrison County, Ohio, April 25, 1848, and came with his mother to Henry County in 1855. He educated himself under many disadvantages. Later he taught school, studied law and was deputy county clerk under David W. Kinsey and Robert B. Carr, succeeding the latter in the office. He was married in 1874 to Emma Cook. They have two sons, Eugene S. and Horace J. After retiring from the clerk's office he practised law for a time in partnership with David W. Chambers, and then went into several manufacturing enterprises. He is now engaged in active business in New Castle, with his son, Eugene S.

MILTON BROWN, JR., was born at Ogden, Henry County, May 12, 1854. When his father. Milton Brown, Sr., was elected recorder, Milton, Jr., assumed the duties of deputy under him. On the death of his father he was appointed to fill the former's unexpired term. Later he was elected county clerk and upon his retirement from that office moved to Garden City, Finney County, Kansas, where he practised law and took an active part in politics. He represented his senatorial district in the Kansas Legislature. Afterward he moved to Topeka, the capital of the State, where he is now engaged in the practise of the law.

ADOLPH ROGERS, born in Henry County, August 16, 1847, is a grandson of Ezekiel Rogers of whom and his family proper biographical reference will be found elsewhere in this History. His father was William A. Rogers, who lost his life in the Civil War and whose name will be found in the Roll of Honor. His mother was Rachel Draper, of the well-known family west of New Castle. He early taught school and was the deputy treasurer under George Hazzard, author of this History, and afterward under Luther W. Modlin. He was for a time part owner and editor of the New Castle Courier. He read law in the office of the late James Brown and is now actively engaged in the practise of his profession in New Castle. He has always taken great interest in educational matters and has been school trustee of New Castle and a member of the county board of education. He was also the first county assessor appointed under the law approved March 6, 1891.

LORING A. WILLIAMS, born in New Castle June 18, 1849, was a son of Simon and Ann J. Williams. He was early left an orphan, his father having been killed in a railroad accident in New Castle, July 27, 1854. He was educated at the New Castle schools and at the Spiceland Academy. Later he taught school, filled several clerical positions, became deputy county clerk under John S. Hedges and then county clerk. He was married in 1881 to Carrie (now deceased) daughter of Rev. W. C. Bowen. He is now one of the rural route mail carriers from the New Castle postoffice.

DOCTOR GEORGE W. BURKE was born in Franklin County, Pennsylvania, February 26, 1841. In 1866 he moved to New Castle. A year later he went to Sulphur Springs, returning to New Castle in 1870. As a physician and surgeon he had a large practise. He was for two terms a member of the New Castle Common Council and for one term school trustee. Governor Albert G. Porter appointed him one of the trustees of the Insane Asylum at Indianapolis. He was the fourth and last clerk to die in office.

JOSEPH MENDENHALL BROWN was born on the home farm in Blue River Township, Henry County, August 10, 1841, a son of Moses and Delphia (Dowell) Brown. Moses Brown was born in Preble County, Ohio, December 1, 1819, and came with his parents to Henry County in 1822, where his father entered land from the government, in Blue River Township. Moses Brown was a man of industry, who by his patient toil and systematic farming, assisted in making Henry County a garden spot out of the wilderness of woods. In 1852 he purchased one hundred and eighty acres of land in Liberty Township, on which he resided during the remainder of his life. He was married March 8, 1839, to Delphia Dowell, born in North Carolina, April 15, 1819, and who came to Henry County when a child, residing with the late Samuel Wells in Liberty Township until her marriage. Eleven children were born to Moses and Delphia (Dowell) Brown, of whom Joseph M. was the second child. Moses Brown died August 5, 1883, and his wife died June 13, 1893.

Joseph M. Brown remained on the farm until he was twenty one years old, attending the township schools during the winter season. In 1862 he responded to the call for volunteers in the Union cause and enlisted as a private in Company I, 69th Indiana Infantry. He participated in the severe engagement between the Union and Confederate forces at Richmond, Kentucky, August 30, 1862, where he was only slightly wounded, but reported as killed. The battle was very disastrous to the Federal forces. Most of the 69th Indiana and other regiments were captured. Brown was also taken prisoner but he escaped and made his way to Louisville, Kentucky, from which place he wrote to his parents. He was held at Louisville for about three weeks, when he was furloughed home.

Meantime the report had reached his home that he had been killed in the engagement at Richmond, Kentucky, and he was mourned as one dead by his parents and friends, the letters which he had written home from Louisville having failed to reach their destination. At daylight one morning late in September, 1862, he knocked at the door of his parents' home in Liberty Township. His mother admitted him and was so overcome with surprise at his appearance that she grasped him in her arms and shed tears of excessive joy on his shoulder. His father was sick with what was thought to be a fatal illness, but he leaped from his bed and joined in the general rejoicing at the soldier son's return and rapidly regained good health from that time. The Federal troops captured at Richmond, Kentucky, were paroled and the 69th Indiana was ordered to old Camp Wayne, Richmond, Indiana, where it was reorganized and held until exchanged, and where Mr. Brown rejoined it, when it was again ordered to the front. Later Mr. Brown was seized with an attack of the measles and was taken to the military hospital at Indianapolis. Being unfit for further military duty he was honorably discharged May 26, 1863, and again returned home. His military record is set out in full elsewhere in this History.

In September, 1863, Joseph M. entered the New Castle Academy, then in charge of Professor Henry M. Shockley, and remained until the following spring. Afterward during the winter months he taught a term of school in Harrison Township and several terms in Liberty Township, until in 1866 he entered the law office of Brown and Polk as a student. In January, 1871, he opened a law office at Knightstown and remained there two years. Returning to New Castle in January, 1873, he formed a law partnership with the late James Brown, the latter's partner, Robert L. Polk, having been elected judge of the Common Pleas Court. This partnership continued for about four and one-half years, when he was elected Prosecuting Attorney of the Eighteenth Judicial Circuit and discharged the duties of that office for one term of two years. In 1884 he became the law partner of Rollyn Warner, now a leading attorney of Muncie. In 1889 he and Samuel Hadley Brown formed a law partnership which continued until Joseph M. was appointed county clerk to succeed Doctor George W. Burke, deceased, in October, 1901, to which office he was elected in 1902 for a four years' term.

He was married October 5, 1874, to Rachel Stout, daughter of David Stout, of Franklin County. A son, Charles Stout Brown, was born to them August 11, 1881. He is now and has been for six years past, connected with Levi A. Jennings, a leading manufacturer and hardware merchant of New Castle. Rachel (Stout) Brown died May 3, 1886. Mr. Brown was again married, May 12, 1892, to Martha, daughter of William and Ruth (Bond) Nicholson, of Liberty Township, born January 10, 1846, who has proved in every way a fitting marital companion and their home in the eastern part of New Castle is a very happy one, where their friends delight to meet and partake of the generous hospitality of the host and hostess.

Mr. Brown while practising law was called upon several times to serve as a member of the School Board and while serving in that capacity was largely instrumental in causing the erection of the present commodious school buildings in New Castle—one on Fourteenth Street and the other on Twenty first Street. As a lawyer he has always taken front rank at the bar and in the discharge of the duties of citizenship has ever proved faithful and efficient. In addition to the duties of his office he finds time to successfully manage a large farm which he has brought to a high state of cultivation and in the supervision of which he finds great enjoyment.

The first public employment Mr. Brown had was that of collector of delinquent turnpike taxes, under George Hazzard, the author of this History, when the latter was treasurer of Henry County, 1869-71. The exacting duties of this position Mr. Brown discharged with fidelity and zeal.

COUNTY AUDITOR.

By an act of the General Assembly, approved February 12, 1841, the office of county auditor was created. Prior to this period the position of clerk to the board of county commissioners had been filled by the clerk of the circuit court, the duties of clerk to the county board so far as they went being somewhat similar to the duties now performed by the county auditor, although not nearly so extensive as those that now devolve upon him. Indeed, the records of the first twenty years' transactions of the clerk to the board of county commissioners are not equal to those recorded for one quarter of a year at the present day. Some estimate may be formed of the duties of the office and the necessities of a county auditor from the fact that Rene Julian, the first county clerk, was allowed but seventeen dollars for his labors as clerk of the board for four terms of the commissioners' court in 1822. Today the duties of the county auditor require the unremitting labor of three and sometimes four persons from early morning, every working day in the year. The term of the office until the new constitution became effective was five years, when it was reduced to four years. No man other than a Whig or Republican ever filled the office.

AUDITORS.

James Iliff, commissioned from 1841 to 1846; re-elected and commissioned from 1846 to 1851.

Thomas Rogers, commissioned from 1851 to November 1, 1855.

James S. Ferris, commissioned from November 1, 1855, to November 1, 1859; re-elected and commissioned from November 1, 1859, to November 1, 1863.

Thomas Rogers, commissioned from November 1, 1863, to November 1, 1867.

Seth S. Bennett, commissioned from November 1, 1867, to November 1, 1871; re-elected and commissioned from November 1, 1871, to November 1, 1875.

William W. Cotteral, commissioned from November 1, 1875, to November 1, 1879; re-elected and commissioned from November 1, 1879, to November 1, 1883.

Joshua I. Morris, commissioned from November 1, 1883, to November 1, 1887; re-elected and commissioned from November 1, 1887, to November 1, 1891.

Richmond Wisehart, commissioned from November 1, 1891, to November 1, 1895; re-elected and commissioned from November 1, 1895, to November 1, 1899.

Mark Davis, commissioned from November 1, 1899, to November 1, 1903. Here the term of county officers had been made by an act of the General Assembly to begin on the uniform date of January 1, which made a vacancy in the office from the time Mr. Davis' commission expired to the beginning of the new year. Davis was appointed to fill the vacancy from November 1, 1903, to January 1, 1904, when the term of his successor began.

John M. Bundy, commissioned from January 2, 1904, to January 1, 1908; present incumbent.

The first four incumbents of the office were ministers of the Gospel. James Iliff was a Wesleyan Methodist preacher; Thomas Rogers and James S. Ferris were ministers of the Methodist Episcopal Church, and Seth S. Bennett, a minister of the Disciples or Christian Church, formerly called Campbellites.

The first auditor, James Iliff, served longer than any other man, two full terms of five years each under the old constitution. The author regrets that he has been unable to secure more information regarding Mr. Iliff.

James S. Ferris, a well-known school teacher of New Castle, was a member of the lower house of the General Assembly before being elected auditor. After his term as auditor expired he moved to Iowa. A few years later he removed to Winchester, Indiana, where he died. Elsewhere in this History will be found a full biographical sketch of Dr. Samuel Ferris, in which reference is made to his brother, James S. Ferris.

Seth S. Bennett and Richmond Wisehart were soldiers in the Civil War whose respective services will be found appropriately set out elsewhere in this History.

THOMAS ROGERS was the only auditor re-elected after an intervening term. He was born in Ireland, December 14, 1822, and came with his parents to the United States in 1824, settling in Philadelphia. In 1837 they moved to Indiana, locating in Richmond. Later, in 1839, they moved to Milton, Wayne County. In 1846 Thomas Rogers was married to Joanna Willits and soon thereafter settled on a farm on Flatrock in Henry County, a few miles from New Castle. Mr. Rogers early became a school teacher, which profession he followed in Wayne and Henry counties until 1849, when he settled in New Castle and on August 1 of that year became deputy auditor under James Iliff. He was a very religious man who early identified himself with the Methodist Episcopal Church and later, in 1866, became a regularly ordained minister of that denomination. He served for several years as school examiner and afterward as county school superintendent. The last years of his life were spent on a farm of two hundred and fifty acres about a mile west of New Castle, where he built a spacious brick residence. The rolling mill has since been located near there. Mr. Rogers was known as the "marrying deacon," he having tied more nuptial knots than any other minister in Eastern Indiana, or probably in the State; persons bent on matrimony coming from all parts of the county to be united in marriage by him. He left a record showing that he had joined in wedlock more than 1,200 couples. His wife died March 26, 1895, and he did not long survive her, dying July 11, 1895. Both are buried in South Mound Cemetery, New Castle.

SETH S. BENNETT was the "learned blacksmith." During the Civil War he lived in Laporte County, entering the army from there. After the close of the war he moved again to Henry County, settling at Ogden, where he followed his trade. He was a man of argumentative disposition and possessed of much general information. Aside from preaching on Sunday and on other occasions while working at his trade he took an active part on the stump in all political campaigns, having been an ardent Republican. He was a great advocate of George W. Julian during the latter's Congressional career. During his second term as auditor, in 1874, he married Isabella, sister of David W. Chambers. After his term of office expired he moved to Enterprise, Volusia County, Florida, where he died of yellow fever November 20, 1887, his wife dying ten days later of the same disease. Both are buried in Florida.

WILLIAM W. COTTERAL was a resident of Middletown for many years prior to his election as county auditor. While there he was respectively merchant, postmaster and railroad agent. His wife was a daughter of Chauncey H. Burr, one of the oldest, most progressive and most highly esteemed citizens of Middletown and one of the original incorporators of the town, for many years a justice of the peace there. She was also the aunt of the present sheriff of the county. Mr. Cotteral during his term as auditor was a member of the State Board of Agriculture and clerk to the board. Soon after his term of office expired he moved to Garden City, Finney County, Kansas, where he resided for some time, later removing to Guthrie, Logan County, Oklahoma, where he now lives and where his son, John H., is a leading attorney.

JOSHUA I. MORRIS is a resident of New Castle. Elsewhere in this History, in connection with a biographical sketch of his brother, Judge John M. Morris, will be found full biographical reference to the entire Morris family.

RICHMOND WISEHART is a member of the well-known family of that name who have lived for so many years in Fall Creek Township. In Chapter XIII of this History in connection with a biographical sketch of his brother, Philander Wisehart, the first soldier from Henry County killed in the Civil War, will be found full biographical reference to the Wisehart family. He has recently moved to Pasadena, California.

MARK DAVIS was born December 1, 1851, in a log cabin on the farm four miles north of New Castle. His parents were Aquilla and Linna (Harvey) Davis, splendid types of early settlers of Henry County. Mark first attended the primitive school at Hillsboro and afterward pursued his studies in the graded academy at New Castle. In 1872 he went to Salina City, California, near San Francisco, and while there took a thorough course in Heald's Business College, San Francisco. He returned to the old Henry County farm in 1874 and in that year married Miss Jennie Allender, a most estimable young lady, daughter of a prominent pioneer family of Hillsboro. They continued to reside on the farm until 1879 when Mark moved his family to New Castle and engaged in the grain business with Davis and Loer, where he remained for two years. He then associated himself with the late Peter P. Rifner in the grain business at Mount Summit for two years. Returning to New Castle he established a grocery store on East Broad Street which he conducted for several years. While thus engaged he was elected Trustee of Henry Township, which office he filled to the entire satisfaction of the people for five years. Richmond Wisehart selected him as deputy during his incumbency of the office and later Mr. Davis was elected auditor as above noted. After he retired from that office he opened a shoe store on East Broad Street, New Castle, which is conducted by his son. Another son, Ray, is deputy under Auditor Bundy, while Mr. Davis is now serving in that capacity in the office of County Treasurer White.

JOHN M. BUNDY was born September 20, 1856, in Greensboro Township, the son of Josiah and Maria Jane Bundy, among the best known and most respected citizens of Henry County. Josiah Bundy was born in Wayne County in 1823; died in New Castle January 6, 1894. Maria Jane Bundy died in New Castle May 9, 1887. Both are buried in South Mound Cemetery. Josiah Bundy was a genial, jovial, whole-souled man, long the landlord of the Bundy hotel in New Castle. Associated with him were his sons, Charles, John M., (for one year), Frank and Orla P., and under his careful training each of the boys was fitted to assume the cares and responsibilities of honorable citizenship. After his death Frank and Orla P. assumed the management of the Bundy hotel and by their genial manner and splendid business ability the patronage has grown until it is second to none in Indiana and their names are familiar as household words to that portion of the traveling public so fortunate as to have enjoyed their hospitality. Charles is engaged in the livery business in New Castle where he enjoys a large and lucrative trade. The subject of this sketch, John M. Bundy, resided with his parents in Greensboro until about his eighth year when he accompanied them to their new home on a farm near Minneapolis, Minnesota. There they remained for about seven years when they returned to Indiana and purchased a farm near and east of Spiceland. About two years afterward they moved to a farm on Flatrock in Franklin Township where they lived for six years and then settled in New Castle, having purchased the well-known hotel then known as the Taylor House, from George Hazzard, author of this History, the name of which was changed to the Bundy House. In October, 1877, John M. Bundy was married to Jennie Healey, daughter of Welborn and Huldah Healey, of Franklin Township, and granddaughter of Jesse H. Healey, first sheriff of Henry County. They lived at the Healey homestead for about three years when they moved to Greensboro where Mr. Bundy engaged in the dry goods business with his brother, Lorenzo D. This partnership continued for six years when John M. went into the grocery business in the same town, being associated with William S. Moffett. His first wife died in Greensboro April 8, 1886. Two years later he was married to Adaline Reece, daughter of Absalom and Priscilla Reece. Soon thereafter they moved to Knightstown and he became clerk in the clothing store of Carroll and Barker of that town where he remained for about eleven years. Ill health compelled him to retire from that business and a year later, in 1902, he was elected auditor of the county. While engaged in business in Greensboro he was elected to the office of Trustee of Greensboro Township, the duties of which he discharged to the complete satisfaction of his constituents from 1886 to 1890. Since taking charge of the auditor's office he has shown great capability in conducting that intricate branch of the county's financial affairs, coupled with an affable and obliging disposition which renders it a pleasure for those who have business to transact there. In the management of the office he is ably assisted by two very competent lieutenants, Charles W. Vuncannon and Ray Davis, deputy auditors.

COUNTY RECORDER.

While the earliest records in the recorder's office were kept with precision so far as the recording of instruments was concerned, yet they were not kept so as to indicate precisely when Rene Julian, county clerk, ceased to act as recorder ex-officio, and when Thomas Ginn, the first elected county recorder, assumed the duties of the office. The constitutional term of the office being seven years, and Ginn having been succeeded by Dr. Joel Reed August 14, 1834, the presumption is that Ginn was elected and authorized to begin the duties of the office in August, 1827, thus giving him a full term of seven years. The office was not at that time regarded as a valuable one, its duties being considered rather as a burden and as taking one from his other vocations. Probably Ginn, having been elected as stated, neglected to assume the duties of the office until the death of County Clerk Julian, August 9, 1828, which was considered as being an opportune time to begin. The preponderance of the record seems to show that Julian acted as recorder ex-officio until his death. For the reasons above related the date when Ginn began as recorder of the county is left blank. The term of this office under the new constitution was reduced to four years. No man other than a Whig or Republican, with the possible exception of Thomas Ginn, ever filled the office.

RECORDERS.

Rene Julian, county clerk and ex officio recorder, commissioned from July 5, 1822, to July 5, 1829; died in office August 9, 1828.

Thomas Ginn, commissioned from ———— to August 14, 1834.

Joel Reed, commissioned from August 14, 1834, to August 14, 1841.

James A. McMeans, commissioned from August 14, 1841, to August 14, 1848; re-elected and commissioned from August 21, 1848, to August 21, 1855; re-elected and commissioned from August 21, 1855, to August 21, 1859.

Butler Hubbard, commissioned from August 21, 1859, to August 21, 1863; re-elected and commissioned from August 21, 1863, to August 21, 1867.

Enos Bond, commissioned from August 21, 1867, to August 21, 1871; died in office April 28, 1868.

Butler Hubbard, appointed vice Enos Bond, deceased, serving from April 28, 1868, to October 27, 1868.

Levi Bond, commissioned from October 28, 1868, to October 28, 1872.

Milton Brown, Sr., commissioned from October 28, 1872, to October 28, 1876; died in office May 12, 1876.

Milton Brown, Jr., appointed to fill the unexpired term of his father, serving to October 31, 1876.

Thomas B. Reeder, commissioned from October 31, 1876, to October 31, 1880.

James T. J. Hazelrigg, commissioned from October 31, 1880, to October 31, 1884; died in office September 27, 1884.

Thomas H. Hazelrigg, appointed vice James T. J. Hazelrigg, his uncle, deceased, serving to October 31, 1884.

Jonathan C. Boone, commissioned from October 31, 1884, to October 31, 1888.

Richard J. Edleman, commissioned from October 31, 1888, to October 31, 1892.

William B. Bock, commissioned from October 31, 1892, to October 31, 1896.

Hoy Bock, appointed October 31, 1896, serving to November 15, 1896. This appointment was rendered necessary from the fact that Daniel Neff, who was elected and commissioned to serve from October 31, 1896, to October 31, 1900, died May 30, 1895, before entering upon the duties of his office.

Mark M. Morris, commissioned from November 15, 1896, to November 15, 1900.

Adam V. Harter, commissioned to serve from November 15, 1900, to November 15, 1904; died in office December 4, 1904. By a change in the law his successor was not commissioned until January 1, 1905.

Floyd Elliott, appointed vice Adam V. Harter, deceased, serving from December 5, 1904, to January 1, 1905.

Thomas W. Gronendyke, commissioned from January 1, 1905, to January 1, 1909; present incumbent.

BIOGRAPHICAL.

The foregoing facts regarding county recorders show that there has been quite a relationship sustained between some of the respective incumbents of the office. Enos Bond, who died in office, was a brother of Levi Bond, who succeeded to the office subsequent to the appointment of Butler Hubbard. Milton Brown, Sr., was succeeded by his son, Milton Brown, Jr. James T. J. Hazelrigg was succeeded by his nephew, Thomas H. Hazelrigg. William B. Bock was succeeded by his son, Hoy Bock. Adam V. Harter, the last recorder to die in office, was succeeded by his brother-in-law, Floyd Elliott.

James A. McMeans held the office in all eighteen years; two terms, fourteen years, under the old constitution and one term, four years, under the constitution of 1851. Butler Hubbard held the office three terms, twice by election and once by appointment.

There seems to have been a great fatality connected with this office, as five of the incumbents died during their term of office—Rene Julian (recorder ex officio), Enos Bond, Milton Brown, Sr., James T. J. Hazelrigg and Adam V. Harter, and Daniel Neff, who was elected and commissioned, died before assuming the duties of the office.

Enos Bond, Levi Bond, Thomas B. Reeder, James T. J. Hazelrigg, Richard J. Edleman, William B. Bock, Mark M. Morris and Thomas W. Gronendyke were soldiers in the Civil War whose respective services will be found appropriately set out elsewhere in this History.

Three recorders, Rene Julian, Thomas Ginn and Milton Brown, Jr., respectively, filled the office of county clerk and brief biographical mention of them will be found under that head.

DR. JOEL REED, during his long and active life was more widely known in Henry County than any other citizen. He was the prominent man and eminent physician of the county. He was born near Cincinnati, Ohio, May 15, 1796, and in early childhood moved with his parents to a farm in Warren County, Ohio, near Lebanon, where he continued to live until he reached his majority, doing his part of the farm labor and acquiring such education as he could from the ordinary schools of the community. Leaving the farm, young Reed moved to Wayne County, Indiana, where for five or six years in the winter months he taught school, thus securing some extra means with which to commence the study of medicine under Dr. Samuel W. Waldo, at Jacksonburg, Wayne County, the leading physician of that period in that section of the country. He remained with Dr. Waldo for three years, assisting his preceptor in the practise of his profession, and, in 1826, moved to New Castle, where he remained until his death, February 17, 1869.

In 1830, Dr. Reed purchased of Asahel Woodward and Miles Murphey the two lots in New Castle, beginning with the present Wayman block, fronting on East Broad Street, and extending one hundred and sixty five feet, one half the distance from Fourteenth to Fifteenth streets, for sixty dollars. On this corner Dr. Reed built a log cabin and lived there until 1837, when he built in its stead a two-story frame edifice, which at the time was considered one of the most pretentious dwellings in New Castle. About that time he also built just east of his residence a one-story house containing two offices, one of which he used for his "doctor shop" during the remainder of his life. A Chinese laundry now occupies one of these rooms and a millinery store the other. These two lots are now worth, unimproved, two hundred and fifty dollars a front foot.

As a physician, Dr. Reed was eminently successful. His practise in the early period was almost co-extensive with the county. He never failed to respond to a call for his services, if able for duty, and it is impossible to adequately describe the labor, fatigue and exposure he endured in the discharge of his professional duties. More than this, as has been aptly said by one who knew him well during all of his life: "Dr. Reed was never known to inquire whether his patients were able to pay and in his practise of more than forty years never enforced payment in a single instance."

Dr. Reed was, in the Autumn of 1827, united in marriage with Emeline Jobs. She was born September 9, 1808, and died February 17, 1862. To them were born two children: Loring Waldo, born September 21, 1828, died at Greencastle, Indiana, May 10, 1848; Miles Listen, born February 6, 1831, died April 6, 1901.

Notwithstanding Dr. Reed's almost constant duty as a practising physician, he found time to consider local, State and National affairs and became subsequently a prominent factor in the politics of the county. He was elected Recorder and served as above stated. The office during his term was located in his own office and his deputy, who performed all the duties of Recorder, was Judge Martin L. Bundy, of whom proper biographical mention is made in Chapter IX.

Following the expiration of his term as Recorder, Dr. Reed was twice elected a member of the lower house of the General Assembly, as is fully set out under that head in this History. He never after this filled any other public office, but this fact did not deter him from taking, until his death, an active, determined interest in all the questions which agitated the public mind, and especially so as relates to the period preceding, during and following the Civil War. In 1838 he joined the Methodist Episcopal Church, of which he was a consistent member until his death. He was a decided and aggressive antagonist to the evils of intemperance, and moral, upright and strictly honorable in all his dealings. For many years he was the patriarch of the physicians of the county and no man was held in higher esteem by the members of that profession. He was liberal, kind-hearted, sympathetic and rigidly adhered to the Golden Rule.

LORING WALDO REED was an excellent young man and his death just on the verge of manhood was a severe blow to his parents. He was a diligent student, having graduated at the "old seminary" in New Castle and had fairly entered upon a collegiate course at Asbury University (now De Pauw) at Greencastle, Indiana, when death claimed him.

MILES LISTEN REED obtained his early education in the "old seminary;" afterward attended Asbury University (now De Pauw) at Greencastle, Indiana, and Farmers College, on College Hill, near Cincinnati, Ohio. He subsequently read law and began the practise at New Castle, and was for several years district attorney of the Court of Common Pleas, as is fully shown in treating of that court elsewhere in this History. During the last year of his official life as prosecuting attorney the Civil War broke out and in September following the firing on Fort Sumter, he entered the army and served in two organizations and then served in the navy, all of which is appropriately set out elsewhere in this History. He was finally discharged at the close of the war and returned to his home in New Castle, where he resumed the practise of the law. Henry County sent no more gallant soldier to the front than Miles Listen Reed. His service in three enlistments covered nearly the entire period of the conflict and he was always at the front. Shortly after the close of the war Mr. Reed was appointed United States Assessor of Internal Revenue for Henry County, and afterward was for a short time employed as a clerk in the pension office at Washington City. He spent two years (1872-3) under an appointment from the government as a teacher in the Ponca tribe of Indians in the then territory of Dakota. In 1881 he founded the Richmond (Indiana) Enquirer, which he conducted for about fifteen months, at the expiration of which time he disposed of the plant and once more resumed the practise of his profession in New Castle. Subsequently he purchased the New Castle Democrat and successfully published that paper for several years. He was married at Centreville, Wayne County, Indiana, January 17, 1856, to Catharine Woods. She was the daughter of James and Harriet Woods, pioneers of Wayne County, and was born August 16, 1832; died June 26, 1858. Catharine (Woods) Reed was an accomplished woman, highly educated and a successful teacher of music. They were the parents of two children, Loring, (deceased), and Gertrude, now Mrs. William Beard, of Dayton, Ohio. Mr. Reed was again married. at New Castle, January 1, 1868, to Jerusha Lawhead. She still survives and is now residing at New Castle. They had one child, Laura, now the widow of Banning Lake. Mrs. Lake is an accomplished music teacher and· while pursuing her profession makes her home with her mother. All of the foregoing who are deceased, except Miles L. Reed, his son Loring, and Mr. Lake, are buried in the old cemetery at New Castle. Miles L. is buried in South Mound Cemetery, his son Loring in Lawrence County, Indiana, where he died, and Banning Lake is buried at LaFayette, Alabama, where he died May 11, 1900.

JAMES A. McMEANS was a son of Thomas E. McMeans, a native of Tennessee, who came to Union County, Indiana, in 1819, and being a man of affairs served as sheriff of that county. In 1834 he moved to Henry County with his family and settled in Franklin Township. James A. and his twin brother, Nathaniel, were born in Union County about the year 1819. The other children were Laban, Marshall E., Elliott,· Alfred L., Seldon R. and Edghill B., and two daughters, Emily, afterward Mrs. Hugh Rogers, and Lunissa, afterward Mrs. Scott, whose son, James M., was a soldier in Company G, Eighty Fourth Indiana Infantry, and was killed at the battle of Chickamauga, September 20, 1863. James A. McMeans married Maria, daughter of John and Ann Taylor. After his term of office expired he moved to Richmond, Wayne County, and during the Civil War was chief clerk in the office of Isaac Kinley, provost marshal for the Fifth District. After the war he sought the office of recorder of Wayne County and later moved to Lincoln, Nebraska. A few years afterward he moved to Fairbury, Jefferson County, Nebraska, where for the remainder of his life he kept hotel, and where he died and is buried. His widow survived him many years, dying within the past year in California. Mr. McMeans was born July 25, 1819.

BUTLER HUBBARD at the time of his election lived in Knightstown, where he had been a resident for many years, following the trade of harness maker. He was a member of the lower house of the General Assembly, serving in the thirty fifth regular session, 1850, having as his colleague the late Russell Jordan, of Stony Creek Township. He was a genial, companionable man, well educated and possessed of a great sense of humor. He had several daughters and one son, Horace G., now and for many years past connected with the Cincinnati Times Star. Butler Hubbard and his wife continued to reside in New Castle until their deaths.

Having made brief biographical reference to the several county recorders down to the Civil War period, the author finds it necessary to leave mention of those serving since that time to some future history.

COUNTY SHERIFF.

The first sheriff of Henry County, Jesse H. Healey, was not elected by the people. On December 31, 1821, Jonathan Jennings, Governor of Indiana, approved the law organizing Henry County, the same to become effective June 1, 1822. On January 1, 1822, he appointed Jesse H. Healey, sheriff, for the proposed new county. This shows that the law then was that whenever it was determined to organize a new county it was the duty of the Governor to immediately appoint a sheriff in order that the territory embraced in the proposed new county might have a chief peace officer. The term of the sheriff's office under both the old and the new constitution was made the same—two years—yet Jesse H. Healey served more than that term, as the first sheriff was not elected until at the August election, 1824.

The record of "Commissions Issued" in the office of the Secretary of State, at Indianapolis, relating to the sheriff's office in Henry County, from Jesse H. Healey, January 1, 1822, to Joshua Chappell's second commission, August 23, 1845, gives the date only on which the commission was issued, failing to specify the term for which the person commissioned was to serve, therefore the term for which the incumbent named served, until August 23, 1845, is made up by having the preceding term end on the day when the succeeding officer was commissioned, which is approximately correct.

SHERIFFS.

Jesse H. Healey, commission dated January 1, 1822; served to September 27, 1824.

John Dorrah, commission dated September 8, 1824; died in office.

Thomas Ginn, appointed vice John Dorrah, deceased; commission dated January 14, 1825; refused to qualify.

Ezekiel Leavell, appointed vice Thomas Ginn, refused to qualify; commission dated February 19, 1825, served to August 16, 1825.

Jesse H. Healey, elected to vacancy vice John Dorrah, died in office; vice Thomas Ginn, refused to qualify; vice Ezekiel Leavell, appointed to the vacancy to serve until the next general election, which was on the first Monday in August, 1825; commission dated August 16, 1825; served to August 19, 1826.

Ezekiel Leavell, commission dated August 19, 1826; served to August 28, 1828; re-elected; commission dated August 28, 1828; served to December 12, 1828; resigned.

Jacob Thornburgh, appointed vice Ezekiel Leavell, resigned; commission dated December 12, 1828; served to August 14, 1829.

Jesse Forkner, commission dated August 14, 1829; served to August 19, 1831; re-elected; commission dated August 19, 1831; served to August 5, 1833.

Moses Robertson, commission dated August 5, 1833; served to August 20, 1835; re-elected; commission dated August 20, 1835; served to August 21, 1837.

Tabor W. McKee, commission dated August 21, 1837; served to August 13, 1839.

Thomas Ginn, commission dated August 13, 1839; served to August 2, 1841.

Tabor W. McKee, commission dated August 2, 1841; served to August 7, 1843.

Joshua Chappell, commission dated August 7, 1843; served to August 23, 1845; re-elected and commissioned from August 23, 1845, to August 23, 1847.

Jesse H. Healey, commissioned from August 23, 1847, to August 23, 1849; re-elected and commissioned from August 23, 1849, to August 23, 1851.

Joshua Johnson, commissioned from August 23, 1851, to August 23, 1853.

Winford W. Shelley, commissioned from August 23, 1853, to August 23, 1855; re-elected and commissioned from August 23, 1855, to August 23, 1857.

Peter Shroyer, commissioned from August 23, 1857, to August 23, 1859.

Vincent Shelley, commissioned from August 23, 1859, to August 23, 1861.

John W. Vance, commissioned from August 23, 1861, to August 23, 1863; re-elected and commissioned from August 23, 1863, to August 23, 1865.

Robert B. Carr, commissioned from August 23, 1865, to August 23, 1867; re-elected and commissioned from August 23, 1867, to August 23, 1869.

William S. Bedford, commissioned from August 23, 1869, to August 23, 1871.

Hugh L. Mullen, commissioned from August 23, 1871, to August 23, 1873; re-elected and commissioned, from August 23, 1873, to August 23, 1875.

Hiram R. Minor, commissioned from August 23, 1875, to August 23, 1877; re-elected and commissioned, from August 23, 1877, to August 23, 1879.

Joel Hazelton, commissioned from August 23, 1879, to August 23, 1881; re-elected and commissioned, from August 23, 1881, to August 23, 1883.

George H. Cain, commissioned from August 23, 1883, to August 23, 1885; re-elected and commissioned, from August 23, 1885, to August 23, 1887.

COMPANY C, 36th INDIANA INFANTRY.

... ... and the new constitution was made ... ... more than that term, as the first ... ... election, 1824.

... in the office of the Secretary of State, at ... office in Henry County, from Jesse H. Healey, ... second commission, August 23, 1845, gives the ... was issued, failing to specify the term for which ... therefore the term for which the incumbent ... is made up by having the preceding term end on ... was commissioned, which is approximately correct.

SHERIFFS.

dated January 1, 1822; served to September 27, 1824. ...d September 8, 1824; died in office.

John Dorrah, deceased; commission dated January

...ice Thomas Ginn, refused to qualify; commission . ... August 16. 1825.

...ance vice John Dorrah, died in office; vice Thomas ...e: Leavell, appointed to the vacancy to serve until ...as on the first Monday in August, 1825; commission August 19, 1826.

dated August 19, 1826; served to August 28, 1828; ... 28, 1828; served to December 12, 1828; resigned.

vice Ezekiel Leavell, resigned; commission dated st 14, 1829.

ated August 14, 1829; served to August 19, 1831; st 19, 1831; served to August 5, 1833.

dated August 5, 1833; served to August 20, 1835; re- 20, 1835; served to August 21, 1837.

dated August 21, 1837; served to August 13, 1839.. ed August 13, 1839; served to August 2, 1841.

dated August 2, 1841; served to August 7, 1843.

lated August 7, 1843; served to August 23, 1845; re- zust 23, 1845, to August 23, 1847.

ad from August 23, 1847, to August 23, 1849; re-. ust 23, 1849, to August 23, 1851.

l from August 23, 1851, to August 23, 1853.

sioned from August 23, 1853, to August 23, 1855; August 23, 1855, to August 23, 1857.

from August 23, 1857 to August 23, 1859.

from August 23, 1859, to August 23, 1861.

d from August 23, 1861 to August 23, 1863; re- gust 23, 1863, to August 23, 1865.

d from August 23, 1865, to August 23, 1867; re- just 23, 1867, to August 23, 1869.

ned from August 23, 1869, to August 23, 1871.

d from August 23, 1871, to August 23, 1873; re- gust 23, 1873, to August 23, 1875.

d from August 23, 1875, to August 23, 1877; re- igust 23, 1877, to August 23, 1879.

rom August 23, 1879, to August 23, 1881; re-elected

COMPANY C, 36th INDIANA INFANTRY.

William H. Macy, commissioned from August 23, 1887, to August 23, 1889; re-elected and commissioned, from August 23, 1889, to August 23, 1891.

William Rhinewalt, commissioned from August 23, 1891, to August 23, 1893.

George W. Tompkins, commissioned from August 23, 1893, to August 23, 1895; re-' elected and commissioned, from August 23, 1895, to August 23, 1897.

John James, commissioned from August 23, 1897, to August 23, 1899; re-elected and commissioned, from August 23, 1899, to August 23, 1901.

Here the term of the office had been made, by an act of the General Assembly, to begin January 1, 1902, thus creating a vacancy from the time John James' commission expired until the date when Charles M. Christopher, who had been elected as James' successor, was commissioned to serve.

Charles M. Christopher, appointed vice vacancy as above, served from August 23, 1901, to January 1, 1902; commissioned from January 1, 1902, to January 1, 1904; re-elected and commissioned, from January 1, 1904, to January 1, 1906.

Chauncey H. Burr, commissioned from January 1, 1906, to January 1, 1908; present incumbent.

BIOGRAPHICAL.

Jesse H. Healey served longer than any other sheriff, his four terms, once by appointment and three times by election, comprising seven years, eight months and twenty six days.

Charles M. Christopher was next in point of service, his three terms, once by appointment and twice by election, comprising four years, four months and seven days. The rule has been to give the sheriff two terms, and since the tenure of John W. Vance, 1861-5, William S. Bedford and William Rhinewalt are the only two not re-elected. Bedford was defeated for re-nomination by an accident, in consequence of which he was afterward made treasurer. Rhinewalt was not a candidate for a second term.

Since political lines were drawn in the county, about 1835-7, Joshua Johnson, of Henry Township, Democrat, is the only man other than a Whig or Republican to hold the office, with the exception of Thomas Ginn.

Peter Shroyer, Robert B. Carr, William S. Bedford, Hugh L. Mullen, Hiram R. Minor, George H. Cain, William H. Macy, William Rhinewalt and John James were soldiers in the Civil War, whose respective services will be found appropriately set out elsewhere in this History.

John Dorrah was the only sheriff to die in office. He was the father of Joseph Dorrah, who lived for many years two miles north of New Castle, and was for a long time assessor of Henry Township.

Further reference to some of the earlier sheriffs is as follows:

JESSE H. HEALEY came with his family from North Carolina to Wayne County prior to the year 1820. In 1821 he moved to Henry County. His father, Hugh Healey, who had been a Revolutionary soldier, accompanied his son to Indiana. He died in New Castle about the year 1827. Jesse H. Healey cut as great a figure in Henry County as any other man who ever lived in the county. He was an all around man of affairs and held respectively the offices of Sheriff, Tax Collector, Member of the Legislature, Probate Judge and County Commissioner, his term of service in these offices being fully set out under their several heads. He died about the year 1855. His son, Welborn Healey, was for many years a leading and influential citizen of Henry County, residing in Franklin Township. There may be somewhere in the archives of the Henry County Historical Society a biographical sketch of this early pioneer, but the author has been unable to find it. Eugene Healey, of Knightstown, is a grandson and has recently presented to the Historical Society some of the early commissions issued to his grandfather.

THOMAS GINN is referred to in the list of county clerks.

EZEKIEL LEAVELL was the agent of Henry County for the sale of the town lots in New Castle, and in the chapter devoted to Towns and Villages under the head of New Castle will be found brief biographical reference to Mr. Leavell.

JACOB THORNBURGH was one of the very early merchants of New Castle, coming here from Wayne County, and in Chapter XI, of this History, in connection with a biographical sketch of his son, John, will be found full reference to Jacob Thornburgh and his family and the part he took in the affairs of Henry County.

JESSE FORKNER and his brother, Isaac, came from Wayne County about the year 1822, and settled in Liberty Township, two miles south of Millville. Isaac Forkner was the grandfather of Judge Mark E. Forkner, of New Castle, and elsewhere in this History will be found biographical sketches of Judge Forkner and his brother, John L., containing full information of the Forkner family in general.

MOSES ROBERTSON came to Henry County in company with the two Forkner brothers above mentioned, from Wayne County. In addition to filling the office of sheriff he was county collector, an early justice of the peace and a member of the board of justices governing the county from 1824 to 1827, and was in general a public spirited citizen who had the confidence of the public to a large degree. He was one of the original promoters of the railroad from Richmond to New Castle, now a part of the Panhandle Railway. Late in life he moved to Hagerstown, Wayne County, where he died and is buried.

TABOR W. MCKEE, of Harrison Township, married Sarah Elliott, sister of Judge Jehu T. Elliott, and in the biographical sketch of Judge Elliott, elsewhere in this History, will be found reference to him.

JOSHUA CHAPPELL was a driving, energetic Henry County pioneer, who for a long time kept the old log and frame hotel in New Castle that stood on the site now occupied by the Bundy House. On his retirement from the hotel he moved to Madison County, where he spent the remainder of his life on a farm.

JOSHUA JOHNSON, of Henry Township, is above referred to as being the only Democrat to hold the office since political lines were drawn in the county. He died soon after leaving the office.

WINFORD W. SHELLEY AND VINCENT SHELLEY were brothers. Winford W., commonly called "Dykesey" Shelley, was a versatile auctioneer whose services were greatly in demand and in his time he was probably better known and knew more people in Henry County than any other man who ever lived in the county. Vincent Shelley moved to Iowa about the beginning of the Civil War. The Shelleys were a numerous family, who early came to Henry County from North Carolina.

THE SHROYER FAMILY came to Henry County from Greene County, Pennsylvania, in 1835. There were three brothers, Henry, John and Peter, and five sisters, Mrs. John Taylor, Mrs. Robert C. Kinsey, Mrs. Thomas, Mrs. Hipes and Miss Maria Shroyer. The family was well known in Wayne and Henry counties. Peter was a harness maker and worked at that trade in New Castle until he was elected sheriff. After his return from the Civil War he conducted a store at Sulphur Springs. Later he moved to Chatsworth, Livingstone County, Illinois, where he engaged in merchandising and lived there until his death. He married in New Castle, Mary Benbow, and they raised an interesting family.

JOHN W. VANCE was for many years a carpenter and farmer near Greensboro before he became sheriff. After retiring from the sheriff's office he moved to Iowa, where he died and is buried.

The author having made brief biographical reference to all the sheriffs down to the Civil War and mentioned all those who served in that struggle, must leave the others to some future history.

COUNTY TREASURER.

There is no record in the office of the Secretary of State at Indianapolis of commissions issued to treasurers of Henry County until Lorenzo D. Meek, who seems to have been the first one commissioned under the new constitution to serve for the term of two years, from August 5, 1853. In the earlier days of Henry County and the State, the office of county treasurer was not as important as it is now. The law was such that from the organization of the county until 1841-2 the county treasurer had nothing to do with the collection of the taxes and there is no tax duplicate in the county treasurer's office prior to the one for the fiscal year 1842. There was a county collector whose duty it was to collect the taxes and turn them over to the county treasurer, whose only duty it was to disburse them according to law. Until the office of county collector was abolished, in 1841-2, the county treasurer was appointed by the board of county commissioners.

Under an act approved February 12, 1841, entitled, "An act prescribing the duties of county treasurers," it was provided that this officer "shall be elected on the first Monday of August next and tri-ennially thereafter," by the qualified voters of the respective counties. Thus it happened that Joshua Holland was the first treasurer of Henry County elected directly by the people. He was also the last county collector appointed by the board of county commissioners.

The author has been unable to find any satisfactory record of the precise term of the county treasurers who preceded Joshua Holland, all of whom were appointed in the language of the law "by the board doing county business;" neither is their precise term essential, therefore the author takes the list from William Shannon to Joshua Holland, as made up by Elwood Pleas, in "Henry County Past and Present; 1821-71," a small but highly valuable volume of one hundred and fifty pages.

As Joshua Holland assumed the duties of the office, August 5, 1841, as above shown, the term of this office began with each new incumbent on August 5, from Joshua Holland, 1841-4, to John A. Cook, commissioned to serve from August 5, 1895, to August 5, 1897, but whose term was extended by law to January 1, 1898. Under the present constitution the term of this office was reduced from three to two years.

TREASURERS.

William Shannon, 1822; Benjamin Harvey, 1824; Isaac Bedsaul, 1825; Matthew Williams, 1826; Isaac Bedsaul, 1826 to 1833; Miles Murphey, 1833; Jehu T. Elliott, 1834 to 1839; Samuel Hazzard, 1839 to 1841.

Joshua Holland, commissioned from August 5, 1841, to August 5, 1844.

Martin L. Bundy, commissioned from August 5, 1844, to August 5, 1847.

John C. Hudelson, commissioned from August 5, 1847, to August 5, 1850; reelected and commissioned from August 5, 1850, to August 5, 1853.

Lorenzo D. Meek, commissioned from August 5, 1853, to August 5, 1855.

Henry C. Grubbs, commissioned from August 5, 1855, to August 5, 1857; died in office, March 26, 1857.

John W. Grubbs, appointed vice Henry C. Grubbs, deceased, serving from March 30, 1857, to August 5, 1857.

Caleb Johnson, commissioned from August 5, 1857, to August 5, 1859; re-elected and commissioned, from August 5, 1859, to August 5, 1861.

Emsley Julian, commissioned from August 5, 1861, to August 5, 1863; re-elected and commissioned, from August 5, 1863, to August 5, 1865.

Morgan James, commissioned from August 5, 1865, to August 5, 1867.

Robert M. Grubbs, commissioned from August 5, 1867, to August 5, 1869.

George Hazzard (author of this History), commissioned from August 5, 1869, to August 5, 1871.

Rotheus Scott, commissioned from August 5, 1871, to August 5, 1873.

Thomas S. Lines, commissioned from August 5, 1873, to August 5, 1875.

William S. Bedford, commissioned from August 5, 1875, to August 5, 1877.

Thomas I. Howren, commissioned from August 5, 1877, to August 5, 1879.

Frank M. Millikan, commissioned from August 5, 1879, to August 5, 1881.

Luther W. Modlin, commissioned from August 5, 1881, to August 5, 1883.

James P. Dykes, commissioned from August 5, 1883, to August 5, 1885.

Frank J. Vestal, commissioned from August 5, 1885, to August 5, 1887.

Dayton L. Fenstamaker, commissioned from August 5, 1887, to August 5, 1889.

William H. Harden, commissioned from August 5, 1889. to August 5, 1891.
Albert W. Saint, commissioned from August 5, 1891, to August 5, 1893.
Cornelius M. Moore, commissioned from August 5, 1893, to August 5, 1895.
John A. Cook, commissioned from August 5, 1895, to August 5, 1897.
Here the law was changed, making the term of the office begin on the uniform date of January 1, which extended Cook's term to January 1, 1898.
Clarkson Gordon, commissioned from January 1, 1898, to January 1, 1900.
William C. Hess, commissioned from January 1, 1900, to January 1, 1902.
John O. Holtsclaw, commissioned from January 1, 1902, to January 1, 1904.
Lewis E. Cloud, commissioned from January 1, 1904, to January 1, 1906.
Edgar T. White, commissioned from January 1, 1906, to January 1, 1908; present incumbent.

BIOGRAPHICAL.

From the foregoing roster of county treasurers it appears that three brothers have respectively held the office—Henry C. Grubbs, John W. Grubbs, and Robert M. Grubbs; also that father and son respectively held the office—Samuel Hazzard and his son, George, the author of this History. Henry C. Grubbs was the only treasurer to die in office.

Some of Henry County's most distinguished citizens in their younger days filled the office of county treasurer, notably Colonel Miles Murphey, Judge Jehu T. Elliott, Judge Martin L. Bundy, John C. Hudelson and John W. Grubbs.

Since Morgan James held the office, (1865-7), to the present time, the position has been considered a "one-term" office. This arises from the fact that during and immediately succeeding the Civil War, on account of the excessive war taxation, the office was the most remunerative of any in the county, the treasurer then being paid a per cent. on his total collections. Many county treasurers have tried for renomination, but all have failed. Notwithstanding the fact that the emoluments of the office have been greatly reduced, first by taxation getting on a peace basis, and later by the office being made a salaried one, yet the "one-term" idea has grown so firmly fixed in the minds of the people that a renomination has been impossible.

Morgan James, Robert M. Grubbs, George Hazzard, William S. Bedford, Thomas I. Howren, Albert W. Saint, Cornelius M. Moore and Clarkson Gordon were soldiers in the Civil War, whose respective services will be found appropriately set out elsewhere in this History.

Since the term of Miles Murphey, then a Democrat (1833), no man other than a Whig or Republican has held the office of county treasurer. At that time political lines were not drawn in the county. From the repeal of the Missouri Compormise, in 1854, until after the close of the Civil War, Miles Murphey was a Republican, and from that time a Democrat until the end of his life.

Elsewhere in this History will be found proper biographical mention of Miles Murphey, Jehu T. Elliott, Joshua Holland, Martin L. Bundy, John C. Hudelson and John W. Grubbs (as founder of the New Castle Courier), and the author having made proper reference to the military service of those who were in the Civil War now finds it necessary to leave biographical mention of such as are not above included, excepting Samuel Hazzard and his son, George, the author of this History, to some future history.

SAMUEL HAZZARD was a native of Delaware, where he was born, August 10, 1815, There were several brothers who emigrated about 1835 to Indiana, settling in the Whitewater Valley. David stopped at Laurel, in Franklin County, where he lived for many years as a merchant and general'trader. Henry became a resident of Cambridge City. Samuel located at New Castle in 1835, and opened a general country store in a primitive frame building which stood where the First National Bank building now stands. Later he was joined by his younger brother, George W., who was appointed to West Point and served in the Regular Army, as is elsewhere properly referred to in this History. On February 14, 1839, Samuel Hazzard was married to Vienna Woodward, second daughter and second child of Asahel and Catharine Woodward. · Vienna.

(Woodward) Hazzard was born April 20, 1818, in Preble County, Ohio; died January 30, 1858. In Chapter XVII of this History will be found full biographical reference to the parents of Mrs. Samuel Hazzard.

Samuel and Vienna (Woodward) Hazzard were the parents of nine children, namely: Clarinda, born December 6, 1839, married to Jacob Sims, whom she survived; she afterwards became the wife of Dr. William G. Armstrong, a leading physician of La Fontaine, Wabash County, Indiana, now deceased; Mrs. Armstrong now resides in Wabash, Indiana, with her daughter, Nettie (Sims) Sisson; Elizabeth, born October 25, 1841, and married to Alonzo 'S. Gear; she is now a resident of Tacoma, Washington, and is one of the best known women educators in the Puget Scund basin; Rachel M., born November 24, 1843, died March 20, 1845; George (author of this History), born July 22, 1845; John W., born May 6, 1847, died January 27, 1887, a soldier of the Civil War in Company H, 147th Indiana Infantry; Belle Jane, born June 30, 1849, married to Ed. E. Hopkins, of Hendricks County, Indiana, afterward moved to near Laoti, Wichita County, Kansas, where she died March 11, 1905, and where she is buried; James V., born October 26, 1851; Leander E., born March 19, 1854, killed by the Indians while a soldier in the United States Army; memorial stone erected in South Mound Cemetery; date of death and place of burial unknown; Walter, born January 25, 1858, died in infancy. All of the above, who are deceased, excepting Belle Jane and Leander E., are buried in South Mound Cemetery, New Castle.

Samuel Hazzard was a natural merchant whose business ability was equal to that of any man that ever lived in Henry County. He is well remembered in New Castle, where his career is identified with the early growth of the town and county and in the prosperity of both he was a leading factor, not only as a citizen and business man, but also in an official capacity. He died January 25, 1867.

No family of Hazzards ever lived in Henry County, excepting that of Samuel Hazzard and his family; therefore, wherever the name is mentioned it refers to this family, and George Hazzard is the only one so named that ever lived in Henry County, save his uncle, George W., appointed to West Point as above mentioned. This fact makes sufficient biographical reference to the author, as his name properly appears from time to time in these pages.

GEORGE HAZZARD, the author of this History, was married June 30, 1870, to Maria Eudora, eldest daughter and child of the Reverend Reuben and Adaline Tobey, the former a Methodist minister, at one time stationed in New Castle, both of whom are now deceased. She was born May 30, 1849. To George and Maria E. Hazzard were born four children, all natives of New Castle, namely: Adaline V., died in infancy; Elizabeth G., born April 28, 1872, married to Frank L. Hale, at Tacoma, Washington, November 27, 1895, by the Reverend Preston Barr; died near Tacoma, October 31, 1903; buried in the Tacoma Cemetery; George Howard Hazzard, assistant superintendent of the Washington and Columbia River railroad, with headquarters at Walla Walla, Washington, born July 28, 1874, married to Alice M. Dodge (born March 17, 1875), of Tacoma, Washington, March 18, 1901; they have one child, a daughter, named Marian Elizabeth, born October 6, 1903; Julia Anna, born February 1, 1877, married to John C. R. Cootes, of Tacoma, Washington, February 5, 1896; they have three children, Sarah Marian, born April 6, 1897; George H., born September 10, 1902, and the youngest son, named for his father, born April 5, 1904. Mr. Cootes and family reside at Hedley, British Columbia, where he is electrical superintendent for the Daily gold and silver mines, operated at that place.

George Hazzard has resided in Tacoma, Washington, since June, 1883. He only returned to his native county temporarily to write this History, and for the writing and publishing thereof is more entitled, in his opinion, to public favor than to any other act of his life. His career is known of all men, not only in Indiana, but also in the State of Washington.

63

COUNTY ASSESSOR.

Under an ·act of the General Assembly, entitled "an act concerning taxation," approved March 6, 1891, the office of·county assessor was created. The duty of this officer is to act in an advisory capacity to the township assessors, look after omitted and sequestered property and report the same to the county auditor to be placed on the duplicate for taxation. He has the power to issue citations to all persons, executors, administrators, guardians, trustees and officers of corporations whom he desires to examine in regard to omitted or sequestered property to appear before him, and in case of failure to so appear to compel their attendance by process issued through the sheriff.

Nathan H. Ballenger informs the author that in the earlier days of the county this office existed and that he was once elected and discharged the duties of the office, serving from January 1, 1849, to January 1, 1850. He assessed the whole county at a compensation of $1.50 per day, and made a formal report in May, 1850. The present term of the office is four years.

ASSESSORS.

Adolph Rogers, appointed June 2, 1891, serving to November, 1892.

Daniel W. Saint, commissioned from November, 1892, to November, 1896.

William N. Clift, commissioned from November, 1896, to November, 1900. /

Thomas J. Burchett, commissioned November 16, 1900, to November 16, 1904.

By an act of the General Assembly of 1903, the terms of all county assessors were extended to January 1, 1907, to which time Mr. Burchett's term of office extends, when the term will again be for four years.

BIOGRAPHICAL.

ADOLPH ROGERS, the first county assessor appointed under the act creating the office was for several years editor of the New Castle Courier, when that newspaper was owned principally by George Hazzard, author of this History. Mr. Rogers was county clerk from October 29, 1884, to October 29, 1888, and additional reference is made to him in that list.

DANIEL W. SAINT was a well known citizen of the county residing at Greensboro, where he died and is buried.

WILLIAM N. CLIFT has a large acquaintance as an auctioneer and a man of affairs in New Castle.

THOMAS J. BURCHETT was a soldier in the Civil War, whose service will be found appropriately set out elsewhere in this History.

COUNTY COLLECTOR.

From the organization of Henry County until the approval by the Governor, February 12, 1841, of an act entitled "an act prescribing the duties of the county treasurer," which law made the county treasurer the collector of the taxes as well as the disburser thereof, and also abolished the office of county collector, there was a collector appointed by the board of county commissioners whose duty it was to receive annually from the county clerk, acting as clerk to the board of county commissioners, the tax duplicate. Whereupon the collector would travel over the county from village to village, from house to house, with his tax duplicate, collecting the taxes due from the respective property owners and turning the same over to the county treasurer, whose only duty it was to disburse the same according to law.

The sheriff of the county in the absence of a collector otherwise appointed was ex officio tax collector, but it appears that Jesse H. Healey was the only sheriff who actually performed the duties of tax collector.

COLLECTORS.

Jesse H. Healey, 1822-3; Joseph Craft, 1824; John Anderson, 1825; Joseph Craft, 1826; Jesse Forkner, 1827; John Harris, 1828-9; Moses Robertson, 1830-3; Wesley Goodwin, 1834-5; Moses Robertson, 1836-8; Andrew G. Small, 1839; Joshua Holland, 1840-1.

BIOGRAPHICAL.

JESSE FORKNER AND MOSES ROBERTSON graduated from the office of tax collector into that of sheriff, and further reference is made to them and to Jesse H. Healey, also in that list.

JOSHUA HOLLAND was the last county collector and the first county treasurer elected by the people.

WESLEY GOODWIN, a well known Democrat in his day, was county collector in 1834-5. This was about the time political lines began to be finally drawn in the politics of the county. Goodwin became the owner of the school section, one mile west of New Castle, where the rolling mill now stands, and was the father of George W. Goodwin, a full biographical sketch of whom will be found in Volume I, Chapter IX, of this History, appended to that of his father-in-law, Colonel Miles Murphey.

When Jesse H. Healey was sheriff and was ex officio tax collector as above stated, the capital of the State was at Corydon. After he had collected the taxes in 1823, he walked to Corydon, a distance of about one hundred and fifty miles, paid over the amount due the State, and then walked back to New Castle. The total amount collected from the citizens of Henry County in that year was $112.00, for all purposes.

COUNTY COMMISSIONERS.

When Henry County was organized, in 1822, the "board doing the county business" was the board of county commissioners. Later, in July, 1824, the General Assembly changed the law, abolished the board of county commissioners, and constituted the justices of the peace in the respective counties as a "board doing the county business." This plan was found not to be satisfactory; therefore, in 1827, the board of county commissioners was restored and has since continued until the present time as the "board doing the county business."

During the time that the justices of the peace were ex officio the board of county commissioners, James Johnston was president of the board in 1825, James Gilmore in 1826, and Abraham Elliott in 1827.

On account of the uncertainty as to precise dates when the respective county commissioners assumed the duties of their office the author is forced to content himself with giving the years only in which the respective commissioners served until the law became effective making all county officers assume their duties on the uniform date of January 1, which applies only to the three last named commissioners.

In the earlier days of the county the term of commissioner was for only one year. Later it was extended to two years and is now three years.

COMMISSIONERS 1822-4.

Allen Shepherd, 1822-3; Samuel Goble, 1822-4; Elisha Shortridge, 1822-4; William Shannon, 1823-4.

BOARD OF JUSTICES, 1824-7.

James Johnston, 1824-5; William Shannon, 1824-7; James Gilmore, 1824-6; Samuel Batson, 1824-7; Robert Thompson, 1824-7; Thomas Wadkins, 1824-7; Abraham Heaton, 1824-7; Sampson Smith, 1825-6; John Harris, 1825-7; Lewis Tacket, 1825-7; Abraham Elliott, 1825-7; Moses Robertson, 1825-7; Abraham Louthain, 1826-7; John Freeland, 1826-7; Jesse Daily, 1826-7; Joseph Craft, 1827; Levi Cropper, 1827; Thomas Ellison, 1827.

COMMISSIONERS FROM 1827 TO 1909.

James Fort, 1827-8; Elisha Shortridge, 1827-9; Abraham Heaton, 1827-8; John Whitacre, 1828-31; John S. Cooper, 1828-9; Solomon Brown, 1829-34; Robert Murphey, 1829-36; Joseph Robbins, 1831-4; J. R. Leonard, 1831-4; Tabor W. McKee, 1834-6; John

Whitacre, 1835-6; Jesse Forkner, 1836-7; Jesse W. Baldwin, 1836-8; David C. Shawhan, 1837-40; George Corwine, 1838-41; Jesse H. Healey, 1840-3; James Ball, 1838-9; Mathew McKimmey, 1839-42; Nathan Hunt, 1841-4; Nelson Sharp, 1842-8; Aquilla Barrett, 1843-5; Jacob Elliott, 1844-7; William S. Yost, 1844-5; Preserved L. W. McKee, 1845-6; Elisha Clift, 1846-53; Jason Williams, 1847-50; James T. Snodgrass, 1848-51; David Palmer, 1850-3; Jesse Paul, 1851-4; John Cooper, 1853-6; Samuel B. Binford, 1854-60; Thomas R. Stanford, 1854-60; William L. Boyd, 1856-62; Morris F. Edwards, 1860-6; John Minesinger, 1861-7; Elias Phelps, 1862-8; Andrew Harrold, 1867-70; Andrew Pierce, 1867-70; Williams Nicholson, 1868-71; Thomas N. White, 1870-6; Jabish Luellen, 1870-6, died in office January 19, 1876, Newton B. Davis appointed to the vacancy; Robert H. Cooper, 1871-4; Elias Phelps, 1874-7; Ithamer W. Stuart, 1877-83; William D. Cooper, 1877-80; Cyrus Van Matre, 1877-83; Peter Shaffer, 1881-4; Joshua Holland, 1883-6; Cheniah Covalt, 1883-6; Thomas N. Wilhoit, 1884-90; Thomas C. Phelps, 1886-9; Andrew J. Fletcher, 1887-90; Eli Brookshire, 1889-95; Nathan Nicholson, 1890-6; John W. Whitworth, 1891-4; Newton B. Davis, 1894-7; Harvey B. Chew, 1895-8; White Heaton, 1896-9; John W. Whitworth, 1897-1904; William D. Pierce, 1898-1905; Edwin Hall, 1899-1903; Robert M. Russell, January 1, 1903, to January 1, 1909, two terms; Charles D. Mohler, January 1, 1904, to January 1, 1907; John M. Huff, January 1, 1905, to January 1, 1908. The three last named are present incumbents.

BIOGRAPHICAL.

But one commissioner, Jabish Luellen, died in office. A perusal of the list of those who have filled the office will show the high character of the citizens who have been called upon to discharge the duties of this responsible public trust. It will be seen that many of the commissioners filled other important positions in the county, notably Tabor W. McKee, Jesse Forkner and Jesse H. Healey, who filled the office of sheriff, either before or after being county commissioner. Thomas N. White was a member of the lower house of the General Assembly after serving as commissioner. Thomas R. Stanford filled the office of associate justice and represented the county for several years in both branches of the General Assembly. He was also county surveyor. Joshua Holland was a commissioner forty years after he had been county collector and county treasurer. Morris F. Edwards and Elias Phelps were commissioners during the Civil War period, as was also John Minesinger. They began the construction of the original part of the present court house and their names are chiseled in stone over the Goddess of Justice on the east front of the tower.

Cyrus Van Matre, Eli Brookshire, Nathan Nicholson, John W. Whitworth, Harvey B. Chew and White Heaton were soldiers in the Civil War, whose respective services will be found appropriately set out in Volume one of this History.

THOMAS C. PHELPS, who was commissioner in 1886-9, is a son of Elias Phelps, who filled the office during the Civil War period and afterward. Nathan Nicholson was also one of the successors of his father, Williams Nicholson.

ABRAHAM ELLIOTT, who was president of the board of justices when it was the "board doing the county business," was afterward county clerk and then associate justice.

ABRAHAM HEATON, who was one of the board of justices governing the county in 1824-7, was afterward a commissioner. William Shannon, who was a commissioner in 1823-4, was one of the board of justices in 1824-7. Joseph Craft, who was county collector in 1824, was one of the board of justices in 1827. John Harris, who was one of the board of justices in 1825-7, was county collector in 1828-9. Moses Robertson, who was one of the board of justices in 1825-7, was county collector in 1828-9, and county sheriff in 1833-7.

Since political lines were drawn in the county about 1835-7, no Democrat has filled the office.

COUNTY CORONER.

The record of "Commissions Issued" in the office of the Secretary of State relating to the office of coroner in Henry County, from Ezekiel Leavell, September 8, 1824, to

Josiah Needham, August 18, 1845, gives the date only on which the commission was issued, failing to specify the time the person commissioned was to serve. Therefore, the term which the incumbent named served in the office of coroner until August 8, 1845, is made up by having the preceding term end on the day when the succeeding officer's commission is dated, which is approximately correct.

CORONERS.

Ezekiel Leavell, commission dated September 8, 1824; resigned January 24, 1825.

William Dixon, commission dated August 16, 1825, served to September 24, 1827; re-elected and commission dated September 24, 1827; served to August 14, 1829.

John Rozell, commission dated August 14, 1829, served to August 19, 1831.

John Baldwin, commission dated August 19, 1831, served to August 5, 1833.

James Conley, commission dated August 5, 1833, served to August 20, 1835.

Andrew Smith, commission dated August 20, 1835, served to August 21, 1837.

James Pierson, commission dated August 21, 1837, served to August 13, 1839.

Nathan Swafford, commission dated August 13, 1839, served to August 2, 1841.

William McDowell, commission dated August 2, 1841, served to August 7, 1843; re-elected and commission dated August 7, 1843, served to August 18, 1845.

Josiah Needham, commissioned from August 18, 1845, to August 18, 1847.

William McDowell, commissioned from August 18, 1847, to August 23, 1849; re-elected and commissioned from August 23, 1849, to August 23, 1851.

Thomas Henderson, commissioned from August 23, 1851, to August 23, 1853.

William McDowell, commissioned from August 23, 1853, to August 23, 1855; re-elected and commissioned eleven consecutive terms, serving from August 23, 1855, to August 7, 1876.

Thomas C. Hiatt, commissioned from August 7, 1876, to August 7, 1878.

Harrison Hoover, commissioned from August 7, 1878, to August 7, 1880.

Henry C. Baer, commissioned to serve from August 7, 1880, to August 7, 1882. Mr. Baer, whoever he was, failed to qualify, and on December 15, 1880, the Secretary of State issued a commission to Lewis Fouts. This shows that Fouts had been appointed by the Board of County Commissioners soon after the beginning of the term to which Baer had been elected.

Lewis Fouts, appointed to serve vice Baer, failed to qualify, from December 15, 1880, to November 13, 1882; elected and commissioned from November 13, 1882, to November 13, 1884.

Robert Smith, commissioned from November 13, 1884, to November 13, 1886.

Lewis Fouts, commissioned from November 13, 1886, to November 13, 1888; re-elected and commissioned for four full terms, from November 13, 1888, to November 13, 1896.

Charles P. Seward, commissioned to serve from November 13, 1896, to November 13, 1898; resigned, exact date not stated.

Ora O. Graff, appointed vice Seward, resigned, serving from January 13, 1898, to November 17, 1898.

George H. Smith, commissioned from November 17, 1898, to November 17, 1900.

Osa R. Summers, commissioned from November 17, 1900, to November 17, 1902.

Here the law was changed by an act of the General Assembly to make the term of county offices begin on the uniform date of January 1, and accordingly Summers served until January 1, 1903.

James E. Pierce, commissioned to serve from January 1, 1903, to January 1, 1905; died in office, January 9, 1904.

Charles W. Wright, appointed vice Pierce, deceased, from January 16, 1904, to January 1, 1905; elected and commissioned from January 1, 1905, to January 1, 1907; present incumbent.

WILLIAM McDOWELL, who was commonly known as "Uncle Billy Mack," served longer as coroner than any of his predecessors or successors—in fact so long that he came to be regarded as *The Coroner.*

The office of coroner is a position of more dignity and importance and of less pay than is generally known. The incumbent may be called on to fill the sheriff's office when that officer is a party to a suit. He is also a peace officer with the same powers as the sheriff, and in case of a vacancy in the office or disqualification of the sheriff, he becomes sheriff *de facto.*

EZEKIEL LEAVELL is the man who, on the authority of Judge Martin L. ·Bundy, named New Castle after New Castle, Henry County, Kentucky. He was the agent of the county to sell the town lots, and was once, by appointment and twice by election, sheriff of Henry County, to whom additional reference is made in the brief history of New Castle, printed elsewhere in this History.

HARRISON HOOVER was a soldier in the Civil War, whose service will be found appropriately set out elsewhere in this History.

COUNTY SURVEYOR.

As stated under the head of county sheriff, the law was approved December 31, 1821, organizing Henry County, the same to be effective June 1, 1822, and that on January 1, 1822, Governor Jonathan Jennings appointed Jesse H. Healey, sheriff. Afterwards, on May 9, 1822, he appointed William McKimmey, surveyor for the proposed new county, which shows that he had authority to appoint officers other than the sheriff. At that time the office of county surveyor was a highly important one when it is considered that every acre of land in Henry County belonged to the public domain. The land was taken up rapidly by settlers and the metes and bounds not only of every section but in many cases every subdivision thereof had to be officially determined.

The record of "Commissions Issued" in the office of the Secretary of State from December 28, 1825, the date of Henry Lewelling's commission, to November 8, 1852, the date of Isaac Kinley's commission and the beginning of his term of office, fails to show a commission issued to any one for the office of county surveyor in Henry County. Yet the county records relating to this office now in possession of Omar E. Minesinger, Surveyor of Henry County, show that Thomas R. Stanford acted as county surveyor from 1832 to 1846; George H. Ballengall from 1846 to 1849; Stephen G. Mendenhall from 1849 to 1851. The probabilities are that there was no one elected surveyor in Henry County for the time above mentioned, thus leaving a vacancy which the Board of County Commissioners filled by naming Stanford, Ballengall and Mendenhall respectively to perform the duties of the office.

William McKimmey, commissioned from May 9, 1822, to December 28, 1825.

Henry Lewelling, commissioned from December 28, 1825, served presumably to 1832.

Thomas R. Stanford, appointed in 1832, serving to 1846.

George H. Ballengall, appointed in 1846, serving to 1849.

Stephen G. Mendenhall, appointed in 1849, serving to 1851.

Isaac Kinley, commissioned from November 6, 1852, to November 6, 1854; re-elected and commissioned from November 6, 1854, to November 6, 1856.

John F. Polk, commissioned from November 6, 1856, to November 6, 1858; re-elected and commissioned from November 6, 1858, to November 6, 1860.

James M. Clements, commissioned from November 6, 1860, to November 6, 1862; re-elected, commissioned and served four full terms from November 6, 1862, to November 6, 1870.

Noah Hayes, commissioned to serve from November 6, 1870, to November 6, 1872; resigned in May, 1871, to join Professor Hall's Polaris expedition in search of the North Pole.

INDIANA SOLDIE

November 6. 1854; re-elected

INDIANA SOLDIERS.

William R. Harrold, appointed to fill the vacancy vice Hayes, resigned, serving to November 6, 1872; elected and commissioned from November 6. 1872, to November 6. 1874.

Joseph Unthank, commissioned to serve from November 6, 1874. to November 6. 1876; resigned in June, 1875.

John H. Hewit, appointed vice Unthank, resigned, serving to November 6, 1876.

Daniel K. Cook, commissioned from November 6, 1876, to November 6, 1878; re-elected and commissioned from November 6, 1878, to November 6, 1880.

Robert I. Morrison, commissioned from November 13. 1880, to November 13. 1882; re-elected and commissioned from November 13, 1882, to November 13, 1884.

Daniel K. Cook, commissioned from November 13, 1884, to November 13, 1886; re-elected, commissioned and served two full terms, from November 13, 1886, to November 13, 1890.

Omar E. Minesinger, commissioned from November 13, 1890, to November 13, 1892; re-elected,·commissioned and served two full terms, from November 13, 1892, to November 13, 1896.

Ulysses S. Cook, commissioned from November 13 ,1896, to November 13, 1898.

Solomon A. Robe, commissioned from November 13, 1898, to November 13, 1900; re-elected and commissioned from November 13. 1900, to November 13, 1902. Here the law was changed by an act of the General Assembly to make the terms of all county officers begin on the uniform date of January 1, thus extending Mr. Robe's second term to January 1, 1903. He died in office December 31, 1902, the day prior to the expiration of his second term, he having been elected and commissioned for another full term from January 1, 1903, to January 1, 1905.

Omar E. Minesinger, appointed vice Solomon A. Robe, deceased, serving from January 5, 1903, to January 1, 1905; elected and commissioned from January 1, 1905, to January 1, 1907; present incumbent.

BIOGRAPHICAL.

Many of the men who have served as surveyors of Henry County have cut a very important figure in the history of the county. Thomas R. Stanford was one of the first two associate justices, afterward a member of the lower house of the General Assembly for three terms and then a State Senator. His precise term as a legislator will be found set out under the title of The General Assembly elsewhere in this History.

Dr. George H. Ballengall was one of the three delegates from Henry County to the convention which framed the present constitution of this State, and is referred to in the introduction to this chapter.

Isaac Kinley was a disinguished soldier of the Civil War; first as Captain of Company D, 36th Indiana Infantry, then Major of the regiment. Afterward he was Provost Marshal of the Fifth Indiana district.

John F. Polk. a brother of Judge Robert L. Polk, was one of Henry County's leading educators, a native of Greensboro. now residing in Nebraska.

James M. Clements. who served five consecutive terms in the office. was for many years civil engineer of the town of New Castle. Elsewhere in this History will be found farther reference to him.

Noah Hayes was a gallant soldier in the Civil War—first in Company E. 36th Indiana Infantry, and then in Company A. 30th Indiana Infantry, reorganized, serving four years, all the time at the front. After returning from the North Pole expedition he had an appointment in the treasury department at Washington during which time he read medicine and graduated. He then located in Seneca, Nemaha County, Kansas, where he is now engaged in the practise of his profession.

Daniel K. Cook filled the office for five full terms of two years each, but not consecutively. His son, Ulysses S. Cook. was one of his successors. The Cooks. both father and son, were for years civil engineers of the town of New Castle—the father for sixteen years and the son for .two years. Daniel K. Cook drew the plans and specifications for the present sanitary sewer system of New Castle. costing about $100,000. and superintended its construction. He, assisted by his son, made the surveys through the counties of Marion, Hancock, Henry and Randolph, and made the plans, profiles and estimates for the proposed Indianapolis, New Castle and Toledo Electric railway.

OMAR E. MINESINGER is the grandson of John Minesinger, who was county commissioner during the Civil War and who was the civil engineer in charge of the construction of the first railroad built through New Castle, the present Panhandle railway. Mr. Minesinger, when he completes his present term, will have filled the office five full terms, but not consecutively. As civil engineer he made the surveys, plans and specifications for the Dunreith and New Castle branch of the Indianapolis and Eastern Railway, the first electric line constructed in Henry County.

SOLOMON A. ROBE was the only surveyor to die in office. He was a descendant of the family of that name who for so many years have lived in and around Luray and in the northern part of Prairie Township. The family is one of the oldest in that part of Henry County.

SUPERINTENDENT OF COUNTY SCHOOLS.

Beginning about the time the present constitution of the State became effective, November 1, 1851, the law provided that there should be in each county a school or county examiner whose duties consisted in examining applicants who desired to become teachers. Whenever the applicant was found possessed of the requisite knowledge the examiner issued a certificate to him or her to teach for a determinate period, not exceeding two years, regulated by the proficiency which the applicant might display. The county examiner was also authorized to visit the various schools, but no compensation was provided therefor. Before 1852 there was in each county a board of school examiners, consisting of three members, who performed the same duties as subsequently devolved upon the school examiners.

From 1852 to 1873 the following named persons acted as county examiner and from the fact that no official record of their terms can be found it is not possible to state the exact time that any of them served, viz: James S. Ferris, Simon T. Powell, Russell B. Abbott, Isaac Kinley, Thomas Rogers, William M. Watkins, Henry M. Shockley, Daniel Newby and Clarkson Davis.

In 1873 the General Assembly provided for the election of a county superintendent with enlarged powers and fixed compensation. From time to time since 1873 the General Assembly has increased the power and compensation of this officer to keep pace with the growing school demands until now the office is an important one and is regarded as a very desirable position, the superintendent having an office in the court house the same as any other county official. The present term of office is four years and he is elected by the township trustees.

Since 1873 the following persons have held the office of county superintendent in the order named: Enos Adamson, 1873-5; George W. Hufford, 1875-7; Timothy Wilson, 1877-83; William R. Wilson, 1883-9; Fassett A. Cotton, 1889-95; Joseph A. Greenstreet, 1895-7; William F. Byrket, 1897-1901; Joseph A. Greenstreet, 1901-3; William F. Byrket, 1903-5.

THE COUNTY COUNCIL.

The county council was created by an act of the General Assembly approved March 3 1899 It is composed of seven members, three from the county at large and one each from four districts into which it is made the duty of the board of county commissioners to divide the county, without, however, dividing any townships, which districts can only be changed once in six years. The members of the first council were appointed by William O. Barnard, judge of the circuit court, as provided by section 48 of the law and held office until 1900, when their successors were elected at the general election in November to serve until 1902, as provided in section 5, since which time the term of office of a member of the county council has been for four years, the third board of councilmen being in office at this time.

On May 1, 1899, the board of county commissioners established the four councilmanic districts as follows: 1st—Henry and Prairie Townships. 2d—Greensboro, Harrison, Fall Creek and Jefferson Townships. 3d—Stony Creek, Blue River, Liberty, Dudley and Franklin Townships. 4th—Spiceland and Wayne Townships.

The council appointed by Judge Barnard was as follows: For the county at large—Thomas C. Phelps, of Harrison Township; Sanford M. Bouslog, of Prairie Township; Alpha Langston, of Dudley Township. By districts—1st—John C. Livezey, of Henry Township; 2d—Imla W. Cooper, of Fall Creek Township; 3d—David M. Brown, of Franklin Township; 4th—Nathan T. Nixon, of Wayne Township.

The council chosen at the regular election on November 8, 1900, was: For the county at large—Benjamin F. Koons, of Blue River Township; Thomas C. Phelps, of Harrison Township; Milton Edwards, of Wayne Township. By districts.—1st—John F. Luellen, of Henry Township; 2d—Levi Cook, of Greensboro Township; 3d—Ephraim Leakey, of Dudley Township; 4th—Harper F. Sullivan, of Wayne Township. This council under the provisions of section 5 of the law served only two years.

At the general election in November, 1902, a new council was elected for the full term of four years, as follows: For the county at large—Thomas C. Phelps, of Harrison Township; Milton Edwards, of Wayne Township; William E. Kerr, of Blue River Township. By districts.—1st—Evan H. Peed, of Henry Township; 2d—Presley E. Jackson, of Greensboro Township; 3d—Ephraim Leakey, of Dudley Township; 4th—Harper F. Sullivan, of Wayne Township. A new council will be chosen at the general election in November, 1906.

The pay of members under section 3 of the law is fixed by the population of the county and in Henry county is $10 per annum for each councilman. Sections 7 and 8 of the law provide for an annual meeting of the council to be held on the first Tuesday after the first Monday in September for the purpose of fixing the tax levy and making appropriations and for such special meetings as may be called by the auditor upon proper personal notice and publication. The officers are a president and a president pro tem. elected by the members. The County Auditor is the clerk of the council and keeps a record of its proceedings. The County Sheriff, in person or by deputy, must attend its meetings and execute its orders. A majority of all members shall constitute a quorum and a majority vote is necessary to pass an ordinance, except at called meetings when a two thirds vote is necessary. A two thirds vote is also required to expel a member. A member of the council can hold no other office and must be a qualified voter and resident freeholder in the district which he represents. No councilman is permitted to be interested in any contract with the county under penalty of a fine not to exceed $1,000.

Secion 15 of the law sets out the duties of the council, in a general way, as the power of fixing the rate of taxation for county purposes and of making appropriations of money to be paid out of the county treasury, and except as is otherwise expressly provided, no money shall be drawn from the county treasury only in pursuance of appropriations so made. The cases in which money may be paid out of the county treasury without being appropriated by the council are specifically defined in another section of the law.

The board of county commissioners must submit through the county auditor as their clerk, an estimate of the various amounts that will be required to meet each and all of the various items of county expenditure during the ensuing year, to the council at its regular annual meeting in September. This estimated list is considered by the council and either approved, modified or overruled. No county officer is permitted to disburse funds in excess of such appropriations, under heavy penalties. The board of county commissioners make up their estimates from many sources, such as bridges, public buildings, expenses of the poor, salaries, books, stationery, care of insane and of criminals and scores of other items, all relating to every form of county expenditure. Each county officer is required to make and file with the Auditor of the county an itemized statement of the needs of his office for the ensuing year, before the Thursday following the first Monday in August of each year. It is from all these sources, so arranged and tabulated as to be readily understood, that the county commissioners first, and then the county council as the highest fiscal authority, finally makes up the annual budget of appropriations for county expenditures.

TOWNSHIP ADVISORY BOARDS.

By an act of the General Assembly, approved February 27, 1899, an Advisory Board consisting of three resident freeholders and qualified voters in each of the townships in every county of the State was provided. The duties and powers of this board with respect to township business are the same as those of the county council relating to county business. The board's annual meeting to fix the rates of township taxation for the several purposes is held on the first Tuesday of each year, at which time a chairman is selected, and special meetings may be held upon call of the township trustee or chairman of the board. The township trustee must make an itemized statement of the various amounts of money that will likely be required for the ensuing year. This estimate must be presented at the annual meeting for the board's approval, modification or rejection.

The first township boards were named by the judges of the several circuit courts of the State, each judge naming the boards for the township within his judicial circuit, at the first term of court held in the county in which the townships are situated, after the taking effect of the law. These appointees held office until the November election in 1900, at which time their successors were elected for two years. At the November election in 1902, a new board was elected for the full term of four years.

Albert D. Ogborn, joint senator from Henry, Fayette and Union counties, and George W. Williams, representative from Henry County, in the General Assembly, voted in the affirmative for both the county council and advisory boards, two important measures of legislation.

COUNTY ATTORNEY.

Prior to 1877 the prosecuting attorney was regarded as the legal adviser to the Board of County Commissioners, since which time it has been deemed necessary to have regularly employed counsel in consequence of the increased court duties of the prosecuting attorney and the growing business and more intricate and complicated affairs of the county coming before the commissioners on account of turnpikes, ditches, highways, public buildings, bridges, etc., etc. Therefore since 1877 the board has employed legal counsel and three New Castle lawyers have held the office of county attorney, namely:

Joshua H. Mellett, from 1877 to 1893; Adolph Rogers, from 1893 to 1903; Fred C. Gause, from 1903; present incumbent.

At first the salary was only $150 annually. From March 1, 1895, to the close of 1903 it was $300, since which time it has been $400.

DRAINAGE COMMISSIONERS.

The office of drainage commissioners was created by an act of the General Assembly, approved April 6, 1885, providing for the appointment of a drainage commissioner by the Board of County Commissioners to serve for two years or until his successor is qualified. The county surveyor is by virtue of his office also a drainage commissioner.

Since the law has been in operation a great number of costly and important ditches have been constructed in Henry County under its provisions and thousands upon thousands of dollars collected and disbursed. During this time Blue River has been straightened, deepened and dredged from its headwaters to within less than a mile of Stone Quarry mill in Greensboro Township. Flatrock has been straightened and dredged its entire length in Henry County; Big Buck Creek has been dredged, straightened and made deeper, and many other streams of the county have been improved in the same way. Under the provisions of the law the costs of such drainage is paid by assessments levied on the lands through which the drainage passes or which are directly benefited by it. The owners of the lands benefited are given their option to pay their assessments in cash without additional costs or in ten annual payments of one tenth per year with six per cent. interest, the principal and interest being payable at the office of the county treasurer, the money to pay for the work being provided by the sale of bonds and the interest charged to those who take the ten year plan of payment in order to recoup the county for the interest it must pay on the bonds.

The drainage commissioner is allowed three dollars a day for the time actually employed. The county surveyor, who is also the engineer in charge of the work, is allowed a sum not to exceed four dollars per day for every day that he is employed in the surveying of the ditches, establishing the levels, making the diagrams, etc. All expenses of officers, advertising, court charges. attorneys fees and labor in connection with the surveys, are added to the estimated cost of construction, the benefits to each tract of land being assessed by three disinterested freeholders of the county. Damages are also allowed where sustained.

The following have served as Drainage Commissioners:

William O. Bogue, of Spiceland Township, from 1885 to 1887.

Robert Cluggish, of Henry Township, from 1887 to 1893.

Henry Fadely, of Fall Creek Township, from 1893 to 1904.

Luther M. Anderson, of Greensboro Township, since May, 1904.

Considering the large number of land owners and their many conflicting opinions and interests the work of drainage and the assessment and collection of the large amount of money which it has cost, has been accomplished with very little friction, ill will or litigation.

COURT HOUSE JANITOR.

For many years the care of the court house and county offices devolved upon the sheriff, excepting during terms of the courts when the court bailiff had charge of the court room, but since the completion of the court house in 1868 the building and grounds have been cared for by a janitor appointed annually by the Board of County Commissioners. There is no fixed salary, the janitor being employed by contract from year to year.

The following have served as janitors. (The names of those who served between Shopp and Kirk are not now obtainable): Henry L. Shopp, Allen T. Kirk, Nathan Upham, Ephraim Burk. William J. C. Crandall, William T. Corya and the present janitor, William Barnett. The duties of the janitor now include the care of the court house and grounds. Janitors in recent years have received from $350 to $456 per year. The recent completion of an addition to the court house, almost doubling its size, adds greatly to the labors of the janitor. The contract with the janitor for the fiscal year ending June 1, 1905, was $456.00, since which time the salary has been continued on the same terms, $38 per month.

COURT BAILIFFS.

The following have acted as bailiffs to the several courts in Henry County:

William McDowell, John Alexander. Miles E. Anderson, Harvey W. Swaim, John W. Brattain. George H. Cain and William H. Macy. William McDowell was the bailiff of the first grand jury impaneled in the county and continued as such officer of the courts of the county for a period covering fifty years, when, at his own request. he was in 1873 relieved by Judge Joshua H. Mellett, who appointed John Alexander, his successor.

CHAPTER XLIV.

From the organization of the State until the court of common pleas was finally abolished by act of the General Assembly, March 6, 1873, there were two courts in each county, since which time there has been but one, the Circuit Court having jurisdiction and discharging all the duties theretofore performed by the different courts in the county during the period of their existence. Until the new constitution became effective, November 1, 1851, the court of highest jurisdiction in the respective counties was, as it is now, the Circuit Court, which then consisted of three judges—a presiding judge whose duty extended over the entire circuit and two associate judges, or as they were then commonly called "side judges" for each county. The presiding judge was a man supposed to be "learned in the law," who traveled over his circuit from county to county and presided with the associate judges, one on each side. From this fact in early times came the expression "riding the circuit." There were no railroads or other means of communication between points in the circuit, except by horseback. The presiding judge would "ride the circuit" accompanied usually by some of the leading lawyers of the judicial circuit who went from one county seat to another in search of business. It is from this state of affairs that so many attorneys from the different counties in central and eastern Indiana, who afterward became famous in the State or Nation were practising attorneys before the early courts of Henry County, as is mentioned in the article on the "First Courts," set out in the preceding chapter in this History.

The "presiding judges" before the advent of the present constitution were elected by the joint vote of the two houses of the General Assembly. The associate judges were elected by the direct vote of the electors of the respective counties. In early days an associate judge who was a lawyer was the exception rather than the rule. They were men who had the confidence of their fellow citizens,

HENRY COUNTY JUDGES

ING THE CIRCUIT—JUDICIAL CIR-
S—REGISTERS OF AND BIOGRAPH-
TING AND DISTRICT ATTORNEYS.
ES—THE GENERAL ASSEMBLY
IONS OF THE GENERAL ASSEM-
IN CONGRESSIONAL DISTRICTS
FOR PRESIDENT, 1832
THE PRESIDENT IN 1904—
OF INDIANA—

court of common pleas was
March 6, 1873, there were
has been but one, the Circuit
the duties theretofore performed
period of their existence. Until
r 1, 1851, the court of highest
is now, the Circuit Court, which
re whose duty extended over the
they were then commonly called
judge was a man supposed to be
cuit from county to county and
side. From this fact in early
There were no railroads or
except by horseback.
usually by some of
went from one county seat to
state of affairs that so many at-
eastern Indiana who afterward
tising attorneys before the early
the "First Courts."

present constitution were
General Assembly. The as-
the electors of the respective
was the exception
confidence of their fellow citizens.

HENRY COUNTY JUDGES.

and were elected for their honesty and their common sense, regardless of the fact that they were "unlearned in the law." Since the present constitution became effective all judges have been elected by the direct vote of the people. In the absence of the presiding judge the associate judges had the power to hold their respective county courts. More than this, when the presiding judge was presiding, he had but one vote in three, and in order to have his decision stand as that of the court he had to carry one associate judge with him. It was sometimes the case that the associate judges joined together and outvoted the presiding judge. In the earlier law reports of Indiana instances can be found of causes taken to the Supreme Court on an appeal from a decision made by the two associate judges, with the presiding judge dissenting, in which the court of last resort affirmed the decision of the lower court.

Under the old constitution the term of office for the presiding and associate judges was seven years, but in some instances on account of a change of circuit, or the election of the presiding judge to a more important office, or from an occasional resignation, the office itself being finally abolished by the present constitution, no one presiding judge, excepting Judge Jehu T. Elliott, presided for the full term of seven years over the Henry Circuit Court; and from various causes more fully explained under the head of "Associate Judges," all of such judges in Henry County except Anderson and Crowley served less than the full term of seven years. The judges of probate were elected for the term of seven years. Under the present constitution the "side judges" were dispensed with and the presiding judge was made sole judge and the title of his office changed to Judge of the Henry Circuit Court; the term of office was reduced to six years. The probate court was also abolished. The term of office of the judge of the common pleas court, from the time it was established until it was finally legislated out of existence, was four years. Henry County alone now constitutes the Fifty Third Judicial Circuit.

JUDICIAL CIRCUITS.

When Henry County was organized and "attached" to the Third Judicial Circuit, this circuit embraced practically one fourth of the territorial limits of the State of Indiana. Beginning with Switzerland County on the Ohio river and extending northward to the Michigan line and west of the Ohio State line, it took in the counties of Ohio (since organized, in 1844, out of Dearborn), Dearborn, Ripley, Jennings, Franklin, Union, Fayette, Rush, Henry, Wayne, Randolph and Delaware, and the unorganized territory, "attached for judicial purposes," which embraced what is now Jay, Blacktord, Adams, Wells, Allen (although Allen was then organized as a "detached" county), DeKalb, Steuben and all that part of Grant, Huntington, Whitley, Noble and LaGrange counties lying east of the line extending north on the western boundary of Henry County.

It is recorded by former United States Senator Oliver H. Smith in his book entitled, "Early Indiana Trials and Sketches," published in 1857, that in the Fall of 1825 as a young attorney "riding the circuit," in company with James Rariden, of Centreville, they accompanied Presiding Judge Miles C. Eggleston, of the Third Judicial Circuit, to Fort Wayne, to hold court. At that time all the territory north of Delaware (the first county so named), and Randolph counties was "unorganized" territory with the exception of Allen County, which was organized practically with its present boundaries. The reader must keep in mind the fact that there have been two Delaware counties—the "unorganized" county, which embraced all of the new purchase, organized January 22, 1820, and the present county of Delaware, organized January 26, 1827. By the term "unorganized" county is meant that certain described territory in a new State, embraced in what is designated as a county, although having no "organized" county civil government.

Indiana was first organized into counties by beginning at the Ohio River and extending northward, organization of new counties being made from contiguous territory, except in the case of Allen County, which was organized as a "detached" county from the fact that one of the earlier frontier forts, known as Fort Wayne, was established at the confluence of the St. Joseph and St. Mary's rivers, the two forming the Maumee River at Fort Wayne. There was an early settlement around this point, which led to the early organization of the county, which was named after the revolutionary hero, Ethan Allen, its principal town taking the name of the fort which had been named in honor of "Mad Anthony" Wayne. At the time mentioned by Oliver H. Smith, Fort Wayne contained a mixed population of about two hundred people and the entire county of Allen contained less than one hundred voters.

In 1830 the organization of counties was begun on the Michigan line and extended southward. The first two counties so organized were St. Joseph and Elkhart, by an act of the General Assembly approved January 29, 1830, which fact has direct reference to the history of Henry County, because Elkhart County was attached for judicial purposes to the Sixth Judicial Circuit, of which Henry County formed a part. From this time until all of the unorganized territory of the State was embraced in counties the organization of counties proceeded southward from the Michigan line as well as northward, as before mentioned. So much space has already been given to the formation of the Third Judicial Circuit that briefer reference must be made to the other early circuits, of which Henry County was a part.

The Fifth Judicial Circuit embraced the counties of Henry, Bartholomew, Decatur, Hamilton, Hendricks, Johnson, Marion, Monroe, Morgan, Rush and Shelby. Looking at the present map of Indiana, showing the populous county of Marion, containing the capital city with its numerous steam and electric lines diverging in every direction, the adjoining and contiguous counties teeming with industry, with the thrifty county towns of New Castle, Columbus, Greensburg, Noblesville, Danville, Franklin, Bloomington, Martinsville, Rushville and Shelbyville (Hancock was not then organized), it is difficult to realize that only three quarters of a century have elapsed since this territory was so sparsely populated, so lacking in wealth and so meagre in legal and official business that it could all be combined in one judicial circuit.

The Sixth Judicial Circuit was composed of the counties of Henry, Allen, Delaware, Elkhart, Fayette, Randolph, Rush, Union and Wayne. Mention has been made of the fact that Elkhart County when organized was attached to this circuit for judicial purposes. As has been stated, Elkhart and St. Joseph were the first two counties organized on the Michigan line. At this time (1830) practically the northern half of the State of Indiana was a dense wilderness, peopled by the Delaware, Kickapoo, Miami, Pottawatomie and Ottawa Indian tribes. An authorized map of the State of Indiana, published in 1827, shows not a county in the State other than Allen organized north of the northern boundary of Henry County extending east and west across the State, excepting Randolph (1818), Delaware (1827), Madison (1823), Hamilton (1823), Montgomery (1822), Fountain (1825), and Vermilion (1824). The now populous county of Boone on a line across the State as mentioned is not named on this map of 1827, as it was not organized until 1830. Elkhart County was attached to the Sixth Judicial Circuit in name only and the presiding judge of the circuit probably never in the county for the purpose of holding court. Afterward (1832), La Grange County, which is the first county east of Elkhart, was also attached to this district for judicial purposes. The presiding judge was probably never in La Grange County for the purpose of holding court.

PRESIDING JUDGES.

THIRD JUDICIAL CIRCUIT

Miles C. Eggleston, of Brookville, afterward of Centreville, commissioned April 21, 1822, presiding judge, to supply the vacancy occasioned by the resignation of Alexander A. Meek; again commissioned December 18, 1823, for the full term of seven years. He succeeded himself and was re-commissioned December 18, 1830. The circuit was composed of the counties of Dearborn, Delaware, Fayette, Franklin, Jennings, Randolph, Ripley, Rush, Switzerland, Union and Wayne, as contiguous territory and all unorganized territory north to the Michigan line, which included the "attached" but organized county of Allen. When Henry County was organized it was "attached" for judicial purposes to this circuit. Within three years a new circuit, the Fifth, was created and Henry County was made a part of it.

FIFTH JUDICIAL CIRCUIT.

Bethuel F. Morris, of Indianapolis, commissioned July 20, 1825, was presiding judge. He succeeded himself, being re-commissioned January 22, 1829. This circuit was composed of the counties of Henry (until it was transferred to the Sixth Circuit), Bartholomew, Decatur, Hamilton, Hendricks, Johnson, Marion, Morgan, Rush and Shelby.

SIXTH JUDICIAL CIRCUIT.

Charles H. Test, of Centreville, commissioned January 23, 1830, as presiding judge; resigned December 30, 1835, to take effect January 20, 1836.

Samuel Bigger, of Rushville, commissioned presiding judge vice Charles H. Test, resigned, to fill out his unexpired term from January 20, 1836, to January 23, 1837. Judge Bigger succeeded himself, being re-commissioned for the full term beginning January 23, 1837. He was elected Governor of Indiana on the "first Monday in August," 1840, for the term of three years, and accordingly resigned the office of presiding judge.

James Perry, of Richmond, commissioned as presiding judge December 9, 1840, to fill the unexpired term of Judge Bigger, resigned, which ended December 23, 1844.

Jehu T. Elliott (Whig), of New Castle, elected "Tuesday, December 19, 1843," and commissioned as presiding judge for the full term beginning January 23, 1844. As has been stated, the presiding judges were elected by both houses of the General Assembly, in joint session. The vote stood: Jehu T. Elliott, 83; Samuel E. Perkins, of Richmond, 36; Andrew Davidson, of Greensburg, 24; scattering, 3; total, 146. The Legislature was Democratic. Samuel E. Perkins, the Democratic candidate, afterward moved to Indianapolis and became a justice of the Supreme Court, 1846-55. He was for many years prominent in political and legal pursuits. He served again as a justice of the Supreme Court, 1877-9, by appointment from Governor Williams.

On January 14, 1851, the General Assembly, a majority of whose members were Democrats, was again in joint session to elect a successor to Judge Elliott, who, as, stated above, was a Whig. A distinguished citizen of New Castle, then a Democrat, was a candidate for the succession. The first ballot stood: William Grose, 70; Jehu T. Elliott, 68; blank, 7; total, 145. Grose lacked three votes of an election. Second ballot: William Grose, 67; Jehu T. Elliott, 75; blank, 4; total, 146.

Judge Elliott resigned, presumably early in 1851, to accept the presidency of the then proposed and partially located Cincinnati, Logansport and Chicago railway, the principal office of which was at New Castle. At this time work on the road was barely begun at Richmond, and it was not until "1854 that the cars ran into the depot door" at New Castle. The statement "presumably early in 1851" is used for the reason that on February 25, 1851, the General Assembly in joint session elected Oliver P. Morton, Indiana's future great war governor, as presiding judge to fill the vacancy caused by Judge Elliott's resignation. William Dudley Foulke, of Richmond, in his admirable life of Oliver P. Morton, says, Volume 1, page 17: "When, in 1852, a vacancy occurred in the circuit which embraced Wayne County, Morton was, on February 23 of that year, elected judge by that body (the General Assembly) without opposition." Mr. Foulke is plainly mistaken, as to the year, for the reason that the present constitution became effective November 1, 1851, after which time the power to elect circuit judges was taken from the General Assembly and placed directly with the people by popular vote and has since continued until this day. Morton continued as judge for a short time only, when he resigned and returned to the practise of law. A judgeship was hardly congenial to Indiana's future great citizen and the new constitution coming into effect changed somewhat the whole court procedure.

The Sixth Judicial Circuit from the time it was first organized in 1830, underwent many changes. At first it consisted of the counties of Henry, Allen, Delaware, Elkhart, Fayette, Randolph, Rush, Union and Wayne. As has been stated, when La Grange County was organized (1832), it was "attached" to this circuit for judicial purposes. As population increased the number of counties comprised in a judicial circuit decreased, and when Judge Elliott resigned, in 1851, the district was composed of the counties of Henry, Delaware, Fayette, Grant, Randolph, Rush, Union and Wayne; and so ends the sixth and last judicial circuit of which Henry County was a part under the constitution of 1816.

BIOGRAPHICAL.—PRESIDING JUDGES.

MILES C. EGGLESTON presided at only a partial term of the court in Henry County, and perhaps for but one day, from the fact that he proceeded to decide the first question that came before the court without consultation with the "side judges," whereupon Judges Stanford and Long, both very pronounced men, held a brief whispered consultation and then announced that the opinion of Judge Eggleston, just rendered, was not the judgment of the court. Judge Eggleston immediately left the bench and, taking his hat in hand, made a profound bow to the lawyers present, saying: "Gentlemen, I see you have a court of your own here, and hence have no use for a judge, so that I will take my departure," which he immediately did, and never returned. Judge Eggleston lived first at Brookville, and later at Centreville.

BETHUEL F. MORRIS was an early pioneer lawyer, settling at Indianapolis, where he lived until his death, which occurred about the beginning of the Civil War period. He was a presiding judge for a long time after Henry County ceased to be a part of his circuit. His son, Samuel V. Morris, now residing in Minneapolis, Minnesota, married twice; both of his wives were sisters of ex-President Benjamin Harrison.

CHARLES H. TEST, of Centreville, was a son of John Test, of Brookville, who for three terms represented in Congress the district of which Henry County was a part, as is shown under the head of "Congressional Districts." The cause of Judge Test's resignation was that he moved to Mobile, Alabama, to engage in the practise of the law, but within a year returned to Centreville and in 1849 was elected Secretary of State by the General Assembly, serving a full term, 1849-53. Afterward he moved to LaFayette, where he served for twelve years as judge of the circuit court. Later he took up his residence in Indianapolis and served a term as judge of the Marion Criminal Court. Late in life he moved to Vincennes, where he died in 1884, at the age of eighty four years, at the home of his son, and is buried in the cemetery at Vincennes. General John Coburn, of Indianapolis, married Judge Test's daughter.

SAMUEL BIGGER, of Rushville, was a distinguished citizen, a leading jurist and one of Indiana's most famous chief executives. While serving as judge of the judicial circuit, of which Henry County was a part, he was in 1840 elected Governor of Indiana by the Whigs and served a term of three years. His history is a part of that of the State of Indiana.

JAMES PERRY, of Richmond, was a lawyer of note and a man of affairs. During the Civil War period he took an active part as an advocate and supporter of Governor Morton. His son, General Oran Perry, now quartermaster general of Indiana, distinguished himself as Colonel of the 69th Indiana Infantry, and biographical mention is made of him in a full account of that famous regiment published elsewhere in this History.

JEHU T. ELLIOTT's biography will be found in full in the succeeding chapter.

OLIVER P. MORTON's history is familiar to all as Indiana's great war governor.

ASSOCIATE JUDGES.

Term Beginning July 5, 1822, to July 5, 1829.

Thomas R. Stanford, commissioned from July 5, 1822, to July 5, 1829; resigned June 21, 1825.

Elisha Long, commissioned from July 5, 1822, to July 5, 1829; resigned May 22, 1826.

John Anderson, elected to vacancy vice Stanford, resigned; commissioned from August 16, 1825, to July 5, 1829.

Byram Cadwallader, elected to vacancy vice Long, resigned; commissioned from August 19, 1826, to July 5, 1829.

Term Beginning July 5, 1829, to July 5, 1836.

John Anderson, commissioned from July 5, 1829, to July 5, 1836.

Byram Cadwallader, commissioned from July 5, 1829, to July 5, 1836; resigned in the summer of 1834, exact date not given.

Jacob Thorp, elected to the vacancy vice Cadwallader, resigned; commissioned from August 15, 1834, to July 5, 1836.

Term Beginning July 5, 1836, to July 5, 1843.

John Anderson, commissioned from July 5, 1836, to July 5, 1843; died in office, probably in December, 1838, as the record of executive proceedings on file in the office of the Secretary of State shows the following entry: "January 1, 1839, a writ of election is issued to the sheriff of Henry County for the election of an associate judge vice John Anderson, deceased."

Jacob Thornburgh, elected to vacancy vice Anderson, deceased; commissioned from February 19, 1839, to July 5, 1843; died in office February 16, 1840.

Gabriel Cosand, elected to vacancy vice Thornburgh, deceased; commissioned April 16, 1840, to July 5, 1843.

Term Beginning July 5, 1843, to July 5, 1850.

Abraham Elliott, commissioned from July 5, 1843, to July 5, 1850; died in office September 14, 1848.

William W. Williams, elected to vacancy vice Abraham Elliott, deceased; commissioned from January 17, 1849, to July 5, 1850.

James W. Crowley, commissioned from July 5, 1843, to July 5, 1850.

Abraham Elliott, who sat as an associate judge from July 5, 1843, until his death, was the father of the presiding judge, Jehu T. Elliott.

Term Beginning July 5, 1850, to July 5, 1857.

William W. Williams, commissioned from July 5, 1850, to July 5, 1857.

Joseph Farley, commissioned from July 5, 1850, to July 5, 1857.

The office of associate judge ceased to exist November 1, 1851, when the present constitution became effective.

Regarding the salary paid associate judges, Judge Martin L. Bundy informs the author that it was first two dollars a day, for the time actually employed; later it was increased to three dollars a day.

After political lines were drawn in the county (1835-7) no man other than a Whig held the office.

BIOGRAPHICAL—ASSOCIATE JUDGES.

THOMAS R. STANFORD was respectively associate judge, for several terms a member of the lower house of the General Assembly, State senator, county commissioner and acted as county surveyor for many years. His record as a county official in point of service is only equaled by that of Jesse H. Healey. Judge Martin L. Bundy says of him: "In my opinion, Judge Thomas R. Stanford must be regarded as the foremost citizen of the county during the period in which he lived." He was born in Virginia, November

64

23, 1794. When a child he came with his parents to Warren County, Ohio, where he lived until his marriage, January 16, 1817, to Mary Arnét, when he immigrated to Wayne County, Indiana, near Economy. In 1820, he moved to Madison County, settling near Pendleton. In 1822 he came to Henry County and settled about three miles east of New Castle on what is now known as the Millikan farm. He was elected one of the first probate judges within a few months after he came into the county and continued most active in public affairs until he retired from the office of county commissioner, in 1860. He died January 4, 1869, and is buried beside his wife in the Batson Cemetery, Liberty Township. The late Dr. William M. Kerr, of Rogersville, married his eldest daughter and child, Narcissa, and Mrs. Lycurgus L. Burr, of New Castle, is his granddaughter. Her son, Horace L. Burr, has filed with the Henry County Historical Society an exhaustive sketch of Judge Stanford and to this the reader is referred for additional information concerning him.

ELISHA LONG'S name with biographical reference will be found in the Senatorial list.

JOHN ANDERSON was a farmer, living at Raysville. His death occurred while he was in the prime of life and his remains were interred in the cemetery at Raysville.

BYRAM CADWALLADER lived on what is now known as the Hudelson farm, three miles north of New Castle. In 1832 he moved to Laporte County, where he died and is buried.

JACOB THORP, the old bell maker, lived two miles south of Millville. In early days it was the custom to bell the cows and other stock running at large, and Thorp made the bells.

JACOB THORNBURGH'S biographical reference will be found published in connection with that of his son, John Thornburgh, in Chapter XI of this History.

GABRIEL COSAND was a son of Benjamin and Mary Cosand, who came from North Carolina to Henry County about 1825. The family, which was a large one, settled in the northern part of Franklin Township, about half way between New Castle and Lewisville. Samuel, John, Elias, Nathan and William were brothers of Gabriel; and a sister named Miriam married Cyrus Wright; they resided in Wayne County, two miles north of Richmond. Gabriel Cosand was born in North Carolina, February 13, 1799. On November 21, 1833, he was married to Sarah Wickersham, a daughter of Caleb and half sister of Jethro Wickersham, the latter now living in Franklin Township. They were the parents of ten children, three of whom died in infancy. The others were: Benjamin F., now residing in Kansas; Ellen M., now deceased, married to Joseph H. White; Eunice, residing in New Castle; Cornelius W., a resident of Franklin Township, who was a gallant soldier in the Civil War and whose record will be found elsewhere in this History; Lydia, now deceased, who was married to Elvin Greenstreet, of Howard County; Miriam, died at the age of twenty two years, and Aaron T., now living in New Castle. Gabriel Cosand was a man of sterling integrity and great purity of character. No man ever lived in Franklin Township who left at his death a more enviable reputation. After serving as associate judge he was for several years trustee of Franklin Township. He died May 22, 1881, and his wife died March 6, 1883. Both are buried in Rich Square Cemetery.

ABRAHAM ELLIOTT'S biographical reference will be found in connection with that of his son, Judge Jehu T. Elliott, published in the succeeding chapter.

WILLIAM W. WILLIAMS' name with biographical reference will be found in the Senatorial list.

JAMES W. CROWLEY was a merchant at Greensboro, where he was postmaster for four years, as is shown in Chapter I of this History. He moved from Greensboro to Howard County.

JOSEPH FARLEY was a farmer residing in Dudley Township, not far from the home of Isaac Parker, in Franklin Township. The two men were close friends and it was probably through the influence of Parker that Farley was elected associate judge. Biographical reference to Isaac Parker will be found elsewhere in this History.

JUDICIAL CIRCUITS UNDER THE PRESENT CONSTITUTION.

Seventh Judicial Circuit.

The General Assembly early under the present constitution enacted a law dividing the State into ten judicial circuits. The Seventh Circuit consisted of the counties of Henry, Blackford, Delaware, Grant, Jay, Randolph and Wayne. At the October election, 1852, Joseph Anthony, of Muncie, was elected judge and commissioned to serve for a full term of six years, to November 12, 1858. His competitor for the judgeship was Jacob B. Julian, of Centreville. Judge Anthony was badly afflicted physically, walked with great difficulty supported by two crutches and had to be assisted to and from the bench. From this cause and possibly from others, the arrangement was highly unsatisfactory; accordingly, in 1855, when the State was re-districted for judicial purposes, a special point was made to assign Henry County to a new circuit.

Tenth Judicial Circuit.

This circuit was created by act of the General Assembly, approved January 9, 1855, and was composed of the counties of Henry, Jay, Randolph and Wayne. February 25, 1855, Governor Joseph A. Wright commissioned Jeremiah Smith, of Randolph County, to serve as judge "until his successor was elected and qualified." At the October election, 1855, Jehu T. Elliott, of New Castle, was elected as Judge Smith's successor and commissioned to serve for six years, from October 20, 1855, to October 20, 1861. It is pertinent to state that annual elections prevailed under the present constitution until about 1870, since which time all elections have been biennial.

At the October election, 1861, Judge Elliott was elected his own successor without opposition, and commissioned to serve for six years, from October 21, 1861, to October 21, 1867. He resigned January 1, 1865, having been elected at the previous October election a justice of the Supreme Court to serve for the full term of six years, from January 3, 1865.

Silas Colgrove, of Winchester, was commissioned by Governor Morton, January 2, 1865, to fill the vacancy occasioned by Elliott's resignation "until the next general election." Colgrove was well known in Henry County, having been prosecuting attorney of the circuit 1852-4. In the Civil War he was lieutenant colonel of the Eighth Indiana Infantry, three months' service, and afterward colonel of the 27th Indiana Infantry. He greatly distinguished himself and at the close of the war he was made a brevet brigadier general for gallant and meritorious services. At the October election, 1865, Judge Colgrove was elected without opposition to succeed himself and commissioned for the full term, from November 23, 1865, to November 23, 1871.

In 1867 the General Assembly created a new judicial circuit, or rather re-arranged the existing circuits, which removed Henry County from the Tenth to the Seventh Circuit.

Seventh Judicial Circuit.

This circuit was created by a re-arrangement of the counties by an act of the General Assembly, approved February 26, 1867, and was composed of the counties of Henry, Delaware, Hancock and Grant. Joseph S. Buckles, of Muncie, had at the general election of 1864 been elected judge of the Seventh Circuit, as it was then constituted, and commissioned for a full term of six years, from December 22, 1864.

Joshua H. Mellett, of New Castle, was at the October election, 1870, elected judge and commissioned for six years from October 24, 1870. He had no opposition in the district.

Eighteenth Judicial Circuit.

This circuit was created by an act of the General Assembly, approved March 6, 1875, and consisted of the counties of Henry and Hancock, Judge Mellett continuing as judge of the new circuit.

Robert L. Polk, of New Castle, was elected at the October election, 1876, and commissioned for six years from October 24, 1876. He died in office, May 7, 1881.

Mark E. Forkner, of New Castle, was appointed judge until the next general election, when he succeeded himself, being commissioned for six years from November 17, 1882. Here, by constitutional amendment, the election had been changed from the second Tuesday in October to the first Tuesday after the first Monday in November.

William H. Martin, of Greenfield, was elected at the November election, 1888, and commissioned for six years from November 17, 1888.

Fifty Third Judicial Circuit.

By an act of the General Assembly, approved February 22, 1889, Henry County alone was thereafter to be known "as the Fifty Third Judicial Circuit;" whereupon Governor Alvin P. Hovey commissioned Eugene H. Bundy, of New Castle, judge, "to hold until the next general election."

Eugene H. Bundy was elected as his own successor at the November election, 1890, and commissioned for a full term of six years from November 17, 1890.

William O. Barnard, of New Castle, was elected at the November election, 1896, and commissioned for six years from November 17, 1896.

John M. Morris, of New Castle, was elected at the election in November, 1902, and commissioned for six years from November 17, 1902; present incumbent.

Judge Eugene H. Bundy, above mentioned, is the son of Judge Martin L. Bundy, who was for two terms of four years each judge of the Common Pleas Court for Henry County. His wife is the daughter of the late Judge Joshua H. Mellett, for six years judge of the Henry Circuit Court. He is also a nephew of the late Judge Jehu T. Elliott and a grandson of the latter's father, Judge Abraham Elliott, associate judge of Henry County, 1843-8.

In 1851 the annual salary of a circuit judge was eight hundred dollars; the present annual salary of the judge of the Henry Circuit Court is twenty-five hundred dollars.

The author has not ascertained the political complexion of either Judge Eggleston or Judge Bethuel F. Morris; indeed, when they first held the office of judge there was but one political party in the country, as is shown in the introduction to the preceding chapter. Judge Morris' successor, Charles H. Test, became a Whig and all of his successors with but two exceptions were of that political faith, or Republicans. The exceptions were Oliver P. Morton, who held the office for a short time in 1851, and who did not leave the Democratic party until after the repeal of the Missouri Compromise, in 1854, and Judge Jeremiah Smith, Democrat, appointed February 25, 1855, by Joseph A. Wright, then the Democratic Governor of Indiana.

BIOGRAPHICAL—CIRCUIT COURT JUDGES.

Joseph Anthony, Jeremiah Smith, Silas Colgrove, Joseph S. Buckles and William H. Martin never resided in Henry County, hence this History will not go into biographical mention of them.

Joshua H. Mellett, Mark E. Forkner, Eugene H. Bundy, William O. Barnard and John M. Morris are included in full and appropriate biographical reference in the succeeding chapter.

ROBERT L. POLK was born near Greensboro, Henry County, October 12, 1841. He was the son of Robert H. and Hannah (Hodgin) Polk, who came from North Carolina in the year in which Robert L. was born. His father was a farmer and at the same time followed his trade of a gunsmith, which was very important in those days, the use of fire arms being general in the early settlement of the county. In 1853 the family located in New Castle, from which time young Polk made the best of his educational privileges by attending the old seminary, then in charge of Ferris and Abbott. Subsequently he attended a commercial college at Cleveland, Ohio, and later Whitewater College at Centreville, Indiana, from which he graduated. Meantime, he was studying for the legal profession and was admitted as a member of the Henry County bar in 1863. Soon thereafter he formed a partnership with his legal preceptor, James Brown, which continued until 1872, in which year he was elected judge of the Common Pleas Court for the district of Henry, Hancock and Madison counties, which position he filled until the court was abolished, as is shown under the head of Common Pleas Court in this chapter. Leaving the bench, he resumed the practise of law in New Castle and continued until he was elected judge of the Henry Circuit Court, as is shown in this article. He died in office, May 7, 1881, and is buried in South Mound Cemetery. He was an active member of the Methodist Episcopal Church and his death was mourned by a large circle of friends, by whom he was regarded as a model man, an excellent lawyer and a just judge. He was married in New Castle, November 28, 1865, to Harriet, born October 22, 1844, daughter of Reverend Milton and Eliza (Dorsey) Mahin, the former being at that time pastor of the Methodist Episcopal Church and long one of the most earnest, eloquent and sincere ministers of that great denomination, now retired and living in New Castle, enjoying, with his excellent wife in their declining years, the comfort that comes to those whose lives have been devoted to ennobling thoughts and Christian deeds. Robert L. and Harriet (Mahin) Polk were the parents of five children—Paul; Mary, now Mrs. Dr. R. H. Ritter; George; Catharine, now Mrs. Dr. W. J. Sandy; and Dudley. Mrs. Polk still survives and is living in New Castle.

PROBATE COURT.

The constitution of 1816 provided, Article 5, Section 1, that "the judicial power of the State is in a supreme court, circuit courts and such other inferior courts" as the General Assembly may establish. Accordingly there was established in the respective counties probate courts, which, as the name implies, had jurisdiction of all wills, testaments, executors, administrators, guardians and trustees for persons *non compos mentis;* in short, of all matters relating to decedents' estates. A judge of this court also had authority to take acknowledgements, administer oaths, solemnize marriages, etc., etc.

This court was first established in Henry County in 1829. The term of office was seven years. The court ceased to exist when the present constitution became operative, November 1, 1851.

JUDGES OF PROBATE.

Jesse H. Healey, commissioned from August 14, 1829, to August 14, 1836.
Samuel Hoover, commissioned from August 14, 1836, to August 14, 1843.
Ralph Berkshire, commissioned from August 14, 1843, to August 14, 1850.
Milton Wayman, commissioned from August 14, 1850, to August 14, 1857.
No man other than a Whig ever held the office.
The salary of the probate judge was principally fees, with probably a small annual compensation.

BIOGRAPHICAL—PROBATE JUDGES.

Jesse H. Healey, Samuel Hoover and Ralph Berkshire are elsewhere appropriately referred to in this History.

MILTON WAYMAN was born in Covington, Kentucky, August 9, 1813. While yet a young man he came with his brother, William, to Henry County, and settled on Blue River, three miles north of New Castle, where they engaged in farming. Later they moved to New Castle and engaged in the dry goods trade. During this time Milton was elected probate judge. After the office was abolished he, having always been a very religious man, entered the ministry of the Methodist Episcopal Church, joined the regular conference and was called away from New Castle to the pastorate of a church at some other place. At the time of his death, which occurred March 10, 1896, he was superanuated and resided at Hillisburg, Clinton County, Indiana. His remains are buried at Ridgeville, Randolph County, Indiana. His daughter, Mary Belle, is the wife of Charles J. Keesling and they reside in New Castle. Dr. James V. Wayman, a noted physician and surgeon, formerly of New Castle and later of Cambridge City, was a brother. William Wayman, above mentioned, was born July 7, 1817, in Campbell County, Kentucky. He died in New Castle, April 26, 1856. His wife, Fidelia (Clawson) Wayman, was a noble Christian woman, who long survived him, dying in New Castle, February 2, 1904, at the age of eighty four years, having been born January 30, 1820. He is buried in the old cemetery and she in South Mound Cemetery, New Castle. They were the parents of a large and interesting family. Dr. John C. Wayman, of New Castle, the eldest son, was as gallant a soldier in the Civil War as ever shouldered a musket. His full military record is set out in this History. Another son is the retired grocer, Alonzo R. Wayman, of New Castle.

PROSECUTING ATTORNEYS.

Under the constitution of 1816 the office of prosecuting attorney was a statutory one. The term of office at first appears to have been for one year, and later it was for two years, perhaps three. Under the present constitution the office became a constitutional one, as is provided in Article 7, Section 11, the term of office being for two years.

The names of prosecuting attorneys for the several judicial circuits, of which Henry County was at any time a part, together with the names of their respective counties and the dates of service, are as follows:

Lot Bloomfield, (Wayne), 1822; James Gilmore, (Henry), 1823; Abraham Elliott, (Henry), 1824; Harvey Grigg, (Marion), 1825; Calvin Fletcher, (Marion), 1826; James Whitcomb, (Monroe), 1827; Charles H. Test, (Wayne), 1828; Samuel C. Sample, (Wayne), 1828; William W. Wick, (Fayette), 1829; James Perry, (Wayne), 1830; William J. Brown, (Rush), 1831-7; Samuel W. Parker, (Fayette), 1837-9; David Macy, (Henry), 1839-41; Martin M. Ray, (Wayne), 1841-3; Jehu T. Elliott, (Henry), 1843; Samuel E. Perkins, (Wayne), 1844; Jacob B. Julian, (Wayne), 1844-6; John B. Stitt, (Wayne), 1846-8; Joshua H. Mellett, (Henry), 1848-52; Silas Colgrove, (Randolph), 1852-4; Elijah B. Martindale, (Henry), 1855; Thomas M. Browne, (Randolph), 1855-62; James N. Templar, (Delaware), 1862-7; Lemuel W. Gooding, (Hancock), 1867; David W. Chambers, (Henry), 1868-73; Charles M. Butler, (Henry), 1873-5; William F. Walker, (Henry), 1875-7; Joseph M. Brown, (Henry), 1877-9; Charles M. Butler, (Henry), 1879-81; Leonidas P. Newby, (Henry), 1881-3; George W. Duncan, (Hancock), 1883-7; William O. Barnard, (Henry), 1887-93; Frank E. Beach, (Henry), 1893-7; Wrighter R. Steele, (Henry), 189?-1901; Ed. Jackson, (Henry), from January 1, 1901, to January 1, 1906; George M. Barnard, (Henry), commissioned from January 1, 1906, to January 1, 1908; present incumbent. He is the son of William O. Barnard, who held the office 1887-93.

The change of the term of this office in Henry County was occasioned very often by change of the judicial circuit. In the earlier history of the county some of the prosecuting attorneys above mentioned were appointed for a term of court or more on account of the absence of the regularly elected prosecuting attorney. It has been found impossible on account of the many changes in this office from the causes above mentioned to set out the term of the office with the same precision as that of the circuit judge.

Since political lines were drawn in elections (1835-7), no man other than a Whig or Republican has ever held the office in any judicial circuit of which Henry County was a part with the exception of Charles M. Butler, of Knightstown, in 1873-5, and again in 1879-81. The circumstances regarding Mr. Butler's two elections were briefly as follows: When he was first elected the Republican candidate was Eli N. Smith, of Knightstown, the manner of whose nomination gave much offense to the Republicans of the circuit (Henry and Hancock counties), with the result that he was defeated. Mr. Butler's second election was brought about by the fact that there was a disagreement among the Republicans of the two counties as to which county should have the candidate. Joseph M. Brown, of Henry, and Alexander Black, of Hancock, were both candidates, which gave the election to Mr. Butler. The salary of the prosecuting attorney is five hundred dollars per annum and fees.

Silas Colgrove, Thomas M. Browne, David W. Chambers, Charles M. Butler, Joseph M. Brown and William F. Walker were soldiers in the Civil War. The last four named were from Henry County and their service will be found appropriately set out elsewhere in this History.

Lot Bloomfield, James Gilmore and Abraham Elliott were among the first attorneys to practise law in New Castle.

David Macy, Jehu T. Elliott, Joshua H. Mellett, David W. Chambers and Leonidas P. Newby represented Henry County in the General Assembly.

Charles H. Test, James Perry, Jehu T. Elliott, Silas Colgrove, Joshua H. Mellett and William O. Barnard became judges of the Henry Circuit Court, Abraham Elliott an associate judge, and Elijah B. Martindale judge of the Common Pleas Court.

Jehu T. Elliott and Samuel E. Perkins became justices of the Supreme Court of Indiana.

William W. Wick, Samuel W. Parker and Thomas M. Browne became members of Congress, the two last named for the district of which Henry County was a part. Browne represented Randolph County in the State Senate and after the Civil War was United States District Attorney for Indiana and Republican candidate for Governor in 1872.

James Whitcomb became Governor of Indiana during the Mexican War period and was afterward United States Senator. His statue is one of the four on the circle surrounding the great Soldiers' and Sailors' Monument in Indianapolis.

David W. Chambers, Charles M. Butler, Joseph M. Brown, Leonidas P. Newby, William O. Barnard, Frank E. Beech, Ed. Jackson and George M. Barnard are now living in Henry County and all of them engaged in the practise of the law with the exception of Joseph M. Brown, who is the clerk of the Henry Circuit Court.

Harvey Grigg, Calvin Fletcher, Samuel C. Sample, William J. Brown, Martin M. Ray and Jacob B. Julian, not above mentioned, were eminent men in their respective counties.

John B. Stitt, James N. Templar, Lemuel W. Gooding and George W. Duncan were prominent legal lights in their several localities and were active practitioners at a later period than the pioneer lawyers last mentioned.

COMMON PLEAS COURT.

The present constitution of Indiana provides: Article 7, Section 1, that "the judicial power of the State shall be vested in a supreme court, in circuit courts and in such other courts as the General Assembly may establish." Accordingly, the General Assembly, at its first session under the present constitution, by an act approved May 14, 1852, established the common pleas court, which was intended to cover practically the same functions exercised by the old probate court. The office of district attorney was also created and attached to this court, the term of office being two years. However, the jurisdiction of this court was afterward from time to time much enlarged. The term of office was four years. Henry County alone was made a district by the act above mentioned.

Martin L. Bundy, commissioned from November, 1852, to November, 1856. The candidates for the office were Martin L. Bundy, Edmund Johnson and Ralph Berkshire.

Martin L. Bundy was re-elected without opposition and commissioned from November, 1856, to November, 1860.

The district attorneys during Judge Bundy's term of eight years were Elijah B. Martindale, James Brown, Thomas B. Redding and Miles L. Reed, each having been elected to serve for two years; it appears, however, that Redding resigned and Reed was appointed in his place and afterward elected.

By the time of the October election, 1860, the district had been enlarged to consist of the counties of Henry, Hancock, Decatur, Madison, and Rush. William Grose was elected. He resigned in the Autumn of 1861 to enter the army as colonel of the 36th Indiana Infantry. Elijah B. Martindale was appointed to fill the vacancy until the next general election, October, 1861. David S. Gooding, of Greenfield, was elected to fill the unexpired term of Judge Grose.

The district attorneys under Judges Grose, Martindale and Gooding were William R. Hough, of Greenfield, and Daniel W. Comstock and James B. Martindale, of New Castle. The first two were elected to serve for two years each. Comstock resigned in December, 1863, to enter the army, as a private, in Company E, Ninth Indiana Cavalry, and Martindale was appointed to the vacancy.

William R. West, of Anderson, was elected at the October election, 1864, and commissioned from November, 1864, to November, 1868. He was re-elected in 1868, and commissioned from November, 1868, to November, 1872. During Judge West's first term the district was made to consist of Henry, Hancock and Madison counties and so continued until the court was abolished.

The district attorneys during Judge West's two terms were James B. Martindale, of New Castle; Calvin D. Thompson, of Anderson, and William F. Walker and Joseph W. Worl, of New Castle. Calvin D. Thompson was the only Democrat who ever held the office.

At the October election, 1872, Robert L. Polk, of New Castle, was elected and commissioned from November, 1872, to November, 1876.

This court was abolished by an act of the General Assembly approved March 6, 1873, all business being transferred to the Circuit Court.

Washington Sanders, of Anderson, was elected district attorney in 1872, and served until the court was abolished.

The annual salary of the Common Pleas Judge in 1852 was $800. In 1860 it was increased to $1,000. When the court was abolished, in 1873, it was $1,500. The salary of the district attorney was principally fees, with a small annual compensation.

BIOGRAPHICAL—COMMON PLEAS COURT.

David S. Gooding, William R. Hough, William R. West, Calvin D. Thompson and Washington Sanders, either judge or district attorney of the Common Pleas Court, never lived in Henry County. Biographical mention of them is therefore omitted.

William Grose, Miles L. Reed, Daniel W. Comstock and William F. Walker were soldiers in the Civil War. Their service is appropriately set out elsewhere in this History.

Martin L. Bundy, Ralph Berkshire, William Grose, James Brown, Miles L. Reed and Daniel W. Comstock are the subjects of biographical reference in another part of this History.

EDMUND JOHNSON was born at Plainfield, Windham County, Connecticut, November 20, 1813. He received an excellent education, first attending the common school at Plainfield, afterward Brownsville Academy, in his native State, and later the famous Yale College. He came to New Castle in 1839, after having spent about one year at Centreville, Indiana, where he taught one or two terms of school, and for a part of the time was a surveyor on the Whitewater Canal, and also read law with the late Martin M. Ray. He at once began the practise of the law in New Castle and the late Judge Joshua H. Mellett was a student in his office. He stood very high in the legal profession; was a fluent conversationalist; physically, was an exceptionally fine specimen of manhood, and had a personal bearing which, while genial and kindly, forbade undue familiarity. He took great delight in gentlemanly discussion of political and current events, and socially and professionally was held in greatest regard by his acquaintances and friends. He was not a member of any religious denomination, nor of any secret organization. In political affiliation he was a life-long Democrat and recognized by his party associates as a leader. In 1862 and again in 1874, he was the nominee of his party for a seat in Congress from the district of which Henry County was a part, but was defeated. He was a charter member and stockholder of the First National Bank and later one of the organizers and directors of the Citizens' State Bank, of New Castle. In the later years of his life he devoted his attention to the care and cultivation of his two farms, one southwest of New Castle near the corporation line, and the other in Rush County, about two miles south of Lewisville. In 1846 he was married to Frances Cborne, who was born in Rush County in 1831; her parents were George and Mary (Perryman) Cborne, who settled in Rush County in 1828. Eight children were born to Edmund and Frances (Cborne) Johnson—Aggeiliese, died in infancy; India M., now deceased. married to Asa Hatch; Mary C., wife of Jacob C. Cope, residing at Cambridge City; George S., deceased; Olive W., now deceased, married to George R. Murphey, of New Castle; Frances S., deceased; Bertha B., a resident of New Castle, and Edmund P., engaged in business in Chicago. Edmund Johnson died March 23, 1876, his widow surviving him many years, dying December 27, 1896. Both are buried in South Mound Cemetery.

ELIJAH B. MARTINDALE, judge, and his brother, James B., district attorney, were sons of the Reverend Elijah Martindale, who came from Wayne County in 1832 and settled on Flatrock, four miles southeast of New Castle. The elder Martindale was a pioneer minister of the Disciples or Christian Church, formerly called Campbellites, and was for fifty years, until his death, the central figure in that denomination in Henry County. He and his wife lived to a ripe old age, dying in New Castle and were buried in South Mound Cemetery. Elijah B. Martindale was born in Wayne County, Indiana, August 22, 1828. At the age of sixteen he was apprenticed to John Taylor, whose daughter, Emma, he subsequently married, to learn the trade of a harness maker. While working at this trade he acquired a fair education and studied law under the tutelage of Judge Joshua H. Mellett, whose law partner he subsequently became. He was in 1855 prosecuting attorney of the district of which Henry County was a part. In May, 1862, he moved to Indianapolis, where he has since continued to reside and where he is widely and favorably known.

JAMES B. MARTINDALE was born in Henry County March 30, 1836, and died in Brooklyn, New York, May 17, 1904. In September, 1857, he married Ann Elizabeth, daughter of James and Charlotte McAfee, who was born July 29, 1837, and died in September, 1872. James B. read law with his brother above mentioned and practised his profession in New Castle. In 1868 he organized the Martindale Law and Collection Association, which in 1871 he transferred to Indianapolis, a few years later to Chicago and afterward to New York, where the agency is now conducted under the name of The Martindale Mercantile Agency by his two sons, George B. and Barton W. S. From the small beginning in New Castle in 1868 this agency has grown to be one of the leading mercantile companies in the United States. James B. Martindale and his wife are buried in South Mound Cemetery.

THOMAS B. REDDING was born in Henry County, December 27, 1831. His parents, Iredell and Anna (Nixon) Redding, were among the early immigrants to the county, coming from North Carolina. After attending the common schools and the Henry County Seminary he entered Asbury University, where he graduated in 1854. He began his career as a school teacher at the age of sixteen. After leaving college he taught school in Richmond, Indiana, for one year. He next took charge of the New Castle Seminary for one year and at the expiration of that time became editor of the New Castle Courier. Meantime he had been reading law and abandoned school teaching to practise his profession. In 1858 he located in Chicago, but two years later returned to New Castle, where he continued to reside until his death, April 11, 1895. He served as trustee of Asbury, now DePauw, University, at Greencastle, Indiana, and always exhibited a deep interest in educational matters. He was a very religious man and spent a great deal of his time and money in the furtherance of the cause of the Methodist Episcopal Church with which he was so long actively identified. On December 2, 1858, he was married to Sarah W., daughter of Reverend Elijah Corrington, of the Central Illinois Methodist Episcopal Conference. She was born in 1831 and died August 17, 1887. They were the parents of three daughters—Ailsie, born March 5, 1861, died in infancy; Rosa Mary, born July 28, 1862; Alice Gray, born July 14, 1865, died August 18, 1870. Mr. Redding, his wife and deceased daughters are buried in South Mound Cemetery. Rosa Mary Redding was married June 24, 1886, to Charles N. Mikels, a leading attorney of New Castle, who was interested with Charles S. Hernly in locating the Indianapolis, New Castle and Toledo electric railway line. Mrs. Mikels is a graduate of the New Castle High School and DePauw University and is now and has been for fifteen years principal of the New Castle High School. She is universally conceded to be the most competent lady educator who ever held that position. Mr. and Mrs. Mikels have one daughter, Ailsie Hester, born March 14, 1888. In 1866-7 George Hazzard, the author of this History, read law in New Castle in the office of Thomas B. Redding.

WILLIAM F. WALKER is a son of Alvius Walker, who was one of the early settlers of Henry County, locating in Franklin Township where William F. was born about 1835. The latter was educated in the country schools and in early manhood studied law in the office of James Brown at New Castle. He pursued his studies in a Cincinnati law school and began the practisé of his profession in New Castle. He was married about 1860 to a sister of Robert B. Carr, former sheriff and clerk of Henry County. In 1879 he moved to Wichita, Kansas, where he now resides.

JOSEPH W. WORL is a native of Liberty Township. His father was John Worl, a farmer who so long lived in the neighborhood of old Chicago, where he was so well and favorably known and where he accumulated several hundred acres of rich farming land. Joseph W. attended school at Dublin, Wayne County, then in New Castle and later entered the law office of Thomas B. Redding as a student. After practising his profession in New Castle until 1877, during which time he served as prosecuting attorney, he moved to Nebraska. There he engaged in the banking and grain business for several years in the towns of Firth and Sterling. Later he located in Oklahoma Territory, where he now resides and is engaged in operating a cotton gin, conducting a bank and buying grain. He is widely known in the territory as a public-spirited, successful and broad-minded citizen.

THE GENERAL ASSEMBLY.

The first constitution, effective November 7, 1816, when Indiana became a State, but not recognized by Congress until December 11, 1816, provided, article 3, section 1, that the "legislative authority of this State shall be vested in a General Assembly, which shall consist of a Senate and House of Representatives, both to be elected by the people."

Section 3 provided for the election of Representatives as follows: "The Representatives shall be chosen annually by the qualified electors of each county respectively on the first Monday of August."

Section 5 provided for the election of Senators as follows: "The Senators shall be chosen for thrée years on the first Monday in August by the qualified votes for Representatives."

Section 25 provided that the "first session of the General Assembly shall commence on the first Monday of November next (1816), and forever after the General Assembly shall meet on the first Monday in December every year and at no other period unless directed by law or provided for by this constitution." The convention which framed the first constitution of the State, at Corydon, was presided over by Jonathan Jennings, afterwards the first Governor. This convention concluded its labors June 29, 1816. The date first above given, November 7, 1816, is the day when Indiana was first declared a State by the General Government.

While the term of office of a State Senator was for three years, yet some of them did not serve for that period as representatives of Henry County. Amaziah Morgan, of Rush County, in his second term, represented Henry County in but two of the three annual sessions of the General Assembly, from the fact that Henry County was taken out of the district with Rush and placed in a new district composed of Henry, Hancock and Madison counties. Elisha Long, of Henry County, was elected in 1831 and re-elected in 1834, yet he served in but one annual session of the three for which he was elected in his second term.

The author, having made an examination of all the data bearing on this subject, finds that Long resigned after having served in the first annual session of his second term and then moved to Brookville, Franklin County. Mr. Long, or General Long as he was called on account of his connection with the Indiana Militia, was appointed one of the State Commissioners, having charge of the proposed internal improvements then about to be undertaken by the State. He was assigned to take personal charge of the construction of the old Whitewater Canal, from Connersville to Cincinnati, and in order that he might have the matter under his personal supervision he resigned and went to Brookville as above stated. He afterwards became a member of the General Assembly from Franklin County, and also served as treasurer of said county. He was a son of the old Revolutionary soldier, Christopher Long, who is buried near the Boyd school house in Liberty Township, and was the father of Judge Elisha Van Buren Long, now of Los Vegas, New Mexico.

Thomas Bell, of Madison County, who was elected as Long's successor, possibly to fill the unexpired term, represented Henry County in but one session, that of 1835, when Hancock and Madison counties were made a separate district and Henry alone for the first time constituted a Senatorial district.

From this time until the formation of the new constitution, Henry County alone was continued as a Senatorial district and each of the Senators served full terms of three years. All sessions of the General Assembly under the old constitution were continued into the year succeeding that in which they began.

STATE SENATORS UNDER THE FIRST CONSTITUTION.

James Gregory, of Shelby County, elected in 1823. Served in the eighth, ninth and tenth sessions of the General Assembly, 1823-4-5. The Eighth session was the last held at Corydon, the first capital of the State. It was during the Ninth session that the capital was moved to Indianapolis. The first entry of public business at Indianapolis is dated January 10, 1825. The district represented by Gregory consisted of the counties of Henry, Hamilton, Johnson, Marion, Madison, Rush and Shelby.

Amaziah Morgan, of Rush County, elected in 1826. Served in the Eleventh and Twelfth sessions, 1826-7. District, Henry, Allen, Randolph and Rush counties. At this time there was no organized county north of Randolph to Allen, and the latter was the only organized county in the State north of the line drawn east and west in the present boundary on the north of Randolph County. Morgan also represented the same district, with Delaware County added, in the thirteenth regular session, 1828. Delaware County (unorganized) embraced the whole of the New Purchase, by act of the General Assembly, January 2, 1820, but the present county of Delaware was not organized until January 16, 1827, by an act of the General Assembly. The New Purchase was a vast tract of land in the center and on the east side of the State, relinquished by the Indians to the General Government and the State of Indiana. Morgan was again elected in 1829 and served in the Fourteenth and Fifteenth sessions, 1829-30; district composed of Henry and Rush counties.

Elisha Long, of Henry County, elected in 1831. Served in the Sixteenth, Seventeenth and Eighteenth sessions, 1831-2-3; district, Henry, Hancock and Madison counties; re-elected in 1834; served in the Nineteenth regular session, 1834; district same as above; resigned as previously stated.

Thomas Bell, of Madison County, elected in 1835. Served in the Twentieth session, 1835; district, Henry, Hancock and Madison counties.

Thomas R. Stanford, of Henry County, elected in 1836. Served in the Twenty first, Twenty second and Twenty third sessions, 1836-7-8, Henry County alone constituting the district, as it continued to do until the adoption of the new constitution in 1851.

Jehu T. Elliott, elected in 1839. Served in the Twenty fourth, Twenty fifth and Twenty sixth sessions, 1839-40-1.

Thomas R. Stanford, elected in 1842. Served in the Twenty seventh, Twenty eighth and Twenty ninth sessions, 1842-3-4.

Eli Murphey elected in 1848. Served in the Thirtieth, Thirty first and Thirty second sessions, 1845-6-7.

George Evans elected in 1848. Served in the Thirty third, Thirty fourth and Thirty fifth sessions, 1848-9-50.

Ezekiel T. Hickman elected in 1851. Served in the Thirty sixth session only. He was the last State Senator serving under the constitution of 1816, and the last Democrat, since 1834, when General Long résigned, to represent Henry County in the Senate. But for the adoption of the new constitution, 1851, he would have served two years longer.

THE GENERAL ASSEMBLY UNDER THE NEW CONSTITUTION.

The present constitution of the State which became effective November 1, 1851, provides, article 4, section 1: "The legislative authority of the State shall be vested in the General Assembly which shall consist of a Senate and House of Representatives. The style of every law shall be, 'Be it enacted by the General Assembly of the State of Indiana,' and no law shall be enacted except by bill."

Section 2. "The Senate shall not exceed fifty nor the House one hundred members."

Section 3. "Senators shall be elected for the term of four years and Representatives for the term of two years from the day next after the general election."

Members of the General Assembly were first elected on the second Tuesday of October, until 1881, when the constitution was changed making the general election fall on the first Tuesday after the first Monday in November.

Section 9. "The sessions of the General Assembly shall be held biennially- on the Thursday next after the first Monday in January, 1853, and every second year thereafter * * * * the Governor * * * * may * * call a special session.

From Senator William W. Williams to Senator Luther W. Hess, Henry County alone constituted a Senatorial district.

The biennial sessions of the Legislature are limited to sixty days.

STATE SENATORS UNDER THE PRESENT CONSTITUTION.

William W. Williams, elected in 1852. Served in the Thirty seventh and Thirty eighth regular sessions 1853-5.

Isaac Kinley, elected in 1856. Served in the Thirty ninth regular session, 1857; in a special session November 20 to December 15, 1858, and in the Fortieth regular session, 1859.

Joshua H. Mellett, elected in 1860. Served in the Forty first regular session, 1861; in a special session April 24 to June 2, 1861, and in the Forty second regular session, 1863.

Milton Peden, elected in 1864. Served in the Forty third regular session, 1865; resigned at the close of the session to accept the Colonelcy of the 147th Regiment Indiana Infantry.

Thomas Reagan, elected in October, 1865. to fill the vacancy occasioned by the resignation of Colonel Peden. Served first in a special session which convened November 15 to December 22, 1865, and in the Forty fourth regular session, 1867.

Luther W. Hess, elected in 1868. Served in the Forty fifth regular session, 1869; in a special session April 8 to May 17, 1869, and in the Forty sixth regular session, 1871; district composed of Henry and Hancock counties. This district continued through the Senatorial terms of William R. Hough and Benjamin Shirk.

William R. Hough, of Hancock County, elected in 1872. Served first in a special session November 13 to December 22, 1872, and afterwards in the Forty seventh and Forty eighth regular sessions, 1873-5, and later in a special session, March 9 to March 14, 1875.

Benjamin Shirk elected in 1876. Served in the Forty ninth regular session, 1877; in a special session March 8 to March 15, 1877, and in the Fiftieth regular session, 1879. At the Fiftieth regular session the district was changed to that represented by Senator Bundy.

Eugene H. Bundy, elected in 1880. Served in the Fifty first regular session, 1881; in a special session March 8 to April 15, 1881, and in the Fifty second regular session, 1883; district, Henry, Delaware and Randolph counties. This district continued during the first session of Senator Macy's term.

John W. Macy, of Randolph County, elected in 1884. Served in the Fifty third regular session, 1885, and in a special session March 10 to March 13, 1885.

James N. Huston, of Fayette County, elected in 1884 to represent the counties of Rush, Fayette and Union. The State was redistricted at the session of 1885 and a new district formed consisting of the counties of Henry and Fayette, and thus Senator Huston represented Henry and Fayette counties in the Fifty fourth regular session in 1887. This district continued through the Senatorial term of William Grose.

William Grose, elected in 1888. Served in the Fifty fifth and Fifty sixth regular sessions, 1889-91.

Leonidas P. Newby, elected in 1892. Served in the Fifty seventh and Fifty eighth regular sessions, 1893-5; re-elected in 1896. Served in the Fifty ninth and Sixtieth regular sessions, 1897-9; district Henry, Fayette and Union counties. This district continued through the Senatorial term of Albert D. Ogborn.

Albert D. Ogborn, elected in 1900. Served in the Sixty first and Sixty second regular sessions, 1901-3.

Edward E. Moore, of Fayette County, elected in 1904. Served in the Sixty third regular session, 1905; term of office extends through the Sixty fourth regular session, 1907. However, Senator Moore will not represent Henry County, as at the Sixty third regular session a new district was formed consisting of the counties of Henry and Madison. A Senator will be elected for the district at the November election, 1906.

BIOGRAPHICAL.

JAMES GREGORY and Amaziah Morgan, the first and second Senatorial representatives of Henry County, were very closely identified with the early history of the State.

GENERAL ELISHA LONG is fully mentioned in the text preceding the list of State Senators.

THOMAS BELL was a well known citizen of Madison County.

THOMAS R. STANFORD was respectively associate judge, county commissioner, member of the lower house of the General Assembly and county surveyor. He was one of the earlier citizens of the county who seemed to have possessed in a full degree the confidence of the people. Further reference is made to him under the head of Associate Judges.

JEHU T. ELLIOTT was the eminent jurist so long Judge of the Henry Circuit Court and afterward a Justice of the State Supreme Court. A full biographical sketch of Judge Elliott will be found elsewhere in this History.

ELI MURPHEY was born in North Carolina May 5, 1811, and came with his parents to Henry County in 1823. He was identified with the growth of the county seat from its inception and gave largely of his time and talent to its material prosperity. He studied law together with the late Judge Jehu T. Elliott at Centreville and began the practise of his profession at the age of 22 in New Castle. During the cholera epidemic of 1833 he was a faithful and constant attendant upon the suffering. While a member of the State Senate in 1845 he reported and advocated the bill chartering the New Castle and Richmond railroad, was earnest in his efforts to build the road and after its completion acted as treasurer of the company for some time. In the various official positions to which his fellow citizens elected him he was a very capable man and the records in the county clerk's office written by him are models of conciseness and beautiful penmanship. For forty years he was an earnest, honest, enterprising citizen and his life work was always well and faithfully carried out. He was for nearly ten years clerk of Henry County, and served three sessions (1845-6-7) in the State Senate to which he was elected as a Whig but later in life became a Democrat. He was married in 1835 to Rebecca Carpenter, and five children were born to them—one daughter, Caroline, now deceased, and four sons, namely, William H., Henry C., Charles P. and George R. Henry C. is engaged

in business in Chicago and the three other sons are prominent in the business life of New
Castle; William H. is a manufacturer, George R. cashier of the First National Bank, and
Charles P., a prominent jeweler. Eli Murphey died September 11, 1877, and Rebecca
(Carpenter) Murphey died September 11, 1899. Both are buried in South Mound
Cemetery.

GEORGE EVANS was a rugged Henry County pioneer who emigrated from North
Carolina and lived for many years in Spiceland Township. Politically he was early
classed as a moderate Whig. In 1848 the Whigs of Henry County nominated as their
candidate for State Senator, Robert M. Cooper, of Raysville. The manner of Mr. Cooper's
nomination, or at least some facts connected with it, caused much dissatisfaction and
accordingly Mr. Evans became an independent candidate. This was the year when
the Free Soil Democrats, the Free Soil Whigs and the Abolitionists joined in a convention at Buffalo, New York, and nominated ex-President Martin Van Buren for President
and Charles Francis Adams (Whig) for Vice President. After this convention, the
Democrats of Henry County determined to support Evans for State Senator, he having
in the meantime issued an address to the people of the county which was received with
much favor by the Democrats. Evans was elected by a small majority. While in the
State Senate he was considered a moderate Democrat and acted with that party. On
the formation of the Republican party he became a Republican and so continued until
his death. He was an active member of the Friends' Church at Spiceland. Owen Evans,
who prior to the Civil War moved to Minnesota and went into the army from that State—
his military service being elsewhere in this History appropriately set out—was his son.
After the war Owen Evans returned to Henry County and was for nearly six years deputy
auditor under Seth S. Bennett. Later he moved to Arkansas, where he died and is buried.

EZEKIEL T. HICKMAN came from West Virginia to Henry County about 1831, identical with the time that the Beavers, Hickman, Ice, Mellett and Veach families came, so
numerously, from Monongalia and Marion counties, West Virginia, and settled in Prairie
Township. Senator Hickman was for many years, and at the time of his election, a prosperous farmer living on the main road to Muncie at the upper end of what is known as
the Harvey neighborhood, eight miles north of New Castle, his election to the Senate
being due to the fusion movement fully set out in the introduction to the preceding chapter. He was always an uncompromising Democrat and as such was the only Democratic
representative from Henry County in the State Senate, excepting George Evans just
above mentioned, since party lines were drawn in the county (1835-7). The author is
unable to classify the politics of Senators Gregory, Morgan and Bell. Aside from these,
Senators Long, Evans (independent) and Hickman are the only Democratic Senators.
Late in life Mr. Hickman sold his farm and moved to New Castle, where he remained
until his death, leaving behind him an enviable reputation. His two sons are highly
prosperous business men, at present conducting a department store in Muncie.

WILLIAM W. WILLIAMS was a prominent citizen and active Whig who lived first at
Knightstown, where he operated a tanyard and then at Ogden in the mercantile business.
He was one of the last associate judges, serving from January 17, 1849, until the office
was abolished. See Associate Judges in this chapter. He moved to Madison County and
died there.

ISAAC KINLEY was one of Henry County's most distinguished Civil War soldiers.
In Chapter XVI of this History will be found full biographical reference to him.

JOSHUA H. MELLETT was one of Henry County's most distinguished citizens and
foremost lawyers. Elsewhere in this History will be found a full biographical sketch of
Judge Mellett.

MILTON PEDEN was another of the county's distinguished soldiers. In Chapter
XXII of this History will be found a full biographical sketch of Colonel Peden. His wife
died July 3, 1905, and is buried in the old cemetery, Knightstown, Indiana.

THOMAS REAGAN and other members of the Reagan family came to Greensboro at a
very early day from North Carolina. The first and second postmasters at Greensboro,
as shown in Chapter I of this History, were William and Thomas Reagan, brothers of
Wiley Reagan, who was the father of the Senator. Immediately preceding the Civil War,

in business in ...   . business life of New
Castle; Willia...   ...   ... National Bank, and
Charles P., a   ...   ... 1, 1877 and Rebecca
(Carpenter)   ...   ... in South Mound
Cemetery.

GEORGE ...   . emigrated from North
Carolina and   ...   ... he was early
classed as a   ...   ... nominated as their
candidate for   ...   ... manager of Mr. Cooper's
nomination, ... dissatisfaction and
accordingly   ...   ... was the year when
the Free S...   ...   ... joined in a convention at B...   ...   ... for President
and Cha...   ...   ... this convention, the
Democra...   ...   ... State Senator, he having
in the m...   ...   ... which was received with
much fa...   ...   .jority. While in the
State Se...   ...   ... with the party. On
the form...   ...   ... continued until
his dea...   ...   ... Owen Evans.
who pr...   ...   ... that State—
his military service being elsewhere in this ...   ... as his son.
After the war Owen Evans returned to Henry ...   .s deputy
auditor ... for Seth S. Bennett, later ... buried.

...T. HOSKMAN came from ...   ... identical w... ...me that the ...   .He came, so
num... Marshall ...   .ed in Prairie
Tow...   ...   .lection, a prosper...   ... Morton of ...   ... that is known as
the   ... ...outh of N...   ... ...on to the Senate
bei...   ... ...duction ... the preceding chapter ...   .ing ... as such was the only Democratic
re...   ...   ... except...George Evans just

COMPANY D, 36th INDIANA INFANTRY.

Senator Reagan built the fine residence and large store room at Greensboro which still stands as a monument to his enterprise. In the Winter of 1881-2, Thomas Reagan and Morgan James organized at Greensboro an emigration movement to Nebraska. The party consisted of the following named persons and their families, all of whom settled in Polk County, Nebraska, near Osceola, the county seat: Thomas Reagan, Morgan James (father of Leander M. James, the well-known auctioneer of New Castle), Ambrose B. Barnard, Harper Byers, Cornelius Dillee, Josiah Fentress, Jasper James, Frank Wilson, Lewis Walton and perhaps others. Thomas Reagan resided there until his death. Morgan James returned to New Castle after about twenty years and died at the home of his son, Leander M. James, November 2, 1897, and is buried in Addison Cemetery in Rush County, two and one-half miles south of Knightstown. Mr. Barnard returned to Greensboro, where he now lives, the owner of a saw mill, and is also engaged in farming. The others all remained in Nebraska. Thomas Reagan in company with Milton Peden, Daniel Harvey, George W. Goodwin, Isaac Howard, George W. Woods and others comprised a party who sought the gold fields of California in 1849. They returned within two years. Mr. Reagan was a merchant in Greensboro from that time until he moved to Nebraska.

LUTHER W. HESS was born in Morgantown, West Virginia, December 12, 1821, of which State his parents, Thomas and Matilda (Scott) Hess, were natives. Thomas Hess was born in 1790 and his wife in 1789. They came to Henry County about 1829 and settled in Prairie Township, afterward moving to Harrison Township, where the mother died in 1868 and the father in 1870. Luther W. Hess began the study of medicine in the office of Dr. Horn at Middletown, in 1845, where he practised his profession until 1852, when he moved to Cadiz and throughout the remainder of his life enjoyed an extensive practise. He was an earnest, honest, intelligent man who had the respect and confidence of the people throughout Henry County. July 4, 1847, he was married to Phoebe A. Pickering. Of their four children but two are living: Angelina M., born December 20, 1852, widow of Dr. Walter A. Boor, of New Castle, to whom she was married September 24, 1873, and Frank C., born June 1, 1856, who was married November 30, 1882, to Lena, daughter of Daniel and Malinda Harvey, pioneers of Henry County. Frank C. succeeded to his father's practise on the death of the latter which occurred March 8, 1883, and stands high in his profession and in the esteem of the people of Harrison Township.

WILLIAM R. HOUGH was, and is now, a leading attorney residing in Greenfield.

BENJAMIN SHIRK was for eight years clerk of the Henry Circuit Court. Biographical reference to him will be found elsewhere in this History.

EUGENE H. BUNDY was, in 1884, the Republican candidate for Lieutenant Governor, afterward Judge of the Henry Circuit Court and is now one of the leading attorneys of New Castle. A full biographical sketch of Senator Bundy will be found elsewhere in this History.

JOHN W. MACY was an attorney residing at Winchester and is the present judge of the Randolph Circuit Court. In the Civil War he was a gallant soldier in Company A, 84th Indiana Infantry.

JAMES N. HUSTON was a resident of Connersville and for several years chairman of the Republican National Committee. He was Treasurer of the United States under President Benjamin Harrison.

WILLIAM GROSE reached the highest rank of any soldier from Henry County in the Civil War. In Chapter IX of this History will be found a full biographical sketch of him.

LEONIDAS P. NEWBY is the well-known lawyer, banker and politician residing at Knightstown.

ALBERT D. OGBORN was a Captain in the Spanish-American War. In Chapter XXXI of this History will be found a full biographical sketch of him.

EDWARD E. MOORE, at the time of his election, was editor of the Weekly Courier at Connersville.

In April, 1864, Colonel George W. Lennard, then in the field with his regiment, the 57th Indiana Infantry, was nominated by the Republicans, or as they then styled themselves, the Union party, for State Senator. He would have been elected at the October election following, but unfortunately he was killed at Resaca, Georgia, May 14, 1864, and

Milton Peden, then Captain of Company K, 36th Indiana Infantry, was nominated vice Lennard. In Chapter XXIX of this History will be found a full biographical sketch of Colonel Lennard.

HOUSE OF REPRESENTATIVES UNDER THE FIRST CONSTITUTION.

Thomas Hendricks, of Shelby County, elected in 1823. Served in the Eighth regular session, 1823; re-elected in 1824. Served in the Ninth regular session, 1824; district Henry, Decatur, Rush and Shelby counties, which continued the same through the Tenth regular session.

Thomas R. Stanford, elected in 1825. Served in the Tenth regular session, 1825.

Elisha Long, elected in 1826. Served in the Eleventh regular session, 1826; re-elected in 1827. Served in the Twelfth regular session, 1827; re-elected in 1828. Served in the Thirteenth regular session, 1828; district, Henry, Hamilton, and Madison counties; re-elected in 1829. Served in the Fourteenth regular session, 1829; district, Henry, Hamilton, Hancock and Madison counties, and all the country north to the State line not attached to any other district. Long was re-elected in 1830. Served in the Fifteenth regular session, 1830; district same as in 1829.

William Conner, of Hamilton County, was the joint representative in the Fourteenth regular session, 1829.

Thomas Bell, of Madison County, was the joint representative in the Fifteenth regular session, 1830.

Thomas R. Stanford, elected in 1831. Served in the Sixteenth regular session, 1831; re-elected in 1832. Served in the Seventeenth regular session, 1832; re-elected in 1833. Served in the Eighteenth regular session, 1833; re-elected in 1834. Served in the Nineteenth regular session, 1834. Henry County alone constituted the district for the four terms above, as also through the Twentieth regular session.

David Macy, elected in 1835. Served in the Twentieth regular session, 1835.

David Macy and Richard Henderson, elected jointly in 1836. Served in the Twenty first regular session, 1836. Henry County alone constituted the district and so continued with joint representatives in all succeeding sessions under the first constitution, except the last one, for which session there was but one representative elected, Isaac H. Morris.

David Macy and Miles Murphey, elected jointly in 1837. Served in the Twenty second regular session, 1837.

Robert M. Cooper and Jesse H. Healey, elected jointly in 1838. Served in the Twenty third regular session, 1838.

Ralph Berkshire and Robert M. Cooper, elected jointly in 1839. Served in the Twenty fourth regular session, 1839.

Thomas R. Stanford and David C. Shawhan, elected jointly in 1840. Served in the Twenty fifth regular session, 1840.

Robert M. Cooper and Joel Reed, elected jointly in 1841. Served in the Twenty sixth regular session, 1841.

Isaac Parker and Simon Summers, elected jointly in 1842. Served in the Twenty seventh regular session, 1842.

Robert I. Hudelson and Joel Reed, elected jointly in 1843. Served in the Twenty eighth regular session, 1843.

John W. Grubbs and Isaac Parker, elected jointly in 1844. Served in the Twenty ninth regular session, 1844.

Marble S. Cameron and Samuel Coffin, elected jointly in 1845. Served in the Thirtieth regular session, 1845.

John Powell and Simon Summers, elected jointly in 1846. Served in the Thirty first regular session, 1846.

Samuel Coffin and Jesse W. Baldwin, elected jointly in 1847. Served in the Thirty second regular session, 1847.

Martin L. Bundy and William A. Rifner, elected jointly in 1848. Served in the Thirty third regular session, 1848.

Samuel W. Stuart and Simon Summers, elected jointly in 1849. Served in the Thirty fourth regular session, 1849.

Isaac H. Morris, elected in 1851. Served in the Thirty sixth regular session, 1851.

Butler Hubbard and Russell Jordan, elected jointly in 1850. Served in the Thirty fifth regular session, 1850.

HOUSE OF REPRESENTATIVES UNDER THE PRESENT CONSTITUTION.

Joseph Yount and James S. Ferris, elected jointly in 1852. Served in the Thirty seventh regular session, 1853. During this and all subsequent sessions under the present constitution, Henry County alone constituted the district, unless otherwise specified.

Luther ·C. Mellett and Milton Peden, elected jointly in 1854. Served in the Thirty eighth regular session, 1855.

Nathan H. Ballenger and William Grose, elected jointly in 1856. Served in the Thirty ninth regular session, 1857.

Joshua H. Mellett, elected in 1858. Served in a special session from November 20 to December 15, 1858, and in the Fortieth regular session, 1859.

Martin L. Bundy, elected in 1860. Served in the Forty first regular session, 1861, and in a special session April 24 to June 2, 1861.

Charles D. Morgan, elected in 1862. Served in the Forty second regular session, 1863.

David W. Chambers, elected in 1864. Served in a special session November 13 to December 22, 1864, and in the Forty third regular session, 1865; re-elected in 1866. Served in the Forty fourth regular session, 1867.

John R. Millikan, elected in 1868. Served in the Forty fifth regular session, 1869, and in a special session April 8 to May 17, 1869.

George F. Chittenden, of Madison County, elected in 1868. Served in the Forty fifth regular session, 1869, and in a special session April 8 to May 17, 1869; district, Henry and Madison counties. This representation was in addition to the member (John R. Millikan) elected from Henry County alone. Thomas S. Lines, John O. Hardesty, Addison R. A. Thompson, Joseph T. Smith and Exum Saint were respectively members from this joint district, in addition to the member elected from Henry County alone.

John R. Millikan, elected in 1870. Served in the Forty sixth regular session, 1871.

Thomas S. Lines, elected in 1870. Served in the Forty sixth regular session, 1871.

John Hedrick, elected in 1872. Served in a special session November 13 to December 22, 1872, and in the Forty seventh regular session, 1873.

John O. Hardesty, of Madison County, elected in 1872. Served in a special session November 13 to December 22, 1872, and in the Forty seventh regular session, 1873.

Mark E. Forkner, elected in 1874. Served in the Forty· eighth regular session, 1875, and in a special session March 9 to March 14, 1875.

Addison R. A. Thompson, elected in 1874. Served in the Forty eighth regular session, 1875, and in a special session March 9 to March 14, 1875.

Charles S. Hubbard, elected in .1876. Served in the Forty ninth regular session, 1877, and in a special session March 6 to March 14, 1877.

Joseph T. Smith, of Madison County, elected in 1876. Served in the Forty ninth regular session, 1877, and in a special session March 6 to March 14, 1877.

Charles S. Hubbard, elected in 1878. Served in the Fiftieth regular session, 1879.

Exum Saint, elected in 1878. Served in the Fiftieth regular session, 1879.

William M. Bartlett, elected in 1880. Served in the Fifty first regular session, 1881, and in a special session March — to April 16, 1881.

Isaac Franklin, of Madison County, elected in 1880. Served in the Fifty first regular session, 1881, and in a special session March 8 to April 16, 1881; district, Henry, Hancock and Madison counties. This district continued through the terms of joint representatives, Henry Marsh and Joseph Franklin, the representation being in· addition to that of Henry County alone.

John A. Deem, elected in 1882. Served in the Fifty second regular session, 1883.

Henry Marsh, of Hancock County, elected in 1882. Served in the Fifty second regular session, 1883.

65

John A. Deem, elected in 1884. Served in the Fifty third regular session, 1885, and in a special session March 10 to April 13, 1885.

Joseph Franklin, of Madison County, elected in 1884. Served in the Fifty third regular session, 1885, and in a special session, March 10 to April 13, 1885.

William A. Brown, elected in 1886. Served in the Fifty fourth regular session, 1887.

William Grose, elected in 1886. Served in the Fifty fourth regular session, 1887; district, Henry and Fayette counties. The district continued through the two terms of Jefferson H. Claypool.

William A. Brown, elected in 1888. Served in the Fifty fifth regular session, 1889.

Jefferson H. Claypool, of Fayette County, elected in 1888. Served in the Fifty fifth regular session, 1889.

John M. Morris, elected in 1890. Served in the Fifty sixth regular session, 1891.

Jefferson H. Claypool, of Fayette County, elected in 1890. Served in the Fifty sixth regular session, 1891. There was no joint representative from this district again until 1896, when Francis T. Roots was elected.

Thomas N. White, elected in 1892. Served in the Fifty seventh regular session, 1893.

Erastus L. Elliott, elected in 1894. Served in the Fifty eighth regular session, 1895; re-elected in 1896. Served in the Fifty ninth regular session, 1897.

Francis T. Roots, of Fayette County, elected in 1896. Served in the Fifty ninth regular session, 1897.

George W. Williams, elected in 1898. Served in the Sixtieth regular session, 1899.

Benjamin S. Parker, elected in 1900. Served in the Sixty first regular session, 1901.

Otho Williams, elected in 1902. Served in the Sixty second regular session, 1903.

Levi Ulrich, elected in 1904. Served in the Sixty third regular session, 1905.

The last session of the General Assembly, the one which convened in January, 1905, is numbered on the journal of the General Assembly and was referred to generally in the public press as the Sixty fourth regular session. · This is an error, and the session last held should be numbered the Sixty third regular session. This error in numbering the sessions has been continuous since 1861 and arose from the fact that the special session, April 24 to June 2, 1861, was numbered the Forty second regular session, whereas it should have had no number but should have been treated as a special session of the Forty first regular session. In the report of Union B. Hunt, Secretary of State in 1902, page 363, he called attention to this error and attempted to correct it, but notwithstanding this the sessions have continued to be erroneously numbered.

BIOGRAPHICAL.

Elsewhere in this History will be found biographical reference to Thomas R. Stanford, Elisha Long, Miles Murphey, Jesse H. Healey, Ralph Berkshire, Joel Reed, Isaac Parker, John W. Grubbs, John Powell, Jesse W. Baldwin, Martin L. Bundy, Joseph Yount, James S. Ferris, Milton Peden, Nathan H. Ballenger, William Grose, Joshua H. Mellett, Charles D. Morgan, David W. Chambers, John R. Millikan, Mark E. Forkner, John A. Deem, William A. Brown, Erastus L. Elliott and Benjamin S. Parker.

The following who have represented Henry County as a part of a joint district in the lower branch of the General Assembly never lived in Henry County, therefore this History has no concern with their biographies: Thomas Hendricks, Shelby County; William Connor, Hamilton County; Thomas Bell, George F. Chittenden, John O. Hardesty, Joseph T. Smith, Isaac Franklin and Joseph Franklin, Madison County; Henry Marsh, Hancock County; Jefferson H. Claypool and Francis T. Roots, Fayette County.

DAVID MACY, born in North Carolina, December 25, 1810, was one of the early attorneys of New Castle, coming from Wayne County in 1832, and was very decidedly a man of affairs. During his service as a representative in the General Assembly from Henry County he was a leading advocate of internal improvements then undertaken by the State, such as building canals, opening highways across the State, etc. (railroads not then being considered). In 1838 he was elected prosecuting attorney of the Sixth Judicial

District of which Henry County was a part. In 1840 he moved to Lawrenceburg, where he resided until 1852, when he moved to Indianapolis. During his residence in Lawrenceburg he was mayor of the city and represented Dearborn County in the General Assembly. At Indianapolis he formed a law partnership with David McDonald. In 1855 he was elected president of the Indianapolis and Peru railway, now a part of the Lake Erie and Western system. From this time until he retired from active business he gave his attention to railroads and banking. He died May 29, 1892. His only daughter, Caroline, is the wife of Volney T. Malott, a leading banker and very wealthy citizen of Indianapolis.

RICHARD HENDERSON was a well-known citizen of Greensboro, where he was postmaster for nearly ten years, being succeeded in the office by his wife, as is shown in Chapter I of this History. He was the father of Isom P., Richard T. and Henry H. Henderson, three as gallant soldiers as went from Henry County to the Civil War or as ever wore the uniform of their country. The military record of each of the three is appropriately set out in this History.

ROBERT M. COOPER was a lawyer who lived in Raysville for twenty five years, until his death in 1849. He had a brother named Silas who for many years lived in Ogden and was justice of the peace, notary public, and later an attorney.

DAVID C. SHAWHAN resided in Fall Creek Township, where he was a farmer and general trader and in his day a very active man. He served as County Commissioner from 1837 to 1840.

SIMON SUMMERS was a farmer and leading citizen of Fall Creek Township and a man very highly esteemed. He belonged to the well-known family of that name long so prominent and influential in and around Middletown.

ROBERT I. HUDELSON came from Kentucky and settled first in Rush County just south of Ogden. Later he moved to Ogden, where he lived when he was elected to the General Assembly. He afterward moved to Knightstown, where he lived at the time of his death. He married a daughter of Waitsel M. Cary, original proprietor of Knightstown, and was himself interested in two additions to that town. John Waitsel Hudelson, a soldier of the Civil War in Company A, 57th Indiana Infantry, now living in Knightstown, is his son.

MARBLE S. CAMERON was an enterprising citizen of Knightstown. His three sons, William M., John D. and Joseph B. Cameron, whose service is elsewhere appropriately set out, were soldiers in the Civil War. The first two named are deceased. Joseph B. was deputy treasurer of Henry County under Robert M. Grubbs, is a musician of excellent attainment and is now connected with a leading wholesale music house in Indianapolis.

SAMUEL COFFIN lived for many years in Stony Creek Township. Late in life he moved to Minnesota, where he died and is buried.

SAMUEL W. STEWART was a pioneer resident of Dudley Township and a leading member of the Society of Friends.

RUSSELL JORDAN resided for a long time about a mile southwest of Blountsville. He was a man of much influence and greatly respected throughout the county. His daughter, Mrs. Erastus Burch, whose husband was a soldier in the Civil War, now lives on the home farm. A son, Anthony W. Jordan, who was also a soldier in the Civil War, lives in Blountsville.

ISAAC H. MORRIS, who was elected under the fusion of 1851, was the only Democrat to represent Henry County since Miles Murphey, then a moderate Democrat, was elected in 1837. He was from Wayne Township, a brother of John Morris, father of John M. Morris, present Judge of the Henry Circuit Court. He was the only member elected from Henry County who died while the legislature was in session.

LUTHER C. MELLETT was a member of the well-known family of that name in Prairie Township. A general biography of the Mellett family will be found elsewhere in this History in a biographical sketch of the late Judge Joshua H. Mellett, who was a brother of Luther C. George W. Woy, who was a soldier in the Civil War, married a daughter of Luther C. Mellett, and Randolph H. Mellett, who served in the navy on a gunboat in the Mississippi River, is a son, who now lives near Denver, Colorado.

THOMAS S. LINES, commonly called "Uncle Tommy," was a Baptist minister who moved from Fayette County, where he was once sheriff, and settled in the northern part of Prairie Township, about 1850. He served as Treasurer of Henry County in 1873-5, and continued to reside in New Castle for several years thereafter. He then returned to Prairie Township, where he lived until his death. His son, Elijah H., died at home near Luray while a soldier in the Civil War, serving as a private in Company C, 5th Indiana Cavalry, and whose name will be found in the Roll of Honor in this History. Wilson R. and Squire N., sons of Elijah H. Lines, reside in the village of Messick and each has served as postmaster there. The first-named is a well-known stock buyer, the other is the merchant of the village.

JOHN HEDRICK lived in Franklin Township, three miles northwest of Lewisville, where the family has been prominent for many years. Soon after serving in the General Assembly he moved to Tecumseh, Johnson County, Nebraska, where he became a merchant and took an active part in politics. He died and is buried there.

ADDISON R. A. THOMPSON lived for many years on a farm immediately south of Blountsville. He was a large landholder in Henry, Wayne and Randolph counties and was possessed of much personal property; indeed he was considered one of the wealthy men of the county. During the Civil War, he was very active in support of the State and National governments and as a token of his admiration for the great war governor he named his son, Oliver P. Morton Thompson. This son inherited largely of his father's property but died soon after his father passed away. A son of Oliver P. M. Thompson now lives on the old home farm above mentioned. About 1870 Mr. Thompson became dissatisfied with the Republican party and joined the Granger and Greenback movements in which he was very active. In a fusion of the Democrats and other elements opposed to the Republican party he was elected to the General Assembly. Exum Saint, a lawyer in New Castle, can be classed politically with Mr. Thompson. Neither of them can be designated a Democrat.

CHARLES S. HUBBARD has exemplified throughout his long and useful career the value of time carefully spent and of well directed ambition, that has made that part of the great world in which he has lived the better, happier and more prosperous for his being a part of it. Born in Milton, Wayne County, Indiana, September 1, 1829, the second of twelve children of Richard and Sarah (Swain) Hubbard, although bereft from birth of a right hand, the indomitable will that has characterized his life early displayed itself, so that from the age of ten years when with his parents he came to Henry County and located just east of Knightstown he has steadfastly and courageously carried out his carefully planned determination to prosper and be of benefit to mankind. Notwithstanding the infirmity spoken of he was able as a boy to plow, chop wood and do almost all kinds of work on the farm. This same energy enabled him to acquire a fair education and by teaching school in the Winter months he earned enough money to enter the Friends' boarding school, now Earlham College, Richmond, where he remained for three terms, at the end of which he entered his father's store in Raysville as a clerk. Later he purchased his father's interest in the store and conducted the business until 1862 when he sold out and retired. A year later he and Timothy Harrison, of Richmond, opened a dry goods store in Knightstown, and for several years they did a large and successful business. He was for four years one of the trustees of the Soldiers' and Sailors' Orphans' Home, a State institution about two miles south of Knightstown. In 1868 as one of the board of managers of Earlham College, he canvassed several States and raised a large sum of money as an endowment fund for that institute of learning. He was for a number of years one of the directors of the First National Bank of Knightstown. While a member of the General Assembly, he procured the passage of a bill providing a home for feeble minded children of the State and locating it in connection with the Soldiers' and Sailors' Orphans' Home above mentioned, which has since been detached, moved to Fort Wayne and much enlarged. He has for a great many years been active and indefatigable in church and Sunday school work, a life-long member of the Society of Friends and for a number of years was a minister in that church. Since 1890 he has been vice-president and organizing agent of the American Humane Education

Society of Boston, Massachusetts. It is his duty to travel and organize humane societies and bands of mercy among the children in the public schools. In this capacity he has traveled throughout all New England, every State in the South except Florida, and generally throughout the West. The brick residence that he now occupies in Raysville was built by him forty seven years ago and he has occupied it continuously ever since. Mr. Hubbard had four brothers in the Civil War—Henry, Edwin, George and Joseph B. The military record of all of them is appropriately set out in this History. Henry was killed in battle and his name and the circumstances of his death will be found in the Roll of Honor.

Mr. Hubbard was married in November, 1850, to Martha, daughter of Toms and Millicent White, of Washington County, Indiana. Two sons and four daughters were born to them: Francis T., born January 9, 1852, now in the railway mail service and residing at Benton Harbor, Michigan; Mary Alice, born January 6, 1854, now Mrs. Matthew S. Lowden, of Dakota City, Iowa; Ellen, born May 31, 1856, a most accomplished stenographer holding a position with the Drainage Board in Chicago at a salary of $1,200 a year; Henry, born February 26, 1865, died in infancy; Elizabeth T., born December 8, 1868, residing at home with her parents; Estella H., born March 20, 1870, now the wife of Aubrey C. Wilkinson, who is associated in business in Knightstown with his father, Thomas B. Wilkinson. Mr. Hubbard has seven grandchildren and two great grandchildren living, the latter being the grandchildren of his son, Francis T.

WILLIAM M. BARTLETT was born May 15, 1826, in Clermont County, Ohio, of sturdy English-Scottish stock. In 1839 he came with his parents to Milroy, Rush County, Indiana. Here making the most of his meagre opportunities he acquired a fair education. He taught school for a time and at the age of eighteen began the study of medicine and in 1847 "hung out his shingle" in Raleigh, Rush County. There on April 20, 1848, he was married to Elizabeth J. Shepler, born October 2, 1832. They were the parents of six children, namely: Laura, now of Indianapolis, widow of Thomas W. Hall, a former prominent business man of Lewisville, whose remains are buried in the cemetery there; Rebecca, who died at the age of six years; Claudius G., one of the leading physicians of Lewisville; Hala (Bartlett) Cortelyow, of Bentonville, Fayette County, who has three children, Laura, Rilla and Helen; Andrew C., who married Sebbie M. Wood, of Richmond, and who was at the time of his death, July 10, 1904, a successful physician of New Castle; James A., a prominent farmer of Franklin Township, who married Jennie Vernon, of Lewisville; they have one son, Claude M., who is assistant cashier of the First National Bank of Lewisville, and two daughters, Maude and Hazel Fern; William E. is the youngest son. Dr. William M. Bartlett moved from Rush County to Lewisville in 1864 and continued the practise of medicine. He built up a large practise and was not only one of the most successful medical practitioners of the county but also a man who had great influence in molding public opinion on all questions affecting local, State and National interests. He was a very liberal man, but believed also in accumulating a sufficiency of this world's goods to provide for the proverbial rainy day and at the time of his death which occurred May 26, 1892, he was possessed of several hundred acres of fine farming land in addition to other valuable property. His wife died April 13, 1898, and their remains rest in the cemetery at Raleigh, Rush County, five miles south of Lewisville.

THOMAS N. WHITE was born in North Carolina October 25, 1818. He became an orphan at an early age and came with an elder brother to Henry County in 1832. He remained with his brother for many years and about the age of twenty one years began to farm on his own account. In 1843 he bought the farm in Franklin Township on which he resided at the time of his death, April 2, 1899. He was married April 25, 1844, to Lydia Parker, a daughter of Robert and Marian (Bell) Parker, who were among the early settlers of Wayne County, where Mrs. White was born April 15, 1827. Eleven children were born to them—Maria J., deceased; Mary A., widow of Professor William W. White, now living in Germantown, Pennsylvania; Alpheus E., who lives on the old home farm; Esther A., married to Professor George White, but is now deceased; Robert A., a farmer living one mile northeast of Lewisville; David O., a farmer living in Hancock County; Rebecca E., deceased; Dora, now Mrs. Absalom Knight, living in Oklahoma Territory; Thomas W., a farmer living two miles northeast of Lewisville; Edward N., a farmer living two miles northwest of New Castle; one child died in infancy. Mr. White was industrious and methodical and was held in high regard throughout the county. He gave the same intelligent and honest care to all affairs of the people when serving in an official capacity that he rigidly adhered to in private life. He served as county commissioner for six years, as is shown under the head of County Commissioners in the preceding chapter. Thomas N. and Lydia (Parker) White were members of the Society of Friends. The latter died November 15, 1898. Both are buried in Rich Square Cemetery, in Franklin Township.

GEORGE W. WILLIAMS was born on a farm near Cleveland, Hancock County, October 14, 1846. His father, Richard Williams, was a substantial pioneer farmer of that county who died when the son was but three years old, leaving the early education and training of the latter to the pious and gentle though firm and thorough care of the mother, and it was largely through her tender and solicitous guardianship that he received that moral training which has remained as his guiding star through life. He was educated in the common schools of Greenfield and Knightstown with a year's course in the high school. At the age of seventeen he was a teacher in a district school and for about ten years thereafter devoted the Summer months to farming and the Winter time to teaching. He married, in 1869, Sarah E. Barnett, of Knightstown. In 1872, in partnership with his brother, Ellison Williams, and his mother's brother, John O. Hatfield, he engaged in the mercantile business in Knightstown. This establishment he has continued with changing partnership, up to the present time. The firm now consists of himself and two sons, Charles and Edward B. Williams. They do a large retail business, amounting in volume to at least seventy five thousand dollars a year and have occupied one location, the southeast corner of Main and Jefferson streets in Knightstown since 1872. Recently in consequence of fire destroying the old building, a new and modern structure to accommodate the growing trade of the firm has taken its place.

OTHO WILLIAMS was born and reared in Wayne County. He early embraced the religious faith commonly known as the Disciples or Christians, formerly called Campbellites, of which denomination he became a minister, preaching at Mooreland and perhaps at other points in the county. After his election to the General Assembly he took up his residence in New Castle, but in the Fall of 1904 he moved to New Mexico, where he now resides.

LEVI ULRICH, present incumbent, is a well-known citizen and business man of Greensboro.

SESSIONS OF THE GENERAL ASSEMBLY, TERRITORIAL AND STATE.

TERRITORIAL—DATE OF MEETING.

First session at Saint Vincennes, January 12, 1801; Second, at Saint Vincennes, January 30, 1802; Third, at Saint Vincennes, February 16, 1803; Fourth, (data not obtainable); Fifth, at Borough of Vincennes, July 29, 1805; Sixth, at Borough of Vincennes, November 3, 1806; Seventh, (data not obtainable); Eighth, at Town of Vincennes, September 26, 1808; Ninth, (data not obtainable); Tenth, at Town of Vincennes, November 12, 1810; Eleventh, at Town of Vincennes, November 11, 1811; Twelfth, at Town of Vincennes, —————, 1812; Thirteenth, at Town of Vincennes, February 12, 1813; adjourned meeting at Corydon, December 6, 1813; Fourteenth, at Corydon in August, 1814; Fifteenth, at Corydon, December 4, 1815.

GENERAL AND SPECIAL SESSIONS UNDER THE CONSTITUTION OF 1816.

The sessions from the first to the eighth, inclusive, were held at Corydon; all other sessions were held at Indianapolis. All dates are inclusive.

First session, November 4, 1816, to January 3, 1817; Second, December 1, 1817, to January 29, 1818; Third, December 7, 1818, to January 2, 1819; Fourth, December 6,

1819, to January 22, 1820; Fifth, November 27, 1820, to January 9, 1821; Sixth, November 19, 1821, to January 3, 1822; Seventh, December 22, 1822, to January 11, 1823; Eighth, December 1, 1823, to January 31, 1824; Ninth, January 10, 1825, to February 12, 1825; Tenth, December 5, 1825, to January 21, 1826; Eleventh, December 4, 1826, to January 7, 1827; Twelfth, December 3, 1827, to January 24, 1828; Thirteenth, December 1, 1828, to January 24, 1829; Fourteenth, December 7, 1829, to January 30, 1830; Fifteenth, December 6, 1830, to February 10, 1831; Sixteenth, December 5, 1831, to February 3, 1832; Seventeenth, December 3, 1832, to February 4, 1833; Eighteenth, December 2, 1833, to February 3, 1834; Nineteenth, December 1, 1834, to February 9, 1835; Twentieth, December 7, 1835, to February 8, 1836; Twenty first, December 5, 1836, to February 6, 1837; Twenty second, December 4, 1837, to February 19, 1838; Twenty third, December 3, 1838, to February 16, 1839; Twenty fourth, December 2, 1839, to February 24, 1840; Twenty fifth, December 7, 1840, to February 15, 1841; Twenty sixth, December 6, 1841, to January 31, 1842; Twenty seventh, December 5, 1842, to February 13, 1843; Twenty eighth, December 4, 1843, to January 15, 1844; Twenty ninth, December 2, 1844, to January 13, 1845; Thirtieth, December 1, 1845, to January 20, 1846; Thirty first, December 7, 1846, to January 28, 1847; Thirty second, December 6, 1847, to February 17, 1848; Thirty third, December 4, 1848, to January 5, 1849; Thirty fourth, December 3, 1849, to January 21, 1850; Thirty fifth, December 3, 1850, to February 14, 1851; Thirty sixth, December 1, 1851, to June 21, 1852. As this was the last session preceding the adoption of the new constitution it was probably prolonged on that account.

REGULAR SESSIONS UNDER PRESENT CONSTITUTION.

Thirty seventh session, January 6, 1853, to March 7, 1853; Thirty eighth, January 4, 1855, to March 5, 1855; Thirty ninth, January 8, 1857, to March 9, 1857; Fortieth, January 6, 1859, to March 7, 1859; Forty first, January 10, 1861, to March 11, 1861; Forty second, January 8, 1863, to March 9, 1863; Forty third, January 5, 1865, to March 6, 1865; Forty fourth, January 10, 1867, to March 11, 1867; Forty fifth, January 7, 1869, to March 8, 1869; Forty sixth, January 5, 1871, to February 27, 1871; Forty seventh, January 9, 1873, to March 10, 1873; Forty eighth, January 7, 1875, to March 8, 1875; Forty ninth, January 4, 1877, to March 5, 1877; Fiftieth, January 9, 1879, to March 10, 1879; Fifty first, January 6, 1881, to March 7, 1881; Fifty second, January 4, 1883, to March 5, 1883; Fifty third, January 8, 1885, to March 9, 1885; Fifty fourth, January 6, 1887, to March 7 ,1887; Fifty fifth, January 10, 1889, to March 11, 1889; Fifty sixth, January 8, 1891, to March 9, 1891; Fifty seventh, January 5, 1893, to March 6, 1893; Fifty eighth, January 10, 1895, to March 11, 1895; Fifty ninth, January 9, 1897, to March 8, 1897; Sixtieth, January 5, 1899, to March 6, 1899; Sixty first, January 10, 1901, to March 11, 1901; Sixty second, January 8, 1903, to March 9, 1903; Sixty third, January 5, 1905, to March 6, 1905.

SPECIAL SESSIONS UNDER THE PRESENT CONSTITUTION.

(1) November 20, 1858, to December 15, 1858; (2) April 24, 1861, to June 2, 1861; (3) November 13, 1865, to December 22, 1865; (4) April 8, 1869, to May 17, 1869; (5) November 13, 1872, to December 22, 1872; (6) March 9, 1875, to March 14, 1875; (7) March 6, 1877, to March 15, 1877; (8) March 11, 1879, to March 31, 1879; (9) March 8, 1881, to April 16, 1881; (10) March 10, 1885, to April 13, 1885.

For explanation of variance in numbering the sessions of the General Assembly, see page 1023 of this History, immediately following the name of Levi Ulrich, present Representative from Henry County.

HENRY COUNTY IN CONGRESSIONAL DISTRICTS.

Henry County has formed a part of the several Congressional districts and has been represented in Congress as follows:

THIRD DISTRICT, 1822 TO 1831.

Henry, Dearborn, Delaware, Fayette, Franklin, Randolph, Ripley, Switzerland, Union and Wayne counties. Representatives—John Test, Whig, Brookville, 18th and

19th Congress, March 4, 1823, to March 4, 1827; Oliver H. Smith, Whig, Connersville, 20th Congress, March 4, 1827, to March 4, 1829; John Test, Whig, Brookville, 21st Congress, March 4, 1829, to March 4, 1831.

THIRD DISTRICT. 1831 TO 1833.

Henry, Allen, Decatur, Delaware, Dearborn, Franklin, Fayette, Randolph, Ripley, Rush, Switzerland, Union and Wayne counties. (To this district was attached all the unorganized territory now embraced in the counties of Jay, Blackford, Adams, Wells, Whitley, Noble, DeKalb, Steuben, LaGrange and a part of Grant and Huntington.) Representative—Jonathan McCarty, Whig, Connersville, 22d Congress, March 4, 1831, to March 4, 1833.

FIFTH DISTRICT, 1833 TO 1843.

Henry, Allen, Delaware, Fayette, Grant, Huntington, LaGrange, Randolph, Union and Wayne counties. (This district when first organized embraced the unorganized territory afterward incorporated into the counties of Jay, Blackford, Wells, Adams, Whitley, DeKalb, Noble and Steuben). Representatives—Jonathan McCarty, Whig, Connersville, 23d and 24th Congress, March 4, 1833, to March 4, 1837; James Rariden, Whig, Centreville, 25th and 26th Congress, March 4, 1837, to March 4, 1841; Andrew Kennedy, Democrat, Muncie, 27th Congress, March 4, 1841, to March 4, 1843.

FOURTH DISTRICT. 1843 TO 1853.

Henry, Fayette, Union and Wayne counties. Representatives—Caleb B. Smith, Whig, Connersville,, 28th, 29th and 30th Congress, March 4, 1843, to March 4, 1849; George W. Julian, Free Soiler, Centreville, 31st Congress, March 4, 1849, to March 4, 1851; Samuel W. Parker, Whig, Connersville, 32d Congress, March 4, 1851, to March 4, 1853.

FIFTH DISTRICT, 1853 TO 1869.

Henry, Delaware, Fayette, Randolph, Union and Wayne counties. Representatives —Samuel W. Parker, Whig, Connersville, 33d Congress, March 4, 1853, to March 4, 1855; David P. Holloway, Whig, Richmond, 34th Congress, March 4, 1855, to March 4, 1857; David Kilgore, Republican, Yorktown, 35th and 36th Congress, March 4, 1857, to March 4, 1861; George W. Julian, Republican, Centreville, 37th, 38th, 39th and 40th Congress, March 4, 1861, to March 4, 1869.

NINTH DISTRICT, 1869 TO 1875.

Henry, Adams, Allen, Blackford, Delaware, Jay, Randolph and Wells counties. Representative—John P. C. Shanks, Republican, Portland, 41st, 42d and 43d Congress, March 4, 1869, to March 4, 1875.

SIXTH DISTRICT. 1875 TO 1881.

Henry, Delaware, Grant, Hancock, Johnson, Madison and Shelby counties. Representatives—Milton S. Robinson, Republican, Anderson, 44th and 45th Congress, March 4, 1875, to March 4, 1879; William R. Myers, Democrat, Anderson, 46th Congress, March 4, 1879, to March 4, 1881.

SIXTH DISTRICT, 1881 TO 1893.

Henry, Delaware, Fayette, Randolph, Rush and Wayne counties. Representatives— Thomas M. Browne, Republican, Winchester, 47th, 48th, 49th, 50th and 51st Congress, March 4, 1881, to March 4, 1891; Henry U. Johnson, Republican, Richmond, 52d Congress, March 4, 1891, to March 4, 1893.

Henry, Delaware, Fayette, Randolph, Union and Wayne counties. Representatives—Henry U. Johnson, Republican, Richmond, 53d, 54th, and 55th Congress, March 4, 1893, to March 4, 1899; James E. Watson, Republican, Rushville, 56th Congress, March 4, 1899, to March 4, 1901.

SIXTH DISTRICT, 1901 TO PRESENT TIME.

Henry, Decatur, Fayette, Franklin, Hancock, Rush, Shelby, Union and Wayne. Representative—James E. Watson, Republican, Rushville, 57th, 58th and 59th Congress, March 4, 1901, to March 4, 1907.

From the foregoing it will be seen that Henry County never had a member of Congress and only in one instance since the county was organized has a citizen of the county been the nominee of the dominant party for the office—General William Grose, Republican, who was defeated by William R. Myers, Democrat, of Anderson, in 1878. The minority party has been more favorable to Henry County citizens. In 1852 General Grose, then a Democrat, was a candidate against Samuel W. Parker, Whig. Edmund Johnson was three times the Democratic candidate; in 1856, against David Kilgore; in 1862, against George W. Julian, and in 1874 against Milton S. Robinson. In 1866, Judge Martin L. Bundy was the independent Republican candidate against George W. Julian. Bundy was supported by the independent Republicans and the Democrats, all then designated as the supporters of Andrew Johnson. In 1876 David W. Chambers was the Democratic candidate against Milton S. Robinson. In 1894 the Democrats nominated Nimrod R. Elliott to oppose Henry U. Johnson.

The politics of each congressman is designated from the beginning of the history of the county. Notwithstanding the Whig party was not in existence until 1832, as is shown in the introduction to the preceding chapter, yet the representatives before that time afterward became Whigs. Since division on party lines, 1835-7, no man other than a Whig or Republican has represented in Congress the district of which Henry County was a part, excepting in two instances, namely, Andrew Kennedy, Democrat, Muncie, 27th Congress, 1841-3, and William R. Myers, Democrat, Anderson, 46th Congress, 1879-81.

For biographical information regarding any of the above members of Congress, see Biographical Congressional Directory, printed by the U. S. Government in 1904. The book can be obtained for a nominal sum from the superintendent of documents in the office of the Public Printer, Washington, D. C. It contains biographical mention of every member of Congress from the beginning to the present time.

HENRY COUNTY'S VOTE FOR PRESIDENT.

The first presidential election in which Henry County participated was in 1824, when the candidates were John Quincy Adams, Henry Clay, William H. Crawford and Andrew Jackson. The vote of the county at this election is not obtainable, neither is it obtainable for the election of 1828, when the candidates were John Quincy Adams and Andrew Jackson. The vote at the succeeding elections was as follows:

1832—Henry Clay, Whig, 767; Andrew Jackson, Democrat, 580; total, 1347.

1836—William Henry Harrison, Whig, 1394; Martin Van Buren, Democrat, 712; total, 2106.

1840—William Henry Harrison, Whig, 1652; Martin Van Buren, Democrat, 839; total, 2491.

1844—Henry Clay, Whig, 1458; James K. Polk, Democrat, 1005; James G. Birney, Free Soiler, 188; total, 2651.

1848—Zachary Taylor, Whig, 1115; Lewis Cass, Democrat, 1005; Martin Van Buren, Free Soiler, 455; total, 2575.

1852—Winfield Scott, Whig, 1559; Franklin Pierce, Democrat, 1225; John P. Hale, Free Soiler, 456; total, 3240.

1856—John C. Fremont, Republican, 2741; James Buchanan, Democrat, 1229; Millard Filmore, American party, commonly called "Know Nothings," 49; total, 4019.

1860—Abraham Lincoln, Republican, 2726; Stephen A. Douglas, Democrat, 1296; John C. Breckenridge, pro slavery Democrat, 90; John Bell, independent conservative, 16; total, 4128.

1864—Abraham Lincoln, Republican, 3027; George B. McClellan, Democrat, 1057; total, 4084.

1868—Ulysses S. Grant, Republican, 3432; Horatio Seymour, Democrat, 1412; total, 4824.

1872—Ulysses S. Grant, Republican, 3355; Horace Greeley, independent Republican, 1615; total, 4970.

1876—Rutherford B. Hayes, Republican, 3631; Samuel J. Tilden, Democrat, 1924; total, 5555.

1880—James A. Garfield, Republican, 3784; Winfield S. Hancock, Democrat, 2031; scattering votes, 252; total, 6067.

1884—James G. Blaine, Republican, 3671; Grover Cleveland, Democrat, 2096; Benjamin F. Butler, People's party, 232; John P. St. John, Prohibitionist, 77; total, 6076.

1888—Benjamin Harrison, Republican, 3849; Grover Cleveland, Democrat, 2277; Andrew J. Streeter, Union Labor, 51; Clinton B. Fiske, Prohibitionist, 230; total, 6407.

1892—Benjamin Harrison, Republican, 3330; Grover Cleveland, Democrat, 1861; James B. Weaver, People's party, 604; Bidwell, Prohibitionist, 232; total, 6027.

1896—William McKinley, Republican, 3991; William J. Bryan, Democrat, 2971; John M. Palmer, gold Democrat, 6; Levering, Prohibitionist, 48; scattering votes, 54; total, 7070.

1900—William McKinley, Republican, 4047; William J. Bryan, Democrat, 2754; John G. Woolley, Prohibitionist, 316; Eugene V. Debs, Socialist, 6; total, 7123.

1904—Theodore Roosevelt, Republican, 4391; Alton B. Parker, Democrat, 2482; Silas C. Swallow, Prohibitionist, 403; scattering votes, 46; total, 7322.

Vote of State of Indiana for President: Roosevelt, 368,289; Parker, 274,345; Swallow, Prohibitionist, 23,496; Debs, Socialist, 12,013; scattering, 4042; total vote, 682,185.

Vote of United States for President: Roosevelt, 7,624,489; Parker, 5,082,754; Debs, Socialist, 402,286; Swallow, Prohibitionist, 258,787; Watson, Populist, 117,935; Corrigan, Socialist Labor, 32,088; total vote, 13,519,169.

HENRY COUNTY'S VOTE FOR GOVERNOR.

The first election for Governor in which Henry County participated was in 1825. Under the constitution of 1816 the governor was elected on "the first Monday in August" for the term of three years, the General Assembly met annually on the first Monday in December and the governor was to hold his office as provided in article 4, section 3, as follows: "The governor shall hold his office during three years from and after the third day of the first session of the General Asesmbly next ensuing his election and until a successor shall be chosen and qualified and shall not be capable of holding it longer than six years in any term of nine years." The present constitution provides, article 5, section 9, as follows: "The official term of the governor * * * shall commence on the second Monday of January, 1853, and every four years thereafter," he having been previously elected on "the second Tuesday in October" until 1880, since which time he has been elected on the first Tuesday after the first Monday in November. He is not eligible to the office until he has reached the age of thirty years and is ineligible for re-election until a term has intervened.

The term "Free Soiler" implied opposition to slavery in the territories and that no more slave States should be admitted.

The vote in detail was as follows:

1825—James B. Ray, 303; Isaac Blackford, 66; total, 369.

1828—James B. Ray, 479; Conley, 68; Moore, 37; total, 584.

1831, 1834, 1837—The vote is not obtainable.

1840—Samuel Bigger, Whig, Rushville, 1579; Tilghman Howard, Democrat, Rockville, 846; total, 2426.

1843—Samuel Bigger, Whig, Rushville, 1140; James Whitcomb, Democrat, Bloomington, 902; Elizur Deming, Free Soiler, 191; total, 2233.

1846—Joseph Marshall, Whig, Madison, 1180; James Whitcomb, Democrat, Bloomington, 814; total, 1994.

1849—John A. Matson, Whig, Brookville, 1437; Joseph A. Wright, Democrat, Rockville, 1287; John H. Cravens, Free Soiler, Versailles, 115; total, 2839.

1852—Nicholas McCarty, Whig, Indianapolis, 1527; Joseph A. Wright, Democrat,
Rockville, 1179; Andrew L. Robinson, Free Soiler, 358; total, 3064.

1856—Oliver P. Morton, Republican, Centreville, 2486; Ashbel P. Willard, Democrat, New Albany, 1328; total, 3814.

1860—Henry S. Lane, Republican, Crawfordsville, 2797; Thomas A. Hendricks,
Democrat, Shelbyville, 1328; total, 4125.

1864—Oliver P. Morton, Republican, Indianapolis, 3008; Joseph E. McDonald, Democrat, Indianapolis, 1123; total, 4131.

1868—Conrad Baker, Republican, Evansville, 3373; Thomas A. Hendricks, Democrat, Indianapolis, 1516; total, 4889.

1872—Thomas M. Browne, Republican, Winchester, 3399; Thomas A. Hendricks,
Democrat, Indianapolis, 1730; total, 5129.

1876—Benjamin Harrison, Republican, Indianapolis, 3663; James D. Williams, Democrat, Vincennes, 1881; total 5544.

1880—Albert G. Porter, Republican, Indianapolis, 3774; Franklin Landers, Democrat, Indianapolis, 2066; Richard Griggs, Prohibitionist, 248; total, 6088.

1884—William H. Calkins, Republican, Laporte, 3648; Isaac P. Gray, Democrat,
Union City, 2108; Hiram Z. Leonard, Prohibitionist, 218; Robert S. Dwiggins, Union
Labor, 96; total, 6070.

At this election (1884) one of Henry County's citizens, Eugene H. Bundy, of New
Castle, was the Republican candidate for lieutenant governor.

1888—Alvin P. Hovey, Republican, Mount Vernon, 3844; Courtland C. Matson,
Democrat, Greencastle, 2284; Jasper S. Hughes, Prohibitionist, Indianapolis, 237; John
B. Milroy, Socialist, 51; total, 6416.

1892—Ira J. Chase, Republican, Indianapolis, 3323; Claude Matthews, Democrat,
Clinton, 1861; Aaron Worth, Prohibitionist, Bryant, 261; Leroy Templeton, People's
party, Indianapolis, 593; total, 6038.

1896—James A. Mount, Republican, Crawfordsville, 3997; Benjamin F. Shively,
Democrat, South Bend, 2824; scattering votes, 196; total, 7017.

1900—Winfield T. Durbin, Republican, Anderson, 4018; John W. Kern, Democrat,
Indianapolis, 2735; Charles Eckhart, Prohibitionist, Auburn, 312; scattering votes, 18;
total, 7083.

1904—J. Frank Hanly, Republican, La Fayette, 4310; John W. Kern, Democrat,
Indianapolis, 2479; Felix T. McWhirter, Prohibitionist, Indianapolis, 391; scattering
votes, 41; total, 7221.

The vote of the State of Indiana for governor was: Hanly, 359,362; Kern, 274,998;
McWhirter, Prohibitionist, 22,690; scattering, 14,493; total vote, 671,543.

GOVERNORS OF INDIANA.

(TERRITORIAL.)

Arthur St. Clair, governor (Northwest Territory), from 1787 to 1800.
John Gibson (acting), from July 4, 1800, to January 10, 1801.
William H. Harrison, from 1801 to 1812 (a).
Thomas Posey, from 1812 to 1816.

(STATE.)

Jonathan Jennings, from 1816 to 1822 (b).
Ratliff Boon, from September 12 to December 5, 1822.

William Hendricks, from 1822 to 1825.

James B. Ray (acting), February 12 to December 11, 1825 (c).

James B. Ray, from 1825 to 1831.

Noah Noble, from 1831 to 1837.

David Wallace, from 1837 to 1840.

Samuel Bigger, from 1840 to 1843.

James Whitcomb, from 1843 to 1848.

Paris C. Dunning (acting), from 1848 to 1849 (d).

Joseph A. Wright, from 1849 to 1857.

Ashbel P. Willard, from 1857 to 1860.

Abram A. Hammond (acting), from 1860 to 1861 (e).

Henry S. Lane, from January 14 to January 16, 1861 (f).

Oliver P. Morton (acting), from 1861 to 1865.

Oliver P. Morton, from 1865 to 1867.

Conrad Baker (acting), from 1867 to 1869 (g).

Conrad Baker, from 1869 to 1873.

Thomas A. Hendricks, from 1873 to 1877.

James D. Williams, from 1877 to 1880.

Isaac P. Gray (acting), from 1880 to 1881 (h).

Albert G. Porter, from 1881 to 1885.

Isaac P. Gray, from 1885 to 1889.

Alvin P. Hovey, from 1889 to 1891 (i).

Ira J. Chase (acting), from November 24, 1891, to January 9, 1893.

Claude Matthews, from 1893 to 1897.

James A. Mount, from 1897 to 1901.

Winfield T. Durbin, from 1901 to 1905.

J. Frank Hanly, from 1905 to 1909.

(a) Governor Harrison was appointed early in the year 1800, but was not sworn into office until January 10, 1801. John Gibson, the Secretary of the Territory, acted as Governor until his arrival.
(b) Jonathan Jennings, having been elected to Congress before the end of his second term, resigned the office of Governor September 18, 1822, and was succeeded by Ratliff Boon, who served until December 5 of the same year.
(c) Governor Hendricks, having been elected a Senator of the United States, resigned his office on the 12th day of February, 1825, and was succeeded by James B. Ray, the President of the State Senate, who served as Governor during the remainder of the term.
(d) Governor Whitcomb was elected a Senator of the United States December 27, 1848, and Paris C. Dunning, Lieutenant-Governor, served as Governor during the remainder of the term.
(e) Governor Willard died on the third day of October, 1860, and Abram A. Hammond, the Lieutenant-Governor, served as Governor during the remainder of the term.
(f) Governor Lane was elected a Senator of the United States January 16, 1861, and Oliver P. Morton, the Lieutenant-Governor, served as Governor the remainder of the term.
(g) Governor Oliver P. Morton was elected Senator of the United States on the 23d day of January, 1867. On the day following he resigned his office, and Conrad Baker, the Lieutenant-Governor, served as Governor during the remainder of the term.
(h) Governor Williams died November 20, 1880, and Isaac P. Gray, Lieutenant-Governor, served as Governor the remainder of the term.
(i) Governor Hovey died November 23, 1891, and Lieutenant-Governor Ira J. Chase served as Governor the remainder of the term.

POPULATION OF HENRY COUNTY, 1830 TO 1900.

The following table shows the population of Henry County, properly divided between sex and color, at every United States Census, from 1830 to 1900, inclusive:

	WHITE			COLORED			Total Male Population	Total Female Population	Total Population
Census	Male	Female	Total	Male	Female	Total			
1830	3,316	3,141	6,457	31	10	41	3,347	3,151	6,498
1840	7,721	7,262	14,983	82	63	145	8,803	7,325	15,128
1850	8,722	8,596	17,318	148	139	287	8,870	8,735	17,b05
1860	10,092	9,744	19,836	149	134	283	10,241	9,878	20,119
1870	(a)	(a)	22,686	(a)	(a)	441	11,688	11,298	23,127
1880	(a)	(a)	23,332	(a)	(a)	684	12,118	11,898	24,016
1890	11,735	11,390	23,325	262	292	554	11,997	11,882	23,879
1900	12,521	12,088	24,609	235	244	479	12,756	12,332	25,088

(a). Not given by sex.

CHAPTER XLV.

In Chapter XL of this History, entitled "The First Courts and First Attorneys" and again in Chapter XLIII, entitled "Henry County Official Register," may be found mention of a number of legal practitioners who have adorned the bar of Henry County, many of whom possessed not only a local celebrity among their contemporaries but achieved State and even National renown.

The prescribed limits of this work will hardly permit of a fuller treatment of a subject so important and interesting to laymen as well as to members of the profession itself. It is, however, just and proper to remark that the profession has always had within its ranks in the county, men of rare forensic skill, great learning and distinguished intellectual ability, and they have usually been among the most progressive and public spirited of citizens.

Many of them when called to the bench have exhibited a rare fitness for the position and have displayed a soundness of judgment and legal acumen that have enhanced the reputation of the bench and bar of Indiana.

In this chapter is presented the life history of a few of the county's eminent lawyers and judges to the end that a fitting tribute be paid to a profession which is of such vast importance to the affairs of the people of today and which has always attracted to its ranks so large a proportion of the best intellect of the country.

BIOGRAPHICAL SKETCH OF JEHU TINDLE ELLIOTT.

LAWYER, LEGISLATOR, JURIST.

The pioneer lawyers of Eastern Indiana, a district composed in part of the counties of Henry, Delaware, Fayette, Franklin, Jay, Randolph, Rush, Union and Wayne,
were a notable body of men, a number of whom in later years occupied high and honorable positions, not only in their own county or district but in the State and the Nation
as well. This sketch relates especially to Jehu Tindle Elliott, who from 1834 to the
time of his death, February 12, 1876, was probably the most eminent member of the
"Whitewater Valley Bar."

Jehu Tindle Elliott was the seventh child and the third son of Abraham Elliott,
senior, and his wife, Jean (Alexander) Elliott. Abraham Elliott was born March 10,
1780, and died September 15, 1848. His wife was born February 14, 1782, and died
August 29, 1833. He was a native of Guilford County, North Carolina, and emigrated
from there to Ohio, settling on the banks of the Miami River, where the town of
Waynesville now stands. In 1806 he moved from there to Wayne County, Indiana, settling near Richmond. He was the first lawyer to locate there and was one of the most
prominent citizens of that locality. His son Stephen says: "He cut the first stick of
timber ever cut by a white man where Richmond now stands." In 1809 he removed to
Greensfork, then known as Washington, where he resided until 1817, when he went to
Jacksonburg. While a resident of the latter place, where he sold goods, he was elected
Sheriff of Wayne County. This was about the year 1820 and at that time he also got
the contract to carry the Winchester, Randolph County, mail. His son Stephen says
of this: "I was then a boy fourteen years old and was put to carrying the mail. My
starting point was old Salisbury, three miles east of Centreville, thence by way of
Jacksonburg to Washington (Greensfork), and then on to Winchester through a wilderness, having for the last ten miles but one cabin on the way." He says further: "I
very often went to Winchester with empty mail bags but had to go to see if there was
anything to bring back."

Abraham Elliott left Wayne County in 1823 and came to Henry County, where he
settled on what is now known as the Elliott farm, about two miles south of New Castle.
He soon afterwards opened a law office in the latter place. He was a self-made man;
physically vigorous; possessed of a strong and active mind; and for several years did a
large share of the legal business of the county. He served for a term as a justice of
the peace, and from 1843 to 1848 he was one of the associate judges, sitting on the
bench during this period with his son, Jehu T. Elliott, who was then the presiding
judge. He died in office, September 14, 1848.

Abraham and Jean (Alexander) Elliott were the parents of twelve children, namely:
William, born August 29, 1800; died July 14, 1848; Sarah, born October 3, 1802, died
May 20, 1885; Mary, born November 10, 1804, died April 4, 1868; Stephen, born Decem-
ber 26, 1806, died December 4, 1896; Elizabeth, born February 14, 1809, date of death not
obtainable; Jehu T., born February 7, 1813, died February 12, 1876; Abraham (junior),
born April 3, 1815, died April 6, 1884; Zimri, born May 13, 1817, died August 14, 1835;
Jane, born May 10, 1819, died September 7, 1864; Amanda, born April 7, 1821, died
July 30, 1903; Theresa, born August 8, 1823, died January 19, 1901.

Of these children, William Elliott resided at Cambridge City, Wayne County. His
wife was Elisa (Branson) Elliott, who was a sister of Hannah Scott (Branson) Elliott,
wife of the late Judge Jehu T. Elliott. They were the parents of the late Calvin B.
Elliott, of that place, and of Dewitt C. Elliott, deceased, William H. Elliott and Jehu T.
Elliott, junior, all three of Logansport, Indiana, and of Harriet (Elliott) Murphey, deceased, who was the wife of the late Benjamin F. Murphey, of Chicago.

Mary Elliott married Daniel Bradbury, a prominent citizen of Wayne County, who
lived near Greensfork. He was largely interested in and identified with the building of
the Cincinnati, Logansport and Chicago railway, now a part of the Panhandle road, and
was the grandfather of Albert D. Ogborn and Edwin C. Ogborn, of New Castle. His
wife was an excellent woman and was held in the highest regard by her relatives,
friends and neighbors.

Randolph, Rush, Union and Wayne,
later years occupied high and honor-
:rict but in the State and the Nation
indle Elliot., who from 1834 to the
.y the most eminent member of the

d the thi.. son of Abraham Elliott,
.braham Elliott was born March 10,
s born February 14, 1782, and died
unty, North Carolina, and emigrated
e Miam: River, where the town of
here to Wayne County, Indiana, set-
ocate .here and was one of the most
ien say "He cut the first stick of
now ...b." In 1809 he removed to
res.... ntil 1817, when he went to
where he sold goods, he was elected
...... and at that time he also got
...... .ail. His son Stephen says
i was .. to carrying the mail. My
t ..' C. .reville. thence by way of
.n .. .. Winchester through a wil-
on, th. way." He says further: "I
es ho .ad to go to see if there was

ad came to Henry County, where he
.bout .wo miles south of New Castle.
er place. He was a self-made man;
.e m..d and for several years did a
.e served for a term as a justice of
the .....late judges, sitting on the
.lliott. who was then the presiding

a paren.. .of twelve children, namely:
: Sarah born October 3, 1802, died
April 4, 1856; Stephen, born Decem-
Februar. .t, 1809, date of death not
bruary 1., 1876; Abraham (junior),
May 13, 1..7, died August 14, 1835;
Amanda. .orn April 7, 1821, died
uary 19, 190..
ambridge City, Wayne County. His
of Hannah Scott (Branson) Elliott,
. the parents of the late Calvin B.
sed, William H. Elliott and John T.
.t of Harriet (Elliott) Murphey, de-
.urphey, of Chicago.
.inent citizen of Wayne County, who
and identified with the building of
. a part of the Panhandle road, and

On October 19, 1820, Sarah Elliott married Tabor W. McKee, a pioneer of Harrison Township, Henry County, but at an early day they moved from there to near Indianola, Iowa, where they continued to abide until death. He was born January 2, 1801, and died July 14, 1871. Mr. McKee had been prominent in the affairs of Henry County prior to his removal to Iowa, and there he was quickly recognized as a leading man of affairs, entitled to the confidence and support of the people. He was elected sheriff of Warren County, Iowa, in 1857, and served for two years (1858-1859); he was elected treasurer and recorder (one office) in 1861 and served four years (1862-1865).

Stephen Elliott's life is intimately connected with the history of New Castle. For nearly ninety years he went in and out before its people and was always regarded as one of the leading citizens of the town and of the county. He was a sturdy and stalwart man, energetic and industrious, and noted for his honesty and probity. His memory will always be cherished.

Elizabeth Elliott was married in Wayne County, Indiana, to the late James Peed, a native of Kentucky. They came to Henry County in 1834 and settled on a farm in Liberty Township. She was a noble woman, beloved by all who knew her. She was the mother of several children, among them being Evan H. Peed, of New Castle, whose fine character makes him a fitting representative of his father.

Matilda Elliott became the wife of Niles Gregory, and after her marriage resided with her husband at Plymouth, Indiana. After the death of her first husband, she was married to Reuben Swain, of Greensboro, Henry County, and resided there until her death.

Abraham Elliott, junior, lived for a number of years on a farm, two miles south of New Castle, but shortly after the exodus of so many people from Indiana to Iowa began, he with his family removed to that State, where he lived until his death. He was a farmer but gave much attention to the politics of the "Hawkeye State," and for many years attended the sessions of the Iowa Legislature, as a member of the "Third House." He was a positive man, tenacious of his opinions and when necessary, very demonstrative.

The youngest son, Zimri, died while a young man. Jane Elliott married James Black and resided with him until his death, at Laporte, Indiana, where he conducted successfully a large tannery. After his death, the widow moved to New Castle, where she lived until her death. She was the mother of Amanda V. (Black) Hudelson, who was the wife of John C. Hudelson, of New Castle; of the late Nathaniel E. Black, for many years a prominent merchant of New Castle; and of Kate (Black) McMeans, widow of the late Edghill B. McMeans.

Amanda Elliott married Judge Martin L. Bundy, a sketch of whose life appears in another place in this History. She was a woman of noble character, devoted to her family and beloved by a wide circle of relatives and friends.

Theresa Elliott, the youngest of the children, spent the greater portion of her life in New Castle. She was first the wife of the late Henry Clay Grubbs, who was at one time connected with the New Castle Courier and who afterwards became treasurer of Henry County. After his death, she became the wife of Samuel McCrady, and following his decease was married to the late Josiah Needham, for many years a justice of the peace, who preceded her to the grave.

The family was a noted one in the early history of Henry County and a long line of descendants continues to honor the name.

JEHU TINDLE ELLIOTT.

Jehu Tindle Elliott was one of a large family and as his father was not financially strong in the pioneer days, each of his children, as they grew in strength and understanding, found it necessary to shift for themselves. The subject of this sketch early became a school teacher and continued in that employment for one or two years, until he was about twenty years of age, when he entered the office of Martin M. Ray at Centreville to study law. But little is known of the history of Martin M. Ray. He was one of the first lawyers to settle in Eastern Indiana and one of the first to be admitted to the Henry County bar. He was regarded as an able lawyer and had a large and lucrative practise for the times. Jehu T. Elliott studied day and night with steady persistence and at the end of a year or so was admitted to the bar. Then just barely of age, he returned to his home at New Castle, "hung out his shingle," and entered upon the practise of law.

On October 24, 1833, at Centreville, Wayne County, he was united in marriage with Hannah Scott Branson, the ceremony being performed by Nathan Smith. She was a daughter of Owen and Hannah Branson and was born January 3, 1817; she died November 14, 1902. Her parents were natives of Maryland, from near Baltimore, where her father had been a market gardener. They came to Indiana in the pioneer days. They were members of the Quaker or Friends' Church. Hannah Scott (Branson) Elliott was a sister of Eliza (Branson) Elliott, above mentioned, and of Margaret (Branson) Brenneman, who was the wife of the late Jacob Brenneman, one of New Castle's early and prominent pioneers.

To the union of Jehu Tindle Elliott and Hannah Scott (Branson) Elliott were born nine children, four of whom, Milton Sapp, born June 3, 1835; Henry Clay, born May 25, 1837; Edward, born July 22, 1847; and Emma Lillian, born May 13, 1851, died in infancy. The other children were: Eliza Josephine, born November 1, 1838, now the wife of John Thornburgh, of New Castle; Helen Mary, born November 14, 1841, died July 5, 1871. She married Leander E. Murphey, of Chicago, who died March 18, 1904. Both are buried in South Mound Cemetery, New Castle. William Henry, born July 4, 1844, now editor of the New Castle Courier; Jane, who was married May 12, 1869, to Lieutenant Commander Archibald N. Mitchell, U. S. N., and after his death to John T. Reichard, also now deceased, of Monmouth, Illinois; and Carrie May, born January 1, 1858, now the wife of James L. McAfee, of Chicago, Illinois.

Jehu T. Elliott's connection with the Henry County bar was rather as a judge than as a practitioner, his elevation to the bench occurring in 1844, about eleven years after his admission to the bar. Prior to this, however, in 1834, he had been elected Treasurer of Henry County, by the board of county commissioners, in which the authority was then vested, and served until 1839. In 1833 he had also been elected assistant secretary of the lower house of the General Assembly of Indiana and in 1837 he was elected secretary of the same body. In 1838 he was elected prosecuting attorney for the Sixth Judicial District, composed of the counties of Henry, Delaware, Fayette. Grant, Randolph, Rush, Union and Wayne, Samuel Bigger, afterward Governor of Indiana, being at that time judge of the circuit. In August, 1839, he was elected State Senator and served the full term of three years, acceptably to his constituents and with credit to himself. He was afterwards, when but thirty one years of age, elected circuit judge by the General Assembly of Indiana. In 1851 he was re-elected to the same position for the term of seven years, but he soon resigned to become president of the Cincinnati, Logansport and Chicago railway, then in process of construction from Richmond to New Castle and northwest to Chicago. For about two years he gave his time and ability to the completion of that projected road. In this work he was greatly assisted by his fellow townsmen, Martin L. Bundy, Eli Murphey, John Powell, John W. Grubbs, Joshua Holland, John C. Hudelson, Samuel Hazzard, the father of the author of this History, and others, including the late Daniel Bradbury, of Wayne County. He resigned this position in 1854 and resumed the practise of the law, but in 1855 he was again elected judge of the circuit court, by the people. In this capacity he served with unusual ability until 1865, when he was elected, along with James S. Frazer, of Warsaw, Robert C. Gregory, of La Fayette, and Charles A. Ray, of Indianapolis, a judge of the Supreme Court of Indiana. He took his place on the Supreme Bench, January 3, 1865, and served with honor and distinction until the expiration of his term of office, in 1871.

The career of Judge Jehu T. Elliott, as lawyer and judge, covered a period of some thirty seven years, of which twenty four years were spent on the bench, eighteen as circuit and six as supreme court judge. He was contemporary with such lawyers and jurists as James Rariden, Charles H. Test, John S. Newman, Samuel E. Perkins, James Perry, Oliver P. Morton, Nimrod H. Johnson, John F. Kibbey, William A. Peele, Jesse

P. Siddall, William A. Bickle, Charles H. Burchnall and George W. and Jacob B. Julian, of the Wayne County bar; Pleasant A. Hackleman, George Cox; George B. Kingsley and Samuel Bigger, of the Rush County bar; Caleb B. Smith, Samuel W. Parker and Benjamin F. Claypool, of the Fayette County bar; David Kilgore, Andrew Kennedy, Walter March, Joseph S. Buckles and Thomas J. Sample, of the Delaware County bar; Silas Colgrove, Jeremiah Smith, Thomas M. Browne, Leander J. Monks and Albert O. Marsh, of the Randolph County bar; John Yaryan and Thomas W. Bennett, of the Union County bar; Joseph Robinson and Andrew Davidson, of the Decatur County bar; John D. Howland and George Holland, of the Franklin County bar; John P. C. Shanks, of the Jay County bar; and Martin L. Bundy, William Grose, David Macy (afterwards of Indianapolis), Joshua H. Mellett, James Brown, Thomas B. Redding, Elijah B. Martindale (now of Indianapolis), James B. Martindale (afterwards of New York City), Miles Listen Reed, and Charles D. Morgan, of the Henry County bar.

The foregoing is not a complete list of those who practised with or before Judge Elliott, but in this array of the bar of Eastern Indiana will be noted the names·of many who became judges of the courts, senators and representatives in Congress, secretaries of State, and generals in the Civil War, and one who became the great "War Governor· of Indiana. Many of them filled minor offices of more or less importance, while nearly all of them were eminent in the profession of the law. A previous biographer has said that "it was the opinion of these men that, as a circuit judge, the ability of Judge Elliott was of the highest order and that it is certain no judge ever gave greater satisfaction than he." Moreover, "his popularity was such that no one ever opposed him for the place successfully, and when it was known that he was a candidate, an election naturally followed."

Turning back the pages of memory to the pioneer days of Indiana and comparing the judges and lawyers of that time with those of the present day, it will be found that in learning, in ability, in honesty, in integrity and in stability of character, the former were fully the equals of the latter. The several histories of Indiana have not failed to give to these men, learned in law, just and honorable mention, and it is worth something to know that from the organization of the State down to the present time, the bench and bar of Indiana has maintained a position hardly second to that of any other commonwealth of the Union. Another author touching upon this matter has also well said that "the court houses of Indiana were in the early days the training schools in good citizenship," and that "the people appreciated the teaching and their teachers."

The author of this History well remembers when the lawyers traveled the "circuit" and with what eclat they were welcomed to the straggling village of New Castle. They nearly always came on horseback, frequently over roads next to impassable, and alighting at the "tavern door," entered the barroom—then the real thing—took off their muddy green leggins and otherwise fitted themselves out for the business on hand. It was indeed a time of great excitement, and to be admitted to the inner circle, where one could look into the faces and hear the talk of the lawyers, was something to be proud of and remembered in years to come. Sometimes the lawyers would doff their professional dignity, at the close of the day's litigation, and gathering in a semi-circle about the big, blazing logs in the wide-mouthed fireplace, these men of the law told stories and indulged in such arguments and repartee as was well calculated to excite the interest or mirth of those privileged to be present. Traveling "circuit" is now but a memory and the generations which have since come upon the stage can never obtain more than a shadowy impression of its hardships, privations and dangers as well as its joys. Judge Elliott traveled the "circuit" of his then large judicial district, and in the later years of his life was never more happy than when relating his experiences. The saddle-bags used by him are still retained by his family as souvenirs of those early times. They are large and roomy and well preserved. In traveling "circuit," one side was used as a receptacle for a few law books, papers, etc., while in the other side were stored a few changes of linen and other clothing.

General John Coburn, of Indianapolis, still living and now quite aged, in writing his "Sketches of the Old Indiana Supreme Court Bar," after referring descriptively to

Caleb B. Smith, a member of.President Lincoln's first cabinet, Samuel W. Parker, David Kilgore, the "Delaware Chief," James Rariden, John S. Newman, James Perry, Charles H. Test, Pleasant H. Hackleman, and others, speaks of Judge Elliott as being "a great supreme judge of the State" who "was ruddy of face, an English beef-eating looking man with big round head and massive body, mild and genial in manner, a very sound and able lawyer, an honest, conscientious and capable man. Few better have ever appeared at the bar of Indiana. Scorning the quibbles and technicalities of the practise, he stood on the bedrock of general principles. His opinions are among the best of Indiana judges, concise, pointed and luminous."

Judge Jehu T. Elliott was absolutely impartial in the dispensation of the law. He knew no distinction among litigants. Relationship, friendship nor other tie could swerve him from the proper interpretation of the law, and to the determination of-cases, whether of greater or lesser importance, he brought the entire strength of his mind. Though frequently solicited to take part in the political battles of his time, he stead-fastly declined, believing that the bench should be absolutely free from the semblance of partisanship, yet he was strong in his political faith and always kept well informed as to the political situation. During the Civil War, no man gave the existing condition of affairs more earnest or more serious thought and study. He was a strong supporter of the government and stood hand in hand with Governor Morton in the conduct of the affairs of the State of Indiana.

Immediately succeeding the expiration of his term as judge of the supreme court of Indiana, Jehu T. Elliott re-entered the practise of the law at New Castle and continued in the profession until his death, which came suddenly and almost without warning, though he had been ill for several days. The funeral took place on Tuesday, February 15, 1876, and was attended by a large number of the representative men of the State, among them being Horace P. Biddle, John U. Pettit, Alexander C. Downey, James L. Worden and Samuel H. Buskirk, Justices of the Supreme Court; James S. Frazer, ex-judge of the Supreme Court; John S. Newman, of Indianapolis; John F. Kibbey, Charles H. Burchnall, Daniel W. Comstock, John L. Rupe, Lewis D. Stubbs and John W. Grubbs, of Richmond; Richard J. Hubbard, of Milton; Benjamin F. Claypool, of Connersville; Howell D. Thompson, of Anderson, and Captain Reuben A. Riley, of Green-field. These were supplemented by a full attendance of the Henry County bar, which included General William Grose, Judge Robert L. Polk, Judge Joshua H. Mellett, James Brown and many others. The pall bearers were Judge Joshua H. Mellett, General William Grose, Howell D. Thompson, Reuben A. Riley, Benjamin F. Claypool, Alexander C. Downey, Samuel H. Buskirk, Horace P. Biddle and Joseph L. Worden. The religious services were conducted by Elder Mahin of the Methodist Episcopal Church, assisted by the Reverend J. Colclazer, of the same denomination.

Referring to the death of Judge Elliott, a writer has well said:

"As a lawyer and judge, Jehu T. Elliott had few superiors. His mind was naturally judicial and his innate love of justice gave him a front rank among jurists. No higher tribute can be paid to his abilities than the statement made by one of his successors on the Supreme bench, that there has never yet been occasion for reversing a decision of his. As a man, a citizen, a neighbor, his character was without reproach. He possessed all the domestic virtues, was a good citizen and was ever ready to assist the needy. His generous encouragement of the young, especially the younger members of his profession, will ever be kindly remembered. His character is worthy of emulation."

At the meeting of the Henry County bar held to take appropriate action regarding the death of Judge Elliott, his former associate on the Supreme Bench, James S. Frazer, was made president, and Robert L. Polk, secretary. Upon assuming the chair, Judge Frazer, among other things, said: "Judge Elliott, for half a century or more, by his bearing at the bar, by his fidelity to the public in positions of trust in political and judicial life, by his qualities as a neighbor, as a husband and as a father, won the esteem and approbation of all."

Among the resolutions prepared by the committee of the bar and adopted was the following:

"His long service as circuit judge, his promptness, the accuracy and clearness of his decisions, his courteous and dignified bearing towards the members of the bar, his generous encouragement of the young and diffident, and above all his clear conception of and love for the right, and an impartial administration of the law, earned for him the well deserved title, 'The Model Judge.' "

General Grose, chairman of the committee, in presenting the resolutions, said:

"I have known Judge Elliott intimately for thirty years. In private and social life he had no superior. I never knew him in mixed company to introduce any topic that might prove disagreeable to anyone present. He could discuss differences of opinion with an opponent without for a moment losing his temper or evincing a want of respect for his adversary, and when it is added that in the conversation of the deceased there was never anything low or vulgar, but that rather intellect, refinement and good taste marked all that he ever said, we contemplate a character whose amiability, high breeding and politeness will ever command our respect and admiration."

John S. Newman, between whom and Judge Elliott there existed a bond of love and attachment which could not be broken, said many beautiful things touching the life and character of the deceased and from his remarks are culled the facts that "we were as intimate as brothers for about forty five years—from 1830—up to his death," and that "he wrote a very good hand;" that he was "genial and cheerful," and that "I took him into the Clerk's office (Centreville, Wayne County), with me and he made up many of the records for me. While in the Clerk's office with me, he boarded in my family (Mr. Newman was then just married) and he was one of the most pleasant and agreeable gentlemen that ever entered my abode." He said further: "I can bear witness to the great kindness and the many good qualities of the man, cheerful, pleasant and always practising the gentle courtesies of life, such as endear any man and all men in our age to the confidence and good will of his neighbors and friends. The old adage holds true, 'We shall never look upon his like again.' " Again he said:

"He had no personal foes. He overcame even the party spirit that might be supposed to be engendered. As judge, I practised under him and he always maintained the most perfect courtesy towards the members of the bar, old and young. It seemed to be to him a peculiar pleasure to extend courtesy to all. He seemed to be deeply interested in trying to smooth the asperities that arose in the practise under him. If a young man was embarrassed and desponding, he always seemed to be kindly extending his hand to him, not to give success to what was wrong, but through a natural kindness and to enable such a one to properly present his case."

Richard J. Hubbard, of Wayne County, said:

"I have known Judge Elliott for forty years. I was with him in the General Assembly when he was first elected assistant secretary. I was there with him as a member of that body four winters. I became well acquainted with him. * * * * During all that time I never heard him utter a vulgar or improper word or knew him to say anything to hurt anybody's feelings. I roomed with him during this time at Indianapolis and had a good opportunity to know him well. Since then, I have been acquainted with him as a judge and have served on the jury in this (Henry) County, when he was the judge, as well as in Wayne County, where I live, and he was always remarkable for the respect he showed to everybody. All men felt safe when he was on the bench."

Benjamin F. Claypool, of Connersville, said:

"I look upon Judge Elliott a little different from any others. I regarded him as peculiarly adapted to the bench; a man of quick perception and remarkably clear head. He seemed at the very first presentation of a question to grasp the strong points of the case. He seemed to get at the very marrow of the matter at the start and his conclusions were nearly always sustained by law and reason, and I think the bench was the place where he won the most distinguished honors. I would quote in regard to him the language of the poet:

'He has builded a monument more lasting than brass;
Loftier than the royal seat of the pyramids
Which neither the wasting rain nor the innumerable series of years
Nor the flight of time shall be able to overturn;
He shall not die altogether, but the greater part of him shall avoid death;'

and until we shall be called to final account, one of the freshest memories will be the thousand kindnesses that came from Judge Elliott."

There were others who passed upon the life and character of Judge Elliott, but the citations are closed with the following words from Judge Joshua H. Mellett, who has since followed his friend to the grave. Judge Elliott and Judge Mellett were bosom friends and companions. In many ways they were similar in character and their bond of friendship was as lasting as time. Judge Mellett said with a voice of emotion and tears suffusing his eyes:

"I became acquainted with Judge Elliott when I was an orphan boy of seventeen. For some cause, almost directly after my acquaintance with him, he became almost a father to me, and from the time I grew to manhood until now, he has been all to me that a brother could have been and what I say in regard to him may be considered as the words of a brother speaking of a deceased brother. If he had faults, I overlooked them and did not see them or forgot them as a brother would. If he was not an honest man, a truthful man, a faithful friend, if not a man who believed in the truth and one who hated a lie and loved all mankind, then I never knew one. The circumstances are such that it is not proper that I say more; in fact, I am incapable of saying more."

Probably, as between man and man, no stronger friendship ever existed than that which bound together the lives of Judge Jehu T. Elliott and Judge Martin L. Bundy. The wife of the latter—a most estimable woman—was the sister of Judge Elliott. From the pioneer days, beginning with the organization of Henry County and the establishment of its seat of government at New Castle, the lives of these two were as one. Their intimacy was as close and binding as that which exists between loving brothers. Martin L. Bundy is still living, aged eighty eight years, and is the last link between the dead past—the pioneer days of New Castle—and the living present.

Judge Elliott was always calm, cool and deliberate and slow to anger. He never rendered a decision in even the smallest cause, without giving the matter the fullest consideration. He was strong mentally and physically and a tireless worker. The author of this sketch has known him to sit up all night or until the morning sun streaked with light the eastern heavens, delving into books of law, scattered about on desk and table and chairs, each opened at some particular page, writing and compiling his opinion in some important case. At such times his library—a fine one—was his castle, and for the time he was oblivious of time and place. His closest companion in these searches of authorities was his favorite "brierwood" pipe, from which he seemed to draw an inspiration which gave light and life to opinions which are still regarded as models in the interpretation and expounding of the law.

During his professional life he found leisure in which to read high class literature, preferring such well known authors as Shakespeare, Dickens, Thackeray, Scott, and other eminent writers. He also, as opportunity offered, attended the theatre to see and hear such actors as Booth, Forrest, Macready, Barrett and the now immortal Joseph Jefferson, whose "Rip Van Winkle" he witnessed some five or six times.

He had a special liking for mechanics and would have made a good architect and builder. He had a mechanical eye and could readily detect defects in the construction of buildings or other works requiring precision. In early times, he made his own shoe lasts, a very difficult piece of work, and was an expert in the making and fashioning of the old style hickory axe-handles.

After his marriage, Judge Elliott and his wife began housekeeping in a story and a half log cabin with one room on the ground floor, which he had previously purchased, situate on the lot now occupied by the Maxim block, opposite the Court House Square in New Castle. To this cabin he added a frame, one-story building, adjoining it on the east and an office building of one room, adjoining it on the west. He lived with his family in this home until 1850, when he moved to what is known as the "Elliott homestead," at the then west end of Church Street. Here he lived during the remainder of his life.

The domestic life of Judge Elliott was a very happy one. He delighted in his home and his great love and devotion to his wife and children was beautiful to behold.

His companion, who survived him a number of years, was a faithful, loving wife and a devoted mother. Their happiness was her happiness. She was a very domestic woman and incessant in her labors. She believed in the old adage, "cleanliness is next to godliness." She was notable for her charities. She could herself bear suffering, but her sympathies and her helping hand went out freely to all who were in sorrow or distress.

BIOGRAPHICAL SKETCH OF JOSHUA HICKMAN MELLETT.

LAWYER, LEGISLATOR, JURIST.

No member of the Henry County Bar or of the Bar of Eastern Indiana stood higher in the ranks of the legal profession than the late Judge Joshua Hickman Mellett, of New Castle. The law was his life's study and his life's duty and the author of this History has heard him say frequently that he regarded the practise of his profession as more to be desired than any other position of honor, trust or responsibility. As a member of the bench and bar of Indiana, he was the peer of any who preceded or followed him. He was eager in his pursuit of legal knowledge and zealous and persistent in following his chosen path.

Joshua Hickman Mellett was born in Monongalia County, Virginia, now West Virginia, April 9, 1824. His parents were John and Mary A. (Hickman) Mellett. They came from Virginia in the Fall of 1830 and settled on a farm in Prairie Township, Henry County, in the vicinity of what is now known as the village of Springport. At that time Joshua H. Mellett was a young boy, six years of age, but already the seed of ambition had been implanted within him which grew and flourished with his growth in intellectual stature until it placed him at the head of the legal profession.

His early education was obtained in the common country schools of the pioneer. days when the mastery of reading, writing and arithmetic distinguished the individual as of superior attainments; but when he had finished those branches of education, he advanced a step higher and for a year or more attended school at the "Old Seminary," in New Castle, over which had presided, for a number of years, such teachers as John Barrett, Simon T. Powell, Isaac Kinley and Dr. John Rea. Leaving school at the age of sixteen, he commenced the study of the law with the late Colonel Edmund Johnson, then a prominent member of the Henry County bar. Young Mellett pursued his studies with the same fixedness of purpose as afterwards marked the whole course of his professional career and such was his diligence and persistency that in a very brief time he applied for admision to the bar, passed the rigid examination then required with perfect ease, and in 1844, when less than twenty years of age, received his license to practise. This was a proud moment to him, but he did not rest; rather he took another step forward and went to the then small village of Muncie, Delaware County, Indiana, where he formed a law partnership with the late Judge Joseph S. Buckles, who, like Mellett, was a young and aspiring attorney. This arrangement not proving in all respects satisfactory, the partnership was dissolved and Mr. Mellett returned to New Castle, where, in 1845, he began the practise of the law, which, barring a few years of official life, he followed with eminent success until his death, October 1, 1893. During his practise of the profession in New Castle, he had at different times as partners, each of the following named distinguished members of the Henry County bar, namely: William Grose, Jehu T. Elliott, Elijah B. Martindale (now of Indianapolis), Mark E. Forkner and Eugene H. Bundy.

Mr. Mellett never, in any sense of the word, sought political preferment. He loved his profession and during all of his active life gave to it his close and undivided attention. To the numerous pleadings of his friends that he enter the arena of politics, he always turned a deaf ear, adhering firmly and steadfastly to his dominant passion for the law. Public service at any time was at the sacrifice of his own inclinations and showed a high regard for public duty. Probably the most congenial position held by him, because in line with his profession, was the office of prosecuting attorney for the sixth judicial circuit, composed of the counties of Henry, Delaware, Fayette, Grant, Rush, Randolph, Union and Wayne, which he held from 1848 to 1852. He was the last prosecutor under the old constitution and this was the first office held by him in either the county or the district. The opportunities afforded by the position for acquiring a broader, surer and more practical knowledge of the law, caused this office to be eagerly sought by members of the profession.

To Joshua H. Mellett, as to other men of force and character, came at length the demand that he serve the political interests of the community, and in October, 1858,

the Bar of Eastern Indiana stood higher
late Judge Joshua Hickman Mellett, of
his life's duty and the author of this
regarded the practise of his profession
of honor, trust or responsibility. As a
is the peer of any who preceded or fol-
ll knowledge and zealous and persistent

onongalia County, Virginia, now West
and Mary 1. (Hickman) Mellett. They
ettled on a farm in Prairie Township,
known as the village of Springport. At
ix years of age, but already the seed of
h grew and flourished with his growth
been of the legal profession.

common country schools of the pioneer,
neighbors distinguished the individual
in the three branches of education, he
attended school at the "Old Seminary."
among its years, such teachers as John
John Be.   Leaving school at the age
with his uncle Colonel Edmund Johnson;
bar Joshua Mellett pursued his studies
as teacher the whole course of his proper to that in a very brief time he
id examination then required with per-
s of he received his license to practise.
of his father he took another step for-
ing, Delaware County, Indiana, where
as Jesse B. Buckles, who, like Mellett,
ligenent not proving in all respects sat-
Mellett returned to New Castle, where,
barring a few years of official life, he
, October 1892   During his practise
ifferent times as partners, each of the
Henry County bar, namely: William
low of Indianapolis), Mark E. Forkner

l, sought political preferment. He loved
gave to it his close and undivided at-
nds that he enter the arena of politics,
nd steadfastly to his dominant passion
the sacrifice of his own inclinations and
ly the most congenial position held by
he office of prosecuting attorney for the
s of Henry, Delaware, Fayette, Grant,
ld from 1848 to 1852. He was the last
was the first office held by him in either
fforded by the position for acquiring a
the law, caused this office to be eagerly

force and character, came at length the

at the biennial election, he was chosen to represent Henry County in the General Assembly. He served in a special session from November 20 to December 15, 1858, and in the fortieth regular session, which convened in January, 1859, a session not marked by anything out of the usual order, but Mr. Mellett took an active and conspicuous part in all of its deliberations. Following this service in the lower house of the General Assembly, he was in October, 1860, elected State Senator for the full term of four years, and served in the forty-first regular session, convened in 1861; in the special session, convened April 24, 1861; and in the forty-second regular session, convened in January, 1863. The two last named were distinctively war sessions and the proceedings of the General Assembly were full of interest and often marked by great excitement. Party feeling ran high and party lines were never so closely drawn. Mr. Mellett was an acknowledged leader of the majority in the General Assembly during these sessions. He was intensely loyal and did everything within his power to uphold the cause of the Union. He was a chief adviser of Governor Morton and was by him regarded as one of the ablest men in the State. It was to such men as Joshua H. Mellett, Jehu T. Elliott, Martin L. Bundy, John F. Kibbey, Charles H. Burchnall and others prominent in the history of Eastern Indiana that Governor Morton attributed much of his success in the conduct of affairs during the trying and perilous period of 1861-1865.

So important were Mr. Mellett's services that although tendered a commission as colonel of volunteers, by Governor Morton, it was deemed best that he decline the commission, it being evident that he could best serve the country at home. Through the whole period of the war, therefore, he devoted himself to the fostering of patriotism and to the upholding of the State and National governments in their mighty efforts to preserve the Union. Of him and of the times, another writer has well said: "His services as State Senator from 1860 to 1864 were of great value to the State and Nation. Some of his speeches in the Senate in those dark days were among the most powerful pleas made for the Union cause by any citizen of the State. There his power of invective against the wrong had its full force, and the men who plotted to add Indiana to the Southern Confederacy were never more thoroughly exposed nor made to feel that the lash of justice could sting more deeply than they were by Senator Mellett. Most of the actors in those stormy dramas preceded him to the tomb and the old bitterness has been softened by the all-compelling touch of time, but the story of his services to State and country in those trying days is a part of our war history that the people of Henry County should never forget."

In the opinion of the author, his leadership of the majority in the State Senate, during the Civil War, was high water mark in the career of Joshua H. Mellett.

After the Civil War had been brought to a close and the affairs of the country adjusted, Mr. Mellett, more absorbed than ever in the practise of law, was persuaded almost against his will, to become a candidate for judge of the seventh judicial circuit, and was elected in October, 1870, for the full term of six years. He had no opposition in Henry County. The district was composed of the counties of Henry, Delaware, Hancock and Grant. He filled the position with honor to himself, honor to the district, honor to the bar and honor to Henry County. In 1876, his term of office having expired, he absolutely declined a re-election and at once resumed the practise of the law in which he continued to the end of his life. Though he never again held office, he was more or less active in politics and was often chosen by the Republican party, of which he was a lifelong member, to represent it in county, district, State and National conventions. He was a delegate to the National convention in 1884 that nominated James G. Blaine for the presidency, and took part in the exciting campaign which followed the nomination.

Joshua H. Mellett regarded the legal profession as his life work and gave to it all the resources of his mind. He never ceased to be a student and to every case gave the most earnest and most serious consideration. He was always prepared and it was seldom, if ever, that he was "caught napping," or that he had left open any loop hole by which an adversary might gain advantage. He brought to the bench and bar not only keen intellectual ability, but that personal dignity as well which characterized the lawyers of the early days. For the legal shyster or the dishonest lawyer, Judge Mellett

had the utmost contempt—a contempt which he never tried to conceal—and in denounc-
ing such characters no words from the lips of man could be more bitter or more severe.
He despised demagoguery and looked with undisguised disgust upon those who practised such arts. He believed in honor, truth and the brotherhood of man. He did not
covet fame but valued above all things a good name. He was not a truckler to power,
but was open in all his dealings and knew no distinction between men because of their
wealth or their poverty.

Among those who knew him best, Judge Mellett was a companionable man, and
for the suffering or distress of others he had the utmost sympathy and kindness. He
was a versatile reader and gained great store of knowledge from such authors as
Dickens, Bulwer, Thackeray, Dumas and others. He could not abide tragedy, but for
comedy he had the greatest liking, feeling that it was better to laugh than to cry—better
to rejoice than to mourn. He believed in the teachings of the Bible and lived up to and
practised its precepts. He was a member of the Methodist Episcopal Church, and though
not demonstrative of his religion, was possessed of that larger faith "that links the
whole world around the feet of God with chains of love and hope."

Judge Mellett was the moving spirit in the formation and organization of "The
Henry County Historical Society," and was its first president. He took great interest
in all of its meetings, doing what he could during his life to put the society on a firm
and lasting basis.

Joshua H. Mellett and Catharine (Shroyer) Mellett were united in marriage November 16, 1847. The union was a very happy one. To them were born five children,
namely: Elizabeth Mary (Bettie), born January 1, 1849, now the wife of Judge Eugene H.
Bundy; William, born March 11, 1853, died July 3, 1853; Harry S., born October 25,
1855, died June 18, 1888; another child also named William, born in 1857 and died in
infancy; Charles, born April 14, 1859, died November 15, 1880. Harry S. and Charles
were in the flower of young manhood and their deaths were a severe affliction to their
parents. Their remains, together with those of the father and mother, lie side by side in
South Mound Cemetery, New Castle. The parents of Judge Mellett, as previously stated,
emigrated from Virginia to Henry County and settled in Northern Prairie Township in
1830. They were married May 2, 1811. The father died July 18, 1838, and the mother,
November 8, 1853. Their remains are buried in Lebanon Cemetery, two miles southeast of Springport. The first of the Melletts to emigrate from old Virginia to Henry
County after John Mellett, the father of the subject of this sketch, was his brother
Jesse. Joshua Hickman, an uncle of Judge Mellett, came also at this time (1830) and
located in the same neighborhood. John Mellett's father was also named John. He
died in Loudoun County, Virginia, in 1790. The mother's maiden name was "Suiter," and
a son of Luther Mellett, brother of Judge Mellett, was named "Suiter," after his grandmother.

In 1833 Charles Mellett, father of the late Arthur C. Mellett, the first Governor of
South Dakota, who died in Kansas but whose remains are interred at Watertown, South
Dakota, and James T. Mellett, of New Castle, Indiana, made their first visit to Henry
County in company with John, who had gone back to Virginia on a visit. Jesse Mellett
above mentioned, the eldest brother of John, accompanied by his two sons-in-law, John
Reed and Thomas Veach, and his sister, with her husband, came to the wilds of Indiana
to found new homes. Jesse entered a quarter section of land which afterwards became
known as the site of East Lebanon Church, in Prairie Township, for which he donated
the ground. Later his brothers, John and William, followed and settled two miles
further west. Arthur, another brother, the grandfather of James T. Mellett, came to
Henry County in 1835. The early settlement of the Mellett family in Prairie Township
in conjunction with the high character and reputation maintained by the family made
them a power in the township and the impress of their lives will remain to mark their
long, industrious and honorable careers in that locality. Their influence was wholly
for good in the community in which they so long abided. They left behind them a long
line of descendants, who emulate the spirit and example of their worthy ancestors.

Eugene H. Bundy and Elizabeth Mary (Bettie) Mellette, the only daughter of
Judge Joshua H. and Catharine (Shroyer) Mellett, were married July 6, 1870, the Rev-

erend Milton Mahin, of the Methodist Episcopal Church, performing the ceremony. To their union was born one child, a daughter, Nellie Catharine, born January 1, 1875. To his daughter and granddaughter Judge Mellett was most devotedly attached.

ANCESTRY OF MRS. CATHARINE (SHROYER) MELLETT.

The parents of Catharine (Shroyer) Mellett were John and Elizabeth (Kincaid) Shroyer. They were married in December, 1828, at Jefferson, Greene County, Pennyslvania, and in October, 1835, came to New Castle, Henry County, where they resided until their deaths. John Shroyer was born March 11, 1806, and died August 29, 1873. His wife died February 19, 1866. Both are buried in South Mound Cemetery. They were the parents of six children, of whom Catharine was the eldest. Of the surviving children, Mary, now the widow of the late Isaac R. Howard, resides at Richmond, Indiana; James, resides at New Castle, Henry County, and John at Richmond. Catharine (Shroyer) Mellett died Sunday morning, January 23, 1898. John Shroyer was for many years one of the prominent business men of New Castle. He was a painter and chairmaker by trade and successfully conducted that line of business for a number of years, but finally united with his brother, the late venerable Henry Shroyer, in the drygoods trade. During this partnership the firm erected the building known as the "Shroyer Corner," which was at the time of its construction (1860) one of the largest and best business houses in Eastern Indiana.

Mr. Shroyer was a quiet, unobtrusive man, very careful in business affairs, and strictly economical. He was an extremely temperate man who never drank spirituous liquors nor used tobacco in any form. He was a moral, upright man, and a good citizen, who left behind a record for honor and probity, unexcelled. His wife is remembered with great affection by those, now living, who knew her in New Castle.

BIOGRAPHICAL SKETCH OF JAMES BROWN.

DISTINGUISHED LAWYER AND PROMINENT CITIZEN.

James Brown, who was for many years a prominent attorney, practising in the courts of Henry and the adjoining counties and in the Supreme Court of the State, was a member of a remarkable family. His parents were Isaac and Mary (Mendenhall) Brown, and he was the sixth child in a family of nine, all of whom grew to be men and women of strong character and sterling worth in the various communities in which they lived, and most of them were so well known and respected in the county that it seems proper to recall their names here. They were: Tamar, born September 9, 1816, afterwards the wife of Neziah Davis; Moses, born December 12, 1819, long one of the best-known citizens of the county, and in every way a worthy and upright man; Rachel, born March 19, 1822, afterwards the wife of Dr. Isaac Mendenhall; she and her husband were long among the most influential people of New Castle, Dr. Mendenhall enjoying a large practise as a physician and surgeon; she, with her husband's assistance, was practically the founder of the Friends' meeting in New Castle, and furnished a room in their brick business and residence building, at the corner of Broad and Fourteenth Streets, for its use, where its meetings were held until the erection of the neat brick church on North Main Street. Jacob, born January 17, 1824, never married; Anna, born December 27, 1825, afterwards the wife of James Pressnall; James, born August 17, 1827, the subject of this sketch; Isaac, born July 30, 1829, a prominent farmer of Harrison Township, and for many years a justice of the peace; Samuel, born August 10, 1833, a successful farmer of Liberty Township, and a leading member of the Friends' Church on Flatrock; Thaddeus, the last child, born March 3, 1837.

The parents of this family were persons of great energy and strength of character. The father, Isaac Brown, was a native of North Carolina, where he was born March 9, 1797. He immigrated early in the last century to the neighborhood of Stillwater, Ohio, where he was married to Mary Mendenhall, a lady who was two years older than himself, sne having been born September 28, 1795. Like him, she was a person of strong native sense, rugged health, great industry and conscientious devotion to the tenets of morality and religion. Both husband and wife were possessed of those sterling qualities which were characteristic of the pioneers of the Middle West, of which steadfastness of purpose and quiet courage were prominent features.

Mary (Mendenhall) Brown, the mother of the subject of this sketch, used to relate that when she came to Henry County, Indiana, with her husband and family, in the year 1825, they settled in that part of the county which was afterwards organized into Liberty Township, in a round-log cabin with no shutter to the door, other than a blanket or quilt to keep out the rain and cold. Her husband was often kept away from home, either all night or until a late hour in the night, especially when he went to the mill at Milton, Wayne County, for meal or flour for the family use. At home with her five children, the oldest being but nine years of age, the wolves howling about the cabin and even snapping and snarling upon its roof, she often found it necessary to barricade the door with their meagre furniture and guard the safety of her little ones until morning came or her weary husband returned from his hard journey through the woods.

Isaac Brown had learned the blacksmith's trade in his old home and soon opened a shop in the Henry County wilderness, where he also made coffins in which to bury the dead, and wagons to do the settlers' hauling. He was a master of the blacksmith trade, as it was then followed, and it was said of him that he could weld a wagon tire so perfectly that the weld could not be detected. His education, like that of the majority of his day, was very limited, but he knew how to keep accounts and possessed a native acumen and business foresight which caused him to value correctly the opportunities about him for acquiring ownership of the new lands in his neighborhood. His blacksmithing business furnished him largely with the means to carry out his ideas; but he was also a successful farmer and knew the best methods of making money from the new fields, and in addition to his home farm, now known as the Pleasant M. Koons farm, he became the owner of many tracts of land in his part of the county, some of which he afterwards sold, but the greater part of them was divided among his children.

many years a prominent attorney, practising in the
counties and in the Supreme Court of the State, was
y. His parents were Isaac and Mary (Mendenhall)
d in a family of nine, all of whom grew to be men
l sterling worth. in the various communities in which
e so well known and respected in the county that it
s here. They were: Tamar. born September 9, 1816,
vis; Moses, born December 12. 1819, long one of the
and in every way a worthy and upright man; Rachel,
e wife of Dr. Isaac Mendenhall; she and her husband
lial people of New Castle, Dr. Mendenhall enjoying
nd surgeon; she, with her husband's assistance, was
iends' meeting in New Castle, and furnished a room
ne building. at the corner of Broad and Fourteenth
sings were held until the erection of the neat brick
on. born January 17, 1824, never married; Anna, born
w..fe of James Pressnall; James, born August 17, 1827,
born July 30, 1829, a prominent farmer of Harrison
justice of the peace; Samuel, born August 10, 1833, a
ship, and a leading member of the Friends' Church on
8. born March 3, 1837.

ere persons of great energy and strength of character.
we are of North Carolina, where he was born March
the last century to the neighborhood of Stillwater,
by Vanderson, a lady who was two years older than
a house on a 1825. Like him, she was a person of
great industry and conscientious devotion to the
res. Our hero and wife were possessed of those sterling
the pioneers of the Middle West, of which stead-
s as prominent features.

the subject of this sketch, used to relate
to live with her husband and family, in the
woods which was afterwards organized into
a shelter to the door, other than a blanket
band was often kept away from home,
more especially when he went to the mill
to do the family use. At home with her five
she heard the wolves howling about the cabin
and she was found it necessary to barricade
the window ensure the safety of her little ones until
her husband from his journey through the woods.
He was settled a home and soon opened
farm. He made the coffins in which to bury
the dead. He was master of the blacksmith
every one of them, and he could weld a wagon tire
with the best. His occupation, like that of the majority
the time to keep accounts and possessed a native
ability and keen sense to choose correctly the opportunities
of trade which abounds in his neighborhood. His blacksmith work gave him the means to carry out his ideas; but he
knew the best methods of making money from the
land which was known as the Pleasant M. Koons farm,
one of the best in this part of the county, some of which
part of it has was divided among his children.

James Browns

Isaac Brown and his wife were members of the Society of Friends, or Quakers, and zealous believers in its doctrines of peace and good will, and were among the founders of the Flatrock Meeting of Friends and the Flatrock School, where his children, in. cluding James Brown, were educated. He was a great friend to education and gave freely both to his church and to the support of the school. He often said: "I can't preach, but I know how to make money, and it is my duty to give to those who can preach and teach;" and he did give freely, as attested by many instances of his kind. ness to the ministers of his society, who were mostly poor men and women, who traveled and preached for conscience sake.

A number of young men learned the blacksmith's trade with him in his little, old country shop, who later became prominent in the affairs of the county, as so many of the early blacksmiths did. Among them were John K. Millikan and his own son, James Brown.

JAMES BROWN.

James Brown, the son of Isaac and Mary (Mendenhall) Brown, was born August 17, 1827. Though his father was liberal in the matter of primary education, it is not likely that he gave much thought to the higher education of the colleges and academies, at least none of his children seem to have enjoyed the advantages of such schools. Thus the school days of James Brown were confined to the Flatrock School, which, as a neighborhood school, was superior to the majority of those surrounding it.

As already stated, each child of Isaac Brown received a farm as a start in life. James Brown, however, cherished other aspirations and the longing for the career of a lawyer had grown so strong by the time he had reached the age of twenty two years that he sold his land back to his father, took off his leather apron, threw down his sledge, and came to New Castle, where he entered the law office of William Grose and Joshua H. Mellett, and began to read law. He devoted himself so closely to his studies that, at the end of two years, he was admitted to the bar and soon afterwards became the law partner of William Grose, the firm of Grose and Mellett having been dissolved. The partnership of Grose and Brown continued, with a large and increasing practise, until Mr. Brown was elected district attorney, in 1855, when it was dissolved.

He filled the district attorneyship with ability and after retiring from that office formed a partnership with Robert L. Polk. The firm of Brown and Polk continued with marked success from 1863 to 1872, when the junior partner was elected judge of the Court of Common Pleas of Henry County. Mr. Brown then took into partnership his nephew, Joseph M. Brown, who had been practising for some time, after completing his studies in his uncle's office; and the firm name became J. and J. M. Brown, or, in brief, Brown and Brown. In 1876, Joseph M. Brown was elected prosecuting attorney and James Brown continued the business alone for a few years. He then took his son, William A. Brown, into partnership and this firm continued under the old name of Brown and Brown until the death of James Brown, when the business fell to and is still maintained by the son.

During the last thirty years of James Brown's career as a lawyer he controlled a large and lucrative business, appearing on one side or the other of almost every important action in the circuit court, and also doing a large business in the Superior, Appellate and Supreme courts of the State, and in the United States District and Circuit courts. He was an advocate of singular persistence in behalf of his clients. Once thoroughly interested in behalf of a client, he clung to his cause and fought it out, inch by inch, as long as he could see a reasonable hope of success, often winning his point in the court of last resort. He made no pretenses to oratory and never built upon the chance of carrying a jury away by some impassioned appeal not justified by the logic of the case as disclosed by the evidence. If the evidence was bad for his client's cause, he either assailed it and the witness who gave it, with denunciation and ridicule, or sought to render it nugatory by a logical analysis of the whole evidence given, which seemed to render the unfavorable testimony so highly improbable as to destroy its weight. He was a fighter before a jury and contested every movement that even remotely hinted of danger to his client. It was this quality of armed watchfulness and steadfastness to his clients that made him a successful advocate whose services were always in demand.

Among those who read law under Mr. Brown may be mentioned his former partner, Robert L. Polk; two nephews, Joseph M. and Samuel Hadley Brown, sons of his oldest brother, Moses Brown; George L. Koons, John C. Denny, William O. Barnard, John C. Billheimer, Edwin E. Parker, Adolph Rogers, Charles S. Hernly, William A. Brown, his son, and many others.

James Brown was married to Elizabeth Alice Carpenter, a daughter of William Carpenter, of Wayne County, Indiana, in 1852. She seems to have been admirably fitted to be the life companion of a studious, aspiring man like Mr. Brown, and with her he lived happily all the remainder of his life. Mrs. Brown did not long survive her husband. She died at the beautiful home of the family on East Broad Street, New Castle, Indiana, August 9, 1897, five months and seventeen days after the death of her husband.

James and Elizabeth Alice (Carpenter) Brown were the parents of three children, namely: Mary A. Brown, who married William H. Albright, a gallant Union soldier of Company F, 84th Indiana Infantry, who, after the conclusion of peace, was a photographer in New Castle, with whom she lived happily until his death, March 14, 1905, and whom she survives; William Asbury Brown, the only son; and Fannie A. Brown, now Mrs. Percy W. Liveston, of Indianapolis, Indiana, who for some time held a responsible position with her father's firm, and was his amanuensis and typewriter up to the time of his demise.

James Brown was greatly attached to his home, which he had established at the northeast corner of Broad and Nineteenth streets, in New Castle, where he erected a commodious house and filled the large yard with trees, improving it, year after year, until it had become one of the prettiest and most desirable homes in the little city, fully justifying his affection for and pride in it, and there his children were reared in the midst of pleasant and happy surroundings.

In 1867 the old frame house which he owned east of the northeast corner of Main and Broad streets, New Castle, in which his office was situated, burned down, throwing him out of an office; but his father urged him to rebuild and offered him the necessary assistance, so that joining with his brother-in-law, Dr. Isaac Mendenhall, the twain erected the two-story brick building, known as the Brown and Mendenhall Block, upon the second floor of which the Brown and Brown law office has been so long maintained. James Brown, like his father, pinned his financial faith to real estate and acquired two good farms, one a mile west of New Castle, known as the Slatter farm, and another two miles south of New Castle, both of which he improved and still owned at the time of his death.

In politics he was in early life an old-time Whig, but always opposed the institution of slavery and its encroachments upon free territory, hence he naturally fell into the Republican party, upon its first organization, and engaged actively in the propagation of its views, upon the stump and otherwise. During the war for the preservation of the Union, he was an active supporter of the government and so continued after the war, supporting the reconstruction measures, including the constitutional amendments. In the early 'seventies, however, he became at variance with his party and its measures, and though never as active in politics thereafter as before, he gave his support to the Democracy during the remainder of his life.

In religion he was more a believer in the religion of life and character than of creed, and was never active in church membership, though endorsing the high morality and uplifting power of the law of love taught by the New Testament.

The death of Mr. Brown came without warning on February 22, 1897. He and his daughter, Fannie A., were at the residence of his son, William A. Brown, across Broad Street from their home, where he was dictating a brief to her, which she was typewriting rapidly, when suddenly the dictation ceased and the daughter looked up questioningly only to meet the silent stare of her dead father. His heart had ceased to act and thus, without warning and without pain, had the busy lawyer passed on from the activities and cares of life.

The funeral was held at the family home on February 24, 1897, and was very largely attended by members of the bar from Henry and adjoining counties. On the day of the funeral a largely attended meeting of the bar was held in the court room at New Castle, which was presided over by David W. Chambers. Speeches were made, appreciative of the life, character and professional career of Mr. Brown, by Martin L. Bundy, of New Castle; Charles G. Offutt and Ephraim Marsh, of Greenfield; Benjamin F. Mason, of Wayne County; Eugene H. Bundy, Mark E. Forkner, David W. Chambers, James T. Mellett, Horace L. Burr, Leander P. Mitchell, and Charles N. Mikels, of the Henry County bar, and Messrs. Offutt, Marsh, Mason, Eugene H. Bundy, Chambers, and Judge George L. Koons, of the Delaware Circuit Court, were selected as pall bearers. The funeral was conducted by the Reverend H. J. Norris, of the Methodist Episcopal Church, and the interment was at South Mound Cemetery.

At the meeting of the bar, an appropriate memorial, reported and read by Adolph Rogers, was adopted by a rising vote of all persons present, which, after speaking of the high abilities of the deceased, declared that "his fame as a lawyer is secure," and added its endorsement of his life as a citizen, his interest in public affairs, his patriotism and spoke of his interest in and love for the writings of the best authors, in which "he often surprised his hearers by apt quotations; and while he made no pretense to oratory, he was logical and convincing before a jury, being possessed of certain peculiarities of manner and thought which made his personality a marked one." It closed with the following tribute to his personal character:

"But it was in his home life that he appeared at his best. His tenderness and love for his wife and children and grandchildren were deep and abiding. No sacrifice was too great for him to make for them. To see them happy was the object of his life. The deep, parental pride which he felt in the success of his son and partner in the law was a marked and touching trait in his character. In return his family lavished upon him their purest affections. His life work is done. He achieved success, as the world notes success. He had reached the topmost round in his profession and had won success in its broadest sense, in that he had led a just and upright life, and after life's arduous labors, he rests in peace."

The New Castle Weekly Courier of February 25, 1897, said of Mr. Brown: "Possessed of a wonderfully analytic legal mind, he was a skillful and competent lawyer and his opinions were much sought after by others of his profession, and his death will be a great loss to those who sought his counsel and to the bar of Eastern Indiana."

A contributor to the New Castle Courier, in its issue of March 14, 1897, spoke of Mr. Brown's knowledge of literature and noted especially his love for the poetry of George Crabbe, an English poet, now much neglected, and said that while he had the same love of liberty and the same aversion to slavery as John G. Whittier, yet he did not care for that poet's ringing and impassioned verse. Had that contributor known that Robert Burns was also a favorite of Mr. Brown's, he might have been confused to account for his love for two poets of such opposite qualities as Crabbe and Burns, while rejecting a poet like Whittier, whose genius was so near akin to that of Burns. But here again was one of those peculiarities of Mr. Brown's tastes and habits of thought which tended to make him conspicuous among men.

The same contributor said further:

"It would surprise many to know the extent of Mr. Brown's reading and researches in religious matters and his thoughtful and careful consideration of the historical evidences of Christianity. Few men seemed to be more at home in the discussion of such matters than he, yet he did not intrude his knowledge of and peculiar views concerning them upon unwilling ears."

Speaking of his want of scholastic training and wondering what he might have attained to had his educational opportunities been better, the same writer added this conclusion:

"But no college training, no favoring condition could have made a Franklin, a Cromwell, an Abraham Lincoln, or a Hugh Miller: neither could it have made the country lawyer, James Brown, who, by dint of his individuality and indomitable perseverance, wrote his name high upon the roster of professional success."

WILLIAM ASBURY BROWN.

(*Son.*)

William Asbury Brown, the only son of James and Elizabeth Alice (Carpenter) Brown, who was born at New Castle, Indiana, March 13, 1854, has himself won a fine success at the bar and in politics. He was his father's efficient partner during the later years of his legal career, and succeeds the old firm of Brown and Brown and retains its large practise. In 1887 and again in 1889, he was elected a member of the lower house of the General Assembly of Indiana and served both terms with credit to the county and with distinction to himself. He is now in possession of a large and lucrative legal practise in the Circuit and higher courts.

His wife is a beautiful and accomplished lady who commands the friendship and respect of the entire community. She is a daughter of William Ribble, of Delaware County, Indiana. Mr. and Mrs. William A. Brown are the parents of an interesting family of children, two sons and two daughters. The eldest son, Paul, is now engaged in his father's office and seems likely to uphold the reputation of the family in its chosen field of the law. The younger son bears the name of his grandfather, James. The two daughters are named respectively Ruth and Winifred.

Mark E. Forkner

BIOGRAPHICAL SKETCH OF MARK E. FORKNER.

LAWYER, LEGISLATOR AND JUDGE.

The Forkner family, according to tradition, are of Welsh descent, but just when this family emigrated to America is not definitely known. It is certain, however, that William Forkner, the great-grandfather of Mark E. Forkner, settled at a very early period in North Carolina and was of some prominence in the affairs of that State. Isaac Forkner, the grandfather, moved from Surrey County, North Carolina, about 1812, to Grayson County, Virginia, where the family abided for several years and where Micajah Forkner, father of Mark E., was born in 1814. In 1819 Isaac Forkner moved from Virginia to Indiana, settling near Centreville, in Wayne County. In 1822 he once more moved, this time to Henry County, Indiana, settling in Liberty Township on a farm now owned and occupied by Frank Phelman, one mile south of the present site of Millville. He was a soldier of the War of 1812-15 and for his service in that conflict received a government land warrant.

Jesse Forkner, uncle of Mark E., came to Henry County at the same time as his father, Isaac, and located on what was afterwards known as the John B. Crull farm, in Liberty Township. The lands entered by him are described as follows: east half, southwest quarter, section twenty-four, entered November 12, 1821; and the west half, southwest quarter, section 24, entered December 10, 1827; the whole comprising one hundred and sixty acres. Jesse Forkner was collector for Henry County in 1827 and was sheriff of the county for two terms, August 14, 1829, to August 19, 1831, and from August 19, 1831, to August 5, 1833: During his official career as sheriff he was very persistent in collecting fines assessed against non-combatants for refusal to perform militia service and thereby incurred the displeasure of the Friends or Quakers, who were conscientiously opposed to bearing arms and who would rather lose their all than to engage in conflict with their own or their country's enemies. A great change in such matters has taken place among the Friends since those days. During the Civil War, the government had no warmer supporters than the Quakers and most of the peculiarities that distinguished them in those early times have been discarded by the Friends of the present day.

Micajah Forkner, the father of the subject of this sketch, was twice married, first, in 1835, to Elizabeth Allen, who died in 1849. His second wife was Margaret A. Jordan, to whom he was married in 1852. The children by the first wife were: Granville H., now a resident of Auburn, Indiana; William B., now a resident of Hartford City, Indiana; Thomas Benton, deceased; Mary A., widow of the late Samuel Winings, who now resides in New Castle; John Larue, commonly called "Jack," of Anderson, Indiana; Mark E., the subject of this sketch; and one child, Allen, who died in infancy. Granville H. Forkner has resided for a number of years at Auburn and was at one time the postmaster of the place. William B., of Hartford City, was elected and served one term as treasurer of Blackford County, and John Larue (Jack) has had honors thrust upon him by the city of Anderson and the people of Madison County. He is now the very popular mayor of that city and his name has been mentioned as one that might head the Democratic ticket for Governor of the State. Thomas B., prior to his death, was a young practising physician and had before him a promising future. Of the four living brothers, it should be noted as a rather remarkable fact that two, Granville H. and Mark E., are Republicans, while the other two, William B. and John Larue, are Democrats, and to this should be added the further unusual circumstance that all four held official positions in their several communities. at nearly the same time.

The children of Micajah Forkner by his second wife were: Elizabeth Caroline, now Mrs. John Thornburgh, of Hagerstown, Indiana; Belle, now Mrs. Lue Hoover, of Indianapolis; Morna, now Mrs. Hiram Eshelman, of Greenfield. Indiana; Charles, of Hagerstown, Indiana; and two boys, Lawrence and Burk, both of whom died in early childhood. Lawrence was an unusually bright and interesting child and his death was a source of great sorrow to his parents. The grandfather, the father and the children, who are deceased, are buried in the Chicago Cemetery, about two miles southeast of Millville, on Symons Creek; the mother is buried in Salem Baptist Church Cemetery, on Martindale Creek, in Wayne County.

MARK E. FORKNER.

Mark E. Forkner was born in Liberty Township, Henry County, Indiana, January 26, 1846. His childhood days were like those of the average country boy. He was a stout and sturdy youth, endowed with good, common sense and possessed of a natural ambition which gradually shaper the course of his life. His education was begun in the country or district schools and was completed by attendance for three years at the then well known New Castle Academy. While attending the last named school, he was also engaged in reading law in the office of Joshua H. Mellett, and to secure the means to complete his education, he also, for about three months of each year, taught school, first, at the Stout schoolhouse, east of New Castle; then at the schoolhouse at that time located a little north of the present town of Mooreland; and lastly, at Greensboro, in 1866, where he was associated with Joseph W. Worl, now of Oklahoma Territory.

Under his able and distinguished preceptor, he prosecuted the study of the law with such characteristic zeal and energy that he was admitted to the bar in 1866 and entered at once upon a professional career. By close application to his profession, he steadily advanced in the esteem of his brother lawyers and of the people of the community, until he now stands in the front rank, not only of the bar of Henry County, but of the bar of Central and Eastern Indiana as well.

In the Winter of 1866-7, he was appointed deputy district attorney for the county of Henry, and in the Spring of 1867, he formed a partnership with his former preceptor, Joshua H. Mellett, and this association continued until 1870, when the latter was elected judge of the Thirteenth Judicial Circuit, which comprised the counties of Henry, Delaware, Grant and Hancock. This partnership had been very agreeable to both of the partners and especially profitable to Mr. Forkner, bringing him not only financial gain, but also a greatly widened experience in practical affairs.

Soon after the dissolution of his partnership with Mr. Mellett, by reason of the latter's elevation to the bench, Mr. Forkner and Eugene H. Bundy associated themselves together in the practise of the law. Born in the same year and destined to similar public careers, this period of their lives may well be considered one of happy augury to each. Pitting themselves against the veterans of the profession, they conducted a practise of constantly increasing size and importance and established their standing and reputation as able lawyers and skillful practitioners. Besides this, each had gained that invaluable knowledge of men and of affairs which has so well illustrated their later careers. This partnership was destined to be dissolved after six years of the most agreeable relations. In 1876, upon the retirement of Judge Joshua H. Mellett from the bench, Mr. Bundy withdrew from the firm to enter partnership with Mellett, and Mr. Forkner continued the practise alone until he was appointed judge, as noted below.

Mark E. Forkner has always been a Republican in politics and from his first entry into public affairs has taken a more or less active part in political campaigns, local, State and National. In 1874 he was elected by the Republicans of Henry County as a member of the lower house of the General Assembly of Indiana, forty eighth session, serving one term. He took part in all of the deliberations of that body and discharged his duties with fidelity to his constituents and with credit to himself. He also served in a special session, March 9 to March 14, 1875. Now he, who by his own unaided efforts had achieved an enviable position in his profession and stood well in the councils of his party, was ready for higher honors. When Robert Lindsey Polk died, May 7, 1881, and the office of judge of the Eighteenth Judicial Circuit, composed of Henry and Hancock counties, thereby became vacant, Mr. Forkner, on May 11th following, was appointed by Governor Albert G. Porter to fill the vacancy, and at the ensuing election, in the Fall of 1882, he was chosen for the full term of six years. This high and honorable position he filled with signal ability and to the entire satisfaction of the people whom he so ably and impartially served. The fact has already been pointed out elsewhere in this History that the citizens of Henry County, who have been raised to the bench, have uniformly,

since the organization of the county, maintained a standard of excellence in their positions, second to the judiciary of no other county of the State, and it is with commendable
pride that the names of Jehu T. Elliott, Josnua H. Mellett, Robert Lindsey Polk, Mark
E. Forkner, Eugene H. Bundy, William O. Barnard and the present judge of the Henry
Circuit Court, John M. Morris, are mentioned.

Upon his retirement from the bench, Judge Forkner, still young in years, resumed
the practise of the law and from that time his career as a lawyer and advocate has been
one of great activity. His practise extends to all parts of Central and Eastern Indiana.
He also has an extensive practise before the United States Circuit and District Courts
at Indianapolis. He now has, as a partner in his business, his son, George D. Forkner,
of whom mention is again made at another point in this sketch.

Judge Forkner is a quick thinker and a fast talker, when on his feet. He is a powerful speaker and his talents are not confined to legal arguments nor to appeals to court
and jury. So well informed and happily trained in his mind that he illumines any
subject which may be presented for his consideration.

On June 22, 1869, Mark E. Forkner married Rebecca Donahoo, at the residence of
Stephen and Caroline (Donahoo) Elliott, two miles south of New Castle, the ceremony
being performed by the Reverend Milton Mahin. This was a union of two happily dis-
positioned people and the whole course of their married life has been marked by mutual
love, regard and esteem. The door of their home is always open and within its portals
their friends are given cordial welcome and from their table is dispensed the old fashioned hospitality of our forefathers which is now seldom known.

Judge and Mrs. Forkner are the parents of two children, namely: George Donahoo,
born March 28, 1876, and Caroline, born October 14, 1879. These two children are both
graduates of the High School, New Castle, and of the Indiana State University, Bloomington. They are thoroughly educated and accomplished young people, gracious in manner, delightful entertainers and general favorites. The son, George Donahoo, during his
attendance at the Indiana State University, pursued not only the regular college course,
but at the same time studied law in the law department of the university. After his
graduation from college, he returned to his home and finished his law studies in the
office of his father. He was admitted to the bar in October, 1899, and is now the junior
member of the law firm of Forkner and Forkner. Like his father at his age, he has tne
world before him in which to lose or conquer. Elsewhere in this History will be found
a full biographical sketch of John L. Forkner, wherein further reference is made to
the Forkner family.

ANCESTRY OF REBECCA (DONAHOO) FORKNER.

The parents of Mrs. Mark E. (Donahoo) Forkner were Jeremiah and Caroline.
(Parkinson) Donahoo. They came to Indiana from Licking County, Ohio, and settled
north of Anderson, Madison County, but later moved to that city, where they lived the
remainder of their lives. To them were born three children, namely: Rebecca, now the
wife of Mark E. Forkner, the subject of this sketch; Almeda, now the wife of Nathan
Nicholson, a retired farmer, living in New Castle; and Martha, now the wife of Jacob
Lowe, a well known and prosperous farmer, living north of New Castle.

On December 6, 1859, after the death of her first husband, Mrs. Caroline (Parkinson) Donahoo was united in marriage with the late Stephen Elliott, a Henry County
pioneer, residing two miles south of New Castle. They had one child, Mary, now the wife
of William C. Bond, manufacturer of handles, New Castle, Indiana. Mrs. Elliott died
November 22, 1885, and Mr. Elliott died December 4, 1896. The former is buried in South
Mound Cemetery and the latter in the Elliott Cemetery.

BIOGRAPHICAL SKETCH OF EUGENE HALLECK BUNDY.

LAWYER, LEGISLATOR AND JUDGE.

Eugene Halleck Bundy is a native Hoosier, having been born at New Castle, Indiana, October 10, 1846. His father, Judge Martin L. Bundy, was one of the earliest pioneers of Eastern Indiana and is the oldest living member of the Henry County bar. Of him it can be said that no man, other than himself, has done so much to preserve the history of Henry County. He is possessed of a marvelous memory and recalls without effort events of long ago with perfect accuracy as to names and dates. He wields a ready pen and has furnished the community, which his long and honorable life has so signally honored, with an invaluable fund of information relating to the early affairs of the county, civil and political, which would otherwise be irretrievably lost. For nearly ninety years or almost a century has he gone in and out before this people and has left the impress of his vigorous personality upon their minds and hearts. In honoring him, posterity honors itself.

Amanda (Elliott) Bundy, the mother of Eugene Halleck Bundy, was a daughter of Abraham Elliott, who was admitted to the bar at the first term of the Henry Circuit Court in 1823; in 1825 he was appointed a master in chancery; he was a member of the board of justices from 1825 to 1827, and associate judge, from 1843 to 1849. She was a sister of the late Jehu T. Elliott, who was for many years a judge of the Henry Circuit Court and of the Supreme Court of the State of Indiana.

Eugene Halleck Bundy early became a student. His primary education was obtained in the common and academic schools of New Castle and in September, 1864, he entered Miami University, Oxford, Ohio, where he spent two years. He then went to Union College, Schenectady, New York, where he entered the Sophomore class and remained for a year. He then returned to Miami University, where he completed the regular classical course and graduated in June, 1869.

After graduation, young Bundy returned to his home in New Castle and began the study of the law in the office of his father, which was then in the rear room of the First National Bank, of which the latter was president. He was a diligent student and made such rapid progress in his studies that he was admitted to the bar in 1870, and then began a practise which has grown from day to day, and from year to year. His natural capacity, his eagerness to learn things and his laudable ambition to excel, coupled with the friendly rivalry of boyhood companions, so many of whom had, like himself, entered the arena of the law, caused him to strive with unabated energy for the honors of his profession, until he now stands in the first rank.

In his boyhood he had shown a decided bent toward political life and at the age of fifteen years he was appointed a page in the House of Representatives of the General Assembly of Indiana, by Cyrus M. Allen, of Vincennes, then Speaker of the House. This was in 1861, when the General Assembly (forty first and special sessions) was known and is now historically referred to as the "War Legislature." Great events were coming; civil war was casting its mighty shadow athwart the country; the Union of our fathers was threatened; the rope that bound the Commonwealths together was like to prove a rope of sand; on either side was heard the fife's shrill note and the drum's loud alarm calling the people to arms. It was amid such forboding scenes that young Bundy gained his first experience in governmental affairs and their lasting impression upon his mind has been demonstrated in many ways. It was at this time he came in contact with the then president elect, Abraham Lincoln, who was making his famous journey to Washington City for inauguration. His first stop was at Indianapolis, where he was tendered a reception, which was held in the parlor of the old Bates House, which stood on the southeast corner of Illinois and Washington streets, where the Claypool Hotel now stands. A part of the ceremony was to consist of the presentation of the members of the General Assembly to the president elect and for that purpose they formed in line, headed by John R. Cravens, of Jefferson County, President of the Senate, and Cyrus M. Allen, of Knox County, Speaker of the House. It was the privilege of this young page to stand at the head of the line and, as each member advanced, to announce his name to Mr. Lincoln.

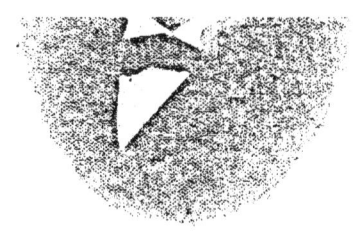

having been born at New Castle, In-
... L. Bundy, was one of the earliest
... member of the Henry County bar.
...self, has done so much to preserve the
marvelous memory and recalls without
... as to names and dates. He wields a
... his long and honorable life has so
... rmation relating to the early affairs of
... rwise be irretrievably lost. For nearly
... and out before this people and has left
ir minds and hearts. In honoring him,

... gene Hallorg Bundy, was a daughter of
at the first term of the Henry Circuit
... in chancery; he was a member of the
... lodge from 1843 to 1849. She was a
... a judge of the Henry Circuit
...

... His private education was ob-
... New Castle and in September, 1864, he
... spent one year. He then went to
... enter the Sophomore class and re-
... University where he completed the
1869.

his home to New Castle and began the
... was then in the rear room of the
... ident. He was a diligent student and
... was admitted to the bar in 1870, and
... to day, and from year to year. His
... his laudable ambition to excel, coupled
... so many of whom had, like himself,
... with unabated energy for the honors
...

... toward political life and at the age of
... of Representatives of the General As-
... then Speaker of the House. This
... and special sessions) was known
... Legislature." Great events were com-
... the country; the Union of our
... Commonwealths together was like to
... shrill note and the drum's loud
... spreading scenes that young Bundy
... and their lasting impression upon
... war at this time he came in contact
... was making his famous journey to
... Indianapolis, where he was ten-
... Bates House, which stood on
... where the Claypool Hotel now
... presentation of the members of the
... purpose they formed in line, headed
... of the Senate, and Cyrus M. Allen,
... privilege of this young page to
... advanced, to announce his name to

In 1861 Martin L. Bundy was appointed and commissioned, by President Lincoln, Major and Paymaster, United States Volunteers, and in the latter part of 1862, Eugene H. became one of his father's clerks and remained with him until September, 1864, when he entered Miami University. During most of their service, they were stationed at Indianapolis, Cincinnati, Chicago and Detroit. These two years of army service were strenuous in character and were important in that they gave the subject of this sketch a business training and education of great importance to him in after life.

Eugene Halleck Bundy and Elizabeth Mary (Bettie) Mellett, only daughter of Judge Joshua H. and Catharine (Shroyer) Mellett, were united in marriage, at the home of the bride's parents in New Castle, Indiana, July 6, 1870, the ceremony being performed by the Reverend Milton Mahin. They are the parents of one child, a daughter, Nellie Catharine, a very charming and accomplished young lady, who gracefully adorns the home and delightfully entertains her many friends.

Not long after his admission to the bar Mr. Bundy entered into a partnership with Mark E. Forkner, under the firm name of Forkner and Bundy. They had a large and lucrative practise for a period of six years, when the firm was dissolved and Mr. Bundy became a partner with his father-in-law, Judge Mellett, who had just retired from the bench. The partnership of Mellett and Bundy continued for thirteen years and was regarded as one of the strongest legal firms in Eastern Indiana.

In the Fall of 1880, Eugene H. Bundy was elected State Senator for the district composed of the counties of Henry, Delaware and Randolph. He served in the fifty first regular and special sessions of 1881 and in the fifty second regular session of 1883. He was an active member of the Senate and took a prominent part in its deliberations, establishing for himself a name which later warranted his nomination for Lieutenant Governor of the State by the Republican State convention in 1884. The candidate for Governor was William H. Calkins, of Laporte. The ticket was defeated, but that result in no wise lessened the estimation in which Mr. Bundy was held by the people. He had made a complete campaign throughout the State and was everywhere recognized as a powerful advocate of the principles of the Republican party.

In 1887 when the State was erecting additional hospitals for the insane at Richmond, Logansport and Evansville, Governor Isaac P. Gray appointed Eugene H. Bundy, a member of the board of commissioners, to which the construction of the buildings was intrusted. He held this responsible position until the completion of the hospital. He was appointed a member of this commission in the place of General William Grose, who had resigned because of his election to the State Senate.

The General Assembly, by an act approved February 22, 1889, having erected Henry County into a separate judicial circuit, designated as the fifty third, Governor Alvin P. Hovey, under authority of the act, appointed Eugene H. Bundy judge of the circuit, to hold until the next general election in November, 1890.. When the election was held, he was chosen to succeed himself and served for the full term of six years. Judge Eugene H. Bundy's career on the bench was entirely satisfactory to the people of the county, and it is unquestioned that he fully maintained the high reputation of the Henry Circuit Court as established by his honorable predecessors.

The life of Judge Bundy, from the time of his first public service while still a boy in his "teens" until the present, has been one of continuous activity. He retired with honor from the bench and at once resumed the practise of the law in partnership with Judge John M. Morris. This association continued until the latter in 1896 was elected judge of the Henry Circuit Court to succeed Judge William O. Barnard. Since that time Judge Bundy has continued to practise his profession alone.

During the term of years that Charles S. Hernly, of Henry County, was Chairman of the Republican State Central Committee, Judge Bundy was a member and chairman of the Executive Committee of that organization and contributed greatly to the success of the party in the campaigns of 1898 and 1900. He has always been a Republican in politics, not merely a voter of the party ticket, but an active and aggressive worker. In all campaigns, local, State and National, except during his incumbency of the bench when he upheld the best traditions of the judiciary by refraining from politics. he has been a conspicuous figure in the councils of his party. As an orator he ranks high and is a forcible campaign speaker who is always eagerly sought for. He is a close observer of political conditions and possesses the ability to clearly expound his well grounded opinions touching matters of importance to the State and Nation.

He has been an active member of the Henry County Historical Society since its organization and is now one of the three trustees of that important institution which has for its main object the preservation of the historical materials of the county. He is also a member of the Knights of Pythias, Crescens Lodge, Number 33; of the Improved Order of Red Men, Iroquois Tribe, Number 97; and of the Benevolent Protective Order of Elks, New Castle Lodge, Number 484. He is not a member of any church, but is closely identified by birth and association with the Methodist Episcopal denomination.

Judge Bundy has grown in years, yet he is, comparatively speaking, not an old man. He is physically sound and mentally well balanced and the future, no doubt, has in store for him many years of usefulness as well as preferment and honors. He is noted for his genial disposition, his fine social qualities and the enduring nature of his friendships. As a young man, he started under the best auspices and throughout his career has made the very best of his opportunities. His whole life has been a success. He enjoys the distinction of having been one of his father's successors on the bench of Henry County, the only case of the kind in the county and one of the very few in the State. It is true, however, that when his uncle, Jehu T. Elliott, was presiding judge of the Henry Circuit Court, his father, the grandfather of Judge Bundy, Abraham Elliott, was associate judge of the county and sat on the bench with his son who was the presiding judge. Judge Bundy is also one of the successors on the bench of his father-in-law, Joshua H. Mellett, who was a judge of the Henry Circuit Court.

In chapter nine of volume one of this History is published a full biographical sketch of Judge Martin L. Bundy and his family, which should be read in connection with this sketch of his son for details of the family not mentioned here. Reference should also be made to the biographical sketch of his father-in-law, Judge Joshua H. Mellett, published in this volume.

William O. Barnard

re not at that time Quakers but became so
e fact of their early removal and settlement
it removal of the family to North Carolina,
ers clearly points, however, to Quaker con-
h Carolina has not been kept and the next
ramily relate to the emigration from North
is the chain of ancestry. The religious and
at of African slavery caused him to move
in Union County, three miles east of

Matilda Gardner in North Carolina about
He died in March, 1858, and his wife
at Poplar Ridge, near Everton, Fay-
the parents of the following named chil-
aged seventy two years, and is buried
Richmond, Indiana, in 1880, and is buried
Mrs. Eli Stanton, now deceased; Mary
buried at her home in Kansas; Isaac,
and is buried at his home in Iowa;
there; Barzillai, who married and reared
at Rushville, Indiana; Margaret, after-
ceased and buried at her home near Oska-
Trusler, sister of Colonel Nelson and
buried at Connersville, Indiana; Melinda,
is now past eighty two years of age;
ried Maria Piper, near Connersville, Indiana,
father of the subject of this sketch.

BARNARD.

child, but the superstition as to that number
fails, as he has been singularly fortunate
ce of the Black Art, however, may have a
virtues of the number "seven," he being the
in Union County, Indiana, on his father's
log cabin of the period. On April 10, 1850,

BIOGRAPHICAL SKETCH OF WILLIAM OSCAR BARNARD.

SCHOOL TEACHER, LAWYER AND JUDGE.

The Barnard family is a notable one and traces its origin back to colonial days in America. The family is of English origin but genealogical information regarding the family in the mother country is lacking. The lineal representatives of seven genera. tions of this family in America, given in their order, are as follows: Thomas, Nathaniel, Ebenezer, William, Tristram, William, and Sylvester, father of William Oscar Barnard, the subject of this sketch. Thomas, Nathaniel, Ebenezer and the first William were all residents of the Island of Nantucket, famous in the annals of the early colonists and which figures prominently in later American History, and where even to this day still survive many of the quaint customs and peculiar forms of government of the seven. teenth century which have become obsolete elsewhere. Thomas Barnard was a soldier in the Colonial Army and was killed by the Indians during King Philip's War, in 1675.

The first white settler of Nantucket was Thomas Macy, whose descendants became connected with the Gardner and Barnard families by intermarriage. The Barnards and Macys first settled on the mainland in the Plantation of Plymouth, but they are said to have been Quakers, who came under the ban of the Puritans,. owing to the religious intolerance of the times, and were driven for safety to take refuge on the Island. As Thomas Barnard rendered military service and lost his life in the Indian Wars, it is possible that the Barnard family at least were not at that time Quakers but became so afterwards. However obscure the reasons, the fact of their early removal and settlement on Nantucket is indisputable. The subsequent removal of the family to North Carolina, where there was a large settlement of Quakers clearly points, however, to Quaker connections. The date of their removal to North Carolina has not been kept and the next known fact regarding the movements of this family relate to the emigration from North Carolina of the second William, named above in the chain of ancestry. The religious and political dislike of the Quakers to the institution of African slavery caused him to move his family in 1818 to Indiana, where they settled in Union County, three miles east of Liberty, the county seat of the county.

The last named William Barnard married Matilda Gardner in North Carolina about the year 1805, but the exact date is not obtainable. He died in March, 1858, and his wife in July, 1845, and both are buried in the cemetery at Poplar Ridge, near Everton, Fayette County, Indiana. This pioneer couple were the parents of the following named children: Lydia G., who died at Spiceland, Indiana, aged seventy two years, and is buried in the Spiceland Cemetery; Paul, who died at Richmond, Indiana, in 1880, and is buried there in Earlham Cemetery; Eunice, afterwards Mrs. Eli Stanton, now deceased; Mary B., afterwards Mrs. Shubal Swain, now deceased and buried at her home in Kansas; Isaac, who married Alvira Swain, died in August, 1880, and is buried at his home in Iowa; Phoebe, who died at Poplar Ridge and is buried there; Barzillai, who married and reared a large family, died and is buried in the cemetery at Rushville, Indiana; Margaret, afterwards Mrs. Richard D. Taylor, who is now deceased and buried at her home near Oskaloosa, Iowa; William D., who married Mary Jane Trusler, sister of Colonel Nelson and Milton Trusler, died in February, 1881, and is buried at Connersville, Indiana; Melinda, who lives at Spiceland, on Academy Avenue, and is now past eighty two years of age; Anderson, who died young; Byron, who married Maria Piper, near Connersville, Indiana, now lives at Halstead, Kansas; and Sylvester, father of the subject of this sketch.

SYLVESTER BARNARD.

Sylvester Barnard was the thirteenth child, but the superstition as to that number being unlucky, in his case at least, completely fails, as he has been singularly fortunate and has lived a very successful life. Devotees of the Black Art, however, may have a ready explanation of this in the mysterious virtues of the number "seven," he being the seventh son. He was born March 31, 1828, in Union County, Indiana, on his father's farm, three miles east of Liberty, in a typical log cabin of the period. On April 10, 1850, he was married, at the home of the bride in Fayette County, nine miles southeast of Connersville, to Lavina Myer, daughter of Jacob and Sarah Myer. Jacob Myer came from Pennsylvania and his wife from Virginia and settled in Union County, near Boston, Wayne County. They were known as Pennsylvania Dutch, an appellation not used derisively but to distinguish a class of people, very many of whom came early to Indiana and by their efforts and those of their descendants have helped to bring the Hoosierland to its present state of prosperity.

Sylvester and Lavina (Myer) Barnard are the parents of the following named children: Edna Ann, who married John Meckel, an architect of Anderson, Indiana, but is now deceased; William Oscar, the subject of this sketch; Isaac Myer, who is a farmer in Rush County, near Knightstown, Henry County; Jacob Newton, who was formerly a teacher and then a dry goods merchant, but is now a banker at Daleville, Delaware County, Indiana; Lawrence Carlton, formerly a school teacher but now connected with one of the large department stores at Muncie, Indiana; and Pliny Colfax, a popular practising physician at Oakville, Delaware County, about ten miles north of New Castle.

Mr. and Mrs. John Meckel became the parents of four children: Frank, Grace, Nellie, deceased, and Maud. The family of Mr. and Mrs. William O. Barnard are treated of fully below; Mr. and Mrs. Isaac M. Barnard, are the parents of Carl W., Helen, and Joseph S.; Mr. and Mrs. Lawrence C. Barnard are the parents of Elliott and Boyd T.; and Mr. and Mrs. Pliny C. Barnard are the parents of one child; Harry L. Of these grandchildren of Sylvester Barnard and wife, two, Frank and Grace Meckel, are married. Frank and his wife are the parents of two children, Edna and Orion; and Grace, and her husband, John Bernard, are the parents of two children, Paul and Ruth.

Sylvester Barnard, for the greater part of his life, has been a farmer. His boyhood was spent amid the difficulties and dangers of pioneer surroundings. He has always been an industrious man and is now enjoying the fruits of a well spent life at his beautiful home in Middletown, Henry County, Indiana. Throughout their married life, Mrs. Barnard has been a sympathetic and helpful companion. In politics he was first a Whig, but when that organization ceased to exist, he became a firm adherent of the Republican party. He has belonged to the Independent Order of Odd Fellows for forty five years, and is now a member of Olive Branch Lodge, Number 89, Dublin, Indiana. He was initiated into the mysteries of the order and conducted through the ceremonies by Milton Trusler, of Everton Lodge, Number 139, Fayette County, Indiana. Mr. and Mrs. Barnard were Quakers until their removal to Middletown in 1892, but as there was no church of that denomination at that place, they took membership in the Methodist Episcopal Church, of which they are consistent and faithful members. They are devoted to their children and their descendants; have many warm friendships; are free givers to charitable objects; and strive in all ways to do the will of Him whom to rightfully serve brings joy and peace everlasting.

Following the advent of the Barnard family into Union County, Indiana, where they resided for a number of years, they removed to the adjoining county of Fayette, where in March, 1858, William, the father of Sylvester, died. He was an influential member of the Society of Friends or Quakers and during his life took an active personal interest in all matters relating to the management of the church and its affairs.

The relationshhip by intermarriage of the Barnard, Gardner and Macy families has already been casually mentioned. Matilda Gardner, the mother of Sylvester Barnard, was the daughter of Isaac and Eunice (Macy) Gardner, who were consequently his grandparents. The line of descent in the Gardner family runs thus. Richard, first, Richard, second, Solomon, Stephen, Isaac, husband of Eunice Macy, Matilda, mother of Sylvester Barnard. The line of descent in the Macy family runs thus: Thomas Macy, the first, who was the first white settler of Nantucket Island, John, Thomas, second, Joseph, Paul, Eunice, who married Isaac Gardner. Sylvester Barnard is consequently a descendant on the maternal side of the first settler of Nantucket.

Tristram, the grandfather of Sylvester and the great grandfather of William O. Barnard, married Margaret Folger, daughter of Latham Folger, and thus relationship by intermarriage is established between the Barnard and Folger families. The line of descent of the Folger family begins with Peter Folger, who was the first Clerk of Nantucket, and runs thus: Peter, John, Jonathan, Latham, Margaret (wife of Tristram Barnard).

WILLIAM OSCAR BARNARD.

William Oscar Barnard, son of Sylvester and Lavina (Myer) Barnard, was born near Liberty, Union County, Indiana, October 25, 1852, but when he was two years of age, his parents moved to Dublin, Wayne County, Indiana. The family remained for a couple of years at that quiet place in Western Wayne County, which preceding the Civil War was noted as one of the stations on the underground railroad where negroes, fleeing from slavery, stopped for safety on their way to Canada. The family left Dublin in 1856 and moved to Fayette County, where they settled on a farm not far from Connersville. It was there that William O. Barnard passed the greater part of his boyhood, performing his share of the duties pertaining to life in the country. The modern conveniences, which make the life of the farmer one of comparative ease, did not prevail when the embryo judge was trudging along behind the single plow or with measured step was dropping the corn, sowing the wheat and swinging the scythe.

In 1866 he came with his parents to Henry County, Indiana, settling in Liberty Township, where he grew to manhood. His education up to this time was such as the average country boy secures, but after coming to Henry County, he entered as a student at the well known Spiceland Academy, where he had the good fortune to come under the guidance of that foremost of teachers, the late Clarkson Davis, whose fine character and remarkable ability as an educator have made a lasting impression upon the community. His students will never cease to honor and cherish his memory as well as that of his noble wife, Hannah Davis.

After leaving school, William O. Barnard became an educator himself. He taught in several of the district schools of the county and was for a year principal of the school at Economy, Wayne County, Indiana; also for a term or more, he taught in the public schools at New Castle.

He was now somewhat past the age of manhood and was confronted with the ever present question, "What shall I do in the world?" He was strongly inclined toward the legal profession and in 1876 commenced to read law with the late James Brown, of New Castle. He was admitted to the Henry County bar in 1877 and at once began the practise, being at first associated, for a short time, as partner with Captain David W. Chambers.

Now fairly launched on the busy sea of professional life, William O. Barnard slowly but surely advanced along the way to success. The discouragements of his profession he brushed aside, its difficulties he overcame, until today he has the uniform regard and esteem of his friends and neighbors and the confidence of the whole bar, and enjoys a well earned reputation as a judge and jurist. While practising his profession, he was for two years the treasurer of the Corporation of New Castle. He afterwards served a term of six years, from 1887 to 1893, as prosecuting attorney, a part of this time for the eighteenth judicial circuit, which comprised the counties of Henry and Hancock, and later for the fifty third judicial circuit, which comprised the county of Henry alone. The fact may have been elsewhere mentioned, but it will bear repetition that the office of prosecuting attorney has in many instances proved the stepping stone to judicial honors, and this was so in the case of Mr. Barnard, who was elected judge of the fifty third judicial circuit and was commissioned for six years from November 17, 1896. At the time of his election, he was forty four years of age and it is a notable circumstance that since the time when Robert L. Polk sat on the bench, the judges of the Henry Circuit Court have been comparatively young men. Judge Polk was but thirty five years of age when he assumed the duties of the office in 1876. He was followed by Judge Mark E. Forkner, in 1881, at the age of thirty-five; Judge Eugene H. Bundy, in 1889, at the age of forty three; Judge William O. Barnard, in 1896, at the age already stated; and the present judge, John M. Morris, at the age of forty five.

Among a law abiding people the position of judge is always an exalted one. In the stately language of Bishop Hooker, "of the law no less can be acknowledged than that her seat is the bosom of God," and unquestionably the judicial position demands of its occupant the loftiest regard for truth, inflexible honesty and unimpeachable integrity. The true judge is an interpreter and administrator of the law, who ignores all earthly ties of kinship and affection, in the discharge of his duties, and who inflicts the just penalties of the law without fear, favor or hope of reward; and it may be said of the judiciary of Henry County that its members, one and all, have been men of such high ideals; and of Judge Barnard, in particular, that during his term upon the bench, he upheld its best traditions and administered the law with the same abiding sense of responsibility as his predecessors.

William Oscar Barnard was united in marriage with Mary V., daughter of Nathan H. and Margaret (Hubbard) Ballenger, December 22, 1876. To them have been born four children, namely: Paul, who occupies a responsible position with the Chicago, Cincinnati and Louisville railroad, which is a part of the Cincinnati, Hamilton and Dayton system, and resides at Peru, Indiana; George Murphey, who is a practising attorney at New Castle; Ralph Waldo, who is in charge of a branch office of the Western Union Telegraph Company, at Indianapolis; and Ruth, a bright and intelligent young lady who is a general favorite among her companions and who lives at home with her parents.

ANCESTRY OF MRS. WILLIAM O. (BALLENGER) BARNARD.

Mary V., daughter of Nathan Hunt and Margaret (Hubbard) Ballenger, was born in Wayne Township, Henry County, Indiana, September 8, 1850, and lived with her parents on a farm, two miles north of Knightstown, until 1863, when the family moved to Spiceland to secure better educational advantages for the children. There she was educated under the direction and care of that splendid scholar and most excellent of men, Clarkson Davis, and graduated from the Spiceland Academy in 1871. She then followed the profession of teaching for a number of years, principally as a grammar and high school teacher. Among the schools in which she taught may be noted the Spiceland Academy, from which she had graduated, the Wabash and Evansville high schools, and the New Castle Grammar School. She was an excellent teacher and imparted learning to a very large number of scholars, who to day hold her in the highest regard. She was married to William O. Barnard, at New Castle, Indiana, December 22, 1876, and that place has ever since been her home.

Mrs. Barnard, on her father's side, is descended from the Ballengers and Hunts of North Carolina, sturdy Quaker families of that State. The Ballengers emigrated from Wales and the Hunts from Scotland at an early period. On her mother's side, she is descended from the Hubbards, a Virginia family, which, according to tradition, is descended from Pocahontas. Her mother was a sister of the well known Charles S. Hubbard, of Raysville, whose whole life has been one of untiring activity in the cause of his fellow men. He has been, during all of his busy life, a member of, and for a number of years, a minister in the Society of Friends. Jeremiah Hubbard, the great grandfather of Mrs. Barnard, was a renowned Quaker preacher. Her maternal grandmother was a daughter of Dr. George Swain, of North Carolina, a man who was prominent in his day and whose ancestors were among the first settlers of Nantucket Island. Mrs. Barnard is a Friend in religious belief, inheriting her religious views from a long and distinguished line of Quaker ancestors. A complete biographical sketch of her father, Nathan Hunt Ballenger, and his family appears elsewhere in this History, to which reference should be made for further information with regard to her family.

GEORGE MURPHEY BARNARD.

(Son).

George Murphey Barnard, second son of Judge William O. and Mary V. (Ballenger) Barnard, was born in New Castle, Henry County, Indiana, June 6, 1881. There he grew to manhood and was educated in the public schools. He graduated from the New Castle High School in May, 1899, and September 21, 1900, he entered the law department of the University of Michigan, at Ann Arbor, in that State, and graduated from that institution, June 21, 1903. Returning from the university to New. Castle, he there entered upon the practise of the law. He was soon afterwards appointed by the Board of Commissioners of Henry County as attorney for the poor and is still filling the position. On July 30, 1904, he received the special nomination for prosecuting attorney of the fifty third circuit, and was elected at the regular Presidential election in the November following. He enters upon the duties of the office January 1, 1906. He is the youngest and the only unmarried man ever nominated and elected to this responsible office in Henry County. His life up to the present time has been one largely of preparation, but in the light of the past it would seem that the future has much of encouragement and promise in store for him. He is one of the successors of his father in the office of prosecuting attorney, which is the only instance in the county of father and son holding that office.

BIOGRAPHICAL SKETCH OF JOHN MONTFORT MORRIS.

LAWYER, LEGISLATOR, JUDGE.

There came to Wayne Township, Henry County, Indiana, in 1833, Lewis Morris, the head of the family of that name, who settled on a piece of land containing fifty six acres, which he entered, situated between what are now known as the villages of Grant City and Elizabeth City. Lewis Morris was a native of Pennsylvania and his wife, Rebecca Hoskins, was a native of Virginia. After their marriage in the latter State, in 1812, they moved to Belmont County, Ohio, where they lived until 1833, when they came to Indiana, as above stated. During their residence in Ohio, they became the parents of seven children, namely: Alpheus, Nancy, Julia Ann, Isaac H., Lewis, Susannah Rachel and John, and after their removal to Indiana, two more children were born, Joshua and Rebecca.

In 1833 there were but few settlements on the road cut through the forest between Knightstown and their home in the wilderness, and Knightstown was only a straggling village. When the family left Ohio and came to Indiana, they were not possessed of much of this world's goods but they had health and strength and an earnestness of purpose which enabled them to subdue all obstacles. They were three weeks, with a two-horse team and wagon, making the journey from Ohio to their Indiana destination. They were in the midst of what seemed to be an interminable forest which the foot of white man had thus far scarcely trod. Their first and probably most important undertaking was to cut out a cleared space whereon to build a log cabin; and next to clear away the forest and prepare the ground for cultivation. In this respect the experience of Lewis Morris and his family was in no wise different from that of hundreds of others, "who came, who saw and who conquered." The pioneers toiled from early morn to late eve; they bore with Spartan fortitude the privations and sufferings of the backwoods; but with it all, the great majority of them saw the forests disappear and the lands wet with the sweat of their brows, blossom and bloom as the rose.

It was amid such primitive conditions that the family of Lewis and Rebecca (Hoskins) Morris grew up and from which they each went forth to his or her own destiny. William, a brother of Lewis Morris, joined the family after the removal of the former to Indiana. Lewis Morris died March 14, 1858, aged sixty eight years, ten months and twenty one days; his wife, Rebecca Morris, died May 16, 1866, aged eighty years and two months. They are buried in the Old Cemetery adjoining Glencove Cemetery, Knightstown. Of the children, three were married in Ohio prior to coming to Indiana, namely: Alpheus to Rebecca Minor; Nancy to Stephen Green; and Julia Ann to Joseph Williams. The rest of the children were married in Indiana.

JOHN MORRIS.

John Morris, the seventh child and the fourth son of Lewis and Rebecca (Hoskins) Morris, was born in Belmont County, Ohio, April 18, 1824, and came with his parents to Henry County, Indiana, as above stated. At this time he was about nine years old and like all farmer boys of that early period, he worked manfully in assisting to clear the forest, destroy the wilderness and prepare the ground for cultivation. While thus laboring, he obtained a limited education in the old fashioned and oft described log cabin school house. His first teacher, according to his own recollection, was Joseph Williams, who had married Mr. Morris' sister, Julia Ann, in Ohio, and immigrated to Indiana with the Morris' family. All in all, John Morris lived the life of the real pioneer, the one who cut the first timber, helped to build the first log cabin, planted and garnered the first crop, endured all the hardships, shared all the joys, partook thankfully of the plain fare and gave praise to Him who guides and controls the destiny of all mankind.

At the age of manhood, following the custom of the period, when both men and women believed in early marriages, John Morris was united in matrimony with Hannah, a daughter of Elisha and Hannah Scovell, January 16, 1845. Elisha Scovell, born April 13, 1796, was one of the early settlers of Wayne Township, his home being situated about

BIOGRAPHICAL SKETCH OF JOHN MONTFORT MORRIS.

LAWYER, LEGISLATOR, JUDGE.

There came to Wayne Township, Henry County, Indiana, in 1833, Lewis Morris, the head of the family of that name, who settled on a piece of land containing fifty six acres, which he entered, situated between what are now known as the villages of Grant City and Blountsville City. Lewis Morris was a native of Pennsylvania and his wife, Rebecca Hoskins, was a native of Virginia. After their marriage in the latter State, in 1812, they moved to Belmont County, Ohio, where they lived until 1833, when they came to Indiana, as above stated. During their residence in Ohio, they became the parents of seven children, namely: Alpheus, Nancy, John Ann, Isaac H., Lewis, Susannah Rachel and John, and after their removal to Indiana, two more children were born, Joshua and Rebecca.

In 1833 there were but few settlements on the road cut through the forest between Knightstown and their home in the wilderness, and Knightstown was only a straggling village. When the family left Ohio and came to Indiana, they were not possessed of much of this world's goods but they had health and strength and an earnestness of purpose which enabled them to subdue all obstacles. They were three weeks, with a two-horse team and wagon, making the journey from Ohio to their Indiana destination. They were in the midst of what seemed to be an interminable forest which the foot of white man had thus far scarcely trod. Their first and probably most important undertaking was that but a cleared space whereon to build a log cabin; and next to clear away the forest and prepare the ground for cultivation. In this respect the experience of Lewis Morris and his family was in no wise different from that of hundreds of others, "who came who saw and who conquered." The pioneers toiled from early morn to late eve; they bore with Spartan fortitude the privations and sufferings of the backwoods; but with it all, the great majority of them saw the forests disappear and the lands wet with the sweat of their brows, blossom and bloom as the rose.

It was amid such primitive conditions that the family of Lewis and Rebecca (Hoskins) Morris grew up and from which they each went forth to his or her own destiny. William, a brother of Lewis Morris, joined the family after the removal of the former to Indiana. Lewis Morris died March 14, 1868, aged sixty eight years, ten months and twenty one days; his wife, Rebecca Morris died May 16, 1866, aged eighty years and two months. They are buried in the Old Cemetery adjoining Glencove Cemetery, Knights-town. Of the children, three were married in Ohio prior to coming to Indiana, namely: Alpheus to Rebecca Minor; Nancy to Stephen Hines and Julia Ann to Joseph Williams. The rest of the children were married in Indiana.

JOHN MORRIS

John Morris, the seventh child and the fourth son of Lewis and Rebecca (Hoskins) Morris, was born in Belmont County, Ohio, April 16, 1820, and came with his parents to Henry County, Indiana, as above stated. At this time he was about nine years old and like all young men of that early period, he worked manfully in assisting to clear the forest, develop the wilderness and prepare the ground for cultivation. While thus laboring, he gained a limited education in the old fashioned and oft described log cabin school house. His first teacher, according to his own recollection, was Joseph Williams, who had married Mr. Morris' sister, Julia Ann, and who had immigrated to Indiana with the Morris family. All in all, John Morris lived the life of a real pioneer, the one who cut the first timber, helped to build the first log cabin, planted and garnered the first crop, endured all the hardships, shared all the joys, but was thankfully of the plain fare and gave praise to God who guides and controls the destiny of all mankind.

At the age of manhood, following the custom of the period, when both men and women believed in early marriages, John Morris was united in matrimony with Hannah, a daughter of Elisha and Hannah Scovell, January 16, 1845. Elisha Scovell, born April 13, 1796, was one of the early settlers of Wayne Township, his home being situated about

John M. Morris

two miles north of Knightstown. There he lived until near the time of his death which occurred in Knightstown about 1862. There were several of the Scovell brothers, one of whom, Ezra, also of Wayne Township, born December 19, 1798, and died March 2, 1873, left a large estate which, under the administration of John Morris, increased in value from $44,000 to $120,000. The ancestor of the Scovells was Orr Scovell, who was an early settler in Henry County. He was a Revolutionary soldier, who served in a New Jersey or Connecticut regiment. He was the great grandfather of Judge John M. Morris, now of the Henry Circuit Court. At the time of his death, he was living on what is now known as the Graham farm, near the "Old Stone Quarry Mill," in Spiceland Township. The Morris and Scovell families were justly regarded as lively, energetic and successful business men and have left their impress upon the generations following, as is plainly discernable to those who have followed the careers of their descendants.

After their marriage, John Morris and wife commenced housekeeping in a little cabin on his father's farm, where they lived for about two years. He prospered and bought land of his own and continued to add to his holdings, from time to time, until he was the possessor of a considerable estate. After his father's death, in 1858, he acquired the several interests of the heirs in the old homestead and improved his property until in 1874 he was the owner of two hundred and twelve acres of highly improved land, located where the family first settled in 1833. In 1874 he moved to his present beautiful home, which is situated about one mile north of and in plain view of Knightstown, and is surrounded by fifty five acres of splendid farm land, highly cultivated, which he had purchased in 1866. It is on this latter place with its beautiful surroundings that John Morris, now past eighty one years of age, is enjoying to the full the sunset of life. It is here that he delights to meet his numerous descendants, his neighbors and his friends, and it is from there that he expects to go some time to that "better land" and receive the reward promised those who have "kept the faith."

Politically, Mr. Morris, when he became of age, allied himself with the Democratic party. He cast his first vote for Lewis Cass and his last vote as a Democrat for the "Little Giant," Stephen A. Douglas. Since that time he has as a rule acted with the Republican party. In religion he adheres to the tenets of the Presbyterian Church and he is one of the ruling elders in the presbytery at Knightstown, and is ever faithful in the discharge of his church duties. He was, during the Civil War, a warm and active supporter of the Government and did all he could as a citizen of the Republic to restore the authority of the nation in the seceded States. He is a charitable man and many there be, who in the hour of need have been relieved by his helping hand. His estimable wife, the proud mother of his children, after a happy wedded life of more than thirty two years, died May 31, 1877, and is buried in Glencove Cemetery, near Knightstown.

To John and Hannah (Scovell) Morris were born the following children: Joshua Irving, born March 28, 1847, who resides in New Castle; Ann Elizabeth, born December 17, 1848, now the widow of Dayton L. Heritage, to whom she was married January 3, 1893, who lives with and keeps house for her father; Alpheus Orlando, born January 9, 1851; Elisha Pierce, born May 25, 1853, died November 20, 1883, and is buried in Glencove Cemetery; Josephine, born April 16, 1855, died August 26, 1898, and is buried in Glencove Cemetery; John Monfort, born April 22, 1857; Stephen Douglas, born January 5, 1861; Lew Wallace, born November 26, 1862, died October 15, 1863, and is buried in the Old Cemetery adjoining Glencove Cemetery; Rosa Belle, born February 26, 1866, died February 21, 1898, and is buried in Glencove Cemetery

JOHN MONFORT MORRIS.

The young man, who starts out in life with the firm determination to win name and fame and who steadily and resolutely follows the path laid out for himself, has at the beginning won half of the battle. Such a course is akin to that of Ulysses S. Grant, who said on a memorable occasion during the Civil War: "I will fight it out on this line, if it takes all Summer." It was this determination, this high resolve, which actuated John Monfort Morris, the principal subject of this sketch.

John Monfort Morris was born on his father's farm in Wayne Township, Henry County, Indiana, where he remained until he was about seventeen years of age. During his early life he attended the country schools at Grant City and Elizabeth City, neighboring villages, and also the public schools at Knightstown for about two months during each of the years 1872, 1873 and 1874. After reaching the age of seventeen, he also clerked for a year or two in a general store owned by his father and brother, Alpheus O., in Knightstown. Early in 1876, young Morris went to Chicago, Illinois, where he attended for a short time the Bryant and Stratton Commercial Business College, after which April 19, 1876, he came to New Castle and entered at once upon the study of the law, having for his preceptors, the well known legal firm of Forkner and Bundy. He pursued his studies with unsurpassed diligence and at the end of two years, April 22, 1878, the twenty first anniversary of his birth, he was admitted to the Henry County bar, Robert Lindsey Polk at that time being the presiding judge of the circuit court. At that time the leading members of the bar were Martin L. Bundy, William Grose, Joshua H. Mellett, Thomas B. Redding, James Brown, David W. Chambers, Eugene H. Bundy, Mark E. Forkner, Joseph M. Brown, James T. Mellett, William H. Elliott and Leander P. Mitchell.

Mr. Morris at once opened an office in New Castle in the room now occupied by Judge Eugene H. Bundy, in the Elliott Block, immediately north of the courthouse. He was not overburdened with business at the start of his professional career, but he was always at his office and exhibited such tenacity of purpose that he gradually but surely obtained the recognition of his legal ability and attainments for which he had so earnestly striven. The author of this History well remembers the advent of young Morris into New Castle and it was his pleasure to meet him often and to extend an encouraging word which is of so much value to young men.

The first official position held by Mr. Morris was as a member of the Board of Town Trustees of New Castle, he having been chosen by said board to succeed Thomas B. Loer, who died May 11, 1885. He was afterwards elected to succeed himself and was for a period of two years president of the board. At the Fall election of 1890, Mr. Morris was elected to the lower house of the General Assembly of Indiana and sat in the fifty sixth session, which convened in January, 1891. In the same session sat Jefferson H. Claypool, joint representative from the counties of Fayette and Henry, and William Grose, joint senator from Fayette and Henry counties. Mason J. Niblack, Democrat, was speaker of the House, the Republicans being in the minority. Mr. Morris was a member of the Judiciary Committee and of the Committee on Drains and Drainage, and did all that he could for the interests of his constituency and the State.

From the time of his admission to the bar, Mr. Morris had steadily followed the practise of the law and had established a large clientage. In 1896 he formed a partnership with his former preceptor, Judge Eugene H. Bundy, who had just retired from the bench, and under the firm name of Bundy and Morris, they were recognized as one of the leading law firms of Henry County and Eastern Indiana. This partnership continued in perfect harmony and with distinguished success until Mr. Morris was elected in 1902, for the full term of six years, Judge of the Henry Circuit Court, which alone comprises the Fifty Third Judicial District, and the firm of Bundy and Morris was then dissolved. Judge Morris is now filling the honorable position of Judge with credit to himself and to the satisfaction of the people of the county. In accordance with a proper and praiseworthy ambition, Judge John Monfort Morris has thus achieved a reputation hardly surpassed in Henry County.

Prior to coming of age and ever since, Judge Morris has been an active Republican, and in every campaign until he became a judge of the court, has given of his time and energy in support of the policies and principles of that great political organization. While thus a Republican, Judge Morris has at no time forgotten the amenities due to opposing parties, but willingly accords them the right to their honest opinions touching local, State and National affairs.

As a lawyer with full understanding of his responsibilities, Judge Morris has filled many offices of trust, especially those relating to the adjustment and settlement of estates, in which matters his efforts have given uniform satisfaction. He was one of the organizers of the Central Trust and Savings Company, of New Castle, holding several shares of its stock, and he is now the vice president of that thriving institution and the chairman of its finance committee. He is now and has been for some years vice president of the Citizens' State Bank, New Castle. He is also interested in the New Castle Light, Heat and Power Company as well as other corporations, and has always taken a lively interest in all that pertains to the growth and advancement of the town of New Castle and the County of Henry. Not the least of Judge Morris' duties are those connected with the management of several farms, which comprise in all about seven hundred and fifty acres, in which he has large interests and to which he necessarily gives a great deal of attention. Judge Morris is a member of the Knights of Pythias; of the Improved Order of Red Men; of the Benevolent Protective Order of Elks, and of the Presbyterian Church.

On January 15, 1879, John Monfort Morris and Cora L. Heritage, daughter and only child of Dayton L. and Susan (Lively) Heritage, were married at the home of her parents, Knightstown, Indiana, the ceremony being performed by the Reverend W. A. Hutchinson, pastor of the Presbyterian Church, of that place. This event was attended by more than one hundred invited guests, many of them from New Castle and other points throughout the State. The twenty sixth anniversary of this wedding was duly celebrated January 15, 1905, by Judge and Mrs. Morris, at which were present as many of the guests at their marriage as could be called together for the occasion. Shortly after their marriage, Mr. and Mrs. Morris began housekeeping in their new home erected by Mr. Morris on South Fourteenth Street, New Castle, where they lived happily until their recent removal to their new residence, one of the finest in Eastern Indiana, on South Main Street. To their union have been born four children, namely: Jay Dayton, died in infancy; Bessie Joye, born February 15, 1883, married to Lennard H. Mitchell, June 23, 1904; John Heritage, born January 29, 1892; and Susan Leone, born January 11, 1900.

ANCESTRY OF MRS. CORA L. (HERITAGE) MORRIS.

Dayton L. Heritage, father of Mrs. Morris, was born at Miamisburg, Ohio, September 13, 1836, and died at his home in Knightstown, Indiana, July 19, 1901. While a boy, he came from Miamisburg, with his parents, to Cambridge City, Wayne County, Indiana, where his father, Joseph Heritage, embarked in a small way in the grocery business. He clerked for his father a while and later entered the employ of H. M. Conklin and Company, of the same place, dealers in hardware. He remained with them for several years and acquired that business acumen which distinguished him in later years. During his early career in Cambridge City, he attended the public schools of that place and acquired an education fully commensurate with the school facilities of that period.

On Thanksgiving Day, 1858, he married Susan Lively, daughter of George and Susan Lively, well known and highly respected citizens of near New Lisbon, Henry County, Indiana. Mr. Heritage and his wife remained at Cambridge City a few years after their marriage and then in 1866 moved to Knightstown, where he continued to reside until his death. Susan (Lively) Heritage, his wife, died January 7, 1891. Both are interred in Glencove Cemetery.

Dayton L. Heritage, after his removal to Knightstown, became one of its most prominent business men and at the time of his death was regarded as one of Henry County's wealthy men. He was a shrewd business man, economical and saving. His will bearing date November 30, 1900, and witnessed by Mark M. Morris and George D. Forkner, disposed of his property, having made provision for his surviving widow, as follows: "To my sister, Mary A. Lackey, I bequeath $500; to my granddaughter, Bessie Joye Morris, $10,000; to my grandson, John Heritage Morris, $10,000; to my grand-daughter, Susan Leone Morris, $10,000; to my son-in-law, John M. Morris, $1,000, and to my daughter, Cora (Heritage) Morris, all of the rest, residue and remainder of my estate, both real and personal." Mrs. Cora (Heritage) Morris was constituted the sole executrix of her father's estate, with full authority to sell real estate, without the order of the court.

Susan (Lively) Heritage, the first wife of Dayton L. Heritage and the mother of his only child, was born in Lancaster County, Pennsylvania, September 30, 1835, and when but two years old came with her parents to Springfield, Ohio; thence, a few years later, they moved to Henry County, Indiana, settling on a farm near New Lisbon. There she grew to young womanhood under the loving care of her parents and was thus prepared to assume the responsibilities of life. She was a noble, Christian woman, devoted to her family and especially kind to her many friends and neighbors. It is worthy of mention that Mrs. John M. Morris, as a memorial to her father and mother, presented to the Presbyterian Church of New Castle the fine, handsome pipe organ now in use in that church, which was Dedicated Thanksgiving Night, 1901, the eminent organist, Professor Charles T. Hanson, of Indianapolis, officiating. The church in a fitting manner expressed its full appreciation of Mrs. Morris' generosity.

BROTHERS OF JOHN M. MORRIS.

Of the brothers of Judge John M. Morris, the eldest, Joshua Irving, remained at the parental home until he reached his eighteenth year when he became a clerk in a store at Ladoga, Indiana, where he remained until the Fall of 1865. In March, 1869, he formed a partnership with his father in the grocery business at Knightstown. In 1874 Joshua I. entered business in Indianapolis and was succeeded in the partnership by his brother, Alpheus O., the style of the firm being "John Morris and Son." This partnership continued until 1877, when Alpheus O. went to Rushville, Indiana, to engage in the same business at that point and was succeeded in the firm by Joshua I., who had in the meantime returned from Indianapolis to Knightstown and engaged in the dry goods business. At this time the father, John Morris, also retired from the firm in favor of his son, Elisha P., and the style of the firm was changed to "Morris Brothers." The two brothers continued in partnership until January 1, 1883, when Joshua I. sold his interest to his brother, Elisha P., and in June, 1883, moved to New Castle. Elisha P. continued the business alone until his death, November 20, 1883. In the meantime, at the November election, 1882, Joshua I. Morris was elected Auditor of Henry County, the duties of which position he assumed November 1, 1883, serving the full term of four years so acceptably that he was re-elected for another term. On November 18, 1868, he was married to Kate, daughter of John and Agnes Slack, natives of Ohio. To them were born two children: Leone, who married Robert H. McIntyre, but has since died and is buried in Glencove Cemetery, Knightstown; and Blanche, who resides with her parents in New Castle. Mr. and Mrs. Morris and their surviving daughter are members of the Presbyterian Church. Mr. Morris is a member of the several Masonic Orders, Blue Lodge, Royal Arch Chapter, Knights Templar, and is also a Thirty Second Degree or Scottish Rite Mason. He is an active Republican, a good neighbor and a good citizen.

Alpheus Orlando Morris, at one time a partner in the above mentioned firm of John Morris and Son, but who had withdrawn from the firm and started in business at Rushville, returned to Knightstown from that place in 1879 and there again entered the grocery business on his own account and has continued in the same line down to the present time. From a small beginning, the business has so expanded that his annual sales now amount to nearly $150,000. He was married January 30, 1878, to Augusta Virginia Welborn, daughter of Peter C. and Eliza (Scott) Welborn, of the well known family of that name in southwestern Henry County.

Stephen Douglas Morris, the seventh child and fifth son, has emulated his brother, John M. Having reached his majority, he left the farm where with his brothers and sisters he had labored from boyhood to manhood, and went to Indianapolis, where he entered the law office of the well known firm of Harrison (President Benjamin Harrison), Hines and Miller. He applied himself zealously to the study of his profession from July, 1882, to August, 1883, when on account of ill health, he went to Knoxville, Tennessee, where he practised his profession from September, 1883, to September, 1885, after which he returned to Indiana and located at Rushville in October, 1885, where he has since continued in the practise of the law. In October, 1892, he was married to Pamela A., daughter of Mr. and Mrs. Jesse J. Spann, the former a State Senator from Rush County. At the general election in November, 1898, Mr. Morris was elected Judge of the Eighth Judicial Circuit, composed of the counties of Rush and Decatur, which was afterwards in

1899 changed to the Sixteenth Judicial Circuit, embracing the counties of Rush and Shelby. He served the full term of six years during which he fulfilled intelligently and impartially the duties of this honorable position. It is a remarkable coincidence that these two brothers, John M. and Stephen D. Mòrris, should at the same time have served as judges of the Circuit Court in adjoining districts. They are only separated politically, John M. being a Republican, while Stephen D. is an equally earnest Democrat.

From the preceding sketch of Judge John Monfort Morris and his immediate branch of the family, it will be noted that they have been in many respects important factors in the affairs of Henry County. The dead of the family are remembered for their probity of character and for public and private duties well performed, while the living, judging the future by the past, will undoubtedly continue to advance in honor and usefulness, adding to their well earned reputations and meriting and receiving from a just and confiding public that meed of praise due to honest worth.

CHAPTER XLVI.

BANKS AND BANKING—NEWSPAPERS, PAST AND PRESENT—STATISTICAL INFORMA-
TION—HENRY COUNTY HISTORICAL SOCIETY.

BANKS AND BANKING IN HENRY COUNTY.

From its organization in 1822 and continuing through the period of the Civil
War to 1865 the banking business of Henry County may properly be designated
as the "coon skin" period; that is, the banking facilities of the county were conducted by individuals without regularly organized charters to do the financial
business and without maintaining regular banking houses. It was a money-lending
operation, pure and simple, in which there were none of the many features, so
necessary in present day banking. A citizen who had succeeded in accumulating
a surplus of cash was the money lender in his neighborhood; to him applied his
neighbors when in want of funds to conduct various enterprises of the earlier
days and frequently these transactions were carried on by the simple word of
obligation of the borrower—no note or mortgage security was required. A miller,
for instance, would take in the wheat of a farmer, give him a receipt for the
number of bushels delivered and the farmer could call on him and get funds as
his needs required; a merchant would carry his farmer customers for all the goods
needed by the latter's family through the year, the farmer paying the merchant
about the holiday season when he sold his hogs, and this latter transaction was
conducted by the stock buyer and for many years the pork packer who would buy
the hogs and when returns were received from the purchasers in Cincinnati or
from the sale of the manufactured products of the packing establishment to
foreign buyers, the farmer would receive credit for the gross number of pounds
he had delivered and get pay for the same. During the period of the old State
Bank system it is fair to presume that our small capitalists (there were no large
ones in the confines of the county in those days) did not look with favor on the
"wild cat" system of banking that prevailed in other sections of the State, and
farther than the loss in handling the money which these banks issued and which
went to the bad when a banking institution failed, it is not recorded that any of
our capitalists were otherwise financially interested in the solvency of the concerns. The nearest branch of the old State Bank system was in Richmond. This
condition of affairs continued until about the close of the Civil War when the
present national banking system was introduced in Henry County by the organization of "The First National Bank of New Castle," which began business January
2, 1865. Its history and that of the other banks organized in the county after
that date follow.

BANKS AND BANKING IN HENRY COUNTY.

ganization in 1822 and continuing through the period of the Civil
' banking business of Henry County may properly be designated
n" period ; that is, the banking facilities of the county were con-
iduals without regularly organized charters to do the financial
1out maintaining regular banking houses. It was a money-lending
and simple, in which there were none of the many features, so
:ent day banking. A citizen who had succeeded in accumulating
' was the money lender in his neighborhood ; to him applied his
in want of funds to conduct various enterprises of the earlier
ally these transactions were carried on by the simple word of
borrower—no note or mortgage security was required. A miller,
uld take in the wheat of a farmer, give him a receipt for the
'ls delivered and the farmer could call on him and get funds as
d : a merchant would carry his farmer customers for all the goods
tter's family through the year, the farmer paying the merchant
v season when he sold his hogs, and this latter transaction was
stock buyer and for many years the pork packer who would buy
returns were received from the purchasers in Cincinnati or
the manufactured products of the packing establishment to
farmer would receive credit for the gross number of pounds
get pay for the same. During the period of the old State
presume that our small capitalists (there were no large
of the county in those days) did not look with favor on the
banking that prevailed in other sections of the State, and
handling the money which these banks issued and which
banking institution failed. it is not recorded that any of
otherwise financially interested in the solvency of the con-
1st branch of the old State Bank system was in Richmond. This
continued until about the close of the Civil War when the
banking system was introduced in Henry County by the organiza-
National Bank of New Castle," which began business January
ary and that of the other banks organized in the county after

NEW CASTLE.

ROBERT M. NIXON.

NEW CASTLE.

ALEXANDER R. SHROYER.

KNIGHTSTOWN.

CHARLES D. MORGAN.

MIDDLETOWN.

NIMROD R. ELLIOTT.

NEW CASTLE.

THOMAS B. MILLIKAN.

NEW CASTLE.

DAVID W. KINSEY.

MIDDLETOWN.

ERASTUS L. ELLIOTT.

HENRY COUNTY BANKERS.

THE FIRST NATIONAL BANK OF NEW CASTLE.

This bank began business January 2, 1865, with a paid-in capital of $100,000. Its present capital and surplus profits are:

Capital stock paid in.....................................$100,000.00
Surplus fund.. 40,000.00
Undivided profits... 8,000.00

Following are the names of all its officers and stockholders from the organization of the bank:

Presidents: Martin L. Bundy, Jehu T. Elliott, William Murphey, William F. Boor, Eli B. Phillips, J. Ward Maxim, George B. Morris.

Vice Presidents: Edmund Johnson, Miles Murphey, Benjamin Shirk, Simon T. Powell, William Murphey, William F. Boor, Mark E. Forkner, George B. Morris, Joshua I. Morris.

Cashiers: Daniel Murphey, John Thornburgh, Robert M. Nixon, Eli B. Phillips, William F. Byrket, George R. Murphey.

Assistant Cashiers: Augustus E. Bundy, Charles C. Powell, Percy G. Phillips, William J. Murphey.

Bookkeepers: Alexander R. Shroyer, John Thornburgh, John R. Peed, Josiah M. Hickman, Loring Bundy, Asa Hatch, Miles M. Canaday, Lena Wisehart, Henry H. Stuart, Hov Bock, the last two named being present incumbents.

First Board of Directors: Martin L. Bundy, Jehu T. Elliott, Edmund Johnson, Miles Murphey, Milton M. Murphey.

Present Board of Directors: William F. Boor, John Ehman, J. Ward Maxim, George B. Morris, Joshua I. Morris, George R. Murphey, William J. Murphey, Nathan Nicholson, Eli B. Phillips.

Stockholders who have been directors but not included in above are: Waterman Clift, Robert H. Cooper, Mark E. Forkner, George Hazzard (author of this History), Ed. Kahn, Leander Livezey, Clement Murphey, Eli Murphey, William Murphey, Robert M. Nixon, William Peper, Marcus A. Pickering, Charles C. Powell, Simon T. Powell, Benjamin Shirk, Edward K. Strattan, James M. Wyatt.

Original stockholders: William F. Boor, Martin L. Bundy, Waterman Clift, Jehu T. Elliott, George W. Goodwin, John W. Grubbs, Isaac R. Howard, Edmund Johnson, James McWhinney, Benjamin F. Murphey, Daniel Murphey, Miles Murphey, Milton M. Murphey, William Murphey, Simon T. Powell, Benjamin Shirk, John Shroyer.

Stockholders September 1, 1905: Mary M. Bond, William F. Boor, Belle S. Burke, John Ehman, Jehu T. Elliott heirs, Sophronia J. Elliott, Barbara Heller, Frank P. Ice, Sallie H. Klein, Sallie H. Klein, guardian, Leander Livezey, Mary C. Livezey, J. Ward Maxim, George B. Morris, Joshua I. Morris, Joshua I. Morris, trustee, Ada G. Murphey, Ellen Murphey, George R. Murphey, George R. and William H. Murphey, William J. Murphey, Almeda D. Nicholson, Nathan Nicholson, Eli B. Phillips, Charles C. Powell heirs, Louie M. Salmon, Victoria Salmon, John Shroyer heirs, Hannah Strattan.

Former stockholders since the organization of the bank were: Cora Bowers, Elisha Clift, Waterman Clift, Robert H. Cooper, DeWitt C. Elliott, Mark E. Forkner, John W. Griffin, George Hazzard (author of this History), Moses Heller, Isaac R. Howard, Simon P. Jennings, Ed. Kahn, Edmund Laurence, Nathan Livezey, A. Warren Murphey, Caroline Murphey, Clement Murphey, Eli Murphey, Elizabeth Murphey, Hulda Murphey, William C. Murphey, Robert M. Nixon, William Peper, Martha G. Phillips, Marcus A. Pickering, Martin L. Powell, Bushrod W. Scott, Sophia Snyder, Edward K. Strattan, Eliza Taylor, Frank J. Vestal, Morris M. White.

As provided by the national banking act the bank was re-chartered January 2, 1885, for twenty years and again re-chartered January 2, 1905, for the same period.

A statement of its condition August 25, 1905, is printed herewith:

Report of the condition of The First National Bank, of New Castle, in the State of Indiana, at the close of business, August 25, 1905:

RESOURCES.		
Loans and discounts.........$224,142.45		
Overdrafts, secured and unse-		
cured	1,507.16	
U. S. bonds to secure circula-		
tion	100,000.00	
Stocks, securities, etc.........	31,552.61	
Banking house, furniture and		
fixtures	6,000.00	
Due from approved reserve		
agents	42,437.84	
· Checks and other cash items..	243.72	
Notes of other National Banks.	8,000.00	
Fractional paper currency, nick-		
els and cents..............	1,398.89	
Lawful money reserve in bank,		
viz:		
Specie ....$ 1,943.00		
Legal tender notes.. 12,000.00	13,943.00	
Redemption fund with ·U. S.		
Treasurer (5 per cent. of cir-		
culation)	5,000.00	

LIABILITIES.		
Capital stock paid in.........$100,000.00		
Surplus fund..................	40,000.00 ·	
Undivided profits, less expenses		
and taxes paid..............	8,020.24	
National Bank notes outstand-		
ing	100,000.00	
Due to trust companies and sav-		
ings banks..................	466.48	
Individual deposits subject to		
check $141,541.92		
Demand certificates		
of deposit...........44,197.03	185,738.95	

Total ....$434,225.67   Total ..·....................$434,225.67

State of Indiana, County of Henry, ss:

I, George R. Murphey, cashier of the above-named bank, do solemnly swear that the above statement is true to the best of my knowledge and belief.

George R. Murphey, Cashier.   Correct attest: John Ehman, W. J. Murphey, Nathan Nicholson, Directors.

Subscribed and sworn to before me, this 30th day of August, 1905.

W. E. JEFFREY, Notary Public.

ROBERT MILTON NIXON, CASHIER.

Robert Milton Nixon, third cashier of the First National Bank of New Castle, was born in New Castle, June 9, 1842, the only child of Jesse R. and Mary Esther (Leonard) Nixon. Jesse R. Nixon was born February 2, 1815, in Surrey County, North Carolina, and came with his parents to Henry County in 1830, settling on a farm four miles south-west of New Castle, now owned by John C. Hudelson. Jesse R. learned the carpenter's trade, at which he worked for some time. He was married September 19, 1841, to Mary Esther Leonard, of this county. For several years he conducted a dry goods store in New Castle and later, after the Civil War, with his son, Robert M., established a drug store with which he was connected until his death. He died July 26, 1884, and his wife died March 5, 1889, each aged sixty-nine years. Both are buried in South Mound Cemetery. They were greatly respected for the probity and purity of their lives.

Robert M. Nixon obtained his education in the schools of New Castle, having been a student at the old academy under those eminent instructors, Ferris and Abbott. He responded to the call for volunteers in the Civil War and enlisted, as a musician of the first class, in the 36th Indiana Infantry, in August, 1861, and was mustered in September 16th of that year. In consequence of the general order abolishing regimental bands, he was discharged. Elsewhere in this History his military service will be found appro-priately set out. Returning home in the Spring of 1862, he became a clerk in the drug store of Dr. John Darr, where he remained until early in 1864, when he went to In-dianapolis and accepted a like position in the wholesale drug house of W. I. Hasket and Company, Mr. Hasket having gone from New Castle to engage in that business. While at Indianapolis he took a course in a commercial college and for a time was a clerk

W. E. JEFFREY, Notary Public.

·

HER.

tional Bank of New Castle, was
: R. and Mary Esther (Leonard)
Surrey County, North Carolina,
line on a farm four miles south-
Jesse R. learned the carpenter's
married September 19, 1841, to
he conducted a dry goods store
and Robert M., established a
it He died July 26, 1884, and
both are buried in South Mound
of purity of their lives.
sole of New Castle, having been
doctors Ferris and Abbott. He
d enlisted, as a musician of the
and was mustered in September
abolishing regimental bands, he
's service will be found appro-
he became a clerk in the drug
in 1864, when he went to In-

in the office of Major Martin L. Bundy, paymaster U. S. V. In October, 1865, he returned to New Castle and resumed his old position in the drug store of Dr. Darr, with whom he soon became a partner, the business being conducted under the name of John Darr and Company. In a short time Dr. Darr retired and was succeeded by Jesse R. Nixon, and the firm became Jesse R. and Robert M. Nixon and later Nixon and Son. Early in the seventies the firm built the commodious block on Broad Street, long occupied by Nixon and Son as a drug and book store, and since by their successors, Beam and Lynn, in the same business. In 1874 Robert M. was elected cashier of the First National Bank, succeeding John Thornburgh, and remained in that position for nearly eleven years, when, in connection with the present vice president of the United States, Charles W. Fairbanks, he largely aided in securing the right of way for the Indiana, Bloomington and Western Railway, now a part of the Big Four system, from Indianapolis to Springfield, Ohio. In August, 1890, President Harrison appointed him deputy comptroller of the currency, a position for which he was thoroughly fitted and the duties of which office he discharged with entire satisfaction for nearly three years, until after President Harrison's term of office expired, (March 4, 1893), when the directors of the Fifth National Bank of Cincinnati, Ohio, prevailed on him to take the presidency of that institution. His career as president of this bank illustrated the energy and splendid business ability of Robert M. Nixon, for within a year or so after he took charge the bank was placed on a solid basis and became one of the leading financial institutions of that city. Perhaps it was the great labor attached to this undertaking that impaired his health, for in the Winter of 1895, his former rugged physical strength gave way to severe indisposition. He was brought to his home in New Castle and lived but a short time thereafter, passing away on the night of January 18, 1896.

Robert M. Nixon and Celestina Beam were married in New Castle, October 15, 1872. Four children were born to them, namely: Frank, Horace, Mary and Estella. The sons are engaged in business in New Castle—Frank is conducting a real estate, loan and insurance office and Horace is connected with the Krell Auto-Grand Piano Company. The two daughters and both sons live with their mother at the elegant home on the corner of Church and Main streets.

Robert M. Nixon was a man of culture and refinement; a student of and thorough master of music; of somewhat reserved nature but genial with friend and acquaintance; habitually industrious and a man who found in his home life the greatest happiness. Vice President Fairbanks paid a beautiful tribute to Robert M. Nixon's memory, at his bier, in which, among other things, he said: "In the meridian of his usefulness, night came upon him. He was not old in years, but in good deeds he was venerable. No day with him was complete without some kindly service performed. He was a lover of his fellowmen and never put upon others burdens he could bear himself." Another friend has said: "If every one for whom he did a kindness were to throw a blossom on his grave he would sleep beneath a pyramid of flowers."

THE ATTEMPTED ROBBERY OF THE FIRST NATIONAL BANK.

"November 1, 1869.—The following resolution was unanimously adopted: Resolved, that the thanks of the stockholders and directors of the First National Bank of New Castle are hereby returned to the citizens of New Castle who so gallantly and heroically defended the bank from burglars on the night of the 29th of October, and particularly to Thomas L. Campbell, who gave the first alarm of the attack.

"JOHN THORNBURGH. Cashier.   MARTIN L. BUNDY. President."

The few pen scratches required to write the above, which is taken from the minutes of the directors' meeting of the First National Bank on the date stated, furnish a slight clew to the curious, but by no means reveal the thrilling features of the story of that much-talked-of incident in local history. No doubt the main incidents of the occurrence are familiar to many who read this sketch, either through personal knowledge or tradition, but an event which had so much importance and note throughout the county, can lose nothing in the repetition.

The night selected for the robbery was one of calm, brilliant serenity, such as is only possible in the crisp atmosphere of Mid-autumn. The moon shone clear and bright over the deserted streets of sleeping New Castle.

It was not yet the day of dynamite, when a small hole quickly drilled, a charge, a fuse, a light, and the money, are all that are required. Dynamite was an unthought-of power. He who would follow the cracksman's wary life must have a strong arm and a true eye to carry out his daring work. Wedges were used to force open the doors, and with these the men expected to pry their way to a fortune.

Then, as now, New Castle had a midnight train on the Panhandle, and it has always been supposed that the two men interested in the affair came in on that train, broke open the tool house door and secured the crow bar with which they pried open the rear entrance of the bank and thus gained admittance to the building.

They lost very little time after their arrival, but began work at once. With all their precautions, however, they had neglected to consider that the noise might arouse someone nearby, or else, having considered it, thought the risk not great, and thus provided for their failure.

In those days, the big store of Mowrer, Murphey and Company occupied that part of the Murphey block now divided into a drug store, barber shop and confectionery store. Thomas L. Campbell, who was at that time a clerk in the store, slept at night on the floor above in the rear of the Murphey building with his bed near the wall against the opposite side of which the safe stood on the bank floor below.

Mr. Campbell was aroused by the first stroke of the hammer and realized almost immediately what was taking place, but stood for some time before deciding on any plan of action, for he had no means of knowing how many men there were or how and where guards might be stationed. That someone was on watch, seemed clearly evident, for at one time the pounding suddenly ceased and soon after, Mr. Campbell, looking from the window, saw a local young man pass by on his way home from a "sparking" trip. He feared to signal him, however, lest he give the alarm to the would-be robbers, and the pounding was, in a short time, resumed.

Having finally planned his course of action, the young man crept carefully down stairs to the front door, then of solid oak without glass, carrying his shoes with him. It seemed as if every sound would alarm the robbers, but the pounding kept uninterruptedly on, and with each stroke his courage rose. Putting on his shoes, he slid the bolts fastening the door and slowly opened it. He at once remarked a pressure against it and perceived through the small opening he had made that a heavy object leaned on it. This, he at first thought, was a man, and grabbed at what he took to be the hand. His relief can be imagined when he found it only a four-foot stick of fire wood, placed there, no doubt, that it might fall and give the alarm should the door be opened.

It was the work of a moment to slip through the opening, close the door and replace the stick, after which the thoroughly aroused young man sped down the street with winged, yet silent feet, to Adam Beam's residence on the corner of Twelfth and Race streets, where he then boarded. Here he quickly aroused George Beam, acquainted him with the situation, and engaged his assistance. The two then awakened Calvin Bond, who lived just across the street on the present Alcazar Theatre site. In low but rapid words, he, too, was informed of the robbery and was told to hasten to the corner of Main and Church streets, where Alexander Chambers lived, on the site of Dr. Oliver J. Gronendyke's present residence, and there await the assembling of others.

In a similar manner, a hasty trip was made down South Main Street, resulting in the assembling at the designated corner of John Thornburgh, cashier of the bank; 'Squire Alvin Burr, William Hoover, Nicholas Mowrer, and James Mowrer, Judge Martin L. Bundy, president of the bank; Augustus E. Bundy, assistant cashier; Clement Murphey, a director; Alexander Chambers, John A. Heichert and Sampson Jetmore, together with a few others whose names can not be learned. In all about a dozen men had collected, armed with various styles of weapons.

The party was quickly divided, one part going east to Fourteenth, thence north to Race, there again subdividing, half going west on Race to the rear and half around on

Broad to the front of the building. The other division marched down Main Street, making a similar separation at Race Street and joined their corresponding parties at the rear and front.

The robbers were thus effectually hemmed in and would have no doubt been captured had not some one of the pursuing party inadvertently made a noise which attracted their attention. The burglars were using a candle, which was at once extinguished, leaving the room in total darkness. One of them ran to the front door and the other to the rear, thus commanding the attention of both parties, though they knew not where nor how many their besiegers were.

As the larger of the two men ran to the rear and out of the door, Alexander Chambers, who stood in the shadow of a wood pile just outside the door, fired his revolver at him, upon which the fellow cried, with an oath, "Take that," and discharged a ball from his revolver into Chambers' hip. He continued firing as he ran to the gate and William Hoover, who was one of the best shots in town, fired a shotgun at him just as he reached it. In his nervousness, however, he aimed high, and the bold robber escaped unharmed. The action was so rapid and the firing so brisk that the man was gone almost before they realized it. Pursuit was begun, but they were kept at bay by his revolver and he escaped. John Alexander, who lived by the old Methodist parsonage, was awakened by the shooting and came to the door in time to see the escaping man as he stood for a moment, bareheaded and coatless, undecided which way to turn, on the corner now occupied by the new Methodist Church, then a vacant lot used as a play ground for school children. Realizing in a moment what was up, it is said, he cried, "Here he is; come and take him."

The hunted man leaped forward and cried and as he ran, "Why don't you take me yourself," firing a parting shot by way of emphasis, and though the search was long continued, nothing more was ever seen or heard of him, unless a discarded shoe, found next morning in one of the lots now occupied by the school house grounds, may count.

With the little man, who started out by way of the front of the bank, things fared not so well. His troubles began when James M. Mowrer hurled a big boulder through the front door at him, informing him of the enemy's presence in front, and on turning, he found that he had left the middle door locked, thus cutting off his escape to the rear.

Mowrer, Campbell and Thornburgh, seconded by others, followed up the attack closely and were almost on the man when he turned at bay and began firing. Mowrer had a revolver but could not use it to advantage for fear of shooting one of the crowd. Thornburgh had a pistol, but for some reason, it failed to go off. One of the fellow's shots struck Campbell in the right arm just under the shoulder and at the same moment the desperate man made a dash for liberty, knocking Campbell down as he did so. Campbell scrambled to his feet only to find his arm useless and at once grew sick. He was taken to Mowrer, Murphey and Company's store, where Dr. Samuel Ferris was called to attend him, and for several weeks he was confined in bed at Mr. Beam's with his wounded arm.

Meanwhile, "John Henry," as he later styled himself, dashed across to the lot where the Burr block now stands, and across Main Street, followed closely by the pursuing crowd, led by James M. Mowrer, and attempted to cross a lot just north of the Shroyer building. Here difficulties again beset him for he tumbled unexpectedly into an unseen cellar, left by the burning down of a saloon. This gave Mowrer a chance to gain on him and by the time he climbed out of the hole and started to run again Mowrer was so close that the final accident was all that was required to make his capture a certainty. A few yards from the cellar, a ditch was being constructed to the Shroyer building and into this the unfortunate man tumbled, headlong, while Mowrer jumped in on top of him. The crowd quickly secured the robber and removed him to the jail, where every effort to get him to reveal his own and his partner's identity failed, his only information being that his name was "John Henry." He was one of the coolest men ever placed in jail here and absolutely refused to be scared by the crowd, who even went so far as to threaten to hang him if he did not tell.

The town people had by this time been aroused by the noise and about fifty people were at the jail. A considerable amount of "shin-plasters" which had been lying in the outer part of the safe was found in the prisoner's bootleg. The outer doors of the safe had been pried open with a most-approved set of burglar's tools and the inner door was almost ready to come open when the men were interrupted, so nearly in fact that it was possible to touch the money with the finger tips through the opening. A few more strokes, and they would have had the money, about $15,000, and made their escape. They left their tools on the floor and the instruments were for a long time prized as relics by the participants in the affray.

"John Henry" sent for Judge Mellett to act as his attorney and informed him where he could write to make arrangements for his fee for defending him. The letter was never answered, however, for the man's clever escape a week later put a stop to all proceedings. The escape was unique, daring, and very ingeniously planned. The night was dark and rainy, as Jailor William N. Clift, who occupied that position under Sheriff William S. Bedford, gave the order for the prisoner to go into his cell. Henry, being the only inmate, slipped around to the rear of his cell and pulled the door shut with a previously arranged string. He had, meanwhile, stuffed paper into the hole for the pin to drop into so that it did not click as it should when it fell. The doors were all locked by a lever, operated by the jail keeper from the outside. When the pin dropped, it did not click properly, however, and Mr. Clift went in to see what was the matter with it, thinking, of course, that the man was in his cell. It was less than twenty feet to the door of the cell, and he left his keys in the door. "Henry" meanwhile, was coming toward the door in the rear of the cell as Mr. Clift went away from it. A sudden dash, and before he realized it, Mr. Clift was a prisoner. The key to the outer door was snatched from Mrs. Clift and the door was locked. After expressing his thanks in the coolest possible manner for the kind treatment he had received, he hastened away and was never again seen in New Castle, except by Martin L. Powell, who met him as he hastened away, but not having seen him before, did not know of his identity until too late. A long search was made but it proved fruitless and he made good his escape. The bank, later, gave Mr. Campbell $500 for his services, which served as his first capital from which he made his start in business in New Castle, where he now lives a highly respected and prosperous citizen.

THE CITIZENS' STATE BANK OF NEW CASTLE.

This, the largest bank in Henry County, began business July 3, 1873. It was organized by George Hazzard, author of this History, who was also the author and largely instrumental in having the present efficient laws governing State banks passed by the General Assembly, and was the first State examiner under the law. It was the outgrowth of a private bank, known as the Citizens' Bank, operated under the firm name, first of George Hazzard and Company, and afterward as Hazzard, Murphey and Company, the latter firm being composed of George Hazzard, William C. Murphey and Reverend Reuben Tobey, the last named being the father-in-law of George Hazzard. This firm was located first in a little front room upstairs in the brick building now occupied by the grocery store of Murphey Brothers and Company, later in the south room of the Murphey block, now occupied by a restaurant. It was in this room that the Citizens' State Bank first began business. This bank, which began business October 2, 1871, was conducted successfully until it was succeeded by the above named institution. The Citizens' State Bank was started with its present capital, which, with its accumulated surplus, is as follows:

Capital stock paid in $130,000.00
Surplus fund 32,500.00

Presidents—George Hazzard, John R. Millikan, William M. Pence.

Vice Presidents—Daniel Murphey, George Hazzard, Benjamin Shirk, William M. Pence, John M. Morris.

Cashiers—William C. Murphey, David W. Kinsey (Since September 9, 1874).

Assistant Cashiers—David W. Kinsey, Thomas B. Millikan (Since July 14, 1874).

Bookkeepers—Benjamin F. Pitman, Lewis E. Kinsey, Will E. Davis, Kittie Peed, Ethel Davis, Frank Pence, Fred Saint, Ella Davis, Edna J. Goudy, John R. Millikan, Jr., the last five named being present bookkeepers.

First Board of Directors—George Hazzard, Luther W. Hess, Edmund Johnson, Isaac Mendenhall, John R. Millikan, Daniel Murphey, John Payne, William M. Pence, Benjamin Shirk.

Present Board of Directors—Enoch S. Bouslog, David W. Kinsey, Thomas B. Millikan, John M. Morris, Charles F. Payne, John W. Payne, William M. Pence, Orlando C. Saffel.

Stockholders who have been directors but not included in above are: Andrew C. Bartlett, Calvin Bond, George M. Byer, Nathan T. Clawson, William D. Cooper, James Goudy, Simeon B. Hayes, Nathan Millikan, Nathan T. Nixon.

Original stockholders—Seth S. Bennett, Calvin Bond, Enos Bond, Jesse Bond, Henry Brenneman, George M. Byer, Nathan T. Clawson, William D. Cooper, Thaddeus H. Gordon, Simeon B. Hays, George Hazzard, Luther W. Hess, John Hunt, A. J. and E. T. Ice, Edmund Johnson, David W. Kinsey, Lewis Kinsey, Clarinda Lennard, James Loer, Charles McDorman, Nathaniel S. McMeans, Isaac Mendenhall, John R. Millikan, Nathan Millikan, Daniel Murphey, William C. Murphey, Nathan T. Nixon, John Payne, William M. Pence, Robert H. Polk, Martin L. Powell, Thomas B. Redding, William A. Rifner, Henry Shaffer, Benjamin Shirk, Clarinda H. Sims, Jehu Stanley, Edward K. Strattan, John H. Terhune, Reuben Tobey, William B. Whitworth, Wilson Wisehart, Asahel Woodward.

Stockholders September 1, 1905—Andrew C. Bartlett estate; Angelia Boor, Enoch S. Bouslog, Henry Brenneman heirs, William A. Brown, George M. Byer estate, George B. Clawson, Ruth Cooper, Mary M. Gause, George W. Goodwin heirs, Miranda Goudy, Strauther Hays, Phebe Hess, Ella Hodson, David W. Kinsey, Martin Kinsey, Margaret McCaffrey, Valentine M. Mendenhall, Eli A. Millikan, Frank M. Millikan, James C. Millikan, Thomas B. Millikan, John M. Morris, Nathan T. Nixon, Charles F. Payne, John W. Payne, William M. Pence, Martha G. Phillips, Charles C. Powell estate, Orlando C. Saffel, Elizabeth C. Stafford, Edward K. Strattan, Hannah Strattan, Sarah J. Wisehart.

Former stockholders since the organization of the bank were: Jonathan K. Bond, Thomas J. Burk, Joel Harvey, Calvin Hinshaw, Isaac Hinshaw, Lewis Kinsey, Thomas S. Lines, Thomas W. Millikan, Nathan Payne, Charles C. Powell, Julia Ann Shroyer, Albert C. Shute, Nettie E. Sims, Charles A. Stafford, Horace Stafford, Frederick Tykle, Frank J. Vestal, Alice Williams.

In accordance with article XI, section 10 of the constitution of the State, the bank was rechartered for twenty years June 5, 1893, to take effect July 3, 1893.

The last official published statement, August 25, 1905, follows:

Report of the condition of the Citizens State Bank, at New Castle, in the State of Indiana, at the close of its business, August 25, 1905:

RESOURCES.		LIABILITIES.	
Loans and discounts	$500,203.01	Capital stock paid in	$130,000.00
Overdrafts	4,111.06	Surplus fund	32,500.00
Bonds	46,791.27	Discount, exchange and interest.	4,107.54
Real estate	4,415.00	Deposits	678,323.13
'Current expenses	550.01		
Premiums	4,415.00		
Due from banks $189,678.66			
U. S. bonds.................	50,780.00		
Gold 12,120.00			
Currency 30,311.00			
Silver 1,238.09			
Exchange 317.57			
	284,445.32		
Total	$844,930 67	Total	$844.930.67

STATE OF INDIANA, COUNTY OF HENRY, ss:

I, David W. Kinsey, cashier of the Citizens' State Bank of New Castle, Indiana, do solemnly swear that the above statement is true.   DAVID W. KINSEY, Cashier.

Subscribed and sworn to before me, this 30th day of August, 1905.

GEORGE A. ELLIOTT, Notary Public.

THE CENTRAL TRUST AND SAVINGS COMPANY.

This is among the latest acquisitions to the financial institutions of the county and shows a steady and healthful increase in business from the time it opened its doors. It began operations January 1, 1903, with a capital of $50,000. This amount was increased July 1, 1905, to $75,000. At this date it shows:

Capital stock paid in $75,000.00
Surplus fund 6,500.00

President, Leonidas P. Newby; Vice President, John M. Morris; Secretary, Robert H. McIntyre; Assistant Secretary, Miles M. Canaday; Bookkeeper, Mary Peed.

First board of directors: Omar H. Barrett, Walter S. Chambers, Robert H. Cooper, Adolph Cooper, Leander P. Mitchell, John M. Morris, Robert H. McIntyre, Leonidas P. Newby, John W. Whitworth.

Present board of directors: David M. Brown, Walter S. Chambers, Robert H. Cooper, John H. Hewit, Robert H. McIntyre, John M. Morris, Leander P. Mitchell, Leonidas P. Newby, John W. Whitworth.

Stockholders before the capital stock was increased. (An asterisk thus * after a name indicates that the person no longer owns stock): Arthur L. Alshouse, Mrs. Rose Barrett, Omar H. Barrett,* Clarence H. Beard, Felton A. Bolser. David M. Brown, William A. Brown,* Eugene H. Bundy, Omar Bundy, Mrs. John J. Campbell, Thomas L. Campbell, Miles M. Canaday, Aaron E. Carroll,* Walter S. Chambers, Charles M. Christopher, John M. Clawson. J. Milton Cook, Adolph Cooper, Robert H. Cooper, David R. Frazier, Charles Haney,* Joseph Harlan,* Waitsel M. Heaton, Elizabeth Heritage, John H. Hewit, James Hinshaw, Ed Jackson,* James H. Jones,* Benjamin F. Koons,* Martin L. Koons, Elihu T. Mendenhall, Leander P. Mitchell, John M. Morris, George F. Mowrer, Robert H. McIntyre, Leonidas P. Newby, Charles F. Payne, Frederick Phelps, Frank Phelman, Edward Smith, John E. Stinson, Louis Taylor, Frank L. Thornburgh,* Lydia J. and Beulah A. Vaughan. John W. Whitworth, John W. Williams, Mathew Williams.

Stockholders not included in the above who subscribed to the new stock: Frank H. Cleveland, Sylvester Davis. Joseph E. Fleming, H. Edgar French, Will M. Goodwin, Warren Hinshaw, David L. Hinshaw, J. Jacob Hoover, Willard Ice, Pleasant M. Koons, John F. Luellen, Charles D. Mohler, John H. Myers, Willard Myers, Felix O. Peckinpaugh, Mrs. Henry L. Powell, Alexander E. Painter, Josiah D. Painter, Thomas M. Painter, William J. Painter, Nathan Ridgway, John W. Rodgers, Leonidas Rodgers, Edgar T. White.

The published statement of the bank August 25, 1905, follows:

Report of the condition of the Central Trust and Savings Company of New Castle, Indiana, at close of business August 25, 1905:

RESOURCES.		LIABILITIES.	
Real estate, furniture and fix-		Capital stock	$75,000.00
tures ....$	10,168.35	Deposits	99,078.70
Loans	142,422.83	Discount and exchange	1,011.91
Cash	11,039.51	Surplus and undivided profits....	6,568.22
Due from banks	17,733.20		
Expense	294.94		
Total ....$	181,658.83	Total ....$	181,658.83

I, Robert H. McIntyre, secretary of the Central Trust and Savings Company, do solemnly swear that the above statement is true.

ROBERT H. McINTYRE, Secretary.

Subscribed and sworn to before me, this 30th day of August, 1905.

ALBERT D. OGBORN, Notary, Public.

In 1867 Martin L. Bundy retired from the presidency of the First National Bank of New Castle, which bank he organized in 1864, and started a private bank called the Union Bank. It was located in the Taylor House, now the Bundy House, in the room which since the hotel was rebuilt has for many years been used as a barber shop. The bank was a success from its inception and did a large business. However, early in 1869 its business and good will were transferred to the First National Bank and Mr. Bundy again became a large stockholder and president of the latter institution, where he remained until in 1873, when he once more retired and instituted a private bank, called the Bundy Bank. On November 9, 1874, it was converted into the Bundy National Bank, with a capital stock of $50,000. Its officers were Martin L. Bundy, president, and Loring Bundy, cashier. First board of directors: Martin L. Bundy, Thomas B. Redding, Addison R. A. Thompson, Jacob S. Elliott and Nathaniel E. Black. In 1877, Martin L. Bundy disposed of his stock and Simon T. Powell was elected president, and in 1879, Loring Bundy resigned as cashier and John C. Livezey was chosen in his stead. The bank continued to do a fairly prosperous business until 1881, when its stockholders, believing that there was not business enough in the town at that time to justify its continuance, determined to wind up its affairs. Accordingly, it ceased to exist, its stockholders receiving quite a premium over the par value of their holdings.

THE FIRST NATIONAL BANK OF KNIGHTSTOWN.

The above named bank was organized January 7, 1865, but did not begin business until April 25, 1865. Its capital stock was originally $100,000 and so remained until January 7, 1885, when the bank was re-chartered with a capital stock of $50,000. Its charter was again renewed January 7, 1905, for twenty years. It stands No. 2 among the national banks in Indiana and No. 201 among those of the United States, as an institution having the largest surplus fund and undivided profits in proportion to its capital stock. A complete list of the officers and stockholders of the bank from the date of organization to and including the present time follows:

Capital stock paid in.......................................$50,000.00
Surplus fund... 50,000.00
Undivided profits... 30,000.00

Presidents: Robert Woods, Charles D. Morgan.
Cashiers: Charles D. Morgan, William Penn Hill, Noah W. Wagoner.
Assistant cashier: Erie C. Morgan.
Bookkeepers: Noah W. Wagoner, Wayne F. Wallace.
First board of directors: John H. Bales, Thomas C. Hill, Charles S. Hubbard, Hugh L. Risk, John T. White, Ellison Williams, Robert Woods.
Present board of directors: Aaron E. Carroll, Charles D. Morgan, Erie C. Morgan, Alpheus O. Morris, Noah W. Wagoner.
Original stockholders: John H. Bales, Gordon Ballard, Jacob Elliott, Amos B. Fithian, Mary A. Furgason, Mary M. Heaton, Charles Henly, Thomas Henly, Thomas C. Hill, William Penn Hill, Charles S. Hubbard, Charles D. Morgan, Henry Morris, William S. T. Morton, John Power, Hugh L. Risk, Charles Rock, James Silver, Charles White, Edmund White, John T. White, Toms White, Joseph M. Whitesel, Ellison Williams, Robert Woods, Joel Wright.
Stockholders September 1, 1905: Aaron E. Carroll, Nancy H. Crouse, Eunice Dunn, William P. Henly, Ann M. Hill, Eliza Hill, Herbert B. Hill, Lillian J. Hill, Margaret Hill, Florence A. Kerwood, Charles D. Morgan, Erie C. Morgan, Alpheus O. Morris, Caroline Righter, Fannie M. Swain, Noah W. Wagoner, Francis T. White, Morris M. White, Mrs. Ellison Williams, Hannah Woodnut, Mary M. Woods.
A statement of the assets and liabilities of the bank, as required by law, showing its condition at the close of business August 25, 1905, is appended:

Report of the condition of The First National Bank at Knightstown, in the State of Indiana, at the close of business, August 25, 1905:

RESOURCES.		LIABILITIES.	
Loans and discounts..........$185,742.91		Capital stock paid in..........$50,000.00	
Overdrafts, secured and unsecured 1,489.94		Surplus fund................. 50,000.00	
U. S. bonds to secure circulation 12,500.00		Undivided profits less expenses and taxes paid....... 30,928.70	
U. S. bonds on hand......... 200.00		National Bank notes outstanding 12,500.00	
Banking house, furniture and fixtures 5,000.00		Individual deposits subject to check 220,639.27	
Due from National Banks (not reserve agents)............. 63,679.04		Demand certificates of deposit. 54,251.32	
Due from State Banks and Bankers 1,114.10			
Due from approved reserve agents 77,493.82			
Notes of other National Banks. 3,000.00			
Fractional paper currency, nickels and cents.............. 444.48			
Lawful money reserve in Bank, viz:			
Specie 65,000.00			
Legal tender notes........... 2,000.00			
Redemption fund with U. S. Treasurer (5 per cent. of circulation) 625.00			

Total ....$418,319.29   Total $418,319.29

State of Indiana, County of Henry, ss:

I, N. W. Wagoner, cashier of the above-named bank, do solemnly swear that the above statement is true to the best of my knowledge and belief.

N. W. Wagoner, Cashier. Correct attest: A. O. Morris, C. D. Morgan, A. E. Carroll, Directors.

Subscribed and sworn to before me this 30th day of August, 1905.

R. L. HARRISON, Notary Public.

The first bank organized in Henry County was the private bank started by Robert Woods and Charles D. Morgan at Knightstown under the name of Robert Woods and Company, several years prior to the organization of The First National Bank. After the passage of the national banking act it was succeeded by the above institution of which its proprietors became respectively president and cashier. Elsewhere in this History will be found a biographical sketch of Charles D. Morgan in which full reference is made to this private bank and to this sketch the reader is referred for farther information.

CITIZENS' STATE BANK OF KNIGHTSTOWN.

On November 7, 1888, this bank, having previously completed its organization, was opened for the transaction of business. Its capital and earnings are:

Capital stock paid in......................................$50,000.00
Surplus fund.. 7,600.00
Undivided profits.. 18,100.00

Presidents: Elnathan Wilkinson, Leonidas P. Newby.

Vice presidents: Gershon D. Porter, Tilghman Fish.

Cashiers: John A. Craft, Frank J. Vestal.

Assistant cashiers: Frank J. Vestal, John A. Sample, Arthur L. Stage.

Bookkeeper: Pearl M. Hibben.

First board of directors: William H. Beard, John A. Craft, William B. Gilson, John C. Hardin, Moses Heller, Leonidas P. Newby, Gershon D. Porter, Jerome F. Sadler, Elnathan Wilkinson.

Present board of directors: Omar H. Barrett, John A. Craft, Tilghman Fish, John C. Hardin, Waitsel M. Heaton, Olin E. Holloway, Leonidas P. Newby, Frank J. Vestal, Thomas B. Wilkinson.

Original stockholders: James O. Addison, Morton Allison, Cyrus C. Barrett, Omar H. Barrett, William H. Beard, Lewis A. Bell, Lycurgus L. Boblett, Robert F. Brewington, Seth S. Copeland, John A. Craft, John A. Deem, William Edgerton, Thomas L. Gilson, William B. Gilson, Thaddeus H. Gordon, Alpheus W. Green, John C. Hardin, Viola A. Heaton, Waitsel M. Heaton, Moses Heller, Mathew Hibben, Melinda Hinchman, Olin E. Holloway, William Hodson, Ed. Kahn, Rufus Lindsey, James Mills, John Mitchell, James A. Moffett, David Monticue, Andrew H. Morris, Leonidas P. Newby, Barbara Porter, Gershon D. Porter, William F. Reeves, Jerome F. Sadler, Lewis L. Sadler, Asa E. Sample, Martin V. Scovell, Jane E. Sims, John M. Sims, George D. Smith, Emily A. Thornton, Julius B. Thornton, Charles H. Thrawley, John W. Vandenbark, Frank J. Vestal, John Weaver, Elnathan Wilkinson, Thomas B. Wilkinson, George W. Williams.

Stockholders September 1, 1905: Morton Allison, Sarah Allison, Omar H. Barrett, Lycurgus L. Boblett, Aaron E. Carroll, John A. Craft, Tilghman Fish, Barbara E. Fort, Oscar Fort, Marcella J. Green, Charles H. Haney, John C. Hardin, John C. Hardin and sons, Viola A. Heaton, Waitsel M. Heaton, Moses Heller estate, Melinda Hinchman, Olin E. Holloway, Alice James, Leonidas P. Newby, Mary Peden estate, Ominda Peden, Irvin Porter, Lewis L. Sadler, Martha A. Sadler, Martin V. Scovell, Mary Shaw, Jane E. Sims, George G. Smith, Arthur L. Stage, Emily A. Thornton, Charles H. Thrawley estate, Moses W. Vandenbark, Frank J. Vestal, Thomas B. Wilkinson.

Appended is the official statement of the resources and liabilities of the bank August 25, 1905:

Report of the condition of the Citizens' State Bank at Knightstown, in the State of Indiana, at the close of business, August 25, 1905:

RESOURCES.		LIABILITIES.	
Loans and discounts	$149,127.40	Capital stock paid in	$ 50,000.00
Overdrafts	291.11	Surplus fund	7,600.00
Other stocks, bonds and mort-		Undivided profits	18,400.00
gages	8,193.53	Discount, exchange and interest	10,284.29
Due from banks and bankers	73,852.37	Individual deposits on demand.	156,432.56
Banking house	4,000.00	Due to banks and bankers	11,267.58
Furniture and fixtures	1,400.00		
Current expenses	2,174.06		
Taxes paid	473.14		
Cash on hand—Currency, $4,-			
560; specie, $9,805.56	14,365.56		
Cash items	107.18		
Total	$253,984.35	Total	$253,984.35

State of Indiana, County of Henry, ss:

I, Arthur L. Stage, Assistant Cashier of the Citizens' State Bank at Knightstown, Indiana, do solemnly swear that the above statement is true.

ARTHUR L. STAGE.

Subscribed and sworn to before me, this 30th day of August, 1905.

FLOYD J. NEWBY,
Notary Public.

THE FARMERS' STATE BANK OF MIDDLETOWN.

When this bank was first organized, May 22, 1882, it was under the name of "The Farmers' Bank. "Under the constitution of the State, it is provided, article XI, section 10, "that every bank or banking company * * * shall be required to close its business within twenty years." The bank was therefore reorganized May 22, 1902, and the word "State" was added to distinguish the new from the old organization.

Its capital and surplus earnings are:

Capital stock paid in.....................................$30,000.00
Surplus fund.. 18,000.00
Presidents: Nimrod R. Elliott, Adolph Cooper.
Vice presidents: Thomas Wilhoit, Adolph Cooper, William H. Keesling.
Cashier: Erastus L. Elliott.
Assistant cashier: Benjamin H. Davis.
Bookkeepers: Henry J. Van Matre, Ola Cummins, Porter W. Cooper.
First board of directors: Nimrod R. Elliott, George W. Tarkleson, R. A. Andes, John Davis, William H. Keesling, Cyrus Van Matre, Thomas Wilhoit.
Present board of directors: Adolph Cooper, John Davis, Erastus L. Elliott, William H. Keesling, Willis Wisehart.
Original stockholders: Mary A. Andes, R. A. Andes, William Burner, Andrew Bushong, Henderson Cummins, Josiah Cromer, Mary A. Cummins, Nathan Cummins, Benjamin H. Davis, John Davis, Erastus L. Elliott, Nimrod R. Elliott, Elliott and Cooper, John B. Hupp, William H. Keesling, Joseph A. Painter, George W. Tarkleson, Frederick Tykle, Cyrus Van Matre, James H. Welsh, Thomas Wilhoit, Willis Wisehart.

Stockholders September 1, 1905: Arthur L. Alshouse, Victor Alshouse, Adolph Cooper, Imla W. Cooper, Mary J. Cummins, John Davis, Erastus L. Elliott, William H. Keesling, Jane H. Elliott, Tabitha Jackson, Ida F. Thurston, Anna D. Welsh, Charles C. Wilhoit, Willis Wisehart.

The bank's official statement of resources and liabilities as shown by the books August 25, 1905, is as follows:

Report of the condition of the Farmers' State Bank at Middletown, in the State of Indiana, at the close of its business on the 25th day of August, 1905:

RESOURCES.		LIABILITIES.	
Loans and discounts.. ....$167,250.88		Capital stock paid in..........$ 30,000.00	
Overdrafts 5,259.54		Surplus fund................. 18,000.00	
Bonds 21,791.60		Discount, exchange and interest 943.52	
Due from banks and bankers.. 38,113.13		Individual deposits on demand 197,771.52	
Banking house, real estate, furniture and fixtures.......... 4,500.00			
Current expenses and taxes paid 238.25			
Currency 4,500.00			
Specie 4.886.25			
Interest paid 175.39			
Total $246,715.04		Total $246,715.04	

State of Indiana, County of Henry, ss:
I, E. L. Elliott, cashier of the Farmers' State Bank, of Middletown, Indiana, do solemnly swear that the above statement is true.   E. L. ELLIOTT, Cashier.
Subscribed and sworn to before me, this 30th day of August, 1905.
GEORGE L. SWAIN, Notary Public.

In October, 1873, Nimrod R. Elliott, George Hazzard, author of this History, and John H. Terhune formed a partnership and established the Farmers' Bank of Middletown, each party contributing to its capital stock the sum of $10,000. Nimrod R. Elliott was president, George Hazzard vice president and John H. Terhune cashier. After several months, in order to reach a larger field of operation, the bank was moved to Anderson, where it became The Madison County Bank, with a capital of $100,000, of which John E. Corwin was president, Nimrod R. Elliott vice president, John H. Terhune cashier and John W. Pence assistant cashier. Later this bank became The Madison County National Bank, but before that time Elliott and Hazzard had disposed of their interests to Corwin. In time this last named bank was succeeded by The Citizens' Bank of Anderson, in which John H. Terhune still retains an interest.

THE HENRY COUNTY BANK OF SPICELAND.

This is a private bank in which some of the best known and wealthiest citizens of Spiceland Township are interested. It was organized September 3, 1895, and its present capital and surplus are:

Capital stock paid in.....................................$10,000.00
Surplus fund.. 1,000.00

President, Wm. H. Beard; vice president, William L. Cory; cashiers. Murray S. Wildman, Herbert T. Baily; bookkeeper, Lena Rayle.

First board of directors: William H. Beard, William Edgerton, Oliver Greenstreet, John William Griffin, Lilburn White.

Present board of directors: Herbert T. Bailey, William H. Beard, William L. Cory, Oliver Greenstreet, John William Griffin.

Original stockholders and those of September 1, 1905: Herbert T. Bailey, William H. Beard, Peter S. Cory, William L. Cory, Caroline Edgerton, William Edgerton, Oliver Greenstreet, John S. Griffin, John William Griffin, John A. Ratliff, Lilburn White, Martha A. White, Murray S. Wildman.

Below is a statement of the condition of the bank on August 25, 1905:

Report of the condition of the Henry County Bank at Spiceland, in the State of Indiana, at the close of its business on August 25, 1905:

RESOURCES.		LIABILITIES.	
Loans and discounts	$48,295.78	Capital paid in	$10,000
Overdrafts	319.64	Surplus fund	1,000.00
Due from banks and bankers	18,524.46	Discount, exchange and interest	588.96
Banking house	2,000.00	Individual deposits on demand.	65,398.99
Furniture and fixtures	500.00		
Current expenses	255.54		
Cash on hand—			
Currency $2,802.00			
Specie 4,290.53	7,092.53		
Total	$76,987.95	Total	$76,987.95

State of Indiana, County of Henry, ss:

I, H. T. Baily, cashier of the Henry County Bank of Spiceland, Indiana, do solemnly affirm that the above statement is true.

H. T. BAILY, Cashier.

Subscribed and affirmed before me, this 31st day of August. 1905.

O. H. NIXON, Notary Public.

THE FIRST NATIONAL BANK OF LEWISVILLE.

Although its capital is the smallest authorized under the national banking law the above bank has done a very large business from its inception. It was organized September 10, 1900, and its present status is:

Capital stock paid in......................................$25.000.00
Surplus fund... 5,000.00
Undivided profits.. 3,300.00

Presidents, David M. Brown, Oliver Greenstreet; vice presidents, Oliver Greenstreet, Horace H. Elwell, Robert Hall; cashier, Luther F. Symons; Assistant cashiers, Charles C. Brown, Claud M. Bartlett.

First board of directors: David M. Brown, Horace H. Elwell, Oliver Greenstreet, Hawley Hall, Robert Hall.

Present board of directors: Oliver Greenstreet. Hawley Hall, Robert Hall, Thomas J. Martin, Otis A. Stubbs.

Original stockholders: Sarah B. Alf, Joseph Ballard, William M. Bartlett, William Beard, William A. Bennett, Ephraim R. Bridgman, Charles C. Brown, David M. Brown,

Allen Butler, Leburn Butler, Albert L. Canaday, Charles F. Custer, Morris B. Cole, Benjamin D. Copeland, Wilson T. Dobbins, Horace H. Elwell, John Foster, Clara Freeman, John J. Gilbert, Frederick E. Glidden, Oliver P. Gotschall, Oliver Greenstreet, Hawley Hall, Lee F. Hall, Luther G. Hall, Robert Hall, Andrew J. Harrold, Edgar Heacock, John Hendricks, Lewis Hoff, William M. Jackson, John Leonberger, Ella V. Loder, William Macy, George W. Manlove, James R. Martin, Thomas J. Martin, Willard W. Martin, William M. Mills, John Myer, John McFarland, Marshall Newhouse, Simeon W. Pickering, Morris Reynolds, Orrin J. Richardson, Samuel S. Riggle, Samuel J. A. Shipley, Philo Southwick, Albert Stewart, Charles Stewart, Otis A. Stubbs, Henry W. Suders, Luther F. Symons, Robert P. White, Thomas W. White.

Stockholders.September 1, 1905: Sarah B. Alf, Joseph Ballard, Claud M. Bartlett, William Beard, Leburn Butler, Albert L. Canaday, Morris B. Cole, Charles F. Custer, Wilson T. Dobbins, Horace H. Elwell, John Foster, Mrs. Frederick E. Glidden, John J. Gilbert, Oliver Greenstreet, Hawley Hall, Lee F. Hall, Robert Hall, Mrs. William C. Hall, Andrew J. Harrold, Edgar Heacock, Lewis Hoff, William M. Jackson, Minnie Kettner, John Leonberger, Lewisville Lodge, Independent Order of Odd Fellows, William A. Macy, George W. Manlove, James R. Martin, Thomas J. Martin, Willard W. Martin, John Myer, Arthur W. Osborne, Simeon W. Pickering. Carrie B. Prine, Morris Reynolds, Samuel S. Riggle, Albert Stewart, Charles Stewart, Otis A. Stubbs, Henry W. Suders, Luther F. Symons, Robert P. White.

A statement of the condition of the bank August 25, 1905, is printed below:

Report of the condition of the First National Bank at Lewisvlile, in the State of Indiana, at the close of business, August 25, 1905:

RESOURCES.		LIABILITIES.	
Loans and discounts.	$ 91,707.17	Capital stock paid in	$ 25,000.00
Overdrafts, secured and unsecured	670.40	Surplus fund	5,000.00
U. S. bonds to secure circulation	10,000.00	Undivided profits, less expenses and taxes paid	3,014.00
Premiums on U. S. bonds	462.50	National Bank notes outstanding	10,000.00
Banking house, furniture and fixtures	3,456.81	Individual deposits subject to check	104,700.73
Due from approved reserve agents	40,493.55	Demand certificates of deposit.	6,481.50
Checks and other cash items..	1,145.95		
Notes of other National Banks	1,206.00		
Fractional paper currency, nickels and cents	122.50		
Lawful money reserve in bank, viz:			
Specie $2,537.35			
Legal tender notes.. 1,900.00	4.437.35		
Redemption fund with U. S. Treasurer (5 per cent. circulation)	500.00		
Total	$154,196.23	Total	$154,196.23

State of Indiana, County of Henry, ss:

I, L. F. Symons, cashier of the above-named bank, do solemnly swear that the above statement is true to the best of my knowledge and belief.

L. F. Symons, Cashier. Correct attest: O. Greenstreet, Robert Hall Otis A. Stubbs, Directors.

Subscribed and sworn to before me this 2d day of September, 1905.

JOHN C. KELLER, Notary Public.

THE MOORELAND STATE BANK OF MOORELAND.

An organization was effected and this bank began business September 8, 1902. Its capital stock, surplus fund, officers and stockholders are set out below:

Capital stock paid in $25,000.00
Surplus fund 750.00

President, Henry Brown; Vice Presidents, George R. Koons, James S. Luellen; Cashier, George F. Keever. ·

First Board of Directors—Enoch G. Bouslog, Henry Brown, Eli Holaday, David W. Kinsey, Thomas B. Millikan, William M. Pence, Elisha Shaffer.

Present Board of Directors—Henry Brown, William Covalt, James W. Current, Eli Holaday, David W. Kinsey, Thomas B. Millikan, William M. Pence.

Original Stockholders—Alvus D. Adams, Henry Brown, Joseph Barnhart, Enoch G. Bouslog, Reuben H. Brown, Elizabeth Conway, Ferdinand Covalt, William Covalt, James W. Current, Charles H. Daniels, Ellen Haynes, George W. Hodson, Eli Holaday, Sylvester H. Huffman, William H. Jones, William E. Kerr, George F. Keever, David W. Kinsey, Benjamin F. Koons, George R. Koons, James C. Lamar, Wilson R. Lines, Henry Main, Thomas B. Millikan, David A. Niccum, William M. Pence, Mary P. Replogle, Christian Richardson, Elisha Shaffer, Hattie S. Smith, Larkin C. Smith, Oliver T. Waltz, Harvey L. Williams.

Stockholders September 1, 1905—Alvus D. Adams, Henry Brown, Eli M. Conwell, Ferdinand Covalt, William Covalt, James W. Current, Eli Holaday, George F. Keever, David W. Kinsey, James S. Luellen, Thomas B. Millikan, William M. Pence, Mary P. Replogle, Elizabeth Ridgway, Larkin C. Smith, Harvey L. Williams.

The bank's resources and liabilities are given below, as shown August 25, 1905:

Report of the condition of the Mooreland State Bank, at Mooreland, in the State of Indiana, at the close of its business on August 25, 1905:

RESOURCES.		LIABILITIES.	
Loans and discounts	$47,334.83	Capital stock paid in	$25,000.00
Overdrafts	160.23	Surplus fund	750.00
Due from banks and bankers	26,366.84	Discount, exchange and interest..	382.20
Furniture and fixtures	600.00	Individual deposits on demand..	53,983.52
Current expenses	79.33		
Cash on hand, currency.. $4,125.00			
Specie 1,449.49			
	5,574.49		
Total	$80,115.72	Total	$80,115.72

State of Indiana, County of Henry, ss:

I, G. F. Keever, cashier of the Mooreland State Bank, do solemnly swear that the above statement is true.   G. F. KEEVER, Cashier.

Subscribed and sworn to before me this 31st day of August, 1905.

IONA T. CHRISTNER, Notary Public.

THE SHIRLEY BANK OF SHIRLEY.

This is a private bank, owned by Mark E. Wood. It began business December 20, 1899. Its capital and surplus are.

Capital stock paid in $10,000.00
Surplus fund 1,000.00

Cashier, Mark E. Wood; Assistant Cashier, Thomas J. De Mund.

A statement of its assets and liabilities as published August 25, 1905, is given herewith:

Report of the condition of the Shirley Bank, at Shirley, in the State of Indiana, at the close of business on August 25, 1905:

RESOURCES.

Loans and discounts $48,628.34
Due from banks and bankers 11.248.86
Furniture and fixtures 3,000.00
Cash on hand, currency..$4,823.00
Specie 924.10 5,747.10
Cash items 164.17

Total $68,788.47

LIABILITIES.

Capital paid in $10,000.00
Discount, exchange and interest.   830.73
Individual deposits 57,957.74

Total $68,788.47

STATE OF INDIANA, COUNTY OF HANCOCK, SS:

I, Mark E. Wood, cashier of the Shirley Bank, at Shirley, Indiana, do solemnly swear that the above statement is true.   MARK E. WOOD, Cashier.

Subscribed and sworn to before me this 1st day of September, 1905.

SYLVESTER HAMILTON. Notary Public.

THE FIRST STATE BANK OF SHIRLEY.

This is the most recent acquisition to the banking institutions of Henry County, and began business August 10, 1904.

Capital stock paid in $25,000.00

Presidents, Frank J. Vestal, William W. Beeson; Vice Presidents, William W. Beeson, Leander A. Johnson; Cashier, John R. Kitterman; Bookkeeper, J. Vernis Kitterman.

First and Present Board of Directors—William W. Beeson, Edward B. Byrket, Leander A. Johnson, John R. Kitterman, Allen Sherry, Frank J. Vestal, Ross Wilkinson.

Stockholders, September 1, 1905—William W. Beeson, Charles E. Byrket, Edward B. Byrket, Citizens' State Bank of Knightstown, William H. Collier, Enoch Courtney, Charles H. Elliott, Alison Frazer, Ezra C. Gebhart, Frank Gebhart, Charles Grunden, Thurza Grunden, Thomas B. Jackson, Verlie Jackson, Jesse M. Johnson, Leander A. Johnson, Floyd Kitterman, John R. Kitterman, Francis E. Pickering, Curtis Riggs, Elwood Riggs, John A. Riggs, Russell Riggs, Alvenus Sherry, Isaac N. Trail, William Trail, John W. Warrick, Robert Ulmer, Alexander Wilkinson, George Q. Wilkinson, Isaac Wilkinson, Joseph Wilkinson, Ross Wilkinson, Thomas Wilkinson estate, Prudence White.

Below is a statement of the bank's resources and liabilities under date of August 25, 1905:

Report of the condition of the First State Bank, at Shirley, in the State of Indiana, at the close of its business on August 25, 1905:

RESOURCES.

Loans and discounts $40,187.59
Due from banks and bankers.... 21,719.10
Banking house 1,625.00
Furniture and fixtures 1,850.00
Current expenses 1,219.28
Cash on hand 6,412.03

Total $73,013.00

LIABILITIES.

Capital stock paid in $25,000.00
Discount, exchange and interest. 1,066.97
Individual deposits on demand.. 46,946.03

Total $73,013.00

STATE OF INDIANA. COUNTY OF HANCOCK. SS:

I. John R. Kitterman, cashier of the First State Bank, at Shirley, do solemnly swear that the above statement is true.   JOHN R. KITTERMAN.

Subscribed and sworn to before me, this 5th day of September, 1905.

SYLVESTER HAMILTON. Notary Public.

In 1869 a private bank, known as The Citizens' Bank, was instituted at Dunreith with a capital of $25,000, by Strattan, Harrold and Company, consisting of Edward K. Straffan, Andrew Harrold. Caleb Johnson and perhaps others, whose names are not now obtainable. Its transactions during the first year of its existence were satisfactory and profitable, but in December, 1870, the bank was burglariously robbed of about $6,000, which so materially interfered with its usefulness that its proprietors within a short time thereafter wound up its affairs.

HENRY COUNTY EDITORS.

The following is a recapitulation of the assets and liabilities of the eleven banks in Henry County, including those of Shirley, as shown by their official statements, August 25, 1905:

ASSETS.		LIABILITIES.	
Loans and discounts	$1,789,358.00	Capital stock	$530,000.00
Real estate, furniture and fix-		Surplus earnings	235,909.00
tures	44,515.00	Deposits	1,945,430.00
Cash ·on hand and in other			
banks	877,466.00		

NUMBER OF BANKS IN INDIANA.

On September 1, 1905, there were 683 banks in Indiana, divided as follows:

National Banks	184
State Banks	175
Private Banks	260
Trust and Savings Banks	64
Total	683

NEWSPAPERS, PAST AND PRESENT, IN HENRY COUNTY.

After a period of evolution, during which the local press has struggled valiantly to gain a permanent foothold, it may be safely asserted that the newspapers of Henry County have found a profitable abiding place in the hearts and patronage of the people. It has been said that "of the making of books there is no end," and that remark may, with striking force, be applied to the many newspapers that have been started to "fill a long-felt want" in this county, only to expire after a few months' or years' struggle and apparently without having left a vacuum in any locality save·in that of the publisher's pocket. From the early days of the county, men with ambition to found a newspaper have not been backward in putting their energy and ability in that direction to the test. The number of names in the long list of newspapers that have existed in Henry County, at various times in a period of sixty years and are now but memories, tells the story of mistaken ideas held by their publishers as to the profitableness of the enterprises. But during all these years, the county has grown in wealth and population amazingly, and who shall say that its newspapers, although many of them were compelled by stress of circumstances to "give up the ghost" because their publishers were powerless to "make the ghost walk" regularly on weekly pay days, were not largely instrumental in helping along this prosperity? In the main, the newspapers of Henry County have been published and edited by men of excellent business and literary ability, —men who afterward reaped golden returns from other fields of business venture. The number of newspapers in the county is less than it was a quarter of a century ago; the process of planting printing presses and of weeding them out has been slow, but sure. The county seat now has but two newspaper offices—*The Courier*, both daily and weekly, and *The Democrat*, weekly. In addition there are weekly newspapers published in Middletown, Mooreland, Lewisville, Spiceland, Knightstown and Shirley, so that all sections of the county are represented by local publications. All of them give most of their space to news of their particular localities and their patrons seem to appreciate and generously support the local publications. The advent of trolley lines, the numerous steam railroads that traverse the county, and the low price of the metropolitan daily and weekly newspapers, which these lines are enabled to deliver at every farm house each week day in the year through the medium of the rural free delivery of mail system, has not lessened the circulation of the local press—on the contrary, every newspaper now published in the county has perhaps the largest patronage in its history.

The honor of having the first newspaper in the county belongs to Knightstown. In 1832 "The Federal Union" was issued by Grant and Mitchell. John W. Grubbs, long identified with "The New Castle Courier," and afterward, until his death, a leading wholesale grocer of Richmond, got his first lessons in the art of printing in this primitive office, and has stated that its publication ceased within a year for want of sufficient patronage. About four years later, perhaps early in 1836, Thomas J. Langdon edited and printed a sheet called "The Banner." It gave up the struggle within six months. In 1837, Tisdale D. Clarkson launched "The Indiana Sun," and a year later sold the plant to Hannum and Grubbs. Hannum abandoned his interest in 1840 and John W. Grubbs became sole proprietor. In 1841, he moved the office to New Castle and changed the name of the paper to "The Indiana Courier." In 1859, Tisdale D. Clarkson again started a newspaper in Knightstown, which he called "The Citizen." Will C. Moreau and A. M. Woodin were connected with this paper at intervals during its short but eventful life, which came to a close in 1861. Isaac Kinley, afterward a distinguished officer in the Civil War, published a literary magazine of thirty two pages, called "The Beech Tree," for a few months in 1859, but it lacked pecuniary support and ceased to exist. In 1865 John A. Deem published an agricultural magazine, "The Western Ruralist," for five months. In the same year R. F. Brown moved the "Henry County Times" from New Castle and continued its publication for about five months. In May, 1867, John A. Deem established "The Knightstown Banner," which seemed to prosper from the start, for its publication still continues, although under other management, and it is regarded as firmly established and profitable newspaper property. In 1877 he sold the establishment to his brother, Thomas B. Deem, and March 23, 1883, Reverend Robert F. Brewington purchased a half interest in the paper, which Deem and Brewington continued to publish until December 3, 1884, when the former bought out the latter. Hunter Bradford purchased the paper October 2, 1885, and Benjamin S. Parker, Henry County's poet and author, became its editor and so continued until June 16, 1888, when Reverend Robert F. Brewington succeeded him and filled the position until November 9, 1888. On May 1, 1892, Wallace K. Deem (born in Knightstown, September 21, 1863, a son of John A. Deem, founder of the paper), purchased "The Banner" and has since remained its editor and proprietor. Mr. Deem is a thorough newspaper man and "The Banner" is one of the excellent county newspapers of the State.

John C. Riddell started "The City Chronicle" in 1870, which appeared periodically and semi-occasionally under his management until 1876. He then sold out to Frank I. Grubbs (now deputy Secretary of State), who changed the name of the paper to "The Knightstown Herald" and it died within six months. Fleming Ratcliff launched "The Knightstown Journal" in 1876, but in the Spring of 1877 it joined the other "has beens." From this date until some time in 1879, "The Banner" was the only paper published in Knightstown, then "The Shield" appeared, conducted by Frank I. Grubbs and Charles Moore. At the end of a year Moore retired and Leonidas P. Newby, now a banker and formerly member of the General Assembly from Henry County, purchased his interest. Newspaper life must have been too strenuous for Leonidas P., for he retired in the Fall of 1880 and "The Shield" was consolidated with "The Banner" under the name of "The Knightstown Banner-Shield." Four months later the publication of both papers was resumed. Grubbs continued to publish "The Shield" until March, 1883, when the plant was purchased by "The Banner" and "The Shield" discontinued. On December 18, 1885, Wallace K. Deem established "The Knightstown Sun" and published it until August 1, 1891, at which time Clarence H. Beard and his brother, Charles A., bought the paper and caused the "Sun" to shine until the Summer of 1895, when they leased the plant to William E. Newby, Joseph H. Hinshaw and William A. Keelum, who remained in charge until July 1, 1903, on which date Roy W. Steele became proprietor. Previous to this, August 19, 1899, "The Daily Journal" was started by Steele. On purchasing the "Sun" he adopted the name of "The Journal-Sun" for the weekly and continued to publish

"The Daily Journal" until January 31, 1904, when it ceased to exist. The name of "Sun" was dropped March 1, 1905, and the "Journal" continued to be published semi-weekly from that date until September 29, 1905, when it was discontinued and the office turned into a job printing establishment. Roy W. Steele is a young man of superior newspaper ability, industrious and earnest in all his undertakings. His brother, Walter B., was associated with him in the management of the "Journal" for a short time preceding its discontinuance.

"The Knightstown Daily News" was started November 11, 1897, with Harry C. Newby as publisher, and William E. Newby as editor. After a lively existence of eleven months it expired.

JOHN A. DEEM—FORMER EDITOR, THE KNIGHTSTOWN BANNER.

The subject of this sketch was born in Greene County, Ohio, on March 9, 1840, and came with his parents, Thomas and Phoebe (Hutzler) Deem, to Spiceland Township, in the Fall of 1848. He acquired a fair education in the district schools during the Winter time, devoting the Spring and Summer seasons to farm work. Later he taught a number of terms of school in the neighborhood. In 1862 he was married to Elizabeth, daughter of Joel and Annie (Gorton) Cloud. Three children were born to them—Wallace K., now editor of "The Knightstown Banner;" Ernest C., and Nora M. In the Spring of 1867, having previously spent some time in learning the printing business, he established "The Knightstown Banner," which he published for ten years and which, under his management, was one of the leading newspapers of the county. In 1877 he disposed of the "Banner" to his brother, Thomas B. Deem, and in 1880 went into the farming and stock-raising business in Spiceland Township, one mile north of Ogden, where he now resides, and has proved as thorough a farmer as he was a newspaper man. In 1882 he was elected to the lower house of the General Assembly and was re-elected in 1884. He was a useful, competent, upright and fearless member of that body and served his constituents most faithfully. The voters of Spiceland Township honored him by giving him the largest vote ever given to a candidate for office. While a citizen of Knightstown he was three times elected trustee of Wayne township and as such was largely instrumental in causing the erection of the splendid high school building of that town.

NEWSPAPERS OF NEWCASTLE.

The first newspaper printed at the county seat appeared in 1836 and was named "The New Castle Banner." James B. Swayze was the publisher and Reverend Alfred J. Cotton the editor. It survived for a half year. The publisher went into the newspaper business in Hagerstown and the Reverend Cotton moved to Dearborn County, where he became a judge of the court.

In 1841 John W. Grubbs moved the plant of "The Indiana Courier" from Knightstown to New Castle and continued its publication under that name. In 1843 his brother, Henry Clay Grubbs, became associated with him. About the middle of the year 1846 the office was sold to Cornelius V. Duggins. Mr. Duggins died in 1850, and for a short time James Comstock, his executor, managed the paper. But in March of the same year John W. Grubbs, the former publisher, took charge of it.

In January, 1853, George W. Lennard purchased the office. A few months later he took Coleman Rogers into partnership, and the two published the paper until the end of the year.

Another change of owners took place in January, 1854, at which time Nation and Ellison purchased the "Courier." This administration began with Henry C. Grubbs as chief editor, and David Nation, local editor. Mr. Grubbs soon retired, and David Nation became the managing editor. In the latter part of 1854 Wrigley and Lyle became the proprietors, and in 1856 they sold out to Charles E. Harwood and Thomas B. Redding.

Elijah B. Martindale was the next owner, but continued as such only a short time, selling out in the beginning of the year 1857, to Isaac S. Drake. Mr. Drake was editor and proprietor until some time in 1859, when Walton P. Goode became his partner. In about a year Goode became sole proprietor, and the "Courier" continued to be published

by him until November, 1862. The paper was then bought by Elwood Pleas, who conducted it nearly six years and a half, selling out in March, 1869, to Maurice E. Pleas and
Harrison Hoover. May 15, 1870, Alfred G. Wilcox, as the representative of the Telegram
Printing Company, of Richmond, bought the "Courier." He conducted it until September, then sold an interest to Calvin R. Scott.

In July, 1872, Adolph Rogers purchased the paper, and soon after Elwood Pleas
secured an interest. Rogers and Pleas continued to own and manage the "Courier"
for two years and six months: Then a stock company purchased it for the sum of
$10,000, and employed Adolph Regers as editor. The following gentlemen composed the
company: Adolph Rogers, Elwood Pleas, George Hazzard, author of this History; John W.
Griffin, Seth S. Bennett, John R. Millikan, Calvin R. Scott and Alexander S. McDowell.
Mr. Rogers continued as editor until January, 1877. Under him the editorial department
was conducted with ability and a high literary character given to the contents of the paper.
With the first number of the year 1877, William H. Elliott, the present editor and manager, took charge of the "Courier." At that time the paper had a circulation of 950 copies,
and its financial condition was anything but prosperous. Without previous experience in
journalism, Mr. Elliott soon succeeded in bringing about a change for the better, and from
that time until the present the "Courier" has steadily grown in prosperity and influence.
It is now among the best weeklies in Eastern Indiana.

In 1896 Mr. Elliott established "The Little Courier," a small daily newspaper of
four pages, five columns to the page, but deemed sufficient to meet the wants of the
public at that time. From this small beginning "The Daily Courier" has grown to its
present size, an eight page, six columns to the page, newspaper, published six days in
the week and giving every week-day afternoon very full and complete accounts of the
local happenings of the county in addition to several columns of telegraphic news from
all parts of the world. It is now the only daily paper published in the county. In 1899
Mr. Elliott disposed of the "Courier" to Mark O. Waters and Joseph A. Greenstreet, who
continued to publish the paper until 1902, when Greenstreet retired and Waters conducted the publication alone. In 1903, George A. Elliott, son of William H., purchased a
half interest in the plant and in 1904 the office went into the control of William H. and
George A. Elliott, who now publish both the daily and weekly "Courier." During
General Elliott's absence from the newspaper, he was first an officer in the navy while
the Spanish-American war continued, and later was a government official in Porto
Rico, as will be found fully set out in another part of this History. The "Courier" was
first a Whig newspaper and has steadfastly supported Republican policies since that
party was organized.

In February, 1852, "The Democratic Banner" was flung to the breeze in New
Castle by J. Fenwick Henry. He published the paper for eighteen months and sold the
property to Nelson Abbott, who changed the name to "The New Castle Banner." It
ceased to exist in 1855. "The Henry County Times" appeared in October, 1865, conducted by R. F. Brown, who moved the office from Connersville to New Castle. The
"Times" did a thirty days' stunt at the county seat and then located in Knightstown, as
is mentioned elsewhere.

Henry L. Shopp and Harrison Hoover started a paper styled "The Henry County
Independent," in April, 1867. Twenty four numbers of the paper were issued by them,
when the office was sold to a company of Democratic citizens and placed under the
editorial charge of Leonard H. Miller. In January, 1868, its name was changed to
"The Signs of the Times." Mr. Miller continued to edit the "Times" until April, 1868,
when S. S. Darling, of Hamilton, Ohio, succeeded him. It seems to have been the fashion
to change the name of this paper with the advent of each new editor, and on the 27th
of May, 1868, the paper was christened "The New Castle Examiner." Lewis L. Dale
then assumed editorial charge. The following May, there being an opening for a Democratic newspaper in Cambridge City, the office was moved thither and the "Examiner"
became "The Democratic Times." The paper was published in Cambridge City only a
few months, and the office was then re-established in New Castle. In December, 1870,
Loring Bundy and William Johnson bought "The Democratic Times" and it was conducted

by them for two years. Jesse M. Hiatt and Harrison Hoover were the next proprietors, taking charge in December, 1872. They changed the name and politics of the paper, making it Republican and styling it "The New Castle Times." About six months later Mr. Hoover sold his interest to James M. Kissell; and he, in the latter part of 1873, sold out to Benjamin S. Parker, a gentleman of well-known literary ability. In January, 1875, Mr. Hiatt disposed of his interest to Arthur E. Wickersham. At the same date the name of the paper was changed again, becoming "The New Castle Mercury." The "Mercury" was conducted by Parker and Wickersham until April 10, 1882, when Elwood Pleas and Company succeeded to the ownership. The publication of the "Mercury" was discontinued in 1884, and the office sold to the owners of "The Muncie Herald," a Democratic newspaper.

"The Henry County Republican" was inaugurated by Elwood and Maurice E. Pleas in August, 1870. In July, 1872, the "Republican" was consolidated with the "Courier."

A Democratic paper, "The New Castle News," was started early in 1877, the proprietors, Thomas J. Higgs and Josiah Crawford, moving the outfit from Connersville. It suspended publication in about nine months.

Colonel James D. Williams began the publication of a Democratic paper in January, 1878, called "The Indiana Statesman," but the venture was not successful and the "Statesman" pulled up stakes in less than six months.

In January, 1878, "The New Castle Democrat," with John M. Goar as publisher, appeared on the scene. It was conducted with varying success by him for several years, and in 1884 Miles L. Reed assumed proprietorship and editorship of the paper, which he successfully published until 1891, when Peter M. Gillies took charge. During Gillies' management of the office he published also a daily evening paper, called the "News," for several months in 1894, but its publication was suspended in that year. In August, 1895, Walter S. Chambers bought the "Democrat" and in the intervening years has placed the paper on a firm footing, having its own building, a substantial brick structure on East Broad street, new and modern presses and other machinery and all the up-to-date material that is required in a first-class printing office of the present day. The "Democrat" has attained a list of nearly 2,500 paying subscribers, who appreciate the paper in the highest degree.

A Greenback-Labor party organ appeared in 1881, published by Henry W. Burtch, called "The Henry County Argus." In 1883 William R. Sanborn became its proprietor, and in March, 1884, it died for want of sufficient circulation, a thing which newspapers as well as individuals require in order to exist.

Charles F. Sudwarth, now of Washington, D. C., started a paper which was a very interesting sheet during its existence of about two years from 1885. It was called "The New Castle Crescent."

On February 20, 1891, a number of men, connected with the Farmers' Alliance or Grange, financed a paper which was named "The People's Press," and placed William W. Prigg in charge as editor. In July, 1893, Walter S. Chambers and Arthur W. Tracy bought the plant and changed the name of the paper to "The New Castle Press." The daily "Press" was started by them January 1, 1895. In July of that year they sold the daily and weekly "Press" to Clarence H. and Charles A. Beard, who changed the name of the weekly to "The Henry County Republican," still continuing the daily "Press." The plant again changed ownership in 1897, two gentlemen of Winona, Minnesota, Messrs. Cameron and Dodge, becoming proprietors. They were succeeded in 1899 by Claude S. Watts, and July 31, 1900, Fleming Ratcliff took charge and consolidated the papers under the name of "The New Castle Tribune," he having in 1897 established a paper by that name. The daily "Tribune" not proving profitable, was discontinued in 1902, but the weekly "Tribune" was continued under his management until the Spring of 1903, when Charles S. Hernly and Otho Williams bought the office, changed the name of the paper back to the "Press" and started a handsome and lively eight-page daily under that name with the well-known and charming writer, John Thornburgh, as editor-in-chief, a position which he very ably and satisfactorily filled during the life of the paper. Mr. Williams soon retired and Charles S. Hernly continued the business alone until February 1, 1904, when the publications not proving profitable, they ceased to exist and the office material was sold to "The New Castle Courier."

In June, 1903, Fleming Ratcliff again revived "The New Castle Tribune," which he continued to publish until July, 1905, when he moved the office to Spiceland and changed the name of the paper to "The Henry County Tribune." Since the establishment of "The Spiceland Reporter," in 1873, of which he was editor, with the exception of a few years in the eighties, when he was depot agent of the Indiana, Bloomington and Western Railroad, at New Castle, Fleming Ratcliff has been identified with the newspapers of Henry County almost continuously at Spiceland, Knightstown and New Castle. His ability as a newspaper man has long been recognized. He is a fluent and forcible writer, an indefatigable newsgatherer and so long has he been connected with newspapers that he will probably continue his life-work to the end in the editorial harness.

ELWOOD PLEAS—FORMER EDITOR, THE NEW CASTLE COURIER.

Editor, Philosopher, Naturalist and Good Citizen.

Elwood Pleas, son of Aaron L. and Lydia (Gilbert) Pleas, was born at Richmond, Indiana, May 4, 1831, and died at his home near Spiceland, Indiana, December 31, 1897. Mr. Pleas' father was of a New York family and his mother was a daughter of Josiah Gilbert, one of the three Gilbert brothers, Josiah, Joel and Thomas, who came from North Carolina to the Hopewell neighborhood, in Dudley Township, Henry County, Indiana, and who, with their families at one time owned so great a portion of the lands of that township and were so prominent in the Friends' meetings of Eastern Indiana. He was married to Sarah Ann, daughter of Joseph and Rebecca Griffin, of near Spiceland, on April 26, 1854. She is a sister of John William Griffin, a biographical sketch of whom appears elsewhere in this History, to which reference should be had for information as to the Griffin family.

Elwood and Sarah Ann (Griffin) Pleas were the parents of six children, two daughters and four sons, of whom one daughter, Mary B., now the wife of George Beckett, and three sons survive their father. Mrs. Beckett and her husband make their home with her mother, Mrs. Sarah A. Pleas, on the old Pleas' homestead. One son, Dr. Edgar Pleas, is a popular physician of Indian Territory; another, Robert J. Pleas, is a business man of Spiceland; and a third, Charles Earl Pleas, is a photographer and fruit grower at Chipley, Florida. There are seven grandchildren in the Pleas family: Mr. and Mrs. Becket have two grown daughters, one of them the wife of Evert Henshaw; Dr. Edgar Pleas and his first wife, who died some years ago, had two daughters; his present wife, Lucy, daughter of William W. Wilson, of Spiceland, was before her marriage a prominent Henry County club woman, so that the two little girls are happily situated in their father's southwestern home; Robert J. Pleas and his wife are the parents of two boys and one girl.

Elwood Pleas was in early life a carpenter, cabinet-maker, a farmer, and always a lover and student of Nature. His opportunities for gaining an education were comparatively meagre, but he made good use of such as he possessed. He was a reader of books and a student of principles and conditions. He was convinced of the great evils of slavery early in life, and made war upon it from and after reaching maturity. When called to the editorship of "The New Castle Courier," in 1862, he made it a power in local politics and speedily made a State reputation as a daring and able newspaper man. Under his management, the "Courier" was a financial, as well as political, success. Benjamin S. Parker, writing of the life and work of Mr. Pleas, says:

"When I first knew him, he was selling Hinton Rowan Helper's "Impending Crisis," from house to house, not as the ordinary agent sells books for his own profit, but to help forward the mighty wave of protest against the extension of slavery, that was then sweeping over the North. That was in the fifties, several years before the war. It was this same enthusiasm for liberty that carried him into the newspaper business during the progress of the war, and a little later led him for a time into the army. He understood very well that he could do the country more effective service with his news-paper than he could hope to do in the ranks of war, but he felt that the editor who so strongly upheld the war for the Union should share its dangers with those whom his words, probably, helped to lead into the service, and thus establish the truth of his convictions by his courage."

In the Civil War he served faithfully as a soldier in Company B, 139th Indiana Infantry, as is appropriately set out elsewhere in this History. His other newspaper enterprises besides the "Courier" were "The Henry County Republican," a second owner-ship or partnership in the "Courier," and last, a connection with "The New Castle Mercury," which did not turn out so well financially, though each and all of them were well sustained editorially and were superior publications.

It was in the field of biological research and investigation that he was at his best, his special lines of work lying mostly in geology and practical entomology. His collection was the best and most representative of any private collection in Eastern Indiana, and his scientific correspondence was very large. It was beginning to yield him good financial returns, as well as many honors, when the illness that was to speedily end his life fell upon him and left his tasks unfinished.

He was a forceful writer and an entertaining speaker. His addresses before the Henry County Historical Society, which he did so much to establish, were always looked forward to as its most interesting and profitable occasions. Elwood Pleas was undoubt-edly one of the few strong men who have stood out clearly as above and beyond the high average level of the county's intelligent manhood. This is apparent in so many pages of our history that he needs no lengthy eulogium at the hands of a biographer. But more than all and better than all, was he the upright citizen and the loving, con-siderate husband and affectionate parent and generous friend. What better can any man be?

Elwood Pleas must also be given consideration as Henry County's first historian. In 1871, he issued "Henry County, Past and Present," which was a brief history of the county from 1821 to 1871. The book is a small volume, containing less than one hun-dred and fifty pages, but it is worth its weight in gold as an historical document and as a first effort to preserve the history of the county. The author of this History ac-knowledges himself to be greatly indebted to this little book of Elwood Pleas, and many of the most valuable of the early historical facts of the county would have been lost had it not been for the careful, methodical and painstaking work of Mr. Pleas. Long may his memory be cherished.

NEWSPAPERS OF SPICELAND.

"The Spiceland Reporter" was started in July, 1873, by James W. Harvey, pro-prietor, and Fleming Ratcliff, editor. About eighteen months later Harvey gave up the publication of the paper, not finding it profitable. The citizens, however, determined to keep the paper running and the "Reporter" company was formed with about $2,700 capital and Mr. Ratcliff continued as editor. Lewis Woods, Elisha B. Ratcliff, Dr. J. B. Cochrane, Joseph E. Bogue and S. E. Unthank constituted the stock company. In July, 1876, Mr. Ratcliff retired from the editorship. His successors in that position were Professor Nathan Newby, Clarkson Davis, Charles P. Butler and others. In July, 1880, the paper was sold at receiver's sale and bought by Clarkson Davis and W. S. Chamness. It expired in November, 1880. For about eighteen months prior to that time James M. Kissell was the publisher.

Recently, in July, 1905, Fleming Ratcliff moved the plant of "The New Castle Tribune" to Spiceland, changed its name to "The Henry County Tribune," and is pub-lishing the paper from an office in that town.

THE MIDDLETOWN NEWS.

The "News" enjoys a unique position in the history of Henry County newspaper-dom from the fact that it was the first newspaper published in Middletown and has occupied the field alone since its inception. It was founded in April, 1885, by J. A.

Wertz. In a short time George W. Rodecap became associated with him and in September, 1885, the latter assumed proprietorship. On November 29, 1886, Joseph O. Lambert took charge and published the paper until July 7, 1893, when he sold out to Willis L. McCampbell, present postmaster at Middletown. In January, 1894, Joseph O. Lambert and Charles B. Unger bought the office and continued in partnership until January, 1902, when Lambert became sole proprietor and has so continued to the present time. Mr. Lambert is a pungent and forceful writer and the "News" very capably caters to its many patrons in and around Middletown. Mr. Lambert is now and has been for several years chairman of the Republican County Central Committee.

NEWSPAPERS OF LEWISVILLE.

The first number of "The Lewisville Democrat was issued November 29, 1877, by William F. Taylor and Lee L. Poarch. Dr. Nelson G. Smith acted as editor for about three months and was succeeded by Thomas W. Hall, for a few weeks; after this, Taylor and Poarch were both editors and proprietors. In January, 1880, the paper passed into the hands of Dr. Nelson G. Smith, who conducted it a few weeks. William A. Dale then became editor and proprietor and after six months the enterprise was abandoned.

In June, 1900, Ursa Martin and Edmund W. Robeson started "The Lewisville Enterprise," and continued its publication for about three months, when Martin succeeded to the business. In December, 1901, he sold the plant to William D. Fancher, who discontinued the publication of the paper. Ursa Martin again purchased the office in November, 1903, and revived the "Enterprise" in March, 1904. On August 28, 1905, he sold out to Edmund W. Robeson, who is now editor and publisher.

NEWSPAPERS OF SHIRLEY.

"The Shirley Enterprise" was started by Benjamin F. Martindale in October, 1900, who continued to publish it until November, 1903, when he sold the office to Joseph H. C. Denman, who changed the name of the paper to the "Gazette," and so continued it until in May, 1904, when Martindale again took charge and published the paper as the "Enterprise."

In the Summer of 1903, J. E. McClain started a paper which he called "The Shirley-Wilkinson News." In June, 1904, it was purchased by Martindale and consolidated with the "Enterprise." In April, 1905, Carl Shafer bought the office and changed the name of the paper to "The Shirley News," and still continues to publish it.

"The Shirley Hustler" was started in April, 1900, by Noble B. Van Matre, who published it about two and one-half years, then engaged in other business and the paper was suspended.

THE MOORELAND RECORD.

This is a weekly newspaper published by Harold C. Burton, by whom it was established July 28, 1905. It is the most recent claimant for the patronage of the reading public of that portion of Henry County.

COMPANY F, 199th PENNSYLVANIA INFANTRY

in a short time George W. Rodecap became associated with him and in September 1885, the latter assumed proprietorship. On November 29, 1886, Joseph O. took charge and published the paper until July 7, 1893, when he sold out to M. McCampbell, present postmaster at Middletown. In January, 1894, Joseph O. and Charles B. Unger bought the office and continued in partnership until 1902, when Lambert became sole proprietor and has so continued to the present Lambert is a pungent and forceful writer and the "News" very capably caters patrons in and around Middletown. Mr. Lambert is now and has been for years chairman of the Republican County Central Committee.

NEWSPAPERS OF LEWISVILLE.

The number of "The Lewisville Democrat was issued November 29, 1877, by William Taylor and Lee L. Poarch. Dr. Nelson G. Smith acted as editor for about three months, was succeeded by Thomas W. Hall, for a few weeks; after this, Taylor and Poarch both editors and proprietors. In January, 1880, the paper passed into the hands of Nelson G. Smith, who conducted it a few weeks. William A. Dale then became and proprietor and after six months the enterprise was abandoned.

In June Mac and Edmund W. Robeson started "The Lewisville Enterprise," and for about three months, when Martin succeeded to the business the plant to William L. Faucher, who discontinued Martin again purchased the office in November, 1903, and March, 1904. On August 28, 1905, he sold out to Edmund W. is the editor and publisher.

NEWSPAPERS OF SHIRLEY.

"The Shirley Enterprise" was started by Benjamin F. Martindale in October, 1900, who continued to publish it until November, 1903, when he sold the office to Joseph H. C. Denman, who changed the name of the paper to the "Gazette," and so continued it until in May, 1904, when Martindale again took charge and published the paper as the "Enterprise."

In the Summer of 1901, E. McClain started a paper which he called "The Shirley-Wilkinson News." In June 1904, it was purchased by Martindale and consolidated with the "Enterprise." In April Carl Shafer bought the office and changed the name of the paper to "The Shirley News" and still continues to publish it.

"The Shirley Hustler" was started in April, 1900, by Noble B. Van Matre, who published it about two and one-half years, then engaged in other business and the paper was suspended

NEWSPAPERS AND RECORD.

This is a weekly newspaper owned by Harry C. Warren, by whom it was established July 28, 1905. It is the weekly claimant for the patronage of the reading public of that portion of Henry County.

COMPANY B, 139th INDIANA INFANTRY.

STATISTICAL INFORMATION.

Total comparative value of property of all kinds in Henry County, as shown by the several townships and towns combined assessed for taxation for the years 1842, 1870 and 1904:

Townships.	1842.	1870.	1904.
Blue River	Not organized.	358,040	825,270
Dudley	275,320	797,600	1,494,380
Fall Creek	207,995	990,960	1,639,540
Franklin	308,319	870,180	1,440,480
Greensboro	157,753	589,300	1,076,380
Harrison	142,292	672,330	1,196,650
Henry	237,183	1,512,770	4,017,650
Jefferson	Not organized	562,550	996,690
Liberty	302,421	1,042,890	1,497,610
Prairie	251,279	825,570	1,299,800
Spiceland	Not organized	802,960	1,426,720
Stony Creek	168,142	330,550	562,420
Wayne	468,660	1,685,620	2,613,790
Total	$2,519,364	$11,041,320	$20,087,380

Total comparative amounts of taxes levied for all purposes in Henry County as shown by the several townships and towns combined for the years 1842, 1870 and 1904:

Townships.	1842.	1870.	1904.
Blue River	Not organized.	3,208.07	13,267.09
Dudley	1,180.62	7,144.68	20,254.76
Fall Creek	961.99	7,937.26	28,404.57
Franklin	1,306.12	8,246.14	20,626.66
Greensboro	668.14	6,179.50	19,259.59
Harrison	627.02	5,805.30	20,828.12
Henry	1,015.14	12,637.84	82,864.85
Jefferson	Not organized.	5,249.98	13,269.00
Liberty	1,282.47	9,192.21	20,354.80
Prairie	1,120.47	7,762.47	18,750.44
Spiceland	Not organized.	6,247.77	21,988.26
Stony Creek	762.49	3,159.72	9,383.63
Wayne	1,974.31	15,258.12	50,879.69
Total	$10,898.77	$98,029.06	$340,631.46

Total comparative value of personal property, of all kinds, in Henry County, as shown by the several townships and towns combined assessed for taxation for the years 1842, 1870 and 1904:

Townships.	1842.	1870.	1904.
Blue River	Not organized.	88,790	190,620
Dudley	50,251	249,970	332,240
Fall Creek	43,080	412,280	476,850
Franklin	47,229	332,260	368,870
Greensboro	25,118	196,330	269,850
Harrison	16,908	217,390	314,560
Henry	39,988	609,400	1,182,760
Jefferson	Not organized.	188,050	214,200
Liberty	50,609	325,410	301,570
Prairie	48,799	258,650	287,290
Spiceland	Not organized.	296,310	393,160
Stony Creek	31,266	112,380	141,740
Wayne	85,078	692,550	824,850
Total	$438,326	$3,979,720	$5,298,560

Total comparative value of all lands, exclusive of town-lots, without the improvements thereon, in Henry County, as shown by the several townships assessed for taxation for the years 1842, 1870 and 1904:

Townships.	1842.	1870.	1904.
Blue River	Not organized.	221,980	458,220
Dudley	119,873	414,460	637,600
Fall Creek	93,387	392,280	659,780
Franklin	150,626	390,190	591,820
Greensboro	76,408	284,120	514,320
Harrison	97,006	338,970	781,280
Henry	118,028	544,630	912,810
Jefferson	Not organized	281,430	543,460
Liberty	135,375	575,940	843,720
Prairie	123,356	467,840	686,730
Spiceland	Not organized.	333,620	453,590
Stony Creek	88,907	178,940	333,010
Wayne	178,810	500,940	694,530
Total	$1,181,776	$4,924,880	$8,090,970

Total comparative value of all improvements on lands, exclusive of improvements on town lots, in Henry County, as shown by the several townships, assessed for taxation for the years 1842, 1870 and 1904:

Townships.	1842.	1870.	1904.
Blue River	Not organized	47,270	37,070
Dudley	102,042	127,660	111,850
Fall Creek	67,338	129,890	124,090
Franklin	95,604	111,060	88,720
Greensboro	44,737	80,730	72,760
Harrison	27,848	106,040	102,200
Henry	52,542	139,720	230,020
Jefferson	Not organized.	77,860	73,010
Liberty	116,437	136,950	104,130
Prairie	78,609	91,370	71,090
Spiceland	Not organized.	123,840	101,410
Stony Creek	45,838	34,810	43,910
Wayne	119,962	163,830	119,560
Total	$750,957	$1,371,030	$1,279,820

The reader should not fail to note that the appraisement of these improvements for the year 1870 is more than $91,000 greater than in 1904, thirty four years later. This may be accounted for in the possibly different ways of making the appraisement for the years mentioned. Then it is a fact that as the wealth of the county has increased, the tendency has been to consolidate and enlarge the farms. The prosperous neighbor has purchased the farm of his less prosperous one; thus, as the farms have increased in size, the value of improvements, so far as houses are concerned, has decreased. The smaller the farms the more valuable the improvements in the aggregate.

Total comparative value of all town lots, without improvements thereon, in Henry County, as shown by towns and townships, assessed for taxation for the years 1859, 1870 and 1904:

Townships.	1859.	1870.	1904.
Blue River			9,160
Dudley	600	890	14,410
Fall Creek	4,420	16,140	79,690
Franklin	6,290	6,290	26,400
Greensboro	3,015	6,070	16,610
Harrison	610	1,100	4,250
Henry	29,980	81,850	677,040
Jefferson	1,160	3,590	2,310
Liberty	580	900	970
Prairie	2,840	2,900	6,900
Spiceland	5,960	10,680	24,550
Stony Creek	2,610	2,040	3,480
Wayne	61,700	110,610	172,260
Total	$119,765	$243,060	$1,047,940

Total comparative value of all improvements in town lots in Henry County, as shown by towns and townships assessed for taxation for the years 1859, 1870 and 1904:

Townships.	1859.	1870.	1904.
Blue River			32,160
Dudley	2,100	4,620	27,560
Fall Creek	22,170	40,370	127,410
Franklin	14,300	30,380	29,330
Greensboro	11,835	22,050	65,820

Harrison	4,780	8,830	14,450
Henry	71,290	137,170	611,130
Jefferson	6,110	11,620	19,890
Liberty	3,500	4,150	3,120
Prairie	8,960	4,810	25,470
Spiceland	16,960	38,510	60,830
Stony Creek	5,140	2,430	10,140
Wayne	102,310	217,690	357,570
Total	$269,455	$522,630	$1,384,880

Total comparative value of all lands (farms and town-lots combined) and improvements thereon, in Henry County, as shown by the several townships and towns combined, assessed for taxation for the years 1842; 1870 and 1904:

Townships.	1842.	1870.	1904.
Blue River	Not organized.	269,250	536,610
Dudley	225,069	547,630	791,420
Fall Creek	164,915	578,680	990,880
Franklin	261,090	537,920	746,370
Greensboro	132,635	392,970	669,510
Harrison	125,384	454,940	882,180
Henry	197,195	903,370	2,431,000
Jefferson	Not organized	374,500	638,670
Liberty	251,812	717,480	951,940
Prairie	202,480	566,920	790,190
Spiceland	Not organized	506,650	640,380
Stony Creek	138,876	218,220	390,540
Wayne	353,582	993,070	1,343,920
Total	$2,081,038	$7,061,600	$11,803,610

Total comparative value of all railroad properties in Henry County, as shown by townships and towns combined, assessed for taxation for the years 1860, 1880 and 1904, steam and electric lines combined for the year 1904:

Townships.	1860.	1880.	1904.
Blue River	No railroad	No railroad	98,040
Dudley	26,250	65,050	370,720
Fall Creek	4,310	56,250	171,810
Franklin	23,330	46,200	325,240
Greensboro	No railroad	No railroad	137,020
Harrison	No railroad	No railroad	No railroad.
Henry	3,190	53,280	403,890
Jefferson	3,560	48,390	143,820
Liberty	4,690	77,470	244,100
Prairie	1,690	50,490	222,920
Spiceland	21,250	44,140	393,180
Stony Creek	No railroad	No railroad	30,140
Wayne	29,660	60,480	445,020
Total	$117,930	$501,750	$2,985,300

Total amount of taxes levied for all purposes in Henry County on the tax duplicate for the year 1842:

State tax	$ 6,078.73
County tax	3,559.36
Road tax	1,259.69
Total	$ 10,897.78
Add delinquent taxes	320.98
Grand total	$ 11,218.76

Total amount of taxes levied for all purposes in Henry County on the tax duplicate for the year 1870:

State tax	$ 18,658.93
State school tax	19,413.55
State sinking fund tax	11,041.29
County tax	12,788.79
Road tax	8,686.45
Township tax	845.61
Special school tax	18,622.54
Special school tuition tax	5,035.56
Corporation tax. Lewisville, Middletown and Sulphur Springs	720.26
Other taxes	104.23
Dog tax	2,108.75
Total	$ 98,029.06
Add delinquency carried forward from duplicate, 1869	3,454.99
Grand total	$ 101,484.05

The county tax of $12,788.79, levied for the year 1870, is not a fair index of county expenditures for the fiscal year ending May 31, 1871. There was a surplus, then, in the treasury of, approximately, $50,000, which had been accumulating through several years on account of the heavy taxation of the last years of the Civil War and for the building of the new courthouse. This surplus the county commissioners determined to use for county purposes; therefore the rate for 1870, approximately, eleven mills on the dollar, was very low.

The total county tax collected on the duplicate, for the preceding year, 1869, and for the fiscal year, ending May 31, 1870, was $51,495.32. The total tax levied in the county for the same period, for all purposes, was $194,330.89, to which was added, as a delinquency carried forward from the preceding duplicate, 1868, of $4,784.66, making a grand total for the duplicate of 1869, of $199,075.55. It was from the funds collected on this duplicate that the final payments were made for the new courthouse and the county jail.

On the tax duplicate for the year 1871 and for the fiscal year ending May 31, 1872, the total levy, for county purposes, was $35,172.24, a part of the surplus above referred to being carried over to be used for county purposes for this period. The total taxes levied on the duplicate of 1871, for all purposes, was $99,768.55, to which was added a delinquency carried forward from the preceding year, 1870, of $4,043.32, making a grand total of $103,811.87.

TOTALS FOR THE TAX DUPLICATE, 1870.

Value of lands, $4,924,880; value of improvements, $1,371,030; total..$6,295,910
Value of lots, $243,060; value of improvements, $522,630; total..765,690
Value of personal property of all kinds...3,979,720
Total value of taxables of all kinds, no mortgage exemption...11,041,320
Total polls, 3,495, tax levied on all males between the ages of 21 and 50 years.........................6,199

On the tax duplicates, at this time, the value of railroad property for taxation was not carried forward so as to make it appear separately in the grand recapitulation of taxes for the entire county. On the duplicate for 1870, the railroads were assessed at $3,500 per mile, main line, which included side tracks and rolling stock, and for the year mentioned the total thereof is included in the total value of taxables as above set forth.

TOTALS FOR THE TAX DUPLICATE OF 1904.

Value of lands, $8,090,970; value of improvements, $1,279,820; total.....................................$ 9,370,790
Value of lots, $1,047,940; value of improvements, 1,384,880; total...2,432,820
Value of personal property of all kinds..5,298,560
Value of railroad property, including electric lines...2,985,300
Value of taxables, $20,087,470, less mortgage exemption, $568,680...19,518,790
Total polls, 4,588. Tax levied on all males between the ages of 21 and 50 years...................10,500.50

Total amount of taxes levied for all purposes in Henry County on the tax duplicate for the year 1904:

state tax...$ 19,846.87	Tax for lighting streets (incorporated towns only)..	3,811.59
Tax for State benevolent institutions.......9,763.61	Tax for street improvements (incorporated towns only).......................	3,255.50
Tax for State debt sinking fund.............5,555.16		
State school tax...23,752.38	School library tax (New Castle and Wayne township only)....................	869.52
Tax for State educational institutions...5,369.97		
County tax for free gravel road repairs 17,574.51	Cemetery tax (New Castle corporation only)..	1,193.96
County tax for ordinary purposes...........41,815.32		
Township poor tax..5,286.89		
Local tuition tax...37,258.23	Water works tax (Knightstown corporation only)............................	1,374.40
special school tax.....................................39,822.11		
Road tax other than free gravel road repairs 42,830.57	Courthouse tax (new addition).*............	19,527.16
Township tax...16,093.63	Total $339,631.46	
Bridge tax...9,763.46	Add delinquency carried forward from duplicate of 1903.........................	3,710.61
Corporation tax (incorporated towns only) 23,987.02		
Corporation bond tax (incorporated towns only..10,606.60	Grand total...............................$343,342.07	

* The total levy of courthouse tax for the addition, on the tax duplicate for the year 1903, was $19,293.16. The total cost of the addition and all improvements there-

with will be found elsewhere in this History in the article treating of public buildings. There will be an additional tax levied for this purpose on the duplicate of 1905 of approximately $19,000.

Total county expenditures for Henry County for the fiscal year ending May 31, 1843:

Expenses, jury fees	$ 645.39	Expenses of buildings	318.75
Expenses, roads	294.34	Interest paid on orders	49.31
Assessing revenue	502.87	Specific allowance	709.25
County officers	627.40	Expenses of roads by receipts as filed	901.45
Expenses of criminals	150.16	State delinquent tax paid	189.75
Expenses of elections	39.87		
Expenses of poor	554.75	Total	$4,983.29

Total county expenditures for Henry County for the fiscal year ending May 31, 1871:

Expense of deaf and dumb	$ 8.60	Delinquent land redeemed	945.44
Taxes refunded, erroneously collected	19.65	Expense of criminals	1,029.71
Justice's mileage	22.60	Public printing, other than county records and stationery	1,030.85
Henry County Teachers' Institute	50.00	County records and stationery	1,356.85
Void sale for taxes, money refunded	59.20	Specific allowances	1,660.10
Docket fees, not collected and paid the State	71.00	Assessing the revenue, paid township assessors	1,801.00
Expense of elections	89.05	Bailiffs' fees, court bailiffs and riding bailiffs for Sheriff and grand jury	1,880.05
Expense of blind	114.06	Jury fees, petit juries and grand juries	3,867.38
Damage money	150.00	County officers, salaries	6,157.89
Coroner's inquests	171.02	Expense of public buildings. Final payments on courthouse and jail	7,272.17
Congressional township interest. Not collected and paid State	195.12	Expense of poor in county asylum and elsewhere	14,257.56
Roads and highways	227.05		
Common school fund interest. Not collected and paid State	242.45	Total	$43,463.12
Expense of insane	345.07		
House of Refuge. Expense of boys in Plainfield Reform School	439.25		

Total county expenditures for Henry County for the fiscal year ending December 31, 1904:

Justices' mileage. Allowed Justices of the Peace for making reports and turning in fines	$ 11.40	ship, and at a private orphans' home, known as the Julia E. Work Training School, at Plymouth, Indiana	1,492.95
Specific allowances, not otherwise classified	112.08	Commissioners' Court. Includes salaries of Commissioners, ($1,050); sheriffs' per diem attending Commissioners' Court; salary of County Attorney and other incidental expense	1,524.00
Historical Society Building. Sums paid for fuel, water and general repairs	131.75		
Delinquent lands redeemed	165.02		
Preliminary expense of ditches, which includes all of the cost of original survey and publication of notices. The money to be collected and refunded to the county by the Ditch Commissioners	279.50	County jail. Includes expense of heat, light, water, boarding prisoners and ordinary repairs	2,165.39
		Expense of elections	2,380.92
Benevolent institutions. For maintenance and transportation of inmates of Blind and Deaf and Dumb Asylums, Reform School for Boys, Reform School for Girls, Asylum for Feeble Minded Youth and Woman's Prison	352.34	Township poor. Sums advanced by the Board of County Commissioners to respective townships and then, by them, afterwards refunded	2,737.48
		Assessing the revenue. This is the amount in the aggregate paid the respective township assessors	2,801.30
Burial of soldiers and soldiers' wives and widows	532.50	County Asylum. This includes fuel, light, maintenance of inmates, salary of superintendent and matron, physician, hired help and general repairs	3,421.45
Insanity proceedings. Includes per diem of Justices of the Peace; witness fees; physician's service; transportation and amount paid by the county, annually, to Eastern Insane Asylum, at Richmond, for maintenance of inmates	546.00	Street assessments. The county's proportion of expense, building streets surrounding courthouse square, under the Barrett act and street improvement on other properties owned by the county in New Castle	4,003.91
Civil engineering. Preliminary work, plans and specifications for bridges	665.18	Circuit Court. Includes all allowances made by the court for grand and petit jury fees; court bailiffs and all specific allowances made by the court, including stationery and law books	4,173.62
Interest on common school fund. Interest on the money borrowed by the Board of County Commissioners for general county purposes from the common school fund	972.39	Courthouse. Includes expense of light, heat, water, janitor and all ordinary repairs	4,929.61
Miscellaneous expenditures. Expense Board of Review; Farmers' Institutes; pauper's attorney; teacher's institutes; ditch assessment and other items not otherwise specified	1,050.28	County officers. Back pay allowed clerks and sheriffs under a decision of the Supreme Court	5,057.83
Public printing. All advertising for public lettings; notice to tax payers; publishing delinquent tax list; Circuit Court allowances and allowances of Commissioners, for other printing	1,087.90	County officers. Including salaries, supplies, stationery and otherwise, for auditor, treasurer, clerk, recorder, sheriff, county assessor, county superintendent, surveyor, coroner and Secretary County Board of Health	17,868.85
Expense of orphans. Maintaining orphan children at the German Baptist Orphans' Home, in Jefferson town-		Total	$58,463.65

The salaries of the judge of the circuit court and of the county prosecuting attorney are not included in the above item, "County Officers," as their salaries are paid directly by the State, from the State Treasury, at Indianapolis.

For the year ending December 31, 1904, the county clerk collected in fees and paid into the treasury as county revenue, $3,158.96; the recorder, $2,844.45; the sheriff, $724.44, and the auditor, $435.90; total, $7,163.75.

John W. Bell, superintendent of the county farm and asylum, paid into the treasury for the year ending December 31, 1904, as county revenue, $1,496.00, proceeds of the farm.

Table showing the amount of taxes levied for county purposes in Henry County, by townships, for the years 1842, 1845, 1855, 1860, 1865, 1870, 1880, 1890, 1900 and 1904:

TOWNSHIPS.	1842.	1845.	1855.	1860.	1865.	1870.	1880.	1890.	1900.	1904.
Blue River	**	**	$ 354.43	$ 387.37	$ 3,865.60	$ 420.53	$ 1,211.94	$ 2,270.16	$ 1,369.08	$ 1,688.20
Dudley	$ 383.82	$ 439.22	781.78	776.14	8,025.10	913.10	2,210.72	2,681.14	2,648.12	3,071.47
Fall	325.00	287.20	669.41	807.97	0197.40	1144.46	2,637.17	4,616.50	3,604.24	3,482.05
Franklin	421.32	263.96	777.58	764.95	8,389.60	987.18	2,304.65	3,750.95	2,495.54	2,969.74
Greensboro	215.75	248.00	553.72	543.01	5,706.30	694.30	1,743.95	3,185.0	1,896.62	2,284.78
Harrison	079	217	564.82	643.0	0409.20	814.83	2,273.50	3,541.14	2,090.94	2,458.25
Henry	329.68	405.54	1,073.20	1,185.0	11,362.60	1,713.76	5,115.60	9,105.34	5,851.60	8,378.16
Jefferson	**	165.07	334.63	502.61	5,076.30	055	651.94	2,925.46	1,869.56	2,063.57
Liberty	414.42	435.76	914.15	937.37	10,084.10	1,139.33	2,780.72	4,533.49	2,788.98	3,067.28
Prairie	371.78	301.47	744.39	825.47	7,951.59	961.0	2,384.31	4,194.96	2,379.58	2,631.05
Spiceland	**	292.24	690.93	738.79	8,065.20	93.046	2,327.74	3,845.0	2,553.06	2,969.18
Stony Creek	255.14	295.56	337.52	344.94	3,406.50	358.05	1.04 032	1,961.46	985.54	1,177.41
Wayne	635.66	578.41	1,378.14	1, 3.37	13,889.10	1,951.12	5,174.79	8,036.43	4,971.04	5,496.18
Totals	$3,559.36	$3,934.60	$9,219.70	$9,750.75	$101,458.80	$12,783.79	$32,857.35	$56,647.75	$35,473.90	$41,815.32

**Not Organized.

The growth of taxation for county purposes, from less than $10,000 in 1860 to more than $100,000 in 1865, was occasioned by the Civil War. The small levy for the year 1870 has already been explained from there being a surplus of county funds in the treasury from preceding years.

This statement shows other facts regarding the census of Henry County which are not set forth in the table entitled "Population of Henry County, 1830 to 1900," published in this History on page 1,036.

CENSUS OF 1900.

Foreign-born population	359.	Number of part owners of farms	417.
Number of dwellings	6,376.	Number of cash tenants	181.
Population by families	24,811.	Number of share tenants	663.
Average size of families	3.09	Estimated population of county, 1905	30,000.
Number of farms	2,601.	Total vote, Tuesday, Nov. 8, 1904, for	
Average size in acres	90.06	Secretary of State	7,217.
Number owning farms	1,269.		

RAILROAD STATISTICS, 1905.

Main line of steam roads, approximately, miles	100	Assessed, per mile, side track, Big Four	3,000
Side tracks of steam roads, approximately, miles	25	Assessed, per mile, rolling stock, Big Four	2,000
Assessed, per mile, main line, Pennsylvania Lines	23,000	Assessed, per mile, main line, L. E. & W.	13,000
Assessed, per mile, side track, Pennsylvania Lines	4,500	Assessed, per mile, side track, L. E. & W.	3,000
Assessed, per mile, rolling stock, Pennsylvania Lines	5,000	Assessed, per mile, rolling stock, L. E. & W.	2,000
Assessed, per mile, main line, Big Four	14,000	Main line of electric roads, complete, approximately, miles	31
		Assessed, per mile, main line	9,000
		Assessed, per mile, rolling stock	600

DOG TAX.

The dog tax is now collected by the township assessors and is turned over to the respective township trustees. This fund is used to pay for sheep killed by dogs and the remainder, if any, not so used, is turned into the school fund.

THE HENRY COUNTY HISTORICAL SOCIETY.

The above is claimed to be the pioneer county historical society of the State, having for its purposes the preservation of the history of the county and State, including the political, pioneer, educational, military ,industrial, social and religious history of the county; its natural history, biography, etc., with collections to illustrate the same.

The first organization of the society was secured by obtaining the signatures of a number of interested persons to a written compact or article of association. Among those who were instrumental in the formation of the society and whose names were attached to the article were: Martin L. Bundy, Nathan H. Ballenger, Eugene H. Bundy, William H. Elliott, Joshua H. Mellett, John R. Millikan, Benjamin S. Parker, Elwood Pleas, Thomas B. Redding, Daniel H. Stafford and several others. Women were, with men, alike eligible to membership and all the privileges of the society, and have been equally active in and helpful to its work. The first meeting was held in April, 1886, at which a committee was appointed to draft a constitution and laws and report at a meeting to be held in the following October.

Pending the adoption of the constitution, an announcement that such a society had been established and would meet in October of that year was made at the annual meeting of the old settlers in September, with an appeal that all should take an interest in the new society and its proposed work. At this meeting a committee was named to work in co-operation with that already appointed, who at once took and afterward maintained a lively interest in the organization.

Perhaps the earliest movement for such a society was made by Martin L. Bundy, through communications to the local papers and by a call or two made by him for a meeting to organize a historical society, which failed, through no fault of the caller, to bring out a sufficient number of people for the purpose; hence the plan adopted by the movers in the new organization to secure its formation before attempting to hold a meeting.

The constitution was reported to the meeting in October, 1886, and adopted by it. Joshua H. Mellett was the first president and William H. Elliott, the first secretary. The society started out with enthusiasm and good promise of usefulness and success. A very large number of interesting historical papers have been prepared for and read before it and a large amount of most valuable historical data collected. For ten years of its earlier history it was without any permanent home or place where such papers or historical collections might be preserved. The New Castle Courier and other local papers, however, printed most of the papers and thus a wealth of the most interesting local history and biography has been preserved that would otherwise have been entirely lost. Among those who have contributed papers and addresses may be mentioned Elwood Pleas, with a large number of valuable geological, biological and other papers; Thomas B. Redding, with a history of the mounds and mound builders and papers upon other themes connected with the early life of Eastern Indiana; Adolph Rogers, with histories of the New Castle schools and papers upon the Mexican War and other themes; Captain Pyrrhus Woodward, experiences in the Mexican War; Daniel H. Stafford, on the earlier pioneer life of the county; Martin L. Bundy, many papers on various themes connected with local history, biographies and sketches of great interest and value; Mrs. Hannah E. Davis, Mrs. Rosa Mikels, Mrs. Rose Pickering, Mrs. Helen V. Austin, Mrs. Carrie Jeffries, Mrs. Mattie E. S. Charles, Mrs. Bell C. Estes, Mrs. Elizabeth Gillies, Mrs. Milton S. Reddick, Mrs. Flora B. Weir and many other ladies with papers and sketches covering various matters connected with the life of the county and State. Others who have made large contributions to its work have been Joshua H. Mellett, Nathan H. Ballenger, Seth Stafford, Dr. John W. White, and Dr. Milton H. Chappell, each with exceptionally valuable contributions; Colonel Milton Peden, Daniel Harvey and others with papers on pioneer adventures; Winchester H. Adams, on the early timber of the county and early life in Liberty Township; Eugene H. Bundy, Mark E. Forkner, Benjamin S. Parker, Albert W. Saint, William O. Barnard and many others with speeches, sketches and biographies; Albert W. Saint and John W. Shockley with poems; John Thornburgh, on "The Delaware Indians," "The Newspapers of Henry County," and other papers, many of them of a reminiscent character. In addition to this, many distinguished people from other parts of the State have appeared at its meetings with timely addresses and papers, among whom may be mentioned Dr. John Clark Ridpath, Amos W. Butler, Will Cumback, Mrs. Virginia C. Meredith, Professor Tice and Judge Abbott. The foregoing is but a partial list of the work which has been done by and before the society and doubtless many names of persons who have rendered equally as valuable services as those mentioned to the county, through its meetings have been unintentionally omitted.

The General Assembly of 1901 having passed a law authorizing county councils, upon the recommendation of the county commissioners, to make appropriations for the construction of buildings or rooms for the use of county historical societies to the amount of $5,000.00, the Henry County Council made the necessary appropriation, late in that year, and the fine large homestead of the late General William Grose on South Fourteenth Street in New Castle was purchased for that purpose for the use of the Henry County society. Much progress has been made since this purchase was concluded and a large and valuable collection of such things as illustrate the history of the county— books of reference, portraits of pioneers, valuable papers, memoirs, natural history specimens, etc., has already been made and located in the building. Mr. and Mrs. Thaddeus H. Coffin are now the custodians, and the place is well kept and a delightful one for the visitor in search of information or pleasure. The members of the society are looking forward to the attainment of many of their hopes and desires in the rapid increase and perfecting of their collection and a great advance in the already inestimable value of the society and its work.

An interesting branch of the society was for a time maintained at Knightstown before which many excellent papers were read by citizens of the town. The society's purpose is to secure histories of every township, town and country neighborhood, school, church, benevolent society, club or other organization, fair, etc., and as far as practicable of every family of long standing in the county; and it should have the aid of all the people in carrying out its purposes. It meets twice each year, on the last Saturday in April and October, at the society building in New Castle, when not otherwise determined.

CHAPTER XLVII.

BIOGRAPHICAL.

·Biographical Sketches of Nathan Hunt Ballenger and Family—Frank Bundy and Family—Robert Holiday Cooper and Family—Nimrod Richard Elliott and Family—Samuel Ferris and Family—John Larue Forkner and Family—John William Griffin and Family—Charles Slaten Hernly and Family—John Craig Hudelson and Family—Levi Allen Jennings and Family—Simon Peter Jennings and Family—David Wagner Kinsey and Family—Benjamin Franklin Koons and Family—Albert Krell and Family—Josiah Ward Maxim and Family—John Russell Millikan and Family—Charles Dayton Morgan and Family—Charles Weimert Mouch and Family—Isaac Parker and Family—Leonidas Perry Newby and Family—John Powell and Family—Simon Titus Powell and Family—John Rea and Family—Henry Shroyer and Family.

This concluding chapter of the History of Henry County consists of sketches of the lives and works of many of the county's pioneers, merchants, manufacturers, bankers, lawyers, physicians, and men of affairs, most of whom have been in the forefront of progress for more than a generation. In the lines of activity in which they were or are engaged, they displayed an ability and enterprise equal to that of any similar group of men in the State or Nation, and the growth of the county's primitive settlements into a highly complex industrial community, rich in material resources and in intellectual and social life, is owing largely to their unsparing endeavors and fine public spirit. The improved farms, solid financial institutions and magnificent manufactories of the county are a testimonial to their wisdom and well directed efforts; and the law abiding reputation of the community rests upon the high character of the legal profession so long maintained by the bar of the county to which so many of these honored citizens belong.

No praise of the living, no eulogy of the dead can give them a more abiding fame than is already theirs. Their long and useful careers in the county are an enduring monument to their worth.

Nathan H. Ballenger

his own bet...
almo.t t...

a native of G.......
. . . ...
were .. .. ..
is the attack ....
Continental forces a...
he visited the scene of
ville, Indiana, an..
He ..lso at this earl.

On ...li t.. ..
. packing ..
...n..y, in a four-bo...
settled ... .
to the State ...   Thi.
three sons and two large
as body guar.. ...ough
They tracked our
Of .. .. ..
seem.. ....iting an

River.

...
.hankfulness that th.. we...

of but ...

then start.. ...
Wayne.. .. ...
i.. .. thick forest, ..
t.. ..
                .Ther.
Na.....l Road v...
... ..

reith is now located
poet cou'd .. ..
behind
byw.. ..
S.m...
     The .. ..
cabin erecte.. ...

they came from N.

allergen

BIOGRAPHICAL SKETCH OF NATHAN HUNT BALLENGER.

PIONEER, FARMER, MINISTER.

It is not what a man can do but it is, rather, what a man has done that entitles him to consideration. Nathan Hunt Ballenger has been a doer of things. He has kept his eyes open to the possibilities of life and accomplished a great deal in the way of his own betterment and the welfare of his neighbors and the whole community. For almost three quarters of a century, he has been prominent in Henry County affairs.

His parents were Henry and Rebecca (Hunt) Ballenger, the former of whom was a native of Guilford County, North Carolina, where he was born January 9, 1772. Henry Ballenger was of Welsh, and Rebecca Hunt, his wife, of Scotch descent. Both were by birth subjects of King George, the Third, and among his earliest recollections is the attack made by Lord Cornwallis and the British upon General Greene and the Continental forces at Guilford Court House. In after years he saw Washington when he visited the scene of that famous battle. In 1821 he attended the land sales at Brookville, Indiana, and there bought a quarter section of land located near Knightstown. He also at this early date rode to Indianapolis when there was not a settler between Raysville and the first named point, and no road except an Indian trail.

On April 11, 1832, Henry Ballenger sold most of his possessions in North Carolina and, packing the few household articles that had been reserved for the use of the family, in a four-horse wagon and a one-horse carryall, started for Indiana, where he settled his family on the land in Henry County purchased by him on his former visit to the State in 1821. This little party of immigrants comprised the father, the mother, three sons, and two large dogs, the latter highly prized for their supposed usefulness as body guards through the anticipated dangers that might beset them on the way. They tracked across the Blue Ridge range of mountains, passing through Magita Gap. Of this part of the journey, Nathan H. Ballenger, in his reminiscences, says: "The scenery was enchanting and I was lost in wonder, every day witnessing new scenes, the whole being climaxed, when we reached the celebrated Hawk's Nest on the Kanawha River."

From the Kanawha they passed down to the Ohio River, which they crossed in "a very unsafe ferryboat and our load was nearly too much for its floating capacity." They landed on the Ohio side of the river in safety and it was with "much relief and thankfulness that they were at last on soil not cursed by slavery, having been used in the old home to seeing droves of slaves driven to a more southern market, like beasts of burden." The party arrived at Richmond, Wayne County, Indiana, May 10, 1832, where they remained for a day or two at the home of a sister of Henry Ballenger, and then started for Henry County, passing through old Salisbury, the first county seat of Wayne; thence to Centreville, and thence along the National Road to their future home in a thick forest, two miles north of Raysville, in Wayne Township, Henry County, where they arrived May 15, 1832. The journey from Centreville is thus described by Nathan H. Ballenger: "There was no Cambridge City then. Milton had a few houses. The National Road was then being used for travel, but it was in a very imperfect condition. We well nigh stuck fast in fording Flatrock at the point where Lewisville now stands. In a short time we came to the fortieth mile, as it was called, just east of where Dunreith is now located. I shall attempt no description of this noted spot; neither sage nor poet could do it justice. Here a man on horseback, riding at full speed, blew a trumpet behind us, warning us to get out of the way of the United States Express Mail. This bugle blast also served to notify the man at the next station to be ready to receive Uncle Sam's mail and to hasten it on."

The newcomers were heartily welcomed and given shelter in the primitive log cabin erected and occupied by Alfred M. Brittain, who had married Malinda, a sister of Nathan H. Ballenger. She was born January 11, 1810, and married Mr. Brittain in 1825; they came from North Carolina to Henry County, Indiana, in 1826. The arrival of the Ballengers greatly over peopled the little cabin, but they soon learned to adapt themselves to circumstances. Relating to this period, Nathan H. Ballenger says: "There was much work at hand finishing the clearing for planting in corn;" and further that he "used to drop the seed in hills, following close after the plow that marked out the rows, and two persons followed with hoes to cover;" that "no one had ever heard of a corn-planter and that such a thing could not have been used anyway." He also says: "Our wheat was sown in the corn and plowed in with single bull tongues. We harvested with hand reaphooks and a man could put about·one acre per day in shock. It was trodden out with horses, often on a dirt floor, and the chaff was blown out, the wind being generated by the flapping of sheets. Two men or women held the corners of the sheets, while a third person poured the wheat in front of the blast thus artificially produced." Continuing he says that "there was little rest from toil either for men or women. The heavy forest must be taken off the land by axe and fagot, the soil broken up by a plow with wooden mould-board, having enough iron on it for a share. Sometimes we used a bull tongue to break the ground." "Our recreations," he says, "were to be had at log rollings, cabin building, barn raisings, corn huskings and quilting bees, but with it all we were a very happy people."

Henry Ballenger cleared and improved his·land and remained upon it until his death in 1865, at the age of ninety three years. His wife survived him until 1870, when she died at the same venerable age. Both are buried at Spiceland. Henry and Rebecca (Hunt) Ballenger were the parents of the following named children: Elizabeth, afterwards Mrs. William Albright; William; Elijah; Malinda; Henry; and Nathan H., the subject of this sketch, whose parents remained with him until their deaths.

NATHAN HUNT BALLENGER.

Nathan Hunt Ballenger was born in Guilford County, North Carolina, February 13, 1823. His early education was obtained at New Garden, North Carolina, in a little schoolhouse built on a forty acre tract of land which had been donated by his grandfather, John Ballenger, to the Friends of North Carolina so long as it should be used for church and school purposes, and it was upon this piece of land that the first Friends' Yearly Meeting House in the State of North Carolina was erected. On this same tract, Guilford College, formerly the "North Carolina Boarding School," was also located. The first schooling that young Ballenger received after coming to Henry County was obtained in an old log cabin which had slab scantlings for seats and for a writing desk had a slab fastened on pins driven into the side of the cabin wall over which the light was admitted by cutting out a log and pasting greased paper over the opening thus made.

There were few roads in that early time, even the "corduroy", and traveling was done by paths "blazed" through the interminable forests. They did· not suffer for food. The woods were full of game and no game laws then· existed. They had venison in plenty; wild turkeys, pheasants, quail, wild pigeons in countless numbers, squirrels, raccoons, opossums, and bear meat, besides vegetables, mostly corn and potatoes, hog and hominy, and the ever pleasing, ever inviting, healthful, muscle-making, old fashioned "corn dodger" for bread.

During this early period of his life, Mr. Ballenger states there was a mysterious disease prevalent among the settlers, called "milk sickness", which then as now baffled the treatment of the physicians; fortunately the disease is now almost unknown; chills and fever were epidemic; doctors were scarce and the few who practised "rode night and day through forest and swamp to relieve the sick and the distressed."

At the age of fifteen he began teaching school, taking the place of a pedagogue who, because of bad conduct, had to give up his charge. He finished the school and received for his compensation the sum of twelve dollars and a half per month. He afterwards taught many pioneer schools and was regarded as a very successful teacher.

Mr. Ballenger was elected assessor of Henry County at the August election, 1848, and served a year from January 1, 1849, and in 1856 he was elected by the then newly organized Republican party as a member of the lower house of the Indiana General Assembly. He served during the thirty ninth regular session which convened January 8, 1857, having for his colleague, William Grose, who was afterwards a general in the

Civil War and of whom a full biographical sketch will be found elsewhere in this History. Mr. Ballenger was an attentive and conscientious member and assisted materially
in shaping the legislation of that period. Previous to the formation of the Republican
party, he had been a warm supporter of William Henry Harrison in the campaign of
1840 and in 1844 was a supporter of Henry Clay, the great leader of the Whig party.
Of Clay he says: "I saw him at Knightstown and heard him speak at Indianapolis,
and always regarded him as the Cicero of America." Mr. Ballenger took a prominent
part in the great temperance agitation of 1840. He delivered many speeches and lectures on the subject and was instrumental in bringing many men to reform.

Mr. Ballenger is a birthright member of the Friends' Church and was for more than
twenty years an able and active minister of that Society. Touching his ministry he
says: "In the Winter of 1867 I inaugurated the first protracted meeting at Spiceland
that was ever held among Friends in modern times, so far as I know. The Lord blessed
us with a marvelous revival and scores of young people were converted, resulting in
nearly one hundred accessions to the church. There are those now living who well remember the early manner of worship of the Friends' Church with all of its positive
restrictions as compared with its present liberality, and it is with satisfaction that they
note the change which now enables the Friends to cordially unite and affiliate with all
other denominations that base their belief on God's Holy Writ and the Christian religion as exemplified in the life, death and resurrection of Jesus Christ."

His whole life has been one of activity and enterprise. As a moral teacher he has
worked earnestly for the betterment of mankind. As a man of affairs, he has had an
important part in the growth and prosperity of the county. He early favored internal
improvements and was interested in the old Whitewater canal, which in its day was a
great avenue of transportation and for a time made Cambridge City a busy mart of
trade. He was a stockholder in the first railroad that entered Henry County and a
stockholder in the first turnpike in the county; he built the first warehouse at Knightstown and was the builder of a flour mill on Blue River besides being part owner of two
others. He had other large interests, among them being a "title to five hundred acres
of land in the best part of the State of Kansas and one hundred and sixty acres of the
best land in Henry County." He was prosperous, out of debt and happy; blessed in
health and strength and possessed of wondrous vigor and power of endurance; but bad
investments and losses incurred by going security for friends swept his property away.
Death also entered upon the scene and took his well beloved son and soon afterwards
came the demise of his beloved and honored wife, of whom it may be said that "her children arise up and call her blessed; her husband also, and he praiseth her."

No one, probably, was more instrumental in bringing about the organization of the
"Old Settlers' Association of Henry County" than Mr. Ballenger. This association has
for a number of years held annual meetings and has been active in the preservation
of many facts relating to the early history of the county which would otherwise have
perished. Mr. Ballenger, when health and strength permitted, has not missed any of
these annual gatherings. He was also associated with Martin L. Bundy, Joshua H. Mellett, Thomas B. Redding, Simon T. Powell, Elias Phelps, Seth Stafford, Benjamin S.
Parker, Elwood Pleas, and others, in founding in 1885 the "Henry County Historical
Society," an institution which has grown in merit and which now has its own beautiful
home in New Castle, on the property hitherto known as the General Grose residence.
Mr. Ballenger has been president of this society several times, and has been constant
in attendance upon its meetings. He has also furnished the society with a number of
interesting papers relating to the early history of Henry County and Eastern Indiana.

His career has been an useful one to the community and entitles him to be considered one of the county's public spirited citizens. Though weighted with more than
the four score years allotted as the span of life, he has not given up his interest in the
moral and material welfare of the people. His sympathies are broad and enduring
and he has always been active in advancing the civilization of his own time. As pioneer, farmer and minister of the Gospel, he has not lived in vain.

On November 28, 1849, Nathan Hunt Ballenger was married to Margaret Hubbard,
daughter of Richard J. and Sarah (Swain) Hubbard. She was a sister of the well known

Henry County citizen, Charles S. Hubbard, now and for many years a resident of Raysville and Knightstown, and noted over a large part of the country for his ability as a
preacher of the Society of Friends, for his philanthropy and for his earnestness of
purpose. Nathan H. and Margaret (Hubbard) Ballenger were the parents of the following children: Mary V., now the wife of Judge William O. Barnard, of New Castle;
Oliver H., deceased; Emma G., widow of the late William S. Seaford; Charles W., of
Spiceland; Albert N., of Old Mexico; Rhoda M., wife of Dr. Charles Cunningham, of
Indianapolis; Walter, deceased; and Edward L. S., of Arizona.

Margaret (Hubbard) Ballenger was a woman of remarkable intelligence, sweet
disposition, hospitable, charitable and devoted to her family. For a number of years,
as a minister of the Society of Friends, she preached the Word of God with a fervent
zeal that brought conversion and comfort to many hearts and imbued all of her hearers
with that love of God which passeth all understanding. She died August 26, 1880, and
is buried in Spiceland Cemetery. Nathan H. Ballenger married again on November 5,
1885, his second wife being Martha Kelley, who has been a faithful companion to him.
One child named Marguerite has been born to them.

Mr. Ballenger was named after Nathan Hunt, who was in his day one of the
ablest ministers of the Friends' Church. He traveled much and died an old man at his
home in North Carolina. Relating to a contemporary of Nathan Hunt, the
following is taken from a Friend's historical record: "Jeremiah Hubbard, whom some
among the old people still living yet recollect, was a contemporary of Nathan Hunt and
was considered one of the most learned and eloquent men of his day. He was an educator, traveled much in the ministry and was many years in advance of his generation
in the liberality of his views. He was one fourth Cherokee Indian, six feet and six
inches in height, long black hair and a striking, dignified figure, and the revivalist
of his day. His death occurred in Wayne County, Indiana, in 1850." Further reference
is made to Jeremiah Hubbard in the sketch of Mary V. Barnard, which is appended
to the sketch of her husband, William O. Barnard, published elsewhere in this History.

Frank Bundy

hundred and sixt

Ben

BIOGRAPHICAL SKETCH OF FRANK BUNDY.

LANDLORD AND PUBLIC SPIRITED CITIZEN.

The paternal grandparents of Frank Bundy, the subject of this sketch, were George and Kerene (Elliott) Bundy, and his parents were Josiah and Maria J. (Stanley) Bundy. Josiah Bundy was born April 21, 1823, in Wayne County, Indiana, and with his parents came to Henry County in 1835 and settled at Greensboro, where his father very soon afterwards sickened and died. Josiah remained at home with his mother until his marriage in 1844 to Maria J., daughter of John and Elizabeth Stanley. He then engaged in farming for a brief period, after which he began to keep hotel at Greensboro and continued in the hotel business until 1862, when he disposed of his possessions and moved his family to Minnesota, where he settled on a fine body of land consisting of one hundred and sixty acres, near the city of Minneapolis. Here he remained until 1868, when he sold his farm and returned to Henry County, Indiana.

The Minnesota venture is the nucleus of an e'er true tale. When Mr. Bundy purchased the land and even after he had disposed of it, it remained for several years outside the limits of Minneapolis, but, as time moved on apace, the city began to grow and spread, a movement which continued until it embraced the whole of the Bundy farm. The land is now worth very many times more than the sixteen thousand dollars which Mr. Bundy received for it from Colonel William S. King, a prominent Minnesotan of that day. The sale was not one of necessity on Mr. Bundy's part but was made with deliberate intention to return to Indiana, no matter at what sacrifice. He did not like Minnesota, especially its severe winters, but he did love, as he himself said repeatedly, "the old Hoosier State." He never regretted the change and in the end found his consolation in the fact that he had lived to know that his several sons were more than able to take care of themselves. He was a fond father, proud of his children, and to him their success was his greatest comfort and happiness. After his return to Indiana, he purchased a farm near Spiceland, where he continued to live until 1876, when he sold the farm to George Hazzard, the author of this History, and going to New Castle bought what then became the Bundy Hotel, formerly called the Taylor House.

Charles Jamison kept a hotel in New Castle in 1824 and is, therefore, apparently the first hotel keeper there. He died in 1835. There has been a hotel in New Castle, on the corner now occupied by the Bundy, ever since the organization of the town. The several landlords were Joshua Chappell, who in 1840 and for several years thereafter kept the Exchange Hotel; and after him came David Murphey, George B. Rogers, Thomas W. Fawcett, Jeremiah Page, and others, until in 1859 John Taylor became the proprietor and changed the name to the Taylor House. He conducted the business until 1869, when he sold to T. B. French, who in 1870 sold to Oliver H. Welborn, of Knightstown, who in turn sold to George Hazzard. Mr. Hazzard leased the hotel to Wilson Cunningham, father of Will Cunningham, the present manager of the "Claypool" at Indianapolis. Mr. Cunningham successfully conducted the hotel until 1872, when the property was sold by George Hazzard, to Colonel John S. Hoover. Colonel Hoover in 1876 re-sold it to Mr. Hazzard, who in a short time transfered it to Josiah Bundy in part payment for the farm above mentioned, and from that time to the present the house has been known as the "Bundy Hotel." It was first conducted by Bundy and Sons; then by the Bundy brothers, Charles, Frank and Orla; and then by a corporation operated by the two last named and managed exclusively by Frank.

The hotel kept by Joshua Chappell was a two-story frame, quite unpretentious but large enough for the time. It was replaced by a brick structure commenced by Jeremiah Page in 1856, but prior to completion transferred to Wesley Goodwin and by him to Elijah B. Martindale, now of Indianapolis, and by him to his father-in-law, John Taylor, who conducted the same as above mentioned. This building was destroyed by fire in 1888, which was a serious loss to the Bundy brothers; but with the pluck and energy that have always characterized them, they went to work and in a brief period had erected at a cost of more than thirty thousand dollars what is now the main portion of the Bundy Hotel. The property is now owned by a corporation with a capital of fifty five thousand dollars and is leased to Frank Bundy. The building has been added to and otherwise so changed that it is now one of the leading hotels of Indiana and is considered by the host of traveling men, who journey to and fro in the State, an ideal stopping place.

In the early times of New Castle there was also a hotel on the corner now occupied by the Citizens' State Bank. The landlords were John Taylor, Samuel Hazzard, James Calvert, John G. Welch, Isaac R. Howard, and others, whose names cannot now be recalled. With the exception of the "Junction House," located in a part of the depot of the present Panhandle and Lake Erie and Western railroads, but long since abandoned for hotel purposes, the Bundy has been the only first class hotel operated in New Castle, until the recent completion of the "Imperial."

During the partnership of Frank and Orla Bundy, they also had charge for several years of the McFarlan Hotel at Connersville, the same being managed by Orla Bundy. Under them this hotel also had a well deserved reputation, commensurate with the name of the Bundy brothers as hotel men. It has been thoroughly demonstrated that it is not every man who can successfully run a hotel, but in this case it seems that as "mine host," no man is better fitted for the business than Frank Bundy.

Josiah and Maria J. (Stanley) Bundy were the parents of seven children, namely: Kerene, afterwards the wife of William Woods, but now deceased; Charles, the well known liveryman of New Castle; David C., deceased; Lorenzo D., deceased; John M., the present auditor of Henry County, who, prior to his election to that office, resided at Knightstown; Frank, the subject of this sketch; and Orlistus (Orla) P.

Josiah Bundy was something more than the ordinary man. He had a wide acquaintance, especially in Eastern Indiana, and was noted for his excellent social qualities, his urbane manners, his generous hospitality and his hearty sympathy with the poor and needy. He was like a brother in his friendships and had no word of censure for such few as may have been his enemies. He overflowed with genial good humor and delighted in hearing and telling a good story. In his family relations, he was an affectionate husband and a kind father. To his wise oversight and to the loving care of the mother may be largely attributed the sterling character of the children who were reared to honor their parents and to respect the rights of others. Josiah Bundy died January 6, 1894, and Maria J. (born November 14, 1826), his wife, died May 9, 1887. Both are buried in South Mound Cemetery, New Castle.

FRANK BUNDY.

Counting by years, Frank Bundy, who was born April 25, 1861, is a comparatively young man, but from his youth up his life has been one of strenuous exertion. His early and continued connection with the hotel business of New Castle has been narrated in the preceding part of this sketch, and to that may be added that in truth he was born and grew up in the business, and that his apprenticeship as well as his later independent career in the business has been marked by a careful watchfulness, coupled with genial and pleasing manners, that have made him one of the leading landlords of the State. He has the mind to direct and the hand to execute which have made him a master of his profession.

It requires administrative ability of a high order, constant supervision and rigid economy to successfully manage a hotel; every avenue of waste must be closed, and the welcoming, feeding and speeding of the guests is an art in itself. A selfish public, often unreasoning and hard to propitiate, adds greatly to the troubles of the landlord, yet in the face of these manifold difficulties Mr. Bundy has won the confidence and good will of his many patrons. He is possessed of executive ability, well balanced judgment and shrewd discernment, and his mind is open to every opportunity in his business. Personally, he is polite and suave, extending a warm welcome to the coming and speeding the parting guest on his way with the hearty invitation, "come again, we will treat you well."

Mr. Bundy's connection with the hotel business in New Castle covers a period of thirty years, from 1876, when he was but fifteen years of age, to the present time. His career has been a successful one from both a personal and a financial standpoint. Outside of the hotel business, he owns and cultivates three hundred and thirty two acres of land and in connection with it gives a great deal of attention to the raising of fine cattle and hogs. His reward has been commensurate with his labors.

In politics he is strong in his attachment to the principles of the Republican party and in a quiet but effective manner gives that party his fullest support. He and his wife are members of the Presbyterian Church of New Castle and give freely of their time and means for religious purposes. Mr. Bundy is also a member of New Castle Lodge, Number 91, Ancient Free and Accepted Masons; of Crescens Lodge, Number 33, Knights of Pythias; of the Benevolent Protective Order of Elks, New Castle Lodge, Number 484; and of Iroquois Tribe, Number 97, Improved Order of Red Men, New Castle.

On January 21, 1885, Frank Bundy was married to Ella, daughter of David M. and Julia E. (Morris) Brown, of Lewisville, Henry County, Indiana. To them has been born one child, a daughter, named Frances Maria, born January 21, 1900. Little Frances is a very lovable child and is the light and life of her parents.

ANCESTRY OF MRS. FRANK (BROWN) BUNDY.

Ella (Brown) Bundy, wife of Frank Bundy, is the daughter of David Monroe Brown and his wife, Julia E. (Morris) Brown. John Brown, the father of David M., came to Indiana from Pennsylvania in 1833 and settled first in Henry County, but afterwards removed to Rush County. David M. was born at Lewisville, Henry County, March 10, 1841, and from the age of nineteen has made his own way in the world. Most of his life has been spent in agricultural pursuits, in which he has been phenomenally successful. He was married in June, 1864, to Julia E., daughter of Joseph R. and Margaret D. (Minor) Morris, a well educated and highly accomplished young lady of Franklin Township. Mr. Brown was connected for several years with the First National Bank of Lewisville, of which he was one of the organizers and of which he was for a time the president and a director. He is now one of the principal stockholders and a director of the Central Trust and Savings Company of New Castle.

David M. and Julia E. (Morris) Brown are the parents of the following named children: Ella, born January 31, 1866, now the wife of Frank Bundy; George M., now of Indianapolis, his wife being Valeta, a daughter of Mr. and Mrs. Samuel Arnold, of New Castle; and Margaret E., who died in infancy.

BIOGRAPHICAL SKETCH OF ROBERT HOLIDAY COOPER.

FARMER, COUNTY OFFICIAL AND BANK DIRECTOR.

Among the men who have risen to local distinction in Henry County, no one is more worthy than Robert Holiday Cooper. His grandparents were John and Ann (Hayes) Cooper, who were natives of Pennsylvania, where the former was born about 1763 and the latter in 1765. They were members of the Society of Friends. They were married in their native State and had four sons, named Caleb, William, father of the subject of this sketch, John and Imla. They removed to Harrison County, Ohio, when their sons were young men and there the father died in 1825. His widow survived him a number of years and died in 1855 in Henry County, Indiana, where she had removed with her sons, all of whom became settlers in that county. She is buried in the Quaker Church Cemetery, Cadiz.

William Cooper, born November 11, 1793, was married in Ohio to Nancy, the fifth child of Robert and Rebecca Holiday. She was born in Pennsylvania, March 3, 1802, but the family afterwards moved to Harrison County, Ohio, where the parents died at an advanced age. William Cooper and family removed in 1835 from Ohio to Indiana and settled in Harrison Township, Henry County, where he purchased eighty acres of land, just south of the present site of Cadiz, upon which he built a log cabin home and here prospered and reared a large family of eleven children, seven of whom were born in Ohio and four in Henry County, Indiana, namely: Ann, afterwards the wife of Joel Hiatt; Rebecca, afterwards the wife of Jehu Weesner; John P., who married Eliza Jane, daughter of Tabor W. McKee; Mary, whose first husband was William McKee and who after his death married Joshua Hiatt; Lewessa, afterwards wife of William P. Newby; Robert H., subject of this sketch; Jane H., widow of the late Nimrod R. Elliott; Israel; Eliza M., afterwards wife of M. A. Pickering, of Cadiz; Caleb and Imla W. The survivors of this family are Robert H., Israel, of Cadiz, where he attends to his large farming interests, and Imla W., of Mechanicsburg, a one-time partner of the late Nimrod R. Elliott and now a retired farmer. Caleb, one of the dead sons, was a splendid young man, affable in demeanor, companionable, polite and popular. He was a gallant cavalry officer who served his country well until the close of the Civil War, first as Second Lieutenant of Company E, 9th Indiana Cavalry and afterwards as First Lieutenant of the same company. He was mustered out of the service August 28, 1865. His military record will be found set out elsewhere in this History. In civil life he was a promising attorney of the Henry County bar. He died December 14, 1867. Imla W. was also a soldier of the Civil War and his record will be found elsewhere in this History in connection with Company D, 147th Indiana Infantry, of which he was a member. William Cooper died August 17, 1876, and his widow, Nancy (Holiday) Cooper, died March 19, 1893.

ROBERT HOLLIDAY COOPER.

Robert Holiday Cooper was born in Harrison County, Ohio, May 6, 1827, and came to Indiana with his parents in 1835. The educational advantages of the pioneers and their children were very meagre, but he acquired a knowledge of reading, writing and arithmetic in the district schools of the neighborhood, and being naturally endowed with a large fund of common sense has always found his education equal to his needs. He spent most of his boyhood on his father's farm and there accumulated a practical experience which determined him to follow farming as a business. His first venture for himself was on a forty acre tract of land, not far from Cadiz, which had been given to his wife, Harriet (Hiatt) Cooper, by her father. She suffered from ill health for some two or three years, which finally resulted in her death. Mr. Cooper then sold this land for seven hundred dollars, but the sickness and death of his wife, combined with other misfortunes in his family, had already consumed this for the times large sum of money, compelling him to start life anew. His second wife had some means of her own and this he used to purchase eighty acres of land on which he once more began farming, which he continued with such success that he has been able in his later years to retire from active work with a competency.

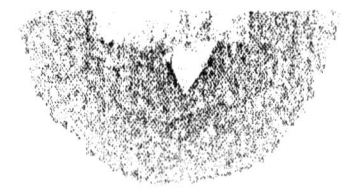

ROBERT HOLIDAY COOPER.

AL AND BANK DIRECTOR.

cal distinction in Henry County, no one is
r His grandparents were John and Ann
sylvania, where the former was born about
mbers of the Society of Friends. They were
sons, named Caleb, William, father of the
v removed to Harrison County, Ohió, when
ther died in 1825. His widow survived him
ry County, Indiana, where she had removed
in that county. She is buried in the Quaker

23 was married in Ohio to Nancy, the fifth
n born in Pennsylvania, March 3, 1802, but
ounty, Ohio, where the parents died at an

R. H. Cooper

As early as 1856 Mr. Cooper became interested in political questions and during that critical period of great political changes allied himself with the Republican party and was a warm supporter of General John C. Fremont, its first candidate for the presidency. In 1860 he was again in line for the principles and party of Abraham Lincoln and has from that time to the present been an earnest advocate of the party and its policy. In Harrison Township he is prominent in the party councils He served four years as assessor of the township and has served one term (1871-4) as commissioner of Henry County for the middle district, having for his colleagues on the board, Williams Nicholson, Thomas N. White and Jabish Luellen. Mr. Cooper made an excellent record in this important office.

About 1874 Mr. Cooper became a stockholder and director in the First National Bank of New Castle and remained with the institution for a number of years. He subsequently became one of the organizers of the Central Trust and Savings Company, of New Castle, of which he is a stockholder and director. He takes a fatherly interest in that institution and uses his influence by word and deed to strengthen its hold upon the business of the community.

For a number of years he was a stockholder in the Henry County Agricultural Society, New Castle, and during a great portion of the time was its president. From the beginning he was recognized as a prime factor in the society and helped in many ways to make a success of its annual exhibitions.

Some three or four years ago Mr. Cooper under the pressure of advancing years retired from the active duties of life and rented his farm, which had grown from eighty to four hundred acres of the best land in Henry County. He removed to New Castle, where he expects to pass the remaining years of a hitherto very busy life.

Mr. Cooper during his whole life has been an industrious, hard working man and has exercised a vigilant economy in his affairs but while looking after his own interests he has not been amiss in his duty to friends and neighbors nor chary of extending a helping hand. He is a public spirited citizen of honest and upright life and it is to the labors of such men as he that the county is indebted for its exalted position among the counties of the State.

He has been for a number of years a member of the Christian Church and a worker in the cause of the Master. He has been liberal of his time and means in promoting the work of the church and in supporting its charities. Mr. Cooper finds support for his religious views in the Masonic fraternity, which has for its cornerstone. faith in God, the King. He is a member of New Castle Lodge, Number 91, Ancient Free and Accepted Masons and of New Castle Chapter, Number 50, Royal Arch Masons.

On February 22, 1847, when but twenty years of age, Robert H. Cooper married Harriet Hiatt, a daughter of David and Ruth (Ratliff) Hiatt. She was born June 15, 1830, and died March 29, 1853. They were the parents of two children: Eldred M., born March 11, 1849; and David L., born March 8, 1851; died May 3, 1874. Eldred M. married Allie Trueblood, daughter of Edward Trueblood, and lives on his farm situated on the line between Henry and Madison counties. Eldred M. is a successful farmer as in early manhood he was a successful teacher.

After the death of his first wife, Robert H. Cooper married Margaret Haworth, daughter of James and Amelia Haworth. She was born June 6, 1837, at Wilmington, Ohio, and afterwards came with her parents to New London, Howard County, Indiana, where she was married to Mr. Cooper. They were the parents of eight children, namely: Belle, born January 20, 1857, who afterwards married John C. McLucas, now of Fairbury, Nebraska; Ida J., born September 3, 1858; married Edmund H. Hinshaw; Frank W., born July 24, 1860; married Emma Depboye; Harriet E., born June 12, 1862, married Luther M. Nelson; Amelia H., born June 22, 1864; married Alvin J. Frazier; Minnie M., born September 25, 1866; married Dr. Edgar S. Ferris; Milton O., born July 24, 1869, married Bessie Woods; Bennie, born December 8, 1875; married Professor Charles R. Atkinson.

John C. McLucas is a son of the late Wilson T. McLucas and was born near Cadiz. He is now a resident of Fairbury, Nebraska, where he has been in the employ of the Rock Island railroad for about twenty years. He also gives his attention to the buying and shipping of live stock.

Edmund Howard Hinshaw was born on a farm near Greensboro, Henry County, Indiana. His father was Lindsey Hinshaw and the late Seth Hinshaw, the well known philanthropist, was his great-uncle. He was educated in the home schools; at the Spiceland Academy and at Butler University, Indianapolis, graduating from the last named in 1885. He taught school for several years, among other places at Cadiz, where he became acquainted with Ida J. Cooper, whom he subsequently married. He afterwards moved to Fairbury, Nebraska, where he was for a time superintendent of the public schools, but finally declined to serve longer in that position. He was admitted to the bar in 1887 and soon became prominent in the practise of the law. He then entered politics and held several municipal and county offices. In 1898 he was nominated for Congress by the Republicans but was unable to overcome the fusion plurality. In 1901 he was candidate for United States Senator but after a contest which lasted three months he and all the other candidates withdrew and a new man was chosen. He was again nominated for Congress from the fourth Nebraska district in the Spring of 1902 and after a spirited contest was elected to the Fifty Eighth Congress. He was reelected to the Fifty Ninth Congress by 7,700 majority and is now serving in that body. His district is composed of eleven counties, viz: Butler, Fillmore, Gage, Hamilton, Jefferson, Polk, Saline, Saunders, Seward, Thayer and York, the population of which is nearly 200,000. Mr. Hinshaw is a well informed and polished gentleman who has the confidence and good will of his constituency and, if he lives, will doubtless receive still higher honors from his adopted State.

Frank W. Cooper is a farmer of Fall Creek Township; he resides at Middletown and has charge of the estate of Mrs. Anna D. Welsh. Luther M. Nelson, husband of Harriet E. Cooper, is a son of Joseph R. Nelson. He was born at Cadiz, but is now a resident of Fairbury, Nebraska, where he has been for a number of years assistant cashier of the Harbine Bank of that city. Alvin J. Frazier is a druggist at Muncie, Indiana. Dr. Edgar S. Ferris is a son of the late Dr. Samuel Ferris and is one of the successful practising physicians of New Castle. He gives special attention to diseases of the eye and ear. Milton O. Cooper is a farmer who lives four and a half miles southwest of New Castle, in the Clear Springs neighborhood. Charles R. Atkinson is superintendent of schools at Sheridan, Wyoming. Before going to Sheridan, he was for a number of years superintendent of schools at York, Nebraska. He is one of the prominent educators of the Great West.

Robert H. Cooper has been blessed beyond all other things in his children, and has every reason to be proud of them and their successes in life. They are all capable and honorable men and women and useful citizens. They are fathers and mothers themselves and children and grandchildren alike always meet with a delightful welcome when they visit the old home.

Margaret (Haworth) Cooper, the second wife of Mr. Cooper, died April 6, 1889. He was again married on June 18, 1890, his present wife, who is a most estimable woman, being Mrs. Mary (Booth) Widup. Charles, her son by her first marriage, resides in New Castle.

Mr. Cooper enjoys a distinction hardly surpassed and probably not equaled in Indiana. In the presidential campaign of 1904, which resulted in the election of Theodore Roosevelt as President and Charles W. Fairbanks as Vice-President, he voted for the successful candidates, as did three of his sons, six of his sons-in-law, five grandsons and his youngest daughter, the wife of Professor Atkinson, of Sheridan, Wyoming, in which State the payment of a poll tax of two dollars admits women to the franchise. Before the election took place, the political preferences of the family were printed in the local papers and brought to the attention of President Roosevelt, who addressed to Mr. Cooper the following interesting communication:

"My Dear Mr. Cooper: "OYSTER BAY, N. Y., August 30, 1904.

"I have just received the enclosed clipping. Evidently you are the kind of an American in whom I believe, and I want to write and congratulate you on your family, while congratulating myself on the fact that I have your and their support. I have a great regard for your son-in-law, Representative Hinshaw.

"Sincerely yours,

"THEODORE ROOSEVELT."

E. H.

Edmund Howard Hinshaw was born on a farm near Greensboro, Henry County, Indiana. His father was Lindsey Hinshaw and the late Seth Hinshaw, the well known philanthropist, was his great-uncle. He was educated in the home schools; at the Spiceland Academy and at Butler University, Indianapolis. graduating from the last named in 1885. He taught school for several years, among other places at Cadiz, where he became acquainted with Ida J. Cooper, whom he subsequently married. He afterwards moved to Fairbury, Nebraska, where he was for a time superintendent of the public schools, but finally declined to serve longer in that position. He was admitted to the bar in 1887 and soon became prominent in the practice of the law. He then entered politics and held several municipal and county offices. In 1898 he was nominated for Congress by the Republicans but was unable to overcome the fusion plurality. In 1901 he was candidate for United States Senator but after a contest which lasted three months he and all the other candidates withdrew and a new man was chosen. He was again nominated for Congress from the fourth Nebraska district in the Spring of 1902 and after a spirited contest was elected to the Fifty-Eighth Congress. He was re-elected to the Fifty-Ninth Congress by 7,700 majority and is now serving in that body. His district is composed of eleven counties, viz: Butler, Fillmore, Gage, Hamilton, Jefferson, Polk, Saline, Saunders, Seward, Thayer and York, the population of which is nearly 200,000. Mr. Hinshaw is a well informed and polished gentleman who has the confidence and good will of his constituents and if he lives will doubtless receive still higher honors from his adopted State.

Frank W. Cooper is a farmer of Fall Creek Township; he resides at Middletown and has charge of the estate of Mrs. Enos D. Woody. Luther M. Nelson, husband of Harriet R. Cooper, is a son of Joseph P. Nelson. He was once at Cadiz, but is now a resident of Fairbury, Nebraska, where he has been for a number of years assistant cashier of the Harbine Bank of that city. John J. Frazier is a druggist at Muncie, Indiana. Dr. Enos M. Ferris is a son of the late Dr. Samuel Ferris and is one of the successful practising physicians of New Castle. He gives special attention to diseases of the eye and ear. Milton C. Cooper is a farmer who lives four and a half miles south-west of New Castle in the Clear Springs neighborhood. Charles R. Atkinson is superintendent of schools at Sheridan, Wyoming. Before going to Sheridan, he was for a number of years superintendent of schools at York, Nebraska. He is one of the prominent educators of the Great West.

Robert B. Cooper has been blessed beyond all other things in his children, and has every reason to be proud of them and their successes in life. They are all capable and honorable men and women and useful citizens. They are fathers and mothers themselves and children and grandchildren alike always meet with a delightful welcome when they visit the old home.

Margaret (Beeson) Cooper the second wife of Mr. Cooper, died April 6, 1889. He was again married on June 18, 1890, his present wife, who is a most estimable woman, being Mrs. Mary (Booth) Widup. Charles, her son by her first marriage, resides in New Castle.

With the exception of a satisfaction hardly surpassed and probably not equalled in any national campaign of 1904, which resulted in the election of Theodore Roosevelt and Charles W. Fairbanks as Vice President, he voted for his two sons and three of his sons, six of his sons-in-law, five grandsons and one daughter, the wife of Professor Atkinson, of Sheridan, Wyoming, in accordance with the political preferences of the family admits women to the franchise. When these political preferences of the family were printed in the papers and brought to the attention of President Roosevelt, who addressed to the family the following interesting communication:

My Dear Mr. Cooper: "Oyster Bay, N. Y., August 30, 1904.

"I have just received the enclosed clipping. Evidently you are the kind of an American in whom I believe and I want to write and congratulate you on your family, while congratulating myself on the fact that I have ever had their support. I have a great regard for your congressman, Representative Hinshaw.

"Sincerely yours,

"THEODORE ROOSEVELT."

E. H. Hinshaw

BIOGRAPHICAL SKETCH OF NIMROD RICHARD ELLIOTT.

FARMER, MERCHANT, BANKER.

Every man's success or failure in life depends to a large extent upon his own ef. forts. How true is the common expression, "every man is the architect of his own fortune." The man of substance and weight in his own particular community is usually one who has risen above the common level by sheer industry and economy, supported by a laudable ambition to excel. The present Governor of Indiana, J. Frank Hanly, was a poor boy who started in life as an humble digger of ditches but, while wielding the pick-axe and shovel, he was looking forward. He was a good ditcher and step by step arose until he found the honors and dignities of the governorship of a great State awaiting him. Such as he not only illustrate the equality of opportunity but indicate the sure pathway to success.

Nimrod Richard Elliott may be taken as another example in point. As a boy he was wholly dependent upon his own exertions but he was animated by a fixity of purpose that in the end brought him to the goal of his ambition. His life work was done mainly among his neighbors in Henry County and his story should be interesting and profitable to the generation of to day.

He was the son of Ephraim B. and Eliza (Harden) Elliott. His father was born in North Carolina, January 12, 1781, and his mother in Georgia, May 3, 1786. They were married in North Carolina in 1810. On June 20, 1829, they started from their old home in North Carolina for Wayne County, Indiana, reaching their destination near Greensfork, after a two months' journey through mountain passes and over bridgeless streams. They did not tarry long in Wayne but in September, 1833, moved to Henry County and settled about two miles northwest of the site of the present town of Cadiz, in Harrison Township. Ephraim B. Elliott and his wife were the parents of seven children, four sons and three daughters, all of whom were born in North Carolina. Nimrod R., the youngest of the family, was born in Perquimans County, that State, May 4, 1826, and was about three years of age when the family came to Indiana. His parents were poor people at the time of their coming west but were in this particular not very different from most of their neighbors who had come to the new country for the express purpose of bettering their condition. Ephraim B. Elliott died February 16, 1859. After the death of her husband, his widow lived with her son, Nimrod R., until the time of her death, November 18, 1861. Nimrod R. Elliott died January 15, 1905. All are buried in the cemetery at Mechanicsburg, Henry County, Indiana.

While a young man working at the carpenter trade, he said to his comrade at the bench, "I intend some day to be worth ten thousand dollars." He was then a poor man working for low wages and the sum mentioned by him was then regarded as a very large one, indeed. Compared with the colossal fortunes of the present day, that sum seems very insignificant. Before learning his trade, young Elliott had attended the district schools of his neighborhood and when sixteen years of age was examined and licensed to teach. He met with merited success as a teacher and was able to save some money, but he was not altogether satisfied with the meagre earnings of the profession in those days and abandoned it for the carpenter's bench, where he made money much more rapidly and soon had enough ahead to embark in his first mercantile venture, a desire which he had long cherished.

In 1851 he opened a country or general store at Mechanicsburg, Henry County, having as partner, Ezra Swain, of that village, the style of the firm being Elliott and Swain. After several years of successful business, Ezra Swain sold his interest in the business to his brother, Elihu Swain, the firm name remaining unchanged. During the Civil War, Mr. Elliott became the sole proprietor. He continued the business alone until 1873, when Imla W. Cooper, a brother of Mr. Elliott's wife, became his partner. This association continued until 1891, when Mr. Elliott again became the sole owner and continued the business alone until 1895, when he retired and from that time on gave his exclusive attention to the management of his farms, banking and other interests. At the time of his death, he owned seven hundred and fifty acres of land in

Harrison and Fall Creek townships, all of it being well improved and in a high state of cultivation. He left an estate of an estimated value of $125,000.

Thus for a period of more than half a century, Mr. Elliott was a very busy and a very successful man 'and ·his fortune at the end far outran the highest hopes of his youth. In 1851, when he went to Mechanicsburg, then a straggling village, the outlook could not be called promising. The locality was in a measure isolated; the country comparatively new, and there were no improved roads and but few improved farms. He lived, however, to see the surrounding country become almost a garden. He pros.pered with the community which has always given him its confidence and to day is united in honoring his excellent name and in keeping green the memory of his good deeds, his good citizenship and his long, unselfish and useful life. In the galaxy of eminent men of Henry County, from its organization to the present time, must be included the name of Nimrod R. Elliott.

In 1850 Nimrod R. Elliott, while working as a carpenter in and around Cadiz, married Jane H., daughter of William Cooper, and in 1851 moved to Mechanicsburg as already stated. His accumulated fortune was mostly invested in farm lands in that locality, but he embraced other opportunities for investment, among the first in im.portance being the establishment of the Farmers' Bank at Middletown, Henry County, in 1873. This bank, with a capital of thirty thousand dollars, was organized by George Hazzard, the author of this History, John H. Terhune, now of Anderson, and Nimrod R. Elliott. It was conducted for several months at Middletown and then, in order to reach a larger field of operations, was moved to Anderson, where it became the Madison County Bank, with a capital of $100,000. The officers of the Farmers' Bank at Middle.town were Nimrod R. Elliott, president, George Hazzard, vice-president, and John H. Terhune, cashier. The officers of the Madison County Bank were John E. Corwin, presi.dent, Nimrod R. Elliott, vice-president, John H. Terhune, cashier, and John W. Pence, assistant cashier. This bank, at the end of about four years, was converted into the Madison County National Bank, which subsequently went out of business, being suc.ceeded by the present Citizens' Bank of Anderson. Before the organization of 'the Madison County National Bank, Mr. Elliott had disposed of his stock and in May, 1882, was the prime mover in organizing what became the present Farmers' State Bank of Middletown, of which he was made president, a position held by him until his death; Thomas Wilhoit was vice-president, Erastus L. Elliott, cashier, and Benjamin H. Davis, assistant cashier. The present officers of the bank are Adolph Cooper, president, William H. Keesling, vice-president, and Erastus L. Elliott, cashier. It is one of the best and most successful banks in Henry County, or for that matter, in Eastern Indiana. Further information regarding this institution will be found in the chapter of this History entitled "Banks and Banking."

Politically, Nimrod R. Elliott was a life long Democrat. He was an earnest advo.cate of the principles of that party and gave it his warmest support. In Henry County and in the districts of which it formed a part, he was regarded as one of its prominent leaders and by those of his immediate party constituency, his advice and direction were implicitly followed. He was faithful in attendance upon the meetings and conventions of his party, local, State and National, and, if he failed by any chance to be present, it was cause for remark. A Democratic convention in Henry County without his presence would at any time during his life have been regarded as an anomaly. He was a strict partisan but never permitted feeling to sway his judgment nor did he permit it to come between him and his friends of opposite political views. He advocated and voted for the principles in which he believed, but never permitted politics to interfere with his business. He was a successful candidate for presidential elector in 1884 and cast his vote for Grover Cleveland. He was the Democratic candidate for Congress in 1894, against Henry U. Johnson, and ran several hundred votes ahead of his party ticket in the district. He had often been tendered the nomination before but had always declined. He was also often solicited to lead the county ticket, but he preferred to remain a worker in the ranks of the party. He was once a candidate for joint representative for the counties of Henry and Madison.

For a long time he belonged to but one secret organization, the Masonic, of which he was a member for more than half a century. He joined the fraternity at Middletown

ll improved and in a high state
of $125,000.

. Elliott was a very busy and a
outran the highest hopes of his
a straggling village, the outlook
measure isolated; the country
s and but few improved farms.
ome almost a garden. He pros-
in its confidence and to day is
green the memory of his good
useful life. In the galaxy of
to the present time, must be

carpenter in and around Cadiz,
'5) moved to Mechanicsburg as

N. R. Elliott

in 1852 and when a lodge was formed at Mechanicsburg, he was a charter member and the first Worshipful Master, a position held by him for a number of years. In addition to being a Free and Accepted Mason, he was also a member of New Castle Chapter, Number 50, Royal Arch Masons, and a Sir Knight, belonging to the Knightstown Commandery. He was a thorough believer in the tenets of the order and invariably practised its precepts. Late in life, when the Improved Order of Red Men was organized at Mechanicsburg, he joined the order and was a faithful and consistent member until his death. He was a supporter of the Universalist Church but was in nowise contentious with regard to religious beliefs. As in politics so in religion, it was his belief, but he had no quarrel with those who preferred other denominations. He was earnest in his support of the church and was regular in attendance upon its services and contributed liberally of his means for its support.

During the Civil War, no man in Henry County was more heartily loyal to the government than Nimrod R. Elliott. He did not go personally into the conflict, but he was a power for good in the relief work which had to be done by those who remained at home. He was ever solicitous for the health and comfort of the soldier in the field and the welfare of the families, which through the misfortunes of war, had become in a manner dependent upon their friends and neighbors. In this as in many other directions, he was exceedingly charitable but so modest withal that it will never be known to what extent or in what amount he gave for the relief of the needy and the distressed.

Nimrod Richard Elliott was a self made man. His first and principal asset through life was industry. He did not know what it was to be idle. Another asset was a laudable ambition to work to some purpose. His other assets were honesty, frugality, morality and a firm and lasting faith in Him who determines the destinies of all mankind.

During his entire married life, his wife was his wise counsellor, his sympathetic companion and a helpful presence. She was a worthy helper of her husband. Since his death Mrs. Elliott has had full charge of the estate of her husband and has ably discharged the trust.

Nimrod Richard and Jane H. (Cooper) Elliott were the parents of two children, the first being Ida Florence, and the second, Erastus Leonidas, commonly called "Joe."

On the occasion of the death of Nimrod R. Elliott, Judge Martin L. Bundy, of New Castle, wrote as follows:

"Mr. Elliott I have known for sixty years. In 1844, when Colonel Miles Murphey built the house on South Main Street, now occupied by his daughter, Mrs. George W. Goodwin, Nimrod was a boy about seventeen years of age and carried the brick and mortar for the masons who built the walls and this was probably the first work he had done away from home. He settled in the small village where he had lived so long, managed to get a small stock of goods, gave close attention to his business, and by good judgment and economy, backed by the strictest integrity, won the confidence of the people and made a large fortune. Our relations were always so cordial that I regret exceedingly to part with Nimrod. His example should impress young men with the great advantages of industry, economy and integrity in business, for these are the sure guides to never-failing success. He lived the simple life of a typical American. Nimrod R. Elliott must be regarded as one of Henry County's great citizens."

ANCESTRY OF MRS. NIMROD R. (COOPER) ELLIOTT.

Mrs. Elliott was the daughter of William Cooper, who was the son of John and Ann (Hayes) Cooper, natives of Pennsylvania, where he was born in 1794. The family consisted of the parents and four sons, named Caleb, William (father of Mrs. Elliott), John and Imla. They moved from Pennsylvania to Ohio, where John Cooper, the father, died in 1825. Caleb came to Henry County, Indiana, in 1832; Imla, in 1834; and William and John, with their mother, in 1835.

William was the father of eleven children, seven of whom were born in Harrison County, Ohio, and four in Henry County, Indiana. Jane H., the sixth child and fourth daughter, became the wife of Nimrod R. Elliott.

The Coopers came to Indiana from Harrison County, Ohio, which had for its county seat the town of Cadiz, and it is through this family that the Henry County town of Cadiz and the township of Harrison obtained their names. The family is a very large one and has had from the beginning an important influence upon the history of Harrison Township and the western part of the county of Henry.

Caleb H. Cooper, a brother of Mrs. Elliott, was one of the most promising young men of the county. He was a soldier in the Civil War, being mustered in as Second Lieutenant of Company E, 9th Indiana Cavalry. He was promoted First Lieutenant and served until the close of the war in 1865. His military history will be found in Chapter XII of this History. Elsewhere in this History will be found a full biographical sketch of Robert Holiday Cooper, brother of Mrs. Elliott, to which reference should be made for further information as to the ancestry of Mrs. Elliott.

ERASTUS LEONIDAS ELLIOTT.

(Son.)

Erastus Leonidas Elliott is the only son of the late Nimrod Richard and Jane H. (Cooper) Elliott. He was born at Mechanicsburg, Henry County, Indiana, September 17, 1853. The place of his birth was at that time little more than a backwoods village but the kaleidoscopic changes of the past half century have changed its whole aspect. It is now the center of a rich farming district that is not excelled by any portion of the county.

He obtained his primary education in the common or district school at Mechanicsburg and this was supplemented by two years' (1878-79) study at Spiceland Academy under the influence and direction of that eminent scholar and teacher, Clarkson Davis, who will long be remembered in Henry County as its foremost educator. After leaving the Academy, Mr. Elliott began the study of the law in the office of Mark E. Forkner, of New Castle, where he continued during the years 1880 and 1881. He then entered the law department of Michigan University, at Ann Arbor, and graduated from that institution in 1882. He never engaged in the practise of the law, however, for in 1882 he became the cashier of the Farmers' Bank, Middletown, Indiana, and filled that position until 1902, when the bank was re-organized as the Farmers' State Bank of Middletown and Mr. Elliott became its cashier, a position which he has held to the present time. Twenty three years of his life have thus been spent in the banking business and the phenomenal success of the institutions controlled by him thoroughly attests his financial ability. From the start he was under the most favorable auspices, but it has been his own capacity for labor and keen insight into business which have made the institution so highly prosperous. Further information regarding this banking institution will be found in the chapter of this work relating to "Banks and Banking."

Erastus L. Elliott has twice been a member of the lower house of the General Assembly of Indiana, serving during the fifty ninth and sixtieth sessions, 1894 and 1896. He was during both terms chairman of the committee on banking. He was an active member of the house and took an advanced position as a legislator, in all things doing his full duty toward his constituents.

He was elected trustee of Fall Creek Township in 1886 and served acceptably in that position for two years. He is now and has been for several years president of the board of school trustees for the corporation of Middletown. He has given much attention to the educational affairs of the town and at the present time the Middletown schools are second to none in the county in efficiency. The school building is one of the best, being modern in construction and appointments, handsome in appearance and conveniently arranged for school purposes.

Erastus L. Elliott, following in his father's footsteps, upon his arrival at the age of manhood, allied himself with the Democratic party. In 1892, however, he became a Republican and has ever since supported the policies of that dominant organization. He has been honored by the party in Henry County by election to membership in the General Assembly of the State as above related. He has been active in the support of

, important influence upon the history of
the county of Henry.
tt, was one of the most promising young
Civil War, being mustered in as Second
'. He was promoted First Lieutenant and
military history will be found in Chapter
y will be found a full biographical sketch
liott, to which reference should be made
Mrs. Elliott.

AS ELLIOTT.

of the late Nimrod Richard and Jane H.
burg, Henry County, Indiana, September
ime little more than a backwoods village
century have changed its whole aspect.
t that is not excelled by any portion of

common or district school at Mechanics-
s (1878-79) study at Spiceland Academy
sent scholar and teacher, Clarkson Davis,
as its foremost educator. After leaving
he law in the office of Mark E. Forkner,
years 1880 and 1881. He then entered
at Ann Arbor, and graduated from that
practise of the law, however, for in 1882
Middletown, Indiana, and filled that posi-
d as the Farmers' State Bank of Middle-
sition which he has held to the present
s been spent in the banking business and
ontrolled by him thoroughly attests his
r the most favorable auspices, but it has
ight into business which have made the
ormation regarding this banking institu-
relating to "Banks and Banking."
er of the lower house of the General As-
nth and sixtieth sessions, 1894 and 1896.
ommittee on banking. He was an active
sition as a legislator, in all things doing

wnship in 1886 and served acceptably in
a been for several years president of the
liddletown. He has given much attention
the present time the Middletown schools
The school building is one of the best,
s; handsome in appearance and conven-

er's footsteps, upon his arrival at the
atic party. In 1892, however, he became
policies of that dominant organization.
ounty by election to membership in the
d. He has been active in the support of

E. L. Elliott

the party in all campaigns since 1892 and though a man of positive opinions he has never permitted political feeling to interfere with his social and business obligations. He has numerous friends in both political parties and extends respect to the opinions of others with whom he may differ as to governmental policies.

He is not a member of any church, but leans toward the Universalist denomination of which his father was for a long time a consistent adherent. He is a member of the Masonic fraternity; of the Knights of Pythias; the Order of Elks; and the Improved Order of Red Men.

Erastus L. Elliott is a gentleman of splendid social qualities and delights to entertain his friends. He is a great reader and keeps fully advised as to the trend of current events, whether the same relate to the civil, religious, moral or social affairs of the country. Comparatively, he is still a young man, not much beyond his prime, and barring the uncertainties of life, bids fair to have many·years of usefulness to the community still before him. What he has already accomplished has been from a desire to· be doing something in the world. He has not been pushed onward by the spur of necessity but rather by a fine moral consciousness of his duty toward his fellow men.

IDA FLORENCE (ELLIOTT) THURSTON.

(Daughter.)

Mrs. Thurston is the only daughter of the late Nimrod Richard and Jane H. (Cooper) Elliott, and was born July 14, 1851. She grew to young womanhood at Mechanicsburg, where she attended the public schools and afterwards finishhed her education at the well known New Castle Academy. She was a bright, vivacious and intelligent girl, who was much beloved by the companions of her youth.

On October 19, 1869, she was married, at her home in Mechanicsburg, to Dr. Joseph M. Thurston, the ceremony being performed by the Reverend Asa Huston. To them have been·born two children: Evaleth Mabel, born December 13, 1870; and Richard Elliott, born November 23, 1879, died November 3, 1893, and is buried in Earlham Cemetery, Richmond, Indiana.

The daughter, Evaleth Mabel, was married September 6,.1899, at the home of her parents in Richmond, to Professor Hugo Paul Thieme, by the Reverend William Warbinton, of the Christian Church at Hagerstown, Indiana. Professor and Mrs. Thieme reside at Ann Arbor, Michigan, where the former is assistant professor of French in the University of Michigan. They have one child, Florence Leonie, born May 20, 1902, in Richmond, Indiana.

Dr. Joseph M. Thurston was born in Warren County, Ohio, July 2, 1841, his parents being William Henry and Delilah (Miller) Thurston. He was educated at Washington Court House, Ohio. In 1866 he came to Mechanicsburg, Henry County, Indiana, and there commenced the study of medicine in the office and under the tutelage of the now venerable Dr. Joseph Weeks. In 1866-7 he attended the course of the Physio-Medical College, Cincinnati, Ohio, and in 1868 opened an office in Hagerstown, Indiana, where he began the practise of his profession. In 1888 he removed his family to Richmond, Indiana, where he still resides and has a large practise. From 1875 to 1890 Dr. Thurston was professor of Physiology and Anatomy in the Physio-Medical College at Indianapolis. He is now professor of Nervous Diseases in the same institution.

In the Civil War, he enlisted as a private in Company F, 90th Ohio Infantry, and served until the end of the conflict. He enlisted July 23, 1862, and was mustered out June 26, 1865. He was a participant in the battles of Perryville and Wildcat, Kentucky; Stone's River, Tennessee, and Ringgold and Chickamauga, Georgia. He was taken prisoner in the last named.battle and was confined for a year in Libby Prison, Richmond, Virginia, where he acted as ward master, hospital steward and assistant to the surgeons in charge.

. Dr. Joseph M. Thurston is prominent in his profession and has a wide acquaintance throughout Eastern Indiana, where he enjoys the full confidence and esteem of the people.

71

BIOGRAPHICAL SKETCH OF SAMUEL FERRIS, M. D.

EMINENT PHYSICIAN AND SURGEON AND LEADING CITIZEN OF NEW CASTLE.

No one, except an immediate member of a family, has so intimate a knowledge of the inner life of its circle as the the the attending physician. He is not merely a dispenser of medicines for the cure or alleviation of physical ills; he must also be a healer of minds distressed. How high, indeed, must the standard of honor be among the members of a profession whose duty it is to invade the secret recesses of the mind and heart. Subject only to the judgment of conscience, how constantly must the physician be on his guard to keep inviolate the confidence of his patients. So seldom, too, is this trust and confidence violated that it is a crown of honor to the whole profession. Then, too, see how wonderfully the smiling lip and the kindly word of the true physician quiet the fears of the sick and inspire them with hope, while the scowling countenance and surly demeanor of another counteract the utmost efforts of his skill in the medical art. Every student of this most ancient and honorable profession must be governed by the most exacting rules of ethics illustrated by the unselfish and single minded devotion to duty which has characterized the lives of its eminent practitioners, and by as much as he fails to attain this ideal standard he falls short of being the perfect healer.

Dr. Samuel Ferris possessed those qualities of mind and heart which are so essential to the successful physician and which for the want of a closer analysis are popularly said to make of one a "natural physician." He was an educated gentleman and supplemented his natural abilities by thorough and exhaustive investigation, and during a practise of many years' duration he was constantly alert to the advances being made in medicine and surgery.

He was the lineal descendant, according to the genealogical records of the family, of Jeffrey Ferris, the first of the American family of that name. He is said to have been a native of Leicester, England, who came to America in 1635 and settled in Boston, Massachusetts. He died in 1666. His descendants in order were as follows: James Ferris (the first), who died about 1726; Samuel Ferris (the first), born in September, 1706, died in 1786; Samuel Ferris (the second), born in February, 1733, and was a soldier of the Revolution; Frederick Ferris, the father of Samuel Ferris (the third), subject of this sketch; he was a native of Connecticut, where he married Susannah Nichols. He was born in 1784 and died in 1845; his wife was born in 1791 and died in 1832. They moved from Connecticut in 1813 and settled on a farm, four miles northeast of Brookville, Franklin County, Indiana.

Frederick and Susannah (Nichols) Ferris were the parents of twelve children, namely: William K., Ann D., Susan E., John W., Caroline, Catharine, James S., Mary, Samuel, Allison B., Isaiah, and a daughter who died in infancy. Of these children, the first five named were born in Connecticut and the remainder in Indiana. All of this family are now dead. Catharine became the wife of the late James M. Clements, who was for several years surveyor of Henry County and who was also the father of Courtland C. Clements, of Washington City. Further reference to James M. Clements will be found in Chapter XLIII, and to Courtland C. Clements in Chapter XXVII, of this History. Mrs. Clements was an excellent woman and mother and much beloved of a large circle of relatives and friends. James S. Ferris, the third son, was for several years a teacher in New Castle; he was the first county school examiner and was for eight years, 1856-1863, auditor of Henry County. He died September 23, 1870.

SAMUEL FERRIS.

Samuel Ferris, the fourth son of Frederick and Susannah (Nichols) Ferris, was born on the farm above mentioned in Franklin County, Indiana, March 13, 1822. He remained under the parental roof until he was about eighteen years of age, when in 1840 he became a medical student under the then well known physician, Dr. Ziba Casterline, of Liberty, Union County, Indiana. He remained with Dr. Casterline as student and assistant for two or three years and then located at Cadiz, Henry County, Indiana,

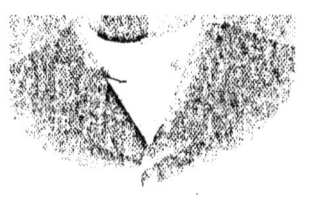

S. Ferris

BIOGRAPHICAL SKETCH OF SAMUEL FERRIS. M. D.

No one, ex . . . . immediate member of a fa . . . . ., has so intimate a knowledge of the inner life o . . . . as the the . . . . He is not merely a dispenser of medicines f . . . . are or alleviation of . . . . he must also be a healer of minds distress . . . . . . High, indeed, ... ard of honor be among the members of a profe . . . . duty it is to . . . . cret recesses of the mind and heart. Subject only . . . . gment of conscience, ... must the physician be on his guard to . . . . the confiden . . . . tients so seldom, too, is this trust and confidenc . . . . that it is a crown . . . . to the whole profession. Then, too, see how won . . . . the smiling lip . . . . ly word of the true physician quiet the fears of . . . . and inspire . . . . while the scowling countenance and surly demea . . . . . . another counteract . . . . efforts of his skill in the medical art. Every stude . . . . ancient or . . . . ble profession must be governed by the most exacti . . . . of ethics illustrated . . . . oselfish and single minded devotion to duty which . . . . ers, and by as much as he fails to . . . . fect healer.

Dr. S . . . . which are so essential to the . . . . is popularly said to m . . . . supplemented h . . . . during a practise o . . . . ade in medicine

He . . . . family, of Jeffre . . . . to have been a r . . . . . . Worcester, Massach . . . . America in 1636 and settled in Boston. Massach . . . . . . He died in 16 . . . . nants in order were as follows: James Ferris . . . . . . who died abo . . . . . . Ferris (the first), born in September, 1706, d . . . . 1786; Samuel Ferris . . . . . . born in . . . . . . 1733, and was a soldier of . . . . revolution; Francis's . . . . . . ther of Samuel Ferris (the third), subject of . . . . he was a native . . . . where he married Susannah Nichols. He wa . . . . 1734 and died in 18 . . . . . . born in 17 . . . and died in 1832. They moved . . . . in 1813 . . . . rm, four miles northeast of Brookville, ... County, Indiana.

. . . . and Susannah (Ni . . . . were the parents of twelve children. nam . . . . Ann . . Susan C . . . . line Ca . . . . . . James S . Mary, Sam . . . . and a daughter . . . . Infancy . . . . the first . . . . n Cornec . . . . fam . . . . ine became . . . . who wa . . . . of Henry . . . . Courtland C. . . . . City. Farmer . . . . will be fo . . . . by Com . . . . of this History to . . . . excellent woman . . . . loved of a large ci . . . . James S. Trish . . . . several years a te . . . . was the first county . . . . ys for eight years, 1 . . . . County. He die . . . . . .

SAMUEL

. . . . the fourth son of . . . . (Nichols) Ferris, was . . . . in Franklin Coun . . . . March 13, 1822. He resided . . . . until he was . . . . years of age, when in 1840 . . . . under the then well known physician, Dr. Ziba Casterline, of Liberty, Union County, In ana. He remained with Dr. Casterline as student and assistant for two or three years and then located at Cadiz, Henry County, Indiana.

S. Ferris

where he practised for about six months. He then entered into partnership with his former preceptor, Dr. Casterline, at Liberty. This partnership continued for two years, after which he located at New Paris, Ohio, where he remained for twelve years. In 1856 he removed to New Castle, Henry County, Indiana, and there continued in the practise of his profession until his retirement in 1898. He died November 4, 1901.

Dr. Samuel Ferris was a man of positive opinions and firm in the discharge of his duties. He was a law-abiding citizen and believed in the strict and impartial enforcement of the law, whether for the prevention of crime, the preservation of health or the elevation of the morals of the community. He was a man of the strictest integrity and demanded like conformity by others to the highest standard of living. He took especial pride in the profession which he adorned and its numerous and onerous demands were met by him with alacrity until worn out in well doing and borne down by the weight of years he was compelled to relinquish to other hands the work he had so long and so faithfully performed. He was a successful physician with a large practise throughout his career and was esteemed by the laity as well as by the profession for his learning and ability. In his profession he was zealous and untiring and endeared himself to the afflicted by his cheerful sympathy and ready aid. He carried rays of sunshine into hundreds of households and departing left behind him an atmosphere charged with confidence and hope. Among his family and friends he was a sociable and companionable man and he was never more delighted than when ministering to their content and happiness.

In addition to his constant practise of medicine, Dr. Ferris was for a number of years health officer of the Corporation of New Castle and during his term in office performed his duties most satisfactorily. He firmly believed that cleanliness is next to godliness. He made frequent personal investigations and enforced observance of his orders by appeal to the law when his instructions were disobeyed or ignored.

Dr. Samuel Ferris, it will be noted, practised his profession in New Castle and contiguous places for more than forty five years. During this time, he was a delegate to the American Medical Association, at Chicago in 1863, from the Henry County Medical Society, which he had helped to organize in 1856, and which was the first society of its kind in the county. He was for many years a member of the State Medical Society of Indiana. In 1882 he was a member of the Board of Trustees of New Castle and in the same year became by appointment one of the board of examining surgeons for pensions which position he filled acceptably for several years. He was the friend of the soldier and while faithfully performing his duty as a member of the board, he always decided doubtful points in favor of the defender of his country.

At New Paris, Preble County, Ohio, March 13, 1845, Dr. Samuel Ferris married Margaret C., daughter of John and Sarah Lohr, of that place. This was a happy union and together they lived in perfect harmony and love for more than fifty six years. She still survives him and though advanced in years, having been born April 17, 1824, she finds consolation in the earnest filial love and devotion of her children. Dr. Samuel and Margaret (Lohr) Ferris were the parents of nine children, of whom but four are now living, namely: William E., Eliza M., now Mrs. James A. Martindale, of New Castle; Luella and Edgar S. William E. Ferris is a practical farmer and gardener, residing two miles north of New Castle, where he gives great attention to the cultivation of the strawberry and other popular fruits. He is an industrious and intelligent worker and his efforts have met with deserved success. Luella lives at home with her mother and manages the household. A sketch of Dr. Edgar S. Ferris follows this article relating to his father.

Dr. Samuel Ferris and his wife were lifelong members of the Methodist Episcopal Church. During his life they were punctual attendants upon its services and liberal contributors to its support. Since his death Mrs. Ferris continues her devotion to the same denomination. Dr. Ferris was not a member of any secret organization, although he had at times expressed a preference for the Masonic order with which his son, Dr. Edgar S. Ferris, is prominently identified.

EDGAR SAMUEL FERRIS, M. D.

Not so many years ago Henry County was noted for its aged practising physicians, most of whom, however, have now passed off the stage, giving place to a new generation. The older generation of physicians followed their profession under the most trying conditions, braving the cold and snows of Winter, the storms and floods of Spring and Summer and facing the most serious difficulties and dangers inseparable from a wild and new land, and they are the real heroes of the early settlement and subsequent development of the country. Such pioneer physicians as Joel Reed, John Darr, William M. Kerr, James V. Wayman, George W. Riddle, William F. Boor, George W. Ballengall, John S. Guisinger, Joseph Weeks, John Rea, William B. Shockley, Luther W. Hess, Joseph W. Whitesel, Isaac Mendenhall, Samuel Ferris, Robert B. Griffis, Roland T. Summers, William M. Bartlett, Jonathan Ross, and others, are each entitled to honorable mention and their names should be forever preserved in the annals of Henry County. The new generation of physicians find their duties comparatively easy and altogether free from the discomforts and dangers which surrounded those who in the language of early times "blazed the way."

Among the younger physicians of the county is Dr. Edgar Samuel Ferris, who is the second son of the late Dr. Samuel and Margaret (Lohr) Ferris. He was born in New Castle, Henry County, Indiana, April 9, 1864, and was educated in the public schools of his native town. He was strongly attracted toward the profession of medicine and like his father began to study the art at the age of eighteen. He pursued his studies under the direction of his father for a couple of years and then entered the Jefferson Medical College, Philadelphia, Pennsylvania, from which he was graduated in 1885. He subsequently took a post-graduate course at the Chicago Polyclinic, having in the meantime entered upon the practise of his profession at New Castle, in partnership with his father. This business union continued uninterruptedly until 1898, when the elder Dr. Ferris retired from active practise. Dr. Edgar S. Ferris continued the business until the Spring of 1902, at which time he concluded to give up the general practise of. medicine and confine himself to diseases of the eye, ear, nose and throat.

He closed his office and went to Philadelphia, where he entered upon a course of study relating to these various organs at the Polyclinic. He subsequently crossed the ocean to London, England, and there attended the lectures at the Royal Opthalmic Hospital and the Central Nose, Throat and Ear College. After his return from London, he established his office at Indianapolis and practised there for several months. He then returned to New Castle, where down to the present time he has given his undivided attention to a constantly increasing and highly successful special practise.

The special branch of the profession to which he gives his attention is a highly important one and requires constant and unceasing study to keep abreast of the developments of modern scientific treatment of disease, and the practitioner has but little time for matters outside of his chosen field; but Dr. Ferris is notably industrious and has no idle moments.. He is a member of the County, State and National Medical societies and was for three years a member of the Board of Trustees of New Castle, in which position he acquitted himself to the complete satisfaction of the community. He was also for several years the very competent secretary of the County Board of Health. Politically he has always been a Republican and is an earnest supporter of the principles of that party. Besides his activity in his profession and in politics, he has also shown a disposition to aid the growth and prosperity of his native town.

Dr. Ferris is an urbane gentleman and by his pleasant manners invites the esteem and confidence of the community. He is quick in decision, quick to act and firm in his opinions. He is a man of fine character, high attainments and increasing reputation in his profession.

On March 23, 1887, at the home of her parents near Cadiz, Henry County, Indiana, Dr. Edgar S. Ferris married Minnie M., the fifth daughter of Robert H. and Margaret (Haworth) Cooper, a sketch of whom appears elsewhere in this History. Dr. and Mrs. Ferris have had born to them one child which died in infancy. They are members of the Methodist Episcopal Church and are constant in attention to their religious duties.

noted for its aged practising physicians
atage, giving place to a new generation
profession under the most trying condi-
' storms and floods of Spring and Sum-
l dangers inseparable from a wild and
irly settlement and subsequent develop-
us Joel Reed, John Darr, William M
/illiam F. Boor, George W. Ballengall,
lliam B. Shockley, Luther W. Hess, Jo-
rris, Robert B. Griffis, Roland T. Sum-
others, are each entitled to honorable
served in the annals of Henry County:
ties comparatively easy and altogether
rounded those who in the language of

uty is Dr. Edgar Samuel Ferris, who
rearet ' Lohr) Ferris. He was born in
4, and was educated in the public
trained toward the profession of medi-
the age of eighteen. He pursued his
length of years and then entered the
which he was graduated in
degree at the Chicago Polyclinic,
of his profession at New Castle, in
continued uninterruptedly until 1898,
case. Dr. Edgar S. Ferris continued the
he concluded to give up the general
of the eye, ear, nose and throat.
where he entered upon a course
the Polyclinic. He subsequently
attended the lectures at the Royal Op-
Ear College. After his return from
practised there for several months.
present time he has given his undi-
successful special practise.
gives his attention to a highly
study to keep abreast of the develop-
the practitioner has but little time
Ferris is notably industrious and has
State and National Medical societies
of New Castle, in which posi-
the community. He was also
the County Board of Health. Politic-
supporter of the principles of
in politics, he has also shown a
town.

manners invites the esteem
quick to act and firm in his
and increasing reputation in

Cadiz, Henry County, Indiana,
daughter of Robert H. and Margaret
where in this History. Dr. and Mrs.
infancy. They are members of
attention to their religious duties.

E S Ferris.

Dr. Ferris is an enthusiastic member of the Masonic Order. He has taken all of the degrees of Ancient Craft Masonry, the Royal Arch Chapter, the Council, the Knights Templar and the Scottish Rite, including the Thirty Second Degree, and is likewise a member of the Mystic Shrine. He has given a great deal of thought and study to Masonic history and is familiar with the unwritten work of the order. He is frequent in his attendance upon its meetings and so far as possible practises its grand precepts and principles. He is also a member of that large sister order, the Knights of Pythias. Counting by years he is still a young man but he is old in experience. Using the term in an entirely complimentary sense, he is "a chip of the old block," and following in the footsteps of his father, Dr. Samuel Ferris, the presumption is that in the coming years, he may more than merit the distinction attaching to the name of that well known and highly honored old school physician.

BIOGRAPHICAL SKETCH OF JOHN LARUE FORKNER.

Home pride is peculiar to no particular locality or people. It prevails, for various reasons, in a greater degree in some communities than in others, perhaps, but nowhere is it wholly absent among the characteristics of a refined and progressive people. Not only are the worthy institutions and enterprises of importance sources of pride in the localities where they have been established, but the men who have by their achievements become prominent, whether at home or abroad, are honored and admired by their fellow citizens. It, therefore, follows that a history of Henry County and its prominent native sons would not be complete without some honorable mention of the subject of this biography.

John Larue Forkner was born in Liberty Township, Henry County, January 20, 1844. His parents were Micajah and Elizabeth (Allen) Forkner, the former a son of Isaac Forkner, who after serving his country in a North Carolina regiment during the war of 1812-15, removed to Virginia and subsequently immigrated to Indiana, locating at Centreville, Wayne County, where he remained for a time, afterwards removing to Henry County with his family. Micajah was born in Virginia in 1812 and was called to his reward at Millville, Henry County, August 11, 1879, honored and respected as an honest, upright citizen by all who knew him.

The early boyhood of John L. Forkner was passed in the midst of rural scenes and was not unlike that of other boys similarly situated in life. He assisted his parents on the farm and attended the district schools until he was twelve years of age, when his parents removed to Millville and engaged in mercantile pursuits. During the time he was not attending school he clerked in his father's store. With an experience of four years as salesman, he left the parental roof and engaged as clerk with Lontz Brothers, merchants, at Hagerstown, Wayne County. In the spring of 1863 he went to Cambridge City and accepted a position as salesman in the store of Lafe Develin. He remained there until 1864, when he was called to represent the interests of an elder brother in the mercantile establishment of Forkner and Allen at Tipton, Indiana.

He remained here until February, 1866, when he went to Madison County, locating at Anderson, where he was employed as salesman in various establishments until 1868. It was during this year that he was elected city clerk and at the expiration of his term of office was re-elected. While serving as city clerk he was also employed as deputy clerk of the circuit court, and held that position until 1872, when he was appointed office deputy by Sheriff Albert J. Ross. He served as deputy sheriff for two years and at the same time discharged the duties of local editor for the Anderson Democrat.

In 1874 he sought and obtained the nomination for auditor on the Democratic ticket, and at the general election that year was elected by a flattering majority. In 1878 he was re-elected and brought to the discharge of the duties of that important office an experience that rendered his service not only highly creditable to himself, but to the party that elected him. During his later term as auditor he purchased a one-third interest in the Exchange Bank of Anderson and upon his retiring from office in 1883 was chosen cashier of that repository. In 1892 the bank was reorganized and converted into a national bank under the title of The National Exchange Bank of Anderson. With the reorganization of the bank he was again chosen cashier by the directors, and although he has been and still is connected with other institutions and enterprises, he has ever since discharged the duties of that position.

In 1891 he was elected to the City Council as a Democrat in a ward that has always returned large Republican majorities. During his term in that office he demonstrated his efficiency and usefulness by securing for the city, electric lights, improved fire protection and many miles of brick-paved streets.

Soon after the discovery of natural gas he took an active part in organizing the Citizens' Gas Company, and served five years as president of that corporation. He was also one of the original promoters of the Anderson Iron and Bolt Company and held a large amount of stock in the Pennsylvania Glass Company. In 1897 he took a promi-

y or people. It prevails, for various
than in others, perhaps, but nowhere
refined and progressive people. Not
f importance sources of pride in the
he men who have by their achieve-
ad, are honored and admired by their
: of Henry County and its prominent
honorable mention of the subject of

wnship, Henry County, January 20,
Allen) Faulkner, the former a son of
North Carolina regiment during the
atly inaugurated to Indiana, locating
for a time afterwards removing to
in Virginia in 1812 and was called to
157. honored and respected as an

war in the midst of rural scenes and
assisted his parents on
years of age, when his
During the time he
With an experience of four
igaged as clerk with Lontz Brothers,
spring of 1883 he went to Cambridge
store of Lafe Develin. He remained
e interests of an elder brother in the
Tipton, Indiana.
he went to Madison County, locating
in various establishments until 1868.
rk and at the expiration of his term
rk he was also employed as deputy
il 1872, when he was appointed office
uty sheriff for two years and at the
the Anderson Democrat.
ion for a spot on the Democratic
elected by a flattering majority. In
e of the duties of that important of-
highly creditable to himself, but to
as auditor purchased a one-third
his interests from office in 1883 was
was reorganized and converted into
change Bank of Anderson. With the
shown by the Directors, and although
income and enterprises, he has ever

Democrat in a ward that has always
to that office he demonstrated his
electric lights, improved fire protection

an active part in organizing the
of that corporation. He was
and Bolt Company and held a
In 1897 he took a promi-

nent part along with Charles L. Henry, at that time a resident of Anderson, and Philip Muller, of Marion, in organizing the Union Traction Company of Indiana, and was treas. urer of the company for two years.

In 1892 he was appointed a trustee of the Northern Asylum for the Insane at Lo. gansport by Governor Matthews and served three years in that capacity, two of which were as president of the official board.

On account of many advantageous circumstances he was selected by his party to make the race for mayor of the city in 1902 and although he had a large majority to overcome, he was elected by a vote that surprised even his most sanguine friends. His administration of public affairs was so satisfactory to the people that in 1904 he was re. elected by a most substantial majority. The most notable undertaking of his adminis. tration, perhaps, was the successful construction of a pure water system for the city. This important public work involved the disbursement of a large sum of money, yet it can be truthfully said to his enduring credit that no man ever had the temerity to in. timate that one dollar was misappropriated.

Among the many honors that have been bestowed upon him by his fellow citizens, and as showing the high esteem in which he is held, it may be mentioned that he was chosen secretary of The Old Settlers' Association of Madison County and served in that capacity for several years, when he was elected president of the association and still holds that honorable position. In 1904 he was elected president of the State Association of Elks and served one year with distinguished credit to himself and the order.

Although entirely pacific in his inclinations, his friends and admirers have bestowed upon him the honorary title of "Colonel," which he will gracefully bear with him through the remainder of his years upon earth.

John Larue Forkner has been married twice. His first wife was Anna B. Hernly, of New Castle, to whom he was married in March, 1873. Three years later she died, leaving one child, Emma, now the wife of Lee C. Newsom, of Anderson. His second and present wife was Mary Carson Watson, daughter of ex-Sheriff David H. Watson, of Anderson, with whom he was united in marriage in 1878. The result of this union has been two children—Wade Hampton Forkner, who died at the age of four years, and Nellie Grant Forkner, at this time the life and sunshine of the Forkner home.

Mayor Forkner, notwithstanding his various business interests and official duties, finds time to devote to the social side of life. He is a member of the Masonic fraternity, the Knights Templar, Improved Order of Red Men, Knights of Honor and the Elks, in each of which he stands deservedly high, and has received all the local honors that these lodges can bestow.

Cherishing a love for the old things that go to make history and seeing the necessity for a complete and intelligent record of the many interesting and important events that have occurred in Madison County since its organization, he in connection with ex-Mayor Byron H. Dyson, of Anderson, wrote and published in 1897 a history of that county that has since been accepted as authority upon all matters of which it treats. The work speaks for itself and will always stand as a proud monument to his memory as an able and faithful chronicler of events.

In matters of politics he has always been a Democrat of the Andrew Jackson type and believing that the world is governed too much, will no doubt continue in the Democratic faith to the end of his career. No man locally stands higher than he in the counsels of his party, and no man takes greater interest in its welfare. He recognizes and appreciates the fact that his party has been generously partial to him in the way of preferment and he is, therefore, ready at all times and under all circumstances to render any service within his ability to promote its success. In his political aspirations he has been successful beyond many, having never been defeated in a contest for office before the people. His methods have always been such that even his opponents could not accuse him of intrigue or indirection. Just and honorable in politics as in business, his record is above reproach.

While not a member of any religious organization, he believes in the good in all religions and stands for the best in good citizenship. With him the Golden Rule is not a mere sentiment, as he illustrates in his daily walk, and in a modest way the fact that he regards it as the safest and best of moral guides.

This in conclusion is the brief history of one of Madison County's most highly respected and popular citizens. As a man of affairs he is pre-eminent in his home city and county, and throughout the State enjoys a reputation in commercial circles inferior to that of no citizen within its borders. Genial and generous, able and conservative, void of vanity and selfishness, candid and conscientious, he is a plain, unpretending gentleman, whose entire life is a conspicuous example of what may be accomplished by untiring industry, honorable methods and right living.

John W. Griffin

The father of John Burgess
hood. John Burgess emigra...
Indiana, and settled on the...
land which is now nearly cov...
old Friends graveyard. near...
their side lies George, the fi...
died in infancy. July 28, 185...

The Caroline Griffins wer...
tradition, came from Wales...
two going south to Rappah...
the Neuse, and others to A...
tor of John W. Griffin going...
is said to have been heir to...
dominating influence the oth...
safety. The emigrating brot...
the family are descended fro...
Wales. who was captured...
in the Tower of London...
above, and that it still ra...

Writing to the subser...
claims to be of his blood...
most of the branch of the...
and States. for several...

BIOGRAPHICAL SKETCH OF JOHN WILLIAM GRIFFIN.

NATIVE CITIZEN, LEADING FARMER, INFLUENTIAL MAN,

John William Griffin, of Dunreith, is a native of Henry County, born December 3, 1831. His parents were Joseph and Rebecca (Burgess) Griffin, who were married in 1830 and at once settled on land which had been entered by Joseph through his father, Jacob Griffin, who lived at Centreville, Wayne County, Indiana. Jacob Griffin was married to Mary Copeland in North Carolina and was a son of James and Hannah Griffin, James being a son of James Griffin and Alice, his wife, all of North Carolina. Joseph Griffin, father of the subject of this sketch, died August 9, 1890, and his widow, Rebecca (Burgess) Griffin, who was born March 16, 1811, died November 22, 1903. Both are buried in Spiceland Cemetery. They had four children, namely: John William, the subject of this sketch; Emily J., who died in middle life, was the wife of the Reverend Thomas Clark, of Wayne County, this State, a graduate of Haverford College, Philadelphia, Pennsylvania; Sarah A. is the widow of Elwood Pleas, the author of the first history of Henry County. She is still living at her old home, south of Spiceland. Mary B. died unmarried at the age of twenty three years.

Rebecca (Burgess) Griffin was the daughter of John and Sarah (Cain) Burgess. The father of John Burgess was born in England but came to America in early manhood. John Burgess emigrated from Paspatank River, South Carolina, to Wayne County, Indiana, and settled on the site of South Richmond, where he entered a half section of land which is now nearly covered by the city. Both himself and wife are buried in the old Friends graveyard, near the ancient yearly meeting house in North Richmond. By their side lies George, the first born child of John William Griffin and his wife, who died in infancy, July 28, 1856.

The Carolina Griffins were descended from one of three brothers who, according to tradition, came from Wales to New York, one of whom settled in that State, the other two going south to Rappahannock River, Virginia, their descendants spreading out to the Neuse, and others to Apalachicola River, and some farther south and west, the ancestor of John W. Griffin going to North Carolina. A fourth brother, who remained in Wales, is said to have been heir to the paternal homestead and ancestral estates, and through his dominating influence the others found the native land not only unwelcome, but of doubtful safety. The emigrating brothers left their native land about 1650. Tradition has it that the family are descended from Llewellyn Ap (son of) Gruyffyd, the last king or prince of Wales, who was captured by Edward I of England about the year 1282 and imprisoned in the Tower of London. On the walls of his cell it is said he scratched his name as above, and that it still remains there.

Writing to the subject of this sketch, one of the Griffins of Ontario, Canada, who claims to be of his blood, as well as name, says: "I believe he was beheaded * * * most of the branch of the family to which I belong were Quakers, in New York (Colony and State), for several generations, and that seems to be another link between your family and ours."

Judge Cyrus Griffin, who was a member of the last Continental Congress at the time of the Revolutionary War (his home being in Virginia), was educated in England. The following is from his family history: "Two brothers named Thomas and Samuel Griffin came to America and settled on the Rappahannock River in Virginia. They were descended from Llewellyn, last king of Wales. They left a brother in Wales who, being the eldest brother, possessed an estate of six hundred pounds sterling per annum. He died without issue, and the youngest brother, Samuel, went over in pursuit of the estate. He also died in England before anything was done with respect to the property. Thomas had an only son, also named Thomas, neither of whom ever left Virginia. They were nearly related to Admiral Griffin, who distinguished himself in the early Dutch wars, for which he was knighted Sir John Griffin. His family, it has always been understood, possess the estate above mentioned. His only daughter was by marriage Baroness Howard de Walden, and when two of Thomas Griffin's grandsons, Cyrus and Samuel, were in England at college they were acknowledged by that family and visited them. Thomas Griffin, Junior, left one son named Leroy, who married Miss Bertrand. They had seven sons and one daughter, whose names were as follows: Thomas Bertrand Griffin married Miss Ball, of Virginia; Corbin Griffin married Miss Berkley, of Virginia; Leroy Griffin; Cyrus Griffin married Lady Christina Stuart, of Scotland; Samuel Griffin married Miss Braxton, of Virginia; William Griffin married Miss Chiswell, of Virginia; John Taylor Griffin married Miss Lightfoot, of Virginia; a daughter who married Mr. Richard Adams, of Virginia. The home of the family was called Zion House, in Lancaster County, Virginia."

John William Griffin, however, never heard a word about this traditional ancestry until in his teens, when a relative, while visiting at his father's was overheard by him in a conversation with his father about "our estate," which attracted his attention and after the guest had departed expressed surprise at being "left in the dark" when the other members of the family were so well posted. "Well," his father replied, "I was in hopes thee would never hear any of the foolishness of throwing away good money in an effort to secure that old estate."

JOHN WILLIAM GRIFFIN.

John William Griffin, the immediate subject of this sketch, was reared on the old homestead, and was educated in the Spiceland schools, this mental training being supplemented by a short term in The Friends Boarding School afterwards Earlham College. Subsequently he engaged as a clerk in a store at Richmond. In 1852, in company with John W. Johnson, a former school mate, he started a small store at Spiceland in a building located where Hoover's block now is, and for two years did quite as much business as their small means would justify, the credit system being in vogue throughout the country. During this time the Panhandle Railroad was built through the southern part of the county and, in company with a cousin, Elihu Griffin, and Caleb Johnson, a former preceptor, a store was also started at Ogden on the new railroad, Elihu Griffin being agent at that point. The firm handled, besides ordinary merchandise, wheat, corn, clover and timothy seeds, and also bought flour by the hundred-barrel lots, from Ogden, Raysville, Carthage and Buck Creek mills. Wool also was bought from the farmers and from Kennard's woolen factory, the grain, wool and flour being bought on commission, the cash being advanced and rates fixed by eastern capitalists, which aided their credit business to stand the strain of a losing or unprofitable credit business. Soon after this the store at Spiceland was sold. Subsequently both the Johnsons and J. W. Griffin sold their interest in the business here and purchased an interest in Nordyke Ham and Company, at Richmond, Indiana, engaged in the manufacture of patent wire cloth flour bolts. This company sent John W. Griffin as its agent to the Chicago Exposition of 1856, where an award of merit was granted the bolt company after passing the closest scrutiny of Committeemen Gage and Haines, mill-owners of the Chicago Mills, the leading mills in the city, and Fulton and Perkins, mill-wrights, who were second to none in importance in the country. Gage and Haines purchased and placed in their mills the new Nordyke and Ham bolts, and the award of the exposition brought orders and inquiries from a large scope of country. Elihu Griffin accompanied John W. Griffin in this labor and proved himself a valuable assistant. Soon after this time, Mr. Griffin sold one-half of his interest in the manufacturing company for three hundred and thirty acres of land in Lake County, this State, which was for him a fortunate transaction. He located on the Lake County land and made his home there for nearly four years, when, his parents desiring to retire from the family homestead owing to the mother's feeble health, he purchased one hundred and ten acres of his father and removed to the place of his birth. He sold out the Lake County interests, taking some other lands in Rush and Madison counties in part payment. He also entered a half section of land in 1853 in Washington County, Iowa. These lands were exchanged for lands and property nearer home, lands were sold, taking mortgages for part payment and other lands bought with these claims, which were of course assigned by the vendor. Quite a little brokerage in real estate was engaged in, when the panic of 1873 caught him with about thirty thousand dollars' worth of paper standing out, and in lieu thereof he had to take the mortgaged lands scattered from Knox to Adams counties, in ten counties in this State. He mortgaged his home property and was thus enabled to clear his outside property of incumbrance so that he could the better handle it. In the course of years he managed to dispose of his outside property, some of it at long time and in one instance at ten years. Eventually he was enabled from these sales to clear himself of debt, though it took him twenty five years to do it. He has made turnpikes, helped make railroads, cut ditches, built tenant houses and barns, cleared lands and made fences. He deserves credit for the manly and successful manner in which he discharged his financial obligations which at one time encumbered him. Think of the amount of interest he has paid and taxes on these over fifteen hundred acres of land carried through hard years.

John William Griffin was married May 2, 1855, to Anna C. Price. She was born September 30, 1832, and died June 1, 1899. She was a most helpful companion to her husband and nobly bore her part in the duties and responsibilities of their lives, always maintaining a perfect trust and confidence in her husband's ability to discharge his financial obligations. To their union were born nine children, of whom five died young. The four surviving children are: Emily, John Scott, Virginia and Susannah P.

Emily Griffin, born November 29, 1859, married Lewis Hyde, October 27, 1903. She and her husband reside at the old Griffin homestead and her father makes his home with them. Mr. Hyde is a practical farmer.

John Scott Griffin, born January 7, 1862, is one of the leading merchants of Spiceland. He was married June 1, 1898, to Ruth, daughter of Jesse and Mary Catharine (McAfee) Nicholson, of New Castle, the ceremony being performed by the Reverend William Mason Jennings, pastor of the Presbyterian Church, New Castle. She was born March 18, 1873. They have three children, namely: Price Nicholson, born March 29, 1899; Louise, born March 8, 1901; and Robert Bond, born January 15, 1904.

Virginia Griffin, born October 10, 1865, was married June 28, 1891, by the Reverend John P. Pennington, to William Littleton Cory, who was born March 25, 1857. Mr. Cory is a prosperous farmer and owns an excellent farm immediately adjoining Dunreith on the south. Mrs. Cory is one of the leading lady educators of the county.

Susannah P. Griffin, born October 26, 1867, was married June 28, 1892, by the Reverend John P. Pennington, to Alta Evans, a leading merchant and citizen of Spiceland, who was born November 12, 1868. They have three children, namely: Ralph Waldo, born June 24, 1893; Anna Louise, born March 10, 1895; and Dorris, born March 11, 1897.

John William Griffin has had a political career in Henry County which is unique in that he has neither sought nor held office yet has wielded a very potent influence in shaping political destinies. For the ten years following 1861, he was the most influential politician in the county and almost revolutionized the policy of the Republican party in the county. He was of Whig antecedents, but was too young by a month to vote for Scott and Graham in 1852 and, as State elections became biennial under the constitution of 1851, he was never able to vote the Whig ticket, for that party had gone out of business before the election of 1854. He gave his support in 1856 to the Republican party ticket, county and State, and voted for its National candidates, Fremont and Dayton, but he declares that he did not at this time sympathize with the abolition sentiments of the party and consequently was not very enthusiastic in its support until 1860.

At the time of his removal to Lake County already mentioned, his cousin, Elihu Griffin, accompanied him and there afterwards became an influential lawyer and politician at Crown Point. The prevailing type of Republicanism in that Congressional district was that often stigmatized in those days in Henry County as "Julianism." "Then," says Mr. Griffin, "I woke up to the dangers of the situation and gave earnest thought to the issues at stake with the result that I became an earnest and zealous Republican of the more radical type." Though not a delegate, he was one of the only two men from Lake County, who attended the Republican National Convention at Chicago, which nominated Lincoln and Hamlin; the other was his cousin, Elihu Griffin, father of the Charles F. Griffin, who was a few years ago, Secretary of State of Indiana. John William Griffin represented The Crown Point Register, and as a representative of the press enjoyed rare facilities for seeing, hearing and knowing all that was going on. He remained throughout the convention and retains the liveliest memories of its impressive scenes and of the overwhelming joy of the western people at the nomination of Lincoln.

He returned to Henry County in 1861 just as the war clouds were beginning to darken the political sky. The county seemed given over to the temporizing policy of those styled "silver gray Republicans," and this condition of things led him to espouse the cause of George W. Julian, whom he had met and learned to respect, and with whose views he was in full accord. Under the old convention system, the rank and file of the new Republican party had no chance to express their real opinions nor to secure the nominations of men of their choice. Hence Mr. Griffin, with others, made a fight for nomination by popular vote, in which they were successful and thus was Mr. Julian given a chance to succeed in Henry County where a majority of the party were his friends. Mr. Griffin's next move was to raise a fund for the purchase of The New Castle Courier by Elwood Pleas, his brother-in-law, who is now generally conceded to have been a man of unusual ability and force of character. This was accomplished in November, 1862, and to condense much in little, George W. Julian became the choice of the Henry County Republicans for Congress and continued so to be until 1872, when he determined to support Horace Greeley for President as against General Grant, and afterwards acted with the Democratic party as did also his loyal friend and supporter, John W. Griffin.

During this period, Mr. Griffin was instrumental in bringing forward and advancing the political fortunes of such men as Seth S. Bennett, who was at the time a poor blacksmith, schoolteacher and preacher, but little known outside of his immediate neighborhood and the local councils of his church, until Mr. Griffin and others induced him to take the stump in answer to Colonel Isaac P. Gray, then a candidate for Congress against George W. Julian. Mr. Bennett was a natural orator and the readiest and most effective stump speaker the county has ever had. His canvass made him many friends and he was urged to run for the General Assembly, when David W. Chambers was nominated and elected; but Mr. Griffin said "No! Bennett needs an office with a better salary to it," and caused his withdrawal and subsequent nomination and election as auditor of the county for two terms of four years each. He also brought forward Captain David W. Chambers for representative in the General Assembly, and Thomas Reagan for senator. So successful was he that during the ten years of his greatest political activity, few, if any, of the men to whom he gave his support failed of success. And yet it may be said to his credit that he never countenanced illegal voting nor encouraged corruption either in nominations or elections. Since 1872 he has acted with the Democratic party, but the feebleness of that party in Henry County has given him no opportunity for the exercise of his political astuteness, and for that reason his Democracy has been of a passive rather than an active character.

John William Griffin was reared in the Quaker faith, but he took an early interest in the Union cause during the Civil War and was convinced that the "non-resistance" theory of the Friends was extreme, and if carried into practise must result in destroying all civil government. When the draft brought him and the other young men of the Society face to face with the issue, he refused to avail himself of the exemption extended by law under certain conditions to persons conscientiously opposed to bearing arms, one of which was the registry of an oath or affirmation, averring conscientious scruples in positive terms. Strong church influences were exerted to convince the young men that duty required them to "plead conscientious," as it was called. To this Mr. Griffin replied that he was not conscientiously scrupulous against taking arms in defense of the Union and of political liberty and he denied that either the New Testament or the authority of the early thinkers and writers of the Society of Friends required or sanctioned the doctrine of "non-resistance" as then insisted upon.

So many of the young men of the Society were already in the army at that time, so many others were ready to volunteer, and still others were refusing to avail themselves of exemption, that it was not deemed wise to enforce the letter of the church discipline against its members who had entered the military service of their country, nor against those who refused to secure exemption by making the conscientious plea. The matter thus remained in statu quo until after the close of the war, probably as much for the reason that the leaders of the Society realized that the anti-slavery attitude of their church had really had the most potent influence upon the action of its young men, as because of the serious loss to the Society involved in cutting off such a large number of its most active and intelligent members. Either view of the case was sufficient to justify the Society when so many of its members looked upon those who urged the more rigid course as "criers of peace, peace! when there is no peace."

After the war was over, the Society, letting bygone differences rest, sought to renew the adhesion of its members to the doctrines of peace and non-resistance, and the Indiana Yearly Meeting appointed a committee composed of some of its ablest men and women to hold conferences in that interest, as opportunity might offer. Such a conference was held in the Friends' meeting house at Spiceland, Indiana, February 9 and 10, 1868. Among the well known members of the committee were such men as Barnabas C. Hobbs, a learned educator and once Superintendent of Public Instruction for Indiana, and Luke Woodard, a preacher of the denomination and a poet of much local repute. Mr. Griffin, with opinions on the question unchanged, attended the conference as a listener, without thought of taking part in its discussions, but much to his surprise received an urgent invitation to join in the discussion and was given an allotment of the time.

With the general results of the debate he was entirely satisfied and felt that he had maintained his position against a strong but courteous opposition, but he then began to doubt the propriety of continuing his membership in a religious society with the expressed views of which he was at variance.

Acting upon this opinion, he sent in his resignation in 1871 to the Spiceland Monthly Meeting of Friends, which was as follows:

"Spiceland Monthly Meeting of Friends:

"Dear Friends: This is to certify that I hereby discontinue my membership in your Society. Of the numerous reasons for so doing, I will only mention the following:

"1· I believe that the Scripture rule found in Matthew, VII, 12, allows civil government to enforce obedience to good laws, even though death ensues. This is denied by the Society.

"2. That the right to take life for treason or willful murder, claimed by William Penn in his laws, is as applicable and right now as in his day. This is denied by the Society.

"3· At the request of members of The Yearly Meeting's Peace Committee, I, with others, met in discussion, February 9 and 10, 1868, and endeavored to show that our view of The Golden Rule was not only sustained by the teachings of Penn, Jonathan Dymond, and other prominent members, but by the general practise of the Society, not only in early times but to day. For this expression of well-grounded opinions, you chose in your answers to the sixth query to complain of us to the yearly meeting.

"4· While complaining of the few Friends whose actions corresponded with their professions, you answered that the rest bore a testimony against bearing arms and all military services; while it was well known to you that nearly all the members of the Society heartily participated in the election of officers sworn to execute the law even though death should ensue; that most members engaged in the year 1868 in electing a military hero to the position of Commander-in-Chief of the Army and Navy, with the full expectation that they would be faithfully used according to their intent and purpose, and it is very well known to many that a prominent member of the Society and the Peace Committee, in February, 1868, in a very public way, pledged the Society to a full vote for General Grant, because of his "well known qualification." It was also well known to you that members of the Society cheerfully paid all military taxes, levies for bounties, for substitutes, and commutation moneys; that the Society employed a police force to protect its sittings and, in short, that its members did everything to support war, except to *risk their own lives*.

"5· Furthermore, the yearly meeting has been levying a tax upon its members for the purpose of supporting a committee in the advocacy of a peace which they *practised not*, and I further believe that the teachings of the committee have a tendency to subvert all civil government and to overturn the power which gives security and protection to the church organization. I further believe that this committee raised and sustained by the church, while enjoying to the fullest extent the security and protection the government affords and all the blessings civil government bestows, denies its right to suppress a wicked rebellion, or maintain its own periled existence, and that the said committee are teaching that a consistent Christian may pray for his government, while it must be left to fight its own battles and take care of itself.

"6. There is a prevailing disposition in the Society, and especially among its public teachers, to denounce all criticism, both public and private, styling such, however kindly meant or conscientiously made, as 'an attack upon the ministry,' a 'pulling down from within,' as 'the works of the devil,' as 'coming from the unregenerate heart,' as 'being among the various forms of infidelity,' 'a persecution of God's faithful servants,' and asserting that such offenders should be 'turned out.' In view of these and many other facts, I prefer to 'go out' where

'There is freedom to him who would read,
There is freedom to him who would write.
There are none so afraid the truth should be heard
As they whom the truth would indict.'

"Yours very truly,
"JOHN W. GRIFFIN."

"September 11, 1871."

A committee of the Society thereupon waited upon him and assured him that he would be welcome to retain his membership with all of its privileges, without recantation. He then said: "Does that mean that I will have entire liberty to express my honest opinions upon all matters of general import to the Society, including that of peace? I can not think so and hence think I had better withdraw." After a moment's consideration, one of the committee responded: "I think thee is in the right of it," to which the committee as well as Mr. Griffin assented. Thus in friendship with and good will for the Society, he surrendered his membership, and after the many years that have passed, he still considers the stand taken and maintained by him during the war to have been the correct one. It was a crucial test of his manhood and integrity of character and he felt it to be far wiser and better to give up his membership than to remain a dissatisfied member, yielding assent to doctrines he could not endorse.

It is not the purpose of this sketch either to affirm or deny the political and religious opinions and actions of Mr. Griffin, as set forth largely in his own language, but simply to give them as having been important factors in his life and character and in the history of the county at a most critical period in its affairs and in the life of the State and of the Nation.

Charles S. Hensley

BIOGRAPHICAL SKETCH OF CHARLES SLATEN HERNLY.

LAWYER, COUNTY OFFICIAL, RAILROAD PROMOTER.

The man who has attained distinction among his fellows is often said to be an "accident," but if an inexorable law of cause and effect orders and governs nature, it must equally apply to the affairs of men, and to the seeker after truth will be revealed the natural causes of human success which are hidden from the unthinking multitude and by them vaguely called "accident.'" Ability to see and to grasp opportunities, wisdom in planning great enterprises, foresight in management, skill in handling men, these are elements of success which remove their possessor from the category of accidents and make him the architect of his own fortune. Charles Slaten Hernly during an extended career has displayed so many of these commanding qualities, united with tireless energy and determination, that he is fairly entitled to be considered one of Henry County's foremost citizens.

To compile an accurate genealogy of this old family would be a voluminous task and for that reason reference to the family in this sketch is confined chiefly to the grandparents and parents of its subject. They were a hardy people, German in speech, and for the most part tillers of the soil. Self reliance has always been a trait of the family, its several members depending for success in life upon their individual efforts.

The records of the Hernly family carry it back to the German cantons of Switzerland whence in 1759 Ulrich Hoernli, as the name appears in the early records, immigrated to America where he settled on a farm near what is now Maabelm, Lancaster County, Pennsylvania. The house there erected by him is still standing, weather beaten but sound, and is still owned in the family, the property never having passed out of the Hernly name. There is hardly a fairer section of country in this broad land than the fertile and marvelously cultivated fields of Lancaster County and they present to the passing traveler a scene of rare agricultural beauty. Ulrich Hoernli (Hernly) purchased the lands upon which he settled of Thomas and Richard Penn, brothers of the more famous William Penn, the friend of a king and the founder of the colony of Pennsylvania. A copy of the original deed of conveyance from the Penn brothers to his ancestor is now in the possession of Charles S. Hernly.

Ulrich Hoernli (Hernly) had four sons, named Christian, Isaac, Abram and John. The last named died young and unmarried. Christian was the great grandfather of Amos B. and Henry B. Hernly, the former of whom is now a resident of New Castle, Indiana, aged eighty one years, and the latter of whom is a resident of Prairie Township, Henry County, four miles north of New Castle, on the Muncie pike. Their father, John, son of Abram Hernly, came to Henry County in 1844 and at one time was the owner of more than thirteen hundred acres of land in the northern part of the county.

John Hernly, son of Isaac Hernly, was the father of Henry Hernly, the last named being the father of Charles Slaten Hernly. The mother of Henry was Barbara (Lichty) Hernly. Both John and Barbara, his wife, lived in Henry County. Upon his death he was buried in the Reiman Cemetery, on Symons Creek, two miles north of Cambridge City, Wayne County, Indiana, and she returned to the family home in Pennsylvania, where she died and is buried.

Henry, father of Charles S., and Maria (Reiman) Hernly, his wife, were both natives of Lancaster County, Pennsylvania, and came to Wayne County, Indiana, in 1844 and settled on Symons Creek, two miles north of Cambridge City, at the Keplinger Mills, where for about ten years he operated a flour mill and distillery combined. In 1855 he purchased the water flour mill, known far and wide as the "Blue River Mills," two and a half miles north of New Castle, Henry County, and to the right of the Muncie pike. He also purchased the farm attached to the mill. He operated this mill, farmed the land and raised fine cattle and hogs, the combined businesses proving both pleasing and profitable. Henry Hernly was a quiet, unassuming man, exceedingly industrious and honest. He was also a man of firm convictions, a good neighbor and a good friend. He believed in Divine Providence and lived a righteous life. He died November 29, 1873, aged fifty-

Charles

BIOGRAPHICAL SKETCH OF CHARLES SLATEN HERNLY.

LAWYER, COUNTY OFFICIAL, RAILROAD PROMOTER.

The man who has attained distinction among his fellows is often said to be an "accident," but if an inexorable law of cause and effect orders and governs nature, it must equally apply to the affairs of men, and to the seeker after truth will be revealed the natural causes of human success which are hidden from the unthinking multitude and by them vaguely called "accident." Ability to see and to grasp opportunities, wisdom in planning great enterprises, foresight in management, skill in handling men, these are elements of success which remove their possessor from the category of accidents and make him the architect of his own fortune. Charles Slaten Hernly during an extended career has displayed so many of these commanding qualities, united with tireless energy and determination, that he is fairly entitled to be considered one of Henry County's foremost citizens.

To compile an accurate genealogy of this old family would be a voluminous task and for that reason reference to the family in this sketch is confined chiefly to the grandparents and parents of its subject. They were a hardy people, German in speech, and for the most part tillers of the soil. Self reliance has always been a trait of the family, its several members depending for success in life upon their individual efforts.

The records of the Hernly family carry it back to the German cantons of Switzerland whence in 1759 Ulrich Hoernli, as the name appears in the early records, immigrated to America where he settled on a farm near what is now Manheim, Lancaster County, Pennsylvania. The house there erected by him is still standing, weather beaten but sound, and is still owned in the family, the property never having passed out of the Hernly name. There is hardly a fairer section of country in this broad land than the fertile and marvelously cultivated fields of Lancaster County and they present to the passing traveler a scene of rare agricultural beauty. Ulrich Hoernli (Hernly) purchased the lands upon which he settled of Thomas and Richard Penn, brothers of the more famous William Penn, the friend of a king and the founder of the colony of Pennsylvania. A copy of the original deed of conveyance from the Penn brothers to his ancestor is now in the possession of Charles S. Hernly.

Ulrich Hoernli (Hernly) had four sons, named Christian, Isaac, Abram and John. The last named died young and unmarried. Christian was the great grandfather of Amos B. and Henry B. Hernly, the former of whom is now a resident of New Castle, Indiana, aged eighty one years, and the latter of whom is a resident of Prairie Township, Henry County, four miles north of New Castle, on the Muncie pike. Their father, John, son of Abram Hernly, came to Henry County in 1844 and at one time was the owner of more than thirteen hundred acres of land in the northern part of the county.

John Hernly, son of Isaac Hernly, was the father of Henry Hernly, the last named being the father of Charles Slaten Hernly. The mother of Henry was Barbara (Lichty) Hernly. Both John and Barbara, his wife, lived in Henry County. Upon his death he was buried in the Reiman Cemetery, on Symons Creek, two miles north of Cambridge City, Wayne County, Indiana, and she returned to the family home in Pennsylvania, where she died and is buried.

Henry, father of Charles S., and Maria (Reiman) Hernly, his wife, were both natives of Lancaster County, Pennsylvania, and came to Wayne County, Indiana, in 1844 and settled on Symons Creek, two miles north of Cambridge City, at the Keplinger Mills, where for about ten years he operated a flour mill and distillery combined. In 1855 he purchased the water flour mill, known far and wide as the "Blue River Mills," two and a half miles north of New Castle, Henry County, and to the right of the Muncie pike. He also purchased the farm attached to the mill. He operated this mill, farmed the land and raised fine cattle and hogs, the combined businesses proving both pleasing and profitable. Henry Hernly was a quiet, unassuming man, exceedingly industrious and honest. He was also a man of firm convictions, a good neighbor and a good friend. He believed in Divine Providence and lived a righteous life. He died November 29, 1872, aged fifty-six years, and his remains are interred in South Mound Cemetery.

After the death of his first wife, Maria (Reiman)Hernly, who died in 1853, and whose remains are buried in the Reiman Cemetery, above mentioned, Henry Hernly married Mary Hoffacker, a native of Maryland, of German descent. She is still living and resides in New Castle where she receives the constant and tender attention of her son, Charles S. Hernly. The children of Henry Hernly by his first wife were: one daughter who died in infancy; John R. and Henry L., both of New Castle; and William, deceased. The children of Henry Hernly by his second wife were: Kate, Rebecca and Homer, all deceased; Frank, who resides at Jonesboro, Indiana, where he is connected with the Indiana Rubber Company; and Charles Slaten Hernly, the subject of this sketch.

The flouring mill heretofore mentioned in this article is no longer known. The race that furnished the water, that gave the power, that turned the wheels, has run dry and the old mill has been moved to another spot, a half mile away, where it stands a melancholy ruin. Not far from the original site of this famous mill are now located the house and grounds of the Country Club of New Castle. The tender memories clinging around the old mill have been embalmed in the sentiment so happily expressed by Charles S. Hernly who called it "the home of the honey bee and the wild flower." It is a romantic spot, set amid rural scenes where youth can disport in plentitude of pleasures and where old age can find relief and rest from the hum of the busy world. The little Blue, fed by innumerable springs of pure, sparkling, invigorating waters, meanders with musical cadence through the valley, which is here circled in a veritable amphitheatre of green and gold, the whole presenting a panoramic, pastoral scene of natural beauty and quiet charm.

CHARLES SLATEN HERNLY.

It was in the rural home, a log cabin with clapboard roof, set almost in the center of the spot above described and not far from the old mill, that Charles Slaten Hernly was born September 23, 1856, and his own description of the place, poetically expressed, is here appropriately inserted. It is entitled "The Old Water Mill" and is as follows:

"I remember the days that have long gone by
    And my thoughts turn back to the place
Where I was born and lived, as a child,
    To the farm and fields by the long mill race
And that log cabin which stood by the rill,
    Just across the road from the Old Water Mill.

"If I had my choice, I would live there now,
    With father and mother and the girls and the boys,
And listen to the song birds singing sweet
    In the big tall trees by that home full of joys,
I say, if I could, I would live there still,
    In that log cabin by the Old Water Mill.

"I have seen the city with its glaring lights
    That shut out the stars and the moon's soft rays,
And my thoughts turn to better things,
    Where I lived as a boy in other days,
With never a care to stagger nor frill
    The mind, in the cabin by the Old Water Mill.

"Life's burdens and sorrows come to us with age,
    And that grim monster, which destroys everything,
Never stops working, but gets in the way
    Of ambition, and strikes with his sting,
I'll be ready to go, if I can rest on the hill
    Where I played as a boy, by the Old Water Mill.

When but a youth of ten or twelve years of age, Charles S. Hernly met with physical misfortune which necessitated the amputation of his left leg, near the hip joint. This naturally more or less affected his career and he became an earnest student, attending with regularity the district or country school and later the schools at New Castle. He also spent a year or more at the Spiceland Academy, under the care of that able teacher, Clarkson Davis. He in time became a teacher himself and followed that profession until 1876, when he entered the office of Brown and Polk, New Castle, and commenced to read law. He was admitted to the bar of the Henry Circuit Court in 1879, Robert L. Polk, who had in the meantime been elected judge of the court, presiding. Mr. Hernly at once entered into partnership with S. Hadley Brown, and during a period of ten or twelve years this firm did a large and lucrative legal business. During this period Mr. Hernly served for four years as clerk of the Board of Trustees of New Castle.

Like the rest of his family, Mr. Hernly is a Republican and his versatile and energetic character soon drew him into the open field of politics. He was for a number of years the committeeman for his precinct and by his activity added greatly to the Republican strength. From precinct committeeman he was advanced to the chairmanship of the Republican County Central Committee and his personality soon recommended him to the party and he became a power in the political affairs of the county, the district and the State. In 1890 his political activity was rewarded by nomination and election to the clerkship of the Henry Circuit Court, a position which he filled acceptably to the people of the county and creditably to himself.

He was now in line for higher political distinction and in 1898 became chairman of the Republican State Central Committee. Mr. Hernly took up the work of this responsible and powerful position with characteristic energy and carried his party triumphantly through the exciting campaigns of 1898 and 1900. No campaigns were ever more systematically fought than these under the leadership of Chairman Hernly and the party success is largely ascribed to his individual efforts. No man could have done more to bring about that unity of action so essential to winning the battle of the ballots. He placed great reliance on precinct organization and with that work well done considered the battle more than half won. His large personal acquaintance was also of great importance. He probably knew more voters by sight and could call more by their full names and locate them by precinct or district than any other person in the State. Cool, calculating and diplomatic, his large grasp of affairs was amply demonstrated in these campaigns and his political reputation greatly increased. He believed in carrying out the pledges of his party and appointed the commission that drafted the present county and township laws of Indiana.

Since that time the qualities shown by him in politics have been turned with equal success to the industrial field. He was an important factor in the organization of the New Castle Industrial Company in 1902 and much of its success may be attributed to his foresight and ability as an organizer. This association was the cause of the subsequent rapid growth of New Castle in population, manufactures and general business. To its activity may be ascribed the location at New Castle of the Krell-French Piano Company, one of the largest concerns of its kind in the world; the Shovel Factory; the Rolling Mill; the Pan-American Bridge Company, and many lesser business interests, almost all of which had their inception after the incorporation of the Industrial Company.

On December 23, 1880, Charles Slaten Hernly was united in marriage with Elizabeth Thornburgh, daughter of the late Hiram and Lydia (Creek) Thornburgh. This has been a happy union and with equal step they have trod the path of life together. To them have been born two children, Frost B. and Mary Victoria. The former is now a young man grown. He is engaged in the activities of life and with added years gives promise of a successful business career. Mary Victoria is now in the heyday of young girlhood. and is the flower of the household. She is fond of music, happy in her studies, quick to learn and a favorite with her many girl friends and associates.

The crowning work of Mr. Hernly's life has so far been the successful promotion in the face of seemingly insurmountable obstacles, and the financing of one of the most important public enterprises ever projected for the benefit of that section of Indiana which embraces the territory extending from Indianapolis to New Castle, to Muncie and

72

to Richmond, and finally terminates in the city of Toledo, Ohio, known as the Indianapolis, New Castle and Toledo Electric Railway. His success in this matter assures to Eastern Indiana a system of interurban railways second in magnitude to that of no other State, and will make New Castle a point of entry and exit next in importance to Indianapolis. His fearless energy and determination have borne down all opposition to this great enterprise and as benefits begin to accrue from it, the importance of his labors will be more and more appreciated in the community in which he lives. He is still a young man, as years are counted, and he may be confidently expected to accomplish still greater things.

Charles S. Hernly is not a member of any religious body but through his wife, who is affiliated with the Methodist Episcopal Church, he gives that denomination his cordial support and in language not to be misunderstood expresses his firm belief in the Christian religion. He is a member of the Masonic fraternity and has taken all the degrees of ancient Craft Masonry including that of Knight Templar, and all of the degrees of Scottish Rite Masonry including the Thirty-Second degree. . He is a Knight of Pythias, a member of the order of Elks and of the Improved Order of Red Men. Socially, he is a hail fellow, well met. As host, he is unequaled; he is liberal to a fault and sympathizes with those who are in trouble and, so far as he is able, cheerfully aids the needy. He believes that bread cast upon the waters will return after many days.

ANCESTRY OF MRS. CHARLES S. (THORNBURGH) HERNLY.

Mrs. Hernly on the paternal side is a great granddaughter of David Hoover, who settled two miles north of Richmond, Wayne County, Indiana, in 1806. Her father, Hiram Thornburgh, was the eldest son of Jacob and Elizabeth (Hoover) Thornburgh. He was born in New Castle, April 14, 1827. No man was probably better known during his life of sixty years in his native town. Everybody was his friend and he was the friend of everybody.

On the maternal side, Mrs. Hernly is a descendant of John Creek, her mother's father, who was born September 13, 1774, and died October 12, 1851. The family came originally from Germany and settled first in Greenbrier County, Virginia, but prior to 1800 moved to Union County, Indiana. The remains of John Creek are buried in the private cemetery on the home farm in Union County. John Creek was married three times and was the father of seventeen children. His third wife was Ann (Collet)Creek, born December 22, 1795. They were married at Brookville, Indiana. The children by his last wife were: Lydia (Creek) Thornburgh, born July 19, 1832, the mother of Mrs. Hernly; Charles C.; John; Margaret; and one child which died in infancy. John Creek farmed on a large scale and also gave great attention to the raising of live stock, horses being his specialty. His son, Charles C., uncle of Mrs. Hernly, is also a farmer and stock raiser. He is the only surviving son of this family of seventeen children and is one of the most prominent agriculturists in Union County, near Liberty, where he has lived all his life. He is the father of Raymond Creek, who now resides with his family in New Castle, where he is engaged with Charles S. Hernly in promoting and building what is known as the Indianapolis, New Castle and Toledo electric railway, which has been poetically, if not appropriately, described as the "Honey Bee and Wild Flower Route." In this enterprise Mr. Hernly's son, Frost B., is also actively engaged and has done much to bring the matter to its present successful stage.

BIOGRAPHICAL SKETCH OF JOHN CRAIG HUDELSON.

FARMER, COUNTY OFFICIAL AND RAILROAD PROMOTER.

The genealogical record of the John Craig Hudelson, branch of the large Henry County family of that name is very incomplete. It is, however, historically correct that Mr. Hudelson's grandfather, John Hudelson, was a native of Pennsylvania, that he was a soldier of the Revolutionary War and that he lost an arm while in the service of his country. There is no record of the birth or death of either of his grandparents, nor of the time of their leaving Pennsylvania and moving into Kentucky. Their remains are buried in the last named State. They were the parents of five sons: David, Samuel, William, James, Alexander, the next to the last named being the father of the subject of this sketch.

James Hudelson, the father, was born in Kentucky, and Esther (Craig) Hudelson, the mother of John Craig Hudelson, was born in Tennessee, the former in 1788 and the latter in 1797. They left Kentucky in 1831 and came to Indiana, where they settled near what is now the village of Ogden, in the southwestern part of Henry County, on the line between Henry and Rush counties. Within twenty days after their arrival in the new country, the father was stricken with typhoid fever and died and was buried near the pioneer home in a special grave, there being at that time no grave yard or cemetery in the settlement. His widow survived him many years, dying in 1879. She is buried in Shiloh Cemetery, Rush County, Indiana. They were the parents of eight children, five boys and three girls, as follows: Mary; John C., the subject of this sketch; Jane; William; James; Samuel; Elizabeth; and David. John C. is the sole survivor of the family.

In answer to questions relating to the condition of the country in 1831, John C. Hudelson says: "It was nothing but a vast forest, no roads, hardly a foot path, no farms, no improvements, no nothing of a civilized character other than an occasional cabin and a bit of clearing." These old pioneers must have been a rugged race, strong of arm and stout of heart to penetrate the wilderness, braving a thousands dangers to carve out homes for themselves in those vast forests hitherto given over to savage animals and still more savage men

JOHN CRAIG HUDELSON.

Amid such surroundings, the fatherless found themselves. A grand and courageous woman must the mother of the bereaved family have been to face a future in the wilderness with no one to provide for them. Upon John C., the eldest son, then a lad only eleven years of age, fell a large share of the burden. He manfully took hold of affairs and the combined efforts of the family established a permanent home, cleared the land and rendered it productive. He was born in Nicholas County, Kentucky, August 24, 1820, and came to Henry County with his parents as above stated. He remained on the farm until he was twenty-seven years of age. In 1843, however, he met with an accident which unfitted him for the physical labors of the farm. Near Mt. Healthy, Ohio, six miles from Cincinnati, while driving with a friend on the way to Kentucky to visit the old home, the horse became frightened by a sharp flash of lightening and loud clap of thunder and whirled about, overturning the buggy which rolled down the hillside until it lodged against a fence. Mr. Hudelson's ankle was broken but fortunately the scene of the accident was near the home of Alice and Phoebe Carey, the well known poet sisters, to which he was carried and where for three or four weeks he was cared for until able to return to his home. The tender care and faithful nursing which he received at "Clover Nook," as the home of the Carey sisters was named, has ever been one of his most cherished memories.

This accident resulted in his quitting the farm after which he for a time drove a team for himself and others. He also engaged in other enterprises among them being a speculation in dried peaches which he purchased in large quantities in Eastern Indiana and peddled through the northern and western parts of the State. The venture proved successful and the profits of his first and probably only trip were sufficient to purchase

BIOGRAPHICAL SKETCH OF JOHN CRAIG HUDELSON.

FARMER, COUNTY OFFICIAL AND RAILROAD PROMOTER.

The genealogical record of the John Craig Hudelson, branch of the large Henry County family of that name is very incomplete. It is, however, historically correct that Mr. Hudelson's grandfather, John Hudelson, was a native of Pennsylvania, that he was a soldier of the Revolutionary War and that he lost an arm while in the service of his country. There is no record of the birth or death of either of his grandparents, nor of the time of their leaving Pennsylvania and moving into Kentucky. Their remains are buried in the last named State. They were the parents of five sons: David, Samuel, William, James, Alexander, the next to the last named being the father of the subject of .s sketch.

James Hudelson, the father, was born in Kentucky, and Esther (Craig) Hudelson, the mother of John Craig Hudelson, was born in Tennessee, the former in 1788 and the latter in 1797. They left Kentucky in 1831 and came to Indiana, where they settled near what is now the village of Ogden, in the southwestern part of Henry County, on the line between Henry and Rush counties. Within twenty days after their arrival in the new country, the father was stricken with typhoid fever and died and was buried near the pioneer home in a special grave, there being at that time no grave yard or cemetery in the settlement. His widow survived him many years, dying in 1879. She is buried in Shiloh Cemetery, Rush County, Indiana. They were the parents of eight children, five boys and three girls, as follows: Mary; John C.; John C., the subject of this sketch; William; James; Samuel; Elizabeth; and David. John C. is the sole survivor of the family.

In answer to questions relating to the condition of the country in 1831, John C. Hudelson says: "It was nothing but a vast forest, no roads, hardly a foot path, no farms, no improvements, no nothing of a civilized character other than an occasional cabin and a bit of clearing." Those old pioneers must have been a rugged race, strong of arm and stout of heart to penetrate the wilderness, braving a thousands dangers to carve out homes for themselves in those vast forests hitherto given over to savage animals and still more savage men.

JOHN CRAIG HUDELSON.

Amid such surroundings, the fatherless found themselves. A grand and courageous woman must the mother of the bereaved family have been to face a future in the wilderness with no one to provide for them. Upon John C., the eldest son, then a lad only eleven years of age, fell a large share of the burden. He manfully took hold of affairs and the combined efforts of the family established a permanent home, cleared the land and rendered it productive. He was born in Nicholas County, Kentucky, August 24, 1820, and came to Henry County with his parents as above stated. He remained on the farm until he was twenty-seven years of age. In 1843, however, he met with an accident which unfitted him for the physical labors of the farm. Near Mt. Healthy, Ohio, six miles from Cincinnati, while driving with a friend on the way to Kentucky to visit the old home, the horse became frightened by a sharp flash of lightening and loud clap of thunder and whirled about, overturning the buggy which rolled down the hillside until it lodged against a fence. Mr. Hudelson's ankle was broken but fortunately the scene of the accident was near the home of Alice and Phoebe Carey, the well known poet sisters, to which he was carried and where for three or four weeks he was cared for until able to return to his home. The tender care and faithful nursing which he received at "Clover Nook," as the home of the Carey sisters was named, has ever been one of his most cherished memories.

This accident resulted in his quitting the farm after which he for a time drove a team for himself and others. He also engaged in other enterprises among them being a speculation in dried peaches which he purchased in large quantities in Eastern Indiana and peddled through the northern and western parts of the State. The venture proved successful and the profits of his first and probably only trip were sufficient to purchase a suit of clothes much more stylish than the home made jeans he had hitherto worn.

His education had suffered because of the necessarily imposed labors of his child-hood and youth, and always remained limited. Referring to the fact that he had been elected justice of the peace, he himself says in his memoirs that "it was a question with me whether to accept the position because of my deficiency in book learning." He managed, however, to learn to read and write and to obtain a knowledge of the primary rules of arithmetic. But his deficiencies in this respect were counterbalanced by keen observation and strong common sense.

While a justice of the peace, he was nominated in 1847 by the Whig party and elected Treasurer of Henry County. He was re-elected in 1850, thus serving two terms of three years each. His election to office necessitated his removal from the farm to New Castle, the county seat, where he has resided continuously to the present time, except a few years spent on his farm southwest of that place. When he assumed the duties of the treasurer's office, he was a young unmarried man. He speedily made the acquaintance of the citizens of the town and the people of the county, and his genial nature, suave deportment and polite speech presently made him the most popular young man in the community. He took "board and lodging" with James Calvert at that time, the land-lord of the Exchange Hotel, which stood on the corner now occupied by the Citizens' State Bank. He made a competent and satisfactory treasurer and retired from the office with, what was in that day, a competency.

After serving the people of Henry County as treasurer for six years, he was in 1853 appointed paymaster of that portion of the Cincinnati, Logansport and Chicago railroad, then under construction, extending from Richmond to Logansport. This road afterwards became the Panhandle branch of the great Pennsylvania System and is now classed under the head of the "Pennsylvania lines." Mr. Hudelson's duties as paymaster carried him from Martindale Creek, in Wayne County, to Sulphur Springs, in Henry County. Upon the completion of the road in 1853-4, he was employed as a conductor and was the first to take a train across Blue River, north of New Castle, in April, 1854. He took a great interest in the building of the road and had so great faith in its future that he and a number of his friends took a large amount of stock, afterwards merged into the bonds of the road, all of which within a few years became valueless. Mr. Hudelson held ten thousand dollars of these worthless bonds and the loss was a severe blow to him.

From a publication issued by George P. Emswiler, of Richmond, Indiana, in 1897, the following with regard to the Panhandle road as it was in 1853-4 is gleaned:

"The first engine that ever ran over the road was called the 'Swinette.' * * * It had no pilot or cow-catcher in front like the engines of to day. No coal was used in firing an engine in those days, wood only being the fuel. The smokestack on the Swinette was a very large affair, spreading out at the top with a large seive covering it to let the sparks and ashes escape. The Swinette coming down the road * * * at night, when she was steamed and her firebox stuffed with dry wood * * * left a string of fire coals stream-ing over her back like the tail of a comet. Painted on her sides was a picture of a man with a pig under his arm, the tail of the pig in his mouth, and the music was invoked, from grunt, basso profundi, to high C, by the strength of the bite inflicted on the tail of his pigship. The Swinette had a twin sister, the Julia Dean. It was, if anything, smaller than the Swinette and as she came sailing along looked like a sugar trough with a stovepipe stuck up in the center of it. If either of these engines ever struck a cow on the track it was simply a question of which went into the ditch. * * * Every town of any importance along the road had an engine named for it. There were the New Castle, the Logansport, the Anderson and the Chicago. These were all handsome engines for the day, but the best of all of them was the "Old Hoosier." She was the favorite of all the engineers who ever traveled the road.

"John Smock was the first engineer who ever ran an engine on the road. * * * Smock was a terrible swearer and it is said could curse the old Swinette until it would begin to move without fire, water or steam. Among the early engineers on the road was a man named Skinner. He for several years ran the old Chicago, a monster engine for that day. He also could swear making the air blue, if anything went wrong." The arti-cle goes on to say that "Tom Clark was the first conductor on the road * * * He knew everybody and everybody knew him. He swore, chewed tobacco, drank good liquor and had a good time generally. * * * There was only one train each way from Richmond to Anderson then. Tom Clark was the only conductor and ran the whole business."

"Then came John C. Hudelson, Charley Lincoln and Elijah Holland, of New Castle. 'Lige' always wore a blue cloth, spiketail coat with brass buttons. * * * Then there were Charley Muchmore, Billy Patterson, a man named Bogart, and others whose names are forgotten." Continuing the article says: "John C. Hudelson is still living (1897) a retired life in New Castle and is one of the largest landowners in Henry County. He has acres and acres of Blue River bottom land that one can see as he nears New Castle on the Panhandle train. It looks like the garden of Eden." Again referring to the "Old Hoosier" it should be stated that "Mark Smith was the engineer who handled her throttle. He was as much a favorite as was his engine. Every man, woman and child on the road knew Mark Smith and loved him. The 'Hoosier' had a whistle that outwhistled all others. People used to say that her whistle, when thrown wide open, would shake the beech nuts off the trees along the road. There are those now living who will remember Mark Smith, John Smock, Tom Clark, Charley Lincoln, whose widow still lives in Richmond, Billy Patterson, Elijah Holland and Charley Muchmore."

From his early youth to within the last few years, Mr. Hudelson has always been interested in political affairs. As a Whig, though too young at the time to vote, he did acceptable work in the campaign of "Tippecanoe and Tyler, too," in 1840, and in 1844 he cast his first presidential vote for the Whig candidate, Henry Clay, who, however, failed of election. This campaign left the party in a weakened condition from which it never recovered. The defeat and final extinction of the old Whig party grieved its many adherents beyond expression. Its chief mourners were such great men as Webster, Clay, Lincoln, Greeley, Seward, John Sherman, Thomas Corwin, Caleb B. Smith, and hundreds of others who had rendered it loyal and willing service. But its mission was ended and from its ashes arose the Republican party which since 1861 has for the most part dominated the affairs of the country.

The doom of the Whig party was foreseen as early as 1852 and the passage of the Kansas-Nebraska bill by Congress which repealed the Missouri Compromise of 1820 was the final blow. Mr. Hudelson was chairman of the Henry County Whig Central Committee in 1854 and with an eye to the inevitable offered a resolution to postpone the convention of that year and await developments. The resolution as he relates "was greeted with groans and hisses and cries of 'traitor, traitor, carry him out,' and so on. The resolution was voted down and a full Whig ticket for the county offices was nominated." Matters moved even more rapidly than he had anticipated. The Indiana Whig members of Congress said, "We must now combine all elements that oppose the further extension of slavery into one great party to resist the common peril." On that basis a State convention was called and the new party which was the forerunner of the Republican party, was organized and temporarily known as the "People's party." It was made up of Whigs, Anti-slavery Democrats, Free Soilers and old-time Abolitionists. The year 1854 was consequently one of great political upheaval. Mr. Hudelson was still in the railroad service but he had kept steadily in touch with the politics of the county and State, and as a result of the advanced stand he had taken on the questions then agitating the public mind, he was in 1855 nominated by the new People's party and elected Clerk of the Henry Circuit Court. He was clerk from November 1, 1855 to November 1, 1859, and filled the position most satisfactorily to the public.

In 1856 Mr. Hudelson assisted in the organization of the Republican party and was an ardent supporter of Fremont and Dayton, the first national standard bearers of the new party. He wrote, talked and made formal speeches favoring the principles of the party and laid special stress upon that part of the platform which advocated the rescue of Kansas and all other territories from the grasp of the slave power. In this campaign, while traveling in the southern part of the county, on a political mission, he received a serious injury in a railroad accident which resulted in the amputation of his lame leg.

His allegiance to the Republican party continued until long after the Civil War and he has always been a warm admirer of the immortal Lincoln. His first difference with his party arose over its financial policies and he joined the short-lived Greenback or Fiat-

Money party. He afterwards joined the Granger or People's party and when that organization was relegated to the graveyard of political parties, he became a Prohibitionist and subsequently a "Free Silverite" under the leadership of William Jennings Bryan. During the preparation of this sketch of himself, when questioned as to his opinion of the present-day policies of the Government, he replied: "I have been delighted with the conduct and policy of the Government as it is now administered by President Theodore Roosevelt." He has always been actuated by principle in his political conduct and has exercised an independence as rare as it is commendable.

John Craig Hudelson has always been a very busy man. Early in life he determined upon farming as his vocation and as soon as able began to buy land. His first purchase consisted of two hundred and forty five acres, two and a half miles southwest of New Castle, where he lived with his family for fifteen years. Since that time he has lived in New Castle. This farm is a fine one, well improved and highly cultivated. It is now occupied by Mr. Hudelson's third son, William Elliott (Ella) Hudelson and family. He next bought of Jacob Shopp what was known as the Thomas Henderson farm, two miles north of New Castle, on the Little Blue River. To this he has added the John Newcomer, the Samuel Hedrick, and a part of the Rufus Mellett farms, comprising in all five hundred and eighty five acres. Assisted by his fourth son, Charles Treat Hudelson, he gives to this farm his close personal attention, in the busy season going to it early in the morning from his home in town and returning late at night. The farm is in the great Blue River Valley amid scenes of rare agricultural beauty. The two farms embrace eight hundred and thirty acres of which more than five hundred are under cultivation. Mr. Hudelson is not financially interested in the numerous industrial enterprises of the day. He is a practical farmer and finds enough to do in keeping abreast of the improved methods of the day in cultivation of the land. He also pays much attention to stock raising, especially cattle and hogs.

John C. Hudelson is the oldest living member of New Castle Lodge, Number 91, Ancient Free and Accepted Masons, and in 1903 was tendered a reception by the lodge in honor of his connection with it of more than fifty years, but at that time he was physically unable to be present and was represented by his son, John C. Hudelson, junior. He warmly indorses the principles of the order which he believes go hand in hand with his duties to the church. He is a communicant of the Methodist Episcopal Church and is a generous supporter of that denomination and a liberal but unostentatious contributor to its charities.

For nearly seventy five years he has been a resident of Henry County and is one of the very few pioneers left to tell the story of its early settlement. There is probably no man in the county who has been more conspicuous in its history. He has always been a man of great industry and perseverance and now oppressed by the weight of years, he remains as industrious, careful and persevering as in his younger days. He is of a positive nature, independent in thought and action, and a man of singular fortitude. The rains of Summer and the snows of Winter may descend but he is not dismayed; he welcomes the sun but fails to see disaster in the clouds; slight of build and apparently not strong physically, he is, nevertheless, fearless of exposure and intent only upon finishing the business to which he may have set his hand.

On July 7, 1859, John Craig Hudelson was united in marriage with Amanda Virginia Black, daughter of Mrs. Jane Black, the ceremony being performed in the Methodist Episcopal Church by the Reverend James S. Ferris. They became the parents of four sons, as follows: James B., born in New Castle, April 20, 1860, died January 4, 1870; John C., junior, born in Henry County, July 4, 1865; William Elliott (Ella) and Charles Treat, twins, born in Henry County, October 7, 1871. James B. was a bright and promising lad and his death was a severe blow to his parents. John C., junior, has been for a number of years a resident of Trinidad, Colorado, where he is cashier of the First National Bank and where he enjoys the confidence and esteem of the entire community. His wife, Kitty, to whom he was married August 19, 1886, by the Reverend James H. Ford, is a native of New Castle. She was the daughter of Mr. and Mrs. Andrew J. Harrison. They have one child, a daughter, named Bessie Gay, who is now a charming young woman, eighteen years of age. Mrs. Harrison is now a widow. She was the daughter of the late Mr. and Mrs. Jacob Mowrer and resides in New Castle.

William Elliott Hudelson, better known as "Ella," was united in marriage with Pearl, daughter of Mr. and Mrs. Gilliam L. Craven, of New Castle, October 12, 1892, by the Reverend Charles H. Brown. They are the parents of one child, Hazel Lee, nine years of age, who is a bright and winning young girl. "Ella" has charge of and resides with his family on the farm southwest of New Castle.

Charles Treat Hudelson was married February 22, 1893, to Bessie W., daughter of Mr. and Mrs. Samuel Fisher, of Henry County, the ceremony being performed by the Reverend Charles H. Brown. They are the parents of five children, namely: Gladys May, Alice Amanda, Howard, John F. and Esther Marie. The family reside in the old Black homestead, which has been so long a landmark at the south end of Main street, New Castle. John C. Hudelson, the father, makes his home with this son, and it is from here that he manages his big farm north of the town.

ANCESTRY OF MRS. JOHN C. (BLACK) HUDELSON.

Mrs. John C. Hudelson, born Amanda Victoria Black, was the daughter of James and Jane (Elliott) Black. She was born at Laporte, Indiana, September 6, 1836, where her father was engaged in the tanning business. James Black, her father, was born at Staunton, Virginia, November 20, 1808, and died at Laporte, August 5, 1849. Her mother, who was born May 10, 1819, was a sister of the late Judge Jehu T. Elliott, of New Castle, and after the death of her husband she moved with her family to that town where she resided with her family until her own death which occurred September 7, 1864. The children of James and Jane (Elliott) Black were Amanda V., Nathaniel Elliott (Ella) and Kate J. The last named is the widow of the late Edghill B. McMeans, who died September 1, 1899. They had no children and since the death of her husband, whose memory will always be very dear to her, she has resided alone in her beautiful home in New Castle.

Nathaniel Elliott (Ella) Black was for a number of years one of the most energetic and successful business men of New Castle and Henry County. He was born with the trading instinct and was far-seeing and prudent in business matters and always ready to grasp opportunity as it came. He was a man of genial disposition, a good story-teller, and held his friends with hooks of steel. He died in September, 1890. His wife was Esther, daughter of the late Mr. and Mrs. Robert C. Kinsey. She was a woman of estimable character who did not long survive her husband but died in February, 1893. They were the parents of two children, namely: Josie, a sweet and lovable child, who died April 22, 1882; and Georgia, who is now Mrs. Herbert H. Hadley, of Indianapolis. She is a charming woman and is devoted to her husband and their children—Elliott Black, Harlan H. and Charles Austin.

Amanda V. (Black) Hudelson was a woman of fine mind, a thoroughly educated and accomplished teacher, and an earnest Christian. At the age of sixteen years, she joined the Methodist Episcopal Church and all of her beautiful life rendered heartfelt devotion to the great truths of religion. She was the life and light of a home rendered delightful by her presence and care. Her death deprived her husband of a source of inspiration and her children of a surpassing affection.

Her remains together with those of her family who are deceased are buried in South Mound Cemetery, New Castle, where from year to year sweet flowers are scattered in their memory.

r
BIOGRAPHICAL SKETCH OF LEVI ALLEN JENNINGS.

MANUFACTURER, MERCHANT AND LEADING CITIZEN.

The industrial methods practiced in Henry County, until after the Civil War, were those of the small shop or local factory of limited capacity. The pioneer in the larger field of modern manufacturing was a young man from Ashland, Ohio, named Levi Allen Jennings, who came to New Castle in 1867 and began business in a modest and unobtrusive way. His initial step was the purchase of an interest in a saw mill for the cutting of the native hardwood and other timber into lumber for building and manufacturing purposes, and, under his lead, the firm of which he had thus become a part also engaged, somewhat tentatively, in the general lumber trade. A few months' experience convinced Mr. Jennings that there was a good field for the lumber, sash, door, blind and general building material trade in New Castle and the surrounding territory.

With this idea in mind, he began buying out his partners, who were too thoroughly grounded in the pioneer way of doing things to adopt his progressive ideas; and in a short time he had secured the entire business and began its expansion into the large and remunerative trade which he has conducted for so many years and to certain branches of which he is, in the afternoon of life, still devoting his energies. He did not attempt to accomplish this at a single bound or by the short cut of doubtful speculations, often leading to financial ruin, but by studying carefully every phase of the question and then by applying to its execution, the most persistent industry. He pushed his undertakings to success by a series of rapid movements while others were prophesying failure, yet he never lost sight of those sound business principles which are so often forgotten or ignored by men of impulsive natures. It has been this close union of care and push that has won for him his splendid success and given him the honorable title of "father of Henry County's Industries."

Levi Allen Jennings was the son of Obadiah and Mary Jennings, of Wayne County, Ohio, who afterwards moved to New Castle, Indiana, where they both died, Mr. Jenning's mother going first and his father a few years later, and their ashes lie in South Mound Cemetery. His paternal ancestors were English and his maternal ancestors were Pennsylvania Dutch. Obadiah and Mary Jennings were both born in Pennsylvania and lived there until their marriage. At an early day thereafter they left Pennsylvania and, braving the dangers of the journey across the Alleghanies, came with all their moveable property in a one horse wagon into the wild woods of Central Ohio to open a farm in the wilderness, where their son, Levi Allen Jennings, was born May 6, 1834.

In this new land he grew up amid the rude surroundings of the log cabin period and was from early boyhood inured to the struggles and privations of the pioneers of the Central West. While these bred in him a certain spirit of discontent and a longing for larger opportunities, they were of inestimable value in teaching him the wise lessons of industry, economy and patient effort. Not content with the rudimentary education furnished by the district schools, young Jennings, in the pursuit of knowledge, read by the light of the evening fire and conned his lessons as he followed the plow in the stumpy fields. The time that other boys lost in idleness or doubtful pleasures, he spent in self-improvement and he was soon so well grounded in the essentials that he was admitted with the consent of his parents to the college at Hayesville, Ohio, where by working mornings and evenings at such tasks as he could find to do, he managed to pay his way for two terms. He then spent two years and a half at the well known high school of Ashland, Ohio, where he mastered much of the mathematical and scientific courses besides giving considerable study to the English language and literature and to Latin and Greek, but his financial needs rendered it necessary for him to leave school and engage in teaching, expecting to return after a time and complete his studies, but the link in his educational life thus broken was never welded. His school days were closed. It was during these years of his studious boyhood that he met another ambitious lad who, under similar difficulties, was eagerly seeking to pass beyond the limits of the narrow life that hedged them in. William B. Allison, afterwards United Sates Senator from Iowa, was reared upon a clear-

BIOGRAPHICAL SKETCH OF LEVI ALLEN JENNINGS.

MANUFACTURER, MERCHANT AND LEADING CITIZEN.

The industrial methods practiced in Henry County, until after the Civil War, were those of the small shop or local factory of limited capacity. The pioneer in the larger field of modern manufacturing was a young man from Ashland, Ohio, named Levi Allen Jennings, who came to New Castle in 1867 and began business in a modest and unobtrusive way. His initial step was the purchase of an interest in a saw mill for the cutting of the native hardwood and other timber into lumber for building and manufacturing purposes, and, under his lead, the firm of which he had thus become a part also engaged, somewhat tentatively, in the general lumber trade. A few months' experience convinced Mr. Jennings that there was a good field for the lumber, sash, door, blind and general building material trade in New Castle and the surrounding territory.

With this idea in mind, he began buying out his partners, who were too thoroughly grounded in the pioneer way of doing things to adopt his progressive ideas; and in a short time he had secured the entire business and began its expansion into the large and remunerative trade which he has conducted for so many years and to certain branches of which he is, in the afternoon of life, still devoting his energies. He did not attempt to accomplish this at a single bound, or to throw money out of doubtful speculations, often leading to financial ruin, but considered carefully every phase of the question and then by applying to its execution the most practical judgment. He pushed his undertakings to success by a series of quick movements while others were prophesying failure, yet he never lost sight of those small economies, punctilios which are so often forgotten or ignored by men of impulsive natures. It has been this close union of care and push that has won for him his splendid success and given him the honorable title of "father of Henry County Industries."

Levi Allen Jennings was the son of Obadiah and Mary Jennings, of Wayne County, Ohio, who afterwards moved to New Castle, Indiana, where they both died. Mr. Jennings' mother going first and his father a few years later, and their ashes lie in South Mound Cemetery. His paternal ancestors were English and his maternal ancestors were Pennsylvania Dutch. Obadiah and Mary Jennings were both born in Pennsylvania and lived there until their marriage. At an early day thereafter they left Pennsylvania and, braving the dangers of the journey across the Alleghanies, came with all their moveable property in a one horse wagon into the wild woods of Central Ohio to open a farm in the wilderness, where their son, Levi Allen Jennings, was born May 6, 1834.

In this new land he grew up amid the rude surroundings of the log cabin period and was from early boyhood inured to the struggles and privations of the pioneers of the central West. While these bred in him a certain spirit of discontent and a longing for larger opportunities, they were of inestimable value in teaching him the wise lessons of industry, economy and patient effort. Not content with the rudimentary education furnished by the district schools, young Jennings, in the pursuit of knowledge, read by the light of the evening fire and conned his lessons as he followed the plow in the stumpy fields. The time that other boys lost in idleness or doubtful pleasures, he spent in self-improvement and he was soon so well grounded in the essentials that he was admitted with the consent of his parents to the college at Hayesville, Ohio, where by working mornings and evenings at such tasks as he could find to do, he managed to pay his way for two years. He then spent two years and a half at the well known high school of Ashland, Ohio, where he mastered much of the mathematical and scientific courses, also giving considerable study to the English language and literature and Latin and Greek, but his financial needs rendered it necessary for him to leave school and engage in teaching, expecting to return after a time to complete his studies, but the link in his educational life thus broken was never welded. His school days were closed. It was during these years of his studious boyhood that he met another ambitious lad who, under similar difficulties, was eagerly seeking to pass beyond the limits of the narrow life that hedged them in. William B. Allison, afterwards United States Senator from Iowa, was reared upon a clear-

ing about three miles distant from the Jennings home in Ohio, and was about four years older than Mr. Jennings, and it is quite probable that his influence upon his more youthful companion was most salutary. The two became united in a friendship that has never been broken.

It was while Levi A. Jennings was teaching that an event occurred which diverted him from scholarly pursuits and induced him to adopt the business career for which he was most admirably fitted. His uncle, J. O. Jennings, then and now a prominent banker of Ashland, Ohio, was a man of great business capacity and possessed a seemingly intuitive knowledge of men. He took an interest in young men whom he found to be studious, efficient and careful and was often pleased to give them opportunities to demonstrate their ability. When the new county of Ashland, Ohio, was formed and the town of Ashland made its county seat, so great was the personal popularity of Jacob O. Jennings that, although the new county was strongly Democratic and he himself a Whig, he was appointed clerk of the courts. His own time being devoted to his private affairs, he appointed William B. Allison, then a law student, his chief deputy, who transacted the business of the office in a masterly manner. Levi A. Jennings was then attending school. At the end of Jacob O. Jennings' term, the dominant political party claimed the office and elected their candidate who proved incompetent and at the next election Mr. Jennings was elected to the office by a large vote. He had naturally been watching the career of his nephew and now sought him out and tendered him the principal deputyship. The position under the circumstances was not a desirable one but after some deliberation was accepted and for three years—the full term—he discharged its duties to the satisfaction of his principal and of the public. He then retired from official life to engage in private business. He remembers his uncle as his good genius in business and in a large sense refers all his successes in life to his kindly assistance and friendly advice in those early days of his career.

He looks upon his life in Ashland as the halcyon days of his career in which youthful enthusiasm made easy the endurance of hard and continuous toil. Among the pleasing incidents of his life there was the renewal and strengthening of his friendship with William B. Allison who was deputy prosecutor for the common pleas and district courts of Ashland County at the same time that he (Jennings) was deputy clerk. Mr. Allison and his first wife, then quite young, boarded at the same hotel as Mr. Jennings. He recalls that the first Mrs. Allison was a most gracious lady, full of kindly impulses and generous sympathies and that her early death was deeply mourned by a wide circle of friends. Mr. Jennings was also well acquainted with the famous Sherman brothers—John and William Tecumseh—who were then young lawyers of a neighboring town and had a large practise in Ashland County. He also knew Columbus Delano, who was then judge of the district court of which Mr. Jennings was deputy clerk, and who afterwards became Secretary of the Treasury of the United States.

The first business venture of Levi A. Jennings in Ashland was an unfortunate one. He entered into a partnership in the boot and shoe business with a man who in a short time proved to be a bankrupt and involved him in considerable loss. The Ball Reaper and Mower Company, which was at that time doing an extensive business in Ohio and Indiana, recognizing his activity and push, then tendered him a position and he entered their employment to sell their machines and establish agencies. He was very successful and continued with them for three years at a remunerative salary, but in his own words he was constantly revolving this problem in his mind: "If I am worth so much to my employers, why may I not be worth more to myself in a business of my own?" As a result of such self-questioning, he resigned his position and soon afterwards appeared in New Castle, Indiana, as heretofore mentioned.

Mr. Jennings has had a remarkably successful career in New Castle. In 1868 he started a planing mill, a sash, door and blind factory and a general lumber yard and building material business which he continued until recently, doing a vast amount of business and giving to it the most scrupulous care in every detail. Like all men of moderate means, he found the dark days of the panic of 1873 exceedingly trying but his business acumen and caution together with a well established credit carried him through safely and enabled him to make money at a time when so many old and established firms were either failing or suffering severe loss.

In 1877 he built his fine brick business block at the southwest corner of Broad and Elm (now Fourteenth) streets, New Castle. It is one hundred and thirty two feet deep and four stories in height, including the basement, and contains three first-class business rooms, running the whole length of the building, with modern conveniences, and many offices and supplementary business rooms on the upper floors, making it one of the most convenient and roomy business blocks in this part of the State. When first completed it seemed in advance of the town and its needs but Mr. Jennings opened in the new building the most extensive stocks of hardware, building materials, furniture, carpets and house furnishing goods in this part of the State. Beginning with the room in the corner and certain of the upper floors, he rapidly enlarged his stock until it occupied the three first floor business rooms and five or six rooms on the upper floors. His trade grew rapidly with the development of his spirit of enterprise until it reached $150,000 per year and so continued until he determined to curtail its volume that he might secure a much needed rest. The town of New Castle has now reached a point at which its store rooms can no longer be called losing ventures, thanks to Mr. Jennings and other enterprising citizens who have dared to take the initiative in making improvements, both public and private.

But to go back to the date of that important event in his life, his marriage—the record shows that Levi A. Jennings was married December 2, 1858, to Martha W. Coffin, of Ashland, Ohio, born in Troy, New York, February 3, 1835, a most excellent lady of a well cultivated mind and pleasing manner, who is a most worthy companion for her enterprising husband. The Coffin family, to which she belongs, was a remarkable one, consisting of eleven members (before death began to thin its ranks),—the father and mother, four sisters and five brothers, all of them people of unusual talent, especially in musical and mechanical lines. All of the brothers possess unusual musical ability and certain of them are fine performers on various instruments. The family has held many reunions, since its members have been scattered abroad from the old Ashland home, which their varied gifts have made very interesting and enjoyable occasions to others as well as to themselves. The name, Coffin, suggests strength and capability, for so far as known, all persons of the name in this section of the country are descended from the famous Coffin family of Nantucket.

Since the removal of Mr. and Mrs. Jennings to New Castle, they have steadily advanced in prosperity and in the good will of the public. After some years, Mr. Jennings secured the rolling grounds upon which the old sulphur spring was located and where the Methodist camp-meetings of an early day were held. There their elegant and commodious home stands upon a gentle elevation overlooking the finest private park in Eastern Indiana, which Mr. Jennings has christened "Idlewild" after the beautiful grounds and former home of the late poet, Nathaniel P. Willis, on the Hudson River. Mr. and Mrs. Jennings' "Idlewild" is of an undulating surface, with a little stream flowing through it and has been made beautiful by green swards, majestic trees and "flowers of all hues and lovelier than their names."

This fine home and park have been the scenes of much generous hospitality. Something of all this and its nearness to the contrasting scenes of the town, in the very heart of which it is located, were condensed ten years ago into the following lines by one of Mr. Jennings' friends who had watched it all develop from the beginning:

IN IDLEWILD.

Cool shadows floating along the grass,
  Like tender sympathies in the air,
Cloud ships, white sailed, that over-pass,
  Their graceful silhouettes gliding where
The summer reigns and the roses blow,
  Or the loit'ring solidaries glow,
Pure gold in the autumn's frosted hair.

Lithe, lissome willows, low trailing down,
  Long, floating streamers of silv'ry spray,

Where the robin, robed in his Quaker brown,
        Sings to the rising or setting day,
    As the birch's poem of classic whites
    And greens and graces the joy recites
        Of the singing season's insistent way;

    And under the maples a lover's walk,
        Where blushes, glances and sighs dispense
    With the dull illusions of sober talk,
        And the irony of our common sense;
    Where voices falter as hearts grow loud,
        While sweet carnations are flushed and bowed,
    And joy bells ring on the lily stalk.

    Here echoes come from the busy town
        That hint of a world of toil and din,
    Of souls that conquer and souls that drown,
        Where all men struggle and few men win.
    They seem to flow from a far-off land,
        Like waves that beat on the shifting sand,
    And soften to song as the winds go down.

    And so we wander in Idlewild,
        And dream of dreams that were born of dreams,
    Of a world of innocence undefiled,
        Of the halcyon land of elysian streams;
    And here with the trees and birds and flowers,
        And comradeship of the happy hours,
    Our souls are rested and reconciled.

Mr. Jennings services to New Castle and the surrounding country have been of the hopeful and encouraging kind and have exerted an inspiring influence in the upbuilding and beautifying of the town and in the improvement of the farmers' homes. He has had faith in New Castle and the surrounding fertile region, and has proved his faith by deeds. Not only did he enter upon a series of substantial improvements to the town when others were halting; not only has he been the pioneer in its manufacturing interests, but from his earliest career in the town he has adhered to the proposition that New Castle is so eligibly situated and its site and environments so inviting that it may and must become one of the finest little cities of the State, until, now, when the sunshine of three score years has silvered his hair and many cares have furrowed his brow, he begins to enjoy the realization of his dream in the substantial growth and prosperity of his adopted town.

Altogether he has built not less than seventy five houses in New Castle. Among the most important, in the popular estimation, are three large brick and brick and steel business blocks on Broad street, containing twelve first floor business rooms—some of them the largest and best adapted to the needs of a large trade of any in the county—with a great number of upper floors and offices, and his extensive four-story brick factory building at the Pennsylvania railroad crossing on Broad Street, opposite the station, which he erected to meet the demands of his large trade in furniture. But the many dwellings he has caused to be constructed, many of which are up-to-date and commodious, have been of even greater importance to the growth of the town.

Besides taking stock in, or giving money directly, to many of the new enterprises that have been organized by other citizens or have come to the town from elsewhere, thus encouraging the development of the town, he has kept "everlastingly at it" himself. One of his methods has been to make large investments in real estate, which he has divided into lots and sold on easy payments to persons seeking to establish homes, or upon which he has first built dwellings and then sold them on like easy terms of payment. In this way a large per cent. of his constructions have passed into the hands of tradesmen, mechanics and workmen who constitute the substantial citizenship of the town.

Mr. Jennings was one of the pioneers of the cultivation of roses and carnations which has rendered New Castle famous as "The City of Roses," and he still makes his greenhouses and grounds the home of great floral loveliness.

He was one of the active promoters, first stockholders, and was president of the Rushville branch of the old Fort Wayne, Muncie and Cincinnati railroad, now one of the "Lake Erie and Western Lines" of the Vanderbilt system. The New Castle and Rushville road was completed in 1882 and Mr. Jennings served as its president for about three years or until its consolidation with the main line, with entire satisfaction to all concerned. During that period the headquarters of both branches of the Fort Wayne, Muncie and Cincinnati road were at New Castle and the offices of the train dispatcher, master of transportation, and other officers were in one of Mr. Jennings' buildings. Elijah Smith, of Boston, was then the president and the largest stockholder in the Fort Wayne, Muncie and Cincinnati road and W. W. Worthington was the general superintendent.

In 1892 he made a visit to the seaboard cities and while in New York attended the annual convention of the American Furniture Dealers' Association, a business organization representing every important trade center of the country.. As the representative of certain interests of the trade in the middle western States, it became necessary for him to speak upon some question before one of the earlier sessions of the convention, which he did in his off-hand, direct manner, to such purpose that he found himself the center of an attention that approached the nature of an ovation and greatly to his surprise resulted in his election as president of the association.

The American Furniture Manufacturers' Association was at that time holding a great exposition in New York and naturally nothing was too good for the "dealers." On the day following Mr. Jennings' election as president, the manufacturers took the dealers on a chartered vessel to Glen Island, where they were treated to that novelty to a western man—an east-shore clambake. On the next day, in ninety landaus escorted by two policemen, they were shown the sights of the greatest of American cities. In the evening a splendid banquet was given at the Metropolitan Hotel, for which a portion of Gilmore's then famous band furnished the music. Taken as a whole, Mr. Jennings regards the days thus spent as among his happiest and most fortunate experiences. Aside from the attentions shown to the furniture dealers and to himself, the open-handedness and general good will displayed on every side made a lasting impression upon him and the advertisement given him by his unexpected elevation to the presidency of the American Furniture Dealers' Association, through its widely extended membership, and. through the flattering notices of the metropolitan press which were copied by the press of the whole country, has been of great value to him in a business way.

In 1893, just prior to the opening of the World's Fair, this association met again, this time in Chicago, and Mr. Jennings, as president, made the principal address of the occasion and acquitted himself with honor, making so many sound and pertinent suggestions that the great newspapers were outspoken in praise and his reputation as a far-seeing, cautious but enterprising leader in business was greatly enhanced. After retiring from the presidency, Mr. Jennings served the association as its treasurer for a number of years.

During the Civil War, Mr. Jennings was a strong supporter of the Union cause and firmly believed that the fate of popular government for ages to come depended upon the result of that struggle. He served as a deputy United States Marshal in Ohio for a time, and was one of the "Squirrel Hunters" who shouldered rifles and went. in ·pursuit of General John H. Morgan during his daring raid in Indiana and Ohio.

In politics he was first a Whig and then a Republican. He has never been an aspirant for office but has given freely toward the payment of the legitimate campaign expenses of his party. Especially has he felt a pride in the presidential candidates of his party who hailed from his native State; Rutherford B. Hayes, James A. Garfield, Benjamin Harrison and William McKinley, all of whom were elected and two of whom fell by the hands of assassins.

During the Garfield campaign in 1880, Senator William B. Allison, of Iowa, and General Stewart L. Woodford, of New York, visited New Castle for the discussion of political issues and Senator Allison became the guest at Idlewild of his boyhood friend, Levi A. Jennings, and their reunion was a most happy one. After the election and inauguration of President Garfield, it was understood that Senator Allison was to be tendered the portfolio of the Treasury Department and it was at that time that he wrote a friendly letter to Mr. Jennings, saying among other things: "What can I do for you? I shall be glad to do anything in my power for you." The Senator's decision to remain in the Senate and the assassination of the President conspired to influence Mr. Jennings against a political career. Otherwise he might have had honorable and responsible political preferment, but the wisdom of his determination few will doubt.

Mr. Jennings is a firm believer in the tenets of the Christian religion. The church of his choice is the Methodist Episcopal, of which he has long been a devoted and active member, donating freely of his means and time to its various charities., He was an earnest promoter of the efforts to build the new church of that denomination in New Castle which was completed in 1904 and his personal contribution to that end was twenty five hundred dollars in cash. He ·has also been a liberal contributor to other denominations and benevolences. Although he has always been a very busy man, even in years when his life was seriously threatened by disease, he has been a student of public affairs, a reader of current literature, an amateur in art and a great lover of trees and flowers and beautiful landscapes as is attested by his elegant home and Idlewild Park.

Both Mr. and Mrs. Jennings have traveled extensively in the United States and Mr. Jennings has visited Cuba and the Bahama Islands. He has long cherished the dream of travel in Europe and the Orient and is now maturing plans for a flight across the great waters. Should his present purpose hold, he will take with him the best wishes of friends and neighbors.

Levi A. and Martha W. (Coffin) Jennings have been the parents of three children, one of whom, a sweet little child, named Birdie, died in infancy, and a daughter, Helen Etta, born April 20, 1861, now Mrs. Joseph Crow, of Omaha, Nebraska; their son, Winslow D., is an active business man and public spirited citizen of New Castle.

Like other active, progressive men, Mr. Jennings has not gone through life without meeting with some misconception and ill will. These, however, are but passing shadows, if the current of life be as pure as it is swift and strong, and in the end the man's real qualities win honor and compensation. Mr. Jennings has won his place in New Castle as the father of its permanent growth and development, and the good will of the people goes out to him and to Mrs. Jennings in no meagre recognition of their services to the city ·and county.

MRS. HELEN ETTA (JENNINGS) CROW.

(*Daughter*).

Helen Etta, daughter of Levi A. and Martha W. (Coffin) Jennings, as a girl, was remarkably bright and promising, possessing the decided musical talent of her mother's family and much of her father's genius for affairs. She is a graduate of the New Castle High School and of the. College of Music' at Cincinnati, Ohio. She also received additional special musical training and sings and plays so well that she has received the merited compliments of professional musicians. Her gentle manners and winning ways made her a wide circle of friends among both young and old.

She was married to Joseph Crow, a young attorney, October 27, 1886. Most of their married life has been spent in Omaha, Nebraska, where Mr. Crow has a large legal practise and where he has also been engaged in business and politics. He was elected to the State Legislature of Nebraska within two or three years after locating at Omaha, and was re-elected, serving the two terms with distinction. He was and is a supporter and close friend of former United States Senator John M. Thurston, and through his influence and that of other friends, he was appointed postmaster at Omaha, by President McKinley, and served for more than four years. Upon his retirement he was presented with a silver service, valued at two hundred and fifty dollars, but of much greater worth to him as a souvenir of the good will of his friends and subordinates in the service.

The home life of Mr. and Mrs. Crow is a happy one and their beautiful residence has been the center of much social enjoyment. They are the parents of five bright and healthy children, one daughter and four sons. The daughter graduated with honors from the Omaha High School, June 16, 1905.

WINSLOW DE VERE JENNINGS.

(Son).

Winslow De Vere Jennings, only son of Levi A. and Martha W. (Coffin) Jennings, was born December 27, 1862. As a boy, he showed great aptitude in all matters involving mechanical skill and was a favorite with the boys of his own age because he could do everything that boys admire from snaring a fish or building a boat to dressing a turtle or cooking a frog ham to a turn.

He was educated in the New Castle High School and De Pauw University, and he learned every branch of his father's extensive business by close application. He possesses a ready intuition as to the grades, qualities and values of goods and to day is considered to be one of the best posted men of the county in his special lines of business. After a long connection with his father's business, he is now engaged in plumbing, brass and lead fitting, installment of electric lighting and hot water systems, and in contracting, and carries a large stock of goods in those lines. He also gives a part of his time to assisting his father in the management of his affairs.

He was one of the promoters and long an active member of "The Rescue Fire Company" of New Castle, and at one time was its chief. His readiness at unravelling a business tangle, in planning a pleasure excursion or in writing a song and singing it after it was written, and in conducting a political glee club, have combined to make him many friends; but it is in serious, practical business that his strength lies. He has a most retentive memory and quick discernment and sound judgment as to the real worth and market values of goods and their acceptability to the public, and it is believed that thus equipped great successes in the business world are within his grasp.

On May 6, 1895, he married Lena M. Brown, of Dublin, Indiana, born June 17, 1875. She is a lady of high standing in her native town and has won a wide circle of friends in New Castle. They have been the parents of only one child, a promising boy, Norman B. Jennings, who was a favorite with all and the idol of his parents and grandparents. He died January 29, 1905, at the age of eight years.

The loss of their little son is not only the greatest sorrow that has come into their lives but is the greatest bereavement that has stricken the hearts of the grandparents. Though nothing may lift the shadow from their lives, the joy and blessing of the few brief years of sunshine which his presence brought will remain with them in memory to make their days sweeter and richer as they pass.

The loss of the little boy has determined his grandfather to carry out the long cherished plan of erecting in South Mound Cemetery a substantial monument of modest but lasting character which will grace and beautify that "city of the dead," and be a loving tribute to the memory of his grandson and to the living members of the family who are to follow.

of at length in the
of English and German
in that part of the
was born and reared
and farm-making
in the meantime
and, at the age of
remained there two
struction as would
studies, he found it
engage in reading.

After leaving
success that he was ten
in the high school American
But he was
teacher in the southern school
with T. C. Fison his brother
two years that time his
New Castle with their family
to join them thereupon

In the
it, of the late
business building
Street to Race
pied by a
could give

Early
brother, I
was organized
nings, in
bought Mr
interest
Jennings
his father
sold out
this period.
brick is place
under construction.

mater occupying

for
lunch
in
large corner shed
Jennings had joined
May 15, 1885, and
some years last

BIOGRAPHICAL SKETCH OF SIMON PETER JENNINGS.

MANUFACTURER, BUSINESS MAN AND EX-PRESIDENT OF THE CITY COUNCIL.

Simon Peter Jennings is the son of Obediah and Mary Jennings, who are spoken of at length in the biography of his elder brother, Levi A. Jennings, and he is, therefore, of English and German origin. He was born August 11, 1840, in Wayne County, Ohio, in that part of the county which has since been incorporated in Ashland County. He was born and reared upon a farm and took part in the hard, exacting labors of farming and farm-making in a new country, until he reached the age of eighteen years. He had in the meantime acquired such an education as the early public schools of Ohio afforded and, at the age of eighteen, entered Otterbein University, near Columbus, Ohio, and remained there two years, taking the regular course and such special studies and instruction as would qualify him for teaching. To provide the means for continuing his studies, he found it necessary to make some breaks in his two years of college life to engage in teaching.

After leaving college, he taught in the common schools of Ohio for a time with such success that he was tendered and accepted the position of instructor of the junior class in the high school, Auburn, Indiana, where he taught for a year with continued success. But he was by nature designed for a business career and at the end of his first year as a teacher in the Auburn school, he entered the grocery trade in that place in partnership with T. C. Elson, his brother-in-law, maintaining with him a successful business for two years. By that time his father and his brother, Levi A. Jennings, had located in New Castle with their families and were preparing to go into business and wished him to join them. He, thereupon, sold his interest in the grocery and came to New Castle.

In the same year, 1867, he purchased the lot, with an old frame store-room upon it, of the late William C. Murphey, upon which he erected in 1875 his two-story brick business building, one hundred and thirty two feet deep, extending south from Broad Street to Race. At the time of its purchase, however, the old frame store-room was occupied by a merchant with a stock of merchandise, and it was sometime before the latter could give possession of the room to its new owner.

Early in 1868 a new firm, consisting of the subject of this sketch, his senior brother, Levi A. Jennings, and a man from Ashland, Ohio, by the name of Andrews, was organized in New Castle and opened up, in the frame store-room of Simon P. Jennings, in the general hardware and stove trade. In about two years, Levi A. Jennings bought Mr. Andrews' interest and soon after that Obediah Jennings purchased the entire interest of his son, Levi A. Jennings, in the business. The firm thus formed of Obediah Jennings and his son, Simon P. Jennings, lasted for some years until Simon P. secured his father's part of the business and continued alone with most satisfactory success. He sold out to his chief clerks, Daniel Monroe and Jason W. Holloway, in 1890. During this period, the only change in the location of the store occurred in 1875, while the new brick building in place of the little old frame which the business had outgrown, was under construction.

In that same year, 1875, Mr. Jennings had entered the lumber and building-material trade, occupying the lot immediately south of the store room, across Race Street, now occupied by the brick and frame buildings, since put up by Henry Adams, for the poultry trade. Upon this lot Mr. Jennings constructed his sheds and stored his lumber, sash, blinds, doors and other material. This lumber business was not included in the sale to Monroe and Holloway but was transferred to the factory building and large lumber sheds on out-lot number seven, on the east side of Fifteenth Street. Mr. Jennings had purchased this lot of the widow and heirs of the late Charles C. Powell on May 15, 1885, and built the main two-story brick factory building upon it in 1886, and some years later, the lumber sheds attached thereto.

It was in this main wing of the factory building that he established his extensive saw and planing mills and sash, door and blind machinery and from 1886 forward carried on a large business in lumber and building materials of all kinds for about three years, when he built the south wing of the factory and otherwise increased its capacity to make room for another branch of the wood manufacturing business, that of sledge, hammer, pick, axe and other short handles, except "D" handles. This required the installment of a large amount of new machinery designed expressly for that line of manufacture and the investment of much additional capital. The business proved to be a profitable one and was pushed with energy until the timber, suitable to the purpose, in the surrounding country was so far exhausted as to greatly curtail the output of the factory. Mr. Jennings then established a branch of their handle business at Charleston, West Virginia, under the management of his second son, Charles W. Jennings, but also continued the business in the home factory. Ample supplies of timber were obtainable at Charleston and the business went on very successfully until 1900, when the factory burned down and the machinery was ruined by the fire.

In the meanwhile the trade in lumber and building material had increased so rapidly at the New Castle factory and lumber yard that Mr. Jennings determined to turn his energies and capital largely in that direction and consequently discontinued the Charleston business. His son, Charles W. Jennings, returned to New Castle and took an interest with his father in the business there. The trade has so rapidly increased that it gives employment to several hands and occupies the time of both Mr. Jennings and his son in its management, though Mr. Jennings now enjoys more leisure than formerly and occasionally takes a well earned rest at some favorite spot in Florida or some other part of picturesque America. As an indication of the magnitude of Mr. Jennings' trade, it may be mentioned that it has for some years amounted to one hundred and fifty carloads of merchandise per year and continues at that figure, if not somewhat more. Mr. Jennings was President of the town council during the years 1896 and 1897, during which many street and other improvements, were made, to all of which he gave his close personal attention and care.

It is evident from the foregoing that Simon P. Jennings' contributions to the growth and prosperity of New Castle fully entitle him to an honored place in the ranks of her leading manufacturers. It would be interesting and profitable, were the statistics at hand, to note his annual outlays in wages and to give the numbers of workmen who have received employment at his hands, and their various occupations. His disbursements in this way have been of the kind which promote the happiness and comfort of the people and the prosperity of the city, and have been of such magnitude that New Castle may well regard him as one of its most active promoters and benefactors and long hold him in cherished remembrance.

Simon P. Jennings married Angeline, born December 2, 1846, daughter of Jacob J. and Mary Pickering, of Henry Township, Henry County, Indiana, March 23, 1870. Miss Pickering was of a good family, which was one of the best known among the pioneers of Eastern Indiana. Her father was a prominent farmer, who took a deep interest in public as well as private affairs. Her mother died while she was yet a child and much of the care of her father's household fell upon her youthful shoulders, a responsibility to which she proved fully equal. Her education was obtained at the neighborhood school and the Spiceland Academy. She was of an observant and thoughtful nature and possessed of more than ordinary intelligence. Her pure and beautiful character and her devotion to her husband, her children and her home, with her patient, painstaking industry made her an ideal companion for a man of Mr. Jennings' active business life and energy, as well as an ideal mother of his children. They were the parents of one daughter, Mary Ada Thornburgh, afterward Mrs. Richard J. Roberts, and three sons, Harry Edmond Jennings, Charles Wesley Jennings and Walter Pickering Jennings. The sons are all living and active in business, but the daughter, Mary Ada, died November 9, 1901.

Mr. and Mrs. Simon P. Jennings' married life covered a period of almost thirty five happy years. The next year after their marriage, 1871, Mr. Jennings purchased the lot at the southeast corner of Broad and Twenty First streets, where the Jennings' homestead now stands, and built a dwelling upon it, which with enlargements and improvements developed into a pretty, commodious home. There their children were born and there, though never pretentious entertainers, they delighted to receive their friends with a modest but sincere hospitality. This place, surrounded by its beautiful grounds, has been the scene of much real happiness.

Mrs. Jennings had been in failing health before the death of her daughter whom she greatly loved. That sad event came as a great shock to both herself and Mr. Jennings; she rallied from it, however, better than her friends anticipated, but during the latter part of 1903, she grew rapidly worse until death came to her with its untold peace, December 31, 1903.

Both Mr. and Mrs. Jennings were brought up under good influences, moral, religious and social. Mr. Jennings' parents were faithful adherents of the religious body, known as United Brethren in Christ, and was reared under its auspices and worshiped with its members in a church near his father's home during his boyhood days, but never connected himself with the denomination, his first church membership having been taken in the Methodist Episcopal Church at New Castle, Indiana, soon after locating there, in 1869. Of that church and congregation he has ever since been an active member.

Mrs. Jennings was reared under Quaker influences, but soon after her marriage to Mr. Jennings she united with the Methodist Episcopal Church which is much the same, in matters of belief regarded as essential, as the Friends, and remained a consistent member of and an active worker in that church and died full of faith in the mercy and goodness of God.

Mr. Jennings is not a man of many words. He attends to his business and greets his friends quietly, but keeps things moving. His business success is more largely due to the persistence of his character and to his tireless industry than to any other causes. He has been and is a successful business man and the lesson of his career is the one so often repeated that success comes not so often to those who make haste as to the sure-footed and steady-going.

MARY ADA (JENNINGS) ROBERTS.

(Daughter).

Mary Ada Jennings was born in New Castle, Indiana, February 1, 1872, and was reared by her parents, Simon P. and Angeline (Pickering) Jennings, with loving care. She was during her life a source of great consolation and happiness to them. She was educated in the public schools of New Castle and graduated from the High School with the class of 1891. She then entered De Pauw University, Greencastle, Indiana, taking the literary and musical courses. From early childhood, she took pleasure in singing and playing for her many friends and was a favorite with young and old. She sang with the choir of the Methodist Episcopal Church, whenever she found it possible to do so, and often appeared in solos, greatly to the pleasure and profit of all who heard her.

She attained to great proficiency on the piano and in the management of the voice, having been endowed by nature with great love for music, a fine voice, and a quick ear for the detection of delicate tones and combinations and the modulations of time in the various movements, to which she added a rare enthusiasm of study. All of these things combined to render her attractive as a singer and efficient as a teacher. She taught music and voice culture, first, at a young ladies' seminary in Orleans, Nebraska, and afterward, at a similar school in Huntsville, Alabama, succeeding finely in both places. She possessed a literary taste and culture which added much to her efficiency as a teacher and especially qualified her for the duties and pleasures of club life in which she was active. In New Castle she was one of the organizers of The College Club and was one or more times its president.

She was married to Professor Richard J. Roberts, of the High School of Shelbyville, Illinois, August 9, 1899, in the Methodist Episcopal Church in New Castle, the ceremony being performed by the Reverend Doctor John P. John, President of De Pauw University. They had become acquainted while students at De Pauw and an attachment sprang up between them which resulted in their union. Their short but happy wedded life was spent in a pleasant home at Shelbyville, Illinois. She died at the home of her parents, regretted by all who knew her, November 9, 1901. The funeral occurred at New Castle amid many evidences of affectionate sorrow and many floral offerings from friends, far and near, and her mortal remains repose in South Mound Cemetery.

73

(Son).

Harry Edmond Jennings, eldest son of Simon P. and Angeline (Pickering) Jennings, was born March 1, 1874, at the homestead on the corner of Broad and Twenty First streets, New Castle, Indiana, where he was reared and educated in the public schools and graduated from the High School with honor. He was brought up from early childhood to take part in his father's business and was connected with it until in May, 1893, when he established a factory for the manufacture of barrel hoops in New Castle, which he has since carried on upon a large scale, finding sale for the output of the factory in all parts of the country, and doing a profitable business.

He was married on January 1, 1896, to Edna, (born July 1, 1874), only child of David W. and Sophia J. (Shirk) Kinsey, of New Castle, Indiana. In the Fall of 1900 and Spring of 1901, he erected the fine dwelling house on east Broad Street, New Castle, recently sold to Thomas B. Millikan, which has been his home ever since and where he and Mrs. Jennings have lived most happily, dispensing a generous and refined hospitality.

His manufacturing plant was once swept away by fire; but scarcely waiting for the ashes to cool, he began replacing it with a new one, receiving the reward of his energy and pluck in an increased business. In February, 1904, he began the manufacture of staves at Milton, Wayne County, Indiana, in conjunction with his brother, Walter P., who is the local manager of the business, and in this he is again scoring a good success. Harry E. and Edna (Kinsey) Jennings are the parents of one child, a very promising little boy, born June 22, 1897, named David Harry, after his grandfather, David W. Kinsey, and his father. Mr. Jennings attends the Methodist Episcopal Church and contributes liberally to its support but has never taken membership in any church.

He is at present engaged with his wife's father, David W. Kinsey, in erecting a large, up-to-date residence for the two families on the east side of south Main Street, New Castle. Though not yet thirty two years of age, Mr. Jennings is regarded as one of New Castle's solid and prosperous business men and as one having still brighter prospects before him.

(Son).

Charles Wesley Jennings, second son of Simon P. and Angeline (Pickering) Jennings, was born at his parents' home in New Castle, February 4, 1876, and, like his elder brother, grew up to his father's business, and, like Harry E., possessed a fondness for machinery and a remarkable readiness in its adjustment and management, which made him a valuable assistant in his father's large manufacturing enterprises. Before taking a permanent place in the business, he passed successfully through the New Castle public schools and graduated from the High School.

His aptitude for the business was such that at the age of twenty two years, he was placed in charge of a branch of the handle business which his father and himself had established at Charleston, West Virginia, in 1898, and he conducted the business with much success until the plant was burned down in 1900, the heat of the fire ruining the machinery. His father's lumber and building material business at New Castle having in the meantime grown rapidly with the growth of the town, he returned to that place and took an interest in the factory on Fifteenth Street, and the several branches of the business connected with it, in which he still continues with decided financial success.

Charles W. Jennings was married on June 25, 1901, to Mabel S. (born March 11, 1882), daughter of Mr. and Mrs. Henry Eastwood, of Charleston, West Virginia, in the State Street Methodist Episcopal Church there by the Reverend Compton. The Eastwood family is an old and prominent one in Charleston. During the Civil War, Mrs. Jennings' grandfather was a staunch Unionist and incurred the enmity of the Confederates who placed him and his family upon a boat and sent them down the Kanawha and

Harry R. Jennings

Jennings, eldest son of Simon P. and Angeline (Pickering) Jennings,
... the homestead on the corner of Broad and Twenty First
Avenue, where he was reared and educated in the public schools
... High School with honor. He was brought up from early child.
... father's business and was connected with it until in May, 1893,
... for the manufacture of barrel hoops in New Castle, which
... on a large scale, finding sale for the output of the factory in
V. and doing a profitable business.
... January 1, 1896, to Edna, (born July 1, 1874), only child of
... (Shirk) Kinsey, of New Castle, Indiana. In the Fall of 1900
... the fine dwelling house on east Broad Street, New Castle,
... B. Millikan; which has been his home ever since and where he
lived most happily, dispensing a generous and refined hospitality.
... plant was once swept away by fire; but scarcely waiting for
... replacing it with a new one, receiving the reward of his
increased business. In February, 1904, he began the manufacture
... county, Indiana, in conjunction with his brother, Walter P.,
... the business, and in this he is again scoring a good suc.
... (Kinsey) Jennings are the parents of one child, a very prom.
... 24, 1897, named David Harry, after his grandfather, David
... Mr. Jennings attends the Methodist Episcopal Church and
... support, but has never taken membership in any church.
... engaged with his wife's father, David W. Kinsey, in erecting a
... for the two families on the east side of south Main Street,
... yet thirty two years of age, Mr. Jennings is regarded as one
... prosperous business men and as one having still brighter

CHARLES WESLEY JENNINGS.

(Son).

Jennings, second son of Simon P. and Angeline (Pickering) Jennings,
... home in New Castle, February 4, 1876, and, like his elder
father's business, and, like Harry E., possessed a fondness for
... readiness in its adjustment and management, which made
... his father's large manufacturing enterprises. Before taking
... business, he passed successfully through the New Castle public
... the High School.
... business was such that at the age of twenty two years, he
... a branch of the handle business which his father and himself
... West Virginia, in 1898, and he conducted the business
the plant was burned down in 1900, the heat of the fire ruining
... lumber and building material business at New Castle hav-
... rapidly, with the growth of the town, he returned to that
... in the factory on Fifteenth Street, and the several branches
... with it, in which he still continues with decided financial

... was married on June 25, 1901, to Mabel S. (born March 11,
... Mrs. Henry Eastwood, of Charleston, West Virginia, in the
Episcopal Church there by the Reverend Compton. The East-
... prominent one in Charleston. During the Civil War, Mrs.
... a staunch Unionist and incurred the enmity of the Confeder.
... family seized a boat and sent them down the Kanawha and

Harry R. Jennings

Ohio rivers, exiles from their home. But when the Union forces took command of the town, they returned and now occupy the old Eastwood mansion in Charleston.

After coming to New Castle, Mr. and Mrs. Jennings occupied a home in the eastern part of the town until the death of his mother, when they moved in with his father in the old home and are making the old place as comfortable and life as happy as possible for Simon P. Jennings as well as for themselves. They are very popular, especially with the young people, in social circles, and Mrs. Jennings has found a warm welcome to "The City of Roses." They are the parents of one child, a bright boy (born April 20, 1905), named Charles Henry. Young, prosperous and happy, their lot in life seems to be a fortunate one.

WALTER PICKERING JENNINGS.

(Son).

Walter Pickering Jennings, third son of Simon P. and Angeline (Pickering) Jennings, was born at the Jennings' homestead in New Castle, Indiana, April 16, 1878, and like his older brothers was brought up to his father's business and like them is a graduate of the New Castle High School, where he showed great proficiency in his studies. Unlike them, however, he is inclined to the office work rather than the mechanical features of the business. Soon after graduation from school, he took charge of the books in his father's office and continued in charge of them to the benefit of the business, until about one year ago, when he formed a partnership with his brother, Harry E., and the new firm established themselves at Milton, Indiana, in the manufacture of barrel staves, Walter locating at that place and taking charge of the business, which has been very profitable up to the present time and promises well for the future, or so long as timber for the making of staves shall be procurable at that point.

Walter P. Jennings is a young, unmarried man, twenty seven years of age, popular with his young associates and with the general public. Like his brothers, he is of high moral character and correct habits and devoted to business, but he is not unmindful of the social amenities and enjoys society and cherishes his friends, who all have high hopes for his continued prosperity and happiness.

BIOGRAPHICAL SKETCH OF DAVID WAGNER KINSEY.

SCHOOL TEACHER, COUNTY OFFICIAL AND BANKER.

The citizens of Henry County have shown commendable enterprise in many channels of business and trade, and not the least deserving are those who have established
and maintained banking facilities in the growing communities within the limits of the
county. Its banking interest, originally small, has been steadily developed under the
able and conservative management of the foremost financiers of the community until
it now possesses a stability of resources that commands the confidence and support of
the people. Among the well known citizens who have worked effectively to this end
is David Wagner Kinsey, cashier of the Citizens' State Bank of New Castle.

Henry Kinsey, the paternal great-grandfather, and Abraham Kinsey, the paternal
grandfather of David Wagner Kinsey, were both natives of Virginia. The latter left
Virginia in 1797, at the age of seventeen years, and became one of the early settlers of
Montgomery County, Ohio, and while a citizen of that State served as a soldier in the
last year of the War of 1812-15. He married Mary Magdalene Wagner, who was born
and reared at Frankstown, Blair County, Pennsylvania. Together they lived for many
years on a farm which now forms part of the Soldiers' Home property at Dayton, Ohio.

In 1835 he sold this farm and moved to Wayne County, Indiana, locating on
Noland's Fork, west of Richmond, where he and his family lived for about six years.
He then bought one hundred and sixty acres of land upon which has since been built
that part of Hagerstown, Indiana, lying north of Main Street in that town, where he
resided until he retired from farming and went to live with one of his sons at Pendleton, Indiana. He died there at the patriarchal age of eighty six years and his remains
lie beside those of his wife in the German Baptist Cemetery, near Hagerstown.

Lewis Kinsey, son of Abraham and father of David Wagner Kinsey, was born on
the Ohio farm, near Dayton, April 6, 1818. He came to Indiana with his parents and
lived with them on the farms at Noland's Fork and Hagerstown until his marriage.
He was united in marriage with Catharine, daughter of Martin and Christena Shultz,
natives of Pennsylvania, December 31, 1837. She was born April 11, 1821. After their
marriage they lived for four years on his father's farm in a house some forty or fifty
rods north of where Lewis Teeter now lives in Hagerstown. He then bought a farm
of eighty acres located a half mile north of the present village of Millville, Liberty
Township, Henry County. In 1847 he sold this farm and bought what was known as the
John Dixon farm, consisting of one hundred and sixty acres located on Flatrock, five
miles east of New Castle, where he lived until 1871, when he moved to a farm three
miles northwest of Hagerstown, Wayne County, where he spent the remainder of his
days.

Lewis Kinsey had two full brothers, Abraham and Philip, and four full sisters:
Mary married Henry Harris; Margaret married Mathew Luse; Susan married Jacob
Heiny; and Anna married Benjamin Conley. He also had two half brothers, David and
Jacob. All of these are dead, excepting Anna Conley, who lives with her daughter, Mrs.
Jesse Mendenhall, in Muncie, Indiana.

Lewis and Catharine (Shultz) Kinsey were the parents of five children, two sons
and three daughters, namely: Martin, born June 12, 1839, who is a farmer living two
and a half miles southeast of New Castle, on the Dublin pike; Anna, born September
27, 1842, was married at her parents' home in Liberty Township, January 3, 1861, to
Benjamin F. Shaffer, a native of Henry County; they moved to Altoona, Iowa, after their
marriage, where he died May 27, 1879, and she died December 20, 1904, both are buried
in the Altoona Cemetery; seven children survive them. David Wagner, born February
1, 1846, is the subject of this sketch; Sarah J., born November 6, 1850, was married
August 7, 1869, to Eli M. Wisehart (born April 14, 1846), at the home of her parents
in Liberty Township, Henry County, the ceremony being performed by the Reverend
Daniel Bowman; they were the parents of eleven children, seven of whom survive.
The last child of Lewis and Catharine (Shultz) Kinsey was Catharine, born August 7,
1857, who died September 14, 1863, and is buried in the German Baptist Cemetery, near

David W. Knox

BIOGRAPHICAL SKETCH OF DAVID WAGNER KINSEY.

SCHOOL TEACHER, COUNTY OFFICIAL AND BANKER.

The citizens of Henry County have shown commendable enterprise in many channels of business and trade, and not the least deserving are those who have established
and maintained banking facilities in the growing communities within the limits of the
county. Its banking interest, originally small, has been steadily developed under the
able and conservative management of the foremost financiers of the community until
it now possesses a stability of resources that commands the confidence and support of
the people. Among the well known citizens who have worked effectively to this end
is David Wagner Kinsey, cashier of the Citizens' State Bank of New Castle.

Henry Kinsey, the paternal great-grandfather, and Abraham Kinsey, the paternal
grandfather of David Wagner Kinsey, were both natives of Virginia. The latter left
Virginia in 1797, at the age of seventeen years, and became one of the early settlers of
Montgomery County, Ohio, and while a citizen of that State served as a soldier in the
last war of the War of 1812-15. He married Mary Magdalene Wagner, who was born
near Hometown, Blair County, Pennsylvania. Together they lived for many
years on a farm which now forms part of the Soldiers' Home property at Dayton, Ohio.

In 1835 he sold this farm and moved to Wayne County, Indiana, locating on
several miles east of Henry and where he and his family lived for about six years.
He then removed to a modern and later acres of land upon which has since been built
the portion of Hagerstown, Indiana, lying north of Main Street in that town, where he
was a retired and living and went to live with one of his sons at Pendleton Indiana. He died there at the patriarchal age of eighty-six years and his remains
are those of his wife in the German Baptist Cemetery, near Hagerstown.

Lewis Kinsey, son of Abraham and father of David Wagner Kinsey, was born on
the old farm, near Dayton, April 6, 1818. He came to Indiana with his parents and
lived with them on the farms on Noland's Fork and Hagerstown until his marriage.
He was united in marriage with Catharine, daughter of Martin and Christena Shultz,
natives of Pennsylvania, December 31, 1837. She was born April 11, 1821. After their
marriage they lived for four years on his father's farm in a house some forty or fifty
rods north of where Lewis Teeter now lives in Hagerstown. He then bought a farm
of forty acres located a half mile north of the present village of Millville, Liberty
Township, Henry County. In 1847 he sold this farm and bought what was known as the
Teeter farm, consisting of one hundred and sixty acres located on Flatrock, five
miles east of New Castle, where he lived until 1871, when he moved to a farm three
miles southwest of Hagerstown, Wayne County, where he spent the remainder of his

Lewis Kinsey had two full brothers, Abraham and Philip, and four full sisters:
Mary married Harris; Margaret married Mathew Luse; Susan married Jacob
Teeter and married Benjamin Conley. He also had two half brothers, David and
Jacob, all of whom are dead, excepting Anna Conley, who lives with her daughter, Mrs.
Muncie, Indiana.

Lewis and Catharine (Shultz) Kinsey were the parents of five children, two sons
and three daughters, namely: Martin, born June 12, 1839, who is a farmer living two
and one-half miles northeast of New Castle, on the Dublin pike; Anna, born September
in 1841 married at her parents' home in Liberty Township, January 3, 1861, five
to Benjamin who was a native of Henry County; they moved to Altoona, Iowa, after their
marriage, she married May 27, 1879, and she died December 29, 1894; both are buried
in the Altoona Cemetery, seven children survive them. David Wagner, born February
1, 1845, is the subject of this sketch; Sarah J., born November 6, 1850, was married
August 1, 1866 to David Wisehart (born April 14, 1846), at the home of her parents
in Liberty Township, Henry County, the ceremony being performed by the Reverend
Daniel Bowman; they were the parents of eleven children, seven of whom survive.
The last child of Lewis and Catharine (Shultz) Kinsey was Catharine, born August 7,
1857, who died September 14, 1863, and is buried in the German Baptist Cemetery, near

David W Kinsey

Hagerstown. Lewis Kinsey died March 3, 1904; his kind and devoted wife preceded him in death, having died May 21, 1899. Both are buried in the German Baptist Ceme- tery, near Hagerstown.

Mr. and Mrs. Kinsey joined the German Baptist, sometims called the Dunkard Church, in the year 1859, and about one year later he was called to the ministry and later was ordained. He had not the advantage of an advanced education, but his natural abilities enabled him to attain a high degree of efficiency in his ministerial work. He traveled and preached much among the different congregations of his church and with Elder George W. Studebaker made the first missionary tour through the southern dis- trict of Indiana and through parts of the Southern States, soon after the close of the Civil War.

His hospitality was unstinted and he was very liberal in answering the demands of charity. He and his faithful wife and helper were very devoted to the church of their choice and gave liberally to its support. He was a good man and a good citizen and was held in the highest esteem by his church, his friends and his neighbors. Two sons, one daughter, nineteen grandchildren, one great-grandchild and one sister survive him.

DAVID WAGNER KINSEY.

David Wagner Kinsey was born February 1, 1846, on his father's farm, near Mill- ville, Henry County, Indiana. His boyhood was spent in the performance of the routine duties of the farm which fell to the lot of the youths of that period. He assisted on the farm in season and attended the public schools of his neighborhood in Winter. In the Winter and Spring of 1861-2 and again in the same seasons of 1862-3, he was a student in the New Castle public schools under Professor E. J. Rice, and in the Winter and Spring of 1863-4 he taught school at the Maple Hill schoolhouse, Blue River Township. The Civil War was then at its height and special efforts were making to strengthen the Union forces at the front. Mr. Kinsey felt it to be his duty to offer his services to the cause and accordingly enlisted as a private in Company B, 139th Indiana Infantry. He was mustered into the service of the United States, June 5, 1864, and was mustered out as a Corporal, September 29, 1864. His military record is set out in full elsewhere in this History in connection with the roster of his company and regiment.

After his discharge from the army, he returned home and immediately resumed the prosecution of his studies under the Reverend Henry M. Shockley at the New Cas- tle Academy. In the Winter of the year 1864, he again began to teach, having secured the assignment to the school at Old Chicago; in the Winter of 1865-6 he taught in Liberty Township and in the same season of 1866-7 he had charge of the Salem school, Franklin Township. At this time he seems to have abandoned the profession of teaching and took up the study of law for the next two years in the office of Brown and Polk, New Castle, and in 1869 was admitted to the Henry County bar. From that time to the present, he has been closely identified with the commercial and social affairs of New Castle and Henry County. He became deputy clerk of the Henry Circuit Court, under Harry H. Hiatt, and upon the latter's death, March 21, 1871, he was appointed to fill the unexpired term. He was also for a short time deputy clerk under his successor in the office, Robert B. Carr. Mr. Kinsey was a very capable and accommodating official and upon his retirement from office bore with him the good will of the court, the bar and the people. Mr. Kinsey enjoys the reputation of being one of the most competent clerks the county has ever had and the records left by him in the Clerk's office are models of neatness and precision.

David W. Kinsey was one of the original stockholders in the Citizens' State Bank of New Castle, and upon its organization in 1873 was chosen assistant cashier and a year later was elected cashier, a position he has held for more than a third of a century. During that time the bank has steadily grown in financial strength, keeping pace with the growth and prosperity of the county, and is now ranked among the leading financial institutions of the State. Its management has been sound and conservative, yet accom- panied by a liberality and a willingness to accommodate the mercantile interests of the county which reflect great credit upon its officers. Mr. Kinsey, during his long career as cashier, has guarded with fidelity the trust reposed in him by his associates and his knowledge of the principles as well as the details of the business is so comprehensive as to gain for him high repute in financial circles. He is a broad gauge man of a kindly and companionable disposition.

The engrossing nature of his position has not prevented him, however, from giving considerable attention to his duties as a citizen. He has at intervals, for a number of years, been a member of the Board of School Trustees of the Corporation of New Castle, and has always been regarded by his colleagues and by the people as a safe and valuable adviser regarding the educational interests of the community. He has been interested in the material progress of the town and connected with several of its important industries, such as the Hoosier Shredder Factory, the Bundy Hotel Company, the Rolling Mill, the Shovel Factory, the New Castle Heat, Light and Power Company, the Pan-American Bridge Company, the Industrial Association, through which was secured to the town the Krell-French Piano Company, an institution which is among the largest of its kind in the United States, and which is of vast importance to the development and growth of New Castle. His connection with these various enterprises shows how fully alive he has always been to the needs and welfare of the town and points him out as one of the county's most public spirited citizens.

On March 2, 1870, at the home of the bride in New Castle, David W. Kinsey was united in marriage with Sophia J., daughter of Benjamin and Frances (Newcomer) Shirk, the ceremony being performed by the Reverend Peter G. Bell, the then pastor of the Lutheran Church, New Castle. They are the parents of one child, a daughter, named Edna, born January 1, 1874. She is now the wife of Harry E. Jennings, the well known manufacturer of New Castle, to whom she was married January 1, 1896, the ceremony being performed by the Reverend Charles Steck. Mr. and Mrs. Jennings have one child, a son, named David Harry Jennings, after his maternal grandfather, David W. Kinsey, and his own father. He was born June 22, 1897, and is a bright lad, who is the favorite of the two households which are now united in the large, commodious residence, erected by Mr. Kinsey and his son-in-law, located on the east side of south Main Street, New Castle, south of Indiana Avenue. A sketch of Harry E. Jennings will be found appended to that of his father, Simon P. Jennings, published elsewhere in this History.

Since attaining his majority, Mr. Kinsey has taken a rational interest in all public questions and in politics has always given his support to the Republican party. He is not a demonstrative man but has always exerted a quiet and beneficial influence upon the organization and policy of his party. He is a charter member of Crescens Lodge, Number 33, Knights of Pythias, New Castle, which was organized and instituted in 1872. He is also a member of the order of Elks, New Castle Lodge, Number 484. Mr. and Mrs. Kinsey have been for many years members of the English Lutheran Church and have contributed liberally of their means for its support.

A distinguished and well merited public honor was conferred upon Mr. Kinsey by his appointment as one of the commissioners from Indiana to the Louisiana Purchase Exposition, which was held at St. Louis in 1904. As a member of this commission, he was chairman of the committee on Publicity and Promotion and was largely instrumental in bringing to perfection the exhibit of the State at what has been rightfully termed the most wonderful and complete exhibition of the world's industries and its arts and sciences that was ever presented to an universal public. He was also an active member of the committee on Building and that its labors were fully appreciated was shown by the general praise bestowed upon the large, commodious and handsome Indiana Building. Mr. Kinsey also served as a member of the committee on Education and of the committee in charge of the Indiana Stone Exhibit. These were marked features of the exposition and attracted much attention by reason of their completeness and merit. Indiana's fame as a manufacturing, industrial and educational State was perfectly sustained at the great exposition through the untiring labors of her commissioners and the perfection of detail in all departments reflects the greatest credit upon the individual commissioners and entitles them to the grateful thanks of the entire State.

Thus for a period of nearly forty years, David W. Kinsey has been an integral part of the history of Henry County and to him and his associates must be attributed much

during the .a . . . .
State. Grau . .
located on .. . .
his days and . . . . Shirk, who . . . .
large family . . . . . .

. . . . . . Sophia Palmer. who . . . .
scent but of w h. . . . . tle. My fath. . was . . . .
and in 1816 h. . . . . of the . . . .
place, and it w. . . . . that I was . . . . .
    Benjam. . . . . the first of s u. . . . .
to the institu. . . . . Keystone St. . . . .
at New Castle . . . . ty, where for . . . .
brick buildi. . . . . use," wh. . .
now occupie. . . . . united St. . . . . north W . . .

    He aft. actory for . . .
ness he . . . . when he . . .
Perhaps . . . . . .
signed . . . . county clerk of . . .
such . . . . four year. .
ex. . . . . . . of his ser. . .
for . . u years.
    After . . . . e formed a partnership
James . . . . . . s . and John M. Fisher, who under the firm style . . . Shirk.
Fisher. . sumed . . . . ufacture of grain cradles. T . .
New C. . . important industri. . . . .

bil ler w. . .
come into genera. . .
farm imp. . . . . . . has given w. . .
perio. that th. grain . . . . . n was the . . . .
fact . . . . s and they w. .
There a. . . . . per cannot . . . .
had . . the c. . . . . them i. . . .

Johnson . . . . . .
of the impleme. . . .
. . . . 1876, Ben. . .
u. . . . . 'enry a. .
in the . . . . on from
re. . . . . ssion, . . . He was a . . .
dem . . . . constituents.
    . . . . part of the prese. .
Shirk w. . . . . sing agent, and for . .
secretary . . . . (South Mound . . . .
. . . . the Enterprise N. . .

of the material and moral advancement of the county. This is especially true of the re-markable development of its financial institutions.

ANCESTRY OF MRS. DAVID W. (SHIRK) KINSEY.

Of his immediate family, Benjamin Shirk, in an autobiographical sketch of him-self, said:

"I am of German descent, my paternal ancestry having emigrated from Germany during the early settlement of Pennsylvania; they located in Lancaster County, in that State. Grandfather Shirk afterward moved with his family into Franklin County and located on a farm three miles east of Chambersburg, where he spent the remainder of his days and it was here my father, Jacob Shirk, who was next to the youngest of a large family of children, was born November 26, 1774. At the age of twenty six years, in 1800, he was joined in marriage with Sophia Palmer, who was also of German de-scent but of whose ancestry I know but little. My father was by occupation a miller and in 1816 he rented and took charge of the Chambersburg Mills, located in that place, and it was here, March 20, 1819, that I was born."

Benjamin Shirk, following the drift of a number of emigrants from Pennsylvania to the inviting West, left the "Keystone State" in 1847, coming to Indiana and settling at New Castle, Henry County, where for a few years he taught school in the one-story brick building, known as the "Little Brick Schoolhouse," which stood on the ground now occupied by the United Brethren Church, on north Fourteenth Street. He was a well educated man and was regarded as a very competent teacher.

He afterwards established a factory for the making of grain cradles. This busi-ness he maintained until 1853, when he became the depot agent of what is now the Panhandle Railroad. He continued in that position for about two years when he re-signed to become deputy clerk of the Henry Circuit Court. He filled this position with such credit that four years later he was elected clerk; he was re-elected and after the expiration of his second term, he served as deputy under his successor, Harry H. Hiatt, for two years.

After this long service in the clerk's office, he formed a partnership in 1871 with James Johnson and John M. Fisher, who under the firm style of Shirk, Johnson and Fisher, resumed the manufacture of grain cradles. This was one of the very first of New Castle's important industries and attained proportions unsurpassed by any similar business concern in the entire country.

When they began the manufacture of grain cradles, the present harvester and binder were unknown, perhaps, unthought of. Since that time, however, they have come into general use and the old fashioned grain cradle, like many another old style farm implement, has given way to modern machinery and appliances. But during the period that the grain cradle was the reaper, the firm of Shirk, Johnson and Fisher manu-factured them by the thousands and they were shipped to all parts of the country. There are still places where the modern reaper cannot be used and recourse must be had to the cradle; and for that reason the business of making them is still carried on at New Castle by John M. Fisher, the only surviving member of the old firm of Shirk, Johnson and Fisher. The business is now a small one and turns out only just enough of the implements to supply a limited demand.

In 1876, Benjamin Shirk was elected to the Indiana State Senate from the dis-trict comprising Henry and Hancock counties. He sat in the forty ninth session, 1877; in the special session from March 8th to 15th of the same year, and in the fiftieth regular session, 1879. He was a thoroughly competent legislator and merited the confi-dence of his constituents.

When the old part of the present county courthouse was building, 1864-8, Mr. Shirk was the disbursing agent, and for a period of about fifteen years he was the secretary of the New Castle (South Mound) Cemetery Association. He was also for a number of years secretary of the Enterprise Natural Gas Company. He was always a public spirited citizen and numbered the whole community among his friends. He was a man of fine social qualities, an entertaining conversationalist and a kindly gentleman. In argument he was quiet and equable, granting to everyone the right to his own honest opinion.

In 1842, Benjamin Shirk married Frances, daughter of John and Agnes (Brindle) Newcomer, who were natives of Franklin County, Pennsylvania. Mr. Shirk came to New Castle, Indiana, in 1847 and in 1851 the Newcomer family followed him to Henry County, where Mr. Newcomer purchased what is now a part of the John C. Hudelson farm, north of New Castle, and there resided until his death. John Newcomer was a farmer all his life and gave that pursuit his undivided attention. John and Agnes (Brindle) Newcomer were the parents of nine children, namely: Joseph, Frances, Mary, Melchor, John, Sarah, Richards, Ann and Benjamin F., the youngest son, who became a member of Company G, 84th Indiana Infantry, during the Civil War, and was killed at Pine Mountain, Georgia, June 18, 1864, while in the service of his country. His name will be found in the Roll of Honor published elsewhere in this History.

To the union of Benjamin and Frances (Newcomer) Shirk were born six children, namely: George W., who was, during the Civil War, a musician in Company C, 36th Indiana Infantry, and was mortally wounded at the battle of Chickamauga, Georgia, September 20, 1863, and died at his home in New Castle, after severe suffering, June 6, 1864; his name appears in the Roll of Honor published elsewhere in this History; Sophia J., now the wife of David W. Kinsey, cashier of the Citizens' State Bank of New Castle; John J., who was born June 3, 1851, and died January 26, 1897; William H., who died in 1892; Anna Rebecca, who is now the wife of Charles M. Harrison, Sioux Falls, South Dakota; and Mary F., who died in childhood. Of this family of six children only two are now living. The marriage and family of Mr. and Mrs. David W. Kinsey are fully mentioned in the sketch of Mr. Kinsey. Mr. and Mrs. Charles M. Harrison, of Sioux Falls, are the parents of three children, namely: Ruth, now Mrs. Frederick Powers, of Sioux Falls; Benjamin Thomas (called Ben Tom), of St. Louis, Missouri, where he is connected with the New York Life Insurance Company; and Florence, who is at home with her parents. John J. Shirk, who was a farmer and stockman, left a widow, Mrs. Barbara (Kinsey) Shirk, and two sons, George and Winters, all of whom are residents of New Castle. William H. Shirk, who was a druggist in New Castle at the time of his death, was an excellent young man and the soul of honor; he was attacked by a fatal disease to which he soon succumbed, and his death was sincerely mourned by his relatives and friends.

Mrs. Frances (Newcomer) Shirk died December 16, 1857, her married life covering the brief period of fifteen years. She was an estimable woman and was devoted to the contentment and happiness of her husband and children. One year after her death, October 25, 1858, Mr. Shirk was united in marriage with Mrs. Johanna F. Wood, widow of the late John F. Wood, who came to Henry County, bringing his wife and family with him in 1849, from Pennsylvania. He located at Hillsboro, then quite a village, where he engaged in mercantile business. He afterwards removed to New Castle and engaged in business there. He died in 1852. Mrs. Wood was the mother of three children by her first husband, namely: Kate, afterwards wife of William M. Pence, but now deceased; James, deceased; and John M., who has been for a number of years a resident of Cincinnati. Benjamin and Joanna (Wood) Shirk were the parents of two children: Martha O., who died in infancy; and Lois, who is a resident of New Castle. Mrs. Benjamin (Wood) Shirk was a loving mother to both her own children and to those of Mr. Shirk by his first marriage. She died September 15, 1903. Benjamin Shirk and both of his wives, together with the father and mother of Mrs. Benjamin (Newcomer) Shirk, are buried in South Mound Cemetery, as are also all of the deceased children, except James Wood, who is buried in the cemetery at Dayton, Ohio.

Benjamin Shirk was a faithful, earnest and consistent member of the English Lutheran Church. He was for many years superintendent, teacher and leader in the Sunday School, and was in all respects a clean, pure man. In politics he was a Republican and as long as he lived did effective work for his party and was honored by election to several positions of public trust. He was one of the oldest, in length of membership, of the members of the Independent Order of Odd Fellows, having joined Fidelity

Martin Kinsey

Lodge, Number 59, New Castle. In 1849. He filled all of the chairs of the lodge from the humblest to the most exalted and was regarded as an authority upon all questions touching the growth, strength and character of the order. In 1896 Mr. Shirk became vice-president of the Citizens' State Bank of New Castle, of which he was one of the original stockholders, and held that position until his death, September 6. 1893. The officers of the bank at a meeting held September 7, 1893, adopted the following resolutions upon his death:

"First. That in the death of Benjamin Shirk, one of the directors, and vice-president of this bank, the bank and the business community have met with an irreparable loss.

"Second. That his long and active career as a business man, a public officer and as an enterprising and public spirited citizen, a Christian gentleman, neighbor, husband, father and friend is worthy to be honored by the old, emulated by the young and affectionately cherished by all."

Mr. Shirk was also one of the original stockholders and a director of The First National Bank of New Castle. His connection with both of these banking institutions will be found in the chapter of this History relating to "Banks and Banking."

MARTIN KINSEY.

Martin Kinsey, eldest son and child of Lewis and Catharine (Shultz) Kinsey, was born June 12, 1839, on his grandfather's farm, which adjoined Hagerstown on the north and which is now a part of that town. Lewis Kinsey and wife lived on this farm during the first four years of their married life. Martin Kinsey remained at home with his parents on the different farms owned by them, as mentioned in the foregoing sketch, until 1864, when he was twenty-four years of age. During his boyhood he attended the country schools and spent one term at the New Castle Academy, when Professor Joseph L. Brady was principal. After he had reached man's estate he assisted his father in the cultivation and management of the farm, in which capacity he was an invaluable aid because of his great industry and practical knowledge in making the soil yield profitable returns. In his twenty-fourth year, March 19, 1864, he was married to Sarah, daughter of Joseph and Christena (Epperly) Replogle, at their home, one mile north of Hagerstown, Wayne County, the marriage ceremony being performed by the Reverend William Lindley. Soon after his marriage Mr. Kinsey bought what was then known as the Jacob Hoover farm, located in Liberty Township, a mile and a half east and north of Old Chicago, then a village, but now long since passed into innocuous desuetude. This farm contained one hundred and forty-five acres. After several years, or in 1878, Mr. Kinsey disposed of this place and purchased the Joseph Replogle farm, then owned by Abraham Replogle, a relative of Mr. Kinsey's wife. This body of land comprised one hundred and twenty acres, situated one mile north of Hagerstown, for which he paid $100 an acre. Subsequently he sold this farm to George Gephart and about the year 1890 purchased the Williams Nicholson farm, containing one hundred and forty acres, situated along the Dublin pike, two and one-half miles southeast of New Castle, and has since continued to reside there. It is a fine body of land, which the present owner has brought to a high state of cultivation. In addition to grain farming he devotes much care and attention to the raising of stock, in which he has been very successful. All of his life has been spent on the farm, and his opinion on all matters pertaining to the tilling of the soil and the raising of profitable stock is very highly regarded. Mr. Kinsey was reared in the faith of the German Baptist or Dunkard Church, and while not a member of that religious body, gives his cordial support to the church. He has always been a Republican and clings to the belief that he will continue to pin his faith to that political party so long as he lives. He cast his first vote for Abraham Lincoln for President in 1860 and rejoices in that fact. In that year he was a member of the "Wide Awakes" and participated in the great Republican demonstration at Middletown, when Thomas Corwin was the orator of the day and General Sol Meredith the grand marshal. He supported Lincoln, Grant and McKinley for two terms each and his last vote was cast for Theodore

Lodge, Number 59, New Castle, in 1849. He filled all of the chairs of the lodge from the humblest to the most exalted and was regarded as an authority upon all questions touching the growth, strength and character of the order. In 1896 Mr. Shirk became vice-president of the Citizens' State Bank of New Castle, of which he was one of the original stockholders, and held that position until his death, September 6, 1893. The officers of the bank at a meeting held September 7, 1893, adopted the following resolutions upon his death:

"First. That in the death of Benjamin Shirk, one of the directors, and vice-president of this bank, the bank and the business community have met with an irreparable loss.

"Second. That his long and active career as a business man, a public officer and as an enterprising and public spirited citizen, a Christian gentleman, neighbor, husband, father and friend is worthy to be honored by the old, emulated by the young and affectionately cherished by all."

Mr. Shirk was also one of the original stockholders and a director of The First National Bank of New Castle. His connection with both of these banking institutions will be found in the chapter of this History relating to "Banks and Banking."

MARTIN KINSEY.

Martin Kinsey, eldest son and child of Lewis and Catharine (Shultz) Kinsey, was born June 12, 1839, on his grandfather's farm, which adjoined Hagerstown on the north and which is now a part of that town. Lewis Kinsey and wife lived on this farm during the first four years of their married life. Martin Kinsey remained at home with his parents on the different farms owned by them, as mentioned in the foregoing sketch, until 1864, when he was twenty-four years of age. During his boyhood he attended the country schools and spent one term at the New Castle Academy, when Professor Joseph L. Brady was principal. After he had reached man's estate he assisted his father in the cultivation and management of the farm, in which capacity he was an invaluable aid because of his great industry and practical knowledge in making the soil yield profitable returns. In his twenty-fourth year, March 19, 1864, he was married to Sarah, daughter of Joseph and Christena (Epperly) Replogle, at their home, one mile north of Hagerstown, Wayne County, the marriage ceremony being performed by the Reverend William Lindley. Soon after his marriage Mr. Kinsey bought what was then known as the Jacob Hoover farm, located in Liberty Township, a mile and a half east and north of old Chicago, then a village, but now long since passed into innocuous desuetude. This farm contained one hundred and forty-five acres. After several years, or in 1878, Mr. Kinsey disposed of this place and purchased the Joseph Replogle farm, then owned by Abraham Replogle, a relative of Mr. Kinsey's wife. This body of land comprised one hundred and twenty acres, situated one mile north of Hagerstown, for which he paid $100 an acre. Subsequently he sold this farm to George Gephart and about the year 1890 purchased the Williams Nicholson farm, containing one hundred and forty acres, situated along the Dublin pike, two and one-half miles southeast of New Castle, and has since continued to reside there. It is a fine body of land, which the present owner has brought to a high state of cultivation. In addition to grain farming he devotes much care and attention to the raising of stock, in which he has been very successful. All of his life has been spent on the farm, and his opinion on all matters pertaining to the tilling of the soil and the raising of profitable stock is very highly regarded. Mr. Kinsey was reared in the faith of the German Baptist or Dunkard Church, and while not a member of that religious body, gives his cordial support to the church. He has always been a Republican and clings to the belief that he will continue to pin his faith to that political party so long as he lives. He cast his first vote for Abraham Lincoln for President in 1860 and rejoices in that fact. In that year he was a member of the "Wide Awakes" and participated in the great Republican demonstration at Middletown, when Thomas Corwin was the orator of the day and General Sol Meredith the grand marshal. He supported Lincoln, Grant and McKinley for two terms each and his last vote was cast for Theodore Roosevelt.

Mrs. Martin Kinsey's father, Joseph Replogle, came from Pennsylvania and her mother, Christena (Epperly) Replogle, came from Virginia. Both were of that sturdy, industrious stock that so largely aided in making Indiana a garden spot where almost impenetrable forests stood. The Replogles constituted a large family, who settled in Wayne and the eastern part of Henry counties. Joseph Replogle and Christena Epperly were married in Wayne County, near Centreville, where Sarah (Replogle) Kinsey was born March 6, 1842. Both her parents are dead. The names and dates of birth of the children of Martin and Sarah (Replogle) Kinsey are as follows: Lewis Elsworth, born November 1, 1864; Joseph Henry, born March 27, 1866; Charles, born November 1, 1867; Nevada Catharine, born March 17, 1869. She was married March 1, 1894, to Luther L. Campbell, at that time a merchant in New Castle, afterward located at Winchester, Randolph County; she died January 9, 1899; Jennie, born March 23, 1872, died January 31, 1877; Benjamin Franklin, born February 9, 1878, died April 18, 1883. All of the above who are deceased are buried in the German Baptist Cemetery near Hagerstown.

LEWIS ELLSWORTH KINSEY.

Lewis Elsworth Kinsey, now a popular business man of New Castle, spent his boyhood on his father's farm, finding time during that period to acquire a good common school education. In January, 1885, he accepted a position with The Citizens' State Bank of New Castle as bookkeeper, which he resigned in 1887 to take a like position with the firm of Baldwin, Roberts and Company, extensive pork packers in New Castle, and remained with them until they retired from the business in 1890. He then went to the Pacific coast and was in southern California and on Puget Sound for about two years. Returning to New Castle, he purchased the old established drug store, then and now located in the room adjoining that occupied by The Citizens' State Bank, April 1, 1892, which he has since conducted, and which under his careful and methodical management has continuously enjoyed a large and lucrative trade. Mr. Kinsey stands high in the business and social circles of New Castle. He is a member of Crescens Lodge, No. 33, Knights of Pythias, Independent Order of Red Men, Blue Lodge, No. 91, Ancient Free and Accepted Masons; No. 484, Benevolent Protective Order of Elks, and Court No. 21, of Ben Hur.

JOSEPH HENRY KINSEY.

Joseph Henry Kinsey remained with his parents on the farm until he reached early manhood, during that time attending the schools of the neighborhood. He took up the study of medicine while at home and afterward became a student in the office of Dr. Joseph M. Thurston, who then resided in Hagerstown. Later he graduated from the Physio-Medical College of Indianapolis and went from that institution to Richmond, where he began the practise of medicine. Dr. Joseph H. Kinsey stands deservedly high in his profession and has a very extensive practise. He built and resides in a handsome home in Richmond, where he is regarded as one of the substantial citizens of that city. He was married April 10, 1889, to Belle Bellis, the ceremony being performed by the groom's grandfather, Elder Lewis Kinsey. They have one child, a daughter named Ruth, now in her fifteenth year.

CHARLES KINSEY

has been for some time employed in the Krell-French Piano Factory in New Castle.

mely: George, Davault, Gasper, John

BIOGRAPHICAL SKETCH OF BENJAMIN FRANKLIN KOONS.

NATIVE CITIZEN, LEADING FARMER, INFLUENTIAL MAN.

It is not necessary that a man should have performed some great deed, formulated and brought to a successful conclusion some great work, or that he should have been especially active in public affairs to warrant the publication of a sketch of his life. It is the few who gain widespread fame or who rise far above their fellows in any locality. Nevertheless, the great majority have been workers in the world's vineyard, many of whom are still living and making their impress upon the communities with which they are identified. Benjamin Franklin Koons is such a man, whose life has been one of activity, chiefly in agricultural pursuits, to which he has brought a practical knowledge and understanding and in which he has shown a tenacity of purpose such as make him one of the leading farmers of Henry County and eastern Indiana.

The Koons family is a very large one and is especially numerous and prominent in the northeastern part of the county. The great-grandparents of Benjamin F. Koons were Davault Koons, a native of Pennsylvania, and Susan (Dicks) Koons, a native of Germany, who lost her first husband at sea while crossing the ocean to America. She sub-sequently married Davault Koons, and to their union were born three sons—Gasper, George and John. Gasper, who was born in Pennsylvania, November 8, 1759, married Mercy Presnall, also a native of Pennsylvania, in 1775. They had seven children, four sons and three daughters, namely: George, Davault, Gasper, John, Martha, Mary and one who died in infancy.

The mother of these children died and in 1797 the father, Gasper Koons,. married Abigail Piggott, a school teacher, the daughter of Jeremiah and Rachel Piggott. They were members of the Friends' or Quaker Church, and the marriage was according to the Friends' ceremony. To the union of Gasper Koons and Abigail Piggott were born twelve children, nine sons and three daughters; the eldest son died in infancy; the others were: Jeremiah, William, Nathan, Henry, Samuel, Joseph, Benjamin, Jesse, Hannah, Rachel and Susannah.

This family moved, about the year 1800, from Pennsylvania to North Carolina, where they settled near Bald Mountain. In the fall of the year 1808 the family left North Carolina and after traveling for fully six weeks, climbing mountains and fording streams and rivers, they arrived safely at Whitewater, near the then village of Richmond, Wayne County, Indiana, and there entered one hundred and sixty acres of land, which now lie just beyond the corporate limits, southeast of the city of Richmond. Gasper Koons and his wife were devout members of the Friends' Church and the considerable body of their co-religionists, who were already settled in Wayne County about Richmond, made the location seem an especially favorable one to them. They attended the meetings of their church at Richmond as long as their healths would permit. Gasper Koons died November 8, 1820, at the age of sixty-one years. His widow followed him to the grave in 1850, aged seventy-eight years. Both are buried in Earlham Cemetery, Richmond.

Joseph, the seventh son of Gasper and Abigail (Piggott) Koons, and father of the subject of this sketch, was born southeast of Richmond, near Greenmount, February 17, 1811. He was married to Lucinda Ray in 1834. She was the daughter of Thomas and Martha Ray, who came from Virginia, and after several removals, finally entered and located a tract of land one mile west of what is now the town of Mooreland, Henry County, Indiana, where he resided with his family until his death in 1845. On this farm his son, the well-known James Ray, of Blue-river Township, lived and died.

To Joseph and Lucinda (Ray) Koons were born the following named children: Sarah, Thomas, Benjamin F., the subject of this sketch; George R., Samuel, Joseph, Pleasant M., Hannah Louisa, John L. and Nancy Ellen. Of these children Benjamin F., George R., Pleasant M. and John L. are living. All of the deceased are buried in the Kissenger Cemetery, two miles north of Mooreland, except Joseph and Hannah Louisa, who are buried in the Mooreland Cemetery. Joseph Koons, the father, died November 10, 1878, and and his widow, Lucinda (Ray) Koons, died November 21, 1880. Both are buried in the Friends' Cemetery, near Franklin, Wayne County, Indiana.

BENJAMIN FRANKLIN KOONS.

Benjamin Franklin Koons, son of Joseph and Lucinda (Ray) Koons, was born November 23, 1839, on a farm two miles southwest of Mooreland, where he lived as boy and man until he moved in 1864 to a farm two miles southeast of Mooreland, where he has continuously lived to the present time. On June 27, 1861, he was married to Mahala, daughter of Jacob and Sophia Deardorff, who came from Ohio and entered the one hundred and sixty acres of land in Blue River Township now owned and occupied by Mr. Koons.

To the union of Benjamin Franklin and Mahala (Deardorff) Koons were born nine children, as follows: John L., James Albert, Thomas Benton, Newton Clay, Cora See, Charley, Harvey L., Robert H. and Perry O. These children are all living except the second son, James Albert, who died in early childhood and is buried in the Mooreland Cemetery by the side of his mother, who died June 21, 1900. John L. and Thomas Benton reside at Muncie, Indiana, where the former is engaged with Ball Brothers, glass manufacturers, and the latter is a member of the Muncie fire department. Both are married and have children. Newton Clay owns and lives on a farm two miles east of Mooreland with his wife and children. Cora See is the wife of Lorenzo D. Adamson and resides in New Castle. Charley, with his wife and one child, and his brother, Perry O., live with their father on the home place. Harvey L. lives one mile and a half south of Losantville, on one of the most beautiful farms in eastern Indiana; his wife, Ina (Thompson) Koons, died in July, 1905, leaving two children and a bereaved husband. Robert H. married Josie Stanley and resides in Mooreland, where he is engaged in business. Fifteen grandchildren contribute very materially to the happiness of Benjamin F. Koons.

Mr. Koons received his primary education in the typical log cabin school house, of which mention is so frequently made in this History. He afterwards, during the winters for several years, attended the common or district schools and worked on the farm in the summers. He also attended the Blountsville High School and sat under the teachings of Newton Kimball, who was afterwards a sergeant in Company I, 124th Indiana Infantry during the Civil War, and subsequently became a prominent physician, with a large practise, at Franklin, Wayne County, Indiana, where he died. He was buried at Blountsville.

After completing his education Mr. Koons himself became a school teacher, beginning when he was eighteen years of age and continuing in that profession for several years after his marriage, until he was past thirty years of age, teaching in the winter and farming during the summer. He then gave up teaching and turned his attention mainly to the settlement of estates, guardianship of orphan children and other business of like character. He was assignee of Clapper, Shaffer and Smith, pork packers, at New Castle, whose failure caused a large financial flurry in middle and northeastern Henry County, and he has been assignee, administrator, executor, guardian, etc., in a great number of cases, and all of his fiduciary duties have been faithfully and satisfactorily performed.

Mr. Koons has been a member of the German Baptist Church since 1863 and his wife, who joined the same church at the same time, continued in that faith until her death. He has been, almost from the beginning of his membership, a deacon in the church and has given freely of his means to its support. For a long time he has been identified officially and otherwise with the Old Settlers' Association of Henry County and is now the president of the organization. He is also a member of the Henry County Historical Society, of which he is now and has been for a number of years the treasurer. An old settlers' gathering or a meeting of the historical society would be incomplete without his cheerful and cheering presence.

Politically Mr. Koons has been from its organization an aggressive and uncompromising member of the Republican party. He was an alternate delegate to the Republican National Convention at Philadelphia in 1900 and to the Chicago convention of 1904. He has been a delegate to many county, district and State conventions, and has for many years been a leader in the politics of Blue River Township. He is a very competent writer and has contributed to the county and other papers exhaustive articles, mainly relating to the different phases of. the financial and political questions of the day. He is a student of affairs and has kept well abreast of current events and opinions and never takes up a subject without exhausting its possibilities.

Mr. Koons assisted in the first organization of the Indianapolis, New Castle and Winchester (electric) Railway and was the first president of the company, which consisted of Charles S. Hernly, Daniel Storms, Union B. Hunt and others. This road is now known as the Indianapolis, New Castle and Toledo (electric) Railway, and is frequently referred to as the "wild flower and honey bee route," and is now in process of construction. When completed it will extend from Indianapolis to New Castle and thence to Muncie, Winchester and Richmond in Indiana, its terminus being Toledo, Ohio.

Mr. Koons is a consistent advocate of temperance and a worker in its cause and it is largely through his influence that the saloon has been prevented from obtaining a foothold in the beautiful town of Mooreland. All in all, Mr. Koons has ever been an active and moving spirit in the affairs of Henry County. He is possessed of strong natural ability and has uniformly observed in all his life work the inspiring command, "Go forward."

BIOGRAPHICAL SKETCH OF ALBERT KRELL,

MANUFACTURER, BUSINESS MAN AND CHIEF PROMOTER OF THE KRELL-FRENCH PIANO COMPANY,
NEW CASTLE.

The man of high aims often reaches the goal of his ambition by persistent and intelligent effort, while the man of lesser ambition more often fails to accomplish anything of lasting value through lack of proper incentive. It is nature's law that the child
must creep before it can walk, but with the first step comes consciousness of a new power
and the bent of the child's mind is disclosed. One makes its first essay with firmness
and determination; another with fear and trembling; in the same family different dispositions manifest themselves, one child, possessed of push and vim, clinging tenaciously
to its rights and boldly elbowing its way through the world, while the more timid nature
is pushed to the wall. The bolder natures smile at reverses that overwhelm the shrinking brother and with redoubled effort press along the pathway to success.

This thought is illumined by the business career of Albert Krell, whose high aims
have been supplemented by a boldness in planning and an energy in executing great
enterprises that entitled him to be considered one of the great industrial leaders of the
day. Should his work now suddenly cease, the business enterprises with which his name
has become so intimately linked would stand as a lasting monument to his sagacity and
push.

THE KRELL-FRENCH PIANO COMPANY.

This company, which owes its existence and prosperity largely to the efforts of Mr.
Krell, is said to be the largest concern of its kind in the world, and the history of its
location in New Castle is an interesting one. At the time of its coming the town was
not dead, but there was little of that bustling activity which pervades towns of similar
size, but with larger manufacturing interests. By individual efforts a sentiment was
gradually aroused in the community in favor of such enterprises which finally crystallized in the organization of the New Castle Industrial Company, with such substantial
and public-spirited citizens as Charles W. Mouch, Eli B. Phillips, James S. McQuinn,
David W. Kinsey, Simon P. Jennings, Eugene H. Bundy, Lycurgus L. Burr as directors
and Charles S. Hernly as secretary, and its influence upon the future of the town is well
known.

Scarcely had this company been organized when it was advised that the plant of
the Krell-French Piano Company, then located at Springfield, Ohio, had been destroyed
by fire, February 10, 1902. Negotiations were at once undertaken and under certain
guaranties, which it is unnecessary to repeat in detail, the company moved from Springfield to New Castle and erected there the most modern and complete piano factory in the
world. One institution has brought another until the industrial prosperity of the town is
assured. The main building of this factory was originally sixty feet wide and ten hundred and fifty feet long and three stories high, all built of brick and with double and
triple floors. Besides the main building there were a boiler and engine house, a veneer
warehouse, a varnish house and three dry kilns. Additions have been made from time
to time and it is in contemplation at an early day to more than double the capacity of
this already great factory, a factory whose magnitude and importance is not fully realized by the town itself. The population of the town has more than doubled since the
coming of this business, and the factory now employs over five hundred workmen, and
its weekly pay-roll will average over six thousand dollars. Its present weekly output of
finished pianos is one hundred and twenty-five, which are shipped to all parts of the
United States and Canada, many also going to foreign lands, but the factory working
to its full capacity, is unable to supply the demand for its instruments.

The capital stock, common and preferred, of this company is $550,000. Its stock-
holders are chiefly individuals who are interested in the piano trade. The officers, all
men of long practical experience, were originally Albert Krell, president; Jesse French,
Sr., a capitalist of St. Louis, Missouri, first vice-president; Otto Bollman, second vice-president; Edwin B. Pfau, secretary, and H. Edgar French, treasurer.

BIOGRAPHICAL SKETCH OF ALBERT KRELL,

MANUFACTURER, BUSINESS MAN AND CHIEF PROMOTER OF THE KRELL-FRENCH PIANO COMPANY,
NEW CASTLE.

The man of high aims often reaches the goal of his ambition by persistent and intelligent effort, while the man of lesser ambition more often fails to accomplish anything of lasting value through lack of proper incentive. It is nature's law that the child must creep before it can walk, but with the first step comes consciousness of a new power and the bent of the child's mind is disclosed. One makes its first essay with firmness and determination; another with fear and trembling; in the same family different dispositions manifest themselves, one child, possessed of push and vim, clinging tenaciously to its rights and boldly elbowing its way through the world, while the more timid nature is pushed to the wall. The holder natures smile at reverses that overwhelm the shrinking brother and with redoubled effort press along the pathway to success.

This thought is illumined by the business career of Albert Krell, whose high aims have been supplemented by a boldness in planning and an energy in executing great enterprises that entitled him to be considered one of the great industrial leaders of the day. Should his work now suddenly cease, the business enterprises with which his name has become so intimately linked would stand as a lasting monument to his sagacity and push.

THE KRELL-FRENCH PIANO COMPANY.

This company, which owes its existence and prosperity largely to the efforts of Mr. Krell, is said to be the largest concern of its kind in the world, and the history of its location in New Castle is an interesting one. At the time of its coming the town was not dead, but there was little of that bustling activity which pervades towns of similar size, but with larger manufacturing interests. By individual efforts a sentiment was gradually aroused in the community in favor of such enterprises which finally crystallized in the organization of the New Castle Industrial Company, with such substantial and public-spirited citizens as Charles W. Mouch, Eli B. Phillips, James S. McQuinn, David W. Kinsey, Simon P. Jennings, Eugene H. Bundy, Lycurgus L. Burr as directors and Charles S. Hernly as secretary, and its influence upon the future of the town is well known.

Scarcely had this company been organized when it was advised that the plant of the Krell-French Piano Company, then located at Springfield, Ohio, had been destroyed by fire, February 10, 1902. Negotiations were at once undertaken and under certain guaranties, which it is unnecessary to repeat in detail, the company moved from Springfield to New Castle and erected there the most modern and complete piano factory in the world. One institution has brought another until the industrial prosperity of the town is assured. The main building of this factory was originally sixty feet wide and ten hundred and fifty feet long and three stories high, all built of brick and with double and triple floors. Besides the main building there were a boiler and engine house, a veneer warehouse, a varnish house and three dry kilns. Additions have been made from time to time and it is in contemplation at an early day to more than double the capacity of this already great factory, a factory whose magnitude and importance is not fully realized by the town itself. The population of the town has more than doubled since the coming of this business, and the factory now employs over five hundred workmen, and a weekly pay-roll will average over six thousand dollars. Its present weekly output of finished pianos is one hundred and twenty-five, which are shipped to all parts of the United States and Canada, many also going to foreign lands, but the factory working to its full capacity, is unable to supply the demand for its instruments.

The capital stock, common and preferred, of this company is $550,000. Its stockholders are chiefly individuals who are interested in the piano trade. The officers, all men of long practical experience, were originally Albert Krell, president; Jesse French, Sr., a capitalist of St. Louis, Missouri, first vice-president; Otto Bollman, second vice-president; Edwin B. Pfau, secretary, and H. Edgar French, treasurer.

The directors were Otto Bollman and Jesse French, Sr., both of St. Louis, Missouri; Charles L. Dengler, H. Edgar French, Albert Krell and Edwin B. Pfau, all of New Castle, Indiana; Henry Dreher, of B. Dreher and Sons, Cleveland, Ohio; E. E. Forbes, of E. E. Forbes Piano Company, Birmingham, Montgomery and Mobile, Alabama; William N. Grunewald Company, Limited, New Orleans, Louisiana; O. K. Houck Piano Company, Memphis, Tennessee, St. Louis, Missouri, and Little Rock, Arkansas; Harvey S. Patterson, C. C. Mellor Company, Pittsburg, Pennsylvania.

What has been said of this company merely outlines its resources and strength. The brains and energy which organized and managed this great industry belonged to Albert Krell, who was its president until the annual meeting of stockholders, August 10, 1905, when he declined to longer serve for the reason that he designed in the future to devote his attention to the manufacture and sale of the Krell Auto-Grand Piano. His arduous labors and his long and successful connection with the management of the Krell-French Piano Company were recognized by that organization upon his retirement from the presidency by the unanimous adoption of the following resolutions:

"Whereas, The phenomenal success of the Krell Auto-Grand Piano Company requires the entire time and attention of our president and he declines to become a candidate for re-election, be it

"Resolved, That, while we regret the necessity of such action, we rejoice in his success and wish him continued prosperity. We therefore hereby tender him our vote of thanks, as well as feel that the success of our company is in a large degree due to his ability and indefatigable industry. But we have induced him to remain in the board to be of such assistance as may be necessary to further the interests of the Krell-French piano."

The present officers of the company are: Jesse French, Sr., president; Otto Bollman, first vice-president; O. K. Houck, second vice-president; Jesse French, Jr., secretary; H. Edgar French, treasurer. Directors: Albert Krell, Henry Dreher, Henry Patterson, W. E. Grunewald, E. E. Forbes, Jesse F. Houck, Olney Davies, Otto Bollman, H. Edgar French, Jesse French, Sr., and O. K. Houck.

THE KRELL AUTO-GRAND PIANO COMPANY.

This company was organized in November, 1904, with the following officers: Albert Krell, president; Edwin B. Pfau, secretary and treasurer; L: A. Krell, vice-president; Peter Welin and Charles L. Dengler, directors. The Krell Auto-Grand Piano is already recognized throughout the civilized world as the acme of musical perfection in the piano line. The completeness of this instrument can hardly be realized except by one who has noted for many years the constant improvement and change going on in so many of the arts and lines of business pursuit. Of the inventor it may be said that like the poet he is born, not made. Who to-day remembers the first crude sewing machine and its predicted failure? Or what old printer forgets the ridicule that greeted the first typesetting machine? Yet the perfected sewing machine is with us to-day and the "lightning compositor" has given way to the Mergenthaler and Linotype machines. So with the typewriter and many other equally wonderful machines, but in none of the arts has there been wrought a more magical change than in that of piano making.

It is a far cry from the simple "spinet" of our mothers, the first one of which to come to Henry County was brought about the year 1835 among the household goods of William Henry, one of the earliest pioneers. The beauty, finish and tone of that "spinet," which is still in existence, compared with the instrument that has taken its place, is as a mouth organ to an Italian harp.

The Krell Auto-Grand Piano is, simply stated, a piano with an attachment which enables even the unskilled musician to manipulate the instrument so as to produce the simplest as well as the most difficult musical compositions for the benefit of himself and of others, and to do so in a manner equal or superior to that of accomplished players. This attachment, as its name implies, is automatic in its action, and all the performer has to do is to work the pedals and by means of stops to increase or decrease, as may be desired, the volume of tone of the instrument, a thing easily learned.

The attention of the musical world has been turned to this problem for years and many devices have been tried to bring about this result, but it has remained for the Krell Auto-Grand Piano Company to perfect the idea and to-day not only is their instrument recognized as the finest product of the skilled pianomaker, but the automatic attachment is considered the highest achievement of inventive genius in musical lines. Many people possessing a high appreciation of the harmony of sound are debarred by lack of musical training from the pleasures of music because they cannot get their fingers to perform the necessary work. For such the piano-playing attachment will produce the most classical music with a technique and finish surpassing the skill of the deftest of human fingers.

The Krell Auto-Grand Piano is a wonderful piece of mechanism, of new and handsome design, and no one looking at its beautiful exterior would imagine that behind it all lies hidden a power which only needs to be invoked to make the piano the prince of musical instruments. The inventor of this automatic attachment is Peter Welin, a musical genius, who has patented some of the most remarkable improvements in piano-players that the world has heard or seen. The Auto-Grand is his latest and greatest production and far excels all other piano-playing devices.

Edwin B. Pfau, formerly secretary of the Krell-French Piano Company, but now secretary and treasurer of the Krell Auto-Grand Piano Company, has been from his boyhood associated with the trade and manufacture of pianos. He is thoroughly versed in the business, knows all about the mechanism of the piano and in the discharge of his duties never loses sight of the two most important features—perfection and durability—of the instruments made and turned out by their great factory.

For the present the Krell Auto-Grand Piano will continue to be manufactured at the works of the Krell-French Piano Company, but it is the intention of its owners to build their own factory on their own ground, thus adding another great industry to those already established in New Castle. In direct reference to this statement a gentleman of observant mind and known soundness of judgment has given it as his opinion that "Mr. Krell's Auto-Grand attachment is worth a cool million of dollars, and I predict that in a few years he will be operating in New Castle a plant as large, if not larger, than the present Krell-French factory, devoted exclusively to the manufacture of the Auto-Grand. The attachment will in time be universally used."

The history of this splendid industry is the history of Albert Krell. Like many other industrial organizations which have had modest beginning, this has grown and waxed great through his fostering care and must ever remain indebted to his energy and push for its present prosperity. Mr. Krell is indefatigable in business and possesses great driving power. He likes to hear the engines' mighty throbbings and the humming of the machinery and to see the wheels turning round. He is all the time doing things himself, watching and overseeing the vast interests under his control.

ALBERT KRELL.

Albert Krell's genealogical record shows that his great-grandfather, Frederick William Krell, was born in 1774 and that he died in 1870, thus having lived for nearly one hundred years. He was a captain in the French army under the great Napoleon and participated in the famous Russian campaign of that illustrious conquerer in 1812, and on the retreat of the grand army from Moscow he was one of the comparatively few soldiers to escape with his life from the terrible deprivations and the dreadful horrors of that midwinter retreat. The grandfather of Albert Krell was Gustave Frederick William, born in 1800; died in 1886. Both of the above died and were buried in Prussia, now the leading State in the German Empire.

Mr. Krell's father was also named Albert Krell, and was born in Prussia in 1832 and died in Cincinnati, Ohio, January 5, 1900.

His wife, the mother of the subject of this sketch, was Alvina (Lindemuth) Krell, who was also born in Prussia and died in Cincinnati, Ohio, in February, 1866. Both of his parents are buried in Walnut Hills Cemetery, Cincinnati. They were the parents of seven sons and one daughter. All are now deceased excepting Albert Krell, the subject of this sketch, and are buried in Walnut Hills Cemetery.

Edwin B. Pfau

Albert Krell, the father, was a leading violinmaker of his time and as such had not only a national but a world-wide reputation. It is said that he and George Gemunder, the latter of New York City, were the only violinmakers of note who lived in the United States during the nineteenth century, and that as a matter of fact there is now no great violinmaker in this country nor in the old world. The violins made by both Mr. Krell and by Mr. Gemunder have an established reputation among connoisseurs and bring fabulous prices.

Albert Krell, the subject of this sketch, was born September 6, 1859, in Cincinnati, and it was there that he received his education and learned his trade as a pianomaker with his father, who was not only a great violinmaker, but had skilled knowledge regarding the mechanism of the piano and many other musical instruments. He was married December 26, 1883, in Cincinnati, Ohio, to Laura Amelia Pfau. Her grandparents on her mother's side were Peter and Wilhelmina Bogen. Her parents were John Michael and Wilhelmina (Bogen) Pfau. Albert and Laura Amelia (Pfau) Krell are the parents of two children, namely: Elsa, born November 21, 1884, and Meda, born September 29, 1887. They are very popular young ladies, prominent in social circles, well educated and highly accomplished. Mr. and Mrs. Krell have also an adopted son, Harold Alexander, the orphan child of Mr. Krell's brother Alexander.

Mr. Krell began pianomaking in 1889 at Cincinnati in company with his brother, Alexander Krell. They started in a small way, having their factory on the top floor of their father's place of business, Number 144 West Fourth Street. The business prospered and in time increased to such proportions that removal to larger quarters became advisable, and in 1890 the premises at Race and Canal streets were leased and the factory established there. Trade continued to increase so rapidly that in 1892 they bought a factory on Ninth, Harriet and Richmond streets, embracing two hundred feet on Harriet, running back two hundred and forty feet on Richmond and Ninth streets. Shortly after their removal to these new quarters Mr. Krell disposed of part of his interest in the factory in 1900 and in the succeeding year, 1901, went to Springfield, Ohio, where, in conjunction with several other parties, a large factory was started, which was then owned and conducted as it is now by the Krell-French Piano Company. "It is an ill wind that blows nobody good." Not long after the establishment of the piano factory at Springfield it was almost totally destroyed by fire, February 10, 1902, and soon afterwards moved to New Castle, Indiana, as above stated.

Although Mr. Krell is personally and financially interested in the Krell-French Piano Company and as anxious as ever for its growth and prosperity, he has, nevertheless, become especially identified with the Krell Auto-Grand Piano Company and is giving to that industry his undivided attention.

Though reared in the Lutheran faith, Mr. Krell is now a member of the Methodist Episcopal Church and, with his family, is a regular attendant upon its services. He is a member of the Masonic fraternity and politically is a strong adherent of the Republican party, giving that organization and its principles and policies his warmest encouragement and support.

EDWIN BOGEN PFAU.

Edwin Bogen Pfau, born June 2, 1867, is the brother-in-law of Albert Krell. He is a son of John M. and Wilhelmina (Bogen) Pfau, the former being a native of Germany and the latter a native of Cincinnati, Ohio. On June 11, 1889, Edwin B. Pfau was united in marriage with Stella S., daughter of Charles W. and Abbie (Brown) Longley. She was born in Sidney, Maine, June 12, 1868. Edwin B. and Stella S. (Longley) Pfau are the parents of three children, namely: Walter L., born October 20, 1891; Helen J., born December 26, 1893, and Mildred, born September 7, 1895.

Mr. Pfau was educated in the schools of Cincinnati and is a graduate of the well-known Woodward High School of that city. He was reared in the Lutheran Church, his parents being members of that great denomination. He is not himself a member of any religious organization, but usually attends the regular services of the Methodist Episcopal Church. He belongs to no secret societies or orders. He is a Republican in politics and uniformly supports the policies of that political organization.

74

Mr. Pfau is a practical accountant and obtained his start in life as accountant and business manager of Buhr, Wendte and Company, wholesale confectioners of Cincinnati, with whom he remained from 1884 to 1895. He then became bookkeeper and cashier of the Krell Piano Company, Cincinnati, which position he occupied until the organization of the Krell-French Piano Company, at Springfield, Ohio, in 1901, when he went to that company. He continued with them, as is related in the foregoing article regarding Mr. Krell, until the organization of the Krell Auto-Grand Piano Company, of which he is now secretary and treasurer, and to which his whole time is devoted.

It is a notable cicumstance that in 1896 Mr. Pfau was elected a director in the Krell Piano Company of Cincinnati, which position he has held from that time to the present. The success of the companies with which Mr. Pfau has been connected as accountant, director and officer is in large measure due to his careful, methodical and prudent business management.

J. W. Maxim

immense beds
oil and medici
colleges, unive
greatly enhanc
among the Sta
The wave
later years ha
attracted to th
possible lowest
East that broug
tle, Henry Cou
interests.
The Max
father of the
year 1750. Fi
grandfather of
about the yea
Ephraim and
Roland, Aud

Taxan

BIOGRAPHICAL SKETCH OF JOSIAH WARD MAXIM.

ONE OF NEW CASTLE'S EARLY MANUFACTURERS AND ENTERPRISING CITIZENS.

It is a far step from the town of Wayne, Maine, to New Castle, Indiana—from the "Pine Tree" to the "Hoosier" State; from "away down East" to the used· to be "away out West"; yet there are those who have made the venture and profited greatly thereby. Emigration from the far eastern States of Maine, Vermont, Connecticut, New Hampshire and Massachusetts to any part of Indiana, especially in the early times, was so infrequent as to be hardly worth mentioning. The movement of the people from those States somehow flowed in another direction, going largely to the northwestern States of Michigan, Wisconsin, Minnesota and later to Illinois, Iowa, Kansas and Nebraska. It was a different class of people who came in pioneer times to Indiana, being representatives, almost entirely, of Pennsylvania, Virginia, North Carolina, Tennessee, Kentucky and Ohio. In later years, however, when the country had been more fully settled and developed, other classes of immigrants came into the State, among them being a number from the old New England States.

In the meantime the Indiana wilderness had given way to splendid farms; a network of railroads had bound together all of the counties of the State; the discovery of immense beds of coal, of fine building stone, underground stores of natural gas, coal oil and medicinal waters led to great manufacturing enterprises; her public schools, colleges, universities and scientific institutions, all bearing a national reputation, had greatly enhanced the reputation of the State and placed it very close to the front rank among the States of the American Union.

The wave of literary activity that has swept over the State and characterized its later years has also disseminated the reputation of Hoosierland to far away points and attracted to the State the keen down-east Yankee looking for favorable locations and possible investments. It was this increased knowledge floating from the West to the East that brought Josiah Ward Maxim from Maine to Indiana. He located at New Castle, Henry County, where he has become identified · with its industrial, civic and social interests.

The Maxims came originally from England and Nathan Maxim, the great-grandfather of the subject of this sketch, was born at Wareham, Massachusetts, about the year 1750. He was a soldier of the Revolutionary War. His son, Ephraim Maxim, the grandfather of Josiah Ward Maxim, was born in Wareham, but moved to Wayne, Maine, about the year 1790. The grandmother, Susan Maxim, was a native of Massachusetts. Ephraim and Susan Maxim were the parents of nine children, namely: Ephraim, Silas, Roland, Andrew, Phoebe, Jemima, Sarah, Clarissa and Ruth. Ephraim (second), the father of the subject of this sketch, was born in Wayne, Maine, in 1800, and married Ruth Bellington, of Concord, New Hampshire, where she was born in 1809. They were married at Wayne in 1829 and to them were born the following children: Leonard H. (1830), Olive A. (1832), Luther (1834), Ephraim H. (1836), George A. (1839), Josiah Ward (1846) and Mary K. (1849).

Josiah Ward Maxim, more generally known as J. Ward Maxim, was born September 19, 1846, and was united in marriage with Florence E. Macomber (born in Winthrop, Maine, August 26, 1853) at Winthrop, December 22, 1878, and the fruits of this union were: Ethel V., born at Wayne, Maine, March 22, 1880; Helen B., born in New Castle, Indiana, April 19, 1884, and Edna L., born in New Castle, December 30, 1890.

J. Ward Maxim with his wife and one child, Ethel V., came directly to New Castle, Indiana, in 1882 from Buckfield, Maine, where he had been engaged in the handle business in partnership with the late Holman W. Waldron, under the firm name of Maxim·and Waldron.• In conjunction with Mr. Waldron he established a handle factory in New Castle, which commenced business January 1, 1883. The partners continued this business until the death of Mr. Waldron in 1888, when Mr. Maxim took· over the business and continued it alone until he disposed of it to William C. Bond in February, 1902. The handle business was a new one in New Castle and Henry County and in it Mr. Maxim was eminently successful. Touching the life and character of his partner,

Mr. Waldron, it may be said that he merited and received that recognition due to genuine worth from all those with whom he had business or social relations. During the Civil War he was a soldier in Company C, 23d Maine Infantry, and in Company E, 32d Maine Infantry. On page 580 of this History his military record will be found appropriately set forth. In this connection it is also worth while to mention the late George H. Maxim, who came to New Castle with his uncle, J. Ward Maxim, and who was during the later years of his young life foreman of the handle factory. He was born on Long Island, New York, and was married June 7, 1893, to Kate, daughter of Captain William F. Shelley, of New Castle, Indiana. They were the parents of one child, which died in infancy. George Maxim died April 17, 1903. He was an excellent young man, attentive to duty and held in the very highest esteem by his numerous friends and associates. He was a member of New Castle Lodge, Number 91, Ancient Free and Accepted Masons; New Castle Chapter, Number 50, Royal Arch Masons, and of New Castle Commandery, Number 44, Knights Templar. He was an enthusiastic working member and delighted in giving to the ceremonies of the order that character designed to make the strongest and most lasting impression.

Ethel V., the eldest daughter of J. Ward Maxim, is a very accomplished young lady, who was married to Joseph A. Greenstreet, June 18, 1902, the Reverend Chauncey King, the then pastor of the Methodist Episcopal Church of New Castle, performing the ceremony. This union has been blessed with one child, a daughter, Dorothy, born December 24, 1904, who is the pride of two households. Joseph A. Greenstreet is a native of Henry County and was for a number of years a teacher. He then became superintendent of the Henry County schools and prior to moving to Richmond, Indiana, where he now resides with his family, he was associated with Mark O. Waters on the New Castle Courier, of which they were editors and proprietors. He is now connected with Mr. Maxim in the Richmond Handle Factory, established in 1902. This concern at its organization consisted of J. Ward Maxim, Joseph A. Greenstreet and George H. Maxim. Mr. Greenstreet now has the sole management of the factory and is doing a very successful business.

Mr. Maxim, who seems to have a predilection for the handle business, is also interested in a handle factory at Lewiston, Maine, under the firm name and style of the Lewiston Handle Factory. This company has a capital of fifty thousand dollars. Its president is Frank B. Norris and its secretary and treasurer is Howard L. Holmes. These two with Mr. Maxim constitute the directorate. The concern is doing a very satisfactory business.

For several years it has been the custom of Mr. Maxim and family to spend the greater portion of their summers at his birthplace in Wayne, Maine, a very popular resort, located near the Androscoggin and Pocasset lakes, both beautiful bodies of water, where fishing is good and boating delightful.

Mr. Maxim has been, from the date of his arrival at New Castle, one of its foremost and active citizens. Every enterprise having for its object the advancement of the interests of the town and county has had his cordial support. He was the prime promoter of the erection of the Maxim Building. which bears his name, and he is the president of the Maxim Building Company, which was organized with a capital of twenty-five thousand dollars, and has twice that amount invested in this fine office building. It is a large, four-story, modern business block, the lower floors being used for mercantile purposes, the second and third floors for offices and the entire fourth floor by the Improved Order of Red Men, Iroquois Lodge, Number 97, New Castle, giving them large and spacious quarters, second in arrangement and fittings to no other in eastern Indiana. The building is a splendid addition to the business center of New Castle, being located immediately south of the public square between the Masonic Temple and the Alcazar Theater on the one hand and the well known Bundy House on the other. This building reflects credit upon the enterprise of Mr. Maxim and his associates.

Mr. Maxim is a member of the Methodist Episcopal Church and that denomination is largely indebted to him for the splendid edifice in which its members now worship. He is a member of New Castle Lodge, Number 91, Ancient Free and Accepted Masons; of New Castle Chapter, Number 50, Royal Arch Masons; of New Castle Commandery, Number 44, Knights Templar, and has taken the Scottish Rite degrees and is a member of the Mystic Shrine. He also belongs to Crescens Lodge, Number 33, Knights of Pythias, New Castle. Mr. Maxim was at one time the president of the First National Bank of New Castle and is now one of the directors of that institution and as such gives to its affairs his careful attention and supervision.

Mr. Maxim and his family occupy a delightful home on South Main Street, New Castle, where he dispenses that genuine hospitality characteristic of those who are reared in the old "Pine Tree" State. That he is a Republican in politics is emphasized by the fact that he is a native of that State which for long years grandly supported the great chieftain, James G. Blaine, of whom it has been often said that he was "the first of American citizens"; of that State about which it was so often proclaimed: "As goes Maine, so goes the Union," and that other equally famous political slogan, "Maine went hell-bent for Governor Kent."

Mr. Maxim is a relative of the world famous inventor, Hiram S. Maxim, who was born in Sangersville, Maine, February 5, 1840, being the son of Isaac W. and Harriet B. Maxim. This family was a very poor one and engaged in an incessant struggle for the necessaries of life. It is said that the mother was an "expert weaver, spinner, dyer and seamstress" and that the father was "a trapper, tanner, miller, blacksmith, carpenter, mason and farmer." Hiram, the son, early exhibited great mechanical skill and with no other tool than the ordinary Yankee jack knife produced such articles of his handiwork as to excite the wonder of the people of the little town where he was born. He became a coach builder, served some time subsequently in a machine shop, labored in a scientific instrument manufactory at Boston, likewise in the Novelty Iron Works Shipbuilding Company at New York, and during all this period of his life made a number of useful inventions, but the one which has secured the foremost place in the estimation of the public is the now celebrated Maxim rapid-fire gun, which automatically loads itself and fires seven hundred and seventy shots a minute. Out of this great invention came the Maxim-Nordenfelt Gun Company with a capital of nine millions of dollars. He has taken out numerous patents of various kinds, more than one hundred of them being for smokeless gunpowder and for petroleum and other motors and autocycles.

In concluding this Sketch of J. Ward Maxim it is pertinent to state that he is far seeing, practical and progressive. He keeps step with the march of improvement, watches with great interest the growth and prosperity of the town and county, the State and the Nation, and so far as possible liberally supports every movement having for its object the good of the community. He is noted for his vigor of mind and body, for his excellent social qualities and for his good citizenship.

BIOGRAPHICAL SKETCH OF JOHN RUSSELL MILLIKAN, HIS ANCESTORS AND
DESCENDANTS.

A PROMINENT AND INFLUENTIAL FAMILY OF HENRY COUNTY.

The Millikan family was one of the most prominent in the early history and development of Henry County and at the present day its numerous descendants are still contributing to the material, moral and intellectual life and prosperity of the county in no
small degree, particularly in that part of it which comprises Liberty Township, the largest and in some respects the most highly improved and richest section of the county.
This township is noted for its well-to-do citizens, past and present, many of whom have
had more than local fame and reputation, while of the present generation, a number have
reached positions of trust and responsibility in the community and have been honored
with unusual marks of public confidence. This family has always been distinguished by
certain marked characteristics, its several members displaying a quickness of perception,
soundness of judgment and determination to accomplish results, which have kept
them in the van of the county's progress.

The ancestors of the Millikan family were William and Eleanor Millikan, who belonged to the colonial period of American History. They were the parents of the following named children: Alexander, Elihu, George, Solomon, Samuel, Eli, father of the
late Nathan Millikan, William, Hannah, afterwards wife of William Canaday, and Nellie,
afterwards wife of Jesse Howell. All of the above are deceased.

Alexander Millikan, son of William and Eleanor Millikan, was born in North Carolina in 1788 and was taken by his parents to East Tennessee in 1793, where he grew
to manhood and married Elizabeth Russell. They were the parents of the following
named children: Edith, afterwards wife of Abraham Chaney, both deceased; John Russell; Matilda, afterwards wife of Wesley Stubblefield, both deceased; Hannah, afterwards
wife of George Koons, Sr., but now deceased; David, recently deceased; Eli B., deceased;
Jane, afterwards wife of Thomas J. Bland, but now deceased; Matthew R., a resident
of New Castle; Esther, widow of George H. Messick, now living in New Castle; Malinda,
widow of William Hobson, now living in Kansas; Keziah, now wife of Nathan F. Allen,
of Indianapolis; Polly, afterwards wife of William Hedrick, both deceased, parents of
Elihu Hedrick, one of the best known and most respected citizens of Liberty Township;
and one child which died in infancy.

In 1837, more than sixty eight years ago, Alexander Millikan (born January 18,
1788) immigated to Indiana and settled in Blue River Township, Henry County, about
six miles northeast of New Castle, on land which now adjoins the town of Messick, near
where his son, John R., and his daughters, Edith and Matilda, with their husbands, were
already located. He purchased some land on which a log cabin had already been erected
and a few acres of which had been cleared, and there he remained throughout the pioneer
days, redeeming the land from the wilderness and from time to time adding other acres
to his possessions until he had a farm second to none in the northeastern part of the
county. At last, full of years, he relinquished the farm and went to live in Liberty
Township with his son, David, where he remained until his death, August 18, 1880, at the
ripe old age of ninety-two years. He was buried in Batson Cemetery.

JOHN RUSSELL MILLIKAN.

During a life of more than sixty years in Henry County, John Russell Millikan, was
one of its best citizens. He was a fine type of that rugged band of North Carolinians and
East Tennesseans who at a very early period left the South, mostly because of their
antipathy to slavery, and made their way into the wilderness and established new homes
amid the forests of Indiana. He was born in Jefferson County, Tennessee, April 27,
1814. His father, Alexander, was of Scotch. and his mother, Elizabeth Russell, of Irish
descent. He was a splendid specimen, physically, of American manhood, and when, at the
age of twenty one years, he cut the cords that bound him to his Southern home, he was
in fine condition to battle his way to that success which eventually rewarded his energy.

AND INFLUENTIAL FAMILY OF HENRY COUNTY.

is one of the most prominent in the early history and devel.
d at the present day its numerous descendants are still con-
oral and intellectual life and prosperity of the county in no
that part of it which comprises Liberty Township, the larg-
e most highly improved and richest section of the county.
ts well-to-do citizens, past and present, many of whom have
d reputation, while of the present generation, a number have
ad responsibility in the community and have been honored
u confidence. This family has always been distinguished by
es. its several members displaying a quickness of percep-
and determination to accomplish results, which have kept
ity's progress.
illikan family were William and Eleanor Millikan, who be-
l of American History. They were the parents of the fol-
xander. Elihu. George. Solomon, Samuel, Eli, father of the
u. Hannah, afterwards wife of William Canaday, and Nellie,
eli. All of the above are deceased.
of William and Eleanor Millikan, was born in North Caro-
by his parents to East Tennessee in 1795, where he grew
izabeth Russell. They were the parents of the following
rwards wife of Abraham Chaney, both deceased; John Rus-
of Wesley Stubblefield, both deceased; Hannah, afterwards
t now deceased; David, recently deceased; Eli B., deceased;
omas J. Bland, but now deceased; Matthew R., a resident
of George H. Messick, now living in New Castle; Malinda,
w living in Kansas; Keziah, now wife of Nathan F. Allen,
vards wife of William Hedrick, both deceased, parents of
t known and most respected citizens of Liberty Township;
fancy.
y eight years ago, Alexander Millikan (born January 18,
and settled in Blue River Township, Henry County, about
sue, on land which now adjoins the town of Messick, near
is daughters, Edith and Matilda, with their husbands, were
l some land on which a log cabin had already been erected
een cleared, and there he remained throughout the pioneer
a the wilderness and from time to time adding other acres
d a farm second to none in the northeastern part of the
s, he relinquished the farm and went to live in Liberty
where he remained until his death, August 18, 1880, at the
rs. He was buried in Batson Cemetery.

JOHN RUSSELL MILLIKAN.

a sixty years in Henry County, John Russell Millikan, was
a a fine type of that rugged band of North Carolinians and
ery early period left the South, mostly because of their
their way into the wilderness and established new homes
He was born in Jefferson County, Tennessee, April 27,
and his mother, Elizabeth Russell, of Irish
physically of American manhood, and when, at the
that bound him to his Southern home, he was
success which eventually rewarded his energy.

When he cast his lot with the early pioneers of Henry County, he had a realizing sense of the herculean task before him in wresting a home from the stubborn wilderness, but he took up the task with a resolution and an energy to which everything must yield. Like that of all pioneers, his life consisted largely of clearing, cultivating and improving lands hitherto undisturbed by the hand of man. Of John R. Millikan, another has said: "His mission was labor and work was scarce. He did not repine at his surroundings. He had brawn and brains in happy alliance." He brought to Indiana, as his sole earthly possessions, a horse, ten dollars in cash, and a few clothes. His chief capital was strength and pluck, and they never failed him. He chopped cordwood at thirty seven and a half cents a cord, and did whatever came to his hand to do with all his might but always bearing in mind the saying, "there is a better day coming." Steadily but surely, as time came and went, prosperity smiled upon his way. He accumulated a large property and in doing so never forfeited the confidence and warm regard of his friends and neighbors. He was always accounted a good man and a good citizen, straight-forward, honest and sincere.

After coming to Indiana, he was first a farmer, then a farmer and blacksmith, and to these employments he afterwards added that of raising fine stock, principally cattle and hogs. He spent several Winters in killing hogs and packing pork, having for his associate in the business, and acting as agent for his friend, Abner D. Bond, of Cambridge City, Wayne County, whose subsequent death threw into Mr. Millikan's hands, as administrator, the settlement of his estate, valued at one hundred and fifty thousand dollars. He was also guardian of the children. He administered this trust for nearly twenty five years in a manner most satisfactory to the parties in interest and was honorably discharged by the court at the final settlement of the estate. Before being associated with Abner D. Bond as above stated he had gained experience in the business mentioned by having been connected in New Castle with Miles, Eli and Clement Murphey. Afterward, in 1874-5, he was for a short time associated in pork packing in New Castle with Smith, Clapper and Shaffer.

Mr. Millikan served as a justice of the peace for eight years with a fairness, firmness and impartiality that met with general approval. Politically, he was in accord with the Democratic party until the repeal of the Missouri Compromise in 1854, when he left that party and joined the Republicans. He was active in support of the latter and was often a delegate to its various political conventions. In 1868 he was elected a member of the lower house of the General Assembly of Indiana, and was re-elected in 1870, serving during the forty sixth and forty seventh regular and special sessions of that body. He was a watchful member and a careful legislator and discharged his duties to the complete satisfaction of his constituents.

He was one of the original stockholders of the Citizens' State Bank of New Castle, and assisted in its organization in 1873. He was made president of the bank and held that position until his death. He was a strong advocate of education, having himself felt the lack of instruction in his youth, and was one of the prime movers in securing the adoption of the system of free schools for the county.

On August 5, 1838, John Russell Millikan was married to Martha, daughter of George and Mary (Eller) Koons, who came to Indiana from North Carolina about 1820 and settled on Flatrock, in Liberty Township. John R. and Martha (Koons) Millikan were the parents of the following named children: James W., who sacrificed his young life in defense of his country, the record of whose service in the Civil War will be found in Chapter XVI of this History, and whose name also appears in the Roll of Honor for Henry County; Sarah Jane, wife of Thomas Benton Hunt; Davault K.; Mary Elizabeth, wife of Hamilton Z. Beck; Frank M.; Thomas Benton; Isaac N.; and one child which died in infancy.

Thomas Benton and Sarah Jane (Millikan) Hunt were the parents of: Clay C.; John M.; Clemmie, died at the age of sixteen years; James R.; and George W. (commonly called "Web"), who is the representative at Columbus, Ohio, of the Remington Typewriter Company. Clay C. Hunt has for a number of years been identified with the political and social history of Henry County and is now the Register in Bankruptcy for the district composed of the counties of Delaware, Fayette, Franklin, Hancock, Henry,

Randolph, Rush, Shelby, Union and Wayne, with his principal office at New Castle. James R. Hunt is a well known traveling salesman of Indiana, who resides at New Castle, and John M. Hunt lives with his parents on the farm in Liberty Township.

Davault K. Millikan was born May 7, 1844, on the farm of his father in Hancock County, Indiana, where his parents lived for a short time. He married Gertrude, daughter of the late William L. Boyd, a one-time prominent citizen of Henry County. To this marriage have been born two children, a son, Glenn R., and a daughter, Florence.

Hamilton Z. and Mary Elizabeth (Millikan) Beck are the parents of Ray M. Beck, who resides at Indianapolis, where he is connected with the Smith Premier Typewriter Company, and Frank Willard Beck, who resides at Fort Wayne, where he represents the Smith Premier Typewriter Company in seven counties of northeastern Indiana.

Isaac N. Millikan is a prominent agriculturist and resides on the old home farm in Liberty Township. His wife, Narcissa, is a daughter of James M. and Pamelia (Hunt) Boyd, pioneers of Henry County. They are the parents of one living child, Imogene, born January 16, 1889. Two children, Margaret and Wayne, died in infancy.

The home life of John R. Millikan and wife was marked by real happiness. He was a loving husband and father and his children still do honor to his memory, sanctified by a thousand kindnesses. She was a pattern of wifely devotion and by precept and example taught the beauty and holiness of a Christian life. Under the care of this good woman, the children learned the lessons of virtue and morality which have marked their footsteps through life.

In 1881, Mr. and Mrs. Millikan left their delightful home in the country, where they had lived so long and so happily, and moved to New Castle, where they continued to reside until their deaths. They were for many years members of the Christian Church, to which large and influential religious body they gave their earnest support. Mr. Millikan was a member of the Old Settlers' Association and of the Henry County Historical Society. He served as president of each of those organizations and always took great interest in their maintenance and support.

One of the most pleasing incidents in the long lives of Mr. and Mrs. Millikan was the observance of their golden wedding, August 5, 1888. This event was celebrated at the home farm in Liberty Township and was attended by more than two hundred relatives and friends. An elaborate dinner was served at six long tables, each accommodating twenty six guests, and each presided over by one of their six surviving children, Mrs. Thomas Benton Hunt, Mrs. Hamilton Z. Beck, Davault K., Frank M., Thomas Benton and Isaac N. Millikan.

John R. Millikan died September 12, 1895, and his wife, Martha (Koons) Millikan, died June 25, 1900. Both are buried in Batson Cemetery, Liberty Township. He lived some years beyond the allotted three score and ten of man and his loss was most deeply and sincerely mourned by a large circle of relatives, neighbors and friends. The directors of the Citizens' State Bank of New Castle, among others, expressed the sentiment of the community at his loss in the following resolutions:

"Resolved, that in his long career of nearly sixty years spent in the county as mechanic, farmer, business man and banker, legislator, public spirited citizen, husband, father, neighbor, friend and Christian gentleman, he has ever been actuated by noble impulses and has maintained the strictest integrity of purpose and character. Able, honest, industrious and sincere, his life has been successful and has earned for him and he has received the respect and love of the entire community. His career is worthy the emulation of old and young. He has walked in virtue's path and his sun has set in peace."

During the Civil War, he was very active in support of the government and was one of the trusted advisers of Governor Morton. In addition to sending his own son to the front, he aided in recruiting for the army and was solicitous of the welfare of the wives and children of those who were serving their country in the ranks. Up to the time of his death his children all resided in the same neighborhood with him which was a source of great consolation and enjoyment to him. It will be noted, too, that up to the present time there have been only two deaths among his children.

Frank M. Millikan

father's far... ...rty Township... ...Indiana, nea
son of John M... ...former of Sc
of German de... ...c. Millikan... ...his ancestry, ...
sessing in gr... ...those ...ments of ...rves and brawn
and ennoblin... ...one of life and in
of citizenship.

He receiv... ...that ... in common schools of
academies of N... ...Salketup... ...institutions were
their societies of... ...His Millic for
tracted the atte...
elected to the ...
Academy. He p...
farm and attending...

While the a... ...were than the college, youn...
cation made us f... ...b.c.., besides he had acquired
nature which has... ...greatly to his success in life—som
in the university on... ...ad for which no amount of Greek
To read men and fa... ...r motives is to a certain extent
adds largely to such... ...ents, and in business it is a qualifi
gree valuable, preve... ...mize mistakes and often so...ma no
human affairs. Mr... ...man's ambition was to be one of t
attending ... her sch...
tention of Thomas ...
he becaus... ...ep...
and Thomas ... How...
as prom... business   ...ctanti...
the people appreci...   ...idence of wh...
Henry County, wh...   ...ted him for as own... .y
plurality over his c...   ...s when to l i...
afterwards elected

Mr. Millika...   ...been a stude...
tering zeal for ...   of his owe.
1884 he was appi...
in that capacity ...
1898. He was l...
chairman of the
identified with   ...sitions of P...tic...

Frank M. Millikan

FRANK M. MILLIKAN.

(*Son.*)

Frank M. Millikan, a citizen of Indianapolis, was born December 2, 1851, on his father's farm in Liberty Township, Henry County, Indiana, near New Castle. He is the son of John R. and Martha (Koons) Millikan, the former of Scotch-Irish and the latter of German descent. Mr. Millikan is fortunate in his ancestry, no race combination possessing in greater degree those elements of brain and brawn which exert a healthy and ennobling influence in solving the problems of life and in elevating the standard of citizenship.

He received his early education in the common schools of Henry County and the academies of New Castle and Spiceland. These institutions were semi-collegiate and had their societies of which he was a member. His aptitude for acquiring knowledge attracted the attention of his teachers, and at the early age of seventeen years he was elected to the position of teacher, over one of his then preceptors in the New Castle Academy. He engaged in teaching for several terms, meanwhile working on his father's farm and attending the academies to secure a more thorough education.

While the academy rated lower than the college, young Millikan's business education made up for every deficiency, besides he had acquired a knowledge of human nature which has contributed greatly to his success in life—something that is not found in the university curriculum, and for which no amount of Greek or Latin is a substitute. To read men and fathom their motives is to a certain extent intuitive, but. experience adds largely to such acquirements, and in business it is a qualification in the highest degree valuable, preventing serious mistakes and often solving most complex problems in human affairs. Mr. Millikan's early ambition was to become a lawyer. He contemplated attending a law school for that purpose, but his business qualifications attracted the attention of Thomas S. Lines, ex-representative and treasurer-elect of Henry County, and he became his deputy treasurer, serving in that capacity also under William S. Bedford and Thomas I. Howren, succeeding treasurers, in which position he became well known as prompt in business and courteous in demeanor, qualities of head and heart which the people appreciated, an evidence of which was manifested by the Republicans of Henry County, who nominated him for county treasurer, April 1, 1878, by a large plurality over his competitors, when but twenty six years of age, to which office he was afterwards elected.

Mr. Millikan has always been a staunch Republican. He has worked with unfaltering zeal for the welfare of his party, and his abilities have been appreciated. In 1884 he was appointed a member of the Republican State Executive Committee, serving in that capacity and as secretary of the Republican State Committee until January, 1898. He was its secretary from July, 1889, to January, 1894, of that period, and was chairman of the executive committee in the great campaign of 1896. He was closely identified with both nominations of President Harrison in the campaigns of 1888 and 1892, and likewise with the nomination and election of William McKinley as president in 1896. In the Republican State Convention of 1896, Mr. Millikan was elected delegate-at-large from Indiana to the St. Louis Convention by a large representative vote, receiving the full delegate vote of twenty eight counties and one half or more of the delegate vote of twenty five other counties, an evidence of popularity and confidence of which, he might feel justly proud; but Mr. Millikan, having chosen business pursuits for his life work, has not sought, by election or appointment, preferment in political life.

In December, 1893, he accepted the responsible position. of special loan agent for Indiana of the Northwestern Mutual Life Insurance Company, of Milwaukee, Wisconsin, which position be still occupies, lending a million or more dollars annually for said company, whose business has prospered in his field until the aggregate of its loans in the State is from five to six millions of dollars. Such facts bear eloquent testimony regarding Mr. Millikan's business qualifications and his fealty to the great institution which he represents.

Mr. Millikan is a man whose superb physique would attract attention anywhere, and bespeaks robust health, incalculable endurance and application to business, and these are characteristic attributes of him. He is a member of the Columbia Club of Indianapolis. In social life he responds to all its amenities in a way that makes his beautiful home on North Delaware Street, Indianapolis, the center of elegant refinement.

On September 16, 1874, Mr. Millikan was married to Emma F. Boyd, daughter of William and Hannah (Peed) Boyd, of Henry County. One son, Harry Boyd Millikan, blessed this union, who as a member of the 27th Battery, Indiana Volunteers—old Battery A, of Indianapolis—under Captain Curtis, served his country creditably in the war with Spain, and had a taste of soldier life in Porto Rico. Mrs. Millikan, the mother of Harry, died August 22, 1888. On February 25, 1897, Mr. Millikan married Elma Elliott Barbour, daughter of Evans Elliott, deceased, who was a Mexican War soldier, and who died a merchant, resident at Shelbyville, Indiana.

Honorable and upright in all his dealings, blessed with a competency, Mr. Millikan's career has been bright in business as well as in a political way, and socially he and his family stand deservedly high, having many friends throughout the State and country. He has proved himself a worthy and influential citizen in all respects, and being yet comparatively a young man, has before him a future in which still further to emulate those attributes of character which make one esteemed and honored by one's neighbors and fellow citizens.

He is a member of Crescens Lodge, Number 33, Knights of Pythias, New Castle, Indiana, it being a matter of pride with him to keep his membership in his old home lodge, and was a trustee of the lodge from 1884 until he took up his legal residence in Indianapolis. While serving as a trustee the financial condition of the lodge, largely through his efforts, improved to such an extent that the order undertook the construction of and completed its magnificent building in New Castle. From the foregoing it will be seen that Mr. Millikan's business and political associations in the Capital City date back nearly twenty years, yet he did not give up New Castle and make his legal residence in Indianapolis until 1897, soon after his second marriage. A sketch is appended to this article relating to Emma Florence (Boyd) Millikan and her ancestry. Also appended is a sketch of their son, Harry Boyd Millikan.

THOMAS BENTON MILLIKAN.

(Son.)

Thomas Benton Millikan, the fourth son of John R. and Martha (Koons) Millikan, was born on his father's farm in Liberty Township, Henry County, Indiana, March 28, 1854. He was reared on the farm and as a boy did his proper share of the farm work. He obtained his early education in the common or district school and afterwards attended the public schools of New Castle, at the time they were under the efficient direction of Professor George W. Hufford, now of Indianapolis, and for many years a teacher in the Shortridge High School of that city. Mr. Millikan also attended the Holbrook Normal School at Lebanon, Ohio. His school days ended in 1874 and in September of that year, he entered the service of the Citizens' State Bank of New Castle, as assistant cashier.

In 1891, when James N. Huston, of Connersville, Indiana, resigned the treasurership of the United States and Enos H. Nebeker, of Covington, Indiana, was appointed to succeed him, the latter selected Thomas B. Millikan as his representative to count with others the cash in the United States Treasury, preliminary to the transfer of the office to Mr. Nebeker. This selection was highly complimentary to Mr. Millikan, who accepted the trust and spent the time from May 20 to July 1, 1891, in Washington, D. C., ascertaining the balance in the treasury and during that period handled funds or their equivalent, amounting to over $614,000,000.

From 1894 to 1902, both inclusive, he served as the State Bank Examiner of Indiana, an office, the duties of which are very onerous and responsible, involving a complete examination into the condition of each of the several State banks. Mr. Millikan discharged the duties of this position with such signal ability that during his eight years' incumbency only one or two such institutions of the State failed in business.

ietic attributes of him. He is a member of the Columbia Club of
social life he responds to all its amenities in a way that makes his
North Delaware Street, Indianapolis, the center of elegant refinement.
16, 1874, Mr. Millikan was married to Emma F. Boyd, daughter of
ah (Peed) Boyd, of Henry County. One son, Harry Boyd Millikan,
who as a member of the 27th Battery, Indiana Volunteers—old
napolis—under Captain Curtis, served his country creditably in the
and had a taste of soldier life in Porto Rico. Mrs. Millikan, the
died August 22, 1888. On February 25, 1897, Mr. Millikan married
our, daughter of Evans Elliott, deceased, who was a Mexican War
and a merchant, resident at Shelbyville, Indiana.
upright in all his dealings, blessed with a competency, Mr. Milli-
en bright in business as well as in a political way, and socially he
and deservedly high, having many friends throughout the State and
proved himself a worthy and influential citizen in all respects, and
lively a young man, has before him a future in which still further
tributes of character which make one esteemed and honored by one's
w citizens.

er of Crescens Lodge, Number 33, Knights of Pythias, New Castle,
matter of pride with him to keep his membership in his old home
cause of the lodge from 1884 until he took up his legal residence
his serving as a trustee the financial condition of the lodge, largely
improved to such an extent that the order undertook the construction its magnificent building in New Castle. From the foregoing it
Millikan's business and political associations in the Capital City
many years, yet he did not give up New Castle and make his legal
residence until 1897, soon after his second marriage. A sketch is
relating to Emma Florence (Boyd) Millikan and her ancestry.
sketch of their son, Harry Boyd Millikan.

THOMAS BENTON MILLIKAN.

(Son.)

Millikan, the fourth son of John R. and Martha (Koons) Millikan,
her's farm in Liberty Township, Henry County, Indiana, March 28,
on the farm and as a boy did his proper share of the farm work.
his education in the common or district school and afterwards
schools of New Castle, at the time they were under the efficient
of George W. Hufford, now of Indianapolis, and for many years a
bridge High School of that city. Mr. Millikan also attended the
school at Lebanon, Ohio. His school days ended in 1874 and in
he entered the service of the Citizens' State Bank of New
Castle.
James N. Huston, of Connersville, Indiana, resigned the treasurership and Peter J. Nybaker, of Covington, Indiana, was appointed
and selected Thomas B. Millikan as his representative to count
the New United States Treasury, preliminary to the transfer of the
This selection was highly complimentary to Mr. Millikan, who
spent the time from May 20 to July 1, 1891, in Washington, D. C.,
here the treasury and during that period handled funds or their
of over $614,000,000.
both inclusive, he served as the State Bank Examiner of
the duties of which are very onerous and responsible, involving a
into the condition of each of the several State banks. Mr.
the duties of this position with such signal ability that during his
they only one or two such institutions of the State failed in

Mr. Millikan's long familiarity with the banking business was very useful to him as State Bank Examiner and as the personal representative of Mr. Nebeker in taking over the funds of the United States Treasury. While making these several incursions into other fields, he retained his position with the Citizens' State Bank and counts thirty two years of continuous service with that institution, during all of which time he has been associated with Mr. David W. Kinsey, the cashier of the bank. It means a great deal to be thus identified for so many years with a single business, especially when it is a bank. The continued trust and confidence of the stockholders and depositors and the esteem of the general public have been uniformly extended to him during that long period of time and his best years have been freely given to the growth and prosperity of that institution. He has never lost an opportunity to advance its interests and is entitled to no small measure of credit for the popularity which the bank enjoys.

Aside from his duties as a banker, which ordinarily absorb the energy of the individual engaged in that pursuit, his life has been a busy one. He is a man of positive character and has made his influence felt not only within the boundaries of his home county but throughout the State. He is animated by a laudable ambition for the widest public usefulness and his motto has always been, "do something all the time." He is a man of even temper and calm and deliberate in his actions, with a pleasing deportment which enables him to smooth over the rough places and to avoid unpleasant antagonisms.

Ever since attaining his majority, he has been a member of the Republican party and very active in support of the party principles and policies. In the Republican State Convention of 1902, he was a prominent candidate for the nomination of Treasurer of the State of Indiana. There were four candidates for this position and though Mr. Millikan was unsuccessful in his candidacy, he stood next in order on the ballot to the winner of the nomination. He has been for twenty two years continuously a member of the Henry County Republican Central Committee. He is still comparatively a young man and with his assured standing in financial and political circles, his future career bids fair to equal, if it does not surpass, that of any of his contemporaries. He is an attendant upon the services of the Christian Church and is a member of the fraternal orders, belonging to Crescens Lodge, Number 33, Knights of Pythias, of which he served for several years as trustee; he is also a member of Iroquois Tribe, Number 97, Improved Order of Red Men, and of New Castle Lodge, Number 484, Benevolent Protective Order of Elks.

On October 26, 1877, Thomas Benton Millikan and Alice, daughter of the late James C. and Martha Jane (Boyd) Peed, were united in marriage, the ceremony being performed by Elder William J. Howe, of the Christian Church. James C. Peed was the son of the late well known James Peed, and Martha Jane (Boyd) Peed was the daughter of Robert and Narcissa Boyd, old settlers of Liberty Township, Henry County, and a sister of James M. Boyd, now on the staff of the rural route carriers, with headquarters at New Castle.

Thomas B. and Alice (Peed) Millikan were the parents of three children, namely: John R., born September 8, 1884, who is now an employe of the Citizens' State Bank of New Castle; Louise, born April 5, 1892; and Martha Janet, born March 10, 1897; the daughters are each accomplished far beyond their years and are possessed of delightful dispositions, happy amid their pleasant surroundings and the pride of their father, who since the death of their mother has given to them and to their education his loving and devoted attention. They are admired and beloved by all who know them.

Alice (Peed) Millikan, his beloved wife, died July 25, 1902. She joined the Flatrock Christian Church in 1870. She was educated in the country schools of Liberty Township and in the New Castle High School. In 1874-5 she taught school in the Boyd school house in Liberty Township. She was a woman of high character but of a domestic disposition and was wrapped up in the happiness of her family; and when the light of her life went out, grief and sorrow filled the household; she too rests in that most beautiful of rural cities of the dead, Batson Cemetery, where, with but one or two exceptions, all of the dead of the Millikan family are buried. Further reference might be made to the Peed family and to the ancestry of Mrs. Alice (Peed) Millikan, but as the

civil history of Liberty Township can never be properly considered nor written without
extended notice of the Peed and Boyd families, further reference to them is not made
here.

ANCESTRY OF EMMA FLORENCE (BOYD) MILLIKAN.

The Boyd family came originally from Mason County, Kentucky, at an early day
and settled in Wayne County, Indiana, near the village of Jacksonburg. The head of
the family in Wayne County was Samuel Boyd, who was the father of five sons and six
daughters. One of the sons was named Robert, born October 24, 1798, who moved from
Wayne to Henry County in 1826, prior to which time he was married in the former
county to Narcissa Stevenson. He located in Liberty Township, Henry County, six
miles southeast of New Castle, which locality has ever since been known and recognized
as the Boyd neighborhood. It was here that Robert Boyd and his estimable wife, Narcissa (Stevenson) Boyd, born November 1, 1796, lived until their respective deaths.
Robert Boyd died February 22, 1853, and his wife died October 20, 1885. Both are
buried in the Batson Cemetery. They were the parents of six children, three sons and
three daughters. One son, Alcander, died in infancy. The other children were William
L., James M., Martha Jane, afterward wife of James C. Peed; Louisa, who after the
death of her sister, Martha Jane, married her husband, James C. Peed; and Mary, who
married Henry T. Bond, of Wayne County. All of the above named are dead, except
Henry T. Bond, who still resides in Wayne County, near Jacksonburg, and James M.
Boyd, who is now a resident of New Castle, and connected with the rural route mail
service.

William L. Boyd, eldest of Robert and Narcissa (Stevenson) Boyd's children, was
born March 12, 1822, and was married first to Hannah Ann, daughter of the late well
known James Peed, father of Evan H. Peed, of New Castle, August 18, 1846. They were
the parents of Emma Florence Boyd, who subsequently became the wife of Frank M.
Millikan. She was born at the farm home east of New Castle, October 18, 1850, and
died at her home in New Castle, August 22, 1888. Her mother, Hannah Ann (Peed)
Boyd, died October 28, 1852, when Emma was but two years of age. Frank M. Millikan
and Emma F. Boyd were married September 16, 1874, and to them was born one son,
Harry B., now a resident of Indianapolis. Following the death of his first wife, William L. Boyd was again married, his second wife being Martha J. Hixson, of Daviess
County, Indiana. She died and he subsequently married Harriet A. Carter, of Henry
County, January 31, 1865. The latter still survives her husband, who died August 12,
1898, and she now resides at her well appointed home on South Twelfth Street, New
Castle. William L. Boyd, aside from his daughter, Emma Florence (Boyd) Millikan,
was the father of Augustus, born November 20, 1848; Gertrude, born November 1,
1856, now Mrs. Davault K. Millikan; Anna Martha, born November 23, 1862; Lynn C.,
born April 7, 1868; Horace W., born May 22, 1870; and Walter H., born February 16,
1882. All of the foregoing children are now living in New Castle, except Augustus, who
resides in Columbus, Indiana, and Walter H., who resides on the old home farm in
Liberty Township. In private as well as public life, William L. Boyd was the ideal
citizen. He was a model farmer and public spirited man. When called upon to serve
the people in an official capacity, he discharged the duties appertaining to the office with
the same fidelity and zeal as characterized his whole life. He was one of Nature's
noblemen every day in the year. Among the public duties he performed, were those of
a member of the board of county commissioners, as is shown by the register of Henry
County officials elsewhere in this History, and during the Civil War, he was military
agent for Liberty Township, a highly important position.

Too much cannot be said in praise of the sweet, gentle and saintly character of
Emma Florence (Boyd) Millikan. Deprived of a mother's love and protection at an
early age, the great responsibilities of caring for her father's household, on the death
of his second wife, devolved upon her when she was twelve years old, but with a brave
heart she took up the duties and carried forward the work in all of its departments
with skill beyond her years. She was the light and life of the household and her young
womanhood was crowned with deeds of love and labor performed for those near and

marriage
denomina
her memb
ƒu 186
well remem
the

n val to New Castle sl
loyal member
h the Flatrock chur
attended the New C
ducator the Reveren
emy when Professo

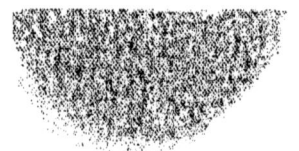

dear to her. In the few brief years of wifehood and motherhood that were allotted her, she was all in all, so that when Death claimed her, it was hard, indeed, for those who loved her so to realize that her bright smile and cheery words and loving kindnesses were gone from their lives forever, and as was said by one of the members of the Woman's Working Society of the Christian Church, of which she was a devoted mem. ber, "the voice of one of our sweetest singers is hushed to earth's music. Her remains as well as those of all of the above who are deceased are buried in the Batson Cemetery.

In September, 1867, she united with the Christian Church at Flatrock and after her marriage and removal to New Castle she was an attendant and supporter of the same denomination there and a loyal member of its societies but until her death she retained her membership with the Flatrock church with which she first pledged her faith to God.

In 1868-9 she attended the New Castle Academy, then under the direction of that well remembered educator, the Reverend Henry M. Shockley. In 1870-1 she taught in the New Castle Academy when Professor George W. Hufford, now of Indianapolis, was principal. In the Winter of 1871-2 and again in 1872-3, she taught school at Millville, in Liberty Township, being associated as teacher in the school for both terms with her future husband, Frank M. Millikan. In the Summer of 1872, she taught a private or subscription school at Millville. Prior to the winter school at Millville, in 1871-2, she taught two subscription schools in her home neighborhood at the old Devon church.

. No woman ever lived in Henry County who left a wider circle of friends than Emma Florence (Boyd) Millikan. To know her was to love her.

HARRY BOYD MILLIKAN.

(*Grandson.*)

Harry Boyd Millikan, son of Frank M. and Emma (Boyd) Millikan, was born in New Castle, Indiana, June 28, 1875. After reaching school age, he began his education in the public schools of New Castle. His mother died August 22, 1888, and Harry resided with his cousin, Clay C. Hunt, for about two years, and then with his grandfather, John R. Millikan, still continuing his studies in the public school until the Fall of 1894, when he entered Miami University at Oxford, Ohio, where he remained during two collegiate years, at the expiration of which he joined his father in Indianapolis, the latter having taken up legal residence there in 1897. Young Millikan at once began a business career and was appointed to the responsible position of general agent of the National Surety Company of New York for the State of Indiana in August, 1897, and was the first general agent that company had in this State. Early in 1898 he joined the Indiana Militia and became a private in Battery A of the Indiana National Guard. When the Spanish-American War began, this battery became the 27th Indiana Battery of Light Artillery, U. S. V., of which James B. Curtis, of Indianapolis, formerly speaker of the Indiana House of Representatives, was the captain. Briefly the history o. this battery is as follows:

The 27th Battery of Light Artillery, Indiana Volunteers, was Battery A, 1st Artillery, Indiana National Guard. The battery arrived at Camp Mount, Indianapolis, April 26, 1898, under orders from the Governor, for the purpose of being mustered into the service of the United States. After the officers and men had undergone the physical examination necessary, they were mustered into the volunteer service on May 10, 1898. The date of enrollment of officers and men was April 26, 1898, the day they were ordered to Camp Mount. They left Indianapolis, May 15, and proceeded to Camp Thomas, Chickamauga Park, Georgia, arriving there May 17. At Camp Thomas the battery was assigned to a brigade of artillery consisting of eleven batteries commanded by General Williston, U. S. V. They left Camp Thomas, July 24, arrived at Newport News, Virginia, and embarked for Porto Rico, July 28, arriving at Arroyo, Porto Rico, August 4; marched to Guayma, Porto Rico, August 11, and were on the firing line on the San Juan road when news of the peace protocol having been signed was received. They marched to Ponce, Porto Rico, August 28, and embarked for the United States September 7, reached New York, September 15, and traveled by rail to Indianapolis, reaching there September 17 under orders for muster out. The battery was furloughed for two months on September 23 and was finally mustered out and discharged November 25, 1898.

At Newport News, Private Millikan was detached and joined the United States warship St. Paul, under Captain Charles D. Sigsbee, who commanded the Maine when that vessel was blown up in the harbor at Havana, Cuba. The St. Paul landed at Arroyo, Porto Rico, arriving there two days in advance of the transport bearing the 27th Battery, which private Millikan rejoined about August 5, and remained in Porto Rico with the battery until September, 1898, when the Spanish-American war being practically ended, the battery was ordered to Indianapolis, as above stated, and private Millikan was given an honorable discharge September 22, 1898, his discharge being endorsed under the head of remarks, "service honest and faithful," by order of the Secretary of War. Private Millikan did not take advantage of the two months furlough allowed before final muster out of the battery, but received his discharge in order that he might return to business pursuits. The statement published on page 678 of this History in connection with the Spanish-American war, that private Millikan was discharged on account of disability is an error, as he passed a perfect physical examination both at muster in and muster out.

After his return to Indianapolis, young Millikan again took up employment with the National Surety Company and so continued until October, 1899, when he went to Helena, Montana, as confidential clerk with Palmer, Cooper and Company, bankers, where he remained until June, 1900. Again returning to Indianapolis, he entered the loan department of the Northwestern Mutual Life Insurance Company of Milwaukee, Wisconsin, and was connected with that company until February, 1902, when he became associated with the Advance Veneer and Lumber Company of Indianapolis, one of the largest concerns of the kind in the State, with a capital of $50,000. He is now secretary, treasurer and acting general manager of the company. Following in the footsteps of his father, he has taken an active part in politics and in the campaign of 1896 had charge of the bureau of the Republican State Committee for bringing home absent voters. In the campaign of 1900, he had charge of the bureau for the assignment of speakers. He is a young man of correct habits and quick to make friends, his social qualities being most excellent. His broad comprehension of business details added to his untiring industry give sure indications of his future success in the business and social world.

He was married May 3, 1905, to Ruth Johnson, of Bloomington, Indiana, daughter of Mr. and Mrs. William Johnson. Mr. Johnson is the owner of the Chicago-Bloomington Stone Company and is also heavily interested in the Johnson-Matthews Stone Company, both of which are prominent in the Bedford stone industry.

BIOGRAPHICAL SKETCH OF CHARLES DAYTON MORGAN.

LAWYER, BANKER, LEGISLATOR, PATRIOTIC AND PROSPEROUS CITIZEN.

Charles Dayton Morgan was born at Richmond, Indiana, July 31, 1829. His father, Nathan Morgan, was a pioneer of Wayne County, Indiana, who removed from New Jersey to the neighborhood of Richmond soon after that town was laid out in 1806. He was a farmer and cabinet maker, having served an apprenticeship to that trade in Philadelphia, Pennsylvania. He had also been a boatman on the Delaware River in his early manhood, and retained the memory of his old sailor days through life. Mr. Morgan remembers that when delirious during his last illness, which occurred when he was ninety years old, his father imagined himself to be a boatman again and gave the orders of command as he was wont to do so many years before. Nathan Morgan came to Indiana with his little family and such household goods as he possesed in a one-horse wagon, but he was industrious and frugal and soon accumulated a competency. He was twice married and was the father of a large family of children, who like himself were prosperous people and good citizens.

Charles D. Morgan's mother was Nathan Morgan's second wife. Her maiden name was Margaret Holloway. She was a sister of the late David P. Holloway, who was, for many years, editor of The Richmond Palladium, and was once a member of Congress from the old Fifth District of Indiana, and who was also commissioner of patents under President Abraham Lincoln. She was a woman of great force of character and notable for her motherly tenderness and sympathy. Mr. Morgan's great-grandmother on the maternal side was a daughter of Rowland Richards, who came over with William Penn, and seems to have had much to do with the early life of the Quaker colony in Pennsylvania.

In a sketch of Mr. Morgan's life in a book entitled "Men of Progress of Indiana," published by The Indianapolis Sentinel Company in 1899, it is said that "the ancestors of the family, on both the paternal and maternal sides, were Welsh, traced back for two hundred years." Since that was written, however, the record has been followed much further back and it is believed that, on the mother's side, there is an almost, if not wholly, unbroken line of descent extending back to Charlemagne. Mrs. Francis Swain, wife of President Joseph Swain of Swarthmore College, Pennsylvania, and former president of Indiana University, who is Mr. Morgan's daughter, has recently made many researches in Wales, in England, and on the continent of Europe, on the descent and lineage of the family, and has visited many of the places occupied by her father's ancestors, one of which is the famous old seat of the Townsends, from whom Mr. Morgan's mother was descended, and one member of which family, John Townsend, made a notable journey across the American continent, from east to west, and by vessel to the Sandwich Islands, about 1838, following much the same route as that followed earlier in the century by Lewis and Clark. Returning to Philadelphia, Mr. Townsend published an account of his expedition in 1839, which very interesting volume is among Mr. Morgan's most highly prized books. Mr. Morgan's interest in these matters of genealogy is only such as any right-minded American citizen should cherish for their historical value and because family relationships, lineage and antecedents are really very important matters, which in the hard struggles of the immediate past the American people have for the most part greatly neglected.

Of his father's immediate family there were five sons and five daughters, of whom the one best known in this section of Indiana, next to the subject of this sketch, was the late Nathan Morgan, of Richmond, Indiana. Charles D. Morgan was educated in the public school of Richmond and graduated from the high school of that city. After completing his school life he entered the law office of William A. Bickle, of Richmond, as a student of the law and spent two years with Mr. Bickle, followed by one year's study in the office of James Perry, one of the old time circuit judges, who was held in much esteem for his learning and impartiality.

Mr. Morgan was admitted to the practise of the law by the Wayne Circuit Court in 1850. He opened an office in Richmond, but two years later, in 1852, removed to

Knightstown, Henry County, Indiana, and entered upon the practise of his profession at that place, which has been his home ever since. He found it advisable to piece out his income from the law by other labors, and accepted the place of operator for the company that owned the first telegraph line in Eastern Indiana, which line ran along the National Road. Mr. Morgan had to learn telegraphy from the start, but soon mastered it sufficiently to manage the office, which was located in the book store of a young friend of his, Tilghman Fish, and held the place for a year.

In the year 1852 the Henry County turnpike, the first gravel road in the county, was completed through the county on the line of the National Road, and the Indiana Central Railway, now the first division of The Pennsylvania System, west of Pittsburg, was in course of construction. The old flat-bar railroad from Knightstown to Shelbyville and on to Madison on the Ohio River, was still doing business, and Knightstown was the most important business point in the county. The men then prominent in the affairs of the bustling town have nearly all passed away; but among them were such men as Joel B. Lowe, James Woods, Robert Woods, John Weaver, Harvey Bell, George S. Lowery, Peter C. Welborn, Moses Heller, Lemuel Murray, Morris F. Edwards and others, who have departed, while a few, like Sol Hittle, John W. White and Tilghman Fish, remain. In the surrounding country were such well remembered people as Gordon Ballard, Edward Lewis, John H. Bales and many another honored pioneer.

Mr. Morgan was a young man of great intellectual as well as business activity, of correct morals, good habits and possessed of positive convictions on moral and political questions and business propositions. Especially was he an earnest champion of the temperance reform which in the early fifties swept over the country like a mighty tide. Being a captivating public speaker and possessed of a fine presence, he was called for, far and near, to address Washingtonian gatherings or to make speeches at celebrations of the Sons of Temperance. His Sundays were particularly devoted to that line of work for several years. It brought him little or no immediate pay, but it won for him many friends, whose faithful adherence through a long and active life has been of inestimable value to him, which he has endeavored to reciprocate. He also made literary and educational addresses and political speeches, as occasion offered, or his political convictions required.

In the law he was a safe counselor and a reliable adviser. He has always despised shystering and crooked practices and has maintained a sincere contempt for the arts and subterfuges to which dishonest attorneys sometimes resort. When Mr. Morgan made a successful banker and financier of himself he evidently accomplished it at the expense of the popular and able jurist which he would otherwise have been.

Charles Dayton Morgan was married November 13, 1856, to Alvira Holland Woods, daughter of Robert and Hannah Woods, of Knightstown, by the Reverend David Monfort. Mrs. Morgan was a refined and noble woman and the twain lived happily and prosperously together until April 17, 1889, when she died after an illness of many months' duration and was laid to rest in beautiful Glencove Cemetery, Knightstown. They were the parents of six children, three of whom died in infancy. The three who remain are Frances, wife of Joseph Swain, president of Swarthmore College, Philadelphia, Pennsylvania; Raymond C., a farmer and stockman at Knightstown, and Erie C., assistant cashier of The First National Bank of Knightstown.

Among the diversions of his early career before locating in Knightstown Mr. Morgan recalls with pleasure a few days spent in carrying the chain for the engineers who were establishing the grade of the Indiana Central Railway.

The inconvenience caused by the want of banking facilities—for there was then no bank in the county—early called Mr. Morgan's attention to the subject of banking, and as a result he was mainly instrumental in establishing and was the manager of the first bank started in Henry County. It was what is now known as a private bank and was opened in 1859 under the firm name of R. Woods and Company. This bank continued to do a good business and to be a great convenience to the business men of Knightstown and the surrounding parts of Henry, Hancock and Rush counties until the establishment by Mr. Morgan and others of The First National Bank of Knightstown in 1865, which is its lineal successor.

The first officers of the national bank were Robert Woods, president; Charles D. Morgan, cashier, and William P. Hill, assistant cashier, or teller. To anticipate a little here: The career of The First National Bank of Knightstown, which has from its start been practically under the management of Mr. Morgan, has been a most remarkable one in three respects; first, for its unprecedented record as a sound and stable institution; second, for its undoubted preparation and readiness, in the times of panic and financial craze through which it has passed, to have met every legal demand against it from cash in its own vaults; and, third, for the few changes that have occurred in its official household. The American Financier in its Bank Roll of Honor, made up from the verified statistical reports, for many years placed The First National Bank of Knightstown at the head of the Indiana banks. For the past two years, however, The First National Bank of Washington, Indiana, has surpassed it slightly in certain particulars, so that the Knightstown bank now stands second in the State in proportion to the amount of its surplus to its capital stock.

The first change in the bank's household was made when Noah P. Wagoner was added to the force. Upon the death of Robert Woods Mr. Morgan became president, Mr. Hill cashier and Mr. Wagoner teller. After the demise of William Penn Hill, Noah P. Wagoner became cashier and the three men, Charles D. Morgan, Noah P. Wagoner and Erie C. Morgan are now its working force. While so few changes have occurred in the official roll of the bank during its forty years of existence, all the original stockholders except two have passed away.

Charles D. Morgan was early in life a Whig of anti-slavery convictions. With the political revolution that swept over the Northern States after the passage of the Kansas-Nebraska bill by Congress and the opening of Kansas and Nebraska to the incursions of slavery, he was one of that great host of young men, who in Indiana broke away from old party lines and in 1854 carried the State for a party of protest, known as the "People's Party," which two years later formed the nucleus of the young Republican Party, into the support of which he threw the strength and force of his young manhood. From 1856 to 1896 Mr. Morgan was an active and earnest supporter of the Republican Party, but since the latter date he has acted independently, voting for the men and measures of his choice.

It was as a champion of the Union cause during the Civil War that his most signal public service was rendered. Mr. Morgan had been elected in October, 1862, to represent Henry County in the lower house of the General Assembly—Joshua H. Mellett being the senator from the county at that time. When the session opened January 8, 1863, the old distinctions between Republican and Democrat seemed to be in abeyance and the lines of political conflict were drawn between supporters and opponents of the Civil War. The latter had elected so large a majority of the General Assembly as to permit the carrying of its measures over the vetoes of Governor Morton, but in the lower house the anti-war party lacked a few votes of a two-thirds majority and could not maintain a quorum in the absence of the supporters of the Governor. This crisis called for courage, wisdom and prompt action to meet the responsibilities of the hour, qualities granted in abundant measure to the supporters of the war and to none more than to the senator and representative from Henry.

The majority, under the leadership of Bayless W. Hanna, on February 5, 1863, proposed an enactment depriving the Governor of the military authority vested in him by the State constitution and vesting it in a commission of State officers opposed to the Governor and the conduct of the war, to be known and designated as The Executive Council. Numerous other bills and resolutions were introduced by the majority, the adoption of which must have resulted in crippling the powers of the State and Federal administrations in their efforts to sustain the Union.

Fortunately the Federal army under General Rosecrans had won a signal victory at Stone's River, December 31, 1862, and January 1-2, 1863, just before the meeting of the General Assembly, which elated the friends of the government and dampened the ardor of its opponents, who could not in the face of victory discountenance the soldiers and their achievements. To put the matter to the test, Mr. Morgan, of Henry, on the afternoon of the first day of the session, introduced a resolution "tendering the thanks of

57

the House to Major General Rosecrans and the officers and privates under him for their heroic conduct at the late battle at Stone's River and that we sincerely sympathize with the friends and relatives of the many patriots who there sacrificed their lives on behalf of their country, and that the clerk transmit a copy of this resolution to the commander of each regiment engaged in that battle." The result was as Mr. Morgan anticipated; the anti-war party refused to vote in the negative and the resolution was adopted by an affirmative vote of ninety-two.

The ground was fought over day after day and the session became one of continued anxiety and dread to the friends of the government and supporters of the war. At length, on February 25, 1863, when the military bill of Mr. Hanna reached engrossment, and was to be put on final passage, in compliance with a predetermined program, a sufficient number of the minority to break the quorum walked out and, taking a train to Madison, on the Ohio River, remained there until the expiration of the session. The risk involved was great and the attitude of the minority required great moral courage, but the action taken by them blocked and eventually defeated a course most injurious to the best interests of the State and Nation.

The subsequent failure of appropriations and the enhanced difficulties of the administration resulting from this session of the General Assembly are matters pertaining more particularly to State and National history. How the counties and people of the State rallied to the aid of Governor Morton and how the great banking house of Winslow, Lanier and Company—former citizens of Madison, Indiana—evinced their faith in Hoosier honesty by large and unsecured loans which enabled the Governor and his patriotic advisers to continue their active and effective support of the National administration, are most interesting details of this stormy period in State history; but beyond all doubt the salvation of the State from graver internal troubles was due to the courageous action of the minority in breaking the power of the majority in the General Assembly of 1863, and for the part he bore in this memorable crisis Henry County loves Charles D. Morgan and honors him as a man of sterling ability and character and a good citizen. Mr. Morgan has always regarded David C. Brannum, of Jefferson County, as a most able and conscientious leader of the minority in that historic session. Others of the strong men of the minority were Thomas J. Carson, of Boone; David R. Van Buskirk, of Decatur, and John S. Tarkington, of Marion.

Charles D. Morgan is of Quaker origin and was reared in that faith and though he does not now claim membership in that society, its principles of peace, probity and good will more nearly accord with his own thought and life than do the more pretentious creeds. He is an Odd Fellow of probably fifty years' standing and because that society's teachings and ministrations are such as meet his approval he is and has ever been an active and earnest member of the Knightstown Lodge, to whom the performance of the duties it imposes is a pleasure. During the Civil War he gave freely and liberally to the Union cause through many channels. Through life he has been steadfast in his friendships, as a husband and parent, true and tender, and as a citizen, beyond reproach.

Mr. Morgan is a great reader and lover of books and his library attests his taste for the best literature as well as his devotion to history and the masterpieces of forensic effort. both ancient and modern. Nothing delights him more than a walk with a friend who has a regard for books and for nature. It is exceedingly pleasant to stroll with him on such occasions and listen to him as he unfolds the wonderful stores that are retained by his clear and appreciative memory.

He has never lacked the confidence and esteem of his neighbors and both have been worthily bestowed. While he loves the entire State and country, Knightstown, where he has lived so long and well, is to him the one best spot of all the world. He has always been a lover of the soil and while his accumulations in other lines of property have been large, he has invested in a number of good farms in the vicinity of Knightstown, not only for his own profit and pleasure, but as the best investment for his heirs.

Charles D. Morgan was married a second time, his present wife being Rebecca F., daughter of the late William Brinkley and Margaret Ann (McCabe) Gray, of Knightstown, Indiana. Mrs. Morgan is a lady of sprightly intellect and kindly disposition, who has a wide circle of friends and seems well suited to be the partner of a thoughtful man of affairs like Mr. Morgan.

FRANCES (MORGAN) SWAIN.

(Daughter).

Frances Morgan, the eldest living child of Charles Dayton and Alvira Holland (Woods) Morgan, was born at Knightstown, Indiana, May 20, 1860. She was educated in the Knightstown public schools and The Indiana University and Leland Stanford, Jr., University of California, from which she was graduated with honor, and is a lady of many attainments. She was married at the residence of her parents to Joseph Swain, son of Woolston and Mary Ann (Thomas) Swain, honored pioneers of Madison County, living near Pendleton, Indiana, on September 22, 1885, by the Rev. H. N. Herrick of the Methodist Episcopal Church.

Mr. Swain was educated in the local schools, near his father's home, and in The Indiana University, from which he was graduated in June, 1883, receiving the degree of Master of Science in 1885, and that of Doctor of Laws from Wabash College in 1893. He has been associate professor of mathematics in Indiana University, professor of mathematics in the same and in Leland Stanford, Jr., University, of California; he spent one year of study at the University of Edinburgh, Scotland; he has also been president of Indiana University, and is now at the age of forty-eight years president of Swarthmore College, near Philadelphia, Pennsylvania, besides having held important positions in many educational associations, traveled largely both in Europe and America and lectured on educational themes in every county of Indiana. Mrs. Swain has also traveled much in her own country and in the lands beyond the Atlantic. She has been president of the Indiana Federation of Clubs and done much effective work among the young women in college. They have no children.

RAYMOND C. MORGAN.

(Son).

Raymond C. Morgan, son of Charles Dayton and Alvira Holland (Woods) Morgan, was born December 23, 1868, in Knightstown, Indiana. He studied in the schools of his native town, and afterwards taking a course in mathematics and civil engineering at Leland Stanford, Jr., University of California. He was married to Bertha V., daughter of Joshua S. and Elizabeth (McKeehan) Jayne, of near Queensville, Jennings County, Indiana, by the Reverend J. F. Baird. They are the parents of three children—Charles Townsend, born August 12, 1897; Donald Swain, born September 20, 1899, and Raymond Stewart, born January 21, 1904. Mr. and Mrs. Raymond Morgan with their little family live in Knightstown, where Mr. Morgan is a successful farmer and stockman of the progressive type.

ERIE C. MORGAN.

(Son).

Erie C. Morgan, son of Charles Dayton and Alvira Holland (Woods) Morgan, was born in Knightstown, Indiana, September 21, 1871. He attended the public schools of Knightstown and Indiana University, Bloomington. He early developed an aptitude for business and was given a clerkship in The First National Bank of Knightstown, of which he is now the assistant cashier. He was married to Emma Dale, daughter of John Riley and Sarah Alvira McCann, October 4, 1893, by the Reverend Robert F. Brewington.

They are the parents of two children—Rowland Richard, born May 30, 1896, and Alfred Dale, born May 12, 1905. Mrs. Morgan is a lady of fine natural endowments, heightened by cultivation and study. Before her marriage to Mr. Morgan she had won an honorable reputation as a recitationist and mistress of the art of expression. Mr. and Mrs. Erie C. Morgan are in the enjoyment of an elegant and happy home at Knightstown.

BIOGRAPHICAL SKETCH OF CHARLES WEIMERT MOUCH.

A PROGRESSIVE YOUNG BUSINESS MAN, SUCCESSFUL MANUFACTURER AND ENTERPRISING CITI-
ZEN.

The rapid development of industries and industrial methods in all parts of the
United States has not only given great impetus to the productive energies of the nation,
but has also opened many new avenues of promotion or advancement to young men
of capacity and perseverance.   As a consequence of this new condition of things in the
manufacturing world, it has become very common to find young men at the front in
the largest of our industrial enterprises, but to find them in actual ownership is not of
such frequent occurrence.

The subject of this sketch, however, is the chief owner as well as the general
manager of one of the most important enterprises in this section of the country.   It embraces under the one management the several operations of making and finishing shovels
of many kinds and patterns for a wide diversity of uses.   This practically includes the
several operations of the rolling mill, the shovel factory proper, and of the handle factory, and in addition thereto a large business is done in the rolling, cutting and finishing of steel disks for harrows and cultivators.   All of these varied branches of a great
manufacturing business with all of their accessory industries are under the general
management of Charles Weimert Mouch, a young man, forty two years of age, who was
practically thrown upon his own resources at a very early age, without means and with
only such meagre educational advantages as a few terms of winter school in an Ohio
village could bestow upon him.

Charles Weimert Mouch was born at Wapakoneta, Ohio, on July 6, 1863.   He was
the son of Matthias and Mary (Weimert) Mouch, and was, as is amply testified by
the names of his parents, as well as his own, of that sturdy Teutonic origin which has
contributed so much of its best blood to the development of America's soils and industries and to the rapid growth of its commercial character and spirit.

The opportunities of Mr. Mouch's childhood were limited to such as an humble
home in a struggling new town might afford to a little boy whose parents were economizing and toiling to earn a living and get a start in the world.   As already stated
a few months of schooling at the town school, during the earlier years of his life, constituted his entire educational outfit so far as it was obtained from the schools.   He must,
however, have made good use of such limited opportunities as were given him and
improved upon them afterwards, for he seems to be a ready and accurate accountant,
amply able to look after the financial side of an extensive and complicated business,
and also seems to be well informed in commercial affairs of many kinds, which necessarily involve the possession of an extensive fund of general information.

He was placed in charge of a team of horses and a wagon at the age of twelve
years and from that time until he was seventeen years of age he was a teamster, doing
general hauling about his native town and supporting his father, who was then disabled
from earning his own living.   At the age of seventeen years he entered the office of the
master mechanic of the Scioto Valley Railroad to learn telegraphy.   He says that the
conditions were such as to inspire him to the utmost industry in his quest for practical
knowledge, and so closely did he apply himself that in five months he had so mastered
his instrument and had become so proficient in its details that he was made telegraph
operator for the Scioto Valley Railroad at Portsmouth, Ohio, one of the road's most
important stations.   He served in that position so satisfactorily to all parties in interest that he soon attained to the maximum salary of sixty dollars per month.

Then an event occurred which illustrates his foresight.   He was offered the position of operator and agent of the newly constructed Indianapolis and Springfield, Ohio,
branch of the Indianapolis, Bloomington and Western Railroad, now the Peoria and
Eastern division of the Big Four, at the village of Mooreland, Henry County, Indiana,
at the princely salary of thirty-five dollars per month, and promptly accepted it, giving
up his sixty-dollar job in a good town, amid good social and business surroundings, to
do so.   Not many young men would have made such a choice.   But Mr. Mouch, though

Charles. W. Mouch

BIOGRAPHICAL SKETCH OF CHARLES WEIMERT MOUCH.

A PROGRESSIVE YOUNG BUSINESS MAN, SUCCESSFUL MANUFACTURER AND ENTERPRISING CITIZEN.

The rapid development of industries and industrial methods in all parts of the United States has not only given great impetus to the productive energies of the nation, but has also opened many new avenues of promotion or advancement to young men of capacity and perseverance. As a consequence of this new condition of things in the manufacturing world, it has become very common to find young men at the front in the largest of our industrial enterprises, but to find them in actual ownership is not of such frequent occurrence.

The subject of this sketch, however, is the chief owner as well as the general manager of one of the most important enterprises in this section of the country. It embraces under the one management the several operations of making and finishing shovels of many kinds and patterns for a wide diversity of uses. This practically includes the several operations of the rolling mill, the shovel factory proper, and of the handle factory, and in addition thereto a large business is done in the rolling, cutting and finishing of steel disks for harrows and cultivators. All of these varied branches of a great manufacturing business with all of their accessory industries are under the general management of Charles Weimert Mouch, a young man, forty two years of age, who was practically thrown upon his own resources at a very early age, without means and with only such meagre educational advantages as a few terms of winter school in an Ohio village could bestow upon him.

Charles Weimert Mouch was born at Wapakoneta, Ohio, on July 6, 1863. He was the son of Matthias and Mary (Weimert) Mouch, and was, as is amply testified by the names of his parents, as well as his own, of that sturdy Teutonic origin which has contributed so much of its best blood to the development of America's soils and industries and to the rapid growth of its commercial character and spirit.

The opportunities of Mr. Mouch's childhood were limited to such as an humble home in a struggling new town might afford to a little boy whose parents were economizing and toiling to earn a living and get a start in the world. As already stated a few months of schooling at the town school, during the earlier years of his life, constituted his entire educational outfit so far as it was obtained from the schools. He must, however, have made good use of such limited opportunities as were given him and improved upon them afterwards, for he seems to be a ready and accurate accountant, amply able to look after the financial side of an extensive and complicated business, and also seems to be well informed in commercial affairs of many kinds, which necessarily involve the possession of an extensive fund of general information.

He was placed in charge of a team of horses and a wagon at the age of twelve years and from that time until he was seventeen years of age he was a teamster, doing general hauling about his native town and supporting his father, who was then disabled from earning his own living. At the age of seventeen years he entered the office of the master mechanic of the Scioto Valley Railroad to learn telegraphy. He says that the conditions were such as to inspire him to the utmost industry in his quest for practical knowledge, and so closely did he apply himself that in five months he had so mastered his instrument and had become so proficient in its details that he was made telegraph operator for the Scioto Valley Railroad at Portsmouth, Ohio, one of the road's most important stations. He served in that position so satisfactorily to all parties in interest that he soon attained to the maximum salary of sixty dollars per month.

Then an event occurred which illustrates his foresight. He was offered the position of operator and agent of the newly constructed Indianapolis and Springfield, Ohio, branch of the Indianapolis, Bloomington and Western Railroad, now the Peoria and Eastern division of the Big Four, at the village of Mooreland, Henry County, Indiana, at the princely salary of thirty-five dollars per month and promptly accepted it, giving up his sixty-dollar job in a good town, amid good social and business surroundings, to do so. Not many young men would have made such a choice. But Mr. Mouch, though

Charles. W. Morreh

but a boy then, had been so educated in the hard school of adversity and cherished such an ambition to reach pecuniary independence that he thought he saw in the humbler position in a village which then contained less than a dozen houses, far better oppor. tunities to save money than he could hope for in the environments at Portsmouth, and far better reasons to hope for advancement with the new railroad and the new town than were to be found in the better paid position at Portsmouth. He had discovered in time to save himself from it what every poor boy finds out, but often when it is too late, that the character of one's associates and the habits acquired from them have far more to do with his ability to save money and get on in the world than the size of his salary. In Portsmouth he associated with the first young people of the town. The young men were the sons of well-to-do parents, and having plenty of means, were not under an ever present necessity to economize. He could not maintain a respectable standing with such associates, desirable as they were in other respects, and lay up money with which to establish himself in business. For these reasons he accepted the Mooreland agency and by so doing laid the foundation for the remarkable business prosperity that he has enjoyed up to the present time.

Mr. Mouch became the second agent at Mooreland in 1883, when he was but twenty years old, the first agent having served for a few months only. The new village was probably eight miles from any railroad town of local importance and the country surrounding it was and is exceedingly fertile, conditions which more than justified the young man's hope that it might prove a good place in which to advance with the growth of the town. The surroundings were certainly crude enough to give room for development, for the preceding agent, who had filled the position in a sort of desultory way, had kept his office in the box of an old freight car. The original plat of Mooreland was acknowledged August 9, 1882, by the late Miles M. Moore, it having been carved out of a portion of his fine farm. Thus it will be seen that Mr. Mouch practically began his business career in the town with the beginning of the town itself.

It requires much real pluck and nerve and a determined spirit of enterprise to enable a boy of twenty to turn his back upon the comforts and pleasures of a long established community and leave all the friends, acquaintances and familiar scenes of his early life to locate in a town that exists mostly on the blue paper of the engineer's plat, to lead the lonesome yet responsible life of a railroad agent and operator, with all its dull monotony of care and weary rounds of watchfulness; for twenty is an age at which most boys are in the heyday of fun, when the exuberances of irrepressible youth overrun and dominate their lives. Perhaps we may consider that Mr. Mouch's childhood practically ended when he became a teamster at the age of twelve, and that by the time he had reached his twentieth year he had attaind to a maturity of judgment and devotion to business that other men do not reach until ten years later in life. Be that as it may, it seems to be certain that he exercised unusual business foresight and clearness of vision during his entire stay in Mooreland, in all some fourteen years, extending from 1883 to 1897. The first five years spent by him there seem to have been years of quiet devotion to the business of the railroad, except that he served as the village postmaster from February 6, 1886, until after the inauguration of President Benjamin Harrison in 1889, keeping the office most of the time at the railroad station, which is centrally located in the town.

It was in 1887 that he entered the grain and timber trade in Mooreland, using a house of Jacob H. Swearingen, in which to store his grain. He made good profits both in grain and lumber and soon began to loan money on good mortgage and other securities. He always kept close watch of his investments, which though comparatively small at first, grew in proportion to the care bestowed upon them. In the year 1889 the failure of Wisehart and Kent, grain dealers at Mooreland, who had up to that time owned and operated the only elevator in the place, threw it upon the market at assignee's sale. Mr. Mouch improved the opportunity to multiply his facilities for handling grain by purchasing it and thus becoming master of the local trade in cereals. He bought the elevator at Losantville, Randolph County, on the same line of railroad, in 1892, thus preparing himself to handle the grain for a large territory lying in the three counties of Henry, Randolph and Wayne. Each of these movements added greatly to the volume of his trade and his advance was rapid. Another important purchase was made by him in 1890, which added much to his prestige as a far-seeing business man as well as to his substantial possessions. It was the purchase of the Jacob H. Swearingen farm of four hundred and thirty acres, located three and one-half miles northwest from Mooreland, which is recognized as one of the best and most profitable farms in Henry County, and which has doubled in value since his purchase of it.

On October 1, 1893, Charles Weimert Mouch was married to Hattie Estella, born April 18, 1867, daughter of James H. and Emily Louisa Moore, at their home in White County, Indiana, the latter being a daughter of Thomas and Elmira Lamb, formerly of near Dalton, in Wayne County, Indiana. Mrs. Mouch is a most excellent lady and well suited to be the partner of a man of such earnest purpose and active industry as Mr. Mouch. They live happily together and at present occupy their own commodious and elegant home in New Castle, which is reckoned among the best in a city noted for its pretty and well appointed family residences. They are the parents of four children, two of whom died in infancy and two of whom, Lois Hortense, born April 6, 1898, and a son, James Edward, born July 7, 1901, are bright, pretty and promising children. With so much to make them happy, Mr. and Mrs. Mouch are still in the bloom and vigor of youth and their friends are, apparently, warranted in hoping for them many long years of useful and contented life.

To continue the history of Mr. Mouch's life at Mooreland, the elevator at that place burned down in 1894 and was at once rebuilt and equipped as an up-to-date elevator of ample capacity to handle the grain for the Mooreland territory, and the trade continued as before. During the years 1889 to 1897 Mr. Mouch handled an immense amount of grain and logs besides managing the business of the railroad at that point and doing other incidental business. With it all he had amassed a comfortable fortune, such as many men would have been satisfied with. However, it may have been with him, his business activity was only confirmed and strengthened by his past experiences. He turned his Mooreland business over to his brother, Joseph Mouch, and removed to New Castle, which was then just emerging from its old-time, county-seat quietude into the stir and bustle of a manufacturing center, where skilled laborers or successful managers count for as much as the ancient lawyers did, except in the matter of awe-inspiring dignity.

He came to New Castle in 1897 and became a partner with Thomas J. Burk and Eugene Runyan in The New Castle Bridge Works, which were then located on a Big Four track in the western part of the town, and were doing a large business. At the end of eleven months he sold his interest in the bridge works at a fair advance. In 1899, he, with others, organized The Indiana Shovel Works and soon after erected the extensive factory buildings near the Big Four and the Pennsylvania railroads, in the northern part of the town, he being from the start the head and general manager of the company. In the large and well appointed brick factory building the business of making and finishing shovels from the rolled sheets was carried on with good success for three years; but by and through those three years of experience Mr. Mouch learned that the security and profits of the business might be materially increased if the shovel blades could be rolled as well as cut and finished by his company.

A favorable opportunity for carrying this idea into effect occurred in 1902, when the failure of the bottle works, located on the Rogers farm, west of New Castle, threw the buildings and plant upon the market at trustee's sale. Mr. Mouch purchased the grounds and buildings and installed machinery for rolling the sheets from which the blades of the many varieties of shovels turned out by the factory are made. After the new rolling mills were ready for business, early in 1903, some of the heavier machinery and certain portions of the work which had been done before at the shovel factory, north of town, were transferred to the plant west of town, leaving the original buildings to be occupied by the finishing departments. The materials from which the shovel blades have thus far been rolled are broken steel rails and locomotive tires.

In 1904 The Chicago Steel Manufacturing Company, having lost its plant at Hammond, Indiana, by fire, removed to New Castle and built a mill and installed machinery for the manufacture of nails and steel disks for harrows and plows, in close proximity

Jas H Moore

to the shovel company's rolling mills, in order to secure its rolled material from that mill. It began operations early in 1904 and consumed about fifteen tons of rolled steel per day, until November 8th of that year, when it burned down, with so little insurance upon it that the Chicago Steel Company decided not to rebuild it. Mr. Mouch then purchased all the machinery belonging to the plant except that used for the manufacturing of nails, such as presses, shears, rolls, etc., suitable for making harrow and plow disks and added the manufacture of steel disks to the already large business of the shovel factory.

The average annual output of the factory is now placed at sixty thousand dozens of spades and shovels of all kinds and two hundred thousand harrow, plow and grain disks, and the average annual value of the output is placed at five hundred thousand dollars. An average of about two hundred and twenty-five men and boys find employment in the various branches of the business carried on by the combined disk and shovel factories, at the rolling mills and in the original shovel factory buildings, and the wages paid average one hundred and twenty-five thousand dollars per annum. The products of the mills find a ready market in all parts of the United States and in Canada, Mexico, Australia and Cuba, shovels short and long handled, spades, etc., being made in many varied styles and patterns to suit the preferences of purchasers and the various uses to which they are put in the several countries in which they find a market.

Another important feature of Mr. Mouch's large business is that he manufactures his own handles, his factories for this purpose being at present located in western Ohio, the thrifty young or second growth gray ash used for the purpose having been exhausted in the country about New Castle. He regards it as very important to the interests of the business that the factory should control its own sources of supply as far as practicable, so that it may not be subjected to suspensions by failure to obtain some part or parts of the material necessary to its continuous operation.

From the foregoing it will be seen that Charles W. Mouch has probably been a greater factor in promoting the more recent industrial growth of New Castle and the prosperity of the surrounding country than any other man of similar age in the county. When a young man of forty-two years of age, beginning with nothing but industry and perseverance, has struggled upward until he controls an establishment that turns out a half million dollars' worth of finished products annually, and pays out one hundred and twenty-five thousand dollars in wages yearly, it is evident that he is a person of great business capacity and that he is of real service to the community in the dispensation of the means for comfortable livelihood to others, consequently bringing a large increase of business to local merchants and producers of the town and surrounding county.

He has further given tangible expression to his interest in the industrial growth of the town and county by direct money aid to new enterprises, both as a stockholder in them and through The New Castle Industrial Company, of which he is one of the founders, and its vice-president, a company which has been of much service to the local public in the help and encouragement it has given to the location of new manufacturing establishments and by making known to the general business world the fine, healthy location, worthy citizenship and excellent railroad facilities of New Castle.

He was also one of the founders of The Pan-American Bridge Company of New Castle and its first president, and was one of the early stockholders of the Maxim Building Company and is one of its directors.

Charles Weimert Mouch is greatly attached to his wife and children, of whom he is justly proud, and for whose sake he most prizes the early success which has come to him in his business undertakings.

The parents of Mrs. Charles W. Mouch reside in White County, Indiana, nine miles south of Monticello. Her father is a native of Henry County and is a son of the well known pioneer, Philip Moore, upon whose home farm the town of Mooreland was located and named in honor of that family. In 1865 James H. Moore and his brother, Miles M., both of whom were then married, moved from the home farm in Blue River Township to White County, Indiana. After a few years Miles M. returned to Henry County and bought a part of the old home farm, but James H. has continued to reside in White County. Elsewhere in this volume in connection with a brief history of Mooreland will be found biographical reference to Miles M. Moore in particular and to the Moore family in general, and to this sketch the reader is referred. Mrs. Nancy Moore, of Mooreland, is a sister of Mrs. Mouch's mother and her husband was a brother of Mrs. Mouch's father. When Mr. Mouch lived at Mooreland before his marriage he made his home with Mrs. Nancy Moore, and there became acquainted with Mrs. Mouch, who was visiting her aunt. Mr. and Mrs. Mouch were married at the home of the bride's parents in White County.

L. P. Kirby.

ood and the sub

P. Skovby

BIOGRAPHICAL SKETCH OF LEONIDAS PERRY NEWBY,

LAWYER, POLITICIAN, PUBLIC OFFICIAL AND SUCCESSFUL BUSINESS MAN AND FINANCIER.

The Newby family, of which Leonidas Perry Newby is a member, came to Indiana from North Carolina early in the nineteenth century. The early settlements of the ancestral branch of the family in North Carolina were in the counties bordering upon Albemarle Sound, such as Perquimans, Paspitank and Chowan. They were members of the Society of Friends, and certain Friends of the name in those counties are known to have been the owners of large tracts of land and many slaves, whom they treated with kindness and leniency. But when the Society of Friends or Quakers arrived at the conclusion that slavery was sinful and the holding of slaves an offense against the law of God, and late in the eighteenth century the yearly meetings determined that all Friends must liberate their slaves, they obeyed the behest and in carrying it out impoverished themselves, so that the family became widely scattered over the State. Early in the following century many families of the Newby relationship, which was and is a large one, sought the new country north of the Ohio River, and taking up the new lands in Ohio and Indiana, became sturdy pioneers of the two sister States.

The immediate family to which Mr. Newby belongs located in Henry County, Indiana, coming here from Randolph County, North Carolina, in 1837. Mr. Newby's father first engaged in the business of merchant tailoring at Greensboro. In those days the country merchants all sold goods upon long credits, and in fact could sell them in no other way. The system broke up most of the earlier merchants. Mr. Newby's father, whose name was Jacob Newby, and who was a most worthy man, being no exception to the rule. The head of the family, after the loss of his property, went back for a time to the cultivation of the soil for a livelihood, and the subject of this sketch was born upon a farm near Lewisville, Indiana, on April 9, 1855. Mr. Newby's mother was before her marriage Lavina Leonard, and both she and her husband were enthusiastic Methodists of the old-time, earnest and devoted kind, notwithstanding the fact that Jacob Newby's ancestors had been primitive Quakers.

Although Mr. Newby's father and mother were exemplary and industrious people, his father was never a robust man, and though he toiled often beyond his strength, both when farming or when working at his trade, he could accumulate but little, and found that it required all the strength he could muster to support his six children and keep the wolf from the door. Hence it was that Leonidas Perry, who was the youngest of the sons, was thrown upon his own resources early in life, a fact which largely accounts for his business success.

His first ambition seems to have been for knowledge—the attainment of a practical education—hence we find him as a small boy performing the duties of janitor for the Greensboro school to gain the means to supply himself with clothing and books and help the family along, while he was at the same time pursuing his studies in the school and keeping up with, and at times, leading his classes. During the summer months young Newby worked for the neighboring farmers and saved his earnings to aid him in his winter campaigns for knowledge. This course was persevered in until he arrived at the age of sixteen, when the family removed to Knightstown, Indiana, where he entered the high school. The Knightstown school was then under the very efficient superintendency of the late Professor Hewitt, with John I. Morrison as the leading member of the board of trustees, and was one of the foremost town schools in eastern Indiana.

Before he had reached the age of seventeen, Mr. Newby began to teach in the public schools of the neighborhood, thus gaining the means to enable him to pursue his studies in the high school, teaching and attending school alternately. While thus engaged he also began to read law, giving to it whatever time he could spare from his studies in the school or duties in the school room. He graduated from the Knightstown High School with honor in 1875, being its first graduate; but he continued certain lines of study with Professor Hewitt after his graduation and also continued his study of the law, and to keep up his expenses taught for three hours every day in the high school.

The time that was left to him for his legal studies was spent first in the law office of Butler and Swaim, of Knightstown, and later in the office of J. Lee Furgason, of the same place. He was admitted to the practise by the Henry Circuit Court in 1878 and in the same year formed a partnership with the late Walter B. Swaim and opened an office in Knightstown. This partnership with Swaim was terminated at the end of the first year, when Mr. Newby established an office of his own and has continued the practise single-handed ever since.

"The Bench and Bar of Indiana," a valuable and entertaining volume of more than eight hundred pages devoted to the biographies of eminent Indiana lawyers, edited by Charles W. Taylor and published at Indianapolis in 1895, says of Leonidas P. Newby:

"In 1880 he was elected prosecuting attorney of the eighteenth judicial circuit, composed of the counties of Henry and Hancock. His office, however, did not begin until nearly two years had elapsed after his election; but within three months after that event the prosecuting attorney then in office resigned, and Governor Porter appointed Mr. Newby to the vacancy, thus enabling him to hold the office nearly four years. One of his first cases on opening an office was the famous Foxwell murder case at Rushville, Indiana, in which he appeared for the defendant. The ability shown by the young attorney in tnis case received much favorable comment and so placed him on his feet as to give him a good start. In 1886, he was the leading counsel in the celebrated Anderson murder case at Williamstown, Kentucky, and received the credit of making one of the most able speeches ever made at the bar, in closing the argument for the defense. In the prosecution of this cause appeared Hon. M. D. Gray, the county attorney and now the commonwealth attorney for the judicial district; Captain Dejarnette, then commonwealth attorney and now considered one of the most brilliant lawyers in Kentucky; Col. J. J. Landerman, a noted politician and lawyer of Warsaw, of that State, and Hon. W. P. Harden, of Lexington, then the attorney general of that State, and now (1895) a candidate for governor. With Mr. Newby was associated Hon. O. D. McManama, afterwards judge of the criminal court of Frankfort, Kentucky; Hon. L. C. Norman, of Frankfort, now Auditor of State; Capt. John Combs, of Williamstown, Kentucky, and Hon. W. W. Dickerson, since a member of Congress and now a candidate for re-election. In the preliminary trial Hon. W. P. C. Breckinridge appeared for the defendant, but was unable to appear at the trial. "Mr. Newby has been employed in trial cases in all the Middle States as well as in some of the Southern, Western and Eastern ones and has held the greatest part of the practise in the southern part of Henry and the northern part of Rush County."

Since "The Bench and Bar" from which the foregoing is taken was published, Mr. Newby has succeeded the late Judge Joshua H. Mellett, of New Castle, as the Henry County attorney of the Pennsylvania Railroad Company and in conjunction with John L. Rupe, of Richmond, has charge of its extensive and lucrative legal business in Eastern Indiana, which added to his already large practise makes his income from his profession one of the best of those enjoyed by Eastern Indiana lawyers.

The Masonic Advocate, in an article in its issue for May, 1901, speaking of Mr. Newby's legal attainments and successes, said: "Brother Newby has single-handed built up a large and lucrative practise, not only in his home court, but throughout Eastern Indiana, where he stands as the peer of the ablest in his profession." The same journal in addition to the foregoing says: "He has never aspired to the bench but is, however, a favorite when acting as special judge and has frequently been called to the neighboring counties of late years, to hold special terms of court and try causes on change of venue,. having sat as the trial judge in many important cases."

Mr. Newby has been a Republican in politics all his life and is always active in the support of his party and its candidates. He has often been a member of the Republican County Committee and, during two or more presidential campaigns, a member of the executive committee chosen by the Republican State Committee to act in conjunction with its chairman in the immediate direction of the work of the campaign.

. Mr. Newby was nominated and elected to succeed the late General William Grose in the State Senate in 1892 and re-elected in 1896. His activities and services in that body were such that he soon took rank among the able leaders of the Republican party in the

Senate and was for six years the president pro tempore of the Senate. He was also chairman of the judiciary committee for six years. He has been twice a candidate for the nomination by his party for lieutenant governor, but owing to the conflicting interests of candidates for the other State offices he was defeated in convention both times by very narrow margins. He is a hustler, a good mixer and possessed of a rare geniality which with his recuperative powers of mind and spirit enable him to come out of such political contests without having suffered loss of temper and with no sore spots to nurse and no political graveyard to fill. Hence he is a hard man to keep down and, as he is yet young and in fine health and full of mental vigor, he is likely to be heard from in the future.

Mr. Newby has been thus far in life very successful in business, having accumulated a snug fortune. He is the owner of a fine home in Knightstown and quite a number of rental properties as well as some valuable business blocks. He has also some good farms in the neighborhood of his home town in which he takes much pride and greatly enjoys the time which he can give to their oversight. He owns stock in and is president of The Citizens' State Bank of Knightstown and also of The Natural Gas Company, The Electric Light and other business organizations of the town. He is a stockholder, director and vice-president in and of The Columbia National Bank of Indianapolis; a stockholder in The American National Bank of the same city, and one of the largest stockholders in The Security Trust Company of Indianapolis and president of the New Castle Central Trust and Savings Company, and has many other important business interests in various parts of the State. He is also president of the board of trustees of the southern State prison or reformatory for young men and boys, which has rendered such signal service to the State in carrying out reforms in the prison management and making improvements to the buildings and grounds at a saving in money and to the betterment of the inmates as well as to the advantage of the people of the State.

Mr. Newby was united in marriage with Mary Elizabeth, daughter of Robert B. and Julia A. Breckinridge, of Knightstown, Indiana, September 20, 1877. Mrs. Newby's family is a good one, noted for the integrity and energy of its members, her father, the late Robert B. Breckinridge, having been for many years a prominent business man of Knightstown. She is a lady of many accomplishments and graces and skilled in the arts of home-making and in dispensing the genuine courtesies of social life. The married and home life of Mr. and Mrs. Newby have been very happy, surrounded by comforts and refinements, and cheered by a large circle of friends. They are the parents of two children, an accomplished daughter, and a son, who is a member of his father's profession, of whom more will be said further on.

Mr. Newby is a member of several benevolent orders and other social and business societies; but the one society of his choice, in which he has taken most interest and to which he has devoted most time and talent, is the time-tried order of Free and Accepted Masons. He was made a Master Mason in Golden Rule Lodge, Number 16, Knightstown, having been initiated April 12, 1882, passed May 17, and raised June 7, of the same year. The Masonic Advocate traces his advances in and services to Masonry as follows:

"He was made a Royal Arch Mason in Knightstown Chapter, Number 33, receiving the preceding degrees during the months of August, September and October, and the Royal Arch, November 6, 1882. He was High Priest during 1898. He received the degrees of Royal and Select Master in Cryptic Council, Number 29, Knightstown, November 12, 1883. He was created a Knight Templar in Knightstown Commandery, Number 9, January 30, 1883, and worked his way up to Eminent Commander, which position he held during the years 1889 and 1890.

"In the Grand Commandery he started as Grand Sword Bearer in 1895 and by regular advancement became R. E. Grand Commander of Indiana at the recent Annual Conclave, and enjoyed the honor of representing the Grand Commandery in the Grand Encampment of the United States at the tri-centennial conclave at Louisville, Kentucky, in August, 1901.

"He received the grades of the A. A. Scottish Rite, including the Thirty Second Degree, at the annual convocation in 'The Valley of Indianapolis' in March, 1892, and became a 'Shriner' in Murat Temple, March 25, 1892.

"As secretary of the triennial committee of The Grand Commandery, Sir Knight Newby has rendered excellent service in providing quarters for the grand and subordinate commanderies of Indiana at the triennial conclave at Denver, Boston, Pittsburg, Louisville and San Francisco, whereby Indiana has always made a favorable showing with other grand jurisdictions and at a reasonable expense. As a member of the board of trustees of his home lodge and chapter at Knightstown, brother Newby took an active part in the erection of their fine Masonic Temple, which was destroyed by fire October 18, 1899, and also in the erection of the fine and massive new structure which now occupies the place of the old one and is such an adornment to the beautiful little city of Knightstown. As a Mason and as a citizen, in all the walks of life, he stands ready in a public-spirited way to do his full share in promoting the general good. Long may he live in his sphere of usefulness."

Such is the estimate of Mr. Newby as a Mason and a man, made by one who stands high in the "ancient and honorable" order. In addition it may be stated that Mr. Newby is now and has been for the past seven years Inspector General of The Knights Templar of Indiana, and is a life member of the Committee of Jurisprudence of the Knights Templar of the United States.

Mr. and Mrs. Newby have both traveled extensively in their own country and are familiar with many parts of the United States, and Mr. Newby himself has visited Cuba and other islands of the West India group, also Mexico and Central America, and gained much valuable information, and during the Summer of 1905 made a delightful trip to England and Continental Europe in company with Smiley N. Chambers, of Indianapolis, and others, from which he gleaned a great deal of pleasure and profit, and returned to again take up the responsibilities of life in the best county of the best State in the Union and in the town which to him is the best spot of the best county.

THE CHILDREN OF MR. AND MRS. LEONIDAS PERRY NEWBY.

Floss Newby, the only daughter of Mr. and Mrs. Newby, was born May 3, 1879. She was reared in Knightstown, receiving her primary education in the public schools of that town and graduated from its high school. She also studied for three years in De Pauw University and afterwards graduated from Madam Phelps' Young Ladies School at Columbus, Ohio. She has received extensive training in the Greek and Latin languages and in French and German and also in music and has traveled much in her own country and made recently an extended tour of Europe. She is an accomplished young lady, whose genial manners and generous disposition have given her a large circle of friends. She makes her home with her parents at Knightstown.

Floyd J. Newby, the only son of Mr. and Mrs. Newby, was born in Knightstown, January 9, 1881, and grew up in that town, received his early education there and graduated from its high school. After graduation from the Knightstown school, he spent four years in the regular course at De Pauw University and one year at the Indiana State University at Bloomington, in the law course. He has also spent two years in the study of the law in an office where he came in contact with actual practise and the application of legal principles to business. Most of this time was devoted to study in the office of Judge Eugene H. Bundy, of New Castle, Indiana. He was then admitted to the practise by the Henry Circuit Court, upon examination. He is now engaged in the practise in partnership with his father at Knightstown and is in the enjoyment of a prosperous business.

He was united in marriage with Mary H., only child of Judge Henry Clay Lewis, of Greencastle, Indiana, on November 23, 1904. She was educated in the Greencastle public schools, in De Pauw University, and completed her course in the Young Ladies' Seminary at Tarrytown, New York. She is an accomplished lady who stands very high among the best people of Knightstown as well as of her former home. There seem, therefore, to be many reasons to look for a happy and prosperous future for the junior Mr. Newby and his wife.

BIOGRAPHICAL SKETCH OF ISAAC PARKER, A BACKWOODS GENIUS.

FARMER, LEGISLATOR AND MAN OF AFFAIRS.

Isaac Parker, son of Jeremiah and Keren (Newby) Parker, was born in Northampton County, North Carolina, in 1806, where he reached the age of twelve years, with only such opportunities for gaining an education as an occasional term of an "old field school" afforded, before leaving the State. About the year 1818 he removed with his parents to Wayne Count, Indiana, where the family settled upon a tract of timber land on Elkhorn Creek, five or six miles south of Richmond. It is upon this tract of land that the big Elkhorn sulphur spring is situated.

His father was descended from that English family of Parkers who came with, or soon afterward followed, William Penn from England into the wilderness of Pennsylvania, and from which one branch went south and settled in North Carolina, another went to New England, and one remained in Chester and Westmoreland counties, Pennsylvania, where the original settlements of the family were made. The southern branch of the family has contributed many men and women of strong character and influence to the life of the South.

His mother was a daughter of Robert Newby, whose broad acres lay well down to Albemarle Sound, upon the Perquimans River, but who impoverished himself by giving freedom to all of his slaves, of whom the best information obtainable seems to indicate that there were more than one hundred, about one-half of whom he sent to Liberia, and was put to much expense and trouble to prevent the others from being sold back into slavery. Some of these ex-slaves came with the Parker family to Indiana, and one of them, then an old woman, lived in Isaac Parker's family as late as 1859 and 1860.

Mr. Parker's mother was a very active and sprightly woman, with a wonderful memory and strong intellect. She remembered with great clearness scenes and incidents of the Revolutionary period, especially when Greene and Cornwallis were contending for the mastery in the Carolinas, and often rehearsed them to her grandchildren. His father was an invalid from a hurt received in early life, so that the work of making and cultivating the backwoods farm fell upon Isaac and his elder brother, Robert. But the father was not idle. He had learned the shoemaker's trade and was a fine workman in that line. When able to work he was always busy at the bench, for his work was in much demand. He was a gentle, kind-hearted man, but so thoroughly grounded in the peculiar formalities that had grown up among the Friends in country places at that early day that his rule often bore hard upon his son Isaac, who seems to have inherited a broader view of life from his gracious and gifted mother. He venerated and loved his father nevertheless, but he also loved books and poetry and longed for a larger life and opportunities. There were occasional winter terms of school taught at the Orange Meeting House, near the farm and home of the family on Elkhorn Creek, but the teachers were so poorly equipped with learning that little was to be gained from them. A few terms of two to three months in the winter at that school and a single term in a school conducted by Elijah Coffin—so long at the head of The Indiana Yearly Meeting of Friends, and also of the banking interests of eastern Indiana— in which he paid his way by hearing recitations and acting as the master's assistant, constituted his only opportunities for obtaining a school education.

But so eager was he for knowledge that he sought for books in all directions, read them with eagerness and stored their contents in one of the most comprehensive and tenacious of memories. As long as he lived and retained his faculties he could all the day long repeat the beautiful or striking things in oratory, history, poetry and the drama that he had read in his earlier years, or even when well along in life, often having heard or read them but once. Parts of great speeches, sermons, newspaper editorials and a vast fund of anecdote were thus stored in his memory ready for use at any time. But withal the memory was not abnormal and did not affect his originality of character, save in a favorable and pleasing way. It must have been very largely the result of his intense yearning for those things which appeal to the larger and better intelligence of men, and his fervor in their pursuit which literally burned them into his brain and made them part of his being. How did he acquire all that he knew of history, law, biography, romance and poetry? One can but wonder how in that early day, in a backwoods cabin, restrained and restricted by his father's mistrust of books and printed matter that did not emanate from his own religious society, he ever secured the use of the books from which to obtain it, and did so without giving offense or grief to the parent whom he loved.

In the formation of his tastes he was greatly aided by the works of that great English Quaker and profound linguist and scholar, Lindley Murray, whose books, "The English Reader," "The Introduction to the English Reader" and "Murray's English Grammar," were then in use in all the better schools and in even the humblest of the Quaker schools. They were crowded with selections from the writings of the world's great thinkers, from Homer and Demosthenes among the ancient Greeks to Virgil and Cicero among the Romans; the Bible and Josephus, besides the whole broad field of English literature as it existed in the dawn of the nineteenth century. These led him naturally to the great authors of the past and few men of his time knew Plutarch's Lives or Shakespeare's plays better than he, and fewer still, except professional actors, could have rendered from memory so many of the choicest passages in the plays.

His familiarity with English and American verse, including Pope's Translation of Homer; Shakespeare, Milton, Pope, Cowper, Goldsmith, Byron, Crabbe, Heber, Pollok, Scott, Campbell, Moore, Burns, Mrs. Hemans and the earlier American poets such as Freneau, Barlow, Trumble, "The Milford Bard"; Mrs. Sigourney and later in his life, Whittier, Halleck, Bryant, Longfellow, Nathaniel P. Willis and Dr. Oliver Wendell Holmes, was perhaps greater than that of any other person in the eastern half of Indiana. He wrote some verse himself, but most of it was in the way of political satire and has not survived him.

In romance his field of interest was even wider, including everything from Fielding to the latest of Fenimore Cooper's Indian stories. Among his favorites were Bulwer Lytton, Sir Walter Scott, Eugene Sue and Victor Hugo, though Hugo had not then reached his best. He loved to recite from Burns or Shakespeare for the pleasure of his friends and in that way added to the enjoyment of many a neighborhood gathering. In Burns's "Tam O'Shanter's Ride" and "The Address to a Louse" he was at his best.

But to recount a tithe of the striking or beautiful things he knew is not possible in this brief sketch. His poses and attitudes were all peculiar and different from those of the staid people about him, who thought him exceedingly awkward, a charge to which he readily pleaded guilty and which he seemed to enjoy. The keen delight he experienced in reading Macaulay's History of England aloud to the family soon after its first appearance in this country was most remarkable. Its splendid diction stirred him to a lively emotion, such as "The Ballads of Ancient Rome" often awake in a studious boy who is thrilled with a yearning for military glory.

In his early life he longed for a professional career. Medicine or the law he thought would open up to him opportunities for the realization of his dreams, and business seemed to him to point in the same direction, but his father's religious notions were in the way of any such undertaking and more than all else that withheld him was the fact that by the time he had reached the age to begin such studies his father's declining health made it necessary for him—he being the youngest son—to assume the care of his parents and devote himself to their welfare. He bowed to the inevitable, but relaxed not his pursuit after knowledge and the ability to do things well.

He associated with the foremost young men of Wayne County—J. C. Williams, Septimus Smith, David P. Holloway, John Finley, John S. Newman and others who were then coming into notice, were among his advisers and friends who helped him to books and gave him encouragement. When he lay upon his death bed in 1866 John S. Newman, then president of The Indiana Central Railway, spent a day at his bedside, renewing with him the struggles and triumphs of their early lives. Newman was almost the last of his earlier friends.

About the year 1830 the family determined to remove to Henry County, where an eighty-acre tract of land was entered and another purchased later. In 1831 a neat house of hewed logs was built on the first tract, where the farm residence of Robert Hall now stands. Into this house Mr. Parker's parents removed, after selling their Wayne County holdings. When Mr. Parker married he built a round-log cabin nearby, in which he and his young wife, Mary Strattan, began the journey of life together in 1831. He had made her acquaintance in Richmond, Indiana, some years before, she having been the daughter of Benjamin Strattan, a village blacksmith, who was somewhat famous as a fine workman in iron and steel. He was an auger, axe and bellmaker and manufacturer of many kinds of wood workers' tools, his house being not far from the site of the present court house of Wayne County. Mary Strattan proved to be a most intelligent and sympathetic partner for a man of the character and attainments of Isaac Parker. Her father and mother had sold their home in Richmond and purchased a farm in what is now the Hopewell neighborhood, and moved there to spend the evening of their lives, with the homes of their married sons and daughters about them, on neighboring eighties. In the same new Quaker neighborhood of Hopewell settled Robert, brother of Isaac Parker, and his two married sisters.

Another Friends' community was then forming on Flatrock, among whom Jeremiah Parker, father of Isaac, was one of the oldest of the first-comers. A meeting house was built one mile north of his home in the woods, and, at his suggestion, the meeting and the neighborhood, taken as one, were called "Richsquare," after the name of his old home meeting in North Carolina, where it seems to have been a very decided misfit. It was in this church that the first Richsquare schools were taught. A school certificate is still extant which was issued to Isaac Parker to teach "reading, writing and arithmetic to the single rule of three," signed by Jehu T. Elliott, Joel Reed and Martin L. Bundy, the license being in the beautiful handwriting of Mr. Bundy. These three gentlemen were then the county school examiners. The school was taught in the log meeting house in the winter of 1836-7, and it is needless to say that much more was taught than the certificate required, as the school was largely made up of young men and women much further advanced in their studies. The school was a success and another term. was called for. At least one other primary school had been taught in the new neighborhood before, but Parker's first term was the practical inauguration of the very effective school which has been maintained there ever since and which is now the Franklin Township High School.

In his early career in Henry County Isaac Parker was quite a successful, farmer, as farming was done in those days, but as more and more demands were made upon him to undertake the settlement of estates and such public duties as the assessing of property for taxation, the appraisement of real estate, the taking of the census and like services, which occupied his time, the management of the farm fell upon the oldest son, Benjamin S. Parker, and a brother, Edwin E. Parker, eight years younger.

Isaac Parker was also drawn into politics, for which he had a great liking, but for which his temperament unfitted him. Generous and sincere himself, he could not bring himself to understand nor to condone the self-seeking eagerness and often bitter personalities and dissimulations of politicians, great and small, and was wounded and hurt by them so deeply and lastingly that the suffering entailed upon him far exceeded all the gain from office that ever came to him. He was several times the nominee of his party for places of honor, the last time being for delegate to the constitutional convention of 1851. In that instance he was defeated by a curious coalition between the Democrats and Free Soilers of the county. By the terms of the act of the General Assembly providing for the election of delegates to the convention, each county was entitled to as many delegates as it had representatives in the lower House of the General Assembly, and each senatorial district to one member, but there was no difference whatever created between the functions of a senatorial and representative delegate, as all were to serve in the same body upon an equal footing, yet an awkwardness in the wording of the act distinguished them as senatorial and representative delegates and the political parties followed the blunder in making their nominations and printing their tickets. Thus the Whigs nominated Daniel Mason, of Knightstown, for senatorial delegate, and Isaac Parker, of Franklin Township, and Dr. George H. Ballengall, of Middletown, for representative delegates, while the coalition of Democrats and Free Soilers chose Isaac

Kinley, Free Soiler, for senatorial delegate, and Daniel Mowrer and John F. Johnston for representative delegates, and the two tickets were so printed and distributed. The vote was a very close one with the result that Kinley received more votes than Mason, and Mowrer more votes than Parker, while Ballengall scored a few more than either of the opposition candidates for representative delegate, and Parker received more votes than Kinley. As a matter of fact the entire Whig ticket for delegates was elected, Henry County being then entitled to two representatives and one senator; but under the ruling that prevailed, two fusionists, Kinley and Mowrer, and one Whig, Ballengall, were given the certificates of election and served in that memorable body to the approval of the people of the county. It seems proper to say that Major Isaac Kinley who, after a long and highly honorable career as teacher, author, editor, legislator, scholar and soldier, is now an invalid in Los Angeles, California, and unable to leave his bed, is believed to be the only surviving member of the convention that framed our present State constitution.

Isaac Parker was twice elected to the General Assembly and served in the sessions of 1841-2 and 1845-6, with honor to himself and profit to his constituents. In the latter term which was strongly democratic, he managed to so win favor among his democratic colleagues, who were divided among themselves between two democratic candidates, as to secure the election of his personal friend, Jehu T. Elliott, as prosecuting attorney for the circuit of which Henry County was then a part—that officer being chosen by the General Assembly under the old constitution. Politically speaking, that election as prosecutor was the beginning of the career which carried Judge Elliott through several promotions, to the Supreme bench of the State, where he won such well merited distinction and honor.

It was a great sorrow to Mr. Parker that his wife, whose industry and devotion were far beyond her strength, was for years an invalid and that, of a large family of children, only his two sons, Benjamin S., the eldest, and Edwin E., who was born in 1840, lived to be grown. Perhaps the greatest of these severe afflictions occurred in 1858, when Martha and Charles Rollin, aged respectively ten and seven years, fell victims to diphtheria and Edwin E. was paralyzed and made an invalid and sufferer by it for all his after life. Bright, gifted and beautiful were the two children that died. They were the joy and hope of their parents and neither ever recovered from the grief caused by their loss.

Mary Parker, the wife and mother, died in the Spring of 1861, at the age of forty nine years. Edwin E., so far recovered that he taught school in 1861 and volunteered in the 69th Indiana Infantry, in 1862; he saw some service with the regiment and was brought home, as all supposed, to die, but slowly gained strength until he was able to enter a law office at New Castle to study that profession. After raising a cavalry company in conjunction with Volney Hobson, he again sought admission to the service but was refused on account of his physical condition. He was married about that time to Caroline Hubbard, a daughter of Butler Hubbard, who was then County Recorder. They were the parents of four children; one son, now a resident of Richmond, Indiana; a son, who died in childhood; and two daughters, who live with their mother in Fort Wayne, Indiana. After a varied career in Indiana, Ohio and the West, as a teacher, lawyer, reporter, editor and lecturer, Edwin E. Parker died in 1903, and sleeps in the beautiful Linden Wood Cemetery, at Fort Wayne, Indiana. He left a number of poems, essays, and other prose writings that his friends hope to issue in book form at some appropriate time.

It was in the hope of renewing his father's hold upon life that Benjamin S. Parker gave up, for the time being only, as he supposed, his cherished dream of a life divided between agricultural and scholarly pursuits, and engaged in business with his father at Lewisville, where Isaac Parker died in 1866, at the age of sixty years. He and his cherished wife and all of their deceased children, except Edwin E., lie buried in the quiet country graveyard at Richsquare, near their old, and except for the invading sorrow of death, happy home.

Isaac Parker was in youth a man of fine appearance; his hair, eyebrows and beard were very black; his face rosy and his eyes clear and piercing. He was five feet and ten inches in height; his shoulders were broad and his head finely proportioned. He was a good public speaker and had wonderful ways of making and retaining friends, due to his sincerity of character and his obliging disposition. So ready to help others was he that much of his time was taken up by men who wanted aid with their accounts, or in the settlement of estates, always without pay and, possibly, in some cases without thanks. He never had a plow, a horse nor a utensil of any kind that was too good to lend to his neighbors. His home was always open in hospitality such as his means afforded. He belonged essentially to the old, ideal life taught by the sages, prophets and poets of the past, and yet he had his strong ambitions and was somewhat quick of temper in his earlier manhood, and intolerant of meanness and littleness always. Later in life his nature became refined into a silken smoothness which only some untoward offense could rouse into fiery action.

One of the tenderest and most sympathetic of men, anything like brutality and cruelty toward the weak, called forth his severest condemnation. It was characteristic of his tenderness of heart that once, when one of his children died and there was only a farm wagon in which to convey it to the graveyard, he took his seat upon the floor of the wagon, and folding the little coffin in his arms carried it thus to the place of burial and then handed it over to the friends who were to hide it away in the ground.

His close friend and neighbor, Judge Joseph Farley—who was a man of note and for some years an associate judge of the circuit court—and he were once rival candidates for the General Assembly, Farley on the Democratic and Parker on the Whig ticket. They canvassed the county together on horseback, met and conversed with the people in behalf of their respective parties. If anything occurred to keep either of them at home for a day, the other refrained from continuing the canvass until his friendly rival could again participate in it. If any other canvass for office in this county was ever made upon such terms, no record has been kept of it.

Isaac Parker was of such peculiar nature and genius that he could not possibly conform to all the peculiarities of the Quaker sect, then considered essentials by most of their organizations in the new settlements. He loved art, romance, poetry, song and music, as the body of the Society in the West has come to do now to a lesser degree, and yet he was in deep sympathy with the cardinal doctrines of the Society and was by no means a "Hickory Quaker" in the sense of being careless of spiritual things, but was really one of the most reverential and earnest thinkers upon subjects connected with the destiny of the human soul. Indeed his sensitive mind was always alert upon such themes; so much so that insincerity and sham disgusted and grieved him. His neighbors, most of them, respected his attitude upon sacred things and accepted it as one of his peculiarities, little dreaming how soon it was to cease being peculiar even among the Quakers.

In his devotion to books and the larger life of the intellect and the imagination, he found those who best understood him among the lawyers, editors and other professional men of his time and in their company took such delight and imparted so much pleasure in return that it became a common saying among his friends that Parker never left town for the lonely ride to his home through the woods until after sunset.

Looking back upon his life and influence, it seems that he might well have been termed a "backwoods genius." He cannot be compared with other leading men of the local world in which he moved, because he was unique. His genius was radiant, attractive and contagious in its influence with men and women of larger thought, while to the many,—those of whom it may be said as Wordsworth said of one of his characters, Peter Bell, that

> "A daisy on the river's rim,
> A yellow daisy was to him
> And nothing more."

—he was but a common man, yet for his kindness of disposition, gentleness of demeanor and sincere interest in the welfare of all about him, he was ever the good friend to whom they might appeal in either joy or sorrow with a certainty of receiving a sympathetic hearing and wise counsel, if he could give no more.

76

He was the friend of many of the leading men of the State and enjoyed their friendship in return. Had the conditions of his life permitted his genius to become creative instead of spontaneous and, therefore, ephemeral, he might have won an enduring reputation as one of the pioneers in the literature of the new land. It is often said that such men "live before their time" and waste their lives upon the raw, uncultured wilds of pioneer communities; but the better thought is that, unconsciously to themselves and to the world in which they move, they sow the seeds of future grace and beauty and are really among the most effective moulders of public opinion.

During the Civil War, the services of Isaac Parker were much in request by the friends of sick or wounded soldiers to whom, his long acquaintance and friendship with Governor Morton and many of the generals, colonels and men in military authority, enabled him to be of much assistance at a time when the conditions of the service rendered such attentions to individual cases of great value; but he made no charges beyond his expenses. Even deserters came to him and through his good offices were received back into the service with no greater penalty than that they were required to serve out the full time for which they had enlisted.

The war was over and the struggle over reconstruction was upon the country when his health, which had been precarious from and after his wife's decease, grew worse and he died as already stated on October 27, 1866. His funeral was probably the largest that had, up to that time, ever been given to a private citizen in the southeastern part of the county, and so he passed away, as "one in whom the elements were so mixed and mingled that all the world might say, here was a man."

BENJAMIN STRATTAN PARKER.

Editor, Author and Citizen.

Benjamin Strattan Parker, eldest son of Isaac and Mary (Strattan) Parker, was born in "A Cabin in the The Clearing," as related in the biography of his father, on February 10, 1833. He was married on January 21, 1869, to Hulda Wickersham, daughter of Jethro and Mary Wickersham, of Henry County, Indiana. They have lived happily together up to the present time and are the parents of three children. Florence Parker, the eldest, is the well known and popular primary teacher in the New Castle public schools, where she has rendered twelve years of most valuable and effective service. Allegra, the second daughter, is now Mrs. Samuel J. Bufkin, of New Castle, Indiana. She is a woman of many attainments and has been a favorite in club circles; she writes naturally and well and is much interested in birds and bird lore. She is the mother of two bright and promising children, a little girl of three years and an infant boy. The third child and only son, Jethro W. Parker, is also married and at present lives in Rushville, Indiana. He is an active business man, his specialty being the clothing trade, of which he has much knowledge and in which he is considered efficient.

Benjamin S. Parker and his wife are living quietly at their modest, tree-surrounded home, in New Castle, where they take delight in meeting their friends. Mrs. Parker is a generous, kind hearted woman, popular with her friends and respected by the community. She has been somewhat active in religious and social life and in certain benevolent societies. She was the first president of the Henry County Federation of Clubs and was one of the early members of the Woman's Club, but is at present taking a rest from club work, though still much interested therein, and especially in that of the Woman's Club.

Benjamin S. Parker, in addition to what is told of his life in the preceding sketch of his father, has been a teacher, a business man, an editor, a contributor to newspapers and magazines and by a sort of compulsion has practised law a little in years that are past; he has also written and edited and published books and has taken an interest in politics and held office. He taught at various points in Henry and Rush counties, prior to 1863, sold goods and dealt in grain at Lewisville, Indiana, for eleven years prior to 1874 and edited "The New Castle Mercury" from 1875 to 1882. He was the elector for the sixth Congressional district on the Garfield ticket in 1880 and cast the vote of

s the friend of many of the leading men of the State and enjoyed their
in return. Had the conditions of his life permitted his genius to become
tead of spontaneous and, therefore, ephemeral, he might have won an endur.
ion as one of the pioneers in the literature of the new land. It is often
ich men "live before their time" and waste their lives upon the raw, uncul-
of pioneer communities; but the better thought is that, unconsciously to
and to the world in which they move, they sow the seeds of future grace
and are really among the most effective moulders of public opinion.

the Civil War, the services of Isaac Parker were much in request by the
ick or wounded soldiers to whom, his long acquaintance and friendship with
orton and many of the generals, colonels and men in military authority,
1 to be of much assistance at a time when the conditions of the service
ich attentions to individual cases of great value; but he made no charges
expenses. Even deserters came to him and through his good offices were
:k into the service with no greater penalty than that they were required to
e full time for which they had enlisted.

.r was over and the struggle over reconstruction was upon the country
salth, which had been precarious from and after his wife's decease, grew
:e died as already stated on October 27, 1866. His funeral was probably the
had, up to that time ever been given to a private citizen in the southeastern
county, and so he passed away, as "one in whom the elements were so
. ngled that all the world might say, here was a man."

HON. JOHN STRATTAN PARKER.

Editor, Author and Citizen.

.n Strattan Parker, eldest son of Isaac and Mary (Strattan) Parker, was
Cabin in the The Clearing," as related in the biography of his father, on
). 1833 He was married on January 21, 1869, to Hulda Wickersham,
Jethro and Mary Wickersham, of Henry County, Indiana. They have lived
ther up to the present time and are the parents of three children. Florence
eldest, is the well known and popular primary teacher in the New Castle
ls, where she has rendered twelve years of most valuable and effective
egra, the second daughter, is now Mrs. Samuel J. Bufkin, of New Castle,
e is a woman of many attainments and has been a favorite in club circles;
aturally and well and is much interested in birds and bird lore. She is the
:o bright and promising children, a little girl of three years and an infant
.rd child and only son, Jethro W. Parker, is also married and at present
ihville, Indiana. He is an active business man, his specialty being the
e, of which he has much knowledge and in which he is considered efficient.
in S. Parker and his wife are living quietly at their modest, tree-sur.
ie, in New Castle, where they take delight in meeting their friends. Mrs.
generous, kind hearted woman, popular with her friends and respected by
ity. She has been somewhat active in religious and social life and in
rolent societies. She was the first president of the Henry County Federa.
and was one of the early members of the Woman's Club, but is at present
: from club work, though still much interested therein, and especially in
Voman's Club.

in S. Parker, in addition to what is told of his life in the preceding sketch
has been a teacher, a business man, an editor, a contributor to newspapers
as and by a sort of compulsion has practiced law a little in years that are
also written and edited and published books and has taken an interest
1d held office. He taught at various points in Henry and Rush counties,
sold goods and dealt in grain at Lewisville, Indiana, for eleven years prior

Benjamin S Parker

the district for the second martyr-president in the State electoral college. He was appointed United States consul at Sherbrook, Province of Quebec, Canada, by President Chester A. Arthur, in 1882, and filled the place efficiently until 1885. He was elected Clerk of the Henry Circuit Court in 1886, filling the place most satisfactorily for the full term of four years, from 1888 to 1892, although an invalid during much of his term. He was elected representative for Henry County in the General Assembly in 1900 and served with credit during the session of 1901. At an earlier period of his life he had served the town of Lewisville, seven years consecutively, as school trustee, during which time in conjunction with the late Dr. W. M. Bartlett, he was instrumental in building a new schoolhouse in 1866, which was the first schoolhouse in Franklin township of more than one room and which started the remarkable educational advance in that town and its vicinity. He has been an ardent, though never bitter supporter of the Republican party because of its adherence to those principles of freedom and equality in which he believes.

Benjamin S. Parker, in his early years, spoke, lectured or read papers very often before literary societies, teachers' associations, Sunday school gatherings, political meetings and other assemblies of the people. Always of slender build, it was not permitted him to enter the Union service as a soldier, but his services to the cause during the Civil War were so numerous and of so many kinds that he has often. since its close, been a welcome guest at soldiers' reunions, especially of the regiments that were made up in Henry, Rush and Wayne counties, and he was many years ago elected an honorary member of the regimental association of the famous 36th Indiana Regiment.

Like his father, he has always been a great lover of poetry, art and music, and has written extensively in verse, of which his published volumes have been "The Lesson and Other Poems," 1871; "The Cabin in the Clearing," 1887; "Hoosier Bards," etc., in 1891; "Rhymes of Our Neighborhood," in 1895. He also, in collaboration with E. B. Heiney, compiled and edited "The Poets and Poetry.of Indiana," a most valuable addition to Indiana letters, in 1900. His poetry has been widely read and has received many words of approval and praise from critics, scholars and newspaper editors, east and west. But the greater volume of his writings has been in prose and unfortunately for his reputation with the larger world, much of it devoted to local themes.

While his opportunities for gaining a school training were confined to the Richsquare school, which in early times was one of the best in its immediate section, the home life in his father's house was in matters of literary and general information a sort of continuous school and Mr. Parker was so imbued with the idea of a life largely devoted to scholarly pursuits, that it made a student of him and when at an early age he began teaching he did not permit himself to lose much time in idleness which might have been devoted to increasing his knowledge and capabilities; but circumstances, seemingly beyond his control, changed the current of his life and carried him into traffic, in which adverse conditions arose which subjected him to loss and burdened him with debt—a burden which he did not cast off, as he might have done, but for long years has striven with and paid off as best he could, greatly to the detriment of his hopes and aspirations in other directions, until the strain and worry have so broken his health that at times his friends have thought that the end of his career was near at hand; but now at three score years he is as active and alert as ever and still buoyant with hope and works with his hands, his head and his heart as earnestly as in the past.

His affections have been and are centered largely in his native State and county. He was the second president of The Western Association of Writers, and is an honorary member of The Century Club, of Indianapolis, and the Indiana Audubon Society, and with Thomas B. Redding, Elwood Pleas and Martin L. Bundy, founded The Henry County Historical Society nineteen years ago. He was also the first person to introduce the annual decoration of the graves of the soldiers of the Union in Henry County. This was in 1867, several years before it was taken up by the Grand Army of the Republic.

In religion and ethics Mr. Parker has long been impressed with the broader faith and hope, rather than with narrow creeds of any kind, and hence is well disposed towards any form of religious faith which may tend to make humanity better and nobler, the conditions of life more hopeful and the soul more in harmony with the evident purposes of its Author.   .

Among a great many tributes that have been paid to his character and qualities of mind by his friendly contemporaries, the following from his friend of many years, James Whitcomb Riley, has been selected to fittingly close this sketch:

THE CLEARER HAIL.

To Benjamin S. Parker.

Thy rapt song makes of earth a realm of light,
And shadowy, mystical as some dreamland
Arched with unfathomed azure—vast and grand
With splendor of the morn, or dazzling bright
With Orient noon; or strewn with stars of night
Thick as the daisies blown in grasses fann'd
By odorous midsummer breezes and
Showered over by all bird songs exquisite.
This is thy voice's beatific art—
To make melodious all things below,
Calling through them, from far, diviner space,
Thy clearer hail to us. The faltering heart
Thou cheerest, and thy fellow mortal so
Fares onward with uplifted face.

                                        —Armazinda, page 50.

BIOGRAPHICAL SKETCH OF JOHN POWELL.

LEADING PIONEER, PUBLIC OFFICIAL AND WELL REMEMBERED CITIZEN.

The first interrogation one receives upon entering Boston is: "What do you know?" In New York it is: "What are you worth?" In Philadelphia: "Who are your relations?" To answer the last question and show who were the ancestors and who the descendants of John Powell is the purpose of this sketch.

In the principality of Wales, near Brecon, Brecknockshire, Watkin Powell was born. He had three sons—John, Thomas and Watkin, who in 1801 came to the United States of America and settled first at Utica, New York. From that point Watkin Powell went to Spring, Crawford County, Pennsylvania, where he settled and where his descendants are at the present day farmers and stockmen of national reputation. John Powell moved to Virginia and became the head of the southern branch of the Powell family. Thomas Powell, with his wife, Nancy, who was also a native of Wales, and their son, Thomas, who was born in Wales, moved to Port Carbon, Pennsylvania, and there was born to this couple July 22, 1806, a son, John Powell, who is the subject of this sketch.

In 1809 Thomas and Nancy Powell moved with their family to Butler County, Ohio, and settled on a farm near Cincinnati. While located there two more children were born to them, namely: William, born October 15, 1810, and Elizabeth, born July 5, 1814. The latter became the wife of James Wasson and died his widow in Crawfordsville, Indiana, January 17, 1905.

John Powell lived with his parents and worked on the farm until he was eighteen years of age, when he went to Connersville, Indiana, and there served as a tanner's apprentice under Abraham Conwell. When his apprenticeship ended he was master of the business in every detail. Mr. Conwell always bore in remembrance his young apprentice, and when in 1863 Martin L. Powell, son of John, was in Connersville on a visit to Mr. Conwell, the latter called out to some men of his acquaintance, saying: "Here is a boy I want to introduce you to. His father was with me for years and I knew him well. You might fill this room with uncounted money and he would not touch a dollar save his own. I never knew a more honest man."

John Powell moved from Connersville to New Castle in 1827, where he soon afterwards purchased the tanyard of Charles Mitchell and all of the three hundred and thirty feet of land fronting on the south side of Broad Street, east of Mill, or what is now known as Fifteenth Street, for four hundred dollars. The Charles Mitchell referred to was the father of Leander P. Mitchell, the present assistant comptroller of the United States Treasury, and biographical mention is made of him in connection with the sketch of another son, Samuel Alexander Mitchell, which is published elsewhere in this History. This was in reality the beginning of the business career of John Powell. From the time of this purchase until his death no man was more closely identified with the history of New Castle. He was a thorough business man, who seemed to have an intuitive grasp of the principles of trade, and he was an indefatigable worker. He did not depend on the local supply of hides for use in his tannery, but patronized for fully thirty years the markets of Cincinnati, St. Louis and New Orleans.

Mr. Powell was not, however, a man with a single idea, but while steadily conducting his tanning business, he was also looking ahead, and seeing a future full of promise he dealt extensively for the period in real estate. Some of the prices paid for land by him show the remarkable opportunities for money making in that line which existed at that early period. The southwest corner of Fifteenth and Broad streets, eighty-two and a half feet, cost him twenty-five dollars March 10, 1832. It was upon this lot that he built in 1838 the brick house which is still standing, good and solid, and which was at the time the finest in New Castle. It was in this house that his son, Martin L. Powell, and the children following him were born. This lot unimproved is worth to-day probably twelve thousand dollars. On August 12, 1829, Mr. Powell bought the east half of the north side of Broad Street, between Fourteenth and Fifteenth streets, one hundred and sixty-five feet, for ten dollars; the northwest corner of Broad and Fourteenth streets, eighty-two and a half feet, for ten dollars, and the square of five acres, the northeast corner of which is the southwest corner of Seventeenth and Broad streets, for one hundred dollars. These properties are now worth a large fortune.

Mr. Powell was especially noted for his kindly and charitable disposition. He was a truly benevolent man, but never sought publicity or personal commendation for his many benefactions. He was not only charitable, but he also made it a point to assist in a business way many whom he saw in need of such assistance. He was a good judge of men and seemed to know well whom he could trust. Ezekiel T. Ice, of Mount Summit, has the most pleasurable recollections of Mr. Powell's generosity. In 1852, when Ice was a young man, twenty-two years of age, he and the late Joseph Kinsey desired to build a steam saw mill at Mount Summit, for which thirty-five hundred dollars were needed. Ice had eighty acres of not very valuable land and Kinsey had five hundred dollars in cash. They applied to Mr. Powell for aid and he not only made the necessary loan, but agreed to furnish the machinery besides. After a year of almost superhuman toil they found that it would take five hundred dollars more to complete the work. Discouraged, Mr. Ice offered the property to Mr. Powell for the debt, but he instead advanced the needed five hundred dollars and said: "You are young and energetic and can pay two hundred dollars a year and six per cent. interest." They paid the debt. This was during the hard times preceding the great financial panic of 1857 and there was due Mr. Powell from others obligations amounting to more than ten thousand dollars. He did not even take a mortgage from Ice and Kinsey, nor did he foreclose on others when by so doing he could have profited by many thousands of dollars.

When the New Castle and Dublin turnpike was projected and bids asked for the work, Mr. Powell advised the late Robert Cluggish, then a young man, almost fresh from Scotland, to put in a bid. Cluggish had no money, but finally made a successful bid and was furnished the money by Mr. Powell without security. In this as in the previous case, his confidence was not misplaced. He furnished money to Murphey, Goodwin and Company with which to buy hogs. He gave credit to Henry Shroyer, then a young man, in 1834, for all the leather needed by him in his business of saddle and harness making. He gave horses to three preachers unconditionally, but from Charles B. Davidson he took a note payable when he should cease preaching Methodism. This note became due and collectable when Davidson afterwards joined the Presbyterian church at Indianapolis, but was never paid. Old "Daddy" Westlake, of Dublin, Wayne County, being harrassed by officers for debt, Mr. Powell loaned him a horse over sixty years ago. It was never returned. Some persons were given the opportunity by Mr. Powell to work out eighty acres of land at the entry fee of one hundred dollars, and this land is now for the most part worth fifty dollars or more an acre. Others were helped by him to build homes. No one in trouble, financial or otherwise, ever applied to John Powell in vain, whether it was for money or for counsel and advice.

Mr. Powell was a notably eccentric man and no one in Henry County was ever like him in oddity of manners and of speech. He was very quick and active and in the purchase or sale of a farm scarcely a dozen words would be used by him. Probably as large a gift as he ever made was when, although at the time a comparatively poor man, he paid the entire debt of the Methodist Episcopal Church of New Castle, then occupying the frame building which stood on the ground recently purchased and now used by the Board of Trustees of New Castle.

During the great cholera epidemic of 1833 and also that of 1849, when every person who could apparently left New Castle to escape the ravages of that dread disease, John Powell and his wife remained and gave their services to the needy, the sick and the dying. They were without fear and more than all put their trust in God.

Summing up in a general way, it may be said that John Powell was, during his whole life in New Castle, one of its foremost citizens and that he was intensely interested in everything that had for its object the good of the town and of the county at large. He was a progressive man and strongly favored internal improvements. He supported the building of the Whitewater Canal from Hagerstown, Wayne County, to Cincinnati, which was used, however, from Cambridge City only. He gave his personal attention to that enterprise and contributed liberally of his means. That canal is now a memory only, but during its use it gave to Cambridge City a commercial importance which placed it in the front rank of towns in eastern Indiana.

He was also a prominent figure in the building of what has since become the Panhandle Railroad, extending from Richmond to Logansport and thence to Chicago. Associated with him in this enterprise were Judge Jehu T. Elliot, Judge Martin L. Bundy, Colonel Miles Murphey, Joshua Holland, John C. Hudelson, John W. Grubbs, Eli Murphey and Daniel Bradbury, of Greensfork, Wayne County. He was likewise personally identified with what is now the Lake Erie and Western Railroad, extending from Fort Wayne to Cincinnati via New Castle, Cambridge City and Connersville. He favored the building of all the turnpikes which had existence prior to his death. Mr. Powell was a member of the lower House of the General Assembly of Indiana during the session of 1847 and had as his colleague Simon Summers, of Middletown.

Touching his interests in land, it may be stated that he sold to the late Jehu T. Elliott the farm adjoining New Castle, which now belongs to the Elliott heirs; and to Judge Martin L. Bundy the Bundy farm, two miles south of New Castle. Mr. Powell also owned one hundred and sixty acres, four miles north; one hundred and sixty acres northwest; two hundred and fifty acres, three miles west, and eighty acres east of New Castle. He was also the owner of other tracts of land in Henry County and hundreds of acres in Clinton, Grant, Wells and other counties in the northern part of the State. Land which cost him an entrance fee of one dollar and a quarter per acre has since sold for as much as one hundred dollars per acre. Mr. Powell has been heard to say that he could have been worth twice as much as he was had he cared to be, and there is a volume contained in his statement that he was never either plaintiff or defendant in a court of justice. As a taxpayer he was rated the second highest in the county.

Mr. Powell was an uncompromising opponent of the use of liquor and tobacco in any form. He was a true Christian and an active member of the Methodist Episcopal Church, faithful in his attendance upon its worship and liberal in his support of its many benefactions. The passage of Scripture contained in Matthew, 6-33: "Seek ye first the kingdom of God and His righteousness, and all these things shall be added unto you," he made the rule of his life. His last work was the founding, in association with others, of beautiful South Mound Cemetery, New Castle, of which he became, at the early age of fifty-two years, nine months and twenty-five days, May 19, 1859, the first occupant.

On September 28, 1828, soon after coming to New Castle, John Powell was united in marriage with Lydia Collett, of Brookville, Indiana. She lived but a short time, her death occurring March 6, 1830. Subsequently he married Elizabeth, daughter of John Creek, of near Liberty, Union County, Indiana, July 4, 1832. She was born November 30, 1813. To this union were born the following named children: Charles Collett, March 30, 1833; Martin Luther, February 12, 1840; Albert, September 5, 1842; Samantha, June 4, 1845; Sophronia, June 9, 1847, who died August 23, 1865; George, June 30, 1850, and Elizabeth, April 4, 1853. John Powell died May 17, 1859, and his widow, Elizabeth (Creek) Powell, died June 29, 1862.

CHARLES COLLETT POWELL.

(Son.)

Charles Collett Powell, the eldest son of John and Elizabeth (Creek) Powell, was born March 30, 1833, and was united in marriage March 11, 1858, with Mary Ellen Van Winkle, a sister of John Q. Van Winkle, the present general superintendent of the Big Four Railroad. She died the year following her marriage and Mr. Powell subsequently married Mary Jane, daughter of William and Jane Taylor, natives of Virginia, who lived near Frankton, Madison County, Indiana. To Charles Collett and Mary Jane (Taylor) Powell were born four children, namely: Fletcher and Harriet F., who died in New Castle; Mary Ellen, who afterwards married Archibald Coulter; they have one daughter named Ellen; and Sophronia, who now resides with her mother at Walnut Hills, Cincinnati, Ohio. Charles C. Powell died in New Castle May 19, 1883, and is buried in South Mound Cemetery. The funeral took place on May 21, 1883, a day long remembered from the fact that there were six inches of snow on the ground.

Charles C. Powell received a good education and when about twenty-two years of age began his mercantile career at Quincy, now Elwood, Indiana, having for a partner the late Colonel Miles Murphey. They conducted what was then known as a general store and did a successful business for several years. Shortly after the death of his father and because of that event this arrangement was given up and Mr. Powell returned to New Castle, where he lived continuously until his death. He became a large stockholder in the First National Bank of New Castle and was for many years a director of that institution.

Charles C. Powell was a quiet, unassuming man, well informed as to current events, possessed of an excellent judgment, and whose truth, honor and integrity were never questioned. He was a member of the Methodist Episcopal Church from early childhood, and no man was more faithful to his religious duties than he. He was also a member of the Masonic fraternity. Like his father, he was pronounced in his temperance sentiments, and again like his father, he was a quiet and unostentatious supporter of many charities. Mr. Powell, at his death, left his family well provided for, and the surviving members of his family, though living in Cincinnati, have large property interests in New Castle.

MARTIN LUTHER POWELL.

(Son.)

Martin Luther Powell, the second son of John and Elizabeth (Creek) Powell, was born February 12, 1840, and was united in marriage April 30, 1862, with Susan R., daughter of Jacob and Martha Byer. Jacob Byer was born in Fredericksburg, Maryland, April 29, 1803, and was married to Martha Mitchell April 29, 1829. He was by trade a tanner, but became a farmer and moved to lands near Greencastle, Pennsylvania, where himself and family remained until 1849, when they came to New Castle, Henry County, Indiana, where they located on a farm adjoining New Castle on the east, which Mr. Byer purchased from the late Jacob Elliott in the year mentioned. In company with Henry Clunk, who also came from Pennsylvania, Jacob Byer opened the first hardware store in New Castle in 1855. He was a devout member of the United Brethren Church and was one of the principals in the construction of the present church building of that denomination in New Castle and its main support until his death, March 19, 1867. His widow, Martha (Mitchell) Byer, died September 26, 1877.

To Martin Luther and Susan R. (Byer) Powell were born the following children: John Jacob, so named after his two grandfathers; Perry Edward, Archie Albert, Martha Elizabeth, so named after her two grandmothers; Mary Belle, Edgar Byer, Helen Josephine, Arthur Mitchell and George Byer.

John Jacob Powell, the eldest son, is a baker by trade. He served in Porto Rico during the Spanish-American War, in the United States Hospital Corps. He is a member of the Knights of Pythias and of the Odd Fellows. He is unmarried and lives at home with his parents.

Perry Edward Powell, the second son, is a graduate of the New Castle High School, of the Indianapolis Commercial College, of De Pauw University, Greencastle, Indiana, and of the Illinois Wesleyan University, Bloomington, Illinois, where he received the degree of doctor of philosophy. He entered the ministry of the Methodist Episcopal Church and was stationed for four years at Greenfield, Indiana, and during his pastorate there was instrumental in the building of the beautiful church of his denomination in that city. He is now pastor of the Methodist Episcopal Church at Garrett, Indiana, and is one of the most prominent preachers in the Northern Indiana Conference. He married Louise Smith and they have one child, Harriet Emily.

Archie Albert Powell, the third son, married Eva Thornberry, of Mattoon, Illinois, and they are the parents of one child, Maynard. Archie is a prominent dentist and has a good practise in Mattoon. Martha Elizabeth Powell, the eldest daughter, is unmarried and lives at home in New Castle with her parents. Mary Belle Powell, the second daughter, is the wife of Walter B. Runyan, a practical plumber of New Castle. They have one child, Martha Lea. Mary Belle graduated from the New Castle High School with the remarkable record of nine years' attendance in the public schools without being absent or tardy once. Edgar Byer Powell, the fourth son, is a graduate of the New Castle High School and of the Indianapolis Commercial School. In 1902 he graduated from the Rose Polytechnic Institute, Terre Haute, Indiana. He is a civil engineer by profession and for several years has been employed in architectural work on the great steel "skyscrapers" in New York City. Helen Josephine Powell, the third daughter, was for about three years a teacher in the East Ridge schoolhouse, but she is now married to Benjamin H. Baker, of New Castle, where they reside. Arthur Mitchell Powell, the fifth son, is a student at Purdue University, Lafayette, Indiana, and will graduate from that institution in 1908. George Byer Powell, the sixth son, is bookkeeper and collector for the Independent Telephone Company. He is unmarried and lives at home with his parents. This family of nine children has received the best educational advantages of the day and constitutes a group of which the parents may well be proud. The family have a remarkable hygienic record, there not having been a case of sickness among them in a period of forty-four years.

Martin L. Powell is most worthy of honorable mention in this History in connection with the careers of his father and of his elder brother, Charles Collett Powell. He has lived continuously in New Castle for a period of some sixty-six years and is one of its native born citizens. He obtained his education in the schools of the town and for many years was one of the leading business men of the place. He has contributed liberally to its advancement and prosperity and, though now retired, holds it to be his duty to assist in maintaining the prosperity of a town which he has seen spring up from the little country village in which he was born. He is possessed of an excellent memory and is considered an authority regarding the events of half a century ago. He is justly proud of his parentage and of his own descendants. He is a loyal citizen of his native town and enjoys the confidence and esteem of the whole community.

ALBERT POWELL.

(Son.)

Albert Powell, the third son of John and Elizabeth (Creek) Powell, was born September 5, 1842, and has never married. His home has been at New Castle all his life and no name or face is more familiar to its people. He is a well-known horseman and no man has a greater love for the horse than he. He purchased and imported from Scotland the well-known stallion, Glencairn, and thus originated the interest in horse-breeding which has given the county a reputation in that line hardly second to any. Glencairn lived to be twenty-six years old and at the time of his death belonged to Evan H. Peed, now superintendent of the Indiana State Fair. During his life Albert Powell has handled and broken to saddle or harness more than a thousand colts, and in no case did he ever use other than the kindest methods of treatment. Everything was accomplished by persistence and patience.

SAMANTHA (POWELL) PEED.

(Daughter.)

Samantha Powell, the eldest daughter of John and Elizabeth (Creek) Powell, was born June 4, 1845, and was married to Evan H. Peed May 29, 1866, and to their union were born the following children: James A.; Neva; Albert, born December 20, 1873, and died April 14, 1886; Elizabeth, born May 12, 1879; died in infancy; Olive and Nellie. The girls are all graduates of the New Castle High School. James A. was married to Emma, daughter of William Wimmer, of New Castle, November 29, 1899. He is a veterinary surgeon and took his degree in that profession in March, 1892, from the New York Veterinary College, which is a branch of the New York University of Medicine. He and his wife are well-known residents of New Castle.

No man is more esteemed in Henry County by those who know him than Evan H. Peed. He has many of the characteristics of his father, James Peed, who was a typical Kentucky gentleman, well known for his generous hospitality. Evan H. Peed has made a life study of farming and stands in the front rank of the agriculturists of Indiana. For several years he has been the superintendent of the Indiana State Fair Association and to his efforts and to his influence much of the success of that organization must be attributed.

GEORGE POWELL.

(Son.)

George Powell, the youngest son of John and Elizabeth (Creek) Powell, was born June 30, 1850, and was united in marriage November 19, 1873, with Ella, daughter of Jacob and Catharine Mowrer, of New Castle. They have one child, Frederick, born September 17, 1878. The family resides in Indianapolis, where Mr. Powell is engaged in business.

ELIZABETH (POWELL) CAMPBELL.

(Daughter).

Elizabeth Powell, the youngest daughter of John and Elizabeth (Creek) Powell, was born April 4, 1853, and was married to Stephen C. Campbell April 3, 1873. Mr. Campbell is a native of Crawfordsville, Indiana, and it is there, in what is aptly termed the "Athens of Indiana," that they reside. He has been long identified with the business interests of that place.

BIOGRAPHICAL SKETCH OF SIMON TITUS POWELL.

SCHOOL TEACHER, LAWYER AND COUNTY OFFICIAL.

Among the remarkable men who have figured in the history of eastern Indiana was Simon Titus Powell, the subject of this sketch. He was a native of Wayne County, Indiana, having been born August 21, 1821, on a farm which is now a part of Cambridge City. His parents were John and Margaret (Huff) Powell, both of whom were natives of Kentucky, who had removed from that State to Wayne County, Indiana, in 1816. The family remained at Cambridge City for several years and then moved to Illinois, where they settled near Danville. At this time young Powell was about five years of age. He attended school at Danville and Champaign, Illinois, and subsequently became a student at St. Gabriel's College, a Catholic institution at Vincennes, Indiana, where he remained for about three years. While yet a boy he returned to Cambridge City, Indiana, and entered the school then taught by the well-known educator, Reverend Samuel K. Hoshour, whose name is distinguished in Indiana history. He was rightfully regarded as the most capable teacher in eastern Indiana and when Mr. Powell came to New Castle in 1841 he brought with him a recommendation from Mr. Hoshour of such a complimentary character that it secured him employment at once as a teacher in the "old seminary."

Mr. Powell was a successful teacher and for the three years during which he had charge of the seminary he showed in that position the same energy which he displayed in after life, an energy which was resistless. He neither knew nor realized the meaning of the word "fail." The early schools of New Castle were taught by eminent educators and Mr. Powell followed worthily in their footsteps. Richard Huff was the first teacher and his oldest student was Jehu T. Elliott. Other scholars were Rachel Woodward, Mary Carroll, afterwards wife of Stephen Elliott; Martha Bowers, Martha Ward, afterwards Mrs. Andrew J. Lytle, and Vienna Woodward, afterwards the wife of Samuel Hazzard, who were the father and mother of the author of this History. Other teachers were: Abraham Elliott, Jesse H. Healey, Revel Coleman, Jehu T. Elliott, William Way, Caleb H. Cole and Samuel Hoover. William Henry, who taught in 1835-6, had among his pupils Martin L. Bundy, Thomas J. Neal, Luther C. Mellett and Rezin H. Powers. Mr. Powers died August 17, 1905, at his home near Springport, Henry County, aged ninety years. His twin brother preceded him to the grave by only a few months. They were both excellent citizens.

After the retirement of Mr. Henry the late Nimrod H. Johnson, father of Henry U., for years a member of Congress from this district, and of Robert U. Johnson, one of the editors of the Century Magazine, became the teacher. He was a man of fine education, an excellent teacher, polite, always well dressed and a gentleman of the old school. Then came George W. Julian, who was also for years a member of Congress from this district, and who attained a national reputation. Levi Linn, of South Carolina, was also a good teacher, but had a temper which often ran away with his better judgment and caused him to make inordinate use of the rod. Simon T. Powell took charge of the school in 1841, as above stated, and among his scholars were Joshua H. Mellett, Loring and Miles L. Reed, Maria and Mary Taylor, Harriet Parsons, Hiram, John and Jacob Thornburgh, Pyrrhus, Franklin and Clarinda Woodward, John Barrett, Volney Hobson, John D. Meek, Absalom B. Harvey, William H. Murphey, John M. Darr, Adolphus D. Thornton, Coleman F. Rogers, William R. Charles, Marshall G. Henry, Francis Marion McDowell and a number of others, almost all of whom have long since passed over and beyond this "vale of tears." The John Barrett above referred to also became a teacher in the "old seminary" in 1844, as did Isaac Kinley. It was about this time that Mr. Barrett went to South Carolina to investigate the slavery conditions. His action so excited the slaveholders that he was arrested and imprisoned and was only subsequently released through the intervention of friends, but not until his health had been broken down. He died very soon after his return from the South.

After teaching three years Mr. Powell gave up the school and was succeeded by the late Dr. John Rea, Mr. Powell himself becoming deputy clerk of the Henry Circuit Court under the late Samuel Hoover. He had entire supervision of the office and so admirably discharged its various duties that he was himself elected in 1850 to the position of clerk. Counting the time that he was clerk and deputy clerk of the courts, he served the public in that office for a period covering about thirteen years. As clerk of the Henry Circuit, Probate and Common Pleas courts, he performed most of the duties of the office him-self, never having had but one employe, Samuel W. Taylor, who was employed for a very brief period only. Mr. Taylor afterwards moved to Tipton, Tipton County, Indiana, where he became identified with the business interests of the place and was elected and served as State Senator from the counties of Hamilton and Tipton during the special and regular sessions of 1877 and 1879. Mr. Taylor was also the first mayor of New Castle under the law approved January 1, 1849, which substituted a mayor and four council-men for the president and trustees, the charter under this law being surrendered March 30, 1867.

Mr. Powell was well known for his habits of industry and he labored day and night in order that the records of the court proceedings might be, day after day, full and com-plete. He slighted nothing; the work was conscientiously performed and when he left the office at the expiration of his term he left behind an official record, upon which there was neither blot nor stain. This was the only official position to which he was ever elected and upon his retirement from it he turned his attention to the practise of the law. He opened an office with the late Eli Murphey as his partner, and pursued the profession until the breaking out of the Civil War.

He was a thorough Union man and from the time of the first call for troops took a prominent part in the prosecution of the great conflict. He could not personally enter the ranks of volunteers who were hastening to the battlefield because of the loss of the use of his left leg, resulting from cold taken while in swimming, which was a favorite pastime of his; otherwise physically strong and sound, he was compelled from that time to use a crutch and cane; though thus debarred from serving the flag, as he would un-questionably have done, he did the next best thing, giving his willing consent to the entry into the service of his two stalwart sons, Henry L. and Orlistes W. The first named became a member of Company B, 8th Indiana Infantry, three months' service, and was wounded at the battle of Rich Mountain, West Virginia, July 11, 1861, and the wound thus received more than forty years ago has never healed, but requires now, as at first, daily attention. A biographical sketch of Henry L. Powell is published on page 253 of this History and reference should be made thereto for further information regarding that soldier. Orlistes W. Powell was a member of Company C, 36th Indiana Infantry, and arose to the non-commissioned rank of sergeant-major. He was shot through the heart and instantly killed at the battle of Chickamauga, Georgia, September 20, 1863, and his name will be found in the Roll of Honor, published elsewhere in this History. The military career of each of these brave sons of a patriotic father will be found set forth in another part of this History in connection with their respective companies and regi-ments.

It is well known that during the Civil War the executive of each Northern State took great pains in caring for the interests of the general government and at the same time exercised a watchful care over the boys in blue who went into the army from their respective States. In this respect no executive was more vigilant than Governor Oliver P. Morton, of Indiana, and his fame as the friend of the soldier was known throughout the land; and to-day no man's memory is held in so great reverence by the Indiana sol-dier as is that of the "great war Governor." Governor Morton was ever in consultation with the foremost men of the State with regard to the proper measures for the conduct of the war, and among others whose advice and counsel were most welcome was Simon T. Powell, who ably and with whole-souled fervor supported and sustained the great Governor in those trying and perilous times.

In January, 1865, when it seemed that such an institution was imperatively needed, The First National Bank of New Castle was organized with Martin L. Bundy as its first president and Daniel Murphey as its first cashier. Mr. Powell was one of the original stockholders of this bank and a member of its first board of directors. He afterwards became vice-president of the bank and continued in that position for several years. He disposed of his interests in The First National Bank and in 1877 became president of the Bundy National Bank, with which he remained until it went into voluntary liquidation and ceased to do business. As a banker he was distinctively conservative, taking no chances except those entirely warranted by the facts presented. After the winding up of The Bundy National Bank Mr. Powell retired from active business, giving his attention exclusively to his own private affairs, a part of which consisted in looking after and increasing his large farming properties, the whole embracing about one thousand acres, much of which was among the best farm lands in Henry County.

The fact is so well known that it is hardly necessary to state that politically Mr. Powell was an aggressive member of the Republican party. He was, however, first a Whig and regarded Henry Clay as the first of American citizens. In 1868 he was a delegate to the Republican National Convention, which met at Chicago; he was also a delegate to the Philadelphia convention of his party in 1872, and again to the convention at Cincinnati in 1876, where he strenuously advocated the nomination of Governor Morton for President. He was also a delegate to the Chicago convention of 1880 and was one of the stalwart "306," who, under the leadership of Senator Roscoe Conkling, of New York, voted to secure the nomination of Grant for a third term, as President of the United States.

The last official position held by Mr. Powell was that of supervisor of internal revenue for the district composed of the States of Ohio and Indiana, with headquarters at Indianapolis. He received his appointment from President Grant and was commissioned December 14, 1872, and served for a period covering about five years, being succeeded by the late General Thomas W. Brady. Mr. Powell discharged the duties of this office with his accustomed zeal and fidelity to the interests of the government and was one of the coterie of internal revenue officers who were most instrumental in bringing to light and subsequently breaking up the great whisky ring, which had its headquarters at St. Louis, Missouri, and which resulted also in the punishment by fine, imprisonment and discharge from the service of many of those who were guilty participants in that great conspiracy against the government.

On April 5, 1842, Simon Titus Powell was united in marriage with Elizabeth Thornburgh, widow of Jacob Thornburgh. She was a daughter of David Hoover, of near Richmond, Wayne County, Indiana, and came with her husband, Jacob Thornburgh, to New Castle in 1825. By her first husband she was the mother of eight children, only one of whom, John Thornburgh, of New Castle, survives. By her second husband she was the mother of four children, namely: Henry L., Orlistes W., Catharine, afterwards wife of William H. Elliott, and Elizabeth. Of these four children Henry L. Powell alone survives. Elizabeth (Hoover-Thornburgh) Powell died October 8, 1881. She was a noble woman, a devoted wife and a loving mother; she was a great reader, had a retentive memory and was possessed of vivid descriptive powers, which made her recollections of the days of the early pioneers peculiarly interesting.

After the death of his first wife Mr. Powell was married on April 4, 1883, to Melvina, a daughter of William and Eliza (Robertson) Conway, of near Hagerstown, Wayne County, Indiana. Mr. Powell died at his handsome home in New Castle October 5, 1901. He was during the greater part of his life a member of the Methodist Episcopal Church and was also a prominent member of New Castle Lodge, number 59, Independent Order of Odd Fellows. He was for many years identified with the old settlers' organization, of which he was uniformly the treasurer. He was also a member of the Henry County Historical Society, to which he gave during his life a great deal of his attention and on the walls of that institution hangs an excellent portrait of himself, presented to the society by his son, Henry L. Powell.

The will of Simon Titus Powell gave to his surviving widow and to his surviving son, Henry L. Powell, his entire estate, the whole bearing an estimated value of more than $100,000. Since his death his widow, Mrs. Melvina Powell, has placed in the new Methodist Episcopal Church of New Castle a handsome memorial window in honor and out of reverence to his memory. His remains, together with those of his first wife and his deceased children, are buried in South Mound Cemetery, New Castle.

Melvina (Conway) Powell, widow of Simon T. Powell, was the daughter of the late William and Eliza (Robertson) Conway, and was reared at her parents' home, two miles and a half east of Hagerstown, Wayne County, Indiana.

Her father, William Conway, was a native of Kentucky, where he was born January 22, 1817. His parents, Miles and Catharine Conway, were also natives of that State, but removed to Henry County, Indiana, where they settled on a farm. William Conway was of an aspiring and versatile mind, and when a young man undertook, in his usual ardent manner the study of the law and became so well versed in its principles that his friends and neighbors relied upon him as a trusted adviser in legal matters.

He always had a natural love of horses, and became in later years known over the whole State as an expert horseman. He was one of the kindest of men and his heart was of that large mold which is only found in company with a broad mind. He was especially fond of children and young people and his doors were always open to the needy and friendless. His unspoken deeds of charity are almost without number, and many a young person has found his way to success through his assistance.

He was a member of the Newlight or Christian Church, and his religion reached beyond the mere orthodox type. It came directly from the heart. For a number of years he resided at Walnut Level, near Hagerstown, Wayne County, where his wife died May 2, 1901. His last days were spent at the home of his daughter, Mrs. Simon T. Powell, in New Castle, where he died Saturday, March 14, 1903, aged eighty-six years. He was the father of a large family, of whom one son and three daughters survive. Mr. Conway and his wife are buried in the Hagerstown cemetery.

Eliza (Robertson) Conway, the mother of Mrs. Powell, was the daughter of Moses and Polly Robertson. Her father, Moses Robertson, came from Wayne to Henry County in company with Jesse and Isaac Forkner about 1822, and entered land in Liberty Township at the first land sale, August 16, 1822. In addition to filling the office of sheriff for two terms, from August 5, 1833, to August 21, 1837, he was county collector, 1830-1833, and an early justice of the peace and a member of the board of justices governing the county, from 1824 to 1827. He was a public-spirited citizen, who had the confidence of the people to an unusual degree. He was one of the original promoters of the railroad from Richmond to New Castle, now a part of the Panhandle Railroad. Late in life he moved to Hagerstown, Wayne County, where he died and is buried in the cemetery on Symons Creek, near old Chicago. Mrs. Powell thus has as much reason to be proud of her ancestry as any lady living in Henry County, for her grandfather Robertson was certainly one of the county's grand old pioneers.

Mrs. Simon T. Powell was educated in the schools of Hagerstown and resided at home with her parents until her marriage. She was a most excellent and congenial companion to her husband and with rare devotedness made his last days pleasant and happy. She is a lady who is held in high esteem among her friends and acquaintances. Since the death of her husband the considerable property interests which have come into her care have demonstrated that she has business qualities of a high order. The large property has not only been maintained intact, but has been so administered as to greatly increase it.

John Real

BIOGRAPHICAL SKETCH OF JOHN REA, M. D.

A PAPER READ BEFORE THE HENRY COUNTY HISTORICAL SOCIETY BY HIS DAUGHTER, MRS. ELIZA ....

If I were vain of my own poor power to interest and entertain, I should probably br... in your request to prepare a memoir of my father and read it here to-day, a suggestion that as his daughter I should speak from my own knowledge of his life and ... as duty and affection prompt. But I know it is not so and that it is the pioneer and physician you would honor and not m.....li, his child. Knowing this, I have chosen to quote from my father's autobiography, which he began writing in 1878, as follows.

"I have intended for some little time to occupy my spare moments in jotting down the events of my life thinking they might be of some interest to those of my family who will survive me and perhaps give encouragement to some who may have th... way in life to .... in every way, if there be any suggestions in these pages that follow that shall be worthy of emulation or shall tend to making those who read them better and happier citizens .... time has been well spent.

Lexington, a section of county distinguished for .... natural wonder of nature the Natural Bridge. There are many points in my early life that I do not remember, for my parents died before I became anxious to preserve such information .... We were very poor, but well-to-do; they were both hard working and I was necessary, as they had a large family, and the land .... very sterile or productive that the strictest economy I used to enable us to live upon what could be .... made. But my father had good credit and he never abused that .... It was necessary that, as each one should bear his part of the work on the farm and in the house. ....

.... of the truth of the Presbyterians; indeed, the county in which we .... were .... almost entirely by this denomination. We attended meeting mostly at a .... called Hunter church, about two miles from our home. It was built of solid .... a hundred and fifty years ago, and at the present day stands as a monument of the fidelity and loyalty of the early settlers of this country to their religion.

"Our educational advantages at that day were very imperfect, having school only .... than six months in a .... and sometimes only from one to three months. .... younger to work on the farm. While .... opportunities for attending school were limited, each of these years was laid the foundation for future work and a determination for an education was implanted that has continued through my entire life. A part of the road that would scarcely see at times, yet even at this late day I recall with a shudder the many times I had to pass this .... to school or going to mill.

"Time passed until 18.. when we sold our farm of one hundred .... forty acres for $3,... and after selling all our possessions that we could not take with us, we left the State of Virginia in a .... wagon for Indiana in October 18... We were just thirty days making the trip. With most of the journey was .... and we encountered some difficulties but these were all overcome. On our .... sketch .... reached my uncle James Rea's place .... lived near Connersville and who had moved to Indiana about fifteen years before. After spending some little time at his home, we secured a farm near Harrisburg and moved to it. While living here .... attended school in the village and my first teacher in Indiana was Waterman Cliff, who had lately come to that vicinity from New York. The desire for an education grew with my years and I determined was I to obtain more than I worked at odd times, when not .... with my work at home, to get money enough to clothe myself and buy books. In 18.. for one of .... I had access to the county library at Connersville. I read and studied all my .... time day and at night. It was customary in those days to sit by a .... fire place and .... would use the light from this place to save the expense of a candle that ....

BIOGRAPHICAL SKETCH OF JOHN REA, M. D.

A PAPER READ BEFORE THE HENRY COUNTY HISTORICAL SOCIETY BY HIS DAUGHTER, MRS. ELIZA-
BETH REA GILLIES, SATURDAY, OCTOBER 25, 1902.

If I were vain of my own poor power to interest and entertain, I should probably
find in your request to prepare a memoir of my father and read it here to-day, a suggestion that, as his daughter, I should speak from my own knowledge of his life and work
as duty and affection prompt. But I know it is not so and that it is the pioneer and
physician you would honor and not myself, his child. Knowing this, I have chosen to
quote from my father's autobiography, which he began writing in 1878, as follows:

"I have intended for some little time to occupy my spare moments in jotting down
the events of my life, thinking they might be of some interest to those of my family who
will survive me and perchance give encouragement to some who may have their way in
life to make. Or, even beter, if there be any suggestions in these pages that follow that
shall be worthy of emulation, or shall tend to making those who read them better and
happier citizens, my time has been well spent.

. "I was born February 10, 1819, in Rockbridge County, Virginia, near the city of
Lexington, a section of country distinguished for that great wonder of nature, the Natural Bridge. There are many points in my early life that I do not remember, for my
parents died before I became anxious to preserve such information. My parents were
poor, but well-to-do; they were both hard-working and it was necessary, as they had a
large family, and the land not very fertile or productive, that the strictest economy be
used to enable us to live upon what could be thus made. But my father had good credit
and he never abused the trust reposed in him. As has been said, there was a large family and it was necessary that, at an early age, each one should bear his part of the work
on the farm and in the house. My parents were of Scotch-Irish descent and possessed the
intellect and physical characteristics of that ancestry. In religious belief they were firm
and reared the family in the faith of the Presbyterians; indeed, the county in which we
lived was settled almost entirely by this denomination. We attended meeting mostly at
a church called Timber Ridge, about two miles from our home. It was built of solid
stone one hundred and fifty years ago, and at the present day stands as a monument to
the fidelity and loyalty of the early settlers of this country to their religion.

"Our educational advantages at that day were very imperfect, having school not more
than six months of any year and sometimes only from one to three months. My younger
brother and I attended school during the winter months and in the spring we were put
to work on the farm. While our opportunities for attending school were limited, yet in
these years was laid the foundation for future work and a determination for an education was implanted that has continued through my entire life. A part of the road that
led to this school was about one-half mile through a dense forest which was so dark I
could scarcely see at times, and even at this late day I recall with a shudder the many
times I had to pass this way either to school or going to mill.

"Thus time passed until 1833 when my father sold his farm of one hundred and
forty acres for $550, and after selling all our possessions that we could not take with us,
we left the State of Virginia in a four-horse wagon for Indiana on October 1, 1833. We
were just thirty days making the trip. While most of the journey was pleasant, yet we
encountered some difficulties but they were easily overcome. On the 30th of October, we
reached my uncle James Rea's place, who lived near Connersville, and who had moved
to Indiana about fifteen years before. After spending some little time at his home, we
secured a farm near Harrisburg, and moved to it. While living here I attended school
in the village and my first teacher in Indiana was Waterman Clift, who had lately come
to that vicinity from New York. The desire for an education grew with my years and so
determined was I to obtain one that I worked at odd times, when not assisting with the
work at home, to get money enough to clothe myself and buy books. In 1836, for one dollar a year, I had access to the county library at Connersville. I read and studied all my
leisure time and at nights. It was customary in those days to sit by a large fireplace and
in the evenings I would use the light from this place to save the expense of a candle that I

might use what was thus saved towards my one object. About this time the way was not clear as to how I should pursue my studies, for there was no one near from whom I could obtain assistance, or advice, and all I learned had to be studied out alone. One day my father and I went into a store in Connersville and I saw a Natural Philosophy and upon looking into the book I felt I could master it. My father gave his consent for me to purchase it, and I was so delighted that I read and reread it many times, and in this same way I gained a knowledge of chemistry and astronomy.

"In 1838, when nineteen years of age, I was overwhelmed with surprise and aston-ishment, when the trustees from the adjoining district solicited me to teach their school. I objected for I knew my limited knowledge, but they insisted and I was elected teacher for the winter term of three months. I went to Connersville the day after this and passed a creditable examination. Dr. Ryland T. Brown, who was considered one of the finest scholars in the State, was the examiner and you can imagine my embarrassment. The following Monday I began my first school, receiving sixteen dollars per month and board. Nothing unusual occurred during the term. I had to study to keep in advance of my pupils and had no trouble until an arithmetic problem toward the last of the book pre-sented itself. The class was approaching this lesson and I worked and puzzled over it for several days. It was my first and last thought, but to my joy, one morning when I arose, I solved the problem at the first trial and it seemed as clear as day. The patrons of the school were pleased with my work for I was employed the second Winter. I then taught and went to school alternately for several years.

"In 1840 the political excitement ran very high and while I had my own opinions and held to them tenaciously, yet I talked very little upon the subject. It was this year that I cast my first vote for Van Buren.

"In 1842 I was desirous of attending the high school conducted by Samuel K. Hoshour at Cambridge City, Wayne County. My greatest incentive to attend school here was that I might take up the study of Calculus and Conic sections, as I had advanced thus far alone. But to my dismay when I intimated my intention to. Mr. Hoshour, he frankly admitted that he could not teach either of the branches mentioned. In their place I took Geometry and the French language. In Mr. Hoshour I found the person whom I needed. Besides being a fine teacher, he was easily approached and gave such advice as a young man needed, and he seemed to anticipate their needs. The following Winter I taught east of Milton securing sixteen dollars a month and paid one dollar and a quarter a week for my board. According to contract I had to take part of my pay in State script, which at that time was below par, but I had to take it at par.

"My next term of school was taught in Milton, where I made many and valuable friends. While here I became acquainted with Robert Murphey and family, several of his children coming to my school. A son, Benjamin F. Murphey, was clerking in New Castle in his uncle Miles Murphey's store. Through him I learned that the schools of New Castle would soon be without a teacher, and he thought that upon application I might secure the position. This position at Milton has always seemed to have been the stepping stone to my greater success. The school in New Castle was a county seminary and, ac-cording to the constitution, was under the control of trustees specially appointed. Eli Murphey was one of the trustees and he sent me word to come to New Castle, which I did at once. I made the journey on horseback and the first person I met in the town was Winford W. Shelley, who was acting as hostler at the hotel. After dinner I called on Benjamin F. Murphey and there became acquainted with Simon T Powell, who was the former teacher. After meeting the trustees and making my application, at their next meeting I was chosen to fill the place, the term to begin April 7. When I came to New Castle, aside from a few personal effects, such as clothing and books, I had just twenty dollars in canal scrip and it was only worth fifty cents on the dollar. It was at this time that my parents moved from Fayette to Cass County, near Logansport, where they resided till their death.

"I had now arrived at an age when I felt that I must make some choice of a pro-fession or business calling for my life's work, and becoming acquainted with Dr. Thomas B. Woodward, a young physician here, he suggested I study medicine, which suggestion I followed and began the study of medicine at once. I did this in connection with my school work, and put in five hours a day in reading and study outside of my duties in the school, for I was determined to not slight my obligations there. In May, 1847, after three years' study I presented myself to the Thirteenth Medical District Society for examination and a license to practise medicine. This was a regularly organized society and comprised several counties. The president was Dr. Joel Reed and the censors Drs. Thomas Jones, George W. Riddle and Thomas B. Wooward. They issued me a license signed by the president and the censors with the seal of the society and admitted me as a member of said society. I first located in Middletown, on May 9, 1847, and formed a partnership with Dr. Luther W. Hess. I only remained here till November 1st and then removed to Lewisville. I was advised by friends to make the change and it proved a good move. These were dark days to me, for I had but little means and had left a few bills, all of which amounted to something like ten dollars, but it was always a source of great worry to me to be in debt. I did not become discouraged but persevered and took advantage of everything that came my way. About this time the Henry County Turn-pike Company was organized and I was made secretary, which was a financial boon to me. With the amount received from this and the little revenue from my business, I was enabled to liquidate my little bills and live well but economically. In 1848 a division of the "Sons of Temperance" was founded in Lewisville. The place had been rather _disposed to intemperance, but the work of this society made such an impression upon public opinion in regard to the use of spirituous liquors as a beverage, that one hesitated to carry a jug through the streets for fear of being suspected of going for whisky. The educational side of the question for the town was now agitated and it was not long before a stock company was formed, a building erected and we had a good school and a fine teacher. The second teacher was a Miss Remby from Salem, Massachusetts. I now had a lucrative practise and felt I could support a home of my own and on October 9, 1851, I was married to Miss Remby. We started out to live within our means and my wife was a great comfort to me, encouraging me in my dark hours and being a true helpmeet during all our lives. Our oldest child was born on July 28, 1852, which was a source of great joy to us and we now seemed to have everything that made life enjoyable and a new incentive to lay up for the future. In the Fall of 1854, I had my home paid for and money enough laid by to enable me to attend a course of medical lectures in the Ohio Medical College, from which college I graduated in March, 1855. In July of the same year Jacob Mowrer and Dr. Thomas B. Woodward, my preceptor in medicine, wrote me asking that I should move to New Castle. They assured me a good practise, for Dr. Woodward wanted to retire and there was no physician there at that time, who would ride at night. On the 24th of the same month I moved to New Castle. This was an advantageous move in many respects, and I was glad to make my future home in this town. The schools were better here and we could educate our family and give them facilities that we did not have in a smaller place. I very soon purchased my present home on Elm Street and have lived continuously in the one place. My business from the time I moved here was very heavy and in the main lucrative. It was this year I joined the Masonic order, of which I have continued to be a member.

"The years from 1855 to 1860 were among the most pleasant years of my life. During that time I had gained a competence and felt confident that my youthful ambition would be fully realized; that is, I should live to the average age of man and that my decline of life would be comfortable and that I might be able to give my family the pleasures and advantages I had not been able to have; and that together we might enjoy life and its happiness.

"But at this time a dark cloud was arising which threatened to disturb the peace of our nation. War was no longer a conjecture, but a certainty. In January, 1863, there was a call for volunteer surgeons and I was one of a number to respond to the call. We were sent to Nashville, Tennessee, but after a little time they changed our appointments and it was found necessary to take the wounded to Cincinnati, that they might receive better care. I was given full charge of the boat and we reached our destination after many difficulties. I came home sick and lay seriously ill for a long time, but finally recovered and resumed my business, and for many years had uninterrupted health and vigor of constitution. For a number of years I had felt I should identify myself with a

77

Christian church and had considerable exercise of mind and convictions upon the sub. ject. In 1865 I united with the Baptist Church near Springport, Indiana. Within the next few years death entered our home a number of times, taking away from our midst several children.

"The only business venture, aside from my profession that I engaged in, was the dry goods business. In 1873 I formed a partnership with Lee Harvey, and later pur. chased his interest. This was not a success financially as it was the year of the demone. tization of silver which affected business generally. In 1875 I traded the store for a farm of one hundred and sixty acres in Wayne County.

"Our daughter, Ollie, was taken from us by death in 1882 and in 1885 our oldest son, George. These deaths were severe afflictions for they were grown and gave much promise of usefulness.

"I became a member of the examining board of pensions in 1885 and held this place for twelve consecutive years. I had a serious illness in the Winter of 1898 and my recov. ery was a matter of doubt. For the kind and skillful treatment of my brother physicians, Drs. Ferris and Boor, I can never express to them my deep sense of gratitude and also to my fellow Masons who so kindly furnished me with a competent and efficient nurse, Daniel Harvey, my heart goes out in untold appreciation."

Thus briefly have we traced through my father's notes, the principal events of the active period of his life and have now arrived at the point in his history where he was so soon to lay down his pen for the last time. On the day of January 28, 1899, he writes briefly of my mother's illness and the final entry in his journal is dated, Sunday p. m., February 12, 1899, just two days before the beginning of his own last sickness. He was ill but ten days and his chief concern, although suffering greatly, seemed to be his inabil. ity to care for "mother," as he had always before done throughout the long period of their married life. He died on February 24, 1899.—Elizabeth Rea Gillies.

The parents of Dr. John Rea were David and Elizabeth (Adams) Rea, who were both natives of Virginia. They moved with their children from Virginia to Indiana and settled on a farm near Connersville, Fayette County, in 1833, but a few years later sold their possessions there and went to Cass County, Indiana, locating not far from Logansport, where both father and mother died in 1855.

It is difficult to add to or strengthen what Dr. John Rea has himself said touching his life history. The author of this work knew him as one of Henry County's foremost citizens, one who had the respect and esteem of the whole community, a man who followed the strict path of duty and who was keenly alive to the betterment of the civil, social and political conditions of his time. He was devoted to his profession and during his whole life was a student who kept abreast of the advances in the medical art and who received the merited respect of his fellow practitioners.

As a teacher in the old New Castle or Henry County Seminary, in the 'forties, he was eminently successful. He was strict in his government of the school but gained and held the respect and confidence of his scholars. His punctuality in the discharge of his duties was so well known that it is said the people of the town set their watches and clocks by the ringing of teacher Rea's school bell. He was a member of the New Castle school board for over a quarter of a century and no man took greater interest in the cause of education.

In his business affairs, Dr. Rea was wholly successful. He accumulated a considerable property and at his death left his family well provided for. He was devoted to his wife and children and found his greatest comfort within his home. He was a lover of his profession, a dutiful Christian and a loyal member of the Masonic order. He was a member of New Castle Lodge, Number 91, of that order and during nearly all of his long connection with that honorable organization, he was its treasurer.

Doctor Rea was a charitable man, without ostentation, and in his life-long practise, the poor, who needed his assistance, were never disappointed. He was extremely modest and made no pretensions beyond his known character and ability. He was in truth a splendid exemplar of strong and dignified manhood. Shortly after his death a friend wrote of him: "He was a genuine and a manly man; solid, honest, sincere and reliable. He never wore a mask. Deception was not in him. He was out in the open. One always knew where to find him. His heart was large, generous, unselfish." Another wrote: "His good character and upright conduct must have a good influence on all who knew him. There was nothing in his conduct which required explanation or apology. His life was an open book which all could read with profit." He faithfully served the cause of humanity for more than half a century and it will be remembered that upon the occasion of the funeral of this good man, the public schools of New Castle were closed and all business suspended to do honor to his memory.

Mrs. John Rea died April 24, 1899, just two months to the day after the death of her husband. She was a noble wife and mother and gave to her husband and to her children her heart's fullest measure of love. She lived for her family and their comfort was her supreme happiness. She was herself a teacher and an accomplished woman, who was beloved by her friends and neighbors and no words of praise or commendation would be too many touching her life and character.

CHARLES LORING REA. M. D.

(Son.)

Dr. Charles Loring Rea, son of Dr. John and Mary Ella (Remby) Rea, was born August 10, 1859, and was educated in the public schools of New Castle. In 1881-4 he read medicine in the office and under the instruction of his father and in the winters of 1882-3 and 1883-4, while reading medicine, he attended the sessions of the Ohio Medical College at Cincinnati and graduated from that school in 1884. He commenced the practise of medicine at Rogersville, in Henry County, Indiana, where he continued until June, 1891, when he moved to Falmouth, Rush County, Indiana, where he has ever since resided, and where he has steadily and successfully pursued his chosen profession. On November 30, 1898, he was married to Lillie, daughter of Horace H. and Mary Jane (Powell) Elwell, of Rush County. They have no children. •

MRS. ELIZABETH (REA) GILLIES.

(Daughter.)

Mrs. Elizabeth (Rea) Gillies, the eldest daughter of Dr. John and Mary Ella (Remby) Rea, was born June 22, 1857, and was married to Peter M. Gillies April 27, 1892. She is a highly educated and thoroughly accomplished woman and after the death of her parents much of the business relating to the settling and adjustment of the estate was left to her care, a trust which was well and faithfully executed. Mrs. Gillies and her sister, Frances Rea, occupy the old homestead, near the corner of Race and Fourteenth streets. They are both members of the Presbyterian Church of New Castle and both are active in the work of that denomination.

GENEALOGICAL RECORD.

The family record of Dr. John Rea, now in possession of his daughter. Elizabeth (Rea) Gillies, shows the following:

John Rea, born February 10, 1819; Mary Ella (Remby) Rea, born April 5, 1829; John Rea and Mary Ella Remby married October 9, 1851; John Rea died February 24, 1899; his wife died April 24, 1899; both are buried in South Mound Cemetery, New Castle, Indiana.

Dr. John Rea and Mary Ella (Remby) Rea, his wife, were the parents of the following named children:

George Nathaniel Rea, born July 28, 1852; married July 3, 1878, to Ida B. Galliher; he died February 19, 1885; their children were: Clarence Galliher, born April 1, 1880; John Martin, born December 9, 1881, and Rhoda Olive, born November 20, 1884.

Edgar Ives Rea, born March 6, 1855; died March 1, 1858; Elizabeth Rea, born June 22, 1857; married April 27, 1892, to Peter M. Gillies; Charles Loring Rea, born August 10,

1859; married November 30, 1898, to Lillie, daughter of Horace H. and Mary Jane (Powell) Elwell, of Rush County; Olive Rea, born June 9, 1862; died December 26, 1882; John Edgar Rea, born August 19, 1865; died July 12, 1870; David Albert Rea, born September 30, 1866; died February 11, 1867; Frances Rea, born November 15, 1867; Mary Rea, born March 24, 1870; died October 9, 1872; Belle Rea, born May 24, 1872; died July 28, 1872; Arthur Clarence Rea, born September 21, 1873; died August 31, 1874. All of the above children, who are deceased, are buried in South Mound Cemetery.

Henry Shroyer

BIOGRAPHICAL SKETCH OF HENRY SHROYER.

PIONEER MERCHANT, UPRIGHT MAN AND WELL REMEMBERED CITIZEN.

To omit a sketch of the life and character of Henry Shroyer from the history of Henry County would leave a large portion of the record incomplete, unsatisfactory and in a measure unjust. For more than sixty seven years, or from 1835 to 1902, he was a moving spirit in all that concerned the building up, growth and prosperity of the county and its towns. He was supremely active and alert during almost his entire life or until the infirmities of old age took their final and irresistible hold upon him. Up to that time he did not know what it was to be an idle man.

Henry Shroyer was born in Jefferson, Greene County, Pennsylvania, July 28, 1810, and died in New Castle, Indiana, June 18, 1902, at the ripe old age of ninety-two years, eleven months and twenty days. He came to Indiana in 1835 and from that time until his death was a continuous resident of and a prominent factor in the history of New Castle. He was a son of David and Catharine Shroyer, of Jefferson, Pennsylvania, and early in life learned the trade of a saddler and harness maker. Upon his arrival in New Castle, he at once opened and for a number of years successfully conducted the first saddle and harness shop ever established in the town. Mr. Shroyer's father died in 1826 and when he came to New Castle in 1835, he brought with him his mother and his sister, Maria. The mother died in 1838. After following his trade for a period of almost eight years, he disposed of the business and very soon thereafter became a dry goods merchant and continued in that business for a period of over forty years.

Henry Shroyer was married on March 21, 1839, to Esther, the youngest daughter of David Hoover, a well known pioneer settler of near Richmond, Wayne County, Indiana. She was a sister of Elizabeth (Hoover) Thornburgh, widow of Jacob Thornburgh, pioneer merchant (1825) of New Castle, who became after his death the first wife of the late Simon T. Powell. Henry and Esther (Hoover) Shroyer were the parents of seven children, namely: Alexander Rotheus, born March 6, 1840; David, born July 16, 1843, died July 20, 1853; Caroline, now wife of Jehu T. Elliott; Julia, afterwards wife of Thomas B. Loer; Catharine, now wife of William G. Hillock; Lizzie, now wife of Henry Bierhaus; and Fannie, the youngest child, born May 5, 1859, died February 19, 1863. Mr. and Mrs. Bierhaus are graduates of the Deaf Institute, Indianapolis, in which both have also been teachers and where he is now engaged as an instructor. They are both well educated and highly accomplished and are very happily situated in their home at Indianapolis.

No man was better or more familiarly known in Henry County than Henry Shroyer, and to almost everyone, he was for long years "Uncle Henry," an appellation at once affectionate and seemingly appropriate. He was, indeed, New Castle's grand old man whom everybody loved and admired. He was of a humorous turn of mind and a lover of innocent sports, quick in speech and active in his movements. He loved his garden and his plants, his vines and his flowers. He felt the charm of beautiful things and of beautiful scenes. His soul was full of music and sweet, harmonious sounds had for him a special charm. He was big hearted, sympathetic, charitable and a lover of his fellow man. His strong and rugged honesty was never questioned and his word of promise was as sure to be executed as if he had given his bond for the deed.

He was a moral man of whom it can be said that he never swore an oath, never smoked a pipe or cigar, or chewed tobacco, and that he never drank a dram of liquor, except as used for medicinal purposes. He was in all respects an honored citizen, the memory of whose good deeds and good life is enshrined in the hearts of all who knew him. He was an earnest Christian and with his beloved wife was for many years a member of the Methodist Episcopal Church to which denomination they both clung, bearing upon their lips the words "Rock of Ages cleft for me, let me hide myself in Thee." Mr. Shroyer always looked upon the bright side of life. Trouble, care and sorrow he brushed aside, ever holding to the course that had for him joy and peace and comfort and that brought everlasting consolation and satisfaction.

At the time of his death, Mr. Shroyer was probably by reason of his age the oldest Mason in the State, while in membership in that ancient order he had served for nearly or quite fifty years. He was a member of New Castle Lodge, Number 91, Ancient, Free and Accepted Masons, and was ever faithful not only in his attendance upon its meetings but he was alike faithful in the practise of its high moral precepts and principles.

About ten years prior to his death, Mr. Shroyer retired from the active duties of life and thereafter gave his exclusive attention to the cultivation of his garden and the care of his vines and flowers and trees and the beautiful lawn attached to his home. In the last years of his life, he was scarcely able to hear but he never complained and seemingly found his full measure of enjoyment even under such deprivation. No man so enjoyed the society of his friends as did Henry Shroyer and at all social gatherings, when present, he was often the light and life of the assemblage.

Politically, he was a life-long Democrat and gave a strong, willing and conscientious support to his party. He was not a man who aroused antagonisms but in all his beliefs, whether social, religious or political, he was firm and steadfast in his convictions. His life was a busy one and in its battle he was a strenuous participator. His efforts were not in vain and when the end came, it was but the tranquil closing of a long, a happy and a well spent life.

ALEXANDER ROTHEUS SHROYER.

Alexander Rotheus Shroyer, son of Henry and Esther (Hoover) Shroyer, was born March 6, 1840, and died at Logansport, Indiana, May 22, 1901. He received a good common school and academic education in New Castle and then entered upon a business career. He was for a time a clerk in his father's store and afterwards became the first bookkeeper of the First National Bank of New Castle, at the time of its organization. He next went to Fairbury, Illinois, where he spent several years in the employ of Americus L. Pogue, whose wife, Mrs. Fannie Pogue, was the daughter of Henry Shroyer's sister, Emeline Thomas. Mrs. Thomas died in Richmond, Indiana, in August, 1893, and is buried in Earlham Cemetery, at that place.

In 1866 Alexander R. Shroyer went to Logansport, where he and his father in association with Lewis Hicks and Dewitt C. Elliott, purchased the wholesale grocery of Robert P. and William H. Murphey, which they carried on under the name of Hicks, Elliott and Shroyer (1866) until Henry Shroyer and Lewis Hicks disposed of their interests, the first named to Dewitt C. Elliott and the last named to Americus L. Pogue, the style of the firm becoming Elliott, Pogue and Shroyer (1871). Later Jehu T. Elliott, who was an employe of the firm and who represented the interests of Mr. Pogue therein, bought out the latter and the firm style was changed to Elliott, Shroyer and Company (1879). Later to Elliott and Company (1891) and then to The Jehu T. Elliott Company (since 1897).

In 1889 Alexander R. Shroyer disposed of his entire interest in the business to Dewitt C. and Jehu T. Elliott and later, after the death of Dewitt C. Elliott, the firm became Elliott and Company, the interest of the deceased partner passing to his son, William M., and his widow, Sophronia J. Elliott. After a few years, this partnership was dissolved, Jehu T. Elliott, his son, Henry Shroyer Elliott, and his nephew, William Murphey Elliott, becoming and remaining the sole owners of the business, the firm name being "The J. T. Elliott Company."

In this connection it is proper to state that all of the parties, except Americus T. Pogue, who had connection with this first wholesale grocery business in Logansport, were previously (Henry Shroyer continuously) business men of New Castle. Robert P. Murphey was a son of the late Clement Murphey and the son-in-law of the late Eli Murphey; William H. Murphey is the eldest son of Eli Murphey and is now connected with the New Castle Box Factory; Dewitt C. Elliott and Jehu T. Elliott were natives of Wayne County, nephews of Judge Jehu T. Elliott, the eminent Indiana jurist, and were for a long time in the retail grocery business in New Castle; Lewis Hicks was, prior to his removal to Logansport, in the hardware business in New Castle; Mrs. Sophronia J. Elliott is a daughter of the late William Murphey, pioneer merchant of New Castle and for many years president of the First National Bank of that place. She was born and reared in

New Castle and with her son, William M., and daughter, Louie, resides at Logansport. Americus L. Pogue, now and for many years a prominent citizen of Richmond, resided for a short time in Logansport.

Alexander R. Shroyer was a splendid business man, an expert accountant and in the unravelling and straightening out of tangled partnership matters had few if any equals. He had hosts of warm personal friends and held them to him with hooks of steel. He was, if anything, over-generous and no one ever applied to him for assistance and was turned away. He was married to Helen, daughter of Elisha and Charlotte (Jennings) Clift, at New Castle, Indiana, January 12, 1864. To them were born three children: Fannie, now wife of Emil Keller, landlord of the new Barnett hotel, Logansport; Willie, who died in infancy; and Lottie, now wife of Claud Wise, a merchant of Logansport. The latter live with and keep house for their mother who was rendered almost helpless by a stroke of paralysis, several years ago. .

Mr. Shroyer was a senator from Cass County in the Indiana General Assembly, serving during the Fifty fifth and Fifty sixth regular sessions, 1887-1889. He was a prominent Republican of Logansport and Cass County and was delegate to the Republican National Convention at Minneapolis in 1892, when Benjamin Harrison was nomiated for a second term as president. He was a member of the Masonic fraternity, having been initiated into the order by New Castle Lodge, Number 91. One who knew him well has said of his life and character: "He was noted for his kindness of heart, for his sympathy with the distressed and the suffering, for his steadfast friendship, for his generosity, for his honorable dealing and for his unswerving integrity."

MRS. CAROLINE (SHROYER) ELLIOTT.

Caroline, daughter of Henry and Esther (Hoover) Shroyer, is the wife of Jehu T. Elliott, who is mentioned above as engaged in the wholesale grocery business at Logansport. They have three children: Harry, Esther and Arethusie. Harry, the eldest son and child is associated with his father in the grocery business and is also the present clerk of the Cass Circuit Court. He is a very popular official and occupies an enviable position in the social and business life of Logansport. He was married April 19, 1900, to Maude Castle of that place and they are the parents of three children, namely: Jehu T.; Raymond; and Richard, who is named after Richard D. Goodwin, of New Castle. Esther, daughter of Jehu T. and Caroline Elliott, is the wife of Harry Uhl, to whom she was married June 14, 1905. Arethusie, the other daughter, is the wife of Edward Bliss, to whom she was married April 26, 1903.

MRS. JULIA (SHROYER) LOER.

Julia, daughter of Henry and Esther (Hoover) Shroyer, was married to Thomas B. Loer, August 1, 1870, and they were the parents of one daughter, Nina. Thomas B. Loer was born November 4, 1847, and died May 11, 1885. He was the son of James and Joanna (Stout) Loer, Henry County pioneers. He was a man of fine character who enjoyed the regard and respect of a wide circle of friends and acquaintances and who during his brief career was a part of the business life of New Castle and Henry County. He was for a number of years in the dry goods business in New Castle in partnership with his father-in-law and the latter's brother, John Shroyer. At the time of his death he was engaged in the grain business. His remains are at rest in South Mound Cemetery.

Nina, the daughter of this couple, was married November 10, 1892, to Edward E. Pitman, of New Castle. They reside in Logansport, where Mr. Pitman is superintendent and manager of the Pitman-Hillock (William G. Hillock, of New Castle) Handle Factory. Julia (Shroyer) Loer and Nina (Loer) Pitman are each prominent in the social circles of their respective homes.

MRS. CATHARINE (SHROYER) HILLOCK.

Catharine, daughter of Henry and Esther (Hoover) Shroyer, was married to William Gibson Hillock, November 4, 1873. Mr. Hillock came to New Castle in 1868 and from that time to the present has been identified with the business interests of the community. He was for a number of years the leading jeweler of New Castle but he now gives most of his attention to the Safety Corn Husker and Fodder Shredder, one of the leading industrial concerns of New Castle, of which he is the president. He is also largely interested in the New Castle Foundry Company which bids fair to become one of the big manufacturing plants of Eastern Indiana. Mr. and Mrs. Hillock and Mrs. Julia Loer together occupy their beautiful new home on South Fourteenth Street, where it is their pleasure to receive and entertain extensively their many friends.

FAMILY OF DAVID AND CATHARINE SHROYER.

The children of David and Catharine Shroyer were: Catharine (Shroyer) Parkinson (Aunt Kate), who was born, lived and died in Jefferson, Pennsylvania; Mary (Shroyer) Hipes (Aunt Polly), who died in New Castle and is buried in the cemetery at Jacksonburg, Wayne County, Indiana; Elizabeth (Shroyer) Kinsey (Aunt Betsey), wife of Robert C. Kinsey; Ann (Shroyer) Taylor, wife of John Taylor, for many years a popular hotel keeper of New Castle; Emeline (Shroyer) Thomas, whose husband lived and died in Pennsylvania; Aunt Maria Shroyer lived and died in New Castle and is buried in South Mound Cemetery; John Shroyer; Henry Shroyer, the subject of the foregoing sketch; Peter Shroyer, a one-time sheriff of Henry County; and David, a promising young man, who died at New Castle and with his good mother lies buried in the old cemetery on North Fourteenth Street, New Castle. Elizabeth Kinsey, Robert C. Kinsey, Ann Taylor and John Taylor, John Shroyer, Henry Shroyer, and the latter's life-long companion, who died April 7, 1902, are buried in South Mound Cemetery.

This was a large and interesting family, bound together by ties of love which could not be broken. Those of them who came in the early pioneer days to Indiana, settling in Henry and Wayne counties, did much to bring about the present condition of affairs which make the Hoosier name and fame hardly second to any other commonwealth of the nation.

GENERAL INDEX.

Lightning Source UK Ltd.
Milton Keynes UK
UKHW021005031218
333381UK00015B/2256/P